Beginning C++23

From Beginner to Pro

Seventh Edition

Ivor Horton
Peter Van Weert

Apress®

Beginning C++23: From Beginner to Pro

Ivor Horton
Stratford-upon-Avon, Warwickshire, UK

Peter Van Weert
Kessel-Lo, Belgium

ISBN-13 (pbk): 978-1-4842-9342-3
https://doi.org/10.1007/978-1-4842-9343-0

ISBN-13 (electronic): 978-1-4842-9343-0

Managing Director, Apress Media LLC: Welmoed Spahr
Acquisitions Editor: Steve Anglin
Development Editor: James Markham
Editorial Assistant: Gryffin Winkler
Copyeditor: Kim Burton

Cover designed by eStudioCalamar

Cover image by @Harryarts on Freepik (www.freepik.com)

Distributed to the book trade worldwide by Springer Science+Business Media New York, 1 New York Plaza, Suite 4600, New York, NY 10004-1562, USA. Phone 1-800-SPRINGER, fax (201) 348-4505, e-mail orders-ny@springer-sbm.com, or visit www.springeronline.com. Apress Media, LLC is a California LLC and the sole member (owner) is Springer Science + Business Media Finance Inc (SSBM Finance Inc). SSBM Finance Inc is a **Delaware** corporation.

For information on translations, please e-mail booktranslations@springernature.com; for reprint, paperback, or audio rights, please e-mail bookpermissions@springernature.com.

Apress titles may be purchased in bulk for academic, corporate, or promotional use. eBook versions and licenses are also available for most titles. For more information, reference our Print and eBook Bulk Sales web page at http://www.apress.com/bulk-sales.

Any source code or other supplementary material referenced by the author in this book is available to readers on GitHub (github.com/apress). For more detailed information, please visit https://www.apress.com/gp/services/source-code.

Paper in this product is recyclable

For my wonderful family. For all your love and support.
—Peter Van Weert

In memory of my wife, Eve
—Ivor Horton

Table of Contents

About the Authors

Ivor Horton is self-employed in consultancy and writes programming tutorials. He is the author of many programming books. Ivor worked for IBM for many years and holds a bachelor's degree, with honors, in mathematics. Horton's experience at IBM includes programming in most languages (including assembler and high-level languages on a variety of machines), real-time programming, and designing and implementing real-time closed loop industrial control systems. He has extensive experience teaching programming to engineers and scientists (Fortran, PL/1, APL, etc.). Horton is an expert in mechanical, process, and electronic CAD systems; mechanical CAM systems; and DNC/CNC systems.

Peter Van Weert is a Belgian software engineer whose main interests and expertise are application software development, programming languages, algorithms, and data structures.

After graduating summa cum laude, he obtained a PhD from the Declarative Languages and Artificial Intelligence (DTAI) Research Group. During his doctoral studies, he was a teaching assistant for object-oriented programming (Java), software analysis and design, and declarative programming.

Peter then joined Nikon Metrology, where he worked on large-scale, industrial applications in 3D laser scanning and point cloud inspection. Today, Peter is a senior C++ engineer and Scrum master at Medicim, Envista Holdings' R&D unit for digital dentistry software. At Medicim, he codevelops a suite of applications for dental professionals, capable of capturing patient data from a wide range of hardware, with advanced diagnostic functionality and support for implant planning and prosthetic design.

Common themes in his professional career include desktop application development, mastering code bases of millions of lines of C++ code, high-performant, real-time processing of 3D data, interfacing with cutting-edge hardware, and leading agile development teams.

In his spare time, Peter coauthors books on C++ and is a regular expert speaker at and board member of the Belgian C++ Users Group.

About the Technical Reviewer

Marc Gregoire is a software project manager and software architect from Belgium. He graduated from the University of Leuven, Belgium, with a degree in "Burgerlijk ingenieur in de computer wetenschappen" (equivalent to a master of science in engineering in computer science). The year after, he received an advanced master's degree in artificial intelligence, cum laude, at the same university. After his studies, Marc started working for Ordina Belgium, a software consultancy company. As a consultant, he worked for Siemens and Nokia Siemens Networks on critical 2G and 3G software running on Solaris for telecom operators. This required working in international teams stretching from South America and the United States to Europe, the Middle East, Africa, and Asia. Now, Marc is a software architect at Nikon Metrology (`www.nikonmetrology.com`), a division of Nikon and a leading provider of precision optical instruments, X-ray machines, and metrology solutions for X-ray, CT, and 3-D geometric inspection.

His main expertise is C/C++, specifically Microsoft VC++ and the MFC framework. He has experience developing C++ programs running 24/7 on Windows and Linux platforms, such as KNX/EIB home automation software. In addition to C/C++, Marc also likes C#.

Since April 2007, he has received the annual Microsoft MVP (Most Valuable Professional) award for his Visual C++ expertise.

Marc is the founder of the Belgian C++ Users Group (`www.becpp.org`), author of *Professional C++* 2nd, 3rd, 4th, and 5th editions (Wiley/Wrox), coauthor of *C++ Standard Library Quick Reference* 1st and 2nd editions (Apress), technical editor for numerous books for several publishers, and a regular speaker at the CppCon C++ conference. He maintains a blog at `www.nuonsoft.com/blog/` and is passionate about traveling and gastronomic restaurants.

Introduction

Welcome to *Beginning C++23*. This book is a revised and updated version of Ivor Horton's original one called *Beginning ANSI C++*. It teaches the essentials of the C++ language and Standard Library features. We'll start with the basics and gradually guide you to the point where you can write your own C++ applications. We by no means aim to cover every single advanced language feature—properly explaining those you'll need daily will serve you much better—nor could we possibly explore all nooks and corners of C++'s vast and ever-growing Standard Library. Regardless, with the firm foundations and knowledge you'll get from this book, you should have no difficulty extending the depth and scope of your C++ expertise going forward.

We assume no prior programming knowledge. If you are keen to learn and have an aptitude for thinking logically, getting a grip on C++ will be easier than you might imagine. By developing C++ skills, you'll be learning a language that is already used by millions and that provides the capability for application development in just about any context.

C++ is powerful. Very powerful. Arguably, more powerful even than most programming languages. So, yes, like with any powerful tool, you can wield some considerable damage if you use it without proper training. We often compare C++ to a Swiss Army knife: age-old, trusted, incredibly versatile, yet potentially mind-boggling and full of pointy things that could really hurt you. But once someone tells you what all those pointy things are for and teaches you some elementary knife safety rules, you'll never have to look for another pocket knife again.

C++ does not need to be dangerous or difficult at all. C++ today is much more accessible than many assume. The language has come a long way since its conception nearly 40 years ago. We've learned how to wield all its mighty blades and tools in the safest and most effective way possible. And more importantly, the C++ language and its Standard Library have evolved accordingly to facilitate this. The past decade has seen the rise of what is now known as *modern C++*. Modern C++ emphasizes the use of newer, more expressive, and safer language features combined with tried and tested best practices and coding guidelines. Once you know and apply a handful of simple rules and techniques, C++ loses much of its complexity. The key is that someone properly and gradually explains not simply what you *can* do with C++ but rather what you *should* do with C++. And that's where this book comes in!

With every revision of the book, we go to great lengths to keep it in line with the new, modern era of C++ programming we're living in. We pick and choose those improvements and extensions to the language that are most relevant to those beginning C++. The C++ language in this book corresponds to the latest International Organization for Standardization (ISO) standard, commonly referred to as *C++23*. The book introduces all relevant shiny blades and pointy things C++23 has to offer—both old and new—using many hands-on coding samples and exercises. We've made sure to always explain which tool is best to use for which purpose, why that is the case, and how to avoid getting cut. We've made sure that you will begin C++ from day one, using the safe, productive, modern programming style that employers will expect from you tomorrow.

Using the Book

To learn C++ with this book, you'll need a compiler that conforms to the C++23 standard and a text editor suitable for working with program code. Several currently available compilers support, to some extent, C++23 features, many of which are free.

GCC and Clang are free, open source compilers with solid and rapidly increasing support for the latest versions of the language. Installing these compilers and putting them together with a suitable editor can be a little tricky if you are new to this kind of thing. An easy way to install a compiler along with a suitable editor is to download a free integrated development environment (IDEs) such as Code::Blocks or Qt Creator. Such IDEs support complete program development for several compilers, including GCC and Clang.

Another possibility is to use the commercial Microsoft Visual C++ IDE that runs under Microsoft Windows. The Community edition is free for individual use and small professional teams, and its support for C++23 is on par with GCC and Clang. With Visual Studio, you get a comprehensive, easy-to-use professional editor and debugger, as well as support for other languages, such as C# and JavaScript.

There are other compilers that support C++23 as well, which you can find with a quick online search.

▓ **Note**   At the time of writing, no compiler fully supports C++23. If the past is any guide, though, we are confident they will catch up soon. Also, with only a few minimal workarounds, we were able to compile and execute all sample C++23 code with our primary compiler. In the online code repository of the book, you can find an overview of tips and workarounds that should help you get started with either one of the major compilers.

We've organized the material in this book to be read sequentially, so you should start at the beginning and keep going until you reach the end. However, no one ever learned programming by just reading a book. You'll only learn how to program in C++ by writing code, so make sure you key in all the examples—don't just copy them from the download files—and compile and execute the code that you've keyed in. This might seem tedious at times, but it's surprising how much just typing in C++ statements will help your understanding, especially when you're struggling with some of the ideas. If an example doesn't work, resist the temptation to return to the book to see why. Try to figure out from your code what is wrong. This is good practice for what you'll have to do when you are developing C++ applications for real.

Making mistakes is a fundamental part of the learning process, and the exercises should provide you with ample opportunity for that. It's a good idea to dream up a few exercises of your own. If you are unsure how to do something, just have a go before looking it up. The more mistakes you make, the greater the insight you'll have into what can, and does, go wrong. Make sure you attempt all the exercises, and remember, don't look at the solutions until you're sure that you can't work them out yourself. Most of these exercises just involve a direct application of what's covered in a chapter—they're just practice, in other words—but some also require a bit of thought or inspiration.

We wish you every success with C++. Above all, enjoy it!

Ivor Horton
Peter Van Weert

CHAPTER 1

▨ ▨ ▨

Basic Ideas

In this book, we sometimes use certain code in the examples before explaining it in detail. This chapter is intended to help you when this occurs by presenting an overview of the major elements of C++ and how they hang together. We'll also explain a few concepts relating to your computer's representation of numbers and characters.

In this chapter, you'll learn

- What is meant by *modern C++*

- What the terms *C++11*, *C++14*, *C++17*, *C++20*, and *C++23* mean

- What the C++ Standard Library is

- What the elements of a C++ program are

- How to document your program code

- How your C++ code becomes an executable program

- How object-oriented programming differs from procedural programming

- What binary, hexadecimal, and octal number systems are

- What floating-point numbers are

- How a computer represents numbers and letters using nothing but bits and bytes

- What Unicode is

Modern C++

Created in the early 1980s by Danish computer scientist Bjarne Stroustrup, C++ is one of the oldest programming languages still in active use. Despite its age, however, C++ is still standing strong, steadily maintaining its top-five position in popularity rankings for programming languages. Just about any kind of program can be written in C++, from device drivers to operating systems and from payroll and administrative programs to games. Major operating systems, browsers, office suites, email clients, multimedia players, database systems—name one, and chances are it's written at least partly in C++.

Above all else, C++ is best suited for applications where performance matters, such as applications that process large amounts of data, computer games with high-end graphics, or apps for embedded or mobile devices. Programs written in C++ remain many times faster than those written in most other popular languages. C++ is also very effective for developing applications across an enormous range of computing devices and environments, including personal computers, workstations, mainframe computers, tablets, and mobile phones.

© Ivor Horton and Peter Van Weert 2023
I. Horton and P. Van Weert, *Beginning C++23*, https://doi.org/10.1007/978-1-4842-9343-0_1

The C++ programming language may be old, but it's still very much alive and kicking. Or, better yet, it's *again* very much alive and kicking. After its initial development and standardization in the 1980s, C++ evolved very slowly and remained essentially unchanged for decades. But all this changed in 2011 when the International Organization for Standardization (ISO) released a new version of the formal C++ standard. This edition of the standard, commonly referred to as *C++11*, revived C++ and catapulted the somewhat dated language right back into the 21st century. It modernized the language and the way we use it so profoundly that you could almost call C++11 a completely new language.

Programming using the features of C++11 and beyond is referred to as *modern C++*. In this book, we'll show you that modern C++ is about more than simply embracing the language's newer features—lambda expressions (Chapter 19), auto type deduction (Chapter 2), and range-based for loops (Chapter 5), to name a few. More than anything else, modern C++ is about modern ways of programming, the consensus of what constitutes a good programming style. It's about applying an implicit set of guidelines and best practices, all designed to make C++ programming easier, less error-prone, and more productive. A modern, safe C++ programming style replaces traditional low-level language constructs with the use of containers (Chapters 5 and 20), smart pointers (Chapter 6), or other RAII techniques (Chapter 16). It emphasizes exceptions to report errors (Chapter 16), passing objects by value through move semantics (Chapter 18), leveraging algorithms and range adaptors (Chapter 20) instead of writing loops (Chapter 5), and so on. Of course, all this probably means little to nothing to you yet. But not to worry; in this book, we'll gradually introduce everything you need to know to program in C++ today!

The C++11 standard also appears to have revived the C++ community, which has been actively working hard on extending and further improving the language ever since. Every three years, a new version of the standard is published. After C++11 came *C++14, C++17, C++20*, and, most recently, C++23.

After some smaller updates in C++14 and C++17, C++20 was again a major milestone. As C++11 did a decade before, C++20 changed the way we program in C++ forever. Modules (Chapter 11) obsolete C++'s antiquated ways of composing larger programs (Appendix A), ranges revolutionized the way we inspect and manipulate data (Chapter 20), concepts facilitate the creation of easy-to-use templates (Chapter 21), and so on.

The latest update of the language is C++23. While perhaps not as groundbreaking as C++11 or C++20, C++23 does again bring many welcome improvements: the std umbrella module reliefs you from having to remember in which module of the Standard Library everything goes (see later this chapter), std::print() and println() relief you from working directly with streams (Chapter 2), std::expected<> provides an interesting alternative to exceptions (Chapters 9 and 17), ranges::to<>() eases range-container and container-container conversions (Chapter 20), and so on.

The best thing about all these modern features—particularly for someone beginning C++ today—is that they made the language easier, more elegant, and more accessible than ever before.

This book relates to C++ as defined by C++23. All code should work on any compiler that complies with the C++23 edition of the standard. The good news is that most major compilers work hard to keep up with all the latest developments, so if your compiler does not support a particular feature yet, it soon will. In the meantime, our online source code repository also contains pointers on how to work around any missing recent language features.

Standard Libraries

If you had to create everything from scratch every time you wrote a program, it would be tedious indeed. The same functionality is required in many programs—reading data from the keyboard, calculating a square root, sorting data records into a particular sequence, and so on. C++ comes with a large amount of prewritten code that provides facilities such as these, so you don't have to write the code yourself. All this standard code is defined in the *Standard Library*.

The Standard Library is a huge collection of routines and definitions that provide the functionality required by many programs. Examples are numerical calculations, string processing, input and output, concurrency and synchronization, sorting and searching, and organizing and managing data. Over the course of this book, we will introduce key functionality from over 35 submodules of the Standard Library. More than enough to get you going, surely, but only scratching the surface regardless—the C++23 Standard Library contains over 100 modules. The Standard Library is so vast that you need several books to properly elaborate its capabilities. *Beginning STL* (Apress, 2015) is a companion tutorial on using the Standard Template Library, the classical subset of the C++ Standard Library for managing and processing data we also briefly introduce in Chapter 20 (though with far fewer examples). For a compact, comprehensive overview of everything the C++23 Standard Library has to offer, we also recommend the forthcoming book *C++23 Standard Library Quick Reference* (Apress, 2024).

Given the scope of the language and the extent of the library, it's not unusual for a beginner to find C++ somewhat daunting. It is too extensive to learn in its entirety from a single book. However, you don't need to learn all of C++ to be able to write substantial programs. You can approach the language step-by-step, in which case it really isn't difficult. An analogy might be learning to drive a car. You can certainly become a competent and safe driver without necessarily having the expertise, knowledge, and experience to drive in the Indianapolis 500. With this book, you can learn everything you need to program effectively in C++. By the time you reach the end, you'll be confidently writing your own applications. You'll also be well equipped to explore the full extent of C++ and its Standard Library.

C++ Program Concepts

We'll jump straight in with a complete, fully working C++ program. We'll use this example as a base for discussing some more general aspects of C++. However, there will be much more detail on everything we discuss in this section later in the book.

```cpp
// Ex1_01.cpp - A complete C++ program
import std;              // This line makes the entire Standard Library available,
                         // including the std::println() functionality used below
int main()
{
  int answer {42};     // Defines the variable answer with value 42
  std::println("The answer to life, the universe, and everything is {}.", answer);
  return 0;
}
```

Source Files

The file outlined earlier, Ex1_01.cpp, is in the code download for the book. The file extension, .cpp, indicates that this is a C++ *source file* or *implementation file*. Source files contain function bodies and, thus, most of the executable code in a program. The names of source files usually have the extension .cpp, although other extensions such as .cc, .cxx, or .c++ are sometimes used to identify a C++ source file.

For the first ten chapters, all your programs will be small enough to fit in a single C++ source file. Real-life programs, however, are often composed of thousands of files. Not all source files, mind you. In larger programs, you use other kinds of files as well, mostly to separate out the interfaces of the program's various components (function prototypes, class definitions, module interfaces, and so on) from their implementation in a corresponding source file. In Chapter 11, you will learn about the various kinds of files used to define modules, and in Appendix A, we review the old-fashioned *header files* that are used by legacy code to compose larger programs.

Comments and Whitespace

The first line in Ex1_01 is this *comment*:

```
// Ex1_01.cpp - A complete C++ program
```

You add comments that document your program code to make it easier to understand how it works. The compiler ignores everything that follows two successive forward slashes on a line, even if these slashes follow code on a line. The example contains two instances of comments that follow a line of code like that.

▓ **Note**   In this book, we identify the file for each working example by adding the corresponding filename in a comment on the first line (// Ex1_01.cpp - for the first example). These comments are only there for your convenience. In normal coding, there is no need to add them; they only introduce unnecessary maintenance overhead when renaming files.

Any *single-line* // comment (also known as *C++-style* comments) can also be written as a /* */ comment (also known as a *C-style* comment), as follows:

```
/* Ex1_01.cpp - A complete C++ program */
```

One advantage of the /* */ syntax is that you can use it to spread a comment over several lines. Here's an example:

```
/* This comment is
   over two lines.  */
```

Everything between /* and */ will be ignored by the compiler. You can embellish this sort of comment to make it stand out. For instance:

```
/*** Ex1_01.cpp **********\
 * A complete C++ program *
\*************************/
```

You can also use /* */ to add comments at the start or even in the middle of a line of code as well—something you cannot accomplish using // comments. To illustrate the different uses of /* */ comments, here is an even further overembellished version of Ex1_01.

```
import std;        /* This line makes the entire Standard Library available,
                      including the std::println() functionality used below */
int main(/* Not always empty: see Chapter 8... */)
{
  int answer {42};   /* Defines the variable answer with value 42 */
  std::println("The answer to life, the universe, and everything is {}.", answer);
  /* This last line is optional in main(): see later --> */ return 0;
}
```

▓ **Note**   Because you are still learning, we often use code comments in this book to explain even the most basic lines of C++ code. Of course, you should not do this in real life, at least not nearly as extensively as we do here. In real life, for instance, you would never clarify the meaning of "int answer {42};" with a comment as we did in our initial example. Once you know and understand the syntax, well-written code should explain itself. Simply echoing code in a comment is considered bad practice. Ordinarily, you should only add comments to clarify or document aspects of your code that are not immediately obvious to its intended readers (typically you and/or your coworkers).

A concept related to comments is *whitespace*. Whitespace is any sequence of spaces, tabs, newlines, or form feed characters. Whitespace is generally ignored by the compiler, except when it is necessary for syntactic reasons to distinguish one element from another. Anywhere you can add extra whitespace, you can also add /* */ comments.

The Standard Library and Modules

The first non-comment line in Ex1_01.cpp is this *import declaration*:

```
import std;
```

This line *imports* the module named std, thus making all types and functionality that the module named std *exports* available in the Ex1_01.cpp source file. The std module is special in the sense that it comes pre-configured with any C++23-compliant compiler. By importing it, you gain access to everything[1] the *C++ Standard Library* has to offer.

In particular, the std module exports the std::println() function templates used by Ex1_01. If you omit the declaration to import the std module from Ex1_01.cpp, the source file will no longer compile because then the compiler no longer knows what std::println() is.

▓ **Note**   The std module is new in C++23. Prior to C++23, you had to know which of the over 150 modules of the Standard Library to import for each specific functionality. For instance, to use std::println() without importing std, you'd have to import the <print> module (notice the angular brackets). While importing individual modules is certainly still possible, it is far easier to simply import the std umbrella module.

Of course, std and its submodules are not the only modules you can import. In the second half of the book, you'll create and use modules that export types and functions of your own creation. And any non-trivial C++ program will leverage several third-party libraries as well, for instance, to create a graphical user interface, to interact with databases or networks, and so on.

---

[1] Well, *almost* everything. As seen in Appendix A, macros are never exported by a module. Examples include the assert() macro from <cassert>, the feature test macros from <version>, and so on. To use these and other macros, you either need to explicitly include the corresponding *header file* (#include <cassert>) or import the corresponding *header unit* (import <version>;). We refer you to Appendix A for more information on macros, headers, and #include directives. Luckily, you no longer need C-style macros that often, as C++ usually offers equivalent or superior alternatives.

▨ **Note**   For the time being, third-party libraries are not likely to come in the form of modules. To make their functionality available, you therefore have to use `#include` directives instead of `import` declarations. We refer you to Appendix A for more information.

Functions

Every C++ program consists of at least one and usually many more *functions*. A function is a named block of code that carries out a well-defined operation such as "read the input data," "calculate the average value," or "output the results." You execute, or *call*, a function in a program using its name. All the executable code in a program appears within functions. There must be one function with the name `main`, and execution always starts automatically with this function. The `main()` function usually calls other functions, which in turn can call other functions, and so on. Functions provide several important advantages:

- A program that is broken down into discrete functions is easier to develop and test.

- You can reuse a function in several different places in a program, which makes the program smaller than if you coded the operation in each place that it is needed.

- You can often reuse a function in many different programs, thus saving time and effort.

- Large programs are typically developed by a team of programmers. Each team member is responsible for programming a set of functions that are a well-defined subset of the whole program. Without a functional structure, this would be impractical.

The program in `Ex1_01.cpp` consists of just the function `main()`. The first line of the function is as follows:

```
int main()
```

This is called the *function header*, which identifies the function. Here, `int` is a type name that defines the type of value that the `main()` function returns when it finishes execution—an integer. An integer is a number without a fractional component; that is, 23 and –2048 are integers, while 3.1415 and ¼ are not. In general, the parentheses following a name in a function definition enclose the specification for information to be passed to the function when you call it. There's nothing between the parentheses in this instance, but there could be. You'll learn how you specify the type of information to be passed to a function when it is executed in Chapter 8. We'll always put parentheses after a function name in the text—like we did with `main()`—to distinguish it from other things that are code.

The executable code for a function is always enclosed between curly braces. The opening brace follows the function header.

Statements

A *statement* is a basic unit in a C++ program. A statement always ends with a semicolon, and it's the semicolon that marks the end of a statement, not the end of the line. A statement defines something, such as a computation or an action that is to be performed. Everything a program does is specified by statements. Statements are executed in sequence until there is a statement that causes the sequence to be altered. You'll learn about statements that can change the execution sequence in Chapter 4. There are three statements in main() in Ex1_01. The first defines a variable, which is a named bit of memory for storing data of some kind. In this case, the variable has the name answer and can store integer values:

```
int answer {42};    // Defines answer with the value 42
```

The type, int, appears first, preceding the name. This specifies the kind of data that can be stored—integers. Note the space between int and answer. One or more whitespace characters are essential here to separate the type name from the variable name; without the space, the compiler would see the name intanswer, which it would not understand. An initial value for answer appears between the braces following the variable name, so it starts out storing 42. There's a space between answer and {42}, but it's not essential. Any of the following definitions are valid as well:

```
int one{ 1 };
int two{2};
int    three      {
    3
};
```

The compiler mostly ignores superfluous whitespace. However, you should use whitespace in a consistent fashion to make your code more readable.

There's a somewhat redundant comment at the end of the first statement explaining what we just described, but it does demonstrate that you can add a comment to a statement. The whitespace preceding the // is also not mandatory, but it is desirable.

You can enclose several statements between a pair of curly braces, { }, in which case they're referred to as a *statement block*. The body of a function is an example of a block, as you saw in Ex1_01, where the statements in the main() function appear between curly braces. A statement block is also referred to as a *compound statement* because, in most circumstances, it can be considered as a single statement, as you'll see when we look at decision-making capabilities in Chapter 4 and loops in Chapter 5. Wherever you can put a single statement, you can equally well put a block of statements between braces. Consequently, blocks can be placed inside other blocks, which is a concept called *nesting*. Blocks can be nested, one within another, to any depth.

Text Output

As of C++23, the preferred mechanism for outputting text to the computer's screen is through functions such as std::println() and std::print(). We will use these in nearly every example in this book. The second statement in Ex1_01 constitutes the first basic case:

```
std::println("The answer to life, the universe, and everything is {}.", answer);
```

A sequence of characters between double quotes, such as
"The answer to life, the universe, and everything is {}", is called a *string literal*. You will learn all about working with strings in Chapters 5 to 7.

std::println() simply outputs whatever string you pass it, except that all sequences surrounded by curly braces—called *replacement fields*—are substituted with textual representations of one of the subsequent function arguments. In our example, there is only one (empty) replacement field and, correspondingly, only one value to format, answer. The replacement field is therefore substituted with "42", the natural textual representation of the current value of the integer variable answer. The resulting output is as follows:

```
The answer to life, the universe, and everything is 42.
```

In general, you can use any number of replacement fields, and you can add *format specifiers* to the replacement fields to override the default formatting scheme. Here is a sneak preview:

```
std::println("The answer to {} is {:!^12b}", "the ultimate question", answer);
```

Unless you have prior programming experience, :!^12b no doubt looks like some random grawlix[2]. In reality, this format specifier instructs std::println() to output answer as a binary number (b), centered (^) in a field that is 12 characters wide, filling the remainder of the thus overly wide field with exclamation marks (!). The resulting output is therefore as follows:

```
The answer to the ultimate question is !!!101010!!!
```

We explain string formatting in more detail in Chapter 2.

Next to std::println(), we will also regularly use std::print(). The only difference with std::println() is that std::print() does not add a line break at the end. The next four statements are equivalent to our initial std::println() statement:

```
std::print("The answer to life, ");
std::print("the universe, ");
std::print("and everything ");
std::println("is {}", answer);
```

As explained in the section on escape sequences in Chapter 2, you can add line breaks yourself by adding \n anywhere in your string literal. The following std::print() statement is therefore again equivalent to the std::println() statement of Ex1_01:

```
std::print("The answer to life, the universe, and everything is {}.\n", answer);
```

▓ **Caution** Unlike in several other programming languages, you cannot invoke std::print() or std::println() without a format string. That is, you cannot, for instance, use std::println(value) to output only the value of answer. Instead, you use statements of the form std::println("{}", value). You also cannot invoke std::println() without an argument to output a line break, and nothing else. Instead, you use either std::println("") or std::print("\n").

---

[2]A grawlix is a string of symbols, such as "@#$%&!" used in comics to replace swear words.

return Statements

The last statement in main() is a return statement. A return statement ends a function and returns control to where the function was called. In this case, it ends the function and returns control to the operating system. A return statement may or may not return a value. This particular return statement returns 0 to the operating system. Returning 0 to the operating system indicates that the program ended normally. You can return nonzero values, such as 1, 2, and so forth, to indicate different abnormal end conditions. The return statement in Ex1_01.cpp is optional, so you could omit it. This is because if execution runs past the last statement in main(), it is equivalent to executing return 0.

■ **Note**   main() is the only function for which omitting return is equivalent to returning zero. For any other function, the compiler will never presume to know which value to return by default. Any other function with return type int normally ends with an explicit return statement.

You can also end a function without returning a value, for instance, by throwing an exception. We will have more to say about this in Chapter 16.

Namespaces

A large project will involve several programmers working concurrently. This potentially creates a problem with names. The same name might be used by different programmers for different things, which could at least cause some confusion and may, at worst, cause things to go wrong. Accidental use of names from external libraries could also cause problems. The Standard Library alone, for instance, defines a lot of names, more than you can possibly remember. And with every new library release come new names, which, if you're not careful, could start conflicting with names in your own sources. *Namespaces* are designed to overcome these difficulties.

A *namespace* is a family name that prefixes all the names declared within the namespace. The names in the Standard Library are all defined within a namespace that has the name std (short for "standard"). println is a name from the Standard Library, so the full name is std::println. Those two colons together, ::, have a fancy title: the *scope resolution operator*. We'll have more to say about it later. Here, it separates the namespace name, std, from the names in the Standard Library, such as print and println. All names from the C++ Standard Library (except for the names of macros; see Appendix A) are prefixed with std.

The code for a namespace looks like this:

```
namespace my_space {
    // All names declared in here need to be prefixed
    // with my_space when they are referenced from outside.
    // For example, a min() function defined in here
    // would be referred to outside this namespace as my_space::min()
}
```

Everything between the braces is within the my_space namespace. You'll find out more about defining your own namespaces in Chapter 11.

■ **Caution**   The main() function must not be defined within a namespace. Things that are not defined in a namespace exist in the *global namespace*, which has no name.

■ **Tip** C++ Standard Library headers such as `<cmath>` or `<cstddef>` have their roots in the C Standard Library (C++ Standard Library headers that mirror headers of the C Standard Library all have names prefixed with the letter c). If you include these headers, some implementations make the C Standard Library names available both in the global namespace (optional) and in the `std` namespace (required). They do this to ease the porting of C code (C does not have namespaces). Importing the `std` module, however, no longer introduces any names in the global namespace. Everything imported by the `std` module resides in the `std` namespace, including all functionality inherited from the C Standard Library. In legacy code that extensively uses C functions and types (`fopen()`, `size_t`, and so on) without qualifying the `std` namespace, you could consider importing the `std.compat` module instead. Unlike `std`, `std.compat` exports all C library facilities in both the global namespace and the `std` namespace. In new code, we recommend you don't use this backward compatibility option.

Identifiers and Keywords

`Ex1_01.cpp` contains a definition for a variable with the *identifier* `answer`, and it uses the *identifier* `println` defined somewhere by the Standard Library. Lots of things need identifiers in a program, and there are precise rules for defining identifiers. In essence, these rules are:

- An identifier can be any sequence of upper- or lowercase letters, digits, or underscore characters, _.

- An identifier must begin with either a letter or an underscore (although the latter is not recommended; see later).

- Identifiers are case-sensitive.

Here are some identifiers that are clearly valid under these rules:

```
toe_count  shoeSize  Box  doohickey  Doohickey  number1  x2  y2  pValue  out_of_range
```

Uppercase and lowercase are differentiated, so `doohickey` is not the same identifier as `Doohickey`. You can see examples of conventions for writing identifiers that consist of two or more words; you can capitalize the second and subsequent words or separate them with underscores.

The C++ standard allows identifiers to be of any length. At times a particular compiler will impose some sort of limit, but this is normally sufficiently large that it doesn't represent a serious constraint (the smallest limit we found is 2,048 characters…).

Prior to C++23, the standard only required compilers to support letters a to z or A to Z and digits 0 to 9 in identifiers. These antiquated Anglocentric restrictions are all good for using English identifiers, but not everyone is Anglophone. In fact, the vast majority of the world's population is not. And to express yourself using virtually any other language, an alphabet of 63 characters simply does not cut it. In `Ex01_01`, for instance, Francophones may want to use réponse instead of `answer`, Russophones ответ, Sinophones 回答, Arabophones جواب, and so on.

C++23 therefore formally generalized the rules of what constitutes a valid identifier (something most compilers had already done as well, in similar ways). Without going too much into the technicalities, the rules are now roughly as follows:

- An identifier can start with any character that you'd informally refer to as a letter. This still includes the letters a to z and A to Z, but also letters from virtually any other character set. An identifier can also technically start with an underscore (see later).

- The remainder of an identifier allows for these same "letter" characters, as well as underscores, decimal numbers (0 to 9, of course, but also, for instance, ๐ to ๙, or ໐ to ໙), and various other letter-related characters (mostly characters that combine with others to form more complex "letters," such as the ¨ in ö, the ੋ੭ in ਹਿੰਦੀ, etc.).

These rules allow for all the aforementioned identifiers, as well as most words in most languages. As permissive as this is, though, there are still characters you cannot use. Punctuation characters (-, ', ", &, (, ., and so on), spaces, currency symbols, mathematical symbols, superscript and subscript numbers, and emojis (☺...) are but a few examples of character categories that are, as a rule, disallowed. These are some examples of invalid identifiers:

```
quarante-deux   don't  R&B   ∞   x⁴   🙈    $
```

With roughly 131,975 characters to choose from to begin an identifier, however, and an additional 3,078 to use in the remainder of an identifier, we're sure you can easily work around these limitations.

```
quarante_deux  doNot Rhythm_and_Blues  infinity  x4  言わざる  dollar
```

As a final restriction, there are certain words and reserved identifiers that you are not allowed to use as identifiers. *Keywords*, most notably, have a specific meaning in C++, so you must not use them for other purposes. `class`, `int`, `namespace`, `throw`, and `catch` are examples. Other identifiers that you are not supposed to use include the following:

- Identifiers that begin with two consecutive underscores

- Identifiers that begin with an underscore followed by an uppercase letter

- Within the global namespace, all names that begin with an underscore

While compilers often won't really complain if you use these, the problem is that such names might clash either with names generated by the compiler or with names that are used internally by your Standard Library implementation. Notice that the common denominator with these *reserved identifiers* is that they all start with an underscore. To make life simple, our advice is this:

▒ **Tip**   Do not use identifiers that start with an underscore.

Streams

Input and output in C++ are, as a rule, performed using *streams*. To output data, you write it to an *output stream*, and to input data, you read it from an *input stream*. A *stream* is an abstract representation of a source of data or a data sink. When your program executes, each stream is tied to a specific device that is the source of data in the case of an input stream and the destination for data in the case of an output stream. The advantage of having an abstract representation of a source or sink for data is that the programming is then the same regardless of the device the stream represents. You can read a disk file in essentially the same way as you read from the keyboard.

  `std::print()` and `std::println()` are little more than thin layers on top of streams. In essence, the `std::println()` statement in the `main()` function of `Ex1_01` is analogous to either one of these statements:

```
std::cout << std::format("The answer to life, the universe, and everything is {}.", answer)
        << std::endl;
std::cout << "The answer to life, the universe, and everything is " << answer << std::endl;
```

The standard output and input streams in C++ are called `std::cout` and `std::cin`, respectively, and by default, they correspond to your computer's screen and keyboard. You'll be reading input from `std::cin` in Chapter 2 and later chapters.

`std::format()` is similar to `std::print()`, except that instead of streaming directly to the standard output stream, `std::format()` returns the formatted character sequence encapsulated in a `std::string` object (see Chapter 7). This is why `std::print()` is effectively analogous to streaming the result of `std::format()` to `std::cout`, as we did in the first line of our example.

`<<`, finally, is the *stream insertion operator* that transfers data to a stream. In Chapter 2, you'll meet the *stream extraction operator*, `>>`, which similarly reads data from a stream. Whatever appears to the right of each `<<` is transferred to `std::cout`. You can insert as many strings or other values in one statement as you want (we'll clarify how this works exactly in Chapter 13). Inserting `std::endl` to `std::cout` causes a new line to be written to the stream and the output buffer to be flushed. Flushing the output buffer ensures that the output appears immediately.

Compared to working directly with `std::cout`, working with `std::print()` and `std::println()` is generally both more elegant and efficient (see the next chapter for more convincing evidence). This is why we won't use output streams that often anymore as of this edition of the book. But because output streams remain an important concept in C++ in general, we'll briefly return to working with streams at the end of the next chapter to introduce the basic principles.

Classes and Objects

A *class* is a block of code that defines a data type. A class has a name that is the name for the type. An item of data of a class type is an *object*. You use the class type name when you create variables that can store objects of your data type. Defining your own data types enables you to specify a solution to a problem in terms of the problem. If you were writing a program processing information about students, for example, you could define a `Student` type. Your `Student` type could incorporate all the characteristics of a student—such as age, gender, or school record—that were required by the program.

You will learn about creating your own classes and programming with objects in Chapters 12 through 15. Nevertheless, you'll be using objects of specific Standard Library types long before that. Examples include vectors in Chapter 5 and strings in Chapter 7. Even the `std::cout` and `std::cin` streams are technically objects. But not to worry; you'll find that working with objects is easy enough, much easier than creating your own classes, for instance. Objects are usually intuitive because they're mostly designed to behave like real-life entities (although some do model more abstract concepts, such as input or output streams, or low-level C++ constructs, such as data arrays and character sequences).

Templates

You sometimes need several similar classes or functions in a program where the code differs only in the kind of data that is processed. A *template* is a recipe that you create to be used by the compiler to generate code automatically for a function or class customized for a particular type or types. The compiler uses a *function template* to generate one or more of a family of functions. It uses a *class template* to generate classes. Each template has a name that you use when you want the compiler to create an instance of it. The Standard Library uses templates extensively.

Defining function and class templates are the subjects of Chapters 10 and 17; and in Chapter 21, we cover how to make templates safer and easier to use by adding *concept expressions*. But, again, you'll use certain Standard Library templates throughout earlier chapters already, such as instantiations of certain elementary utility function templates such as `std::min()` and `max()`, or of the `std::vector<>` and `array<>` class templates you first encounter in Chapter 5. Even the `std::string` class you'll learn to master in Chapter 7 is an instantiation of a class template (`std::basic_string<>`), although we doubt you'd even notice if we hadn't pointed it out.

Code Appearance and Programming Style

The way in which you arrange your code can have a significant effect on how easy it is to understand. There are two basic aspects to this. First, you can use tabs and/or spaces to indent program statements in a manner that provides visual cues to their logic, and you can arrange matching braces that define program blocks in a consistent way so that the relationships between the blocks are apparent. Second, you can spread a single statement over two or more lines when that will improve the readability of your program.

There are many different styles of code. The following table shows three of many possible options for how a code sample could be arranged.

Style 1	Style 2	Style 3
| ```c++
namespace mine
{
 int gcd(int x, int y)
 {
  if (y == 0)
  {
   return std::abs(x);
  }
  else
  {
   return gcd(y, x % y);
  }
 }
}
``` | ```c++
namespace mine {
 int gcd(int x, int y) {
  if (y==0) {
   return std::abs(x);
  } else {
   return gcd(y, x % y);
  }
 }
}
``` | ```c++
namespace mine {
 int gcd(int x, int y)
 {
  if (y==0)
   return std::abs(x);
  else
   return gcd(y, x % y);
 }
}
``` |

We will use Style 1 for examples in the book. Over time, you will surely develop your own, based either on personal preferences or on company policies. It is recommended, at some point, to pick one style that suits you and then use this consistently throughout your code. Not only does a consistent code presentation style look good, but it also makes your code easier to read.

A particular convention for arranging matching braces and indenting statements is only one of several aspects of one's *programming style*. Other important aspects include conventions for naming variables, types, and functions, and the use of (structured) comments. The question of what constitutes a good programming style can be highly subjective at times, though some guidelines and conventions are objectively superior. The general idea, though, is that code that conforms to a consistent style is easier to read and understand, which helps to avoid introducing errors. Throughout the book, we'll regularly give you advice as you fashion your own programming style.

▒ **Tip**　One of the best tips we can give you regarding good programming style is to choose clear, descriptive names for all your variables, functions, and types.

Creating an Executable

Creating an executable from your C++ source code is basically a three-step process. In the first step, the *preprocessor* processes all preprocessing directives. Traditionally, one of its key tasks was to copy the entire contents of all #included headers into your source files, yet this practice will be phased out with the introduction of modules in C++20. We discuss #include and other preprocessing directives in Appendix
```

A. In the second step, your *compiler* processes each source file to produce an *object file* that contains the machine code equivalent of the preprocessed code. In the third step, the *linker* combines the binary files for a program into a file containing the complete executable program.

Figure 1-1 shows three source files being compiled to produce three *object files* (the preprocessing stage is not shown explicitly). The filename extension that's used to identify object files varies between different machine environments, so it isn't shown here. The source files that make up your program may be compiled independently in separate compiler runs, or most compilers will allow you to compile them in a single run. Either way, the compiler treats each source file as a separate entity and produces one object file for each .cpp file. The link step then combines the object files for a program, along with any library functions that are necessary, into a single executable file.

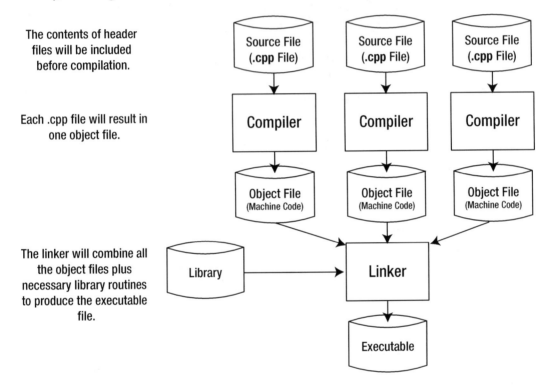

Figure 1-1. *The compile and link process*

In the first half of the book, your programs will consist of a single source file. In Chapter 11, we will show you how to compose a larger program consisting of multiple modules and source files.

▦ **Note**   The concrete steps you must follow to get from your source code to a functioning executable differ from compiler to compiler. While most of our examples are small enough to compile and link through a series of command-line instructions, it is probably easier to use an *integrated development environment* (IDE) instead. Modern IDEs offer a very user-friendly graphical user interface to edit, compile, link, run, and debug your programs. References to the most popular compilers and IDEs can easily be found online.

In practice, compilation is an iterative process because you're almost certain to have made typographical and other errors in the code. Once you've eliminated these from each source file, you can progress to the link step, where you may find that yet more errors surface. Even when the link step produces an executable, your program may still contain logical errors; that is, it doesn't produce the results you expect. To fix these, you must go back and modify the source code and try to compile it once more. You continue this process until your program works as you think it should. As soon as you declare to the world at large that your program works, someone will discover several obvious errors that you should have found. It hasn't been proven beyond doubt so far as we know, but it's widely believed that any program larger than a given size will always contain errors. It's best not to dwell on this thought when flying.[3]

Procedural and Object-Oriented Programming

Historically, procedural programming is the way almost all programs were written. To create a procedural programming solution to a problem, you focus on the process that your program must implement to solve the problem. Here is a rough outline of what you do once the requirements have been defined precisely:

- You create a clear, high-level definition of the overall process that your program will implement.

- You segment the overall process into workable units of computation that are, as much as possible, self-contained. These will usually correspond to functions.

- You code the functions in terms of processing basic types of data: numerical data, single characters, and character strings.

Apart from the common requirement of starting with a clear specification of what the problem is, the object-oriented approach to solving the same problem is quite different:

- From the problem specification, you determine what types of *objects* the problem is concerned with. For example, if your program deals with baseball players, you're likely to identify BaseballPlayer as one of the types of data your program will work with. If your program is an accounting package, you may well want to define objects of type Account and type Transaction. You also identify the set of *operations* that the program will need to carry out on each type of object. This will result in a set of application-specific data types that you will use in writing your program.

- You produce a detailed design for each of the new data types that your problem requires, including the operations that can be carried out with each object type.

- You express the logic of the program in terms of the new data types you've defined and the kinds of operations they allow.

The program code for an object-oriented solution to a problem will be completely unlike that for a procedural solution and almost certainly easier to understand. It will also be a lot easier to maintain. The amount of design time required for an object-oriented solution tends to be greater than for a procedural solution. However, the coding and testing phase of an object-oriented program tends to be shorter and less troublesome, so the overall development time is likely to be roughly the same in either case.

---

[3] The total flight software of a Boeing 787 reportedly consists of about 14 *million* lines of code (about half of which is part of the avionics and online support systems). Knowing that some studies claim you can expect a few or even dozens of defects per *thousand* lines of code. Precisely. Best not to dwell...

To get an inkling of what an objected-oriented approach implies, suppose you're implementing a program dealing with various boxes. A feasible requirement of such a program would be to package several smaller boxes inside another larger box. In a procedural program, you would need to store each box's length, width, and height in a separate group of variables. The dimensions of a new box that could contain several other boxes would need to be calculated explicitly in terms of the dimensions of each box, according to whatever rules you had defined for packaging a set of boxes.

An object-oriented solution might involve first defining a Box data type. This would enable you to create variables that can reference objects of type Box and create Box objects. You could then define an operation that would add two Box objects together and produce a new Box object that could contain them. Using this operation, you could write statements like this:

```
bigBox = box1 + box2 + box3;
```

In this context, the + operation means much more than simple addition. The + operator applied to numerical values will work exactly as before, but for Box objects, it has a special meaning. Each of the variables in this statement is of type Box. The statement would create a new Box object big enough to contain box1, box2, and box3.

Being able to write statements like this is clearly much easier than having to deal with all the box dimensions separately, and the more complex the operations on boxes you take on, the greater the advantage is going to be. This is a trivial illustration, though, and there's a great deal more to the power of objects than you can see here. The purpose of this discussion is just to give you an idea of how readily problems solved using an object-oriented approach can be understood. Object-oriented programming is essentially about solving problems in terms of the entities to which the problems relates rather than in terms of the entities that computers are happy with: numbers and characters.

Representing Numbers

Numbers are represented in a variety of ways in a C++ program, and you need to understand the possibilities. If you are comfortable with binary, hexadecimal, and floating-point number representations, you can safely skip this bit.

Binary Numbers

First, let's consider exactly what a common, everyday decimal number, such as 324 or 911, means. Obviously, what we mean here is "three hundred and twenty-four" or "nine hundred and eleven." These are shorthand ways of saying "three hundreds" plus "two tens" plus "four," or "nine hundred" plus "one ten" plus "one." Putting this more precisely, we really mean this:

- 324 is $3 \times 10^2 + 2 \times 10^1 + 4 \times 10^0$, which is $3 \times 100 + 2 \times 10 + 4 \times 1$.

- 911 is $9 \times 10^2 + 1 \times 10^1 + 1 \times 10^0$, which is $9 \times 100 + 1 \times 10 + 1 \times 1$.

This is called *decimal notation* because it's built around powers of 10. We also say that we are representing numbers to *base 10* here because each digit position is a power of 10. Representing numbers in this way is handy for beings with ten fingers and/or ten toes, or indeed ten of any kind of appendage that can be used for counting. Your PC is rather less handy, being built mainly of switches that are either on or off. Your PC is okay for counting in twos but not spectacular at counting in tens. You're probably aware that this is why your computer represents numbers using base 2 rather than base 10. Representing numbers using base 2 is called the *binary system* of counting. Numbers in base 10 have digits that can be from 0 to 9. In general, for numbers in an arbitrary base, n, the digit in each position in a number can be from 0 to $n-1$. Thus, binary digits can be only 0 or 1. A binary number, such as 1101, breaks down like this:

$$1 \times 2^3 + 1 \times 2^2 + 0 \times 2^1 + 1 \times 2^0, \text{ which is } 1 \times 8 + 1 \times 4 + 0 \times 2 + 1 \times 1$$

This is 13 in the decimal system. In Table 1-1, you can see the decimal equivalents of all (positive) numbers you can represent using eight binary digits. A binary digit is more commonly known as a *bit*.

Table 1-1. *Decimal Equivalents of 8-Bit Binary Values*

Binary	Decimal	Binary	Decimal
0000 0000	0	1000 0000	128
0000 0001	1	1000 0001	129
0000 0010	2	1000 0010	130
...	...	...	...
0001 0000	16	1001 0000	144
0001 0001	17	1001 0001	145
...	...	...	...
0111 1100	124	1111 1100	252
0111 1101	125	1111 1101	253
0111 1110	126	1111 1110	254
0111 1111	127	1111 1111	255

Using the first seven bits, you can represent numbers from 0 to 127, which is a total of 128 different numbers. Using all eight bits, you get 256, or 2^8, numbers. In general, if you have n bits available, you can represent 2^n integers, with positive values from 0 to $2^n - 1$.

Adding binary numbers inside your computer is a piece of cake because the "carry" from adding corresponding digits can be only 0 or 1. This means that very simple—and thus excruciatingly fast—circuitry can handle the process. Figure 1-2 shows how the addition of two 8-bit binary values would work.

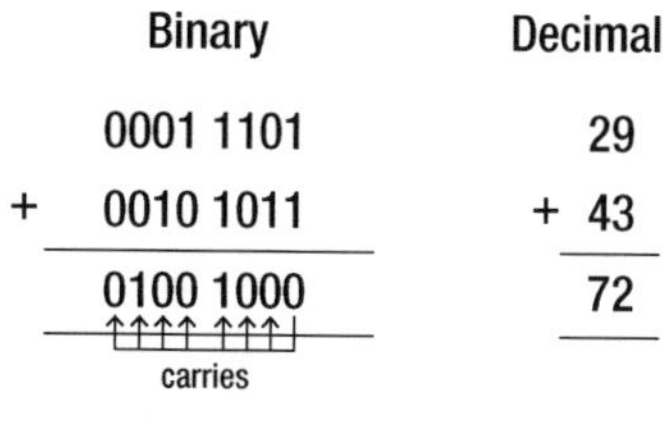

```
        Binary       Decimal

        0001 1101       29
    +   0010 1011     + 43
        ─────────      ────
        0100 1000       72
        ↑↑↑↑ ↑↑↑↓
          carries
```

Figure 1-2. *Adding binary values*

The addition operation adds corresponding bits in the operands, starting with the rightmost. Figure 1-2 shows that there is a "carry" of 1 to the next bit position for each of the first six bit positions. This is because each digit can be only 0 or 1. When you add 1 + 1, the result cannot be stored in the current bit position and is equivalent to adding 1 in the next bit position to the left.

Hexadecimal Numbers

When you are dealing with larger binary numbers, a small problem arises with writing them. Look at this:

1111 0101 1011 1001 1110 0001

Binary notation here starts to be more than a little cumbersome for practical use, particularly when you consider that this in decimal is only 16,103,905—a miserable eight decimal digits. You can sit more angels on the head of a pin than that! Clearly you need a more economical way of writing this, but decimal isn't always appropriate. You might want to specify that the 10th and 24th bits from the right in a number are 1, for example. Figuring out the decimal integer for this is hard work, and there's a good chance you'll get it wrong anyway. An easier solution is to use *hexadecimal notation*, in which the numbers are represented using base 16.

Arithmetic to base 16 is a much more convenient option, and it fits rather well with binary. Each hexadecimal digit can have values from 0 to 15 and the digits from 10 to 15 are represented by the letters A to F (or a to f), as shown in Table 1-2. Values from 0 to 15 happen to correspond nicely with the range of values that four binary digits can represent.

Table 1-2. *Hexadecimal Digits and Their Values in Decimal and Binary*

Hexadecimal	Decimal	Binary	Hexadecimal	Decimal	Binary
0	0	0000	A or a	10	1010
1	1	0001	B or b	11	1011
2	2	0010	C or c	12	1100
3	3	0011	D or d	13	1101
4	4	0100	E or e	14	1110
5	5	0101	F or f	15	1111
6	6	0110			
7	7	0111			
8	8	1000			
9	9	1001			

Because a hexadecimal digit corresponds to four binary digits, you can represent any binary number in hexadecimal simply by taking groups of four binary digits starting from the right and writing the equivalent hexadecimal digit for each group. Look at the following binary number:

1111 0101 1011 1001 1110 0001

Taking each group of four bits and replacing it with the corresponding hexadecimal digit from the table produces the following:

F   5   B   9   E   1

You have six hexadecimal digits corresponding to the six groups of four binary digits. Just to prove that it all works out with no cheating, you can convert F5B9E1 directly from hexadecimal to decimal by again using the analogy with the meaning of a decimal number.

$$15 \times 16^5 + 5 \times 16^4 + 11 \times 16^3 + 9 \times 16^2 + 14 \times 16^1 + 1 \times 16^0$$

Thankfully, this adds up to the same number you got when converting the equivalent binary number to a decimal value: 16,103,905.

The other handy coincidence with hexadecimal numbers is that modern computers store integers in words that are an even number of bytes, typically 2, 4, 8, or 16 bytes. A *byte* is 8 bits, which is exactly two hexadecimal digits, so any binary integer word in memory always corresponds to an exact number of hexadecimal digits.

Negative Binary Numbers

There's another aspect to binary arithmetic that you need to understand: negative numbers. So far, we've assumed that everything is positive—the optimist's view—and so the glass is still half-full. But you can't avoid the negative side of life—the pessimist's perspective—that the glass is already half-empty. But how is a negative number represented in a modern computer? You'll see shortly that the answer to this seemingly easy question is actually far from obvious....

Integers that can be both positive and negative are referred to as *signed integers*. Naturally, you only have binary digits at your disposal to represent numbers. At the end of the day, any language your computer speaks shall consist solely of bits and bytes. As you know, your computer's memory is generally composed of 8-bit bytes, so all binary numbers are going to be stored in some multiple (usually a power of 2) of 8 bits. Thus, you can also only have signed integers with 8 bits, 16 bits, 32 bits, or whatever.

A straightforward representation of signed integers therefore consists of a fixed number of binary digits, where one of these bits is designated as a *sign bit*. In practice, the sign bit is always chosen to be the leftmost bit. Say we fix the size of all our signed integers to 8 bits; then the number 6 could be represented as 00000110, and –6 could be represented as 10000110. Changing +6 to –6 just involves flipping the sign bit from 0 to 1. This is called a *signed magnitude* representation: each number consists of a sign bit that is 0 for positive values and 1 for negative values, plus a given number of other bits that specify the *magnitude* or absolute value of the number (the value without the sign, in other words).

While signed magnitude representations are easy for humans to work with, they have one unfortunate downside: they are not at all easy for computers to work with! More specifically, they carry a lot of overhead in terms of the complexity of the circuits that are needed to perform arithmetic. When two signed integers are added, for instance, you don't want the computer to be messing about, checking whether either or both numbers are negative. What you really want is to use the same simple and very fast "add" circuitry regardless of the signs of the operands.

Let's see what happens when we naively add together the signed magnitude representations of 12 and –8. You almost know in advance that it won't work, but we'll carry on regardless:

12 in binary is	00001100
–8 in binary (you suppose) is	10001000
If you now "add" these together, you get	10010100

This seems to give –20, which isn't what you wanted at all. It's definitely not +4, which you know is 00000100. "Ah," we hear you say, "you can't treat a sign just like another digit." But that is just what you *do* want to do to speed up binary computations!

Virtually all modern computers therefore take a different approach: they use the *two's complement representation* of negative binary numbers. With this representation, you can produce the negative of any positive binary number by a simple procedure that you can perform in your head. At this point, we need to ask you to have a little faith because we'll avoid getting into explanations of why it works. Like a true magician, we won't explain our magic. We'll show you how you can create the two's complement form of a negative number from a positive value, and you can prove to yourself that it does work. For this, let's return to the previous example, in which you need the two's complement representation of –8:

1. You start with +8 in binary: 00001000.

2. You then "flip" each binary digit, changing 0s to 1s, and vice versa: 11110111. This is called the *ones' complement* form.

3. If you now add 1 to this, you get the two's complement form of –8: 11111000.

Note that this works both ways. To convert the two's complement representation of a negative number back into the corresponding positive binary number, you again flip all bits and add one. For our example, flipping 11111000 gives 00000111, and adding one to this gives 00001000, or +8 in decimal. Magic!

But of course, the proof of the pudding is in the eating. The two's complement representation would just be a fun parlor trick if it didn't facilitate binary arithmetic. So, let's see how 11111000 fares with your computer's elementary add circuitry:

+12 in binary is	00001100
The two's complement representation of –8 is	11111000
If you add these together, you get	00000100

The answer is 4—it works! The "carry" propagates through all the leftmost 1s, setting them back to 0. One fell off the end, but you shouldn't worry about that—it's probably compensating for the one you borrowed from the end in the subtraction you did to get –8. In fact, what's happening is that you're implicitly assuming that the sign bit, 1 or 0, repeats forever to the left. Try a few examples of your own; you'll find it always works, like magic. The great thing about the two's complement representation of negative numbers is that it makes arithmetic—and not just addition, by the way—very easy for your computer. And that accounts for one of the reasons computers are so good at crunching numbers.

Octal Values

Octal integers are numbers expressed with base 8. Digits in an octal value can only be from 0 to 7. Octal is used rarely these days. It was useful in the days when computer memory was measured in terms of 36-bit words because you could specify a 36-bit binary value by 12 octal digits. Those days are long gone, so why are we introducing it? The answer is the potential confusion it can cause. You can still write octal constants in C++. Octal values are written with a leading zero, so while 76 is a decimal value, 076 is an octal value that corresponds to 62 in decimal. So, here's a golden rule:

▓ **Caution**   Never write decimal integers in your source code with a leading zero. You'll get a value different from what you intended!

Big-Endian and Little-Endian Systems

Integers are stored in memory as binary values in a contiguous sequence of bytes, commonly groups of 2, 4, 8, or 16 bytes. The question of the sequence in which the bytes appear can be important—it's one of those things that doesn't matter until it matters, and then it *really* matters.

Let's consider the decimal value 262,657 stored as a 4-byte binary value. We chose this value not because it's a prime (that was a pure coincidence) but because in binary, each byte happens to have a pattern of bits that is easily distinguished from the others:

00000000 00000100 00000010 00000001

If you're using a PC with an Intel processor, the number will be stored as follows:

Byte address:	00	01	02	03
Data bits:	00000001	00000010	00000100	00000000

As you can see, the most significant eight bits of the value—the one that's all 0s—are stored in the byte with the highest address (last, in other words), and the least significant eight bits are stored in the byte with the lowest address, which is the leftmost byte. This arrangement is described as *little-endian*. Why on earth, you wonder, would a computer reverse the order of these bytes? The motivation, as always, is rooted in the fact that it allows for more efficient calculations and simpler hardware. The details don't matter much; the main thing is that you're aware that most modern computers these days use this counterintuitive encoding. Most, but not *all*, computers do, though. If you're using a machine based on a Motorola processor, the same data is likely to be arranged in memory in a more logical manner, like this:

Byte address:	00	01	02	03
Data bits:	00000000	00000100	00000010	00000001

Now the bytes are in reverse sequence, with the most significant eight bits stored in the leftmost byte, which is the one with the lowest address. This arrangement is described as *big-endian*. Some processors, such as PowerPC and all recent ARM processors, are *bi-endian*, which means that the byte order for data is switchable between big-endian and little-endian. In practice, however, no operating system tolerates switching endianness at runtime once an application has launched.

▓ **Caution**   Regardless of whether the byte order is big-endian or little-endian, the bits *within each byte* are arranged with the most significant bit on the left and the least significant bit on the right.

This is all very interesting, you may say, but when does it matter? Most of the time, it doesn't. More often than not, you can happily write a program without knowing whether the computer on which the code will execute is big-endian or little-endian. It does matter, however, when you're processing binary data that comes from another machine. You need to know the endianness. Binary data is written to a file or transmitted over a network as a sequence of bytes. It's up to you how you interpret it. If the source of the data is a machine with a different endianness from the machine on which your code is running, you must reverse the order of the bytes in each binary value. If you don't, you have garbage.

For those who collect curious background information, the terms *big-endian* and *little-endian* are drawn from the book *Gulliver's Travels* by Jonathan Swift. In the story, the emperor of Lilliput commanded all his subjects to always crack their eggs at the smaller end. This was a consequence of the emperor's son having cut his finger following the traditional approach of cracking his egg at the big end. Ordinary, law-abiding Lilliputian subjects who cracked their eggs at the smaller end were described as Little Endians. The Big Endians were a rebellious group of traditionalists in the Lilliputian kingdom who insisted on continuing to crack their eggs at the big end. Many were put to death as a result.

▓ **Tip** To determine whether your program is being compiled for a big- or little-endian platform, the C++20 Standard Library introduced `std::endian::native` in the `<bit>` module. In practice, this value always equals either `std::endian::little` or `std::endian::big`. You can consult your favorite Standard Library reference for more details.

Floating-Point Numbers

All integers are numbers, but not all numbers are integers: 3.1415 is no integer, and neither is –0.00001. Most applications will have to deal with fractional numbers at one point or another. So you need a way to represent such numbers on your computer as well, complemented with the ability to efficiently perform computations with them. The mechanism nearly all computers support for handling fractional numbers, as you may have guessed from the section title, is called *floating-point* numbers.

Floating-point numbers do not just represent fractional numbers, though. As an added bonus, they can deal with very large numbers as well. They allow you to represent, for instance, the number of protons in the universe, which needs around 79 decimal digits (though not accurate within one particle, but that's okay—who has the time to count them all anyway?). Granted, the latter is perhaps somewhat extreme, but clearly there are situations in which you'll need more than the ten decimal digits you get from a 32-bit binary integer or even more than the 19 you can get from a 64-bit integer. Equally, there are lots of very small numbers, for example, the amount of time in minutes it takes the typical car salesperson to accept your generous offer on a 2001 Honda (and it's covered only 480,000 miles...). Floating-point numbers are a mechanism that can represent both these classes of numbers quite effectively.

We'll first explain the basic principles using decimal floating-point numbers. Of course, your computer will again use a binary representation instead, but things are much easier to understand for us humans when we use decimal numbers. A so-called normalized number consists of two parts: a *significand* (also called *mantissa, coefficient,* or *fraction*) and an *exponent*. Both can be either positive or negative. The magnitude of the number is the significand multiplied by ten to the power of the exponent. In analogy with your computer's binary floating-point number representations, we'll fix the number of decimal digits of both the significand and the exponent.

It's easier to demonstrate this than to describe it, so let's look at some examples. The number 365 could be written in a floating-point form, as follows:

```
3.650000E02
```

The significand here has seven decimal digits, the exponent two. The E stands for *exponent* and precedes the power of ten that the 3.650000 (the significand) part is multiplied by to get the required value. That is, to get back to the regular decimal notation, you simply have to compute the following product: 3.650000×10^2. This is clearly 365.

Now let's look at a small number:

```
-3.650000E-03
```

This is evaluated as -3.65×10^{-3}, which is –0.00365. They're called floating-point numbers for the fairly obvious reason that the decimal point "floats," and its position depends on the exponent value.

Now suppose you have a larger number, such as 2,134,311,179. Using the same number of digits, this number looks like this:

```
2.134311E09
```

It's not quite the same. You've lost three low-order digits, and you've approximated your original value as 2,134,311,000. This is the price to pay for being able to handle such a vast range of numbers: not all these numbers can be represented with full precision; in general, floating-point numbers are only approximate representations of the exact number.

Aside from the fixed-precision limitation in terms of accuracy, there's another aspect you may need to be conscious of. You need to take great care when adding or subtracting numbers of significantly different magnitudes. A simple example will demonstrate the problem. Consider adding $1.23E-4$ to $3.65E+6$. The exact result is 3,650,000 + 0.000123, or 3,650,000.000123. But when converted to floating-point with seven digits of precision, this becomes the following:

```
3.650000E+06 + 1.230000E-04 = 3.650000E+06
```

Adding the latter smaller number to the former has had no effect whatsoever, so you might as well not have bothered. The problem lies directly with the fact that you carry only seven digits of precision. The digits of the larger number aren't affected by any of the digits of the smaller number because they're all further to the right.

Funnily enough, you must also take care when the numbers are nearly equal. If you compute the difference between such numbers, most numbers may cancel each other out, and you may end up with a result that has only one or two digits of precision. This is referred to as *catastrophic cancellation*, and it's quite easy in such circumstances to end up computing with numbers that are totally garbage.

While floating-point numbers enable you to carry out calculations that would be impossible without them, you must always keep their limitations in mind if you want to be sure your results are valid. This means considering the range of values that you are likely to be working with and their relative values. The field that deals with analyzing and maximizing the precision—or *numerical stability*—of mathematical computations and algorithms is called *numerical analysis*. This is an advanced topic, though, and well outside the scope of this book. Suffice it to say that the precision of floating-point numbers is limited and that the order and nature of arithmetic operations you perform with them can have a significant impact on the accuracy of your results.

Your computer again does not work with decimal numbers; rather, it works with binary floating-point representations. Bits and bytes, remember? Concretely, nearly all computers today use the encoding and computation rules specified by the IEEE 754 standard. Left to right, each floating-point number then consists of a single sign bit, followed by a fixed number of bits for the exponent, and finally, another series of bits that encode the significand. The most common floating-point numbers representations are the *single precision* (1 sign bit, 8 bits for the exponent, and 23 for the significand, adding up to 32 bits in total) and *double precision* (1 + 11 + 52 = 64 bits) floating-point numbers (see also Chapter 2).

Floating-point numbers can represent huge ranges of numbers. A single-precision floating-point number, for instance, can already represent numbers ranging from 10^{-38} to 10^{+38}. Of course, there's a price to pay for this flexibility: the number of digits of precision is limited. You know this already from before, and it's also only logical; not all 38 digits of all numbers in the order of 10^{+38} can be represented exactly using 32 bits. After all, the largest signed integer a 32-bit binary integer can represent exactly is only $2^{31} - 1$, which is about $2 \times 10^{+9}$. The number of decimal digits of precision in a floating-point number depends on how much memory is allocated for its significand. A single-precision floating-point value, for instance, provides approximately seven decimal digits accuracy. We say "approximately" because a binary fraction with 23 bits doesn't exactly correspond to a decimal fraction with seven decimal digits. A double-precision floating-point value corresponds to around 16 decimal digits accuracy.

Representing Characters

Data inside your computer has no intrinsic meaning. Machine code instructions are just numbers. Of course, numbers are just numbers, but so are, for instance, characters. Each character is assigned a unique integer value called its *code* or *code point*. The value 42 can be the atomic number of molybdenum; the answer to life, the universe, and everything; or an asterisk character. It all depends on how you choose to interpret it. You can write a single character in C++ between single quotes, such as 'a' or '?' or '*', and the compiler will generate the code value for these.

ASCII Codes

Way back in the 1960s, the American Standard Code for Information Interchange (ASCII) was defined for representing characters. This is a 7-bit code, so there are 128 different code values. ASCII values 0 to 31 represent various nonprinting control characters such as carriage return (code 15) and line feed (code 12). Code values 65 to 90 inclusive are the uppercase letters *A* to *Z*, and 97 to 122 correspond to lowercase *a* to *z*. If you look at the binary values corresponding to the code values for letters, you'll see that the codes for lowercase and uppercase letters differ only in the sixth bit; lowercase letters have the sixth bit as 1, and uppercase letters have the sixth bit as 0. Other codes represent digits 0 to 9, punctuation, and other characters.

The original 7-bit ASCII is fine if you are American or British, but if you are French or German, you need accents and umlauts in text, which are not included in the 128 characters that 7-bit ASCII encodes. To overcome the limitations imposed by a 7-bit code, extended versions of ASCII were defined with 8-bit codes. Values from 0 to 127 represent the same characters as 7-bit ASCII, and values from 128 to 255 are variable. One variant of 8-bit ASCII you have probably met is Latin-1, which provides characters for most European languages, but there are others for languages such as Russian.

If you speak Korean, Japanese, Chinese, or Arabic, however, even an 8-bit coding is totally inadequate. To give you an idea, modern encodings of Chinese, Japanese, and Korean scripts (which share a common background) cover nearly 88,000 characters—a tiny bit more than the 256 characters you can squeeze out of 8 bits! The Universal Character Set (UCS) emerged in the 1990s to overcome the limitations of extended ASCII. UCS is defined by the standard ISO 10646 and has codes with up to 32 bits. This provides the potential for hundreds of millions of unique code values.

UCS and Unicode

UCS defines a mapping between characters and integer code values called *code points*. It is important to realize that a *code point* is not the same as an *encoding*. A code point is an integer; an encoding specifies how to represent a given code point as a series of bytes or words. Code values less than 256 are popular and can be represented in one byte. It would be inefficient to use four bytes to store code values that require just one byte because other codes require several bytes. Encodings represent code points that allow them to be stored more efficiently.

Unicode is a standard that defines a set of characters and their code points identical to those in UCS. Unicode also defines several different encodings for these code points and includes additional mechanisms for dealing with right-to-left languages, such as Arabic. The range of code points is more than enough to accommodate the character sets for all the languages in the world, as well as many different sets of graphical characters such as mathematical symbols, or even emoticons and emojis. Regardless, the codes are arranged such that strings in most languages can be represented as a sequence of 16-bit codes.

One aspect of Unicode that can be confusing is that it provides more than one *character encoding method*. The most commonly used encodings are UTF-8, UTF-16, and UTF-32, which can represent all the characters in the Unicode set. The difference is in how a given character code point is presented; the numerical code value for any given character is the same in any of the representations. Here's how these encodings represent characters:

- *UTF-8* represents a character as a variable-length sequence between one and four bytes. The ASCII character set appears in UTF-8 as single-byte codes that have the same code values as ASCII. UTF-8 is by far the most popular encoding of Unicode. Most web pages, for example, use UTF-8 to encode text (97.9%, according to a recent study).

- *UTF-16* represents characters as one or two 16-bit values. For some time, Microsoft advocated the use of their native UTF-16–based APIs for Windows. Today the recommended encoding across most platforms, however, is UTF-8.

- *UTF-32*, you guessed it, simply represents all characters as 32-bit values. In practice, UTF-32 is rarely used by applications internally.

In C++, you have four types designed to store Unicode characters: wchar_t, char8_t, char16_t, and char32_t. Because char8_t was only introduced in C++20, though, many legacy applications and APIs will still use char to represent UTF-8–encoded strings as well. You'll learn more about the different character types in Chapter 2.

▓ **Tip** As of C++23, any compiler is required to accept source files encoded in UTF-8 (and prior to C++23, most compilers already did so anyway). We therefore recommend you configure your editor and compiler to use UTF-8 for maximum portability. Even if you don't anticipate the need for non-ASCII characters in identifiers (ASCII characters have the same code unit in virtually any encoding), eventually special characters will creep into string literals or code comments—believe us (think of characters such as °, ², ©, and so on). Without a portable encoding such as UTF-8, your source files then become (partially) illegible to compilers that use a different encoding.

Summary

This chapter's content has been a broad overview to give you a feel for some of the general concepts of C++. You'll encounter everything discussed in this chapter again, and in much more detail, in subsequent chapters. However, some of the basics that this chapter covered are as follows:

- A C++ program consists of one or more functions, one of which is called main(). Execution always starts with main().

- The executable part of a function is made up of statements contained between braces.

- A pair of curly braces enclose a statement block.

- A statement is terminated by a semicolon.

- Keywords are reserved words that have specific meanings in C++. No entity in your program can have a name that coincides with a keyword.

- A C++ program will be contained in one or more files. Source files contain most of the executable code.

- The source files that contain the code defining functions typically have the extension .cpp.

- The Standard Library provides an extensive range of capabilities that supports and extends the C++ language.

- Access to Standard Library functions and definitions is enabled through importing the std module in a source file.

- Input and output are performed using streams and involve the use of the insertion and extraction operators, << and >>. std::cin is a standard input stream that corresponds to the keyboard. std::cout is a standard output stream for writing text to the screen. Both are defined in the <iostream> Standard Library module.

- Object-oriented programming involves defining new data types that are specific to your problem. Once you've defined the data types that you need, a program can be written in terms of the new data types.

- Unicode defines unique integer code values that represent characters for virtually all of the languages in the world as well as many specialized character sets. Code values are referred to as *code points*. Unicode also defines how these code points may be encoded as byte sequences. The most popular Unicode encoding by far is UTF-8.

EXERCISES

The following exercises enable you to try what you've learned in this chapter. If you get stuck, look back over the chapter for help. If you're still stuck after that, you can download the solutions from the Apress website (www.apress.com/book/download.html), but that really should be a last resort.

Exercise 1-1. Create, compile, link, and execute a program that will display the text "Hello World" on your screen.

Exercise 1-2. Create and execute a program that outputs your name on one line and your age on the next line. Define a variable to hold your age first.

Exercise 1-3. The following program produces several compiler errors. Find and correct these errors so the program compiles cleanly.

```
#import std

Int main
{
   std:printn("Holla Mundo!")
)
```

CHAPTER 2

■ ■ ■

Introducing Fundamental Types of Data

In this chapter, we'll explain the fundamental data types that are built into C++. You'll need these in every program. All the object-oriented capabilities are founded on these fundamental data types because all the data types that you create are ultimately defined in terms of the basic numerical data your computer works with. By the end of the chapter, you'll be able to write a simple C++ program of the traditional form: input – process – output.

In this chapter, you'll learn

- What a fundamental data type is in C++

- How you declare, initialize, and reassign variables

- How you can fix the value of a variable

- What integer literals are and how you define them

- How calculations work

- How to work with variables that contain floating-point values

- Which elementary mathematical functions and constants you have at your disposal

- How to convert variables from one type to another

- What the auto keyword does

- How to work with variables that store characters

- How to control the format that is used when printing variables

Variables, Data, and Data Types

A *variable* is a named piece of memory that you define. Each variable stores data only of a particular type. Every variable has a *type* that defines the kind of data it can store. Each fundamental type is identified by a unique type name that, as a rule, consists of one or more *keywords*. Keywords are reserved words in C++ that you cannot use for anything else.

© Ivor Horton and Peter Van Weert 2023
I. Horton and P. Van Weert, *Beginning C++23*, https://doi.org/10.1007/978-1-4842-9343-0_2

The compiler makes extensive checks to ensure that you use the right data type in any given context. It will also ensure that when you combine different types in an operation, such as adding two values, for example, either they are of the same type or they can be made compatible by converting one value to the type of the other. The compiler detects and reports attempts to combine data of different types that are incompatible.

Numerical values fall into two broad categories: integers, which are whole numbers, and floating-point values, which can be nonintegral. There are several fundamental C++ types in each category, each of which can store a specific range of values. We'll start with integer types.

Defining Integer Variables

Here's a statement that defines an integer variable:

```
int apple_count;
```

This defines a variable of type int with the name apple_count. The variable will contain some arbitrary junk value. You can and should specify an initial value when you define the variable, like this:

```
int apple_count {15};                          // Number of apples
```

The initial value for apple_count appears between the braces following the name so it has the value 15. The braces enclosing the initial value are called a *braced initializer*. You'll meet situations later in the book where a braced initializer will have several values between the braces. You don't have to initialize variables when you define them, but it's a good idea to do so. Ensuring variables start out with known values makes it easier to work out what is wrong when the code doesn't work as you expect.

The size of variables of type int is typically four bytes, so they can store integers from –2,147,483,648 to +2,147,483,647. This covers most situations, which is why int is the integer type that is used most frequently.

Here are definitions for three variables of type int:

```
int apple_count {15};                          // Number of apples
int orange_count {5};                          // Number of oranges
int total_fruit {apple_count + orange_count};  // Total number of fruit
```

The initial value for total_fruit is the sum of the values of two variables defined previously. This demonstrates that the initial value for a variable can be an expression. The statements that define the two variables in the expression for the initial value for total_fruit must appear earlier in the source file; otherwise, the definition for total_fruit won't compile.

There are two other ways for initializing a variable: *functional notation* and *assignment notation*. These look like this (yes, a tomato is a fruit):

```
int lemon_count(4);                            // Functional notation
int tomato_count = 12;                         // Assignment notation
```

Most of the time, these three notations—curly braces, functional, and assignment notation—are equivalent. The braced initializer form, however, is slightly safer when it comes to *narrowing conversions*. A narrowing conversion changes a value to a type with a more limited range of values. Any such conversion thus has the potential to lose information. Here is an example:

```
int banana_count(7.5);                         // Typically compiles without warning
int tangerine_count = 5.3;                     // Typically compiles without warning
```

Normally, the initial value you provide will be of the same type as the variable you are defining. If it isn't, though, the compiler will try to convert it to the required type. In our previous example, we specified non-integer initial values for two integer variables. We'll have more to say about floating-point to integer conversions later, but for now believe us when we say that after these variable definitions, banana_count and tangerine_count will contain the integer values 7 and 5, respectively. It's unlikely that this is what the author had in mind.

Nevertheless, as far as the C++ standard is concerned, these two definitions are perfectly legal. They are allowed to compile without even the slightest warning. While some compilers issue a warning about such flagrant narrowing conversions, not all do. If you use the braced initializer form, however, a conforming compiler is required to at least issue a diagnostic message. For instance:

```cpp
int papaya_count{0.3};     // At least a compiler warning, often an error
```

If this statement compiles, papaya_count will be initialized to the integer value 0. But at least the compiler will have warned you that something may be amiss. Some compilers will even issue an error and refuse to compile such definitions altogether.

We believe inadvertent narrowing conversions do not deserve to go unnoticed, as they often are a mistake. In this book, we therefore embrace the braced initializer syntax. This is the most recent syntax that was introduced in C++11 specifically to standardize initialization. Besides providing better safety guarantees when it comes to narrowing conversions, its main advantage is that it enables you to initialize just about everything in the same way—which is why it is also commonly referred to as *uniform initialization.*

▓ **Note** To represent fractional numbers, you typically use floating-point variables rather than integers. We'll describe these later in this chapter.

You can define and initialize more than one variable of a given type in a single statement. Here's an example:

```cpp
int foot_count {2}, toe_count {10}, head_count {1};
```

While this is legal, it's often considered best to define each variable in a separate statement. This makes the code more readable and reduces the risk of mistakes, particularly with variables of pointer types (Chapter 5). It also facilitates end-of-line comments explaining variables whose purpose is not obvious.

You can print the value of any variable of a fundamental type to the standard output stream. Here's a program that does that with a couple of integers:

```cpp
// Ex2_01.cpp - Writing values of variables to the screen
import std;

int main()
{
  int apple_count {15};                            // Number of apples
  int orange_count {5};                            // Number of oranges
  int total_fruit {apple_count + orange_count};    // Total number of fruit

  std::println("The value of apple_count is {}", apple_count);
  std::println("The value of orange_count is {}", orange_count);
  std::println("The value of total_fruit is {}", total_fruit);
}
```

If you compile and execute this, you'll see that it outputs the values of the three variables following some text explaining what they are. The integer values are automatically converted to a character representation for output by `std::println()`. This works for values of any of the fundamental types.

▨ **Tip** The three variables in Ex2_01.cpp do not really need any comments explaining what they represent. Their variable names already make that crystal clear—as they should! In contrast, a lesser programmer might have produced the following, for instance:

```
int n {15};
int m {5};
int t {n + m};
```

Without extra context or explanation, no one would ever be able to guess this code is about counting fruit. You should therefore always choose your variable names as self-descriptive as possible. Properly named variables and functions mostly need no additional explanation in the form of a comment. Of course, this does not mean you should never add comments to declarations. You cannot always capture everything in a single name. A few words or, if need be, a little paragraph of comments can then do wonders in helping someone understand your code. A little extra effort at the time of writing can considerably speed up future development!

Signed Integer Types

Table 2-1 shows the complete set of fundamental types that store signed integers—that is, both positive and negative values. The memory allocated for each type, and hence the range of values it can store, may vary between different compilers. Table 2-1 shows the sizes and ranges used by compilers for all common platforms and computer architectures.

Table 2-1. *Signed Integer Types*

Type Name	Typical Size (Bytes)	Typical Range of Values	Minimum Size (Bytes)
signed char	1	–128 to +127	1
short short int signed short signed short int	2	–32,768 to +32,767	2
int signed signed int	4	–2,147,483,648 to +2,147,483,647	2
long long int signed long signed long int	4 or 8	Same as either int or long long	4
long long long long int signed long long signed long long int	8	–9,223,372,036,854,775,808 to +9,223,372,036,854,775,807	8

Variables of type signed char always occupy one byte (a byte, in turn, is nearly always eight bits). The number of bytes that variables of the other types occupy depends on the compiler, though it will never be less than occupied by the type that precedes it in Table 2-1, nor less than the number listed in the last column.

Where two type names appear in the first column of Table 2-1, the abbreviated name that comes first is more commonly used. That is, you will usually see long used rather than long int or signed long int.

The signed modifier is mostly optional; if omitted, your type will be signed by default. The only exception to this rule is char. While the unmodified type char does exist, it is compiler-dependent whether it is signed or unsigned. We'll discuss this further in the next subsection. For all integer types other than char, however, you are free to choose whether you add the signed modifier. Personally, we normally do so only when we really want to stress that a particular variable is signed.

Unsigned Integer Types

Of course, there are circumstances where you don't need to store negative numbers. The number of students in a class or the number of parts in an assembly is always a positive integer. You can specify integer types that only store non-negative values by prefixing any of the names of the signed integer types with unsigned instead of signed—types unsigned char or unsigned short or unsigned long long, for example. Each unsigned type is a different type from the signed type but occupies the same amount of memory.

Unlike other integer types, type char is a different integer type from both signed char and unsigned char. The char type is intended for variables that store character codes, typically as part of a string. char can be a signed or unsigned type depending on your compiler.[1] We'll have more to say about variables that store characters later in this chapter.

■ **Tip** Use the unmodified char type primarily to store letter characters (as explored further later in this chapter). To store numbers, always use signed char or unsigned char instead. And to represent a byte of raw binary data, you could consider the std::byte Standard Library type (although many APIs likely still use char or unsigned char arrays for binary data, so you may have to be pragmatic here).

With the exception of unsigned char (with possible values 0 to 255) and possibly unsigned short (typically 0 to 65,535), the main motivator for adding the unsigned modifier is rarely to increase the range of representable numbers. It rarely matters, for instance, whether you can represent numbers up to 2,147,483,647 or up to 4,294,967,295. Instead, you mostly add unsigned to make your code more self-documenting, to make it more predictable what values a given variable will or should contain.

■ **Tip** You can also use the keywords signed and unsigned on their own. As Table 2-1 shows, the type signed is considered shorthand for signed int. So naturally, unsigned is short for unsigned int.

---

[1] If need be, you can determine whether char is signed or not on your platform using the expressions std::is_signed_v<char> (a so-called type trait expression), std::signed_integral<char> (a concept expression; see Chapter 21), or std::numeric_limits<char>::is_signed (see also later in this chapter).

Zero Initialization

The following statement defines an integer variable with an initial value equal to zero:

```
int counter {0};                       // counter starts at zero
```

You could omit the 0 in the braced initializer here, and the effect would be the same. The statement that defines counter could thus be written like this:

```
int counter {};                        // counter starts at zero
```

The empty curly braces somewhat resemble the number zero, which makes this syntax easy to remember. *Zero initialization* works for any fundamental type. For all fundamental numeric types, for instance, an empty braced initializer is always assumed to contain the number zero.

Defining Variables with Fixed Values

Sometimes you'll want to define variables with fixed values that must not be changed. You use the const keyword in the definition of a variable that must not be changed. Such variables are often referred to as *constants*. Here's an example:

```
const unsigned toe_count {10};         // An unsigned integer with fixed value 10
```

The const keyword tells the compiler that the value of toe_count must not be changed. Any statement that attempts to modify this value will be flagged as an error during compilation; cutting off toes is a definite no-no, growing extra is challenging! You can use the const keyword to fix the value of variables of any type.

░ **Tip**   If nothing else, knowing which variables can and cannot change their values along the way makes your code easier to follow. So, we recommend you add the const specifier whenever applicable.

░ **Note**   Modern C++ offers three more keywords that sound related to const: constexpr, consteval, and constinit. We'll discuss these and their (fairly limited) relation to const in Chapters 8 and 12. For now it suffices to know that, in our opinion, const remains the primary keyword to specify immutability, even in modern C++.

Integer Literals

Constant values of any kind, such as 42, 2.71828, 'Z', or "Mark Twain", are referred to as *literals*. These examples are, in sequence, an *integer literal*, a *floating-point literal*, a *character literal*, and a *string literal*. Every literal will be of some type. We'll first explain integer literals and introduce the other kinds of literals in context later.

Decimal Integer Literals

You can write integer literals in a very straightforward way. Here are some examples of decimal integers:

```
-123L    +123    123    22333    98u    -1234LL    12345ULL
```

Unsigned integer literals have u or U appended. Literals of types long and type long long have L or LL appended, respectively, and if they are unsigned, they also have u or U appended. If there is no suffix, an integer constant is of type int. The U and L or LL can be in either sequence.

▩ **Tip**   You can use lowercase for the L and LL suffixes, but we recommend that you don't because lowercase l is easily confused with the digit 1.

You could omit the + in the second example, as it's implied by default, but if you think putting it in makes things clearer, that's not a problem. The literal +123 is the same as 123 and is of type int because there is no suffix.

The fourth example, 22333, is the number that you might write, depending on local conventions as 22,333; 22 333; or 22.333 (though other formatting conventions also exist). You cannot use commas or spaces in a C++ integer literal, though, and adding a dot would turn it into a floating-point literal (as explained later). Since C++14, however, you can use the single quote character, ', to make numeric literals more readable. Here are some examples:

```
22'333    -1'234LL    12'345ULL    15'000'000
```

Note that there are no restrictions on how to group the digits. Most Western conventions group digits per three, but this is not universal. Natives of the exotic subcontinent of India, for instance, would typically write the literal for 15 million as follows (using groups of two digits except for the rightmost group of three digits):

```
1'50'00'000
```

Here are some statements that use some of these integral literals to initialize a variable:

```
unsigned long age {99UL};            // 99ul or 99lU would be OK too
unsigned short price {10u};          // There is no specific literal type for short
long long distance {15'000'000LL};   // Common digit grouping of the number 15 million
```

So far, we have been very diligent in adding literal suffixes—u or U for unsigned literals, L for literals of type long, and so on. In practice, however, you'll rarely add these in variable initializers of this form. The reason is that no compiler will ever complain if you simply type this:

```
unsigned long age {99};
unsigned short price {10};           // There is no specific literal type for short
long long distance {15'000'000};     // Common digit grouping of the number 15 million
```

While all these literals are technically of type (signed) int, your compiler will happily convert them to the correct type for you. As long as the target type can represent the given values without loss of information, there's no need to issue a warning.

▩ **Note**   While relatively uncommon, there are situations where you need to add the correct literal suffixes; for instance, when you initialize a variable with type auto (explained later in this chapter) or when calling overloaded functions with literal arguments (see Chapter 8).

An initializing value should always be within the permitted range for the type of variable, as well as from the correct type. The following two statements violate these restrictions. They require, in other words, narrowing conversions:

```
unsigned char high_score { 513U };   // The valid range for unsigned char is [0,255]
unsigned int high_score { -1 };      // -1 is a literal of type signed int
```

As we explained earlier, both these braced initialization statements will result in at least a compiler warning, if not a compilation error, depending on which compiler you use.

Hexadecimal Literals

You can write integer literals as hexadecimal values. You prefix a hexadecimal literal with 0x or 0X, so 0x999 is a hexadecimal number of type int with three hexadecimal digits. Plain old 999, on the other hand, is a decimal value of type int with decimal digits, so the value will be completely different. Here are some more examples of hexadecimal literals:

Hexadecimal literals:	0x1AF	0x123U	0xAL	0xcad	0xFF
Decimal literals:	431	291U	10L	3245	255

A major use for hexadecimal literals is to define particular patterns of bits. Each hexadecimal digit corresponds to four bits, so it's easy to express a pattern of bits as a hexadecimal literal. The red, blue, and green components (RGB values) of a pixel color, for instance, are often expressed as three bytes packed into a 32-bit word. The color white can be specified as 0xFFFFFF because the intensity of each of the three components in white has the same maximum value of 255, which is 0xFF. The color red would be 0xff0000. Here are some examples:

```
int turquoise {0x0ff1ce};            // Unsigned int hexadecimal literal - decimal 1,044,942
unsigned mask {0XFF00FF00u};         // Four bytes specified as FF, 00, FF, 00
unsigned long value {0xDEADlu};      // Unsigned long hexadecimal literal - decimal 57,005
```

Octal Literals

You can also write integer literals as octal values—that is, using base 8. You identify a number as octal by writing it with a leading zero.

Octal literals:	0657	0443U	012L	06255	0377
Decimal literals:	431	291U	10L	3245	255

■ **Caution** Don't write decimal integer values with a leading zero. The compiler will interpret such values as octal (base 8), so a value written as 065 will be the equivalent of 53 in decimal notation.

Binary Literals

Binary literals were introduced by the C++14 standard. You write a binary integer literal as a sequence of binary digits (0 or 1) prefixed by either 0b or 0B. As always, a binary literal can have L or LL as a suffix to indicate it is type long or long long, and u or U if it is an unsigned literal. Here are some examples:

Binary literals:	0B110101111	0b100100011u	0b1010L	0B110010101101	0b11111111
Decimal literals:	431	291u	10L	3245	255

We have illustrated in the code fragments how you can write various combinations for the prefixes and suffixes, such as 0x or 0X and UL, LU, or Lu, but it's best to stick to a consistent way of writing integer literals.

As far as your compiler is concerned, it doesn't matter which number base you choose when you write an integer value. Ultimately it will be stored as a binary number. The different ways for writing an integer are there just for your convenience. You choose one or other of the possible representations to suit the context.

▓ **Tip**   You can use a single quote as a separator in any integer literal to make it easier to read. This includes hexadecimal or binary literals. For instance: 0xFF'00'00'FFu or 0b11001010'11011001.

Calculations with Integers

To begin with, let's get some bits of terminology out of the way. An operation such as addition or multiplication is defined by an *operator*—the operators for addition and multiplication are + and *, respectively. The values that an operator acts upon are called *operands*, so in an expression such as 2 * 3, the operands are 2 and 3. Operators such as multiplication that require two operands are called *binary operators*. Operators that require one operand are called *unary operators*. An example of a unary operator is the minus sign in the expression -width. The minus sign negates the value of width, so the result of the expression is a value with the opposite sign to that of its operand. This contrasts with the binary multiplication operator in expressions such as width * height, which acts on two operands, width and height.

Table 2-2 shows the basic arithmetic operations that you can carry out on integers.

Table 2-2. *Basic Arithmetic Operations*

Operator	Operation
+	Addition
-	Subtraction
*	Multiplication
/	Division
%	Modulo (the remainder after division)

The operators in Table 2-2 are all binary and work largely in the way you would expect. Two operators may need a little explanation: the somewhat lesser-known modulo operator and the division operator. Integer division is slightly idiosyncratic in C++. When applied to two integer operands, the result of a division operation is always again an integer. Suppose, for instance, that you write the following:

```
int numerator{ 11 };
int quotient{ numerator / 4 };
```

Mathematically speaking, the result of the division 11/4 is 2.75 or 2¾; that is, two and three-quarters. But 2.75 is clearly no integer, so what to do? Any sane mathematician would suggest that you round the quotient to the nearest integer, so 3. But, alas, that is *not* what your computer will do. Instead, your computer will simply discard the fractional part, 0.75, altogether. No doubt this is because proper rounding would require more complicated circuitry and hence also more time to evaluate. This means that, in C++, 11/4 will always give the integer value 2. Figure 2-1 illustrates the effects of the division and modulo operators on our example.

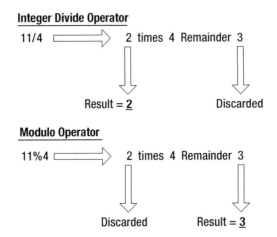

Figure 2-1. *Contrasting the division and modulo operators*

Integer division returns the number of times that the denominator divides into the numerator. Any remainder is discarded. The modulo operator, %, complements the division operator in that it produces the *remainder after integer division*. It is defined such that, for all integers x and y, $(x / y) * y + (x \% y) = x$. For negative operands, the modulo operator therefore also obeys this identity: $-x \% y = x \% -y = -(x \% y)$.

The result of both the division and modulo operator is undefined when the right operand is zero—what'll happen depends, in other words, on your compiler and computer architecture.

Compound Arithmetic Expressions

If multiple operators appear in the same expression, multiplication, division, and modulo operations always execute before addition and subtraction. Here's an example of such a case:

```
long width {4};
long length {5};
long area { width * length };          // Result is 20
long perimeter {2*width + 2*length};   // Result is 18
```

You can control the order in which more complicated expressions are executed using parentheses. You could write the statement that calculates a value for `perimeter` as follows:

```
long perimeter{ (width + length) * 2 };   // Result is 18
```

The subexpression within the parentheses is evaluated first. The result is then multiplied by two, which produces the same end result as before. If you omit the parentheses here, however, the result would no longer be 18. The result, instead, would become 14:

```
long perimeter{ width + length * 2 };     // Result is 14
```

The reason is that multiplication is always evaluated before addition. So, the previous statement is actually equivalent to the following one:

```
long perimeter{ width + (length * 2) };
```

Parentheses can be nested, in which case subexpressions between parentheses are executed in sequence from the innermost pair of parentheses to the outermost. This example of an expression with nested parentheses will show how it works:

```
2*(a + 3*(b + 4*(c + 5*d)))
```

The expression `5*d` is evaluated first, and `c` is added to the result. That result is multiplied by 4, and b is added. That result is multiplied by 3, and a is added. Finally, that result is multiplied by 2 to produce the result of the complete expression.

We will have more to say about the order in which such *compound expressions* are evaluated in the next chapter. The main thing to remember is that whatever the default evaluation order is, you can always override it by adding parentheses. And even if the default order happens to be what you want, it never hurts to add some extra parentheses just for the sake of clarity:

```
long perimeter{ (2*width) + (2*length) };   // Result is 18
```

Assignment Operations

In C++, the value of a variable is fixed only if you use the `const` qualifier. In all other cases, the value of a variable can always be overwritten with a new value:

```
long perimeter {};
// ...
perimeter = 2 * (width + length);
```

This last line is an *assignment statement*, and the = is the *assignment operator*. The arithmetic expression on the right of the assignment operator is evaluated, and the result is stored in the variable on the left. Initializing the perimeter variable upon declaration may not be strictly necessary—as long as the variable is not read prior to the assignment, that is—but it's considered good practice to always initialize your variables nevertheless. And zero is often as good a value as any.

You can assign a value to more than one variable in a single statement. Here's an example:

```
int a {}, b {}, c {5}, d{4};
a = b = c*c - d*d
```

The second statement calculates the value of the expression c*c - d*d and stores the result in b, so b will be set to 9. Next the value of b is stored in a, so a will also be set to 9. You can have as many repeated assignments like this as you want.

It's important to appreciate that an assignment operator differs from an = sign in an algebraic equation. The latter implies equality, whereas the former specifies an action—specifically, the act of overwriting a given memory location. A variable can be overwritten as many times as you want, each time with different, mathematically nonequal values. Consider the assignment statement in the following:

```
int y {5};
y = y + 1;
```

The variable y is initialized with 5, so the expression y + 1 produces 6. This result is stored back in y, so the effect is to increment y by 1. This last line makes no sense in common math; as any mathematician will tell you, y can never equal y + 1 (except of course when y equals infinity...). But in programming languages such as C++ repeatedly incrementing a variable with one is extremely common. In Chapter 5, you'll find that equivalent expressions are, for instance, ubiquitous in loops.

Let's see some of the arithmetic operators in action in an example. This program converts distances that you enter from the keyboard and in the process illustrates using the arithmetic operators:

```
// Ex2_02.cpp - Converting distances
import std;

int main()
{
  unsigned int yards {}, feet {}, inches {};

  // Convert a distance in yards, feet, and inches to inches
  std::print("Enter a distance as yards, feet, and inches ");
  std::println("with the three values separated by spaces: ");
  std::cin >> yards >> feet >> inches;

  const unsigned feet_per_yard {3};
  const unsigned inches_per_foot {12};

  unsigned total_inches {};
  total_inches = inches + inches_per_foot * (yards*feet_per_yard + feet);
  std::println("This distance corresponds to {} inches.", total_inches);

  // Convert a distance in inches to yards, feet, and inches
  std::print("Enter a distance in inches: ");
  std::cin >> total_inches;
```

```
feet    = total_inches / inches_per_foot;
inches  = total_inches % inches_per_foot;
yards   = feet / feet_per_yard;
feet    = feet % feet_per_yard;
std::println("This distance corresponds to {} yards {} feet {} inches.",
          yards, feet, inches);
}
```

The following is an example of typical output from this program:

```
Enter a distance as yards, feet, and inches with the three values separated by spaces:
9 2 11
This distance corresponds to 359 inches.
Enter a distance in inches: 359
This distance corresponds to 9 yards 2 feet 11 inches.
```

The first statement in main() defines three integer variables and initializes them with zero. They are type unsigned int because in this example the distance values cannot be negative. This is an instance where defining three variables in a single statement is reasonable because they are closely related.

The next two statements prompt for user input. We split this over two statements mainly because we are bound by the width of a page. But you could combine them into a single statement as well. While overly long lines of code are generally discouraged, no one would object to putting such a somewhat longer println() statement on a single line of code. Another option is given in the following tip.

▓ **Tip**   You can break up a longer string literal into several lines of code, as follows:

```
std::println("Enter a distance as yards, feet, and inches "
            "with the three values separated by spaces: ");
```

Two or more consecutive string literals separated only by whitespace are glued together as one string literal very early on in the compilation process.

The print statements prompting for user input are followed by a statement that reads values from std::cin and stores them in the variables yards, feet, and inches. The type of value that the >> operator expects to read is determined by the type of variable in which the value is to be stored. So, in this case, unsigned integers are expected to be entered. The >> operator ignores spaces, and the first space following a value terminates the operation. This implies that you cannot read and store spaces using the >> operator for a stream, even when you store them in variables that store characters. The input statement in the example could also be written as three separate statements:

```
std::cin >> yards;    // Read unsigned integer from standard input and store it in yards
std::cin >> feet;     // Read unsigned integer from standard input and store it in feet
std::cin >> inches;   // Read unsigned integer from standard input and store it in inches
```

The effect of these statements is the same as the original.

You define two variables, inches_per_foot and feet_per_yard, that you need to convert from yards, feet, and inches to just inches, and vice versa. The values for these are fixed, so you specify the variables as const. You could use explicit values for conversion factors in the code, but using const variables is much better because it is then clearer what you are doing. The `const` variables are also positive values, so you define them as type `unsigned int`. You could add u or U modifiers to the integer literals if you prefer, but there's no need. The conversion to inches is done in a single assignment statement:

```
total_inches = inches + inches_per_foot * (yards*feet_per_yard + feet);
```

The expression between parentheses executes first. This converts the `yards` value to feet and adds the feet value to produce the total number of feet. Multiplying this result by `inches_per_foot` obtains the total number of inches for the values of `yards` and `feet`. Adding `inches` to that produces the final total number of inches, which you output using this statement:

```
std::println("This distance corresponds to {} inches.", total_inches);
```

Converting a value from inches to yards, feet, and inches requires four statements:

```
feet   = total_inches / inches_per_foot;
inches = total_inches % inches_per_foot;
yards  = feet / feet_per_yard;
feet   = feet % feet_per_yard;
```

You reuse the variables that stored the input for the previous conversion to store the results of this conversion. Dividing the value of `total_inches` by `inches_per_foot` produces the number of whole feet, which you store in `feet`. The % operator produces the remainder after division, so the next statement calculates the number of residual inches, which is stored in `inches`. The same process is used to calculate the number of yards and the final number of feet.

Notice the use of whitespace to nicely outline these assignment statements. You could've written the same statements without spaces as well, but that simply does not read very fluently:

```
feet=total_inches/inches_per_foot;
inches=total_inches%inches_per_foot;
yards=feet/feet_per_yard;
feet=feet%feet_per_yard;
```

We generally add a single space before and after each binary operator, as it promotes code readability. Adding extra spaces to outline related assignments in a semitabular form doesn't harm either.

There's no `return` statement after this final output statement because it isn't necessary. When the execution sequence runs beyond the end of `main()`, it is equivalent to executing `return 0`.

The op= Assignment Operators

In `Ex2_02.cpp`, there was a statement that you could write more economically:

```
feet = feet % feet_per_yard;
```

This statement could be written using an op= assignment operator. The op= *assignment operators* or *compound assignment operators* are so called because they're composed of an operator and an assignment operator =. You could use one to write the previous statement as follows:

```
feet %= feet_per_yard;
```

This is the same operation as the previous statement.

In general, an op= assignment is of the following form:

```
lhs op= rhs;
```

lhs represents a variable of some kind that is the destination for the result of the operator. rhs is any expression. This is equivalent to the following statement:

```
lhs = lhs op (rhs);
```

The parentheses are important because you can write statements such as the following:

```
x *= y + 1;
```

This is equivalent to the following:

```
x = x * (y + 1);
```

Without the implied parentheses, the value stored in x would be the result of x * y + 1, which is quite different.

You can use a range of operators for op in the op= form of assignment. Table 2-3 shows the complete set, including some operators you'll meet in Chapter 3.

Table 2-3. *op= Assignment Operators*

Operation	Operator	Operation	Operator
Addition	+=	Bitwise AND	&=
Subtraction	-=	Bitwise OR	|=
Multiplication	*=	Bitwise exclusive OR	^=
Division	/=	Shift left	<<=
Modulo	%=	Shift right	>>=

Note that there can be no spaces between op and the =. If you include a space, it will be flagged as an error. You can use += when you want to increment a variable by some amount. For example, the following two statements have the same effect:

```
y = y + 1;
y += 1;
```

The shift operators that appear in the table, << and >>, look the same as the insertion and extraction operators that one uses with streams. The compiler can figure out what << or >> means in a statement from the context. You'll understand how it is possible that the same operator can mean different things in different situations later in the book.

Incrementing and Decrementing Integers

You've seen how you can increment a variable with the += operator and we're sure you've deduced that you can decrement a variable with -=. There are two other operators that can perform the same tasks. They're called the *increment operator* and the *decrement operator*, ++ and --, respectively.

These operators are more than just other options. You'll see a lot more of them, and you'll find them to be quite an asset once you get further into C++. In particular, you'll use them all the time when working with arrays and loops in Chapter 5. The increment and decrement operators are unary operators that you can apply to an integer variable. The following three statements that modify count have exactly the same effect:

```
int count {5};
count = count + 1;
count += 1;
++count;
```

Each statement increments count by 1. Using the increment operator is clearly the most concise. The action of this operator is different from other operators that you've seen in that it directly modifies the value of its operand. The effect in an expression is to increment the value of the variable and then to use the incremented value in the expression. For example, suppose count has the value 5 and you execute this statement:

```
total = ++count + 6;
```

The increment and decrement operators execute before any other binary arithmetic operators in an expression. Thus, count will be incremented to 6, and then this value will be used in the evaluation of the expression on the right of the assignment. total will therefore be assigned the value 12.

You use the decrement operator in the same way:

```
total = --count + 6;
```

Assuming count is 6 before this statement, the -- operator will decrement it to 5, and then this value will be used to calculate the value to be stored in total, which will be 11.

You've seen how you place a ++ or -- operator before the variable to which it applies. This is called the *prefix form* of these operators. You can also place them after a variable, which is called the *postfix form*. The effect is a little different.

Postfix Increment and Decrement Operations

The postfix form of ++ increments the variable to which it applies after its value is used in context. For example, you can rewrite the earlier example as follows:

```
total = count++ + 6;
```

With an initial value of 5 for count, total is assigned the value 11. In this case, count will be incremented to 6 only *after* being used in the surrounding expression. The preceding statement is thus equivalent to the following two statements:

```
total = count + 6;
++count;
```

In an expression such as a++ + b, or even a+++b, it's less than obvious what you mean, or indeed what the compiler will do. These two expressions are actually the same, but in the second case, you might have meant a + ++b, which is different—it evaluates to one more than the other two expressions. It would be clearer to write the preceding statement as follows:

```
total = 6 + count++;
```

Alternatively, you can use parentheses:

```
total = (count++) + 6;
```

The rules that we've discussed in relation to the increment operator also apply to the decrement operator. For example, suppose count has the initial value 5 and you write this statement:

```
total = --count + 6;
```

This results in total having the value 10 assigned. However, consider this statement:

```
total = 6 + count--;
```

In this instance, total is set to 11.

You should take care applying these operators to a given variable more than once in an expression. Suppose count has the value 5 and you write this:

```
total = ++count * 3 + count++ * 5;
```

The result of this statement is undefined because the statement modifies the value of count more than once using increment operators. Even though this expression is undefined according to the C++ standard, this doesn't mean that compilers won't compile them. It just means that there is no guarantee for consistency in the results.

Now consider the following statement:

```
k = k++ + 5;
```

In the expression on the right, you're incrementing the value of the variable that also appears on the left of the assignment operator. So you're again modifying the value of k twice. Prior to C++17, the effects of such statements used to be undefined as well. With k equal to 10 prior to this statement, we have seen both 15 and 16 as possible outcomes with older compilers.

Informally, the C++17 standard added the rule that all side effects of the right side of an assignment (including compound assignments, increments, and decrements) are fully committed before evaluating the left side and the actual assignment. Meaning that with C++17, our statement should take k from 10 to 15.

Nevertheless, the rules of when precisely an expression is defined or undefined remain subtle, even in C++17 and beyond. So our advice remains unchanged:

▓ **Tip**   Modify a variable only once within a statement and access the prior value of the variable only to determine its new value—that is, do not attempt to read a variable again after it has been modified in the same statement.

The increment and decrement operators are usually applied to integers, particularly in the context of loops, as you'll see in Chapter 5. You'll see later in this chapter that you can apply them to floating-point variables too. In later chapters, you'll explore how they can also be applied to certain other data types, in some cases with rather specialized (but very useful) effects.

Floating-Point Variables

You use floating-point variables whenever you want to work with values that are not integral. Here are some statements that define floating-point variables:

```
float pi {3.1415926f};                  // Ratio of circle circumference to diameter
double inches_to_mm {25.4};
long double root2 {1.4142135623730950488L};  // Square root of 2
```

As you see, you define floating-point variables just like integer variables. The types float, double, and long double are the three standard floating-point data types supported by any C++ compiler. We cover these in the next subsection. As of C++23, compilers may additionally offer *extended floating-point data types*, with precisions ranging from 16 to 128 bit. We introduce these newer types in a second subsection.

Standard Floating-Point Data Types

Table 2-4 shows the three floating-point data types that are supported by any C++ compiler. As explained in Chapter 1, the term *precision* refers to the number of digits in the significand. The *range* of numbers that can be represented by a particular type is determined by the range of possible exponents.

Table 2-4. *Standard Floating-Point Data Types and Their Typical Sizes*

Data Type	Format	Bit Size	Significand Precision	Exponent
float	Single-precision floating-point	32	24	8
double	Double-precision floating-point	64	53	11
long double	Extended-precision floating-point	64 or 80	53 or 64	11 or 15

▓ **Note** You cannot use the unsigned or signed modifiers with floating-point types; floating-point types are always signed.

The precision and range of the float, double, and long double types aren't prescribed by the C++ standard. In principle, they therefore depend both on your compiler and on the floating-point representations supported by the hardware that you are targeting.[2] The standard only guarantees that the precision of type long double will not be less than that of type double, and that of type double not less than that of type float.

---

[2] You typically compile executables to run on your own computer, or at least on computers with the same basic architecture. But in general you can create executables for other hardware as well (this is called *cross-compilation*). The target hardware could, for instance, be some mobile or embedded device, supporting significantly different native data types and processor instructions.

In practice, though, virtually all compilers and computer architectures today use floating-point numbers and arithmetic as specified by the IEEE 754 standard introduced in Chapter 1. Type float thus normally provides about seven decimal digits of precision (due to its significand of 24 bits, of which 23 are stored[3]), and type double nearly 16 digits (53-bit significand, 52 bits stored).

In practice, only the precision and range of type long double varies significantly between compilers and target architectures. The x86 CPU architecture of most desktop and laptop computers, notably, natively supports 80-bit floating-point numbers with a significand precision of 64 bit (which amounts to about 18 to 19 decimal digits of precision). Several x86 compilers therefore use that 80-bit extended-precision floating-point format for type long double—several, but not all. Microsoft Visual C++, for instance, implements long double using the same double-precision format as double, and Intel C++ requires a compiler switch to enable 80-bit precision. When targeting architectures other than x86, long double is likely represented differently as well.

Table 2-5 shows typical ranges of values that you can represent with the floating-point types on a x86 processor.

Table 2-5. *Typical Decimal Precisions and Ranges of Standard Floating-Point Types*

Type	Precision (Decimal Digits)	Range (+ or –)
float	7	$\pm 1.18 \times 10^{-38}$ to $\pm 3.4 \times 10^{38}$
double	15 (nearly 16)	$\pm 2.22 \times 10^{-308}$ to $\pm 1.8 \times 10^{308}$
long double	18-19	$+3.65 \times 10^{-4932}$ to $\pm 1.18 \times 10^{4932}$

The numbers of digits of precision in Table 2-5 are approximate. Zero can be represented exactly with each type, but values between zero and the lower limit in the positive or negative range can't be represented, so the lower limits are the smallest possible nonzero values.

▓ **Tip**   Type double is more than adequate in the majority of circumstances. When you use float, you always need to be more vigilant that the resulting loss of precision is acceptable for your application. You therefore typically use float only when speed or data size is of the essence.

Extended Floating-Point Data Types

While single- and double-precision IEEE 754 floating-point numbers are by far the most common floating-points formats, they are by no means the only formats in use by modern hard- and software. Hardware capable of processing 16-bit floating-point data is becoming more and more widely available. In acknowledgment of this evolution, C++23 added the possibility to support some of these alternative floating-point formats in a standardized manner. The names of these *extended floating-point data types* are listed in Table 2-6.

---

[3] In the IEEE 754 schema binary floating-point numbers are normalized to the form ±1....e±.... Since the leading bit of these normalized significands is always 1, there is no need to explicitly store it. Note that this is also why the numbers in Table 2-4 seemingly leave no room for the sign bit.

Table 2-6. *Optional Extended Floating-Point Data Types*

Data Type	Format	Bit Size	Significand Precision	Exponent
`std::float16_t`	IEEE half-precision floating-point	16	11	5
`std::float32_t`	IEEE single-precision floating-point	32	24	8
`std::float64_t`	IEEE double-precision floating-point	64	53	11
`std::float128_t`	IEEE quadruple-precision floating-point	128	113	15
`std::bfloat16_t`	"Brain Floating-Point"	16	8	8

The support for these extended floating-point data types is optional. Your compiler's documentation should tell you which, if any, of these types it supports. If available, however, their layout and behavior is fully prescribed by the C++ standard. Most of the extended floating-point data types again follow the IEEE 754 standard. The only exception is `std::bfloat16_t`, which follows a floating-point scheme developed by Google Brain, an artificial intelligence research group at Google.

▓ **Note** Even though `std::float32_t` and `std::float64_t` will often use the exact same representation and CPU instructions as `float` and `double`, they are distinct C++ types (that is, they are not simply type aliases for `float` and `double`: see Chapter 3 for the concept of type aliases).

The main advantage of `std::float32_t` and `std::float64_t` is portability. Your code will produce results that are (even) more predictable across all compilers that offer these types.

▓ **Caution** Even when using `std::float32_t` or `std::float64_t`, you still should not expect different implementations and/or processors to produce the exact same results for a given program. The IEEE floating-point standard, much like the C++ standard, allows for some implementation freedom, meaning different instruction sets and/or compiler optimizations may always produce slightly different results for floating-point calculation sequences. Of course, unless your calculations are particularly numerically unstable, these differences should only impact lesser significant bits.

You use `std::float16_t` and `std::bfloat16_t` when handling larger amounts of data in contexts where a lower precision is acceptable. Typical application areas for these data types include machine learning and image processing. `std::bfloat16_t` has the exact same range as single-precision floating-point numbers (both have an 8-bit exponent size), which of course means it offers a particularly small precision (only 2–3 decimal digits; see Table 2-7). `std::float16_t`, on the other hand, has a reduced range (5-bit exponent), resulting in a somewhat more balanced precision.

`std::float128_t`, finally, obviously targets situations where a higher precision is required, and/or where you need to represent numbers that are either very small or very large.

Table 2-7. *Half- and Quadruple-Precision Floating-Point Decimal Precisions and Ranges*

Type	Precision (Decimal Digits)	Range (+ or −)
std::float16_t	3	$\pm6.1\times 10^{-5}$ to $\pm65,504$
std::bfloat16_t	2-3	$\pm1.18 \times 10^{-38}$ to $\pm3.4 \times 10^{38}$
std::float128_t	34	$\pm3.36 \times 10^{-4932}$ to $\pm1.19 \times 10^{4932}$

▓ **Note**   We won't use the extended floating-point data types in this book. The portability argument for the 32- and 64-bit formats is not too relevant for us (and will also only truly begin to apply once sufficient compilers and libraries support the new C++23 data types), and the 16- and 128-bit formats are obviously intended for more specialized applications.

Floating-Point Literals

A floating-point literal includes either a decimal point or an exponent, or both; a numeric literal with neither is an integer. Here are some examples:

```
const float solar_mass{ 1.98847e30f }; // Decimal point, (positive) exponent, f suffix
const double ronto_gram{ 1e-27 };      // Negative exponent, no decimal point, no suffix
const std::float128_t plastic_number{ 1.324717957244746025960908854478097341F128 };
```

Floating-point literals without a suffix are of type double, float literals have f (or F) appended, and long double L (or l). Similar suffixes are defined for any available extended floating-point data type. Table 2-8 provides an overview.

Table 2-8. *Floating-Point Literal Suffixes*

Data Type	Literal Suffix	Data Type	Literal Suffix
float	f or F	std::float16_t	f16 or F16
double	(no suffix)	std::float32_t	f32 or F32
long double	l or L	std::float64_t	f64 or F64
		std::float128_t	f128 or F128
		std::bfloat16_t	bf16 or BF16

▓ **Tip**   Like with integer literals, we don't recommend the use of l as a suffix for long double literals because the letter l is easily confused with the number 1.

An exponent is optional in a floating-point literal and represents a power of 10 that multiplies the value. An exponent must be prefixed with e or E and follows the value. Here are some floating-point literals that include an exponent:

5E3 (5000.0)   100.5E2 (10050.0)   2.5e-3 (0.0025)   -0.1E-3L (-0.0001L)   .345e1F (3.45F)

The value between parentheses following each literal with an exponent is the equivalent literal without the exponent. Exponents are particularly useful when you need to express very small or very large values (such as 1.66e-27 or 1.988e30, the mass in kilograms of respectively a hydrogen atom and the sun).

As always, most compilers will happily initialize floating-point variables with literals that lack a matching suffix, or even with integer literals. If the literal value falls outside the representable range of the variable's type, though, your compiler should at least issue a warning regarding a narrowing conversion.

Finding the Limits

You have seen tables of the upper and lower limits for various types. The `<limits>` module of the Standard Library makes this information available for all the fundamental data types so you can access this for your compiler. For example, to display the maximum value you can store in a variable of type double, you could write this:

```
std::println("Maximum value of type double is {}", std::numeric_limits<double>::max());
```

The expression `std::numeric_limits<double>::max()` produces the value you want. By putting different type names between the angled brackets, you can obtain the maximum values for other data types. You can also replace `max()` with `min()` to get the minimum value that can be stored, but the meaning of minimum is different for integer and floating-point types. For an integer type, `min()` results in the true minimum, which will be a negative number for a signed integer type. For a floating-point type, `min()` returns the minimum positive value that can be stored.

▓ **Caution** `std::numeric_limits<double>::min()` typically equals 2.225e-308, an extremely tiny *positive* number. For floating-point types, `min()` thus does not give you the complement of `max()`. To get the lowest *negative* value a type can represent, you should use `lowest()` instead. For instance, `std::numeric_limits<double>::lowest()` typically equals -1.798e+308, a hugely negative number. For integer types, `min()` and `lowest()` always evaluate to the same number.

The following program displays the maximums and minimums for some of the numerical data types:

```
// Ex2_03.cpp - Finding maximum and minimum values for data types
import std;

int main()
{
  std::println("The range for type short is from {} to {}",
    std::numeric_limits<short>::min(), std::numeric_limits<short>::max());
  std::println("The range for type unsigned int is from {} to {}",
    std::numeric_limits<unsigned int>::min(), std::numeric_limits<unsigned int>::max());
  std::println("The range for type long long is from {} to {}",
    std::numeric_limits<long long>::min(), std::numeric_limits<long long>::max());
  std::println("The positive range for type float is from {} to {}",
    std::numeric_limits<float>::min(), std::numeric_limits<float>::max());
  std::println("The full range for type float is from {} to {}",
    std::numeric_limits<float>::lowest(), std::numeric_limits<float>::max());
```

```
  std::println("The positive range for type double is from {} to {}",
    std::numeric_limits<double>::min(), std::numeric_limits<double>::max());
}
```

You can easily extend this to include additional numeric types (see also Exercise 2-1). On our test system, the results of running Ex2_03 are as follows:

```
The range for type short is from -32768 to 32767
The range for type unsigned int is from 0 to 4294967295
The range for type long long is from -9223372036854775808 to 9223372036854775807
The positive range for type float is from 1.1754944e-38 to 3.4028235e+38
The full range for type float is from -3.4028235e+38 to 3.4028235e+38
The positive range for type double is from 2.2250738585072014e-308 to
1.7976931348623157e+308
```

Finding Other Properties of Fundamental Types

You can retrieve many other items of information about various types. The number of binary digits, or bits, for example, is returned by this expression:

```
std::numeric_limits<type_name>::digits
```

For floating-point types, you'll get the number of bits in the significand. For signed integer types, you'll get the number of bits in the value, that is, excluding any sign bit (remember, though, most integer representations today no longer use a sign bit). You can also find out what the range of the exponent component of floating-point values is, whether a type is signed or not, and so on. You can consult a Standard Library reference for the complete list.

The sizeof Operator

Notably absent from std::numeric_limits<> (see previous section) is a means to obtain the total binary size occupied by a type. The reason, of course, is that there exists a built-in operator for this. To obtain the number of bytes occupied by a type, by a variable, or by the result of any expression, you can use the sizeof operator instead. Here are some examples:

```
int height {74};
std::println("Type 'long double' occupies {} bytes.", sizeof(long double));
std::println("The height variable occupies {} bytes.", sizeof height);
std::println("The result of the expression height * height/2 occupies {} bytes",
                                              sizeof(height * height/2));
```

To use sizeof to obtain the memory occupied by a type (fundamental or otherwise), the type name must be between parentheses. You also need parentheses around an expression with sizeof. You don't need parentheses around a variable name, but there's no harm in putting them in either. In short, if you always use parentheses with sizeof, you can't go wrong.

The result of operator `sizeof` has type `std::size_t`. `std::size_t` is a Standard Library alias for an unspecified fundamental unsigned integer type (typically `unsigned long` or `unsigned long long`). As you'll learn in Chapter 3, a *type alias* is a different name for an existing type—much like cougar, puma, mountain lion, catamount, and panther are all aliases for one and the same animal[4]. The type of `std::size_t` monikers differs from compiler to compiler. The idea is that as long as you use `std::size_t` your code will compile with any compiler.

■ **Tip** As of C++23, you can define integer literals of type `std::size_t` using a suffix consisting of both u or U and z or Z (that is, uz, uZ, Uz, UZ, zu, zU, Zu, or ZU).[5]

■ **Tip** In older code, you will often find `size_t` used without its `std` namespace qualifier. The reason is that the `size_t` name originates from the C Standard Library, and C does not have the concept of namespaces. With `import std;`, however, the name `size_t` should normally only be made available in the `std` namespace. If you can't or don't feel like adding `std::` qualifiers all over a legacy code base, yet still want the convenience of importing the entire Standard Library in one go, you should therefore use `import std.compat;`. As noted also in Chapter 1, importing the `std.compat` module does the same as importing the `std` module except that it makes functionality from the C Standard Library available in both the `std` and the global namespace.

Floating-Point Calculations

You write floating-point calculations in the same way as integer calculations. Here's an example:

```
const double pi {3.141592653589793}; // Circumference of a pizza divided by its diameter
double a {0.2};                       // Thickness of proper New York-style pizza (in inches)
double z {9};                         // Radius of large New York-style pizza (in inches)
double volume {};                     // Volume of pizza - to be calculated
volume = pi*z*z*a;
```

The modulo operator, %, can't be used with floating-point operands, but all the other arithmetic operators that you have seen, +, -, *, and /, can be. You can also apply the prefix and postfix increment and decrement operators, ++ and --, to a floating-point variable with essentially the same effect as for an integer; the variable will be incremented or decremented by 1.0.

■ **Tip** The equivalent of the modulo operator % for floating-point calculations is `std::fmod()`, one of many mathematical functions offered by the Standard Library (more examples follow later). `std::fmod(7.4, 3.1)`, for example, evaluates to `1.2` (because $7.4 = 2 \times 3.1 + 1.2$, the remainder after integer division of 7.4 by 3.1 is 1.2; or, in mathematical speak, 7.4 is *congruent* to 1.2 modulo 3.1).

---

[4] The animal formally known as Puma concolor proudly holds the Guinness record for the animal with the highest number of different aliases, with over 40 aliases in the English language alone. It also holds the record for highest jump by a mammal from a standstill (23 ft, or 7 m!).
[5] If not combined with u or U, a z or Z suffix defines a literal of the signed integer type with the same size as `std::size_t` (until further notice, C++ defines no alias for this signed version of `std::size_t`).

Mathematical Constants

In the previous example, we computed the volume of a New York-style pizza using a self-defined constant pi:

```
const double pi {3.141592653589793};  // Circumference of a pizza divided by its diameter
```

But this number has other applications as well. You can use it to compute the volume of Neapolitan-style pizzas, California-style pizzas, Chicago-style pizzas, Greek pizzas, and so on—though not that of Sicilian- or Detroit-style pizzas. In fact, some even use this number outside of Italian cuisine as well. It is known among mathematicians as Archimedes' constant, and generally denoted by the Greek letter π.

Given its many uses in Italian cuisine and scientific computations alike, it would be a shame if every developer had to reinvent this wheel over and over again (or, rather, reinvent the ratio of this wheel's circumference to its diameter over and over again). The Standard Library therefore provides definitions for π and several other common mathematical constants. Table 2-9 lists some of the most well-known examples. You can consult a Standard Library reference for the complete list (look for the <numbers> module).

Table 2-9. *Examples of Numerical Constants Defined by the Standard Library*

Constant	Description	Approximate Value
std::numbers::e	The base of the natural logarithm	2.71828...
std::numbers::pi	π	3.14159...
std::numbers::sqrt2	The square root of 2	1.41421...
std::numbers::phi	The golden ratio constant φ	1.618...

All these constants have type double and are as accurate as possible for double-precision floating-point numbers (so up to about 17 decimal digits, typically). If you need these constants in a different precision, you append _v<T> to the constant's name, substituting T with the desired floating-point type. Examples of this are std::numbers::pi_v<std::float16_t> and std::numbers::sqrt_2_v<long double>.[6]

▓ **Tip**   Prefer predefined constants over self-defined ones. And if you do need to define some new constant, make sure to use the appropriate precision. All too often have we encountered legacy code that defines π as, say, 3.14159, with needlessly inaccurate results as a consequence!

Mathematical Functions

The Standard Library defines a large selection of mathematical functions that you can use in your programs. These functions range from the most basic to some of the most advanced mathematical functions (examples of the latter category include beauties such as cylindrical Neumann functions, associated Laguerre polynomials, and, our favorite, the Riemann zeta function). In this section, we introduce some of the basic functions that you are likely to use on a regular basis, but know that there are many, many more. You can consult a Standard Library reference for a complete list (look for the <cmath> header).

---

[6] These are examples of *variable templates,* a lesser-used flavor of templates. The principle is the same as with the function and class templates we explain in Chapters 10 and 17.

Table 2-10 presents some commonly used mathematical functions. As always, all the function names defined are in the std namespace. All listed functions accept arguments that can be of any floating-point or integral type. Unless otherwise noted, the outcome has type double if any argument has an integer type, and the same type of the (largest) floating-point argument otherwise.

Table 2-10. *Numerical Functions of the* <cmath> *Standard Library Header*

Function	Description
abs(arg)	Computes the absolute value of arg. Unlike all other standard math functions, std::abs() returns an integer type if arg is an integer (all other standard math functions effectively convert integer inputs to type double).
ceil(arg)	Computes the floating-point value nearest to the smallest integer greater than or equal to arg, so std::ceil(2.5) produces 3.0 and std::ceil(-2.5) produces -2.0.
floor(arg)	Computes the floating-point value nearest to the largest integer less than or equal to arg, so std::floor(2.5) results in 2.0 and std::floor(-2.5) results in -3.0.
trunc(arg)	Simply put, trunc()—short for *truncate*—zeros out (as much as possible) the fractional part of a floating-point number when written as a decimal number, so std::trunc(2.5) is 2.0 and std::trunc(-2.5) is -2.0.
round(arg) lround(arg) llround(arg)	Rounds arg to the nearest integer. The result of round() is a floating-point number, even for integer inputs, whereas, the results of lround() and llround() are of type long and long long, respectively. Halfway cases are rounded away from zero.[7] In other words, std::round(0.5f) gives 1.0f, and std::lround(-1.5) gives -2L.
pow(arg1, arg2)	Computes the value of arg1 raised to the power arg2, or $arg1^{arg2}$. arg1 and arg2 can be integer or floating-point types. The result of std::pow(2, 3) is 8.0, std::pow(1.5f, 3) equals 3.375f, and std::pow(4, 0.5) is equal to 2.0.
sqrt(arg)	Computes the square root of arg.
exp(arg)	Computes the value of e^{arg}. (Euler's number e raised to the power arg.)
log(arg)	Computes the natural logarithm (to base e) of arg. In math, this function is commonly written as $\ln(arg)$ or $\log_e(arg)$.
cos(arg) sin(arg) tan(arg)	Computes the cosine, sine, and tangent of arg, where arg is an angle measured in radians. The inverse trigonometric functions, acos(), asin(), and atan(), are available as well (returning, of course, an angle measured in radians).

---

[7] Usually, the rounding behavior of std::round() will suit you just fine. But just so you know, the Standard Library also offers the std::nearbyint() and std::rint() functions for which you can configure the rounding behavior through std::fesetround(). Available options include rounding halfway cases toward zero, toward negative infinity, and so on. You can consult a Standard Library reference for further details in the unlikely event that your need this flexibility.

Let's look at some examples of how these are used. Here's how you can calculate the cosine of an angle in radians:

```
double angle {1.5};                              // In radians
double cosine_value {std::cos(angle)};
```

If the angle is expressed in degrees, you simply convert it to radians first using the π constant:

```
const double pi_degrees {180};                   // pi radians equals 180 degrees
double angle_deg {60.0};                         // Angle in degrees
double cosine_value {std::cos(angle_deg * std::numbers::pi / pi_degrees)};
```

If you know the height of a church steeple is 100 feet and you're standing 50 feet from its base, you can calculate the angle in radians of the top of the steeple, like this:

```
double height {100.0};                           // Steeple height in feet
double distance {50.0};                          // Distance from base in feet
double angle {std::atan(distance / height)};  // Result in radians
```

You can use this value in `angle` and the value of `distance` to calculate the distance from your toe to the top of the steeple:

```
double toe_to_tip {distance / std::sin(angle)};
```

Of course, fans of Pythagoras of Samos could obtain the result much more easily, like this:

```
double toe_to_tip {std::sqrt(std::pow(distance, 2) + std::pow(height, 2))};
```

▓ **Tip**   The problem with an expression of form `std::atan(a / b)` is that by evaluating the division `a / b`, you lose information about the sign of a and b. This does not matter much in our example, as both `distance` and `height` are positive, but in general, you may be better off calling `std::atan2(a, b)`. Because `atan2()` knows the signs of both a and b, it is capable of properly reflecting this in the resulting angle. You can consult a Standard Library reference for the detailed specification.

Let's try a floating-point example. Suppose that you want to construct a circular pond in which you will keep fish. Having looked into the matter, you know that you must allow two square feet of pond surface area for every six inches of fish length. You need to figure out the diameter of the pond that will keep the fish happy. Here's how you can do it:

```
// Ex2_04.cpp - Sizing a pond for happy fish
import std;

int main()
{
  // 2 square feet pond surface for every 6 inches of fish
  const double fish_factor { 2.0/0.5 };  // Area per unit length of fish
  const double inches_per_foot { 12.0 };
```

```
double fish_count {};              // Number of fish
double fish_length {};             // Average length of fish

std::print("Enter the number of fish you want to keep: ");
std::cin >> fish_count;
std::print("Enter the average fish length in inches: ");
std::cin >> fish_length;
fish_length /= inches_per_foot;    // Convert to feet
std::println("");

// Calculate the required surface area
const double pond_area {fish_count * fish_length * fish_factor};

// Calculate the pond diameter from the area in feet
const double pond_diameter {2.0 * std::sqrt(pond_area / std::numbers::pi)};

// Convert to feet and inches
const double pond_diameter_feet{ std::floor(pond_diameter) };
const double pond_diameter_inch{
    std::round((pond_diameter - pond_diameter_feet) * inches_per_foot) };

std::println("Pond diameter required for {} fish is {} feet {} inches.",
            fish_count, pond_diameter_feet, pond_diameter_inch);
}
```

With input values of 20 fish with an average length of 9 inches, this example produces the following output:

```
Enter the number of fish you want to keep: 20
Enter the average fish length in inches: 9
Pond diameter required for 20 fish is 8 feet 9 inches.
```

You first define two const variables in main() that you'll use in the calculation. Notice the use of a constant expression to specify the initial value for fish_factor. You can use any expression for an initial value that produces a result of the appropriate type. You specify fish_factor and inches_per_foot as const because their values are fixed and should not be altered.

Next, you define the fish_count and fish_length variables in which you'll store the user input. Both have an initial value of zero. The input for the fish length is in inches, so you convert it to feet before you use it in the calculation for the pond. You use the /= operator to convert the original value to feet.

You define a variable for the area of the pond and initialize it with an expression that produces the required value:

```
const double pond_area {fish_count * fish_length * fish_factor};
```

The product of fish_count and fish_length gives the total length of all the fish in feet, and multiplying this by fish_factor gives the required area for the pond in square feet. Once computed and initialized, the value of pond_area will and should not be changed anymore, so you might as well declare the variable const to make that clear.

The area of a circle is given by the formula πr^2, where r is the radius. You can therefore calculate the radius of the circular pond by dividing the area by π and calculating the square root of the result. The diameter is twice the radius, so the whole calculation is carried out by this statement:

```
const double pond_diameter {2.0 * std::sqrt(pond_area / std::numbers::pi)};
```

You obtain the square root using the standard `sqrt()` function.

Of course, you could calculate the pond diameter in a single statement like this:

```
const double pond_diameter
    {2.0 * std::sqrt(fish_count * fish_length * fish_factor / std::numbers::pi)};
```

This eliminates the need for the `pond_area` variable so the program will be smaller and shorter. It's debatable whether this is better than the original, though, because it's far less obvious what is going on.

Either way, the variable `pond_diameter` now holds the pond's diameter in feet. To showcase `std::floor()` and `round()`, Ex2_04 then converts this nonintegral number of feet (roughly 8.74 feet for the inputs that we used earlier) to integral feet and inches values (8 feet 9 inches) using these two statements:

```
const double pond_diameter_feet{ std::floor(pond_diameter) };
const double pond_diameter_inch{
    std::round((pond_diameter - pond_diameter_feet) * inches_per_foot) };
```

To obtain the correct integral number of feet, you can round down `pond_diameter` using `std::floor()`. In our running example, this turns the diameter of about 8.74 feet into 8.0 feet—still a value of type `double`, but then without a fractional part. Had you used `std::round(pond_diameter)` instead, the result would've been 9.0—one foot too many.

To compute the integral number of remaining inches, on the other hand, `std::round()` is better suited that `std::floor()`. In our running example, subtracting `pond_diameter_feet` (8.0) from `pond_diameter` results in a residual distance of roughly 0.74 foot or 8.88 inches (the latter is obtained by multiplying with the `inches_per_foot` constant). And, clearly, rounding 8.88 to 9.0 is more accurate than flooring it to 8.0.

▓ **Caution**   In Ex2_04, `std::floor()` is only correct because ponds rarely have a negative diameter. When converting a negative number of feet to feet and inches, though, `std::floor()` gives undesired results. `std::floor(-8.74)`, for instance, equals -9.0, while the natural conversion of -8.74 feet is -8 feet 9 inches. One solution is to use `std::trunc()`: `std::trunc(±8.74)` gives the desired ±8.0. Another is to convert to an integer using the type casting operator explained later in this chapter.

Invalid Floating-Point Results

So far as the C++ standard is concerned, the result of division by zero is undefined. Nevertheless, floating-point operations are, as you know, mostly implemented according to the IEEE 754 standard. So in practice, compilers generally behave quite similarly when dividing floating-point numbers by zero.

The IEEE floating-point standard defines special values having a binary significand of all zeros and an exponent of all ones to represent `+infinity` or `-infinity`, depending on the sign bit. When you divide a positive nonzero value by zero, the result will be `+infinity`, and dividing a negative value by zero will result in `-infinity`. Evaluating for instance `std::log(0)` will result in `-infinity` as well.

Another special floating-point value defined by the IEEE standard is called *not-a-number*, usually abbreviated to NaN. This represents a result that isn't mathematically defined, such as when you divide zero by zero, or when you apply `std::sqrt()` to a negative number.

Any operation in which either or both operands are NaN results in NaN. Similarly, once an operation results in ±infinity, this will pollute all subsequent operations in which it participates as well. Table 2-11 summarizes all the possibilities (value in the table is any nonzero value).

Table 2-11. *Floating-Point Operations with NaN and ±infinity Operands*

Operation	Result	Operation	Result
±value / 0	±infinity	0 / 0	NaN
±infinity ± value	±infinity	±infinity / ±infinity	NaN
±infinity * value	±infinity	infinity - infinity	NaN
±infinity / value	±infinity	infinity * 0	NaN

▓ **Tip**   You can obtain a floating-point value that represents either infinity or NaN through the `std::numeric_limits<>` template seen earlier. Concretely, you can use expressions like `std::numeric_limits<float>::infinity()`, `-std::numeric_limits<std::bfloat16_t>::infinity()`, and `std::numeric_limits<double>::quiet_NaN()`. For the three standard floating-point types, NaN values can also be obtained through `std::nanf("")`, `std::nan("")`, and `std::nanl("")`.[8]

A discussion about the difference between quiet and signaling NaN values, or what other string arguments are valid for the `std::nan()` functions, is outside the scope of this brief introduction. If you're interested, you can always consult your Standard Library documentation.

You can discover how these values are printed by plugging the following code into `main()`:

```
double a{ 1.5 }, b{}, c{ -1 };
double result { a / b };
std::println("{} / {} = {}", a, b, result);
std::println("{} + {} = {}", result, a, result + a);
std::println("sqrt({}) = {}", c, std::sqrt(c));
```

The result should be:

```
1.5 / 0 = inf
inf + 1.5 = inf
sqrt(-1) = -nan
```

---

[8] The C standard library also defines the INFINITY and NAN float constants. These don't become available with `import std;` (or even with `import std.compat;`), though, because they are defined in the form of macros (see Appendix A). We therefore recommend you use equivalent C++ constructs instead.

▓ **Tip** To check whether a given number is either infinity or NaN, you can use the `std::isinf()` and `std::isnan()` Standard Library functions. (What you can do with the Boolean values you obtain from these classification functions, though, will only be disclosed in Chapter 4...)

Pitfalls

You need to be aware of the limitations of working with floating-point values. It's not difficult for the unwary to produce results that may be inaccurate or even incorrect. As you'll recall from Chapter 1, common sources of errors when using floating-point values include the following:

- Many decimal values don't convert exactly to binary floating-point values. The small errors that occur can easily be amplified in your calculations to produce large errors.

- Taking the difference between two nearly identical values will lose precision. If you take the difference between two values of type `float` that differ in the sixth significant digit, you'll produce a result that will have only one or two digits of accuracy. The other digits in the significand will be garbage. In Chapter 1, we already named this phenomenon *catastrophic cancellation*.

- Working with values that differ by several orders of magnitude can lead to errors. An elementary example of this is adding two values stored as type `float` where one value is 10^8 times larger than the other. You can add the smaller value to the larger as many times as you like, and the larger value will be unchanged.

Mixed Expressions and Type Conversion

You can write expressions involving operands of different types. For example, you could have defined the variable to store the number of fish in Ex2_04 like this:

```
unsigned int fish_count {};        // Number of fish
```

The number of fish is certainly an integer, so this makes sense. The number of inches in a foot is also integral, so you would want to define the variable like this:

```
const unsigned int inches_per_foot {12};
```

The calculation would still work okay despite the variables now being of differing types. Here's an example (available in Ex2_04A):

```
fish_length /= inches_per_foot;    // Convert to feet
const double pond_area{fish_count * fish_length * fish_factor};
```

Technically, all binary arithmetic operands require both operands to be of the same type. Where this is not the case, however, the compiler will arrange to convert one of the operand values to the same type as the other. These are called *implicit conversions*. The way this works is that the variable of a type with the more limited range is converted to the type of the other. The `fish_length` variable in the first statement is of type double. Type double has a greater range than type `unsigned int`, so the compiler will insert a conversion for the value of inches_per_foot to type double to allow the division to be carried out. In the second statement, the value of fish_count will be converted to type double to make it the same type as fish_length before the multiply operation executes.

With each operation with operands of different types, the compiler chooses the operand with the type that has the more limited range of values as the one to be converted to the type of the other. If we omit the extended floating-point data types for brevity (which follow similar conversion rules), it effectively ranks the types in the following sequence, from high to low:

1. long double	4. unsigned long long	7. long
2. double	5. long long	8. unsigned int
3. float	6. unsigned long	9. int

The operand to be converted will be the one with the lower rank. Thus, in an operation with operands of type long long and type unsigned int, the latter will be converted to type long long. An operand of type char, signed char, unsigned char, short, or unsigned short is always converted to at least type int. (Remember this. It'll become relevant in the next chapter!)

Implicit conversions can produce unexpected results. Consider these statements:

```
unsigned int x {20u};
int y {30};
std::println("{}", x - y);
```

You might expect the output to be -10, but it isn't. The output will be 4294967286! This is because the value of y is converted to unsigned int to match the type of x, so the result of the subtraction is an unsigned integer value. And -10 cannot be represented by an unsigned type. For unsigned integer types, going below zero always wraps around to the largest possible integer value. That is, for a 32-bit unsigned int type, -1 becomes 2^{32} - 1 or 4294967295, -2 becomes 2^{32} - 2 or 4294967293, and so on. This then of course means that -10 indeed becomes 2^{32} - 10, or 4294967286.

▨ **Note** The phenomenon where the result of a subtraction of unsigned integers wraps around to very large positive numbers is sometimes called *underflow*. In general, underflow is something to watch out for (we'll encounter examples of this in later chapters). Naturally, the converse phenomenon exists as well, and is called *overflow*. Adding the unsigned char values 253 and 5, for instance, will not give 258—the largest value a variable of type unsigned char can hold is 255! Instead, the result will be 2, or 258 modulo 256.

▨ **Caution** The outcome of over- and underflow is only defined for unsigned integers. With variables of signed integer types, the outcome of going beyond the bounds of what their type can represent is undefined—that is, it depends on your compiler and its target computer architecture.

The compiler will also insert an implicit conversion when the expression on the right of an assignment produces a value that is of a different type from the variable on the left. Here's an example:

```
int y {};
double z {5.0};
y = z;            // Requires an implicit narrowing conversion
```

The last statement requires a conversion of the value of the expression on the right of the assignment to allow it to be stored as type int. The compiler will insert a conversion to do this, but since this is a narrowing conversion, it may issue a warning message about possible loss of data. Compilers rarely look beyond the statement at hand when warning about type conversions they perceive as dangerous, and in general assigning a double to an integer will for sure result in a loss of precision (even if we disregard the unavoidable loss of the fractional part, the range of values that a double can typically hold, $\pm1.8 \times 10^{308}$, is ever so slightly larger than that of a 32-bit signed int, $\pm2.1 \times 10^{9}$).

Conversely, you also need to take care converting integers to floating-point values. With a significand of 53 bits, IEEE double-precision floating-point values can (easily) represent all 32-bit integer values exactly, but not all 64-bit integers. Single-precision floating-point values cannot even hold all 32-bit integers; a significand of 24 bits is not nearly enough to represent all 32-bit integers. Loss of precision may therefore occur when representing larger integers as lower-precision floating-point values. The IEEE single-precision floating-point value nearest to the integer 1'000'000'160, for instance, is 1'000'000'128.f.

```
int y {1'000'000'160};
float z {};
z = y;              // z holds 1'000'000'128.f after implicit narrowing conversion
```

Implicit type conversions may thus not always produce the result you want. It is therefore considered good practice to only use the *explicit type conversion* expressions we explain in the next sections. Most compilers offer optional compilation warnings that can help enforce such conventions.

Explicit Type Conversion

To explicitly convert the value of an expression to a given type, you write the following:

```
static_cast<type_to_convert_to>(expression)
```

The static_cast keyword reflects the fact that the cast is checked statically, that is, when the code is compiled. Later, when you deal with class types, you'll meet *dynamic casts*, where the conversion is checked dynamically, that is, when the program is executing. The effect of the cast is to convert the value that results from evaluating expression to the type that you specify between the angle brackets. The expression can be anything from a single variable to a complex expression involving lots of nested parentheses. You could eliminate any warning that arises from assignments such as those in the previous section by writing it as follows:

```
y = static_cast<int>(z);       // Never a compiler warning this time
```

Adding an explicit cast signals the compiler that a narrowing conversion is intentional. If the conversion is not narrowing, you'd rarely add an explicit cast. Here's another example of the use of static_cast<>():

```
double value1 {10.9};
double value2 {15.9};
int whole_number {static_cast<int>(value1) + static_cast<int>(value2)};   // 25
```

The initializing value for whole_number is the sum of the integral parts of value1 and value2, so they're each explicitly cast to type int. whole_number will therefore have the initial value 25. Note that as with integer division, casting from a floating-point type to an integral type uses *truncation* (similar to the std::trunc() function explained earlier). That is, it simply discards the entire fractional part of the floating-point number.

■ **Tip** Functions such as `std::round()`, `lround()`, and `llround()` (see earlier this chapter) allow you to round floating-point numbers to the nearest integer. In many cases rounding is better than the truncation used by (implicit or explicit) casting.

The casts in our previous example do not affect the values stored in `value1` and `value2`, which will remain as `10.9` and `15.9`, respectively. The values 10 and 15 produced by the casts are just stored temporarily for use in the calculation and then discarded. Although both casts cause a loss of information, the compiler always assumes you know what you're doing when you explicitly specify a cast.

Of course, the value of `whole_number` would be different if you wrote this:

```
int whole_number {static_cast<int>(value1 + value2)};                    // 26
```

The result of adding `value1` and `value2` will be `26.8`, which results in 26 when converted to type `int`. This is again different from what you would obtain if you instead wrote this:

```
int whole_number {static_cast<int>(std::round(value1 + value2))};   // 27
```

As always with braced initializers, without the explicit type conversion in this statement, the compiler will either refuse to insert or at least warn about inserting implicit narrowing conversions.

This example converts a length in yards as a decimal value to yards, feet, and inches using mostly explicit type conversions:

```cpp
// Ex2_05.cpp - Using explicit type conversions
import std;

int main()
{
  const unsigned feet_per_yard {3};
  const unsigned inches_per_foot {12};
  const unsigned inches_per_yard { feet_per_yard * inches_per_foot };

  double length {};        // Length as decimal yards
  unsigned int yards{};    // Whole yards
  unsigned int feet {};    // Whole feet
  unsigned int inches {};  // Whole inches

  std::print("Enter a length in yards as a decimal: ");
  std::cin >> length;

  // Get the length as yards, feet, and inches
  yards  = static_cast<unsigned int>(length);
  feet   = static_cast<unsigned int>((length - yards) * feet_per_yard);
  inches = static_cast<unsigned int>(
            std::round(std::fmod(length * inches_per_yard, inches_per_foot)));

  std::println("{} yards converts to {} yards {} feet {} inches.",
            length, yards, feet, inches);
}
```

This is the typical output from this program:

```
Enter a length in yards as a decimal: 2.8
2.8 yards converts to 2 yards 2 feet 5 inches.
```

The first three statements in `main()` define unsigned integer constants to convert between yards, feet, and inches. You declare these as `const` to prevent them from being modified accidentally. The variables that will store the results of converting the input to yards, feet, and inches are of type `unsigned int` and initialized with zero.

The statement that computes the whole number of yards from the input value is as follows:

```
yards = static_cast<unsigned int>(length);
```

The cast discards the fractional part of the value in `length` and stores the integral result in `yards`. You could omit the explicit cast here and leave it to the compiler to take care of, but it's always better to write an explicit cast in such cases. If you don't, it's not obvious that you realized the need for the conversion and the potential loss of data. Many compilers will then issue a warning as well.

You obtain the number of whole feet with this statement:

```
feet = static_cast<unsigned int>((length - yards) * feet_per_yard);
```

Subtracting `yards` from `length` produces the fraction of a yard in the length as a double value. The compiler will arrange for the value in `yards` to be converted to type `double` for the subtraction. The value of `feet_per_yard` will then be converted to `double` to allow the multiplication to take place, and finally, the explicit cast converts the result from type `double` to type `unsigned int`.

The final part of the calculation obtains the residual number of whole inches:

```
inches = static_cast<unsigned int>(
            std::round(std::fmod(length * inches_per_yard, inches_per_foot)));
```

Quite a lot is happening here. We'll work our way from the inside to the outside:

Starting from `length`, this expression first computes the total number of inches by multiplying `length` with `inches_per_yard`. Because `length` is of type `double`, `inches_per_yard` will implicitly be converted to type `double` as well before calculating this product.

Next, `std::fmod()` determines the number of residual inches—for now, still as a floating-point number. As noted earlier, `std::fmod()` is the equivalent of the % operator for floating-point calculations. In our example of 2.8 yards, the `std::fmod()` subexpression evaluates from `std::fmod(2.8 * 36, 12)` over `std::fmod(100.8, 12)` to eventually 4.8 (100.8 = 8×12 + 4.8).

At this point, all that remains is converting the resulting nonintegral number of inches (4.8) to an integer value of type `unsigned int` (ideally, in this case, 5u). Naturally, we could again cast to `unsigned int` directly using `static_cast<unsigned int>(4.8)`. But since casting truncates, doing so would result in a remainder of 4 inches instead of the preferred 5 inches. We therefore compute `std::round(4.8)` first, and only then cast the rounded floating-point value (5.0) to the desired type `unsigned int`.

░ **Note**   Had the target type been `long` or `long long` instead of `unsigned int`, we could have avoided the explicit cast by invoking `std::lround()` or `std::llround()`. But since there is no standard function to round to an `unsigned int` directly, we had to combine rounding with an explicit type conversion.

Old-Style Casts

Prior to the introduction of static_cast<> into C++ around 1998—so a very, very long time ago—explicit casts were written like this:

```
(type_to_convert_to)expression
```

The result of expression is cast to the type between the parentheses. For example, the statement to calculate feet in the previous example could be written like this:

```
feet = (unsigned int)((length - yards) * feet_per_yard);
```

This type of cast is a remnant of the C language and is referred to as a *C-style cast*. Several kinds of casts in C++ are now differentiated, but the old-style casting syntax covers them all. Because of this, code using the old-style casts is more prone to errors. It isn't always clear what you intended, and you may not get the result you expected. Also, the round parentheses blend in too much with the surrounding (compound) expressions—the static_cast<>() operator is far easier to spot visually.

▓ **Tip** You'll still see old-style casts at times because it's still part of the language, but we strongly recommend you do not use them in new code. One should never use C-style casts in C++ code. Period. That is why this is also the last time we mention this syntax in this book.

The auto Keyword

You use the auto keyword to indicate that the compiler should deduce the type of a variable. Here are some examples:

```
auto m {10};               // m has type int
auto n {200UL};            // n has type unsigned long
auto p {std::numbers::pi}; // p has type double
```

The compiler will deduce the types for m, n, and p from the initial values you supply. You can use functional or assignment notation with auto for the initial value as well:

```
auto m = 10;               // m has type int
auto n = 200UL;            // n has type unsigned long
auto p(std::numbers::pi);  // p has type double
```

Having said that, this is not really how the auto keyword is intended to be used. When defining variables of fundamental types, you often might as well specify the type explicitly. You'll meet the auto keyword again later in the book where it is more appropriately and much more usefully applied.

■ **Caution**   In JavaScript, you can declare variables using the `var` or `let` keywords without immediately assigning them a value. You *cannot* do the same in C++ using the `auto` keyword.

```
auto v1;           /* Not allowed! */
auto v2{};         /* Not allowed! */
```

Every variable in C++ requires a type from the get-go. The `auto` keyword simply saves you from having to spell out the type of a variable yourself. It instructs the compiler to deduce its type for you from that of the initial value. In C++, the deduction of this type happens exclusively at compile-time, where in JavaScript this may happen at runtime as well whenever you assign a value to a variable.

Be careful when using braced initializers with the `auto` keyword. For example, suppose you write this (notice the equals sign!):

```
auto m = {10};              // m has type std::initializer_list<int>
```

Then the type deduced for m will not be `int`, but `std::initializer_list<int>`. To give you some context, this is the same type you would get if you'd use a list of elements between the braces:

```
auto list = {1, 2, 3};     // list has type std::initializer_list<int>
```

You will see later that such lists are typically used to specify the initial values of containers such as `std::vector<>`. As of C++17, this is the only minor quirk you need to be aware of. [9] Here's an overview:

```
auto i {10};                // i has type int
auto pi = {3.14159};        // pi has type std::initializer_list<double>
auto list1{1, 2, 3};        // error: does not compile!
auto list2 = {4, 5, 6};     // list2 has type std::initializer_list<int>
```

To summarize, you can use braced initialization to initialize any variable with a single value, provided you do not combine it with an assignment.

Working with Character Variables

Variables of type char occupy one byte, and typically store a code for a single character. You define variables of type char in the same way as variables of the other types that you've seen. Here's an example:

```
char letter;                // Uninitialized - so junk value
char yes {'Y'}, no {'N'};   // Initialized with character literals
char ch {33};               // Integer initializer equivalent to '!'
```

---

[9] For those of you still using C++11 or C++14 compilers, never use braced initializers with auto type deduction because the results are simply too unpredictable. Instead, either explicitly state your variable types or use assignment or functional notation.

You can initialize a variable of type char with a character literal between single quotes or by an integer. An integer initializer must be within the range of type char—remember, it depends on the compiler whether it is a signed or unsigned type.

Variables of type char are numeric; after all, they store integer codes that represent characters. They can therefore participate in arithmetic expressions, just like variables of type int or long. Here's an example:

```
char ch {'A'};
char letter {ch + 2};        // letter is 'C'
++ch;                        // ch is now 'B'
ch += 3;                     // ch is now 'E'
```

When you write a char variable using std::print() functions, it is by default output as a character, not as an integer. If you want to see it as a numerical value, one option is to cast it to another integral type first. Here's an example:

```
std::println("ch is '{}' which is code {}", ch, static_cast<int>(ch));
```

This produces the following output:

```
ch is 'E' which is code 69
```

> **Note** Instead of casting, std:println() also allows you to format characters as numbers directly by overriding the default formatting. We'll see an example of this later in this chapter in Ex2_08.

Working with Unicode Characters

The encoding used for char and the corresponding string literals is implementation-defined. It may be a variable-length encoding (typically UTF-8; see Chapter 1), but it may also simply be the single-byte ASCII encoding or 8-bit extension thereof.

> **Note** If supported, you should consider configuring your compiler to use UTF-8 for encoding character and string literals (if it does not do so already by default).

Single-byte characters are generally adequate for representing English text (à propos, even that statement is already a bit naïve…). However, if you want to handle character sets for non-English languages, a repertoire of 128- or 256-character codes doesn't go nearly far enough. And as you know from Chapter 1, Unicode is the most commonly used answer to this problem.

Next to char, C++ defines four more character types: wchar_t, char8_t, char16_t, and char32_t. Types char8_t, char16_t, or char32_t are intended to store characters encoded as UTF-8, UTF-16, or UTF-32, respectively, and their sizes are the same on all common platforms (we're sure you can guess what these sizes are…). Here are some example variables of these types:

```
char8_t dollar {u8'$'};
char16_t delta {u'Δ'};
char32_t ya {U'я'};
```

The prefixes u8, u, and U to the literals indicate that they are UTF-8, UTF-16, and UTF-32, respectively. Because UTF-8 and UTF-16 are variable-width encodings, not all letters can be represented by a single character. The Greek letter Δ, for instance, needs a sequence of two bytes to be encoded in UTF-8.

```
char8_t delta8 {u8'Δ'}; /* Error: Δ (code point U+0394) encoded as 2 UTF-8 code units */
```

▓ **Note**   Because the char8_t type was introduced in C++20, most legacy code and libraries still use type char to represent UTF-8 encoded letters. This can be confusing, at times, because the same type is used to store different encodings as well (be it single-byte or multi-byte). New code should shift toward using char8_t as much as possible.

Type wchar_t is an older fundamental type intended for character sets where a single character does not fit into one byte. Hence its name. wchar_t derives from *wide char*acter, because it is "wider" than the usual one-byte character. By contrast, type char is referred to as "narrow."

You define wide-character literals similarly to literals of type char, but you prefix them with L. Here's an example:

```
wchar_t cc {L'ç'};
```

This defines cc as type wchar_t and initializes it to the wide-character representation for the letter c-cedilla (a letter commonly used in, for instance, French, Catalan, and Portuguese).

The size of wide characters and the encoding used for wide-character literals is again implementation-specific. Both generally correspond to the preferred wide-character encoding of the target platform. For Windows, wchar_t is typically 16-bit wide and wide-character literals are encoded with UTF-16; for most other platforms, wchar_t is 32-bit wide and wide-character literals are encoded with UTF-32. While that makes wchar_t perfectly suited for interacting with native Unicode APIs, it does not lend itself to writing code that is portable across different platforms.

The Standard Library provides standard input and output streams std::wcin and std::wcout for reading and writing characters of type wchar_t, and std::print() and std::format() functions are capable of formatting wide characters as well. Unfortunately, there is no such provision within the library for handling char8_t, char16_t, or char32_t character data yet.

We briefly return to processing Unicode characters in Chapter 7, where we discuss strings.

Unicode Literals and Source File Encodings

The encoding of your source files is orthogonal to the encoding that the compiler uses to transcode literals. Recall these examples from the previous section:

```
char8_t dollar {u8'$'};   // Compiled to a UTF-8 code unit
char16_t delta {u'Δ'};    // Compiled to a UTF-16 code unit
char32_t ya {U'я'};       // Compiled to a UTF-32 code unit
```

In your source file these three characters are encoded using one and the same encoding (never mix different encodings within the same source file!). In the executable, though, the compiler writes code points of three different encodings, each of a different size. Suppose you use UTF-8 to encode your source files (as recommended in Chapter 1, for maximum portability). Then the Δ character is encoded as two 8-bit code units in your source file (1100111010010100 in binary form). Compiled, though, the literal results in a single UTF-16 code unit (0000001110010100 in binary form).

Escape Sequences

Certain characters are inherently problematic within character or string literals. Obviously, you can't enter characters such as newline directly in literals, as they'll just do what they're supposed to do: go to a new line in your source code file (the only exception to this rule are raw string literals, which are covered in Chapter 7). You can enter these problem characters in literals by means of an *escape sequence*, though. An escape sequence is an indirect way of specifying a character, and it always begins with a backslash. Table 2-12 shows the most commonly used escape sequences.

Table 2-12. *The Most Commonly Used Escape Sequences*

Escape Sequence	Character
\n	Newline
\r	Carriage return (part of the \r\n newline sequence for Windows)
\t	Horizontal tab
\\	Backslash (\)
\"	Double quote (") in string literals
\'	Single quote (') in character literals

The first three escape sequences in Table 2-12 represent various line breaks or whitespace characters. The last three characters, however, are more regular, yet at times problematic to represent directly in code. Clearly, the backslash character itself is difficult because it signals the start of an escape sequence, and the single and double quote characters because they are used as delimiters for literals, as in the constant 'A' or the string "text". This program that uses escape sequences outputs a message to the screen. To see it, you'll need to enter, compile, link, and execute the code:

```
// Ex2_06.cpp - Using escape sequences
import std;

int main()
{
  std::println("\"Least \'said\' \\\n\t\tsoonest \'mended\'.\"");
}
```

When you manage to compile, link, and run this program, you should see the following output displayed:

```
"Least 'said' \
                soonest 'mended'."
```

The output is determined by what's between the outermost double quotes in the following statement:

```
std::println("\"Least \'said\' \\\n\t\tsoonest \'mended\'.\"");
```

The outer double quote characters are *delimiters* that identify the beginning and end of the string literal; they aren't part of the string. In principle, *everything* between these delimiters gets printed. Each escape sequence, though, will be converted to the character it represents by the compiler, so that character will be sent to `std::println()`, not the escape sequence itself. A backslash in a string literal *always* indicates the start of an escape sequence, so the first character that's printed is a double quote character. Least followed by a space is output next. This is followed by a single quote character, then `said`, followed by another single quote. Next is a space, followed by the backslash specified by `\\`. Then a newline character corresponding to `\n` is printed so the cursor moves to the beginning of the next line. You then presented two tab characters with `\t\t`, so the cursor will be moved two tab positions to the right. The word `soonest` is output next followed by a space and then `mended` between single quotes. Finally, a period is output followed by a double quote.

▓ **Tip**   If you're no fan of escape sequences, Chapter 7 introduces an interesting alternative to them called *raw string literals*.

The truth is, in our enthusiasm for showcasing character escaping, we may have gone a bit overboard in `Ex2_06.cpp`. You actually do not have to escape the single quote character, `'`, inside string literals; there's already no possibility for confusion. So, the following statement would have worked just fine:

```
std::println("\"Least 'said' \\\n\t\tsoonest 'mended'.\"");
```

It's only when within a character literal of the form `'\''` that a single quote really needs escaping. Conversely, double quotes don't need a backslash then; your compiler will happily accept both `'\"'` and `'"'`.

▓ **Note**   The `\t\t` escape sequences in Ex2_06 are, strictly speaking, not required either—you could in principle type tabs in a string literal as well (as in `"\"Least 'said' \\\n          soonest 'mended'.\""`). Using `\t\t` is nevertheless recommended; the problem with tabs is that one generally cannot tell the difference between a tab, "   ", and a number of spaces, "   ", let alone properly count the number of tabs. Also, some text editors tend to convert tabs into spaces upon saving. It's therefore not uncommon for style guides to require the use of the `\t` escape sequence in string literals.

Escaping Unicode Characters

Tabs, line breaks, quotes, and backslashes are not the only characters that may need escaping. The Unicode standard, for instance, defines at least a few dozen different whitespace characters, all even harder to type and distinguish in your editor than tabs (see earlier). Your keyboard also only has a limited number of keys, so typing foreign or non-letter characters will always be challenging. Or perhaps you simply prefer to use plain 7-bit ASCII to encode your source files to increase portability even further (although we can't imagine any editor or compiler not supporting UTF-8 these days…). Either way, you can use various escape sequences to encode any Unicode character you want. Here are some examples:

```
char8_t dollar {u8'\44'};       // Octal escape code for the dollar sign ($)
char16_t delta {u'\x394'};      // Hexadecimal escape code for Greek Delta (Δ)
char32_t ya {U'\u044f'};        // UTF-16 character code for Cyrillic letter ya (я)
wchar_t cc {L'\U000000E7'};     // UTF-32 character code for c-cedilla (ç)
```

The values between the single quotes are an escape sequence that specifies the octal or hexadecimal representation of the character code. The backslash always indicates the start of the escape sequence. Table 2-13 lists the different forms of escape sequences in C++.

Table 2-13. *Numerical Escape Sequences and Universal Character Names*

Escape Sequence	Numeric Values	Example (ß character)
\ddd	1 to 3 octal digits	\337
\o{d...}	Any number of octal digits	\o{337}
\xd...	Any number of hexadecimal digits	\xDF, \x00DF
\x{d...}	Any number of hexadecimal digits	\x{DF}, \x{00DF}
\udddd	4 hexadecimal digits (UTF-16 code unit)	\u00DF
\u{d...}	Any number of hexadecimal digits	\u{DF}, \u{00DF}
\Udddddddd	8 hexadecimal digits (UTF-32 code unit)	\u000000DF
\N{*name*}	Universal character name	\N{LATIN SMALL LETTER SHARP S}

Octal codes are rarely used, with the notable exception of \0 often used to enter the null terminating character of C-style strings; see Chapter 7. For the most part, you'll use one of the other escape sequence formats. There are various websites where you can find the hexadecimal codes and names of all Unicode characters.

▒ **Note** The \u, \U, and \N sequences can also be used to escape characters outside of character or string literals should you want to (in identifiers, for instance, or in code comments; see Chapter 1); \, \o, and \x are valid only within literals. In practice, though, this difference rarely matters.

Escape sequences of the form \o{}, \x{}, and \u{} are new in C++23. They are mostly useful in Unicode string literals (see Chapter 7), where \o{} and \x{} in particular allow you to sidestep ambiguities when the next character happens to be a valid octal or hexadecimal digit as well.

The option to use the full universal character name is new in C++23 as well. While verbose, it generally leads to more human readable code[10]. When using any other escape sequence, you'll often find yourself clarifying what character you encoded with a comment (and/or a well-chosen variable name):

```
const auto cat {U'\U0001F638' }; // Grinning cat face with smiling eyes emoji
```

▒ **Note** Unlike in C++ identifiers (see Chapter 1), any Unicode character is allowed within character and string literals, including emojis, currency symbols, mathematical symbols, and so on. Unless you use raw literals (see Chapter 7), and if you use a proper source file encoding, the only characters that you really have to escape are the backslash (\\), new line (\n, \r), and quote characters (\' or \").

---

[10] Granted, "Latin Small Letter Sharp S" in Table 2-13 is perhaps not the best example for selling you on the use of the Unicode name, given that ß is probably better known by its less formal name, "eszett"...

Formatting

Earlier in this chapter, we produced a highly sophisticated scientific program to recommend the optimal diameter for new fish ponds. For 20 fish with an average length of nine inches, Ex2_04 and Ex2_04A produced the following output:

```
Pond diameter required for 20 fish is 8 feet 9 inches.
```

Suppose that instead of converting pond_diameter to integer feet and inch values, we simply print it directly using the following statement (see Ex2_04B):

```
std::println("Pond diameter required for {} fish is {} feet.",
             fish_count, pond_diameter);
```

Then for the same shoal of 20 fish, the program's recommendation becomes:

```
Pond diameter required for 20 fish is 8.740387444736633 feet.
```

Evidently, std::println() by default prints the complete decimal representation of floating-point numbers such as pond_diameter. More specifically, it prints the shortest string that still ensures a *lossless round-trip*. Or, in other words, the shortest string that when converted back to a floating-point number of the same type gives the exact same value as the one you started with. For a double this can result in strings with up to 16 or 17 decimal digits, as in our example. Of course, not all doubles require that many digits for a lossless round-trip. The default formatting of double value 1.5, for instance, is simply "1.5".

For Ex2_04B, the precision of 8.740387444736633 may be a tad excessive: even the most meticulous pond enthusiast rarely measures his digs up to sub-femtometer precision—a precision about a million times smaller than your average atom. Most fish really aren't all that fussy either.

So how to tune Ex2_04B to print pond_diameter with a more sensible precision? You could attempt to round each number up to the desired number of decimals yourself prior to printing it (that would make for an interesting exercise, actually!). But surely there must be a better solution? Let's explore.

Modern Formatting

To repeat what you already know from Chapter 1: the first argument to std::println() is the *format string*. This string contains any number of *replacement fields*, each surrounded with a pair of curly braces, {}. The format string is followed by zero or more additional *arguments*, generally one per replacement field. In Ex2_04B, for instance, there are two variables to format: fish_count and pond_diameter. The result is that std::println() prints the format string to the standard output stream with each field replaced with a textual representation of one the additional arguments, followed by a line break. If you don't want the line break, you use std::print() instead.

By default, replacement fields are paired with the arguments after the format string in *left-to-right* order, after which the argument values are converted to text using a fixed set of *default formatting* rules. For integer and floating-point numbers these default formatting rules boil down to a lossless conversion to a decimal representation.

But of course, you can override the default formatting. You do so by adding a *format specifier* between the curly braces of a replacement field. We discuss this in the next subsection. After that, we'll explain how to override the default left-to-right order and how to output the same value more than once.

■ **Note** The `std::format()` family of functions we briefly introduced in Chapter 1 accept the same format specifiers as `std::print()` and `std::println()`. We don't use `std::format()` that often in this book, though, so we'll focus on `std::print()` and `std::println()` in this section as well.

Format Specifiers

A format specifier is a seemingly cryptic sequence of numbers and characters, introduced by a colon, telling `std::format()`, `std::print()` or `std::println()` how you would like the corresponding data to be formatted. To tune floating-point precision, for instance, you add, after the mandatory colon, a dot followed by an integer number:

```
std::println("Pond diameter required for {} fish is {:.2} feet.",
             fish_count, pond_diameter);
```

By default, this integer specifies the *total number of significant digits* (2 in our example), counting digits both before and after the decimal point. The result thus becomes (see `Ex2_04C.cpp`):

```
Pond diameter required for 20 fish is 8.7 feet.
```

You can instead make the precision specify the number of digits *after* the decimal point—the *number of decimal places* in other words—by enabling "fixed-point" formatting of floating-point numbers. You do so by appending the letter f to the format specifier. If you replace `{:.2}` with `{:.2f}` in our running example, it produces the following output instead (see `Ex2_04D.cpp`):

```
Pond diameter required for 20 fish is 8.74 feet.
```

Here is the (slightly simplified) general form of the format specifiers for fields of fundamental and string types:

```
[[fill]align][sign][#][0][width][.precision][type]
```

The square brackets are for illustration purposes only and mark optional *formatting options*. Not all options are applicable to all field types. precision, for instance, is only applicable to floating-point numbers (as you already know) and strings (where it defines how many characters will be used from the string).

■ **Note** If you specify an unsupported formatting option, or if you make any syntactical mistake in one of the format specifiers, `std::print()`, `std::println()`, and `std::format()` (should) fail to compile. For instance, you can try this by adding a second `.2` format specifier to our favorite format string:

```
std::println("Pond diameter required for {:.2} fish is {:.2} feet.",
             fish_count, pond_diameter);
```

Because `fish_count` is an integer (ever since `Ex2_04A`), you are not allowed to specify a precision for that field. And so the previous `std::println()` statement should fail to compile. Unfortunately, at the time of writing, the error messages produced by the various implementations of `std::println()` rarely excel in clarity, and as such may not assist you much in diagnosing your mistakes. We can only hope this improves as the implementations of C++'s formatting libraries mature.

Formatting Tabular Data

The following formatting options (highlighted in Bold) allow you to control the width and alignment of each field. We regularly use them in this book to output text that resembles a table.

[[fill]align][sign][#]**[0][width]**[.precision][type]

    width is a positive integer that defines the *minimum field width*. If needed, extra characters are inserted into the formatted field to reach this minimum width. Which characters are inserted and where depends both on the field's type and which other formatting options are present:

- For numeric fields, if the width option is preceded with 0 (zero), extra 0 characters are inserted before the number's digits, but after any sign character (+ or -) or prefix sequence (such as 0x for hexadecimal numbers; see later). 0 has no effect if combined with any of the align options discussed shortly.

- Otherwise, the *fill character* is inserted. The default fill character is a space, but you can override this with the fill formatting option. The align option determines where this fill character is inserted. A field can be *left-aligned* (<), *right-aligned* (>), or *centered* (^). The default alignment depends on the field's type.

    You cannot specify the fill character without specifying an alignment as well. Note also that the fill, align, and 0 options have no effect unless you also specify a width.

    Still with us? Or is your head starting to spin? We know we just threw a lot of formatting options at you all at once. High time we made it all concrete with some code. We recommend that you take your time to analyze this next example (perhaps you can try to predict what the output will look like?), and to play with its format specifiers to see the effects of the different formatting options.

```cpp
// Ex2_07.cpp - The width, alignment, fill, and 0 formatting options of std::println()
import std;

int main()
{
  // Default alignment: right for numbers, left otherwise
  std::println("{:7}|{:7}|{:7}|{:7}", 1, -.2, "str", 'c');
  // Left and right alignment + custom fill character
  std::println("{:*<7}|{:*<7}|{:*>7}|{:*>7}", 1, -.2, "str", 'c');
  // 0 formatting option for numbers + centered alignment
  std::println("{:07}|{:07}|{:^7}|{:^7}", 1, -.2, "str", 'c');
}
```

Because we use the same width, 7, for all fields, the result resembles a table. More specifically, the result looks as follows:

```
      1|   -0.2|str    |c
1******|-0.2***|****str|******c
0000001|-0000.2|  str  |   c
```

From the first line, you see that the default alignment of fields is not always the same. By default, numeric fields align to the right, whereas string and character fields align to the left.

For the second line, we mirrored all default alignments using the < and > alignment options. We also set the fill character of all fields to *.

The third line showcases two more options: centered alignment (^) and the special 0 filling option for numeric fields (0 may only be used for numeric fields).

Formatting Numbers

These four remaining options are mostly relevant to numeric fields:

[[fill]align]**[sign][#]**[0][width]**[.precision][type]**

precision you already know, but there is much more to formatting numbers than that. Like in the previous section, there is a lot to take in here, and we will make it more concrete with an example after.

- Fixed-point formatting (f; see earlier) is not the only supported type option for formatting floating-point numbers. Others are *scientific formatting* (e), *general formatting* (g), and even *hexadecimal formatting* (a).

- Integer fields are mostly equivalent to floating-point fields, except that the precision option is not allowed. Supported types include *binary formatting* (b) and *hexadecimal formatting* (x).

- Adding a # character toggles the *alternate form*. For integers, the alternate form adds a *base prefix* (0x or 0b); for floating-point numbers it causes the output to always contain a decimal point, even if no digit follows it.

- The E, G, A, B, and X formatting types are equivalent to their lowercase equivalents, except that any letter in the output is capitalized. This includes base prefixes (0X or 0B), hexadecimal digits (A through F), and values for infinity and NaN values (INF and NAN instead of inf and nan).

- The sign option is a single character that determines what is printed in front of non-negative numbers. Negative numbers are always preceded with a – character. Possible values for sign include + (instructs to put a + in front of non-negative numbers) and a space character (put a space in front of non-negative numbers).

The following example should clarify these points (the different bullets from earlier are illustrated more or less in order):

```
// Ex2_08.cpp - Formatting numeric values with std::println()
import std;

int main()
```

```
{
  const double pi{ std::numbers::pi };
  std::println("Default: {:.2}, fixed: {:.2f}, scientific: {:.2e}, general: {:.2g}",
             pi, pi, pi, pi);
  std::println("Default: {}, binary: {:b}, hex.: {:x}", 314, 314, 314);
  std::println("Default: {}, decimal: {:d}, hex.: {:x}", 'c', 'c', 'c');
  std::println("Alternative hex.: {:#x}, binary: {:#b}, HEX.: {:#X}", 314, 314, 314);
  std::println("Forced sign: {:+}, space sign: {: }", 314, 314);
  std::println("All together: {:*<+10.4f}, {:+#09x}", pi, 314);
}
```

Here is the expected outcome:

```
Default: 3.1, fixed: 3.14, scientific: 3.14e+00, general: 3.1
Default: 314, binary: 100111010, hex.: 13a
Default: c, decimal: 99, hex.: 63
Alternative hex.: 0x13a, binary: 0b100111010, HEX.: 0X13A
Forced sign: +314, space sign:  314
All together: +3.1416***, +0x00013a
```

You should be able to understand most of this yourself. Only the different formatting options for floating-point numbers may warrant some more explanation.

Scientific formatting (e or E) always adds an exponent component to the output, precisely like we did in Chapter 1 when explaining floating-point numbers. You can use the same exponent notation also when entering floating-point literals. Exponents are mostly interesting either for very small numbers (such as 2.50e-11, the radius of a hydrogen atom), or for very large numbers (such as 1.99e30, the mass of the sun).

For more regular-sized numbers, always adding an exponent component is typically not ideal, as seen in our example (where pi has exponent +00). This is where the *general formatting* option (g or G) comes in handy; by default, it is equivalent to fixed-point formatting (f or F), only for very small or large numbers (the exact heuristic is not that important), it switches to scientific formatting (e or E) and adds the exponent. You can give it a run by assigning different values (large or small) to the pi constant in Ex2_08.

▪ **Caution** The default "shortest decimal round-trip" formatting of floating-point values uses exponent notation if this leads to a (strictly) shorter representation. We can illustrate this with the following example (the trailing dots turn the literals into floating-point values of type double):

```
std::println("{}, {}, {}, {}", 1'000., 10'000., 100'000., 100'001.);
```

The output of this statement is "1000, 10000, 1e+05, 100001". For 100'000, the string "1e+05" is one character shorter than "100000", making "1e+05" the shortest string that ensures a lossless round-trip. For 10'000, "1e+04" is tied in length with "10000", and so default formatting prefers "10000".

Argument Indexes

Being the perceptive, critical reader that you are, you have likely been wondering why we put a colon in front of each format specifier. The reason is that there is still something that you can add to the left of this colon as well. And that something is an *argument index*. Until now all replacement fields were matched with arguments of std::println() in a left-to-right order. You can override this, however, by adding an argument index to each replacement field. To illustrate, consider the following variation of our favorite println() statement.

```
std::println(
    "{1:.2f} feet is the optimal diameter for a pond with {0} fishes.",
    fish_count, pond_diameter
);
```

By rephrasing our English sentence, we have swapped the order of the two replacement fields. To then keep the order of the other two arguments, fish_count and pond_diameter, the same, we had to add an argument index to both replacement fields. This index is separated from the format specifier by a colon. If no format specifier is required, the index is not followed by a colon.

The semantics of an argument index should be rather straightforward. The only thing to watch out for is that you must start counting at zero: the first argument, fish_count, has index 0, the second index 1, and so on. This may seem odd at first, but that is just the way indexes always work in C++. In Chapter 5, you'll encounter the same phenomenon again when working with arrays.

▓ **Note**   In our toy example, the argument indexes are not required. You could instead simply swap the order of the fish_count and pond_diameter arguments. It would even make the code clearer to do so. But the need for out-of-order formatting does arise in real-life scenarios, where you, as a developer, are not necessarily the one supplying the (final) format string. Instead, a technical writer may be entering user-facing text (where the order may change for grammatical reasons), or a translator may be providing translated messages (where the order may even differ between different languages). It would be a shame if a program had to be reworked each time one of these texts changes.

Besides reordering fields, you can also use argument indexes to format the same input value more than once. The second print statement of Ex2_08, for instance, could be written as follows (see Ex2_08A for similar rewrites of all print Ex2_08's statements):

```
std::println("Default: {0}, binary: {0:b}, hex.: {0:x}", 314);
```

Formatting Stream Output

You can change the way an output stream such as std::cout formats data using *stream manipulators* (see Chapter 1 for a brief introduction on streams). You apply a stream manipulator by inserting it into the stream using its << operator together with the data itself. With the setprecision() manipulator, for instance, you can tweak the number of decimal digits the stream uses to format floating-point numbers. Here is an example (see Ex2_04E.cpp).

```
std::cout << "Pond diameter required for " << fish_count << " fish is "
          << std::setprecision(2) << std::fixed << pond_diameter << " feet."
          << std::endl;
```

This drawn-out statement is equivalent to the more concise std::println() statement we wrote earlier in Ex2_04D.cpp:

```
std::println("Pond diameter required for {} fish is {:.2f} feet.",
        fish_count, pond_diameter);
```

See how much more compact '{:.2f}' is compared to '<< std::precision(2) << std::fixed'? And how much easier is it to determine what will be printed if the format string is not interleaved with the arguments to format and various stream manipulators?

The standard <ios> and <iomanip> modules define many more stream manipulators. Examples include std::hex (produces hexadecimal numbers), std::scientific (enables exponent notation for floating-point numbers), and std::setw() (used to format tabular data). We do not discuss stream manipulators in detail here, however, because in this book we will use std::print() functions instead. The reason is that, compared to stream manipulators, the more modern formatting functions are more powerful, tend to result in more compact and readable code, and are often faster in execution. You can consult a Standard Library reference to learn more about stream manipulators. Doing so should be a walk in the park now that you know about format specifiers, as stream manipulators operate using the same concepts (width, precision, fill characters, and so on).

Summary

In this chapter, we covered the basics of computation in C++. You learned about most of the fundamental types of data that are provided in the language. The essentials of what we've discussed up to now are as follows:

- Constants of any kind are called literals. All literals have a type.

- You can define integer literals as decimal, hexadecimal, octal, or binary values.

- A floating-point literal must contain a decimal point or an exponent or both. If there is neither, you have specified an integer.

- The fundamental types that store integers are short, int, long, and long long. These store signed integers, but you can also use the type modifier unsigned preceding any type names to produce a type that occupies the same number of bytes but stores unsigned integers.

- The standard floating-point data types are float, double, and long double. As of C++23, compilers optionally also support more specialized floating-point types, such as std::float16_t or std::float128_t.

- Uninitialized variables generally contain garbage values. Variables may be given initial values when defined, and it's good programming practice to do so. A braced initializer is the preferred way of specifying initial values.

- A variable of type char can store a single character and occupies one byte. Type char may be signed or unsigned, depending on your compiler. You can also use variables of the types signed char and unsigned char to store integers. Types char, signed char, and unsigned char are different types.

- Type wchar_t stores a wide character and occupies either two or four bytes, depending on your compiler. Types char8_t, char16_t, and char32_t may be better for handling Unicode characters cross-platform.

- You can fix the value of a variable by using the const modifier. The compiler will check for any attempts within the program source file to modify a variable defined as const.

- The four main mathematic operations correspond to the binary +, -, *, and / operators. For integers, the modulo operator % gives you the remainder after integer division.

- The ++ and -- operators are special shorthand for adding or subtracting one from a numeric variable. Both exist in postfix and prefix forms.

- You can mix different types of variables and constants in an expression. The compiler will arrange for one operand in a binary operation to be automatically converted to the type of the other operand when they differ.

- The compiler will automatically convert the type of the result of an expression on the right of an assignment to the type of the variable on the left when these are different. This can cause loss of information when the left-side type isn't able to contain the same information as the right-side type—double converted to int, for example, or long converted to short.

- You can explicitly convert a value of one type to another using the static_cast<>() operator.

- The std::format() and std::print() functions offer a multitude of options to tune the formatting of textual output.

EXERCISES

The following exercises enable you to try what you've learned in this chapter. If you get stuck, look back over the chapter for help. If you're still stuck after that, you can download the solutions from the Apress website (www.apress.com/book/download.html), but that really should be a last resort.

Exercise 2-1. Print the number of bytes occupied by values of all integral and floating-point types seen in this chapter. (You may skip the extended floating-point types if your compiler does not support them yet.) If a type has multiple equivalent names, group them all together on a single line. Only the std::size_t deserves an extra line of output, even though it is technically also just an equivalent name for one of the fundamental unsigned integer types—only this time an alias defined by the Standard Library instead of a predefined C++ keyword sequence.

Exercise 2-2. Create a program that converts a person's weight from SI to imperial units. Concretely, ask users for their (potentially nonintegral) weight in kilograms and output how much they weigh in stones and pounds. The number of pounds should be given as an integral value. Can you think of at least two ways to accomplish this? If you're unfamiliar with the SI and/or imperial units, 1 stone equals 14 pounds, and 1 pound equals 0.45359237 kg.

Exercise 2-3. Write a program that will compute the area of a circle. The program should prompt the radius of the circle to be entered from the keyboard. Calculate the area using the formula area = pi * radius * radius, and then display the result.

Exercise 2-4. For your birthday, you've been given a long tape measure and an instrument that measures angles (the angle between the horizontal and a line to the top of a tree, for instance). If you know the distance, d, you are from a tree, and the height, h, of your eye, when peering into your angle-measuring device, you can calculate the height of the tree with the formula h + d*tan(angle). Create a program to read h in inches, d in feet and inches, and angle in degrees from the keyboard, and output the height of the tree in feet.

■ **Note**　There is no need to chop down any trees to verify the accuracy of your program. Just check the solutions on the Apress website!

Exercise 2-5. Your body mass index (BMI) is your weight, w, in kilograms divided by the square of your height, h, in meters (w/(h*h)). Write a program to calculate the BMI from a weight entered in pounds and a height entered in feet and inches. A kilogram is 2.2 pounds, and a foot is 0.3048 meters.

Exercise 2-6. Knowing your BMI with a precision higher than one decimal digit after the decimal point is pointless. Adjust the program in Exercise 2-6 accordingly.

Exercise 2-7. Reproduce Table 2-9 with a program, without hard-coding the numeric values or filling spaces. If your command-line interface does not support Unicode characters (perfectly possible), you can replace π with "pi" and omit φ (the Greek letter "phi," in case you were wondering).

Exercise 2-8. Add a row to your table in Exercise 2-7 for sin(π/4), showing the result with exponent notation and five digits after the decimal point. Make sure the exponent component begins with a capital E, not a lowercase e.

Exercise 2-9. Here's an extra exercise for puzzle fans. Write a program that prompts the user to enter two different positive integers and then prints out the value of the larger integer first, followed by that of the smaller one. Using the decision-making facilities from Chapter 5 would be like stealing a piece of cake from a baby while walking in the park. What makes this a tough brain teaser is that you can do this solely with the operators you've learned about in this chapter!

CHAPTER 3

■ ■ ■

Working with Fundamental Data Types

In this chapter, we expand on the types that we discussed in the previous chapter and explain how variables of the basic types interact in more complicated situations. We also introduce some new features of C++ and discuss some of the ways that these are used.

In this chapter, you'll learn

- How the execution order in an expression is determined

- What the bitwise operators are and how you use them

- What variable scope is and what its effects are

- What the storage duration of a variable is and what determines it

- How you can define a new type that limits variables to a fixed range of possible values

- How you can define alternative names for existing data types

Operator Precedence and Associativity

You already know that there is a priority sequence for executing arithmetic operators in an expression. You'll meet many more operators throughout the book, including a few in this chapter. In general, the sequence in which operators in an expression are executed is determined by the *precedence* of the operators. Operator precedence is just a fancy term for the priority of an operator.

Some operators, such as addition and subtraction, have the same precedence. That raises the question of how an expression such as a+b-c+d is evaluated. When several operators from a group with the same precedence appear in an expression in the absence of parentheses, the execution order is determined by the *associativity* of the group. A group of operators can be *left-associative*, which means operators execute from left to right, or they can be *right-associative*, which means they execute from right to left.

Nearly all operator groups are left-associative, so most expressions involving operators of equal precedence are evaluated from left to right. The only right-associative operators are all unary operators, the various assignment operators, and the conditional operator. Table 3-1 shows the precedence and associativity of all the operators in C++. You haven't met most of these operators yet, but when you need to know the precedence and associativity of any operator, you'll know where to find it.

© Ivor Horton and Peter Van Weert 2023
I. Horton and P. Van Weert, *Beginning C++23*, https://doi.org/10.1007/978-1-4842-9343-0_3

Table 3-1. *The Precedence and Associativity of C++ Operators*

Precedence	Operators	Associativity
1	::	Left
2	() [] -> . Postfix ++ and --	Left
3	! ~ Unary + and - Prefix ++ and -- Address-of & and indirection * C-style cast (type) sizeof co_await (related to coroutines, not discussed in this book) new new[] delete delete[]	Right
4	.* ->* (pointers-to-members, not discussed in this book)	Left
5	* / %	Left
6	Binary + and -	Left
7	<< >>	Left
8	<=>	Left
9	< <= > >=	Left
10	== !=	Left
11	&	Left
12	^	Left
13	|	Left
14	&&	Left
15	||	Left
16	?: (conditional operator) = *= /= %= += -= &= ^= |= <<= >>= throw co_yield (related to coroutines, not discussed in this book)	Right
17	, (comma operator)	Left

Each row in Table 3-1 is a group of operators of equal precedence, and the rows are in precedence sequence, from highest to lowest. Let's see a simple example to make sure that it's clear how all this works. Consider this expression:

```
x*y/z - b + c - d
```

The * and / operators are in the same group with precedence that is higher than the group containing + and -, so the expression x*y/z is evaluated first, with a result of r, say. The operators in the group containing * and / are left-associative, so the expression is evaluated as though it was (x*y)/z. The next step is the evaluation of r - b + c - d. The group containing the + and - operators is also left-associative, so this will be evaluated as ((r - b) + c) - d. Thus, the whole expression is evaluated as though it was written as follows:

```
((((x*y)/z) - b) + c) - d
```

Remember, nested parentheses are evaluated in sequence from the innermost to the outermost. You probably won't be able to remember the precedence and associativity of every operator, at least not until you have spent a lot of time writing C++ code. Whenever you are uncertain, you can always add parentheses to make sure things execute in the sequence you want. And even when you *are* certain (because you happen to be a precedence guru), it never hurts to add some extra parentheses to clarify a complex expression.

Bitwise Operators

As their name suggests, *bitwise operators* enable you to operate on an integer variable at the bit level. You can apply the bitwise operators to any type of integer, both signed and unsigned, including type char. However, they're usually applied to unsigned integer types. A typical application is to set individual bits in an integer variable. Individual bits are often used as *flags*, which is the term used to describe binary state indicators. You can use a single bit to store any value that has two states: on or off, male or female, true or false.

You can also use the bitwise operators to work with several items of information stored in a single variable. For instance, color values are usually recorded as three 8-bit values for the intensities of the red, green, and blue components in the color. These are typically packed into three bytes of a 4-byte word. The fourth byte is not wasted either; it usually contains a value for the transparency of the color. This transparency value is called the color's *alpha* component. Such color encodings are commonly denoted by letter quadruples such as RGBA or ARGB. The order of these letters then corresponds to the order in which the red (R), green (G), blue (B), and alpha (A) components appear in the 32-bit integer, with each component encoded as a single byte. To work with individual color components, you need to be able to separate the individual bytes from a word, and the bitwise operators are just the tool for this.

Let's consider another example. Suppose you need to record information about fonts. You might want to store the style and the size of each font and whether it's bold or italic. You could pack all of this information into a 2-byte integer variable, as shown in Figure 3-1.

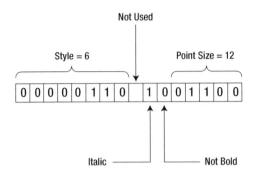

Using Bits to Store Font Data

Figure 3-1. *Packing font data into two bytes*

Here one bit records whether the font is italic—1 signifies italic, and 0 signifies normal. Another bit specifies whether the font is bold. One byte selects one of up to 256 different styles. Five bits could record the point size up to 31 (or 32, if you disallow letters of size zero). Thus, in one 16-bit word you have four separate pieces of data. The bitwise operators provide you with the means of accessing and modifying the individual bits and groups of bits from an integer very easily so they provide you with the means of assembling and disassembling the 16-bit word.

The Bitwise Shift Operators

The bitwise *shift operators* shift the contents of an integer variable by a specified number of bits to the left or right. These are used in combination with the other bitwise operators to achieve the kind of operations we described in the previous section. The >> operator shifts bits to the right, and the << operator shifts bits to the left. Bits that fall off either end of the variable are lost.

All the bitwise operations work with integers of any type, but we'll use type short, which is usually two bytes, to keep the figures simple. Suppose you define and initialize a variable, number, with this statement:

```
unsigned short number {16'387};
```

You can shift the contents of this variable with this statement:

```
auto result{ static_cast<unsigned short>(number << 2) };  // Shift left two bit positions
```

■ **Caution**   If you want result to have the same type as number, namely unsigned short, you have to add an explicit type conversion using static_cast<>. The reason is that the expression number << 2 evaluates to a value of type int, despite the fact that number starts out as type short. There are technically no bitwise or even mathematical operators for integer types smaller than int (that is, the same would happen for, say, number + 1). If their operands are either char or short, they are always implicitly converted to int first. Signedness is not preserved during this conversion either.

The left operand of the left shift operator, <<, is the value to be shifted, and the right operand specifies the number of bit positions by which the value is to be shifted. Figure 3-2 shows the effect.

Decimal 16,387 in binary is: | 0 | 1 | 0 | 0 | 0 | 0 | 0 | 0 | 0 | 0 | 0 | 0 | 0 | 0 | 1 | 1 |

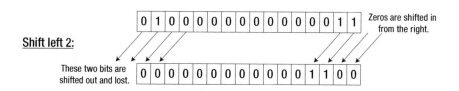

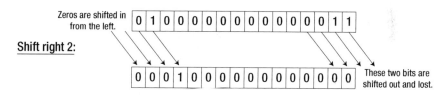

Figure 3-2. *Shift operations*

As you can see from Figure 3-2, shifting 16,387 two positions to the left produces the value 12. The rather drastic change in the value is the result of losing the high-order bits (technically, these high-order bits are only lost here during the static_cast from int back to unsigned short, as we'll show later in this section).

This statement similarly shifts number right two bit positions:

```
result = static_cast<unsigned short>(number >> 2);   // Shift right two bit positions
```

The result is 4,096, so shifting right two bits effectively divides the value by 4. As long as bits aren't lost, shifting *n* bits to the left is equivalent to multiplying by 2, *n* times. In other words, it's equivalent to multiplying by 2*n*. Similarly, shifting right *n* bits is equivalent to dividing by 2*n*. But beware: as you saw with the left shift of number, if significant bits are lost, the result is nothing like what you would expect. However, this is not different from the "real" multiply operation. If you multiplied the 2-byte number by 4, you would get the same result, so shifting left and multiplying are still equivalent. The incorrect result arises because the result of the multiplication is outside the range of a 2-byte integer.

When you want to modify the original value of a variable using a shift operation, you can do so using the >>= or <<= operator. Here's an example:

```
number >>= 2;                              // Shift right two bit positions
```

This is equivalent to the following:

```
number = static_cast<unsigned short>(number >> 2);  // Shift right two bit positions
```

There's no confusion between these shift operators and the insertion and extraction operators for input and output to streams. In this case, as far as the compiler is concerned, the meaning is clear from the context. But sometimes you do need to be careful. For example, suppose you want to verify that, for number equal to 16,387, the expression number << 2 does indeed result in 12, as seen in Figure 3-2, by inserting it into the standard output stream, std::cout. Then you could write the following very reasonable-looking statement:

```
std::cout << number<<2 << std::endl;       // Prints 163872 ("16387" followed by "2")
```

Unfortunately, the compiler interprets this shift operator as a stream insertion operator, so you do not get the intended result. To fix this, you need to add extra parentheses:

```
std::cout << (number<<2) << std::endl;     // Prints 65548
```

Of course, std::println() does not suffer from such operator precedence issues:

```
std::println("{}", number << 2);           // Prints 65548
```

While the result of these two latest statements is already better than the 163872 that we got before, they still do not produce the predicted outcome 12. Instead, they print 65548, which happens to be 16,387 times 4. The reason is that prior to shifting its bits to the left, the value of number is again implicitly promoted from a value of type unsigned short to a value of type (signed) int. And int, unlike unsigned short, is more than large enough to represent the exact result, 65,548. To obtain 12, as in Figure 3-2, you can use static_cast<> to explicitly cast the int result back to an unsigned short:

```
std::println("{}", static_cast<unsigned short>(number << 2));   // Prints 12
```

Shifting Signed Integers

You can apply the bitwise shift operators to both signed and unsigned integers. As you know from previous chapters, C++20 always encodes signed integers using the two's complement notation. In this section you'll learn how bit shifting works with numbers using this encoding.

For negative numbers, right shift operators introduce 1 bits at the left to fill vacated bit positions; for positive numbers, 0 bits. This is known as *sign extension*, as in both cases the added bits are equal to the sign bit. The sign bit is propagated to maintain consistency between a right shift and a divide operation. We can illustrate this with these two variables of type signed char.

```
signed char positive {+104};               // 01101000
signed char negative {-104};               // 10011000
```

(Remember, to obtain the two's complement binary encoding, you must first flip all bits of the positive binary value and then add one.)

You can shift both values two bits to the right with these operations:

```
positive >>= 2;  // Result is 00011010, or +26, which is +104 / 4
negative >>= 2;  // Result is 11100110, or -26, which is -104 / 4
```

The results are shown in the comments. In both cases, two 0s are shifted out at the right end, and the value of the sign bit is inserted twice at the left. The decimal value of the resulting values is ±26, which is the same as if you had divided by 4, as you would expect.

With bitwise shift operations on unsigned integer types, the sign bit is not propagated, and 0s are always inserted on the left.

▒ **Tip** Do not use `signed` integer types (or `char`) if your goal is to manipulate the bits of binary data. This avoids the high-order bit from being propagated. Also, for this and similar reasons, you should use the `std::byte` Standard Library type over `unsigned char` to manipulate binary data.

Left shift operations are more straightforward; they shift the bits of a two's complement number in exactly the same way as they would for the unsigned number represented with the same bit sequence. This has one interesting consequence. Suppose we use the same two variables as before, again equal to ±104, but this time we shift their bits two positions to the left instead of to the right:

```
positive <<= 2;  // Result is 10100000, or -96 (+104 * 4 = +416, or 01'10100000)
negative <<= 2;  // Result is 01100000, or  96 (-104 * 4 = -416, or 10'01100000)
```

The results are shown in the comments. As with unsigned integers, shifting to the left drops bits on the left and adds zeros to the right. This example shows that once significant bits start dropping off at the left, a left shift operation may change the sign of an integer. This occurs if the corresponding multiplication with a power of two—shown in parentheses in the comments—results in an integer that falls outside of the range of the signed integer type.

Logical Operations on Bit Patterns

Table 3-2 shows the four bitwise operators that modify bits in an integer value.

Table 3-2. *Bitwise Operators*

Operator	Description
~	The *bitwise complement operator* is a unary operator that inverts the bits in its operand, so 1 becomes 0, and 0 becomes 1.
&	The *bitwise AND operator* ANDs corresponding bits in its operands. If the corresponding bits are both 1, then the resulting bit is 1; otherwise, it's 0.
^	The *bitwise exclusive OR operator* or *XOR operator* exclusive-ORs corresponding bits in its operands. If the corresponding bits are different, then the result is 1. If the corresponding bits are the same, the result is 0.
|	The *bitwise OR operator* ORs corresponding bits in its operands. If either bit is 1, then the result is 1. If both bits are 0, then the result is 0.

The operators appear in Table 3-2 in order of precedence, so the bitwise complement operator has the highest precedence, and the bitwise OR operator has the lowest. The shift operators << and >> are of equal precedence, and they're below the ~ operator but above the & operator.

Using the Bitwise AND

You'll typically use the bitwise AND operator to select particular bits or groups of bits in an integer value. Suppose you are using a 16-bit integer to store the point size, font style, and whether it is bold and/or italic, as illustrated in Figure 3-1. Suppose further that you want to define and initialize a variable to specify a 12-point, italic, style 6 font (the same one illustrated in Figure 3-1). In binary, the style will be 00000110 (binary 6), the italic bit will be 1, the bold bit will be 0, and the size will be 01100 (binary 12). Remembering that there's an unused bit as well, you need to initialize the value of the font variable to the binary number 0000 0110 0100 1100. Because groups of four bits correspond to a hexadecimal digit, the most compact way to do this is to specify the initial value in hexadecimal notation:

```
unsigned short font {0x064C};                     // Style 6, italic, 12 point
```

Of course, ever since C++14, you also have the option to simply use a binary literal instead:

```
unsigned short font {0b00000110'0'10'01100};   // Style 6, italic, 12 point
```

Note the creative use of the digit grouping character here to signal the borders of the style, italic/bold, and point size components.

To work with the size afterward, you need to extract it from the font variable; the bitwise AND operator will enable you to do this. Because bitwise AND produces a 1 bit only when both bits are 1, you can define a value that will "select" the bits defining the size when you AND it with font. You need to define a value that contains 1s in the bit positions that you're interested in and 0s in all the others. This kind of value is called a *mask*, and you can define such a mask with one of these statements (both are equivalent):

```
unsigned short size_mask {0x1F};
// unsigned short size_mask {0b11111};
```

The five low-order bits of font represent its size, so you set these bits to 1. The remaining bits are 0, so they will be discarded. (Binary 0000 0000 0001 1111 is hexadecimal 1F.)

You can now extract the point size from font with the following statement:

```
auto size {static_cast<unsigned short>( font & size_mask )};
```

Where both corresponding bits are 1 in an & operation, the resultant bit is 1. Any other combination of bits results in 0. The values therefore combine like this:

font	0000 0110 0100 1100
size_mask	0000 0000 0001 1111
font & size_mask	0000 0000 0000 1100

We have shown the binary values in groups of four bits just to make it easy to identify the hexadecimal equivalent; it also makes it easier to see how many bits there are in total. The effect of the mask is to separate out the five rightmost bits, which represent the point size.

You can use the same mechanism to select the font style, but you'll also need to use a shift operator to move the style value to the right. You can define a mask to select the left eight bits as follows:

```
unsigned short style_mask {0xFF00};        // Mask for style is 1111 1111 0000 0000
```

You can obtain the style value with this statement:

```
auto style {static_cast<unsigned short>( (font & style_mask) >> 8 )};
```

The effect of this statement is as follows:

font	0000 0110 0100 1100
style_mask	1111 1111 0000 0000
font & style_mask	0000 0110 0000 0000
(font & style_mask) >> 8	0000 0000 0000 0110

You should be able to see that you could just as easily isolate the bits indicating italic and bold by defining a mask for each. Of course, you still need a way to test whether the resulting bit is 1 or 0, and you'll see how to do that in the next chapter.

Another use for the bitwise AND operator is to turn bits off. You saw previously that a 0 bit in a mask will produce 0 in the result of the AND operator. To just turn the italic bit off in font, for example, you bitwise-AND font with a mask that has the italic bit as 0 and all other bits as 1. We'll show you the code to do this after we've shown you how to use the bitwise OR operator, which is next.

Using the Bitwise OR

You can use the bitwise OR operator for setting one or more bits to 1. Continuing with your manipulations of the font variable, it's conceivable that you would want to set the italic and bold bits on. You can define masks to select these bits with these statements:

```
unsigned short italic {0x40};                   // Seventh bit from the right
unsigned short bold   {0x20};                   // Sixth bit from the right
```

Naturally, you could again use binary literals to specify these masks. In this case, however, using the left shift operator is probably easiest:

```
auto italic {static_cast<unsigned short>( 1u << 6 )};   // Seventh bit from the right
auto bold   {static_cast<unsigned short>( 1u << 5 )};   // Sixth bit from the right
```

▓ **Caution**   Do remember that to turn on the *n*th bit, you must shift the value 1 to the left by *n*-1 bits! To see this, it's always easiest to think about what happens if you shift with smaller values: shifting 1 by *zero* gives you the *first* bit, shifting by *one* the *second*, and so on.

This statement then sets the bold bit to 1:

```
font |= bold;          // Set bold
```

The bits combine like this:

font	0000 0110 0100 1100
bold	0000 0000 0010 0000
font | bold	0000 0110 0110 1100

Now font specifies that the font is bold as well as italic. Note that this operation will set the bit on regardless of its previous state. If it was on, it remains on.

You can also OR masks together to set multiple bits. The following statement sets both the bold and italics bits:

```
font |= bold | italic;   // Set bold and italic
```

▓ **Caution** It's easy to fall into the trap of allowing language to make you select the wrong operator. Because you say "Set italic *and* bold," there's the temptation to use the & operator, but this would be wrong. ANDing the two masks would result in a value with all bits 0, so you wouldn't change anything.

Using the Bitwise Complement Operator

As we said, you can use the & operator to turn bits off—you just need a mask that contains 0 at the bit position you want to turn off and 1 everywhere else. However, this raises the question of how best to specify such a mask. To specify it explicitly, you need to know how many bytes there are in the variable you want to change (not exactly convenient if you want the program to be portable). However, you can obtain the mask that you want using the bitwise complement operator on the mask that you would use to turn the bit on. You can obtain the mask to turn bold off from the bold mask that turns it on:

bold	0000 0000 0010 0000
~bold	1111 1111 1101 1111

The effect of the complement operator is to flip each bit, 0 to 1 or 1 to 0. This will produce the result you're looking for, regardless of whether bold occupies two, four, or eight bytes.

▓ **Note** The bitwise complement operator is sometimes called the *bitwise NOT operator* because for every bit it operates on, what you get is not what you started with.

Thus, all you need to do to turn bold off is to bitwise-AND the complement of the bold mask with font. The following statement will do it:

```
font &= ~bold;              // Turn bold off
```

You can set multiple bits to 0 by combining several inverted masks using the & operator and bitwise-ANDing the result with the variable you want to modify:

```
font &= ~bold & ~italic;   // Turn bold and italic off
```

This sets both the italic and bold bits to 0 in font. No parentheses are necessary here because ~ has a higher precedence than &. However, if you're ever uncertain about operator precedence, use parentheses to express what you want. It certainly does no harm, and it really does good when they're necessary. Note that you can accomplish the same effect using the following statement:

```
font &= ~(bold | italic);  // Turn bold and italic off
```

Here the parentheses are required. We recommend you take a second to convince yourself that both statements are equivalent. If this doesn't come naturally yet, rest assured, you'll get more practice working with similar logic when learning about Boolean expressions in the next chapter.

Using the Bitwise Exclusive OR

The outcome of the bitwise *exclusive OR operator*—or *XOR operator* for short—contains a 1 if and only if precisely one of the corresponding input bits is equal to 1, while the other equals 0. Whenever both input bits are equal, even if both are 1, the resulting bit is 0. The latter is where the XOR operator differs from the regular OR operator. Table 3-3 summarizes the effect of all three binary bitwise operators.

Table 3-3. *Truth Table of Binary Bitwise Operators*

x	y	x & y	x | y	x ^ y
0	0	0	0	0
1	0	0	1	1
0	1	0	1	1
1	1	1	1	0

One interesting property of the XOR operator is that it may be used to *toggle* or *flip* the state of individual bits. With the font variable and the bold mask defined as before, the following toggles the bold bit—that is, if the bit was 0 before, it now becomes 1, and vice versa:

```
font ^= bold;              // Toggles bold
```

This implements the notion of clicking the Bold button in a typical word processor. If the selected text is not bold, it simply becomes bold. If the selection is already bold, however, its font reverts to the regular, nonbold style. Let's take a closer look at how this works:

font	0000 0110 0100 1100
bold	0000 0000 0010 0000
font ^ bold	0000 0110 0110 1100

If the input is a font that is not bold, the result thus contains 0 ^ 1, or 1. Conversely, if the input already would be bold, the outcome would contain 1 ^ 1, or 0.

The XOR operator is used less frequently than the & and | operators. Important applications arise, however, in cryptography, random number generation, and computer graphics, for instance. XOR is also used to back up hard disk data by certain RAID technologies. Suppose you have three similar hard drives, two with data and one to serve as backup. The basic idea is to ensure that the third drive always contains the XOR'ed bits of all contents of the two other drives, like so:

Drive one	... 1010 0111 0110 0011 ...
Drive two	... 0110 1100 0010 1000 ...
XOR drive (backup)	... 1100 1011 0100 1011 ...

If any of these three drives is lost, its contents can be recovered by XOR'ing the other two drives. Suppose, for instance, that you lose your second drive because of some critical hardware failure. Then its contents are easily recovered as follows:

Drive one	... 1010 0111 0110 0011 ...
XOR drive (backup)	... 1100 1011 0100 1011 ...
Recovered data (XOR)	... 0110 1100 0010 1000 ...

Notice that even with such a relatively simple trick, you already need only *one* extra drive to back up *two* others. The naïve approach would be to simply copy the contents of each drive onto another, meaning you'd need not three but four drives. The XOR technique is thus already a tremendous cost saver!

Using the Bitwise Operators: An Example

It's time we looked at some of this stuff in action. This example exercises bitwise operators:

```cpp
// Ex3_01.cpp - Using the bitwise operators
import std;

int main()
{
  const unsigned int red{ 0xFF0000u };    // Color red
  const unsigned int white{ 0xFFFFFFu }; // Color white - RGB all maximum
```

```
  std::println("Try out bitwise complement, AND and OR operators:");
  std::println("Initial value:      red = {:08X}", red);
  std::println("Complement:        ~red = {:08X}", ~red);

  std::println("Initial value:    white = {:08X}", white);
  std::println("Complement:      ~white = {:08X}", ~white);

  std::println("Bitwise AND: red & white = {:08X}", red & white);
  std::println("Bitwise  OR: red | white = {:08X}", red | white);

  std::println("\nNow try successive exclusive OR operations:");
  unsigned int mask{ red ^ white };
  std::println("mask = red ^ white = {:08X}", mask);
  std::println("        mask ^ red = {:08X}", mask ^ red);
  std::println("      mask ^ white = {:08X}", mask ^ white);

  unsigned int flags{ 0xFF };            // Flags variable
  unsigned int bit1mask{ 0x1 };          // Selects bit 1
  unsigned int bit6mask{ 0b100000 };     // Selects bit 6
  unsigned int bit20mask{ 1u << 19 };    // Selects bit 20

  std::println("Use masks to select or set a particular flag bit:");
  std::println("Select bit 1 from flags  : {:08X}", flags & bit1mask);
  std::println("Select bit 6 from flags  : {:08X}", flags & bit6mask);
  std::println("Switch off bit 6 in flags: {:08X}", flags &= ~bit6mask);
  std::println("Switch on bit 20 in flags: {:08X}", flags |= bit20mask);
}
```

If you typed the code correctly, the output is as follows:

```
Try out bitwise complement, AND and OR operators:
Initial value:      red = 00FF0000
Complement:        ~red = FF00FFFF
Initial value:    white = 00FFFFFF
Complement:      ~white = FF000000
Bitwise AND: red & white = 00FF0000
Bitwise  OR: red | white = 00FFFFFF

Now try successive exclusive OR operations:
mask = red ^ white = 0000FFFF
        mask ^ red = 00FFFFFF
      mask ^ white = 00FF0000
Use masks to select or set a particular flag bit:
Select bit 1 from flags  : 00000001
Select bit 6 from flags  : 00000020
Switch off bit 6 in flags: 000000DF
Switch on bit 20 in flags: 000800DF
```

The code uses `std::println()` to conveniently display all values as hexadecimal values. To make it easier to compare printed values, we also arrange for them to have the same number of digits and leading zeros using the `{:08X}` replacement fields throughout the program. Their 0 prefixes set the fill character to `'0'`, the 8s toggle the field width, and the X suffixes result in integers being formatted using hexadecimal notation with uppercase letters. If you use x instead of X, the integers will be formatted using lowercase hexadecimal digits.

To see the effect of the 0 and X components of the `{:08X}` replacement fields, you can, for instance, replace the replacement field in the "Initial value" print statement as follows:

```
std::println("Initial value:     red = {:8x}", red);  // {:08X} --> {:8x}
```

The formatted string for red will then use lowercase letters and will no longer start with a sequence of leading zeros (the default fill character is the space character):

```
Initial value:     red =     ff0000
Complement:       ~red = FF00FFFF
...
```

But enough about string formatting—let's get back to the matter at hand: bitwise operators. In Ex3_01, you first define constants red and white as unsigned integers and initialize them with hexadecimal color values. After some initial print statements, you then combine red and white using the bitwise AND and OR operators with these two statements:

```
std::println("Bitwise AND: red & white = {:08X}", red & white);
std::println("Bitwise  OR: red | white = {:08X}", red | white);
```

If you check the output, you'll see that it's precisely as discussed. The result of ANDing two bits is 1 if both bits are 1; otherwise, the result is 0. When you bitwise-OR two bits, the result is 1 unless both bits are 0.

Next, you create a mask to use to flip between the values red and white by combining the two values with the XOR operator. The output for the value of mask shows that the exclusive OR of two bits is 1 when the bits are different and 0 when they're the same. By combining mask with either color values using exclusive OR, you obtain the other. This means that by repeatedly applying exclusive OR with a well-chosen mask, you can toggle between two different colors. Applying the mask once gives one color, and applying it a second time reverts to the original color. This property is often exploited in computer graphics when drawing or rendering using a so-called XOR mode.

The last group of statements demonstrates using a mask to select a single bit from a group of flag bits. The mask to select a particular bit must have that bit as 1 and all other bits as 0. To select a bit from flags, you just bitwise-AND the appropriate mask with the value of flags. To switch a bit off, you bitwise-AND flags with a mask containing 0 for the bit to be switched off and 1 everywhere else. You can easily produce this by applying the complement operator to a mask with the appropriate bit set, and bit6mask is just such a mask. Of course, if the bit to be switched off was already 0, it would remain as 0.

The Lifetime of a Variable

All variables have a finite *lifetime*. They come into existence from the point at which you define them, and at some point, they are destroyed—at the latest, when your program ends. How long a particular variable lasts is determined by its *storage duration*. There are four different kinds of storage duration:

- Variables defined within a block that are not defined to be `static` have *automatic storage duration*. They exist from the point at which they are defined until the end of the block, which is the closing curly brace, }. They are referred to as *automatic variables* or *local variables*. Automatic variables are said to have *local scope* or *block scope*. All the variables you have created so far have been automatic variables.

- Variables defined using the `static` keyword have *static storage duration*. They are called *static variables*. Static variables exist from the point at which they are defined and continue in existence until the program ends. You'll learn about static variables in Chapters 8 and 12.

- Variables for which you allocate memory at runtime have *dynamic storage duration*. They exist from the point at which you create them until you release their memory to destroy them. You'll learn how to create variables dynamically in Chapter 5.

- Variables declared with the `thread_local` keyword have *thread storage duration*. Thread local variables are an advanced topic, though, so we won't be covering them in this book.

Another property that variables have is *scope*. The scope of a variable is the part of a program in which the variable name is valid. Within a variable's scope, you can refer to it, set its value, or use it in an expression. Outside of its scope, you can't refer to its name. Any attempt to do so will result in a compiler error message. Note that a variable may still exist outside of its scope, even though you can't refer to it. You'll see examples of this situation later, when you learn about variables with static and dynamic storage duration.

▓ **Note** Remember that the *lifetime* and *scope* of a variable are different things. Lifetime is the period of execution time over which a variable survives. Scope is the region of program code over which the variable name can be used. It's important not to get these two ideas confused.

Global Variables

You have great flexibility in where you define variables. The most important consideration is what scope the variables need to have. You should generally place a definition as close as possible to where the variable is first used. This makes your code easier for another programmer to understand. In this section, we'll introduce a first example where this is not the case: global variables.

You can define variables outside all of the functions in a program. Variables defined outside of all blocks and classes are also called *globals* and have *global scope* (which is also called *global namespace scope*). This means they're accessible in all the functions in the source file following the point at which they're defined. If you define them at the beginning of a source file, they'll be accessible throughout the file. In Chapter 11, we'll show how to declare variables that can be used in multiple files.

Global variables have *static storage duration* by default, so they exist from the start of the program until execution of the program ends. Initialization of global variables takes place before the execution of `main()` begins, so they're always ready to be used within any code that's within the variable's scope. If you don't initialize a global variable, it will be zero-initialized by default. This is unlike automatic variables, which contain garbage values when uninitialized.

Figure 3-3 shows the contents of a source file, `Example.cpp`, and illustrates the extent of the scope of each variable in the file.

Program File Example.cpp

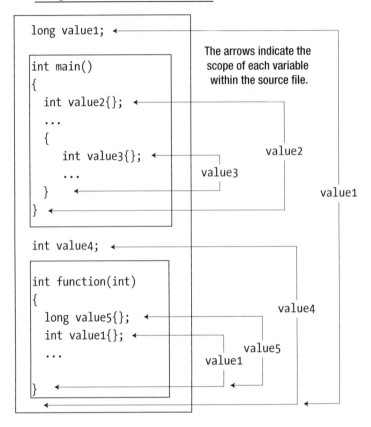

Figure 3-3. *Variable scope*

The variable value1 at the beginning of the file is defined at global scope, as is value4, which appears after the definition of main(). They will be initialized with zero by default. Remember, only global variables have default initial values, not automatic variables. The lifetime of global variables is from the beginning of program execution to when the program ends. Global variables have a scope that extends from the point at which they're defined to the end of the file. Even though value4 exists when execution starts, it can't be referred to in main() because main() isn't within its scope. For main() to use value4, you would need to move the definition of value4 to the beginning of the file.

The local variable called value1 in function() will hide the global variable of the same name. If you use the name value1 in the function, you are accessing the local automatic variable of that name. To access the global value1, you must qualify it with the scope resolution operator, ::. Here's how you could print the values of the local and global variables that have the name value1:

```
std::println("Global value1 = {}", ::value1);
std::println("Local value1 = {}", value1);
```

Because global variables continue to exist for as long as the program is running, you might be wondering, "Why not make all variables global and avoid messing around with local variables that disappear?" This sounds attractive at first, but there are serious disadvantages that completely outweigh any advantages. Real programs are composed of a huge number of statements, a significant number of functions, and a great many variables. Declaring all variables at global scope greatly magnifies the possibility of accidental, erroneous modification of a variable. It makes it hard to trace which part of the code is responsible for changes to global variables. It also makes the job of naming them sensibly quite intractable. Global variables, finally, occupy memory for the duration of program execution, so the program will require more memory than if you used local variables where the memory is reused.

By keeping variables local to a function or a block, you can be sure they have almost complete protection from external effects. They'll only exist and occupy memory from the point at which they're defined to the end of the enclosing block, and the whole development process becomes much easier to manage.

■ **Tip**   Common coding and design guidelines dictate that global variables are typically to be avoided, and with good reason. Global constants—global variables declared with the `const` keyword—are a noble exception to this rule. It is recommended to define all your constants only once, and global variables are perfectly suited for that.

Here's an example that shows aspects of global and automatic variables:

```
// Ex3_02.cpp - Demonstrating scope, lifetime, and global variables
import std;

long count1{999L};          // Global count1
double count2{3.14};        // Global count2
int count3;                 // Global count3 - default initialization

int main()
{ /* Function scope starts here */
  int count1{10};           // Hides global count1
  int count3{50};           // Hides global count3
  std::println("Value of outer count1 = {}", count1);
  std::println("Value of global count1 = {}", ::count1);
  std::println("Value of global count2 = {}", count2);

  { /* New block scope starts here... */
    int count1{20};            // This is a new variable that hides the outer count1
    int count2{30};            // This hides global count2
    std::println("\nValue of inner count1 = {}", count1);
    std::println("Value of global count1 = {}", ::count1);
    std::println("Value of inner count2 = {}", count2);
    std::println("Value of global count2 = {}", ::count2);

    count1 = ::count1 + 3;     // This sets inner count1 to global count1+3
    ++::count1;                // This changes global count1
    std::println("\nValue of inner count1 = {}", count1);
    std::println("Value of global count1 = {}", ::count1);
    count3 += count2;          // Increments outer count3 by inner count2
```

```
    int count4 {};
  } /* ...and ends here. */

// std::println("{}", count4);        // count4 does not exist in this scope!

  std::println("\nValue of outer count1 = {}", count1);
  std::println("Value of outer count3 = {}",   count3);
  std::println("Value of global count3 = {}", ::count3);

  std::println("Value of global count2 = {}", count2);
} /* Function scope ends here */
```

The output from this example is as follows:

```
Value of outer count1 = 10
Value of global count1 = 999
Value of global count2 = 3.14

Value of inner count1 = 20
Value of global count1 = 999
Value of inner count2 = 30
Value of global count2 = 3.14

Value of inner count1 = 1002
Value of global count1 = 1000

Value of outer count1 = 10
Value of outer count3 = 80
Value of global count3 = 0
Value of global count2 = 3.14
```

We've duplicated names in this example to illustrate what happens—of course, it's not at all a good approach to programming. Doing this kind of thing in a real program is confusing and totally unnecessary, and it results in code that is error-prone.

There are three variables defined at global scope, count1, count2, and count3. These exist as long as the program continues to execute, but the names will be masked by local variables with the same name. The first two statements in main() define two integer variables, count1 and count3, with initial values of 10 and 50, respectively. Both variables exist from this point until the closing brace at the end of main(). The scope of these variables also extends to the closing brace at the end of main(). Because the local count1 hides the global count1, you must use the scope resolution operator to access the global count1 in the print statement in the first group of std::println() statements. Global count2 is accessible just by using its name.

The second opening brace starts a new block. count1 and count2 are defined within this block with values 20 and 30, respectively. count1 here is different from count1 in the outer block, which still exists, but its name is masked by the second count1 and is not accessible here; global count1 is also masked but is accessible using the scope resolution operator. The global count2 is masked by the local variable with that name. Using the name count1 following the definition in the inner block refers to count1 defined in that block.

The first line of the second block of output is the value of the count1 defined in the inner scope—that is, inside the inner braces. If it was the outer count1, the value would be 10. The next line of output corresponds to the global count1. The following line of output contains the value of local count2 because you are using just its name. The last line in this block prints global count2 by using the :: operator.

The statement assigning a new value to count1 applies to the variable in the inner scope because the outer count1 is hidden. The new value is the global count1 value plus three. The next statement increments the global count1, and the following two print statements confirm this. The count3 that was defined in the outer scope is incremented in the inner block without any problem because it is not hidden by a variable with the same name. This shows that variables defined in an outer scope are still accessible in an inner scope as long as there is no variable with the same name defined in the inner scope.

After the brace ending the inner scope, count1 and count2, which are defined in the inner scope, cease to exist. Their lifetime has ended. Local count1 and count3 still exist in the outer scope, and their values are displayed in the first two lines in the last group of output. This demonstrates that count3 was indeed incremented in the inner scope. The last lines of output correspond to the global count3 and count2 values.

Enumerated Data Types

You'll sometimes need variables that have a limited set of possible values that can be usefully referred to by name—the days of the week, for example, or the months of the year. An *enumeration* provides this capability. When you define an enumeration, you're creating a new type, so it's also referred to as an *enumerated data type*. Let's create an example using one of the ideas we just mentioned—a type for variables that can assume values corresponding to days of the week. You can define this as follows:

```
enum class Day {Monday, Tuesday, Wednesday, Thursday, Friday, Saturday, Sunday};
```

This defines an enumerated data type called Day, and variables of this type can only have values from the set that appears between the braces, Monday through Sunday. If you try to set a variable of type Day to a value that isn't one of these values, the code won't compile. The symbolic names between the braces are called *enumerators*.

Each enumerator will be automatically defined to have a fixed integer value of type int by default. The first name in the list, Monday, will have the value 0, Tuesday will be 1, and so on, through to Sunday with the value 6. You can define today as a variable of the enumeration type Day with the following statement:

```
Day today {Day::Tuesday};
```

You use type Day just like any of the fundamental types. This definition for today initializes the variable with the value Day::Tuesday. When you reference an enumerator, it must be qualified by the type name.

To print the value of today, you must convert it to a numeric type because the string formatting library will not recognize the type Day. The obvious way to do this is using static_cast<>:

```
std::println("Today is {}", static_cast<int>(today));
```

As of C++23, though, the recommended way to convert an enumeration type to its underlying integer type is the std::to_underlying() function template (std::to_underlying() ensures the conversion is safe, even if the underlying type changes):

```
std::println("Today is {}", std::to_underlying(today));
```

Either way, these statements will print "Today is 1".

By default, the value of each enumerator is one greater than the previous one, and by default, the values begin at 0. However, you can make the implicit values assigned to enumerators start at a different integer value. This definition of type Day has enumerator values 1 through 7:

```
enum class Day {Monday = 1, Tuesday, Wednesday, Thursday, Friday, Saturday, Sunday};
```

Monday is explicitly specified as 1, and subsequent enumerators will always be one greater than the preceding one. You can assign any integer values you like to the enumerators, and assigning these values is not limited to the first few enumerators either. The following definition, for instance, results in weekdays having values 3 through 7, Saturday having value 1, and Sunday having value 2:

```
enum class Day {Monday = 3, Tuesday, Wednesday, Thursday, Friday, Saturday = 1, Sunday};
```

The enumerators don't even need to have unique values. You could define Monday and Mon as both having the value 1, for example, like this:

```
enum class Day {Monday = 1, Mon = 1, Tuesday, Wednesday, Thursday, Friday, Saturday,
Sunday };
```

You can now use either Mon or Monday as the first day of the week. A variable, yesterday, that you've defined as type Day could then be set with this statement:

```
yesterday = Day::Mon;
```

You can also define the value of an enumerator in terms of a previous enumerator. Throwing everything you've seen so far into a single example, you could define the type Day as follows:

```
enum class Day { Monday,                      Mon = Monday,
                 Tuesday   = Monday + 2,      Tues = Tuesday,
                 Wednesday = Tuesday + 2,     Wed = Wednesday,
                 Thursday = Wednesday  + 2,   Thurs = Thursday,
                 Friday    = Thursday + 2,    Fri = Friday,
                 Saturday = Friday  + 2,      Sat = Saturday,
                 Sunday    = Saturday + 2,    Sun = Sunday
               };
```

Now variables of type Day can have values from Monday to Sunday and from Mon to Sun, and the matching pairs of enumerators correspond to the integer values 0, 2, 4, 6, 8, 10, and 12. Values for enumerators must be *compile-time constants*, that is, constant expressions that the compiler can evaluate. Such expressions include literals, enumerators that have been defined previously, and variables that you've specified as const. You can't use non-const variables, even if you've initialized them using a literal.

The enumerators can be an integral type that you choose rather than the default type int. You can also assign explicit values to all the enumerators. For example, you could define this enumeration:

```
enum class Punctuation : char {Comma  = ',', Exclamation = '!', Question='?'};
```

The type specification for the enumerators goes after the enumeration type name and is separated from it by a colon. You can specify any integral data type for the enumerators—including character types and the Boolean type you will learn about in the next chapter. The possible values for variables of type Punctuation are defined as char literals and will correspond to the code values of the symbols. Thus, the values of the enumerators are 44, 33, and 63, respectively, in decimal, which also demonstrates (again) that the values don't have to be in ascending sequence.

So far, we have always used capitalized names for our enumerations and enumerators, but you are free to use any valid identifier you like for either:

```
enum class casing { camelCase, PascalCase, snake_case, UPPER_CASE, CRaZyCaS3 };
```

As always, we recommend you eventually adopt some fixed style for your enumeration identifiers, and then consistently use it. If you code C++ professionally, it is not unlikely that your company already has such coding conventions in place.

Here's an example that demonstrates some of the things you can do with enumerations:

```
// Ex3_03.cpp - Operations with enumerations
import std;

int main()
{
  enum class Day { Monday, Tuesday, Wednesday, Thursday, Friday, Saturday, Sunday };
  Day yesterday{ Day::Monday }, today{ Day::Tuesday }, tomorrow{ Day::Wednesday };
  const Day poets_day{ Day::Friday };

  enum class Punctuation : char { Comma = ',', Exclamation = '!', Question = '?' };
  Punctuation ch{ Punctuation::Comma };

  std::println("yesterday's value is {}{} but poets_day's is {}{}",
    std::to_underlying(yesterday), std::to_underlying(ch),
    std::to_underlying(poets_day), std::to_underlying(Punctuation::Exclamation));

  today = Day::Thursday;          // Assign new ...
  ch = Punctuation::Question;     // ... enumerator values
  tomorrow = poets_day;           // Copy enumerator value

  std::println("Is today's value({}) the same as poets_day({}){}",
      std::to_underlying(today), std::to_underlying(poets_day), std::to_underlying(ch));

// ch = tomorrow;               /* Uncomment any of these for an error */
// tomorrow = Friday;
// today = 6;
}
```

The output is as follows:

```
yesterday's value is 0, but poets_day's is 4!
Is today's value(3) the same as poets_day(4)?
```

We'll leave you to figure out why. Note the commented statements at the end of main(). They are all illegal operations. You should try them to see the compiler messages that result.

Enumeration types defined with enum class are called *scoped enumerations*. By default, you cannot use their enumerators without specifying the type's name as a scope. In Ex3_03, for instance, you could not simply write Friday (as in the commented-out code); you have to add Day:: as a scope. You can bypass this sometimes tedious requirement with a using enum or using declaration. The following snippet explains how these declarations work. You can add it to the end of Ex3_03.

```
using enum Day;            // All Day enumerators can be used without specifying 'Day::'
today = Friday;            // Compiles now (of course, Day::Friday would still work as well)

using Punctuation::Comma;  // Only Comma can be used without 'Punctuation::'
ch = Comma;                // 'ch = Question;' would still result in a compile error
```

▓ **Note**   Scoped enumerations obsolete the older kind of enumerations—now called *unscoped enumerations*. These are defined only with the enum keyword, without the extra `class` keyword. For example, you could define an unscoped Day enumeration like this:

```
enum Day {Monday, Tuesday, Wednesday, Thursday, Friday, Saturday, Sunday};
```

Your code will be less error-prone if you stick to scoped enumeration types. And not just because their names do not leak into the surrounding scope. Old-style enumerators also convert to values of integral or floating-point types without an explicit cast, which can easily lead to mistakes.

▓ **Tip**   It's not because you *can* use unqualified enumerators now that you *should* start adding using declarations everywhere. Just as with namespaces (see the upcoming sidebar titled "Using for Namespaces"), we recommend that you only use using sporadically, as locally as possible, and only within scopes where the repetition of the type's name would otherwise reduce code legibility.

USING FOR NAMESPACES

Just as with scoped enumerations, there are times were repeatedly specifying the name of a (nested) namespace can become tedious or even hamper code readability. You can eliminate the need to qualify a specific name with the namespace in a source file with a using *declaration*. Here's an example:

```
using std::println;   // Make println available without qualification
```

With this declaration before the main() function definition, you can write println() instead of std::println(), which can save typing and make the code look a little less cluttered. Notice that you may not include any parentheses in a using declaration for a function; all you specify is a qualified name.

You could include these using declarations at the beginning of most of our examples thus far and avoid the need to qualify cin, print(), and println():

```
using std::cin;
using std::print;
using std::println;
```

You can apply using declarations to names from any namespace, not just std.

A `using` *directive* imports all the names from a namespace. Here's how you could use any name from the `std` namespace without the need to qualify it:

```
using namespace std; // Make all names in std available without qualification
```

With this at the beginning of a source file, you don't have to qualify any name that is defined in the `std` namespace. At first sight, this seems an attractive idea. The problem is it defeats a major reason for having namespaces. It is unlikely that you know all the names that are defined in `std`, and with this `using` directive, you have increased the probability of accidentally using a name from `std`.

We'll use a `using` directive for the `std` namespace occasionally in examples in the book where the number of `using` declarations that would otherwise be required is excessive. We recommend that you use `using` directives only when there's a good reason to do so.

Aliases for Data Types

You've seen how enumerations provide one way to define your own data types. The `using` keyword enables you to specify a *type alias*, which is your own data type *name* that serves as an alternative to an existing type name. Using `using`, you can define the type alias `BigOnes` as being equivalent to the standard type `unsigned long long` with the following statement:

```
using BigOnes = unsigned long long; // Defines BigOnes as a type alias
```

It's important you realize this isn't defining a new type. This just defines `BigOnes` as an alternative name for type `unsigned long long`. You could use it to define a variable `mynum` with this statement:

```
BigOnes mynum {};                    // Define & initialize as type unsigned long long
```

There's no difference between this definition and using the standard type name. You can still use the standard type name as well as the alias, but it's hard to come up with a reason for using both.

There's an older syntax for defining an alias for a type name as well, which uses the `typedef` keyword. For example, you can define the type alias `BigOnes` like this:

```
typedef unsigned long long BigOnes; // Defines BigOnes as an alias for unsigned long long
```

Among several other advantages,[1] however, the newer syntax is more intuitive, as it looks and feels like a regular assignment. With the old `typedef` syntax, you always had to remember to invert the order of the existing type, `unsigned long long`, and the new name, `BigOnes`. Believe us, you would have struggled with this order each time you needed a type alias—we certainly have! Luckily, you'll never have to experience this as long as you follow this simple guideline:

---

[1] The other advantages of the `using` syntax over the `typedef` syntax manifest themselves only when specifying aliases for more advanced types. Using `using`, for instance, it's much easier to specify aliases for function types. You'll see this in Chapter 19. The `using` keyword moreover allows you to specify type alias templates, or parameterized type aliases, something that is not possible using the old `typedef` syntax. We'll show you an example of an alias template in Chapter 19 as well.

░ Tip   Always use the `using` keyword to define a type alias. In fact, if it weren't for legacy code, we'd be advising you to forget the keyword `typedef` even exists.

Because you are just creating a synonym for a type that already exists, this may appear to be a bit superfluous. This isn't the case. A major use for this is to simplify code that involves complex type names. For example, a program might involve a type name such as `std::map<std::shared_ptr<Contact>, std::string>`. You'll discover what the various components of this complex type mean later in this book, but for now, it should already be clear that it can make for verbose and obscure code when such long types have to be repeated too often. You can avoid cluttering the code by defining a type alias, like this:

```
using PhoneBook = std::map<std::shared_ptr<Contact>, std::string>;
```

Using `PhoneBook` in the code instead of the full type specification can make the code more readable. Another use for a type alias is to provide flexibility in the data types used by a program that may need to be run on a variety of computers. Defining a type alias and using it throughout the code allows the actual type to be modified by just changing the definition of the alias.

Still, type aliases, like most things in life, should be used with moderation. Type aliases can surely make your code more compact, yes. But compact code is never the goal. There are plenty of times when spelling out the concrete types makes the code easier to understand. Here's an example:

```
using StrPtr = std::shared_ptr<std::string>;
```

`StrPtr`, while compact, does not help clarify your code. On the contrary, such a cryptic and unnecessary alias just obfuscates your code. Some guidelines go as far as forbidding type aliases altogether. We certainly wouldn't go that far; just use common sense when deciding whether an alias either helps or obfuscates, and you'll be fine.

Summary

These are the essentials of what you've learned in this chapter:

- You don't need to memorize the operator precedence and associativity for all operators, but you need to be conscious of it when writing code. Always use parentheses if you are unsure about precedence.

- The bitwise operators are necessary when you are working with flags—single bits that signify a state. These arise surprisingly often—when dealing with file input and output, for example. The bitwise operators are also essential when you are working with values packed into a single variable. One common example is RGB-like encodings, where three to four components of a given color are packed into one 32-bit integer value.

- By default, a variable defined within a block is automatic, which means that it exists only from the point at which it is defined to the end of the block in which its definition appears, as indicated by the closing brace of the block that encloses its definition.

- Variables can be defined outside of all the blocks in a program, in which case they have global namespace scope and static storage duration by default. Variables with global scope are accessible from anywhere within the program file that contains them, following the point at which they're defined, except where a local variable exists with the same name as the global variable. Even then, they can still be reached by using the scope resolution operator (::).

- Type-safe enumerations are useful for representing fixed sets of values, especially those that have names, such as days of the week or suits in a pack of playing cards.

- The using keyword has many uses:

  - It allows you to refer to (specific or all) enumerators of scoped enumerations without specifying the enumeration's name as scope.

  - It allows you to refer to (specific or all) types and functions of a namespace without specifying the namespace's name as scope.

  - It allows you to define aliases for other types. In legacy code, you might still encounter typedef being used for the same purpose.

EXERCISES

The following exercises enable you to try what you've learned in this chapter. If you get stuck, look back over the chapter for help. If you're still stuck, you can download the solutions from the Apress website (https://www.apress.com/gp/services/source-code), but that really should be a last resort.

Exercise 3-1. Create a program that prompts for the input of an integer and stores it as an int. Invert all the bits in the value and store the result. Output the original value, the value with the bits inverted, and the inverted value plus 1, each in hexadecimal representation and on one line. On the next line, output the same numbers in decimal representation. These two lines should be formatted such that they look like a table where the values in the same column are right aligned in a suitable field width. All hexadecimal values should have leading zeros so eight hexadecimal digits always appear.

Note: Flipping all bits and adding one—ring any bells? Can you perhaps already deduce what the output will be before you run the program?

Exercise 3-2. Write a program to calculate how many square boxes can be contained in a single layer on a rectangular shelf with no overhang. The dimensions of the shelf in feet and the dimensions of the side of the box in inches are read from the keyboard. Use variables of type double for the length and depth of the shelf and type int for the length of the side of a box. Define and initialize an integer constant to convert from feet to inches (1 foot equals 12 inches). Calculate the number of boxes that the shelf can hold in a single layer of type long and output the result.

Exercise 3-3. Without running it, can you work out what the following code snippet will produce as output?

```
auto k {430u};
auto j {(k >> 4) & ~(~0u << 3)};
std::println("{}", j);
```

Exercise 3-4. Write a program to read four characters from the keyboard and pack them into a single integer variable. Display the value of this variable as hexadecimal. Unpack the four bytes of the variable and output them in reverse order, with the low-order byte first.

Exercise 3-5. Write a program that defines an enumeration of type Color where the enumerators are red, green, yellow, purple, blue, black, and white. Define the type for enumerators as an unsigned integer type and arrange for the integer value of each enumerator to be the RGB combination of the color it represents. (You can easily find the hexadecimal RGB encoding of any color online.) Create variables of type Color initialized with enumerators for yellow, purple, and green. Access the enumerator value and extract and output the RGB components as separate values.

Exercise 3-6. We'll conclude with one more exercise for puzzle fans (and *exclusively* so). Write a program that prompts for two integer values to be entered and store them in integer variables, a and b, say. Swap the values of a and b *without* using a third variable. Output the values of a and b.

Hint: This is a particularly tough nut to crack. To solve this puzzle, you *exclusively* need one single compound assignment operator.

CHAPTER 4

■ ■ ■

Making Decisions

Decision-making is fundamental to any kind of computer programming. It's one of the things that differentiates a computer from a calculator. It means altering the sequence of execution depending on the result of a comparison. In this chapter, you'll explore how to make choices and decisions. This will allow you to validate program input and write programs that can adapt their actions depending on the input data. Your programs will be able to handle problems where logic is fundamental to the solution.

In this chapter, you'll learn

- How to compare data values

- How to alter the sequence of program execution based on the result of a comparison

- What logical operators and expressions are and how you apply them

- How to deal with multiple-choice situations

Comparing Data Values

To make decisions, you need a mechanism for comparing things, and there are several kinds of comparisons. For instance, a decision such as "If the traffic signal is red, stop the car" involves a comparison for equality. You compare the color of the signal with a reference color, red, and if they are equal, you stop the car. On the other hand, a decision such as "If the speed of the car exceeds the limit, slow down" involves a different relationship. Here you check whether the speed of the car is greater than the current speed limit. Both comparisons are similar in that they result in one of two values: *true* or *false*. This is precisely how comparisons work in C++.

You can compare data values using two new sets of operators, namely *relational* and *equality operators*. Table 4-1 lists the six classical operators for comparing two values.

Table 4-1. *Relational and Equality Operators*

Operator	Meaning
<	Less than
<=	Less than or equal to
>	Greater than
>=	Greater than or equal to
==	Equal to
!=	Not equal to

© Ivor Horton and Peter Van Weert 2023
I. Horton and P. Van Weert, *Beginning C++23*, https://doi.org/10.1007/978-1-4842-9343-0_4

▧ **Caution**　The equal-to operator, ==, has two successive equals signs. This is not the same as the assignment operator, =, which consists of a single equals sign. It's a common beginner's mistake to use one equals sign instead of two to compare for equality. This will not necessarily result in a warning message from the compiler because the expression may be valid but just not what you intended, so you need to take particular care to avoid this error.

Each of these operators compares two values and results in a value of type bool. The name bool is short for *Boolean*. It is an homage to George Boole, the father of Boolean algebra, the study of logical operations on the truth values *true* and *false*. Accordingly, variables of type bool can only have two possible values as well: true and false. true and false are keywords and are literals of type bool.

You create variables of type bool just like other fundamental types. Here's an example:

```
bool valid {true};    // Define and initialize a logical variable to true
```

This defines the variable valid as type bool with an initial value of true. If you initialize a bool variable using empty braces, {}, its initial value is false:

```
bool correct {};      // Define and initialize a logical variable to false
```

While explicitly using {false} here could arguably improve the readability of your code, it is good to remember that wherever numeric variables would be initialized to zero, Boolean variables will be initialized to false.

Applying the Comparison Operators

You can see how comparisons work by looking at a few examples. Suppose you have integer variables i and j, with values 10 and –5, respectively. Consider the following expressions:

```
i > j       i != j       j > -8       i <= j + 15
```

All of these expressions evaluate to true. Note that in the last expression, the addition, j + 15, executes first because + has a higher precedence than <=.

You could store the result of any of these expressions in a variable of type bool. Here's an example:

```
valid = i > j;
```

If i is greater than j, true is stored in valid; otherwise, false is stored. You can compare values stored in variables of character types, too. Assume that you define the following variables:

```
char first {'A'};
char last {'Z'};
```

You can write comparisons using these variables:

```
first < last       'E' <= first       first != last
```

Here you are comparing code values (recall from Chapter 1 that characters are mapped to integral codes using standard encoding schemes such as ASCII and Unicode). The first expression checks whether the value of first, which is 'A', is less than the value of last, which is 'Z'. This is always true. The result of the second expression is false because the code value for 'E' is greater than the value of first. The last expression is true, because 'A' is definitely not equal to 'Z'.

The next example illustrates that the printing values of type bool are as straightforward as always:

```
// Ex4_01.cpp - Comparing data values
import std;

int main()
{
  char first {};        // Stores the first character
  char second {};       // Stores the second character

  std::print("Enter a character: ");
  std::cin >> first;

  std::print("Enter a second character: ");
  std::cin >> second;

  std::println("The value of the expression {} < {} is {}",
               first, second, first < second);
  std::println("The value of the expression {} == {} is {}",
               first, second, first == second);
}
```

Here's an example of output from this program:

```
Enter a character: ?
Enter a second character: H
The value of the expression ? < H is true
The value of the expression ? == H is false
```

The prompting for input and reading of characters from the keyboard you have seen before. And with std::println(), printing the resulting Boolean values is just as straightforward as printing integers or floating-point values. The only thing new in Ex4_01 is therefore the first < second and first == second expressions that compare the first and second characters that the user entered.

▓ **Tip**   Modern C++ formatting functions such as std::println() and std::format() represent the Boolean values true and false as "true" and "false" by default. To format them as "1" and "0" instead, you can specify any integer presentation type in the corresponding replacement fields. Sensible options include {:b} or {:d}, where b is short for *binary* and d short for *decimal*.

■ **Caution** Unlike more modern formatting functionality, Standard Library output streams such as std::cout represent true and false as "1" and "0" by default. You override this inconstant (and usually undesired) default by inserting the std::boolalpha stream manipulator into a stream as follows:

```
std::cout << std::boolalpha; // From now on, print "true"/"false" instead of "1"/"0"
```

You can restore the default behavior by inserting std::noboolalpha. The same defaults and stream manipulators apply to input streams such as std::cin as well.

```
std::cin << std::boolalpha; // From now on, read "true"/"false" instead of "1"/"0"
bool b {};
std::cin >> b;
```

To output an expression such as first < second with the stream insertion operator <<, you need to surround it with parentheses. To understand why you can review the operator precedence rules from the beginning of the previous chapter. The correct equivalent of the first std::println() statement in Ex4_01, for instance, is therefore the following somewhat more complex statement:

```
std::cout << std::boolalpha
          << "The value of the expression " << first << " < " << second
          << " is " << (first < second) << std::endl;
```

If you omit the parentheses around first < second on the last line, the compiler outputs an error message. Notice also again how much more readable the std::println() statement of Ex4_01 is compared to this jumble of " and < characters!

Comparing Floating-Point Values

Of course, you can also compare floating-point values. Let's consider some slightly more complicated numerical comparisons. First, define variables with the following statements:

```
int i {-10};
int j {20};
double x {1.5};
double y {-0.25e-10};
```

Now consider the following logical expressions:

```
-1 < y        j < (10 - i)        2.0*x >= (3 + y)
```

The comparison operators are all of lower precedence than the arithmetic operators, so none of the parentheses are strictly necessary, but they do help make the expressions clearer. The first comparison evaluates to true because y has a very small negative value (–0.000000000025), which is greater than –1. The second comparison results in false because the expression 10 - i has the value 20, which is the same as j. The third expression is true because 3 + y is slightly less than 3.

One peculiarity about floating-point comparisons is that not-a-number values are neither less than, greater than, nor equal to any other number. They're not even equal to another not-a-number value. Let the nan variable be defined as follows (see Chapter 2 for the numeric_limits template):

```
const double nan{ std::numeric_limits<double>::quiet_NaN() };
```

Then all of the following expressions evaluate to false:

```
i < nan        nan > j        nan == nan
```

You now know you can use relational and equality operators to compare values of any of the fundamental types. When you learn about classes, you'll see how you can arrange for the comparison operators to work with types that you define, too. All you need now is a way to use the result of a comparison to modify the behavior of a program. We'll look into that shortly. But first, a visit from outer space...

The Spaceship Operator

In C++20 a new operator was added to the language to compare values: the *three-way comparison operator*, denoted <=>. This new operator is better known using its informal name: *spaceship operator*. It gets this nickname from the fact that the character sequence <=> somewhat resembles a flying saucer[1].

In a way, <=> behaves as <, ==, and > all squished into one. Simply put, a <=> b determines, in a single expression, whether a is less than, equal to, or greater than b. It's easiest to explain the basic working of <=> through some code. The following example reads an integer and then uses <=> to compare that number to zero:

```
// Ex4_02.cpp - Three-way comparison of integers
import std; // Required also for using operator <=> (even for fundamental types)

int main()
{
  std::print("Please enter a number: ");
  int value;
  std::cin >> value;

  std::strong_ordering ordering{ value <=> 0 };

  std::println("value < 0: {}", ordering == std::strong_ordering::less);
  std::println("value > 0: {}", ordering == std::strong_ordering::greater);
  std::println("value == 0: {}", ordering == std::strong_ordering::equal);
}
```

For integer operands the <=> operator evaluates to a value of type std::strong_ordering, a type that resembles an enumeration type (see Chapter 3) with possible values less, greater, and equal[2]. Based on the value of ordering, you can then determine how value is ordered compared to the number zero.

---

[1] More specifically, the term "spaceship operator" was coined by Perl expert Randal L. Schwartz because it reminded him of the spaceship in the 1970s text-based strategy video game *Star Trek*.
[2] There's technically a fourth value as well—called equivalent—but more on that shortly...

At this point, you may wonder what's the point of this operator. And rightfully so. As with all alien encounters, the spaceship operator appears somewhat strange and puzzling at first. After all, the last four statements of Ex4_02 can be written much more economically as follows:

```
std::println("value < 0: {}", value < 0);
std::println("value > 0: {}", value > 0);
std::println("value == 0: {}", value == 0);
```

A lot less typing, and just as efficient (as if performance even matters for integer comparisons). And so, indeed, when comparing variables of fundamental types, in isolation, the <=> operator makes little to no sense.

The <=> operator does become interesting, though, when comparing variables of more complex types. Comparing larger arrays or data structures can be arbitrarily expensive. In such cases, it may pay off to compare these values only once (as in Ex4_02) instead of two to three times (as in Ex4_01). In Chapter 7, we'll see examples of that with string objects.

Another raison d'être for the spaceship operator is seen in Chapter 13: by defining a single <=> operator you can make one of your own data types support multiple comparison operators (<, >, <=, and >=) all at once. But before we can get to that point, we'll need to cover some more groundwork in the next two subsections.

Comparison Categories

The <=> operator does not always evaluate to type std::strong_ordering as it did in Ex4_02. The type it evaluates to depends on the type of its operands. Table 4-2 shows the three types that can be used for three-way comparisons.

Table 4-2. *Comparison Category Types*

	less	greater	equal	equivalent	unordered	Usage
strong_ordering	✔	✔	✔	✔		Integers and pointers
partial_ordering	✔	✔		✔	✔	Floating-point numbers
weak_ordering	✔	✔		✔		User-defined operators only

▓ **Note**　The three comparison category types are defined by the <compare> module of the Standard Library. Whenever you use the <=> operator, even with operands of fundamental types, you must make sure to import these definitions. The easiest, as always, is to simply import the complete std module.

When comparing integers, Booleans, characters, or pointers, <=> always evaluates to type strong_ordering. For floating-point operands, however, <=> evaluates to type partial_ordering. The reason is that floating-point numbers are not *strongly ordered* (or *totally ordered*, as this is more commonly called in mathematics); they are only *partially ordered*. That is, not all pairs of floating-point numbers are comparable. Concretely, as seen in the previous section, *not-a-number* values are not ordered with respect to any other number. For that reason, f1 <=> f2 evaluates to std::partial_ordering::unordered if (and only if) f1 and/or f2 is not-a-number.

A textbook example of another partial ordering would be comparing collections of data through a <=> operator that implements a subset relation (⊆ in mathematical notation). Obviously such an operator would result in unordered when comparing disjoint or partially overlapping collections.

The ability for two values to be unordered with respect to one another is not all that sets std::partial_ordering apart from std::strong_ordering. As you can see in Table 4-2, partial_ordering uses the term equivalent where strong_ordering uses equal. Formally *equality* implies *substitutability*, whereas *equivalence* does not. And *substitutability*, in turn, more or less means that whenever a == b is true, f(a) == f(b) must be true for any function f. For floating-point values, for instance, even though -0.0 == +0.0 in C++, std::signbit(-0.0) != std:signbit(+0.0) (std::signbit() returns—you guessed it—the sign bit of a floating-point number). In other words: -0.0 and +0.0 are very nearly *equal*, but not quite; they are, however, for all intents and purposes, *equivalent*.

■ **Note** std::strong_ordering::equivalent equals std::strong_ordering::equal. We recommend you mostly use the latter, as it better expresses the semantics of a strong ordering.

As long as both operands of <=> only involve values of fundamental or Standard Library types—and this includes strings, arrays, vectors, pairs, and optional values comprised of these types—the rule of thumb remains analogous: <=> evaluates to strong_ordering, except when floating-point numbers are involved. As soon as floating-point numbers enter the equation, <=> by default evaluates to partial_ordering.

User-defined overloads of the <=> operator (see Chapter 13) may evaluate to any of the three comparison categories, including the not yet discussed std::weak_ordering. An example of a weak ordering would be the ordering of points based on their Euclidian distance to the origin. With such a comparison operator, all points would be ordered (unlike std::partial_ordering, std::weak_ordering has no unordered option; see Table 4-2), but not strongly so (non-equal points (3, 4), (4, -3), and (0, 5), for instance, would all compare equivalent to each other as they all lie at Euclidian distance 5 from the origin).

Values of type strong_ordering implicitly convert to both weak_ and partial_ordering, and weak_ordering values implicitly convert to partial_ordering—with the obvious results. partial_ordering values, however, cannot be converted to either of the other types. (Think about it. What would you do with unordered values otherwise?)

■ **Note** While the comparison category types of Table 4-2 may *act* like enumeration types, they are actually class types. Consequences include that you cannot use these types in using enum (Chapter 3) or switch statements (introduced later in this chapter).

Named Comparison Functions

You can write the last three lines of Ex4_02 more compactly as follows (see Ex4_02A):

```
std::println("value < 0: {}", std::is_lt(ordering));  // is less than
std::println("value > 0: {}", std::is_gt(ordering));  // is greater than
std::println("value == 0: {}", std::is_eq(ordering)); // is equivalent
```

The std::is_lt(), is_gt(), and is_eq() are *named comparison functions*. Three more such functions exist, namely std::is_neq() (is not equal/equivalent), std::is_lteq() (is less than or equal/equivalent), and std::is_gteq() (is greater than or equal/equivalent). The last two especially can save you some typing. To express std::is_lteq(ordering), for instance, you'd otherwise have to compare ordering to both less and equal and combine the results using the logical OR operator you'll encounter later in this chapter.

The named comparison functions can be used with all three comparison category types of Table 4-2, and behave exactly as you would expect.

That concludes what we needed to say about the spaceship operator. As said, we'll venture deeper into this particular space in Chapters 7 and 13. But for now, let's get back safely to Earth and explore what you can do with Booleans beyond printing them as "true" and "false" (or, of course, as "1" and "0").

The if Statement

The basic if statement enables you to choose to execute a single statement, or a block of statements, when a given condition is true. Figure 4-1 illustrates how this works.

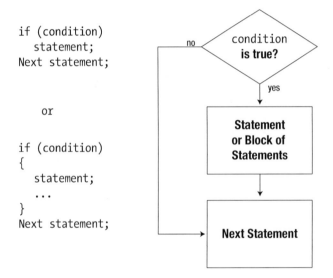

The statement or block of statements that follows
the **if** is only executed if **condition** is **true**.

Figure 4-1. *Logic of the simple if statement*

Here is an example of an if statement that tests the value of a char variable, letter:

```
if (letter == 'A')
  std::println("The first capital, alphabetically speaking."); // Only if letter equals 'A'

std::println("This statement always executes.");
```

If letter has the value 'A', the condition is true, and these statements produce the following output:

```
The first capital, alphabetically speaking.
This statement always executes.
```

If the value of letter is not equal to 'A', only the second line appears in the output. You put the condition to be tested between parentheses immediately following the keyword, if. We adopt the convention to add a space between the if and the parentheses (to differentiate visually from function calls), but this is not required. As usual, the compiler will ignore all whitespace, so the following are equally valid ways to write the test:

```
if(letter == 'A')        if( letter == 'A' )
```

The statement following the if is indented to indicate that it executes only as a result of the condition being true. The indentation is not necessary for the program to compile, but it does help you recognize the relationship between the if condition and the statement that depends on it. Sometimes, you will see simple if statements written on a single line, like this:

```
if (letter == 'A') std::println("The first capital, alphabetically speaking.");
```

▓ **Caution**   Never put a semicolon (;) directly after the condition of the if statement. Unfortunately, doing so compiles without errors (at best, the compiler will issue a warning). But it rarely means what you intended—quite the contrary, in fact:

```
if (letter == 'A');   // Oops... An erroneous semicolon...
  std::println("The first capital, alphabetically speaking.");
```

The semicolon on the first line introduces a so-called *null statement* or *empty statement*. Superfluous semicolons, and therefore null statements, are allowed to appear pretty much anywhere within a series of statements. The following, for instance, is legal C++:

```
int i = 0;; i += 5;; ; std::println("{}", i); ;
```

Usually, such null statements have no effect at all. But when added immediately after the condition of an if, a semicolon binds the statement that is executed if the condition evaluates to true. In other words, writing a semicolon after the if (letter == 'A') test has the same effect as writing this:

```
if (letter == 'A') { /* Do nothing */ }
std::println("The first capital, alphabetically speaking.");   // Always executes!
```

So this states, if letter equals 'A', then do nothing. But what is worse is that the second line always executes, unconditionally, even if letter is different from 'A'—precisely what the if statement intended to prevent. Therefore, take care to never put a semicolon directly after a conditional test because it essentially nullifies the test!

You could extend the code fragment to change the value of letter if it contains the value 'A'.

```
if (letter == 'A')
{
  std::println("The first capital, alphabetically speaking.");
  letter = 'a';
}

std::println("This statement always executes.");
```

All the statements in the block will be executed when the if condition is true. Without the braces, only the first statement would be the subject of the if, and the statement assigning the value 'a' to letter would always be executed. Of course, each of the statements in the block is terminated by a semicolon. No semicolon is necessary, though, after the closing brace of the block. You can have as many statements as you like within the block; you can even have nested blocks. If and when letter has the value 'A', both statements within the block will be executed, so its value will be changed to 'a' after the same message as before is displayed. Neither of these statements executes if the condition is false. The statement following the block always executes.

If you cast true to an integer type, the result will be 1; casting false to an integer results in 0. Conversely, you can also convert numerical values to type bool. Zero converts to false, and any nonzero value converts to true. When you have a numerical value where a bool value is expected, the compiler will insert an implicit conversion to convert the numerical value to type bool. This is useful in decision-making code.

Let's try an if statement for real. This program will range check the value of an integer entered from the keyboard:

```
// Ex4_03.cpp - Using an if statement
import std;

int main()
{
  std::print("Enter an integer between 50 and 100: ");
  int value {};
  std::cin >> value;

  if (value)
    std::println("You have entered a value that is different from zero.");

  if (value < 50)
    std::println("The value is invalid - it is less than 50.");

  if (value > 100)
    std::println("The value is invalid - it is greater than 100.");

  std::println("You entered {}.", value);
}
```

The output depends on the value that you enter. For a value between 50 and 100, the output will be something like the following:

```
Enter an integer between 50 and 100: 77
You have entered a value that is different from zero.
You entered 77.
```

Outside the range of 50 to 100, a message indicating that the value is invalid will precede the output showing the value. If it is less than 50, for instance, the output will be as follows:

```
Enter an integer between 50 and 100: 27
You have entered a value that is different from zero.
The value is invalid - it is less than 50.
You entered 27.
```

After prompting for and reading a value, the first `if` statement checks whether the value entered is different from zero:

```
if (value)
  std::println("You have entered a value that is different from zero.");
```

Recall that any number is converted to `true`, except 0 (zero)—which is converted to `false`. So, the value always converts to `true`, except if the number you entered is zero. You will often find such a test written like this, but if you prefer, you can easily make the test for zero more explicit as follows:

```
if (value != 0)
  std::println("You have entered a value that is different from zero.");
```

The second `if` statement then checks if your input is less than 50:

```
if (value < 50)
  std::println("The value is invalid - it is less than 50.");
```

The output statement is executed only when the `if` condition is `true`, which is when `value` is less than 50. The next `if` statement checks the upper limit in essentially the same way and outputs a message when it is exceeded. Finally, the last output statement is always executed, and this prints the value. Of course, checking for the upper limit being exceeded when the value is below the lower limit is superfluous. You could arrange for the program to end immediately if the value entered is below the lower limit, like this:

```
if (value < 50)
{
  std::println("The value is invalid - it is less than 50.");
  return 0;              // Ends the program
}
```

You could do the same with the `if` statement that checks the upper limit. You can have as many `return` statements in a function as you need.

If you conditionally end the program like that, though, the code after both if statements is no longer executed. That is, if the user enters an invalid number and one of these return statements is executed, then the last line of the program will no longer be reached. To refresh your memory, this line was as follows:

```
std::println("You entered {}.", value);
```

Later this chapter, we will see other means to avoid the upper limit test if value was already found to be below the lower limit—means that do not involve ending the program.

Nested if Statements

The statement that executes when the condition in an if statement is true can itself be an if statement. This arrangement is called a nested if. The condition of the inner if is tested only if the condition for the outer if is true. An if that is nested inside another can also contain a nested if. You can nest ifs to whatever depth you require. We'll demonstrate the nested if with an example that tests whether an entered character is alphabetic:

```
// Ex4_04.cpp - Using a nested if
import std;

int main()
{
  char letter {};                    // Store input here
  std::print("Enter a letter: ");    // Prompt for the input
  std::cin >> letter;

  if (letter >= 'A')
  {                                  // letter is 'A' or larger
    if (letter <= 'Z')
    {                                // letter is 'Z' or smaller
      std::println("You entered an uppercase letter.");
      return 0;
    }
  }

  if (letter >= 'a')                 // Test for 'a' or larger
    if (letter <= 'z')
    {                                // letter is >= 'a' and <= 'z'
      std::println("You entered a lowercase letter.");
      return 0;
    }
  std::println("You did not enter a letter.");
}
```

Here's some typical output:

```
Enter a letter: H
You entered an uppercase letter.
```

After creating the char variable letter with initial value zero, the program prompts you to enter a letter. The if statement that follows checks whether the character entered is 'A' or larger. If letter is greater than or equal to 'A', the nested if that checks for the input being 'Z' or less executes. If it *is* 'Z' or less, you conclude that it is an uppercase letter and display a message. You are done at this point, so you execute a return statement to end the program.

The next if, using essentially the same mechanism as the first, checks whether the character entered is lowercase, displays a message, and returns. You probably noticed that the test for a lowercase character contains only one pair of braces, whereas the uppercase test has two. The code block between the braces belongs to the inner if here. In fact, both sets of statements work as they should—remember that if (condition) {...} is effectively a single statement and does not need to be enclosed within more braces. However, the extra braces do make the code clearer, so it's a good idea to use them.

The output statement following the last if block executes only when the character entered is not a letter, and it displays a message to that effect. You can see that the relationship between the nested ifs and the output statement is much easier to follow because of the indentation. Indentation is generally used to provide visual cues to the logic of a program.

This program illustrates how a nested if works, but it is not a good way to test for characters. Using the Standard Library, you can write the program so that it works independently of the character coding. We'll explore how that works in the next subsection.

Character Classification and Conversion

The nested ifs of Ex4_04 rely on these three built-in assumptions about the codes that are used to represent alphabetic characters:

- The letters *A* to *Z* are represented by a set of codes where the code for 'A' is the minimum and the code for 'Z' is the maximum.

- The codes for the uppercase letters are contiguous, so no nonalphabetic characters lie between the codes for 'A' and 'Z'.

- All uppercase letters in the alphabet fall within the range *A* to *Z*.

While the first two assumptions will hold for any character encoding used in practice today, the third is definitely not true for many languages. The Greek alphabet, for instance, knows uppercase letters such as Δ, Θ, and Π; the Russian one contains Ж, Ф, and Щ; and even Latin-based languages such as French often use capital letters such as É and Ç whose encodings won't lie at all between 'A' and 'Z'. It is therefore not a good idea to build these kinds of assumptions into your code because it limits the portability of your program. Never assume that your program will be used only by fellow Anglophones!

To avoid making such assumptions in your code, the C and C++ Standard Libraries offer the concept of *locales*. A locale is a set of parameters that defines the user's language and regional preferences, including the national or cultural character set and the formatting rules for currency and dates. A complete coverage of this topic is beyond the scope of this book, though. We only cover the character classification functions provided by the <cctype> header of the Standard Library, listed in Table 4-3. As always, these functions are all defined in the std namespace.

Table 4-3. *Functions for Classifying Characters*

Function	Operation
isupper(c)	Tests whether c is an uppercase letter, by default 'A' to 'Z'.
islower(c)	Tests whether c is a lowercase letter, by default 'a' to 'z'.
isalpha(c)	Tests whether c is an uppercase or lowercase letter (or any alphabetic character that is neither uppercase nor lowercase, should the locale's alphabet contain such characters).
isdigit(c)	Tests whether c is a digit, '0' to '9'.
isxdigit(c)	Tests whether c is a hexadecimal digit, either '0' to '9', 'a' to 'f', or 'A' to 'F'.
isalnum(c)	Tests whether c is an alphanumeric character; same as isalpha(c) || isdigit(c).
isspace(c)	Tests whether c is whitespace, by default a space (' '), newline ('\n'), carriage return ('\r'), form feed ('\f'), or horizontal ('\t') or vertical ('\v') tab.
isblank(c)	Tests whether c is a space character used to separate words within a line of text. By default either a space (' ') or a horizontal tab ('\t').
ispunct(c)	Tests whether c is a punctuation character. By default, this will be either a space or one of the following: _ { } [ ] # ( ) < > % : ; . ? * + - / ^ & | ~ ! = , \ " '
isprint(c)	Tests whether c is a printable character, which includes uppercase or lowercase letters, digits, punctuation characters, and spaces.
iscntrl(c)	Tests whether c is a control character, which is the opposite of a printable character.
isgraph(c)	Tests whether c has a graphical representation, which is true for any printable character other than a space.

The functions in Table 4-3 all expect a single character to test as input, and they all return a value of type int as a result. The reason that these functions return an int rather than a bool is because they originate from the C Standard Library and predate the introduction of a Boolean data type into C by over a decade (_Bool and its alias bool were only added to C in 1999). Regardless, you can normally treat these functions precisely as if they did in fact return values of type bool, as the return value will be nonzero (true) if the character is of the type being tested for, and 0 (false) if it isn't.

You could for instance use these character classification functions to implement Ex4_04 without any hard-coded assumptions about either the character set or its encoding. The character codes in different environments are always taken care of by the Standard Library functions. An additional advantage is that these functions also make the code simpler and easier to read. You'll find the adjusted program under the name Ex4_04A.cpp.

```
if (std::isupper(letter))    // Equivalent to 'if (std::isupper(letter) != 0)'
{
  std::println("You entered an uppercase letter.");
  return 0;
}

if (std::islower(letter))    // Equivalent to 'if (std::islower(letter) != 0)'
{
  std::println("You entered a lowercase letter.");
  return 0;
}
```

To conclude, the same Standard Library header also provides the two functions shown in Table 4-4 (again in the std namespace) for converting between uppercase and lowercase characters. The result will be returned as type int, so you need to explicitly cast it if you want to store it as type char, for instance.

Table 4-4. *Functions for Converting Characters Provided by the* <cctype> *Header*

Function	Operation
tolower(c)	If c is uppercase, the lowercase equivalent is returned; otherwise, c is returned.
toupper(c)	If c is lowercase, the uppercase equivalent is returned; otherwise, c is returned.

▓ **Note** All standard character classification and conversion functions except for std::isdigit() and std::isxdigit() operate according to the rules of the current locale. The examples given in Table 4-3 are for the default "C" locale, which is a set of preferences similar to those used by English-speaking Americans. The C++ Standard Library offers an extensive library for working with other locales and character sets. You can use these to develop applications that work correctly irrespective of the user's language and regional conventions. This topic is a bit too advanced for this book, though. Consult a Standard Library reference for more details.

The if-else Statement

The if statement that you have been using executes a statement or block of statements if the condition specified is true. Program execution then continues with the next statement in sequence. Of course, you may want to execute one block of statements when the condition is true and another set when the condition is false. An extension of the if statement called an if-else statement allows this.

The if-else combination provides a choice between two options. Figure 4-2 shows its general logic.

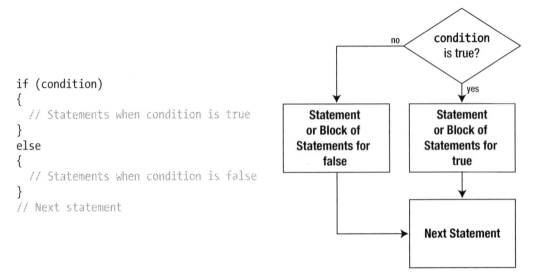

```
if (condition)
{
    // Statements when condition is true
}
else
{
    // Statements when condition is false
}
// Next statement
```

One of the two blocks in an if-else statement is always executed.

Figure 4-2. *The if-else statement logic*

The flowchart in Figure 4-2 shows the sequence in which statements execute, depending on whether the if condition is true or false. You can always use a block of statements wherever you can put a single statement. This allows any number of statements to be executed for each option in an if-else statement.

You could write an if-else statement that would report whether the character stored in the char variable letter was alphanumeric:

```
if (std::isalnum(letter))
{
  std::println("It is a letter or a digit.");
}
else
{
  std::println("It is neither a letter nor a digit.");
}
```

This uses the std:isalnum() function you saw earlier. If letter contains a letter or a digit, isalnum() returns a positive integer. This will be implicitly converted to a bool value, which will be true, so the first message is displayed. If letter contains something other than a letter or a digit, isalnum() returns 0, which converts to false so the output statement after else executes. The braces are again not mandatory here because they contain single statements, but it's clearer if you put them in. The indentation in the blocks is a visible indicator of the relationship between various statements. You can clearly see which statement is executed for a true result and which is executed for false. You should always indent the statements in your programs to show their logical structure.

Here's an example of using if-else with a numerical value:

```cpp
// Ex4_05.cpp - Using the if-else statement
import std;

int main()
{
  long number {};       // Stores input
  std::print("Enter an integer less than 2 billion: ");
  std::cin >> number;

  if (number % 2)       // Test remainder after division by 2 (equivalent: number % 2 == 1)
  {                     // Here if remainder is 1
    std::println("Your number is odd.");
  }
  else
  {                     // Here if remainder is 0
    std::println("Your number is even.");
  }
}
```

Here's an example of output from this program:

```
Enter an integer less than 2 billion: 123456
Your number is even.
```

After reading the input into number, the program tests this value in the if condition. This is an expression that produces the remainder that results from dividing number by 2. The remainder will be 1 if number is odd, or 0 if it's even, and these values convert to true and false, respectively. Thus, if the remainder is 1, the if condition is true, and the statement in the block immediately following the if executes. If the remainder is 0, the if condition is false, so the statement in the block following the else keyword executes.

You could also specify the if condition as number % 2 == 0, in which case the sequence of blocks would need to be reversed because this expression evaluates to true when number is even.

Nested if-else Statements

You have already seen that you can nest if statements within if statements. You have no doubt anticipated that you can also nest if-else statements within ifs, ifs within if-else statements, and if-else statements within other if-else statements. This provides you with plenty of versatility (and considerable room for confusion), so let's look at a few examples. Taking the first case, an example of an if-else nested within an if might look like the following:

```cpp
if (coffee == 'y')
  if (donuts == 'y')
    std::println("We have coffee and donuts.");
  else
    std::println("We have coffee, but not donuts.");
```

This would be better written with braces, but it's easier to make the point we want to make without. coffee and donuts are variables of type char that can have the value 'y' or 'n'. The test for donuts executes only if the result of the test for coffee is true, so the messages reflect the correct situation in each case. The else belongs to the if that tests for donuts. However, it is easy to get this confused.

If you write much the same thing but with incorrect indentation, you can be trapped into the wrong conclusion about what happens here:

```
if (coffee == 'y')
  if (donuts == 'y')
    std::println("We have coffee and donuts.");
else                              // This is indented incorrectly...
  std::println("We have no coffee...");  // ...Wrong!
```

The indentation now misleadingly suggests that this is an if nested within an if-else, which is not the case. The first message is correct, but the output as a consequence of the else executing is quite wrong. This statement executes only if the test for coffee is true, because the else belongs to the test for donuts, not the test for coffee. This mistake is easy to see here, but with larger and more complicated if structures, you need to keep in mind the following rule about which if owns which else:

▓ **Caution**　An else always belongs to the nearest preceding if that's not already spoken for by another else. The potential for confusion here is known as the *dangling else problem*.

Braces will always make the situation clearer:

```
if (coffee == 'y')
{
  if (donuts == 'y')
  {
    std::println("We have coffee and donuts.");
  }
  else
  {
    std::println("We have coffee, but not donuts.");
  }
}
```

Now it's absolutely clear. The else definitely belongs to the if that is checking for donuts.

Understanding Nested ifs

Now that you know the rules, understanding an if nested within an if-else should be easy:

```
if (coffee == 'y')
{
  if (donuts == 'y')
    std::println("We have coffee and donuts.");
}
```

```
else if (tea == 'y')
{
  std::println("We have no coffee, but we have tea.");
}
```

Notice the formatting of the code here. When an else block is another if, writing else if on one line is an accepted convention. The braces enclosing the test for donuts are essential. Without them the else would belong to the if that's looking out for donuts. In this kind of situation, it is easy to forget to include the braces and thus create an error that may be hard to find. A program with this kind of error compiles without a problem, as the code is correct. It may even produce the right results some of the time. If you removed the braces in this example, you'd get the right results only as long as coffee and donuts were both 'y' so that the check for tea wouldn't execute.

Nesting if-else statements in other if-else statements can get very messy, even with just one level of nesting. Let's beat the coffee and donuts analysis to death by using it again:

```
if (coffee == 'y')
  if (donuts == 'y')
    std::println("We have coffee and donuts.");
  else
    std::println("We have coffee, but not donuts.");
else if (tea == 'y')
  std::println("We have no coffee, but we have tea, and maybe donuts...");
else
  std::println("No tea or coffee, but maybe donuts...");
```

The logic here doesn't look quite so obvious, even with the correct indentation. Braces aren't necessary, as the rule you saw earlier will verify, but it would look much clearer if you included them:

```
if (coffee == 'y')
{
  if (donuts == 'y')
  {
    std::println("We have coffee and donuts.");
  }
  else
  {
    std::println("We have coffee, but not donuts.");
  }
}
else
{
  if (tea == 'y')
  {
    std::println("We have no coffee, but we have tea, and maybe donuts...");
  }
  else
  {
    std::println("No tea or coffee, but maybe donuts...");
  }
}
```

There are much better ways of dealing with this kind of logic. If you put enough nested `if`s together, you can almost guarantee a mistake somewhere. The next section will help to simplify things.

Logical Operators

As you have seen, using `if`s where you have two or more related conditions can be cumbersome. You have tried your `iffy` talents on looking for coffee and donuts, but in practice, you may want to check much more complex conditions. For instance, you could be looking for someone who is older than 21, younger than 35, is female, has a bachelor's or master's degree, is unmarried, and speaks Hindi or Urdu. Defining a test for this with what you know now already would involve the mother of all nested `if`s.

Luckily, the logical operators provide a neat and simple solution. Using logical operators, you can combine a series of comparisons into a single expression so that you need just one `if`, almost regardless of the complexity of the set of conditions. What's more, you won't have trouble determining which one to use because there are just the three shown in Table 4-5.

Table 4-5. *Logical Operators*

Operator	Description
&&	Logical AND
||	Logical OR
!	Logical negation (NOT)

The first two, && and ||, are binary operators that combine two operands of type `bool` and produce a result of type `bool`. The third operator, !, is unary, so it applies to a single operand of type `bool` and produces a `bool` result. In the following pages we'll explain first how each of these is used; then we'll demonstrate them in an example. Finally, we'll compare these logical operators with the bitwise operators you learned about earlier.

Logical AND

You use the AND operator, &&, when you have two conditions that must both be `true` for a `true` result. For example, you want to be rich *and* healthy. Earlier, to determine whether a character was an uppercase letter, the value had to be both greater than or equal to `'A'` *and* less than or equal to `'Z'`. The && operator *only* produces a `true` result if both operands are `true`. If either or both operands are `false`, then the result is `false`. Here's how you could test a `char` variable, `letter`, for an uppercase letter using the && operator:

```
if (letter >= 'A' && letter <= 'Z')
{
  std::println("This is an uppercase letter.");
}
```

The output statement executes only if both of the conditions combined by && are `true`. No parentheses are necessary in the expression because the precedence of the comparison operators is higher than that of &&. As usual, you're free to put parentheses in if you want. You could write the statement as follows:

```
if ((letter >= 'A') && (letter <= 'Z'))
{
  std::println("This is an uppercase letter.");
}
```

Now there's no doubt that the comparisons will be evaluated first. Still, experienced programmers probably wouldn't put these extra parentheses here.

Logical OR

The OR operator, ||, applies when you want a true result when either or both of the operands are true. The result is false only when both operands are false.

For example, you might be considered creditworthy enough for a bank loan if your income was at least $100,000 a year or if you had $1,000,000 in cash. This could be tested like this:

```
if (income >= 100'000.00 || capital >= 1'000'000.00)
{
  std::println("Of course, how much do you want to borrow?");
}
```

The response emerges when either or both of the conditions are true. (A better response might be "*Why* do you want to borrow?" It's strange how banks will only lend you money when you don't need it.)

Notice also that we've used digit separators to increase the readability of the integer literals; it is far more obvious that 1'000'000.00 equals one million than that 1000000.00 does. Would you even spot the difference between 100000.00 and 1000000.00 without the separators? (Should the bank ever make mistakes filling in either one of these numbers, you'd surely want it to be in your favor!)

Logical Negation

The third logical operator, !, applies to single bool operand and inverts its value. So, if the value of a bool variable, test, is true, then !test is false; if test is false, then !test results in the value true.

Like all logical operators, you can apply logical negation to any expressions that evaluate to true or false. Operands can be anything from a single bool variable to a complex combination of comparisons and bool variables. For example, suppose x has the value 10. Then the expression !(x > 5) evaluates to false because x > 5 is true. Of course, in that particular case, you may be better off simply writing x <= 5. The latter expression is equivalent, but because it does not contain the negation, it is probably easier to read.

▓ **Caution** Let foo, bar, and xyzzy be variables (or any expressions if you will) of type bool. Then beginning C++ programmers, such as yourself, often write statements like this:

```
if (foo == true) ...
if (bar == false) ...
if (xyzzy != true) ...
```

While technically correct, it is generally accepted that you should favor the following equivalent, yet shorter, `if` statements instead:

```
if (foo) ...
if (!bar) ...
if (!xyzzy) ...
```

Combining Logical Operators

You can combine conditional expressions and logical operators to any degree to which you feel comfortable. This example implements a questionnaire to decide whether a person is a good loan risk:

```cpp
// Ex4_06.cpp - Combining logical operators for loan approval
import std;

int main()
{
  int age {};              // Age of the prospective borrower
  int income {};           // Income of the prospective borrower
  int balance {};          // Current bank balance

  // Get the basic data for assessing the loan
  std::print("Please enter your age in years: ");
  std::cin >> age;
  std::print("Please enter your annual income in dollars: ");
  std::cin >> income;
  std::print("What is your current account balance in dollars: ");
  std::cin >> balance;

  // We only lend to people who are at least 21 years of age,
  // who make over $25,000 per year,
  // or have over $100,000 in their account, or both.
  if (age >= 21 && (income > 25'000 || balance > 100'000))
  {
    // OK, you are good for the loan - but how much?
    // This will be the lesser of twice income and half balance
    int loan {};                // Stores maximum loan amount
    if (2*income < balance/2)
    {
      loan = 2*income;
    }
    else
    {
      loan = balance/2;
    }
    std::println("\nYou can borrow up to ${}", loan);
  }
```

```
  else    // No loan for you...
  {
    std::println("\nUnfortunately, you don't qualify for a loan.");
  }
}
```

Here's some sample output:

```
Please enter your age in years: 25
Please enter your annual income in dollars: 28000
What is your current account balance in dollars: 185000

You can borrow up to $56000
```

The interesting bit is the if statement that determines whether a loan will be granted. The if condition is as follows:

```
age >= 21 && (income > 25'000 || balance > 100'000)
```

This condition requires that the applicant's age be at least 21 and that either their income is larger than $25,000 or their account balance is greater than $100,000. The parentheses around the expression (income > 25'000 || balance > 100'000) are necessary to ensure that the result of OR'ing the income and balance conditions together is AND'ed with the result of the age test. Without the parentheses, the age test would be AND'ed with the income test, and the result would be OR'ed with the balance test. This is because && has a higher precedence than ||, as you can see from the table in Chapter 3. Without the parentheses, the condition would have allowed an 8-year-old with a balance over $100,000 to get a loan. That's not what was intended. Banks never lend to minors or mynahs.

If the if condition is true, the block of statements that determine the loan amount executes. The loan variable is defined within this block and therefore ceases to exist at the end of the block. The if statement within the block determines whether twice the declared income is less than half the account balance. If it is, the loan is twice the income; otherwise, it is half the account balance. This ensures the loan corresponds to the least amount according to the rules.

▓ **Tip**   When combining logical operators, it is recommended to always add parentheses to clarify the code. Suppose for argument's sake that the bank's condition for allowing a loan was as follows:

```
(age < 30 && income > 25'000) || (age >= 30 && balance > 100'000)
```

That is, for younger clients, the decision depends entirely on their yearly salary—yes, even toddlers get a loan, as long as they can submit proof of sufficient income. More mature clients, though, must already have sufficient savings. Then you could also write this condition as follows:

```
age < 30 && income > 25'000 || age >= 30 && balance > 100'000
```

Both expressions are perfectly equivalent. But surely you'll agree that the one with parentheses is much easier to read than the one without. When combining && and ||, it is therefore recommended to always clarify the meaning of the logical expression by adding parentheses, even when it strictly speaking is not necessary.

Logical Operators on Integer Operands

In a way, logical operators can be—and actually fairly often are—applied to integer operands instead of Boolean operands. For instance, earlier you saw that the following can be used to test whether an int variable value differs from zero:

```
if (value)
  std::println("You have entered a value that is different from zero.");
```

Equally frequently, you will encounter a test of the following form:

```
if (!value)
  std::println("You have entered a value that equals zero.");
```

Here, logical negation is applied to an integer operand—not to a Boolean operand as usual. Similarly, suppose you have defined two int variables, value1 and value2; then you could write the following:

```
if (value1 && value2)
  std::println("Both values are non-zero.");
```

Because these expressions are so short, they are popular among C++ programmers. Typical use cases of such patterns occur if these integer values represent, for instance, the number of elements in a collection of objects. It is therefore important that you understand how they work. Every numeric operand to a logical operator in expressions such as these is first converted to a bool using the familiar rule: zero converts to false, and every other number converts to true. Even if all operands are integers, the logical expression still evaluates to a bool, though.

Logical Operators vs. Bitwise Operators

It's important not to confuse the logical operators—&&, ||, and !—that apply to operands that are convertible to bool with the bitwise operators &, |, and ~ that operate on the bits within integral operands.

From the previous subsection, you'll remember that logical operators always evaluate to a value of type bool, even if their operands are integers. The converse is true for bitwise operators; they always evaluate to an integer number, even if both operands are of type bool. Nevertheless, because the integer result of a bitwise operator always converts back to a bool, it may often seem that logical and bitwise operators can be used interchangeably. The central test in Ex4_06 to test whether a loan is admissible, for instance, could in principle be written like this:

```
if (age >= 21 & (income > 25'000 | balance > 100'000))
{
    ...
}
```

This will compile and have the same end result as before when && and || were still used. In short, what happens is that the bool values that result from the comparisons are converted to ints, which are then bitwise combined into a single int using the bitwise operators, after which this single int is again converted to a bool for the if statement. Confused? Don't worry, it's not really all that important. Such conversions back and forth between bool and integers are rarely a cause for concern.

What *is* important, though, is the second, more fundamental difference between the two sets of operators; namely, unlike bitwise operators, the binary logical operators are *short-circuit* operators.

Short-Circuit Evaluation

Consider the following code snippet (x is of type int):

```
if (x < 0 && (x*x + 632*x == 1268))
{
  std::println("Congrats: {} is the correct solution!", x);
}
```

Quickly, is x = 2 the correct solution? Of course not. 2 is not less than 0! It does not matter whether 2*2 + 632*2 equals 1268 or not (it does, if you must know). Whenever x < 0, the first operand of the AND operator in the if statement, is false, the end result will be false as well. After all, false && true remains false; the only case where the AND operator evaluates to true is true && true.

Similarly, in the following snippet, it should be instantly clear that x = 2 is a correct solution:

```
if (x == 2 || (x*x + 632*x == 1268))
{
  std::println("Congrats: {} is a correct solution!", x);
}
```

Because the first operand is true, you immediately know that the full OR expression will evaluate to true as well. There's no need to even compute the second operand.

Naturally, a C++ compiler knows this as well. Therefore, if the first operand to a binary logical expression already determines the outcome, the compiler will make sure not to waste time evaluating the second operand. This property of the logical operators && and || is called *short-circuit evaluation*. The bitwise operators & and |, on the other hand, do not short-circuit. For these operators, both operands are always evaluated.

This short-circuiting semantics of logical operators is often exploited by C++ programmers:

- If you need to test for multiple conditions that are glued together with logical operators, then you should put the cheapest ones to compute first. Our two examples in this section already illustrate this to a point, but this technique only really pays off if one of the operands is truly expensive to calculate.

- Short-circuiting is more commonly utilized to prevent the evaluation of right-hand operands that would otherwise fail to evaluate—as in cause a fatal crash. This is done by putting other conditions first that short-circuit whenever the other operands would fail. As we will see later in this book, a popular application of this technique is to check that a pointer is not null before dereferencing it.

We will see several more examples of logical expressions that rely on short-circuit evaluation in later chapters. For now, just remember that the second operand of && is evaluated only after the first operand evaluates to true, and the second operand of || only after the first evaluates to false. For & and |, both operands are always evaluated.

Oh yes, in case you were wondering, the one and only correct solution for our logical expression x < 0 && (x*x + 632*x == 1268) from earlier is x = -634. Obviously.

Logical XOR

There is no counterpart of the bitwise XOR—short for eXclusive OR—operator, ^, among the logical operators. This is in part, no doubt, because short-circuiting this operator makes no sense (both operands must always be evaluated to know the correct outcome of this operator; best take a second to think about this). Luckily, the XOR operator, like any of the bitwise operators, can simply be applied to Boolean operands as well. The following test, for instance, passes for most youngsters and millionaires. Adults with a normal bank balance will not pass the cut, though, and neither will teenage millionaires:

```
if ((age < 20) ^ (balance >= 1'000'000))
{
    ...
}
```

In other words, this test is equivalent to either one of the following combinations of logical operators:

```
if ((age < 20 || balance >= 1'000'000) && !(age < 20 && balance >= 1'000'000))
{
    ...
}
```

```
if ((age < 20 && balance < 1'000'000) || (age >= 20 && balance >= 1'000'000))
{
    ...
}
```

We recommend you take the time to convince yourself that these three if statements are indeed equivalent. It makes for a very nice little exercise in Boolean algebra.

The Conditional Operator

The *conditional operator* is sometimes called the *ternary operator* because it involves three operands—the only operator to do so. It parallels the if-else statement, in that instead of selecting one of two statement blocks to execute depending on a condition, it selects the value of one of two expressions. Thus, the conditional operator enables you to choose between two values. Let's consider an example.

Suppose you have two variables, a and b, and you want to assign the value of the greater of the two to a third variable, c. The following statement will do this:

```
c = a > b ? a : b;    // Set c to the higher of a and b
```

The conditional operator has a logical expression as its first operand—in this case, a > b. If this expression is true, the second operand—in this case, a—is selected as the value resulting from the operation. If the first operand is false, the third operand—in this case, b—is selected as the value. Thus, the result of the conditional expression is a if a is greater than b, and b otherwise. This value is stored in c. The assignment statement is equivalent to the if statement:

```
if (a > b)
{
  c = a;
}
else
{
  c = b;
}
```

Similarly, in Ex4_06, you used an if-else to decide the value of the loan; you could use this statement instead:

```
loan = 2*income < balance/2 ? 2*income : balance/2;
```

This produces the same result. The condition is 2*income < balance/2. If this evaluates to true, then the expression 2*income evaluates and produces the result of the operation. If the condition is false, the expression balance/2 produces the result of the operation.

You don't need parentheses because the precedence of the conditional operator is lower than that of the other operators in this statement. Of course, if you think parentheses would make things clearer, you can include them:

```
loan = (2*income < balance/2) ? (2*income) : (balance/2);
```

The general form of the conditional operator, which is often represented by ?:, is as follows:

condition ? *expression1* : *expression2*

As usual, all whitespace before or after both the ? or the : is optional and ignored by the compiler. If condition evaluates to true, the result is the value of expression1; if it evaluates to false, the result is the value of expression2. If condition is an expression that results in a numerical value, then it is implicitly converted to type bool.

Note that only one of expression1 or expression2 will be evaluated. Similar to the short-circuiting evaluation of binary logical operands, this has significant implications for expressions such as the following:

```
divisor ? (dividend / divisor) : 0;
```

Suppose both divisor and dividend are variables of type int. For integers, division by zero results in undefined behavior in C++. This means that, in the worst case, dividing an integer by zero may cause a fatal crash. If divisor equals zero in the previous expression, however, then (dividend / divisor) is not evaluated. If the condition to a conditional operator evaluates to false, the second operand is not evaluated at all. Instead, only the third operand is evaluated. In this case, this implies that the entire expression trivially evaluates to 0. That is a much better outcome indeed than a potential crash!

You can use the conditional operator to control output depending on the result of an expression or the value of a variable. You can vary a message by selecting one text string or another depending on a condition.

```
// Ex4_07.cpp - Using the conditional operator to select output.
import std;

int main()
{
  int mice {};     // Count of all mice
  int brown {};    // Count of brown mice
  int white {};    // Count of white mice

  std::print("How many brown mice do you have? ");
  std::cin >> brown;
  std::print("How many white mice do you have? ");
  std::cin >> white;
```

```
  mice = brown + white;

  std::println("You have {} {} in total.", mice, mice == 1 ? "mouse" : "mice");
}
```

The output from this program might be as follows:

```
How many brown mice do you have? 2
How many white mice do you have? 3
You have 5 mice in total.
```

The only bit of interest is the output statement that is executed after the numbers of mice have been entered. The expression using the conditional operator evaluates to "mouse" if the value of mice is 1, or "mice" otherwise. This allows you to use the same output statement for any number of mice and select singular or plural as appropriate.

There are many other situations in which you can apply this sort of mechanism, such as when selecting between "is" and "are" or between "he" and "she" or indeed in any situation in which you have a binary choice. You can even combine two conditional operators to choose between three options. Here's an example:

```
std::println("{}", a < b ? "a is less than b." :
                  (a == b ? "a is equal to b." : "a is greater than b."));
```

This statement outputs one of three messages, depending on the relative values of a and b. The second choice for the first conditional operator is the result of another conditional operator.

The switch Statement

You're often faced with a multiple-choice situation in which you need to execute a particular set of statements from a number of choices (that is, more than two), depending on the value of an integer variable or expression. The switch statement enables you to select from multiple choices. The choices are identified by a set of fixed integral literals or enumerators, and the selection of a particular choice is determined by an expression of an integral or enumeration type (integral types also include character types).

The choices in a switch statement are called *cases*. A lottery where you win a prize depending on your number coming up is an example of where it might apply. You buy a numbered ticket, and if you're lucky, you win a prize. For instance, if your ticket number is 147, you win first prize; if it's 387, you can claim a second prize; and ticket 29 gets you a third prize; any other ticket number wins nothing. The switch statement to handle this situation would have four cases: one for each of the winning numbers, plus a "default" case for all the losing numbers. Here's a switch statement that selects a message for a given ticket number:

```
switch (ticket_number)
{
case 147:
  std::println("You win first prize!");
  break;
case 387:
  std::println("You win second prize!");
  break;
```

```
case 29:
  std::println("You win third prize!");
  break;
default:
  std::println("Sorry, you lose.");
  break;
}
```

The switch statement is harder to describe than to use. The selection of a particular case is determined by the value of the integer expression between the parentheses that follow the keyword switch. In this example, it is simply the integer variable ticket_number.

▓ **Note** You can only switch on values of integral (int, long, unsigned short, etc.), character (char, etc.), and enumeration types (see Chapter 2). Technically, switching on Boolean values is allowed as well, but instead of a switch on Booleans you should just use if/else statements. Unlike some other programming languages, however, C++ does not allow you to create switch() statements with conditions and labels that contain expressions of any other type. A switch that branches on different string values, for instance, is not allowed (we'll discuss strings in Chapter 7).

The possible choices in a switch statement appear in a block, and each choice is identified by a case value. A *case value* appears in a *case label*, which is of the following form:

```
case case_value:
```

It's called a case *label* because it labels the statements or block of statements that it precedes. The statements that follow a particular case label execute if the value of the selection expression is the same as that of the case value. Each case value must be unique, but case values don't need to be in any particular order, as the example demonstrates.

In practice, case values are nearly always[3] either integer literals, integer constants, or enumerator values (enumeration types were introduced in Chapter 3). Naturally, all case values must either be of the same type as the condition expression inside the preceding switch() or be convertible to that type.

The default label in the example identifies the *default case*, which is a catchall that is selected if none of the other cases is selected. If present, the default label does not have to be the last label. In principle, it can appear anywhere among the regular case labels. You also don't have to specify a default case. If you don't and none of the case values is selected, the switch does nothing.

The break statement that appears after each set of case statements is essential for the logic here. Executing a break statement breaks out of the switch and causes execution to continue with the statement following the closing brace. If you omit the break statement for a case, the statements for the following case will execute. Notice that we don't *need* a break after the final case (usually the default case) because execution leaves the switch at this point anyway. It's good programming style to include it, though, because it safeguards against accidentally falling through to another case that you might add to a switch later. switch, case, default, and break are all keywords.

---

[3] In principle, case values can be any appropriately typed compile-time-evaluated expression. We refer you to Chapter 8 for more information on such so-called constant expressions.

This example demonstrates the switch statement:

```cpp
// Ex4_08.cpp - Using the switch statement
import std;

int main()
{
  std::println("Your electronic recipe book is at your service.");
  std::println("You can choose from the following delicious dishes:");
  std::println(" 1. Boiled eggs");
  std::println(" 2. Fried eggs");
  std::println(" 3. Scrambled eggs");
  std::println(" 4. Coddled eggs");

  std::print("\nEnter your selection number: ");
  int choice {};   // Stores selection value
  std::cin >> choice;

  switch (choice)
  {
  case 1:
    std::println("Boil some eggs.");
    break;
  case 2:
    std::println("Fry some eggs.");
    break;
  case 3:
    std::println("Scramble some eggs.");
    break;
  case 4:
    std::println("Coddle some eggs.");
    break;

  default:
    std::println("You entered a wrong number - try raw eggs.");
    break;
  }
}
```

After laying out the available options in the first series of output statements and reading a selection number into the variable choice, the switch statement executes with the selection expression specified simply as choice in parentheses, immediately following the keyword switch. The possible choices in the switch are between braces and are each identified by a case label. If the value of choice corresponds with any of the case values, then the statements following that case label execute.

If the value of choice doesn't correspond with any of the case values, the statements following the default label execute. If you hadn't included a default case here and the value of choice was different from all the case values, then the switch would have done nothing, and the program would continue with the next statement after the switch—effectively executing return 0; because the end of main() has been reached.

The empty line we added before the default case is entirely optional. As are the line breaks after each case label. The following more compact code formatting, for instance, is therefore equally valid:

```
switch (choice)
{
case 1: std::println("Boil some eggs.");      break;
case 2: std::println("Fry some eggs.");       break;
case 3: std::println("Scramble some eggs."); break;
case 4: std::println("Coddle some eggs.");    break;
default: std::println("You entered a wrong number - try raw eggs."); break;
}
```

You have only one statement plus a break statement for each case in this example, but in general, you can have as many statements as you need following a case label, and you generally don't need to enclose them between braces. The cases where you do need to add braces are discussed in one of the next sections.

As we said earlier, each of the case values must be a compile-time constant and must be unique. The reason that no two case values can be the same is that if they are, the compiler has no way of knowing which statements should be executed when that particular value comes up. However, different case values don't need to have unique actions. Several case values can share the same action, as the following example shows:

```
// Ex4_09.cpp - Multiple case actions
import std;

int main()
{
  char letter {};
  std::print("Enter a letter: ");
  std::cin >> letter;

  if (std::isalpha(letter))
  {
    switch (std::tolower(letter))
    {
    case 'a': case 'e': case 'i': case 'o': case 'u':
      std::println("You entered a vowel.");
      break;
    default:
      std::println("You entered a consonant.");
      break;
    }
  }
  else
  {
    std::println("You did not enter a letter.");
  }
}
```

Here is an example of some output:

```
Enter a letter: E
You entered a vowel.
```

135

The if condition first checks that you really do have a letter and not some other character using the std::isalpha() classification function from the Standard Library. The integer returned will be nonzero if the argument is alphabetic, and this will be implicitly converted to true, which causes the switch to be executed. The switch condition converts the value to lowercase using the Standard Library character conversion routine, std::tolower(), and uses the result to select a case. Converting to lowercase avoids the need to have case labels for uppercase and lowercase letters. All of the cases that identify a vowel cause the same statements to be executed. You can see that you can just write each of the cases in a series, followed by the statements any of these cases is to select. If the input is not a vowel, it must be a consonant, and the default case deals with this.

If std::isalpha() returns 0, which converts to false, the switch doesn't execute because the else clause is selected; this outputs a message indicating that the character entered was not a letter.

In Ex4_09.cpp, we put all case labels with vowel values on a single line. This is not required. You are allowed to add line breaks (or any form of whitespace, for that matter) in between the case labels as well. Here's an example:

```
switch (std::tolower(letter))
{
  case 'a':
  case 'e':
  case 'i':
  case 'o':
  case 'u':
    std::println("You entered a vowel.");
    break;
...
```

A break statement is not the only way to move control out of a switch statement. If the code following a case label contains a return statement, control instantly exits not only the switch statement but the surrounding function as well. So, in principle, you could rewrite the switch statement in Ex4_09 as follows:

```
switch (std::tolower(letter))
{
case 'a': case 'e': case 'i': case 'o': case 'u':
  std::println("You entered a vowel.");
  return 0;       // Ends the program
}

// We did not exit main() in the above switch, so letter is not a vowel:
std::println("You entered a consonant.");
```

With this particular variant, we also again illustrate that a default case is optional. If you enter a vowel, the output will reflect this, and the return statement in the switch statement will terminate the program. Note that after a return statement, you should never put a break statement anymore. If you enter a consonant, the switch statement does nothing. None of these cases apply, and there is no default case. Execution continues after the statement and outputs that you have in fact entered a consonant—remember, if you would've entered a vowel, the program would've terminated already because of the return statement.

The code for this variant is available as Ex4_09A. We created it to show a few points, though, not because it necessarily reflects good programming style. The use of a default case is surely recommended over continuing after a switch statement after none of the cases executed a return.

Fallthrough

The break statement at the end of each group of case statements transfers execution to the statement after the switch. You could demonstrate the essential nature of the break statements by removing them from the switch statements of examples Ex4_08 or Ex4_09 and seeing what happens. You'll find that the code beneath the case label directly following the case without a break statement then gets executed as well. This phenomenon is called *fallthrough* because, in a way, we "fall through" into the next case.

More often than not, a missing break statement signals an oversight and therefore a bug. To illustrate this, let's return to our example with the lottery numbers:

```
switch (ticket_number)
{
case 147:
  std::println("You win first prize!");
case 387:
  std::println("You win second prize!");
  break;
case 29:
  std::println("You win third prize!");
  break;
default:
  std::println("Sorry, you lose.");
  break;
}
```

You'll notice that this time, we have "accidentally" omitted the break statement after the first case. If you executed this switch statement now with ticket_number equal to 147, the output would be as follows:

```
You win first prize!
You win second prize!
```

As ticket_number equals 147, the switch statement jumps to the corresponding case, and you win first prize. But since there is no break statement, execution simply goes on with the code underneath the next case label, and you win second prize as well—huzza! Clearly, this omission of break must be an accidental oversight.

Because a missing break statement is such a common source of mistakes, most compilers[4] issue a warning if a nonempty switch case is not followed by either a break or a return statement (maybe you noticed this already when removing a break statement from Ex4_08 or Ex4_09 as suggested earlier?). And a good thing, too; such bugs could otherwise easily creep in unnoticed, especially if the case that falls through incorrectly occurs only rarely.

But, of course, fallthrough does not always mean a mistake was made. Empty switch cases, notably, are common enough not to warrant compiler warnings. We already saw an example of those in Ex4_09 (where we used a sequence of empty switch cases to check for vowels). But even for a case label that is followed by

---

[4] For the Visual Studio C++ compiler, notably, this compiler warning is disabled by default. You can, and probably should, enable it, though, through the /w15262 or /Wall compiler flags.

one or more statements you can at times purposely employ fallthrough. Suppose that our lottery produces multiple winning numbers for second and third prize (two and three winners, respectively) and that one of the third prize winners gets a special bonus prize. Then we could express this logic as follows:

```
switch (ticket_number)
{
case 147:
  std::println("You win first prize!");
  break;
case 387:
case 123:
  std::println("You win second prize!");
  break;
case 929:
  std::println("You win a special bonus prize!");
  // This is where we purposely fall through to the next case(s)...
case 29:
case 78:
  std::println("You win third prize!");
  break;
default:
  std::println("Sorry, you lose.");
  break;
}
```

The idea is that if your ticket_number equals 929, the outcome should be the following:

```
You win a special bonus prize!
You win third prize!
```

If your number is either 29 or 78, however, you'd only win third prize.

The only downside is the intentional use of fallthrough triggers compiler warnings as well. And, as any self-respecting programmer, you want to compile all your programs free of warnings—as you should.

▪ **Tip** Compiler warnings should, as a rule, not be ignored. If your compiler supports it, and most do, we recommend you configure it so that all compiler warnings are treated as errors (and therefore halt compilation).

You can always eliminate fallthrough by rewriting the switch statement. In our lottery example, for instance, doing so involves repeating the statement that prints "You win third prize!" at the end of case 929, followed by an extra break statement. While it's worth noting that such a rewrite could surely be beneficial (it may very well lead to simpler and clearer code), it does inevitably involve duplicating one or more statements. And code duplication, as a rule, is something that you normally want to avoid as well.

The solution is to signal both the compiler and anyone reading your code that you are intentionally falling through to the next case by adding a [[fallthrough]] statement in the same place where you would otherwise add a break statement:

```
switch (ticket_number)
{
...
case 929:
  std::println("You win a special bonus prize!");
  [[fallthrough]];
case 29:
case 78:
  std::println("You win third prize!");
  break;
...
}
```

For empty cases, such as the one for number 29, a [[fallthrough]] statement is allowed but not required. As said, compilers already do not issue warnings for this.

Switching on Enumeration Values

In practice, many if not most switch statements operate on values of an enumeration type. After all, it's a match made in heaven. An enumeration type restricts expressions to a predictable, limited set of possible values (as seen in Chapter 3), precisely the kind of expressions a switch statement is designed for. Naturally, the case values for such switch statements are then enumerators of the corresponding enumeration type. Here is a small example of a typical switch statement on an enumeration variable that should require no further explanation.

```
// Ex4_10.cpp - Switching on enumeration values
import std;

int main()
{
  enum class Color { red, green, blue };

  Color my_color = Color::red;

  std::print("Today, I'm feeling ");
  switch (my_color)
  {
  case Color::red:   std::println("loving"); break;
  case Color::green: std::println("jealous"); break;
  case Color::blue:  std::println("sad"); break;
  }
}
```

▓ **Tip** To avoid having to qualify the enumerators in the different `case` labels with the name of the enumeration type (the `Color::` qualifiers in Ex4_10, for instance), you can add a `using enum` declaration (see also Chapter 3) at the start of a `switch` statement. Here is an example based on Ex4_10:

```
switch (my_color)
{
using enum Color;  // No need to qualify 'Color::' within this switch statement
case red:  std::println("loving"); break;
case green: std::println("jealous"); break;
case blue: std::println("sad"); break;
}
```

If there is no `default` case, most compilers[5] warn you if the `case` labels of a `switch` statement do not exhaustively list all possible enumerators of an enumeration type. You can try this in Ex4_10 by adding, say, enumerators named yellow and/or orange (which, of course, should map to feeling frightened and lonely, respectively). This leads us to the following important advice:

▓ **Tip** Avoid `default` cases when switching on enumeration values. Instead, always exhaustively list as many `case` labels as there are enumerators, even if that means adding a series of empty cases that all fall through to the same (default) code. That way, whenever you add a new enumerator to an enumeration type, you can leverage the aforementioned compiler warnings to revisit all relevant `switch` statements and, in doing so, ensure that all relevant `switch` statements have a correct `case` for the new enumerator. In `switch` statements with a `default` case, on the other hand, new enumerators are always silently huddled under that `default` case. Without the assistance of the compiler warnings, it then becomes very easy to end up with `switch` statements where you forgot to add `case`s for newer enumerators (that is, where the `default` behavior is not correct for new enumerators).

Statement Blocks and Variable Scope

A `switch` statement has its own block between braces that encloses the `case` statements. An `if` statement also often has braces enclosing the statements to be executed if the condition is `true`, and the `else` part may have such braces too. These statement blocks are no different from any other blocks when it comes to variable scope. Any variable declared within a block ceases to exist at the end of the block, so you cannot reference it outside the block.

---

[5] If your compiler doesn't warn about missing enumerator cases you may need to configure it to be more informative. For the Visual C++ compiler, for instance, this warning is disabled by default, but it can be enabled through the /w34062 or /Wall compiler flags. We recommend you enable as many compiler warnings as is practicable, especially for new code bases.

For example, consider the following rather arbitrary calculation:

```
if (value > 0)
{
  int savit {value - 1};    // This only exists in this block
  value += 10;
}
else
{
  int savit {value + 1};    // This only exists in this block
  value -= 10;
}
std::println("{}", savit);  // This will not compile! savit does not exist
```

The output statement at the end causes a compiler error message because the savit variable is undefined at this point. Any variable defined within a block can be used only within that block, so if you want to access data that originates inside a block from outside it, you must define the variable storing that information in an outer block.

Variable definitions within a switch statement block must be reachable in the course of execution, and it must not be possible to bypass them by jumping to a case after the declaration and within the same scope; otherwise, the code will not compile. Most likely, you don't understand at all yet what we mean. It'll be much easier to explain, though, by means of an example. The following code illustrates how illegal declarations can arise in a switch:

```
int test {3};
switch (test)
{
  int i {1};                // ILLEGAL - cannot be reached

case 1:
  int j {2};                // ILLEGAL - can be reached but can be bypassed
  std::println("{}", test + j);
  break;

  int k {3};                // ILLEGAL - cannot be reached

case 3:
{
  int m {4};                // OK - can be reached and cannot be bypassed
  std::println("{}", test + m);
  break;
}

default:
  int n {5};                // OK - can be reached and cannot be bypassed
  std::println("{}", test + n);
  break;
}
std::println("{}", j);      // ILLEGAL - j doesn't exist here
std::println("{}", n);      // ILLEGAL - n doesn't exist here
```

Only two of the variable definitions in this switch statement are legal: the ones for m and n. For a definition to be legal, it must first be possible for it to be reached and thus executed in the normal course of execution. Clearly, this is not the case for variables i and k. Second, it must not be possible during execution to enter the scope of a variable while bypassing its definition, which is the case for the variable j. If execution jumps to either the case with label 3 or the default case, it enters the scope in which the variable j was defined while bypassing its actual definition. That's illegal. Variable m, however, is only "in scope" from its declaration to the end of the enclosing block, so this declaration cannot be bypassed. And the declaration of variable n cannot be bypassed because there are no cases after the default case. Note that it's not because it concerns the default case that the declaration of n is legal; if there were additional cases following the default one, the declaration of n would've been just as illegal.

Initialization Statements

Consider the following code snippet:

```
auto lower{ static_cast<char>(std::tolower(input)) };
if (lower >= 'a' && lower <= 'z') {
  std::println("You've entered the letter '{}'", lower);
}
// ... more code that does not use lower
```

We convert an input character to lowercase character lower and use the outcome first to check whether the input was a letter and then, if so, to produce some output. For illustration's sake, ignore the fact that we could—*should* even—be using the portable std::isalpha() function here instead. You've learned all about that in this chapter already. The key point that we want to make with this example is that the lower variable is used only by the if statement and not anymore by any of the code that follows the snippet. In general, it is considered good coding style to limit the scope of variables to the region in which they are used, even if this means adding an extra scope as follows:

```
{
  auto lower{ static_cast<char>(std::tolower(input)) };
  if (lower >= 'a' && lower <= 'z') {
    std::println("You've entered the letter '{}'", lower);
  }
}
// ... more code (lower does not exist here)
```

The result is that, for the rest of the code, it is as if the lower variable never existed. Patterns such as this, where an extra scope (and indentation) is introduced to bind local variables to if statements, are relatively common. In fact, they are common enough for modern C++ to have a specialized syntax for it. The general syntax is as follows:

```
if (initialization; condition) ...
```

The additional initialization *statement* is executed prior to evaluating the `condition` expression, the usual Boolean expression of the `if` statement. You will use such initialization statements mainly to declare variables local to the `if` statement. With this, our earlier example becomes the following:

```
if (auto lower{ static_cast<char>(std::tolower(input)) }; lower >= 'a' && lower <= 'z') {
  std::println("You've entered the letter '{}'", lower);
}
// ... more code (lower does not exist here)
```

Variables declared in the initialization statement can be used both in the `if` statement's condition expression and in the statement or block that immediately follows the `if`. For `if-else` statements, they can be used in the statement or block that follows the `else` as well. But for any code after the `if` or `if-else` statement, it is as if these variables never existed.

For completeness, C++ also supports a similar syntax for `switch` statements:

```
switch (initialization; condition) { ... }
```

Summary

In this chapter, you added the capability for decision-making to your programs. You now know how *all* the decision-making statements in C++ work. The essential elements of decision-making that you have learned about in this chapter are as follows:

- You can compare two values using the comparison operators. This will result in a value of type `bool`, which can be either `true` or `false`.

- You can convert a `bool` value to an integer type—`true` will convert to `1`, and `false` will convert to `0`.

- Numerical values can be converted to type `bool`—a zero value converts to `false`, and any nonzero value converts to `true`. When a numerical value appears where a `bool` value is expected—such as in an `if` condition—the compiler will insert an implicit conversion of the numerical value to type `bool`.

- The `if` statement executes a statement or a block of statements depending on the value of a condition expression. If the condition is `true`, the statement or block executes. If the condition is `false`, it doesn't.

- The `if-else` statement executes a statement or block of statements when the condition is `true` and executes another statement or block when the condition is `false`.

- `if` and `if-else` statements can be nested.

- The logical operators `&&`, `||`, and `!` are used to string together more complex logical expressions. The arguments to these operators must either be Booleans or values that are convertible to Booleans (such as integral values).

- The conditional operator, `?:`, selects between two values depending on the value of a Boolean expression.

- The `switch` statement provides a way to select one from a fixed set of options, depending on the value of an expression of integral or enumeration type.

```
                            EXERCISES
```

The following exercises enable you to try what you've learned in this chapter. If you get stuck, look back over the chapter for help. If you're still stuck after that, you can download the solutions from the Apress website (https://www.apress.com/gp/services/source-code), but that really should be a last resort.

Exercise 4-1. Write a program that prompts for two integers to be entered and then uses an if-else statement to output a message that states whether the integers are the same.

Exercise 4-2. Write another program that prompts for two integers to be entered. This time, any negative number or zero is to be rejected. Next, check whether one of the (strictly positive) numbers is an exact multiple of the other. For example, 63 is a multiple of 1, 3, 7, 9, 21, or 63. Note that the user should be allowed to enter the numbers in any order. That is, it does not matter whether the user enters the largest number first or the smaller one; both should work correctly!

Exercise 4-3. Create a program that prompts for input of a number (nonintegral numbers are allowed) between 1 and 100. Use a nested if, first to verify that the number is within this range and then, if it is, to determine whether it is greater than, less than, or equal to 50. The program should output information about what was found.

Exercise 4-4. It's time to make good on a promise. Somewhere in this chapter, we said we'd look for someone "who is older than 21, younger than 35, is female, has a bachelor's or master's degree, is unmarried, and speaks Hindi or Urdu." Write a program that prompts the user for these qualifications and then outputs whether they qualify for these very specific requirements. To this end, you should define an integer variable age, a character variable gender (to hold 'm' for male, 'f' for female, etc.), a variable degree of an enumeration type AcademicDegree (possible values: none, associate, bachelor, professional, master, doctor), and three Boolean variables: married, speaksHindi, and speaksUrdu. Emulate a trivial online job interview, ignore any and all flagrant age and sex discrimination issues, and query your applicant for input on all these variables. People who enter invalid values do not qualify, of course, and should be ruled out as early as possible (that is, immediately after entering any invalid value; ruling them out precognitively prior to entering invalid values, sadly, is not possible yet in Standard C++).

Exercise 4-5. Add some code to the end of the main() function of Ex4_07.cpp to print an additional message. If you have exactly one mouse, output a message of the form "It is a brown/white mouse." Otherwise, if you have multiple mice, compose a grammatically correct message of the form "Of these mice, N is a/are brown mouse/mice." If you have no mice, no new message needs to be printed. Use an appropriate mixture of conditional operators and if/else statements.

Exercise 4-6. Write a program that determines, using only the conditional operator, if an integer that is entered has a value that is 20 or less, is greater than 20 but not greater than 30, is greater than 30 but not exceeding 100, or is greater than 100.

Exercise 4-7. Implement a program that prompts for the input of a letter. Use a library function to determine whether the letter is a vowel and whether it is lowercase or not, and output the result. Finally, output the lowercase letter together with its character code as a binary value. As a bonus exercise, you could try to do the latter by printing to std::cout without the use of the formatting capabilities of the std::print() or std::format() family of functions.

Hint: Even though C++ supports binary integral literals (of the form 0b11001010; see Chapter 2), C++ streams do not support outputting integral values in binary format. Besides the default decimal formatting, they only support hexadecimal and octal formatting (for std::cout, for instance, you can use the std::hex and std::oct output manipulators). So, to stream a character in binary format without the assistance of std::format(), you'll have to write some code yourself. It shouldn't be too hard, though; a char only has eight bits, remember? You can stream these bits one by one, even without knowing about loops (see the next chapter). Perhaps binary integer literals can also be helpful—why else would we have mentioned them at the start of this hint?

Exercise 4-8. Create a program that prompts the user to enter an amount of money between $0 and $10 (decimal places allowed). Any other value is to be rejected politely. Determine how many quarters (25c), dimes (10c), nickels (5c), and pennies (1c) are needed to make up that amount. For our non-American readers, one dollar ($) equals 100 cents (c). Output this information to the screen and ensure that the output makes grammatical sense (for example, if you need only one dime, then the output should be "1 dime" and not "1 dimes"). Naturally, the goal is to pay with as few coins as possible.

CHAPTER 5

Arrays and Loops

An array enables you to work with several data items of the same type using a single name, the array name. The need for this occurs often—when working with a series of temperatures or the ages of a group of people, for example. A loop is another fundamental programming facility. It provides a mechanism for repeating one or more statements as many times as your application requires. Loops are essential in the majority of programs. Using a computer to calculate the company payroll, for example, would not be practicable without a loop. There are several kinds of loop, each with their own particular area of application.

In this chapter, you'll learn

- What an array is and how you create an array
- How to use a for loop
- How the while loop works
- What the merits of the do-while loop are
- What the break and continue statements do in a loop
- How to use nested loops
- How to create and use an array container
- How to create and use a vector container

Arrays

The variables you have created so far can store only a single data item of the specified type—an integer, a floating-point value, a character, or a bool value. An array stores several data items of the same type. You can create an array of integers or characters (or an array of any type of data), and there can be as many as the available memory will allow.

Using an Array

An *array* is a variable that represents a sequence of memory locations, each storing an item of data of the same data type. Suppose, for instance, you've written a program to calculate the average temperature. You now want to extend the program to calculate how many samples are above that average and how many are below. To do this, you'll need to retain the original sample data, but storing each data item in a separate variable would be tortuous to code and highly impractical. An array provides you with the means of doing this easily. You could store 366 temperature samples in an array defined as follows:

```
double temperatures[366];        // Define an array of 366 temperatures
```

© Ivor Horton and Peter Van Weert 2023
I. Horton and P. Van Weert, *Beginning C++23*, https://doi.org/10.1007/978-1-4842-9343-0_5

This defines an array with the name temperatures to store 366 values of type double. The data values are called *elements*. The number of elements specified between the brackets is the *size* of the array. The array elements are not initialized in this statement, so they contain junk values.

The size of an array must always be specified using a *constant integer expression*. Any integer expression that the compiler can evaluate at compile time may be used, although mostly this will be either an integer literal or a const integer variable that itself was initialized using a literal.

You refer to an array element using an integer called an *index*. The index of a particular array element is its offset from the first element. The first element has an offset of 0 and therefore an index of 0; an index value of 3 refers to the fourth array element—three elements from the first. To reference an element, you put its index between square brackets after the array name, so to set the fourth element of the temperatures array to 99.0, you would write the following:

```
temperatures[3] = 99.0;                    // Set the fourth array element to 99
```

While an array of 366 elements nicely illustrates the need for arrays—just imagine having to define 366 distinct variables—creating figures with that many elements would be somewhat cumbersome. Let's therefore look at another array:

```
unsigned int height[6];                    // Define an array of six heights
```

As a result of this definition, the compiler will allocate six contiguous storage locations for storing values of type unsigned int. Each element in the height array contains a different number. Because the definition of height doesn't specify any initial values for the array, the six elements will contain junk values (analogous to what happens if you define a single variable of type unsigned int without an initial value). You could define the array with proper initial values like this:

```
unsigned int height[6] {26, 37, 47, 55, 62, 75};  // Define & initialize array of 6 heights
```

The braced initializer contains six values separated by commas. These might be the heights of the members of a family, recorded to the nearest inch. Each array element will be assigned an initial value from the list in sequence, so the elements will have the values shown in Figure 5-1. Each box in the figure represents a memory location holding a single array element. As there are six elements, the index values run from 0 for the first element through to 5 for the last element. Each element can therefore be referenced using the expression above it.

height [0]	height [1]	height [2]	height [3]	height [4]	height [5]
26	37	47	55	62	75

Figure 5-1. An array with six elements

▓ **Note** The type of the array will determine the amount of memory required for each element. The elements of an array are stored in one contiguous block of memory. So if the unsigned int type is 4 bytes on your computer, the height array will occupy 24 bytes.

The initializer must not have more values than there are elements in the array; otherwise, the statement won't compile. There can be fewer values in the list, however, in which case the elements for which no initial value has been supplied will be initialized with 0 (false for an array of bool elements). Here's an example:

```
unsigned int height[6] {26, 37, 47};        // Element values: 26 37 47 0 0 0
```

The first three elements will have the values that appear in the list. The last three will be 0. To initialize all the elements with 0, you can just use an empty initializer:

```
unsigned int height[6] {};                  // All elements 0
```

To define an array of values that cannot be modified, you simply add the keyword const to its type. The following defines an array of six unsigned int constants:

```
const unsigned int height[6] {26, 37, 47, 55, 62, 75}
```

Any modification to either one of these six array elements (be it an assignment, increment, or any other modification) will now be prevented by the compiler.

Array elements participate in arithmetic expressions like other variables. You could sum the first three elements of height like this:

```
unsigned int sum {};
sum = height[0] + height[1] + height[2];    // The sum of three elements
```

You use references to individual array elements such as ordinary integer variables in an expression. As you saw earlier, an array element can be on the left of an assignment to set a new value, so you can copy the value of one element to another in an assignment, like this:

```
height[3] = height[2];                       // Copy 3rd element value to 4th element
```

However, you can't copy all the element values from one array to the elements of another in an assignment. You can operate only on individual elements. To copy the values of one array to another, you must copy the values one at a time. What you need is a loop.

Understanding Loops

A *loop* is a mechanism that enables you to execute a statement or block of statements repeatedly until a particular condition is met. Two essential elements make up a loop: the statement or block of statements that is to be executed repeatedly forms the so-called *body* of the loop, and a *loop condition* of some kind that determines when to stop repeating the loop. A single execution of a loop's body is called an *iteration*.

A loop condition can take different forms to provide different ways of controlling the loop. For example, a loop condition can do the following:

- Execute a loop a given number of times

- Execute a loop until a given value exceeds another value

- Execute a loop until a particular character is entered from the keyboard

- Execute a loop for each element in a collection of elements

You choose the loop condition to suit the circumstances. You have the following varieties of loops:

- *The* for *loop* primarily provides for executing the loop a prescribed number of times, but there is considerable flexibility beyond that.

- *The range-based* for *loop* executes one iteration for each element in a collection of elements.

- *The* while *loop* continues executing as long as a specified condition is true. The condition is checked at the beginning of an iteration, so if the condition starts out as false, no loop iterations are executed.

- *The* do-while *loop* continues to execute as long as a given condition is true. This differs from the while loop in that the do-while loop checks the condition at the end of an iteration. This implies that at least one loop iteration always executes.

We'll start by explaining how the for loop works.

The for Loop

The for loop generally executes a statement or block of statements a predetermined number of times, but you can use it in other ways too. You specify how a for loop operates using three expressions separated by semicolons between parentheses following the for keyword. This is shown in Figure 5-2.

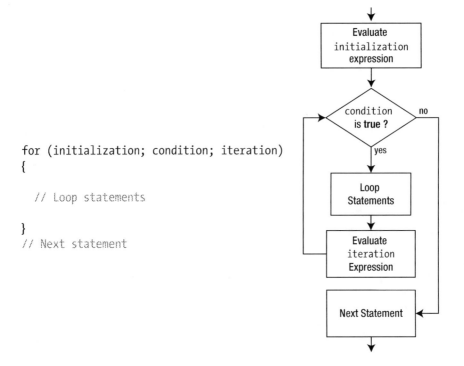

```
for (initialization; condition; iteration)
{

    // Loop statements

}
// Next statement
```

Figure 5-2. *The logic of the for loop*

You can omit any or all of the expressions controlling a for loop, but you must always include the semicolons. We'll explain later in this chapter why and when you might omit one or other of the control expressions. The initialization expression is evaluated only once, at the beginning of the loop. The loop condition is checked next, and if it is true, the loop statement or statement block executes. If the condition is false, the loop ends, and execution continues with the statement after the loop. After each execution of the loop statement or block, the iteration expression is evaluated, and the condition is checked to decide whether the loop should continue.

In the most typical usage of the for loop, the first expression initializes a counter, the second expression checks whether the counter has reached a given limit, and the third expression increments the counter. For example, you could copy the elements from one array to another like this:

```
double rainfall[12] {1.1, 2.8, 3.4, 3.7, 2.1, 2.3, 1.8, 0.0, 0.3, 0.9, 0.7, 0.5};
double copy[12] {};
for (std::size_t i {}; i < 12; ++i)  // i varies from 0 to 11
{
  copy[i] = rainfall[i];                  // Copy ith element of rainfall to ith element of copy
}
```

The first expression defines i as type std::size_t with an initial value of 0. You might remember the size_t type from the values returned by the sizeof operator (see Chapter 2). This alias for one of the fundamental unsigned integer types is not only commonly used for sizes of things, but also for counting and indexing things. As i will be used to index the rainfall and copy arrays, using std::size_t makes sense.

The loop condition i < 12 is obviously true as long as i is less than 12, so the loop continues while i is less than 12. When i reaches 12, the expression will be false, and the loop ends.

The third expression, ++i, increments i at the end of each loop iteration, so the loop block that copies the ith element from rainfall to copy will execute with values of i from 0 to 11.

■ **Caution**   Array index values are not checked to verify that they are valid. It's up to you to make sure that you don't reference elements outside the bounds of the array. If you store data using an index value that's outside the valid range for an array, you'll either inadvertently overwrite something in memory or cause a so-called *segmentation fault* or *access violation* (these terms are synonymous and denote an error that is raised by the operating system if and when it detects unauthorized memory access). Either way, your program will almost certainly come to a sticky end.

As always, the compiler ignores all whitespace within the for statement. Also, if the loop's body consists of only a single statement, the curly braces are again optional. So, if you like, you could format the for loop from before like this:

```
for( std::size_t i {} ; i<12 ; ++i )  // i varies from 0 to 11
  copy[i] = rainfall[i];                  // Copy ith element of rainfall to ith element of copy
```

In this book, we will put a single space after the for keyword (to differentiate loops from function calls), put no spaces before the two semicolons (like with any other statement), and mostly use curly braces even for single-statement loop bodies (for better visual identification of loop bodies). You are free to follow any coding style you prefer, of course.

Not only is it *legal* to define variables such as i within a for loop initialization expression, it is common. This has some significant implications. A loop defines a scope. The loop statement or block, including any expressions that control the loop, falls within the scope of a loop. Any automatic variables declared within the scope of a loop do not exist outside it. Because i is defined in the first expression, it is local to the loop, so when the loop ends, i will no longer exist. When you need to be able to access the loop control variable after the loop ends, you just define it before the loop, like this:

```
std::size_t i {};
for (i = 0; i < 12; ++i)              // i varies from 0 to 11
{
  copy[i] = rainfall[i];              // Copy ith element of rainfall to ith element of copy
}
// i still exists here...
```

Now you can access i after the loop—its value will then be 12 in this case. i is initialized to 0 in its definition, so the first loop control expression is superfluous. You can omit any or all of the loop control expressions, so the loop can be written as follows:

```
std::size_t i {};
for ( ; i < 12; ++i)                  // i varies from 0 to 11
{
  copy[i] = rainfall[i];              // Copy ith element of rainfall to ith element of copy
}
```

The loop works just as before. We'll discuss omitting other control expressions a little later in this chapter.

■ **Note**   At the end of the previous chapter we introduced the initialization statements for if and switch statements. These initialization statements are modeled after, and are therefore completely analogous to, those of for loops. The only difference is that with a for loop you cannot omit the first semicolon when forsaking the initialization statement.

Avoiding Magic Numbers

One minor problem with the code fragments in the preceding section is that they involve the "magic number" 12 for the array sizes. Suppose they invented a 13th month—Undecimber—and you had to add a rainfall value for that month. Then it wouldn't be unthinkable that, after increasing the size of the rainfall array, you'd forget to update the 12 in the for loop. This is how bugs creep in!

A safer solution is to define a const variable for the array size and use that instead of the explicit value:

```
const std::size_t size {12};
double rainfall[size] {1.1, 2.8, 3.4, 3.7, 2.1, 2.3, 1.8, 0.0, 0.3, 0.9, 0.7, 0.5};
double copy[size] {};
for (std::size_t i {}; i < size; ++i) // i varies from 0 to size-1
{
  copy[i] = rainfall[i];                // Copy ith element of rainfall to ith element of copy
}
```

This is much less error-prone, and it is clear that size is the number of elements in both arrays.

■ **Tip** If the same constant is scattered around your code, it is easy to make a mistake by forgetting to update some of them. Therefore, define magic numbers, or any constant variable for that matter, only once. If you then have to change the constant, you must do so in only one place.

Let's try a for loop in a complete example:

```cpp
// Ex5_01.cpp - Using a for loop with an array
import std;

int main()
{
  const std::size_t size {6};                       // Array size
  unsigned height[size] {26, 37, 47, 55, 62, 75};   // An array of heights

 unsigned total {};                                 // Sum of heights
  for (std::size_t i {}; i < size; ++i)
  {
    total += height[i];
  }

  const auto average {static_cast<double>(total)/size}; // Calculate average height
  std::println("The average height is {:.1f}.", average);

  unsigned count {};
  for (std::size_t i {}; i < size; ++i)
  {
    if (height[i] < average) ++count;
  }
  std::println("{} people are below average height.", count);
}
```

The output is as follows:

```
The average height is 50.3
3 people are below average height.
```

The definition of the height array uses a const variable to specify the number of elements. The size variable is also used as the limit for the control variable in the two for loops. The first for loop iterates over each height element in turn, adding its value to total. The loop ends when the loop variable i is equal to size, and the statement following the loop is executed, which defines the average variable with the initial value as total divided by size. In this statement, total is converted to type double first to avoid truncation of this quotient due to integer division (see Chapter 2).

After outputting the average height, the second for loop iterates over the elements in the array, comparing each value with average. The count variable is incremented each time an element is less than average, so when the loop ends, count will contain the number of elements less than average.

Incidentally, you could replace the if statement in the loop with this statement:

```cpp
count += height[i] < average;
```

This works because the `bool` value that results from the comparison will be implicitly converted to an integer. The value `true` converts to 1, and `false` converts to 0, so `count` will be incremented only when the comparison results in `true`. However, while this new code is clever and fun, just the fact that it needs to be explained should be enough to stick with the original `if` statement instead. Always choose code that reads (almost) like plain English over clever code![1]

Defining the Array Size with the Braced Initializer

You can omit the size of the array when you supply one or more initial values in its definition. The number of elements will be the number of initial values. Here's an example:

```
int values[] {2, 3, 4};
```

This defines an array with three elements of type `int` that will have the initial values 2, 3, and 4. It is equivalent to writing this:

```
int values[3] {2, 3, 4};
```

The advantage of omitting the size is that you can't get the array size wrong; the compiler determines it for you.

Determining the Size of an Array

You saw earlier how you can avoid magic numbers for the number of elements in an array by defining a constant initialized with the array size. You also don't want to be specifying a magic number for the array size when you let the compiler decide the number of elements from the braced initializer list. You need a fool-proof way of determining the size when necessary.

The easiest and recommended way is to use the `std::size()` function provided by the Standard Library. Suppose you've defined this array:

```
int values[] {2, 3, 5, 7, 11, 13, 17, 19, 23, 29};
```

Then you can use the expression `std::size(values)` to obtain the array's size, 10.

Note The `std::size()` function doesn't only work for arrays; it's also an alternative means to obtain the size of just about any collection of elements defined by the Standard Library, including the `std::vector<>` and `std::array<>` containers we will introduce later in this chapter.

---

[1]Without going too much into the specifics, "clever" C++ coders concoct statements such as
`count += height[i] < average;` because they assume they will run faster than the original conditional statement, `if (height[i] < average) ++count;`. The reason is that the latter contains an obvious so-called branching statement. And branching statements generally slow down execution. Any self-respecting compiler, however, will already rewrite this `if` statement for you in a similar manner. Our advice is to leave the cleverness to the compiler, and to always strive for clear and correct code instead.

Before the handy std::size() was added to the Standard Library, people often used a different technique based on the sizeof operator. You know from Chapter 2 that the sizeof operator returns the number of bytes that a variable occupies. This works with an entire array as well as with a single array element. Thus, the sizeof operator provides a way to determine the number of elements in an array; you just divide the size of the array by the size of a single element. Let's try both:

```
// Ex5_02.cpp - Obtaining the number of array elements
import std;

int main()
{
  int values[] {2, 3, 5, 7, 11, 13, 17, 19, 23, 29};

  std::println("There are {} elements in the array.", std::size(values));

  int sum {};
  const std::size_t old_school_size = sizeof(values) / sizeof(values[0]);
  for (std::size_t i {}; i < old_school_size; ++i)
  {
    sum += values[i];
  }
  std::println("The sum of the array elements is {}.", sum);
}
```

This example produces the following output:

```
There are 10 elements in the array.
The sum of the array elements is 129
```

The number of elements in the values array is determined by the compiler from the number of initializing values in the definition. In the first output statement, we use the std::size() function—clear and simple. For the old_school_size variable, we instead use the sizeof operator to calculate the number of array elements—far less clear and simple. The expression sizeof(values) evaluates to the number of bytes occupied by the entire array, and sizeof(values[0]) evaluates to the number of bytes occupied by a single element (any element will do, but usually one takes the first element). The right-side expression sizeof(values) / sizeof(values[0]) divides the number of bytes occupied by the whole array by the number of bytes for one element, so this evaluates to the number of elements in the array.

Clearly, std::size() is much easier to use and understand than the old sizeof-based expression. So, if possible, you should always use std::size(). (Or, better yet, use a std::array<> container and its size() function instead, as explained later in this chapter.)

The for loop itself determines the sum of the array elements. None of the control expressions has to be of a particular form. You have seen that you can omit the first control expression. In the for loop in the example, you could accumulate the sum of the elements within the third loop control expression. The loop would then become the following (let's use std::size() as well, as recommended):

```
int sum {};
for (std::size_t i {}; i < std::size(values); sum += values[i++]);
```

The third loop control expression now does two things: it adds the value of the element at index i to sum, and then it increments the control variable, i. Note that earlier i was incremented using the prefix ++ operator, whereas now it is incremented using the postfix ++ operator. This is essential here to ensure the element selected by i is added to sum before i is incremented. If you use the prefix form, you get the wrong answer for the sum of the elements; you'll also use an invalid index value that accesses memory beyond the end of the array.

The single semicolon at the end of the line is an empty statement that constitutes the loop's body. In general, this is something to watch out for; you should never add a semicolon prior to a loop's body. In this case, however, it works because all calculations occur within the loop's control expressions already. An alternative, clearer way of writing a loop with an empty body is this:

```
int sum {};
for (std::size_t i {}; i < std::size(values); sum += values[i++]) {}
```

▓ **Caution**   Performing actions beyond adjusting the loop index variable in the for loop's increment expression (the last component between the round parentheses) is unconventional, to say the least. In our example, it is far more common to simply update the sum variable in the loop's body, as in Ex5_02. We only showed you these alternatives here to give you a feeling of what is possible in principle. In general, however, you should always choose conventional and clear code over code that is compact and clever!

Controlling a for Loop with Floating-Point Values

The for loop examples so far have used an integer variable to control the loop, but you can use anything you like. The following code fragment uses floating-point values to control the loop:

```
for (double radius {2.5}; radius <= 20.0; radius += 2.5)
{
  std::println("radius = {:4.1f}, area = {:7.2f}",
               radius, std::numbers::pi * radius * radius);
}
```

This loop is controlled by the radius variable, which is of type double. It has an initial value of 2.5 and is incremented at the end of each loop iteration until it exceeds 20.0, whereupon the loop ends. The loop statement calculates the area of a circle for the current value of radius, using the standard formula πr^2, where r is the radius of the circle. The :4.1f and :7.2f format specifications give each output value a fixed width (4 and 7) and precision (1 and 2). The widths ensure that the printed values line up vertically (values are aligned right by default), the precision controls the number of digits after the decimal period. The f suffix, finally, toggles the fixed-point presentation type for floating-point numbers, thus disallowing exponent notation.

You need to be careful when using a floating-point variable to control a for loop. Fractional values may not be representable exactly as a binary floating-point number. This can lead to some unwanted side effects, as this complete example demonstrates:

```
// Ex5_03.cpp - Floating-point control in a for loop
import std;
```

```
int main()
{
  const unsigned values_per_line {3}; // Outputs per line
  unsigned values_current_line {};     // Number of outputs on current line
  for (double radius {0.2}; radius <= 3.0; radius += 0.2)
  {
    const auto area{ std::numbers::pi * radius * radius };
    std::print("radius = {:4.2f}, area = {:5.2f}; ", radius, area);
    if (++values_current_line == values_per_line)  // When enough values written...
    {
      std::println("");              // ...start a new line...
      values_current_line = 0;       // ...and reset the line counter
    }
  }
  std::println("");
}
```

On our test system, this produces the following output:

```
radius = 0.20, area =  0.13; radius = 0.40, area =  0.50; radius = 0.60, area =  1.13;
radius = 0.80, area =  2.01; radius = 1.00, area =  3.14; radius = 1.20, area =  4.52;
radius = 1.40, area =  6.16; radius = 1.60, area =  8.04; radius = 1.80, area = 10.18;
radius = 2.00, area = 12.57; radius = 2.20, area = 15.21; radius = 2.40, area = 18.10;
radius = 2.60, area = 21.24; radius = 2.80, area = 24.63;
```

The loop includes an if statement to output three sets of values per line. You would expect to see the area of a circle with radius 3.0 as the last output. After all, the loop should continue as long as radius is less than or equal to 3.0. But the last value displayed has the radius at 2.8; what's going wrong?

The loop ends earlier than expected because when 0.2 is added to 2.8, the result is greater than 3.0. This is an astounding piece of arithmetic at face value, but read on! The reason for this is a very small error in the representation of 0.2 as a binary floating-point number. 0.2 cannot be represented exactly in binary floating-point. The error is in the last digit of precision, so if your compiler supports 15-digit precision for type double, the error is of the order of 10^{-15}. Usually, this is of no consequence, but here you depend on adding 0.2 successively to get *exactly* 3.0—which doesn't happen.

You can see what the difference is by changing the loop to output just one circle area per line and to display the difference between 3.0 and the next value of radius (see also Ex5_03A online):

```
for (double radius {0.2}; radius <= 3.0; radius += 0.2)
{
  std::println("radius = {:4.2f}, area = {:5.2f}, radius + 0.2 = 3.0 + {}",
      radius,
      std::numbers::pi * radius * radius,
      (radius + 0.2) - 3.0
  );
}
```

On our machine, the last line of output is now this:

```
radius = 2.80, area = 24.63, radius + 0.2 = 3.0 + 4.440892098500626e-16
```

As you can see, radius + 0.2 is greater than 3.0 by around 4.44×10^{-16}. This causes the loop to terminate before the next iteration.

■ **Note** No number that is a fraction with an odd denominator can be represented exactly as a binary floating-point value.

While this example may seem a tad academic, rounding errors do cause analogous bugs in practice. One of the authors remembers a real-life bug with a for loop similar to that of Ex5_03. A bug that very nearly resulted in the destruction of a high-tech piece of hardware worth well over $10,000—just because the loop occasionally (not always!) ran for one iteration too many. Conclusion:

■ **Caution** Comparing floating-point numbers can be tricky. You should always be cautious when comparing the result of floating-point computations directly using operators such as ==, <=, or >=. Rounding errors almost always prevent the floating-point value from ever becoming exactly equal to the mathematically precise value.

For the for loop in Ex5_03, one option is to introduce an integral counter i specifically for controlling the loop. Another option is to replace the loop's condition with one that anticipates rounding errors. In this particular case, it suffices to use something like radius < 3.0 + 0.001. Instead of 0.001, you can use any number sufficiently greater than the expected rounding errors yet sufficiently less than the loop's .2 increment. A corrected version of the program can be found in Ex5_03B.cpp. Most math libraries as well as so-called unit test frameworks will offer utility functions to aid you with comparing floating-point numbers in a reliable manner.

More Complex for Loop Control Expressions

You can define and initialize more than one variable of a given type in the first for loop control expression. You just separate each variable from the next with a comma. Here's a working example that uses that:

```cpp
// Ex5_04.cpp - Multiple initializations in a loop expression
import std;

int main()
{
  unsigned int limit {};
  std::print("This program calculates n! and the sum of the integers up to n ");
  std::print("for values 1 to limit.\nWhat upper limit for n would you like? ");
  std::cin >> limit;

  // Output column headings
  std::println("{:>8} {:>8} {:>20}", "integer", "sum", "factorial");

  for (unsigned long long n {1}, sum {}, factorial {1}; n <= limit; ++n)
  {
    sum += n;            // Accumulate sum to current n
    factorial *= n;      // Calculate n! for current n
    std::println("{:8} {:8} {:20}", n, sum, factorial);
```

```
    }
}
```

The program calculates the sum of the integers from 1 to n for each integer n from 1 to `limit`, where `limit` is an upper limit that you enter. It also calculates the factorial of each n. (The factorial of an integer n, written n!, is the product of all the integers from 1 to n; for example, 5! = 1 × 2 × 3 × 4 × 5 = 120.)

Best not to enter large values for `limit`. Factorials grow rapidly and easily exceed the capacity of even a variable of type `unsigned long long`. Typically, the largest factorial that can be represented by `unsigned long long` is 20!, or 2,432,902,008,176,640,000. Note that there will be no warning if a factorial value cannot be accommodated in the memory allocated; the result will just be incorrect. (Just give it a try. The correct value of 21! is 51,090,942,171,709,440,000... As you probably already knew...)

Here's some typical output:

```
This program calculates n! and the sum of the integers up to n for values 1 to limit.
What upper limit for n would you like? 10
  integer    sum        factorial
        1      1                 1
        2      3                 2
        3      6                 6
        4     10                24
        5     15               120
        6     21               720
        7     28              5040
        8     36             40320
        9     45            362880
       10     55           3628800
```

First, we read the value for `limit` from the keyboard after displaying a prompt. The value entered for `limit` will not be large, so type `unsigned int` is more than adequate.

Next, we print a line representing the table's header. We give each column a fixed width, and force right alignment using the > alignment option (strings, unlike numbers, align to the left by default).

The `for` loop, finally, takes care of the lion share of the work. The first control expression defines and initializes not one, but three variables of type `unsigned long long`: n, the loop counter; sum, to accumulate the sum of integers from 1 to the current n; and `factorial` to store n!. At the end of every iteration, we also add a new row to our printed table, using the same field widths as we used for the header.

▨ **Note** The optional initialization statement of `if` and `switch` statements we introduced in the previous chapter is completely equivalent to that of `for` loops. So there too you can define multiple variables of the same type at once if you want.

The Comma Operator

Although the comma looks as if it's just a humble separator, it is actually a binary operator. It combines two expressions into a single expression, where the value of the operation is the value of its right operand. This means that anywhere you can put an expression, you can also put a series of expressions separated by commas. For example, consider the following statements:

```
int i {1};
int value1 {1};
int value2 {1};
int value3 {1};
std::println("{}", (value1 += ++i, value2 += ++i, value3 += ++i));
```

The first four statements define four variables with an initial value 1. The last statement outputs the result of three assignment expressions that are separated by the comma operator. The comma operator is left associative and has the lowest precedence of all the operators, so the expression evaluates like this:

```
(((value1 += ++i), (value2 += ++i)), (value3 += ++i));
```

The effect will be that value1 will be incremented by two to produce 3, value2 will be incremented by three to produce 4, and value3 will be incremented by four to produce 5. The value of the composite expression is the value of the rightmost expression in the series, so the value that is output is 5. You could use the comma operator to incorporate the calculations into the third loop control expression of the for loop in Ex5_04.cpp:

```
for (unsigned long long n {1}, sum {1}, factorial {1}; n <= limit;
                            ++n, sum += n, factorial *= n)
{
  std::println("{:8} {:8} {:20}", n, sum, factorial);
}
```

The third control expression combines three expressions using the comma operator. The first expression increments n as before, the second adds the incremented n to sum, and the third multiplies factorial by that same value. It is important here that we *first* increment n and only *then* perform the other two calculations. Notice also that we initialize sum to 1 here, where before we initialized it to 0. The reason is that the third control expression is executed only for the first time *after* the first execution of the loop's body. Without this modification, the first iteration would start by printing out an incorrect sum of zero. If you replace the loop in Ex5_04.cpp by this new version and run the example again, you'll see that it works as before (the resulting program is available online as Ex5_04A).

The Range-Based for Loop

The *range-based* for *loop* iterates over all the values in a range of values. This raises the immediate question: What is a range? An array is a range of elements, and a string is a range of characters. The *containers* provided by the Standard Library are all ranges as well. We'll introduce two Standard Library containers later in this chapter, and more in Chapter 20. This is the general form of the range-based for loop:

```
for ([initialization;] range_declaration : range_expression)
  loop statement or block;
```

The square brackets are for reference only, and they indicate that the initialization part is optional. The initialization statement in range-based for loops is, apart from the fact that it is optional, completely analogous to that of regular for loops. You can use it to initialize one or more variables you can then use in the remainder of the range-based for loop.

The range_expression identifies the range that is the source of the data, and the range_declaration identifies a variable that will be assigned each of the values in this range in turn, with a new value being assigned on each iteration. This will be clearer with an example. Consider these statements:

```
int values [] {2, 3, 5, 7, 11, 13, 17, 19, 23, 29};
int total {};
for (int x : values)
  total += x;
```

The variable x will be assigned a value from the values array on each iteration. It will be assigned values 2, 3, 5, and so on, in succession. Thus, the loop will accumulate the sum of all the elements in the values array in total. The variable x is local to the loop and does not exist outside of it.

A braced initializer list itself is a valid range, so you could write the previous code even more compactly as follows:

```
int total {};
for (int x : {2, 3, 5, 7, 11, 13, 17, 19, 23, 29})
  total += x;
```

Of course, the compiler knows the type of the elements in the values array, so you could also let the compiler determine the type for x by writing the former loop like this:

```
for (auto x : values)
  total += x;
```

Using the auto keyword causes the compiler to deduce the correct type for x. The auto keyword is used often with the range-based for loop. This is a nice way of iterating over all the elements in an array or other kind of range. You don't need to be aware of the number of elements. The loop mechanism takes care of that.

Note that the values from the range are *assigned* to the range variable, x. This means you cannot modify the elements of values by modifying the value of x. For example, this doesn't change the elements in the values array:

```
for (auto x : values)
  x += 2;
```

This just adds 2 to the local variable, x, not to the array element. The value stored in x is overwritten by the value of the next element from values on the next iteration. In the next chapter, you'll learn how you *can* change values within a range-based for loop by using a reference variable.

The while Loop

The while loop uses a logical expression to control execution of the loop body. Figure 5-3 shows the general form of the while loop.

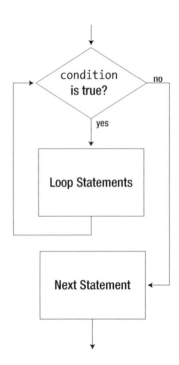

This expression is evaluated at the beginning of each loop iteration. If it is **true,** the loop continues, and if it is **false,** execution continues with the statement after the loop.

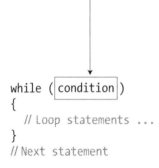

```
while ( condition )
{
    // Loop statements ...
}
// Next statement
```

Figure 5-3. *How the while loop executes*

The flowchart in Figure 5-3 shows the logic of this loop. You can use any expression to control the loop, as long as it evaluates to a value of type bool or can be implicitly converted to type bool. If the loop condition expression evaluates to a numerical value, for example, the loop continues as long as the value is nonzero. A zero value ends the loop.

You could implement a version of Ex5_04.cpp using a while loop to see how it differs:

```
// Ex5_05.cpp - Using a while loop to calculate the sum of integers from 1 to n and n!
import std;

int main()
{
  unsigned int limit {};
  std::print("This program calculates n! and the sum of the integers up to n ");
  std::print("for values 1 to limit.\nWhat upper limit for n would you like? ");
  std::cin >> limit;

  // Output column headings
  std::println("{:>8} {:>8} {:>20}", "integer", "sum", "factorial");

  unsigned int n {};
  unsigned int sum {};
  unsigned long long factorial {1ULL};
```

```
  while (++n <= limit)
  {
    sum += n;           // Accumulate sum to current n
    factorial *= n;     // Calculate n! for current n
    std::println("{:8} {:8} {:20}", n, sum, factorial);
  }
}
```

The output from this program is the same as Ex5_04.cpp. The variables n, sum, and factorial are defined before the loop. Here the types of the variables can be different, so n and sum are defined as unsigned int. The maximum value that can be stored in factorial limits the calculation, so this remains as type unsigned long long. Because of the way the calculation is implemented, the counter n is initialized to zero. The while loop condition increments n and then compares the new value with limit. The loop continues as long as the condition is true, so the loop executes with values of n from 1 up to limit. When n reaches limit+1, the loop ends. The statements within the loop body are the same as in Ex5_04.cpp.

■ **Note**   Any for loop can be written as an equivalent while loop, and vice versa. For instance, a for loop has the following generic form:

```
for (initialization; condition; iteration)
    body
```

This can typically[2] be written using a while loop as follows:

```
{
  initialization;
  while (condition)
  {
    body
    iteration;
  }
}
```

The while loop needs to be surrounded by an extra pair of curly braces to emulate the way the variables declared in the *initialization* code are scoped by the original for loop.

■ **Note**   while and do-while loops (see next section) do not allow for an *initialization;* component within the round parentheses. The reason, no doubt, is that you can simply use a for loop instead if you need a loop with an *initialization;* component.

---

[2] If the for loop's *body* contains continue statements (covered later in this chapter), you'll need some additional work rewriting the loop to a while loop. Concretely, you'll have to ensure a copy of the *iteration* code is added prior to every continue statement.

The do-while Loop

The do-while loop is similar to the while loop in that the loop continues for as long as the specified loop condition remains true. The only difference is that the loop condition is checked at the *end* of the do-while loop, rather than at the beginning, so the loop statement is always executed at least once.

Figure 5-4 shows the logic and general form of the do-while loop. Note that the semicolon that comes after the condition between the parentheses is absolutely necessary. If you leave it out, the program won't compile.

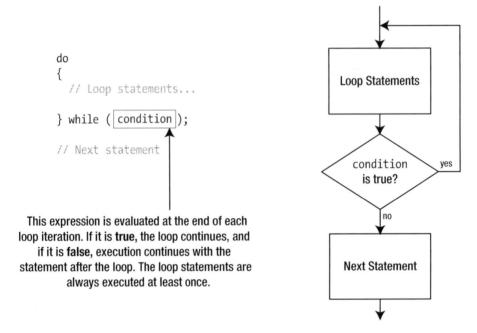

Figure 5-4. *How a do-while loop executes*

This kind of logic is ideal for situations where you have a block of code that you *always* want to execute once and may want to execute more than once. We can tell that you're not convinced that this is something that you'd ever need to do, so let's look at another example.

This program will calculate the average of an arbitrary number of input values—temperatures, for example—without storing them. You have no way of knowing in advance how many values will be entered, but it's safe to assume that you'll always have at least one, because if you didn't, there'd be no point to running the program. That makes it an ideal candidate for a do-while loop. Here's the code:

```cpp
// Ex5_06.cpp - Using a do-while loop to manage input
import std;

int main()
{
  char reply {};                        // Stores response to prompt for input
  unsigned int count {};                // Counts the number of input values
```

```
double temperature {};                        // Stores an input value
double total {};                              // Stores the sum of all input values
do
{
  std::print("Enter a temperature reading: "); // Prompt for input
  std::cin >> temperature;                    // Read input value

  total += temperature;                       // Accumulate total of values
  ++count;                                    // Increment count

  std::print("Do you want to enter another? (y/n): ");
  std::cin >> reply;                          // Get response
} while (std::tolower(reply) == 'y');

std::println("The average temperature is {:.3}", total/count);
}
```

A sample session with this program produces the following output:

```
Enter a temperature reading: 53
Do you want to enter another? (y/n): y
Enter a temperature reading: 65.5
Do you want to enter another? (y/n): y
Enter a temperature reading: 74
Do you want to enter another? (y/n): Y
Enter a temperature reading: 69.5
Do you want to enter another? (y/n): n
The average temperature is 65.5
```

(For our non-American readers: The temperature readings we entered here are in degrees Fahrenheit, not Celsius, and are therefore not at all that extraordinary...)

This program deals with any number of input values without prior knowledge of how many will be entered. After defining four variables that are required for the input and the calculation, the data values are read in a do-while loop. One input value is read on each loop iteration, and at least one value will always be read, which is not unreasonable. The response to the prompt that is stored in reply determines whether the loop ends. If the reply is y or Y, the loop continues; otherwise, the loop ends.

We ensure either uppercase or lowercase is accepted by using the std::tolower() function. As an alternative, you could also express this same condition as reply == 'y' || reply == 'Y'. This ORs the two bool values that result from the comparisons so that either an uppercase or lowercase y entered will result in true.

▧ **Caution**   While the semicolon after a do-while statement is required by the language, you should normally never add one after the while() of a regular while loop:

```
while (condition);   // You rarely want a semicolon here!!
  body
```

This creates a `while` loop with a null statement as its body. In other words, it is equivalent to the following:

```
while (condition) {} /* Do nothing until condition becomes false (if ever) */
body
```

Two things may happen if you accidentally add such a semicolon: either *body* becomes executed exactly once or never at all. The former would happen, for instance, if you add a semicolon to the `while` loop of Ex5_05. In general, however, it is more likely that a `while` loop's *body* is supposed to, after one or more iterations, make the evaluation of its *condition* flip from `true` to `false`. Adding an erroneous semicolon then causes the `while` loop to go on indefinitely.

Nested Loops

You can place a loop inside another loop. In fact, you can nest loops within loops to whatever depth you require to solve your problem. Furthermore, nested loops can be of any kind. You can nest a `for` loop inside a `while` loop inside a `do-while` loop inside a range-based `for` loop, if you have the need. They can be mixed in any way you want.

Nested loops are often applied in the context of arrays, but they have many other uses. We'll illustrate how nesting works with an example that provides lots of opportunity for nesting loops. Multiplication tables are the bane of many children's lives at school, but you can easily use a nested loop to generate one.

```cpp
// Ex5_07.cpp - Generating multiplication tables using nested loops
import std;

int main()
{
  int table {};            // Table size
  const int table_min {2};  // Minimum table size - at least up to the 2-times
  const int table_max {12}; // Maximum table size
  char reply {};           // Response to prompt

  do
  {
    std::print("What size table would you like ({} to {})? ", table_min, table_max);
    std::cin >> table;      // Get the table size

    // Make sure table size is within the limits
    if (table < table_min || table > table_max)
    {
      std::println("Invalid table size entered. Program terminated.");
      return 1;
    }
    std::println("");

    // Create the top line of the table
    std::print("{:>6}", '|');
    for (int i {1}; i <= table; ++i)
```

```
    {
       std::print(" {:3} |", i);
    }
    std::println("");

    // Create the separator row
    for (int i {}; i <= table; ++i)
    {
       std::print("------");
    }
    std::println("");

    for (int i {1}; i <= table; ++i)
    {    // Iterate over rows
       std::print(" {:3} |", i);        // Start the row

       // Output the values in a row
       for (int j {1}; j <= table; ++j)
       {
          std::print(" {:3} |", i*j);  // For each column
       }
       std::println("");                // End the row
    }

    // Check if another table is required
    std::print("\nDo you want another table (y or n)? ");
    std::cin >> reply;

  } while (std::tolower(reply) == 'y');
}
```

Here's an example of the output:

```
What size table would you like (2 to 12)? 4
      |   1 |   2 |   3 |   4 |
----------------------------
   1 |   1 |   2 |   3 |   4 |
   2 |   2 |   4 |   6 |   8 |
   3 |   3 |   6 |   9 |  12 |
   4 |   4 |   8 |  12 |  16 |

Do you want another table (y or n)? y
What size table would you like (2 to 12)? 10

      |   1 |   2 |   3 |   4 |   5 |   6 |   7 |   8 |   9 |  10 |
----------------------------------------------------------------
   1 |   1 |   2 |   3 |   4 |   5 |   6 |   7 |   8 |   9 |  10 |
   2 |   2 |   4 |   6 |   8 |  10 |  12 |  14 |  16 |  18 |  20 |
   3 |   3 |   6 |   9 |  12 |  15 |  18 |  21 |  24 |  27 |  30 |
   4 |   4 |   8 |  12 |  16 |  20 |  24 |  28 |  32 |  36 |  40 |
   5 |   5 |  10 |  15 |  20 |  25 |  30 |  35 |  40 |  45 |  50 |
```

6		6		12		18		24		30		36		42		48		54		60	
7		7		14		21		28		35		42		49		56		63		70	
8		8		16		24		32		40		48		56		64		72		80	
9		9		18		27		36		45		54		63		72		81		90	
10		10		20		30		40		50		60		70		80		90		100	

```
Do you want another table (y or n)? n
```

The input value for the size of the table is stored in `table`. A table will be output presenting the results of all products from 1 × 1 up to `table` × `table`. The value entered is validated by comparing it with `table_min` and `table_max`. A table less than `table_min` doesn't make much sense, and `table_max` represents a size that is the maximum that is likely to look reasonable when it is output. If `table` is not within range, the program ends with a return code value of 1 to indicate it's not a normal end.

(Granted, terminating the program after a bad user input is a tad drastic. Perhaps you could try to make it so that the program asks the user to try again instead?)

The multiplication table is presented in the form of a rectangular table—what else? The values along the left column and the top row are the operand values in a multiplication operation. The value at the intersection of a row and column is the product of the row and column values. The `table` variable is used as the iteration limit in the first `for` loop that creates the top line of the table. Vertical bars are used to separate columns, and the use of field widths in the format specifiers makes all the columns the same width. Note that all numbers are right-aligned by default, but the | character of the top-left cell of the table had to be right-aligned explicitly.

The next `for` loop creates a line of dash characters to separate the top row of multipliers from the body of the table. Each iteration adds six dashes to the row. By starting the count at zero instead of one, you output `table + 1` sets—one for the left column of multipliers and one for each of the columns of table entries.

The final `for` loop contains a nested `for` loop that outputs the left column of multipliers and the products that are the table entries. The nested loop outputs a complete table row, right after the multiplier for the row in the leftmost column is printed. The nested loop executes once for each iteration of the outer loop, so `table` rows are generated.

The code that creates a complete table is within a `do-while` loop. This provides for as many tables to be produced as required. If `y` or `Y` is entered in response to the prompt after a table has been output, another iteration of the `do-while` loop executes to allow another table to be created. This example demonstrates three levels of nesting: a `for` loop inside another `for` loop that is inside the `do-while` loop.

Skipping Loop Iterations

Situations arise where you want to skip one loop iteration and press on with the next. The `continue` statement does this:

```
continue;        // Go to the next iteration
```

When this statement executes within a loop, execution transfers immediately to the end of the current iteration. As long as the loop control expression allows it, execution continues with the next iteration. This is best understood in an example. Let's suppose you want to output a table of characters with their character codes in hexadecimal and decimal formats. Of course, you don't want to output characters that don't have a graphical representation—some of these, such as tabs and newline, would mess up the output. So, the program should output just the printable characters. Here's the code:

```cpp
// Ex5_08.cpp - Using the continue statement to display ASCII character codes
import std;

int main()
{
  // 3 cols., 11 wide, centered (^)
  std::println("{:^11}{:^11}{:^11}", "Character", "Hexadecimal", "Decimal");

  // Output 7-bit ASCII characters and corresponding codes
  for (int ch {}; ch <= 127; ++ch)
  {
    if (!std::isprint(ch))  // If it's not printable...
      continue;             // ...skip this iteration
    std::println("{0:^11}{0:^11X}{0:^11d}", static_cast<char>(ch)); // Print 3 times
  }
}
```

This displays a handy table of the codes for all 95 printable ASCII characters. From Chapter 1 you may recall that ASCII is a 7-bit encoding, meaning all ASCII code values lie between 0 and 127 (both inclusive).

Character	Hexadecimal	Decimal
	20	32
!	21	33
"	22	34
#	23	35
⋮	⋮	⋮
}	7D	125
~	7E	126

We generate a table with three columns, each of width 11 and each with their values centered (as dictated by the ^ alignment options). The first std::println() statement prints the table's header, the second the rows of the table's body. Even though the table has three columns, we only pass one extra argument to the std::println() statement inside the for loop. This works because in the corresponding format string, "{0:^11}{0:^11X}{0:^11d}", we use the positional argument identifier 0 (to the left of the colons) to format this same argument three times: once as a letter, once as an uppercase hexadecimal number (thanks to the X suffix), and once as a decimal number (thanks to the d suffix—which could be omitted, as decimal output is the default).

The interesting bit here, though, is the (conditional) continue statement. You don't want to print details of characters that do not have printable representations. The std::isprint() character classification function helps with that; it only returns nonzero (true) for printable characters. By negating its result, the continue statement thus only executes for non-printable characters. Whenever this happens, the continue statement skips the rest of the code for the current loop iteration.

■ **Tip**　You should use `continue` statements judiciously. The loop of Ex5_08, for instance, becomes more readable if written as follows:

```
for (int ch {}; ch <= 127; ++ch) {
  if (std::isprint(ch))  // If the character is printable...
    std::println("{0:^11}{0:^11X}{0:^11d}", static_cast<char>(ch)); // Print 3 times
}
```

Looking back, the original logic essentially stated "if the character is *not* printable, do *not* print a row". Even the most experienced programmer needs at least some fraction of a second to work out that double negation. The new loop body, on the other hand, simply reads "if the character is printable, print a row". Crystal clear. In general, we recommend you always consider replacing a `continue` statement with an equivalent `if` statement if that simplifies your code (even if that means introducing a negation in the condition). The main advantage `continue` statements occasionally bring to the table is that they can help sidestep overly complex, nested `if-else` blocks.

Maybe you wondered why the loop control variable in Ex5_08, ch, is of type `int` and not of the more obvious type char? That is, since we're looping over characters, why not simply write the loop as follows?

```
for (char ch {}; ch <= 127; ++ch)  /* Caution: could be an indefinite loop! */
{
  if (std::isprint(ch))                     // If the character is printable...
    std::println("{0:^11}{0:^11X}{0:^11d}", ch); // Nice: no static_cast<char>()!
}
```

The reason is that the loop then likely carries on indefinitely if char is a signed type. Because 127 is the largest possible value for signed 8-bit integers (see Chapter 2), ch <= 127 likely never becomes `false` if char is signed. We said *likely*, twice, because technically the behavior of ++ch is undefined for ch equal to 127 if char is signed. As seen in Chapter 2, the behavior of integer overflow is only defined for unsigned integer types. It's fairly *likely*, though, that a signed char value of +127 loops around to -128 if you increment it. If that happens, the loop will then increment ch back all the way up to +127, loop around to -128 a second time, and so on. Indefinitely. In Ex5_08 we sidestepped this problem by using the larger `int` type for the `for` loop's driving variable.

■ **Caution**　Take care not to write loops with stop conditions that are always `true`!

Breaking Out of a Loop

Sometimes, you need to end a loop prematurely; something might arise within the loop statement that indicates there is no point in continuing. In this case, you can use the `break` statement. Its effect in a loop is much the same as it is in a `switch` statement; executing a `break` statement within a loop ends the loop immediately, and execution continues with the statement following the loop. The `break` statement is often used with an *indefinite loop*, so let's look next at what one of those looks like.

Indefinite Loops

An *indefinite loop* can potentially run forever. Omitting the second control expression in a for loop results in a loop that potentially executes an unlimited number of iterations. There has to be some way to end the loop within the loop block itself; otherwise, the loop repeats indefinitely.

Indefinite loops have many practical uses, such as programs that monitor some kind of alarm indicator, for instance, or that collect data from sensors in an industrial plant. An indefinite loop can be useful when you don't know in advance how many loop iterations will be required, such as when you are reading a variable quantity of input data. In these circumstances, you code the exit from the loop within the loop block, not within the loop control expression.

In the most common form of the indefinite for loop, all the control expressions are omitted, as shown here:

```
for (;;)
{
  // Statements that do something...
  // ... and include some way of ending the loop
}
```

You still need the semicolons (;), even though no loop control expressions exist. The only way this loop can end is if some code within the loop terminates it.

You can have an indefinite while loop, too:

```
while (true)
{
  // Statements that do something...
  // ... and include some way of ending the loop
}
```

The loop condition is always true, so you have an indefinite loop. This is equivalent to the for loop with no control expressions. Of course, you can also have a version of the do-while loop that is indefinite, but it is not normally used because it has no advantages over the other two types of loops.

The obvious way to end an indefinite loop is to use the break statement. You could have used an indefinite loop in Ex5_07.cpp to allow several tries at entering a valid table size, instead of ending the program immediately. This loop would do it:

```
const int max_tries {3};        // Max. number of times a user can try entering a table size
do
{
  for (int count {1}; ; ++count)  // Indefinite loop
  {
    std::print("What size table would you like ({} to {})? ", table_min, table_max);
    std::cin >> table;            // Get the table size

    // Make sure table size is within the limits
    if (table >= table_min && table <= table_max)
    {
      break;                      // Exit the input loop
    }
```

```
    else if (count < max_tries)
    {
      std::println("Invalid input - try again.");
    }
    else
    {
      std::println("Invalid table size entered - yet again!");
      std::println("Sorry, only {} allowed - program terminated.", max_tries);
      return 1;
    }
  }
}
...
```

This indefinite for loop could replace the code at the beginning of the do-while loop in Ex5_07.cpp that handles input of the table size. This allows up to max_tries attempts to enter a valid table size. A valid entry executes the break statement, which terminates this loop and continues with the next statement in the do-while loop. You'll find the resulting program in Ex5_07A.cpp.

Here's an example that uses an indefinite while loop to sort the contents of an array in ascending sequence:

```cpp
// Ex5_09.cpp - Sorting an array in ascending sequence using an indefinite while loop
import std;

int main()
{
  const std::size_t size {1000};   // Array size
  double data[size] {};            // Stores data to be sorted
  std::size_t count {};            // Number of values in array

  while (true)
  {
    double input {};               // Temporary store for a value
    std::print("Enter a non-zero value, or 0 to end: ");
    std::cin >> input;
    if (input == 0)
      break;

    data[count] = input;

    if (++count == size)
    {
      std::println("Sorry, I can only store {} values.", size);
      break;
    }
  }

  if (count == 0)
  {
    std::println("Nothing to sort...");
    return 0;
  }
```

```
  std::println("Starting sort...");

  while (true)
  {
    bool swapped{ false };              // Becomes true when not all values are in order
    for (std::size_t i {}; i < count - 1; ++i)
    {
      if (data[i] > data[i + 1])        // Out of order so swap them
      {
        const auto temp{ data[i] };
        data[i] = data[i+1];
        data[i + 1] = temp;
        swapped = true;
      }
    }

    if (!swapped)                       // If there were no swaps
      break;                            // ...all values are in order...
  }                                     // ...otherwise, go round again.

  std::println("Your data in ascending sequence:");
  const unsigned perline {10};          // Number output per line
  unsigned n {};                        // Number on current line
  for (size_t i {}; i < count; ++i)
  {
    std::print("{:8.1f}", data[i]);
    if (++n == perline)                 // When perline have been written...
    {
      std::println("");                 // Start a new line and...
      n = 0;                            // ...reset count on this line
    }
  }
  std::println("");
}
```

Typical output looks like this:

```
Enter a non-zero value, or 0 to end: 44
Enter a non-zero value, or 0 to end: -7.8
Enter a non-zero value, or 0 to end: 56.3
Enter a non-zero value, or 0 to end: 75.2
Enter a non-zero value, or 0 to end: -3
Enter a non-zero value, or 0 to end: -2
Enter a non-zero value, or 0 to end: 66
Enter a non-zero value, or 0 to end: 6.7
Enter a non-zero value, or 0 to end: 8.2
Enter a non-zero value, or 0 to end: -5
Enter a non-zero value, or 0 to end: 0
Starting sort.
Your data in ascending sequence:
    -7.8     -5.0     -3.0     -2.0      6.7      8.2     44.0     56.3     66.0     75.2
```

The code limits the number of values that can be entered to size, which is set to 1,000. Only users with amazing keyboard skill and persistence will fill out this entire array. This is thus rather wasteful with memory, but you'll learn how you can avoid this in such circumstances later in this chapter.

Data entry is managed in the first while loop. This loop runs until either 0 is entered or the array, data, is full because size values have been entered. In the latter instance, the user will see a message indicating the limit.

Each value is read into the variable input. This allows the value to be tested for zero before it is stored in the array. Each value is stored in the element of the array data at index count. In the if statement that follows, count is pre-incremented and thus incremented *before* it is compared to size. This ensures that it represents the number of elements in the array by the time it is compared to size.

The elements are sorted in ascending sequence in the next indefinite while loop. Ordering the values of the array elements is carried out in the nested for loop that iterates over successive pairs of elements and checks whether they are in ascending sequence. If a pair of elements contains values that are not in ascending sequence, the values are swapped to order them correctly. The bool variable, swapped, records whether it was necessary to interchange any elements in any complete execution of the nested for loop. If it wasn't, the elements are in ascending sequence, and the break statement is executed to exit the while loop. If any pair had to be interchanged, swapped will be true, so another iteration of the while loop will execute, and this causes the for loop to run through pairs of elements again.

This sorting method is called the *bubble sort* because elements gradually "bubble up" to their correct position in the array. It's not the most efficient sorting method, but it has the merit that it is very easy to understand, and it's a good demonstration of yet another use for an indefinite loop.

░ **Tip**   In general, indefinite loops, or even just break statements inside loops, should be used judiciously. They are sometimes considered bad coding style. As much as possible, you should put the conditions that determine when a loop terminates between the round parentheses of the for or while statement. Doing so increases code readability because this is where every C++ programmer will look for such conditions. Any (additional) break statements inside the loop's body are much easier to miss and can therefore make code harder to understand.

Controlling a for Loop with Unsigned Integers

You probably didn't notice, but Ex5_09 actually contains a perfect example of a rather crucial caveat regarding controlling a for loop with unsigned integers, such as values of type std::size_t. Suppose we omit the following check from the program in Ex5_09.cpp:

```
if (count == 0)
{
  std::println("Nothing to sort...");
  return 0;
}
```

What would happen then, you think, if the user decides not to enter any values? That is, if count equals 0? Something bad, I'm sure you already guessed. And, of course, you guessed correctly! Concretely, the execution would enter the following for loop with count equal to 0:

```
for (std::size_t i {}; i < count - 1; ++i)
{
  ...
}
```

Mathematically speaking, if count equals 0, count - 1 should become -1. But since count is an unsigned integer, it cannot actually represent a negative value such as -1. Instead, subtracting one from zero gives std::numeric_limits<std::size_t>::max(), a very large unsigned value. On our test system, this equals 18,446,744,073,709,551,615—a number well over 18 *quintillion*. So if count equals 0, this effectively turns the loop into the following:

```
for (std::size_t i {}; i < 18'446'744'073'709'551'615; ++i)
{
  ...
}
```

While technically not an indefinite loop, it would take even the fastest computer a fair amount of time to count to 18 quintillion (and change). In our case, though, the program will crash long before the counter i comes even close to that number. The reason is that the loop counter i is used in expressions such as data[i], which means that the loop will quickly start accessing and overwriting parts of memory it has no business touching.

▓ **Caution** Take care when subtracting from unsigned integers. Any value that, mathematically speaking, should be negative then wraps around to become a huge positive number. These types of errors can have catastrophic results in loop control expressions.

A first solution is to test that count does not equal zero prior to entering the loop, as we did in Ex5_09. Other options include casting to a signed integer or rewriting the loop so it no longer uses subtraction:

```
// Cast to a signed integer prior to subtracting
for (int i {}; i < static_cast<int>(count) - 1; ++i)
  ...

// Rewrite to avoid subtracting from unsigned values
for (std::size_t i {}; i + 1 < count; ++i)
  ...
```

Similar caveats lurk when using a for loop to traverse an array in reverse order. Suppose we have an array my_array, and we want to process it starting with the last element and working our way back to the front of the array. Then an understandable first attempt could be a loop of the following form:

```
for (std::size_t i = std::size(my_array) - 1; i >= 0; --i)
  ... // process my_array[i] ...
```

Let's assume that we know for a fact that my_array always contains at least one value and that we can ignore the truly awful things that would happen if my_array were of length 0. Even then, we are in serious trouble here. Since the index variable i is of an unsigned type, i is, by definition, always greater than or equal to zero. That's what unsigned means. The loop's termination condition, i >= 0, therefore always evaluates to true, effectively turning this buggy reverse loop into an indefinite one.

■ **Caution**   Take care not to write loops with stop conditions that are always `true`! (Déjà vu?)

The most elegant workaround here is to use C++20's `std::ssize()` instead of `std::size()`. This function, whose name is short for *signed size*, returns the same number as `std::size()`, but then as a signed instead of an unsigned integer (generally of the same byte size as `std::size_t`).

```
for (auto i{ std::ssize(my_array) - 1 }; i >= 0; --i)
    ... // process my_array[i] ...
```

With `i` now of a signed type, `--i` will eventually make `i >= 0` false. An added bonus is that if `my_array` is now an empty array, `std::ssize(my_array) - 1` will simply start out at `-1`, and the loop's body will never execute. Neat.

Arrays of Characters

An array of elements of type `char` can have a dual personality. It can simply be an array of characters, in which each element stores one character, *or* it can represent a string. In the latter case, the characters in the string are stored in successive array elements, followed by a special string termination character called the *null character* that you write as `'\0'`. The null character marks the end of the string.

A character array that is terminated by `'\0'` is referred to as a *C-style string*. This contrasts with the `string` type from the Standard Library, which we'll explain in detail in Chapter 7. Objects of type `string` are much more flexible and convenient for string manipulation than using arrays of type `char`. For the moment, we'll introduce C-style strings in the context of arrays in general and return to them and type `string` in Chapter 7.

You can define and initialize an array of elements of type `char` like this:

```
char vowels[5]  {'a', 'e', 'i', 'o', 'u'};
```

This isn't a string—it's just an array of five characters. Each array element is initialized with the corresponding character from the initializer list. As with numeric arrays, if you provide fewer initializing values than there are array elements, the elements that don't have explicit initial values will be initialized with the equivalent of zero, which is the null character, `'\0'` in this case. This means that if there are insufficient initial values, the array will effectively contain a string. Here's an example:

```
char vowels[6]  {'a', 'e', 'i', 'o', 'u'};
```

The last element will be initialized with `'\0'`. The presence of the null character means that this can be treated as a C-style string. Of course, you can still regard it as an array of characters.

You could leave it to the compiler to set the size of the array to the number of initializing values:

```
char vowels[] {'a', 'e', 'i', 'o', 'u'};    // An array with five elements
```

This also defines an array of five characters initialized with the vowels in the braced initializer.

You can also declare an array of type `char` and initialize it with a *string literal*, as follows:

```
char name[10] {"Mae West"};
```

This creates a C-style string. Because you're initializing the array with a string literal, the null character will be stored in the element following the last string character, so the contents of the array will be as shown in Figure 5-5.

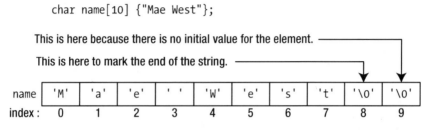

```
char name[10] {"Mae West"};
```

This is here because there is no initial value for the element. ⎯⎯⎯⎯⎯⎯⎯⎯⎯⎯⎯

This is here to mark the end of the string. ⎯⎯⎯⎯⎯⎯⎯⎯⎯⎯

name	'M'	'a'	'e'	' '	'W'	'e'	's'	't'	'\0'	'\0'
index :	0	1	2	3	4	5	6	7	8	9

Figure 5-5. *An array of elements of type char initialized with a string literal*

You can leave the compiler to set the size of the array when you initialize it with a string literal:

```
char name[] {"Mae West"};
```

This time, the array will have nine elements: eight to store the characters in the string, plus an extra element to store the string termination character. Of course, you could have used this approach when you declared the vowels array:

```
char vowels[] {"aeiou"};      // An array with six elements
```

There's a significant difference between this and the previous definition for vowels without an explicit array dimension. Here you're initializing the array with a string literal. This has '\0' appended to it implicitly to mark the end of the string, so the vowels array will contain six elements. The array created with the earlier definition will have only five elements and can't be used as a string.

You can print a string stored in an array just by using the array name. The string in the name array, for example, could be printed with this statement:

```
std::println("{}", name);
```

This will display the entire string of characters, up to the '\0'. There *must* be a '\0' at the end. If there isn't, println() will continue to print characters from successive memory locations, which almost certainly contain garbage, until either a null character happens to turn up or an illegal memory access occurs.

This example analyzes an array of elements of type char to work out how many vowels and consonants are used in it:

```
// Ex5_10.cpp - Classifying the letters in a C-style string
import std;

int main()
{
  const std::size_t max_length {100}; // Array size
  char text[max_length] {};           // Array to hold input string

  std::println("Enter a line of text:");
```

```
// Read a line of characters including spaces
std::cin.getline(text, max_length);
std::println("You entered:\n{}", text);

unsigned int vowels {};          // Count of vowels
unsigned int consonants {};      // Count of consonants
for (std::size_t i {}; text[i] != '\0'; i++)
{
  if (std::isalpha(text[i]))  // If it is a letter...
  {
    switch (std::tolower(text[i]))
    {                            // ...check lowercase...
      case 'a': case 'e': case 'i': case 'o': case 'u':
        ++vowels;                // ...it is a vowel
        break;

      default:
        ++consonants;           // ...it is a consonant
    }
  }
}
std::println("Your input contained {} vowels and {} consonants.",
            vowels, consonants);
}
```

Here's an example of the output:

```
Enter a line of text:
A rich man is nothing but a poor man with money.
You entered:
A rich man is nothing but a poor man with money.
Your input contained 14 vowels and 23 consonants.
```

The text array of type char elements has the size defined by a const variable, max_length. Because a C-style string array is always terminated by a null character, text can only store strings of at most max_length - 1 proper characters.

You can't use the extraction operator to read the input because it won't read a string containing spaces; any whitespace character terminates the input operation with the >> operator. The getline() function for std::cin reads a sequence of characters, including spaces. By default, the input ends when a newline character, '\n', is read, which will be when you press the Enter key. The getline() function expects two arguments between the parentheses. The first argument specifies where the input is to be stored, which in this case, is the text array. The second argument specifies the maximum number of characters that you want to store. This includes the string termination character, '\0', which will be automatically appended to the end of the input.

▧ **Note** The period between the name of the `cin` object and that of its so-called member function `getline()` is called the *direct member selection* operator. This operator is used to access members of a class object. You will learn all about defining classes and member functions from Chapter 12 onward.

Although you haven't done so here, you can optionally supply a *third* argument to the `getline()` function. This specifies an alternative to `'\n'` to indicate the end of the input. If you want the end of the input string to be indicated by an asterisk, for example, you could use this statement:

```
std::cin.getline(text, max_length, '*');
```

This would allow multiple lines of text to be entered because the `'\n'` that results from pressing Enter would no longer terminate the input operation. Of course, the total number of characters that you can enter in the read operation is still limited by `max_length`.

Just to show that you can, the program outputs the string that was entered using just the array name, `text`. The `text` string is then analyzed in a straightforward manner in the `for` loop. The second control expression within the loop will be `false` when the character at the current index, `i`, is the null character, so the loop ends when the null character is reached.

Next, to work out the number of vowels and consonants, you only need to inspect alphabetic characters, and the `if` statement selects them; `isalpha()` only returns `true` for alphabetic characters. Thus, the `switch` statement executes only for letters. Converting the `switch` expression to lowercase avoids having to write cases for uppercase as well as lowercase letters. Any vowel will select the first case, and the `default` case is selected by anything that isn't a vowel, which must be a consonant, of course.

By the way, because the null character `'\0'` is the only character that converts to the Boolean `false` (analogous to 0 for integral values), you could write the `for` loop in `Ex5_10` like this as well:

```
for (std::size_t i {}; text[i]; i++)
{
  ...
```

Multidimensional Arrays

All the arrays so far have required a single index value to select an element. Such an array is called a *one-dimensional array* because varying one index can reference all the elements. You can also define arrays that require two or more index values to access an element. These are referred to generically as *multidimensional arrays*. An array that requires two index values to reference an element is called a *two-dimensional array*. An array needing three index values is a *three-dimensional array*, and so on, for as many dimensions as you think you can handle.

Suppose, as an avid gardener, that you want to record the weights of the carrots you grow in your small vegetable garden. To store the weight of each carrot, which you planted in three rows of four, you could define a two-dimensional array:

```
double carrots[3][4] {};
```

This defines an array with three rows of four elements and initializes all elements to zero. To reference a particular element of the carrots array, you need two index values. The first index specifies the row, from 0 to 2, and the second index specifies a particular carrot in that row, from 0 to 3. To store the weight of the third carrot in the second row, you could write the following:

```
carrots[1][2] = 1.5;
```

Figure 5-6 shows the arrangement of this array in memory. The rows are stored contiguously in memory. As you can see, the two-dimensional array is effectively a *one*-dimensional array of three elements, each of which is a one-dimensional array with four elements. You have an array of three arrays that each has four elements of type double. Figure 5-6 also indicates that you can use the array name plus a *single* index value between square brackets to refer to an entire row.

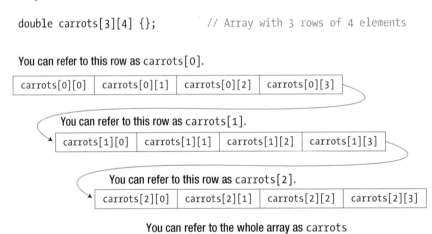

Figure 5-6. *Elements in a two-dimensional array*

You use two index values to refer to an element. The second index selects an element within the row specified by the first index; the second index varies most rapidly as you progress from one element to the next in memory. You can also envisage a two-dimensional array as a rectangular arrangement of elements in an array from left to right, where the first index specifies a row and the second index corresponds to a column. Figure 5-7 illustrates this. With arrays of more than two dimensions, the rightmost index value is always the one that varies most rapidly, and the leftmost index varies least rapidly.

```
double carrots [3][4] {};
```

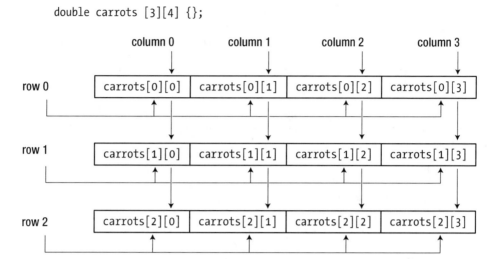

Figure 5-7. Rows and columns in a two-dimensional array

Defining an array of three dimensions just adds another set of square brackets. You might want to record three temperatures per day, seven days a week, for 52 weeks of the year. You could declare the following array to store such data as type int:

```
int temperatures[52][7][3] {};
```

The array stores three values in each row. There are seven such rows for a whole week's data and 52 sets of these for all the weeks in the year. This array will have a total of 1,092 elements of type int. They will all be initialized with zero. To display the middle temperature for day 3 of week 26, you could write this:

```
std::println("{}", temperatures[25][2][1]);
```

Remember that all the index values start at 0, so the weeks run from 0 to 51, the days run from 0 to 6, and the samples in a day run from 0 to 2.

Initializing Multidimensional Arrays

You have seen that an empty braced initializer initializes an array with any number of dimensions to zero. It gets a little more complicated when you want initial values other than zero. The way in which you specify initial values for a multidimensional array derives from the notion that a two-dimensional array is an array of one-dimensional arrays. The initializing values for a one-dimensional array are written between braces and separated by commas. Following on from that, you could declare and initialize the two-dimensional carrots array with this statement:

```
double carrots[3][4] {
                    {2.5, 3.2, 3.7, 4.1},    // First row
                    {4.1, 3.9, 1.6, 3.5},    // Second row
                    {2.8, 2.3, 0.9, 1.1}     // Third row
                };
```

Each row is a one-dimensional array, so the initializing values for each row are contained within their own set of braces. These three lists are themselves contained within a set of braces because the two-dimensional array is a one-dimensional array of one-dimensional arrays. You can extend this principle to any number of dimensions—each extra dimension requires another level of nested braces enclosing the initial values.

A question that may immediately spring to mind is, "What happens when you omit some of the initializing values?" The answer is more or less what you might have expected from past experience. Each of the innermost pairs of braces contains the values for the elements in the rows. The first list corresponds to carrots[0], the second to carrots[1], and the third to carrots[2]. The values between each pair of braces are assigned to the elements of the corresponding row. If there aren't enough to initialize all the elements in the row, then the elements without values will be initialized to 0.

Let's look at an example:

```
double carrots[3][4] {
                 { 2.5, 3.2      },      // First row
                 { 4.1           },      // Second row
                 { 2.8, 2.3, 0.9 }       // Third row
             };
```

The first two elements in the first row have initial values, whereas only one element in the second row has an initial value, and three elements in the third row have initial values. The elements without initial values in each row will therefore be initialized with 0, as shown in Figure 5-8.

carrots[0][0]	carrots[0][1]	carrots[0][2]	carrots[0][3]
2.5	3.2	0.0	0.0

carrots[1][0]	carrots[1][1]	carrots[1][2]	carrots[1][3]
4.1	0.0	0.0	0.0

carrots[2][0]	carrots[2][1]	carrots[2][2]	carrots[2][3]
2.8	2.3	0.9	0.0

Figure 5-8. *Omitting initial values for a two-dimensional array*

You can easily verify this yourself by printing the contents of the carrots array with std::println(). With carrots initialized as indicated last, the statement std::println("{}", carrots) should produce the following output (we'll discuss how to control the formatting of data ranges at the end of the chapter):

```
[[2.5, 3.2, 0, 0], [4.1, 0, 0, 0], [2.8, 2.3, 0.9, 0]]
```

If you don't include sufficient sets of braces to initialize all of the rows in the array, the elements in the rows without braces enclosing initializing values will all be set to 0. If you include several initial values in the braced initializer but omit the nested braces enclosing values for the rows, values are assigned sequentially to the elements, as they're stored in memory—with the rightmost index varying most rapidly. For example, suppose you define the array like this:

```
double carrots[3][4] {1.1, 1.2, 1.3, 1.4, 1.5, 1.6, 1.7};
```

Then the first four values in the list initialize elements in row 0, the last three values in the list initialize the first three elements in row 1, and the remaining elements are initialized with zero. If you print this array, you'd therefore see this output:

```
[[1.1, 1.2, 1.3, 1.4], [1.5, 1.6, 1.7, 0], [0, 0, 0, 0]]
```

■ **Note** If `std::println()` or `std::format()` do not support formatting of arrays yet in the Standard Library implementation of your compiler (which, at the time of writing, is fairly likely), you can write something like this instead to display an array.

```
for (std::size_t i {}; i < std::size(carrots); ++i)        // Iterate over all rows
{
  for (std::size_t j {}; j < std::size(carrots[i]); ++j) // Iterate over items in row i
  {
    std::print("{:5}", carrots[i][j]);
  }
  std::println("");                                        // Add line break after each row
}
```

You can use range-based `for` loops here as well. However, to write the outer loop as a range-based `for`, you'll first need to learn about references. You'll do so in the next chapter.

The loops we wrote in this note don't add square brackets around the array and each of its rows as `std::println()` does, nor does it add commas between the elements and rows. Instead, it prints each number in a field of width 5, and adds a line break after each row (the latter, incidentally, is not possible with `std::println()`). (Mimicking `std::println()` more closely with nested loops makes for an excellent exercise for you!)

Setting Dimensions by Default

You can let the compiler determine the size of the first (leftmost) dimension of an array with any number of dimensions from the set of initializing values. The compiler, however, can determine only *one* of the dimensions in a multidimensional array, and it has to be the first. You could define the two-dimensional carrots array with this statement:

```
double carrots[][4] {
                    {2.5, 3.2       },   // First row
                    {4.1            },   // Second row
                    {2.8, 2.3,  0.9 }    // Third row
                  };
```

The array will have three rows, as before, because there are three sets of braces within the outer pair. If there were only two sets, the array would have two rows. The number of inner pairs of braces determines the number of rows.

What you cannot do is have the compiler deduce any dimension other than the first one. Up to a point, this makes sense. If you were to supply 12 initial values for a two-dimensional array, for instance, there's no way for the compiler to know whether the array should be three rows of four elements, six rows of two elements, or indeed any combination that amounts to 12 elements. Still, this does mean that, rather unfortunately, array definitions such as the following should result in a compiler error as well:

```
double carrots[][] {                 /* Does not compile! */
                    {2.5, 3.2, 3.7, 4.1},   // First row
                    {4.1, 3.9, 1.6, 3.5},   // Second row
                    {2.8, 2.3, 0.9, 1.1}    // Third row
                   };
```

You always have to explicitly specify all array dimensions except the first one. Here's an example of defining a three-dimensional array:

```
int numbers[][3][4] {
                     {
                       { 2,  4,  6,  8},
                       { 3,  5,  7,  9},
                       { 5,  8, 11, 14}
                     },
                     {
                       {12, 14, 16, 18},
                       {13, 15, 17, 19},
                       {15, 18, 21, 24}
                     }
                    };
```

This array has three dimensions of sizes 2, 3, and 4. The outer braces enclose two further sets of braces, and each of these, in turn, contains three sets, each of which contains the four initial values for the corresponding row. As this simple example demonstrates, initializing arrays of three dimensions or more gets increasingly complicated, and you need to take great care when placing the braces enclosing the initial values. The braces are nested to as many levels as there are dimensions in the array.

Multidimensional Character Arrays

You can define arrays of two or more dimensions to hold any type of data. A two-dimensional array of type char is interesting because it can be an array of C-style strings. When you initialize a two-dimensional array of char elements with string literals, you don't need the braces around the literal for a row—the double quotes delimiting the literal do the job of the braces in this case. Here's an example:

```
char stars[][80] {
                  "Robert Redford",
                  "Hopalong Cassidy",
                  "Lassie",
                  "Slim Pickens",
                  "Boris Karloff",
                  "Oliver Hardy"
                 };
```

This array will have six rows because there are six string literals as initial values. Each row stores a string containing the name of a movie star, and a terminating null character, '\0', will be appended to each string. Each row will accommodate up to 80 characters according to the row dimension you've specified. We can see this applied in the following example:

```
// Ex5_11.cpp - Working with strings in an array
import std;

int main()
{
  const std::size_t max_length{80};    // Maximum string length (including \0)
  char stars[][max_length] {
                          "Fatty Arbuckle",  "Clara Bow",
                          "Lassie",          "Slim Pickens",
                          "Boris Karloff",   "Mae West",
                          "Oliver Hardy",    "Greta Garbo"
                        };
  unsigned choice {};

  std::print("Pick a lucky star! Enter a number between 1 and {}: ", std::size(stars));
  std::cin >> choice;

  if (choice >= 1 && choice <= std::size(stars))
  {
    std::println("Your lucky star is {}", stars[choice - 1]);
  }
  else
  {
    std::println("Sorry, you haven't got a lucky star.");
  }
}
```

This is some typical output from this program:

```
Pick a lucky star! Enter a number between 1 and 8: 6
Your lucky star is Mae West
```

Apart from its incredible inherent entertainment value, the main point of interest in the example is the definition of the array, stars. It's a two-dimensional array of char elements, which can hold multiple strings, each of which can contain up to max_length characters, including the terminating null that's automatically added by the compiler. The initializing strings for the array are enclosed between braces and separated by commas. Because the size of the first array dimension is omitted, the compiler creates the array with the number of rows necessary to accommodate all the initializing strings. As you saw earlier, you can omit the size of only the first dimension; you must specify the sizes of any other dimensions that are required.

The if statement arranges for the output to be displayed. Its condition checks that the integer that was entered is within range before attempting to display a name. When you need to reference a string for output, you only need to specify the first index value. A single index selects a particular 80-element subarray, and because this contains a string, the operation will output the contents of each element up to the terminating null character. The index is specified as choice-1 because the choice values start from 1, whereas the index values need to start from 0. This is quite a common idiom when you're programming with arrays.

Allocating an Array at Runtime

The C++ standard does not permit an array dimension to be specified at runtime. That is, the array dimension must be a constant expression that can be evaluated by the compiler. However, some current C++ compilers do allow setting variable array dimensions at runtime because the C standard permits this, and a C++ compiler will typically compile C code too.

These so-called variable-length arrays can be a useful feature, so in case your compiler supports this, we'll show how it works with an example. Keep in mind, though, that this is not strictly in conformance with the C++ language standard. Suppose you want to calculate the average height for a group of people, and you want to accommodate as many people as the user wants to enter heights for. As long as the user can input the number of heights to be processed, you can create an array that is an exact fit for the data that will be entered, like this:

```cpp
std::size_t count {};
std::print("How many heights will you enter? ");
std::cin >> count;
int height[count];              // Create the array of count elements
```

The height array is created when the code executes and will have count elements. Because the array size is not known at compile time, you cannot specify any initial values for the array.

Here's a working example using this:

```cpp
// Ex5_12.cpp - Allocating an array at runtime
import std;

int main()
{
  std::size_t count {};
  std::print("How many heights will you enter? ");
  std::cin >> count;
  int height[count];            // Create the array of count elements

  // Read the heights
  std::size_t entered {};
  while (entered < count)
  {
    std::print("Enter a height (in inches): ");
    std::cin >> height[entered];
    if (height[entered] > 0)    // Make sure value is positive
    {
      ++entered;
    }
    else
    {
      std::println("A height must be positive - try again.");
    }
  }

  // Calculate the sum of the heights
  unsigned int total {};
  for (size_t i {}; i < count; ++i)
```

```
  {
    total += height[i];
  }
  std::println("The average height is {:.1f}", static_cast<float>(total) / count);
}
```

Here's some sample output:

```
How many heights will you enter? 6
Enter a height: 47
Enter a height: 55
Enter a height: 0
A height must be positive - try again.
Enter a height: 60
Enter a height: 78
Enter a height: 68
Enter a height: 56
The average height is 60.7
```

The height array is allocated using the value entered for count. The height values are read into the array in the while loop. Within the loop, the if statement checks whether the value entered is positive. If so, the entered variable that counts the number of values entered so far is incremented. When the value is zero or negative, a message is output, and the next iteration executes without incrementing entered. Thus, the new attempt at entering a value will be read into the current element of height, which will overwrite the value that was read on the previous iteration. A straightforward for loop aggregates the total of all the heights, and this is used to output the average height. You could have used a range-based for loop here:

```
for (auto h : height)
{
  total += h;
}
```

Alternatively, you could accumulate the total of the heights in the while loop and dispense with the for loop altogether. This would shorten the program significantly. The while loop would then look like this (this variant can also be found in Ex5_12A):

```
  unsigned int total {};
  std::size_t entered {};
  while (entered < count)
  {
    std::print("Enter a height (in inches): ");
    std::cin >> height[entered];
    if (height[entered] > 0)              // Make sure value is positive
    {
      total += height[entered++];
    }
    else
    {
      std::println("A height must be positive - try again.");
    }
  }
```

Using the postfix increment operator in the expression for the index to the `height` array when adding the most recent element value to `total` ensures the current value of `entered` is used to access the array element before it is incremented for the next loop iteration.

■ **Note**   If your compiler does not allow variable-length arrays, you can achieve the same result—and much more—using a `vector`, which we'll discuss shortly.

Alternatives to Using an Array

The Standard Library defines a rich collection of data structures called *containers* that offer a variety of ways to organize and access your data. You'll learn more about these different containers in Chapter 20. In this section, however, we briefly introduce you to the two most elemental containers: `std::array<>` and `std::vector<>`. These form a direct alternative to the plain arrays built into the C++ language, but they are much easier to work with, are much safer to use, and provide significantly more flexibility than the more low-level, built-in arrays. Our discussion here won't be exhaustive, though; it's just enough for you to use them like the built-in arrays you've seen thus far. More information will follow in Chapter 20.

Like all containers, `std::array<>` and `std::vector<>` are defined as *class templates*—two C++ concepts you're not yet familiar with. You'll learn all about classes from Chapter 12 onward and all about templates in Chapters 10 and 17. Still, we prefer to introduce these containers here because they're so important and because then we can use them in the examples and exercises of upcoming chapters. Also, given a clear initial explanation and some examples, we're certain that you'll be able to successfully use these containers already. After all, these containers are specifically designed to behave analogously to built-in arrays and can thus act as near drop-in replacements for them.

The compiler uses the `std::array<T,N>` and `std::vector<T>` templates to create a concrete type based on what you specify for the template parameters, `T` and `N`. For example, if you define a variable of type `std::vector<int>`, the compiler will generate a `vector<>` container class that is specifically tailored to hold and manipulate an array of `int` values. The power of templates lies in the fact that any type `T` can be used. We'll mostly omit both the namespace `std` and the type parameters `T` and `N` when referring to them generically in text, as in `array<>` and `vector<>`.

Using array<T,N> Containers

An `array<T,N>` container is a fixed sequence of `N` elements of type `T`, so it's just like a regular array except that you specify the type and size a little differently. Here's how you create an `array<>` of 100 elements of type `double`:

```
std::array<double, 100> values;
```

This creates an object that has 100 elements of type `double`. The specification for the parameter `N` must be a constant expression—just like in declarations of regular arrays. In fact, for most intents and purposes, a variable of type `std::array<double, 100>` behaves in *exactly* the same manner as a regular array variable declared like this:

```
double values[100];
```

If you create an `array<>` container without specifying initial values, it will contain garbage values as well—just like with a plain array. Most Standard Library types, including `vector<>` and all other containers, always initialize their elements, typically to the value zero. But `array<>` is special in the sense that it is specifically designed to mimic built-in arrays as closely as possible. Naturally, you can initialize an `array<>`'s elements in the definition as well, just like a normal array:

```
std::array<double, 100> values {0.5, 1.0, 1.5, 2.0}; // 5th and subsequent elements are 0.0
```

The four values in the initializer list are used to initialize the first four elements; subsequent elements will be zero. If you want all values to be initialized to zero, you can use empty braces:

```
std::array<double, 100> values {};       // Zero-initialize all 100 elements
```

As of C++17, the compiler is capable of deducing the template arguments—the values between the angle brackets—from a given initializer list—the values between the curly braces. Here is an example:

```
std::array values {0.5, 1.0, 1.5, 2.0};  // Deduced type: std::array<double, 4>
```

Of course, the deduced array size will be 4 here, and not 100 as we used earlier.

Note that the type of `values` does not become `std::array`—it remains `std::array<double, 4>`. Whenever you refer to this array object later in the program, you must use the full, deduced type again. You are only ever allowed to write `std::array` without specifying the template argument list when initializing a new variable from one or more given values.

For template argument deduction to work, the initializer list also has to be non-empty, obviously, and consist of values of exactly the same type:

```
std::array oopsy {};                      // Error: cannot deduce type without values
std::array daisy {0.5, 1, 1.5, 2};        // Error: mixed types (double and int)
```

You can easily set all the elements to any other given value as well using the `fill()` function for the `array<>` object. Here's an example:

```
values.fill(std::numbers::pi);            // Set all elements to pi
```

The `fill()` function belongs to the `array<>` object. The function is a so-called member of the class type, `array<double, 100>`. All `array<>` objects will therefore have a `fill()` member, as well as several other members. Executing this statement causes all elements to be set to the value you pass as the argument to the `fill()` function. Obviously, this must be of a type that can be stored in the container. You'll understand the relationship between the `fill()` function and an `array<>` object better after Chapter 12.

The `size()` function for an `array<>` object returns the number of elements as type `std::size_t`. With our latest `values` variable from before, the following statement outputs 4:

```
std::println("{}", values.size());
```

In a way, the `size()` function provides the first real advantage over a standard array because it means that an `array<>` object always knows how many elements there are. You'll only be able to fully appreciate this, though, after Chapter 8, where you learn all about passing arguments to functions. You'll learn that passing a regular array to a function in such a way that it preserves knowledge over its size requires some advanced, hard-to-remember syntax. Even programmers with years of experience—yours truly included—mostly don't know this syntax by heart. Many, we're sure, don't even know that it exists. Passing an `array<>` object to a function, on the other hand, will turn out to be straightforward, and the object always knows its size by means of the `size()` function.

Accessing Individual Elements

You can access and use elements using an index in the same way as for a standard array. Here's an example:

```
values[3] = values[2] + 2.0 * values[1];
```

The fourth element is set to the value of the expression that is the right operand of the assignment. As another example, this is how you could compute the sum of all elements in the values object:

```
double total {};
for (std::size_t i {}; i < values.size(); ++i)
{
  total += values[i];
}
```

Because an array<> object is a range, you can use the range-based for loop to sum the elements more simply:

```
double total {};
for (auto value : values)
{
  total += value;
}
```

Accessing the elements in an array<> object using an index between square brackets doesn't check for invalid index values. The at() function for an array<> object does and therefore will detect attempts to use an index value outside the legitimate range. The argument to the at() function is an index, the same as when you use square brackets, so you could write the for loop that totals the elements like this:

```
double total {};
for (std::size_t i {}; i < values.size(); ++i)
{
  total += values.at(i);
}
```

The values.at(i) expression is equivalent to values[i] but with the added security that the value of i will be checked. For example, this code is guaranteed to fail:

```
double total {};
for (std::size_t i {}; i <= values.size(); ++i)
{
  total += values.at(i);
}
```

The second loop condition now using the <= operator allows i to reference beyond the last element. This will result in the program terminating at runtime with a message relating to an exception of type std::out_of_range being thrown. Throwing an exception is a mechanism for signaling exceptional error conditions. You'll learn more about exceptions in Chapter 16. If you code this using values[i], the program will likely silently access the element beyond the end of the array and add whatever it contains to total. The at() function provides a further advantage over standard arrays.

The array<> template also offers convenience functions to access the first and last elements. Given an array<> variable values, the values.front() expression is equivalent to values[0], and values.back() is equivalent to values[values.size() - 1].

Operations on array<>s As a Whole

You can compare entire array<> containers using any of the comparison operators as long as the containers are of the same size and they store elements of the same type. Here's an example:

```
std::array these {1.0, 2.0, 3.0, 4.0};      // Deduced type: std::array<double, 4>
std::array those {1.0, 2.0, 3.0, 4.0};
std::array them  {1.0, 1.0, 5.0, 5.0};

if (these == those) std::println("these and those are equal.");
if (those != them)  std::println("those and them are not equal.");
if (those > them)   std::println("those are greater than them.");
if (them < those)   std::println("them are less than those.");
```

Containers are compared element by element. For a true result for ==, all pairs of corresponding elements must be equal. For inequality, at least one pair of corresponding elements must be different for a true result. For all the other comparisons, the first pair of elements that differ produces the result. This is essentially the way in which words in a dictionary are ordered, where the first pair of corresponding letters that differ in two words determines their order. All the comparisons in the code fragment are true, so all four messages will be printed when this executes.

To convince you of how truly convenient this is, let's try exactly the same thing with plain arrays:

```
double these[] {1.0, 2.0, 3.0, 4.0};       // Deduced type: double[4]
double those[] {1.0, 2.0, 3.0, 4.0};
double them[]  {1.0, 1.0, 5.0, 5.0};

if (these == those) std::println("these and those are equal.");
if (those != them)  std::println("those and them are not equal.");
if (those > them)   std::println("those are greater than them.");
if (them < those)   std::println("them are less than those.");
```

This code still compiles (at least, it probably does; see the upcoming note). So that looks promising. However, running this on our test system now produces the following disappointing result:

```
those and them are not equal.
```

While those and them are indeed not equal, we had hoped to see all four messages like before. You can try it for yourself by running Ex5_13.cpp. The results differ depending on which compiler you use, but it's unlikely that you'll see all four messages appear as desired. So what exactly is going on here? Why does comparing regular arrays not work as expected? You'll find out in the next chapter. (You see, it's not just comics and television shows that know how to employ a cliffhanger.) For now, just remember that applying comparison operators to plain array names is not at all that useful.

■ **Note** Comparison of C-style array types using <, >, <=, >=, ==, or ! = is deprecated as of C++20. This means that for now compilers are advised to issue a warning if you write code such as that of our earlier example, and that at some point in the future such code will no longer be allowed at all.

Unlike standard arrays, you can also assign one array<> container to another, as long as they both store the same number of elements of the same type. Here's an example:

```
them = those;                    // Copy all elements of those to them
```

Moreover, array<> objects can be stored inside other containers. Regular arrays cannot. The following, for instance, creates a vector<> container that can hold array<> objects as elements, each in turn containing three int values:

```
std::vector<std::array<int, 3>> triplets;
```

The vector<> container is discussed in the next section.

Conclusion and Example

The takeaway should be clear by now: always choose array<> containers in your code over standard arrays. We've given you plenty of reasons already—at least seven by our count. And what's more, there's absolutely no disadvantage to using array<> either. Using an array<> container carries no performance overhead at all compared to a standard array. (That is, unless you use the at() function instead of the [ ] operator of array<>—bounds checking may come at a small runtime cost.)

■ **Note** Even if you use std::array<> containers in your code, it remains perfectly possible to call legacy functions that expect plain arrays as input. You can always access the built-in array that is encapsulated within the array<> object using its data() member.

Here's an example that demonstrates array<> containers in action:

```
// Ex5_14.cpp - Using array<T,N> to create Body Mass Index (BMI) table
// (BMI = weight/(height*height), with weight in kilograms, height in meters)
import std;

int main()
{
  const unsigned min_wt {100};      // Minimum weight in table (in pounds)
  const unsigned max_wt {250};      // Maximum weight in table
  const unsigned wt_step {10};
  const unsigned wt_count {1 + (max_wt - min_wt) / wt_step};

  const unsigned min_ht {48};       // Minimum height in table (inches)
  const unsigned max_ht {84};       // Maximum height in table
  const unsigned ht_step {2};
  const unsigned ht_count { 1 + (max_ht - min_ht) / ht_step };
```

```
  const double lbs_per_kg {2.2};         // Pounds per kilogram
  const double ins_per_m {39.37};        // Inches per meter
  std::array<unsigned, wt_count> weight_lbs {};
  std::array<unsigned, ht_count> height_ins {};

  // Create weights from 100lbs in steps of 10lbs
  for (unsigned i{}, w{ min_wt }; i < wt_count; w += wt_step, ++i)
  {
    weight_lbs[i] = w;
  }
  // Create heights from 48 inches in steps of 2 inches
  for (unsigned i{}, h{ min_ht }; h <= max_ht; h += ht_step)
  {
    height_ins.at(i++) = h;
  }
  // Output table headings
  std::print("{:>8}", '|');
  for (auto w : weight_lbs)
    std::print("{:^6}|", w);
  std::println("");

  // Output line below headings
  for (unsigned i{1}; i < wt_count; ++i)
    std::print("--------");
  std::println("");

  const unsigned inches_per_foot {12u};
  for (auto h : height_ins)
  {
    const unsigned feet = h / inches_per_foot;
    const unsigned inches = h % inches_per_foot;
    std::print("{:2}'{:2}\" |", feet, inches);

    const double h_m = h / ins_per_m;      // Height in meter
    for (auto w : weight_lbs)
    {
      const double w_kg = w / lbs_per_kg; // Weight in kilogram
      const double bmi = w_kg / (h_m * h_m);
      std::print(" {:2.1f} |", bmi);
    }
    std::println("");
  }
  // Output line below table
  for (size_t i {1}; i < wt_count; ++i)
    std::print("--------");
  std::println("\nBMI from 18.5 to 24.9 is normal");
}
```

We leave you to run the program to see the output because it takes quite a lot of space. There are two sets of four const variables defined that relate to the range of weights and heights for the BMI table. The weights and heights are stored in array<> containers with elements of type unsigned (short for unsigned int) because all the weights and heights are integral. The containers are initialized with the appropriate values in for loops. The second loop that initializes height_ins uses a different approach to setting the values just to demonstrate the at() function. This is appropriate in this loop because the loop is not controlled by the index limits for the container, so it's possible that a mistake could be made that would use an index outside the legal range for the container. The program would be terminated if this occurred, which would not be the case using square brackets to reference an element.

The next two for loops output the table column headings and a line to separate the headings from the rest of the table. The table is created using nested range-based for loops. The outer loop iterates over the heights and outputs the height in the leftmost column in feet and inches. The inner loop iterates over the weights and outputs a row of BMI values for the current height.

Using std::vector<T> Containers

The vector<T> container is a sequence container that may seem much like the array<T,N> container, but that is in fact far more powerful. There's no need to know the number of elements a vector<> will store in advance at compile time. In fact, there is even no need to know the number of elements it will store in advance at runtime. That is, the size of a vector<> can grow automatically to accommodate any number of elements. You can add some now and then some more later. You can remove some in the middle and then insert some more. It's all very easy with a vector<> container. A vector<> will grow as you add more and more elements; additional space is allocated automatically whenever required. There is no real maximum number of elements either—other than the one imposed by the amount of memory available to your process, of course—which is the reason you need only the type parameter T. There's no need for the N with a vector<>.

Here's an example of creating a vector<> container to store values of type double:

```
std::vector<double> values;
```

This typically has no space for elements allocated yet, so memory will need to be allocated dynamically when you add the first data item. You can add an element using the push_back() function for the container object. Here's an example:

```
values.push_back(3.1415);        // Add an element to the end of the vector
```

The push_back() function adds the value you pass as the argument—3.1415 in this case—as a new element at the end of the existing elements. Since there are no existing elements here, this will be the first, which probably will cause memory to be allocated for the first time.

You can initialize a vector<> with a predefined number of elements, like this:

```
std::vector<double> values(20);     // Vector contains 20 double values - all zero
```

Unlike a built-in array or an array<> object, a vector<> container *always* initializes its elements. In this case, our container starts out with 20 elements that are initialized with zero. If you don't like zero as the default value for your elements, you can specify another value explicitly:

```
std::vector<long> numbers(20, 99L); // Vector contains 20 long values - all 99
```

The second argument between the parentheses specifies the initial value for all elements, so all 20 elements will be 99L. Unlike most other array types you've seen so far, the first argument that specifies the number of elements—20 in our example—does *not* need to be a constant expression. It could be the result of an expression executed at runtime or read in from the keyboard. Of course, you can add new elements to the end of this or any other vector using the push_back() function.

A further option for creating a vector<> is to use a braced list to specify initial values:

```
std::vector<int> primes { 2, 3, 5, 7, 11, 13, 17, 19 };
```

The primes vector container will be created with eight elements with the given initial values.

For a vector<> with at least one given initial value the compiler can again deduce the template type argument, which may save you some typing. Here are two examples where this works:

```
std::vector primes { 2, 3, 5, 7, 11, 13, 17, 19 }; // Deduced type: std::vector<int>
std::vector numbers(20, 99L);                       // Deduced type: std::vector<long>
```

▨ **Caution** You may have noticed that we didn't initialize the values and numbers vector<> objects using the usual braced initializer syntax but instead using round parentheses:

```
std::vector<double> values(20);       // Vector contains 20 double values - all zero
std::vector<long> numbers(20, 99L);   // Vector contains 20 long values - all 99
```

This is because using braced initializers here has a significantly different effect, as the comments next to the statements explain:

```
std::vector<double> values{20};       // Vector contains 1 double value: 20
std::vector<long> numbers{20, 99L};   // Vector contains 2 long values: 20 and 99
```

When you use curly braces to initialize a vector<>, the compiler always interprets it as a sequence of initial values. This is one of only few occasions where the so-called uniform initialization syntax is not quite so uniform. To initialize a vector<> with a given number of identical values—without repeating that same value over and over, that is—you cannot use curly braces. If you do, it is interpreted by the compiler as a list of one or two initial values.

You can use an index between square brackets to set a value for an existing element or just to use its current value in an expression. Here's an example:

```
values[0] = std::numbers::pi;        // Pi
values[1] = 5.0;                     // Radius of a circle
values[2] = 2.0*values[0]*values[1]; // Circumference of a circle
```

Index values for a vector<> start from 0, just like a standard array. You can always reference existing elements using an index between square brackets, but you cannot create new elements this way. For that, you need to use, for instance, the push_back() function. The index values are not checked when you index a vector like this. So, you can accidentally access memory outside the extent of the vector and store values in such locations using an index between square brackets. The vector<> object again provides the at() function as well, just like an array<> container object, so you could consider using the at() function to refer to elements whenever there is the potential for the index to be outside the legal range.

Besides the at() function, nearly all other advantages of array<> containers directly transfer to vector<> as well:

- Each vector<> knows its size and has a size() member to query it.

- Passing a vector<> to a function is straightforward (see Chapter 8).

- Each vector<> has the convenience functions front() and back() to facilitate accessing the first and last elements of the vector<>.

- Two vector<> containers can be compared using the <, >, <=, >=, ==, !=, and <=> operators, provided the individual elements can be compared using these same operators. Unlike with array<>, this even works for vectors that do not contain the same number of elements. The semantics then is the same as when you alphabetically compare words of different length. We all know that *aardvark* precedes *zombie* in the dictionary, even though the former has more letters. Also, *love* comes before *lovesickness*—both in life and in the dictionary. The comparison of vector<> containers is analogous. The only difference is that the elements are not always letters but can be any values the compiler knows how to compare using <, >, <=, >=, ==, !=, and <=>. In technical speak, this principle is called a *lexicographical comparison*. We'll have more to say about lexicographical comparisons in Chapter 7 when we discuss how you can compare strings.

- Assigning a vector<> to another vector<> variable copies all elements of the former into the latter, overwriting any elements that may have been there before, even if the new vector<> is shorter. If need be, additional memory will be allocated to accommodate more elements as well.

- A vector<> can be stored inside other containers, so you can, for instance, create a vector of vectors of integers.

A vector<> does not have a fill() member, though. Instead, it offers assign() functions that can be used to reinitialize the contents of a vector<>, much like you would when initializing it for the first time:

```cpp
std::vector numbers(20, 99L);    // Vector contains 20 long values - all 99
numbers.assign(99, 20L);         // Vector contains 99 long values - all 20
numbers.assign({99L, 20L});      // Vector contains 2 long values - 99 and 20
```

Deleting Elements

As of C++20, you can delete all occurrences of an element from a vector<> with std::erase(). Unlike the other operations with vector<> you've seen so far, std::erase() is a nonmember function. You invoke it like this:

```cpp
std::vector numbers{ 7, 9, 7, 2, 0, 4 };
std::erase(numbers, 7);    // Erase all occurrences of 7; numbers becomes { 9, 2, 0, 4 }
```

You can also remove all elements from a vector<> at once by calling the clear() member function of the vector object. Here's an example:

```cpp
std::vector data(100, 99);    // Contains 100 integers initialized to 99
data.clear();                 // Remove all elements
```

▓ **Caution**   vector<> also provides an empty() function, which is sometimes wrongfully called in an attempt to clear a vector<>. But empty() does not empty a vector<>; clear() does. Instead, the empty() function checks whether a given container is empty. That is, empty() does not modify the container. Instead, it evaluates to a Boolean value of true if and only if the container is empty. The following statement is therefore almost certainly a mistake:

```
data.empty();        // Remove all elements... or so I thought...
```

Fortunately, as of C++20 the definition of the empty() function is such that compilers are encouraged to issue a warning if you write code like that (give it a try!).

You can remove the last element from a vector object by calling its pop_back() function. Here's an example:

```
std::vector numbers{ 7, 9, 7, 2, 0, 4 };
numbers.pop_back();   // Remove the last element; numbers becomes { 7, 9, 7, 2, 0 }
```

This is by no means all there is to using vector<> containers. For instance, we showed you only how to remove all occurrences of an element, or elements at the back, while it's perfectly possible to erase any single element at any position. Similarly, we only showed you how to add elements at the back of a vector<>, while it's perfectly possible to insert elements at arbitrary positions. And so on. You'll learn more about working with vector<> containers in Chapter 20.

Example and Conclusion

You are now in a position to create a new version of Ex5_09.cpp that uses only the memory required for the current input data:

```
// Ex5_15.cpp - Sorting an array in ascending sequence using a vector<T> container
import std;

int main()
{
  std::vector<double> data; // Stores data to be sorted

  while (true)
  {
    double input {};         // Temporary store for a value
    std::print("Enter a non-zero value, or 0 to end: ");
    std::cin >> input;
    if (input == 0)
      break;

    data.push_back(input);
  }
```

```cpp
  if (data.empty())
  {
    std::println("Nothing to sort...");
    return 0;
  }

  std::println("Starting sort.");

  while (true)
  {
    bool swapped{ false };           // Becomes true when not all values are in order
    for (std::size_t i {}; i < data.size() - 1; ++i)
    {
      if (data[i] > data[i + 1])     // Out of order so swap them
      {
        const auto temp{ data[i] };
        data[i] = data[i+1];
        data[i + 1] = temp;
        swapped = true;
      }
    }

    if (!swapped)                    // If there were no swaps
      break;                         // ...all values are in order...
  }                                  // ...otherwise, go round again.

  std::println("Your data in ascending sequence:");
  const unsigned perline {10};       // Number output per line
  unsigned n {};                     // Number on current line
  for (std::size_t i {}; i < data.size(); ++i)
  {
    std::print("{:8.1f}", data[i]);
    if (++n == perline)              // When perline have been written...
    {
      std::println("");             // Start a new line and...
      n = 0;                        // ...reset count on this line
    }
  }
  std::println("");
}
```

The output will be the same as Ex5_09.cpp. Because the data is now stored in a container of type vector<double>, there is no longer a maximum of 1,000 elements imposed onto our more diligent users. Memory is allocated incrementally to accommodate whatever input data is entered. We also no longer need to track a count of the values the user enters; the vector<> already takes care of that for us.

Other than these simplifications, all other code inside the function remains the same as before. This shows that you can use a std::vector<> in the same manner as you would a regular array. But it gives you the added bonus that you do not need to specify its size using a compile-time constant. This bonus comes at a small cost, though, as we're sure you'll understand. Luckily, this small performance overhead is rarely a cause for concern, and you'll soon find that std::vector<> will be the container you use most frequently. We'll return to this in more detail later, but for now just follow this simple guideline:

■ **Tip**   If you know the exact number of elements at compile time, and you don't need to move this data around once assigned (see also Chapter 18), use `std::array<>`. Otherwise, use `std::vector<>`.

Formatting Ranges

As of C++23, the `std::format()` and `std::print()` functions can format containers such as `std::array<>` or `std::vector<>` directly. Just like they can directly format C-style arrays, as demonstrated earlier already (in the section on multidimensional arrays). In general, any range can be formatted—in other words, you can format the exact same entities that you can use in a range-based `for` loop (see Chapter 20 for more explanation on the range concept). The only restriction, for obvious reasons, is that the individual elements of the range must be formattable as well.

■ **Note**   You cannot output containers or arrays directly into streams such as `std::cout`. Of course, you can always turn them into a string first using, for instance, `std::format()`.

As always, you control the formatting of ranges and their elements through format specifiers. Slightly simplified,[3] the general syntax for these specifiers looks as follows:

`[[fill]align][width][n][:element format specifier]`

The following example will help us explain the available formatting options:

```
// Ex5_16.cpp - Format specifiers for containers
import std;

int main()
{
  std::vector v{ 1, 2, 3, 4 };                        // Deduced type: std::vector<int>
  std::println("Default formatting: {}", v);          // [1, 2, 3, 4]
  std::println("No braces: {:n}", v);                 // 1, 2, 3, 4
  std::println("Curly braces: {{{:n}}}", v);          // {1, 2, 3, 4}
  std::println("Format range only: {:*^20}", v);      // ****[1, 2, 3, 4]****
  std::println("Format elements only: {::*<3}", v);   // [1**, 2**, 3**, 4**]
  std::println("All at once: {:*^20n:03b}", v);       // *001, 010, 011, 100*
}
```

By default, `println()` simply formats all elements using their own default formatting rules, separated by `", "` delimiters, and surrounds this entire range with square brackets. That is, `println()` uses square brackets to represent a range, even though in C++ code you define a range with curly braces. You cannot directly change the type of braces used by the formatting of ranges. The only direct control you have over

---

[3] We omitted the optional `type` option at the end of the range's format specifier (right before the optional nested specifier). The available `type` options only apply to ranges of specific element types, though. We'll discuss these as and if they become relevant in later chapters.

the brackets is that you can remove them by adding the letter n to the range's format specifier, which allows you to indirectly replace the square brackets with, for instance, curly ones, as shown by the third println() statement of Ex5_16. (To use curly braces in a format string, you must escape them by doubling: {{ and }}. Otherwise, curly braces introduce replacement fields.)

■ **Tip**   You cannot override the " , " delimiters used by the standard range formatting either. So to separate elements in any other way, you'll have to write some extra code. A first, somewhat laborious option is to loop over all elements yourself and print them one by one (similar to what we did for instance in Ex5_14 to use " | ", or in Ex15_15 to inject line breaks every so many elements). A second, at times more elegant option is to use the string replacement facilities introduced in Chapter 7 to replace the " , " substrings in the range representation produced by std::format().

Getting back to Ex5_16, the fourth print statement shows the effect of the width, fill, and align options when applied to a range field. These options are entirely analogous to the ones seen in Chapter 2. The only thing you need to realize is that if placed after a first colon, they apply to the entire field and not to the individual elements. We emphasize this because you can tune the formatting of the individual elements as well. The fifth print statement, for example, applies the same width, fill, and align options to the numeric elements instead of to the entire range by placing them in a *nested format specifier*, introduced by a second colon. A nested format specifier can be any valid specifier for the elements of the range.

Naturally, you can also combine formatting options for the entire field with formatting options for its elements. This is exemplified by the last line of Ex5_16. After a first colon, the range format specifier there instructs to center (^) the formatted range in a field that is (at least) 20 wide, and to fill any excess space with asterisks (*). Next, after a second colon, the nested specifier stipulates to print the range's elements as binary numbers in sub-fields of width 3, each filled according to the rules of the special 0 fill option for integers (see Chapter 2).

■ **Tip**   Format specifiers can be nested multiple levels deep if the elements of a range are again ranges. Examples include nested containers (vectors of vectors and such), as well as the multidimensional C-style arrays you learned about earlier in this chapter. You could, for instance, tune the formatting of our favorite carrots array (as displayed in Figure 5-8) using the following statement:

```
std::println("{:n::.1f}", carrots);  // Third level of nested specifiers...
```

The result would then be [2.5, 3.2, 0.0, 0.0], [4.1, 0.0, 0.0, 0.0], [2.8, 2.3, 0.9, 0.0]. The n option only removes the square brackets surrounding the outer range. The inner ranges (the rows of the multidimensional array) retain their square brackets. Should you want to remove those as well, you'd have to add a second n after the second colon. The elements themselves, finally, are printed using a fixed-point (f) precision of 1 (which forces, for instance, the trailing .0s in the zero elements).

Summary

You will see further applications of containers and loops in the next chapter. Almost any program of consequence involves a loop of some kind. Because they are so fundamental to programming, you need to be sure you have a good grasp of the ideas covered in this chapter. These are the essential points you learned in this chapter:

- An array stores a fixed number of values of a given type.

- You access elements in a one-dimensional array using an index value between square brackets. Index values start at 0, so in a one-dimensional array, an index is the offset from the first element.

- An array can have more than one dimension. Each dimension requires a separate index value to reference an element. Accessing elements in an array with two or more dimensions requires an index between square brackets for each array dimension.

- A loop is a mechanism for repeating a block of statements.

- There are four kinds of loops that you can use: the while loop, the do-while loop, the for loop, and the range-based for loop.

- The while loop repeats for as long as a specified condition is true.

- The do-while loop always performs at least one iteration and continues for as long as a specified condition is true.

- The for loop is typically used to repeat a given number of times and has three control expressions. The first is an initialization expression, executed once at the beginning of the loop. The second is a loop condition, executed before each iteration, which must evaluate to true for the loop to continue. The third is executed at the end of each iteration and is normally used to increment a loop counter.

- The range-based for loop iterates over all elements within a range. An array is a range of elements, and a string is a range of characters. The array and vector containers define a range so you can use the range-based for loop to iterate over the elements they contain.

- Any kind of loop may be nested within any other kind of loop to any depth.

- Executing a continue statement within a loop skips the remainder of the current iteration and goes straight to the next iteration, as long as the loop control condition allows it.

- Executing a break statement within a loop causes an immediate exit from the loop.

- A loop defines a scope so that variables declared within a loop are not accessible outside the loop. In particular, variables declared in the initialization expression of a for loop or a range-based for loop are not accessible outside the loop.

- The array<T,N> container stores a sequence of N elements of type T. An array<> container provides an excellent alternative to using the arrays that are built into the C++ language.

- The vector<T> container stores a sequence of elements of type T that increases dynamically in size as required when you add elements. You use a vector<> container instead of a standard array when the number of elements cannot be determined in advance.

EXERCISES

The following exercises enable you to try what you've learned in this chapter. If you get stuck, look back over the chapter for help. If you're still stuck after that, you can download the solutions from the Apress website (https://www.apress.com/gp/services/source-code), but that really should be a last resort.

Exercise 5-1. Write a program that outputs the squares of the odd integers from 1 up to a limit that is entered by the user.

Exercise 5-2. Write a program that uses a while loop to accumulate the sum of an arbitrary number of integers entered by the user. After every iteration, ask the user whether they are done entering numbers. The program should output the total of all the values and the overall average as a floating-point value.

Exercise 5-3. Create a program that uses a do-while loop to count the number of nonwhitespace characters entered on a line. The count should end when the first # character is found.

Exercise 5-4. Use std::cin.getline(...) to obtain a C-style string of a maximum of 1,000 characters from the user. Count the number of characters the user entered using an appropriate loop. Next, write a second loop that prints out all characters, one by one, but in reverse order.

Exercise 5-5. Write a program equivalent to that of Exercise 5-4, except for the following:

- If before you used a for loop to count the characters, you now use while, or vice versa.

- This time you should first reverse the characters in the array before printing them left to right (for the sake of the exercise, you could still use a loop to print out the characters one by one).

Exercise 5-6. Create a vector<> container with elements containing the integers from 1 to an arbitrary upper bound entered by the user. Output the elements from the vector that contain values that are not multiples of 7 or 13. Output them ten on a line, aligned in columns.

Exercise 5-7. Write a program that will read and store an arbitrary sequence of records relating to products. Each record includes three items of data—an integer product number, a quantity, and a unit price. For product number 1001, the quantity is 25, and the unit price is $9.95. Because you do not yet know how to create compound types, simply use three different array-like sequences to represent these records. The program should output each product on a separate line and include the total cost. The last line should output the total cost for all products. Columns should align, so the output should be something like this:

Product	Quantity	Unit Price	Cost
1001	25	$9.95	$248.75
1003	10	$15.50	$155.00
			$403.75

Exercise 5-8. The famous Fibonacci series is a sequence of integers with the first two values as 1 and the subsequent values as the sum of the two preceding values. So, it begins 1, 1, 2, 3, 5, 8, 13, and so on. This is not just a mathematical curiosity. The sequence also regularly appears in biological settings, for instance. It relates to the way shells grow in a spiral, and the number of petals on many flowers is a number from this sequence. Create an `array<>` container with 93 elements. Store the first 93 numbers in the Fibonacci series in the array and then output them one per line. Any idea why we'd be asking you to generate 93 Fibonacci numbers and not, say, 100?

CHAPTER 6

■ ■ ■

Pointers and References

The concepts of pointers and references have similarities, which is why we have put them together in a single chapter. Pointers are important because they provide the foundation for allocating memory dynamically. Pointers can also make your programs more effective and efficient in other ways. Both references and pointers are fundamental to object-oriented programming.

In this chapter, you'll learn

- What pointers are and how they are defined

- How to obtain the address of a variable

- How to create memory for new variables while your program is executing

- How to release memory that you've allocated dynamically

- The many hazards of raw dynamic memory allocation and what the much safer alternatives are that you have at your disposal

- The difference between raw pointers and smart pointers

- How to create and use smart pointers

- What a reference is and how it differs from a pointer

- How you can use a reference in a range-based for loop

What Is a Pointer?

Every variable in your program is located somewhere in memory, so they all have a unique *address* that identifies where they are stored. These addresses depend on where your program is loaded into memory when you run it, so they may vary from one execution to the next. A *pointer* is a variable that can store an address of another variable, of some piece of data elsewhere in memory. Figure 6-1 shows how a pointer gets its name: it "points to" a location in memory where some other value is stored.

© Ivor Horton and Peter Van Weert 2023
I. Horton and P. Van Weert, *Beginning C++23*, https://doi.org/10.1007/978-1-4842-9343-0_6

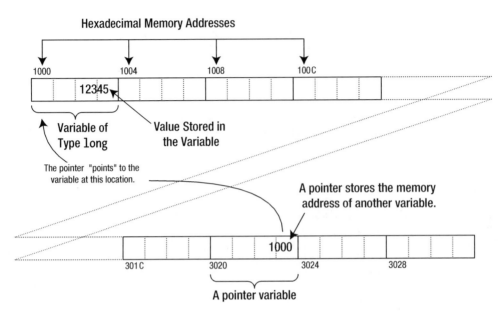

Figure 6-1. *What a pointer is*

As you know, an integer has a different representation from a floating-point value, and the number of bytes occupied by an item of data depends on what it is. So, to use a data item stored at the address contained in a pointer, you need to know the type of the data. If a pointer were nothing more than the address of some arbitrary data, it would not be all that interesting. Without knowing the type of data, a pointer is not of much use. Each pointer therefore points *to a particular type of data item at that address*. This will become clearer when we get down to specifics, so let's look at how to define a pointer. The definition of a pointer is similar to that of an ordinary variable, except that the type name has an asterisk following it to indicate that it's a pointer and not a variable of that type. Here's how you define a pointer called pnumber that can store the address of a variable of type long:

```
long* pnumber {};              // A pointer to type long
```

The type of pnumber is "pointer to long," which is written as long*. This pointer can only store an address of a variable of type long. An attempt to store the address of a variable that is other than type long will not compile. Because the initializer is empty, the statement initializes pnumber with the pointer equivalent of zero, which is a special address that doesn't point to anything. This special pointer value is written as nullptr, and you could specify this explicitly as the initial value:

```
long* pnumber {nullptr};
```

You are not obliged to initialize a pointer when you define it, but it's reckless not to. Uninitialized pointers are more dangerous than ordinary variables that aren't initialized.

■ **Tip**   As a rule, you should always initialize a pointer when you define it. If you cannot yet give it its intended value, initialize the pointer to nullptr.

It's relatively common to use variable names beginning with p for pointers, although this convention has fallen out of favor lately. Those adhering to what is called Hungarian notation—a somewhat dated naming scheme for variables—argue that it makes it easier to see which variables in a program are pointers, which in turn can make the code easier to follow. We will occasionally use this notation in this book, especially in more artificial examples where we mix pointers with regular variables. But in general, to be honest, we do not believe that adding type-specific prefixes such as p to variable names adds much value at all. In real code, it is almost always clear from the context whether something is a pointer or not.

In the examples earlier, we wrote the pointer type with the asterisk next to the type name, but this isn't the only way to write it. You can position the asterisk adjacent to the variable name, like this:

```
long *pnumber {};
```

This defines precisely the same variable as before. The compiler accepts either notation. The former is perhaps more common because it expresses the type, "pointer to long," more clearly.

However, there *is* potential for confusion if you mix definitions of ordinary variables and pointers in the same statement. Try to guess what this statement does:

```
long* pnumber {}, number {};
```

This defines two variables: one called pnumber of type "pointer to long," which is initialized with nullptr, and one called number of type long—not pointer to long!—which is initialized with 0L. The fact that number isn't simply a second variable of type long* no doubt surprises you. The fact that you're surprised is no surprise at all; the notation that juxtaposes the asterisk and the type name makes it less than clear what the type of the second variable will be to say the least. It's a little clearer already if you define the two variables in this form:

```
long *pnumber {}, number {};
```

This is a bit less confusing because the asterisk is now more clearly associated with the variable pnumber. Still, the only good solution really is to avoid the problem in the first place. It's much better to always define pointers and ordinary variables in separate statements:

```
long number {};            // Variable of type long
long* pnumber {};          // Variable of type 'pointer to long'
```

Now there's no possibility of confusion, and there's the added advantage that you can append comments to explain how the variables are used.

Note that if you did want number to be a second pointer, you could write the following:

```
long *pnumber {}, *number {};  // Define two variables of type 'pointer to long'
```

You can define pointers to any type, including types that you define. Here are definitions for pointer variables of a couple of other types:

```
double* pvalue {};          // Pointer to a double value
char16_t* char_pointer {};  // Pointer to a 16-bit character
```

No matter the type or size of the data a pointer refers to, though, the size of the pointer variable itself will always be the same. To be precise, all pointer variables *for a given platform* will have the same size. The size of pointer variables depends only on the amount of addressable memory of your target platform. To find out what that size is for you, you can run this little program:

```
// Ex6_01.cpp - The size of pointers
import std;

int main()
{
  // Print out the size (in number of bytes) of some data types
  // and the corresponding pointer types:
  std::println("{} > {}", sizeof(double), sizeof(char16_t));
  std::println("{} == {}", sizeof(double*), sizeof(char16_t*));
}
```

On our test system, the result is as follows:

```
8 > 2
8 == 8
```

For nearly all platforms today, the size of pointer variables will be either 4 bytes or 8 bytes (for 32- and 64-bit computer architectures, respectively—terms you've no doubt heard about before). Although, in principle, you may encounter other values as well, for instance if you target more specialized embedded systems.

The Address-Of Operator

The *address-of* operator, &, is a unary operator that obtains the address of a variable. You could define a variable, number, and a pointer, pnumber, initialized with the address of number with these statements:

```
long number {12345L};
long* pnumber {&number};
```

&number produces the address of number, so pnumber has this address as its initial value. pnumber can store the address of any variable of type long, so you can write the following assignment:

```
long height {1454L};      // The height of a building
pnumber = &height;        // Store the address of height in pnumber
```

The result of the statement is that pnumber contains the address of height. The effect is illustrated in Figure 6-2.

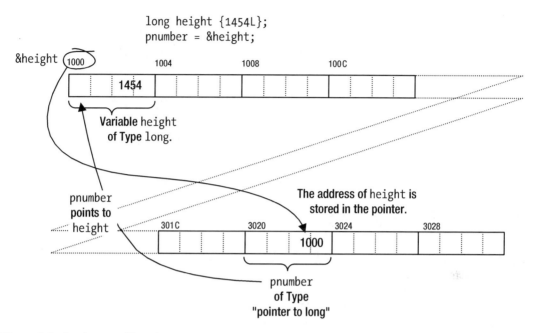

Figure 6-2. *Storing an address in a pointer*

The & operator can be applied to a variable of any type, but you can only store the address in a pointer of the appropriate type. If you want to store the address of a double variable, for example, the pointer must have been declared as type double*, which is "pointer to double."

Naturally, you could have the compiler deduce the type for you as well by using the auto keyword:

```
auto pnumber {&height};    // deduced type: long* (pointer to long)
```

We recommend you use auto* here instead to make it clear from the declaration that it concerns a pointer. Using auto*, you define a variable of a compiler-deduced pointer type:

```
auto* pnumber {&height};
```

A variable declared with auto* can be initialized only with a pointer value. Initializing it with a value of any other type will result in a compiler error.

Taking the address of a variable and storing it in a pointer is all very well, but the really interesting thing is how you can use it. Accessing the data in the memory location to which the pointer points is fundamental, and you do this using the *indirection operator*.

▓ **Tip**   Unlike output streams such as std::cout, std::format() and std::print() don't accept arbitrary pointer type arguments. To print the address stored inside a pointer, you need to cast it to void* first, a special "pointer to anything" type. Here is an example:

```
std::println("Address stored in pnumber: {}", static_cast<void*>(pnumber));
```

Supposing pnumber indeed holds address 1000 as in Figure 6-2, std::println() would then represent this address as the string 0x1000 (the addresses in the figure use hexadecimal formatting). There are no formatting options to override this hexadecimal formatting.

The Indirection Operator

Applying the *indirection operator*, *, to a pointer accesses the contents of the memory location to which it points. The name *indirection operator* stems from the fact that the data is accessed "indirectly." The indirection operator is also often called the *dereference operator*, and the process of accessing the data in the memory location pointed to by a pointer is termed *dereferencing* the pointer. To access the data at the address contained in the pointer pnumber, you use the expression *pnumber. Let's see how dereferencing works in practice with an example. The example is designed to show various ways of using pointers. The way it works will be fairly pointless but far from pointerless:

```
// Ex6_02.cpp - Dereferencing pointers
// Calculates the purchase price for a given quantity of items
import std;

int main()
{
  int unit_price {295};              // Item unit price in cents
  int count {};                      // Number of items ordered
  int discount_threshold {25};       // Quantity threshold for discount
  double discount {0.07};            // Discount for quantities over discount_threshold

  int* pcount {&count};              // Pointer to count
  std::print("Enter the number of items you want: ");
  std::cin >> *pcount;
  std::println("The unit price is ${:.2f}", unit_price / 100.0);

  // Calculate gross price
  int* punit_price{ &unit_price };   // Pointer to unit_price
  int price{ *pcount * *punit_price }; // Gross price via pointers
  auto* pprice {&price};             // Pointer to gross price

  // Calculate net price in US$
  double net_price{};
  double* pnet_price {nullptr};
  pnet_price = &net_price;
  if (*pcount > discount_threshold)
  {
    std::println("You qualify for a discount of {:.0f} percent.", discount * 100);
    *pnet_price = price*(1 - discount) / 100;
```

```
  }
  else
  {
    net_price = *pprice / 100;
  }
  std::println("The net price for {} items is ${:.2f}", *pcount, net_price);
}
```

Here's some sample output:

```
Enter the number of items you want: 50
The unit price is $2.95
You qualify for a discount of 7 percent.
The net price for 50 items is $137.17
```

We're sure you realize that this arbitrary interchange between using a pointer and using the original variable is not the right way to code this calculation. However, the example does demonstrate that using a dereferenced pointer is the same as using the variable to which it points. You can use a dereferenced pointer in an expression in the same way as the original variable, as the expression for the initial value of price shows.

It may seem confusing that you have several different uses for the same symbol, *. It's the multiplication operator and the indirection operator, and it's also used in the declaration of a pointer. The compiler is able to distinguish the meaning of * by the context. The expression *pcount * *punit_price may look slightly confusing, but the compiler has no problem determining that it's the product of two dereferenced pointers. There's no other meaningful interpretation of this expression. If there was, it wouldn't compile. You could always add parentheses to make the code easier to read, though: (*pcount) * (*punit_price).

Why Use Pointers?

A question that usually springs to mind at this point is "Why use pointers at all?" After all, taking the address of a variable you already know about and sticking it in a pointer so that you can dereference it later seems like an overhead you can do without. There are several reasons pointers are important:

- Later in this chapter you'll learn how to allocate memory for new variables dynamically—that is, during program execution. This allows a program to adjust its use of memory depending on the input. You can create new variables while your program is executing, as and when you need them. When you allocate new memory, the memory is identified by its address, so you need a pointer to record it.

- You can also use pointer notation to operate on data stored in an *array*. This is completely equivalent to the regular array notation, so you can pick the notation that is best suited for the occasion. Mostly, as the name suggests, array notation is more convenient when it comes to manipulating arrays, but pointer notation has its merits as well.

- When you define your own functions in Chapter 8, you'll see that pointers are used extensively to enable a function to access large blocks of data that are defined outside the function.

- Pointers are fundamental to enabling *polymorphism* to work. Polymorphism is perhaps the most important capability provided by the object-oriented approach to programming. You'll learn about polymorphism in Chapter 15.

▓ **Note** The last two items in this list apply equally well to references—a language construct of C++ that is similar to pointers in many ways. References are discussed near the end of this chapter.

Pointers to Type char

A variable of type "pointer to char" has the interesting property that it can be initialized with a string literal. For example, you can declare and initialize such a pointer with this statement:

```
char* pproverb {"A miss is as good as a mile"};    /* Never do this! (Deprecated!) */
```

This looks similar to initializing a char array with a string literal, and indeed it is. The statement creates a null-terminated string literal (actually, an array of elements of type const char) from the character string between the quotes and stores the address of the first character in pproverb. This is shown in Figure 6-3.

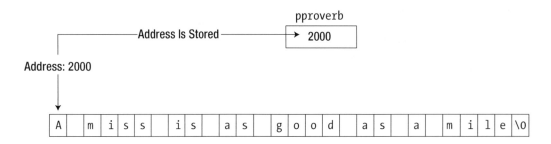

Figure 6-3. *Initializing a pointer of type char**

Unfortunately, all is not quite as it seems. A string literal is a C-style char array that you're not supposed to change. You'll recall from earlier that the const specifier is used for the type of variables that cannot or must not be changed. So, in other words, the type of the characters in a string literal is const. But this is not reflected in the type of our pointer! The statement nevertheless doesn't create a modifiable copy of the string literal; it merely stores the address of the first character. This means that if you attempt to modify the string, there will be trouble. Look at this statement, which tries to change the first character of the string to 'X':

```
*pproverb = 'X';
```

Some compilers won't complain because they see nothing wrong. The pointer, pproverb, wasn't declared as const, so the compiler is happy. With other compilers, you get a warning that initializing pproverb involves a deprecated conversion from type const char* to type char*. In some environments, you'll get an error when you run the program, resulting in a program crash. In other environments, the statement does nothing, which presumably is not what was required or expected either. The reason for this is that the string literal is still a constant, and you're not allowed to change it.

You might wonder, with good reason, why then compilers allow you to assign a pointer-to-const value to a pointer-to-non-const type in the first place, particularly when it causes these problems. The reason is that string literals only became constants with the release of the first C++ standard, and there's a great deal of legacy C-like code that relies on the "incorrect" assignment. Its use is deprecated, and the correct approach is to declare the pointer like this:

```
const char* pproverb {"A miss is as good as a mile"};  // Do this instead!
```

This defines pproverb to be of type const char*. Because it is a pointer-to-const type, the type is now consistent with that of the string literal. Any assignment to the literal's characters through this pointer will now be stopped by the compiler as well. There's plenty more to say about using const with pointers, so we'll come back to this later in this chapter. For now, let's see how using variables of type const char* operates in an example. This is a version of the "lucky stars" example, Ex5_11.cpp, using pointers instead of an array:

```
// Ex6_03.cpp - Initializing pointers with strings
import std;

int main()
{
  const char* pstar1 {"Fatty Arbuckle"};
  const char* pstar2 {"Clara Bow"};
  const char* pstar3 {"Lassie"};
  const char* pstar4 {"Slim Pickens"};
  const char* pstar5 {"Boris Karloff"};
  const char* pstar6 {"Mae West"};
  const char* pstar7 {"Oliver Hardy"};
  const char* pstar8 {"Greta Garbo"};

  std::print("Pick a lucky star! Enter a number between 1 and 8: ");
  unsigned choice {};
  std::cin >> choice;

  switch (choice)
  {
  case 1: std::println("Your lucky star is {}.", pstar1); break;
  case 2: std::println("Your lucky star is {}.", pstar2); break;
  case 3: std::println("Your lucky star is {}.", pstar3); break;
  case 4: std::println("Your lucky star is {}.", pstar4); break;
  case 5: std::println("Your lucky star is {}.", pstar5); break;
  case 6: std::println("Your lucky star is {}.", pstar6); break;
  case 7: std::println("Your lucky star is {}.", pstar7); break;
  case 8: std::println("Your lucky star is {}.", pstar8); break;

  default: std::println("Sorry, you haven't got a lucky star.");
  }
}
```

The output will be the same as Ex5_11.cpp.

Obviously, the original array version is far more elegant, but let's look past that. In this reworked version, the array has been replaced by eight pointers, pstar1 to pstar8, each initialized with a string literal. Because these pointers contain addresses of string literals, they are all specified as const.

A switch statement is easier to use than an if statement to select the appropriate output message. Incorrect values entered are taken care of by the default option of the switch.

Printing a string pointed to by one of the eight pstar pointers, finally, couldn't be easier. You just pass the pointer name as an argument to std::println(). All standard formatting functions know to treat a const char* argument as a pointer to the start of a null-terminated array of char values, and not as, say, a pointer to a single char value.

▨ **Caution**   Of course, this also means that things can go horribly wrong if you try to print a const char* pointer that does *not* point to a null-terminated array of char values. Here are two examples:

```
const char c{ 'c' };
const char unterminated[] { 'b','l','a','h','b','l','a','h' }; // No '\0' at end!
std::println("Double trouble: {} and {}", &c, &unterminated[0]);
```

Both &c and &unterminated[0] have type const char*, yet neither is guaranteed to point to a sequence of characters ending with a null terminator. The formatting procedure, however, can only assume every const char* value points to a null-terminated C-style string. In our example, std::println() therefore faithfully dereferences both const char* pointers, prints the char value it finds there, and then starts scanning subsequent bytes assuming to find more letters and eventually a null terminating character. At best, this printing routine eventually reaches some byte equal to zero in the arbitrary memory beyond both 'c' and the second 'h', and you'll get some garbage output such as this:

Double trouble: c and blahblahâª¬uV¿

Worst case, though, no zero is seen until println() starts accessing parts of memory (the call stack in this case) that the environment's security measures object to, and the program will be terminated. Therefore, make sure all const char* pointers you pass to functions refer to a properly null-terminated string, unless paired for instance with a string length argument. (Incidentally, if you use the std::string class we explain in Chapter 7, you are guaranteed never to run into this problem!)

Arrays of Pointers

So, what have you gained in Ex6_03.cpp? Well, using pointers has eliminated the waste of memory that occurred with the array in Ex5_11.cpp because each string now occupies just the number of bytes necessary. However, the program is a little long-winded now. If you were thinking "Surely, there must be a better way," then you'd be right; you could use an array of pointers:

```
// Ex6_04.cpp - Using an array of pointers
import std;

int main()
{
  const char* pstars[] {
                  "Fatty Arbuckle", "Clara Bow", "Lassie",
                  "Slim Pickens", "Boris Karloff", "Mae West",
```

```
                "Oliver Hardy", "Greta Garbo"
              };

  std::print("Pick a lucky star! Enter a number between 1 and {}: ", std::size(pstars));
  unsigned choice {};
  std::cin >> choice;

  if (choice >= 1 && choice <= std::size(pstars))
  {
    std::println("Your lucky star is {}.", pstars[choice - 1]);
  }
  else
  {
    std::println("Sorry, you haven't got a lucky star.");
  }
}
```

Now you're *nearly* getting the best of all possible worlds. You have a one-dimensional array of pointers defined such that the compiler works out the array size from the number of initializing strings. The memory usage that results from this statement is illustrated in Figure 6-4.

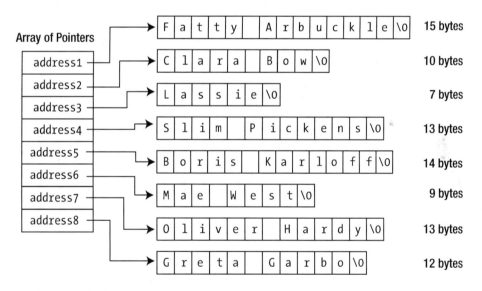

Figure 6-4. An array of pointers

With the char array of Ex5_11, each row had to have at least the length of the longest string, which resulted in quite some wasted bytes. Figure 6-4 clearly shows that by allocating all strings separately this is no longer an issue in Ex6_04. Granted, you do need some extra memory to store the addresses of the strings, typically 4 or 8 bytes per string pointer. And since in our example the difference in string lengths is not that great yet, we might not actually have gained much yet (on the contrary even).

In general, however, the cost of an extra pointer is often negligible compared to the memory required for the strings themselves. And even for our test program this is not entirely unthinkable. Suppose, for instance, that we'd ask you to add the following name as a ninth option: "Rodolfo Alfonso Raffaello Pierre Filibert Guglielmi di Valentina d'Antonguolla" (which is, we kid you not, the real name of an iconic star of the silent movie era)!

Saving space isn't the only advantage that you get by using pointers. In many circumstances, you can save time too. For example, think of what happens if you want to swap "Greta Garbo" with "Mae West" in the array. You'd need to do this to sort the strings into alphabetical order, for example. With the pointer array, you just reorder the pointers—the strings can stay right where they are. With a char array, a great deal of copying would be necessary. Interchanging the string would require the string "Greta Garbo" to be copied to a temporary location, after which you would copy "Mae West" in its place. Then you would need to copy "Greta Garbo" to its new position. All of this would require significantly more execution time than interchanging two pointers. The code using an array of pointers is similar to that using a char array. The number of array elements that is used to check that the selection entered is valid is calculated in the same way.

░ **Note**   In our pursuit of highlighting some of the advantages of pointer arrays, we may have been somewhat overly positive about the use of const char*[ ] arrays. This approach works nicely as long as you know the exact number of strings at compile time and provided all of them are defined by literals. In real applications, however, you're much more likely to gather a variable number of strings, either from user input or from files. Working with plain character arrays then rapidly becomes cumbersome and very unsafe. In the next chapter, you'll learn about a more high-level string type, std::string, which is much safer to use than plain char* arrays and certainly much better suited for more advanced applications. For one, std::string objects are designed to be fully compatible with standard containers, allowing among other things for fully dynamic and perfectly safe std::vector<std::string> containers!

Constant Pointers and Pointers to Constants

In your latest "lucky stars" program, Ex6_04.cpp, you made sure that the compiler would pick up any attempts to modify the strings pointed to by elements of the pstars array by declaring the array using the const keyword:

```
const char* pstars[] {
                "Fatty Arbuckle", "Clara Bow", "Lassie",
                "Slim Pickens", "Boris Karloff", "Mae West",
                "Oliver Hardy", "Greta Garbo"
              };
```

Here you are specifying that the char elements pointed to by the elements of the pstar array are constant. The compiler inhibits any direct attempt to change these, so an assignment statement such as this would be flagged as an error by the compiler, thus preventing a nasty problem at runtime:

```
*pstars[0] = 'X';        // Will not compile...
```

However, you could still legally write the next statement, which would copy the *address* stored in the element on the right of the assignment operator to the element on the left:

```
pstars[5] = pstars[6];          // OK
```

Those lucky individuals due to be awarded Ms. West would now get Mr. Hardy, because both pointers now point to the same name. Of course, this *hasn't* changed the object pointed to by the sixth array element—it has only changed the address stored in it, so the const specification hasn't been contravened.

You really ought to be able to inhibit this kind of change as well, because some people may reckon that good old Ollie may not have quite the same sex appeal as Mae, and of course you can. Look at this statement:

```
const char* const pstars[] {
                        "Fatty Arbuckle", "Clara Bow", "Lassie",
                        "Slim Pickens", "Boris Karloff", "Mae West",
                        "Oliver Hardy", "Greta Garbo"
                    };
```

The extra const keyword following the element type specification defines the elements as constant, so now the pointers *and* the strings they point to are defined as constant. Nothing about this array can be changed.

Perhaps we made it a bit too complicated starting you out with an array of pointers. Because it's important that you understand the different options, let's go over things once more using a basic nonarray variable, pointing to just one celebrity. We'll consider this definition:

```
const char* my_favorite_star{ "Lassie" };
```

This defines an array that contains const char elements. This means the compiler will, for instance, not let you rename Lassie to Lossie:

```
my_favorite_star[1] = 'o';      // Error: my_favorite_star[1] is const!
```

The definition of my_favorite_star, however, does not prevent you from changing your mind about which star you prefer. This is because the my_favorite_star variable itself is not const. In other words, you're free to overwrite the pointer value stored in my_favorite_star, as long as you overwrite it with a pointer that refers to const char elements:

```
my_favorite_star = "Mae West";  // my_favorite_star now points to "Mae West"
my_favorite_star = pstars[1];   // my_favorite_star now points to "Clara Bow"
```

If you want to disallow such assignments, you have to add a second const to protect the content of the my_favorite_star variable:

```
const char* const forever_my_favorite{ "Oliver Hardy" };
```

To summarize, you can distinguish three situations that arise using const when applied to pointers and the things to which they point:

- *A pointer to a constant*: You can't modify what's pointed to, but you can set the pointer to point to something else:

  ```
  const char* pstring {"Some text that cannot be changed"};
  ```

Of course, this also applies to pointers to other types. In Ex6_02, for instance, it would make perfect sense to add const to the definition of the unit_price variable:

```
const int unit_price {295};          // Item unit price in cents
```

If you turn unit_price into a constant (give it a try!), though, you have to change the definition of punit_price accordingly as well:

```
const int* punit_price{ &unit_price }; // Pointer to unit_price
```

This turns punit_price into a pointer to a *constant* (of type pointer-to-const-int), allowing you to initialize it with the address of the unit_price *constant*. You cannot store the address of the const int unit_price in a variable with type pointer to *non*-const int. If you could, you would subsequently be able to modify the unit_price constant through that pointer—and modifying constants really should not be that easy.

```
// Modifying unit_price shouldn't be possible (it is const!),
// yet the following would work if punit_price still had type int*:
*punit_price = -1;
```

What you *can* do, conversely, is assign the address of a non-const variable to a pointer-to-const variable. In Ex6_02, for instance, you could perfectly well add const to the type of pprice without adding const to the definition price as well (maybe give it a try?).

```
const int* pprice {&price};   // Pointer to gross price (&price has type int*)
```

In this case, you make it illegal to modify price through the pointer pprice, even though you can still modify price directly. In general, it's always permitted to strengthen const-ness, but never to weaken it.

- *A constant pointer*: The address stored in the pointer can't be changed. A constant pointer can only ever point to the address that it's initialized with. However, the *contents* of that address aren't constant and can be changed. Suppose you define an integer variable data and a constant pointer pdata:

```
int data {20};
int* const pdata {&data};
```

pdata is const, so it can only ever point to data. Any attempt to make it point to another variable will result in an error message from the compiler. The value stored in data isn't const, though, so you can change it:

```
*pdata = 25;                   // Allowed, as pdata points to a non-const int
```

Again, if data was declared as const, you could not initialize pdata with &data. Pdata can only point to a non-const variable of type int.

- *A constant pointer to a constant*: Here, both the address stored in the pointer and the item pointed to are constant, so neither can be changed. Taking a numerical example, you can define a variable called value like this:

```
const float value {3.1415f};
```

value is a constant, so you can't change it. You can still initialize a pointer with the address of value, though:

```
const float* const pvalue {&value};
```

pvalue is a constant pointer to a constant. You can't change what it points to, and you can't change what is stored at that address.

▓ **Tip**   In some rare cases, the need for even more complex types arises, such as pointers to pointers. A practical tip is that you can read all type names right to left. While doing so, you read every asterisk as "pointer to." Consider this variant—an equally legal one, by the way—of our latest variable declaration:

```
float const * const pvalue {&value};
```

Reading right to left then reveals that pvalue is indeed a const pointer to a const float. This trick always works (even when references enter the arena later in this chapter). You can give it a try with the other definitions in this section. The only complication is that the first const is typically written prior to the element type.

```
const float* const pvalue {&value};
```

So when reading types right to left, you often still have to swap around this const with the element type. It shouldn't be hard to remember, though. After all, "const pointer to float const" just doesn't have the same ring to it!

Pointers and Arrays

There is a close connection between pointers and array names. Indeed, there are many situations in which you can use an array name as though it were a pointer. An array name by itself mostly behaves like a pointer when it's used in an output statement, for instance. That is, if you try to output an array by just using its name, you'll just get the hexadecimal address of the array—unless it's a char array, of course, for which all standard output streams assume it concerns a C-style string. Because an array name can be interpreted as an address, you can use one to initialize a pointer as well:

```
double values[10];
double* pvalue {values};
```

This will store the address of the values array in the pointer pvalue. Although an array name represents an address, it is not a pointer. You can modify the address stored in a pointer, whereas the address that an array name represents is fixed.

Pointer Arithmetic

You can perform arithmetic operations on a pointer to alter the address it contains. You're limited to addition and subtraction for modifying the address contained in a pointer, but you can also compare pointers to produce a logical result. You can add an integer (or an expression that evaluates to an integer) to a pointer, and the result is an address. You can subtract an integer from a pointer, and that also results in an address. You can subtract one pointer from another, and the result is an integer, not an address. No other arithmetic operations on pointers are legal.

Arithmetic with pointers works in a special way. Suppose you add 1 to a pointer with a statement such as this:

```
++pvalue;
```

This apparently increments the pointer by 1. Exactly *how* you increment the pointer by 1 doesn't matter. You could use an assignment or the += operator to obtain the same effect so that the result would be exactly the same with this statement:

```
pvalue += 1;
```

The address stored in the pointer *won't* be incremented by 1 in the normal arithmetic sense, however. Pointer arithmetic implicitly assumes that the pointer points to an array. Incrementing a pointer by 1 means incrementing it by one *element* of the type to which it points. The compiler knows the number of bytes required to store the data item to which the pointer points. Adding 1 to the pointer increments the address by that number of bytes. In other words, adding 1 to a pointer increments the pointer so that it points to the next element in the array. For example, if pvalue is "pointer to double" and type double is 8 bytes, then the address in pvalue will be incremented by 8. This is illustrated in Figure 6-5.

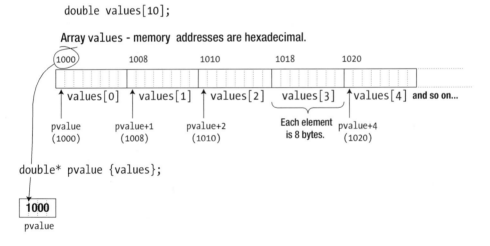

Figure 6-5. Incrementing a pointer

As Figure 6-5 shows, pvalue starts out with the address of the first array element. Adding 1 to pvalue increments the address it contains by 8, so the result is the address of the next array element. It follows that incrementing the pointer by 2 moves the pointer two elements along. Of course, pvalue need not necessarily point to the beginning of the values array. You could store the address of the third element of the array in the pointer with this statement:

```
pvalue = &values[2];
```

Now the expression pvalue + 1 would evaluate to the address of values[3], the fourth element of the values array, so you could make the pointer point to this element with this statement:

```
pvalue += 1;
```

In general, the expression pvalues + n, in which n can be any expression resulting in an integer, will add n * sizeof(double) to the address in pvalue because pvalue is of type "pointer to double."

The same logic applies to subtracting an integer from a pointer. If pvalue contains the address of values[2], the expression pvalue - 2 evaluates to the address of the first array element, values[0]. In other words, incrementing or decrementing a pointer works in terms of the type of the object pointed to. Incrementing a pointer to long by 1 changes its contents to the next long address and so increments the address by sizeof(long) bytes. Decrementing it by 1 decrements the address by sizeof(long).

Of course, you can dereference a pointer on which you have performed arithmetic. (There wouldn't be much point to it, otherwise!) For example, consider this statement:

```
*(pvalue + 1) = *(pvalue + 2);
```

Assuming pvalue is still pointing to values[3], this statement is equivalent to the following:

```
values[4] = values[5];
```

Remember that an expression such as pvalue + 1 doesn't change the address in pvalue. It's just an expression that evaluates to a result that is of the same type as pvalue. On the other hand, the expressions ++pvalue and pvalue += n *do* change pvalue.

When you dereference the address resulting from an expression that increments or decrements a pointer, parentheses around the expression are essential because the precedence of the indirection operator is higher than that of the arithmetic operators, + and -. The expression *pvalue + 1 adds 1 to the value stored at the address contained in pvalue, so it's equivalent to executing values[3] + 1. The result of *pvalue + 1 is a numerical value, not an address; its use in the previous assignment statement would cause the compiler to generate an error message.

Of course, when you store a value using a pointer that contains an invalid address, such as an address outside the limits of the array to which it relates, you'll attempt to overwrite the memory located at that address. This generally leads to disaster, with your program failing one way or another. It may not be obvious that the cause of the problem is the misuse of a pointer.

The Difference Between Pointers

Subtracting one pointer from another is meaningful only when they are of the same type and point to elements in the same array. Suppose you have a one-dimensional array, numbers, of type long defined as follows:

```
long numbers[] {10, 20, 30, 40, 50, 60, 70, 80};
```

Suppose you define and initialize two pointers like this:

```
long *pnum1 {&numbers[6]};        // Points to 7th array element
long *pnum2 {&numbers[1]};        // Points to 2nd array element
```

You can calculate the difference between these two pointers like so:

```
auto difference {pnum1 - pnum2};   // Result is 5
```

221

The difference variable will be set to the integer value 5 because the difference between two pointers is again measured in terms of elements, not in terms of bytes. Only one question remains, though: What will the type of difference be? Clearly, it should be a signed integer type to accommodate for statements such as the following:

```
auto difference2 {pnum2 - pnum1};            // Result is -5
```

As you know, the size of pointer variables such as pnum1 and pnum2 is platform specific—it's typically either 4 or 8 bytes. This, of course, implies that the number of bytes required to store pointer offsets cannot possibly be the same on all platforms either. The C++ language therefore prescribes that subtracting two pointers results in a value of type std::ptrdiff_t, a platform-specific type alias for one of the signed integer types, like so:

```
std::ptrdiff_t difference2 {pnum2 - pnum1};  // Result is -5
```

Depending on your target platform, std::ptrdiff_t is typically an alias for int, long, or long long.

Comparing Pointers

You can safely compare pointers of the same type using the familiar ==, !=, <, >, <=, >=, and <=> operators. The outcome of these comparisons will be compatible with your intuitions about pointer and integer arithmetic. Using the same variables as before, the expression pnum2 < pnum1 will thus evaluate to true, as pnum2 - pnum1 < 0 as well (pnum2 - pnum1 equals -5). In other words, the further the pointer points in the array or the higher the index of the element it points to, the larger the pointer is.

Using Pointer Notation with an Array Name

You can use an array name as though it was a pointer for addressing the array elements. Suppose you define this array:

```
long data[5] {};
```

You can refer to the element data[3] using pointer notation as *(data + 3). This notation can be applied generally so that corresponding to the elements data[0], data[1], data[2], ..., you can write *data, *(data + 1), *(data + 2), and so on. The array name by itself refers to the address of the beginning of the array, so an expression such as data+2 produces the address of the element two elements along from the first.

You can use pointer notation with an array name in the same way as you use an index between square brackets—in expressions or on the left of an assignment. You could set the values of the data array to even integers with this loop:

```
for (std::size_t i {}; i < std::size(data); ++i)
{
  *(data + i) = 2 * (i + 1);
}
```

The expression *(data + i) refers to successive elements of the array. The loop will set the values of the five array elements to 2, 4, 6, 8, and 10. You could sum the elements of the array like this:

```
long sum {};
for (std::size_t i {}; i < std::size(data); ++i)
{
  sum += *(data + i);
}
```

Let's try some of this in a practical context that has a little more meat. This example calculates prime numbers (a prime number is an integer that is divisible only by 1 and itself). Here's the code:

```
// Ex6_05.cpp - Calculating primes using pointer notation
import std;

int main()
{
  const unsigned max {100};                  // Number of primes required
  unsigned long primes[max] {2};             // First prime defined
  unsigned count {1};                        // Count of primes found so far
  unsigned long trial {3};                   // Candidate prime

  while (count < max)
  {
    bool isprime {true};                     // Indicates when a prime is found

    // Try dividing the candidate by all the primes we have
    for (unsigned i {}; i < count && isprime; ++i)
    {
      isprime = trial % *(primes + i) > 0;   // False for exact division
    }

    if (isprime)
    {                                        // We got one...
      *(primes + count++) = trial;           // ...so save it in primes array
    }

    trial += 2;                              // Next value for checking
  }

  // Output primes 10 to a line
  std::println("The first {} primes are:", max);
  for (unsigned i{}; i < max; ++i)
  {
    std::print("{}", *(primes + i));
    if ((i+1) % 10 == 0)                     // Newline after every 10th prime
      std::println("");
  }
  std::println("");
}
```

The output is as follows:

```
The first 100 primes are:
      2       3       5       7      11      13      17      19      23      29
     31      37      41      43      47      53      59      61      67      71
     73      79      83      89      97     101     103     107     109     113
    127     131     137     139     149     151     157     163     167     173
    179     181     191     193     197     199     211     223     227     229
    233     239     241     251     257     263     269     271     277     281
    283     293     307     311     313     317     331     337     347     349
    353     359     367     373     379     383     389     397     401     409
    419     421     431     433     439     443     449     457     461     463
    467     479     487     491     499     503     509     521     523     541
```

The constant max defines the number of primes to be produced. The primes array that stores the results has a first prime defined to start off the process. The variable count records how many primes have been found, so it's initialized to 1.

The trial variable holds the next candidate to be tested. It starts out at 3 because it's incremented in the loop that follows. The bool variable isprime is a flag that indicates when the current value in trial is prime.

All the work is done in two loops: the outer while loop picks the next candidate to be checked and adds the candidate to the primes array if it's prime, and the inner loop checks the current candidate to see whether it's prime. The outer loop continues until the primes array is full.

The algorithm in the loop that checks for a prime is simple. It's based on the fact that any number that isn't a prime must be divisible by a smaller number that *is* a prime. You find the primes in ascending order, so at any point primes contains all the prime numbers lower than the current candidate. If none of the values in primes is a divisor of the candidate, then the candidate must be prime. Once you realize this, writing the inner loop that checks whether trial is prime should be straightforward:

```
// Try dividing the candidate by all the primes we have
for (unsigned i {}; i < count && isprime; ++i)
{
  isprime = trial % *(primes + i) > 0;   // False for exact division
}
```

In each iteration, isprime is set to the value of the expression trial % *(primes + i) > 0. This finds the remainder after dividing trial by the number stored at the address primes + i. If the remainder is positive, the expression is true. The loop ends if i reaches count or whenever isprime is false. If any of the primes in the primes array divides into trial exactly, trial isn't prime, so this ends the loop. If none of the primes divides into trial exactly, isprime will always be true, and the loop will be ended by i reaching count.

■ **Note** Technically you only need to try dividing by primes that are less than or equal to the square root of the number in question, so the example isn't as efficient as it might be.

After the inner loop ends, either because isprime was set to false or because the set of divisors in the primes array has been exhausted, whether or not the value in trial was prime is indicated by the value in isprime. This is tested in an if statement:

```
if (isprime)
{                                  // We got one...
  *(primes + count++) = trial;     // ...so save it in primes array
}
```

If isprime contains false, then one of the divisions was exact, so trial isn't prime. If isprime is true, the assignment statement stores the value from trial in primes[count] and then increments count with the postfix increment operator. When max primes have been found, the outer while loop ends, and the primes are output ten to a line with a field width of seven characters as a result of these statements in a for loop.

Dynamic Memory Allocation

Most code you've written up to now allocates space for data at compile time. The most notable exceptions are the times when you used a std::vector<> container, which dynamically allocates all and any memory it needs to hold its elements. Apart from that, you've mostly specified all variables and arrays that you needed in the code up front, and that's what will be allocated when the program starts, whether you needed the entire array or not. Working with a fixed set of variables in a program can be very restrictive, and it's often wasteful.

Dynamic memory allocation is allocating the memory you need to store the data you're working with at runtime, rather than having the amount of memory predefined when the program is compiled. You can change the amount of memory your program has dedicated to it as execution progresses. Dynamically allocated variables can't be defined at compile time, so they can't be named in your source program. When you allocate memory dynamically, the space that is made available is identified by its address. The obvious and only place to store this address is in a pointer. With the power of pointers and the dynamic memory management tools in C++, writing this kind of flexibility into your programs is quick and easy. You can add memory to your application when it's needed and then release the memory you have acquired when you are done with it. Thus, the amount of memory dedicated to an application can increase and decrease as execution progresses.

In Chapter 3, we introduced the three kinds of storage duration that variables can have—automatic, static, and dynamic—and we discussed how variables of the first two varieties are created. Variables for which memory is allocated at runtime always have *dynamic* storage duration.

The Stack and the Free Store

You know that an automatic variable is created when its definition is executed. The space for an automatic variable is allocated in a memory area called the *stack*. The stack has a fixed size that is determined by your compiler. There's usually a compiler option that enables you to change the stack size, although this is rarely necessary. At the end of the block in which an automatic variable is defined, the memory allocated for the variable on the stack is released and is thus free to be reused. When you call a function, the arguments you pass to the function will be stored on the stack along with the address of the location to return to when execution of the function ends.

Memory that is not occupied by the operating system or other programs that are currently loaded is called the *free store*.[1] You can request that space be allocated within the free store at runtime for a new variable of any type. You do this using the new operator, which returns the address of the space allocated, and you store the address in a pointer. The new operator is complemented by the delete operator, which releases memory that you previously allocated with new. Both new and delete are keywords, so you must not use them for other purposes.

You can allocate space in the free store for variables in one part of a program and then release the space and return it to the free store in another part of the program when you no longer need it. The memory then becomes available for reuse by other dynamically allocated variables later in the same program or possibly other programs that are executing concurrently. This uses memory very efficiently and allows programs to handle much larger problems involving considerably more data than might otherwise be possible.

When you allocate space for a variable using new, you create the variable in the free store. The variable remains reserved for you until the memory it occupies is released by the delete operator. Until the moment you release it using delete, the block of memory allocated for your variable can no longer be used by subsequent calls of new. Note that the memory continues to be reserved regardless of whether you still record its address. If you don't use delete to release the memory, it will be released automatically when program execution ends.

Using the new and delete Operators

Suppose you need space for a variable of type double. You can define a pointer of type double* and then request that the memory is allocated at execution time. Here's one way to do this:

```
double* pvalue {};      // Pointer initialized with nullptr
pvalue = new double;    // Request memory for a double variable
```

This is a good moment to recall that *all pointers should be initialized*. Using memory dynamically typically involves having a lot of pointers floating around, and it's important that they do not contain spurious values. You should always ensure that a pointer contains nullptr if it doesn't contain a legal address.

The new operator in the second line of the code returns the address of the memory in the free store allocated to a double variable, and this is stored in pvalue. You can use this pointer to reference the variable in the free store using the indirection operator, as you've seen. Here's an example:

```
*pvalue = 3.14;
```

Of course, under extreme circumstances it may not be possible to allocate the memory. The free store could be completely allocated at the time of the request. More aptly, it could be that no area of the free store is available that is large enough to accommodate the space you have requested. This isn't likely with the space required to hold a single double value, but it might just happen when you're dealing with large entities

---

[1] A term that is often used as a synonym for the free store is the heap. In fact, it is probably more common to hear the term heap than free store. Nevertheless, some would argue that the heap and the free store are different memory pools. From their point of view, C++'s new and delete operators operate on the free store, whereas C's memory management functions such as malloc and free operate on the heap. While we take no stance in this technical, terminological debate, in this book we consistently use the term free store because this is what the C++ standard uses as well.

such as arrays or complicated class objects. This is something that you may need to consider later, but for now you'll assume that you always get the memory you request. When it does happen, the new operator throws something called an *exception*, which by default will end the program. We'll come back to this topic in Chapter 16 when we discuss exceptions.

You can initialize a variable that you create in the free store. Let's reconsider the previous example: the double variable allocated by new, with its address stored in pvalue. The memory slot for the double variable itself (typically 8 bytes large) still holds whatever bits were there before. As always, an uninitialized variable contains garbage. You could have initialized its value to, for instance, 3.14, though, as it was created by using this statement:

```
pvalue = new double {3.14};          // Allocate a double and initialize it
```

You can also create and initialize the variable in the free store and use its address to initialize the pointer when you create it:

```
double* pvalue {new double {3.14}};  // Pointer initialized with address in the free store
```

This creates the pointer pvalue, allocates space for a double variable in the free store, initializes the variable in the free store with 3.14, and initializes pvalue with the address of the variable.

It should come as no surprise anymore by now that the following initializes the double variable pointed to by pvalue to zero (0.0):

```
double* pvalue {new double {}}; // Pointer initialized with address in the free store
                                // pvalue points to a double variable initialized with 0.0
```

Note the difference with this, though:

```
double* pvalue {};              // Pointer initialized with nullptr
```

When you no longer need a dynamically allocated variable, you free the memory that it occupies using the delete operator:

```
delete pvalue;                  // Release memory pointed to by pvalue
```

This ensures that the memory can be used subsequently by another variable. If you don't use delete and you store a different address in pvalue, it will be impossible to free up the original memory because access to the address will have been lost. The memory will be retained for use by your program until the program ends. Of course, you can't use it because you no longer have the address. Note that the delete operator frees the memory but does *not* change the pointer. After the previous statement has executed, pvalue still contains the address of the memory that was allocated, but the memory is now free and may be allocated immediately to something else. A pointer that contains such a spurious address is sometimes called a *dangling pointer*. Dereferencing a dangling pointer is a sweet recipe for disaster, so you should get in the habit of always resetting a pointer when you release the memory to which it points, like this:

```
delete pvalue;                  // Release memory pointed to by pvalue
pvalue = nullptr;               // Reset the pointer
```

Now pvalue doesn't point to anything. The pointer cannot be used to access the memory that was released. Using a pointer that contains nullptr to store or retrieve data will terminate the program immediately, which is better than the program staggering on in an unpredictable manner with data that is invalid.

> ■ **Tip** It is perfectly safe to apply `delete` on a pointer variable that holds the value `nullptr`. Because the statement then has no effect at all, using `if` tests such as the following is not necessary:
>
> ```
> if (pvalue)        // No need for this test: 'delete nullptr;' is harmless!
> {
>   delete pvalue;
>   pvalue = nullptr;
> }
> ```

Dynamic Allocation of Arrays

Allocating memory for an array at runtime is equally straightforward. This, for instance, allocates space for an array of 100 values of type double and stores its address in data.

```
double* data {new double[100]};        // Allocate 100 double values
```

As always, the memory of this array contains uninitialized garbage values. Naturally, you can initialize the dynamic array's elements just like you would with a regular array:

```
double* data {new double[100] {}};        // All 100 values are initialized to 0.0
int* one_two_three {new int[3] {1, 2, 3}}; // 3 integers with a given initial value
float* fdata{ new float[20] { .1f, .2f }}; // All but the first 2 floats set to 0.0f
```

As with regular arrays, you can also have the compiler deduce the array's dimensions from a given initializer list. (Array size deduction in new-expressions was made possible in C++20; in earlier versions of C++ the following statement was invalid.)

```
int* one_two_three {new int[] {1, 2, 3}};  // 3 integers with a given initial value
```

To remove the array from the free store when you are done with it, you use an operator similar to the delete operator, yet this time the delete has to be followed with [ ]:

```
delete[] data;                         // Release array pointed to by data
```

The square brackets are important because they indicate that you're deleting an array. When removing arrays from the free store, you must include the square brackets, or the results will be unpredictable. Note that you don't specify any dimensions, simply [ ]. In principle you can add whitespace between delete and [ ] as well, should you prefer to do so:

```
delete [] data;                        // Release array pointed to by data
```

It's again good practice to reset the pointer now that it no longer points to memory that you own:

```
data = nullptr;                        // Reset the pointer
```

Let's see how dynamic memory allocation works in practice. Like Ex6_05, this program calculates primes. The key difference is that this time the number of primes is not hard-coded into the program. Instead, the number of primes to compute, and hence the number of elements to allocate, is entered by the user at runtime.

```cpp
// Ex6_06.cpp - Calculating primes using dynamic memory allocation
import std;

int main()
{
  unsigned max {};                           // Number of primes required

  std::print("How many primes would you like? ");
  std::cin >> max;                           // Read number required

  if (max == 0) return 0;                    // Zero primes: do nothing

  auto* primes {new unsigned long[max]};     // Allocate memory for max primes

  unsigned count {1};                        // Count of primes found
  primes[0] = 2;                             // Insert first seed prime

  unsigned long trial {3};                   // Initial candidate prime

  while (count < max)
  {
    bool isprime {true};                     // Indicates when a prime is found

    const auto limit{ static_cast<unsigned long>(std::sqrt(trial)) };
    for (unsigned i {}; primes[i] <= limit && isprime; ++i)
    {
      isprime = trial % primes[i] > 0;       // False for exact division
    }

    if (isprime)                             // We got one...
      primes[count++] = trial;               // ...so save it in primes array

    trial += 2;                              // Next value for checking
  }

  // Output primes 10 to a line
  for (unsigned i{}; i < max; ++i)
  {
    std::print("{:10}", primes[i]);
    if ((i + 1) % 10 == 0)                   // After every 10th prime...
      std::println("");                      // ...start a new line
  }
  std::println("");

  delete[] primes;                           // Free up memory...
  primes = nullptr;                          // ... and reset the pointer
}
```

The output is essentially the same as the previous program, so we won't reproduce it here. Overall, the program is similar but not the same as the previous version. After reading the number of primes required from the keyboard and storing it in max, you allocate an array of that size in the free store using the new operator. The address that's returned by new is stored in the pointer, primes. This will be the address of the first element of an array of max elements of type unsigned long.

Unlike Ex06_05, all statements and expressions involving the primes array in this program use the array notation but only because this is easier; you could equally well use and write them using pointer notation: *primes = 2, *(primes + i), *(primes + count++) = trial, and so on.

Before allocating the primes array and inserting the first prime, 2, we verify that the user did not enter the number zero. Without this safety measure, the program would otherwise write the value 2 into a memory location beyond the bounds of the allocated array, which would have undefined and potentially catastrophic results.

Notice also that the determination of whether a candidate is prime is improved compared to Ex6_05.cpp. Dividing the candidate in trial by existing primes ceases when primes up to the square root of the candidate have been tried, so finding a prime will be faster. The std::sqrt() function first seen in Chapter 2 does this.

When the required number of primes has been output, you remove the array from the free store using the delete[] operator, not forgetting to include the square brackets to indicate that it's an array you're deleting. The next statement resets the pointer. It's not essential here, but it's good to get into the habit of always resetting a pointer after freeing the memory to which it points; it could be that you add code to the program at a later date.

Of course, if you use a vector<> container that you learned about in Chapter 5 to store the primes, you can forget about memory allocation for elements and deleting it when you are done; it's all taken care of by the container. In practice, you should nearly always use std::vector<> to manage dynamic memory for you. In fact, the examples of and exercises on dynamic memory allocation in this book should probably be one of the last occasions at which you should still manage dynamic memory directly. But we're getting ahead of ourselves. We'll return to the risks, downsides, and alternatives to low-level dynamic memory allocation at length later in this chapter!

Multidimensional Arrays

In the previous chapter, you learned how to create arrays of multiple static dimensions. The example we used was this 3 × 4 multidimensional array to hold the weights of the carrots you grow in your garden:

```
double carrots[3][4] {};
```

Of course, as an avid gardener in heart and soul, you plant carrots each year but not always in the same quantity or the same configuration of three rows and four columns. As recompiling from source for each new sowing season is such a drag, let's see how we can allocate a multidimensional array in a dynamic manner. A natural attempt then would be to write this:

```
std::size_t rows {}, columns {};
std::println("How many rows and columns of carrots this year?");
std::cin >> rows >> columns;
auto carrots{ new double[rows][columns] {} };   // Won't work!
...
delete[] carrots;                               // Or delete[][]? No such operator exists!
```

Alas! Multidimensional arrays with multiple dynamic dimensions are not supported by standard C++, at least not as a built-in language feature. The furthest you can get with built-in C++ types are arrays where the value of the first dimension is dynamic. If you are happy always planting your carrots in columns of four, C++ does allow you to write this:

```
std::size_t rows {};
std::println("How many rows, each of four carrots, this year?");
std::cin >> rows;
double (*carrots)[4]{ new double[rows][4] {} };
...
delete[] carrots;
```

The required syntax is plain dreadful, though—the parentheses around *carrots are mandatory—so much so that most programmers won't be familiar with this. But at least it's possible. The good news also is that ever since C++11, you can avoid this syntax altogether using the auto keyword as well:

```
auto carrots{ new double[rows][4] {} };
```

With a bit of effort, it's actually not too hard to emulate a fully dynamic two-dimensional array using regular one-dimensional dynamic arrays either. After all, what is a two-dimensional array if not an array of rows? For our gardening example, one way would be to write this as follows:

```
double** carrots{ new double*[rows] {} };
for (std::size_t i {}; i < rows; ++i)
   carrots[i] = new double[columns] {};
...
for (std::size_t i {}; i < rows; ++i)
   delete[] carrots[i];
delete[] carrots;
```

The carrots array is a dynamic array of double* pointers, each in turn containing the address of an array of double values. The latter arrays, representing the rows of the multidimensional array, are allocated in the free store as well, one by one, by the first for loop. Once you're done with the array, you must deallocate its rows again, one by one, using a second loop, before disposing of the carrots array itself.

Given the amount of boilerplate code required to set up such a multidimensional array and again to tear it down, it's highly recommended to encapsulate such functionality in a reusable class. We'll leave that to you as an exercise after learning all about creating your own class types in upcoming chapters.

▓ **Tip** The naïve technique we presented here to represent dynamic multidimensional arrays is not the most efficient one. It allocates all rows separately in the free store, meaning they are likely not contiguous in memory anymore. Programs tend to run much, much faster when operating on contiguous memory. That's why classes that encapsulate multidimensional arrays generally allocate only a single array of rows * columns elements and then map array accesses at row i and column j to a single index using the formula i * columns + j.

Member Selection Through a Pointer

A pointer can store the address of an object of a class type, such as a vector<T> container. Objects usually have member functions that operate on the object—you saw that the vector<T> container has an at() function for accessing elements and a push_back() function for adding an element, for example. Suppose pdata is a pointer to a vector<> container. This container could be allocated in the free store with a statement such as this:

```
auto* pdata {new std::vector<int>{}};
```

But it might just as well be the address of a local object obtained using the address-of operator.

```
std::vector<int> data;
auto* pdata{ &data };
```

In both cases, the compiler deduces the type of pdata to be std::vector<int>*, which is a "pointer to a vector of int elements." For what follows, it does not matter whether the vector<> is created in the free store or on the stack as a local object. To add an element, you call the push_back() function for the vector<int> object, and you have seen how you use a period between the variable representing the vector and the member function name. To access the vector object using the pointer, you could use the dereference operator, so the statement to add an element looks like this:

```
(*pdata).push_back(66);        // Add an element containing 66
```

The parentheses around *pdata are essential for the statement to compile because the . operator is of higher precedence than the * operator. Because such clumsy looking expressions would otherwise occur very frequently when working with objects, C++ provides an operator that combines dereferencing a pointer to an object and then selecting a member of the object. You can write the previous statement like this:

```
pdata->push_back(66);          // Add an element containing 66
```

The -> operator is formed by a minus sign and a greater-than character and is referred to as the *arrow operator* or *indirect member selection operator*. The arrow is much more expressive of what is happening here. You'll be using this operator extensively later in the book.

Hazards of Dynamic Memory Allocation

There are many kinds of serious problems you may run into when you allocate memory dynamically using new. In this section, we name the most common ones. Unfortunately, these hazards are all too real, as any developer who has worked with new and delete will corroborate. As a C++ developer, a significant portion of the more serious bugs you deal with often boil down to the mismanagement of dynamic memory.

In this section, we will thus paint you a seemingly very bleak picture filled with all kinds of hazards of dynamic memory. But don't despair. We will show you the way out of this treacherous minefield soon enough! Right after this section, we will list the proven idioms and utilities that actually make it easy for you to avoid most, if not all, of these problems. In fact, you already know about one such utility: the std::vector<> container. This container is almost always the better choice over allocating dynamic memory directly using new[]. Other facilities of the Standard Library to better manage dynamic memory are discussed in upcoming sections. But first, let's dwell on all these lovely risks, hazards, pitfalls, and other perils alike that are associated with dynamic memory.

Dangling Pointers and Multiple Deallocations

A *dangling pointer*, as you know, is a pointer variable that still contains the address to free store memory that has already been deallocated by either delete or delete[]. Dereferencing a dangling pointer makes you read from or, often worse, write to memory that might already be allocated to and used by other parts of your program, resulting in all kinds of unpredictable and unexpected results. *Multiple deallocations*, which occur when you deallocate an already deallocated (and hence dangling) pointer for a second time using either delete or delete[], is another recipe for disaster.

We taught you one basic strategy already to guard yourself against dangling pointers, that is, to always reset a pointer to nullptr after the memory it points to is released. In more complex programs, however, different parts of the code often collaborate by accessing the same memory—an object or an array of objects—all through distinct copies of the same pointer. In such cases, our simple strategy rapidly falls short. Which part of the code is going to call delete/delete[]? And when? That is, how do you be sure that no other part of the code is still using the same dynamically allocated memory?

Allocation/Deallocation Mismatch

A dynamically allocated array, allocated using new[], is captured in a regular pointer variable. But so is a single allocated value that is allocated using new:

```
int* single_int{ new int{123} };    // Pointer to a single integer, initialized with 123
int* array_of_ints{ new int[123] }; // Pointer to an array of 123 uninitialized integers
```

After this, the compiler has no way to distinguish between the two, especially once such a pointer gets passed around different parts of the program. This means that the following two statements will compile without error (and in many cases even without a warning):

```
delete[] single_int;        // Wrong!
delete array_of_ints;       // Wrong!
```

What'll happen if you mismatch your allocation and deallocation operators depends entirely on the implementation associated with your compiler. But it won't be anything good.

▓ **Caution**   Every new must be paired with a single delete; every new[] must be paired with a single delete[]. Any other sequence of events leads to either undefined behavior or memory leaks (discussed next).

Memory Leaks

A memory leak occurs when you allocate memory using new or new[] and fail to release it. If you lose the address of free store memory you have allocated, by overwriting the address in the pointer you were using to access it, for instance, you have a memory leak. This often occurs in a loop, and it's easier to create this kind of problem than you might think. The effect is that your program gradually consumes more and more of the free store, with the program potentially slowing increasingly more or even failing at the point when all of the free store has been allocated.

When it comes to scope, pointers are just like any other variable. The lifetime of a pointer extends from the point at which you define it in a block to the closing brace of the block. After that it no longer exists, so the address it contained is no longer accessible. If a pointer containing the address of a block of memory in the free store goes out of scope, then it's no longer possible to delete the memory.

It's still relatively easy to see where you've simply forgotten to use `delete` to free memory when the use of the memory ceases at a point close to where you allocated it, but you'd be surprised how often programmers make mistakes like this, especially if, for instance, `return` statements creep in between the allocation and deallocation of your variable. And naturally, memory leaks are even more difficult to spot in complex programs, where memory may be allocated in one part of a program and should be released in a completely separate part.

One basic strategy for avoiding memory leaks is to immediately add the `delete` operation at an appropriate place each time you use the `new` operator. But this strategy is by no means fail-safe. We cannot stress this enough: humans, even C++ programmers, are fallible creatures. So, whenever you manipulate dynamic memory directly, you *will*, sooner or later, introduce memory leaks. Even if it works at the time of writing, all too often, bugs find their way into the program as it evolves further. `return` statements are added, conditional tests change, exceptions are thrown (see Chapter 16), and so on. And all of a sudden, there are scenarios where your memory is no longer freed correctly!

Fragmentation of the Free Store

Memory fragmentation can arise in programs that frequently allocate and release memory blocks. Each time the `new` operator is used, it allocates a contiguous block of bytes. If you create and destroy many memory blocks of different sizes, it's possible to arrive at a situation in which the allocated memory is interspersed with small blocks of free memory, none of which is large enough to accommodate a new memory allocation request by your program. The aggregate of the free memory can be quite large, but if all the individual blocks are small (smaller than a current allocation request), the allocation request will fail. Figure 6-6 illustrates the effect of memory fragmentation.

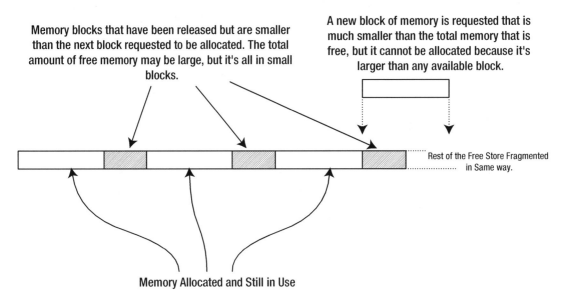

Figure 6-6. *Fragmentation of the free store*

We mention this problem here mostly for completeness because it arises relatively infrequently these days. Virtual memory provides a large memory address space even on quite modest computers. And the algorithms behind `new`/`delete` are clever and designed to counteract such phenomena as much as possible. It's only in rare cases that you need to worry about fragmentation anymore. For instance, for the most performance-critical parts of your code, operating on fragmented memory may seriously degrade performance. The way to avoid fragmentation of the free store is not to allocate many small blocks of memory. Allocate larger blocks and manage the use of the memory yourself. But this is an advanced topic, well outside the scope of this book.

Golden Rule of Dynamic Memory Allocation

After spending more than half a dozen pages learning how to use the new and delete operators, our golden rule of dynamic memory allocation may come as a bit of a surprise. It's nevertheless one of the single most valuable pieces of advice we give you in this book:

▓ **Tip**   Never use the operators new, new[ ], delete, and delete[ ] directly in day-to-day coding. These operators have no place in modern C++ code. Always use either the std::vector<> container (to replace dynamic arrays) or a smart pointer (to dynamically allocate individual objects and manage their lifetimes). These high-level alternatives are much, much safer than the low-level memory management primitives and will help you tremendously by eradicating dangling pointers, multiple deallocations, allocation/deallocation mismatches, and memory leaks from your programs.

The std::vector<> container you already know from the previous chapter, and smart pointers are explained in the next section. The main reason we still teach you about the low-level dynamic memory allocation primitives is not because we'd invite you to use them (often or at all), but because you will surely still encounter them in existing code. This also, unfortunately, implies that you will be tasked with fixing bugs caused by their use. (Bonus tip: a good first step would be to rewrite this code using better, more modern memory management utilities; more often than not, the underlying problem then reveals itself.) In your own code, you should normally avoid manipulating dynamic memory directly.

Raw Pointers and Smart Pointers

All the pointer types we have discussed up to now are part of the C++ language. These are referred to as *raw pointers* because variables of these types contain nothing more than an address. A raw pointer can store the address of an automatic variable or a variable allocated in the free store. A *smart pointer* is an object that mimics a raw pointer in that it contains an address, and you can use it in the same way in many respects. Smart pointers are normally used only to store the address of memory allocated in the free store. A smart pointer does much more than a raw pointer, though. By far the most notable feature of a smart pointer is that you don't have to worry about using the delete or delete[ ] operator to free the memory. It will be released automatically when it is no longer needed. This means that multiple deallocations, allocation/deallocation mismatches, and memory leaks will no longer be possible. If you consistently use smart pointers, dangling pointers will be a thing of the past as well.

Smart pointers are particularly useful for managing class objects that you create dynamically, so smart pointers will be of greater relevance from Chapter 12 on. You can also store them in an array<T,N> or vector<T> container, which is very useful when you are working with objects of a class type.

There are three types of smart pointers, all defined in the std namespace:

- A std::unique_ptr<T> object behaves as a pointer to type T and is "unique" in the sense that there can be only one single unique_ptr<> object containing the same address. In other words, there can never be two or more unique_ptr<T> objects pointing to the same memory address at the same time. A unique_ptr<> object is said to *own* what it points to *exclusively*. This uniqueness is enforced by the fact that the compiler will never allow you to copy a unique_ptr<>.[2]

- A std::shared_ptr<T> object also behaves as a pointer to type T, but in contrast with unique_ptr<T> there can be any number of shared_ptr<T> objects that contain—or, share—the same address. Thus, shared_ptr<> objects allow *shared ownership* of an object in the free store. At any given moment, the number of shared_ptr<> objects that contain a given address in time is known by the runtime. This is called *reference counting*. The reference count for a shared_ptr<> containing a given free store address is incremented each time a new shared_ptr<> object is created containing that address, and it's decremented when a shared_ptr<> containing the address is destroyed or assigned to point to a different address. When there are no shared_ptr<> objects containing a given address, the reference count will have dropped to zero, and the memory for the object at that address will be released automatically. All shared_ptr<> objects that point to the same address have access to the count of how many there are. You'll understand how this is possible when you learn about classes in Chapter 12.

- A std::weak_ptr<T> is linked to a shared_ptr<T> and contains the same address. Creating a weak_ptr<> does not increment the reference count associated with the linked shared_ptr<> object, though, so a weak_ptr<> does not prevent the object pointed to from being destroyed. Its memory will still be released when the last shared_ptr<> referencing it is destroyed or reassigned to point to a different address, even when associated weak_ptr<> objects still exist. If this happens, the weak_ptr<> will nevertheless not contain a dangling pointer, at least not one that you could inadvertently access. The reason is that you cannot access the address encapsulated by a weak_ptr<T> directly. Instead, the compiler will force you to first create a shared_ptr<T> out of it that refers to the same address. If the memory address for the weak_ptr<> is still valid, forcing you to create a shared_ptr<> first ensures that the reference count is again incremented and that the pointer can be used safely again. If the memory is released already, however, this operation will result in a shared_ptr<> containing nullptr.

One use for having weak_ptr<> objects is to avoid so-called reference cycles with shared_ptr<> objects. Conceptually, a reference cycle is where a shared_ptr<> inside an object x points to some other object y that contains a shared_ptr<>, which points back to x. With this situation, neither x nor y can be destroyed. In practice, this may occur in ways that are more complicated. weak_ptr<> smart pointers allow you to break such reference cycles. Another use for weak pointers is the implementation of object caches.

However, as you no doubt already started to sense, weak pointers are used only in more advanced use cases. As they are used only sporadically, we'll not discuss them any further here. The other two smart pointer types, however, you should use literally all the time, so let's dig a bit deeper into them.

---

[2] In Chapter 18, you'll learn that while copying a unique_ptr<> is not possible, you can "move" the address stored by one unique_ptr<> object to another by using the std::move() function. After this move operation the original smart pointer will be empty again.

Using unique_ptr<T> Pointers

A `std::unique_ptr<T>` object stores an address uniquely, so the value to which it points is owned exclusively by the `unique_ptr<T>` smart pointer. Like all smart pointers, a `unique_ptr<>` is mostly used to manage the lifetime of a dynamically allocated object. It always exclusively owns the pointed-to `T` value. It is its (exclusive) *owner*. When the `unique_ptr<T>` is destroyed, so is the value to which it points. A `unique_ptr<>` typically holds a dynamically allocated object that is either not shared by multiple parts of your program or whose lifetime is naturally tied to a single other object. Often `unique_ptr<>` also holds a *polymorphic pointer*, which in essence is a pointer to a dynamically allocated object that can be of any number of related class types.

To cut a long story short, you'll only fully appreciate this smart pointer type after learning all about class objects and polymorphism in Chapters 12 through 15. For now, our examples will simply use dynamically allocated values of fundamental types, which do not really excel in usefulness. What should become obvious already, though, is why these smart pointers are that much safer to use than the low-level allocation and deallocation primitives; that is, they make it impossible for you to forget or mismatch deallocation!

The recommended way to create a `unique_ptr<>` is through the `std::make_unique<>()` function template. Here is a trivial example:

```
std::unique_ptr<double> pdata { std::make_unique<double>(99.9) };
```

Naturally, when defining a local `unique_ptr<>` variable like this, you'll often want to combine the use of `std::make_unique<>()` with that of the `auto` keyword. That way, you only have to type the type of the dynamic variable, `double`, once.

```
auto pdata{ std::make_unique<double>(99.9) };
```

The arguments to `std::make_unique<T>(...)` are exactly those that would otherwise appear in the braced initializer of a dynamic allocation of the form `new T{...}`. In our example, that's the single `double` literal `99.9`.

Granted, there is no functional difference[3] between `std::make_unique<double>(99.9)` and the equivalent `std::unique_ptr<double>(new double{99.9})`. But there are sufficient other reasons to prefer the `std::make_unique<>()` syntax instead. First, it often saves you from typing the type twice. Unlike with containers, template argument deduction does not apply to the creation of smart pointers—that is, `std::unique_ptr(new double{99.9})` will not compile. Second, `std::make_unique<>()` is consistent with the `std::make_shared<>()` function for `shared_ptr<>`s, which, as we'll see shortly, *does* offer functional advantages over allocating the shared memory with `new`. And third, any use of the keyword `new` should prompt a scan for a matching `delete` for anyone reviewing the code. With `std::make_unique<T>()`, it is always instantly clear there is no need for concern. We cannot repeat this enough: the `new` keyword has no place in modern C++. Ever.

▓ **Tip** To create a `std::unique_ptr<T>` object that points to a newly allocated `T` value, always use the `std::make_unique<T>()` function.

---

[3] Not anymore, at least. Prior to C++17 `std::make_unique<>()` offered a crucial additional advantage when used in more complex statements in which other subexpressions could throw exceptions (see Chapter 16). But this advantage no longer applies since C++17 offers better guarantees on the evaluation order of sub-expressions.

You can dereference a unique_ptr<> just like an ordinary pointer, and you can use the result in the same way. With pdata defined like before, the following therefore just works:

```
*pdata = 8888.0;
std::println("{}", *pdata);                    // Prints 8888
```

The big difference is that you no longer have to worry about deleting the double variable from the free store.

You can access the address stored inside a smart pointer by calling its get() function. Here's an example:

```
double* raw_pointer = pdata.get();
```

All smart pointers have a get() function that will return the address that the pointer contains. You should only ever access the raw pointer inside a smart pointer to pass it to functions that use this pointer only briefly, never to functions or objects that would make and hang on to a copy of this pointer. It's not recommended to store raw pointers that point to the same object as a smart pointer because this may lead to dangling pointers again, as well as all kinds of related problems.

You can create a unique pointer that points to an array as well. As before, we recommend you always use std::make_unique<T[]>() for this:

```
auto pvalues{ std::make_unique<double[]>(n) };    // Dynamically create array of n elements
```

pvalues then points to the array of n elements of type double in the free store. Like a raw pointer, you can use array notation with the smart pointer to access the elements of the array it points to:

```
for (std::size_t i {}; i < n; ++i)
  pvalues[i] = static_cast<double>(i + 1);
```

This sets the array elements to values from 1 to n. The static_cast is there to silence any warnings about implicit conversions from std::size_t to double you might otherwise get. You can output the values of the elements in a similar way:

```
for (std::size_t i {}; i < n; ++i)
{
  std::print("{} ", pvalues[i]);
  if ((i + 1) % 10 == 0)
    std::println("");
}
```

This just outputs the values, ten on each line. Thus, you can use a unique_ptr<T[]> variable that contains the address of an array, just like an array name.

▓ **Tip** It is mostly recommended to use a vector<T> container instead of a unique_ptr<T[]> because this container type is far more powerful and flexible than the smart pointer. We refer you to the end of the previous chapter for a discussion of the various advantages of using vectors.

▓ **Tip**   For fundamental types T (such as int and double), the expression std::make_unique<T>() creates a variable of type T that is *initialized to zero*, and std::make_unique<T[]>(n) creates an array of n zero-initialized values. The latter can be especially wasteful (zeroing out blocks of memory takes time), particularly if all these zeros will always be overwritten anyway before they are ever read. Here is a trivial yet fairly typical example:

```
auto one_two_three{ std::make_unique<std::size_t[]>(10'000) }; // Zeroes out array
for (std::size_t i{}; i < 10'000; ++i) one_two_three[i] = i+1;    // Overwrites zeroes
```

As of C++20, you can use std::make_unique_for_overwrite<T>() or make_unique_for_overwrite<T[]>(n) in these cases instead. For fundamental types, these result in one or more uninitialized dynamic T values, similar to what you get when defining variables or arrays on the stack without initializing their values. Of course, as their names suggest, you should only use these functions if you can guarantee to always *overwrite* any uninitialized garbage values before they are read.

You can reset the pointer contained in a unique_ptr<>, or any type of smart pointer for that matter, by invoking its reset() function:

```
pvalues.reset();                  // Address is nullptr
```

pvalues still exists, but it no longer points to anything. This is a unique_ptr<double> object, so because there can be no other unique pointer containing the address of the array, the memory for the array will be released as a result. Naturally, you can check whether a smart pointer contains nullptr by explicitly comparing it to nullptr, but a smart pointer also conveniently converts to a Boolean value in the same manner as a raw pointer (that is, it converts to false if and only if it contains nullptr):

```
if (pvalues)                    // Short for:   if (pvalues != nullptr)
  std::println("The first value is {}", pvalues[0]);
```

You create a smart pointer that contains nullptr either by using empty braces, {}, or simply by omitting the braces:

```
std::unique_ptr<int> my_number;   // Or:   ... my_number{};
                                  // Or:   ... my_number{ nullptr };
if (!my_number)
  std::println("my_number points to nothing yet");
```

Creating empty smart pointers would be of little use, were it not that you can always change the value a smart pointer points to. You can do this again using reset():

```
my_number.reset(new int{ 123 }); // my_number points to an integer value 123
my_number.reset(new int{ 42 });  // my_number points to an integer 42
```

Calling reset() without arguments is thus equivalent to calling reset(nullptr). When calling reset() on a unique_ptr<T> object, either with or without arguments, any memory that was previously owned by that smart pointer will be deallocated. So, with the second statement in the previous snippet, the memory containing the integer value 123 gets deallocated, after which the smart pointer takes ownership of the memory slot holding the number 42.

Next to get() and reset(), a unique_ptr<> object also has a member function called release(). This function is essentially used to turn the smart pointer back into a dumb raw pointer.

```
int* raw_number{ my_number.release() }; // my_number points to nullptr after this
...
delete raw_number;    // The smart pointer no longer does this for you!
raw_number = nullptr; // The smart pointer no longer ensures you only delete once either!
```

Take care, though; when calling release(), it becomes your responsibility again to apply delete or delete[]. You should use this function only when necessary, typically when handing over dynamically allocated memory to legacy code. If you do this, always make absolutely sure that this legacy code effectively releases the memory—if not, get() is what you should be calling instead!

■ **Caution**   Take care with calling release() without capturing the raw pointer that comes out. That is, statements of the following form may very well signal a bug:

```
pvalues.release();
```

Why? Because on its own this statement introduces a whopping memory leak, of course! You release the smart pointer from the responsibility of deallocating the memory, but since you don't capture the raw pointer, there's no way you or anyone else can still apply delete or delete[] to it anymore. While this may seem obvious now, you'd be surprised how often release() is mistakenly called when a reset() statement was intended instead:

```
pvalues.reset();    // Not the same as release()!!!
```

The confusion no doubt stems from the fact that the release() and reset() functions have alliterative names, and both functions put the pointer's address to nullptr. These similarities notwithstanding, there's one rather critical difference: reset() deallocates any memory previously owned by the unique_ptr<>, whereas release() does not.

■ **Tip**   release() is a function you should use only sporadically (typically when interacting with legacy C++ code that does not use smart pointers yet) and with great care not to introduce leaks.

Using shared_ptr<T> Pointers

You can define a shared_ptr<T> object in a similar way to a unique_ptr<T> object:

```
auto pdata{ std::make_shared<double>(999.0) };  // Points to a double variable
```

The type of variable to be created in the free store is specified between the angled brackets. The argument between the parentheses following the function name is used to initialize the double variable it creates. The auto keyword causes the type for pdata to be deduced automatically from the object returned by make_shared<T>(), so it will be shared_ptr<double>.

▓ **Note**   In general, there can be any number of arguments to the `make_shared<>()` and `make_unique<>()` functions, with the actual number depending on the type of object being created. When you are using these functions to create objects in the free store, there will often be two or more arguments separated by commas. You will surely encounter this in the second half of the book.

Once initialized, you can dereference `pdata` to access what it points to or to change the value stored at the address:

```
std::println("{}", *pdata);      // Outputs 999
*pdata = 888.0;
std::println("{}", *pdata);      // Outputs 888
```

Creating a `shared_ptr<T>` object involves a more complicated process than creating a `unique_ptr<T>`, not least because of the need to maintain a reference count[4]. Because allocating and accessing dynamic memory is relatively expensive, `std::make_shared<>()` typically optimizes this process by allocating only a single contiguous memory block in the free store to hold both the shared T value and the reference count variable(s) at once. This is both faster and more economical in memory usage than when you initialize a `std::shared_ptr<>` with operator `new` as follows:

```
auto pdata{ std::shared_ptr<double>{new double(999.0)} };  // Don't do this!
```

▓ **Tip**   To create a `std::shared_ptr<T>` object that points to a newly allocated T value, always use `std::make_shared<T>(...)`. Not only for the same reasons as you should use `std::make_unique<>()` (see earlier) but also because this is more efficient than `std::shared_ptr<T>(new T{...})`.

▓ **Tip**   Like `std::make_unique<>()`, `std::make_shared<>()` uses zero initialization for fundamental types and arrays of fundamental types. While that's mostly fine, on rare occasions, you may want to use C++20's `std::make_shared_for_overwrite<>()` instead to improve performance (see also our explanation on `std::make_unique_for_overwrite<>()`).

You can initialize a `shared_ptr<T>` with another when you define it:

```
std::shared_ptr<double> pdata2 {pdata};
```

`pdata2` points to the same variable as `pdata`. You can also assign one `shared_ptr<T>` to another:

```
std::shared_ptr<double> pdata{ std::make_shared<double>(999.0) };
std::shared_ptr<double> pdata2;  // Pointer contains nullptr
pdata2 = pdata;                  // Copy pointer - both point to the same variable
std::println("{}", *pdata2);     // Outputs 999
```

---

[4] In practice you even need two reference counts: one to count the number of `shared_ptr<T>`s referring to the shared T object, and one to count the number of `weak_ptr<T>`s objects referring to the same object.

Of course, copying pdata, either through the initialization of a second variable or through assignment, increases the reference count. Once copied, both pointers must be reset or destroyed for the memory occupied by the double variable to be released.

Neither copying operation would be possible with unique_ptr<> objects. The compiler never allows you to create two unique_ptr<> objects pointing to the same memory location. At least not unless you bypass the compiler's safety checks by using raw pointers; for instance, by using new or get() (mixing raw pointers and smart pointers is generally a bad idea). With good reason—if it were allowed, multiple unique_ptrs would end up deallocating the same memory, with potentially catastrophic results.

You can also use make_shared<T[]>() to create a shared_ptr<T[]> that holds the address of a newly created array in the free store as follows:

```
auto bools{ std::make_shared<bool[]>(10) }; // Shared dynamic array with 10 times false
```

Another option is to store the address of an array<T,N> or vector<T> container object that you create in the free store. Here's a working example:

```
// Ex6_07.cpp - Using smart pointers
import std;

int main()
{
  std::vector<std::shared_ptr<std::vector<double>>> records; // Temperature records by days

  for (int day{ 1 };; ++day)         // Collect temperatures by day
  {
    // Vector to store current day's temperatures created in the free store
    auto day_records{ std::make_shared<std::vector<double>>() };
    records.push_back(day_records); // Save pointer in records vector

    std::print("Enter the temperatures for day {} separated by spaces. ", day);
    std::println("Enter 1000 to end:");

    while (true)
    { // Get temperatures for current day
      double t{};                    // A temperature
      std::cin >> t;
      if (t == 1000.0) break;

      day_records->push_back(t);
    }

    std::print("Enter another day's temperatures (Y or N)? ");
    char answer{};
    std::cin >> answer;
    if (std::toupper(answer) != 'Y') break;
  }

  for (int day{ 1 }; auto record : records)
  {
    double total{};
    std::size_t count{};
```

```
    std::println("\nTemperatures for day {}:", day++);
    for (auto temp : *record)
    {
      total += temp;
      std::print("{:6.2f}", temp);
      if (++count % 5 == 0) std::println("");
    }

    std::println("\nAverage temperature: {:.2f}", total / count);
  }
}
```

Here's how the output looks with arbitrary input values:

```
Enter the temperatures for day 2 separated by spaces. Enter 1000 to end:
23.2 34 29.9 36.7 1000
Enter another day's temperatures (Y or N)? y
Enter the temperatures for day 2 separated by spaces. Enter 1000 to end:
34.5 35 45.1 43.15 44.44 40 37.73 35 1000
Enter another day's temperatures (Y or N)? Y
Enter the temperatures for day 3 separated by spaces. Enter 1000 to end:
44.55 56 57 45.9 44.44 32 28.5 1000
Enter another day's temperatures (Y or N)? n

Temperatures for day 1:
 23.20 34.00 29.90 36.70
Average temperature: 30.95

Temperatures for day 2:
 34.50 35.00 45.10 43.15 44.44
 40.00 37.73 35.00
Average temperature: 39.37

Temperatures for day 3:
 44.55 56.00 57.00 45.90 44.44
 32.00 28.50
Average temperature: 44.06
```

This program reads an arbitrary number of temperature values recorded during a day, for an arbitrary number of days. The accumulation of temperature records is stored in the records vector, which has elements of type shared_ptr<vector<double>>. Thus, each element is a smart pointer to a vector of type vector<double>.

The containers for the temperatures for any number of days are created in the first for loop. The temperature records for a day are stored in a vector container that is created in the free store by this statement:

```
auto day_records{ std::make_shared<std::vector<double>>() };
```

The day_records pointer type is determined by the pointer type returned by the make_shared<>() function. The function allocates memory for the vector<double> object in the free store along with the shared_ptr<vector<double>> smart pointer that is initialized with its address and returned. Thus, day_records is type shared_ptr<vector<double>>, which is a smart pointer to a vector<double> object. This pointer is added to the records container.

The vector pointed to by day_records is populated with data that is read in the inner while loop. Each value is stored using the push_back() function for the current vector pointed to by day_records. The function is called using the indirect member selection operator. This loop continues until 1000 is entered, which is an unlikely value for a temperature during the day, so there can be no mistaking it for a real value. When all the data for the current day has been entered, the inner while loop ends, and there's a prompt asking whether another day's temperatures are to be entered. If the answer is affirmative, the outer loop continues and creates another vector in the free store. When the outer loop ends, the records vector will contain smart pointers to vectors containing each day's temperatures.

The next loop is a range-based for loop that iterates over the elements in the records vector. The inner range-based for loop iterates over the temperature values in the vector that the current records' element points to. This inner loop outputs the data for the day and accumulates the total of the temperature values. This allows the average temperature for the current day to be calculated when the inner loop ends. Despite having a fairly complicated data organization with a vector of smart pointers to vectors in the free store, accessing the data and processing the data are easy tasks using range-based for loops.

The example illustrates how using containers and smart pointers can be a powerful and flexible combination. This program deals with any number of sets of input, with each set containing any number of values. Free store memory is managed by the smart pointers, so there is no need to worry about using the delete operator or the possibility of memory leaks. The records vector could also have been created in the free store too, but we'll leave that as an exercise for you to try.

▓ **Note**   We've used shared pointers in Ex6_07 mainly for the sake of creating a first example. Normally, you'd simply use a vector of type std::vector<std::vector<double>> instead. The need for shared pointers only really arises when multiple parts of the same program truly share the same object, and it is hard to tell which part should reclaim the memory. Realistic uses of shared pointers hence generally involve objects, as well as more lines of code than is feasible to show in a book.

Understanding References

A reference is similar to a pointer in many respects, which is why we're introducing it here. You'll only get a real appreciation of the value of references, though, once you learn how to define functions in Chapter 8. References become even more important in the context of object-oriented programming later.

A reference is a name that you can use as an alias for another variable. Obviously, it must be like a pointer insofar as it refers to something else in memory, but there are a few crucial differences. Unlike a pointer, you cannot declare a reference and not initialize it. Because a reference is an alias, the variable for which it is an alias must be provided when the reference is initialized. Also, a reference cannot be modified to be an alias for something else. Once a reference is initialized as an alias for some variable, it keeps referring to that same variable for the remainder of its lifetime.

Defining References

Suppose you defined this variable:

```
double data {3.5};
```

You can define a reference as an alias for data like this variable:

```
double& rdata {data};        // Defines a reference to the variable data
```

The ampersand (&) following the type name indicates that the variable being defined, rdata, is a reference to a variable of type double. The variable that it represents is specified in the braced initializer. Thus, rdata is of type "reference to double." You can use the reference as an alternative to the original variable name. Here's an example:

```
rdata += 2.5;
```

This increments data by 2.5. None of the dereferencing that you need with a pointer is necessary—you just use the name of the reference as though it were a variable. A reference always acts as a true alias, otherwise indistinguishable from the original variable. If you take the address of a reference, for instance, the result will even be a pointer to the original variable. In the following snippet, the addresses stored in pdata1 and pdata2 will thus be identical:

```
double* pdata1 {&rdata};     // pdata1 == pdata2
double* pdata2 {&data};
```

Let's ram home the difference between a reference and a pointer by contrasting the reference rdata in the previous code with the pointer pdata defined in this statement:

```
double* pdata {&data};       // A pointer containing the address of data
```

This defines a pointer, pdata, and initializes it with the address of data. This allows you to increment data like this:

```
*pdata += 2.5;               // Increment data through a pointer
```

You must dereference the pointer to access the variable to which it points. With a reference, there is no need for dereferencing; it just doesn't apply. In some ways, a reference is like a pointer that has already been dereferenced, although it also can't be changed to reference something else. Make no mistake, though; given our rdata reference variable from before, the following snippet *does* compile:

```
double other_data{ 5.0 };    // Create a second double variable called other_data
rdata = other_data;          // Assign other_data's current value to data (through rdata)
```

The key is that this last statement does not make rdata refer to the other_data variable. The rdata reference variable is defined to be an alias for data and will forever be an alias for data. A reference is and always remains the complete equivalent of the variable to which it refers. In other words, the second statement acts exactly as if you wrote this:

```
data = other_data;           // Assign the value of other_data to data (directly)
```

A pointer is different. With our pointer pdata, for instance, we can do the following:

```
pdata = &other_data;          // Make pdata point to the other_data variable
```

A reference variable is thus much like a const pointer variable:

```
double* const pdata {&data};  // A const pointer containing the address of data
```

Take care: we didn't say a pointer-to-const variable but a const pointer variable. That is, the const needs to come after the asterisk. Reference-to-const variables exist as well. You define such a reference variable by using the const keyword:

```
const double& const_ref{ data };
```

Such a reference is similar to a pointer-to-const variable—a const pointer-to-const variable to be exact—in the sense that it is an alias through which one cannot modify the original variable. The following statement, for instance, will therefore not compile:

```
const_ref *= 2;               // Illegal attempt to modify data through a reference-to-const
```

In Chapter 8, you'll see that reference-to-const variables play a particularly important role when defining functions that operate on arguments of nonfundamental object types.

Using a Reference Variable in a Range-Based for Loop

You know that you can use a range-based for loop to iterate over all the elements in an array:

```
double sum {};
unsigned count {};
double temperatures[] {45.5, 50.0, 48.2, 57.0, 63.8};
for (auto t : temperatures)
{
  sum += t;
  ++count;
}
```

The variable t is initialized to the value of the current array element on each iteration, starting with the first. The t variable does not access that element itself. It is just a local copy with the same value as the element. Therefore, you also cannot use t to modify the value of an element. However, you can change the array elements if you use a reference:

```
const double F2C {5.0/9.0};   // Fahrenheit to Celsius conversion constant
for (auto& t : temperatures)  // Reference loop variable
  t = (t - 32.0) * F2C;
```

The loop variable, t, is now of type double&, so it is an alias for each array element. The loop variable is redefined on each iteration and initialized with the current element, so the reference is never changed after being initialized. This loop changes the values in the temperatures array from Fahrenheit to Celsius. You can use the alias t in any context in which you'd be able to use the original variable or array element. Another way to write the previous loop, for instance, is this:

```
const double F2C {5.0/9.0};      // Fahrenheit to Celsius conversion constant
for (auto& t : temperatures) {   // Reference loop variable
  t -= 32.0;
  t *= F2C;
}
```

Using a reference in a range-based for loop is efficient when you are working with collections of objects. Copying objects can be expensive on time, so avoiding copying by using a reference type makes your code more efficient.

When you use a reference type for the variable in a range-based for loop, and you don't need to modify the values, you can use a reference-to-const type for the loop variable:

```
for (const auto& t : temperatures)
  std::print("{:6.2}", t);
std::println("");
```

You still get the benefits of using a reference type to make the loop as efficient as possible (no copies of the elements are being made!), and at the same time, you prevent the array elements from being inadvertently changed by this loop.

Summary

You explored some important concepts in this chapter. You will undoubtedly make extensive use of pointers and particularly smart pointers in real-world C++ programs, and you'll see a lot more of them throughout the rest of the book:

These are the vital points this chapter covered:

- A pointer is a variable that contains an address. A basic pointer is referred to as a raw pointer.

- You obtain the address of a variable using the address-of operator, &.

- To refer to the value pointed to by a pointer, you use the indirection operator, *. This is also called the dereference operator.

- You access a member of an object through a pointer or smart pointer using the indirect member selection operator, ->.

- You can add integer values to or subtract integer values from the address stored in a raw pointer. The effect is as though the pointer refers to an array, and the pointer is altered by the number of array elements specified by the integer value. You cannot perform arithmetic with a smart pointer.

- The new and new[ ] operators allocate a block of memory in the free store—holding a single variable and an array, respectively—and return the address of the memory allocated.

- You use the delete or delete[ ] operator to release a block of memory that you've allocated previously using either the new or, respectively, the new[ ] operator. You don't need to use these operators when the address of free store memory is stored in a smart pointer.

- Low-level dynamic memory manipulation is synonymous for a wide range of serious hazards such as dangling pointers, multiple deallocations, deallocation mismatches, memory leaks, and so on. Our golden rule is therefore this: never use the low-level new/new[] and delete/delete[] operators directly. Containers (and std::vector<> in particular) and smart pointers are nearly always the smarter choice!

- A smart pointer is an object that can be used like a raw pointer. A smart pointer, by default, is used only to store free store memory addresses.

- There are two commonly used varieties of smart pointers. There can only ever be one type unique_ptr<T> pointer in existence that points to a given object of type T, but there can be multiple shared_ptr<T> objects containing the address of a given object of type T. The object will then be destroyed when there are no shared_ptr<T> objects containing its address.

- A reference is an alias for a variable. It refers to one and the same memory location from the moment it is initialized.

- You can use a reference type for the loop variable in a range-based for loop to allow the values of the elements in the range to be modified.

- To avoid copying all individual elements one by one while iterating over a range in a range-based for loop, you should use a reference-to-const type for the loop variable.

EXERCISES

The following exercises enable you to try what you've learned in this chapter. If you get stuck, look back over the chapter for help. If you're still stuck after that, you can download the solutions from the Apress website (https://www.apress.com/gp/services/source-code), but that really should be a last resort.

Exercise 6-1. Write a program that declares and initializes an array with the first 50 odd (as in not even) numbers. Output the numbers from the array ten to a line using pointer notation and then output them in reverse order, also using pointer notation.

Exercise 6-2. Revisit the previous exercise, but instead of accessing the array values using the loop counter, this time, you should employ pointer increments (using the ++ operator) to traverse the array when outputting it for the first time. After that, use pointer decrements (using --) to traverse the array again in the reverse direction.

Exercise 6-3. Write a program that reads an array size from the keyboard and dynamically allocates an array of that size to hold floating-point values. Using pointer notation, initialize all the elements of the array so that the value of the element at index position n is $1 / (n + 1)^2$. Calculate the sum of the elements using array notation, multiply the sum by 6, and output the square root of that result.

Test the program with more than 100,000 elements. Do you notice anything interesting about the result?

Note: If the interesting result you see is infinity (printed by std::println() as "inf"): don't worry, it happens to the best of us (yours truly included). While perhaps not the interesting result that we were aiming for, this type of bug is a very interesting learning opportunity in its own right. In fact, try to figure out what went wrong without reading the upcoming tip.

Note: Even if your result is not infinity (congratulations, btw!), maybe it's still worth thinking where and how it could've gone wrong?

Tip: Start by asking yourself: What elementary mathematical operation is often said to lead to infinity? And then: What computational limitation of integer numbers could lead to that situation in this particular case?

Exercise 6-4. Repeat the calculation in Exercise 6-3 but using a `vector<>` container allocated in the free store.

Exercise 6-5. Revisit Exercise 6-3, but this time use a smart pointer to store the array, that is, if you haven't already done so from the start. A good student should've known not to use the low-level memory allocation primitives....

Exercise 6-6. Revisit Exercise 6-4 and replace any raw pointers with smart pointers there as well.

CHAPTER 7

Working with Strings

This chapter is about handling textual data much more effectively and safely than the mechanism provided by a C-style string stored in an array of char elements:

In this chapter, you'll learn

- How to create variables of type string

- What operations are available with objects of type string and how you use them

- How to chain together various bits and pieces to form one single string

- How you can search a string for a specific character or substring

- How you can modify an existing string

- How to convert a string such as "3.1415" into the corresponding number

- How you can work with strings containing Unicode characters

- What a raw string literal is

A Better Class of String

You've seen how you can use an array of elements of type char to store a null-terminated (C-style) string. The <cstring> module provides a wide range of functions for working with C-style strings, including capabilities for joining strings, searching a string, and comparing strings. All these operations depend on the null character being present to mark the end of a string. If it is missing or gets overwritten, many of these functions will march happily through memory beyond the end of a string until a null character is found at some point or some catastrophe stops the process. Even if your process survives, it often results in memory being arbitrarily overwritten. And once that happens, all bets are off! Using C-style strings is therefore inherently unsafe and represents a serious security risk. Fortunately, there's a better alternative.

The C++ Standard Library provides the std::string type, which is much easier to use than a null-terminated string. The string type is defined by a class (or to be more precise, a class template), so it isn't one of the fundamental types. Type string is a *compound type*, which is a type that's a composite of several data items that are ultimately defined in terms of fundamental types of data. Next to the characters that make up the string it represents, a string object typically also contains the number of characters in the string. We'll start by explaining how you create string objects.

Defining string Objects

An object of type `string` contains a sequence of characters of type `char`, which can be empty. This statement defines a variable of type `string` that contains an empty string:

```
std::string empty;                    // An empty string
```

This statement defines a `string` object that you refer to using the name `empty`. In this case, `empty` contains a string that has no characters and so it has zero length.

You can initialize a `string` object with a string literal when you define it:

```
std::string proverb {"Many a mickle makes a muckle"};
```

`proverb` is a `string` object that contains a copy of the string literal shown in the initializer. Internally, the character array encapsulated by a `string` object is always terminated by a null character. This is done to assure compatibility with the numerous existing functions that expect C-style strings.

■ **Tip** You can convert a `std::string` object to a C-style string at no cost using two similar methods. The first is by calling its `c_str()` member function (short for *C-string*):

```
const char* proverb_c_str = proverb.c_str();
```

Because this conversion always results in a C-string of type `const char*`, the resulting pointer cannot be used to modify the characters of the `string`, only to access them. The second option is the `data()` member function:

```
char* proverb_data = proverb.data();
```

Provided `proverb` is of type `std::string` and not `const std::string`[1], `data()` returns a pointer of type `char*`. You can use this to alter the characters in the pointed-to `char` array. You are not allowed to de- or reallocate the array, though, nor can you influence the string's length (say, by writing null characters (`'\0'`) at the tail of the string). The only way to lengthen or shorten this array is through the class's member functions we discuss later.

Still, you should convert to C-style strings only when calling legacy C-style functions. In your own code, we recommend you consistently use `std::string` objects (or equivalents) because these are far safer and far more convenient than plain `char` arrays.

All `std::string` functions, for one, are defined in such a way that you normally never need to worry about the terminating null character. You can also obtain the length of the string for a `string` object using its `length()` function. This length will never include the string termination character.

```
std::println("{}", proverb.length()); // Prints 28
```

This statement calls the `length()` function for the `proverb` object and prints the value it returns. The record of the string length is guaranteed to be maintained by the object itself. That is, to determine the

---

[1] We refer you to Chapter 11 for more details on the relation between `const` objects and `const` member functions.

length of the encapsulated string, the `string` object does not have to traverse the entire string looking for the terminating null character. When you append one or more characters, the length is increased automatically by the appropriate amount and decreased if you remove characters.

Let's get back to creating string objects. There are several more possibilities for initializing a `string` object. You can use an initial sequence from a string literal, for instance:

```
std::string part_literal { "Least said soonest mended.", 5 };  // "Least"
```

The second initializer in the list specifies the length of the sequence from the first initializer to be used to initialize the part_literal object.

You can also initialize a `string` object with a single character between single quotes.

```
std::string vanadium{'V'};
```

This initializes vanadium with the string "V".

▨ **Caution**   To initialize a `string` with a single character value, you cannot use round brackets like this:

```
std::string yttrium('Y'); /* Error: cannot create std::string from single char */
```

The reason is that when initializing a string from a single character surrounded by curly braces, you are initializing the string from an *initializer list*. This initializer list is always surrounded by curly braces, and can contain any number of characters. Here is another example:

```
std::string osmium{'O', 's'};
```

You can also initialize a string with any number of instances of a given character. You can define and initialize a sleepy time `string` object like this:

```
std::string sleeping(6, 'z');
```

The `string` object, sleeping, will contain "zzzzzz". The string length will be 6.

▨ **Caution**   To initialize a `string` with repeated character values, you must not use curly braces like this:

```
std::string sleeping{6, 'z'};
```

The curly braces syntax does compile but certainly won't do what you expect. In our example, the literal 6 would be interpreted as the code for a letter character, meaning sleeping would be initialized to some obscure two-letter word instead of the intended "zzzzzz".[2] If you recall, you already encountered an analogous quirk of C++'s near-uniform initialization syntax with `std::vector<>` in the previous chapter.

---

[2] The character with code 6 is generally a non-printable character—more specifically the transition control character 'ACK' (acknowledge). To better visualize what happens you could, for instance, output the result of `std::string ounce{111, 'z'};`, which is generally the string "oz".

A further option is to use an existing string object to provide the initial value. Given that you've defined proverb previously, you can define another object based on that:

```
std::string sentence {proverb};
```

The sentence object will be initialized with the string literal that proverb contains, so it too will contain "Many a mickle makes a muckle" and have a length of 28.

You can reference characters within a string object using an index value starting from 0, just like an array. You can use a pair of index values to identify part of an existing string and use that to initialize a new string object. Here's an example:

```
std::string phrase {proverb, 0, 13};  // Initialize with 13 characters starting at index 0
```

Figure 7-1 illustrates this process.

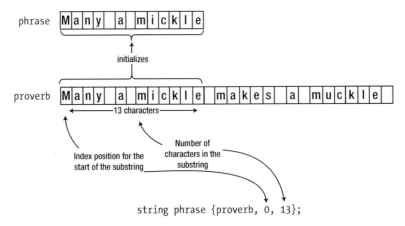

Figure 7-1. *Creating a new string from part of an existing string*

The first element in the braced initializer is the source of the initializing string. The second is the index of the character in proverb that begins the initializing substring, and the third initializer in the list is the number of characters in the substring. Thus, phrase will contain "Many a mickle".

■ **Caution**   The third entry in the {proverb, 0, 13} initializer, 13, is the *length* of the substring, *not an index*. So, to extract for instance the substring "mickle", you should use the initializer {proverb, 7, 6} and not, say, {proverb, 7, 13}. This is a common source of confusion and bugs, especially for those with experience in languages such as JavaScript or Java where substrings are commonly designated using start and end indices.

If you pass only a single integer after the existing std::string object you get a substring starting at the given index, spanning all the way to the end of the original string. Here is an example:

```
std::string tail {proverb, 20};     // a muckle
```

To summarize, this section described no less than eight options for defining and initializing a string object (see a Standard Library reference for the complete list):

1. No initializer (or empty braces, {}):

   ```
   std::string empty;                                          // The string ""
   ```

2. An initializer containing a string literal:

   ```
   std::string proverb{ "Many a mickle makes a muckle" };  // The given literal
   ```

3. An initializer containing an existing string object:

   ```
   std::string sentence{ proverb };                           // Duplicates proverb
   ```

4. An initializer containing a string literal followed by the length of the sequence in the literal to be used to initialize the string object:

   ```
   std::string part_literal{ "Least said soonest mended.", 5 };  // "Least"
   ```

5. An initializer list containing one or more character literals:

   ```
   std::string vanadium{'V'};
   std::string osmium{'O', 's'};
   ```

6. An initializer containing a repeat count followed by the character literal that is to be repeated in the string that initializes the string object (mind the round parentheses!):

   ```
   std::string open_wide(5, 'a');                             // "aaaaa"
   ```

7. An initializer containing an existing string object, an index specifying the start of the substring, and the length of the substring:

   ```
   std::string phrase{proverb, 5, 8};                         // "a mickle"
   ```

8. An initializer containing an existing string object and the start index of the substring:

   ```
   std::string tail{proverb, 20};                             // "a muckle"
   ```

▓ **Caution** The fourth and eighth std::string creation options in this list are dangerously *inconsistent*. The following example clearly illustrates this blatant inconsistency:

```
std::string C_style{"Consistency is the key to success", 11}; // "Consistency"
std::string string{ "Consistency is the key to success" };
std::string Cpp_style{ string, 11 };                          // " is the key to success"
```

That is, when initializing a std::string with a string and an integer, you get a substantially different substring depending on whether you start from a C-style string or another C++ std::string object.

Annoying. But if you look more closely, there is at least some method to this madness. The substring creation starting from C-style strings is no doubt designed to be consistent with functions of the C Standard Library—functions such as `strncpy()` and `strncmp()`, which in turn are consistent with C's low-level memory manipulation functions `memcpy()`, `memcmp()`, and `memmove()`. And the substring creation starting from `std::string` objects, on the other hand, is consistent with other substring functions in C++ world—notably the `substr()` member of `std::string` that we discuss later in this chapter.

Because it's worth getting a feel of what integer arguments you need to correctly mark substrings, we'll look a bit closer at this subject in the next section.

Copying and Marking Substrings

In the previous section we uncovered that there are at least two different, inconsistent ways to mark substrings in standard C++ APIs. Before we can draw any conclusions on this topic, though, there is one more related function that we need to branch out to: `std::string::copy()`. This member function copies a substring of a C++ `std::string` to a C-style string. The following snippet shows it in action.

```
char C_style_copy[100] {};            // Sufficiently large, filled with \0 characters...
proverb.copy(C_style_copy, 4);        // "Many" (terminating null character not copied)
proverb.copy(C_style_copy, 8, 5);     // "a mickle"
proverb.copy(C_style_copy, proverb.length()); // Copy the entire string...
```

The first argument of `copy()` is always a pointer to an array of `char` values. It tells `copy()` where to write the first of the copied characters. This implies that this pointer needs to be of type `char*` and not `const char*`. After the output pointer, you must supply one or two integer arguments. The first, required integer argument determines the (maximum) number of characters to copy; the second, optional integer is the index into the `std::string` of the first character to copy. If the start index is omitted, the copied substring starts at index 0.

■ **Caution** `std::string::copy()` does not append a null terminating character to the copied substring. If you want the target to be a valid C-style string, you must add it yourself. Had we not initialized the buffer with zero values in our earlier example, for instance, then you would have had to add a null terminating character as follows:

```
char C_style_copy[100];            // Sufficiently large, uninitialized (garbage values)
proverb.copy(C_style_copy, 4);     // "Many" (terminating null character not copied)
C_style_copy[4] = '\0';            // Add null terminating character
```

■ **Caution** With `std::string::copy()`, it is your responsibility to ensure that the given C-style string is large enough to receive the entire substring, including—and this is important—the null terminating character if need be (see also the previous caution block).

That said, we are ready to conclude our digression on substrings. Without further ado, here is a rundown on the different ways of marking substrings in the C and C++ Standard Libraries:

■ **Tip**   When marking substrings, always remember:

- *C-style substring marking*: Substrings in C-style char* or const char* strings are marked by a number of characters to copy, optionally followed by a starting index.

- *C++-style substring marking*: Substrings in C++ std::strings are, as a rule, marked by a starting index, optionally followed by a number of characters to copy. The only exception—because why be consistent?—is std::string::copy(), where the substring to copy from the std::string is marked using the C-style substring marking convention.

Both styles thus use the same arguments but in opposite order. The mnemonic we use is that with C-style strings, minding about string lengths is always your *first* priority, and is fundamentally *non-optional*. C++ strings, on the other hand, know their own length, so worrying about their lengths becomes secondary and optional.

Formatting and Reading String Objects

To show the substrings you created earlier, you can print them using std::println(). Here are some examples:

```
std::println("{}", proverb);          // Many a mickle makes a muckle
std::println("{}...{}", phrase, tail); // Many a mickle...a muckle
```

■ **Note**   The format string argument of std::print() and println() must be known at compile time. This allows the library to verify any mistakes in the format string syntax. (We'll explain how this works later in this book.) But it also implies that you cannot print strings such as proverb directly by passing them as the format string:

```
// std::println(proverb);     /* Error: proverb is not a constant expression */
std::println("{}", proverb); // Okay: prints Many a mickle makes a muckle
```

As of C++23, the same holds for std::format(), which is a rare breaking change with C++20, where std::format(proverb) was still a valid expression. We'll have more to say about what other expressions, besides string literals, you can use as format strings in Chapter 8.

The supported format specifier options for string fields are a subset of those for numeric fields seen in Chapter 2:

```
[[fill]align][width][.precision][type]
```

For string fields, the precision option denotes the *maximum* field width; the width option always denotes the *minimum* field width. Consider the following print statement:

```
std::println("{:.13}{:>11}", proverb, tail); // Many a mickle...a muckle
```

Here ".13" specifies that proverb should be printed with a *maximum* width ("precision") of 13. The second format specifier, ".>11", on the other hand, specifies a *minimum* width of 11. Do you see why? If we omit the leading . character, it should be obvious from past examples that ">11" leads to right-alignment (>) in a field that is (at least) 11 characters wide. But the format specifier in this example starts with a . character. Usually, a leading . initiates a precision option, but not in this case. The reason is that in ".>11" the . precedes the alignment option, >, and therefore defines the fill character instead (any character other than { and } may be used as a fill character).

The supported type options for string fields are s (the default) and ?. The ? type option triggers *escaped* formatting. Escaped formatting is typically more suitable for debugging or logging than default formatting. It represents strings similar to how you'd write them as string literals in code; that is, surrounded with " quotes, and with certain special characters escaped. Here is a basic example to illustrate the difference between the two types of string formatting:

```
const std::string alfa_beta{ "α\t\u0392\n" };
std::print("{}", alfa_beta);     // α    β    (followed by a line break)
std::print("{:?}", alfa_beta);   // "α\tβ\n" (no line break)
```

Concretely, the following characters are escaped: whitespace characters except for plain space characters (so \t, \n, \r, and \u{...} for more exotic whitespace characters), double quotes (\"), backslash (\\), and a select number of special characters you're less likely to encounter (these are escaped again as \u{...}). All other valid Unicode characters remain printed unescaped.

▓ **Note**   You can also employ escaped formatting when printing a single character, except that then single quotes are used to surround the (possibly escaped) character.

Of course, you don't just output strings; you can read them as well. Extraction from std::cin is as straightforward for std::string objects as it is for, say, ints or floats:

```
std::string name;
std::print("Enter your name: ");
std::cin >> name;                        // Pressing Enter ends input
```

This reads characters up to the first whitespace character, which ends the input process. Whatever was read is stored in the string object, name. You cannot enter text with embedded spaces with this process. Of course, reading entire phrases complete with spaces is possible as well, just not with >>. We'll explain how you do this later.

Operations with String Objects

Many operations with string objects are supported. Perhaps the simplest is assignment. You can assign a string literal or another string object to a string object. Here's an example:

```
std::string adjective {"hornswoggling"}; // Defines adjective
std::string word {"rubbish"};            // Defines word
word = adjective;                        // Modifies word
adjective = "twotiming";                 // Modifies adjective
```

The third statement assigns the value of `adjective`, which is "hornswoggling", to `word`, so "rubbish" is replaced. The last statement assigns the literal "twotiming" to `adjective`, so the original value "hornswoggling" is replaced. Thus, after executing these statements, `word` will contain "hornswoggling", and `adjective` will contain "twotiming".

Concatenating Strings

You can join strings using the addition operator; the technical term for this is *concatenation*. You can concatenate the objects defined earlier like this:

```
std::string description {adjective + " " + word + " whippersnapper"};
```

After executing this statement, the `description` object will contain the string "twotiming hornswoggling whippersnapper". You can see that you can concatenate string literals with `string` objects using the + operator. This is because the + operator has been redefined to have a special meaning with `string` objects. When one operand is a `string` object and the other operand is either another `string` object or a string literal, the result of the + operation is a new `string` object containing the two strings joined together.

Note that you *cannot* concatenate two string literals using the + operator. One of the two operands of the + operator must always be an object of type `string`. The following statement, for example, won't compile:

```
std::string description {"hornswoggling" + " " + word};    // Wrong!!
```

The problem is that the compiler will try to evaluate the initializer value as follows:

```
std::string description {("hornswoggling" + " ") + word};    // Wrong!!
```

In other words, the first expression that it evaluates is ("hornswoggling" + " "), and the + operator doesn't work with both operands as two string literals. The good news is that you have at least five ways around this:

- Naturally, you can write the first two string literals as a single string literal: {"hornswoggling " + word}.

- You can omit the + between the two literals: {"hornswoggling" " " + word}. Two or more string literals in sequence will be concatenated into a single literal by the compiler.

- You can introduce parentheses: {"hornswoggling" + (" " + word)}. The expression between parentheses that joins " " with `word` is then evaluated first to produce a `string` object, which can subsequently be joined to the first literal using the + operator.

- You can turn one or both of the literals into a std::string object using the familiar initialization syntax: {std::string{"hornswoggling"} + " " + word}.

- You can turn one or both of the literals into a std::string object by adding the suffix s to the literal, such as in {"hornswoggling"s + " " + word}. For this to work, you must first add a `using namespace std::string_literals;` directive. You can add this directive either at the beginning of your source file or locally inside your function. Once this directive is in scope, appending the letter s to a string literal turns it into a std::string object, much like appending u to an integer literal turns it into an unsigned integer, for instance.

That's enough theory for the moment. It's time for a bit of practice. This program reads your first and second names from the keyboard:

```cpp
// Ex7_01.cpp - Concatenating strings
import std;

int main()
{
  std::string first;                      // Stores the first name
  std::string second;                     // Stores the second name

  std::print("Enter your first name: ");
  std::cin >> first;                      // Read first name

  std::print("Enter your second name: ");
  std::cin >> second;                     // Read second name

  std::string sentence {"Your full name is "}; // Create basic sentence
  sentence += first + " " + second + ".";      // Augment with names

  std::println("{}", sentence);           // Print the sentence and its length
  std::println("The string contains {} characters.", sentence.length());
}
```

Here's some sample output:

```
Enter your first name: Phil
Enter your second name: McCavity
Your full name is Phil McCavity.
The string contains 32 characters.
```

After defining two empty string objects, first and second, the program prompts for input of a first name and then a second name. The input operations will read anything up to the first whitespace character. So, if your name consists of multiple parts, say Van Weert, this program won't let you enter it. If you enter Van Weert for the second name, the >> operator will only extract the Van part from the stream. You'll learn how you can read a string that includes whitespace later in this chapter.

After getting the names, you create another string object that is initialized with a string literal. The sentence object is concatenated with the string object that results from the right operand of the += assignment operator:

```cpp
sentence += first + " " + second + ".";            // Augment with names
```

The right operand first concatenates first and " ", then the resulting string with second, and finally the second intermediate string with ".". Afterwards, the += operator appends the concatenated string to sentence. This statement demonstrates that the += operator also works with objects of type string similarly to the basic types. The statement is equivalent to this statement:

```cpp
sentence = sentence + (((first + " ") + second) + "."); // Augment with names
```

Finally, the program uses std::println() to print the contents of sentence first, followed by the length of the string it contains.

■ **Tip** The append() function of a std::string object is an alternative to the += operator. Using this, you could write the previous example as follows:

```
sentence.append(first).append(" ").append(second).append(".");
```

In its basic form, append() is not all that interesting—unless you enjoy typing, that is, or if the + key on your keyboard is broken. But of course there's more to it than that. The append() function is more flexible than += because it allows, for instance, the concatenation of substrings, or repeated characters:

```
std::string compliment("~~~ What a beautiful name... ~~~");
sentence.append(compliment, 3, 22);  // Appends " What a beautiful name"
sentence.append(3, '!');             // Appends "!!!"
```

Concatenating Strings and Characters

Next to two string objects, or a string object and a string literal, you can also concatenate a string object and a single character. The string concatenation in Ex7_01, for example, could also be expressed as follows (see also Ex7_01A.cpp):

```
sentence += first + ' ' + second + '.';
```

Another option, just to illustrate the possibilities, is to use the following two statements:

```
sentence += first + ' ' + second;
sentence += '.';
```

What you cannot do, though, as before, is concatenate two individual characters. One of the operands to the + operand should always be a string object.

To observe an additional pitfall of adding characters together, you could replace the concatenation in Ex7_01 with this variant:

```
sentence += second;
sentence += ',' + ' ';
sentence += first;
```

Surprisingly, perhaps, this code does compile. But a possible session might then go as follows:

```
Enter your first name: Phil
Enter your second name: McCavity
Your full name is McCavityLPhil.
The string contains 31 characters.
```

Notice how the length of the final sentence has dropped from 32 to 31? The third line of this output reveals why: the comma and space characters between McCavity and Phil have somehow mysteriously fused into a single capital letter *L*. The reason this happens is that the compiler does not concatenate two characters; instead, it adds the character codes for the two characters together. Any compiler will use ASCII codes for the basic Latin characters (ASCII encoding was explained in Chapter 1). The ASCII code for ',' is 44, and that of the ' ' character is 32. Their sum, 32 + 44, therefore equals 76, which happens to be the ASCII code for the capital letter 'L'.

Notice that this example would've worked fine if you had written it as follows:

```
sentence += second + ',' + ' ' + first;
```

The reason, analogous to before, is that the compiler would evaluate this statement from left to right, as if the following parentheses were present:

```
sentence += ((second + ',') + ' ') + first;
```

With this statement, one of the two concatenation operands is thus always a std::string. Confusing? Perhaps a bit. The general rule with std::string concatenation is easy enough, though: concatenation is evaluated left to right and will work correctly only as long as one of the operands of the concatenation operator, +, is a std::string object.

■ **Note** Up to this point, we have always used literals to initialize or concatenate with string objects—either string literals or character literals. Everywhere we used string literals, you can also use any other form of C-style string: char[] arrays, char* variables, or any expression that evaluates to either of these types. Similarly, all expressions involving character literals will work just as well with any expression that results in a value of type char.

Concatenating Strings and Numbers

An important limitation in C++ is that you can only concatenate std::string objects with either strings or characters. Concatenation with most other types, such as a double, will generally fail to compile:

```
const double result{ std::numbers::pi };
const auto result_string{ std::string{"result equals: "} + result };   // Compiler error!
```

Worse, such concatenations sometimes compile and produce undesired results, because numbers may again be treated as character codes. Here is an example (the ASCII code for the letter 'E' is 69):

```
std::string song_title{ "Summer of '" };
song_title += 69;
std::println("{}", song_title);   // Summer of 'E
```

This limitation might frustrate you at first, especially if you're used to working with strings in, for instance, Java or C#. In those languages, the compiler implicitly converts values of any type to strings. Not so in C++. In C++, you must explicitly convert these values to strings yourself. There are several ways you might accomplish this. For values of fundamental numeric types, a quick and easy way is the std::to_string() family of functions:

```
const double result{ std::numbers::pi };
const auto result_string{ std::string{"result equals: "} + std::to_string(result) };
std::println("{}", result_string);  // result equals: 3.141593

std::string song_title{ "Summer of '" };
song_title += std::to_string(69);
std::println("{}", song_title);     // Summer of '69
```

The only downside is that you cannot control the format std::to_string(). For floating-point numbers, for instance, std::to_string() will always use fixed-point formatting with precision 6. Of course, if you need more control, you can always use the familiar std::print() or format() functions instead:

```
std::println("result equals: {:.15f}", result);  // result equals: 3.141592653589793
std::println("Summer of '{:x}", 105);             // Summer of '69 (hexadecimal for 105)
```

Accessing Characters in a String

You refer to a particular character in a string by using an index value between square brackets, just as you do with a character array. The first character in a string object has the index value 0. You could refer to the third character in sentence, for example, as sentence[2]. You can use such an expression on the left of the assignment operator, so you can *replace* individual characters as well as access them. The following loop changes all the characters in sentence to uppercase:

```
for (std::size_t i {}; i < sentence.length(); ++i)
  sentence[i] = static_cast<char>(std::toupper(sentence[i]));
```

This loop applies the toupper() function to each character in the string in turn and stores the result in the same position in the string. You best add a static_cast<> here to silence compiler warnings for implicit narrowing (the C function toupper() returns a value of type int, and not of type char as desired). The index value for the first character is 0, and the index value for the last character is one less than the length of the string, so the loop continues as long as i < sentence.length() is true.

A string object is a range, so you could also do this with a range-based for loop:

```
for (char& ch : sentence)
  ch = static_cast<char>(std::toupper(ch));
```

Specifying ch as a reference type allows the character in the string to be modified within the loop.

You can exercise this array-style access method in a version of Ex5_10.cpp that determined the number of vowels and consonants in a string. The new version will use a string object. It will also demonstrate that you can use the getline() function to read a line of text that includes spaces:

```
// Ex7_02.cpp - Accessing characters in a string
import std;

int main()
{
  std::string text;                       // Stores the input
  std::println("Enter a line of text:");
  std::getline(std::cin, text);           // Read a line including spaces
```

```cpp
  unsigned vowels {};                       // Count of vowels
  unsigned consonants {};                   // Count of consonants
  for (std::size_t i {}; i < text.length(); ++i)
  {
    if (std::isalpha(text[i]))              // Check for a letter
    {
      switch (std::tolower(text[i]))        // Convert to lowercase
      {
        case 'a': case 'e': case 'i': case 'o': case 'u':
          ++vowels;
          break;

        default:
          ++consonants;
          break;
      }
    }
  }

  std::println("Your input contained {} vowels and {} consonants.", vowels, consonants);
}
```

Here's an example of the output:

```
Enter a line of text:
A nod is as good as a wink to a blind horse.
Your input contained 14 vowels and 18 consonants.
```

The text object contains an empty string initially. You read a line from the keyboard into text using the getline() function. The version of getline() that you have used previously was a member function of the std::cin input stream (used as std::cin.getline(text, max_length)). The version of getline() we used now is a nonmember function (and thus used as std::getline(std::cin, text)), and reads characters from the stream specified by the first argument, cin in this case, until a newline character is read, and the result is stored in the string object specified by the second argument, which is text in this case. This time you don't need to worry about how many characters are in the input. The string object will automatically accommodate however many characters are entered, and the length will be recorded in the object.

You can change the delimiter that signals the end of the input by using a version of std::getline() with a third argument that specifies the new delimiter for the end of the input:

```cpp
std::getline(std::cin, text, '#');
```

This reads characters until a '#' character is read. Because a newline doesn't signal the end of input in this case, you can enter as many lines of input as you like, and they'll all be combined into a single string. Any newline characters that were entered will be present in the string.

You count the vowels and consonants in much the same way as in Ex5_10.cpp, using a for loop. Naturally, you could also use a range-based for loop instead:

```cpp
for (const char ch : text)
{
  if (std::isalpha(ch))                  // Check for a letter
```

```
{
  switch (std::tolower(ch))                    // Convert to lowercase
  {
    ...
```

This code, available in Ex7_02A.cpp, is simpler and easier to understand than the original. The major advantage of using a string object in this example compared to Ex5_10.cpp, though, remains the fact that you don't need to worry about the length of the string that is entered.

Accessing Substrings

You can extract a substring from a string object using its substr() function. Following the C++-style substring marking convention we identified earlier, the first argument of substr() is the index position where the substring starts, the second is the number of characters in the substring. The returned substring is of type std::string. Here's an example:

```
std::string phrase {"The higher the fewer."};
std::string word1 {phrase.substr(4, 6)};      // "higher"
```

This extracts the six-character substring from phrase that starts at index position 4, so word1 will contain "higher" after the second statement executes. If the length you specify for the substring overruns the end of the string object, then the substr() function returns an object containing the characters up to the end of the string. The following statement demonstrates this behavior:

```
std::string word2 {phrase.substr(4, 100)};  // "higher the fewer."
```

Of course, there aren't 100 characters in phrase, let alone in a substring. In this case, the result will be that word2 will contain the substring from index position 4 to the end, which is "higher the fewer.". You could obtain the same result by omitting the length argument and just supplying the first argument that specifies the index of the first character of the substring:

```
std::string word {phrase.substr(4)};         // "higher the fewer."
```

This version of substr() also returns the substring from index position 4 to the end. If you omit both arguments to substr() (a legal, yet less useful option if you ask us), the whole of phrase will be selected as the substring.

If you specify a starting index for a substring that is outside the valid range for the string object, an *exception* of type std::out_of_range will be thrown, and your program will terminate abnormally—unless you've implemented some code to handle the exception. You don't know how to do that yet, but we'll discuss exceptions and how to handle them in Chapter 16.

Comparing Strings

In example Ex7_02, you used an index to access individual characters in a string object for comparison purposes. When you access a character using an index, the result is of type char, so you can use the comparison operators to compare individual characters. You can also compare entire string objects using any of the comparison operators. These are the comparison operators you can use:

>   >=   <   <=   ==   !=   <=>

You can use these to compare two objects of type string or to compare a string object with a string literal or C-style string. When applied to strings, the <=> operator results in a std::strong_ordering (see Chapter 4)—but more on that in the next subsection. The other six operators, of course, result in a Boolean.

For all seven operators, the operands are compared character by character until either a pair of corresponding characters contains different characters or the end of either or both operands is reached. When a pair of characters differs, numerical comparison of the character codes determines which of the strings has the lesser value. If no differing character pairs are found and the strings are of different lengths, the shorter string is "less than" the longer string. Two strings are equal if they contain the same number of characters and all corresponding character codes are equal. Because you're comparing character codes, the comparisons are case sensitive.

The technical term for this string comparison algorithm is *lexicographical comparison*, which is just a fancy way of saying that strings are ordered in the same manner as they are in a dictionary or phone book[3].

You could compare two string objects using this if statement:

```
std::string word1 {"age"};
std::string word2 {"beauty"};
if (word1 < word2)
  std::println("{} comes before {}.", word1, word2);
else
  std::println("{} comes before {}.", word2, word1);
```

Executing these statements will result in the following output:

```
age comes before beauty.
```

This shows that the old saying must be true.

Let's compare strings in a working example. This program reads any number of names and sorts them into ascending sequence:

```
// Ex7_03.cpp - Comparing strings
import std;

int main()
{
  std::vector<std::string> names;       // Vector of names
  std::string input_name;               // Stores a name

  for (;;)                              // Indefinite loop (stopped using break)
  {
    std::print("Enter a name followed by Enter (leave blank to stop): ");
    std::getline(std::cin, input_name); // Read a name and...
    if (input_name.empty()) break;      // ...if it's not empty...
    names.push_back(input_name);        // ...add it to the vector
  }
```

---

[3] Or, for our younger readers who are no longer familiar with archaic paper relics such as dictionaries and phone books, in the same manner as your contacts are ordered on your smartphone.

```cpp
  // Sort the names in ascending sequence
  bool sorted {};
  do
  {
    sorted = true;                          // remains true when names are sorted
    for (std::size_t i {1}; i < names.size(); ++i)
    {
      if (names[i-1] > names[i])
      { // Out of order - so swap names
        names[i].swap(names[i-1]);
        sorted = false;
      }
    }
  } while (!sorted);

  // Find the length of the longest name
  std::size_t max_length{};
  for (const auto& name : names)
    if (max_length < name.length())
      max_length = name.length();

  // Output the sorted names 5 to a line
  const std::size_t field_width{ max_length + 2 };
  std::size_t count {};

  std::println("In ascending sequence the names you entered are:");
  for (const auto& name : names)
  {
    std::print("{:>{}}", name, field_width); // Right-align + dynamic width
    if (!(++count % 5)) std::println("");
  }

  std::println("");
}
```

Here's a sample session with this program:

```
Enter a name followed by Enter (leave blank to stop): Zebediah
Enter a name followed by Enter (leave blank to stop): Meshach
Enter a name followed by Enter (leave blank to stop): Eshaq
Enter a name followed by Enter (leave blank to stop): Abednego
Enter a name followed by Enter (leave blank to stop): Moses
Enter a name followed by Enter (leave blank to stop): Job
Enter a name followed by Enter (leave blank to stop): Bathsheba
Enter a name followed by Enter (leave blank to stop):
In ascending sequence the names you entered are:
   Abednego  Bathsheba      Eshaq        Job    Meshach
      Moses   Zebediah
```

An indefinite for loop collects names from the user, until an empty line is read. To check for an empty input, we use the empty() function—one of many functions std::string has in common with std::vector<> (see also later in this chapter).

The names are stored in a vector of string elements. As you know, using a vector<> container means that an unlimited number of names can be accommodated. The container also acquires memory as necessary to store the string objects and deletes it when the vector is destroyed. The container will also keep track of how many there are, so there's no need to count them independently.

Sorting is implemented using the same bubble sort algorithm that you have seen applied to numerical values before (in Ex5_09). Because you need to compare successive elements in the vector and swap them when necessary, the for loop iterates over the index values for vector elements; a range-based for loop is not suitable here. The names[i].swap(names[i-1]) statement in the for loop swaps the contents of two string objects; it has, in other words, the same effect as the following sequence of assignments:

```cpp
auto temp{ names[i] };      // Out of order - so swap names
names[i] = names[i-1];
names[i-1] = temp;
```

■ **Tip**   Most Standard Library types offer a swap() member function exactly like the one we used in Ex7_03. Besides std::string, this includes all container types (such as std::vector<> and std::array<>), all smart pointer types, and many more. But the std namespace also defines a nonmember function template you can use to the same effect:

```cpp
std::swap(names[i], names[i-1]);
```

The advantage of this template is that it works for fundamental types such as int or double as well. You could try this for instance in Ex5_09 to swap doubles x[i] and x[i+1].

In the second half of the program, there are two range-based for loops. You can write such loops because a vector<> container represents a range. The first range-based for loop determines the length of the longest name. We need this maximum length in the second loop to align the names vertically. The expression in that loop that formats a single name looks as follows:

```cpp
std::print("{:>{}}", name, field_width)    // Right-align (>) + dynamic width ({})
```

This contains a construct that you haven't encountered yet: a *dynamic width*. That is, the width of the output is not hard-wired into the format string, as you're used to by now, but taken from the second input argument, field_width. You specify a dynamic width using a *nested replacement field*, {}, which is replaced at runtime with one of the arguments of std::print(). Suppose that in our example field_width is equal to, say, 11, then this formatting expression becomes equivalent to the following:

```cpp
std::print("{:>11}", name)                 // Right-align (>) + 11 wide
```

A nested replacement field can optionally contain an argument identifier, to facilitate for instance out-of-order arguments, but no other format specifications. Here is an example where we have swapped the second and third arguments of print():

```cpp
std::print("{1:>{0}}", field_width, name) // Right-align (>) + dynamic width ({0})
```

You can also use nested replacement fields to achieve a *dynamic precision*. Besides the width and the precision, no other part of the format specification can be replaced with a nested replacement field.

Three-Way Comparisons

As you'll recall from Chapter 4, a *three-way comparison* determines, in one single expression, whether one value is less than, greater than, or equal to another. For fundamental types such as integers and floating-point numbers, there was actually little point in doing so. But for compound objects such as strings, three-way comparisons can make sense. To illustrate, look at these lovely lyrical lines of code:

```
std::string s1{ "Little Lily Lovelace likes licking lollipops." };
std::string s2{ "Little Lily Lovelace likes leaping lizards." };

if (s1 < s2) ...
else if (s1 > s2) ...
else ...
```

The moment this program determines that s1 < s2, the condition of its first if statement, is false (because the *i* in li*c*king comes after the *e* in l*e*aping), it could in principle already conclude that s1 > s2 will be true. Nevertheless, to evaluate s1 > s2 the comparison will start all the way back at the beginning again: "Little Lily Lovelace etc.". Three-way comparison functions exist to overcome such inefficiencies.

As of C++20 there are two ways to perform three-way comparisons of string objects: the new <=> operator, and the older compare() function. You could thus improve the performance of our Lovely Little Lily Lovelace comparisons as follows, using either <=> or compare():

`const auto order{ s1 <=> s2; };`
`if (std::is_lt(order))`
`...else if (std::is_gt(order)) ...else ...`
	`const int comp{ s1.compare(s2) };`
	`if (comp < 0) ...else if (comp > 0) ...else ...`

You already know <=>, is_lt(), and is_gt() from Chapter 4, so no surprises there (order is of type std::strong_ordering, as mentioned earlier).

The expression s1.compare(s2) similarly compares the contents of the string object s1 with that of the argument to compare(), s2. Unlike the spaceship operator, the compare() member function returns the result of the comparison as a value of type int. This will be a positive integer if s1 is greater than s2, zero if s1 is equal to s2, and a negative integer if s1 is less than s2.

Both alternatives can compare a string object with either another string object, a string literal, or a C-style string. So which should you prefer? Our vote goes to the spaceship operator, <=>. First and foremost, this operator makes subsequent code more readable, especially to those unfamiliar with the return values of older three-way comparison functions such as compare(). And then there is also the following caveat of compare():

■ **Caution** A common mistake is to write an if statement of the form if (s1.compare(s2)), assuming this condition will evaluate to true if s1 and s2 are equal. But the actual result, of course, is precisely the opposite. For equal operands, compare() returns zero, and zero converts to the Boolean value false. To compare for equality, you should use the == operator instead.

The expression if (s1 <=> s2), on the other hand, does not compile. The type of s1 <=> s2 is std::strong_ordering, a class type that purposely does not convert to a Boolean.

Comparing Substrings Using compare()

The compare() function does have one edge over the <=> operator, though: it is far more flexible. You can for instance use it to compare a substring of a string object with the argument:

```
std::string word1 {"A jackhammer"};
std::string word2 {"jack"};
const int result{ word1.compare(2, word2.length(), word2) };
if (result == 0)
  std::println("{} contains {} starting at index 2", word1, word2);
```

The expression that initializes result compares the four-character substring of word1 that starts at index position 2 with word2. This is illustrated in Figure 7-2.

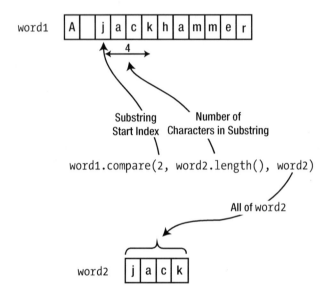

Figure 7-2. *Using compare() with a substring*

The first two arguments mark a substring of word1 using the usual C++-style substring marking. The first argument to compare() is, in other words, the index position of the first character in a substring of word1 that is to be compared with word2. The second argument is the number of characters in the substring, which in our example is sensibly specified as the length of the third argument, word2. Obviously, if the substring length you specify is not the same as the length of the third argument, the substring and the third argument are unequal by definition.

You could use the compare function to search for a substring. Here's an example:

```
std::string text {"Peter Piper picked a peck of pickled peppers."};
std::string word {"pick"};
for (std::size_t i{}; i < text.length() - word.length() + 1; ++i)
  if (text.compare(i, word.length(), word) == 0)
    std::println("text contains {} starting at index {}", word, i);
```

This loop finds word at index positions 12 and 29 in text. The upper limit for the loop variable allows the last word.length() characters in text to be compared with word. This is not the most efficient implementation of the search. When word is found, it would be more efficient to arrange that the next substring of text that is checked is word.length() characters further along, but only if there is still word.length() characters before the end of text. However, there are easier ways to search a string object, as you'll see very soon.

You can compare a substring of one string with a substring of another using the compare() function. This involves passing *five* arguments to compare()! Here's an example:

```
std::string text {"Peter Piper picked a peck of pickled peppers."};
std::string phrase {"Got to pick a pocket or two."};
for (std::size_t i{}; i < text.length() - 3; ++i)
  if (text.compare(i, 4, phrase, 7, 4) == 0)
    std::println("text contains {:?} starting at index {}", phrase.substr(7, 4), i);
```

The two additional arguments are the index position of the substring in phrase and its length. The substring of phrase is compared with the substring of text.

And we're not done yet! The compare() function can also compare a substring of a string object with a null-terminated C-style string.

```
std::string text{ "Peter Piper picked a peck of pickled peppers." };
for (std::size_t i{}; i < text.length() - 3; ++i)
  if (text.compare(i, 4, "pick") == 0)
    std::println("text contains \"pick\" starting at index {}", i);
```

The output from this will be the same as the previous code; "pick" is found at index positions 12 and 29.

Still another option is to select the first n characters from a null-terminated string by specifying the number of characters. The if statement in the loop could be as follows:

```
  if (text.compare(i, 4, "picket", 4) == 0)
    std::println("text contains \"pick\" starting at index {}", i);
```

Luckily, no matter what flavor of compare() you use, the substring marking arguments always follow the conventions we established at the beginning of the chapter. In our latest compare() expression, for instance, "picket" is a C-style string, which means the fourth argument specifies the number of characters from this string to use in the comparison.

■ **Note** You have seen that the compare() function works quite happily with different numbers of arguments of various types. The same was true for the substr() and append() functions we encountered earlier. What you have here are several different functions with the same name. These are called *overloaded functions*, and you'll learn how and why you create them in the next chapter.

Comparing Substrings Using substr()

Of course, if you have trouble remembering the sequence of arguments to the more complicated versions of the compare() function, you can use the substr() function to extract the substring of a string object. You can then use the result with the comparison operators in many cases. For instance, to check whether two substrings are equal, you could write a test as follows:

```
std::string text {"Peter Piper picked a peck of pickled peppers."};
std::string phrase {"Got to pick a pocket or two."};
for (std::size_t i{}; i < text.length() - 3; ++i)
  if (text.substr(i, 4) == phrase.substr(7, 4))
    std::println("text contains {} starting at index {}", phrase.substr(7, 4), i);
```

Unlike the equivalent operation using the compare() function from earlier, this new code is readily understood. Sure, it will be slightly less efficient (because of the creation of the temporary substring objects), but code clarity and readability are far more important here than marginal performance improvements. In fact, this is an important guideline to live by. You should always choose correct and maintainable code over error-prone, obfuscated code, even if the latter may be a few percent faster. You should only ever complicate matters if benchmarking shows a significant performance increase is feasible.

▓ **Tip**   Suppose the creation of the temporary substring objects really bothers you. (It shouldn't, but suppose you're a die-hard C++ developer to whom every byte and clock cycle matters.) You can then replace the first two lines in the preceding example with these:

```
std::string_view text {"Peter Piper picked a peck of pickled peppers."};
std::string_view phrase {"Got to pick a pocket or two."};
```

You will learn all about string_views in Chapter 9, but in a nutshell, string_view allows you to inspect any type of character sequence (in our case, string literals) using the same high-level functions as std::string, but with the additional guarantee that it will never copy any (sub)strings. A string_view object only allows you to *view* a string's characters (hence the name), not to alter, add, or remove them.

Checking the Start or End of a String

At times, the need arises to check whether a string starts or ends with a given substring. Of course, you could do this with either compare() or substr(). Like this, for instance:

```
std::string text {"Start with the end in mind."};
if (text.compare(0, 5, "Start") == 0)
  std::println("The text starts with 'Start'.");
if (text.substr(text.length() - 3, 3) != "end")
  std::println("The text does not end with 'end'.");
```

But this code does not excel in readability, and it's also fairly easy to get those pesky substring indices wrong. Luckily, C++20 introduced two useful member functions to remedy this, starts_with() and ends_with():

```
std::string text {"Start with the end in mind."};
if (text.starts_with("Start"))
  std::println("The text starts with 'Start'.");
if (!text.ends_with("end"))
  std::println("The text does not end with 'end'.");
```

This code is perfectly readable and impossible to get wrong. Besides C-style strings or string objects, both functions work with a single character as well:

```
if (text.ends_with('.'))
  std::println("The text ends with a period.");
```

Moreover, starts_with() and ends_with() are always perfectly safe to use on empty strings (naturally, they both always[4] return false for empty strings). This is not the case with related members such as [], front(), back(), or substr().

Searching Strings

Beyond compare(), you have many other alternatives for searching within a string object. They all involve functions that return an index. We'll start with the simplest sort of search. A string object has a find() function that finds the index of a substring within it. You can also use it to find the index of a given character. The substring you are searching for can be another string object or a string literal. Here's a small example showing these options:

```
// Ex7_04.cpp - Searching within strings
import std;

int main()
{
  std::string sentence {"Manners maketh man"};
  std::string word {"man"};
  std::println("{}", sentence.find(word));  // Prints 15
  std::println("{}", sentence.find("Ma"));  // Prints 0
  std::println("{}", sentence.find('k'));   // Prints 10
  std::println("{}", sentence.find('x'));   // Prints std::string::npos
}
```

In each output statement, sentence is searched from the beginning by calling its find() function. The function returns the index of the first character of the first occurrence of whatever is being sought. In the last statement, 'x' is not found in the string, so the value std::string::npos is returned. This constant represents an illegal character position in a string and is used to signal a failure in a search.

---

[4] Well, almost always, if you're pedantically inclined. Every string begins and ends with the empty string, even empty strings. So, yes, starts_with() and ends_with() technically can return true, but only when called on an empty string with an empty string as argument.

On our computer, Ex7_04 thus produces these four numbers:

```
15
0
10
18446744073709551615
```

As you can tell from this output, std::string::npos is defined to be a very large number. More specifically, it is the largest value that can be represented by the type std::size_t. For 64-bit platforms, this value equals 2^{64}-1, a number in the order of 10^{19}—a one followed by *19* zeros. It is therefore unlikely that you'll be working with strings that are long enough for npos to represent a valid index. To give you an idea, last we counted, you could fit all characters of the English edition of Wikipedia in a string of a mere 24 billion characters—still about 770 *million* times less than npos.

Of course, you can use npos to check for a search failure with a statement such as this:

```cpp
if (sentence.find('x') == std::string::npos)
  std::println("Character not found");
```

▓ **Caution** When used as a Boolean, the std::string::npos constant evaluates to true, not false. The only numeric value that evaluates to false is zero, which is a perfectly valid value for an index. Consequently, you should take care not to write code such as this:

```cpp
if (!sentence.find('x')) // Oops...
    std::println("Character not found");
```

While this if statement may read like something sensible, what it actually does makes considerably less sense. It prints "Character not found" when the character 'x' is found at index 0, that is, for all sentences starting with 'x'.

▓ **Tip** When you are not interested in the index at which that substring or character occurs, but instead simply want to check if a string contains a given substring or character, then you can now also use C++23's contains() function:

```cpp
if (!sentence.contains('x'))        // OK: returns a Boolean (unlike find(): see earlier)
    std::println("Character not found");
if (sentence.contains("substring")) // it won't...
    std::println("sentence contains substring");
```

Searching Within Substrings

An at times interesting variation on the find() function allows you to search part of a string starting from a specified position. For example, with sentence defined as before, you could write this:

```
std::println("{}", sentence.find("an", 1));     // Prints 1
std::println("{}", sentence.find("an", 3));     // Prints 16
```

Each statement searches sentence from the index specified by the second argument, to the end of the string. The first statement finds the first occurrence of "an" in the string. The second statement finds the second occurrence because the search starts from index position 3.

You could search for a string object by specifying it as the first argument to find(). Here's an example:

```
std::string sentence {"Manners maketh man"};
std::string word {"an"};
int count {};    // Count of occurrences
for (std::size_t i {}; i <= sentence.length() - word.length(); )
{
  std::size_t position{ sentence.find(word, i) };
  if (position == std::string::npos)
    break;
  ++count;
  i = position + 1;
}
std::println("{:?} occurs in {:?} {} times.", word, sentence, count); // 2 times...
```

A string index is of type std::size_t, so position that stores values returned by find() is of that type. The loop index, i, defines the starting position for a find() operation, so this is also of type std::size_t. The last occurrence of word in sentence has to start at least word.length() positions back from the end of sentence, so the maximum value of i in the loop is sentence.length() - word.length(). There's no loop expression for incrementing i because this is done in the loop body.

If find() returns npos, then word wasn't found, so the loop ends by executing the break statement. Otherwise, count is incremented, and i is set to one position beyond where word was found, ready for the next iteration. You might think you should set i to be position + word.length(), but this wouldn't allow overlapping occurrences to be found, such as if you were searching for "ana" in the string "ananas".

You can also search a string object for a substring of a C-style string or a string literal. In this case, the first argument to find() is the null-terminated string, the second is the index position at which you want to start searching, and the third is the number of characters of the null-terminated string that you want to take as the string you're looking for. Here's an example:

```
std::println("{}", sentence.find("ananas", 8, 2)); // Prints 16
```

This searches for the first two characters of "ananas" (that is, "an") in sentence, starting from position 8 in sentence (so after Manners). The following variations show the effect of changing the arguments:

```
std::println("{}", sentence.find("ananas", 0, 2)); // Prints 1
std::println("{}", sentence.find("ananas", 8, 3)); // Prints std::string::npos
```

The first search now looks for "an" from the start of sentence, and finds it at index 1. The second search looks for "ana" and fails because that substring isn't in sentence.

Here is a program that searches a `string` object for a given substring and determines how many times the substring occurs:

```
// Ex7_05.cpp - Searching within substrings
import std;

int main()
{
  std::string text;          // The string to be searched
  std::string word;          // Substring to be found
  std::println("Enter the string to be searched and press Enter:");
  std::getline(std::cin, text);

  std::println("Enter the string to be found and press Enter:");
  std::getline(std::cin, word);

  std::size_t count{};       // Count of substring occurrences
  std::size_t index{};       // String index
  while ((index = text.find(word, index)) != std::string::npos)
  {
    ++count;
    index += word.length();  // Advance by full word (discards overlapping occurrences)
  }

  std::println("Your text contained {} occurrences of {:?}.", count, word);
}
```

Here's some sample output:

```
Enter the string to be searched and press Enter:
Smith, where Jones had had "had had", had had "had". "Had had" had had the examiners'
approval.
Enter the string to be found and press Enter:
had
Your text contained 10 occurrences of "had".
```

There are only ten occurrences of "had". "Had" doesn't count because it starts with an uppercase letter. The program searches text for the string in word, both of which are read from the standard input stream using getline(). Input is terminated by a newline, which occurs when you press Enter. The search is conducted in the while loop, which continues as long as the find() function for text does not return npos. A return value of npos indicates that the search target is not found in text from the specified index to the end of the string, so the search is finished. On each iteration when a value other than npos is returned, the string in word has been found in text, so count is incremented, and index is incremented by the length of the string; this assumes that we are not searching for overlapping occurrences. There is quite a lot happening in this loop, so to help you follow the action, the process is shown in Figure 7-3.

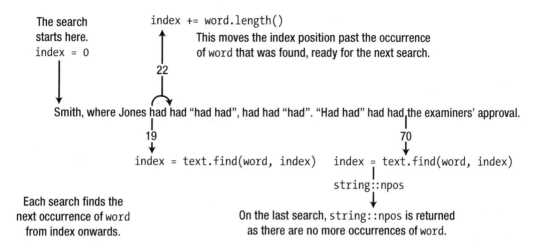

Figure 7-3. *Searching a string*

Searching for Any of a Set of Characters

Suppose you have a string—a paragraph of prose, perhaps—that you want to break up into individual words. You need to find where the separators are, and those could be any of a number of different characters such as spaces, commas, periods, colons, and so on. A function that can find any of a given set of characters in a string would help. This is exactly what the find_first_of() function for a string object does:

```
std::string text {"Smith, where Jones had had \"had had\", had had \"had\"."
                  " \"Had had\" had had the examiners' approval."};
std::string separators {" ,.\""};
std::println("{}", text.find_first_of(separators));        // Prints 5
```

The set of characters sought are defined by a string object that you pass as the argument to the find_first_of() function. The first character in text that's in separators is a comma, so the last statement will output 5. You can also specify the set of separators as a null-terminated string. If you want to find the first vowel in text, for example, you could write this:

```
std::println("{}", text.find_first_of("AaEeIiOoUu"));        // Prints 2
```

The first vowel in text is 'i', at index position 2.

You can search backward from the end of a string object to find the *last* occurrence of a character from a given set by using the find_last_of() function. For example, to find the last vowel in text, you could write this:

```
std::println("{}", text.find_last_of("AaEeIiOoUu"));        // Prints 92
```

The last vowel in text is the second 'a' in approval, at index 92.

You can specify an extra argument to find_first_of() and find_last_of() that specifies the index where the search process is to begin. If the first argument is a null-terminated string, there's an optional third argument that specifies how many characters from the set are to be included.

A further option is to find a character that's *not* in a given set. The find_first_not_of() and find_last_not_of() functions do this. To find the position of the first character in text that isn't a vowel, you could write this:

```cpp
std::println("{}", text.find_first_not_of("AaEeIiOoUu")); // Prints 0
```

The first character that isn't a vowel is clearly the first, at index 0.

Let's try some of these functions in a working example. This program extracts the words from a string. This combines the use of find_first_of() and find_first_not_of(). Here's the code:

```cpp
// Ex7_06.cpp - Searching a string for characters from a set
import std;

int main()
{
  std::string text;                                    // The string to be searched
  std::println("Enter some text terminated by *:\n");
  std::getline(std::cin, text, '*');

  const std::string separators{ " ,;:.\"!?'\n" };      // Word delimiters
  std::vector<std::string> words;                      // Words found
  auto start { text.find_first_not_of(separators) };   // First word start index

  while (start != std::string::npos)                   // Find the words
  {
    auto end{ text.find_first_of(separators, start + 1) }; // Find end of word
    if (end == std::string::npos)                      // Found a separator?
      end = text.length();                             // No, so set to end of text
    words.push_back(text.substr(start, end - start));  // Store the word
    start = text.find_first_not_of(separators, end + 1); // Find first letter of next word
  }

  std::println("Your string contains the following {} words:", words.size());
  unsigned count{};                                    // Number of printed strings
  for (const auto& word : words)
  {
    std::print("{:15}", word);
    if (!(++count % 5)) std::println("");
  }
  std::println("");
}
```

Here's some sample output:

```
Enter some text terminated by *:
To be, or not to be, that is the question.
Whether tis nobler in the mind to suffer the slings and
arrows of outrageous fortune, or by opposing, end them.*
Your string contains the following 30 words:
```

To	be	or	not	to
be	that	is	the	question
Whether	tis	nobler	in	the
mind	to	suffer	the	slings
and	arrows	of	outrageous	fortune
or	by	opposing	end	them

The string variable, text, will contain a string read from the keyboard. The string is read from cin by the getline() function with an asterisk specified as the termination character, which allows multiple lines to be entered. The separators variable defines the set of word delimiters. It's defined as const because these should not be modified. The interesting part of this example is the analysis of the string.

You record the index of the first character of the first word in start. As long as this is a valid index, which is a value other than npos, you know that start will contain the index of the first character of the first word. The while loop finds the end of the current word, extracts the word as a substring, and stores it in the words vector. It also records the result of searching for the index of the first character of the next word in start. The loop continues until a first character is not found, in which case start will contain npos to terminate the loop.

It's possible that the last search in the while loop will fail, leaving end with the value npos. This can occur if text ends with a letter or anything other than one of the specified separators. To deal with this, you check the value of end in the if statement, and if the search did fail, you set end to the length of text. This will be one character beyond the end of the string (because indexes start at 0, not 1) because end should correspond to the position *after* the last character in a word.

Searching a String Backward

The find() function searches forward through a string, either from the beginning or from a given index. The rfind() function, named from reverse find, searches a string in reverse. rfind() comes in the same range of varieties as find(). You can search a whole string object for a substring that you can define as another string object or as a null-terminated string. You can also search for a character. Here's an example:

```
std::string sentence {"Manners maketh man"};
std::string word {"an"};
std::println("{}", sentence.rfind(word));    // Prints 16
std::println("{}", sentence.rfind("man"));   // Prints 15
std::println("{}", sentence.rfind('e'));     // Prints 11
```

Each search finds the last occurrence of the argument to rfind() and returns the index of the first character where it was found. Figure 7-4 illustrates the use of rfind().

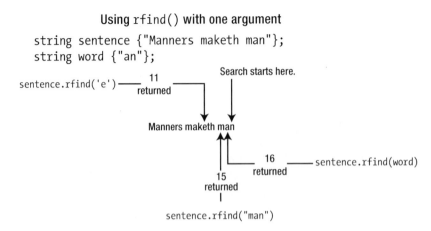

Figure 7-4 content:

Using rfind() with one argument

```
string sentence {"Manners maketh man"};
string word {"an"};
```

sentence.rfind('e') —— 11 returned

Search starts here.

Manners maketh man

16 returned —— sentence.rfind(word)

15 returned

sentence.rfind("man")

As with find(), if the argument is not found,
then the value string::npos is returned.

Figure 7-4. *Searching backward through a string*

Searching with word as the argument finds the last occurrence of "an" in the string. The rfind() function returns the index position of the first character in the substring sought.

If the substring isn't present, npos will again be returned. For example, the following statement will result in this:

```
std::println("{}", sentence.rfind("miners")); // Prints std::string::npos
```

sentence doesn't contain the substring "miners", so npos will be returned and displayed by this statement. The other two searches illustrated in Figure 7-4 are similar to the first. They both search backward from the end of the string looking for the first occurrence of the argument.

Just as with find(), you can supply an extra argument to rfind() to specify the starting index for the backward search, and you can add a third argument when the first argument is a C-style string. The third argument specifies the number of characters from the C-style string that are to be taken as the substring for which you're searching.

Modifying a String

Once you've searched a string and found what you're looking for, you may well want to change the string in some way. You've already seen how you can use an index between square brackets to select a single character in a string object. You can also insert a string into a string object at a given index or replace a substring. Unsurprisingly, to insert a string, you use a function called insert(), and to replace a substring in a string, you use a function called replace(). We'll explain inserting a string first.

Inserting a String

Perhaps the simplest sort of insertion involves inserting a string object before a given position in another string object. Here's an example of how you do this:

```
std::string phrase {"We can insert a string."};
std::string words {"a string into "};
phrase.insert(14, words);
```

Figure 7-5 illustrates what happens. The words string is inserted immediately *before* the character at index 14 in phrase. After the operation, phrase will contain the string "We can insert a string into a string.".

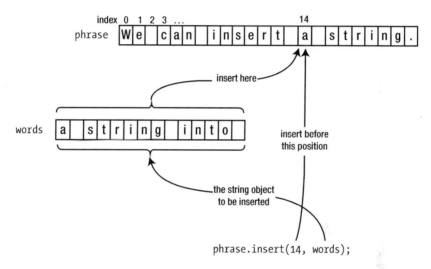

Figure 7-5. *Inserting a string into another string*

You can also insert a null-terminated string into a string object. For example, you could achieve the same result as the previous operation with this statement:

```
phrase.insert(14, "a string into ");
```

Of course, the '\0' character is discarded from a null-terminated string before insertion.

The next level of sophistication is the insertion of a substring of a string object into another string object. In line with the usual *C++-style substring marking* convention, you need to supply two extra arguments to insert(): one specifies the index of the first character in the substring to be inserted, and the other specifies the number of characters in the substring. Here's an example:

```
phrase.insert(13, words, 8, 5);
```

This inserts the five-character substring that starts at position 8 in words, into phrase, preceding index position 13. Given that phrase and words contain the strings as earlier, this inserts " into" into "We can insert a string." so that phrase becomes "We can insert into a string.".

There is a similar facility for inserting a number of characters from a null-terminated string into a `string` object. The following statement produces the same result as the previous one:

```
phrase.insert(13, " into something", 5);
```

As always when marking a substring in C-style strings, 5 indicates the substring length, not an index. This inserts the first five characters of `" into something"` into `phrase` preceding the character at index 13.

There's even a version of `insert()` that inserts a sequence of identical characters:

```
phrase.insert(16, 7, '*');
```

This inserts seven asterisks in `phrase` immediately before the character at index 16. `phrase` will then contain the uninformative sentence `"We can insert a *******string."`.

Replacing a Substring

You can replace any substring of a `string` object with a different string—even if the inserted string and the substring to be replaced have different lengths. We'll return to an old favorite and define `text` like this:

```
std::string text {"Smith, where Jones had had \"had had\", had had \"had\"."};
```

You can replace `"Jones"` with a less common name with this statement:

```
text.replace(13, 5, "Gruntfuttock");
```

Abiding to the usual C++-style substring marking rules, the first argument is the index in `text` of the first character of the substring to be replaced, and the second is the length of the substring. This thus replaces the five characters of `text` that start at index 13 with `"Gruntfuttock"`. If you now output `text`, it would be as follows:

```
Smith, where Gruntfuttock had had "had had", had had "had".
```

A more realistic application of this is to search for the substring to be replaced first. Here's an example:

```
const char substring[] { "Jones" };
text.replace(text.find(substring), std:size(substring), "Gruntfuttock");
```

This finds the position of the first character of `"Jones"` in `text` and passes that as the first argument to `replace()`. The second argument is the length of the substring to replace.

The replacement string can be a `string` object or a null-terminated string. In the former case, you can specify a start index and a length to select a substring as the replacement string. For example, the previous replace operation could have been this:

```
std::string name {"Amos Gruntfuttock"};
text.replace(text.find(substring), std:size(substring), name, 5, 12);
```

These statements have the same effect as the previous use of `replace()` because the replacement string starts at position 5 of `name` (which is the `'G'`) and contains 12 characters.

If the replacement string argument is a C-style string, you must switch to C-style substring marking as well. That is, the next integer argument then specifies the number of characters to use from this replacement string. Here's an example:

```
text.replace(text.find(substring), std:size(substring), "Gruntfuttock, Amos", 12);
```

This time, the string to be substituted consists of the first 12 characters of "Gruntfuttock, Amos", so the effect is the same as the previous replace operation.

A further possibility is to specify the replacement string as multiples of a given character. For example, you could replace "Jones" by three asterisks with this statement:

```
text.replace(text.find(substring), std:size(substring), 3, '*');
```

The result is that text will contain the following:

```
Smith, where *** had had "had had", had had "had".
```

Let's try the replace operation in an example. This program replaces all occurrences of a given word in a string with another word:

```cpp
// Ex7_07.cpp - Replacing words in a string
import std;

int main()
{
  std::string text;                               // The string to be modified
  std::println("Enter a string terminated by *:");
  std::getline(std::cin, text, '*');

  std::string word;                               // The word to be replaced
  std::print("Enter the word to be replaced: ");
  std::cin >> word;

  std::string replacement;                        // The word to be substituted
  std::print("Enter the string to be substituted for {}: ", word);
  std::cin >> replacement;

  if (word == replacement)                        // Verify there's something to do
  {
    std::println("The word and its replacement are the same.\nOperation aborted.");
    return 1;
  }

  std::size_t start {text.find(word)};            // Index of 1st occurrence of word
  while (start != std::string::npos)              // Find and replace all occurrences
  {
    text.replace(start, word.length(), replacement);   // Replace word
    start = text.find(word, start + replacement.length());
  }

  std::println("\nThe string you entered is now:\n{}", text);
}
```

Here's a sample of the output:

```
Enter a string terminated by *:
A rose is a rose is a rose.*
Enter the word to be replaced: rose
Enter the string to be substituted for rose: dandelion

The string you entered is now:
A dandelion is a dandelion is a dandelion.
```

The string that is to have words replaced is read into text by getline(). Any number of lines can be entered and terminated by an asterisk. The word to be replaced and its replacement are read using the extraction operator and therefore cannot contain whitespace. The program ends immediately if the word to be replaced and its replacement are the same.

The index position of the first occurrence of word is used to initialize start. This is used in the while loop that finds and replaces successive occurrences of word. After each replacement, the index for the next occurrence of word in text is stored in start, ready for the next iteration. When there are no further occurrences of word in text, start will contain npos, which ends the loop. The modified string in text is then output.

Removing Characters from a String

You could always remove a substring from a string object using the replace() function; you just specify the replacement as an empty string. But there's also a specific function for this purpose, erase(). As always, you specify the substring to be erased by the index position of the first character and the length. For example, you could erase the first six characters from text like this:

```
text.erase(0, 6);                   // Remove the first 6 characters
```

You would more typically use erase() to remove a specific substring that you had previously searched for, so a more usual example might be as follows:

```
std::string word {"rose"};
std::size_t index {text.find(word)};
if (index != std::string::npos)
  text.erase(index, word.length());  // Second argument is a length, not an index!
```

This searches for word in text and, after confirming that it exists, removes it using erase(). The number of characters in the substring to be removed is obtained by calling the length() function for word.

The erase() function can also be used with either one or no arguments; here's an example:

```
text.erase(5);                      // Removes all but the first 5 characters
text.erase();                       // Removes all characters
```

After this last statement executes, text will be an empty string. Another function that removes all characters from a string object is clear():

```
text.clear();
```

■ **Caution** A common mistake is to call `erase(i)` with a single argument `i` in an attempt to remove a single character at the given index `i`. The actual effect of `erase(i)`, however, is quite different. It removes *all* characters starting from the one at index `i` all the way until the end of the string! To remove a single character at index `i`, you should use `erase(i, 1)` instead.

In C++20 or later, you can easily remove all occurrences of a given character using the nonmember `std::erase()` function. In this example, it is shown gutting a phrase from our favorite tautogram-like movie quote:

```
std::string s{ "The only verdict is vengeance; a vendetta, held as a votive not in vain."};
std::erase(s, 'v');
std::println("{}", s);// The only erdict is engeance; a endetta, held as a otie not in ain.
```

std::string vs. std::vector<char>

We're sure you've noticed that `std::string` is fairly similar to `std::vector<char>`. Both are dynamic arrays of `char` elements, complete with a `[]` operator to emulate plain `char[]` arrays. But the similarity goes well beyond that. A `std::string` object supports nearly all member functions a `std::vector<char>` does. Evidently, this includes `vector<>` functions you already know from Chapter 5:

- A `string` has a `push_back()` function to insert a new character at the end of the string (right before the termination character). It's not used that often, though, as `std::string` objects support the more convenient += syntax to append characters.

- A `string` has an `at()` function that, unlike the `[]` operator, performs bounds checking for the given index.

- A `string` has a `size()` function, which is an alias for `length()`. The latter was added because it's more common to talk about the "length of a string" than the "size of a string."

- A `string` offers `front()` and `back()` convenience functions to access its first and last characters (not counting the null termination character).

- A `string` supports a range of `assign()` functions to reinitialize it. These functions accept argument combinations similar to those you can use between the braced initializers when first initializing a `string`. So, `s.assign(3, 'X')`, for instance, reinitializes s to `"XXX"`, and `s.assign("Reinitialize", 2, 4)` overwrites the contents of the string object s with `"init"`.

If this chapter has made one thing clear, though, then it's that a `std::string` is more than a simple `std::vector<char>`. On top of the functions provided by a `vector<char>`, it offers a wide range of additional, useful functions for common string manipulations such as concatenation, substring access, string searches and replacements, and so on. And of course, a `std::string` is aware of the null character that terminates its char array and knows to take this into account in members such as `size()`, `back()`, and `push_back()`.

▓ **Tip** You can format containers such as std::vector<char> directly using std::print() and format() functions as well. Only by default, character ranges that aren't actually strings are formatted just like any other range; that is, surrounded by [ ] brackets, and with commas between each element. To print such a character range as a string instead, you can specify the s range format type (or ?s if you want escaped string formatting). Some sample code should clarify:

```
std::vector v{ 'N', 'o', 't', ' ', 'a', ' ', 's', 't', 'r', 'i', 'n', 'g' };
std::println("{}", v);     // ['N', 'o', 't', ' ', 'a', ' ', 's', 't', 'r', 'i', 'n', 'g']
std::println("{::}", v);   // [N, o, t,  , a,  , s, t, r, i, n, g] (alternative: {::c})
std::println("{:n:}", v);  // N, o, t,  , a,  , s, t, r, i, n, g (alternative: {:n:c})
std::println("{:s}", v);   // Not a string
std::println("{:?s}", v);  // "Not a string"
```

By default, std::println() uses a format specifier of form ::? (the ? formatting option is applied to any element type that supports it, including type char). To toggle off escaped formatting of the elements, you can use :: or ::c format specifiers (c is the default formatting type of char values); adding an extra n to the range's format specifier removes the [ ] brackets. But this is as close as you can get to regular string formatting, were it not for the s and ?s range formatting types.

Converting Strings into Numbers

Earlier in this chapter you learned that you can use std::to_string() to convert numbers into strings. But what about the other direction? How do you convert strings such as "123" and "3.1415" into numbers? There are several ways to accomplish this in C++, but the easiest option is for sure the std::stoi() function, which, given that its name is short for "string to int," converts a given string to an int:

```
std::string s{ "123" };
int i{ std::stoi(s) };     // i == 123
```

The Standard Library similarly offers stol(), stoll(), stoul(), stoull(), stof(), stod(), and stold() to convert a string into a value of, respectively, type long, long long, unsigned long, unsigned long long, float, double, and long double.

Strings of International Characters

You'll remember from Chapter 1 that, internationally, many more characters are in use than the 128 defined by the standard ASCII character set. French and Spanish, for instance, often use accented letters such as ê, á, or ñ. Languages such as Russian, Arabic, Malaysian, or Japanese use characters that are completely different from those defined by the ASCII standard. The 256 different characters you could potentially represent with a single 8-bit char are not nearly enough to represent all these possible characters. The Chinese script alone consists of many tens of thousands of characters!

Supporting multiple national character sets is an advanced topic, so we'll only introduce the basic facilities that C++ offers—without going into detail about how you apply any of them. Thus, this section is just a pointer to where you should look when working with different national character sets. Potentially, you have four options for working with strings that may contain extended character sets:

- You can define std::wstring objects that contain strings of characters of type wchar_t—the *wide-character type* that is built into your C++ implementation.

- For *n* equal to 8, 16, or 32, you can define std::u*n*string objects to store UTF-*n* encoded strings, using characters of type char*n*_t (of at least, but typically exactly, *n* bits per character).

▒ **Note** All five string types are type aliases for particular instantiations of the same class template, std::basic_string<CharType>. std::string, for instance, is an alias for std::basic_string<char>, and std::wstring is shorthand for std::basic_string<wchar_t>. This explains why all string types offer the same set of functions. You'll understand better how this works after learning about creating your own class templates in Chapter 17.

Strings of wchar_t Characters

The std::wstring type stores strings of characters of type wchar_t. You use objects of type wstring in essentially the same way as objects of type string. You could define a *wide string* object with this statement:

```
std::wstring quote;
```

You write string literals containing characters of type wchar_t between double quotes, but with L prefixed to distinguish them from string literals containing char characters. Thus, you can define and initialize a wstring variable like this:

```
std::wstring aphorism{L"The tigers of wrath are wiser than the horses of instruction."};
```

The L preceding the opening double quote specifies that the literal consists of characters of type wchar_t. Without it, you would have a char string literal, and the statement would not compile.

You can output wide string directly using std::print() or std::println(), but only if the format string is a wide string as well. Here's an example:

```
std::println(L"{}", aphorism);
```

You cannot print wide strings if the format string is a narrow string. The following line therefore does not compile:

```
std::println("{}", aphorism); /* Error: cannot format std::wstring! */
```

Conversely, you *can* format narrow strings if the format string is a wide string. Here is an example (the restrictions for formatting literals are analogous to those for formatting string objects):

```
std::println(L"A {} mind and a {} mouth usually go together.", "narrow", L"wide");
```

std::format() functions support wide strings in an analogous manner. The type of the string object they return matches that of the given format string. std::format(L"...", ...), in other words, produces std::wstring objects instead of std::string objects.

■ **Note**   Standard streams such as std::cout and std::cin do not support wide string input or output. You must use the wide string equivalents of these streams instead. For std::cout and std::cin, these are called std::wcout and std::wcin, respectively.

Nearly all functions we've discussed in the context of string objects apply equally well to wstring objects, so we won't wade through them again. Other functionalities such as the to_wstring() function just take an extra w in their name but are otherwise entirely equivalent. Just remember to specify the L prefix with string and character literals when you are working with wstring objects and you'll be fine!

One problem is that the character encoding used by wide string literals, and expected by functions accepting wide characters strings, is implementation defined, so it can vary from one platform to another. Native APIs of the Windows operating system generally expect strings encoded using UTF-16. So when compiling for Windows, wchar_t strings will normally consist of 2-byte UTF-16 encoded characters as well. Most other implementations, however, use 4-byte UTF-32 encoded wchar_t characters. If you need to support portable multinational character sets, you may be better off using types u8string, u16string, or u32string, which are described in the next section.

Objects That Contain Unicode Strings

The Standard Library defines three further types to store strings of Unicode characters. Objects of type std::u8string / u16string / u32string store strings of characters of type char8_t / char16_t / char32_t respectively. They are intended to contain character sequences that are encoded using UTF-8, UTF-16, and UTF-32, respectively. Like std::wstring objects, you can use a literal of the appropriate type to initialize objects of these types. Here's an example:

```
std::u8string quote{u8"Character is the real foundation of success."};// char8_t characters
std::u16string question {u"Whither atrophy?"};                         // char16_t characters
std::u32string sentence {U"This sentence contains three errars."};     // char32_t characters
```

These statements demonstrate that you prefix a string literal containing char8_t characters with u8, a literal containing char16_t characters with u, and one containing char32_t characters with U. Objects of the u8string, u16string, and u32string types have the same set of functions as the string type.

In principle, you can use the basic std::string type to store strings of UTF-8 characters as well. In fact, prior to C++20, that was the only way you could store UTF-8 strings, because the types char8_t and std::u8string were only introduced in C++20. The problem with this, though, is that you cannot easily differentiate between strings encoded using UTF-8 and strings encoded using the implementation-defined narrow character encoding (which is often, but certainly not always, UTF-8).

■ **Tip**   Ideally, you should always store UTF-*n* encoded strings in std::u*n*string objects, and leave std::string and std::wstring for those cases where portability is not required, and/or for interaction with native APIs of the operating system. Unfortunately, std::string / char have been used to store UTF-8 encoded strings for a very long time, so you may have to be pragmatic when interfacing with legacy APIs that have not yet been upgraded to use std::u8string / char8_t.

One important limitation of the standard Unicode string types is that they know nothing about Unicode encodings. The UTF-8 encoding, for instance, uses between one and four bytes to encode a single character, but the functions that operate on string objects will not recognize this. This means, for instance, that the length() function will return the wrong length if the string includes any characters that require two or three bytes to represent them, as this code snippet illustrates:

```
std::u8string s{u8"字符串"};       // UTF-8 encoding of the Chinese word for "string"
std::println("{}", s.length());   // Length: 9 code units, and not 3 Chinese characters!
```

■ **Tip**   Support for manipulating Unicode strings in the C++23 Standard Library is limited, and even more so in some of its implementations. For one, there are no std::u*n*cout streams, no std::to_u*n*string() functions, no support for formatting char*n*_t strings with std::println() or std::format(), and so on. In C++17, moreover, most functionality that the Standard Library offers to convert between the various Unicode encodings has been deprecated. If producing and manipulating portable Unicode-encoded text is important for your application, you are much better off using a third-party library. Viable candidates include the ICU library, the Boost.Locale library, and Qt's QString.

Raw String Literals

As you know, regular string literals must not contain line breaks or tab characters. To include such special characters, they must be escaped—line breaks and tabs then become \n and \t, respectively. For obvious reasons, the double quote character must also be escaped to \". Because of these escape sequences, the backslash character itself needs to be escaped to \\ as well.

At times, however, you'll find yourself having to define string literals that contain some or even many of these special characters. Having to continuously escape these characters is not only tedious but also renders these literals unreadable. Here are some examples:

```
auto path{ "C:\\ProgramData\\MyCompany\\MySoftware\\MyFile.ext" };
auto escape{ u8"The \"\\\\\" escape sequence is a backslash character, \\." };
auto text{ L"First line.\nSecond line.\nThird line.\nThe end." };
std::regex reg{ "\\*+" };        // Regular expression that matches one or more * characters
```

The latter is an example of a *regular expression*—a string that defines a process for searching and transforming text. Essentially, a regular expression defines patterns that are to be matched in a string, and patterns that are found can be replaced or reordered. C++ supports regular expressions via the <regex> module, though a discussion of this falls outside the scope of this book. The main point here is that regular expression strings often contain backslash characters. Having to use the escape sequence for each backslash character can make a regular expression particularly difficult to specify correctly and very hard to read.

The *raw string literal* was introduced to solve these problems. A raw string literal can include any character, including backslashes, tabs, double quotes, and newlines, so no escape sequences are necessary. A raw string literal includes an R in the prefix, and on top of that, the character sequence of the literal is surrounded by round parentheses. The basic form of a raw string literal is thus R"(...)". The parentheses themselves are not part of the literal. Any of the types of literals you have seen can be specified as raw literals by adding the same prefix as before—L, u, U, or u8—prior to the R. Using raw string literals, our earlier examples thus become as follows:

```
auto path{ R"(C:\ProgramData\MyCompany\MySoftware\MyFile.ext)" };
auto escape{ u8R"(The "\\" escape sequence is a backslash character, \.)" };
auto text
{ LR"(First line.
Second line.
Third line.
The end.)" };
std::regex reg{ R"(\*+)" };        // Regular expression that matches one or more * characters
```

Within a raw string literal, no escaping is required. This means you can simply copy and paste, for instance, a Windows path sequence into them or even an entire play of Shakespeare complete with quote characters and line breaks. In the latter case, you should take care about leading whitespace and all line breaks, as these will be included into the string literal as well, together with all other characters between the surrounding "( )" delimiters.

Notice that not even double quotes need or even can be escaped, which begs the question: What if your string literal itself somewhere contains the sequence)"? That is, what if it contains a) character followed by a "? Here's such a problematic literal:

```
R"(The answer is "(a - b)" not "(b - a)")"   // Error!
```

The compiler will object to this string literal because the raw literal appears to be terminated somewhere halfway already, right after (a - b. But if escaping is not an option—any backslash characters would simply be copied into the raw literal as is—how else can you make it clear to the compiler that the string literal should include this first)" sequence, as well as the next one after (b - a? The answer is that the delimiters that mark the start and end of a raw string literal are flexible. You can use any delimiter of the form "char_sequence(to mark the beginning of the literal, as long as you mark the end with a matching sequence,)char_sequence". Here's an example:

```
R"*(The answer is "(a - b)" not "(b - a)")*"
```

This is now a valid raw string literal. You can basically choose any char_sequence you want, as long as you use the same sequence at both ends:

```
R"Fa-la-la-la-la(The answer is "(a - b)" not "(b - a)")Fa-la-la-la-la"
```

The only limitations are that char_sequence must not be longer than 16 characters and may not contain any parentheses, spaces, control characters, or backslash characters.

Summary

In this chapter, you learned how you can use the string type that's defined in the Standard Library. The string type is much easier and safer to use than C-style strings, so it should be your first choice when you need to process character strings.

The following are the important points from this chapter:

- The `std::string` type stores a character string.

- Like `std::vector<char>`, it is a dynamic array—meaning it will allocate more memory when necessary.

- Internally, the terminating null character is still present in the array managed by a `std::string` object, but only for compatibility with legacy and/or C functions. As a user of `std::string`, you normally do not need to know that it even exists. All `string` functionality transparently deals with this legacy character for you.

- You can store `string` objects in an array or, better still, in a sequence container such as a `vector<>`.

- You can access and modify individual characters in a `string` object using an index between square brackets. Index values for characters in a `string` object start at 0.

- You can use the + operator to concatenate a `string` object with a string literal, a character, or another `string` object.

- If you want to concatenate a value of one of the fundamental numeric types, such as an `int` or a `double`, you must first convert these numbers into a string. Your easiest—though least flexible—option for this is the `std::to_string()` function template. If you need more control over formatting, you can use `std::format()` instead.

- Objects of type `string` have functions to search, modify, and extract substrings.

- `std::stoi()`, `stol()`, `stoll()`, `stoul()`, `stoull()`, `stof()`, `stod()`, and `stold()` convert a `string` into a value of, respectively, type `int`, `long`, `long long`, `unsigned long`, `unsigned long long`, `float`, `double`, and `long double`.

- Objects of type `wstring` contain strings of characters of type `wchar_t`.

- Objects of type `unstring` contain strings of characters of type `charn_t`, for an n equal to 8, 16, or 32.

EXERCISES

The following exercises enable you to try what you've learned in this chapter. If you get stuck, look back over the chapter for help. If you're still stuck after that, you can download the solutions from the Apress website (https://www.apress.com/gp/services/source-code), but that really should be a last resort.

Exercise 7-1. Write a program that reads and stores the first names of any number of students, along with their grades. Calculate and output the average grade and output the names and grades of all the students in a table with the name and grade for three students on each line.

Exercise 7-2. Write a program that reads text entered over an arbitrary number of lines. Find and record each unique word that appears in the text and record the number of occurrences of each word. Output the words and their occurrence counts. Words and counts should align in columns. The words should align to the left; the counts to the right. There should be three words per row in your table.

Exercise 7-3. Write a program that reads a text string of arbitrary length from the keyboard and prompts for entry of a word that is to be found in the string. The program should find and replace all occurrences of this word, regardless of case, by as many asterisks as there are characters in the word. It should then output the new string. Only whole words are to be replaced. For example, if the string is "Our house is at your disposal." and the word that is to be found is "our", then the resultant string should be as follows: "*** house is at your disposal." and not "*** house is at y*** disposal.".

Exercise 7-4. Write a program that prompts for the input of two words and determines whether one is an anagram of the other. An anagram of a word is formed by rearranging its letters, using each of the original letters precisely once. For instance, *listen* and *silent* are anagrams of one another, but *listens* and *silent* are not.

Exercise 7-5. Generalize the program in Exercise 7-4 such that it ignores spaces when deciding whether two strings are anagrams. With this generalized definition, *funeral* and *real fun* are considered anagrams, as are *eleven plus two* and *twelve plus one*, and *desperation* and *a rope ends it*.

Exercise 7-6. Write a program that reads a text string of arbitrary length from the keyboard followed by a string containing one or more letters. Output a list of all the whole words in the text that begin with any of the letters, uppercase or lowercase.

Exercise 7-7. Create a program that reads an arbitrarily long sequence of integer numbers typed by the user into a single string object. The numbers of this sequence are to be separated by spaces and terminated by a # character. The user may or may not press Enter between two consecutive numbers. Next, extract all numbers from the string one by one.

Exercise 7-8. A *tautogram* is a body of text in which all words start with the same letter. In English, an example would be "Truly tautograms triumph, trumpeting trills to trounce terrible travesties." Ask the user for a string, and verify whether it is a tautogram (ignoring casing). If it is, output also the letter by which each word starts.

Note: True tautograms are truly tough to throw together, so perhaps you can bend the rules a bit? Maybe allow short words to glue the text together (such as "a", "to", "is", "are", etc.), or only require a certain percentage of words to begin with the same letter? Have some fun with it!

Exercise 7-9. Extend your solution to Exercise 7-8 to remove all occurrences of the tautogram's beginning letter (ignoring casing). You could do it the easy way (remember the Standard Library function you can use to accomplish this?), but perhaps it's more interesting to do it the hard way and write the complete code yourself?

CHAPTER 8

Defining Functions

Segmenting a program into manageable chunks of code is fundamental to programming in every language. A *function* is a basic building block in C++ programs. So far, every example has had one function, main(), and has typically used functions from the Standard Library. This chapter is all about defining your own functions with names that you choose.

In this chapter, you will learn

- What a function is and why you should segment your programs into functions

- How to declare and define functions

- How data is passed to a function and how a function can return a value

- What the difference is between pass-by-value and pass-by-reference and how to choose between both mechanisms

- What the best way is to pass strings to a function

- How to specify default values for function parameters

- What the preferred way is to return a function's output in modern C++

- How using const as a qualifier for a parameter type affects the operation of a function

- The effect of defining a variable as static within a function

- How to create multiple functions that have the same name but different parameters—a mechanism you'll come to know as *function overloading*

- What recursion is and how to apply it to implement elegant algorithms

Segmenting Your Programs

All the programs you have written so far have consisted of just one function, main(). A real-world C++ application consists of many functions, each providing a distinct, well-defined capability. Execution starts in main(), which must be defined in the global namespace. main() calls other functions, each of which may call other functions, and so on. The functions other than main() can be defined in a namespace that you create.

When one function calls another that calls another that calls another, you have a situation where several functions are in action concurrently. Each that has called another that has not yet returned will be waiting for the function that was called to end. Obviously, something must keep track of from where in memory each function call was made and where execution should continue when a function returns. This information is recorded and maintained automatically in the *stack*. We introduced the stack when we explained free store memory, and the stack is often referred to as the *call stack* in this context. The call stack records all the outstanding function calls and details of the data that was passed to each function. The debugging facilities that come with most C++ development systems usually provide ways for you to view the call stack while your program executes.

Functions in Classes

A class defines a new type, and each class definition will usually contain functions that represent the operations that can be carried out with objects of the class type. You have already used functions that belong to a class extensively. In the previous chapter, you used functions that belong to the string class, such as the length() function, which returns the number of characters in the string object, and the find() function for searching a string. Functions that belong to classes are fundamental in object-oriented programming, which you'll learn about from Chapter 12 onward.

Characteristics of a Function

A function should perform a single, well-defined action and should be relatively short. Most functions do not involve many lines of code, certainly not hundreds of lines. This applies to all functions, including those that are defined within a class. Several of the working examples you saw earlier could easily be divided into functions. If you look again at Ex7_06.cpp, for instance, you can see that what the program does falls naturally into three distinct actions. First the text is read from the input stream, then the words are extracted from the text, and finally the words that were extracted are output. Thus, the program could be defined as three functions that perform these actions, plus the main() function that calls them.

Defining Functions

A *function* is a self-contained block of code with a specific purpose. Function definitions in general have the same basic structure as main(). A function definition consists of a *function header* followed by a block that contains the code for the function. The function header specifies three things:

- The return type, which is the type of value, if any, that the function returns when it finishes execution. A function can return data of any type, including fundamental types, class types, pointer types, or reference types. It can also return nothing, in which case you specify the return type as void.

- The name of the function. Functions are named according to the same rules as variables.

- The number and types of data items that can be passed to the function when it is called. This is called the *parameter list*, and it appears as a comma-separated list between parentheses following the function name.

A general representation of a function looks like this:

```
return_type function_name(parameter_list)
{
  // Code for the function...
}
```

Figure 8-1 shows an example of a function definition. It implements the well-known fundamental mathematical power or exponentiation operation, which for any integral number $n > 0$ is defined as follows.

$$\text{power}(x, 0) = 1$$

$$\text{power}(x, n) = x^n = \underbrace{x * x * \cdots * x}_{n \text{ times}} \qquad \text{power}(x, -n) = x^{-n} = \frac{1}{\underbrace{x * x * \cdots * x}_{n \text{ times}}}$$

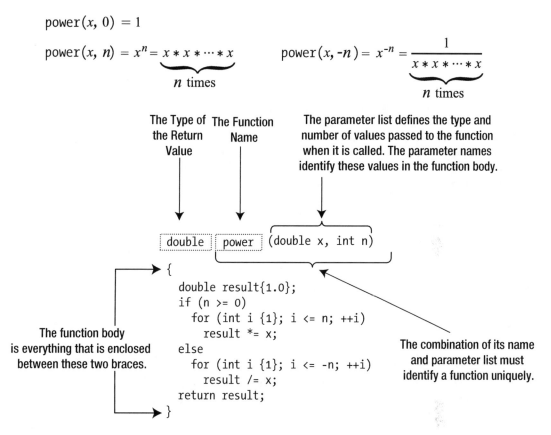

Figure 8-1. *An example of a function definition*

If nothing is to be passed to a function when it is called, then nothing appears between the parentheses. If there is more than one item in the parameter list, they are separated by commas. The power() function in Figure 8-1 has two *parameters*, x and n. The parameter names are used in the body of the function to access the corresponding values that were passed to the function. Our power function could be called from elsewhere in the program as follows:

```
double number {3.0};
const double result { power(number, 2) };
```

When this call to power() is evaluated, the code in the function body is executed with the parameters x and n initialized to 3.0 and 2, respectively, with 3.0 being the value of the number variable. The term *argument* is used for the values that are passed to a function when called. So in our example, number and 2 are arguments, and x and n are the corresponding parameters. The sequence of arguments in a function call must correspond to the sequence of the parameters in the parameter list of the function definition.

More specifically, their types should match. If they do not match exactly, the compiler will apply implicit conversions whenever possible. Here's an example:

```
float number {3.0f};
const double result { power(number, 2) };
```

Even though the type of the first argument passed here is `float`, this code snippet will still compile; the compiler implicitly converts the argument to the type of its corresponding parameter. If no implicit conversion is possible, compilation will, of course, fail.

The conversion from `float` to `double` is lossless since a `double` generally has twice as many bits available to represent the number—and hence the name `double`. So, this conversion is always safe. The compiler will happily perform the opposite conversion for you as well, though. That is, it will implicitly convert a `double` argument when assigned to a `float` parameter. This is a so-called narrowing conversion; because a `double` can represent numbers with much greater precision than a `float`, information may be lost during this conversion. Most compilers will issue a warning when it performs such narrowing conversions.

The combination of the function name and the parameter list is called the *signature* of a function. The compiler uses the signature to decide which function is to be called in any particular instance. Thus, functions that have the same name must have parameter lists that differ in some way to allow them to be distinguished. As we will discuss in detail later, such functions are called *overloaded* functions.

▦ **Tip**   While it made for compact code that fits nicely in Figure 8-1, from a coding style point of view the parameter names x and n used by our definition of `power()` do not particularly excel in clarity. One could perhaps argue that x and n are still acceptable in this specific case because `power()` is a well-known mathematical function and x and n are commonplace in mathematical formulas. That notwithstanding, in general we highly recommend you use more descriptive parameter names. Instead of x and n, for instance, you should probably use base and exponent, respectively. In fact, you should always choose descriptive names for just about everything: function names, variable names, class names, and so on. Doing so consistently will go a long way toward keeping your code easy to read and understand.

Our `power()` function returned a value of type `double`. Not every function, though, has to return a value—it might just write something to a file or a database or modify some global state. The `void` keyword can be used to specify that such a function does not return a value. For instance, after typing `std::println("{}", value)` a gazillion times, surely you'd appreciate a function to print, say, a value of type `double` without having to type `"{}"` first? The following function definition accomplishes precisely that:

```
void println(double value) { std::println("{}", value); }
```

This function simply prints a number to standard output. There is therefore nothing to return. This is expressed by its `void` return type. Note also that it is perfectly fine to reuse the name `println()`, especially since our function is defined outside of the `std` namespace.

▦ **Note**   A function with a return type specified as `void` doesn't return a value, so it can't be used in most expressions. Attempting to use such a function in this way will cause a compiler error message.

> ▓ **Tip** Later in this chapter you'll see how you could add any number of `println()` functions to print `value` arguments of types other than `double` through *function overloading*. And in Chapter 10, you'll see how you could accomplish this for all types at once using a single *function template*.

The Function Body

Calling a function executes the statements in the function body with the parameters having the values you pass as arguments. Returning to our definition of `power()` in Figure 8-1, the first line of the function body defines the `double` variable, `result`, initialized with `1.0`. `result` is an automatic variable so only exists within the body of the function. This means that `result` ceases to exist after the function finishes executing.

The calculation is performed in one of two `for` loops, depending on the value of `n`. If `n` is greater than or equal to zero, the first `for` loop executes. If `n` is zero, the body of the loop doesn't execute at all because the loop condition is immediately `false`. In this case, `result` is left at `1.0`. Otherwise, the loop variable `i` assumes successive values from 1 to `n`, and `result` is multiplied by `x` on each iteration. If `n` is negative, the second `for` loop executes, which divides `result` by `x` on each loop iteration.

The variables that you define within the body of a function and all the parameters are local to the function. You can use the same names in other functions for quite different purposes. The scope of each variable you define within a function is from the point at which it is defined until the end of the block that contains it. The only exceptions to this rule are variables that you define as `static`, and we'll discuss these later in the chapter.

Let's give the `power()` function a whirl in a complete program.

```cpp
// Ex8_01.cpp - Calculating powers
import std;

// Function to calculate x to the power n
double power(double x, int n)
{
  double result {1.0};
  if (n >= 0)
  {
    for (int i {1}; i <= n; ++i)
      result *= x;
  }
  else // n < 0
  {
    for (int i {1}; i <= -n; ++i)
      result /= x;
  }
  return result;
}

int main()
{
  // Calculate powers of 8 from -3 to +3
  for (int i {-3}; i <= 3; ++i)
    std::print("{:10g}", power(8.0, i));

  std::println("");
}
```

This program produces the following output:

```
0.00195312    0.015625     0.125       1       8       64       512
```

All the action occurs in the for loop in main(). The power() function is called seven times. The first argument is 8.0 on each occasion, but the second argument has successive values of i, from –3 to +3. Thus, seven values are outputs that correspond to 8^{-3}, 8^{-2}, 8^{-1}, 8^{0}, 8^{1}, 8^{2}, and 8^{3}.

▪ **Tip** While it is instructive to write your own power() function, there is of course already one provided by the Standard Library. The Standard Library offers a variety of std::pow(base, exponent) functions similar to our version, except that they are designed to work optimally with all numeric parameter types—that is, not just with double and int but also with, for instance, float or long double base values, or noninteger exponents. You should always choose the predefined mathematical functions; they will almost certainly be far more efficient and accurate than anything you could write yourself.

Return Values

A function with a return type other than void *must* return a value of the type specified in the function header. The only exception to this rule is the main() function, where, as you know, reaching the closing brace is equivalent to returning 0. Normally, though, the return value is calculated within the body of the function and is returned by a return statement, which ends the function, and execution continues from the calling point. There can be several return statements in the body of a function with each potentially returning a different value. The fact that a function can return only a single value might appear to be a limitation, but this isn't the case. The single value that is returned can be anything you like: an array, a container such as std::vector<>, or even a container with elements that are containers.

How the return Statement Works

The return statement in the previous program returns the value of result to the point where the function was called. The result variable is local to the function and ceases to exist when the function finishes executing, so how is it returned? The answer is that a *copy* of the double being returned is made automatically, and this copy is made available to the calling function. The general form of the return statement is as follows:

```
return expression;
```

expression must evaluate to a value of the type that is specified for the return value in the function header or must be convertible to that type. The expression can be anything, as long as it produces a value of an appropriate type. It can include function calls and can even include a call of the function in which it appears, as you'll see later in this chapter.

If the return type is specified as void, no expression can appear in a return statement. It must be written simply as follows:

```
return;
```

If the last statement in a function body executes so that the closing brace is reached, this is equivalent to executing a return statement with no expression. In a function with a return type other than void, this is an error, and the function will not compile—except in main(), of course, where omitting a return statement is equivalent to returning 0.

Function Declarations

Ex8_01.cpp works perfectly well as written, but let's try rearranging the code so that the definition of main() *precedes* the definition of the power() function in the source file. The code in the program file will look like this:

```
// Ex8_02.cpp - Calculating powers - rearranged
import std;

int main()
{
  // Calculate powers of 8 from -3 to +3
  for (int i {-3}; i <= 3; ++i)
    std::print("{:10g}", power(8.0, i));

  std::println("");
}

// Function to calculate x to the power n
double power(double x, int n)
{
  double result {1.0};
  if (n >= 0)
  {
    for (int i {1}; i <= n; ++i)
      result *= x;
  }
  else // n < 0
  {
    for (int i {1}; i <= -n; ++i)
      result /= x;
  }
  return result;
}
```

If you attempt to compile this, you won't succeed. The compiler has a problem because the power() function that is called in main() is not defined yet when it is processing main(). The reason is that the compiler processes a source file from top to bottom. Of course, you could revert to the original version, but in some situations, this won't solve the problem. There are two important issues to consider:

- As you'll see later, a program can consist of several source files. The definition of a function that is called in one source file may be contained in a separate source file.

- Suppose you have a function A() that calls a function B(), which in turn calls A(). If you put the definition of A() first, it won't compile because it calls B(); the same problem arises if you define B() first because it calls A().

Naturally, there is a solution to these difficulties. You can *declare* a function before you use or define it by means of a *function prototype*.

▓ **Note**   Functions that are defined in terms of each other, such as the A() and B() functions we described just now, are called *mutually recursive functions*. We'll talk more about recursion near the end of this chapter.

Function Prototypes

A *function prototype* is a statement that describes a function sufficiently for the compiler to be able to compile calls to it. It defines the function name, its return type, and its parameter list. A function prototype is sometimes referred to as a *function declaration*. A function can be compiled only if the call is preceded by a function declaration in the source file. The definition of a function also doubles as a declaration, which is why you didn't need a function prototype for power() in Ex8_01.cpp.

You could write the function prototype for the power() function as follows:

```
double power(double x, int n);
```

If you place function prototypes at the beginning of a source file, the compiler can compile the code regardless of where the function definitions are. Ex8_02.cpp will compile if you insert the prototype for the power() function before the definition of main().

The function prototype shown earlier is identical to the function header with a semicolon appended. A function prototype is always terminated by a semicolon, but in general, it doesn't have to be *identical* to the function header. You can use different names for the parameters from those used in the function definition (but not different types, of course). Here's an example:

```
double power(double value, int exponent);
```

This works just as well. The compiler only needs to know the *type* each parameter is, so you can omit the parameter names from the prototype, like this:

```
double power(double, int);
```

There is no particular merit in writing function prototypes like this. It is much less informative than the version with parameter names. If both function parameters were of the same type, then a prototype like this would not give any clue as to which parameter was which. We recommend that you always include descriptive parameter names in function prototypes.

It could be a good idea to always write prototypes for each function that is defined in a source file—with the exception of main(), which never requires a prototype. Specifying prototypes near the start of the file removes the possibility of compiler errors arising from functions not being sequenced appropriately. It also allows other programmers to get an overview of the functionality of your code.

Passing Arguments to a Function

It is important to understand precisely how arguments are passed to a function. This affects how you write functions and ultimately how they operate. There are also a number of pitfalls to be avoided. In general, the function arguments should correspond in type and sequence to the list of parameters in the function definition. You have no latitude so far as the sequence is concerned, but you do have some flexibility in the argument types. If you specify a function argument of a type that doesn't correspond to the parameter type, then the compiler inserts an implicit conversion of the argument to the type of the parameter where possible. The rules for automatic conversions of this kind are the same as those for automatic conversions in an assignment statement. If an automatic conversion is not possible, you'll get an error message from the compiler. If such implicit conversions result in potential loss of precision, compilers generally issue a warning. Examples of such narrowing conversions are conversions from long to int, double to float, or int to float (see also Chapter 2).

There are two mechanisms by which arguments are passed to functions, *pass-by-value* and *pass-by-reference*. We'll explain the pass-by-value mechanism first.

Pass-by-Value

With the pass-by-value mechanism, the values of variables or constants you specify as arguments are not passed to a function at all. Instead, copies of the arguments are created, and these copies are transferred to the function. This is illustrated in Figure 8-2, using the power() function again.

```
double value {20.0};
int index {3};
double result {power(value, index)};
```

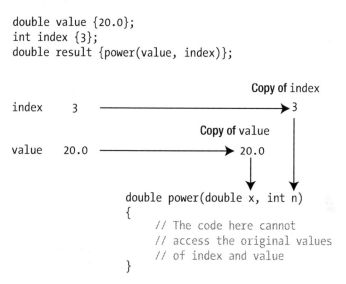

Figure 8-2. *The pass-by-value mechanism for arguments to a function*

Each time you call the power() function, the compiler arranges for copies of the arguments to be stored in a temporary location in the call stack. During execution, all references to the function parameters in the code are mapped to these temporary copies of the arguments. When execution of the function ends, the copies of the arguments are discarded.

We can demonstrate the effects of this with a simple example. The following calls a function that attempts to modify one of its arguments, and of course, it fails miserably:

```
// Ex8_03.cpp - Failing to modify the original value of a function argument
import std;

double changeIt(double value_to_be_changed);    // Function prototype

int main()
{
  double it {5.0};
  double result {changeIt(it)};

  std::println("After function execution, it = {}", it);
  std::println("Result returned is {}", result);
}

// Function that attempts to modify an argument and return it
double changeIt(double it)
{
  it += 10.0;                        // This modifies the copy
  std::println("Within function, it = {}", it);
  return it;
}
```

This example produces the following output:

```
Within function, it = 15
After function execution, it = 5
Result returned is 15
```

The output shows that adding 10 to it in the changeIt() function has no effect on the variable it in main(). The it variable in changeIt() is local to the function, and it refers to a copy of whatever argument value is passed when the function is called. Of course, when the value of it that is local to changeIt() is returned, a copy of its current value is made, and it's this copy that's returned to the calling program.

Pass-by-value is the default mechanism by which arguments are passed to a function. It provides a lot of security to the calling function by preventing the function from modifying variables that are owned by the calling function. However, sometimes you do want to modify values in the calling function. Is there a way to do it when you need to? Sure there is; one way is to use a pointer.

Passing a Pointer to a Function

When a function parameter is a pointer type, the pass-by-value mechanism operates just as before. However, a pointer contains the address of another variable; a copy of the pointer contains the same address and therefore points to the same variable.

If you modify the definition of the first changeIt() function to accept an argument of type double*, you can pass the address of it as the argument. Of course, you must also change the code in the body of changeIt() to dereference the pointer parameter. The code is now like this:

```cpp
// Ex8_04.cpp - Modifying the value of a caller variable
import std;

double changeIt(double* pointer_to_it);     // Function prototype

int main()
{
  double it {5.0};
  double result {changeIt(&it)};                // Now we pass the address

  std::println("After function execution, it = {}", it);
  std::println("Result returned is {}", result);
}

// Function to modify an argument and return it
double changeIt(double* pit)
{
  *pit += 10.0;                               // This modifies the original double
  std::println("Within function, *pit = {}", *pit);
  return *pit;
}
```

This version of the program produces the following output:

```
Within function, *pit = 15
After function execution, it = 15
Result returned is 15
```

Figure 8-3 illustrates the way this works.

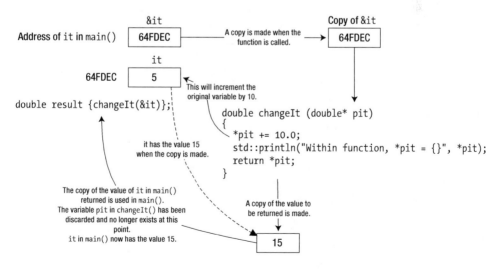

Figure 8-3. *Passing a pointer to a function*

This version of changeIt() serves only to illustrate how a pointer parameter can allow a variable in the calling function to be modified—it is not a model of how a function should be written. Because you are modifying the value of it directly, returning its value is somewhat superfluous.

Passing an Array to a Function

An array name is essentially an address, so you can pass the address of an array to a function just by using its name. The address of the array is copied and passed to the function. This provides several advantages:

- First, passing the address of an array is an efficient way of passing an array to a function. Passing all the array elements by value would be time-consuming because every element would be copied. In fact, you can't pass all the elements in an array by value as a single argument because each parameter represents a single item of data.

- Second, and more significantly, because the function does not deal with the original array variable but with a copy, the code in the body of the function can treat a parameter that represents an array as a pointer in the fullest sense, including modifying the address that it contains. This means you can use the power of pointer notation in the body of a function for parameters that are arrays. Before we get to that, let's try the most straightforward case first—handling an array parameter using array notation.

This example includes a function to compute the average of the elements in an array:

```
// Ex8_05.cpp - Passing an array to a function
import std;

double average(double array[], std::size_t count); // Function prototype

int main()
{
  double values[] {1.0, 2.0, 3.0, 4.0, 5.0, 6.0, 7.0, 8.0, 9.0, 10.0};
  std::println("Average = {}", average(values, std::size(values)));
}

// Function to compute an average
double average(double array[], std::size_t count)
{
  double sum {};                      // Accumulate total in here
  for (std::size_t i {}; i < count; ++i)
    sum += array[i];                  // Sum array elements
  return sum / count;                 // Return average
}
```

This produces the following brief output:

```
Average = 5.5
```

The average() function works with an array containing any number of double elements. As you can see from the prototype, it accepts two arguments: the array address and a count of the number of elements. The type of the first parameter is specified as an array of any number of values of type double. You can pass any one-dimensional array of elements of type double as an argument to this function, so the second parameter that specifies the number of elements is essential. The function will rely on the correct value for the count parameter being supplied by the caller. There's no way to verify that it is correct, so the function will quite happily access memory locations outside the array if the value of count is greater than the array length. With this definition, it is up to the caller to ensure that this doesn't happen.

And in case you were wondering, no, you cannot circumvent the need for the count parameter by using either the sizeof operator or std::size() inside the average() function. Remember, an array parameter such as array simply stores the address of the array, not the array itself. So, the expression sizeof(array) would return the size of the memory location that contains the *address* of the array and not the size of the entire array. A call of std::size() with an array parameter name will simply not compile because std::size() has no way of determining the array's size either. Without the definition of the array, the compiler has no way to determine its size. It cannot do so from only the array's address.

Within the body of average(), the computation is expressed in the way you would expect. There's no difference between this and the way you would write the same computation directly in main(). The average() function is called in main() in the output statement. The first argument is the array name, values, and the second argument is an expression that evaluates to the number of array elements.

The elements of the array that is passed to average() are accessed using normal array notation. We've said that you can also treat an array passed to a function as a pointer and use pointer notation to access the elements. Here's how average() would look in that case:

```
double average(double* array, std::size_t count)
{
  double sum {};                       // Accumulate total in here
  for (std::size_t i {}; i < count; ++i)
    sum += *array++;                    // Sum array elements
  return sum / count;                  // Return average
}
```

For all intents and purposes, both notations are completely equivalent. In fact, as you saw in Chapter 5, you can freely mix both notations. You can, for instance, use array notation with a pointer parameter:

```
double average(double* array, std::size_t count)
{
  double sum {};                       // Accumulate total in here
  for (std::size_t i {}; i < count; ++i)
    sum += array[i];                   // Sum array elements
  return sum / count;                  // Return average
}
```

There really is no difference at all in the way any of these function definitions are evaluated. In fact, the following two function prototypes are considered identical by the compiler:

```
double average(double array[], std::size_t count);
double average(double* array, std::size_t count);
```

We will revisit this later in the section on function overloading.

▓ **Caution** There is a common and potentially dangerous misconception about passing fixed-size arrays to functions. Consider the following variant of the average() function:

```
double average10(double array[10]) /* The [10] does not mean what you might expect! */
{
  double sum {};                     // Accumulate total in here
  for (std::size_t i {}; i < 10; ++i)
   sum += array[i];                  // Sum array elements
   return sum / 10;                  // Return average
}
```

Clearly, this function was written to average exactly ten values; no more, no less. We invite you to replace average() in Ex8_05.cpp with this average10() function and update its main() function accordingly. As the values array in Ex8_05 consists of precisely 10 values of type double, the resulting program should compile and run just fine. But now, let's see what happens if we change the body of main() to pass only 3 values instead of the expected 10:

```
double triplet[] { 1.0, 2.0, 3.0 };  // Only three values!!!
std::println("Average = {}", average10(triplet));
```

The signature of average10()—which unfortunately is perfectly legal C++ syntax—creates the false expectation that the compiler will enforce that only arrays of size ten are passed to this function. You'd therefore expect the compiler to reject this change because triplet clearly contains only 3 values. But sadly, this is not the case. The resulting program, available as Ex8_05A.cpp, will compile just fine. And if you run it, average10() will blindly read beyond the bounds of the triplet array. Obviously, no good can come of this. If the program does not crash, at best it will produce garbage output.

The root of the problem is that, unfortunately, the C++ language dictates that a compiler is supposed to treat a function signature of this form

```
double average10(double array[10])
```

as synonymous with both of the following:

```
double average10(double array[])
double average10(double* array)
```

Because of this, you should never use a dimension specification when passing an array by value; it only creates false expectations. An array that is passed by value is *always* passed as a pointer, and its dimensions are not checked by the compiler. We will see later that you can safely pass given-size arrays to a function using pass-by-reference instead of pass-by-value.

const Pointer Parameters

The average() function only needs to access values of the array elements; it doesn't need to change them. It would be a good idea to make sure that the code in the function does not inadvertently modify elements of the array. Specifying the parameter type as const will do that:

```
double average(const double* array, std::size_t count)
{
  double sum {};           // Accumulate total in here
  for (std::size_t i {}; i < count; ++i)
    sum += *array++;       // Sum array elements
  return sum / count;      // Return average
}
```

By adding this const qualifier, you tell the compiler to verify that the elements of the array are not modified in the body of the function. That is, if you would now accidentally type (*array)++ instead of *array++, for instance, compilation will fail. Of course, you must modify the function prototype to reflect the new type for the first parameter; remember that pointer-to-const types are quite different from pointer-to-non-const types.

Specifying a pointer parameter as const has two consequences: the compiler checks the code in the body of the function to ensure that you don't try to change the value pointed to, and it allows the function to be called with an argument that points to a constant.

▓ **Note**   The other parameter in our latest definition of average(), count, is not const. If a non-pointer parameter is passed by value, it does not need to be declared const, at least not for the same reason. The pass-by-value mechanism makes a *copy* of the argument when the function is called, so you are already protected from modifying the original value from within the function.

That said, it does remain good practice to mark variables as const if they will or should not change during a function's execution. This general guideline applies to *any* variable—including those declared in the parameter list. For that reason, and for that reason only, you might still consider declaring count as const. This would, for instance, prevent you from accidentally writing ++count somewhere in the function's body, which could have disastrous results indeed. But know that you would then be marking *a local copy* as a constant and that it is by no means required to add const to prevent changes to the original value.

Passing a Multidimensional Array to a Function

Passing a multidimensional array to a function is quite straightforward. Suppose you have a two-dimensional array defined as follows:

```
double beans[3][4] {};
```

The prototype of a hypothetical yield() function would look like this:

```
double yield(double beans[][4], std::size_t count);
```

In theory, you could specify the first array dimension in the type specification for the first parameter as well, but it is best not to. The compiler would again simply ignore this, analogous to what happened to the average10() function we discussed earlier. The size of the second array dimension does have the desired effect, though—C++ is fickle that way. Any two-dimensional array with 4 as a second dimension can be passed to this function, but arrays with 3 or 5 as a second dimension cannot.

Let's try passing a two-dimensional array to a function in a concrete example:

```cpp
// Ex8_06.cpp - Passing a two-dimensional array to a function
import std;

double yield(const double values[][4], std::size_t n);

int main()
{
  double beans[3][4] {  { 1.0,    2.0,    3.0,    4.0},
                        { 5.0,    6.0,    7.0,    8.0},
                        { 9.0,   10.0,   11.0,   12.0}  };

  std::println("Yield = {}", yield(beans, std::size(beans)));
}

// Function to compute total yield
double yield(const double array[][4], std::size_t size)
{
  double sum  {};
  for (std::size_t i {}; i < size; ++i)                      // Loop through rows
  {
    for (std::size_t j {}; j < std::size(array[i]); ++j) // Loop through elements in a row
    {
      sum += array[i][j];
    }
  }
  return sum;
}
```

This produces the following output:

```
Yield = 78
```

The first parameter to the yield() function is defined as a const array of an arbitrary number of rows of four elements of type double. When you call the function, the first argument is the beans array, and the second argument is the length of the array. This evaluates to the number of rows in the array.

Pointer notation doesn't apply particularly well with a multidimensional array. In pointer notation, the statement in the nested for loop would be as follows:

```cpp
sum += *(*(array+i)+j);
```

Surely, you'll agree that the computation is clearer in array notation!

▦ **Note**   Because the size of `array[i]` is known to the compiler, you can replace the inner loop of the `yield()` function of Ex8_06 with a range-based `for` loop as follows:

```
for (double val : array[i])      // Loop through elements in a row
{
  sum += val;
}
```

You cannot replace the outer loop with a range-based `for` loop as well, though, nor can you use `std::size()` there. Remember, there is no way for the compiler to know the first dimension of the `double[][4]` array; only the second dimension or higher of an array can be fixed when passing it by value.

Pass-by-Reference

As you may recall, a *reference* is an alias for another variable. You can specify a function parameter as a reference as well, in which case the function uses the *pass-by-reference* mechanism with the argument. When the function is called, an argument corresponding to a reference parameter is not copied. Instead, the reference parameter is initialized with the argument. Thus, it becomes an alias for the argument in the calling function. Wherever the parameter name is used in the body of the function, it is as if it accesses the argument value in the calling function directly.

You specify a reference type by adding & after the type name. To specify a parameter type as "reference to `string`," for example, you write the type as `string&`. Calling a function that has a reference parameter is no different from calling a function where the argument is passed by value. Using references, however, improves performance with objects such as type `string`. The pass-by-value mechanism copies the object, which would be both time- and memory-consuming with a long string. With a reference parameter, there is no copying.

References vs. Pointers

In many regards, references are similar to pointers. To see the similarity, let's use a variation of Ex8_04 with two functions: one that accepts a pointer as an argument and one that accepts a reference instead:

```
// Ex8_07.cpp - Modifying the value of a caller variable - references vs pointers
import std;

void change_it_by_pointer(double* pointer_to_it);      // Pass pointer (by value)
void change_it_by_reference(double& reference_to_it);  // Pass by reference

int main()
{
  double it {5.0};

  change_it_by_pointer(&it);      // Now we pass the address
  std::println("After first function execution, it = {}", it);

  change_it_by_reference(it);     // Now we pass a reference, not the value!
  std::println("After second function execution, it = {}", it);
}
```

```
void change_it_by_pointer(double* pointer_to_it)
{
  *pointer_to_it += 10.0;      // This modifies the original double
}
void change_it_by_reference(double& reference_to_it)
{
  reference_to_it += 10.0;     // This modifies the original double as well!
}
```

The result is that the original it value in main() is updated twice, once per function call:

```
After first function execution, it = 15
After second function execution, it = 25
```

The most obvious difference is that to pass a pointer, you need to take the address of a value first using the address-of operator. Inside the function you then must dereference that pointer again to access the value. For a function that accepts its arguments by reference, you have to do neither. But note that this difference is purely syntactical; in the end, both have the same effect. In fact, compilers will mostly compile references in the same way as pointers.

So, which mechanism should you use, as they appear to be functionally equivalent? That's a fair question. Let's therefore consider some of the facets that play a role in this decision.

The single most distinctive feature of a pointer is that it can be nullptr, whereas a reference must always refer to something. So if you want to allow the possibility of a null argument, you cannot use a reference. Of course, precisely because a pointer parameter can be null, you're almost forced to always test for nullptr before using it. References have the advantage that you do not need to worry about nullptrs.

As Ex8_07 shows, the syntax for calling a function with a reference parameter is indeed no different from calling a function where the argument is passed by value. On the one hand, because you do not need the address-of and dereferencing operators, reference parameters allow for a more elegant syntax. On the other hand, however, precisely the fact that there is no syntactical difference means that references can sometimes cause surprises. And code that surprises is bad code because surprises lead to bugs. Consider, for instance, the following function call:

```
do_it(it);
```

Without a prototype or the definition of do_it(), you have no way of knowing whether the argument to this function is passed either by reference or by value. So, you also have no way of knowing whether the previous statement will modify the it value—provided it itself is not const, of course. This property of pass-by-reference can sometimes make code harder to follow, which may lead to surprises if values passed as arguments are changed when you did not expect them to be.

▨ **Tip** Declare all variables whose value is not supposed to change after initialization as const. This will make your code more predictable and hence easier to read and less prone to subtle bugs. Moreover, and perhaps even more importantly, *always* add const to the type of pointer or reference parameters if the function does not modify the corresponding arguments. First, this makes it easier for programmers to use your functions because they can easily understand what will or will not be modified just by looking at its signature. Second, reference-to-const parameters allow your functions to be called with const values. As we will show in the next section, const values cannot be assigned to a reference-to-non-const parameter.

To summarize, because they are so similar, the choice between pointer or reference arguments is not always clear-cut. In fact, it often is a matter of personal preference which one to use. Here are some guidelines:

- If you want to allow `nullptr` arguments, you cannot use references. Conversely, pass-by-reference can be seen as a contract that a value is not allowed to be null. Note already that instead of representing optional values as a nullable pointer, you may also want to consider the use of `std::optional<>`. We'll discuss this option in Chapter 9.

- Using reference parameters allows for a more elegant syntax but may mask that a function is changing a value. Never change an argument value if it is not clear from the context—from the function name, for instance—that this will happen.

- Because of the potential risks, some coding guidelines advise to never use reference-to-non-`const` parameters and advocate to instead always use pointer-to-non-`const` parameters. Personally, we would not go that far. There is nothing inherently wrong with a reference-to-non-`const`, as long as it is predictable for the caller which arguments may become modified. Choosing descriptive function and parameter names is always a good start to make a function's behavior more predictable.

- Passing arguments by reference-to-`const` is generally preferred over passing a pointer-to-`const` value. Because this is such a common case, we'll present you with a bigger example in the next subsection.

Input vs. Output Parameters

In the previous section, you saw that a reference parameter enables the function to modify the argument within the calling function. However, calling a function that has a reference parameter is syntactically indistinguishable from calling a function where the argument is passed by value. This makes it particularly important to use a reference-to-`const` parameter in a function that does not change the argument. Because the function won't change a reference-to-`const` parameter, the compiler will allow both `const` and non-`const` arguments. But only non-`const` arguments can be supplied for a reference-to-non-`const` parameter.

Let's investigate the effect of using reference parameters in a new version of `Ex7_06.cpp` that extracts words from text:

```
// Ex8_08.cpp - Using a reference parameter
import std;

using std::string;
using std::vector;

void find_words(vector<string>& words, const string& str, const string& separators);
void list_words(const vector<string>& words);

int main()
{
  std::string text;                                // The string to be searched
  std::println("Enter some text terminated by *:");
  std::getline(std::cin, text, '*');

  const std::string separators {" ,;:.\"!?'\n"};   // Word delimiters
  std::vector<std::string> words;                  // Words found
```

```
  find_words(words, text, separators);
  list_words(words);
}

void find_words(vector<string>& words, const string& text, const string& separators)
{
  std::size_t start {text.find_first_not_of(separators)};// First word start index

  while (start != std::string::npos)                      // Find the words
  {
    std::size_t end {text.find_first_of(separators, start + 1)}; // Find end of word
    if (end == string::npos)                              // Found a separator?
      end = text.length();                                // No, so set to end of text

    words.push_back(text.substr(start, end - start));     // Store the word
    start = text.find_first_not_of(separators, end + 1);  // Find 1st character of next word
  }
}

void list_words(const vector<string>& words)
{
  std::println("Your string contains the following {} words:", words.size());
  unsigned count {};                    // Number of outputted words
  for (const auto& word : words)
  {
    std::print("{:>15}", word);
    if (!(++count % 5))
      std::println("");
  }
  std::println("");
}
```

The output is the same as Ex7_06.cpp. Here's a sample:

```
Enter some text terminated by *:
Never judge a man until you have walked a mile in his shoes.
Then, who cares? He is a mile away and you have his shoes!*
Your string contains the following 26 words:
          Never          judge              a            man          until
            you           have         walked              a           mile
             in            his          shoes           Then            who
          cares             He             is              a           mile
           away            and            you           have            his
          shoes
```

There are now two functions in addition to main(): find_words() and list_words(). Note how the code in both functions is the same as the code that was in main() in Ex7_06.cpp. Dividing the program into three functions makes it easier to understand and does not increase the number of lines of code significantly.

The find_words() function finds all the words in the string identified by the second argument and stores them in the vector specified by the first argument. The third parameter is a string object containing the word separator characters.

The first parameter of find_words() is a reference, which avoids copying the vector<string> object. More important, though, it is a reference to a *non*-const vector<>, which allows us to add values to the vector from inside the function. Such a parameter is sometimes called an *output parameter* because it is used to collect a function's output. Parameters whose values are purely used as input are then called *input parameters*.

▓ **Tip**   In principle, a parameter can act as both an input and an output parameter. Such a parameter is called an *input-output parameter*. A function with such a parameter, in one way or another, first reads from this parameter, uses this input to produce some output, and then stores the result into the same parameter. It is generally better to avoid input-output parameters, though, even if that means adding an extra parameter to your function. Code tends to be much easier to follow if each parameter serves a single purpose—a parameter should be either input or output, not both.

The find_words() function does not modify the values passed to the second and third parameters. Both are, in other words, input parameters and should therefore never be passed by reference-to-non-const. Reference-to-non-const parameters should be reserved for those cases where you need to modify the original value—in other words, for output parameters. For input parameters, only two main contenders remain: pass-by-reference-to-const or pass-by-value. And because string objects would otherwise be copied, the only logical conclusion is to declare both input parameters as const string&.

In fact, if you'd declare the third parameter to find_words() as a reference to a non-const string, the code wouldn't even compile. Give it a try if you will. The reason is that the third argument in the function call in main(), separators, is a const string object. You cannot pass a const object as the argument for a reference-to-non-const parameter. That is, you can pass a non-const argument to a reference-to-const parameter but never the other way around. In short, a T value can be passed to both T& and const T& references, whereas a const T value can be passed only to a const T& reference. And this is only logical. If you have a value that you're allowed to modify, there's no harm in passing it to a function that will not modify it—not modifying something that you're allowed to modify is fine. The converse is not true; if you have a const value, you'd better not be allowed to pass it to a function that might modify it!

The parameter for list_words(), finally, is reference-to-const because it too is an input parameter. The function only accesses the argument; it doesn't change it.

▓ **Tip**   Input parameters should usually be references-to-const. Only smaller values, most notably those of fundamental types, should be passed by value. Use reference-to-non-const only for output parameters, and even then you should often consider returning a value instead. We'll study how to return values from functions soon.

Passing Arrays by Reference

At first sight, it may seem that for arrays there would be little benefit from passing them by reference. After all, if you pass an array by value, the array elements themselves already do not get copied. Instead, a copy is made of the pointer to the first element of the array. Passing an array also already allows you to modify the values of the original array—unless you add const, of course. So surely this already covers both advantages typically attributed to passing by reference: no copying and the possibility to modify the original value.

While this is most certainly true, you did already discover the main limitation with passing an array by value earlier, namely, that there is no way to specify the array's first dimension in a function signature, at least not in such a way that the compiler enforces that only arrays of exactly that size are passed to the function. A lesser-known fact, though, is that you *can* accomplish this by passing arrays by reference.

To illustrate, we invite you to again replace the average() function in Ex8_05.cpp with an average10() function, but this time with the following variant:

```cpp
double average10(const double (&array)[10])   /* Only arrays of length 10 can be passed! */
{
  double sum {};                    // Accumulate total in here
  for (std::size_t i {}; i < 10; ++i)
    sum += array[i];                // Sum array elements
  return sum / 10;                  // Return average
}
```

As you can see, the syntax for passing an array by reference is somewhat more complex. The const could in principle be omitted from the parameter type, but it is preferred here because you do not modify the values of the array in the function's body. The extra parentheses surrounding &array are required, though. Without them, the compiler would no longer interpret the parameter type as a reference to an array of doubles but as an array of references to double. Because arrays of references are not allowed in C++, this would then result in a compiler error:

```cpp
double average10(const double& array[10])   // Error: array of double& is not allowed
```

With our new and improved version of average10() in place, the compiler does live up to expectations. Attempting to pass any array of a different length should now result, as desired, in a compiler error:

```cpp
double values[] { 1.0, 2.0, 3.0 };                // Only three values!!!
std::println("Average = {}", average10(values));  // Error...
```

Note, moreover, that if you pass a fixed-size array by reference, it *can* be used as input to operations such as sizeof(), std::size(), and range-based for loops. This was not possible with arrays that are passed by value. You can use this to eliminate the two occurrences of 10 from the body of average10():

```cpp
double average10(const double (&array)[10])
{
  double sum {};                    // Accumulate total in here
  for (double val : array)
    sum += val;                     // Sum array elements
  return sum / std::size(array);    // Return average
}
```

■ **Tip** You have already seen a more modern alternative to working with arrays of fixed length in Chapter 5: std::array<>. Using values of this type, you can just as safely pass fixed-size arrays by reference and without having to remember the tricky syntax for passing plain fixed-size arrays by reference:

```cpp
double average10(const std::array<double, 10>& values)
```

In Chapter 9, we explain another interesting alternative, namely `std::span<double, 10>`, which allows you to write functions that work efficiently for inputs of both C-style arrays of size 10 and `std::array<double, 10>` objects.

We made three variants of this program available to you: Ex8_09A, which uses pass-by-reference; Ex8_09B, which eliminates the magic numbers; and Ex8_09C, to show the use of `std::array<>`.

References and Implicit Conversions

A program often uses many different types, and as you know, the compiler is usually quite happy to assist you by implicitly converting between them. Whether or not you should always be happy about such conversions is another matter, though. That aside, most of the time it is convenient that code such as the following snippet will compile just fine, even though it assigns an `int` value to a differently typed `double` variable:

```cpp
int i{};                    // Declare some differently typed variables
double d{};
...
d = i;                      // Implicit conversion from int to double
```

For function arguments that employ pass-by-value, it is only natural that such conversions occur as well. For instance, given the same two variables i and d, a function with signature `f(double)` can hence be called not only with `f(d)` or `f(1.23)` but also with differently typed arguments such as `f(i)`, `f(123)`, or `f(1.23f)`.

Implicit conversions thus remain quite straightforward for pass-by-value. Let's take a look at how they fare with reference arguments:

```cpp
// Ex8_10.cpp - Implicit conversions of reference parameters
import std;

void double_it(double& it)     { it *= 2; }
void print_it(const double& it) { std::println("{}", it); }

int main()
{
  double d{123};
  double_it(d);
  print_it(d);

  int i{456};
  // double_it(i);          /* error, does not compile! */
  print_it(i);
}
```

We first define two trivial functions: one that doubles `double`s and one that prints them to the standard output, followed by a line break. The first part of `main()` then shows that these work for a `double` variable—obviously, you should thus see the number 246 appear in the output. The interesting parts of this example are its final two statements, of which the first is commented out because it would not compile.

Let's consider the `print_it(i)` statement first and explain why it is in fact already a minor miracle that this even works at all. The function `print_it()` operates on a reference to a `const double`, a reference that as you know is supposed to act as an alias for a double that is defined elsewhere. On a typical system, print_it() will ultimately read the eight bytes found in the memory location behind this reference and print out the 64 bits it finds there in some human-readable format using std::println(). But the value that we passed to the function as an argument is no double; it is an int! This int is generally only four bytes big, and its 32 bits are laid out completely differently than those of a double. So, how can this function be reading from an alias for a double if there is no such double defined anywhere in the program? The answer is that the compiler, before it calls print_it(), implicitly creates a temporary double value somewhere in memory, assigns it the converted int value, and then passes a reference to this temporary memory location to print_it().

Such implicit conversions are only supported for reference-to-const parameters, not for reference-to-non-const parameters. Suppose for argument's sake that the double_it(i) statement on the second-to-last line will compile without error. Surely, the compiler will then similarly convert the int value 456 to a double value 456.0, store this temporary double somewhere in memory, and apply the function body of double_it() to it. Then you'd have a temporary double somewhere, now with value 912.0, and an int value i that is still equal to 456. Now, while in theory the compiler could convert the resulting temporary value back to an int, the designers of the C++ programming language decided that that would be a bridge too far. The reason is that generally such inverse conversions would inevitably mean loss of information. In our case, this would involve a conversion from double to int, which would result in the loss of at least the fractional part of the number. The creation of temporaries is therefore never allowed for reference-to-non-const parameters. This is also why the statement double_it(i) is invalid in standard C++ and should fail to compile.

Default Argument Values

There are many situations in which it would be useful to have default argument values for one or more function parameters. This would allow you to specify an argument value only when you want something different from the default. A simple example is a function that outputs a standard error message. Most of the time, a default message will suffice, but occasionally an alternative is needed. You can do this by specifying a default argument value in the function prototype. You could define a function to output a message like this:

```
void print_error(std::string message)
{
    std::println("{}", message);
}
```

You specify the default argument value like this:

```
void print_error(std::string message = "Program Error");
```

If both are separate, you need to specify default values in the function prototype and not in the function definition. The reason is that when resolving the function calls, the compiler needs to know whether a given number of arguments is acceptable.

To output the default message, you call such functions without the corresponding argument:

```
print_error();        // Outputs "Program Error"
```

To output a particular message, you specify the argument:

```
print_error("Nothing works!");
```

In the previous example, the parameter was passed by value. Of course, you can also specify default values for parameters that are passed by reference-to-`const` in the same manner:

```
void print_error(const std::string& message = "Program Error");  // Better...
```

From what you learned in the previous section, it also should come as no surprise that default values for which the implicit conversion requires the creation of a temporary object—as is in our example—are illegal for reference-to-non-`const` parameters. Hence, the following should not compile:

```
void print_error(std::string& message = "Program Error"); /* Does not compile */
```

Specifying default argument values can make functions simpler to use. Naturally, you aren't limited to just one parameter with a default value.

▦ **Note**   We will have more to say about implicit argument conversions of string literals to temporary `string` objects in Chapter 9. Spoiler alert: `std::string_view` parameters are preferred over reference-to-`const`-`string` parameters because they avoid the creation of temporary `string` objects when passing string literals as arguments, for instance.

Multiple Default Argument Values

All function parameters that have default values must be placed together at the end of the parameter list. When an argument is omitted in a function call, all subsequent arguments in the list must also be omitted. Thus, parameters with default values should be sequenced from the least likely to be omitted to the most likely at the end. These rules are necessary for the compiler to be able to process function calls.

Let's contrive an example of a function with several default argument values. Suppose that you wrote a function to display one or more data values, several to a line, as follows:

```
void print_data(const int data[], std::size_t count, const std::string& title,
                unsigned width, unsigned perLine)
{
  std::println("{}", title);              // Display the title

  // Output the data values
  for (std::size_t i {}; i < count; ++i)
  {
    std::print("{:{}}", data[i], width); // Display a data item
    if ((i+1) % perLine == 0)             // Newline after perLine values
      std::println("");
  }
  std::println("");
}
```

The `data` parameter is an array of values to be displayed, and `count` indicates how many there are. The third parameter of type `const std::string&` specifies a title that is to head the output. The fourth parameter determines the field width for each item, and the last parameter is the number of data items per line. This function has a lot of parameters. It's clearly a job for default argument values! Here's an example:

```
// Ex8_11.cpp - Using multiple default argument values
import std;

// The function prototype including default arguments
void print_data(const int data[], std::size_t count = 1,
                const std::string& title = "Data Values",
                unsigned width = 10, unsigned perLine = 5);
int main()
{
  int samples[] {1, 2, 3, 4, 5, 6, 7, 8, 9, 10, 11, 12};

  int dataItem {-99};
  print_data(&dataItem);

  dataItem = 13;
  print_data(&dataItem, 1, "Unlucky for some!");

  print_data(samples, std::size(samples));
  print_data(samples, std::size(samples), "Samples");
  print_data(samples, std::size(samples), "Samples", 6);
  print_data(samples, std::size(samples), "Samples", 8, 4);
}
```

The definition of print_data() in Ex8_11.cpp can be taken from earlier in this section. Here's the output:

```
Data Values
      -99
Unlucky for some!
       13
Data Values
        1         2         3         4         5
        6         7         8         9        10
       11        12
Samples
        1         2         3         4         5
        6         7         8         9        10
       11        12
Samples
    1     2     3     4     5
    6     7     8     9    10
   11    12
Samples
        1         2         3         4
        5         6         7         8
        9        10        11        12
```

The prototype for print_data() specifies default values for all parameters except the first. There are five ways to call this function: you can specify all five arguments, or you can omit the last one, the last two, the last three, or the last four. You can supply just the first to output a single data item, as long as you are happy with the default values for the remaining parameters.

Remember that you can omit arguments only at the end of the list; you are not allowed to omit the second and the fifth. Here's an example:

```
print_data(samples, , "Samples", 15);                    // Wrong!
```

▩ **Tip**   Default argument values should be predictable, sensible, and safe. The following, for instance, would be a perfectly sensible use of a default argument:

```
void println(double value, const std::string& format = "{}");
```

When you encounter println(1.23) in code, you indeed expect it to print a line containing "1.23". You also never loose precision with default formatting, making this also a safe default. At the other end of the spectrum lies the following function signature:

```
void println(double value, const std::string& format = "{:a}");
```

With this default format specifier, println(1.23) would print "1.3ae147ae147aep+0" (the a type specifier denotes hexadecimal formatting of floating-point numbers)—hardly something anyone would ever expect or want by default. But it does not have to be that extreme. Consider this default:

```
void println(double value, const std::string& format = "{:.6f}");
```

A fixed precision of 6 digits is rarely, if ever, appropriate (which makes it all the more unfortunate that it is, in fact, the default precision used by most older C and C++ formatting functionality, including std::printf(), std::to_string(), and std::cout!). More often than not, 6 digits are more than you want to show to a human reader. And for computer-to-computer communication you should, as a principle, never loose precision, meaning 6 digits is then rarely enough. If most callers of a function end up having to override the default, it's better to not specify a default at all.

Arguments to main()

You can define main() so that it accepts arguments that are entered on the command line when the program executes. The parameters you can specify for main() are standardized; you can define main() either with no parameters, or in the following form:

```
int main(int argc, char* argv[])
{
  // Code for main()...
}
```

The first parameter, argc, is a count of the number of string arguments that were found on the command line. It is type int for historical reasons, not std::size_t or unsigned int as you might expect from a parameter that cannot be negative. The second parameter, argv, is an array of pointers to the command-line arguments, including the program name. The array type implies that all command-line arguments are received as C-style strings. The program name used to invoke the program is normally recorded in the first element of argv, argv[0].[1] The last element in argv (argv[argc]) is always nullptr, so the number of elements in argv will be argc + 1. We'll give you a couple of examples to make this clear. Suppose that to run the program, you enter just the program name on the command line:

```
Myprog
```

In this case, argc will be 1, and argv[] contains two elements. The first is the address of the string "Myprog", and the second will be nullptr.

Suppose you enter this:

```
Myprog  2 3.5  "Rip Van Winkle"
```

Now argc will be 4, and argv will have five elements. The first four elements will be pointers to the strings "Myprog", "2", "3.5", and "Rip Van Winkle". The fifth element, argv[4], will be nullptr.

What you do with the command-line arguments is entirely up to you. The following program shows how you access the command-line arguments:

```cpp
// Ex8_12.cpp - Program that echoes its command line arguments
import std;

int main(int argc, char* argv[])
{
  for (int i {}; i < argc; ++i)
    std::println("{}", argv[i]);
}
```

This lists the command-line arguments, including the program name. Command-line arguments can be anything at all—filenames to a file copy program, for example, or the name of a person to search for in a contact file. They can be anything that is useful to have entered when program execution is initiated.

Returning Values from a Function

As you know, you can return a value of any type from a function. This is quite straightforward when you're returning a value of one of the basic types, but there are some pitfalls when you are returning a pointer or a reference.

Returning a Pointer

When you return a pointer from a function, it must contain either nullptr or an address that is still valid in the calling function. In other words, the variable pointed to must still be in scope after the return to the calling function. This implies the following absolute rule:

---

[1] If, for whatever reason, the operating system cannot determine the name that was used to invoke the program, argv[0] will be an empty string. This does not happen in normal use.

▓ **Caution** *Never* return the address of an automatic, stack-allocated local variable from a function.

Suppose you define a function that returns the address of the larger of two argument values. This could be used on the left of an assignment so that you could change the variable that contains the larger value, perhaps in a statement such as this:

```
*larger(value1, value2) = 100;   // Set the larger variable to 100
```

You can easily be led astray when implementing this. Here's an implementation that doesn't work:

```
int* larger(int a, int b)
{
  if (a > b)
    return &a;       // Wrong!
  else
    return &b;       // Wrong!
}
```

It's relatively easy to see what's wrong with this: a and b are local to the function. The argument values are copied to the local variables a and b. When you return &a or &b, the variables at these addresses no longer exist back in the calling function. You usually get a warning from your compiler when you compile this code.

You can specify the parameters as pointers:

```
int* larger(int* a, int* b)
{
  if (*a > *b)
    return a;   // OK
  else
    return b;   // OK
}
```

If you do, do not forget to also dereference the pointers. The previous condition (a > b) would still compile, but then you'd not be comparing the values themselves. You'd instead be comparing the *addresses* of the memory locations holding these values. You could call the function with this statement:

```
*larger(&value1, &value2) = 100;  // Set the larger variable to 100
```

A function to return the address of the larger of two values is not particularly useful, but let's consider something more practical. Suppose we need a program to normalize a set of values of type double so that they all lie between 0.0 and 1.0, inclusive. To normalize the values, we can first subtract the minimum sample value from them to make them all non-negative. Two functions will help with that, one to find the minimum and another to adjust the values by any given amount. Here's a definition for the first function:

```
const double* smallest(const double data[], std::size_t count)
{
  if (count == 0) return nullptr;   // There is no smallest in an empty array

  std::size_t index_min {};
  for (std::size_t i {1}; i < count; ++i)
```

```
    if (data[index_min] > data[i])
      index_min = i;

  return &data[index_min];
}
```

You shouldn't have any trouble seeing what's going on here. The index of the minimum value is stored in index_min, which is initialized arbitrarily to refer to the first array element. The loop compares the value of the element at index_min with each of the others, and when one is less, its index is recorded in index_min. The function returns the address of the minimum value in the array. It probably would be more sensible to return the index, but we're demonstrating pointer return values among other things. The first parameter is const because the function doesn't change the array. With this const parameter you must specify the return type as const. The compiler will not allow you to return a non-const pointer to an element of a const array.

A function to adjust the values of array elements by a given amount looks like this:

```
double* shift_range(double data[], std::size_t count, double delta)
{
  for (std::size_t i {}; i < count; ++i)
    data[i] += delta;
  return data;
}
```

This function adds the value of the third argument to each array element. The return type could be void so it returns nothing, but returning the address of data allows the function to be used as an argument to another function that accepts an array. Of course, the function can still be called without storing or otherwise using the return value.

You could combine this with the previous function to adjust the values in an array, samples, so that all the elements are non-negative:

```
const auto count {std::size(samples)};                    // Element count
shift_range(samples, count, -(*smallest(samples, count))); // Subtract smallest
```

The third argument to shift_range() calls smallest(), which returns a pointer to the minimum element. The expression negates the value, so shift_range() will subtract the minimum from each element to achieve what we want. The elements in samples are now from zero to some positive upper limit. To map these into the range from 0 to 1, we need to divide each element by the maximum element. We first need a function to find the maximum:

```
const double* largest(const double data[], std::size_t count)
{
  if (count == 0) return nullptr;   // There is no largest in an empty array

  std::size_t index_max {};
  for (std::size_t i {1}; i < count; ++i)
    if (data[index_max] < data[i])
      index_max = i;

  return &data[index_max];
}
```

This works in essentially the same way as smallest(). We could use a function that scales the array elements by dividing by a given value:

```
double* scale_range(double data[], std::size_t count, double divisor)
{
  if (divisor == 0) return data;   // Do nothing for a zero divisor

  for (std::size_t i {}; i < count; ++i)
    data[i] /= divisor;
  return data;
}
```

Dividing by zero would be a disaster, so when the third argument is zero, the function just returns the original array. We can use this function in combination with largest() to scale the elements that are now from 0 to some maximum to the range 0 to 1:

```
scale_range(samples, count, *largest(samples, count));
```

Of course, what the user would probably prefer is a function that will normalize an array of values, thus avoiding the need to get into the gory details:

```
double* normalize_range(double data[], std::size_t count)
{
  shift_range(data, count, -(*smallest(data, count)));
  return scale_range(data, count, *largest(data, count));
}
```

Let's see if it all works in practice:

```
// Ex8_13.cpp - Returning a pointer
import std;

void print_data(const double data[], std::size_t count = 1,
                const std::string& title = "Data Values",
                unsigned width = 10, unsigned perLine = 5);
const double* largest(const double data[], std::size_t count);
const double* smallest(const double data[], std::size_t count);
double* shift_range(double data[], std::size_t count, double delta);
double* scale_range(double data[], std::size_t count, double divisor);
double* normalize_range(double data[], std::size_t count);

int main()
{
  double samples[] {
                    11.0,  23.0,  13.0,   4.0,
                    57.0,  36.0, 317.0,  88.0,
                     9.0, 100.0, 121.0,  12.0
                   };

  const auto count{std::size(samples)};              // Number of samples
  print_data(samples, count, "Original Values");     // Output original values
```

```
  normalize_range(samples, count);                    // Normalize the values
  print_data(samples, count, "Normalized Values", 12); // Output normalized values
}

// Prints an array of double values
void print_data(const double data[], std::size_t count,
                const std::string& title, unsigned width, unsigned perLine)
{
  std::println("{}", title);       // Display the title

  // Print the data values
  for (std::size_t i {}; i < count; ++i)
  {
    // Use dynamic field width and precision (see Chapter 7)
    std::print("{:{}.{}g}", data[i], width, width / 2);
    if ((i + 1) % perLine == 0)    // Newline after perLine values
      std::println("");
  }
  std::println("");
}
```

If you compile and run this example, complete with the definitions of largest(), smallest(), shift_range(), scale_range(), and normalize_range() shown earlier, you should get the following output:

```
Original Values
       11          23        13         4          57
       36         317        88         9         100
      121          12
Normalized Values
  0.0223642   0.0607029   0.028754         0   0.169329
  0.102236            1   0.268371   0.0159744  0.306709
  0.373802    0.0255591
```

The output demonstrates that the results are what was required. The last two statements in main() could be condensed into one by passing the address returned by normalize_range() as the first argument to print_data():

```
print_data(normalize_range(samples, count), count, "Normalized Values", 12);
```

This is more concise but clearly not clearer.

Returning a Reference

Returning a pointer from a function is useful, but it can be problematic. Pointers can be null, and dereferencing nullptr generally results in the failure of your program. The solution, as you will surely have guessed from the title of this section, is to return a *reference*. A reference is an alias for another variable, so we can state the following golden rule for references:

▓ **Caution** *Never* return a reference to an automatic local variable in a function.

By returning a reference, you allow a function call to the function to be used on the left of an assignment. In fact, returning a reference from a function is the only way you can enable a function to be used (without dereferencing) on the left of an assignment operation.

Suppose you code a `larger()` function like this:

```
std::string& larger(std::string& s1, std::string& s2)
{
  return s1 > s2? s1 : s2;      // Return a reference to the larger string
}
```

The return type is "reference to `string`," and the parameters are references to non-`const` values. Because you want to return a reference-to-non-`const` referring to one or other of the arguments, you must not specify the parameters as `const`.

You could use the function to change the larger of the two arguments, like this:

```
std::string str1 {"abcx"};
std::string str2 {"adcf"};
larger(str1, str2) = "defg";
```

Because the parameters are not `const`, you can't use string literals as arguments; the compiler won't allow it. A reference-to-non-`const` parameter permits the value to be changed, and changing a constant is not something the compiler will knowingly go along with. If you make the parameters `const`, you can't use a reference-to-non-`const` as the return type.

We're not going to examine an extended example of using reference return types at this moment, but you can be sure that you'll meet them again before long. As you'll discover, reference return types become essential when you are creating your own data types using classes.

Returning vs. Output Parameters

You now know two ways a function can pass the outcome it produces back to its caller: it can either return a value or put values into output parameters. In `Ex8_08`, you encountered the following example of the latter:

```
void find_words(vector<string>& words, const string& str, const string& separators);
```

Another way of declaring this function is as follows:

```
vector<string> find_words(const string& str, const string& separators);
```

When your function outputs an object, you do not want this object to be copied, especially if it is as expensive to copy as, for instance, a vector of strings. Prior to C++11, the recommended approach then was mostly to use output parameters. This was the only way you could make absolutely sure that all `string`s in the `vector<>` did not get copied when returning the `vector<>` from the function. This advice has changed drastically with C++11, however:

▓ **Tip** In modern C++, you should generally choose to return values over output parameters. This makes function signatures and calls much easier to read. Arguments are for input, and all output is returned. The mechanisms that make this possible are called *move semantics* and *return value optimization*, and are discussed in detail in Chapter 18. In a nutshell, move semantics ensures that objects that manage, say, a dynamic array—such as vectors and strings—can always be returned without copying that entire array (even if return value optimization does not apply). Notable exceptions are arrays of types T[N] or std::array<T,N>, or objects that contain such arrays as member variables. Because arrays cannot be moved efficiently (at least not without allocating them in the free store), it may be better to use output parameters to output into objects of such types.

Return Type Deduction

Just like you can let the compiler deduce the type of a variable from its initialization, you can have the compiler deduce the return type of a function from its definition. You can write the following, for instance:

```
auto getAnswer() { return 42; }
```

From this definition, the compiler will deduce that the return type of getAnswer() is int. Naturally, for a type name as short as int, there is little point in using auto. In fact, it even results in one extra letter to type. But later you'll encounter type names that are much more verbose (iterators are a classic example). For these, type deduction can save you time. Or you may want your function to return the same type as some other function, and for whatever reason you do not feel the need to look up what type that is or to type it out. In general, the same considerations apply here as for using auto for declaring variables. If it is clear enough from the context what the type will be or if the exact type name matters less for the clarity of your code, return type deduction can be practical.

▓ **Note** Another context where return type deduction can be practical is to specify the return type of a function template. You'll learn about this in Chapter 10.

The compiler can even deduce the return type of a function with multiple return statements, provided their expressions evaluate to a value of exactly the same type. That is, no implicit conversions will be performed because the compiler has no way to decide which of the different types to deduce. For instance, consider the following function to obtain a string's first letter in the form of another string:

```
auto getFirstLetter(const std::string& text) // function to get first letter,
{                                             // not as a char but as another string
    if (text.empty())
        return " ";                           // deduced type: const char*
    else
        return text.substr(0, 1);             // deduced type: std::string
}
```

This will fail to compile. The compiler finds one `return` statement that returns a value of type `const char*` and a second that returns a value of type `std::string`. The compiler has no way to decide which of these two types to pick for the return type. To make this definition compile, your options include the following:

- Replace `auto` in the function with `std::string`. This will allow the compiler to perform the necessary type conversion for you.

- Replace the first `return` statement with `return std::string{" "}`. The compiler will then deduce `std::string` as the return type.

▓ **Caution** Do not replace the second `return` statement with `return text.substr(0,1).c_str()`. Sure, that would make the code compile; because `c_str()` returns a `const char*` pointer, the compiler would then happily deduce `const char*` for the return type of `getFirstLetter()`. But the pointer returned by `c_str()` would then refer to the contents of a temporary object—a temporary object that is deleted the moment `getFirstLetter()` returns. The problem becomes more evident if we write this faulty `return` statement in full:

```
else {
  std::string substring{ text.substr(0, 1) };  // Temporary (local) variable
  return substring.c_str();  /* Never return a pointer (in)to a local variable! */
}
```

Note that you would get the same issue when using `data()` instead of `c_str()` (the only difference between these members is that `data()` returns `char*` instead of `const char*` on a non-const string). We can thus generalize our earlier advice as follows: never return a pointer or reference to or into either an automatic local variable or a temporary object.

You need to take care with return type deduction if you want the return type to be a reference. Suppose you write the `larger()` function shown earlier using an auto-deduced return type instead:

```
auto larger(std::string& s1, std::string& s2)
{
  return s1 > s2 ? s1 : s2;  // Return a reference to the larger string
}
```

In this case, the compiler will deduce `std::string` as a return type, not `std::string&`. That is, a copy will be returned rather than a reference. If you want to return a reference for `larger()`, your options include the following:

- Explicitly specify the `std::string&` return type as before.

- Specify `auto&` instead of `auto`. Then the return type will always be a reference.

While discussing all details and intricacies of C++ type deduction is well outside our scope, the good news is that one simple rule covers most cases:

▧ **Caution**   auto always deduces to a value type, never to a reference type. This implies that even when you assign a reference to auto, the value still gets copied. This copy will moreover not be const, unless you explicitly use const auto. To have the compiler deduce a reference type, you can use auto& or const auto&.

Naturally, this rule is not specific to return type deduction. The same holds if you use auto for local variables:

```
std::string test{ "Your powers of deduction never cease to amaze me" };
const std::string& ref_to_test{ test };
auto auto_test{ ref_to_test };
```

In the previous code snippet, auto_test has type std::string and therefore contains a copy of test. Unlike ref_to_test, this new copy isn't const anymore either.

Static Local Variables

In the functions you have seen so far, nothing is retained within the body of the function from one execution to the next. Suppose you want to count how many times a function has been called. How can you do that? One way is to define a variable at file scope and increment it from within the function. A potential problem with this is that *any* function in the file can modify the variable, so you can't be sure that it's being incremented only when it should be.

A better solution is to define a variable in the function body as static. A static variable that you define within a function is created the first time its definition is executed. It then continues to exist until the program terminates. This means you can carry over a value from one call of a function to the next. To specify a variable as static, you prefix the type name in the definition with the static keyword. Let's consider this simple example:

```
unsigned int nextInteger()
{
  static unsigned int count {0};
  return ++count;
}
```

The first time the statement starting with static executes, count is created and initialized to 0.[2] Subsequent executions of the statement have no further effect. This function then increments the static variable count and returns the incremented value. The first time the function is called, it therefore returns 1. The second time, it returns 2. Each time the function is called, it returns an integer that is one larger than the

---

[2] Technically, static local variables of fundamental types are likely initialized already at startup of the program. But it's good to think of them as being initialized only when execution first passes through their declaration, because that is what generally happens with static local variables of more complex types. These are *not* allowed to be initialized during program startup. This property is particularly interesting if initializing such a static variable comes with a cost (dynamic memory allocation, for instance): you then only pay this price if the static local variable is effectively used.

previous value. count is created and initialized only once, the first time the function is called. Subsequent calls simply increment count and return the resulting value. count survives for as long as the program is executing.

You can specify any type of variable as static, and you can use a static variable for anything that you want to remember from one function call to the next. You might want to hold on to the number of the previous file record that was read, for example, or the highest value of previous arguments.

If you don't initialize a static variable, it will be zero-initialized by default. In the previous example, you could therefore omit the {0} initialization and still get the same result. Take care, though, because such zero-initialization does not occur for non-static local variables. If you do not initialize these, they will contain junk values.

Function Overloading

You'll often find that you need two or more functions that do essentially the same thing, but with parameters of different types. The largest() and smallest() functions in Ex8_13.cpp are likely candidates. You would want these operations to work with arrays of different types such as int[], double[], float[], or even string[]. Ideally, all such functions would have the same name: smallest() or largest(). Function overloading makes that possible.

Function overloading allows several functions in a program to have the same name as long as they all have a parameter list that is different from each other. You learned earlier in this chapter that the compiler identifies a function by its *signature*, which is a combination of the function name and the parameter list. Overloaded functions have the same name, so the signature of each overloaded function must be differentiated by the parameter list alone. That allows the compiler to select the correct function for each function call based on the argument list. Two functions with the same name are different if at least one of the following is true:

- The functions have different numbers of parameters.

- At least one pair of corresponding parameters is of different types.

▓ **Note** The return type of a function is not part of the function's signature. To decide which function overload to use, the compiler looks only at the number and types of the function parameters and arguments. If you declare two functions with the same name and parameter list but with a different return type, your program will fail to compile.

Here's an example that uses overloaded versions of the largest() function:

```cpp
// Ex8_14.cpp - Overloading a function
import std;

// Function prototypes
double largest(const double data[], std::size_t count);
double largest(const std::vector<double>& data);
int largest(const std::vector<int>& data);
std::string largest(const std::vector<std::string>& words);

/* The following function overload would not compile:
   overloaded functions must differ in more than just their return type! */
// int largest(const std::vector<std::string>& words);
```

329

```cpp
int main()
{
  double array[] {1.5, 44.6, 13.7, 21.2, 6.7};
  std::vector<int> numbers {15, 44, 13, 21, 6, 8, 5, 2};
  std::vector<double> data{3.5, 5, 6, -1.2, 8.7, 6.4};
  std::vector<std::string> names {"Charles Dickens", "Emily Bronte",
                                  "Jane Austen", "Henry James", "Arthur Miller"};
  std::println("The largest of array is {}", largest(array, std::size(array)));
  std::println("The largest of numbers is {}", largest(numbers));
  std::println("The largest of data is {}", largest(data));
  std::println("The largest of names is {}", largest(names));
}

// Finds the largest of an array of double values
double largest(const double data[], std::size_t count)
{
  double max{ data[0] };
  for (std::size_t i{ 1 }; i < count; ++i)
    if (max < data[i]) max = data[i];
  return max;
}

// Finds the largest of a vector of double values
double largest(const std::vector<double>& data)
{
  double max {data[0]};
  for (auto value : data)
    if (max < value) max = value;
  return max;
}

// Finds the largest of a vector of int values
int largest(const std::vector<int>& data)
{
  int max {data[0]};
  for (auto value : data)
    if (max < value) max = value;
  return max;
}

// Finds the largest of a vector of string objects
std::string largest(const std::vector<std::string>& words)
{
  std::string max_word {words[0]};
  for (const auto& word : words)
    if (max_word < word) max_word = word;
  return max_word;
}
```

This produces the following output:

```
The largest of array is 44.6
The largest of numbers is 44
The largest of data is 8.7
The largest of names is Jane Austen
```

The compiler selects the version of largest() to be called in main() based on the argument list. Each version of the function has a unique signature because the parameter lists are different. It's important to note that the parameters that accept vector<T> arguments are references. If they are not specified as references, the vector object will be passed by value and thus copied. This could be expensive for a vector with a lot of elements. Parameters of array types are different. Only the address of an array is passed in this case, so they do not need to be reference types.

▒ **Note** Did it bother you that several of the largest() functions in Ex8_14.cpp had the exact same implementation, only for a different type? If so, good. A good programmer should always be wary of repeating the same code multiple times—and not just because programmers are a lazy bunch. Later we'll call this *code duplication* and explain to you some other downsides of doing this beyond a lot of typing. To avoid this particular type of duplication—where multiple functions perform the same task but for different parameter types—you need *function templates*. You will learn about function templates in Chapter 10.

Overloading and Pointer Parameters

Pointers to different types are different, so the following prototypes declare different overloaded functions:

```
int largest(int* pValues, std::size_t count);    // Prototype 1
int largest(float* pValues, std::size_t count);   // Prototype 2
```

Note that a parameter of type int* is treated in the same way as a parameter type of int[]. Hence, the following prototype declares the same function as prototype 1 earlier:

```
int largest(int values[], std::size_t count);    // Identical signature to prototype 1
```

With either parameter type, the argument is an address and therefore not differentiated. In fact, you might recall from earlier that even the following prototype declares the same function:

```
int largest(int values[100], std::size_t count); // Identical signature to prototype 1
```

Because such array dimension specifications are completely ignored by the compiler, we argued earlier that they are thus dangerously misleading and advised you to never use this form. If a dimension specification is what you want, the recommended approach instead is either to use std::array<> or to pass arrays by reference.

Overloading and Reference Parameters

You need to be careful when overloading functions with reference parameters. You shouldn't overload a function with a parameter type data_type with a function that has a parameter type (const) data_type&. These prototypes illustrate the problem:

```
void do_it(std::string word);        // These are not distinguishable...
void do_it(const std::string& word); // ...from the argument type
```

While valid C++ (the function signatures are different), these overloads are not particularly useful, because the compiler generally cannot determine which function you want from the argument. Suppose you write the following statements:

```
std::string word {"egg"};
do_it(word);      // Which do_it() function gets called here???
```

The second statement could call either function. The compiler cannot determine which version of do_it() should be called. This invocation of do_it() is said to be *ambiguous*, and will trigger a compiler error of the following form.

```
> error: 'do_it': ambiguous call to overloaded function
> could be 'void do_it(const std::string &)'
> or       'void do_it(std::string)'
> while trying to match the argument list '(std::string)'
```

In fact, you should also be wary when you have overloaded a function where one version has a parameter of type type1 and another has a parameter *reference to* type2—even if type1 and type2 are different. Which function is called depends on the sort of arguments you use, but you may get some surprising results. Let's explore this a little with an example:

```
// Ex8_15.cpp - Overloading a function with reference parameters
import std;

double larger(double a, double b);   // Non-reference parameters
long& larger(long& a, long& b);      // Reference parameters

int main()
{
  double a_double {1.5}, b_double {2.5};
  std::println("The larger of double values {} and {} is {}",
               a_double, b_double, larger(a_double, b_double));

  int a_int {15}, b_int {25};
  std::println("The larger of int values {} and {} is {}", a_int, b_int,
               larger(static_cast<long>(a_int), static_cast<long>(b_int)));
}

// Returns the larger of two floating point values
double larger(double a, double b)
{
```

```
  std::println("double larger() called.");
  return a > b ? a : b;
}

// Returns the larger of two long references
long& larger(long& a, long& b)
{
  std::println("long ref larger() called");
  return a > b ? a : b;
}
```

This produces the following output:

```
double larger() called.
The larger of double values 1.5 and 2.5 is 2.5
double larger() called.
The larger of int values 15 and 25 is 25
```

The third line of output may not be what you were anticipating. You might expect the second output statement in main() to call the version of larger() with long& parameters. This statement has called the version with double parameters—but why? After all, you *did* cast both arguments to long.

That is exactly where the problem lies. The arguments are not a_int and b_int but temporary locations that contain the same values after conversion to type long. As we explained earlier, the compiler will not use a temporary address to initialize a reference-to-non-const.

So, what *can* you do about this? You have a couple of choices. If a_int and b_int were type long, you could remove the type casts, and the compiler will call the version of larger() with parameters of type long&. If the variables can't be type long, you could specify the parameters as references-to-const like this:

```
long larger(const long& a, const long& b);
```

Clearly, you must change the function prototype too. The function works with either const or non-const arguments. The compiler knows that the function won't modify the arguments, so it will call this version for arguments that are temporary values instead of the version with double parameters. Note that you return type long now. If you insist on returning a reference, the return type must be const because the compiler cannot convert from a reference-to-const to a reference-to-non-const.

Overloading and const Parameters

A const parameter is only distinguished from a non-const parameter for references and pointers. For a fundamental type such as int, for example, const int is identical to int. Hence, the following prototypes are not distinguishable:

```
long larger(long a, long b);
long larger(const long a, const long b);
```

The compiler ignores the const attribute of the parameters in the second prototype. This is because the arguments are passed *by value*, meaning that a *copy* of each argument is passed into the function, and thus the original is protected from modification by the function. There is no point to specifying parameters as const in a function prototype when the arguments are passed by value.

Naturally, while it is pointless in a function *prototype*, in a function *definition* it can certainly make sense to declare parameter variables const. You can do this to prevent the function-local *copies* from the arguments from being modified, and you can even do this if some earlier function prototype did not contain the const specifiers. The following is therefore perfectly valid—and even quite sensible:

```
// Function prototype
long larger(long a, long b);              // const specifiers are pointless here

/* ... */

// Function definition for the same function we declared earlier as a prototype
long larger(const long a, const long b)   // local a and b variables are constants
{
  return a > b ? a : b;
}
```

Overloading with const Pointer Parameters

Overloaded functions are different if one has a parameter of type type* and the other has a parameter of type const type*. The parameters are pointers to different things—so they are different types. For example, these prototypes have different function signatures:

```
// Prototype 1: pointer-to-long parameters
long* larger(long* a, long* b);
// Prototype 2: pointer-to-const-long parameters
const long* larger(const long* a, const long* b);
```

Applying the const modifier to a pointer prevents the value at the address from being modified. Without the const modifier, the value can be modified through the pointer; the pass-by-value mechanism does not inhibit this in any way. In this example, the first function shown earlier is called with these statements:

```
long num1 {1L};
long num2 {2L};
long num3 {*larger(&num1, &num2)};       // Calls larger() that has non-const parameter
```

The latter version of larger() with const parameters is called by the following code:

```
const long num4 {1L};
const long num5 {2L};
const long num6 {*larger(&num4, &num5)};  // Calls larger() that has const parameter
```

The compiler won't pass a pointer-to-const value to a function in which the parameter is a pointer-to-non-const. Allowing a pointer-to-const value to be passed through a pointer-to-non-const pointer would violate the const-ness of the variable. The compiler hence selects the version of larger() with const pointer parameters to compute num6.

Two overloaded functions are *the same*, however, if one of them has a parameter of type "*pointer to type*" and the other has a parameter "const *pointer to* type." Here's an example:

```
// Identical to Prototypes 1 and 2, respectively:
long* larger(long* const a, long* const b);
const long* larger(const long* const a, const long* const b);
```

The reason is clear when you consider that the const specifiers after the asterisk (*) of a pointer type make the pointer variables themselves constants. That is, they cannot be reassigned another value. Since a function prototype does not define any code that could be doing such reassignments, it is again pointless to add these const specifiers after the asterisk in a prototype; doing so should again only be considered in a function definition.

Overloading and Reference-to-const Parameters

Reference parameters are more straightforward when it comes to const. Adding const after the ampersand (&), for one, is not allowed. References are already constant by nature, in the sense that they will always keep referring to the same value. And type T& and type const T& are always differentiated, so type const int& is always different from type int&. This means you can overload functions in the manner implied by these prototypes:

```
long& larger(long& a, long& b);
long larger(const long& a, const long& b);
```

Each function will have the same function body, which returns the larger of the two arguments, but the functions behave differently. The first prototype declares a function that doesn't accept constants as arguments, but you can use the function on the left of an assignment to modify one or the other of the reference parameters. The second prototype declares a function that accepts constants and nonconstants as arguments, but the return type is not a reference, so you can't use the function on the left of an assignment.

Overloading and Default Argument Values

You know that you can specify default argument values for a function. However, default argument values for overloaded functions can sometimes affect the compiler's ability to distinguish one call from another. For example, suppose you have two versions of a print_error() function that outputs an error message. Here's a version that has a C-style string parameter:

```
void print_error(const char* message)
{
  std::println("{}", message);
}
```

This version accepts a string argument:

```
void print_error(const std::string& message)
{
  std::println("{}", message);
}
```

You should not specify a default argument for both functions because it would create an ambiguity. The statement to output the default message in either case would be as follows:

```
print_error();
```

335

The compiler has no way of knowing which function is required. Of course, this is a silly example; you have no reason to specify defaults for both functions. A default for just one does everything that you need. However, circumstances can arise where it is not so silly, and overall, you must ensure that all function calls uniquely identify the function that should be called.

Recursion

A function can call itself, and a function that contains a call to itself is referred to as a *recursive function*. Recursion may seem to be a recipe for a loop that executes indefinitely, and if you are not careful, it certainly can be. A prerequisite for avoiding a loop of unlimited duration is that the function must contain some means of stopping the process.

A recursive function call can be indirect. For example, a function fun1() calls another function fun2(), which in turn calls fun1(). In this case, fun1() and fun2() are also called *mutually recursive functions*. We will not see any real examples of mutually recursive functions, though, and restrict ourselves to the easier and far more common case where a single function fun() recursively calls itself.

Recursion can be used in the solution of many different problems. Compilers are sometimes implemented using recursion because language syntax is usually defined in a way that lends itself to recursive analysis. Data that is organized in a tree structure is another example. Figure 8-4 illustrates a tree structure. This shows a tree that contains structures that can be regarded as subtrees. Data that describes a mechanical assembly such as a car is often organized as a tree. A car consists of subassemblies such as the body, the engine, the transmission, and the suspension. Each of these consists of further subassemblies and components until, ultimately, the leaves of the tree are reached, which are all components with no further internal structure.

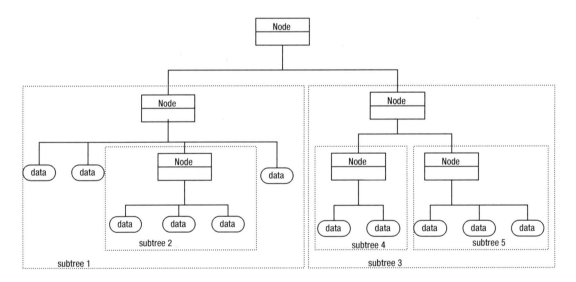

Figure 8-4. *An example of a tree structure*

Data that is organized as a tree can be traversed effectively using recursion. Each branch of a tree can be regarded as a subtree, so a function for accessing the items in a tree can simply call itself when a branch node is encountered. When a data item is encountered, the function does what is required with the item and returns to the calling point. Thus, finding the leaf nodes of the tree—the data items—provides the means by which the function stops the recursive calls of itself.

Basic Examples of Recursion

There are many things in physics and mathematics that you can think of as involving recursion. A simple example is the factorial of a positive integer n (written as $n!$), which is the number of different ways in which n things can be arranged. For a given positive integer, n, the factorial of n is the product $1 \times 2 \times 3 \times \ldots \times n$. The following recursive function calculates this:

```
long long factorial(int n)
{
  if (n == 1) return 1LL;

  return n * factorial(n - 1);
}
```

If this function is called with an argument value of 4, the `return` statement that calls the function with a value of 3 in the expression executes. This will execute the return to call the function with an argument of 2, which will call `factorial()` with an argument of 1. The `if` expression will be `true` in this case, so 1 will be returned, which will be multiplied by 2 in the next level up, and so on, until the first call returns the value $4 \times 3 \times 2 \times 1$.

▓ **Caution**   Consider for a second what would happen if our `factorial()` function is called with zero. The first recursive call would be `factorial(-1)`, the next `factorial(-2)`, and so on. That is, n just becomes more and more negative. This will go on for a very long time, most likely up to the point that the program fails. The lesson here is that you must always ensure that recursion eventually reaches the stopping conditions or you risk running into what is called *infinite recursion*, which generally results in a program crash. A better definition of `factorial()`, for instance, would be the following:

```
unsigned long long factorial(unsigned int n) // n < 0 impossible: unsigned type!
{
  if (n <= 1) return 1;          // 0! is normally defined as 1 as well
  return n * factorial(n - 1);
}
```

Here's another recursive function in a working example—it's a recursive version of the `power()` function you encountered at the beginning of this chapter:

```
// Ex8_16.cpp - A recursive power() function
import std;

double power(double x, int n);

int main()
{
  for (int i {-3}; i <= 3; ++i)      // Calculate powers of 8 from -3 to +3
    std::print("{:10g}", power(8.0, i));

  std::println("");
}
```

```
// Recursive function to calculate x to the power n
double power(double x, int n)
{
  if (n == 0)         return 1.0;
  else if (n > 0)  return x * power(x, n - 1);
  else /* n < 0 */ return 1.0 / power(x, -n);
}
```

The output is as follows:

0.00195312	0.015625	0.125	1	8	64	512

The first line in power() returns 1.0 if n is 0. For positive n, the next line returns the result of the expression x * power(x, n-1). This causes a further call of power() with the index value reduced by 1. If, in this recursive function execution, n is still positive, then power() is called again with n reduced by 1. Each recursive call is recorded in the call stack, along with the arguments and return location. This repeats until n eventually is 0, whereupon 1 is returned and the successive outstanding calls unwind, multiplying by x after each return. For a given value of n greater than 0, the function calls itself n times. For negative powers of x, the reciprocal of x^n is calculated using the same process.

Both with the power() function of Ex8_16 and the factorial() function earlier, the recursive call process is potentially inefficient compared to a loop. If not optimized away[3], every function call involves a lot of housekeeping. Implementing the power() function using loops like we did earlier in this chapter, for instance, would then make it execute a lot faster. Essentially, you need to make sure that the depth of recursion necessary to solve a problem is not itself a problem. For instance, if a function calls itself a million times, a large amount of stack memory will be needed to store copies of argument values and the return address for each call. Even up to the point where your runtime runs out of stack memory, the amount of memory allocated for the call stack is generally fixed and limited; surpassing this limit generally causes a fatal crash. In such cases, it is generally better to use a different approach, such as a loop. However, despite the overhead, using recursion can often simplify the coding considerably. Sometimes this gain in simplicity can be well worth any loss in efficiency that you may get with recursion.

Recursive Algorithms

Recursion is often favored in sorting and merging operations. Sorting data can be a recursive process in which the same algorithm is applied to smaller and smaller subsets of the original data. We can develop an example that uses recursion with a well-known sorting algorithm called *quicksort*. The example will sort a sequence of words. We have chosen this because it demonstrates a lot of different coding techniques and it's sufficiently complicated to tax a few brain cells more than the examples you've seen up to now. The example

---

[3] Most optimizing compilers are perfectly capable of transforming our recursive power() and factorial() algorithms into equivalent loop-based algorithms themselves. They do this precisely to avoid the overhead of performing any recursive function calls. In technical speak, we say that power() and factorial() are *tail recursive*, because all recursive calls happen right before returning from the function. Tail recursion is particularly easy for compilers to optimize away. If more code needs to execute after a recursive call, though, *tail call optimization* does not apply, and you effectively need some form of stack to evaluate the function. The quicksort algorithm we discuss next, for instance, is not tail recursive.

involves more than 100 lines of code, so we'll show and discuss each of the functions in the book separately and leave you to assemble them into a complete working program. The complete program is available in the code download as Ex8_17.cpp.

The Quicksort Algorithm

Applying the quicksort algorithm to a sequence of words involves choosing an arbitrary word in the sequence and arranging the other words so that all those "less than" the chosen word precede it and all those "greater than" the chosen word follow it. Of course, the words on either side of the chosen word in the sequence will not necessarily be in sequence themselves. Figure 8-5 illustrates this process.

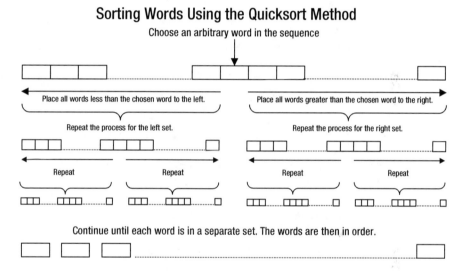

Figure 8-5. *How the quicksort algorithm works*

The same process is repeated for smaller and smaller sets of words until each word is in a separate set. When that is the case, the process ends, and the words are in ascending sequence. Of course, you'll rearrange addresses in the code, not move words around. The address of each word can be stored as a smart pointer to a string object, and the pointers can be stored in a vector container.

The type of a vector of smart pointers to string objects is going to look a bit messy, so it won't help the readability of the code. The following type alias will make the code easier to read:

```
using Words = std::vector<std::shared_ptr<std::string>>;
```

The main() Function

The definition of main() will be simple because all the work will be done by other functions. There will of course be an import directive and several prototypes for the other functions in the application preceding the definition of main():

```cpp
import std;

using Words = std::vector<std::shared_ptr<std::string>>;

void swap(Words& words, std::size_t first, std::size_t second);
void sort(Words& words);
void sort(Words& words, std::size_t start, std::size_t end);
Words extract_words(const std::string& text, const std::string& separators);
void print_words(const Words& words);
std::size_t max_word_length(const Words& words);
```

The Words type alias will make the code less cluttered, including the six function prototypes:

- swap() is a helper function that interchanges the elements at indexes first and second in the words vector.

- The overload of sort() with three function parameters will use the quicksort algorithm to sort a contiguous sequence of elements in words from index start to index end inclusive. Indexes specifying a range are needed because the quicksort algorithm involves sorting subsets of a sequence, as you saw earlier.

- The overload of sort() with one single parameter simply calls the one with three parameters (see later); it is there only for your convenience—to allow you to call sort() with a single vector<> argument.

- extract_words() extracts words from text and returns a vector<> of smart pointers to these words.

- print_words() outputs the words in words.

- max_word_length() determines the length of the longest word in words and is just to help make the output pretty.

The last two functions have reference-to-const parameters for the words vector because they don't need to change it. The others have regular reference parameters because they do. Here's the code for main():

```cpp
int main()
{
  std::string text;                     // The string to be sorted
  const auto separators{" ,.!?\"\n"};   // Word delimiters

  // Read the string to be processed
  std::println("Enter a string terminated by *:");
  getline(std::cin, text, '*');

  Words words{ extract_words(words, text, separators) };
  if (words.empty())
  {
    std::println("No words in text.");
```

```
    return 0;
  }

  sort(words);                                    // Sort the words
  print_words(words);                             // Output the words
}
```

The process in main() is straightforward. It reads some text into the string object text, passes that to the extract_words() function, which builds a vector<> holding pointers to all words in text. We capture the resulting container in the local variable words. After a check to verify that words is not empty, sort() is called to sort the contents of words, and print_words() is called to output the words.

The vector words is passed by reference to sort() and print_words() to avoid copying the vector and/or to allow it to be updated. Forgetting the & in the type parameter of a function such as sort() can lead to a mystifying error. If the parameter to a function that changes words is not a reference, then words is passed by value, and the changes will be applied to the copy of words that is created when the function is called. The copy is discarded when the function returns, and the original vector will be unchanged.

The extract_words() Function

You have seen a function similar to this. Here's the code:

```
Words extract_words(const std::string& text, const std::string& separators)
{
  Words words;

  std::size_t start {text.find_first_not_of(separators)}; // Start index of first word
  while (start != std::string::npos)
  {
    std::size_t end{ text.find_first_of(separators, start + 1) }; // Find end of a word
    if (end == std::string::npos)                        // Found a separator?
      end = text.length();                               // No, so set to end of text
    words.push_back(std::make_shared<std::string>(text.substr(start, end - start)));
    start = text.find_first_not_of(separators, end + 1); // Find start next word
  }

  return words;
}
```

The two parameters are reference-to-const because the function won't change the arguments corresponding to them. The separators object could conceivably be defined as a static variable within the function, but passing it as an argument makes the function more flexible. The process is essentially the same as you have seen previously. Each substring that represents a word is passed to the make_shared() function. The substring is used by make_shared() to create a string object in the free store along with a smart pointer to it. The smart pointer that make_shared() returns is passed to the push_back() function for the words vector to append it as a new element in the sequence.

The swap() Function

There'll be a need to swap pairs of addresses in the vector in several places, so it's a good idea to define a helper function to do this:

```
void swap(Words& words, std::size_t first, std::size_t second)
{
  auto temp{words[first]};
  words[first] = words[second];
  words[second] = temp;
}
```

This just swaps the addresses in words at indexes first and second.

The sort() Functions

You can use swap() in the implementation of the quicksort method because it involves rearranging the elements in the vector. The code for the sorting algorithm looks like this:

```
void sort(Words& words, std::size_t start, std::size_t end)
{
  // start index must be less than end index for 2 or more elements
  if (!(start < end))
    return;

  // Choose middle address to partition set
  swap(words, start, (start + end) / 2);              // Swap middle address with start

  // Check words against chosen word
  std::size_t current {start};
  for (std::size_t i {start + 1}; i <= end; i++)
  {
    if (*words[i] < *words[start])                    // Is word less than chosen word?
      swap(words, ++current, i);                      // Yes, so swap to the left
  }

  swap(words, start, current);                        // Swap chosen and last swapped words

  if (current > start) sort(words, start, current - 1); // Sort left subset if exists
  if (end > current + 1) sort(words, current + 1, end); // Sort right subset if exists
}
```

The parameters are the vector of addresses and the index positions of the first and last addresses in the subset to be sorted. The first time the function is called, start will be 0, and end will be the index of the last element. In subsequent recursive calls, a subsequence of the vector elements is to be sorted, so start and/ or end will be interior index positions in many cases.

The steps in the sort() function code are as follows:

1. The check for start not being less than end stops the recursive function calls. If there's one element in a set, the function returns. In each execution of sort(), the current sequence is partitioned into two smaller sequences in the last two statements that call sort() recursively, so eventually you must end up with a sequence that has only one element.

2. After the initial check, an address in the middle of the sequence is chosen arbitrarily as the pivot element for the sort. This is swapped with the address at index start, just to get it out of the way. You could also put it at the end of the sequence.

3. The for loop compares the chosen word with the words pointed to by elements following start. If a word is *less* than the chosen word, its address is swapped into a position following start: the first into start+1, the second into start+2, and so on. The effect of this process is to position all the words less than the chosen word before all the words that are greater than or equal to it. When the loop ends, current contains the index of the address of the last word found to be less than the chosen word. The address of the chosen word at start is swapped with the address at current, so the addresses of words less than the chosen word are now to the left of current, and the addresses of words that are greater or equal are to the right.

4. The last step sorts the subsets on either side of current by calling sort() for each subset. The indexes of words less than the chosen word run from start to current-1, and the indexes of those greater run from current+1 to end.

With recursion, the code for the sort is relatively easy to follow. And that's not all; if you'd try to implement quicksort without recursion, meaning using just loops, you'd notice that this is not only much harder but also that you need to keep track of a stack of sorts of your own. Consequently, it is quite challenging to be faster with a loop than with recursion for quicksort. So, recursion not only makes for very natural, elegant algorithms, but their performance can be close enough to optimal for many uses as well.

A slight downside of this recursive sort() function is that it requires three arguments; it's slightly unfortunate that sorting a vector requires you to decipher what to pass as second and third arguments. We therefore provide a more convenient single-parameter sort() function you can call instead:

```cpp
// Sort strings in ascending sequence
void sort(Words& words)
{
  if (!words.empty())
    sort(words, 0, words.size() - 1);
}
```

This is actually a fairly common pattern. To get the recursion going, you provide a nonrecursive helper function. Often the recursive function is then not even exposed to the user (you'll learn later to encapsulate or locally define functions).

Mind also the check for empty inputs. Any idea what would happen for empty inputs should you omit it? Precisely. Subtracting one from an unsigned std::size_t value equal to zero would result in a huge number (see, for instance, Chapter 5 for a complete explanation), which in this case would result in the recursive sort() function accessing the vector<> with indices that are massively out of bounds. And the latter, in turn, would almost certainly result in a crash!

The max_word_length() Function

This is a helper function used by the print_words() function:

```
std::size_t max_word_length(const Words& words)
{
  std::size_t max {};
  for (auto& pword : words)
    if (max < pword->length()) max = pword->length();
  return max;
}
```

This steps through the words that the vector elements point to and finds and returns the length of the longest word. You could put the code in the body of this function directly in the print_words() function. However, code is easier to follow if you break it into small, well-defined chunks. The operation that this function performs is self-contained and makes a sensible unit for a separate function.

The print_words() Function

This function outputs the words pointed to by the vector elements. It's quite long because it lists all words beginning with the same letter on the same line, with up to eight words per line. Here's the code:

```
void print_words(const Words& words)
{
  const std::size_t field_width {max_word_length(words) + 1};
  const std::size_t words_per_line {8};
  std::print("{:{}}", *words[0], field_width);     // Output first word

  std::size_t words_in_line {};                    // Number of words in current line
  for (std::size_t i {1}; i < words.size(); ++i)
  { // Output newline when initial letter changes or after 8 per line
    if ((*words[i])[0] != (*words[i - 1])[0] || ++words_in_line == words_per_line)
    {
      words_in_line = 0;
      std::println("");
    }
    std::print("{:{}}", *words[i], field_width); // Output a word
  }
  std::println("");
}
```

The field_width variable is initialized to one more than the number of characters in the longest word. The variable is used for the field width for each word, so they will be aligned neatly in columns. There's also words_per_line, which is the maximum number of words on a line. The first word is output before the for loop. This is because the loop compares the initial character in the current word with that of the previous word to decide whether it should be on a new line. Outputting the first word separately ensures we have a previous word at the start. The rest of the words are output within the for loop. This outputs a newline character when eight words have been written on a line or when a word with an initial letter that is different from the preceding word is encountered.

If you assemble the functions into a complete program, you'll have a good-sized example of a program split into several functions. Here's an example of the output:

```
Enter a string terminated by *:
It was the best of times, it was the worst of times, it was the age of wisdom, it was the
age of foolishness, it was the epoch of belief, it was the epoch of incredulity, it was the
season of Light, it was the season of Darkness, it was the spring of hope, it was the winter
of despair, we had everything before us, we had nothing before us, we were all going direct
to Heaven, we were all going direct the other way—in short, the period was so far like the
present period, that some of its noisiest authorities insisted on its being received, for
good or for evil, in the superlative degree of comparison only.*
Darkness
Heaven
It
Light
age          age          all          all          authorities
before       before       being        belief       best
comparison
degree       despair      direct       direct
epoch        epoch        everything   evil
far          foolishness  for          for
going        going        good
had          had          hope
in           incredulity  insisted     it           it           it           it           it
it           it           it           it           its          its
like
noisiest     nothing
of           of           of           of           of           of           of           of
of           of           of           of           on           only         or           other
period       period       present
received
season       season       short        so           some         spring       superlative
that         the          the          the          the          the          the          the
the          the          the          the          the          the          the          times
times        to
us           us
was          was          was          was          was          was          was          was
was          was          was          way-in       we           we           we           we
were         were         winter       wisdom       worst
```

Of course, words beginning with an uppercase letter precede all words beginning with lowercase letters.

Constant Expressions

Pop quiz. The format string of std::print() (Chapter 2), initializers in enumeration definitions (Chapter 3), case expressions in switch statements (Chapter 4), the size of statically allocated arrays (Chapter 5), non-type template arguments such as N in std::array<N, T> (Chapters 5 and 10). What do all these expressions have in common?

The answer is that the value of all these expressions must be known at compile time. They are *manifestly constant-evaluated*. Until now, we used almost exclusively literals in these expressions, but in general, you can use any expression the compiler can evaluate at compile time in these locations—any *constant expression*. Here are some elementary examples to get us started (all examples of this section are available in Ex8_18.cpp):

```cpp
std::array<int, 1> a1;                                   // Ok: literals are constant expressions

const std::size_t integer_constant{ 2 };
std::array<int, integer_constant> a2; // Ok: integer constants are constant expressions

enum class Size { ONE = 1, TWO = integer_constant, THREE }; // Ok: integer constant
std::array<int, static_cast<std::size_t>(Size::THREE)> a3;  // Ok: enumerator

std::array<int, 2 * integer_constant> a4;               // Ok: constant expression operands
```

No surprises yet. Integer literals, integer constants, enumerators, type conversions, and arithmetic expressions are all expressions that a compiler can evaluate at compile time.

▓ **Note**   The type std::array<int, 2 * integer_constant> we used for variable a4 is 100% identical to type std::array<int, 4>. The compiler evaluates all manifestly constant-evaluated expressions early in the compilation process. After that it is entirely as if you had written the corresponding literals instead.

A *non-const* variable, on the other hand, is never a *const*ant expression. Not even if the variable's current value is trivially deducible.

```cpp
std::size_t variable{ 5 };
std::array<int, variable> a5; /* Error: non-const integers are not constant expressions */
```

Still, hardly a surprise. When validating a program, compilers rarely look further than the type of an expression. And from that limited perspective a non-const variable of type std::size_t sure looks like something that may vary at runtime.

Now, consider the following example:

```cpp
const double floating_constant{ 6 };
/* Error: const non-integers are not constant expressions */
std::array<int, static_cast<std::size_t>(floating_constant)> a6;
```

Surprise! floating_constant is const, and we know static_cast<>() is not an issue (see a3's type earlier), so why does the compiler reject[4] this? Before we explain, we'll first look at the use of functions in constant expressions. After all, this is a chapter on function definitions, not one on variable definitions.

```cpp
std::array<int, std::abs(-7)> a7;       // Ok to use std::abs() (as of C++23)
```

---

[4] At least, it should reject it; at least one major compiler wrongfully accepts the definition of a6.

Evidently, `std::abs(-7)` is a valid constant expression (at least, it should be if your Standard Library implementation is C++23 compliant). Meaning that the compiler is perfectly capable of evaluating function calls at compile time. Remember that writing `std::array<int, std::abs(-7)>` is 100% equivalent to writing `std::array<int, 7>`—`std::abs()` is *abs*olutely never executed at runtime for this statement.

And yet, if we use a function of our own in a constant expression, the compiler rejects it. Suppose we have the following trivial `power()` function:

```
std::size_t power(std::size_t x, unsigned n)
{
  return n == 0 ? 1 : x * power(x, n - 1);
}
```

Then the compiler rejects any use of it in the evaluation of a constant expression:

```
std::array<int, power(2, 3)> a8; /* Error: cannot use power() in a constant expression */
```

It rejects it even if we put the definition of `power()` in the same source file, in plain sight for the compiler to find.

So, what to conclude? Some constants may be used in constant expressions, but not all...? Some functions may be used in constant expressions, but not all...? High time for the big reveal:

▓ **Tip** As a rule, you can only use entities marked with `constexpr` in constant expressions. Notable exceptions are integer, Boolean, enumeration, and character constants[5].

---

constexpr Variables

To make the definition of a6 compile in `Ex8_18.cpp`, you need to add `constexpr` to the definition of `floating_constant` as follows:

```
constexpr const double floating_constant{ 6 };
std::array<int, static_cast<std::size_t>(floating_constant)> a6;
```

The order in which you specify the `constexpr` and `const` keywords does not matter. In fact, because for variable declarations `constexpr` implies `const`, you could omit the `const` keyword as well:

```
constexpr double floating_constant{ 6 };  // const is implied
std::array<int, static_cast<std::size_t>(floating_constant)> a6;
```

▓ **Tip** Explicitly mark variables intended to be usable in constant expressions as `constexpr`, even those of integral types. This is especially relevant for constants defined in module interfaces (Chapter 11) or class definitions (Chapter 12), where `constexpr` then becomes a promise that a constant's definition will forever remain evaluable at compile time. Removing `constexpr` should be treated as a breaking API change.

---

[5] Integral constants were already allowed in manifestly constant-evaluated contexts prior to the introduction of constexpr in C++11.

Obviously, each constexpr variable in turn needs to be initialized with a constant expression. As such, we cannot yet, for instance, use power() to initialize a constexpr variable:

```
constexpr auto p{ power(3, 2) };/* Error: cannot use power() in constant expression */
```

In the next subsection, we show how you may rectify this.

constexpr Functions

To make the definitions of a8 and p in Ex8_18.cpp compile, you need to add constexpr in front of the definition of power():

```
constexpr std::size_t power(std::size_t x, unsigned n)
{
  return n == 0 ? 1 : x * power(x, n - 1);
}
```

▒ **Tip**   Mark functions intended to be usable in constant expressions as constexpr, and only those. constexpr is a promise to the users of your function. It's a promise that the definition will forever remain visible to its callers (in Chapter 11, you'll see how you can move function bodies to different source files), and that it will forever remain evaluable at compile time (more on this shortly). Removing constexpr should be treated as a breaking API change.

▒ **Note**   constexpr is by no means a prerequisite for the compile-time evaluation of functions for program optimization purposes—optimizing compilers evaluate functions at compile time all the time, even outside of manifestly constant-evaluated contexts, and even with functions that are not constexpr. The sole motivation to add constexpr to functions should be to allow their evaluation in manifestly constant-evaluated contexts, because there a compiler needs the reassurance that these functions remain compile-time evaluable in future versions of the program, as well as with any other conforming compiler. Optimizations may come and go, but the compilation of a conforming program should never start failing without breaking changes to an API.

Immediate Functions (consteval Functions)

constexpr functions remain callable at runtime. After adding constexpr to power(), for instance, the following still works:

```
int user_input;    // Impossible to evaluate at compile-time
std::cin >> user_input;
std::println("Runtime power: {}", power(user_input, 2)); // Ok if power() is constexpr
```

To define functions that can only be evaluated at compile time—also known as *immediate functions*—you use the consteval keyword. Suppose, for instance, that you replace the constexpr specifier in the declaration of power() with consteval:

```
consteval std::size_t power(std::size_t x, unsigned n)
{
  return n == 0 ? 1 : x * power(x, n - 1);
}
```

Then the runtime call `power(user_input, 2)` will cease to compile. The compiler generates no binary code for an immediate function, so there simply is no code available in your executable to evaluate `power(user_input, 2)`.

You can only use `consteval` for function definitions, never for variable definitions.

▓ **Note**   A final keyword of the same family as `constexpr` and `consteval` is `constinit`. You can only use it for variable definitions. Like a `constexpr` variable, a `constinit` variable is initialized at compile time. Unlike a `constexpr` variable, though, a `constinit` variable is not `const`. The initial value of a `constinit` variable, in other words, is baked into the executable (as if it were defined by literals), yet you can still alter this value at runtime. Unlike `constexpr`, moreover, you cannot use `constinit` for regular variables at function scope. In technical speak, you can only use `constinit` for variables with static or thread storage duration (see also Chapter 11). Examples of variables with static storage duration are static local variables (seen earlier in this chapter), static class member variables (seen in Chapter 12), and variables defined at namespace scope.

Notice that just now we did not list `const` as being of the "same family" as `constexpr`, `consteval`, and `constinit`. `const` is a distance relative at best. `const` relates to immutability; `constexpr`, `consteval`, and `constinit` relate to compile-time evaluation. Only for variable definitions, `const` and `constexpr` have some loose ties. Here is an overview:

- `const` implies `constexpr` for integral constants for legacy reasons
- `constexpr` implies both `constinit` and `const` in variable definitions
- `constinit` implies neither `const` nor `constexpr`

The fact that `const` relates to an entirely orthogonal concept compared to `constexpr` and `consteval` becomes even more apparent in the context of member function definitions. We'll therefore pick this up again in Chapter 12.

Limitations to Constant Expressions

Ever since C++11, every new standard has relaxed the limitations on what is allowed during the evaluation of constant expressions, up to the point that it is nothing short of amazing what you can accomplish with `constexpr` / `consteval` functions these days.

▓ **Note**   An excellent showcase of the power of constant evaluation is the processing of the format string argument of `std::print()` and `std::format()` statements. Through some clever use of `consteval` and `constexpr` functions, the compiler parses and validates these format strings entirely at compile time. Whenever modern formatting statements compile, you therefore know that the syntax of their format string is valid. Since this feat is realized through `consteval` constructors, though, we postpone further explanations to Chapters 12 and 20.

This section covers some of the remaining, inherent limitations of constant evaluation. Next to these, most other limitations are about prohibiting language features that you don't know yet (throw statements, seen in Chapter 16, goto statements, reinterpret_cast<>() expressions, and so on).

constexpr Function Evaluations Only

During the evaluation of a constant expression, first and foremost, the compiler only evaluates functions that are marked as constexpr. This implies, for one, that you cannot, directly or indirectly, perform any operations that require the assistance of the operating system. So, no file manipulation, no network communication, no concurrency, no launching of processes, no user interaction, and so on.

This limitation notwithstanding, it's important to realize that you can, in fact, call non-constexpr functions from a constexpr function. You can, as long as these non-constexpr functions aren't evaluated during the evaluation of a constant expression. Consider the following example (taken from Ex8_19A.cpp):

```cpp
void logError(const std::string& error);
// Compute the (floor of) the square root of an integer
constexpr int sqrt(int x)
{
  if (x < 0)
  {
    logError("Oh no, this can't be real...");
    return -1;
  }
  int result{ 1 };
  while (result * result <= x) ++result;
  return result - 1;
}
```

This function implements a naïve square root algorithm for integer inputs. While you could study its workings if you want, we mostly want you to focus on the logError() statement. Given that logError() is surely going to be tasked with outputting error messages (to a file, or some other runtime output), it makes perfect sense for logError() to not be constexpr. And yet, evidently, we are allowed to call it from a constexpr function such as sqrt(). The only restriction is that the condition of the if statement must never be met during the evaluation of a constant expression. Out of the following two variable definitions, for instance, only the second one fails to compile.

```cpp
constexpr int a{ sqrt(25) }; // OK
constexpr int b{ sqrt(-1) }; /* Error: logError() is not a constexpr function */
```

Of course, triggering logError() in sqrt() does remain perfectly valid at runtime.

```cpp
int c = sqrt(-1);  // OK: logError() called at runtime
```

Creating constexpr-Ready Functions

For our next point, consider the following sqrt() function (taken from Ex8_19B.cpp):

```cpp
constexpr int sqrt(int x)
{
  if consteval
```

350

```
{
  int result{};
  while (result * result <= x) ++result;
  return result - 1;
}
else
{
  return static_cast<int>(std::sqrt(x)); // Only constexpr as of C++26
}
}
```

This variant of sqrt() no longer logs an error when presented with negative values, but instead returns -1 (again, feel free to verify...). The interesting bit this time is the consteval if statement.

You use consteval if statements (with syntax if consteval or if !consteval) to create functions that behave differently depending on whether they are evaluated for a constant expression, or at runtime. During the evaluation of a constant expression, the if branch of if consteval statements is evaluated; at runtime the (optional) else branch. For if !consteval statements, it's the other way around.

More concretely, you typically use consteval if statements to skip parts of a function body during constant evaluation (for instance, to skip the logging statement in Ex8_19A) or to provide alternate, typically less efficient, implementations of algorithms for use at compile time. Our sqrt() function in Ex8_19B is an example of the latter. The std::sqrt() library function almost certainly uses highly tuned assembler code and/or specialized hardware instructions to calculate the square root. While blazingly fast at runtime, the virtual machine that evaluates constant expressions will not be able to process this code. Which is part of the reason why std::sqrt() is not yet defined as constexpr in C++23.[6] A consteval if statement thus allows you to get the best of both worlds: a function that is blazingly fast at runtime, yet still compile-time evaluable.

```
int b{ sqrt(1'000'000'000) }; // Uses fast version
constexpr int a{ sqrt(100) }; // Uses slow version
```

▒ **Tip** If your compiler does not support constexpr if statements yet, you can use the C++20 library function std::is_constant_evaluated() in a plain if statement. Here is an example:

```
constexpr int sqrt(int x)
{
  if (std::is_constant_evaluated())
  {
    int result{};
    while (result * result <= x) ++result;
    return result - 1;
  }
```

---

[6] In C++26 std::sqrt() is expected to become constexpr, meaning std::sqrt() functions will no doubt start using consteval if statements similar to those in our example (which we'll therefore have to rework in the C++26 edition of the book...).

```
  else
  {
    return static_cast<int>(std::sqrt(x)); // Only constexpr as of C++26
  }
}
```

In fact, since you can use std::is_constant_evaluated() in && or || expressions to create more complex if statements (more complex than easily accomplished using constexpr if statements, that is), std::is_constant_evaluated() remains useful even in C++23.

Dynamic Memory during Constant Evaluation

During constant evaluation you are allowed to, directly or indirectly, allocate dynamic memory using new or new [] (see Chapter 4), as long as all memory is deallocated again using delete or delete [] before the evaluation is done. In other words, the virtual machine that evaluates constant expressions has a free store, but that free store must be empty at the end of the evaluation.

For example, one way to make sqrt(-1) compile-time evaluable in Ex8_19A is to turn logError() into constexpr function using the following useful pattern:

```
constexpr void logError(const std::string& error)
{
  if !consteval
  {
    // ...
  }
}
```

With this constexpr version of logError() in place, you'll notice that the compile-time evaluation of sqrt(-1) will happily evaluate logError("Oh no, this can't be real...") (see Ex8_19C.cpp). In doing so, though, the compiler must convert the "Oh no, this can't be real..." string literal into a std::string object (as explained in the section on references and implicit conversions) at compile time. Internally this std::string object then allocates dynamic memory in the virtual free store to hold a copy of the literal. Since the std::string object is transient (we'll have more to say about this in later chapters), though, its lifetime ends after the evaluation of logError(). At that point, the dynamic memory is deallocated automatically as well (again, more on this in later chapters). And so the virtual free store is empty again when the evaluation of sqrt(-1) ends with the return -1 statement.

A consequence of this restriction on dynamic memory allocation is that there is no way for a constexpr or constinit variable to refer to dynamically allocated memory. A constexpr or constinit variable cannot initialize anything in the runtime free store. The following two variable definitions are therefore invalid:

```
constexpr std::string nok{"People say nothing is impossible, but I do nothing every day"};
constexpr std::vector unsolved{ 12, 6, 3, 10, 5, 16, 8, 4, 2, 1 };
```

Statically allocated arrays, on the other hand, can be constexpr, since these do not reside in the free store:

```
constexpr const char ok[]{ "It always seems impossible until it's done" };
constexpr std::array fine{ 0, 1, 0, 1, 2, 6, 18, 57, 186, 622, 2120, 7338, 25724 };
```

Summary

This marathon chapter introduced you to writing and using functions. This isn't everything relating to functions, though. Chapter 10 covers function templates, and you'll see even more about functions in the context of user-defined types starting in Chapter 12. The following are the important bits that you should take away from this chapter:

- Functions are self-contained compact units of code with a well-defined purpose. A well-written program consists of a large number of small functions, not a small number of large functions.

- A function definition consists of the function header that specifies the function name, the parameters, and the return type, followed by the function body containing the executable code for the function.

- A function prototype enables the compiler to process calls to a function even though the function definition has not been processed.

- The pass-by-value mechanism for arguments to a function passes copies of the original argument values, so the original argument values are not accessible from within the function.

- Passing a pointer to a function allows the function to change the value that is pointed to, even though the pointer itself is passed by value.

- Declaring a pointer parameter as const prevents modification of the original value.

- You can pass the address of an array to a function as a pointer. If you do, you should generally pass the array's length along as well.

- Specifying a function parameter as a reference avoids the copying that is implicit in the pass-by-value mechanism. A reference parameter that is not modified within a function should be specified as const.

- Input parameters should be reference-to-const, except for smaller values such as those of fundamental types. Returning values is generally preferred over output parameters.

- Specifying default values for function parameters allows arguments to be optionally omitted.

- Returning a reference from a function allows the function to be used on the left of an assignment operator. Specifying the return type as a reference-to-const prevents this.

- The signature of a function is defined by the function name together with the number and types of its parameters.

- Overloaded functions are functions with the same name but with different signatures and therefore different parameter lists. Overloaded functions cannot be differentiated by the return type.

- A recursive function is a function that calls itself. Implementing an algorithm recursively can result in elegant and concise code. Sometimes, but certainly not always, this is at the expense of execution time when compared to other methods of implementing the same algorithm.

- During the evaluation of a constant expression the compiler can only evaluate functions or variables marked with constexpr (except for integral constants, which are implicitly constexpr). You can allocate dynamic memory during the evaluation of a constant expression, as long as you deallocate it again before the evaluation ends.

- consteval marks immediate functions, which are functions that can only be evaluated at compile time.

- Use if consteval statements to write functions that behave differently during the evaluation of a constant expression.

EXERCISES

These exercises enable you to try some of what you've learned in this chapter. If you get stuck, look back over the chapter for help. If you're still stuck, you can download the solutions from the Apress website (https://www.apress.com/gp/services/source-code), but that really should be a last resort.

Exercise 8-1. Write a function, validate_input(), that accepts two integer arguments that represent the upper and lower limits for an integer that is to be entered. It should accept a third argument that is a string describing the input, with the string being used in the prompt for input to be entered. The function should prompt for input of the value within the range specified by the first two arguments and include the string identifying the type of value to be entered. The function should check the input and continue to prompt for input until the value entered by the user is valid. Use the validate_input() function in a program that obtains a user's date of birth and outputs it in the form of this example:

```
You were born on the 21st of November, 2012.
```

The program should be implemented so that separate functions, month(), year(), and day(), manage the input of the corresponding numerical values. Don't forget leap years—February 29, 2023, is not allowed!

Exercise 8-2. Write a function that reads a string or array of characters as input and reverses it. Justify your choice of parameter type? Provide a main() function to test your function that prompts for a string of characters, reverses them, and outputs the reversed string.

Exercise 8-3. Write a program that accepts from two to four command-line arguments. If it is called with less than two or more than four arguments, output a message telling the user what they should do and then exit. If the number of arguments is correct, output them, each on a separate line.

Exercise 8-4. Create a function, plus(), that adds two values and returns their sum. Provide overloaded versions to work with int, double, and strings, and test that they work with the following calls:

```
const int n {plus(3, 4)};
const double d {plus(3.2, 4.2)};
const string s {plus("he", "llo")};
const string s1 {"aaa"};
const string s2 {"bbb"};
const string s3 {plus(s1, s2)};
```

Can you explain why the following doesn't work?

```
const auto x {plus(3, 4.2)};
```

Exercise 8-5. Define a function that checks whether a given number is prime. Your primal check does not have to be efficient; any algorithm you can think of will do. In case you have forgotten, a prime number is a natural number strictly greater than 1 and with no positive divisors other than 1 and itself. Write another function that generates a vector<> with all natural numbers less than or equal to a first number and starting from another. By default, it should start from 1. Create a third function that given a vector<> of numbers outputs another vector<> containing all the prime numbers it found in its input. Use these three functions to create a program that prints out all prime numbers less or equal to a number chosen by the user (print, for instance, 15 primes per line). Note: In principle, you do not need any vectors to print these prime numbers; obviously, these extra functions have been added for the sake of the exercise.

Exercise 8-6. Implement a program that queries the user for a number of grades. A grade is an integer number between 0 and 100 (both inclusive). The user can stop at any time by entering a negative number. Once all grades have been collected, your program is to output the following statistics: the five highest grades, the five lowest grades, the average grade, the median grade, and the standard deviation and variance of the grades. Of course, you're to write a separate function to compute each of these statistics. Also, you must write the code to print five values only once. To practice, use arrays to store any five extremes and not, for instance, vectors.

Hint: As a preprocessing step, you should first sort the grades the user enters; you'll see that this will make writing the functions to compute the statistics much easier. You can adapt the quicksort algorithm from Ex8_17 to work with grade numbers.

Caution: Make sure to do something sensible if the user enters less than five or even zero grades. Anything is fine, as long as it does not crash.

Note: The median is the value that appears in the middle position of a sorted list. If there is an even number of grades, there obviously is no single middle value—the median is then defined as the mean of the two middle values. The formulas to compute mean (μ) and standard deviation (σ) of a series of n grades xi are as follows:

$$\mu = \frac{1}{n}\sum_{i=0}^{n-1}x_i \qquad \sigma = \sqrt{\frac{1}{n}\sum_{i=0}^{n-1}(x_i - \mu)^2}$$

The variance is then defined as σ^2. The <cmath> header of the Standard Library defines std::sqrt() to compute square roots.

Bonus: Naturally, the syntax for passing arrays by reference is a bit awkward. Moreover, output parameters are not recommended in modern C++, as you well know. Maybe you can modernize your solution?

Exercise 8-7. The so-called Fibonacci function is popular among lecturers in computer science and mathematics for introducing recursion. This function has to compute the nth number from the famous Fibonacci sequence, named after Italian mathematician Leonardo of Pisa, known also as Fibonacci. This sequence of positive integer numbers is characterized by the fact that every number after the first two is the sum of the two preceding ones. For n ≥ 1, the sequence is defined as follows:

```
1, 1, 2, 3, 5, 8, 13, 21, 34, 55, 89, 144, 233, 377, 610, 987, 1597,
2584, 4181...
```

For convenience, computer scientists mostly define an additional zeroth Fibonacci number as zero. Write a function to compute the nth Fibonacci number recursively. Test it with a simple program that prompts the user for how many numbers should be computed and then prints them out one by one, each on a different line.

Extra: While the naive recursive version of the Fibonacci function is very elegant—the code matches nearly verbatim with common mathematical definitions—it is notorious for being very slow. If you ask the computer to compute, say, 100 Fibonacci numbers, you'll notice that it becomes noticeably slower and slower as n becomes larger. Do you think you can rewrite the function to use a loop instead of recursion? How many numbers can you correctly compute now?

Hint: In each iteration of the loop, you'll naturally want to compute a next number. To do this, all you need are the previous two numbers. So, there should be no need to keep track of the full sequence in, for instance, a vector<>.

Exercise 8-8. If written using a more mathematical notation, the power() functions we wrote in Ex8_01 and especially Ex8_16 both essentially compute a power(x,n) for n > 0, as follows:

```
power(x,n) = x * power(x,n-1)
           = x * (x * power(x,n-2))
           = ...
           = x * (x * (x * ... (x * x)...))
```

Clearly, this method requires exactly n-1 multiplications. It may surprise you, but there is another, much more effective way. Suppose n is even; then you know the following:

```
power(x,n) = power(x,n/2) * power(x,n/2)
```

As both operands of this multiplication are identical, you need to compute this value only once. That is, you have just reduced the computation of power(x,n) to that of power(x,n/2), which obviously at most requires half as many multiplications. Moreover, because you can now apply this formula recursively, you'll need even far fewer multiplications than that—only something in the order of $\log_2(n)$ to be exact. To give you an idea, this means that for n in the order of 1000, you only need in the order of 10 multiplications! Can you apply this idea to create a more efficient recursive version of power()? You can start from the program in Ex8_16.cpp.

Note: This principle is something you'll often see in recursive algorithms. In each recursive call, you reduce a problem to a problem of half the size. If you think back, you'll realize that we applied the same principle in the quicksort algorithm as well, for instance. Because this solution strategy is that common, it also has a name; it's called *divide and conquer*, after the famous phrase of Julius Caesar.

Exercise 8-9. Modify the solution in Exercise 8-8 so that it counts the number of times the call power(1.5,1000) performs a multiplication. Do so by replacing each multiplication with a helper function mult() that takes two arguments, prints a message of how many multiplications have been performed thus far, and then simply returns the product of both arguments. Use at least one static variable.

CHAPTER 9

Vocabulary Types

Some data types will be as much a part of your daily vocabulary as basic types, such as int or double. You'll use them everywhere, all the time: in your function signatures, in your algorithms, as member variables of your classes (see later), and so on. We call such types *vocabulary types*. In modern C++, they are one of the cornerstones of understandable, maintainable, and safe code.

In fact, you already know some vocabulary types, including std::unique_ptr<>, std::shared_ptr<>, std::string, std::array<>, and std::vector<>. So far, these types have one thing in common: they replace certain unsafe and inconvenient types of the core language (raw pointers, const char* strings, low-level dynamic memory, etc.).[1] The three vocabulary types we introduce in this chapter are similar but have slightly different raisons d'être. They are designed to make your code more self-documenting, more efficient, and less repetitive.

In this chapter, you will learn

- How to best encode optional inputs for functions

- How to define functions that may or may not return a value, depending either on their inputs or the current state of the application

- How to best define functions that accept strings that they do not alter

- How to define one single function that can operate on any sequential range you throw at it, be it a C-style array, a vector, or any other sequential container

Working with Optional Values

When writing your own functions, you will often encounter either input arguments that are optional or functions that can return a value only if nothing went wrong. Consider the following example:

```
int find_last(const std::string& s, char char_to_find, int start_index);
```

From this prototype, you can imagine that the find_last() function searches a given string for a given character, back to front, starting from a given start index. Once it's found, it will then return the index of the last occurrence of that character. But what if the character doesn't occur in the string? And what if you want the algorithm to consider the entire string? Would it perhaps work if you pass, say, -1, as the third argument?

---

[1] Other such vocabulary types include std::variant<>, which replaces union types, and std::any, which replaces void* pointers. Because you'll use these less frequently, we'll leave these for you to discover as self-study later on. But don't worry. Once you know std::optional<>, figuring out how to use std::variant<> and std::any should be a walk in the park.

Sadly, without interface documentation or a peek at the implementation code, there is no way of knowing how this function will behave.

A traditional solution is to pick some specific value or values to use when the caller wants the function to use its default settings or to return when no actual value could be computed. And for array or string indices, the typical choice is -1. A possible specification for find_last() would thus be that it returns -1 if char_to_find does not occur in the given string and that the entire string is searched if -1 or any negative value is passed as a start_index. In fact, std::string uses this exact technique for its own find() functions; only instead of -1, it uses the constant std::string::npos (std::size_t is unsigned, so -1 is not a valid value).

The problem is that, in general, it can be hard to remember how every function encodes "input not provided" or "result not computed." Conventions tend to differ between different libraries or even within the same library. Some may return 0 upon failure, others a negative number. Some accept nullptr as input; others don't. And so on.

To aid the users of a function, optional parameters are typically given a valid default value. Here's an example:

```
int find_last(const std::string& s, char char_to_find, int start_index = -1);
```

This technique, however, does not extend to return values. And another problem is that, in general, there may not even be an obvious way of encoding an optional value. The first cause for this may be the optional value's type. Think about it. How would you encode an optional bool, for instance? A second cause may be the specific situation. Suppose, for instance, that you need to define a function to read some configuration file. Then you'd probably define functions of the following form:

```
int read_int_setting(const std::string& fileName, const std::string& settingName);
```

But what should happen if the configuration file does not contain a setting with the given name? Since this is intended to be a generic function, you cannot a priori assume that an int value such as 0, -1, or any other value isn't a valid value for the requested setting. Traditional workarounds include the following:

```
// Return the 'default' value provided by the caller if the setting is not found
int read_int_setting(const string& file, const string& settingName, int default);

// Output setting in output parameter and return true if found; return false otherwise
bool read_int_setting(const string& file, const string& settingName, int& output);
```

While these work, the C++ Standard Library offers a better alternative: std::optional<>. This vocabulary type will make your function declarations much cleaner and easier to read.

▨ **Note** Vocabulary types, and std::optional<> in particular, will be equally useful when defining your own classes in the second half of the book. A Car object can have an optional<SpareTire>, for instance, a Person an optional<string> for its middle name, or a Boat an optional<Engine>. For now, though, we'll just illustrate the new vocabulary types using functions only.

---

std::optional

The Standard Library provides `std::optional<>`, designed to replace all implicit encodings of optional values that we showed earlier. Using this vocabulary type, any optional input or output can be explicitly declared with `std::optional<>` as follows:

```
std::optional<int> find_last(const std::string& s, char c, std::optional<int> startIndex);
std::optional<int> read_int_setting(const std::string& file, const std::string& setting);
```

All optional inputs and outputs are now explicitly marked as such in the function prototype at the code level. No more need for additional documentation or peeking at the implementation to know what is optional. The result is clean, self-documenting function declarations. Your code instantly becomes easier to understand and use.

■ **Note** `std::optional<>` is a class template, just like `std::vector<>` and `std::array<>` were. You can instantiate it with any type, T, resulting in a new optional version of that type. You will learn how to create your own class templates later, but using one should not pose any problems anymore.

Let's take a look at the basic use of `std::optional<>` in some real code:

```
// Ex9_01.cpp - Working with std::optional<>
import std;

std::optional<std::size_t> find_last(
   const std::string& string, char to_find,
   std::optional<std::size_t> start_index = std::nullopt); // or: ... start_index = {});

int main()
{
  const auto string{ "Growing old is mandatory; growing up is optional." };

  const std::optional<std::size_t> found_a{ find_last(string, 'a') };
  if (found_a)
    std::println("Found the last a at index {}", *found_a);

  const auto found_b{ find_last(string, 'b') };
  if (found_b.has_value())
    std::println("Found the last b at index {}", found_b.value());

// Following line gives an error (cannot convert optional<size_t> to size_t)
// const std::size_t found_c{ find_last(string, 'c') };

  const auto found_early_i{ find_last(string, 'i', 10) };
  if (found_early_i != std::nullopt)
    std::println("Found an early i at index {}", *found_early_i);
}

std::optional<std::size_t> find_last(
  const std::string& string, char to_find, std::optional<std::size_t> start_index
)
```

```
{
  // code below will not work for empty strings
  if (string.empty())
    return std::nullopt;       // or: 'return std::optional<std::size_t>{};'
                               // or: 'return {};'
  // determine the starting index for the loop that follows:
  std::size_t index{ start_index.value_or(string.size() - 1) };

  while (true)  // never use while (index >= 0) here, as size_t is always >= 0!
  {
    if (string[index] == to_find) return index;
    if (index == 0) return std::nullopt;
    --index;
  }
}
```

The output produced by this program is as follows:

```
Found the last a at index 46
Found an early i at index 4
```

To showcase `std::optional<>`, we define a variation of the `find_last()` function we used as an example earlier. Notice that because `find_last()` uses unsigned `size_t` indexes instead of `int` indexes, -1 becomes less obvious as a default value for the third parameter. We replaced it with a default value that is equal to `std::nullopt`. This special constant is defined by the Standard Library to initialize `optional<T>` values that do not (yet) have a `T` value assigned. You will see shortly why this is also a useful default value for function parameters.

After the function's prototype, you see the program's `main()` function. In `main()`, we call `find_last()` three times to search for the letters `'a'`, `'b'`, and `'i'` in some sample string. And there is really nothing surprising about these calls themselves. If you want a nondefault start index, you simply pass a number to `find_last()`, as we did in our third call. The compiler then implicitly converts this number to a `std::optional<>` object, exactly like you'd expect. If you're okay with the default starting index, though, you can omit the corresponding argument. The default parameter value then takes care of creating an empty `optional<>`.

These are the two most interesting takeaways from the `main()` function:

- How to check whether an `optional<>` value returned by `find_last()` is empty or whether it was assigned an actual value

- How to subsequently extract this value from the `optional<>`

For the former issue, `main()` shows three alternatives, in this order: you have the compiler convert the `optional<>` to a Boolean for you, you call the `has_value()` function, or you compare the `optional<>` to `nullopt`. For the latter issue, `main()` shows two alternatives: you can either use the `*` operator or call the `value()` function. Assigning the `optional<size_t>` return value directly to a `size_t`, however, would not be possible. The compiler cannot convert values of type `optional<size_t>` to values of type `size_t`.

In the body of `find_last()`, aside from some interesting challenges with empty strings and unsigned index types, pay particular attention to two additional aspects related to `optional<>`. First, notice that returning a value is straightforward. Either you return `std::nullopt`, or you return an actual value. Both will then be converted to a suitable `optional<>` by the compiler. Second, we've used `value_or()` there.

If the optional<> start_index contains a value, this function will return the same as value(); if it does not contain a value, value_or() simply evaluates to the value you pass it as an argument. The value_or() function is therefore a welcome alternative to equivalent if-else statements or conditional operator expressions that would first call has_value() and then value().

▓ **Note** Ex9_01 covers most there is to know about std::optional<>. As always, if you need to know more, please consult your favorite Standard Library reference. One thing to note already, though, is that next to the * operator, std::optional<> also supports the -> operator; that is, in the following example, the last two statements are equivalent:

```
std::optional<std::string> os{
  "Falling in life is inevitable--staying down is optional."
};
if (os) std::println("{}", (*os).size());
if (os) std::println("{}", os->size());
```

Note that while this syntax makes optional<> objects look and feel like pointers, they most certainly aren't pointers. Each optional<> object contains a copy of any value assigned to it, and this copy is not kept in the free store. That is, while copying a pointer doesn't copy the value it points to, copying an optional<> always involves copying the entire value that is stored inside it.

---

std::expected

C++23 added std::expected<T,E>, a vocabulary type very similar to std::optional<T>. A typical use is to return a std::expected<T,E> from a function that is *expected* to return a value of type T, but that may occasionally fail to do so. The difference with std::optional<T> is that std::expected<T,E> is never null. Whenever the expected T value is missing, std::expected<T,E> instead carries an *error* of type E. This error, of course, should provide more information about *why* the T value is missing. At the very least, the error value is some integral error code (as used extensively also in C-style APIs). Ideally, though, the error object carries further information that may help with diagnosing or even recovering from the error (the path of the file that was inaccessible or corrupt, the URL that was unreachable, the line at which parsing an XML file failed, and so on).

▓ **Note** The errors in std::expected<T,E> objects are clearly strongly related to exceptions, which we discuss in Chapter 16. Both serve the exact same purpose: not only to signal that something unexpected/ exceptional occurred, but also, ideally, to inform what, where, and why things went awry. Both error reporting approaches have their merits; neither is perfect. We'll leave it up to you to decide how you report and handle your errors (after reading Chapter 16, of course). What matters most, though, is that you work out a consistent and complete strategy for error handling in your applications. The mechanism you use to report these errors is always secondary to the willingness to invest in systematic, robust error-handling code. At every turn, you must ask yourself what could go wrong, no matter how unlikely, and decide how your application best reacts to this.

The following otherwise nonsensical example (available online in Ex9_02) shows the typical use of std::expected<>:

```
enum class Error { WhoopsADaisy, DisasterStruck, OhMy };
std::expected<std::string, Error> concoctSomeWhatchamacallit(int wobble)
{
  if (wobble < 0)
    return std::unexpected{ Error::WhoopsADaisy };/* Not return Error::WhoopsADaisy; ! */
  else
    return std::string{ "Some superb doohickey" };
}
```

The main takeaway here is that while you can create a std::expected<T,E> from a value of type T (or from any value convertible to type T; the const char[] literal in our example, for instance, first needs to be converted into a std::string object), you *cannot* create a std::expected<T,E> directly from a value of type E. Even if there is no ambiguity between types T and E (as in our example), there is no implicit conversion from E to std::expected<T,E>. Instead, the recommended way to create a std::expected<T,E> holding an error is by creating a value of type std::unexpected<E>.

▨ **Caution**   Unlike std::optional<T>, a default-constructed std::expected<T,E> carries a default-constructed T value. Consequently, where for std::optional<> a statement such as return {}; signals *failure* (it's equivalent to return std::null_opt;), for std::expected<T,E> it signals *success* (and is equivalent to return T{};)!

Besides the ability to carry an error, std::expected<T,E> is mostly analogous to std::optional<T>. The members to access the value, for one, are entirely analogous (has_value(), value(), value_or(), *, ->, and so on). Only one extra member function was added; you can access the embedded error value through the aptly named error() function if (and only if) has_value() is false. As always, refer to a Standard Library reference for a complete list of all available members.

String Views: The New Reference-to-const-string

From the previous chapter, you know that the main motivation for passing input arguments by reference-to-const instead of by value is to avoid unnecessary copies. Copying bigger strings too often, for instance, could become quite expensive in terms of both time and memory. Suppose you have a function that does not alter the strings it receives as input. Then your natural instinct at this point should be to declare the corresponding parameters as const string&. We did this, for example, in Ex8_08 for find_words().

```
void find_words(vector<string>& words, const string& text, const string& separators);
```

Unfortunately, though, const string& parameters are not perfect. While they do avoid copies of std::string objects, they still have their shortcomings. To illustrate why, suppose we slightly alter the main() function of Ex8_08 as follows:

```
int main()
{
  std::string text;       // The string to be searched
  std::println("Enter some text terminated by *:");
  std::getline(std::cin, text, '*');
```

```
// const std::string separators {" ,;:.\"!?'\n"};
   std::vector<std::string> words;      // Words found

   find_words(words, text, " ,;:.\"!?'\n"); /* no more 'separators' constant! */
   list_words(words);
}
```

The only difference is that we no longer store the separator characters in a separate separators constant. Instead, we pass them directly as the third argument to find_words(). You can easily verify that this still compiles and works correctly.

The first question is then: *Why* does this compile and work? After all, the third parameter of find_words() expects a reference to a std::string object, but the argument that we pass now is a string literal of type const char[]—an array of characters—and therefore definitely not a std::string object. Naturally, you recall the answer from the previous chapter: the compiler must be applying some form of implicit conversion. That is, the function's reference will not actually refer to the literal but instead to some *temporary* std::string *object* that the compiler has silently created somewhere in memory. (We will explain in later chapters exactly how such conversions work for nonfundamental types.) In this case, the temporary string object will be initialized with a *copy* of all the characters in the string literal.

Being the careful reader that you are, you now realize why passing strings by reference-to-const is somewhat flawed. Our motivation for using references was to avoid copies. But, alas, string literals still become copied when passed to reference-to-const-std::string parameters. They become copied into temporary std::string objects that emanate from implicit conversions.

And that brings us to the second and real question of this section: How do we create functions that never copy input string arguments, not even string literals or other character arrays? We do not want to revert to const char* for this. Not only would we have to pass the string's length along separately to avoid having to scan for the terminating null character all the time, but we'd also miss out on all the nice and safe functions offered by std::string.

The answer lies with std::string_view, a type defined in the <string_view> module. Values of this type act analogously to values of type const std::string—mind the const!—only with one difference: creating a string_view never involves copying any characters. Not even when created from a string literal. All it uses internally is a copy of the string's length and a pointer to some external character sequence. A string_view does not care where the characters themselves are stored: inside a std::string object, as a string literal, or as a plain C-style string. For a string_view and the code that uses it, this makes absolutely no difference. In a way, the string_view abstracts away the concrete type of textual data you are operating on, allowing you to easily write one single function that can operate efficiently and effectively on such input.

▓ **Tip** Always use the type std::string_view instead of const std::string& for input string parameters. (While there is nothing wrong with using const std::string_view&, you might as well pass std::string_view by value. Because it does not involve copying an entire character array, initializing or copying a string_view is very cheap.)

Because string_views are designed to work for string literals, they do have one important limitation, though: the characters of the underlying string can *never* be modified through the interface of a string_view. string_views are inherently const. Even a non-const string_view does not allow you to alter the characters of the underlying string. To paraphrase "The Boss," you can view, but you cannot touch. But that is often enough, as the example in the next section proves.

> ■ **Note** Next to std::string_view for strings of char elements, std::wstring_view, std::u8string_view, std::u16string_view, and std::u32string_view exist as well for views into strings of wide or Unicode characters. Since they are all instantiations of the same class template (std::basic_string_view<CharType>), their behaviors are completely analogous.

Using String View Function Parameters

To avoid inadvertent copies of string literals and other character sequences, the find_words() function of Ex8_08 is better declared as follows:

```
void find_words(vector<string>& words, string_view text, string_view separators);
```

The std::string_view type can mostly be used as a drop-in replacement for both const std::string& and const std::string. But not quite so in our example. Coincidence? Of course not! We chose this example precisely because it allows us to explain how replacing const std::string& with string_view might go wrong. To make the find_words() function definition compile with its new and improved signature, you have to slightly alter it, like so (the complete program is available as Ex9_02.cpp):

```
void find_words(vector<string>& words, string_view text, string_view separators)
{
  size_t start{ text.find_first_not_of(separators) }; // First word start index
  size_t end{};                                        // Index for end of a word

  while (start != string_view::npos)                   // Find the words
  {
    end = text.find_first_of(separators, start + 1);   // Find end of word
    if (end == string::npos)                            // Found a separator?
      end = text.length();                             // No, so set to end of text

    words.push_back(std::string{text.substr(start, end - start)});
                                                       // Store the word
    start = text.find_first_not_of(separators, end + 1);
                                                       // Find 1st letter of next word
  }
}
```

The modification we had to make is in the second-to-last statement, which originally did not include the explicit std::string{ ... } initialization:

```
    words.push_back(text.substr(start, end - start));
```

The compiler, however, will refuse any implicit conversions of std::string_view objects to values of type std::string (give it a try!). The rationale behind this deliberate restriction is that you normally use string_view to avoid string copy operations, and converting a string_view back to a std::string always involves copying the underlying character array. To protect you from accidentally doing so, the compiler is not allowed to ever implicitly make this conversion. You must always explicitly add the conversion in this direction yourself.

> ▪ **Note** There exist two other cases where a string_view is not exactly equivalent to const string. First, string_view does not provide a c_str() function to convert it to a const char* array. Luckily, it does share with std::string its data() function, though, which for most intents and purposes is equivalent. Second, string_views cannot be concatenated using the addition operator (+). To use a string_view value my_view in a concatenation expression, you must convert it to a std::string first, for instance using std::string{my_view}.

A Proper Motivation

String literals are generally not that big, so you may wonder whether it is really such a big deal if they are copied. Probably not. But a std::string_view can be created from any C-style character array, which can be as big as you want. For instance, you probably did not gain much in Ex9_02 from turning the separators parameter into a string_view. But for the other parameter, text, it could indeed make a difference, as illustrated by this snippet:

```
char* text = ReadHugeTextFromFile();      // last character in text is null ('\0')
find_words(words, text, " ,;:.\"!?'\n");
delete[] text;
```

In this case, the char array is assumed to be terminated by a null character element, a convention common in C and C++ programming. If this is not the case, you'll have to use something more like this form:

```
char* text = ...;                         // again a huge amount of characters...
std::size_t numCharacters = ...;          // the huge amount
find_words(words, std::string_view{text, numCharacters}, " ,;:.\"!?'\n");
delete[] text;
```

The bottom line in either case is that if you use std::string_view, the huge text array is not copied when passing it to find_words(), whereas it would be if you'd use const std::string&.

Spans: The New Reference-to-vector or -array

In Ex8_14, you may have noticed how the first two largest() functions both compute the largest value of sequences of the same element type: double. To refresh your memory, here are their function prototypes:

```
double largest(const std::vector<double>& data);
double largest(const double data[], std::size_t count);
```

Other than the fact that one of them operates on a plain array and the other on a vector, there is very little difference between these two functions.

Back then, we noted that function templates can remedy duplicated function overloads. We will cover that in the next chapter. But for this particular case—function overloads for sequences with the same element type, C++20 offers an interesting alternative called *spans*. The std::span<T> class template allows you to refer to any contiguous sequence of T values—be it a std::vector<T>, std::array<T,N>, or C-style array—without specifying the concrete array or container type.

Let's make that more concrete with an example. You can replace the two aforementioned overloads of largest() in Ex8_14 with a single overload, as follows (see also Ex9_03):

```
// double largest(const std::vector<double>& data);
// double largest(const double data[], std::size_t count);
double largest(std::span<double> data);
```

Apart from the signature, you can implement this new function exactly as you did for the overload for std::vector<double> before:

```
// Finds the largest of a sequence of double values
double largest(std::span<double> data) /* Note: signature is not ideal yet: see later */
{
  double max {data[0]};
  for (auto value : data)
    if (max < value) max = value;
  return max;
}
```

In other words, not only can you use spans in range-based for loops, but they offer a square brackets operator as well, [], which allows you to access individual elements by index. Like string_view objects, span<> objects can be passed to a function by value very efficiently.

▒ **Note** Besides range support and a square bracket operator, std::span<> offers various other functions you already know from std::array<> and std::vector<>: size(), empty(), data(), front(), and back(). Other functions, such as several members to create subspans, are specific to span<>. You can consult a Standard Library reference for the complete list of members.

With this new overload of largest() in place, there is very little that you need to change in the main() function of Ex8_14. Only the expression largest(array, std::size(array)) needs work since largest() now expects a single span object as input instead of a pointer and a size. Luckily, creating a span from a pointer-size pair is trivial. Written in full, the updated output statement looks as follows:

```
double array[] {1.5, 44.6, 13.7, 21.2, 6.7};
// ...
std::println("The largest of array is {}",
             largest(std::span<double>{ array, std::size(array) }));
```

Ouch! That's verbose. Luckily, you can omit the argument type and invoke largest() with only the braced initializer as follows:

```
std::println("The largest of array is {}", largest({ array, std::size(array) }));
```

The compiler knows it must create a span object here because the corresponding function overload is the only one for which this braced initializer works.

But you can use an even shorter expression here. Because the compiler knows the size of array—it is a reference variable of type double(&)[5]—the size argument is redundant.

```
std::println("The largest of array is {}", largest(array));
```

The extra size argument is required only when creating a span<T> object if the first argument is a pointer variable of type T* or const T*, from which the compiler cannot possibly deduce the size for you.

Writing Through a Span

Conceptually, there is one significant difference between a span<T> and a string_view: a span<T>, unlike a string_view, allows you to reassign or change the elements of the underlying array. We can illustrate this by the following code snippet:

```
std::vector<double> my_vector{ 0, 2, 15, 16, 23, 42 };
std::span<double> my_span(my_vector);
my_span.front() = 4;
my_span[1] *= 4;
std::println("{}, {}", my_vector[0], my_vector[1]);   // 4, 8
```

The front(), back(), and operator[] members of std::span<T> all return T& references, referring to non-const elements of the underlying array. This allows you to assign or change these elements. Recall that the equivalent does not work with string_views (no doubt because the character array underlying a string_view will often be a string literal):

```
std::string my_string{
  "Don't accept the limitations of other people who claim things are 'unchangeable'. "
  "If it's written in stone, bring your hammer and chisel."
};
std::string_view my_string_view{ my_string };
// my_string_view[0] = 'W';   /* Error: my_string_view[0] returns const char& */
```

▓ **Note**   While a span<> allows you to reassign or otherwise alter elements, it does not allow you to add or remove any elements. That is, a span<> does not offer members such as push_back(), erase(), or clear(). Otherwise, a span<> could never be created for C-style arrays or std::array<> objects.

Spans of const Elements

The fact that you can modify elements backing a span<T> implies that you should not be able to create one from, for instance, a const container. If you could, this span<> would provide a backdoor to modify the elements of a const container. You can give it a try by attempting to compile this snippet (it will fail):

```
const std::vector<double> my_const_vector{ 4, 8, 15, 16, 23, 42 };
std::span<double> my_span(my_const_vector);  // Should not compile!
my_span[3] = 100;                            // Reason: this should not be possible...
```

Unfortunately, this introduces a seemingly serious problem for the largest() function we created in Ex9_03.cpp. To refresh your memory, here is its declaration:

```
double largest(std::span<double> data);
```

Because a span<double> cannot be created from a const vector, Ex9_03's largest() function is actually not a proper replacement for the original two function overloads at all. For instance, with my_const_vector defined as earlier in this section, the following invocation will not work:

```
auto max{ largest(my_const_vector) };   // Does not compile!
```

Luckily, the solution is easy. To replace const vector<T>&, you should use span<const T> instead of span<T>. That is, you should use a span of const elements. All element accessor functions of a span<const T> (including the [ ] operator) return const T& references, even if the original array or container was non-const. This is illustrated by the following snippet.

```
std::vector<double> my_vector{ 4, 8, 15, 16, 23, 42 };
std::span<const double> my_const_span(my_vector);
// my_const_span[3] = 100;              // Does not compile!
```

▓ **Note** A std::string_view is thus most similar to a std::span<const char>. The key difference is that std::string_view offers extra member functions tailored to working with strings.

The correct prototype for the largest() function is as follows:

```
double largest(std::span<const double> data);
```

Beyond its signature, no other changes are required to the function's definition. You can find the resulting program in Ex9_03A.cpp.

▓ **Tip** Use span<const T> instead of const vector<T>&. Similarly, use span<T> instead of vector<T>&, unless you need to insert or remove elements.

Fixed-Size Spans

You can also use the span<> class template to write a generic function that can operate on fixed-size arrays. All you have to do is add this fixed size as a second argument to the template. You could, for instance, replace the different average10() functions of Ex8_09A, Ex8_09B, and Ex8_09C with a single function as follows:

```
// double average10(const double (&values)[10]);
// double average10(const std::array<double, 10>& values);
double average10(std::span<const double, 10> values);
```

Working out the function definition should be straightforward, so we'll leave that to you as an exercise.

▓ **Tip** Use span<T,N> instead of array<T,N>& or T(&)[N], and span<const T,N> instead of const array<T,N>& or const T(&)[N].

Summary

This shorter chapter introduced you to some of the vocabulary types provided by the modern Standard Library: `std::optional<>`, `std::expected<>`, `std::string_view`, and `std::span<>`.

In summary,

- Use `std::optional<>` to represent values that may or may not be present but require no further explanation as to why they may be missing. Examples are optional inputs to a function, or the result of a function for which returning a null value is quite normal (such as `find_last()` in `Ex9_01`).

- Use `std::expected<>` for values that are normally available but could be missing in unexpected, typically erroneous circumstances. In the latter case, the error value embedded in the `std::expected<>` object provides its consumers with the means to diagnose or even recover from an unexpected situation.

- Use `std::string_view` instead of `const std::string&` to avoid inadvertent copies of string literals or other character arrays.

- Use `std::span<const T>` instead of, for instance, `const std::vector<T>&` parameters to make the same function work as well for C-style arrays, `std::array<>` objects, and so on.

- Similarly, use `std::span<T>` instead of `std::vector<T>&` parameters, unless you need the ability to add or remove elements.

- Use `std::span<(const) T,N>` instead of `(const) std::array<T,N>&` parameters to make the same function work for C-style arrays (or other containers you know to contain at least N elements).

EXERCISES

These exercises enable you to try some of what you've learned in this chapter. If you get stuck, look back over the chapter for help. If you're still stuck, you can download the solutions from the Apress website (`https://www.apress.com/gp/services/source-code`), but that really should be a last resort.

Exercise 9-1. Adjust `Ex9_01` to use `std::string_view`.

Exercise 9-2. Adjust `Ex8_11` to use `std::string_view`.

Exercise 9-3. Adjust `Ex8_13` to use vocabulary types.

Exercise 9-4. Whenever you either read or write code, "What if?" should be your number one go-to question. For instance, consider the `largest()` function of `Ex9_03`. It starts by accessing `data[0]`. But what if `data` is empty? In cases such as this, you have several options.

First, you could add a code comment specifying that `data` may not be empty. This is called a *precondition*. Violating a precondition as a caller results in undefined behavior. All bets are off when you violate a precondition—or, as Ellie Goulding would put it: anything could happen (including a crash).

Second, you could come up with a reasonable behavior for such corner cases. Come up with some result the function could compute for empty input. Say, a not-a-number value for the `largest()` of an empty array?

Both can be viable options at times. But can you, in the spirit of this chapter, work out a third alternative?

Exercise 9-5. As promised, write yet another variant of Ex8_09A, Ex8_09B, and Ex8_09C, where this time the average10() function uses one of the vocabulary types seen in this chapter. Show that this one function can be called both for fixed-size C-style arrays and std::array<> containers and only so for arrays of ten elements.

Exercise 9-6. Suppose you have a vector<>, and you know for a fact that it contains exactly ten elements (or at least ten elements). Can you then call the average10() function of the previous example to compute the average of these ten elements (or the ten first elements)? Not directly, obviously, but it is possible! After all, all the necessary *data* (ten consecutive elements) is present in the vector. You may want to consult a Standard Library reference for this.

CHAPTER 10

■ ■ ■

Function Templates

You may have noticed that some of the overloaded functions in Ex8_15 consisted of exactly the same code. The only difference were the types that appear in the parameter list. It seems an unnecessary overhead to have to write the same code over and over, just because it has to work for different types. And indeed it is. In such situations you can write the code just once, as a *function template*. The Standard Library, for instance, makes heavy use of this feature to ensure that its functions work optimally with any type, including your own custom types, which of course the library cannot know about in advance. This chapter introduces the basics of defining your own function templates that work with any type you desire.

In this chapter, you will learn

- How to define parameterized function templates that generate a family of related functions

- That parameters to function templates are mostly, but not always, types

- That template arguments are mostly deduced by the compiler and how to specify them explicitly when necessary

- How to specialize and overload function templates if the generic function definition provided by the template isn't suited for certain types

- Why return type deduction is really powerful in combination with templates

- How the abbreviated function template syntax makes it even easier to quickly write a basic function template

Function Templates

A *function template* itself it is not a definition of a function; it is a blueprint or a recipe for defining an entire family of functions. A function template is a parametric function definition, where a particular function instance is created by one or more parameter values. The compiler uses a function template to generate a function definition when necessary. If it is never necessary, no code results from the template. A function definition that is generated from a template is an *instance* or an *instantiation* of the template. The parameters of a function template are usually data types, where an instance can be generated for a parameter value of type int, for example, and another with a parameter value of type string. But parameters are not necessarily types. They can be other things such as a dimension, for example. Let's consider a specific example.

In Chapter 8, we defined various overloads of larger(), often for different parameter types. It makes for a good candidate for a template. Figure 10-1 shows a template for these functions.

© Ivor Horton and Peter Van Weert 2023
I. Horton and P. Van Weert, *Beginning C++23*, https://doi.org/10.1007/978-1-4842-9343-0_10

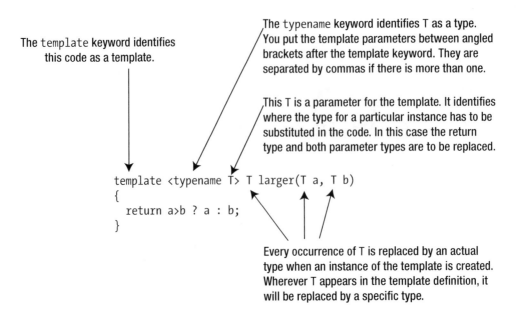

The template keyword identifies this code as a template.

The typename keyword identifies T as a type. You put the template parameters between angled brackets after the template keyword. They are separated by commas if there is more than one.

This T is a parameter for the template. It identifies where the type for a particular instance has to be substituted in the code. In this case the return type and both parameter types are to be replaced.

```
template <typename T> T larger(T a, T b)
{
    return a>b ? a : b;
}
```

Every occurrence of T is replaced by an actual type when an instance of the template is created. Wherever T appears in the template definition, it will be replaced by a specific type.

Figure 10-1. *A simple function template*

The function template starts with the template keyword to identify it as such. This is followed by a pair of angle brackets that contains a list of one or more *template parameters*. In this case, there's only one, the parameter T. T is commonly used as a name for a parameter because most parameters are types, but you can use whatever name you like for a parameter; names such as type, MY_TYPE, or Comparable are equally valid. Especially if there are multiple parameters, using more descriptive names may be recommended.

The typename keyword identifies that T is a type. T is hence called a *template type parameter*. You can also use the keyword class here—the keywords class and typename are synonymous in this context—but we prefer typename because the type argument can be a fundamental type as well, not just a class type.

The rest of the definition is similar to a normal function except that the parameter name T is sprinkled around. The compiler creates an instance of the template by replacing T throughout the definition with a specific type. The type assigned to a type parameter T during instantiation is called a *template type argument*.

You can position the template in a source file in the same way as a normal function definition; you can also specify a prototype for a function template. In this case, it would be as follows:

```
template<typename T> T larger(T a, T b);  // Prototype for function template
```

Either the prototype or the definition of the template must appear in the source file before any statement that results in an instance of the template.

Creating Instances of a Function Template

The compiler creates instances of the template from any statement that uses the larger() function. Here's an example:

```
std::println("Larger of 1.5 and 2.5 is {}", larger(1.5, 2.5));
```

You just use the function in the normal way. You don't need to specify a value for the template parameter T. The compiler deduces the type that is to replace T from the arguments in the larger() function call. This mechanism is referred to as *template argument deduction*. The arguments to larger() are literals of type double, so this call causes the compiler to search for an existing instantiation of larger() with double parameters. If it doesn't find one, the compiler instantiates a new function definition from the template by substituting double for T in the template definition.

The resulting function definition accepts arguments of type double and returns a double value. With double plugged into the template in place of T, the template instance will effectively be as follows:

```
double larger(double a, double b)
{
  return a > b ? a : b;
}
```

The compiler makes sure to generate each template instance only once. If a subsequent function call requires the same instance, then it calls the instance that exists. Your executable only ever includes a single copy of the definition of each instance, even if the same instance is generated in different source files. Now that you are familiar with the concepts, let's road test a function template:

```
// Ex10_01.cpp - Using a function template
import std;

template<typename T> T larger(T a, T b);    // Function template prototype

int main()
{
  std::println("Larger of 1.5 and 2.5 is {}", larger(1.5, 2.5));
  std::println("Larger of 3.5 and 4.5 is {}", larger(3.5, 4.5));

  const int big_int {17011983}, small_int {10};
  std::println("Larger of {} and {} is {}",
              big_int, small_int, larger(big_int, small_int));

  const std::string a_string {"A"}, z_string {"Z"};
  std::println(R"(Larger of "{}" and "{}" is "{}")",
              a_string, z_string, larger(a_string, z_string));
}

// Template for functions to return the larger of two values
template <typename T>
T larger(T a, T b)
{
    return a > b ? a : b;
}
```

This produces the following output:

```
Larger of 1.5 and 2.5 is 2.5
Larger of 3.5 and 4.5 is 4.5
Larger of 17011983 and 10 is 17011983
Larger of "A" and "Z" is "Z"
```

The compiler creates a definition of larger() that accepts arguments of type double as a result of the first statement in main(). The same instance will be called in the next statement. The third statement requires a version of larger() that accepts an argument of type int, so a new template instance is created. The last statement results in yet another template instance being created that has parameters of type std::string and returns a value of type std::string.

Template Type Parameters

The name of a template type parameter can be used anywhere in the template's function signature, return type, and body. It is a placeholder for a type and can thus be put in any context you would normally put the concrete type. That is, suppose T is a template parameter name; then you can use T to construct derived types, such as T&, const T&, T*, and T[][3]. Or you can use T as an argument to a class template, such as in std::vector<T>.

As an example, we can reconsider the larger() function template of Ex10_01. It currently instantiates functions that accept their arguments by value. As witnessed by Ex10_01, however, this template can be instantiated with class types such as std::string as well. In Chapter 8, you learned that passing objects by value results in gratuitous copies of these objects, which is something you should avoid if possible. The standard mechanism for this, of course, is to pass the arguments by reference instead. We would therefore be better off redefining our template as follows:

```
template <typename T>
const T& larger(const T& a, const T& b)
{
    return a > b ? a : b;
}
```

■ **Note** The <algorithm> module of the Standard Library defines a std::max() function template that is completely analogous to our latest definition of larger(). It takes two arguments by reference-to-const and returns a reference-to-const that refers to the largest of the two function arguments. The same module also defines the std::min() template, which of course instantiates functions that determine the smallest of two values.

Explicit Template Arguments

If you add the following statement to main() in Ex10_01.cpp, it will not compile:

```
std::println("Larger of {} and 19.6 is {}", small_int, larger(small_int, 19.6));
```

The arguments to larger() are of different types, whereas the parameters for larger() in the template are of the same type. The compiler cannot create a template instance that has different parameter types. Obviously, one argument could be converted to the type of the other, but you have to code this explicitly; the compiler won't do it. You could define the template to allow the parameters for larger() to be different types, but this adds a complication that we'll discuss later in this chapter: Which of the two do you use for the return type? For now, let's focus on how you can specify the argument for a template parameter explicitly when you call the function. This allows you to control which version of the function is used. The compiler no longer deduces the type to replace T; it accepts what you specify.

You can resolve the problem of using different arguments types with larger() with an *explicit instantiation* of the template:

```
std::println("Larger of {} and 19.6 is {}",
             small_int, larger<double>(small_int, 19.6));        // Prints 19.6
```

You put the explicit type argument for the function template between angle brackets after the function name. This generates an instance with T as type double. When you use explicit template arguments, the compiler has complete faith that you know what you are doing. It will insert an implicit type conversion for the first argument to type double. It will provide implicit conversions, even when this may not be what you want. Here's an example:

```
std::println("Larger of {} and 19.6 is {}",
             small_int, larger<int>(small_int, 19.6));        // Prints 19
```

You are telling the compiler to use a template instance with T as type int. This necessitates an implicit conversion of the second argument to int. The result of this conversion is the value 19, which may not be what you really want in this case. Most compilers will warn you about such dangerous conversions, though not all compilers will.

Function Template Specialization

Suppose that you extend Ex10_01.cpp to call larger() with arguments that are pointers:

```
std::println("Larger of {} and {} is {}",
             big_int, small_int, *larger(&big_int, &small_int)); // May print 10!
```

The compiler instantiates the template with the parameter as type const int*. The prototype of this instance is as follows:

```
const int* larger(const int*, const int*);
```

The return value is an address, and you have to dereference it to output the value. However, the result may very well be 10, which is probably not as intended. The reason is that the comparison is between addresses that are passed as arguments, and not the values at those addresses. Since the compiler is free to rearrange the memory locations of local variables, the actual outcome may vary across compilers. But given that the small_int variable comes second, it is certainly not unthinkable that its address would be larger.

▓ **Note** If the output of the previous snippet is not 10 for your compiler, you can try to rearrange the order in which big_int and small_int are declared. Surely the comparison of two integer values should not depend on the order of their declarations?

In principle, you can define a *specialization* of the template to accommodate a template argument that is a pointer type (although, shortly, we will tell you this is rarely a good idea). For a specific parameter value or set of values in the case of a template with multiple parameters, a template specialization defines a behavior that is different from the standard template. The definition of a template specialization must come after a declaration or definition of the original template. If you put a specialization first, then the program won't compile. The specialization must also appear before its first use.

The definition of a so-called *explicit template specialization* or *full template specialization* (the only type of specialization allowed for function templates; see also Chapter 17) starts with the template keyword, but the parameters are omitted, so the angle brackets following the keyword are empty. The definition for an explicit specialization of larger() for type const int* is as follows:

```
template <>
const int* larger(const int* a, const int* b)
{
  return *a > *b ? a : b;
}
```

The only change to the body of the function is to dereference the arguments a and b so that you compare values rather than addresses. To use this in Ex10_01.cpp, the specialization would need to be placed after the prototype for the template and before main().

Unfortunately, function template specializations have some subtle downsides. As far as we are concerned, they join typedef, new/new [ ], and delete/delete [ ] in the list of discouraged language features:

■ **Tip**   Don't use function template specializations. To customize a function template for specific types, you should overload the function template instead, either with regular functions or different function templates. We introduce both these options in the next section, and we further refer to Chapter 21 for the even more powerful overloading of constrained function templates. Unlike function template specializations, overloaded functions and function templates do always behave intuitively.

Function Templates and Overloading

You can overload a function template by defining other functions with the same name. This allows you to define "overrides" for specific cases without resorting to template specialization. More specific overloads will always be used by the compiler in preference to an instance of a more generic template. As always, each overloaded function must have a unique signature.

Let's reconsider the previous situation in which you need to overload the larger() function to take pointer arguments. Instead of using a template specialization for larger(), you should simply define an overloaded function. The following overloaded function prototype does the trick:

```
const int* larger(const int* a, const int* b); // Function overloading the larger template
```

In place of the specialization definition, you should then use this function definition:

```
const int* larger(const int* a, const int* b)
{
  return *a > *b ? a : b;
}
```

You can even overload the original template with another template specifically for pointer types:

```
template<typename T>
T* larger(T* a, T* b)
{
  return *a > *b ? a : b;
}
```

Note that this is *not* a specialization of the original template but instead a second, distinct template that will be instantiated only for pointer types. If the compiler encounters a call larger(x,y) where x and y are pointers to values of the same type, it will instantiate this second function template; otherwise, it will still instantiate our previous template.

Of course, it's also possible to overload an existing template with another template that generates functions with completely different signatures. For example, you could define a template that overloads the larger() template in Ex10_01.cpp to find the largest value contained in a vector:

```
template <typename T>
const T* larger(const std::vector<T>& data)
{
  const T* result {};        // The largest of an empty vector is nullptr
  for (auto& value : data)
    if (!result || value > *result) result = &value;
  return result;
}
```

The parameter list differentiates functions produced from this template from instances of the original template.

You could extend Ex10_01.cpp to demonstrate this. Add the previous templates to the end of the source file and these prototypes at the beginning:

```
template <typename T> T* larger(T*, T*);
template <typename T> const T* larger(const std::vector<T>& data);
```

The code in main() can then be changed to the following:

```
  const int big_int {17011983}, small_int {10};
  std::println("Larger of {} and {} is {}",
               big_int, small_int, larger(big_int, small_int));
  std::println("Larger of {} and {} is {}",
               big_int, small_int, *larger(&big_int, &small_int));

  const std::vector<double> data {-1.4, 7.3, -100.0, 54.1, 16.3};
  std::println("The largest value in data is {}", *larger(data));

  const std::vector<std::string> words {"The", "higher", "the", "fewer"};
  std::println(R"(The largest word in words is "{}")", *larger(words));
```

We put the complete code in Ex10_02.cpp. This program generates instances of the overloaded templates. If you compile and execute it, the output will be as follows:

```
Larger of 17011983 and 10 is 17011983
Larger of 17011983 and 10 is 17011983
The largest value in data is 54.1
The largest word in words is "the"
```

Function Templates with Multiple Parameters

Until now, you've been using function templates with a single template parameter, but there can be several parameters. Recall from earlier that in the expression larger(small_int, 9.6), the compiler failed to deduce the template type argument because the two function arguments have a different type—int and double, respectively. We solved this before by explicitly specifying the type. But perhaps you were wondering why we could not simply create a larger() template for which the function arguments are allowed to be different? This could then look something like this:

```
template <typename T1, typename T2>
??? larger(const T1& a, const T2& b)
{
  return a > b ? a : b;
}
```

Allowing different types for each function argument is easy enough, and it can often be a good idea to keep your templates as generic as possible. However, in cases such as this, you run into trouble when specifying the return type. That is, in the previous pseudocode, what should we put instead of the three question marks? T1? T2? Neither is correct in general because both could lead to undesired conversions.

The first possible solution is to add an extra template type argument to provide a way of controlling the return type. Here's an example:

```
template <typename ReturnType, typename T1, typename T2>
ReturnType larger(const T1& a, const T2& b)
{
  return static_cast<ReturnType>(a > b ? a : b);
}
```

We added an explicit cast to ReturnType to silence any warnings about implicit conversions.

Template argument deduction works on the basis of the arguments passed in the function's argument list alone. From these arguments, the compiler can easily deduce T1 and T2, but not ReturnType. You must always specify the ReturnType template argument yourself. You can still leave it up to the compiler to deduce T1 and T2, though. In general, if you specify fewer template arguments than the number of template parameters, the compiler will deduce the others. The following three lines are therefore equivalent:

```
std::println("Larger of 1.5 and 2 is {}", larger<int>(1.5, 2));
std::println("Larger of 1.5 and 2 is {}", larger<int, double>(1.5, 2));
std::println("Larger of 1.5 and 2 is {}", larger<int, double, int>(1.5, 2));
```

Clearly, the sequence of parameters in the template definition is important here. If you had the return type as the second parameter, you'd always have to specify both parameters in a call. If you specify only one parameter, it would be interpreted as the argument type, leaving the return type undefined. Because we specified the return type as int, in all three cases, the results of these function calls will all be 2. The compiler creates a function that accepts arguments of type double and int and then converts its result to a value of type int.

While we did illustrate how multiple parameters can be defined and what that means for template argument deduction, you may have noticed that we still haven't found a satisfactory solution that would allow us to write the following:

```
std::println("Larger of {} and 9.6 is {}", small_int, larger(small_int, 9.6));
```

We'll resolve this once and for all in the next section.

Return Type Deduction in Templates

In Chapter 8, you learned about automatic return type deduction for regular functions. In the context of function templates, return type deduction can be a godsend. The return type of a template function with one or more type parameters may depend on the types used to instantiate the template. We have seen this already in the previous section with the following example:

```
template <typename T1, typename T2>
??? larger(const T1& a, const T2& b)
{
  return a > b ? a : b;
}
```

There is no easy way you can specify which type should be returned here. But there is an easy way to have the compiler deduce it for you after instantiating the template:

```
template <typename T1, typename T2>
auto larger(const T1& a, const T2& b)
{
  return a > b ? a : b;
}
```

With this definition, the following statements will compile just fine without the need to explicitly specify any type argument:

```
const int small_int {10};
std::println("Larger of {} and 9.6 is {}",
             small_int, larger(small_int, 9.6));   // deduced return type: double

std::string a_string {"A"};
std::println(R"(Larger of "{}" and "Z" is "{}")",
             a_string , larger(a_string, "Z"));   // deduced return type: std::string
```

With our original definition of larger() in Ex10_01, which had only one type parameter, both of these instantiations would've been ambiguous and thus would've failed to compile. A working program using the two-parameter version is found in Ex10_03.cpp.

decltype(auto)

Using auto as the return type of a function implies this return type will always deduce to a value type. When used as the return type of a function *template*, auto sometimes inadvertently introduces copying.

To illustrate the problem, reconsider the larger<>() template of Ex10_03. Now suppose that it is instantiated with both T1 and T2 equal to std::vector<int>. Then the compiler effectively generates the following instance:

```
auto larger(const std::vector<int>& a, const std::vector<int>& b)
{
  return a > b ? a : b;
}
```

In a next step, the compiler deduces its return type:

```
std::vector<int> larger(const std::vector<int>& a, const std::vector<int>& b)
{
  return a > b ? a : b;
}
```

Because the return type of this template instance was auto, the compiler deduces the *value* type std::vector<int>, rather than the more desirable *reference* type const std::vector<int>&. Unfortunately, this means that this instantiated function then always copies one of its inputs, which could be arbitrarily large vectors. When writing this function in a non-generic way, you'd therefore normally write this instead:

```
const auto& larger(const std::vector<int>& a, const std::vector<int>& b)
{
  return a > b ? a : b;
}
```

The problem is that we cannot use const auto& for the return type in the larger<>() template either because then we'd be returning the address of a temporary value in cases where T1 and T2 differ (and are not related by inheritance; see Chapter 14). That is, using const auto& instead of auto in larger<>() would result in instances such as the following.

```
const auto& larger(const double& a, const int& b)
{
  return a > b ? a : b;    // Warning: returning a reference to a temporary double!!!
}
```

Here a > b ? a : b creates a new temporary value of type double (the *common type* of int and double). And, of course, we taught you better than to return a reference or pointer to a local or temporary variable like that (see Chapter 8)!

The solution to such predicaments, where neither auto nor const auto& is appropriate, is the more advanced decltype(auto) placeholder type. When used as the return type of a function, this placeholder evaluates to the exact type of the expression(s) in the return statement(s). You could therefore create an improved version of the larger<>() template as follows (see also Ex10_03A).

```
template <typename T1, typename T2>
decltype(auto) larger(const T1& a, const T2& b)
{
  return a > b ? a : b;
}
```

For larger<double, int>(), the deduced return type will then still be double, but that of larger<std::vector<int>, std::vector<int>> will be const std::vector<int>&—as desired!

Note that you should only use decltype(auto) in templates. In non-generic code, you should always explicitly choose between the more specific auto or (const) auto& instead.

constexpr If

Since we've started dabbling with more advanced language features (decltype(auto)), we might as well give you a taste of another: constexpr if statements. After all, in our experience, you'll use constexpr if statements far more often than decltype(auto) (albeit still sporadically, of course).

A constexpr if statement is essentially an if statement that is only evaluated at compile time. Although, in principle, you may use constexpr if statements in regular functions as well, you'll mostly use them in templated code. To show how this works, Ex10_04 blends two larger() templates of Ex10_02—the main one and the one for comparing pointers—into one using a basic constexpr if statement. The resulting template looks as follows:

```
template<typename T>
decltype(auto) larger(const T& a, const T& b)
{
  if constexpr (std::is_pointer_v<T>)  // Evaluated only at compile time
    return *a > *b ? a : b;            // Only compiled if T is a pointer type
  else
    return a > b ? a : b;             // Only compiled if T is not a pointer type
}
```

You write a constexpr if statement as if constexpr (...). (Precisely, the other way around! So why do we call it a "constexpr if" statement if the syntax is "if constexpr"? Not quite sure, but it's the official nomenclature, so don't blame us...) As always with if statements, the else branch is optional, and you can add curly braces to branches that contain multiple statements.

▓ **Note**   Unlike with consteval if statements (introduced in Chapter 8), the syntax if !constexpr is invalid (presumably because consteval if statements are far more likely not to have an else branch than consteval if statements).

The expression inside our constexpr if statement, std::is_pointer_v<T>, is a *type trait*—in particular, one offered by the <type_traits> Standard Library module. Fully explaining type traits and how they work would lead us too far. (You need to know about class templates, for one, which we only cover in Chapter 17.) Luckily, you mostly don't need to know how the magic works. You can simply view type traits as functions that operate on types instead of values, and you "invoke" using angular brackets, <>, instead of round brackets, (). Standard type trait constructs whose name end in _v map one or more types onto a compile-time constant (a Boolean for std::is_pointer_v<T>); those ending in _t map one or more types onto another type (you'll encounter an example of such a trait in Chapter 21). The std::is_pointer_v<T> expression, in particular, is a constant expression that evaluates to true if T is a pointer type, and false otherwise.

The test expression of the constexpr if statement itself does not result in runtime code. It's only ever evaluated at compile time. A constexpr if statement simply tells the compiler which statements to compile: those in the if branch or those in the optional else branch. For the branch that is not selected, if any, no code is generated at all either. This is important because, more often than not, the discarded branch contains statements that do not compile for that specific instantiation of the template. So too in our example. Suppose, for instance, that you replace the constexpr if statement with a plain if statement as follows:

```
template<typename T>
decltype(auto) larger(const T& a, const T& b) /* This version won't work! */
{
  if (std::is_pointer_v<T>)    // Evaluated, at least in principle, at runtime
    return *a > *b ? a : b;    // Compiler error if *a and *b are invalid (say, if T is int)
  else
    return a > b ? a : b;
}
```

Now imagine you instantiate this template for T equal to int. Then the compiler effectively generates a function that looks as follows:

```
int larger(const int& a, const int& b)
{
  if (std::is_pointer_v<int>) // Always false. The compiler knows this...
    return *a > *b ? a : b;    // ... yet still this line results in a compilation error!
  else
    return a > b ? a : b;
}
```

In a plain if-else statement, the code in both the if and else branch needs to be valid, even if the compiler knows one of these branches will never be entered (as is the case here). And because *a and *b are not valid if a and b are of type int (these expressions are effectively only valid if T is of a pointer-like type), the compiler has no choice but to cry out error.

If, on the other hand, you instantiate the constexpr if version of the template with T equal to int, the code in the if branch is simply discarded, leaving only the code in the else branch.

```
int larger(const int& a, const int& b)
{
//if constexpr (std::is_pointer_v<int>)  // Evaluates to false at compile time...
//  return *a > *b ? a : b;               // ... so no code is generated here!
//else
    return a > b ? a : b;    // Only statement compiled for this template instantiation
}
```

Because all constexpr if statements need to be evaluated at compile time, it goes without saying that only constant expressions (literals, constants, type trait expressions, constexpr / consteval functions, and so on; see also Chapter 8) may appear inside their condition.

Default Values for Template Parameters

You can specify default values for function template parameters. For example, you could specify double as the default return type in the prototype for the template introduced earlier like this:

```
// Template with default value for the first parameter
template <typename ReturnType=double, typename T1, typename T2>
ReturnType larger(const T1&, const T2&);
```

If you don't specify any template parameter values, the return type will be double. Note that we only use this example to introduce default values for template parameters, not because it is necessarily a good idea to define larger() like this. The reason this is not such a great idea is that this default, double, is not always what you want. The larger() function resulting from the following statement, for instance, accepts arguments of type int and returns the result as type double:

```
std::println("{}", larger(123, 543));
```

The main point we want to convey with this example is that you can specify default values for template arguments at the beginning of the template argument list. You'll recall that, for function parameters, it was only possible to define default values at the end of the list. You have more flexibility when specifying default values for template parameters. In our first example, ReturnType is the first in the list. But you can also specify default values for parameters in the middle of the list or at the end. Here is yet another larger() template to illustrate the latter:

```
// Template with a default value referring to an earlier parameter
template <typename T, typename ReturnType=T>
ReturnType larger(const T&, const T&);
```

In this example, we use the T as the default value for the ReturnType template parameter. Using a template parameter name in the default value of other parameters is possible only if that name, T in our example, appears earlier in the parameter list. This example again mostly serves to illustrate what is possible and less as something that is necessarily a good idea. If the default value for ReturnType does not suit you and you have to specify another type explicitly, you would have to specify all other arguments as well. Nevertheless, it is common practice to specify default values for template parameters at the end of the list. The Standard Library uses this extensively, often also for non-type template parameters. Non-type template parameters are discussed next.

Non-Type Template Parameters

All the template parameters you have seen so far have been types. Function templates can also have *non-type* parameters that require non-type arguments.

You include non-type template parameters in the parameter list along with any type parameters. Suppose you need a function to perform range checking on a value where the limits of the range are fixed beforehand. You could then define a template to handle a variety of types:

```
template <typename T, int lower, int upper>
bool is_in_range(const T& value)
{
  return (value <= upper) && (value >= lower);
}
```

This template has a type parameter, T, and two non-type parameters, lower and upper, both of type int. As of C++20, a template parameter can be of any fundamental type (bool, float, int, and so on), enumeration type, pointer type, or reference type. In theory, class types can be used as the type of a template parameter as well, but the limitations are very restrictive. Restrictive enough for you to disregard this possibility. We'll only consider a few elementary examples here with integer type parameters just to show how it works.

Clearly, the compiler can't deduce all the lower and upper template parameters from the use of our is_in_range() function template. Therefore, the following invocation won't compile:

```
double value {100.0};
std::println("{}", is_in_range(value));                    // Won't compile – incorrect usage
```

Compilation fails because upper and lower are unspecified. To use this template, you must explicitly specify the template parameter values. The correct way to use this is as follows:

```
std::println("{}", is_in_range<double, 0, 500>(value));    // OK – checks 0 to 500
```

The compiler needs to be able to evaluate the arguments corresponding to all non-type parameters at compile time. This means that most non-type template arguments will be composed of either literals or compile-time constants, although any constant expression is allowed (see Chapter 8 for our introduction to constexpr / consteval functions). In the following example, i is a compile-time integer constant, and so both i and i * 100 may be used as non-type template arguments:

```
const int i{ -5 };                                         // OK – compile-time constant
std::println("{}", is_in_range<double, std::abs(i), -i * 10>(value)); // Checks 5 to 50
```

Once you omit the const, however, i is no longer a constant, and the code will fail to compile. All template parameters—both type and non-type—need to be evaluated *at compile time* while generating the concrete function instantiation from the template.

▓ **Note**   std::abs() is only required to be a constexpr function starting from C++23 (together with a selection of other mathematical functions from <cmath> and <cstdlib>). So if your Standard Library implementation is not yet compliant, you may need to omit std::abs() to make the previous example compile. Maybe you can write your own constexpr function to compute the absolute value instead?

One obvious downside of our initial is_in_range() template is that it fixes the type of both lower and upper to int. This is unfortunate if you want to check for non-integral bounds. One solution for this is to use auto as the type of these non-type template parameters instead and have the compiler deduce their types at instantiation time.

```
template <typename T, auto lower, auto upper>
bool is_in_range(const T& value)
{
  return (value <= upper) && (value >= lower);
}
```

Now you can use non-integral bounds as well:

```
const double i{ 0.5 };                                     // OK – compile-time constant
std::println("{}", is_in_range<double, i / 2, i * 10>(value)); // OK – checks 0.25 to 5.0
```

For this particular instantiation, both lower and upper become constant values of type double.

You could also use the name of the template type parameter T as (or in) the type of the other non-type template parameters. The following example will clarify:

```
template <typename T, T lower, T upper>
bool is_in_range(const T& value)
{
  return (value <= upper) && (value >= lower);
}
```

lower and upper now have type T instead of int, making for a potentially interesting variation of our template as well.

In yet another variation, we could put the two non-type template parameters to the left of the template type parameter as follows:

```
template <int lower, int upper, typename T>
bool is_in_range(const T& value)
{
  return (value <= upper) && (value >= lower);
}
```

That way, the compiler is capable of deducing the type argument:

```
std::println("{}", is_in_range<0, 500>(value));  // OK – checks 0 to 500
```

One downside now, though, is that you can no longer refer to T in the types of lower and upper; you can only refer to the names of type parameters declared *to the left* of a non-type parameter.

```
template <T lower, T upper, typename T>                // Error – T has not been declared
bool is_in_range(const T& value);
...
```

All in all, it thus seems that the best variation would be one that puts the type parameter T last (so that this type can be deduced) and uses auto for lower and upper (to avoid hard-coding their type):

```
template <auto lower, auto upper, typename T>
bool is_in_range(const T& value)
{
  return (value <= upper) && (value >= lower);
}
```

That being said, in the case of the limits of is_in_range(), you should probably use regular function parameters over template parameters. Function parameters give you the flexibility of being able to pass values that are calculated at runtime, whereas with template parameters, you must supply the limits at compile time. We used the is_in_range() templates solely to explore the possibilities, not because any of them is an example of the appropriate use of non-type template parameters.

But make no mistake—while relatively rare, non-type template parameters surely have their uses. We discuss one specific use case in the next subsection.

Templates for Functions with Fixed-Size Array Arguments

In Chapter 8, in the section on passing arrays by reference, we defined the following function:

```
double average10(const double (&array)[10])    // Only arrays of length 10 can be passed!
{
  double sum {};                                 // Accumulate total in here
  for (std::size_t i {}; i < 10; ++i)
    sum += array[i];                             // Sum array elements
  return sum / 10;                               // Return average
}
```

Clearly, it would be great if you could create a function that would work for any array size, not just for arrays of exactly ten values. A template with non-type template arguments allows you to do this, as shown next. For good measure, we'll generalize it even further such that it works for arrays of any numerical type as well, not just for arrays of double:

```
template <typename T, std::size_t N>
T average(const T (&array)[N])
{
  T sum {};                                      // Accumulate total in here
  for (std::size_t i {}; i < N; ++i)
    sum += array[i];                             // Sum array elements
  return sum / N;                                // Return average
}
```

Template argument deduction is even powerful enough to deduce the non-type template argument N from the type of the arguments passed to such a template. We can confirm this using a little test program:

```
// Ex10_05.cpp - Defining templates for functions that accept fixed-size arrays
import std;

template <typename T, std::size_t N>
T average(const T (&array)[N]);

int main()
{
  double doubles[2] { 1.0, 2.0 };
  std::println("{}", average(doubles));

  double moreDoubles[] { 1.0, 2.0, 3.0, 4.0 };
  std::println("{}", average(moreDoubles));

  // double* pointer{ doubles };
  // std::println("{}", average(pointer));        /* will not compile */

  std::println("{}", average({ 1.0, 2.0, 3.0, 4.0 }));

  int ints[] { 1, 2, 3, 4 };
  std::println("{}", average(ints));
}
```

This example prints the following:

```
1.5
2.5
2.5
2
```

There are five calls to `average()` inside `main()`, one of which is commented out. The first is the most basic case and proves that the compiler can correctly deduce that T needs to be substituted in the template instance with `double`, and N with 2. The second shows that this even works if you did not explicitly specify the dimension of the array in the type. The compiler still knows that the size of `moreDoubles` is 4. The third call is commented out because it would not compile. Even though arrays and pointers are mostly equivalent, the compiler has no way of deducing the array size from a pointer. The fourth call shows that you can even call `average()` by directly passing the brace-enclosed list as an argument. For the fourth call, the compiler does not have to create another template instance. It will reuse the one generated for the second call. The fifth and final call illustrates that if T is deduced to be `int`, the result will be of type `int` as well—and hence the outcome of an integer division.

While, at least in theory, such templates could lead to code bloat if used with arrays of many different sizes, it is still relatively common to define overloads of functions based on such templates. The Standard Library, for instance, regularly uses this technique.

Abbreviated Function Templates

The syntax to introduce a template is quite verbose. Just take a look at the following straightforward template for functions that square their input:

```
template <typename T>    // <-- Do we really need this?
auto sqr(T x) { return x * x; }
```

It takes two eight-letter keywords, `template` and `typename`, to declare a single template type parameter T. C++20 allows us to write such templates much more compactly, as follows:

```
auto sqr(auto x) { return x * x; }
```

This syntax is a natural extension of the syntax you use to request function return type deduction. Before, you could only use the `auto` keyword as a placeholder for a function's return type, but now you can use it as a placeholder for function parameter types as well. Of course, other placeholder types, such as `auto*`, `auto&`, and `const auto&`, are allowed as well; for instance:

```
auto cube(const auto& x) { return x * x * x; }
```

Even though the `sqr()` and `cube()` definitions now no longer use the `template` keyword, they both remain *function templates*. In fact, semantically, our second definition of `sqr()` is, in every single way, completely equivalent to our original definition. The only difference is that the new syntax is shorter. Hence the name: *abbreviated function template*. The fact that `sqr()`, for instance, is a function template implies that the compiler always needs access to its definition in every compilation unit where you invoke it (we discuss this further in the next chapter). It also implies that you can explicitly instantiate it (`sqr<int>(...)`), specialize it (`template <> auto sqr(int x)`), and so on, should you ever need to.

Every occurrence of auto in the function parameter list of an abbreviated function template effectively introduces an implicit, unnamed template type parameter. The following two prototypes are therefore completely equivalent (notice how the auto in the function return type does *not* give rise to an additional template parameter):

```
const auto& larger(const auto& a, const auto& b);

template <typename T1, typename T2>
const auto& larger(const T1& a, const T2& b);
```

You are even allowed to mix both notations, as shown in this artificial example:

```
// A function template with two template type parameters: one explicit and one implicit
template <typename T>
const T& mixAndMatch(auto* mix, const T& match1, const T& match2);
```

Limitations to Abbreviated Function Templates

If you want your template to instantiate functions where multiple parameters have the same type or related types, you must still use the old syntax.

```
template <typename T>
const T& larger(const T& a, const T& b);
```

Similarly, if you need to refer to one of the parameter type names elsewhere—for instance, in the function body—it remains easier to stick with the old syntax.

```
// Create a vector containing consecutive values in the range [from, to)
template <typename T>
auto createConsecutiveVector(const T& from, const T& to)
{
  std::vector<T> result;  // <-- We mostly need T here
  for (T t{ from }; t < to; ++t)
    result.push_back(t);
  return result;
}
```

Summary

In this chapter, you learned how to define your own parameterized templates for functions and how to instantiate them to create functions. This allows you to create functions that work correctly and efficiently for any number of related types. The important bits that you should take away from this chapter are as follows:

- A function template is a parameterized recipe used by the compiler to generate overloaded functions.

- The parameters in a function template can be type parameters or non-type parameters. The compiler creates an instance of a function template for each function call that corresponds to a unique set of template parameter arguments.

- A function template can be overloaded with other functions or function templates.

- Instead of overloading, you can also introduce specialized code for specific types in a single function template body using a `constexpr if` statement (typically combined with type traits or concept expressions; see also Chapter 21 for the latter).

- Placeholder types such as `auto`, `const auto&`, and `auto*` cannot only be used to enable return type deduction for a function—which can be particularly useful in function templates, as it happens—but when used as the type of a function parameter, they also introduce so-called abbreviated function templates.

EXERCISES

These exercises enable you to try some of what you've learned in this chapter. If you get stuck, look back over the chapter for help. If you're still stuck, you can download the solutions from the Apress website (https://www.apress.com/gp/services/source-code), but that really should be a last resort.

Exercise 10-1. In C++17, the Standard Library <algorithm> module gained the handy std::clamp() function template. The expression clamp(a,b,c) is used to clamp the value a to a given closed interval [b,c]. That is, if a is less than b, the result of the expression will be b; and if a is greater than c, the result will be c; otherwise, a lies within the interval [b,c] and clamp() simply returns a. Write your own my_clamp() function template and try it with a little test program.

Exercise 10-2. Alter the last lines of Ex10_01's main() function as follows:

```
const auto a_string = "A", z_string = "Z";
std::println("Larger of {} and {} is {}",
             a_string, z_string, larger(a_string, z_string));
```

If you now run the program, you may very well get the following output (if not, try rearranging the order in which a_string and z_string are declared):

```
Larger of 1.5 and 2.5 is 2.5
Larger of 3.5 and 4.5 is 4.5
Larger of 17011983 and 10 is 17011983
Larger of A and Z is A
```

What's that? "A" is larger than "Z"? Can you explain what went wrong? Can you fix it?

Hint: To compare two character arrays, you could perhaps first convert them to another string representation.

Exercise 10-3. Write one or more function templates so that you can call plus() functions with two arguments of potentially different types to obtain a value equal to the sum of both arguments. Next, make sure that plus() can be used as well to add the values pointed to by two given pointers.

Extra: Can you now make it so that you can also concatenate two string literals using plus()?

Exercise 10-4. Write your own version of the `std::size()` family of functions called `my_size()` that work not only for fixed-size arrays but also for `std::vector<>` and `std::array<>` objects. You are not allowed to use the `sizeof()` operator or `std::span<>`.

Exercise 10-5. Can you think of a way to verify that the compiler generates only one instance of a function template for any given argument type? Do so for the `larger()` function in `Ex10_01.cpp`.

Exercise 10-6. In Chapter 8, you studied a quicksort algorithm that worked for pointers-to-strings. Generalize the implementation of `Ex8_18.cpp` so that it works for `vectors` of any type (any type for which the `<` operator exists, that is). Write a `main()` function that uses this to sort some `vectors` with different element types. Print both the unsorted and sorted element lists using a function template that prints `vectors` with arbitrary element types with a given field width. Make sure the length of a line never exceeds 80 characters.

CHAPTER 11

■ ■ ■

Modules and Namespaces

While cramming all your code into a single source file is always possible (even for huge programs), a larger code base is far easier to manage if you organize related source code (functions, constants, types, and so on) into logical, composable units, each in their own files. Not least because you and others can then construct different applications out of these same building blocks. As of C++20, the composition unit of choice is a *module*.

The more your code base grows and/or the more third-party libraries you rely on, the more likely it becomes to have two functions, two global variables, two types, and so on, with the same name. Perhaps two independent subsystems inadvertently define their own log() or validate() functions, for instance, or their own ErrorCode enumeration types. Because real-life code bases easily span millions of lines of code, with each subsystem mostly developed by semi-autonomous teams, it is virtually impossible to avoid *name clashes* or *name collisions* without some agreed-upon hierarchical naming scheme. In C++, the recommended approach is that different subsystems declare their names in disjoint *namespaces*.

In this chapter, you'll learn

- How to build composable units of code in the form of modules

- How to export entities from a module so that they can be used in any source file that imports that module

- How to split larger modules into smaller, more manageable units

- The difference between module partitions and submodules

- More about using namespaces and how to define and manage your own

- The relation between modules and namespaces

- How to split a component's interface from its implementation at the level of both modules and namespaces

Modules

At the lowest level of granularity, any C++ program is pieced together from elementary, reusable entities such as functions, types, and variables. And for really small programs—such as the ones you wrote so far—that may be all you need within your own code. But as your code base starts growing, you'll soon notice that you also need some other mechanism to further organize your code at a higher level of granularity. You'll want to group related functionality together, so that you and everyone else knows where to look for it. You'll want to decompose your program into larger, discrete subcomponents, where each component solves one specific piece of the puzzle. Internally, these subcomponents can then use whatever combination of functions, types, and/or other components they may need. As a user of a subcomponent, you do not even

© Ivor Horton and Peter Van Weert 2023
I. Horton and P. Van Weert, *Beginning C++23*, https://doi.org/10.1007/978-1-4842-9343-0_11

need to know how it works internally. In C++20 and beyond, the mechanism of choice is to form self-contained subcomponents of related functionality, called *modules*.

A *module* can *export* any number of C++ entities (functions, constants, types, and so on), which you can then use in any source file that *imports* that module. A module may even export entire other modules. The combination of all entities that a module exports is called the *module interface*. Entities that are not part of the module's interface (directly or indirectly) can only be seen and used from within the module itself.

You of course already know how this works at the consuming end of this relation. For instance, once you *import* the std module, you know that you gain access to all functions, templates, constants, and so on defined by the Standard Library. The std module is said to *export* these entities; you, the *consumer* of the module, *imports* them.

In this chapter, you will learn how to create your own modules. You typically use a separate module for each collection of code that encompasses a common purpose. Each module would represent some logical grouping of types and functions, together with any related global variables. A module could also be used to contain a unit of release, such as a library. Modules thus come in all shapes and sizes. Some essentially export only a single type, a single template, or some constants, whereas larger modules may export a vast library of related types and functions (the std module is a clear example of a larger module). You are free to choose the granularity of your modules.

As some of your modules inevitably grow larger and/or more complex, you may want to further decompose them again into smaller, more manageable subcomponents. We will show you how you can then either decompose such modules internally (using *module partitions*), and/or split them into smaller, loosely related modules (which are then often referred to as *submodules*; this is for instance almost certainly how the std module is essentially realized by your compiler). But before we get to organizing larger modules, we'd better make sure that you can create a smaller one first.

■ **Note**   From this chapter forward, we will use modules to structure our code. While it took some time for compiler vendors to catch up, most major compilers today support modules at least up to some degree. If for some reason you cannot use modules yet, we recommend you read Appendix A after finishing this chapter. After that, converting examples of subsequent chapters to use more traditional means of structuring your code (that is, header files and `#include` directives; see Appendix A) should not be hard. The online code repository of the C++20 edition of the book should help with that as well, as it contains a version of each example and exercise solution that doesn't use modules.

Your First Module

This next file contains the definition of your first module. It is a module named math that exports some features that are glaringly missing from the Standard Library: a template for functions that square a number (deemed too advanced for the Standard Library, which offers only the inverse, `std::sqrt()`), the lambda constant (our homage to one of COVID-19's smartest victims: math's most playful genius, John Horton Conway), and a function to determine the oddity of an integer (a notoriously hard math problem).

```
// math.cppm - Your first module
export module math;

export auto square(const auto& x) { return x * x; }    // An abbreviated function template

export const double lambda{ 1.303577269034296391257 }; // Conway's constant
```

```
export enum class Oddity { Even, Odd };
bool isOdd(int x) { return x % 2 != 0; }  // Module-local function (not exported)
export auto getOddity(int x) { return isOdd(x) ? Oddity::Odd : Oddity::Even; }
```

■ **Note**   At the time of writing, there is no consensus yet on what file extension to use for module files. Each compiler, for as far as they already support modules, uses its own conventions. In this book we use the .cppm extensions for module interface files (.cppm is short for C++—*cee plus plus—module*). Consult your compiler's manual to determine how to best name your module files.

Besides the use of some new keywords,[1] export and module, and the lack of a main() function, this module file looks exactly like any other source file you have seen thus far. In fact, the syntax for creating a basic module is so straightforward that it almost needs no further explanation. Except for perhaps the module declaration on the first line, that is...

Somewhere at the start of every *module file*[2] is a module *declaration*. Every module declaration contains the module keyword followed by the module's name (math in our example). If the module keyword is preceded by the export keyword, the module file is a *module interface file*. Only module interface files may contribute exported entities to the module's interface.

The rules for naming a module are mostly the same as for naming any other entity in C++, except that within a *module name* you may use dots to string together multiple identifiers. Module names are the only names in C++ in which this is allowed. So, not only are math123 and A_B_C valid module names, but so are math.polynomials and a.b.c. Examples of invalid names include 123math, .polynomials, abc., and a..b. We explain later how you can use dotted names to simulate, in essence, hierarchical submodules.

To export an entity from a module, you simply add export in front of its first declaration. In math.cppm you see an example of an exported template, an exported variable, an exported enumeration type, and an exported function, getOddity(). A second function, isOdd(), is purposely not exported. Only module interface files may contain export *declarations*, and only after their module declaration. Only entities that are exported by a module can be used in files that import the module.

---

[1] While export is and has always been a C++ keyword, module and import are technically not keywords. They are merely "identifiers with special meaning." Because module and import weren't keywords at the time modules were introduced in C++20, they could not simply be turned into full-blown keywords anymore—at least not without potentially breaking existing code. You are, as a result, technically still allowed to use module or import as the name of, say, a variable, function, type, or namespace. Of course, we strongly advise against doing so in new code. If you ever do have to use legacy entities named either module or import in module files, you may at times have to add the scope resolution operator :: (introduced later in this chapter) in front of their names to make the compiler accept your code (that is, you then may have to use ::module or ::import instead of module or import).

[2] The C++ standard uses the term *module unit* instead of *module file* because in principle not all code must be delivered through files. In practice, however, every module unit will always correspond to the contents of a module file.

Here is how you import the math module defined by math.cppm and use its exported entities.

```
// Ex11_01.cpp - Consuming your own module
import std;
import math;

int main()
{
  std::println("Lambda squared: {}", square(lambda));

  int number;
  std::print("\nPlease enter an odd number: ");
  std::cin >> number;
  std::println("");

// if (isOdd(number))                /* Error: identifier not found: 'isOdd' */
//   std::println("Well done!");

  switch (getOddity(number))
  {
    using enum Oddity;
    case Odd:
      std::println("Well done! And remember: you have to be odd to be number one!");
    break;
    case Even:
      std::println("Odd, {} appears to be even?", number);
    break;
  }
}
```

■ **Note** Before you can compile a file such as Ex11_01.cpp, you generally have to compile the interface files of all modules that it imports, which in this case includes that of the math module. Compiling a module interface creates a binary representation of all exported entities for the compiler to quickly consult when processing files that import the module. How to compile modules varies between compilers. Consult the documentation of your compiler for further details.

You import the math module by the obvious import math; declaration.

■ **Note** Unlike for header files (see Appendix A), the name that you use to import a module is not based on the name of the file that contains the module interface. Instead it is based on the name that is declared in the export module declaration. While some compilers require the filename to match the name of the module, other compilers allow module interface files with arbitrary names as well. So, even though in this book we always name our module interface files module_name.cppm, do bear in mind that the name of this file is not technically what determines the name you should use in your import declarations.

Once a module is imported, you can use all entities that it exports. The main() function of Ex11_01, for instance, uses all entities exported by our grand and powerful math module: an instantiation of the square<>() function template, the lambda constant, the getOddity() function, and the Oddity enumeration type.

The key, though, is that you can *only* use the exported entities. As an example, you could try to uncomment the if statement that calls isOdd() in Ex11_01.cpp. Your compiler will then signal that it does not know of any function named isOdd(). And there is nothing odd about that. It is not because isOdd() is declared in the module's interface file that it automatically becomes part of the module's interface. To make isOdd() visible from outside the math module, you have to add export in front of its definition as well.

There is nothing new otherwise to the main() program of Ex11_01.cpp. Thanks to the using enum declaration in the switch statement, you can omit Oddity:: from before the enumerator names Even and Odd—yet only within the scope of that switch statement. But you already know this from Chapter 4. Later in this chapter, you will see that you can similarly put other using declarations and using directives at the scope of statements, functions, or namespaces as well.

Export Blocks

In Ex11_01, we exported four different entities, one by one, using as many individual export declarations. You can also export multiple entities all at once by grouping them inside an export *block*. An export block consists of the export keyword followed by a sequence of declarations between curly braces. Here is an alternative definition of the math module of Ex11_01 that uses an export block instead of a sequence of four export declarations (this module file is available from Ex11_01A).

```
// math.cppm - Exporting multiple entities at once
export module math;

bool isOdd(int x) { return x % 2 != 0; }          // Module-local function (not exported)

export
{
  auto square(const auto& x) { return x * x; }

  const double lambda{ 1.303577269034296391257 };  // Conway's constant

  enum class Oddity { Even, Odd };
  auto getOddity(int x) { return isOdd(x) ? Oddity::Odd : Oddity::Even; }
}
```

Separating Interface from Implementation

So far, all entities were always defined directly in the module interface file. And for small functions and types such as those of our mighty math module, that works just fine. Sure, math's interface file is perhaps a bit cluttered already by the module-local isOdd() function, but that is not too distracting yet. In real life, however, function definitions may span dozens of lines each, and you may need several more local functions and types to realize your exported interface. If you're not careful, all these implementation details can obfuscate the module's interface, making it harder for someone to get a quick overview of what a particular module has to offer. In such cases, you should consider separating the module's interface (containing for instance only the prototypes of exported functions) from its implementation (which is then where these exported functions are defined, together with any module-local entities).

Your first option to separate a module's interface from its implementation is to do so within the module interface file itself. This is shown here:

```
// math.cppm - Exporting multiple entities at once
export module math;

export                                          // The module's interface
{
  auto square(const auto& x);

  const double lambda{ 1.303577269034296391257 };   // Conway's constant

  enum class Oddity { Even, Odd };
  auto getOddity(int x);
}

// The implementation of the module's functions (+ local helpers)
auto square(const auto& x) { return x * x; }

bool isOdd(int x) { return x % 2 != 0; }
auto getOddity(int x) { return isOdd(x) ? Oddity::Odd : Oddity::Even; }
```

You can always move function definitions to the bottom of the module interface file like this. You could even move the definition of the enumeration type Oddity down, after first declaring it using enum class Oddity;. We left Oddity's definition in the export block, though, because it is—and needs to be—part of the module's interface (consumers need to know the enumerators to use the module). Constants must be initialized immediately, so the definition of lambda cannot be moved.

Note that you knew most of this already, though, from earlier examples, where we often put all function prototypes at the top of a source file as well (to get a nice overview of the available functions), and all function definitions at the bottom (often after the main() function in which they were used).

The only truly new thing worth noting at this point is that you do not have to repeat the export keyword in front of the definitions at the bottom. You *can*, but you do not have to. That is, you can repeat export in front of the definitions of square<>() and getOddity() at the bottom of math.cppm, but doing so is entirely optional.

What is *not* allowed, however, is to add export in front of the declaration of an entity that was first declared without export. The following sequence of declarations, for instance, would therefore result in a compilation error.

```
bool isOdd(int x);
// ...
export bool isOdd(int x); /* Error: isOdd() was previously declared as not exported! */
```

Module Implementation Files

Instead of putting all your definitions at the bottom of the module interface file, you can mostly move them into a separate source file as well (we discuss some limitations in an upcoming subsection). The module interface file then includes the prototypes of all exported functions, while their definitions along with any module-local entities are moved to one or more *module implementation files*. This approach accentuates a clean separation of interface and implementation—a desirable trait of any software component.

Taking a small break from math modules, here is a slimmed-down module interface file for a module that offers functions to convert between unsigned integers and standard Roman numerals[3].

```
// roman.cppm - Interface file for a Roman numerals module
export module roman;
import std;

export std::string to_roman(unsigned int i);
export unsigned int from_roman(std::string_view roman);
```

While naturally we have no room in this book to lay out truly large modules, we're sure you can appreciate how this single interface file now gives a succinct, clear overview of what the roman module has to offer, free from any clutter caused by local helper functions or other implementation details.

New also in this module file is that it uses another module—the std module of the Standard Library to be precise. The main thing that you need to know about this for now is that in a module file, *all* import declarations must appear *after* the module declaration and *before* any other declaration. (This allows tooling to get an overview of all module dependencies by parsing only the first few lines of all files.) The following module file layout is therefore *not* allowed for the annotated reasons (although some compilers are more lenient about this than others):

```
import std;      /* Error: no imports allowed before the module declaration! */
export module roman;

export std::string to_roman(unsigned int i);

import std;      /* Error: illegal import after declaration of to_roman()! */
export unsigned int from_roman(std::string_view roman);
```

With the roman.cppm module interface file in place, we can now start defining the module's functions. Usually, for a small module such as roman, you would never go further than putting both function definitions into a single module implementation file—say roman.cpp. But just to illustrate the possibility, we will take things one step further and give each function definition its own implementation file. Here is the implementation file that provides the definition of the to_roman() function:

```
// to_roman.cpp - Implementation of the to_roman() function
module roman;

std::string to_roman(unsigned int i)
{
  if (i > 3999) return {}; // 3999, or MMMCMXCIX, is the largest standard Roman numeral
  static const std::string ms[] { "","M","MM","MMM" };
  static const std::string cds[]{ "","C","CC","CCC","CD","D","DC","DCC","DCCC","CM" };
  static const std::string xls[]{ "","X","XX","XXX","XL","L","LX","LXX","LXXX","XC" };
  static const std::string ivs[]{ "","I","II","III","IV","V","VI","VII","VIII","IX" };
  return ms[i / 1000] + cds[(i % 1000) / 100] + xls[(i % 100) / 10] + ivs[i % 10];
}
```

---

[3] Don't worry if you are not that familiar with Roman numerals. This section is about understanding the roman *module,* and not so much about understanding the implementations of the to_roman() and from_roman() functions.

Like all module files, a *module implementation file* contains a module declaration. Unlike module *interface* files, however, the module declaration of a module *implementation* file does *not* begin with the export keyword. Naturally, the implication is that a module implementation file may not export any entities. In fact, you are not even allowed to repeat the export keyword here in front of the definition of to_roman(); you can only add or repeat export in module interface files.

The implementation of the to_roman() function itself contains some clever, compact coding to convert unsigned integers into standard Roman numerals. Having mastered C++ expressions and functions in the first half of this book, we're sure you can work out how it works. As the focus of this section is on modules, we'll thus leave deciphering this function body as an optional exercise for you.

For completeness, here is the second module implementation file for our roman module, which as you know was so massive it could not possibly fit into a single implementation file.

```cpp
// from_roman.cpp - Implementation of the from_roman() function
module roman;

unsigned int from_roman(char c)
{
  switch (c)
  {
    case 'I': return 1;    case 'V': return 5;    case 'X': return 10;
    case 'L': return 50;   case 'C': return 100; case 'D': return 500;
    case 'M': return 1000; default:  return 0;
  }
}

unsigned int from_roman(std::string_view roman)
{
  unsigned int result{};
  for (std::size_t i{}, n{ roman.length() }; i < n; ++i)
  {
    const auto j{ from_roman(roman[i]) };    // Integer value of the i'th roman digit
    // Look at the next digit (if there is one) to know whether to add or subtract j
    if (i + 1 == n || j >= from_roman(roman[i + 1])) result += j; else result -= j;
  }
  return result;
}
```

This second implementation file is similar to the previous one, except that it defines a local helper function to convert a single Roman digit into an integer. This overload of from_roman() is only visible within this source file.

Because switch, for, and if statements are all familiar territory, we again have every faith that you can work out how these from_roman() functions work (should you be interested). We've added some comments to get you started (it's never a bad idea to add such comments in your own code as well, whenever the logic is less than obvious).

Here is a small test program and its output:

```cpp
// Ex11_02.cpp
import std;
import roman;
```

```
int main()
{
  std::println("1234 in Roman numerals is {}", to_roman(1234));
  std::println("MMXXIII in Arabic numerals is {}", from_roman("MMXXIII"));
}
```

```
1234 in Roman numerals is MCCXXXIV
MMXXIII in Arabic numerals is 2023
```

▓ **Note**   With nonmodular code (see Appendix A for more details), there was another, arguably stronger, motivation to not define functions in a header file (which is somewhat akin to a module interface file)—every single change to a header, no matter how small (even fixing a typo in a code comment), generally meant that all code consuming the header (directly or indirectly) had to be recompiled. Worst case, due to recursive `#includes`, that meant rebuilding nearly the entire application over and over during development. Given that the implementation of a function typically changes far more frequently than its prototype, it therefore paid off to consistently move all implementations out of the header file and into a separate source file. Modules, however, do not suffer from this problem. Modules by design are self-contained, independent building blocks. Only changes to the actual module interface impact consumers, and function definitions are purposely *not* part of the module's interface[4] (as discussed in the next subsection). You can thus safely change a function definition in a module interface file, even that of an exported function, without having to worry about recompiling any of the consuming code.

Limitations to Implementation Files

In general, everything that an importer of a module may need to consume an exported entity must be present in a module interface file. The reason is that whenever your compiler processes a source file that consumes that module, it only considers (the precompiled binary representation of) that module's interface. The output of compiled module implementation files is not considered at that time, and instead is only required for the linking stage (linking was briefly explained in Chapter 1). Some entities therefore must always be defined in a module interface file, and not in a module implementation file.

The definitions of all exported templates, for instance, must be part of the module interface. The compiler needs these template definitions to instantiate new template instances for the module's various consumers. You effectively export the entire template, the complete blueprint for future instantiations, and not one particular function prototype (or type definition; see Chapter 17).

All the compiler needs to invoke a regular function, on the other hand, is its prototype. From that it knows what arguments to expect from consumers, and what the resulting type will be. Most function

---

[4] Unless that function is declared as inline with the inline keyword. Definitions of inline functions, like those of templates, *are* part of the module interface. Inline functions are purely a performance optimization that we do not discuss further in this book, though.

definitions can therefore be moved to the module interface file as is. Most, but not all. One example[5] of a function definition that you cannot simply move out of an interface file is that of an exported function with auto return type deduction. For auto return type deduction to work, the compiler needs the function definition to be part of the module interface.

In the math.cppm interface file of Ex11_01, the isOdd() function is the only entity whose definition you could move to a module implementation file as is. Not because isOdd() is the only entity that is not exported, but because square<>() is a template (thanks to its const auto& parameter; see Chapter 10), and because getOddity() uses auto return type deduction.

Implicit Imports in Implementation Files

Being the astute observer that you are, you likely noticed that we didn't import the std module in to_roman.cpp or from_roman.cpp, even though these source files clearly use the std::string, std::string_view, and std::size_t Standard Library types. We invite you to take a quick look back if you missed that. The reason that we can omit these module imports is twofold.

- Every module *implementation file* (that is not a partition file; see later) implicitly imports the module that it belongs to. You can think of this as if a declaration such as module roman; implicitly adds import roman; on the next line. (Explicitly adding import roman; after module roman; is not allowed, by the way.)

- Whenever you import one part of a module into another part of the same module (more on this later), the latter essentially gains access to *all* declarations of the former[6], even to declarations that are not exported. This includes not only declarations of module-local functions, types, and variables, but also imports of other modules, such as import std;.

Combined, these two rules entail that our module implementation files to_roman.cpp and from_roman.cpp both inherit the import declaration for std from the implicitly imported roman.cppm module interface file.

▓ **Caution**   Only module declarations of the exact form module my_module; add an implicit import my_module; declaration (and consequently prohibit explicit import my_module; declarations). Module declarations for module partitions, as seen later, carry no such implications. To gain access to all declarations of the module interface file in partition files, you have to add import my_module; explicitly.

---

[5] Other examples include inline functions (whose definitions are required to be eligible for inlining at the calling sites) and constexpr and consteval functions (whose definitions are required to be eligible for compile-time evaluation; see Chapters 8 and 12).

[6] This is not entirely accurate; entities with *internal linkage* can never be used from outside the file that they are declared in, not even within the same module. But since creating entities with internal linkage is never really required when writing modules (in technical speak, it is far easier to simply give all nonexported entities *module linkage*), we do not discuss that possibility here yet. Refer to Appendix A for more details about the different types of linkage.

Reachability vs. Visibility

When you import a module into a file that is *not* part of the same module, you do *not* implicitly inherit all imports from the module interface file. This is essentially why we had to import the std module in Ex11_02.cpp, even though the module interface file of the imported roman module contained an import declaration for std as well. You can, if you want, explicitly export import declarations from a module—we discuss this option further in an upcoming section. But by default, when you import a module, you do not implicitly gain complete access to all other modules that that module relies on.

And that is a good thing. That is, you really do *not* want all imports in interface files to be exported to consumers willy-nilly. You never want consumers of a module to be affected when that module changes the *implementation* of its interface. Only changes to a module's interface are allowed to impact its consumers. If all imports were exported and imported willy-nilly, any import declaration that you add or remove would ripple through recursively to all code importing that module, either directly or indirectly. And that could most definitely affect consumers; removing an import somewhere deep down could then break other code that came to rely on this import, while adding an import declaration could introduce name clashes. (Headers suffer from these exact problems; see Appendix A for details.)

However, if you give consumers no knowledge about the types that are used in a module's interface, they mostly cannot use that interface anymore. Take the interface of the roman module of Ex11_02, for instance. To invoke from_roman(), you need to know how to create a std::string_view object; and, similarly, to use the result of to_roman(), you need to know at least something about the std::string type.

The fitting compromise that C++ modules offer is to distinguish the *reachability* of an entity's declaration from the *visibility* of its name. We'll clarify what this means with an example. Copy all files of the roman module of Ex11_02 and start a new source file with a blank main() function. In this new source file, you should no longer import the std module like we did earlier in Ex11_02.cpp. The new source file, in other words, should only contain the import declaration for the roman module:

```
// Ex11_03.cpp - Using types with reachable definitions but whose names are not visible
import roman;

int main()
{
// You can put all code used in the remainder of this section here...
}
```

Any declaration (including type definitions) that is *reachable* in an imported module interface file such as roman.cppm (either through local declarations or through imports) is *reachable* in the importing file as well. By importing roman, for instance, the definitions of both std::string and std::string_view therefore become *reachable* in Ex11_03.cpp. Reachability of declarations thus spreads implicitly and recursively to any and all direct and indirect consumers of a module.

First and foremost, implicitly importing the reachability of parameter and return types allows you to invoke exported functions. Here is a minimal example:

```
from_roman("DCLXVI"); // Creates std::string_view object to invoke from_roman(string_view)
to_roman(1234);       // Receives and destructs the string object returned by to_roman(int)
```

In fact, once the definition of a type is reachable, you can, for the most part, use values of that type exactly the way you are used to. You can, for instance, invoke functions on objects whose type definition is reachable. In formal speak, we say that the names of the *members* of a reachable class definition are *visible*. In the following line for Ex11_03.cpp, we can invoke the size() function on the std::string object returned by to_roman(), even though we never imported the module that exports it:

```
const auto num_numerals{ to_roman(1234).size() }; // 8 numerals ("MCCXXXIV")
```

To avoid inadvertent name clashes, however, and to avoid consumers relying on module-local names, the *visibility* of an entity's *name* does not escape a module willy-nilly. The std::string and std::string_view *names* are thus *not* visible in Ex11_03.cpp, and can therefore not be used there.

```
// std::string_view s{ "MMXXIII" };/* Error: the name std::string_view is not visible */
// std::string roman{ to_roman(567) };  /* Error: the name std::string is not visible */
```

Luckily, though, you do not need access to the names of the return types of functions in order to use them. You can always capture a function's result using auto or const auto& as placeholders for that name.

```
const auto roman{ to_roman(789) };              // "DCCLXXXIX"
const auto first_X{ roman.find('X') };          // 4
```

Like the visibility of type names (std::string, std::string_view, and so on), the visibility of function names does not escape a module's borders willy-nilly either. Functions such as std::stoi() and std::to_string(), exported by the same submodule of the Standard Library as std::string, can therefore not be invoked from within Ex11_03.cpp.

```
// auto i{ std::stoi(to_roman(567)); } /* Error: the name std::stoi is not visible */
```

In summary, *reachability* of declarations implicitly and transitively propagates to all consumers of a module—however indirect—but *visibility* of declared names does *not*. Luckily, though, reachable definitions typically suffice for you to use a module's interface without having to import any extra modules, especially since the names of all members of any *reachable* type definition are *visible*.

Exporting Import Declarations

Like with most declarations in a module interface file, you can also add export in front of an import declaration. Any file that imports a module implicitly inherits all import declarations that are exported from that module as well. For instance, suppose in roman.cppm of Ex11_02 you add export in front of its import declaration as follows:

```
// roman.cppm
export module roman;
export import std;

export std::string to_roman(unsigned int i);
export unsigned int from_roman(std::string_view roman);
```

Then you can safely remove the import declaration for std in Ex11_02.cpp, because that file then imports the std module indirectly by importing roman.

You should not systematically export all module imports that you use within a module, though. You should only export an import declaration if you know for a fact that every consumer of a module will need the functions and/or the *names* of the types of that dependent module to be *visible*. As you'll recall from the previous section, *reachability* of type definitions is mostly sufficient to use a module's interface, and for that you do not need to export the corresponding imports.

Another viable reason to export import declarations is to form so-called submodules. We discuss that strategy in the next section.

Managing Larger Modules

The larger a module becomes, or the more complex its functionality, the more the need may arise to further divide its code into smaller, more manageable components.

Of course, your first option then is to split your module into several smaller modules. This works well if its interface can be split into clean, disjoint subinterfaces, whose implementations then are independent as well. One particularly interesting approach then is to split larger modules into several *submodules*. We discuss that option in the first subsection.

Sometimes, however, you do want to keep everything bundled in a single, self-contained module. Maybe it makes no sense to split up its functionality. Or maybe the module interface is already quite small, and you just need a lot of internal machinery to realize it. Not all code needs to be exported to the entire application all the time. Keeping code local within a module has the advantage that you have more flexibility in changing it, without having to worry about external uses. The answer C++ provides for such occasions is *module partitions*. We discuss partitions in a second subsection shortly.

Simulating Submodules

Even though C++ does not formally support the concept of nested *submodules*, you can simulate them quite easily. The principle is probably best explained by example. By creating the following three module interface files (we'll omit the function definitions for brevity), you could split the colossal roman module into two smaller submodules, called roman.from and roman.to (all source files are available under Ex4_04A).

```
// roman.cppm - Module interface file of the roman module
export module roman;
export import roman.from;   // Not: 'export import .from;' (cf. partitions later)
export import roman.to;
```

```
// roman.from.cppm - Module interface file of the roman.from module
export module roman.from;
import std;
export unsigned int from_roman(std::string_view roman);
```

```
// roman.to.cppm - Module interface file of the roman.to module
export module roman.to;
import std;
export std::string to_roman(unsigned int i);
```

It is important to note that, as far as C++ is concerned, roman.from and roman.to are just module names like any other. If you'd like to rename these (sub)modules to from_roman and to_roman, or even cattywampus and codswallop, by all means. The language does not enforce any hierarchical naming scheme at all. It's just that adopting one makes it easier to see the relation between modules and its submodules, and dots were specifically allowed in module names to facilitate such hierarchical naming.

With these three module files in place, you have the following choice in the remainder of the application: either you import individual submodules, or you import them all at once. If you only need to output roman numerals, you can add import roman.to; and gain access to to_roman() only. Or you simply add import roman; and gain access to all submodules at once.

■ **Tip**   Functionally, there is no difference between importing all submodules at once, or only the bits and pieces that you actually need. In fact, from a functional point of view, the former is far more convenient. Potential advantages of more fine-grained submodule imports, however, include improved compilation speeds (fewer dependencies between source files mean more opportunities for parallel compilation) and reduced incremental build times during development (when you alter the interface of a submodule, only files that import that specific submodule need to be rebuilt).

■ **Note**   The `std` and `std.compat` modules are perfect examples of larger modules that are little more than aggregations of submodules. The C++ Standard Library actually consists of well over 100 different modules such as `<string>`, `<string_view>`, `<print>`, `<vector>`, and so on (technically these modules are called *header units*; see Appendix A). While you could import Standard Library modules individually on an as-needed basis if you want (using the `import <...>;` syntax), there is little to no advantage to that as all Standard Library modules are immutable.

Module Partitions

If splitting up a module into multiple (sub)modules does not suit you, *module partitions* offer you the means to bring more structure to otherwise overly large, monolithic module files.

■ **Note**   The key difference between submodules and partitions is that submodules can be imported individually by the rest of the application, whereas partitions are only visible within a module. For the rest of the application, a partitioned module still presents itself as one, self-contained module. You can even completely repartition a module without changing anything else in the remainder of the application.

Module Implementation Partitions

You already know from `Ex11_02` that you can divide a module's implementation across multiple module implementation files. But this is not always enough; sometimes you want to use the same module-local entities within multiple of these source files—preferably without having to declare these implementation details in the shared module interface file. This is what *module implementation partitions*[7] are for.

One example would be the following partition, extracted from our massive roman module. It defines the `from_roman(char)` helper previously defined in `from_roman.cpp` (the complete source for this repartitioned roman module is available as `Ex11_04B`).

```
// roman-internals.cpp - Module implementation file for the
//                       internals partition of the roman module
module roman:internals;
```

---

[7] Module implementation partitions are sometimes also called *internal partitions*.

```
unsigned int from_roman(char c)
{
    // Same switch statement as before...
}
```

The module declaration of a *module partition file* is similar to that of any other module file, except that the name of the *partition* is added after the name of the module, separated by a colon. In our example the name of the partition is thus internals, and clearly it is a partition of the roman module. The lack of an export keyword in the module declaration signals that this is a *module implementation partition*, and that it therefore is not allowed to export any entities. The name internals uniquely identifies this specific file.

▓ **Caution**   No two module partition files can ever share the same *partition name*—not even if one of these files contains a module *interface* partition and the other a module *implementation* partition. A partition name thus always uniquely identifies one single file.

To then use the internals partition and its function in the module implementation file that defines from_roman(string_view), you have to import the partition, as shown next.

```
// from_roman.cpp - Implementation of the from_roman() function
module roman;
import :internals;    // Caution: never 'import roman:internals;'!

unsigned int from_roman(std::string_view roman)
{
    // Same as before... (uses from_roman(char) function from the :internals partition)
}
```

▓ **Caution**   Module partitions can only be imported into other files of the same module, and only using import :partition_name;. The alluring syntax import module_name:partition_name; is never valid (neither outside the module, where the partition cannot be accessed, nor within a module, where the module_name qualification would only be redundant anyway).

Naturally, grouping module-local functionality into implementation partition files only really pays off if these partitions are subsequently reused by multiple other implementation and/or partition files of the same module. If a partition such as internals is only used by one other file, it may not be worth the effort.

Module Interface Partitions

Even module interfaces can at times become large enough to warrant a subdivision in multiple parts. For this you can use *module interface partitions*. The interface of the roman module of Ex11_03, for instance, contains *two* functions. TWO! Clearly way too much for one interface to hold, so we better split this interface into parts.

Creating a module interface partition is easy enough. Here is a first example in which we export and define the to_roman() function (the complete source is available in Ex11_05).

```
// roman-to.cppm – Module interface file for the to partition of the roman module
export module roman:to;
import std;

export std::string to_roman(unsigned int i)
{
  // Same function body as before...
}
```

Like in any module *partition* file, the module declaration of a module interface partition file specifies a unique partition name (to in our case). And like in any module *interface* file, this declaration begins with the keyword export. Using module interface partitions such as roman-to.cppm you can divide your module into multiple parts, each defining some logical subset of the module's functionality.

Of course, using module interface partitions does not preclude separating the interface from the implementation either. To illustrate that, we will move all definitions of our second interface partition, roman:from, to an implementation file.

```
// roman-from.cppm – Module interface file for the from partition of the roman module
export module roman:from;
import std;

export unsigned int from_roman(std::string_view roman);
```

There's just one thing to watch out for now—you cannot, at this point, create a module implementation file that starts with module roman:from;. While this may seem logical, only one file can be created per partition name. So once you create a module *interface* partition named from, you can no longer create a module *implementation* partition with that same name. What you can do, however, is move the partition's function definitions to a regular, unnamed module implementation file (or, if you want, a module implementation partition with a name that is not from). Because we have it lying around, we also reuse the internals partition from Ex11_04 in our implementation.

```
// from_roman.cpp – Module implementation file for the from partition of the roman module
module roman;
import :internals;

unsigned int from_roman(std::string_view roman)
{
  // Same as before... (uses from_roman(char) from the internals partition)
}
```

However you organize your module interface partitions and their implementation, the key is that every *interface partition* must eventually be exported from the module's *primary module interface file*. Remember, to the outside world, a partitioned module still presents itself as a single, self-contained module. Each module must therefore have exactly one primary module interface file that exports its entire interface, even if that interface is internally partitioned across multiple files. This is the primary module file that completes the roman module of our running example, Ex11_05.

```
// roman.cppm - Primary module interface file for the roman module
export module roman;

export import :to;        // Not: 'export import roman:to;'
export import :from;      // Not: 'export import roman:from;'
// export import :internals;  /* Error: only interface partitions can be exported */
```

You cannot export a module implementation partition such as `:internals`; only module interface partitions can (and must) be exported. Outside of the module, a partitioned module can only be imported as a whole (through `import roman;`, for instance); individual partitions can never be imported outside of the module (the syntax `import roman:from;`, as said, is therefore *never* valid). If you want individual parts to be importable from outside the main module, you should turn them into submodules instead.

Namespaces

We briefly introduced *namespaces* in Chapter 1, but there's a bit more to it than we explained then. With large programs, choosing unique names for all the entities can become difficult. When an application is developed by several programmers working in parallel and/or when it incorporates code from various third-party C++ libraries, using namespaces to prevent *name clashes* becomes essential.

A namespace is a block that attaches an extra name—the namespace name—to every entity name that is declared within it. The full name of each entity is the namespace name followed by the scope resolution operator, `::`, followed by the basic entity name. Different namespaces can contain entities with the same name, but the entities are differentiated because they are qualified by different namespace names. You are already aware that Standard Library names are declared within the `std` namespace. In this section you will learn how to define namespaces of your own. But before we dive in to that, first a quick word on the *global namespace*.

The Global Namespace

All the programs that you've written so far have used names that you defined in the *global namespace*. The global namespace applies by default if a namespace hasn't been defined. All names within the global namespace are just as you declare them, without a namespace name being attached.

To explicitly access names defined in the global namespace, you use the scope resolution operator without a left operand, for example, `::power(2.0, 3)`. This is only really required, though, if there is a more local declaration with the same name that *hides* that global name.

■ **Note** A name can be hidden by the name of a totally different kind of entity. In the following function body, for instance, the name of the function parameter power hides that of the afore-alluded-to power() function in the global namespace. To access the latter, you must explicitly add the scope resolution operator (or, of course, rename the function parameter).

```
double zipADee(int power)    // Compute the zip-a-dee of the given power
{
  double doodah = ::power(std::numbers::pi, power);
  // ...
```

With small programs, you can define names within the global namespace without running into any problems. Within larger code bases, the potential for name clashes increases, so you should use namespaces to partition your code into logical groupings. That way, each code segment is self-contained from a naming perspective, and name clashes are prevented.

Defining a Namespace

A namespace definition has the following form:

```
namespace mySpace
{
  // Code you want to have in the namespace,
  // including function definitions and declarations,
  // global variables, enum types, templates, etc.
}
```

Note that no semicolon is required after the closing brace in a namespace definition. The namespace name here is mySpace[8]. The braces enclose the scope for the namespace mySpace, and every name declared within the namespace scope has the name mySpace attached to it.

▓ **Caution** You must not include the main() function within a namespace. The runtime environment expects main() to be defined in the global namespace.

You can extend a namespace scope by adding a second namespace block with the same name. For example, a program file might contain the following:

```
namespace mySpace
{
  // This defines namespace mySpace
  // The initial code in the namespace goes here
}
namespace network
{
  // Code in a new namespace, network
}
namespace mySpace
{
  /* This extends the mySpace namespace
     Code in here can refer to names in the previous
     mySpace namespace block without qualification */
}
```

---

[8] Not to be confused with Myspace™, once the largest social networking site in the world. (We checked: Myspace™ was originally stylized as "MySpace" and now as "myspace"; so, yes, given that namespace names are case-sensitive, mySpace was still available!)

There are two blocks defined as namespace mySpace, separated by a namespace network. The second mySpace block is treated as a continuation of the first, so functions declared within each of the mySpace blocks belong to the same namespace. You can have as many blocks for the same namespace as you want, spread across as many source and module files as you want.

References to names from inside the same namespace do not need to be qualified. For example, names that are defined in the namespace mySpace can be referenced from within mySpace without qualifying them with the namespace name.

The following example illustrates the mechanics of defining and using a namespace:

```cpp
// Ex11_06.cpp
// Defining and using a namespace
import std;

namespace math
{
  const double sqrt2 { 1.414213562373095 };      // the square root of 2
  auto square(const auto& x) { return x * x; }
  auto pow4(const auto& x) { return square(square(x)); }
}

int main()
{
  std::println("math::sqrt2 has the value {}", math::sqrt2);
  std::println("Squared that number equals {}", math::square(math::sqrt2));
  std::println("This should be 0: {}", math::sqrt2 - std::numbers::sqrt2);
}
```

The namespace math in Ex11_06 contains one constant and two (abbreviated) function templates. You can see that it is perfectly okay to define a constant named sqrt2 in the math namespace even though a variable with the same name exists in the std::numbers namespace (std::numbers is a *nested namespace*; we discuss nested namespaces in the next section). As long as you use their qualified names, there is no ambiguity.

Note that you did not have to qualify square() with math:: when calling it (twice) from pow4(). The reason for this is that pow4() is defined in the same namespace as square(). This would still work even if pow4() were defined in a different namespace block than square(), and even if that block were defined in a different file. Of course, you do have to qualify square() with math:: when calling it from outside the math namespace, such as from the main() function of Ex11_06.cpp (a function in the global namespace).

This program produces the following output:

```
math::sqrt2 has the value 1.414213562373095
Squared that number equals 1.9999999999999996
This should be 0: -2.220446049250313e-16
```

The somewhat surprising second and third lines only reaffirms two things: first, that math::sqrt2 and std::numbers::sqrt2 are effectively two different variables with the same base name; and second, that for optimal accuracy you should use predefined constants such as those defined by the Standard Library whenever possible (as recommended in Chapter 2 as well). Believe us, we really did *not* set out for these two constants to be different!

Nested Namespaces

You can define one namespace inside another. The mechanics of this are easiest to understand if we look at a specific context. For instance, suppose you have the following *nested namespaces*:

```
import std;

namespace outer
{
  double min(const std::vector<double>& data)
  {
    // Determine the minimum value and return it...
  }

  namespace inner
  {
    void normalize(std::vector<double>& data)
    {
      const double minValue{ min(data) };   // Calls min() in outer namespace
      // ...
    }
  }
}
```

From within the inner namespace, the normalize() function can call the min() function in the namespace outer without qualifying the name. This is because the declaration of normalize() in the inner namespace is also within the outer namespace. To call min() or normalize() from the global namespace (or any other unrelated namespace), you must qualify both names in the usual way:

```
outer::inner::normalize(data);
const double result{ outer::min(data) };
```

To call outer::inner::normalize() from within the outer namespace, though, it suffices to qualify its name with inner::. That is, you can omit the outer:: qualifier from names in namespaces that are nested inside outer. Here is an example:

```
namespace outer
{
  auto getNormalized(const std::vector<double>& data)
  {
    auto copy{ data };
    inner::normalize(copy);                 // Same as outer::inner::normalize(copy);
    return copy;
  }
}
```

You can add something to a nested namespace directly using the following compact syntax.

```
namespace outer::inner
{
  double average(const std::vector<double>& data) { /* body code... */ }
}
```

410

This is equivalent to—yet far more convenient than—explicitly nesting a block for the inner namespace inside a block for the outer namespace.

```
namespace outer
{
  namespace inner
  {
    double average(const std::vector<double>& data) { /* body code... */ }
  }
}
```

Namespaces and Modules

You typically use a separate namespace within a single program for each collection of code that encompasses a common purpose. Each namespace would represent some logical grouping of types and functions, together with any related global variables. A namespace could also be used to contain a unit of release, such as a library.

If the previous paragraph sounds familiar, it is only because we wrote the exact same passage earlier in this chapter when talking about modules—word for word. And it's true; if you look past some of the differences—modules are composable units of code stored in separate files, whereas namespaces are hierarchical groupings of names, both language features often serve the exact same purpose: they group related code entities to bring structure, order, and overview in an ever-growing code base. Therefore, we also offer the following advice.

▓ **Tip** While not required, it only stands to reason that aligning the names of your modules and namespaces is often a good idea. It would make perfect sense, for instance, to package the three entities of the `math` namespace of `Ex11_06` in a `math` module. That way, you must remember only one name when using a module and its entities.

Even though consistent naming of modules and namespaces may be recommended, the C++ language by no means enforces it. Unlike in other programming languages, namespaces and modules are completely orthogonal in C++. From a single module, you can export entities from as many namespaces as you want, and conversely, entities from the same namespace can be spread across as many modules as you want.

To illustrate this, you could package the `math` namespace of `Ex11_06`, not in a `math` module, but in a `squaring` module instead (see `Ex11_06A`).

```
export module squaring;

namespace math
{
  export const double sqrt2 { 1.414213562373095 };  // the square root of 2
  export auto square(const auto& x) { return x * x; }
  export auto pow4(const auto& x) { return square(square(x)); }
}
```

411

If all entities of a namespace block are to be exported, you can also move the export keyword in front of the namespace keyword. The following is therefore entirely equivalent to our previous squaring module (see Ex11_06B).

```
export module squaring;

export namespace math                        // Exports all nested declarations at once
{
  const double sqrt2 { 1.414213562373095 };    // the square root of 2
  auto square(const auto& x) { return x * x; }
  auto pow4(const auto& x) { return square(square(x)); }
}
```

Either way, besides having to import the squaring module, nothing changes for the main() program of Ex11_06.

Organizing Larger Namespaces and Modules

Here are some strategies you should consider for organizing larger modules and/or namespaces:

- You can divide entities of the same namespace across multiple modules. This is essentially what the Standard Library did for the std namespace.

- You can assign some or all modules a matching (nested) namespace. The <ranges> module of the Standard Library, for instance, uses the std::ranges namespace (as detailed in Chapter 20).

- You can also divide all entities into hierarchical submodules. Suppose the math namespace contains many more entities than those listed in Ex11_06. Then math.squaring would be a good name for the modules of Ex11_06A and Ex11_06B. Other submodules could then be math.polynomials, math.geometry, and so on. Using the techniques discussed earlier, you could then make it so that by importing math, you import all math submodules at once.

- You can combine hierarchical submodules with a parallel hierarchy of nested namespaces (that is, math::squaring, math::polynomials, and so on).

Whichever scheme you choose, our advice is to try to be consistent within your code base. After all, the goal is to bring structure and order in an otherwise chaotic collection of code.

Functions and Namespaces

For a function to exist within a namespace, it is sufficient for the function prototype to appear in a namespace block. Same as with functions in the global namespace, you can then define the function elsewhere—either in the same file or in, for instance, a module implementation file. To define such a function whose prototype was declared earlier, you have two options: either you again enclose the definition in a namespace block, or you use the function's qualified name to introduce its definition.

An example should make things clearer. We start from this module interface file for yet another math module.

```
// math.cppm - Module interface file containing declarations and template definitions
export module math;
import std;

export namespace math
{
  auto square(const auto& x) { return x * x; };

  namespace averages
  {
    double arithmetic_mean(std::span<const double> data);
    double geometric_mean(std::span<const double> data);
    double rms(std::span<const double> data);
    double median(std::span<const double> data);
  }
}
```

As said earlier, separating a module's interface from its implementation allows for a quick and easy overview of a module's content. This particular math module, for example, clearly focuses on the computation of various types of averages.

To export the (abbreviated) square<>() template, its definition must be part of the module interface, as explained earlier as well. You could move its definition either to the bottom of the primary interface file or to an interface partition file, but never to a module implementation file.

The definitions of the functions from the math::averages namespace, on the other hand, can be moved into a module implementation file, as shown next. Of course, you could simply put them at the bottom of the module interface file as well—and there would be nothing wrong with that. For brevity, we have omitted the function bodies in the following outline, but you can find the full code in Ex11_07.

```
// math.cpp - Module implementation file containing function definitions
module math;   // Remember: this implicitly imports the primary module interface...

// Option 1: define in nested namespace block (compact syntax)
namespace math::averages
{
  double arithmetic_mean(std::span<const double>& data) { /* body code... */ }
}

// Option 2: define in nested namespace blocks
namespace math
{
  namespace averages
  {
    double geometric_mean(std::span<const double>& data) { /* body code... */ }
  }
}

// Option 3: define using fully qualified function name
double math::averages::rms(std::span<const double>& data) { /* body code... */ }
```

```
// Option 4: define using qualified name in outer namespace block
namespace math
{
  double averages::median(std::span<const double>& data) { /* body code... */ }
}
```

This implementation file illustrates the different options for defining functions that were previously declared in a (nested) namespace. The first two function definitions are simply placed in equivalent nested namespace blocks. But since all functions have been declared already in their respective namespaces in the implicitly imported module interface file, you no longer have to put their definitions in namespace blocks if you don't want to. You can instead tie the definitions to their declarations by qualifying the function names with the correct namespace names in their definitions. This is illustrated by options 3 and 4 in math.cpp.

It goes without saying that mixing all these different options is not considered good style (and certainly not within one file). Instead, you should pick one option (most commonly option 1 or 3 in math.cpp) and then consistently use that style for all your function definitions.

Using Directives and Declarations

From Chapter 3, you already know that by using a blanket using *directive*, you can reference any name from a namespace without qualifying it with the namespace name:

```
using namespace std;
```

However, this risks defeating the purpose of using namespaces in the first place and increases the likelihood of errors because of the accidental use of a name in the std namespace. It is thus often better to use qualified names or add using declarations for the names from another namespace that you are referencing. A using *declaration*, as you also know from Chapter 3, allows you to use a specific name without its namespace qualification. Here are some examples:

```
using std::vector;
using std::max;
```

These declarations introduce the names vector and max from the namespace std into the current scope or namespace. One using declaration may introduce many different entities. For instance, the using directive for std::max introduces all possible instantiations and overloads of the various std::max<>() templates with a single using declaration.

We have occasionally placed some using declarations and directives already at global scope in some examples. But you can also place them within a namespace, within a function, or even within a statement block. When placed in a namespace, it makes a name from one namespace available within another. Here is a variation of Ex11_06B that uses this technique:

```
// squaring.cppm
export module squaring;
import std;          // For std::numbers::sqrt2

export namespace math
{
  using std::numbers::sqrt2;
  using std::sqrt;    // Never 'using std::sqrt();' or 'using std::sqrt(double);'!
  auto square(const auto& x) { return x * x; }
  auto pow4(const auto& x) { return square(square(x)); }
}
```

By adding the `using std::numbers::sqrt2;` declaration, you ensure that by importing `squaring`, you can qualify the `sqrt2` constant both as `std::numbers::sqrt2` and `math::sqrt2`. Note that if the entire `math` namespace was not exported already, you would have to use `export using std::numbers::sqrt2;` to make this alias visible from outside the `squaring` module.

The second `using` declaration in the exported `math` namespace similarly brings all overloads of the `sqrt()` function into this namespace as well. You cannot pick and choose which overloads of a function to import into a namespace; you can only import a particular *name* (see also the comment in the code). `std::sqrt()`, for instance, has overloads for `double`, `float`, `long double`, and various integral parameters; due to our single `using` declaration, all these overloads are addressable now as `math::sqrt()`.

If you want to introduce all constants (and variable templates) of the `<numbers>` module into the `math` namespace—instead of only the `sqrt2` constant, as we did originally—you can do so by adding (and exporting) the following `using` directive.

```
namespace math
{
  export using namespace std::numbers;
}
```

When adding a `using` directive or declaration at any scope that is not a namespace, analogous aliasing rules apply, but then only within that scope. Take the following function template, for instance, for functions that compute the length of the hypotenuse of a right-angled triangle given the length of the other two sides (using the well-known Pythagorean theorem). Since this `hypotenuse()` template is defined in the global namespace, its body would, by default, have to qualify the `sqrt` and `square` names with `math::`.

```
auto hypotenuse(const auto& x, const auto& y)
{
   using namespace math;
   // Or:
   //    using math::square;
   //    using math::sqrt;      /* Same as, of course: using std::sqrt; */
   return sqrt(square(x) + square(y));
}
```

The declaration or directive applies until the end of the block that contains it.

■ **Caution**   Never use this naïve implementation of `hypotenuse()` in practice. Always use the `std::hypot()` functions of `<cmath>` instead. The reason is that our naïve solution often is fairly inaccurate (it suffers both from underflow and overflow issues). Because creating efficient and numerically stable mathematical primitives is deceptively hard (many scientific articles have been written on algorithms for `hypot()` alone), you should always look for predefined primitives first.

■ **Tip**   What we explained here for `using` directives and declarations also applies to type aliases and `using enum` declarations (both introduced in Chapter 3). They all can be exported from modules and/or brought into a namespace, or applied more locally at function or even statement scopes. You saw an example of a local `using enum` declaration inside the `switch` statement in the `from_roman()` helper function earlier in this chapter.

Personally, we prefer to apply `using` directives and declarations only sparsely, and always as locally as possible. That way, we not only avoid inadvertent name clashes, but we also clarify to the reader of our code from which namespace each entity name originates.

Namespace Aliases

Long namespace names, often originating from deeply nested namespaces, may be unduly cumbersome to use. Having to attach names such as `my_excessively_very_long_namespace_name_version2::` or `MyCompany::MyModule::MySubModule::MyGrouping::` to every function call, for instance, would be more than a nuisance. To get over this, you can define an alias for a namespace name on a local basis. The general form of the declaration you'd use to define an alias for a namespace name is as follows:

```
namespace alias_name = original_namespace_name;
```

You can then use `alias_name` in place of `original_namespace_name` to access names within the namespace. For example, to define aliases for the namespace names mentioned in the previous paragraph, you could write this:

```
namespace v2 = my_excessively_very_long_namespace_name_version2;
namespace MyGroup = MyCompany::MyModule::MySubmodule::MyGrouping;
```

Now you can call a function within the original namespace with a statement such as this:

```
int fancyNumber{ v2::doFancyComputation(MyGroup::queryUserInput()) };
```

Summary

This chapter discussed capabilities that operate between, within, and across program files. C++ programs typically consist of many files, and the larger the program, the more files you must contend with. To keep this code ordered and organized, it's vital that you understand modules and namespaces.

The important points from this chapter include the following:

- Modules allow you to organize your source code into logical, self-contained building blocks.

- Only exported declarations are visible within files that import the module. Other declarations in the module interface files are merely reachable, which mostly suffices to use the module. Declarations and definitions that only exist in module implementation files are unreachable outside of the module.

- You can export basically any declaration from a module: function declarations, variable declarations, type declarations, `using` declarations, `using` directives, module `import` declarations, and so on.

- Only changes in a module's interface (the collection of all exported entities) require you to recompile consumers of the module. Function definitions are not part of the module's interface; only their prototypes are.

- Only module interface files can export declarations, but you can move function definitions and any module-local entities into module implementation files to keep the interface file itself clear and simple.

- At the beginning of every module file is a module declaration. In module interface files, this declaration has the form `export module name;`. In module implementation files, it has the form `module name;`. In these declarations, `name` is normally the name of the module; only in module partition files, this `name` takes the form `module_name:partition_name`.

- Every module has exactly one primary module interface file (starting with `export module module_name;`). Every module interface partition must be exported, directly or indirectly, from the module's primary interface file.

- Partitions cannot be imported outside of the module. If you want parts of a module to be importable like that, you can turn them into submodules instead.

- Namespaces are hierarchical groupings of entity names designed to avoid name clashes within larger code bases (and especially when integrating various third-party libraries). While namespaces and modules are completely orthogonal in C++, it only stands to reason that aligning the names of your namespaces and modules is a sensible idea.

- `using` directives and `using` declarations risk nullifying the advantages of namespaces, and they should therefore only be used sparsely and as locally as possible (ideally even at the level of a function body or statement block).

EXERCISES

The following exercises enable you to try what you've learned in this chapter. If you get stuck, look back over the chapter for help. If you're still stuck after that, you can download the solutions from the Apress website (https://www.apress.com/gp/services/source-code), but that really should be a last resort.

Exercise 11-1. One of the larger programs you have seen thus far is that of `Ex8_17.cpp`. Extract all its functions and put them in a single-file `words` module, with all functions part of a `words` namespace. The module should only export those functions that are relevant to the `main()` function, which, for the most part, should be kept as is. All other functions, and especially the ternary overload of `sort()`, exist solely to support these exported functions.

Exercise 11-2. Retake your solution to Exercise 11-1 and split the module's interface from its implementation by moving all function definitions to an implementation file. Do not use namespace blocks in the implementation file. As part of the exercise, move all nonexported functions out of the `words` namespace and into the global namespace (and then figure out how to still invoke the ternary `sort()` function from the exported unary `sort()` function).

Exercise 11-3. Split the insanely large `words` module of Exercise 11-2 into two aptly named submodules: one submodule containing all *sorting* functionality and one containing any remaining utilities (or *utils*, in programmer speak). Also, put your functions in nested namespaces whose names mirror those of the submodules.

Exercise 11-4. Start again from the Exercise 11-2 solution and move `swap()` and `max_word_length()` into an `internals` module implementation partition.

Exercise 11-5. Go back to the Exercise 11-1 solution, only this time, instead of creating implementation files as in Exercise 11-2, create multiple interface partition files, each still containing their function definitions. One partition again contains all *sorting* functionality, the other the remaining utilities (*utils*). Also, recycle the `internals` partition from Exercise 11-4.

Exercise 11-6. Start once again from Exercise 11-2. Because the length of `words` is exorbitant (five letters, oh my!), make sure that all names in this namespace can also be qualified with `wrds` (four letters, already much better!) and `w` (one letter, perfect!). Use two different techniques for this. (For the record, neither cryptic acronyms such as `wrds` nor one-letter identifiers such as `w` have their place in production-quality code. Clarity always trumps compactness!)

CHAPTER 12

Defining Your Own Data Types

In this chapter, we'll introduce one of the most fundamental tools in the C++ programmer's toolbox: classes. We'll also present some ideas that are implicit in object-oriented programming and show how they are applied.

In this chapter, you'll learn

- What the basic principles in objected-oriented programming are

- How you define a new data type as a class and how you can create and use objects of a class type

- What the different building blocks of a class are—member variables, member functions, class constructors, and destructors—and how to define them

- What a default constructor is and how you can supply your own version

- What a copy constructor is and how to create a custom implementation

- The difference between `private` and `public` members

- What the pointer `this` is and how and when you use it

- What a `friend` function is and what privileges a `friend` class has

- What `const` functions in a class are and how they are used

- What a class destructor is and when you should define it

- What a nested class is and how to use it

Classes and Object-Oriented Programming

You define a new data type by defining a *class*, but before we get into the language, syntax, and programming techniques of classes, we'll explain how your existing knowledge relates to the concept of object-oriented programming. The essence of *object-oriented programming* (commonly abbreviated to *OOP*) is that you write programs in terms of objects in the domain of the problem you are trying to solve, so part of the program development process involves designing a set of types to suit the problem context. If you're writing a program to keep track of your bank account, you'll probably need to have data types such as `Account` and `Transaction`. For a program to analyze baseball scores, you may have types such as `Player` and `Team`.

© Ivor Horton and Peter Van Weert 2023
I. Horton and P. Van Weert, *Beginning C++23*, https://doi.org/10.1007/978-1-4842-9343-0_12

Almost everything you have seen up to now has been *procedural programming*, which involves programming a solution in terms of fundamental data types. The variables of the fundamental types don't allow you to model real-world objects (or even imaginary objects) very well, though. It's not possible to model a baseball player realistically in terms of just an int or double value, or any other fundamental data type. You need several values of a variety of types for any meaningful representation of a baseball player.

Classes provide a solution. A class type can be a composite of variables of other types—of fundamental types or of other class types. A class can also have functions as an integral part of its definition. You could define a class type called Box that contains three variables of type double that store a length, a width, and a height to represent boxes. You could then define variables of type Box, just as you define variables of fundamental types. Similarly, you could define arrays of Box elements, just as you would with fundamental types. Each of these variables or array elements would be called an *object* or *instance* of the same Box class. You could create and manipulate as many Box objects as you need in a program, and each of them would contain their own length, width, and height dimensions.

This goes quite a long way toward making programming in terms of real-world objects possible. Obviously, you can apply this idea of a class to represent a baseball player or a bank account or anything else. You can use classes to model whatever kinds of objects you want and write your programs around them. So, that's object-oriented programming all wrapped up then, right?

Well, not quite. A class as we've defined it up to now is a big step forward, but there's more to it than that. As well as the notion of user-defined types, object-oriented programming incorporates some additional important ideas (famously *encapsulation*, *data hiding*, *inheritance*, and *polymorphism*). We'll give you a rough, intuitive idea of what these additional OOP concepts mean right now. This will provide a reference frame for the detailed programming you'll be getting into in this and the next three chapters.

Encapsulation

In general, the definition of an object of a given type requires a combination of a specific number of different properties—the properties that make the object what it is. An object contains a precise set of data values that describe the object in sufficient detail for your needs. For a box, it could be just the three dimensions of length, width, and height. For an aircraft carrier, it is likely to be much more. An object can also contain a set of functions that operate on it—functions that use or change the properties, for example, or provide further characteristics of an object such as the volume of a box. The functions in a class define the set of operations that can be applied to an object of the class type, in other words, what you can do with it or to it. Every object of a given class incorporates the same combination of things, specifically, the set of data values as *member variables* of the class that characterize an object and the set of operations as *member functions* of the class. This packaging of data values and functions within an object is referred to as *encapsulation*.[1]

Figure 12-1 illustrates this with the example of an object representing a bank loan account. Every LoanAccount object has its properties defined by the same set of member variables; in this case, one holds the outstanding balance, and the other holds the interest rate. Each object also contains a set of member functions that define operations on the object. The object shown in Figure 12-1 has three member functions: one to calculate interest and add it to the balance and two for managing credit and debit accounting entries.

---

[1] In the context of object-oriented programming, you'll find that the term *encapsulation* may refer to two related yet distinct notions. Some authors define encapsulation like we do, namely, as the bundling of data with the functions that operate on that data, while others define it as a language mechanism for restricting direct access to an object's members. The latter is what we refer to as *data hiding* in the next subsection. Enough ink has been spilled debating which definition is right, so we will not go there (although obviously it's ours!). When reading other texts or when discussing with your peers, just keep in mind that encapsulation is often used as a synonym for data hiding.

The properties and operations are all encapsulated in every object of the type LoanAccount. Of course, this choice of what makes up a LoanAccount object is arbitrary. You might define it quite differently for your purposes, but however you define the LoanAccount type, all the properties and operations that you specify are encapsulated within every object of the type.

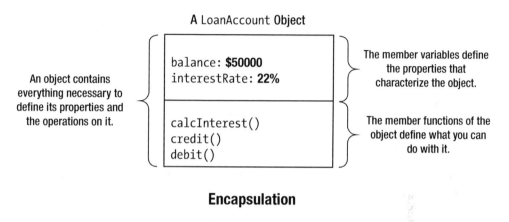

Figure 12-1. *An example of encapsulation*

Note that we said earlier that the data values defining an object needed to be "sufficient for your needs," not "sufficient to define the object in general." A person could be defined just by a name, address, and phone number if you were writing an address book application. But a person as a company employee or as a medical patient is likely to be defined by many more properties, and many more operations would be required. You just decide what you need in the contexts in which you intend to use the object.

Data Hiding

Of course, the bank wouldn't want the balance for a loan account (or the interest rate for that matter) changed arbitrarily from outside an object. Permitting this would be a recipe for chaos. Ideally, the member variables of a LoanAccount object are protected from direct outside interference and are only modifiable in a controlled way. The ability to make the data values for an object generally inaccessible is called *data hiding* or *information hiding*.

Figure 12-2 shows data hiding applied to a LoanAccount object. With a LoanAccount object, the member functions of the object can provide a mechanism that ensures any changes to the member variables follow a particular policy and that the values set are appropriate. Interest shouldn't be negative, for instance, and generally, the balance should reflect the fact that money is owed to the bank, not the reverse.

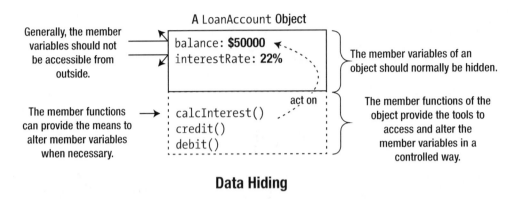

Figure 12-2. *An example of data hiding*

Data hiding is important because it is necessary if you are to maintain the integrity of an object. If an object is supposed to represent a duck, it should not have four legs; the way to enforce this is to make the leg count inaccessible, in other words, to "hide" the data. Of course, an object may have data values that can legitimately vary, but even then, you often want to control the range; after all, a duck doesn't usually weigh 300 pounds, and its weight is rarely zero or negative. Hiding the data belonging to an object prevents it from being accessed directly, but you can provide access through functions that are members of the object, either to alter a data value in a controlled way or to simply to obtain its value. Such functions can check that the change they're being asked to make is legal and within prescribed limits where necessary.

You can think of the member variables as representing the *state* of the object, and the member functions that manipulate them as representing the object's *interface* to the outside world. Using the class then involves programming using the functions declared as the interface. A program using the class interface is dependent only on the function names, parameter types, and return types specified for the interface. The internal mechanics of these functions don't affect the rest of the program that is creating and using objects of the class. That means it's important to get the class interface right at the design stage. You can subsequently change the implementation to your heart's content without necessitating any changes to programs that use the class.

For instance, as a program evolves over time, you may need to change the member variables that constitute an object's state. Instead of storing an interest rate in each LoanAccount object, for example, you may want to change it so that every LoanAccount object refers to an object of a new class AccountType and store the interest rate there instead. Figure 12-3 illustrates this redesigned representation of LoanAccount objects.

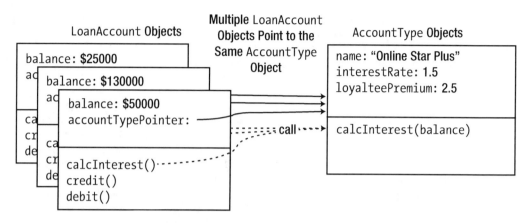

Figure 12-3. *Reworking the representation of the internal state of objects while preserving their interface*

LoanAccount objects now no longer store their interest rate themselves but instead point to an AccountType, which stores all necessary member variables for calculating an account's interest. The calcInterest() member function of LoanAccount therefore calls upon the associated AccountType to do the actual calculation; for this, all the latter needs from an account is its current balance. This more object-oriented design allows you to easily modify the interest rates of all LoanAccounts pointing to the same AccountType all at once or to change the type of an account without re-creating it.

The main point we want to make with this example is that even though both the internal representation (the interestRate member) and the workings (the calcInterest() member) of a LoanAccount have changed drastically, its interface to the outside world remained constant. As far as the rest of the program is concerned, it appears as if nothing has changed at all. Such an overhaul of a LoanAccount's representation and logic would've been much harder if code from outside of its class definition would've been accessing the old, now-removed interestRate member variable of LoanAccounts directly. We would then have had to rework all code using LoanAccount objects as well. Thanks to data hiding, external code can only access member variables through well-defined interface functions. So, all we had to do is to redefine these member functions; we didn't have to worry about the rest of the program.

Notice moreover that because external code could obtain the annual interest only through the calcInterest() interface function, it was trivial for us to introduce an extra "loyalty premium" and use this during interest calculations. This again would've been near impossible if external code would've been reading the old interestRate member directly to calculate interests themselves.

Hiding the data within an object is not mandatory, but it's generally a good idea. In a way, direct access to the values that define an object undermines the whole idea of object-oriented programming. Object-oriented programming is supposed to be programming in terms of *objects*, not in terms of the bits that make up an object. While this may sound rather abstract, we have already seen at least two very good, concrete reasons to consistently hide an object's data and to only access or manipulate it through the functions in its interface:

- Data hiding facilitates maintaining the integrity of an object. It allows you to make sure that an object's internal state—the combination of all its member variables— always remains valid.

- Data hiding, combined with a well-thought-out interface, allows you to rework both an object's internal representation (that is, its *state*) and the implementation of its member functions (that is, its *behavior*) without having to rework the rest of the program as well. In object-oriented speak we say that data hiding reduces the *coupling* between a class and the code that uses it. Interface stability is, of course, even more critical if you are developing a software library that is used by external customers.

A third motivation for accessing member variables only through interface functions is that it allows you to inject some extra code into these functions. Such code could add an entry to a log file marking the access or change, could make sure the data can be accessed safely by multiple callers at the same time, or could notify other objects that some state has been modified (these other objects could then, for instance, update the user interface of your application, say to reflect updates to a LoanAccount's balance), and so on. None of this would be possible if you allow external code to access member variables directly.

A fourth and final motivation is that allowing direct access to data variables complicates debugging. Most development environments support the concept of *breakpoints*. Breakpoints are user-specified points during debugging runs of the code where the execution becomes paused, allowing you to inspect the state of your objects. While some environments have more advanced functionality to pause execution whenever a particular member variable changes, putting breakpoints on function calls or specific lines of code inside functions remains much easier.

In this section, we created an extra AccountType class to facilitate working with different types of accounts. This is by no means the only way to model these real-world concepts into classes and objects. In the next section we'll present a powerful alternative, called *inheritance*. Which design you should use will depend on the exact needs of your concrete application.

Inheritance

Inheritance is the ability to define one type in terms of another. For example, suppose you have defined a BankAccount type that contains members that deal with the broad issues of bank accounts. Inheritance allows you to create the LoanAccount type as a specialized kind of BankAccount. You could define a LoanAccount as being like a BankAccount, but with a few extra properties and functions of its own. The LoanAccount type *inherits* all the members of BankAccount, which is referred to as its *base class*. In this case, you'd say that LoanAccount is *derived* from BankAccount.

Each LoanAccount object contains all the members that a BankAccount object does, but it has the option of defining new members of its own or of *redefining* the functions it inherits so that they are more meaningful in its context. Redefining a base class's function in a derived class is called *overriding*; the latter function is said to *override* the former. This last ability is very powerful, as you'll see.

Extending the current example, you might also want to create a new CheckingAccount type by adding different characteristics to BankAccount. This situation is illustrated in Figure 12-4.

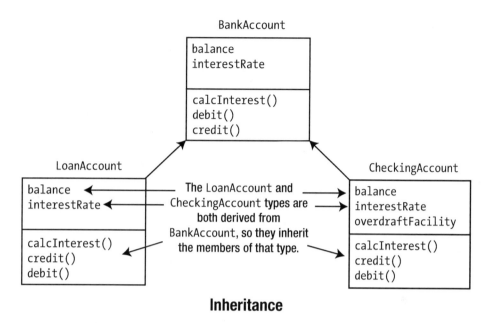

Figure 12-4. *An example of inheritance*

Both the LoanAccount and CheckingAccount types are defined so that they are derived from the type BankAccount. They inherit the member variables and member functions of BankAccount, but they are free to define new characteristics that are specific to their own type.

In this example, CheckingAccount has added a member variable called overdraftFacility that is unique to itself, and both the derived classes can override any of the member functions that they inherit from the base class. It's likely they would override calcInterest(), for example, because calculating and dealing with the interest for a checking account involves something different than doing it for a loan account.

Polymorphism

Polymorphism means the ability to assume different forms at different times. Polymorphism in C++ always[2] involves calling a member function of an object using either a pointer or a reference. Such function calls can have different effects at different times—sort of Jekyll and Hyde function calls. The mechanism works only for objects of types that are derived from a common base type, such as the BankAccount type. Polymorphism means that objects belonging to a "family" of inheritance-related classes can be passed around and operated on using base class pointers and references.

---

[2] Technically speaking, programming language theory distinguishes several different forms of polymorphism. What we refer to here as "polymorphism" is formally known as *subtyping, subtype polymorphism,* or *inclusion polymorphism.* Other forms of polymorphism that are also supported by C++ include *parametric polymorphism* (C++ function and class templates; see Chapters 10 and 17) and *ad hoc polymorphism* (function and operator overloading; see Chapters 8 and 13). In the world of object-oriented programming, however, the term "polymorphism" usually refers solely to subtyping, so that is also the terminology we adopt in this book.

The LoanAccount and CheckingAccount objects can both be passed around using a pointer or reference to BankAccount. The pointer or reference can be used to call the inherited member functions of whatever object it refers to. The idea and implications of this will be easier to appreciate if we look at a specific case.

Suppose you have the LoanAccount and CheckingAccount types defined as before, based on the BankAccount type. Suppose further that you have defined objects of these types, debt and cash, respectively, as illustrated in Figure 12-5. Because both types are based on the BankAccount type, a variable of type *pointer to* BankAccount, such as pAcc in Figure 12-5, can store the address of either of these objects.

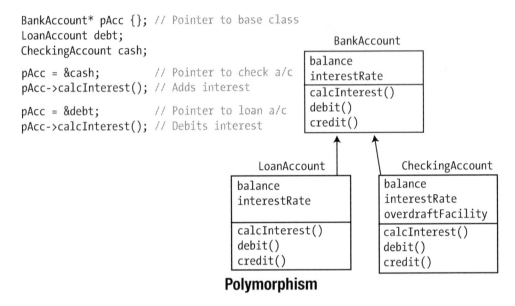

Figure 12-5. *An example of polymorphism*

The beauty of polymorphism is that the function called by pAcc->calcInterest() varies depending on what pAcc points to. If it points to a LoanAccount object, then the calcInterest() function for that object is called, and interest is debited from the account. If it points to a CheckingAccount object, the result is different because the calcInterest() function for that object is called, and interest is credited to the account. The particular function that is called through the pointer is decided at runtime. That is, it is decided not when the program is compiled but when it executes. Thus, the same function call can do different things depending on what kind of object the pointer points to. Figure 12-5 shows just two different types, but in general, you can get polymorphic behavior with as many different types derived from a common base class as your application requires. You need quite a bit of C++ language know-how to accomplish what we've described, and that's exactly what you'll be exploring in the rest of this chapter and throughout the next three chapters.

Terminology

Here's a summary of the terminology that is used when discussing classes. It includes some terms that you've come across already:

- A *class* is a user-defined data type.

- The variables and functions defined within a class are *members* of the class. The variables are *member variables*, and the functions are *member functions*. Member functions are also often called *methods*; member variables are also called *data members, member fields, or just fields*.

- Variables of a class type store *objects*. Objects are sometimes called *instances* of the class. Defining an instance of a class is referred to as *instantiation*.

- *Object-oriented programming* is a programming style based on the idea of defining your own data types as classes. It involves the ideas of *encapsulation*, *data hiding*, *class inheritance*, and *polymorphism*.

When you get into the details of object-oriented programming, it may seem a little complicated in places. Getting back to the basics can often help make things clearer, so use this list to always keep in mind what objects are really about. Object-oriented programming is about writing programs in terms of the objects that are specific to the domain of your problem. All the facilities around classes are there to make this as comprehensive and flexible as possible.

Defining a Class

A *class* is a user-defined type. The definition of a type uses the `class` keyword. The basic organization of a class definition looks like this:

```
class ClassName
{
  // Code that defines the members of the class...
};
```

The name of this class type is `ClassName`. It's a common convention to use the uppercase name for user-defined classes to distinguish class types from variable names. We'll adopt this convention in the examples. The members of the class are all specified between the curly braces. For now, we will include the definitions of all member functions inside the class definition, but later in this chapter we'll see that they can be defined outside the class definition as well. Note that the semicolon after the closing brace for the class definition must be present.

All the members of a class are `private` by default, which means they cannot be accessed from outside the class. This is obviously not acceptable for the member functions that form the interface. You use the `public` keyword followed by a colon to make all subsequent members accessible from outside the class. Members specified after the `private` keyword are not accessible from outside the class. `public` and `private` are *access specifiers* for the class members. There's another access specifier, `protected`, that you'll meet later. Here's how an outline class looks with access specifiers:

```
class ClassName
{
private:
  // Code that specifies members that are not accessible from outside the class...
```

```
public:
  // Code that specifies members that are accessible from outside the class...
};
```

public and private precede a sequence of members that are or are not accessible outside the class. The specification of public or private applies to all members that follow until there is a different specification. You could omit the first private specification here and get the default status of private, but it's better to make it explicit. Members in a private section of a class can be accessed only from functions that are members of the same class. Member variables or functions that need to be accessed by a function that is not a member of the class must be specified as public. A member function can reference any other member of the same class, regardless of the access specification, by just using its name. To make all this generality clearer, we'll start with an example of defining a class to represent a box:

```
class Box
{
public:
  // Function to calculate the volume of a box
  double volume()
  {
    return m_length * m_width * m_height;
  }

private:
  double m_length {1.0};
  double m_width {1.0};
  double m_height {1.0};
};
```

m_length, m_width, and m_height are member variables of the Box class and are all of type double. By popular convention, we add the prefix m_ to the names of all our member variables. While not required—we could just as well use names such as length, _width, or mHeight for member variables—the advantage of adding m_ is that it makes it easy to distinguish member variables from function parameters and local variables. We will follow this relatively standard convention everywhere in this book.

All three member variables of Box are private and therefore cannot be accessed from outside the class. Only the public volume() member function can refer to these private members. Each of the member variables is initialized to 1.0. You don't have to initialize member variables in this way—there are other ways of setting their values, as you'll see in a next section. If member variables of fundamental types are not initialized by some mechanism, though, they will contain junk values.

In our example we grouped all member variables at the end of the class definition. But you do not have to. You can alternate member variables and functions as often as you want. Likewise, you can alternate public and private sections as often as you want and put them in any order you want. Of course, just because you can arbitrarily (dis)arrange your class members does not mean that you should. With modest power comes modest responsibility. Your class definitions become much easier to read and maintain if you consistently group related members together and use the same predictable order across all your classes. In this book, and by popular convention, we will therefore arrange our class members as follows:

- We put all public members first, and all private members last. As a user of a class, you are normally mostly interested in its public interface, and less so in its inner workings. You want to know *what* you can do with a class, not *how* it all works. This is why we prefer to put the public interface first.

- We cluster related members, and put variables after functions. This means that member variables—which are normally private (data hiding!)—can always be found at the end of our class definitions. Nice and predictable.

- Constructors and destructors (both introduced later in this chapter) always come first, before any of the other member functions.

■ **Note** Another way to create a new type is by defining a *structure*. Here is a typical example:

```
struct Student   // A structure with two (public) member variables
{
  std::string name;
  unsigned int age;
};
```

Syntactically the only difference between a structure and a class is the use of the `struct` keyword. Semantically the only difference is that the default access specifier within a structure is always `public` instead of `private` (both for the members and within the base type clause; see the next chapter). Apart from those minor differences, structures and classes are equivalent in C++. The main difference lies in how you typically use them. By convention, you use structures in C++ precisely as you would in C: to encapsulate a series of public member variables; nothing more, nothing less. While in principle you *can* add member functions, private sections, constructors, destructors, and so on, to a C++ structure (none of this is possible in C, by the way), doing so is highly unconventional. For anything beyond the aggregation of public member variables, convention dictates you define a class.

■ **Tip** Prefer defining a dedicated structure over using types such as `std::pair<T1,T2>` or `std::tuple<Types...>` to aggregate two or more variables. The reason is that a structure definition allows you to give a clear, meaningful names to the type and its member variables.

Creating Objects of a Class

Every object of class Box will have its own set of member variables. This is obvious really; if they didn't have their own member variables, all Box objects would be identical. You can create a variable of type Box like this:

```
Box myBox;     // A Box object with all dimensions equal to 1.0
```

The myBox variable refers to a Box object with the default member variable values. You could call the `volume()` member for the object to calculate the volume:

```
std::println("Volume of myBox is {}", myBox.volume());  // Volume is 1
```

The volume will be 1 because the initial values for the three dimensions are 1.0. The fact that the member variables of the Box class are private means that we have no way to set these members. You could specify the member variables as public, in which case you can set them explicitly from outside the class, like this:

```
myBox.m_length = 1.5;
myBox.m_width = 2.0;
myBox.m_height = 4.0;
std::println("Volume of myBox is {}", myBox.volume());  // Volume is 12
```

But it's bad practice to make member variables of a class public. Doing so goes against the data hiding principle. So we need a different mechanism to initialize the private member variables of an object with a given set of values. The special kind of member function responsible for this is called a *constructor*. We discuss constructors at length in the next section.

■ **Note**   As noted in the previous section, a structure typically only aggregates a series of member variables. Nothing more, nothing less. This means that it typically defines no constructors either. Nor does it really need to. After all, C++ offers plenty different means already to initialize a structure without constructors. The following example lists them all:

```
struct Student   // A structure with two (public) member variables
{
  std::string name;
  unsigned int age;
};

Student a; // Default initialization: name is ""; age contains garbage (take care!)
Student b{}; // Value initialization: name is ""; age is zero
Student c{ "Jim", 5 };  // Aggregate initialization: initializes in declaration order
Student d{ "Vicky" };   // Omit variable further down declaration order: age is zero
// Student e{ 25 }; /* Error: cannot omit earlier initializers */
Student f{ .name = "Steven", .age = 20 };  // Designated initializer
Student g{ .name = "Michelle" }; // Omit designator: age is zero
Student h{ .age = 63 };          // You can omit any designator
// Student i{ .age = 19, .name = "Paul" }; /* Out-of-order not allowed */
Student j{ { f.name,0,5 }, 20 }; // Nested initializer: name is "Steve" (substring)
```

---

[3] And to *union types* as well, technically, but we won't cover those in this book. You're better off using std::variant<> anyway in C++, a vocabulary type template similar to the std::optional<> and std::result<> types we discuss in Chapter 9.

We believe the example speaks for itself. It's worth stressing, though, that most of these initialization options (and aggregate and designated initialization in particular) only apply if 1) all member variables are publicly accessible, and 2) there's no constructors defined. In other words, by convention, these initialization options only apply to structures[3]. As we explain next, class types normally hide their member variables and initialize them through constructors.

Constructors

A class *constructor* provides the opportunity to initialize the new object as it is created and to ensure that member variables contain valid values. It is a special kind of function in a class that differs in a few significant respects from an ordinary member function. A class constructor always has the same name as the class. A constructor also does not return a value and therefore has no return type. It is an error to specify a return type for a constructor. Whenever a new instance of the class is defined, a constructor is called. Always, no exception. Objects of a class type can only be created using a constructor.

Default Constructors

Wait, hang on a moment! We created a Box object in the previous section and calculated its volume. How could that have happened? We never defined a constructor? Well, if you don't define a constructor for a class, the compiler supplies a *default default constructor*. And no, the two "defaults" is no typo. Thanks to this default default constructor, or *implicitly-declared constructor*, the Box class effectively behaves as if defined as follows:

```cpp
class Box
{
public:
  // The default constructor that was supplied by the compiler...
  Box()
  {
  // Empty body so it does nothing...
  }

  // Function to calculate the volume of a box
  double volume()
  {
    return m_length * m_width * m_height;
  }

private:
  double m_length {1.0};
  double m_width {1.0};
  double m_height {1.0};
};
```

A *default constructor* is a constructor that can be called without arguments. This constructor is invoked by default if you do not explicitly invoke a constructor with given arguments.

```cpp
Box myBox;    // Invokes the default constructor
```

If you do not define *any* constructor for a class—neither a default constructor nor any other constructor—then the compiler generates one for you: a default constructor. That's why it's called a default default constructor; it is a default constructor that is generated by default. A default default constructor has no parameters and its sole purpose is to allow an object to be created. It does nothing else, so all member variables will have their default values. If no initial value is specified for a member variable of a fundamental type (double, int, bool ...) or pointer type (int*, const Box* ...), it will contain an arbitrary junk value. In the Box class we initialize all member variables to 1.0, so the default default constructor always leaves Box objects in a well-defined initial state.

As soon as you define any constructor, even a nondefault one with parameters, the default default constructor is no longer supplied. There are circumstances in which you need a constructor with no parameters in addition to a constructor that you define that has parameters. In that case, *you* must ensure that there is a definition for the default constructor in the class.

Defining a Class Constructor

Let's extend the Box class from the previous example to incorporate a constructor and then check that it works:

```
// Ex12_01.cpp - Defining a class constructor
import std;

// Class to represent a box
class Box
{
public:
  // Constructor
  Box(double length, double width, double height)
  {
    std::println("Box constructor called.");
    m_length = length;
    m_width = width;
    m_height = height;
  }

  // Function to calculate the volume of a box
  double volume()
  {
    return m_length * m_width * m_height;
  }

private:
  double m_length {1.0};
  double m_width {1.0};
  double m_height {1.0};
};

int main()
{
  Box firstBox {80.0, 50.0, 40.0};              // Create a box
  double firstBoxVolume {firstBox.volume()};  // Calculate the box volume
  std::println("Volume of Box object is {}", firstBoxVolume);

  // Box secondBox;         // Causes a compiler error message
}
```

This produces the following output:

```
Box constructor called.
Volume of Box object is 160000
```

The constructor for the Box class has three parameters of type double, corresponding to the initial values for the m_length, m_width, and m_height member variables of an object. No return type is allowed, and the name of the constructor must be the same as the class name, Box. The first statement in the constructor body outputs a message to show when it's called. You wouldn't do this in production programs, but it's helpful when you're testing a program and to understand what's happening and when. We'll use it regularly to trace what is happening in the examples. The rest of the code in the body of the constructor assigns the arguments to the corresponding member variables.

░ **Note**   Notice how the m_ naming convention pays off nicely inside constructor definitions. If we had used length, width, and height as the names of our member variables instead, we would have had to invent different names for the three parameters of the Box constructor.[4]

The firstBox object is created with this statement:

```
Box firstBox {80.0, 50.0, 40.0};
```

The initial values for the member variables m_length, m_width, and m_height appear in the braced initializer and are passed as arguments to the constructor. Because there are three values in the list, the compiler looks for a Box constructor with three parameters. When the constructor is called, it displays the message that appears as the first line of output, so you know that the constructor that you have added to the class is called.

We said earlier that once you define a constructor, the compiler won't supply a default constructor anymore, at least not by default. That means this statement will no longer compile:

```
Box secondBox;          // Causes a compiler error message
```

If you want to allow Box objects to be defined like this, you must add a definition for a constructor without arguments. We will do so in the next section.

Using the default Keyword

As soon as you add a constructor, *any* constructor, the compiler no longer implicitly defines a default default constructor. If you then still want your objects to be default-constructible, it is up to you to ensure that the class has a default constructor. Your first option is to define one yourself. For the Box class of Ex12_01.cpp, for instance, all you'd have to do is add the following constructor definition somewhere in the public section of the class:

```
Box() {}          // Default constructor
```

---

[4] Some also use statements such as this->length = length; to circumvent such name clashes (the this pointer is discussed later in this chapter), but we prefer the more compact m_ convention.

Because the member variables of a Box are already given a valid value, 1.0, during their initialization, there is nothing left for you to do in the body of the default constructor.

Instead of defining a default constructor with an empty function body, you can also use the default keyword. This keyword can be used to instruct the compiler to generate a default default constructor, even if there are other user-defined constructors present. For Box, this looks as follows:

```
Box() = default;  // Defaulted default constructor
```

Both the equals sign and the semicolon are required. A modified version of Ex12_01 with a defaulted constructor is available online in Ex12_01A.cpp.

While an explicit empty body definition and a defaulted constructor declaration are nearly equivalent, the use of the default keyword is preferred in modern C++ code:

■ **Tip**　If there is nothing to do in a default constructor's body (or initializer list, which we'll encounter later), you should use = default; over { }. Not only does this make it more apparent that it concerns a default default constructor, there are also a few subtle technical reasons that make the compiler-generated version the better choice (see also our section on constexpr members later).

Defining Functions Outside the Class

We said earlier that the definition of a member function can be placed outside the class definition. This is also true for class constructors. The class definition itself then only contains the constructor's signature, not its body. The Box class, for instance, could be defined as follows:

```
// Class to represent a box
class Box
{
public:
  Box() = default;
  Box(double length, double width, double height);

  double volume();   // Function to calculate the volume of a box

private:
  double m_length {1.0};
  double m_width {1.0};
  double m_height {1.0};
};
```

Moving the member definitions outside of the class definition like this makes it easier to get a quick overview of the class's (public) interface. This is particularly interesting for member functions that have longer function bodies, or for classes with a larger number of members.

You can then put the definitions of the members of Box somewhere after the definition of their class. The name of each member must be qualified with the class name so the compiler knows to which class they belong:

```
// Constructor definition
Box::Box(double length, double width, double height)
{
  std::println("Box constructor called.");
  m_length = length;
  m_width = width;
  m_height = height;
}

// Member function definition
double Box::volume()
{
  return m_length * m_width * m_height;
}
```

Ex12_02.cpp puts it all together for you: the Box class definition, followed by these two member definitions, and a main() function. This main() function is the exact same one as in Ex12_01.cpp.

■ **Note** This separation of a class's interface and implementation is completely analogous to that for modules in the previous chapter, in terms of both motivation and technical implications. Unsurprisingly, out-of-class member function definitions can also be moved to implementation files, leaving only the class definition in the interface file (be it a header or a module interface file). We discuss this further later after this section on constructors.

Default Arguments for Constructor Parameters

When we discussed "ordinary" functions, you saw that you can specify *default values* for the parameters in the function prototype. You can do this for class member functions, including constructors. Default parameter values for constructors and member functions always go inside the class, not in an external constructor or function definition. We can change the class definition in the previous example to the following:

```
class Box
{
public:
  // Constructors
  Box() = default;
  Box(double length = 1.0, double width = 1.0, double height = 1.0);

  double volume();      // Function to calculate the volume of a box

private:
  // Same member variables as always...
};
```

If you make this change to Ex12_02, what happens? You get an error message from the compiler, of course! The message basically says that you have multiple default constructors defined. The reason for the confusion is the constructor with three parameters allows all three arguments to be omitted, which is indistinguishable from a call to the default constructor. A constructor for which all parameters have a default value still counts as a default constructor. The obvious solution is to get rid of the defaulted constructor that accepts no parameters in this instance. If you do so, everything compiles and executes okay.

Using a Member Initializer List

So far, you've set values for member variables in the body of a constructor using explicit assignment. You can use an alternative and more efficient technique that uses a *member initializer list*. We'll illustrate this with an alternative version of the Box class constructor:

```
// Constructor definition using a member initializer list
Box::Box(double length, double width, double height)
  : m_length{length}, m_width{width}, m_height{height}
{
  std::println("Box constructor called.");
}
```

The values of the member variables are specified as initializing values in the initialization list that is part of the constructor header. The m_length member variable is initialized with length, for example. The initialization list is separated from the parameter list by a colon (:), and each initializer is separated from the next by a comma (,). If you substitute this version of the constructor in the previous example, you'll see that it works just as well (see Ex12_03.cpp for the resulting program).

This is more than just a different notation, though. When you initialize a member variable using an assignment statement in the body of the constructor, the member variable is first default initialized (using a constructor call if the variable is an instance of a class), after which the assignment is carried out as a separate operation. When you use an initialization list, the correct value is used to initialize the member variable immediately *as it is created*. This can be a much more efficient process, particularly if the member variable is a class instance. This technique for initializing parameters in a constructor is important for another reason. As you'll see, it is the *only* way of setting values for certain types of member variables.

There is one small caveat to watch out for with initializer lists. The order in which the member variables are initialized is always determined by the order in which they are declared in the class definition—so *not* as you may expect by the order in which they appear in the member initializer list. This only matters if the member variables are initialized using expressions for which the order of evaluation matters. Plausible examples would be where a member variable is initialized either by using the value of another member variable or by calling a member function that relies on other member variables being initialized already. Relying on the evaluation order like that in production code can be dangerous. Even if everything is working correctly today, next year someone may change the order in which the variables are declared and inadvertently break the correctness of one of the class's constructors!

■ **Tip** As a rule, it's better to initialize all member variables either directly in their declaration or in the constructor's member initializer list. This is generally more efficient. To avoid any confusion, you ideally put the member variables in the initializer list in the same order as they are declared in the class definition (some compilers will issue a warning if you don't). You should initialize member variables in the body of the constructor only if more complex logic is required or if the order in which the variables are initialized is important.

Using the explicit Keyword

A problem with class constructors with a *single* parameter is that the compiler can use such a constructor as an implicit conversion from the type of the parameter to the class type. This can produce undesirable results in some circumstances. Let's consider a particular situation. Suppose that you define a class that defines boxes that are cubes for which all three sides have the same length:

```
class Cube
{
public:
  Cube(double side);                    // Constructor
  double volume();                      // Calculate volume of a cube
  bool hasLargerVolumeThan(Cube cube);  // Compare volume of a cube with another
private:
  double m_side;
};
```

You can then define the constructor as follows:

```
Cube::Cube(double side) : m_side{side}
{
  std::println("Cube constructor called.");
}
```

Notice that because all constructors (there is only one here) initialize m_side, there is no need to give this member variable an initial value in its declaration.

The definition of the function that calculates the volume will be as follows:

```
double Cube::volume() { return m_side * m_side * m_side; }
```

One Cube object is greater than another if its volume is the greater of the two. The hasLargerVolumeThan() member can thus be defined as follows:

```
bool Cube::hasLargerVolumeThan(Cube cube) { return volume() > cube.volume(); }
```

■ **Note**   Later in this chapter you will see that you would normally pass the cube parameter of hasLargerVolumeThan() by reference-to-const rather than by value. To make that work, however, you first need to know about const member functions, so for now we simply pass cube by value.

The constructor requires only one argument of type double. Clearly, the compiler could use the constructor to convert a double value to a Cube object, but under what circumstances is that likely to happen? You might use the Cube class in the following way (see Ex12_04.cpp):

```
int main()
{
  Cube box1 {7.0};
  Cube box2 {3.0};
```

```
  if (box1.hasLargerVolumeThan(box2))
    std::println("box1 is larger than box2.");
  else
    std::println("Volume of box1 is less than or equal to that of box2.");

  std::println("Volume of box1 is {}.", box1.volume());
  if (box1.hasLargerVolumeThan(50.0))
    std::println("Volume of box1 is greater than 50.");
  else
    std::println("Volume of box1 is less than or equal to 50.");
}
```

Here's the output:

```
Cube constructor called.
Cube constructor called.
box1 is larger than box2.
Volume of box1 is 343.
Cube constructor called.
Volume of box1 is less than or equal to 50.
```

The output shows that the volume of box1 is definitely not less than 50, but the last line of output indicates the opposite. The code presumes that hasLargerVolumeThan() compares the volume of the current object with 50.0. In reality, the function compares two Cube objects. The compiler knows that the argument to the hasLargerVolumeThan() function should be a Cube object, but it compiles this quite happily because a constructor is available that converts the argument 50.0 to a Cube object. The code the compiler produces is equivalent to the following:

```
  if (box1.hasLargerVolumeThan(Cube{50.0}))
    std::println("Volume of box1 is greater than 50.");
  else
    std::println("Volume of box1 is less than or equal to 50.");
```

The function is not comparing the volume of the box1 object with 50.0, but with 125000.0, which is the volume of a Cube object with a side of length 50.0! The result is very different from what was expected.

Fortunately, you can prevent this nightmare from happening by declaring the constructor as explicit:

```
class Cube
{
public:
  explicit Cube(double side);           // Constructor
  double volume();                       // Calculate volume of a cube
  bool hasLargerVolumeThan(Cube cube); // Compare volume of a cube with another
private:
  double m_side;
};
```

With this definition for Cube, Ex12_04.cpp will not compile. The compiler never uses a constructor declared as explicit for an implicit conversion; it can be used only explicitly in the program. By using the explicit keyword with constructors that have a single parameter, you prevent implicit conversions from the parameter type to the class type. The hasLargerVolumeThan() member only accepts a Cube object as an argument, so calling it with an argument of type double does not compile.

▓ **Tip**   Implicit conversions may lead to confusing code; most of the time it becomes far more obvious why code compiles and what it does if you use explicit conversions. By default, you should therefore declare all single-*argument* constructors as explicit. (And, take care: this includes multi-*parameter* constructors that are invokable with just a single *argument* due to default argument values!) Omit explicit only if implicit type conversions are truly desirable. Examples of desirable implicit conversions include the conversion from string literals to std::string, or from T to std::optional<T>.

▓ **Note**   Any constructor that is not a single-argument constructor can be marked as explicit as well; although doing so is significantly less common. Suppose processBox() is a function with a single parameter of type Box or const Box&. Then in modern C++ the expression processBox({ 1.0, 2.0, 3.0 }) is a valid and commonly used shorthand for processBox(Box{ 1.0, 2.0, 3.0 }). To prohibit such shorthand notations, and thus to force the explicit mention of the Box type upon each construction, you can mark the ternary Box(double, double, double) constructor as explicit.

Delegating Constructors

A class can have several constructors that provide different ways of creating an object. The code for one constructor can call another of the same class in the initialization list. This can avoid repeating the same code in several constructors. Here's a simple illustration of this using the Box class:

```cpp
class Box
{
public:
  Box(double length, double width, double height);
  explicit Box(double side);   // Constructor for a cube (explicit!)
  Box() = default;             // Defaulted default constructor

  double volume();             // Function to calculate the volume of a box

private:
  double m_length{1.0};
  double m_width {1.0};
  double m_height{1.0};
};
```

The implementation of the first constructor can be as follows:

```
Box::Box(double length, double width, double height)
  : m_length{length}, m_width{width}, m_height{height}
{
  std::println("Box constructor 1 called.");
}
```

The second constructor creates a Box object with all sides equal, and we can implement it like this:

```
Box::Box(double side) : Box{side, side, side}
{
  std::println("Box constructor 2 called.");
}
```

This constructor just calls the previous constructor in the initialization list. The side argument is used as all three values in the argument list for the previous constructor. This is called a *delegating constructor* because it delegates the construction work to the other constructor. Delegating constructors help to shorten and simplify constructor code and can make the class definition easier to understand. Ex12_05.cpp in the online download contains the following example that illustrates this:

```
int main()
{
  Box box1 {2.0, 3.0, 4.0};                      // An arbitrary box
  Box box2 {5.0};                                // A box that is a cube
  std::println("box1 volume = {}", box1.volume());
  std::println("box2 volume = {}", box2.volume());
}
```

The output is as follows:

```
Box constructor 1 called.
Box constructor 1 called.
Box constructor 2 called.
box1 volume = 24
box2 volume = 125
```

You can see from the output that creating the first object just calls constructor 1. Creating the second object calls constructor 1 followed by constructor 2. This also shows that execution of the initialization list for a constructor occurs before the code in the body of the constructor. The volumes are as you would expect.

You should only call a constructor for the same class in the initialization list for a constructor. Calling a constructor of the same class in the body of a delegating constructor is not the same. Further, you must not initialize member variables in the initialization list of a delegating constructor. The code will not compile if you do. You can set values for member variables in the body of a delegating constructor, but in that case, you should consider whether the constructor should really be implemented as a delegating constructor.

The Copy Constructor

Suppose you add the following statement to main() in Ex12_05.cpp:

```
Box box3 {box2};
std::println("box3 volume = {}", box3.volume());    // box3 volume = 125
```

The output shows that box3 does indeed have the dimensions of box2, but there's no constructor defined with a parameter of type Box, so how was box3 created? The answer is that the compiler supplied a default *copy constructor*, which is a constructor that creates an object by copying an existing object. The default copy constructor copies the values of the member variables of the object that is the argument to the new object.

The default behavior is fine in the case of Box objects, but it can cause problems when one or more member variables are pointers. Just copying a pointer does not duplicate what it points to, which means that when an object is created by the copy constructor, it is interlinked with the original object. Both objects will contain a member pointing to the same thing. A simple example is if an object contains a pointer to a string. A duplicate object will have a member pointing to the same string, so if the string is changed for one object, it will be changed for the other. This is usually not what you want. In this case, *you* must define a copy constructor. We return to the questions of whether, when, and why you should define a copy constructor in Chapters 13 and 18. For now, we'll just focus on the how.

Implementing the Copy Constructor

The copy constructor must accept an argument of the same class type and create a duplicate in an appropriate manner. This poses an immediate problem that you must overcome; you can see it clearly if you try to define the copy constructor for the Box class like this:

```
Box::Box(Box box)    /* Wrong!! */
  : m_length{box.m_length}, m_width{box.m_width}, m_height{box.m_height}
{}
```

Each member variable of the new object is initialized with the value of the object that is the argument. No code is needed in the body of the copy constructor in this instance. This looks okay, but consider what happens when the constructor is called. The argument is passed *by value*, but because the argument is a Box object, the compiler arranges to call the copy constructor for the Box class to make a copy of the argument. Of course, the argument to this call of the copy constructor is passed by value, so another call to the copy constructor is required, and so on. In short, you've created a situation where an unlimited number of recursive calls to the copy constructor will occur. Your compiler won't allow this code to compile.

To avoid the problem, the parameter for the copy constructor must be a *reference*. More specifically, it should be a reference-to-const parameter. For the Box class, this looks like this:

```
Box::Box(const Box& box)
  : m_length{box.m_length}, m_width{box.m_width}, m_height{box.m_height}
{}
```

Now that the argument is no longer passed by value, recursive calls of the copy constructor are avoided. The compiler initializes the parameter box with the object that is passed to it. The parameter should be reference-to-const because a copy constructor is only in the business of creating duplicates; it should not modify the original. A reference-to-const parameter allows const and non-const objects to be copied. If the parameter was a reference-to-non-const, the constructor would not accept a const object as the argument, thus disallowing copying of const objects. You can conclude from this that the parameter type for a copy constructor is *always* a reference to a const object of the same class type. In other words, the form of the copy constructor is the same for any class:

```
MyClass::MyClass(const MyClass& object)
  : // Initialization list to duplicate all member variables
{
    // Possibly some additional code to duplicate the object...
}
```

You can find an example of a Box class with a copy constructor online in Ex12_06. Of course, the copy constructor may also delegate to other, non-copy constructors as well. Here's an example:

```
Box::Box(const Box& box) : Box{box.m_length, box.m_width, box.m_height}
{}
```

▓ **Caution**   You should normally never write this copy constructor of Box yourself. The compiler already generates one just like it by default, so all that could come from defining one yourself are bugs (forgetting to copy one of the member variables) or maintenance issues (forgetting to update the copy constructor if member variables are added). Like we said, this was just to show you *how* you can define one. We'll return to the *when* you should in later chapters. (Spoiler alert: you should do so as little as possible; just let the compiler do all the work!)

Deleting the Copy Constructor

So the compiler normally generates a copy constructor for every class, but what if that is not what you want? What if your Box objects contain highly precious cargo, barred by international copyright and trademark laws from being copied? All kidding aside, there can be any number of good reasons you do not want certain objects to be copied. If so, you can instruct the compiler not to generate a copy constructor by adding = delete; to its declaration in the class definition. For Box, this would look as follows:

```
class Box
{
public:
  Box() = default;
  Box(double length, double width, double height);
  Box(const Box& box) = delete;  // Prohibit copy construction

  // Rest of the class as always...
};
```

Once the copy constructor is deleted, statements such as the following will no longer compile:

```
  Box box3 {box2};   // Error: use of deleted constructor Box(const Box&)
```

442

Note that if any member variable of a class has a deleted or private copy constructor, the default copy constructor of that class is automatically implicitly deleted. In fact, even an explicitly defaulted copy constructor (which you can define using = default;) is then deleted.

■ **Caution** Whenever you delete the copy constructor, you probably also want to delete the *copy assignment operator*. We will tell you more about this in the next chapter.

Defining Classes in Modules

Exporting a class for use outside of a module is no different than exporting a function or a variable. You simply put its definition in the module's interface and add the keyword export in front of it. You can for instance move the definitions of the Box class and its members out of Ex12_03.cpp into a new module interface file of the following form:

```
// Box.cppm - module interface file for a module exporting the Box class
export module box;
import std;

export class Box
{
// Same class definition as before...
};

// Constructor definition
Box::Box(double length, double width, double height)
  : m_length{length}, m_width{width}, m_height{height}
{
  std::println("Box constructor called.");
}

// Member function definition
double Box::volume() { return m_length * m_width * m_height; }
```

Only the definitions of a class may be exported from a module, not those of their members. In fact, it is an error to add the export keyword to the definitions of class members. To use the members of an object, consumers of the module only require access to the (exported) definition of its class.

Of course, you could also have started from the Box class definition of Ex12_01.cpp where the member definitions were still done in-class (see Ex12_07A). There is no semantic difference between defining a member in-class or out-of-class for classes defined in a module file[5]. Separating a class's interface from its implementation does give you a cleaner, uncluttered overview of the module's interface, though.

---

[5] For a class that is defined in a header, however, in-class member function definitions are always (implicitly) inline. For classes defined in a module this no longer holds; a member function in a module is only inline if you explicitly mark it as such. Refer to Appendix A for more information on the differences between headers and modules.

Because member function definitions cannot be exported, they also do not need to be part of the module interface file either. That is, you could put them in a module implementation file instead. For the box module of Ex12_07 such an implementation file would look as shown next (see also Ex12_07B). The import declaration for std can then be removed from the interface file as well.

```
// Box.cpp - module implementation file defining the member functions of Box
module box;
import std;

// Constructor definition
Box::Box(double length, double width, double height)
  : m_length{length}, m_width{width}, m_height{height}
{
  std::println("Box constructor called.");
}

// Member function definition
double Box::volume() { return m_length * m_width * m_height; }
```

Conceptually, there should again be no significant difference between defining members in a module implementation file or defining them all in the module interface file. But it may impact certain optimizations (inlining of the function body at call sites) as well as incremental compilation (will files that import the module need to recompile if you alter a function definition?)—both in the obvious direction.

No matter how you lay out your module files, before you can use Box objects outside of the box module, you must import this module first. Here is a small example program that does precisely that.

```
// Ex12_07.cpp - Exporting a class from a module
import std;
import box;                      // For use of the Box class

int main()
{
  Box myBox{ 6.0, 6.0, 18.5 };   // Create a box
  std::println("My box's volume is {}", myBox.volume());
}
```

Accessing Private Class Members

Inhibiting all external access to the values of private member variables of a class is rather extreme. It's a good idea to protect them from unauthorized modification, but if you don't know what the dimensions of a particular Box object are, you have no way to find out. Surely it doesn't need to be that secret, right?

It doesn't, but that does not mean you should expose the member variables by using the public keyword either. You can provide access to the values of private member variables by adding member functions to return their values. To provide access to the dimensions of a Box object from outside the class, you just need to add these three functions to the class definition:

```
class Box
{
public:
  // Constructors
  Box() = default;
```

```
  Box(double length, double width, double height);

  double volume();        // Function to calculate the volume of a box

  // Functions to provide access to the values of member variables
  double getLength() { return m_length; }
  double getWidth()  { return m_width;  }
  double getHeight() { return m_height; }

private:
  double m_length{1.0};
  double m_width {1.0};
  double m_height{1.0};
};
```

The values of the member variables are fully accessible, but they can't be changed from outside the class, so the integrity of the class is preserved without the secrecy. Functions that retrieve the values of member variables are referred to as *accessor* functions.

Using these accessor functions is simple:

```
Box myBox {3.0, 4.0, 5.0};
std::println("myBox dimensions are {} by {} by {}",
  myBox.getLength(), myBox.getWidth(), myBox.getHeight());
```

You can use this approach for any class. You just write an accessor function for each member variable that you want to make available to the outside world.

There will be situations in which you *do* want to allow member variables to be changed from outside the class. If you supply a member function to do this rather than exposing the member variable directly, you have the opportunity to perform integrity checks on the value. For example, you could add functions to allow the dimensions of a Box object to be changed as well:

```
class Box
{
public:
  // Constructors
  Box() = default;
  Box(double length, double width, double height);

  double volume();        // Function to calculate the volume of a box

  // Functions to provide access to the values of member variables
  double getLength() { return m_length; }
  double getWidth()  { return m_width; }
  double getHeight() { return m_height; }

  // Functions to set member variable values
  void setLength(double length) { if (length > 0) m_length = length; }
  void setWidth(double width)   { if (width > 0)  m_width  = width;  }
  void setHeight(double height) { if (height > 0) m_height = height; }
```

```
private:
  double m_length{1.0};
  double m_width {1.0};
  double m_height{1.0};
};
```

The if statement in each set function ensures that you only accept new values that are positive. If a new value is supplied for a member variable that is zero or negative, it will be ignored. Member functions that allow member variables to be modified are sometimes called *mutators*. Using these simple mutators is equally straightforward:

```
myBox.setLength(-20.0);  // ignored!
myBox.setWidth(40.0);
myBox.setHeight(10.0);
std::println("myBox dimensions are now {} by {} by {}",
  myBox.getLength(),     // 3 (unchanged)
  myBox.getWidth(),      // by 40
  myBox.getHeight()      // by 10
);
```

You can find a complete test program that puts everything together inside Ex12_08.

■ **Note**   By popular convention the accessor function for a member m_member is mostly called getMember() and the function to update that variable is called setMember(). Because of this, these functions are more commonly referred to simply as *getters* and *setters*, respectively. A common exception to this naming convention are accessors for members of type bool, typically named isMember() rather than getMember(). That is, the getter for a Boolean member variable m_valid is usually called isValid() instead of getValid(). And no, this does not mean we're calling them *issers*; these Boolean accessors are still just called *getters*.

The this Pointer

The volume() function in the Box class was implemented in terms of the unqualified class member names. *Every* object of type Box contains these members, so there must be a way for the function to refer to the members of the particular object for which it has been called. In other words, when the code in volume() accesses the m_length member, there has to be a way for m_length to refer to the member of the object for which the function is called, and not some other object.

When a class member function executes, it automatically contains a hidden pointer with the name this, which contains the address of the object for which the function was called. For example, suppose you write this statement:

```
std::println("My box's volume equals {}", myBox.volume());
```

The this pointer in the volume() function contains the address of myBox. When you call the function for a different Box object, this will contain the address of that object. This means that when the member variable m_length is accessed in the volume() function during execution, it is actually referring to this->m_length, which is the fully specified reference to the object member that is being used. The compiler takes care of adding the this pointer name to the member names in the function. In other words, the compiler implements the function as follows:

```
double Box::volume()
{
  return this->m_length * this->m_width * this->m_height;
}
```

You could write the function explicitly using the pointer this if you wanted, but it isn't necessary. However, there are situations where you *do* need to use this explicitly, such as when you need to return the address of the current object.

▪ **Note**   You'll learn about static member functions of a class later in this chapter. These do not contain a this pointer.

C++23 introduces a new syntax that allows you to name the implicit this pointer as an explicit parameter— only then not as a pointer, but typically as a reference. Using this syntax, you could redefine the volume() member of our Box class as follows (provided you adapt the declaration in the class definition accordingly, of course):

```
double Box::volume(this Box& self)  // Or by value: double Box::volume(this Box self)
{
  // Caution: you cannot omit "self." on the next line!
  return self.getLength() * self.getWidth() * self.getHeight();
}
```

An *explicit object parameter* such as self in this example is prefixed with the keyword this, and it must be the first parameter of a (non-static) member function. In general, you can add any number of other parameters after the explicit object parameter. We'll illustrate this by reworking Box::setLength():

```
void Box::setLength(this Box& self, double length)
{
  if (length > 0) self.m_length = length; // Again: you cannot omit "self."!
}
```

You can name the explicit object parameter any way you want, though early convention suggests you name it self. Even though the redefined volume() and setLength() members appear to require an extra input argument, you still invoke them exactly as before (that is, you should not, and cannot, write, say, volume(myBox), or setLength(myBox, 9):

```
myBox.setWidth(9);   // Pointer to &myBox bound to this in setWidth(double) as always
myBox.setLength(9);  // Reference to myBox bound to self
                     // in setLength(this Box&, double)
std::println("{}", myBox.volume()); // Reference to myBox bound to self in volume()
```

The only difference is that &myBox is no longer bound to this inside the function body. Instead, a reference to myBox is bound to the explicit object parameter self. In fact, no this pointer is available inside the body of a function with an explicit object parameter at all, nor can you implicitly access any members of the bound object. You must access all members, both functions and variables, by *explicitly* going through the named explicit object parameter. In our earlier two example function bodies, you therefore cannot omit self.. Of course, if used with plain member functions such as Box::volume() and Box::setLength(), this new syntax provides no advantages at all—quite to the contrary, it's only significantly more verbose. The new syntax is most useful for member function *templates* where the type of the explicit object parameter itself is a template type parameter. We'll show you an example of this in Chapter 17.

Returning this from a Function

If the return type for a member function is a pointer to the class type, you can return this. You can then use the pointer returned by one member function to call another. Let's consider an example of where this would be useful.

Suppose you alter the mutator functions of the Box class from Ex12_08 to return a copy of the this pointer after setting the length, width, and height of a box:

```
export class Box
{
public:
  // ... rest of the class definition as before in Ex12_08

  // Mutator functions
  Box* setLength(double length);
  Box* setWidth(double width);
  Box* setHeight(double height);

private:
  double m_length {1.0};
  double m_width {1.0};
  double m_height {1.0};
};
```

You can implement these new mutators as follows:

```
Box* Box::setLength(double length)
{
  if (length > 0) m_length = length;
  return this;
}
```

```
Box* Box::setWidth(double width)
{
  if (width > 0) m_width = width;
  return this;
}
Box* Box::setHeight(double height)
{
  if (height > 0) m_height = height;
  return this;
}
```

Now you can modify all the dimensions of a Box object in a single statement:

```
Box myBox{3.0, 4.0, 5.0};                               // Create a box
myBox.setLength(-20.0)->setWidth(40.0)->setHeight(10.0); // Set all dimensions of myBox
```

Because the mutator functions return the this pointer, you can use the value returned by one function to call the next. Thus, the pointer returned by setLength() is used to call setWidth(), which returns a pointer you can use to call setHeight(). Isn't that nice?

Instead of a pointer, you can return a reference as well. The setLength() function, for instance, would then be defined as follows:

```
Box& Box::setLength(double length)
{
  if (length > 0) m_length = length;
  return *this;
}
```

If you do the same for setWidth() and setHeight(), you obtain the Box class of Ex12_09. The sample program in Ex12_09.cpp then shows that returning references to *this allows you to chain member function calls together as follows:

```
myBox.setLength(-20.0).setWidth(40.0).setHeight(10.0);   // Set all dimensions of myBox
```

This pattern is called *method chaining*. If the goal is to facilitate statements that employ method chaining, it is commonly done using references. You will encounter several conventional examples of this pattern in the next chapter when we discuss operator overloading.

▓ **Tip** Method chaining is not something you usually do for setters. Being able to set all member variables of an object in a single statement (instead of one statement per variable) is useful, yes, but you already have a mechanism to initialize all members at once; it's called a constructor. If you combine constructors with the *assignment operator* you'll learn about in the next chapter, you can write statements such as this:

```
myBox = Box{-20.0, 40.0, 10.0};  // Reinitialize using construction + assignment
```

Or, even shorter (the compiler will deduce which constructor to use here):

```
myBox = {-20.0, 40.0, 10.0};
```

---

const Objects and const Member Functions

A const variable is a variable whose value cannot be altered. You know this already. Naturally, you can also define const variables of class types. These variables are then called *const objects*. None of the member variables that constitute the state of a const object can be altered. In other words, any member variable of a const object is itself a const variable and thus immutable.

Suppose for a moment that the m_length, m_width, and m_height member variables of our favorite Box class are public (for shame!). Then the following would still not compile:

```
const Box myBox {3.0, 4.0, 5.0};
std::println("The length of myBox is {}", myBox.m_length);   // ok
myBox.m_length = 2.0; // Error! Assignment to a member variable of a const object...
myBox.m_width *= 3.0; // Error! Assignment to a member variable of a const object...
```

Reading a member variable from the const object myBox is allowed, but any attempt to assign a value to one or to otherwise modify such a member variable will result in a compiler error.

From Chapter 8, you'll recall that this principle extends to pointer-to-const and reference-to-const variables as well:

```
Box myBox {3.0, 4.0, 5.0};           // A non-const, mutable Box

const Box* boxPointer = &myBox;      // A pointer-to-const-Box variable
boxPointer->m_length = 2;            // Error!
boxPointer->m_width *= 3;            // Error
```

In the previous snippet, the myBox object itself is a non-const, mutable Box object. Nevertheless, if you store its address in a variable of type pointer-to-const-Box, you can no longer modify the state of myBox using that pointer. The same would hold if you replace the pointer with a reference-to-const.

You'll also recall that this plays a critical role when objects are either passed to or returned from a function by reference or using a pointer. Let printBox() be a function with the following signature:

```
void printBox(const Box& box);
```

Then printBox() cannot modify the state of the Box object; it is passed as an argument, even if that original Box object will be non-const.

In the examples in the remainder of this section, we'll mostly use const objects. Remember, though, that the same restrictions apply when accessing an object through a pointer-to-const or a reference-to-const as when accessing a const object directly.

const Member Functions

To see how member functions behave for const objects, let's go back to the Box class of Ex12_08. In this version of the class, the member variables of a Box object are properly hidden and can be manipulated only through public getter and setter member functions. Suppose now that you change the code in the main() function of Ex12_08 so that myBox is const:

```
const Box myBox {3.0, 4.0, 5.0};
std::println("myBox dimensions are {} by {} by {}",
    myBox.getLength(), myBox.getWidth(), myBox.getHeight());
```

```
myBox.setLength(-20.0);
myBox.setWidth(40.0);
myBox.setHeight(10.0);
```

Now the example will no longer compile! Of course, the fact that the compiler refuses to compile the last three lines in the previous code fragment is exactly what you want. After all, you should not be able to alter the state of a `const` object. We said earlier already the compiler prevents direct assignments to member variables—supposing you have access—so why should it allow indirect assignments inside member functions? The Box object would not be much of an immutable constant if you were allowed to call these setters, now would it?

Unfortunately, however, the getter functions cannot be called on a `const` object either simply because there's the risk that they could change the object. In our example, this means that the compiler will not only refuse to compile the last three lines but also the output statement before that. Similarly, any attempt to call the `volume()` member function on a `const` myBox would result in a compilation error:

```
std::println("myBox's volume is {}", myBox.volume());  // Will not compile!
```

Even though *you* know that `volume()` doesn't alter the object, the compiler does not. At least not at that point in the compilation. All it considers when compiling this `volume()` expression is the function's signature. And even if it does know the function's definition from inside the class definition—as with our three getters earlier—the compiler makes no attempt to deduce whether a function modifies the object's state. All the compiler uses in this setting is the function's signature.

So, with our current definition of the Box class, `const` Box objects are rather useless. You cannot call any of its member functions, not even the ones that clearly do not modify any state. To solve this, you'll have to improve the definition of the Box class. You need a way to tell the compiler which member functions can be called on `const` objects. The solutions are *const member functions*.

First, you need to specify all functions that don't modify an object as `const` in the class definition:

```
export class Box
{
public:
  // Same constructors as before...

  double volume() const;  // Function to calculate the volume of a box

  // Functions to provide access to the values of member variables
  double getLength() const { return m_length; }
  double getWidth() const  { return m_width; }
  double getHeight() const { return m_height; }

  // Functions to set member variable values
  void setLength(double length) { if (length > 0) m_length = length;}
  void setWidth(double width)   { if (width > 0)  m_width  = width; }
  void setHeight(double height) { if (height > 0) m_height = height; }

private:
  // Same member variables as before...
};
```

Next, you must change the out-of-class function definition accordingly:

```
double Box::volume() const
{
  return m_length * m_width * m_height;
}
```

With these changes, all the calls we expect to work for a const myBox object will effectively work. Of course, calling a setter on it remains impossible. A complete example can be downloaded as Ex12_10.

▓ **Tip** For const objects, you can only call const member functions. You should specify all member functions that don't change the object for which they are called as const.

---

const Correctness

For const objects you can only call const member functions. The idea is that const objects must be totally immutable, so the compiler will only allow you to call member functions that do not, and never will, modify them. Of course, this only truly makes sense if const member functions effectively cannot modify an object's state. Suppose you were allowed to write the following (this will not compile!):

```
void setLength(double length) const { if (length > 0) m_length = length; }
void setWidth(double width) const  { if (width > 0)  m_width = width; }
void setHeight(double height) const { if (height > 0) m_height = height; }
```

These three functions clearly modify the state of a Box. So if they were allowed to be declared const like this, you'd again be able to call these setters on const Box objects. This means you would again be able to modify the value of supposedly immutable objects. This would defeat the purpose of const objects. Luckily, the compiler enforces that you can never (inadvertently) modify a const object from inside a const member function. Any attempt to modify an object's member variable from within a const member functions will result in a compiler error.

Specifying a member function as const effectively makes the this pointer const for that function. The type of the this pointer inside our three setters from before, for instance, would be const Box*, which is pointer to a const Box. And you cannot assign to member variables through a pointer-to-const.

Of course, you cannot call any non-const member functions from within a const member function either. Calling setLength() from within a const volume() member would therefore not be allowed:

```
double Box::volume() const
{
  setLength(32);    // Not const (may modify the object): will not compile!
  return m_length * m_width * m_height;
}
```

Calling const member functions, on the other hand, is allowed:

```
double Box::volume() const
{
  return getLength() * getWidth() * getHeight();
}
```

Since these three getter functions are const as well, calling them from within the volume() function is no problem. The compiler knows they will not modify the object either.

The combination of these compiler-enforced restrictions is called *const correctness*—it prevents const objects from being mutated. We'll see one final aspect of this at the end of the next subsection.

Overloading on const

Declaring whether a member function is const is part of the function's signature. This implies that you can overload a non-const member function with a const version. This can be useful and is often done for functions that return a pointer or a reference to (part of) the internal data that is encapsulated by an object. Suppose that instead of the traditional getters and setters for a Box's member variables, we create functions of this form:

```
export class Box
{
public:
  // Rest of the class definition as before...

  double& length() { return m_length; };  // Return references to dimension variable
  double& width()  { return m_width; };
  double& height() { return m_height; };

private:
  double m_length{1.0};
  double m_width{1.0};
  double m_height{1.0};
}
```

These member functions could now be used as follows:

```
Box box;
box.length() = 2;   // References can be used to the right of an assignment
std::println("{}", box.length());  // Prints 2
```

In a way, these functions are an attempt at a hybrid between a getter and a setter. It's a failed attempt thus far, because you can currently no longer access the dimensions of a const Box:

```
const Box constBox;
// constBox.length() = 2;                     // Does not compile: good!
// std::println("{}", constBox.length());     // Does not compile either: bad!
```

You could solve this by overloading the member functions with versions specific for const objects. In general, these extra overloads would have the following form:

```
const double& length() const { return m_length; }; // Return references to const variables
const double& width()  const { return m_width; };
const double& height() const { return m_height; };
```

Because double is a fundamental type, however, one will often return them by value in these overloads rather than by reference:

```
double length() const { return m_length; };   // Return copies of dimension variables
double width()  const { return m_width; };
double height() const { return m_height; };
```

Either way, this enables the overloaded length(), width(), and height() functions to be called on const objects as well. Which of the two overloads of each function gets used depends on the const-ness of the object upon which the member is called. You could confirm this by adding output statements to both overloads. You can find a little program that does exactly this under Ex12_11.

Note that we do not recommend using functions of this form to replace the more conventional getter and setters shown earlier. One reason is that statements of the following form are unconventional and hence harder to read or write:

```
box.length() = 2;   // Less clear than 'box.setLength(2);'
```

Also, and more importantly, by adding public member functions that return references to private member variables, you basically forsake most of the advantages of data hiding mentioned earlier in this chapter. You can no longer perform integrity checks on the values assigned to the member variables (such as checking whether all Box dimensions remain positive), change the internal representation of an object, and so on. In other words, it's almost as bad as simply making the member variables public!

There are certainly other circumstances, though, where overloading on const is recommended. You will encounter several examples later, such as when overloading the array access operator in the next chapter.

■ **Note** To preserve const correctness, the following variation of a Box's getters does not compile:

```
// Attempt to return non-const references to member variables from const functions
double& length() const { return m_length; };   // This must not be allowed to compile!
double& width()  const { return m_width; };
double& height() const { return m_height; };
```

Because these are const member functions, their implicit this pointers are of type const-pointer-to-Box (const Box*), which in turn makes the Box member variable names references-to-const within the scope of these member function definitions. From a const member function, you can thus never return a reference or a pointer to non-const parts of an object's states. And this is a good thing. Otherwise, such members would provide a backdoor to modify a const object.

Casting Away const

Very rarely, circumstances can arise where a function is dealing with a const object, either passed as an argument or as the object pointed to by this, and it is necessary to make it non-const. The const_cast<>() operator enables you to do this. The const_cast<>() operator is mostly used in one of the following two forms:

```
const_cast<Type*>(expression)
const_cast<Type&>(expression)
```

For the first form, the type of expression must be either const Type* or Type*; for the second, it can be const Type&, Type, or Type&.

■ **Caution** The use of const_cast is nearly always frowned upon because it can be used to misuse objects. You should never use this operator to undermine the const-ness of an object. If an object is const, it normally means that you are not expected to modify it. And making unexpected changes is a perfect recipe for bugs. You should only use const_cast where you are absolutely sure the const nature of the object won't be violated as a result. One example could be when someone forgot to add a const in a function declaration in code you cannot modify. Another example is when you implement the idiom we branded const-and-back-again, which you'll learn about in Chapter 17.

Using the mutable Keyword

Ordinarily, the member variables of a const object cannot be modified. Sometimes you want to allow particular class members to be modifiable even for a const object. You can do this by specifying such members as mutable. In Ex12_12, for example, we started again from Ex12_10 and added an extra, mutable member variable to the declaration of Box in Box.cppm as follows:

```cpp
export class Box
{
public:
  // Constructors
  Box() = default;
  Box(double length, double width, double height);

  double volume() const;        // Function to calculate the volume of a box
  void printVolume() const;     // Function to print out the volume of a box

  // Getters and setters like before...

private:
  double m_length{1.0};
  double m_width {1.0};
  double m_height{1.0};
  mutable unsigned m_count{};   // Counts the amount of time printVolume() is called
};
```

The mutable keyword indicates that the m_count member can be changed, even when the object is const. You can thus modify the m_count member in some debugging/logging code inside the newly created printVolume() member function, even though it is declared to be const:

```cpp
void Box::printVolume() const
{
  // Count how many times printVolume() is called using a mutable member in a const function
  std::println("The volume of this box is {}", volume());
  std::println("printVolume() has been called {} time(s)", ++m_count);
}
```

If m_count had not been explicitly declared to be mutable, modifying it from within the const printVolume() function would've been disallowed by the compiler. Any member function, both const and non-const, can always make changes to member variables specified as mutable.

▓ **Caution** You should only need mutable member variables in rare cases. Usually, if you need to modify an object from within a const function, it probably shouldn't have been const. Typical uses of mutable member variables include debugging or logging, caching, and thread synchronization members.

Friends

Under normal circumstances, you'll hide the member variables of your classes by declaring them as private. You may well have private member functions of the class too. Despite this, it is sometimes useful to treat selected functions that are not members of the class as "honorary members" and allow them to access non-public members of a class object. That is, you do not want the world to access the internal state of your objects, just a select few related functions. Such functions are called *friends* of the class. A friend can access any of the members of a class object, however, regardless of their access specification.

▓ **Caution** Friend declarations risk undermining one of the cornerstones of object-oriented programming: data hiding. They should be used only when absolutely necessary, and this need does not arise that often. You'll meet one circumstance where it is needed in the next chapter when you learn about operator overloading. Nevertheless, most classes should not need any friends at all. While that may sound somewhat sad and lonely, the following humorous definition of the C++ programming language should forever remind you why, in C++, one should choose his friends very wisely indeed: "C++: where your friends can access your private parts."

That being said, we will consider two ways a class can declare what its friends are—either an individual function can be specified as a friend of a class or a whole class can be specified as a friend of another class. In the latter case, all the member functions of the friend class have the same access privileges as a normal member of the class. We'll consider individual functions as friends first.

The Friend Functions of a Class

To make a function a friend of a class, you must declare it as such within the class definition using the friend keyword. It's the class that determines its friends; there's no way to make a function a friend of a class from outside the class definition. A friend function can be a global function, or it can be a member of another class. By definition, a function can't be a friend of the class of which it is a member, so access specifiers don't apply to the friends of a class.

The need for friend functions in practice is limited. They are useful in situations where a function needs access to the internals of two different kinds of objects; making the function a friend of both classes makes that possible. We will demonstrate how they work in simpler contexts that don't necessarily reflect a situation where they are required. Suppose that you want to implement a friend function in the Box class to compute the surface area of a Box object. To make the function a friend, you must declare it as such within the Box class definition. Here's a version that does that:

```
export class Box
{
public:
  Box() : Box{ 1.0, 1.0, 1.0} {}                // A delegating default constructor
  Box(double length, double width, double height);

  double volume() const;                        // Function to calculate the volume of a box

  friend double surfaceArea(const Box& box);    // Friend function for the surface area

private:
  double m_length, m_width, m_height;
};
```

You may notice the delegating default constructor that we use for a change. Because of that, all constructors now explicitly initialize all three member variables, and we no longer provide initial values in their declarations either. The definitions of the second constructor and the volume() member, on the other hand, contain nothing that you haven't already seen several times before.

Here is the code to try the friend function:

```
// Ex12_13.cpp - Using a friend function of a class
import std;
import box;

int main()
{
  Box box1 {2.2, 1.1, 0.5};                         // An arbitrary box
  Box box2;                                         // A default box
  auto box3{ std::make_unique<Box>(15.0, 20.0, 8.0) }; // Dynamically allocated Box

  std::println("Volume of box1 = {}", box1.volume());
  std::println("Surface area of box1 = {}", surfaceArea(box1));

  std::println("Volume of box2 = {}", box2.volume());
  std::println("Surface area of box2 = {}", surfaceArea(box2));

  std::println("Volume of box3 = {}", box3->volume());
  std::println("Surface area of box3 = {}", surfaceArea(*box3));
}

// friend function to calculate the surface area of a Box object
double surfaceArea(const Box& box)
{
  return 2.0 * (box.m_length * box.m_width
              + box.m_length * box.m_height + box.m_height * box.m_width);
}
```

Here's the expected output:

```
Box constructor called.
Box constructor called.
Box constructor called.
Volume of box1 = 1.21
Surface area of box1 = 8.14
Volume of box2 = 1
Surface area of box2 = 6
Volume of box3 = 2400
Surface area of box3 = 1160
```

The `main()` function creates one Box object by specifying its dimensions; one object with no dimensions specified, and one dynamically allocated Box object. The last object shows that you can create a smart pointer to a Box object allocated in the free store in the way that you have seen with `std::string` objects. From the output you can see that everything works as expected with all three objects.

You declare the `surfaceArea()` function as a friend of the Box class by writing the function prototype within the Box class definition preceded by the `friend` keyword. The function doesn't alter the Box object that is passed as the argument, so it's sensible to use a `const` reference parameter specification. It's also a good idea to be consistent when placing the `friend` declaration within the definition of the class. You can see that we've chosen to position this declaration at the end of all the public members of the class. The rationale for this is that the function is part of the class interface because it has full access to all class members.

`surfaceArea()` is a global function, and its definition follows that of `main()`. You could put this function in the box module as well because it is related to the Box class, but we wanted to illustrate that friendship in C++ can cross module boundaries. Do note that if you do package the `surfaceArea()` in the box module, you will have to export it.

Notice that you access the member variables of the object within the definition of `surfaceArea()` by using the Box object that is passed to the function as a parameter. A friend function is *not* a class member, so the member variables can't be referenced by their names alone. They each have to be qualified by an object name in the same way as they would be in an ordinary function that accesses public members of a class. A friend function is the same as an ordinary function, except that it can access all the members of a class (even private ones) without restriction.

Although this example demonstrates how you write a friend function, it is not very realistic. You could have used accessor member functions to return the values of the member variables. Then `surfaceArea()` wouldn't need to be a friend function. Perhaps the best option would have been to make `surfaceArea()` a public member function of the class so that the capability for computing the surface area of a box becomes part of the class interface. A friend function should always be a last resort.

Friend Classes

You can declare a whole class to be a friend of another class. All the member functions of a friend class have unrestricted access to all the members of the class of which it has been declared a friend.

For example, suppose you have defined a Carton class and want to allow the member functions of the Carton class to have access to the members of the Box class. Including a statement in the Box class definition that declares Carton to be a friend will enable this:

```
class Box
{
  // Public members of the class...
```

```
  friend class Carton;

  // Private members of the class...
};
```

Friendship is not a reciprocal arrangement. Functions in the Carton class can access all the members of the Box class, but functions in the Box class have no access to the private members of the Carton class. Friendship among classes is not transitive either; just because class A is a friend of class B and class B is a friend of class C, it doesn't follow that class A is a friend of class C.

A typical use for a friend class is where the functioning of one class is highly intertwined with that of another. A linked list basically involves two class types: a List class that maintains a list of objects (usually called *nodes*) and a Node class that defines what a node is. The List class needs to stitch the Node objects together by setting a pointer in each Node object so that it points to the next Node object. Making the List class a friend of the class that defines a node would enable members of the List class to access the members of the Node class directly. Later in this chapter we'll discuss nested classes, a viable alternative for friend classes in such cases.

Arrays of Class Objects

You can create an array of objects of a class type in the same way as you create an array of elements of any other type. Each array element must be created by a constructor, and for each element that does not have an initial value specified, the compiler arranges for a no-arg constructor to be called. You can see this happening with an example. The Box class definition in Box.cppm is as follows:

```
// Box.cppm
export module box;

export class Box
{
public:
  /* Constructors */
  Box(double length, double width, double height);
  Box(double side);          // Constructor for a cube
  Box();                     // Default constructor
  Box(const Box& box);       // Copy constructor

  double volume() const { return m_length * m_width * m_height; };

private:
  double m_length {1.0};
  double m_width {1.0};
  double m_height {1.0};
};
```

The contents of Box.cpp are as follows:

```
module box;
import std;
```

```
Box::Box(double length, double width, double height)   // Constructor definition
  : m_length{length}, m_width{width}, m_height{height}
{
  std::println("Box constructor 1 called.");
}

Box::Box(double side) : Box{side, side, side}          // Constructor for a cube
{
  std::println("Box constructor 2 called.");
}

Box::Box()                                             // Default constructor
{
  std::println("Default Box constructor called.");
}

Box::Box(const Box& box)                               // Copy constructor
  : m_length{box.m_length}, m_width{box.m_width}, m_height{box.m_height}
{
  std::println("Box copy constructor called.");
}
```

Finally, the Ex12_14.cpp source file that defines the program's main() function will contain the following:

```
// Ex12_14.cpp - Creating an array of objects
import std;
import box;

int main()
{
  const Box box1 {2.0, 3.0, 4.0};               // An arbitrary box
  Box box2 {5.0};                               // A box that is a cube
  std::println("box1 volume = {}", box1.volume());
  std::println("box2 volume = {}", box2.volume());
  Box box3 {box2};
  std::println("box3 volume = {}", box3.volume());  // Volume = 125

  std::println("");

  Box boxes[6] {box1, box2, box3, Box {2.0}};
}
```

The output is as follows:

```
Box constructor 1 called.
Box constructor 1 called.
Box constructor 2 called.
box1 volume = 24
box2 volume = 125
```

```
Box copy constructor called.
box3 volume = 125

Box copy constructor called.
Box copy constructor called.
Box copy constructor called.
Box constructor 1 called.
Box constructor 2 called.
Default Box constructor called.
Default Box constructor called.
```

The interesting bit is the last seven lines, which result from the creation of the array of Box objects. The initial values for the first three array elements are existing objects, so the compiler calls the copy constructor to duplicate box1, box2, and box3. The fourth element is initialized with an object that is created in the braced initializer for the array by the constructor 2, which calls constructor 1 in its initialization list. The last two array elements have no initial values specified, so the compiler calls the default constructor to create them.

The Size of a Class Object

You obtain the size of a class object by using the sizeof operator in the same way you have previously with fundamental data types. You can apply the operator to a particular object or to the class type. The size of a class object is generally the sum of the sizes of the member variables of the class, although it may turn out to be greater than this. This isn't something that should bother you, but it's nice to know why.

On most computers, for performance reasons, two-byte variables must be placed at an address that is a multiple of two, four-byte variables must be placed at an address that is a multiple of four, and so on. This is called *boundary alignment*. A consequence of this is that sometimes the compiler must leave gaps between the memory for one value and the next. If, on such a machine, you have three variables that occupy two bytes, followed by a variable that requires four bytes, a gap of two bytes may be left in order to place the fourth variable on the correct boundary. In this case, the total space required by all four is greater than the sum of the individual sizes.

Static Members of a Class

You can declare members of a class as static. Static members are tied to the class itself, not to any individual object. In this section, we discuss how and when to declare both *static member variables* and *static member functions*, in between focusing one specific use of static member variables, namely the definition of class-specific *static constants*.

Static Member Variables

Static member variables of a class are used to provide class-wide storage of data that is independent of any particular object of the class type but is accessible by any of them. They record properties of the class as a whole, rather than of individual objects. When you declare a member variable of a class as static, the static member variable is defined only once and will exist even if no class objects have been created. Each static member variable is accessible in any object of the class and is shared among however many objects there are. An object gets its own independent copies of the ordinary member variables, but only one instance of each static member variable exists, regardless of how many class objects have been defined.

461

You can use static member variables to store constants that are specific to a class (see later), or you could store information about the objects of a class in general, such as how many there are in existence. One such use for a static member variable is to count how many objects of a class exist. You could add a static member variable to the Box class by adding the following statement to your class definition (for static member variables we sometimes use a s_ prefix instead of m_):

```
static inline std::size_t s_object_count {};    // Count of objects in existence
```

Figure 12-6 shows how this member exists outside of any objects but is available to all of them.

```
class Box
{
    private:
        static inline size_t s_object_count {};
        double m_length;
        double m_width;
        double m_height;
        ...
};
```

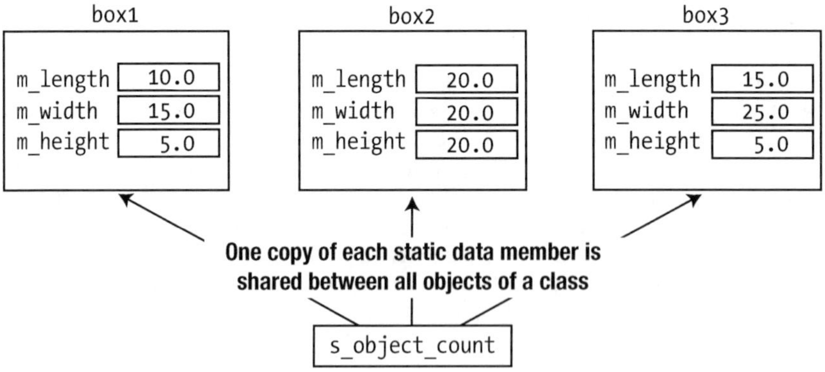

Figure 12-6. *Static class members are shared between objects*

The static s_object_count member is private, so you can't access s_object_count from outside the Box class. Naturally, static members can be either public or protected (see Chapter 14) as well.

The s_object_count variable is furthermore specified to be inline, a requirement that to us feels like a reminiscent of the past (from the time before modules, to be precise). The main thing to remember is that in order to define and initialize a static member variable inside the class definition, you must add this extra inline keyword.

▓ **Note** Before C++17 introduced inline variables, your only option was to declare `s_object_count` as follows (this syntax remains valid today as well):

```
class Box
{
// ...
private:
  static std::size_t s_object_count;
// ...
};
```

Doing so, however, creates somewhat of a problem. How do you initialize a noninline `static` member variable? You don't want to initialize it in a constructor because you want to initialize it only once, not each time a constructor is called. Besides, `s_object_count` must be initialized even if no objects exist (and therefore no constructors have been called). The answer is to initialize each noninline `static` member outside the class with an extra clumsy definition such as this:

```
std::size_t Box::s_object_count {};  // Initialize static member of Box class to 0
```

This *defines* `s_object_count`; the line in the class definition only *declares* that it is a noninline `static` member of the class—a member that is to be *defined* elsewhere. Note that the `static` keyword must not be included in such an out-of-class definition. You do have to qualify the member name with the class name, Box, though, so that the compiler understands that you are referring to a `static` member of the class. Otherwise, you'd simply be creating a global variable that has nothing to do with the class.

Clearly, inline variables are far more convenient, as they can be initialized directly in the class definition without a separate out-of-class definition.

Let's add the `static s_object_count` member variable and the object counting capability to Ex12_14. You need two extra statements in the class definition: one to define the new static member variable and another to declare a function that will retrieve its value.

```
export class Box
{
public:
  Box();                                    // Default constructor
  Box(double side);                         // Constructor for a cube
  Box(const Box& box);                      // Copy constructor
  Box(double length, double width, double height);

  double volume() const { return m_length * m_width * m_height; }

  std::size_t getObjectCount() const { return s_object_count; }

private:
  double m_length {1.0};
  double m_width {1.0};
```

```
  double m_height {1.0};
  static inline std::size_t s_object_count {};    // Count of objects ever created
};
```

The getObjectCount() function has been declared as const because it doesn't modify any of the member variables of the class, and you might want to call it for const or non-const objects.

All constructors of Box need to increment s_object_count (except for those that delegate to another Box constructor, of course; otherwise, the count would be incremented twice). Here is an example:

```
// Constructor definition
Box::Box(double length, double width, double height)
  : m_length {length}, m_width {width}, m_height {height}
{
  ++s_object_count;
  std::println("Box constructor 1 called.");
}
```

We are sure you are more than capable by now to complete the other constructors. You can modify the version of main() from Ex12_14 to output the object count:

```
// Ex12_15.cpp - Using a static member variable
import std;
import box;

int main()
{
  const Box box1{ 2.0, 3.0, 4.0 };                 // An arbitrary box
  Box box2{5.0};                                   // A cube
  std::println("box1 volume = {}", box1.volume());
  std::println("box2 volume = {}", box2.volume());
  Box box3 {box2};
  std::println("box3 volume = {}", box3.volume()); // Volume = 125

  std::println("");

  Box boxes[6] { box1, box2, box3, Box{2.0} };

  std::println("\nThere are now {} Box objects.", box1.getObjectCount());
}
```

This program will produce the same output as before, only this time it will be terminated by the following line:

```
...
There are now 9 Box objects.
```

This code shows that, indeed, only one copy of the static member s_object_count exists, and all the constructors are updating it. The getObjectCount() function is called for the box1 object, but you could use any object including any of the array elements to get the same result. Of course, you're only counting the number of objects that get created. The count that is output corresponds to the number of objects created here. In general, you have no way to know when objects are destroyed yet, so the count won't necessarily reflect the number of objects that are around at any point. You'll find out later in this chapter how to account for objects that get destroyed.

Note that the size of a Box object will be unchanged by the addition of s_object_count to the class definition. This is because static member variables are not part of any object; they belong to the class. Furthermore, because static member variables are not part of a class object, a const member function can modify non-const static member variables without violating the const nature of the function.

Accessing Static Member Variables

Suppose that in a reckless moment, you declared s_object_count as a public class member. You then no longer need the getObjectCount() function to access it. To output the number of objects in main(), just write this:

```
std::println("Object count is {}", box1.s_object_count);
```

There's more. We claimed that a static member variable exists even if no objects have been created. This means that you should be able to get the count *before* you create the first Box object, but how do you refer to the member variable? The answer is that you use the class name, Box, as a qualifier:

```
std::println("Object count is {}", Box::s_object_count);
```

Try it out by modifying the previous example; you'll see that it works as described. You can always use the class name to access a public static member of a class. It doesn't matter whether any objects exist. In fact, it is recommended to always use the latter syntax to access static members precisely because this makes it instantly clear when reading the code that it concerns a static member.

Static Constants

Static member variables are often used to define constants. This makes sense. Clearly there's no point in defining constants as non-static member variables because then an exact copy of this constant would be made for every single object. If you define constants as static members, there is only one single instance of that constant that is shared between all objects.

Some examples are shown in this definition of a class of cylindrical boxes, which is the latest novelty in the boxing world:

```
export module cylindrical;

import std;

export class CylindricalBox
{
public:
  static inline const float s_max_radius { 35.0f };
  static inline const float s_max_height { 60.0f };
  static inline const std::string_view s_default_material { "paperboard" };

  CylindricalBox(float radius, float height,
                 std::string_view material = s_default_material);
  float volume() const;
```

```
private:
  // The value of PI used by CylindricalBox's volume() function
  static inline const float PI { 3.141592f };

  float m_radius;
  float m_height;
  std::string m_material;
};
```

This class defines four inline static constants: s_max_radius, s_max_height, s_default_material, and PI. Note that, unlike regular member variables, there is no harm in making constants public. In fact, it is quite common to define public constants containing, for instance, boundary values of function parameters (such as s_max_radius and s_max_height) or suggested default values (s_default_material). Using these, code outside the class can create a narrow, very high CylindricalBox out of its default material as follows:

```
CylindricalBox bigBox{ 1.23f,
          CylindricalBox::s_max_height, CylindricalBox::s_default_material };
```

Inside the body of a member function of the CylindricalBox class, there is no need to qualify the class's static constant members with the class name:

```
float CylindricalBox::volume() const
{
  return PI * m_radius * m_radius * m_height;
}
```

This function definition uses PI without prepending CylindricalBox::. (Of course, you know better than to define your own PI constant, and that you should be using std::numbers::pi_v<float> here instead...)

You'll find a small test program that exercises this CylindricalBox class in Ex12_16.

▨ **Note** The keywords static, inline, and const may appear in any order you like. For the definition of CylindricalBox, we used the same sequence static inline const four times (consistency is always a good idea!), but all five other permutations would've been valid as well. All three keywords must appear before the variable's type name, though.

Static Member Variables of the Class Type Itself

A static member variable is not part of a class object, so it can be of the same type as the class. The Box class can contain a static member variable of type Box, for example. This might seem a little strange at first, but it can be useful. We'll use the Box class to illustrate just how. Suppose you need a standard "reference" box for some purpose; you might want to relate Box objects in various ways to a standard box, for example. Of course, you could define a standard Box object outside the class, but if you are going to use it within member functions of the class, it creates an external dependency that it would be better to lose. Suppose we only need it for internal use; then you'd declare this constant as follows:

```
class Box
{
  // Rest of the class as before...
```

```
private:
  static const Box s_reference_box;    // Standard reference box
  // ...
};
```

s_reference_box is const because it is a standard Box object that should not be changed. However, you must still define and initialize it outside the class. You could use this line to define s_reference_box:

```
const Box Box::s_reference_box{10.0, 10.0, 10.0};
```

The static keyword is only used with the declaration of a static member, inside the class definition, but not with the definition of that static member:

This calls the Box class constructor to create s_reference_box. Because static member variables of a class are created before any objects are created, at least one Box object will always exist. Any of the static or nonstatic member functions can access s_reference_box. It isn't accessible from outside the class because it is a private member. A class constant is one situation where you might want to make the member variable public if it has a useful role outside the class. As long as it is declared as const, it can't be modified.

Static Member Functions

A *static member function* is independent of any individual class object but can be invoked by any class object if necessary. It can also be invoked from outside the class if it is a public member. A common use of static member functions is to operate on static member variables, regardless of whether any objects of the class have been defined. In general:

▓ **Tip**   If a member function does not access any nonstatic member variables, it may be a good candidate for being declared as a static member function.

A public static member function can be called even if no class objects have been created. Declaring a static function in a class is easy. You simply use the static keyword as you did with s_object_count. As an example, you could for instance turn the getObjectCount() function into a static member in the example earlier. Note that you then also have to remove the const qualifier, for the following reason:

▓ **Caution**   Static member functions cannot be const. Because a static member function isn't associated with any class object, it has no this pointer, so const-ness doesn't apply.

You call a static member function using the class name as a qualifier. Here's how you could call the static getObjectCount() function:

```
std::println("Object count is {}", Box::getObjectCount());
```

Of course, if you have created class objects, you can call a static member function through an object of the class in the same way as you call any other member function. Here's an example:

```
std::println("Object count is {}", box1.getObjectCount());
```

While the latter is certainly valid syntax, it is not recommended. The reason is that it needlessly obfuscates the fact that it concerns a static member function.

A static member function has no access to the object for which it is called. For a static member function to access an object of the class, it would need to be passed as an argument to the function. Referencing members of a class object from within a static function must then be done using qualified names (as you would with an ordinary global function accessing a public member variable).

A static member function is a full member of the class in terms of access privileges, though. If an object of the same class is passed as an argument to a static member function, it can access private as well as public members of the object. It wouldn't make sense to do so, but just to illustrate the point, you could include a definition of a static function in the Box class, as shown here:

```
static double edgeLength(const Box& aBox)
{
  return 4.0 * (aBox.m_length + aBox.m_width + aBox.m_height);
}
```

Even though you are passing the Box object as an argument, the private member variables can be accessed. Of course, it would make more sense to do this with an ordinary member function.

Destructors

Just like a variable of a fundamental type, a class object is destroyed if the delete operator is applied to it, or if the end of a block in which a class object is created is reached. When an object is destroyed, a special member of the class called a *destructor* is executed to deal with any cleanup that may be necessary. A class can have only one destructor. If you don't define one, the compiler provides a default version of the destructor that does nothing. The definition of the default destructor looks like this:

```
~ClassName() {}
```

The name of the destructor for a class is always the class name prefixed with a tilde, ~. The destructor cannot have parameters or a return type. The default destructor in the Box class is therefore as follows:

```
~Box() {}
```

Of course, if the definition is placed outside the class, the name of the destructor would be prefixed with the class name:

```
Box::~Box() {}
```

If the body of your destructor is to be empty, you are again better off using the default keyword:

```
Box::~Box() = default;        // Have the compiler generate a default destructor
```

The destructor for a class is always called automatically when an object is destroyed. The circumstances where you need to call a destructor explicitly are so rare you can ignore the possibility. Calling a destructor when it is not necessary can cause problems.

You only need to define a class destructor when something needs to be done when an object is destroyed. A class that deals with physical resources such as a file or a network connection that needs to be closed is one example; and, if memory is allocated by a constructor using new, the destructor is the place to release the memory. In Chapter 18, we'll argue that defining a destructor should in fact be reserved for only a small minority of your classes—those specifically designated to manage a given resource. This notwithstanding, the Box class in Ex12_15 would surely definitely benefit from a destructor implementation as well, namely, one that decrements s_object_count:

```
class Box
{
public:
  // Same constructors as before...

  ~Box();                                      // Destructor

  // Rest of the class as before...

  static std::size_t getObjectCount() { return s_object_count; }

private:
  // ...

  static inline std::size_t s_object_count {};   // Count of objects in existence
};
```

The destructor has been added to decrement s_object_count, and getObjectCount() is now a static member function (without a const qualifier!). The implementation of the Box destructor can be added to the Box.cpp file from Ex12_15 as follows. It outputs a message when it is called so you can see when this occurs:

```
Box::~Box()                                      // Destructor
{
  std::println("Box destructor called.");
  --s_object_count;
}
```

The following code will check the destructor operation out:

```
// Ex12_17.cpp - Implementing a destructor
import std;
import box;

int main()
{
  std::println("There are now {} Box objects.", Box::getObjectCount());

  const Box box1 {2.0, 3.0, 4.0};                // An arbitrary box
  Box box2 {5.0};                                // A box that is a cube

  std::println("There are now {} Box objects.", Box::getObjectCount());

  for (double d {} ; d < 3.0 ; ++d)
  {
    Box box {d, d + 1.0, d + 2.0};
    std::println("Box volume is {}", box.volume());
  }

  std::println("There are now {} Box objects.", Box::getObjectCount());
```

```
  auto pBox{ std::make_unique<Box>(1.5, 2.5, 3.5) };
  std::println("Box volume is {}", pBox->volume());
  std::println("There are now {} Box objects.", Box::getObjectCount());
}
```

The output from this example is as follows:

```
There are now 0 Box objects.
Box constructor 1 called.
Box constructor 1 called.
Box constructor 2 called.
There are now 2 Box objects.
Box constructor 1 called.
Box volume is 0
Box destructor called.
Box constructor 1 called.
Box volume is 6
Box destructor called.
Box constructor 1 called.
Box volume is 24
Box destructor called.
There are now 2 Box objects.
Box constructor 1 called.
Box volume is 13.125
There are now 3 Box objects.
Box destructor called.
Box destructor called.
Box destructor called.
```

This example shows when constructors and the destructor are called and how many objects exist at various points during execution. The first line of output shows there are no Box objects at the outset. s_object_count clearly exists without any objects because we retrieve its value using the static getObjectCount() member. box1 and box2 are created as in Ex12_15, and the output shows that there are indeed two objects in existence. The for loop created a new object on each iteration, and the output shows that the new object is destroyed at the end of the current iteration, after its volume has been output. After the loop ends, there are just the original two objects in existence. The last object is created by calling the make_unique<Box>() function template. This calls the Box constructor that has three parameters to create the object in the free store. You can see the output from the three destructor calls that occur when main() ends and that destroy the remaining three Box objects.

You now know that the compiler will add a default constructor, a default copy constructor, and a destructor to each class when you don't define these. There are other members that the compiler can add to a class, and you'll learn about them in Chapters 13 and 18.

constexpr Member Functions

You can add constexpr or consteval in front of any member function, constructor, or destructor declaration just like with regular functions (as seen in Chapter 8). The semantics is entirely analogous as well; members can only be evaluated during the compile-time evaluation of a constant expression if they are either constexpr or consteval, and consteval members moreover can *only* be evaluated at compile time.

Suppose, for instance, that we want the following constant definition to compile:

```
constexpr double milk_carton_volume{ Box{ 2.75, 2.75, 7.4 }.volume() };
```

As you may recall from Chapter 8, constexpr variables must be initialized at compile time so that, by the time the program executes, it is as if milk_carton_volume was initialized with the double literal 55.9625 (or 2.75 * 2.75 * 7.4). As always, during the compile-time evaluation of the initializer of this constexpr variable, the compiler can only evaluate functions that are either constexpr or consteval.

The expression Box{ 2.75, 2.75, 7.4 }.volume() in question constructs a transient Box object, invokes volume() on it, and then immediately discards the object again without it ever being bound to a named variable. It accomplishes, in other words, the same as the getVolume() call in the following snippet, where the transient Box object is created on the call stack as a named local variable instead:

```
constexpr double getVolume(double length, double width, double height)
{
   const Box temporary{ length, width, height};
   return temporary.volume();
}
constexpr double milk_carton_volume{ getVolume(2.75, 2.75, 7.4) };
```

Either way, the compiler needs to evaluate three members of the Box class to initialize milk_carton_volume: a constructor, the volume() function, and (don't forget!) the destructor. A definition of a Box class that allows the compiler to do this at compile time therefore looks as follows:

```
class Box
{
public:
  Box() = default;    // Explicitly defaulted -> implicitly constexpr
  constexpr Box(double length, double width, double height);
  // Implicitly compiler-generated destructor -> implicitly constexpr

  constexpr double volume() const;  // Function to calculate the volume of a box
  // ...
private:
  double m_length {}, m_width {}, m_height {};
};
```

Any member generated by the compiler is constexpr when possible. Since all member variables of the Box class are of type double, both the explicitly defaulted default constructor and the implicitly generated destructor will thus be constexpr. Of course, if one or more member variables have a non-constexpr constructor or destructor, the corresponding compiler-generated members will not be constexpr either.

▓ **Caution**   If you define a default constructor or destructor with empty curly braces, then the member is only constexpr if you explicitly add the constexpr keyword.

```
Box() {}  // Not constexpr -> prefer  Box() = default;
~Box() {} // Not constexpr -> prefer ~Box() = default;
```

Therefore, as said before, use = default; over {}.

You need to repeat constexpr in front of the definitions of constexpr members. Here is an example:

```
constexpr double Box::volume() const
{
  return m_length * m_width * m_height;
}
```

This definition of volume() again clearly underlines that constexpr and const are, for the most part, orthogonal concepts: constexpr relates to compile-time evaluation, const to immutability. If you need both, you need to add both. constexpr only implies const for variable definitions (such as our milk_carton_volume constant from earlier, which is implicitly const, and therefore immutable).

■ **Note** If the Box class were exported from a module, the definitions of both constexpr members would have to be part of the module interface file. Without access to the definitions, the compiler would otherwise be unable to evaluate these functions at compile time.

■ **Note** You cannot overload on constexpr or consteval like you can for instance on const. To make members behave differently depending on whether they are evaluated at compile time or at runtime you can use consteval if statements or the std::is_constant_evaluated() library function, as seen in Chapter 8.

---

consteval Constructors

To guarantee that any invalid format strings are caught at compile time, functions such as std::format() and std::print() use some clever tricks based on (non-explicit) consteval constructors. Because this is by far the most impressive use of compile-time evaluation in the Standard Library, we believe it makes for a fitting conclusion to our exposition on constexpr and consteval. These functions truly showcase some of the amazing things you can accomplish with creative use of consteval and constexpr (member) functions. Because they do also rely on some more advanced language features (variadic templates, forwarding references, etc.), we cannot go into too much detail here, but instead focus only on those aspects that relate to compile-time evaluation.

For starters, the first parameter of std::format() and std::print() functions is not of type std::string_view, as you may expect, but of a type instantiated from the std::format_string<> template. For the following statement of Ex12_17, for instance, the first parameter will be of type std::format_string<std::size_t> (because Box::getObjectCount() is of type std::size_t):

```
std::println("There are now {} Box objects.", Box::getObjectCount());
// First argument could be created explicitly as:
//    std::format_string<std::size_t>{ "There are now {} Box objects." }
```

All constructors of std::format_string<> types are consteval, forcing the compiler to always evaluate these constructors at compile time. This explains why you can invoke them with little more than string literals as well (although, naturally, any constant expression that evaluates to a string is acceptable). During the compile-time evaluation of these std::format_string<> constructors, the format string is scanned for replacement fields, all format specifiers are verified and processed, and their contents stored in the member variables of the specialized std::format_string<> type for faster retrieval during the eventual runtime formatting of the string. Because this all happens entirely at compile time, no time is wasted on parsing the format string at runtime anymore. This makes the modern formatting functions not only more powerful, but also more efficient than the old ones.

The final part of the clever `consteval` trickery is that whenever the format string is invalid, the `std::format_string<>` constructor throws an exception of type `std::format_error`. You'll learn all about exceptions in Chapter 16, but for now it suffices to know that compile-time evaluation fails whenever it encounters a statement that throws an exception (even if that exception is caught). This closes the deal. Not only are the modern formatting functions more powerful and more efficient, they are also far safer than many of the older string formatting functions. (They are far safer than, notably, the `std::printf()` family of functions. Never use these again!) And all that in no small part due to the clever use of `consteval` constructors.

▓ **Tip**   You can even extend the formatting framework so that `std::print()` and `std::format()` can directly format values of your own types, complete with custom format specifier flags. As an example, we'll have you formatting Box objects (what else?) in the Chapter 20 exercises. (You first need to know more about inheritance (Chapter 14), exceptions (Chapter 16), class template specialization (Chapter 17), and iterator manipulation and range algorithms (Chapter 20), though, so be patient.)

Using Pointers as Class Members

Real-life programs generally consist of large collections of collaborating objects, linked together using pointers, smart pointers, and references. All these networks of objects need to be created, linked together, and in the end destroyed again. To make sure all objects are deleted in a timely manner, smart pointers help tremendously:

- A `std::unique_ptr<>` makes sure that you can never accidentally forget to delete an object allocated from the free store.

- A `std::shared_ptr<>` is invaluable if multiple objects point to and use the same object—either intermittently or even concurrently—and it is not a priori clear when they will all be done using it. In other words, it is not always clear which object should be responsible for deleting the shared object because there may always be other objects around that still need it.

▓ **Tip**   In modern C++ you should normally never need the `delete` keyword anymore. A dynamically allocated object should always be managed by a smart pointer instead. This principle is called *Resource Acquisition Is Initialization*—RAII for short. Memory is a resource, and to acquire it you should initialize a smart pointer. We'll return to the RAII principle in Chapter 16 where we'll have even more compelling reasons to use it!

Detailing the object-oriented design principles and techniques required to set up and manage larger programs consisting of many classes and objects would lead us too far here. In this section, we'll walk you through a first somewhat larger example and, while doing so, point out some of the basic considerations you need to make—for instance when choosing between the different pointer types or the impact of `const` correctness on the design of your classes. Concretely, we'll define a class with a member variable that is a pointer and use instances of the class to create a *linked list* of objects.

The Truckload Example

In this example, a Box object represents a unit of a product to be delivered, and a collection of Box objects represents a truckload of boxes to be delivered. We'll call the class that manages the latter Truckload, and represent the collection of Box objects as a linked list. A linked list can be as long or as short as you need it to be, and you can add objects anywhere in the list. The class will allow a Truckload object to be created from a single Box object or from a vector of Box objects. It will provide for adding and deleting a Box object and for listing all the Box objects in the Truckload.

A Box object has no built-in facility for linking it with another Box object. Changing the definition of the Box class to incorporate this capability would be inconsistent with the idea of a box—boxes aren't like that. One way to collect Box objects into a list is to define another type of object, which we'll call Package. A Package object will have two members: a pointer to a Box object and a pointer to another Package object. The latter will allow us to create a chain of Package objects.

Figure 12-7 shows how each Package object points to a Box object—SharedBox will be a type alias for std::shared_ptr<Box>—and forms a link in a chain of Package objects that are connected by pointers. This chain of Package objects forms a data structure that is known as a *linked list.* The list can be of unlimited length. As long as you can access the first Package object, you can access the next Package through the m_next pointer it contains, which allows you to reach the next through the m_next pointer that it contains, and so on, through all objects in the list. Each Package object can provide access to the Box object through its m_box member. This arrangement is superior to the Package class having a member that is of type Box, which would require a new Box object to be created for each Package object. The Package class is just a means of tying Box objects together in a linked list, and each Box object should exist independently from the Package objects.

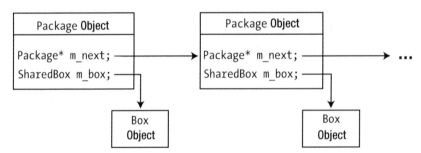

Figure 12-7. *Linked Package objects*

A Truckload object will create and manage a list of Package objects. A Truckload object represents an instance of a truckload of boxes. There can be any number of boxes in a truckload, and each box will be referenced from within a package. A Package object provides the mechanism for the Truckload object to access the pointer to the Box object it contains. Figure 12-8 illustrates the relationship between these objects.

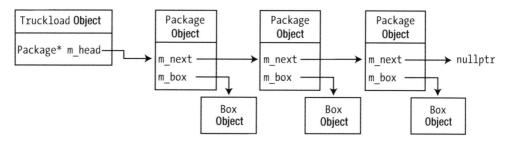

Figure 12-8. *A Truckload object managing a linked list of three Package objects*

Figure 12-8 shows a Truckload object that manages a list of Package objects; each Package object contains a Box object and a pointer to the next Package object. The Truckload object only needs to keep track of the first Package object in the list; the m_head member contains its address. By following the m_next pointer links, you can find any of the objects in the list. In this elementary implementation, the list can only be traversed from the start. A more sophisticated implementation could provide each Package object with a pointer to the previous object in the list, which would allow the list to be traversed backward as well as forward. Let's put the ideas into code.

▧ **Note**　You should not create your own classes for linked lists. Proper linked list types are already defined by the Standard Library (concretely, std::list<> and std::forward_list<>). Moreover, as we'll discuss in Chapter 20, in most cases you are better off using a std::vector<> instead. Defining your own class for a linked list is very educational, though, so we'll go ahead and do it regardless.

The Box Class

The contents of the module file for the Box class definition will be as follows:

```
// Box.cppm
export module box;
import std;

export class Box
{
public:
  Box() = default;
  Box(double length, double width, double height)
    : m_length{length}, m_width{width}, m_height{height} {};

  double volume() const
  {
    return m_length * m_width * m_height;
  }
```

```
  int compare(const Box& box) const
  {
    if (volume() < box.volume()) return -1;
    if (volume() == box.volume()) return 0;
    return +1;
  }

  friend std::string to_string(const Box& box)
  {
    return std::format("Box({:.1f},{:.1f},{:.1f})",
                       box.m_length, box.m_width, box.m_height);
  }

private:
  double m_length {1.0};
  double m_width {1.0};
  double m_height {1.0};
};
```

We have omitted the basic getters because we don't need them in this example. All we need is a means to convert a Box object to a string. As you can see, we opted for a friend function to_string() for this, which you use as follows:

```
Box box{ 1, 2, 3 };
std::println("{}", to_string(box));  // Calls non-member (friend) function to_string()
```

We modeled our non-member to_string() function after the various std::to_string() overloads in the Standard Library that serve a similar purpose. (You may recall using some of these std::to_string() functions already in Chapter 7 to convert numbers to strings.) If you prefer, though, you could define to_string() as a member function as well. The only difference then is that you'd have to use it as follows:

```
std::println("{}", box.to_string()); // Calls member function Box::to_string()
```

This alternate approach would be more akin to Java's toString() or C#'s ToString() methods, in case you're familiar with those. Both approaches work just fine.

▓ **Tip** To convert objects to a textual representation in C++, it is at least as common, if not more common, to instead overload the stream insertion operator, <<. A stream insertion operator allows you to output objects to any stream directly, without creating a transient std::string object first (which obviously comes with the small overhead of allocating character arrays in the free store).

```
std::cout << box << std::endl; // Stream a Box directly by overloading <<
```

Moreover, once you have a stream insertion operator, you can always build a std::string object if need be by streaming to a std::stringstream (consult a Standard Library reference to learn how). You'll learn how to overload the stream insertion operator in Chapter 13.

■ **Note**   A more modern alternative to to_string() functions or overloaded stream insertion operators is to provide custom *formatters* for the std::format() and std::print() family of functions so that they can process replacement fields for values of your own types directly as well.

```
std::println("{:.1f}", box);   // Format a Box directly via a custom formatter
```

As said, you'll be able to write custom formatters of your own by the end of Chapter 20. Until then, we'll manage just fine converting our objects to strings first through functions such as to_string().

The SharedBox Type Alias

To make the rest of the code a bit less cluttered, we first define the type alias SharedBox as shorthand for std::shared_ptr<Box>. Because consumers of the truckload module need access to this alias as well, we define the SharedBox alias in its own tiny module interface partition.

```
// SharedBox.cppm - Minor interface partition exporting the SharedBox type alias
export module truckload:shared_box;
import std;
import box;
export using SharedBox = std::shared_ptr<Box>;
```

By using shared_ptr<> pointers for all Box objects, we make sure that, at least in theory, we can share these same Boxes with the rest of the program without having to worry about their lifetime—that is, without having to worry which class should delete the Box objects and when. As a consequence, the same Box object could, hypothetically, be shared among a Truckload, a truck's destination manifest, the online shipment tracking system for customers, and so on. If these Boxes are only referred to by the Truckload class, a shared_ptr<> wouldn't be the most appropriate smart pointer. A std::unique_ptr<> would then be more appropriate. But let's say that in this case our Truckload classes are to become part of a larger program entirely built around these Boxes and that this justifies the use of std::shared_ptr<>.

Defining the Package Class

Based on the preceding discussion, the Package class can be defined in a module implementation partition as follows:

```
// Package.cpp - Module implementation partition defining the Package class
module truckload:package;
import :shared_box;

class Package
{
public:
  Package(SharedBox box) : m_box{box}, m_next{nullptr} {}   // Constructor
  ~Package() { delete m_next; }                              // Destructor

  // Retrieve the Box pointer
  SharedBox getBox() const { return m_box; }
```

```
// Retrieve or update the pointer to the next Package
Package* getNext() { return m_next; }
void setNext(Package* package) { m_next = package; }

private:
  SharedBox m_box;      // Pointer to the Box object contained in this Package
  Package* m_next;      // Pointer to the next Package in the list
};
```

The SharedBox member of the Package class will store the address of a Box object. Every Package object refers to exactly one Box object. Note that to use the SharedBox alias, we must first import the corresponding module partition (because Package.cpp is a partition file as well, it does not implicitly import the truckload module).

The m_next member variable of a Package will point to the next Package object in the list. The m_next member for the last Package object in a list will contain nullptr. The constructor allows a Package object to be created that contains the address of the Box argument. The m_next member will be nullptr by default, but it can be set to point to a Package object by calling the setNext() member. The setNext() function updates m_next to the next Package in the list. To add a new Package object to the end of the list, you pass its address to the setNext() function for the last Package object in a list.

Packages themselves are not intended to be shared with the rest of the program. Their sole purpose is to form a chain in one Truckload's linked list. A shared_ptr<> is therefore not a good match for the m_next member variable. Normally, you should consider using a unique_ptr<> pointer for this member. The reason is that, in essence, every Package is always pointed to by exactly one object, either by the previous Package in the list or, for the head of the list, by the Truckload itself. And if the Truckload is destroyed, so should all its Packages be. However, in the spirit of the current chapter, we decided to use a raw pointer here instead and thus to grab this opportunity to show you some examples of nondefault destructors.

If a Package object is deleted, its destructor deletes the next Package in the list as well. This in turn will delete the next one, and so on. So, to delete its linked list of Packages, all a Truckload has to do is delete the first Package object in the list, which is the head; the rest of the Packages in the list will then be deleted, one by one, by the destructors of the Packages.

■ **Note** For the last Package in the list, m_next will be nullptr. Nevertheless, you don't need to test for nullptr in the destructor before applying delete. That is, you don't need to write the destructor like this:

```
~Package() { if (m_next) delete m_next; }  // 'if (m_next)' is not required!
```

You'll often encounter such overly cautious tests. But they are completely redundant. The delete operator is defined to simply do nothing when passed a nullptr. Also noteworthy is that, in this destructor, there is little value in setting m_next to nullptr after the deletion. We told you earlier that, in general, it is considered good practice to reset a pointer to null after deleting the value it points to. You should do so to avoid further use of dangling pointers, which includes accidentally deleting the same object twice. But since the m_next member can no longer be accessed once the destructor is done executing (the corresponding Package object no longer exists!), there is little point in doing it here.

Defining the Truckload Class

A Truckload object will encapsulate a list of Package objects. The class must provide everything necessary to create a new list and to extend the list and delete from it, as well as the means by which Box objects can be retrieved. A pointer to the first Package object in the list as a member variable will allow you to get to any Package object in the list by stepping through the chain of m_next pointers, using the getNext() function from the Package class. The getNext() function will be called repeatedly to step through the list one Package object at a time, so the Truckload object will need to track what object to retrieve next. It's also useful to store the address of the last Package object because this makes it easy to add a new object to the end of the list. Figure 12-9 shows this.

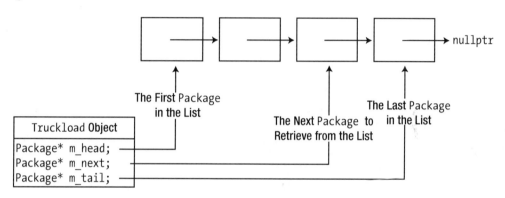

Figure 12-9. *Information needed in a Truckload object to manage the list*

Consider how retrieving Box objects from a Truckload object could work. Naturally, this inevitably involves stepping through the linked list of Packages. You could start by defining a getFirstBox() member in the Truckload class to retrieve the SharedBox stored in the first Package (which in turn is pointed to by m_head). Next, you could add getNextBox() to retrieve, one by one, any and all other SharedBox pointers. Both these members will use m_next to keep track of which Package the next SharedBox is stored in (if any). Other essential capabilities include adding or removing SharedBoxes to or from the list, so you'll need member functions to do that as well. addBox() and removeBox() certainly sound like suitable names for these. A member function to print all the Box objects in the list will also be handy.

Here's the file defining the Truckload class based on these ideas:

```
// Truckload.cppm - Module interface of the truckload module
export module truckload;

export import :shared_box;
import :package;
import std;

export class Truckload
{
public:
  Truckload() = default;          // Default constructor - empty truckload

  Truckload(SharedBox box)        // Constructor - one Box
  { m_head = m_tail = new Package{box}; }
```

```
Truckload(const std::vector<SharedBox>& boxes);    // Constructor - vector of Boxes
Truckload(const Truckload& src);                   // Copy constructor

~Truckload() { delete m_head; }                    // Destructor: clean up the list

SharedBox getFirstBox();                           // Get the first Box
SharedBox getNextBox();                            // Get the next Box
void addBox(SharedBox box);                        // Add a new SharedBox
bool removeBox(SharedBox box);                      // Remove a Box from the Truckload
void printBoxes() const;                            // Output the Boxes

private:
  Package* m_head {};                              // First in the list
  Package* m_tail {};                              // Last in the list
  Package* m_next {};                              // The package whose Box to retrieve next
};
```

The member variables are private because they don't need to be accessible outside the class. The getFirstBox() and getNextBox() members provide the mechanism for retrieving Box objects. Each of these needs to modify the m_next pointer, so they cannot be const. The addBox() and removeBox() functions also change the list so they cannot be const either.

There are four constructors. The default constructor defines an object containing an empty list. You can also create an object from a single pointer to a Box object, from a vector of pointers, or as a copy of another Truckload. The destructor of the class makes sure the linked list it encapsulates is properly cleaned up. As described earlier, deleting the first Package will trigger all other Packages in the list to be deleted as well.

The definitions of the constructor that accepts a vector of pointers to Box objects, the copy constructor, and the other member functions of the class will be placed in a Truckload.cpp module implementation file. We discuss the definitions of these functions in the upcoming subsections.

Traversing the Boxes Contained in a Truckload

Before we look at how the linked list is constructed, we'll look at the member functions that traverse the list. We start with the const member function called printBoxes() that outputs the contents of the Truckload object, which could be implemented like this:

```
void Truckload::printBoxes() const
{
  const std::size_t boxesPerLine{ 4 };
  std::size_t count {};
  for (Package* package{m_head}; package; package = package->getNext())
  {
    std::print(" {}", to_string(*package->getBox()));
    if (! (++count % boxesPerLine)) std::println("");
  }
  if (count && count % boxesPerLine) std::println("");
}
```

The central for loop steps through the Package objects in the linked list, one by one, starting with m_head, until package becomes nullptr (either because m_head was nullptr, or because calling getNext() on the previous Package returned nullptr). The loop's body retrieves the encapsulated SharedBox from each linked Package, dereferences that smart pointer through its unary * operator, and converts the resulting

Box to a string through its (non-member) friend function to_string(). Box objects are printed four on a line, separated by a single space. The one statement after the for loop outputs an extra line break when the last line contains output for fewer than four Box objects.

If you want, you could also write this for loop as a while loop:

```
void Truckload::printBoxes() const
{
  const std::size_t boxesPerLine{ 4 };
  std::size_t count {};
  Package* currentPackage{m_head};
  while (currentPackage)
  {
    std::print(" {}", to_string(*currentPackage->getBox()));
    if (! (++count % boxesPerLine)) std::println("");
    currentPackage = currentPackage->getNext();
  }
  if (count && count % boxesPerLine) std::println("");
}
```

Both loops are completely equivalent, so you're free to use either pattern to traverse linked lists. Arguably, the for loop is somewhat nicer because there is a clearer distinction between the initialization and advancement code of the package pointer (nicely grouped in front of the body, between the round brackets of the for loop) and the core logic of the listing algorithm (the for loop's body is uncluttered by list traversal code).

To allow code outside the Truckload class to traverse the SharedBoxes stored in a Truckload in a similar fashion, the class offers the getFirstBox() and getNextBox() member functions. Before we discuss their implementation, it's better to give you an idea how these functions are intended to be used. The pattern used to traverse the Boxes in a Truckload by external code will look similar to that of the printBoxes() member function (of course, an equivalent while loop could be used as well):

```
Truckload truckload{ ... };
...
for (auto box{truckload.getFirstBox()}; box; box = truckload.getNextBox())
{
  ...
}
```

The getFirstBox() and getNextBox() functions operate using the m_next member variable of Truckload. Once getFirstBox() initializes m_next to the first Package in the list, this pointer must point to the Package whose Box is to be returned next by getNextBox(). Such an assertion is known as a *class invariant*—a property of the member variables of a class that must hold at all times. Before returning, all member functions should make sure that all class invariants hold again. Conversely, they can trust that the invariants hold at the start of their execution. Other invariants for the Truckload class include that m_head points to the first Package in the list and that m_tail points to the last one (see also Figure 12-9). With these invariants in mind, implementing getFirstBox() and getNextBox() is actually not that hard:

```
SharedBox Truckload::getFirstBox()
{
  m_next = m_head;      // nullptr only for an empty truckload
  return getNextBox();
}
```

```
SharedBox Truckload::getNextBox()
{
  if (!m_next)                        // If there's no next...
    return nullptr;                   // ...return nullptr

  SharedBox result = m_next->getBox(); // Extract the box to return shortly
  m_next = m_next->getNext();          // Move to the next Package
  return result;
}
```

The getFirstBox() function is a piece of cake—just two statements. First, we assign the address stored in m_head—that of the first Package object in the list—to m_next—the address of the Package from which the next invocation of getNextBox() will retrieve its SharedBox. Once m_next is set correctly, we can delegate to getNextBox() to retrieve the first SharedBox for us.

If m_next is nullptr at the start of getNextBox(), we made it past the end of the list, and nullptr is returned. Otherwise, m_next points to a valid Package, and getNextBox() retrieves the next SharedBox from it. Next, getNext() advances m_next to prepare for the next call to getNextBox(). Do mind the order, though; before you advance m_next to point to the next Package, you must first call getBox() on the old m_next pointer (the one that we also checked for nullptr). And because we need the resulting SharedBox for the return statement at the end of the function, we need to store it briefly in a local variable.

When called from getFirstBox(), m_next is nullptr only if the Truckload is empty (in which case m_head is nullptr). If the Truckload is not empty, the idea is that after getFirstBox() you call getNextBox() a number of times (in a loop, typically, as outlined earlier) to retrieve all remaining boxes in the Truckload, until eventually m_next inevitably does become nullptr.

Adding and Removing Boxes

We'll start with the easiest of the remaining members: the vector<>-based constructor definition. This creates a list of Package objects from a vector of smart pointers to Box objects:

```
Truckload::Truckload(const std::vector<SharedBox>& boxes)
{
  for (const auto& box : boxes)
  {
    addBox(box);
  }
}
```

The parameter is a reference to avoid copying the argument more than necessary. The vector elements are of type SharedBox, which is an alias for std::shared_ptr<Box>. The loop iterates through the vector elements, passing each one to the addBox() member of the Truckload class, which will create and add a Package object on each call.

The copy constructor simply iterates over all packages in the source Truckload and calls addBox() for each box to add it to the newly constructed Truckload:

```
Truckload::Truckload(const Truckload& src)
{
  for (Package* package{src.m_head}; package; package = package->getNext())
  {
    addBox(package->getBox());
  }
}
```

■ **Note** This copy constructor only copies `shared_ptr<>`s, it does not copy the Box objects themselves. It initializes, in other words, a new Truckload object that shares the exact same set of Box objects with the original Truckload. This procedure is sometimes referred to as a *shallow copy*, compared to a *deep copy* in which new Box objects would be created as well. To make our Truckload constructor perform a deep copy instead, you could replace the addBox() statement in the for loop with the following:

```
addBox(std::make_shared<Box>(*package->getBox())); // Copy-constructs new shared Box
```

How deeply you copy your object trees depends on the needs of your application.

Both of these constructors are made easy because all the heavy lifting is delegated to addBox(). The definition of this member will be as follows:

```
void Truckload::addBox(SharedBox box)
{
  auto package{ new Package{box} }; // Create a new Package

  if (m_tail)                       // Check list is not empty
    m_tail->setNext(package);       // Append the new object to the tail
  else                              // List is empty
    m_head = package;               // so new object is the head

  m_tail = package;                 // Either way: the latest object is the (new) tail
}
```

The function creates a new Package object from the box pointer in the free store and stores its address in a local pointer, package. For an empty list, both m_head and m_tail will be null. If m_tail is non-null, then the list is not empty, and the new object is added to the end of the list by storing its address in the m_next member of the last Package that is pointed to by m_tail. If the list is empty, the new Package is the head of the list. In either case, the new Package object is at the end of the list, so m_tail is updated to reflect this.

The most complicated of all Truckload member functions is removeBox(). This function must also traverse the list, looking for the Box to remove. The initial outline of the function is therefore as follows:

```
bool Truckload::removeBox(SharedBox boxToRemove)
{
  Package* current{m_head};
  while (current)
  {
    if (current->getBox() == boxToRemove)       // We found the Box!
    {
      // remove the *current Package from the linked list...

      return true;                              // Return true: we found and removed the box
    }
    current = current->getNext();               // Move along to the next Package
  }

  return false;                                 // boxToRemove was not found: return false
}
```

You know this pattern already from the previous section. Once current points to the Package that needs to be removed, the only challenge remaining is how to correctly remove this Package from the linked list. Figure 12-10 illustrates what needs to be done.

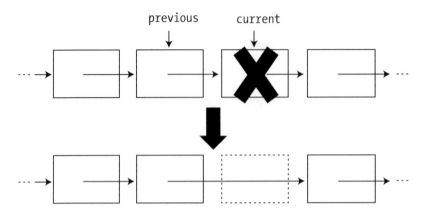

previous   current

Figure 12-10. *Removing a package from the linked list*

Figure 12-10 clearly shows that in order to remove a Package somewhere in the middle of the linked list, we need to update the m_next pointer of the *previous* Package in the list. In the figure, this is the Package pointed to by previous. This is not yet possible with our initial outline of the function. The current pointer has moved past the Package that needs to be updated, and there is no way to go back.

The standard solution is to keep track of both a previous and a current pointer while traversing the linked list, with previous always pointing to the Package that precedes the one pointed to by current. The previous pointer is sometimes called a *trailing pointer* because it always trails one Package behind the traversal pointer, current. The full function definition looks as follows:

```
bool Truckload::removeBox(SharedBox boxToRemove)
{
  Package* previous {nullptr};                 // No previous yet
  Package* current {m_head};                    // Initialize current to the head of the list
  while (current)
  {
    if (current->getBox() == boxToRemove)       // We found the Box!
    {
      // If there is a previous Package make it point to the next one (Figure 12-10)
      if (previous) previous->setNext(current->getNext());

      // Restore class invariants by updating impacted member variable pointers:
      if (current == m_head) m_head = current->getNext(); // Removing first box
      if (current == m_tail) m_tail = previous;           // Removing last box
      if (current == m_next) m_next = current->getNext(); // Removing "next" box

      current->setNext(nullptr);       // Disconnect the current Package from the list
      delete current;                  // and delete it

      return true;                     // Return true: we found and removed the box
    }
```

```
                                     // Move both pointers along (mind the order!)
    previous = current;              //  - first current becomes the new previous
    current = current->getNext();    //  - then move current along to the next Package
  }

  return false;                      // Return false: boxToRemove was not found
}
```

Adjusting the loop outlined earlier to also keep track of the trailing pointer, previous, is not hard; and neither is disconnecting the Package containing boxToRemove from the linked list, as shown in Figure 12-10, once you have access to this trailing pointer. (Do mind the case where there is no previous package; that is, where the Package to remove is the head of the list!)

Once the Package is disconnected from the linked list, though, you must first preserve the class invariants governing m_head, m_tail, and m_next. In particular, you need to update these variables whenever the removed Box is stored in the Package they point to.

Finally, because we used raw pointers for the linked list (ill-advised, as admitted earlier), you mustn't forget to delete the Package object that you've just dislodged from the list yourself. Also, before you can safely do that, it is important that you first set its m_next pointer to null. Otherwise, the destructor of the Package would start deleting the entire list of Packages that used to follow the deleted Package, starting with the Package pointed to by its m_next member.

▓ **Tip** removeBox() is by far the hardest function to get right in this example. It therefore makes for an excellent exercise to delete its function body from Truckload.cpp in Ex12_18 and then try to reconstruct it yourself from scratch!

Generating Random Boxes

To fill a truck, you need Boxes. Your average truck could easily fit hundreds of them. Now you could type in a lot of random Box dimensions yourself, or you could be smart and have the computer generate them for you. The <random> module of the Standard Library provides all that you need for this (and much, much more). Here is a small module that exports two functions to generate random boxes:

```
export module box.random;
import box;
import std;

// Creates a pseudorandom number generator (PRNG) for random doubles between 0 and max
auto createUniformPseudoRandomNumberGenerator(double max)
{
  std::random_device seeder;       // True random number generator to obtain a seed (slow)
  std::default_random_engine generator{seeder()};       // Efficient pseudo-random generator
  std::uniform_real_distribution distribution{0.0, max}; // Generate in [0, max) interval
  return std::bind(distribution, generator);            //... and in the darkness bind them!
}
```

```
export Box randomBox()
{
  const int dimLimit {100};                       // Upper limit on Box dimensions
  static auto random{ createUniformPseudoRandomNumberGenerator(dimLimit) };
  return Box{ random(), random(), random() };
}
export auto randomSharedBox()
{
  return std::make_shared<Box>(randomBox());      // Uses copy constructor
}
```

We named the module box.random, to remind you that module names are allowed to contain a dot even if they are not submodules (box.random is not exported from box as it would be if it were a proper submodule; see Chapter 11).

The module-local createUniformPseudoRandomNumberGenerator() function does most of the work. It uses various concepts that you are not familiar with yet—in particular function objects, which you'll learn about in Chapters 13 and 19—so do not worry if you do not understand it fully yet. For now, you can just blindly copy this function and the way it's used. Nevertheless, we'd like to give you at least some notion of how this all works. While it is not our goal to teach you every in and out of the standard <random> module either, here are some of the basic concepts used by createUniformPseudoRandomNumberGenerator():

- A random_device is an object capable of producing a truly random stream of bits. That is, there is absolutely no way to ever predict which bit sequence will come out next, and every possible bit sequence has an equal likelihood of appearing. This device relies on special hardware instructions to accomplish this. Because these instructions are fairly slow, though, you typically do not want to use a random_device directly to generate larger number sequences.

- A *pseudorandom number generator* (*PRNG*) (or *random number engine*, in the terminology of the <random> module) generates, you guessed it, pseudorandom numbers—pseudorandom unsigned integers to be exact in the case of <random>'s engines. A PRNG can be (and always should be) initialized to some initial value (called the *seed*), after which it starts producing a deterministic yet seemingly random sequence of new numbers. That is, if you know the inner workings of such a generator, you can perfectly predict which number will come out next, yet the stream of numbers that comes out does appear random to an uninformed consumer.

- A *distribution* transforms a given (pseudo)random unsigned integer (typically ranging from 0 to some impractically large maximum) into a value taken from some more interesting statistical distribution. A uniform distribution, in particular, produces values in a specified integer or floating-point interval, where each number in that interval has the same likelihood of being produced. Other distributions exist as well, where for instance larger numbers are more likely to be produced than smaller, or where numbers near the middle of an interval are more likely.

To get a feeling of how this all works, you could imagine a naïve PRNG being built based on the mathematical formula n = (n * 41 + 7) % 100. If we then initialize n to something truly random, say, 5, this PRNG generates the following integer sequence: 5, 12 (= 5 * 41 + 7 % 100 = 212 % 100), 99, 66, 13, 40, 47, 34, and so on. Suppose now that instead of an integer between 0 and 100, as produced by our naïve PRNG, we want one between 10 and 25. Then we could add a distribution that applies n % 15 + 10 to the result of the PRNG, and thus obtain the sequence 15, 22, 19, 16, 23, 20, 12, 14, and so on.

In createUniformPseudoRandomNumberGenerator(), we similarly combine concrete, more advanced instances of these three concepts to form what we need. First, we create random_device and use it to produce a truly random seed value to initialize a PRNG of type std::default_random_engine. The output of this PRNG (a sequence of unsigned integers) is then transformed into floating-point numbers in the half-open interval [0, max) by a std::uniform_real_distribution. The PRNG and the distribution are bound together using std::bind(). The end result returned by createUniformPseudoRandomNumberGenerator() is thus a randomly seeded PRNG that generates doubles between 0 and a given maximum.

The <random> module of the Standard Library offers several more engines and distributions, but whichever combination you choose, they are always initialized and combined using these same steps. If you ever need random numbers with slightly different requirements, it should be easy enough to adjust the four lines of createUniformPseudoRandomNumberGenerator() to suit your needs.

Putting It All Together

With the truckload module and its implementation files in place, you can try the Truckload class using the following code:

```
// Ex12_18.cpp - Using a linked list
import box.random;
import truckload;
import std;

int main()
{
  Truckload load1;  // Create an empty list

  // Add 12 random Box objects to the list
  const std::size_t boxCount {12};
  for (std::size_t i {} ; i < boxCount ; ++i)
    load1.addBox(randomSharedBox());

  std::println("The first list:");
  load1.printBoxes();

  // Copy the truckload
  Truckload copy{load1};
  std::println("The copied truckload:");
  copy.printBoxes();

  // Find the largest Box in the list
  SharedBox largestBox{load1.getFirstBox()};

  SharedBox nextBox{load1.getNextBox()};
  while (nextBox)
  {
    if (nextBox->compare(*largestBox) > 0)
      largestBox = nextBox;
    nextBox = load1.getNextBox();
  }

  std::println("\nThe largest box in the first list is {}", to_string(*largestBox));
  load1.removeBox(largestBox);
  std::println("\nAfter deleting the largest box, the list contains:");
  load1.printBoxes();
```

```
const std::size_t nBoxes {16};        // Number of vector elements
std::vector<SharedBox> boxes;         // Array of Box objects

for (std::size_t i {} ; i < nBoxes ; ++i)
  boxes.push_back(randomSharedBox());

Truckload load2{boxes};
std::println("\nThe second list:");
load2.printBoxes();

auto smallestBox{ load2.getFirstBox() };
for (auto box{ load2.getNextBox() }; box; box = load2.getNextBox())
  if (box->compare(*smallestBox) < 0)
    smallestBox = box;

std::println("\nThe smallest box in the second list is {}", to_string(*smallestBox));
}
```

Here's some sample output from this program:

```
The first list:
 Box(34.9,22.8,5.1) Box(29.1,18.6,2.8) Box(73.1,40.9,92.2) Box(36.6,15.7,5.9)
 Box(74.7,71.5,21.2) Box(45.7,9.5,12.9) Box(69.5,46.6,75.9) Box(49.0,23.1,84.0)
 Box(88.2,58.4,57.2) Box(14.6,66.5,43.0) Box(99.2,31.9,79.0) Box(60.3,84.9,7.9)
The copied truckload:
 Box(34.9,22.8,5.1) Box(29.1,18.6,2.8) Box(73.1,40.9,92.2) Box(36.6,15.7,5.9)
 Box(74.7,71.5,21.2) Box(45.7,9.5,12.9) Box(69.5,46.6,75.9) Box(49.0,23.1,84.0)
 Box(88.2,58.4,57.2) Box(14.6,66.5,43.0) Box(99.2,31.9,79.0) Box(60.3,84.9,7.9)

The largest box in the first list is Box(88.2,58.4,57.2)

After deleting the largest box, the list contains:
 Box(34.9,22.8,5.1) Box(29.1,18.6,2.8) Box(73.1,40.9,92.2) Box(36.6,15.7,5.9)
 Box(74.7,71.5,21.2) Box(45.7,9.5,12.9) Box(69.5,46.6,75.9) Box(49.0,23.1,84.0)
 Box(14.6,66.5,43.0) Box(99.2,31.9,79.0) Box(60.3,84.9,7.9)

The second list:
 Box(70.4,77.8,29.8) Box(23.7,58.0,47.0) Box(26.7,50.5,48.7) Box(89.1,80.9,50.1)
 Box(98.8,50.4,44.6) Box(85.5,39.6,30.0) Box(86.5,54.2,75.0) Box(66.1,8.3,11.8)
 Box(59.9,61.8,47.6) Box(14.3,34.7,76.0) Box(92.5,0.8,74.6) Box(5.2,45.9,54.3)
 Box(52.9,9.9,95.3) Box(100.0,71.0,37.2) Box(73.5,5.2,58.4) Box(72.7,69.0,75.3)

The smallest box in the second list is Box(72.7,69.0,75.3)
```

The main() function first creates an empty Truckload object, adds Box objects in the for loop, and then makes a copy of this Truckload object. It then finds the largest Box object in the list and deletes it. The output demonstrates that all these operations are working correctly. Just to show it works, main() creates a Truckload object from a vector of pointers to Box objects. It then finds the smallest Box object and outputs it. Clearly, the capability to list the contents of a Truckload object is also working well.

Nested Classes

The Package class was designed to be used specifically within the Truckload class. It would make sense to ensure that Package objects can only be created by member functions of the Truckload class. Granted, because the Package class is not exported from the module, the rest of the world already cannot use it. But in general, you may want to go one step further, and employ a mechanism where Package objects are private to Truckload class members and not available to the rest of the module. You can do this by using a *nested class*.

A nested class is a class that has its definition inside another class definition. The name of the nested class is within the scope of the enclosing class and is subject to the member access specification in the enclosing class. We could put the definition of the Package class inside the definition of the Truckload class, like this:

```
export module truckload;
import box;
import std;

// We no longer need the truckload:shared_box partition (or any other partition file)
export using SharedBox = std::shared_ptr<Box>;

export class Truckload
{
public:
  // Exact same public member functions as before...

private:
  class Package
  {
  public:

    SharedBox m_box;      // Pointer to the Box object contained in this Package
    Package* m_next;      // Pointer to the next Package in the list

    Package(SharedBox box) : m_box{box}, m_next{nullptr} {} // Constructor
    ~Package() { delete m_next; }                           // Destructor
  };

  Package* m_head {};     // First in the list
  Package* m_tail {};     // Last in the list
  Package* m_next {};     // The package whose Box to retrieve next
};
```

The Package type is now local to the scope of the Truckload class definition. Because the definition of the Package class is in the private section of the Truckload class, Package objects cannot be created or used from outside the Truckload class. Because the Package class is entirely private to the Truckload class, there's also no harm in making all its members public. Hence, they're directly accessible to member functions of a Truckload object. The getBox(), getNext(), and setNext() members of the original Package class are no longer needed. All of the Package members are directly accessible from Truckload objects but inaccessible outside the class.

The definitions of the member functions of the Truckload class need to be changed to access the member variables of the Package class directly. This is trivial. Just replace all occurrences of getBox(), getNext(), and setNext() in Truckload.cpp with code that directly accesses the corresponding member variable. The resulting Truckload class definition with Package as a nested class will work with the Ex12_18.cpp source file. A working example is available in the code download as Ex12_19.

▨ **Note** Nesting the Package class inside the Truckload class simply defines the Package type in the context of the Truckload class. Objects of type Truckload aren't affected in any way—they'll have the same members as before.

Member functions of a nested class can directly reference static members of the enclosing class, as well as any other types or enumerators defined in the enclosing class. Other members of the enclosing class can be accessed from the nested class in the normal ways: via a class object or a pointer or a reference to a class object. When accessing members of the outer class, the member functions of a nested class have the same access privileges as member functions of the outer class; that is, member functions of a nested class are allowed to access the private members of objects of the outer class.

Nested Classes with Public Access

You could put the Package class definition in the public section of the Truckload class. This would mean that the Package class definition was part of the public interface so it *would* be possible to create Package objects externally. Because the Package class name is within the scope of the Truckload class, you can't use it by itself. You must qualify the Package class name with the name of the class in which it is nested. Here's an example:

```
Truckload::Package myPackage{ myBox };    // Define a Package object
```

Of course, making the Package type public in the example would defeat the rationale for making it a nested class in the first place! That said, there can be other circumstances where a public nested class makes sense. We'll see one such example in the next subsection.

A Better Mechanism for Traversing a Truckload: Iterators

The getFirstBox() and getNextBox() members allowed you to traverse all Boxes stored in a Truckload. It is not unheard of to add analogous members to a class—we have encountered it on at least two occasions in real code—but this pattern has some serious flaws. Perhaps you can already think of one?

Suppose you find—rightfully so—that the main() function of Ex12_18 is too long and crowded and you decide to split off some of its functionality in reusable functions. A good first candidate would then be a helper function to find the largest Box in a Truckload. A natural way to write this is as follows:

```
SharedBox findLargestBox(const Truckload& truckload)
{
  SharedBox largestBox{ truckload.getFirstBox() };

  SharedBox nextBox{ truckload.getNextBox() };
  while (nextBox)
  {
```

```
    if (nextBox->compare(*largestBox) > 0)
      largestBox = nextBox;
    nextBox = truckload.getNextBox();
  }

  return largestBox;
}
```

Unfortunately, however, this function does not compile! Can you see why not? The root cause of the problem is that both getFirstBox() and getNextBox() have to update the m_next member inside truckload. This implies that they both must be non-const member functions, which in turn implies that neither of these functions can be called on truckload, which is a reference-to-const argument. Nevertheless, using a reference-to-const parameter is the normal thing to do here. Nobody would or should expect that searching for the largest Box requires a Truckload to be modified. As it stands, however, it is impossible to traverse the content of a const Truckload, which renders const Truckload objects nearly useless. A proper const Truckload& reference should allow code to traverse the Boxes contained in it, but at the same time prevent it from invoking either AddBox() or RemoveBox().

▨ **Note** You could try to work around the problem by making the m_next member variable of the Truckload class mutable. That would then allow you to turn both getFirstBox() and getNextBox() into const members. While this may be interesting for you as a bonus exercise, this solution still suffers some drawbacks. First, you'd run into problems with nested loops over the same collection. Second, you can probably imagine that using the mutable approach would never allow for concurrent traversals by multiple threads of execution either. In both cases, one m_next pointer would be required per traversal—not one per Truckload object.

The correct solution to this problem is the *iterator pattern*. The principle is easy enough. Instead of storing the m_next pointer inside the Truckload object itself, you move it to another object that is specifically designed and created to traverse the Truckload. Such an object is called an *iterator*.

▨ **Note** In Chapter 20 you'll learn that the containers and algorithms of the Standard Library make extensive use of iterators as well. While Standard Library iterators have a slightly different interface than the Iterator class we are about to define for Truckload, the underlying principle is the same. Iterators allow external code to traverse the content of a container without having to know about the data structure's internals.

Let's see what that could look like for us. We'll start from the Truckload class of Ex12_19—the version where Package is already a nested class—and add a second nested class called Iterator. Just to show you the possibility, we will also define both nested classes outside of the definition of the outer class.

```
export module truckload;
import box;
import std;

export using SharedBox = std::shared_ptr<Box>;
```

```
export class Truckload
{
public:
  // Exact same public members as before,
  // only this time without getFirstBox() and getNextBox()...

  class Iterator;       // Declaration of a public nested class, Truckload::Iterator

  Iterator getIterator() const;

private:
  class Package;        // Declaration of a private nested class, Truckload::Package

  Package* m_head {};  // First in the list
  Package* m_tail {};  // Last in the list
};

// Out-of-class definition of the nested Iterator class (part of the module interface)
class Truckload::Iterator
{
public:
  SharedBox getFirstBox();  // Get the first Box
  SharedBox getNextBox();   // Get the next Box

private:
  Package* m_head;          // The head of the linked list (needed for getFirstBox())
  Package* m_next;          // The package whose Box to retrieve next

  friend class Truckload;   // Only a Truckload can create an Iterator
  explicit Iterator(Package* head) : m_head{head}, m_next{nullptr} {}
};

// Out-of-class definition of the nested Package class (implementation detail)
class Truckload::Package
{
public:
  SharedBox m_box;    // Pointer to the Box object contained in this Package
  Package* m_next;    // Pointer to the next Package in the list

  Package(SharedBox box) : m_box{box}, m_next{nullptr} {} // Constructor
  ~Package() { delete m_next; }                           // Destructor
};
```

Defining nested classes (or *member classes*) out-of-class is analogous to defining other members out-of-class; all you need to remember is to prefix the member name (in this case Iterator or Package) with the name of the containing class (Truckload) followed by two colons. In fact, because Package is only required within the definition of other members, you could move its definition into an implementation file together with that of these members. The definition of the Iterator class, however, should be part of the module interface; the consumers of the module need it to traverse a Truckload's contents.

Here is the definition of the getIterator() member:

```
Truckload::Iterator Truckload::getIterator() const { return Iterator{m_head}; }
```

There are two things worth noting here. First, the function's return type, Truckload::Iterator, must be prefixed with Truckload:: as well. Only within the function body or parameter list, this is not required. And, second, because we defined Iterator out-of-class, the definition of the getIterator() member must be out-of-class as well, and put after that of Iterator. The reason is that the body of getIterator() needs the definition of the Iterator class to invoke its constructor. Of course, we start the iteration at the head of the linked list.

The m_next, getFirstBox(), and getNextBox() members have been moved from Truckload into its nested Iterator class. Both functions are implemented in the same manner as before, except that now they no longer update the m_next member variable of a Truckload object. Instead, they operate using the m_next member of an Iterator object specifically created to traverse this Truckload by getIterator(). As multiple Iterators can exist at the same time for a single Truckload, each with their own m_next pointer, both nested and concurrent traversals of the same Truckload become possible. Moreover, and more importantly, creating an iterator does not modify a Truckload, so getIterator() can be a const member function. This allows us to properly implement the findLargestBox() function from earlier with a reference-to-const-Truckload parameter:

```
SharedBox findLargestBox(const Truckload& truckload)
{
  auto iterator{ truckload.getIterator() };  // Type of iterator is Truckload::Iterator
  SharedBox largestBox{ iterator.getFirstBox() };

  SharedBox nextBox{ iterator.getNextBox() };
  while (nextBox)
  {
    if (nextBox->compare(*largestBox) > 0)
      largestBox = nextBox;
    nextBox = iterator.getNextBox();
  }

  return largestBox;
}
```

▦ **Caution**   One consequence of moving m_next from Truckload to Truckload::Iterator is that Truckload::removeBox() can no longer update this pointer if an iterator's "next" Package is deleted. That is, removeBox() could, unknowingly, turn the m_next pointer of any number of Iterator instances into *dangling pointers* (as defined in Chapter 6). Obviously, any continued use of such an Iterator could then result in disaster. In technical speak, we say that removeBox() *invalidates* any Iterator that points to the removed Package, and that any use of an invalidated iterator results in undefined behavior. Virtually any realization of the container-iterator idiom—including that of the Standard Library (see Chapter 20)—shares these same limitations. Adding or removing elements to or from a container may invalidate iterators, meaning you need to stop using these iterators. In the exercises at the end of the chapter we hint at a (partial) solution to this limitation (see also the Altering Containers During Iteration section of Chapter 20).

We'll leave the completion of this example to you as an exercise (see Exercise 12-7). Before we conclude the chapter, though, let's first take a closer look at the access rights within the definition of Truckload and its nested classes. Iterator is a nested class of Truckload, so it has the same access privileges as Truckload member functions. This is fortunate because otherwise it couldn't have used the nested Package class, which is declared to be for private use only within the Truckload class. Naturally, Iterator itself must be a public nested class; otherwise, code outside of the class would not be able to use it. Notice that we did decide to make the primary constructor of the Iterator class private, however, because external code cannot (it never has access to any Package objects) and should not create Iterators that way. Only the getIterator() function will be creating Iterators with this constructor. For it to access this private constructor, however, we need a friend declaration. Even though you can access private members of the outer class from within a nested class, the same does not hold in the other direction. That is, an outer class has no special privileges when it comes to accessing the members of an inner class. It is treated like any other external code. Without the friend declaration, the getIterator() function would therefore not have been allowed to access the private constructor of the nested Iterator class.

▓ **Note**   Even though external code cannot create a new Iterator using our private constructor, it does remain possible to create a new Iterator object as a copy of an existing one. The default copy constructor generated by the compiler remains public.

Summary

In this chapter, you learned the basics of defining and using class types. However, although you covered a lot of ground, this is just the start. There's a great deal more to implementing the operations applicable to class objects, and there are subtleties in this too. In subsequent chapters, you'll be building on what you learned here, and you'll see more about how you can extend the capabilities of your classes. In addition, you'll explore more sophisticated ways to use classes in practice. The key points to keep in mind from this chapter are as follows:

- A *class* provides a way to define your own data types. Classes can represent whatever types of *objects* your particular problem requires.

- A class can contain *member variables* and *member functions*. The member functions of a class always have free access to the member variables of the same class.

- Objects of a class are created and initialized using member functions called *constructors*. A constructor is called automatically when an object declaration is encountered. Constructors can be overloaded to provide different ways of initializing an object.

- A copy constructor is a constructor for an object that is initialized with an existing object of the same class. The compiler generates a default copy constructor for a class if you don't define one.

- Members of a class can be specified as public, in which case they are freely accessible from any function in a program. Alternatively, they can be specified as private, in which case they may be accessed only by member functions, friends of the class, or members of nested classes.

- Member variables of a class can be static. Only one instance of each static member variable of a class exists, no matter how many objects of the class are created.

- Although static member variables of a class are accessible in a member function of an object, they aren't part of the object and don't contribute to its size.

- Every non-static member function contains the pointer this, which points to the current object for which the function is called.

- static member functions can be called even if no objects of the class have been created. A static member function of a class doesn't contain the pointer this.

- const member functions can't modify the member variables of a class object unless the member variables have been declared as mutable.

- Using references to class objects as arguments to function calls can avoid substantial overheads in passing complex objects to a function.

- A destructor is a member function that is called for a class object when it is destroyed. If you don't define a class destructor, the compiler supplies a default destructor.

- A nested class is a class that is defined inside another class definition.

EXERCISES

The following exercises enable you to try what you've learned in this chapter. If you get stuck, look back over the chapter for help. If you're still stuck after that, you can download the solutions from the Apress website (https://www.apress.com/gp/services/source-code), but that really should be a last resort.

Exercise 12-1. Create a class called Integer that has a single, private member variable of type int. Provide a class constructor that outputs a message when an object is created. Define member functions to *get* and *set* the member variable and to print its value. Write a test program to create and manipulate at least three Integer objects and verify that you can't assign a value directly to the member variable. Exercise all the class member functions by getting, setting, and outputting the value of the member variable of each object. Make sure to create at least one const Integer object and verify which operations you can and cannot apply on it.

Exercise 12-2. Modify the Integer class in the previous exercise so that an Integer object can be created without an argument. The member value should then be initialized to zero. Can you think of two ways to do this? Also, implement a copy constructor that prints a message when called.

Next, add a member function that compares the current object with an Integer object passed as an argument. The function should return –1 if the current object is less than the argument, 0 if the objects are equal, and +1 if the current object is greater than the argument. Try two versions of the Integer class, one where the compare() function argument is passed by value and the other where it is passed by reference. What do you see output from the constructors when the function is called? Make sure you understand why this is so. You can't have both functions present in the class as overloaded functions. Why not?

Exercise 12-3. Implement member functions add(), subtract(), and multiply() for the Integer class that will add, subtract, and multiply the current object by the value represented by the argument of type Integer. Demonstrate the operation of these functions in your class with a version of main() that creates several Integer objects encapsulating integer values and then uses these to calculate the value of $4×5^3+6×5^2+7×5+8$. Implement the functions so that the calculation and the output of the result can be performed in a single statement.

Exercise 12-4. Update your solution for Exercise 12-3 such that $4×5^3+6×5^2+7×5+8$ is guaranteed to be computed at compile time.

Exercise 12-5. Change your solution for Exercise 12-2 so that it implements the compare() function as a friend of the Integer class. Afterward, ask yourself whether it was really necessary for this function to be a friend.

Exercise 12-6. Implement a static function printCount() for the Integer class that you created earlier in Exercise 12-2 that outputs the number of Integers in existence. Modify the main() function such that it tests that this number correctly goes up and down when needed.

Exercise 12-7. Finish the nested Truckload::Iterator class that we started at the end of the chapter. Starting from Ex12_19, add the Iterator class to its definition as listed earlier and implement its member functions. Use the Iterator class to implement the findLargestBox() function as outlined earlier (perhaps you can do it without looking at the solution?) and rework the main() function of Ex12_19 to make use of this. Do the same with an analogous findSmallestBox() function.

Exercise 12-8. Modify the Package class in the Exercise 12-7 solution so that it contains an additional pointer to the previous object in the list. This makes it a doubly linked list—naturally, the data structure we were using before is called a *singly-linked list*. Modify the Package, Truckload, and Iterator classes to make use of this, including providing the ability to iterate through Box objects in the list in reverse order and to list the objects in a Truckload object in reverse sequence. Devise a main() program to demonstrate the new capabilities.

Hint: Because an iterator now needs the capability to move both forward and backward, maintaining a m_next pointer as its primary state variable is no longer ideal. We recommend switching over to a m_current pointer instead, with as primary invariant that this pointer always refers to the Package whose SharedBox was retrieved last.

Note: This exercise nicely illustrates the value of data hiding (private members): due to evolving requirements (we needed to be able to traverse truckloads backward), you had to update the data structure powering the Truckload class from a singly to a doubly linked list. And in the process, if took our hint to hart, you updated the way the Iterator realizes existing functionality (moving forward) as well. But since all public members of the class remained unchanged, both in signature and semantics, you didn't have to change any existing code in the main() function. Existing code just kept on rolling, none the wiser that under the hood the Truckload class received a brand-new engine. Now imagine the impact of these same updates if there were a lot more existing code, all of which accessed, say, the old m_next pointer of the Iterator class directly... Now imagine that the moment you're done updating your code base to work with the doubly linked list, you need to replace it again, only this time with a std::vector<>, to meet even more requirements (say, optimally sorting of the boxes stored in a truckload). Data hiding allows you to overhaul the internal representation of objects without breaking existing code.

Exercise 12-9. A scrutinous analysis of the main() function of Ex12_18 (and thus also that of Ex12_19 and the solutions of the previous two exercises) reveals the following performance flaw. To remove the largest Box, we perform two linear traversals of the linked list. First, we look for the largest Box, and then inside removeBox() we look for the Package to unlink. Devise a solution based on the Iterator class in Exercise 12-8 to avoid this second search.

Hint: The solution hinges on a member function with the following signature:

```
bool removeBox(Iterator iterator);
```

Try not to duplicate any code between the different removeBox() function overloads.

Bonus exercise: This new removeBox() overload (or a variation thereof) also presents a golden opportunity to at least partially address the limitation that Iterators are invalidated after removing the SharedBox / Package that it points to...

CHAPTER 13

Operator Overloading

In this chapter, you'll learn how to add support for operators such as + and < to your classes so that they can be applied to objects. This will make the types that you define behave more like fundamental data types and offer a more natural way to express some of the operations between objects. You've already seen how classes can have member functions that operate on the member variables of an object. Operator overloading enables you to write member functions that enable the basic operators to be applied to class objects.

In this chapter, you will learn

- What operator overloading is

- Which operators you can implement for your own data types

- How to implement member functions that overload operators

- How and when to implement operator functions as ordinary functions instead

- How to implement custom comparison and arithmetic operators for a class

- How the spaceship operator greatly simplifies defining comparison operators

- How to have the compiler generate comparison operators for you

- How overloading the << operator allows objects of your own type to be streamed out to, for instance, std::cout

- How to overload unary operators, including the increment and decrement operators

- How to overload the array subscript operator (informally known as the square brackets operator, [ ]) if your class represents a collection of values

- How to define type conversions as operator functions

- What copy assignment is and how to implement your own assignment operator

Implementing Operators for a Class

The Box class in the previous chapter could've been designed for an application that is primarily concerned with the volume of a box. For such an application, you obviously need the ability to compare boxes based on their volume so that you can determine their relative sizes. In Ex12_18, there was this code:

```
if (nextBox->compare(*largestBox) > 0)
  largestBox = nextBox;
```

© Ivor Horton and Peter Van Weert 2023
I. Horton and P. Van Weert, *Beginning C++23*, https://doi.org/10.1007/978-1-4842-9343-0_13

Wouldn't it be nice if you could write the following instead?

```
if (*nextBox > *largestBox)
  largestBox = nextBox;
```

Using the greater-than operator is much clearer and easier to understand than the original. You might also like to add the volumes of two Box objects with an expression such as box1 + box2 or multiply Box as 10 * box1 to obtain a new Box object that has the capacity to hold ten box1 boxes. We'll explain how you can do all this and more by implementing functions that overload the basic operators for objects of a class type.

Operator Overloading

Operator overloading enables you to apply standard operators such as +, -, *, <, and many more, to objects of your own class types. In fact, you have used several such overloaded operators already with objects of Standard Library types, probably without realizing that these were implemented as overloaded functions. For instance, you have compared std::string objects using operators such as < and ==, concatenated strings using +, and sent them to the std::cout output stream using the overloaded << operator. This underlines the beauty of operator overloading. If applied properly, it leads to very natural, elegant code—the kind of code that you intuitively would want to write and can read without a moment's thought.

To define an operator for objects of your own type, all you need to do is write a function that implements the desired behavior. For the most part, operator function definitions are the same as any other function definition you have written so far. The main difference lies in the function name. The name of a function that overloads a given operator is composed of the operator keyword followed by the operator that you are overloading. The best way to understand how operator overloading works is to step through an example. In the next section, we'll start by explaining how you implement the less-than operator, <, for the Box class.

Implementing an Overloaded Operator

A binary operator that is implemented as a class member has *one* parameter. We'll explain in a moment why there is only one. Here's the member function to overload the < operator in the Box class definition:

```
class Box
{
public:
  bool operator<(const Box& aBox) const;       // Overloaded 'less-than' operator

  // The rest of the Box class as before...
};
```

Because you're implementing a comparison, the return type is bool. The operator<() function will be called as a result of comparing two Box objects using <. The function will be called as a member of the object that is the left operand, and the argument will be the right operand, so this will point to the left operand. Because the function doesn't change either operand, the parameter and the function are specified as const. To see how this works, consider the following statement:

```
if (box1 < box2)
  std::println("box1 is less than box2");
```

The if expression will result in the operator function being called. The expression is equivalent to the function call box1.operator<(box2). If you were so inclined, you could write it like this in the if statement:

```
if (box1.operator<(box2))
  std::println("box1 is less than box2");
```

This shows you that an overloaded binary operator is indeed, for the most part, just a function with two special properties; it has a special name, and the function may be called by writing the operator in between its two operands.

Knowing how the operands in the expression box1 < box2 map to the function call makes implementing the overloaded operator easy. Figure 13-1 shows the definition.

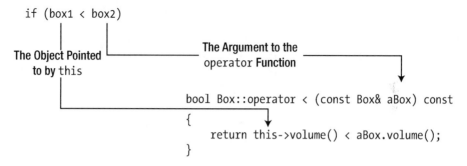

Figure 13-1. *Overloading the less-than operator*

The reference function parameter avoids unnecessary copying of the argument. The return expression calls the volume() member to calculate the volume of the object pointed to by this and compares that with the volume of aBox using the basic < operator. Thus, true is returned if the object pointed to by this has a smaller volume than the object passed as the argument—and false otherwise.

▒ **Note** We used the this pointer in Figure 13-1 just to show the association with the first operand. It isn't necessary to use this explicitly here.

Let's see if this works in an example. Here's how Box.cppm looks:

```
// Box.cppm
export module box;

export class Box
{
public:
  // Constructors
  Box() = default;
  Box(double l, double w, double h) : m_length{l}, m_width{w}, m_height{h} {}

  double volume() const { return m_length * m_width * m_height; }
```

```
// Accessors
double getLength() const { return m_length; }
double getWidth()  const { return m_width; }
double getHeight() const { return m_height; }

bool operator<(const Box& aBox) const        // Less-than operator
{ return volume() < aBox.volume(); }
private:
  double m_length {1.0};
  double m_width {1.0};
  double m_height {1.0};
};
```

All member functions, including the operator function, are defined inside the class. You could implement the operator function outside the class as well. In that case, the function definition would have to look like the one shown in Figure 13-1. That is, the Box:: qualifier must immediately precede the operator keyword.

Here is a little program to exercise the less-than operator for Boxes:

```
// Ex13_01.cpp - Implementing a less-than operator
import std;
import box;

int main()
{
  std::vector boxes {Box {2.0, 2.0, 3.0}, Box {1.0, 3.0, 2.0},
                     Box {1.0, 2.0, 1.0}, Box {2.0, 3.0, 3.0}};
  Box smallBox {boxes[0]};
  for (const auto& box : boxes)
  {
    if (box < smallBox) smallBox = box;
  }

  std::println("The smallest box has dimensions {} x {} x {}",
               smallBox.getLength(), smallBox.getWidth(), smallBox.getHeight());
}
```

This produces the following output:

```
The smallest box has dimensions 1x2x1
```

The main() function first creates a vector initialized with four Box objects. You arbitrarily assume that the first array element is the smallest and use it to initialize smallBox, which will involve the copy constructor, of course. The range-based for loop compares each element of boxes with smallBox, and a smaller element is stored in smallBox in an assignment statement. When the loop ends, smallBox contains the Box object with the smallest volume. If you want to track calls of the operator<() function, add an output statement to it.

Notice that the smallBox = box; statement shows that the assignment operator works with Box objects. This is because the compiler supplies a default version of operator=() in the class that copies the values of the members of the right operand to the members of the left operand, just like it did for the copy constructor. This is not always satisfactory, and you'll see later in this chapter how you can define your own version of the assignment operator.

Nonmember Operator Functions

In the previous section, you learned that an operator overload can be defined as a member function. Most operators can be implemented as a regular, nonmember function as well. For instance, because the volume() function is a public member of the Box class, you could easily implement operator<() as an ordinary function as well. The definition would then be as follows:

```
export bool operator<(const Box& box1, const Box& box2)
{
  return box1.volume() < box2.volume();
}
```

With the operator defined in this way, the previous example would work in the same way. Of course, you must not declare this version of the operator function as const; const only applies to functions that are members of a class. The operator definition is exported so that it may be used from outside the box module.

Even if an operator function needs access to private members of the class, it's still possible to implement it as an ordinary function by declaring it as a friend of the class. Generally, though, if a function must access private members of a class, it is best to define it as a class member whenever possible.

▨ **Tip** Always define nonmember operators in the same namespace as the class of the objects they operate on. Because our Box class is part of the global namespace, the previous operator<() should be as well.

Implementing Full Support for an Operator

Implementing an operator such as < for a class creates expectations. You can write expressions like box1 < box2, but what about box1 < 25.0 or 10.0 < box2? The current operator<() won't handle either of these. When you implement overloaded operators for a class, you need to consider the likely range of circumstances in which the operator might be used.

▨ **Caution** In Chapter 12, we urged you to add the keyword explicit to most single-parameter constructors. Otherwise, these constructors are used for implicit conversions, which may lead to surprising results—and thus bugs. Suppose, for instance, that you define a nonexplicit single-parameter constructor for Box like so:

```
Box(double side) : Box{side,side,side} {}   // Constructor for cube-shaped Boxes
```

Then an expression such as box1 < 25.0 would compile because the compiler would be injecting an implicit conversion from double to Box. But box1 < 25.0 would then compare the volume of box1 not with a volume of 25.0 but instead with that of a Box of dimensions 25×25×25. So, clearly, the constructor for cube-shaped Boxes must be explicit indeed, just like we concluded before! Since you cannot rely on implicit conversions to facilitate comparisons between Box objects and numbers, you'll thus have to put in some extra work to support expressions such as box1 < 25.0.

You can easily support these possibilities for comparing Box objects by adding extra overloads for operator<(). We'll first add a function for < where the first operand is a Box object and the second operand is of type double. You need to add the following member specification to the public section of the Box class definition:

```
bool operator<(double value) const;      // Compare Box volume < double value
```

The Box object that is the left operand will be accessed in the function via the implicit pointer this, and the right operand is value. Implementing this is as easy as the first operator function; there's just one statement in the function body:

```
// Compare the volume of a Box object with a constant
bool Box::operator<(double value) const
{
  return volume() < value;
}
```

Dealing with an expression such as 10.0 < box2 isn't harder; it's just different. A *member* operator function always provides the this pointer as the left operand. In this case, the left operand is type double, so you can't implement the operator as a member function. That leaves you with two choices: to implement it as an ordinary operator function or to implement it as a friend function. Because you don't need to access private members of the class, you can implement it as an ordinary function:

```
// Function comparing a constant with volume of a Box object
export bool operator<(double value, const Box& aBox)
{
  return value < aBox.volume();
}
```

You now have three overloaded versions of the < operator for Box objects to support all three less-than comparison possibilities. Let's see that in action. We'll assume you have modified Box.cppm as described. We also ask you to add a to_string() nonmember function in the style of Ex12_18 to help with printing Boxes.

Here's a program that uses the new comparison operator functions for Box objects:

```
// Ex13_02.cpp - Using the overloaded 'less-than' operators for Box objects
import std;
import box;

int main()
{
  std::vector boxes {Box {2.0, 2.0, 3.0}, Box {1.0, 3.0, 2.0},
                     Box {1.0, 2.0, 1.0}, Box {2.0, 3.0, 3.0}};
  const double minVolume{6.0};

  std::println("Objects with volumes less than {} are:", minVolume);
  for (const auto& box : boxes)
    if (box < minVolume) std::println("{}", to_string(box));

  std::println("Objects with volumes greater than {} are:", minVolume);
  for (const auto& box : boxes)
    if (minVolume < box) std::println("{}", to_string(box));
}
```

You should get this output:

```
Objects with volumes less than 6 are:
Box(1.0, 2.0, 1.0)
Objects with volumes greater than 6 are:
Box(2.0, 2.0, 3.0)
Box(2.0, 3.0, 3.0)
```

The output shows that the overloaded operators are working. Again, if you want to see when they are called, put an output statement in each definition. Of course, you don't need separate functions to compare Box objects with integers. When this occurs, the compiler will insert an implicit cast to type double before calling one of the existing functions.

Operators That Can Be Overloaded

Most operators can be overloaded. Although you can't overload every single operator, the restrictions aren't particularly oppressive. Notable operators that you cannot overload include, for instance, the conditional operator (?:) and sizeof. Nearly all other operators are fair game, though, which gives you quite a bit of scope. Table 13-1 lists all operators that you can overload.

Table 13-1. *Operators That Can Be Overloaded*

Operators	Symbols	Nonmember
Binary arithmetic operators	+ - * / %	Yes
Unary arithmetic operators	+ -	Yes
Bitwise operators	~ & | ^ << >>	Yes
Logical operators	! && ||	Yes
Assignment operator	=	No
Compound assignment operators	+= -= *= /= %= &= |= ^= <<= >>=	Yes
Increment/decrement operators	++ --	Yes
Comparison operators	< > <= >= == != <=>	Yes
Array subscript operator	[]	No
Function call operator	()	No
Conversion-to-type-T operator	T	No
Address-of and dereferencing operators	& * -> ->*	Yes
Comma operator	,	Yes
Allocation and deallocation operators	new new[] delete delete[]	Only
User-defined literal operator	"" _	Only

Most operators can be overloaded either as a class member function or as a nonmember function outside of a class. These operators are marked with Yes in the third column of Table 13-1. Some can be implemented only as a member function, though (marked with No), whereas others can be implemented only as nonmember functions (marked with Only).

In this chapter, you will learn when and how to overload nearly all of these operators, all except the bottom four categories in the table. The address-of and dereferencing operators are mostly used to implement pointer-like types such as the `std::unique_ptr<>` and `std::shared_ptr<>` smart pointer templates you encountered earlier. In part because the Standard Library already offers excellent support for such types, you will not often have to overload these operators yourself. The bottom three categories are overloaded even less frequently in user code.

Restrictions and Key Guideline

While operator overloading is flexible and can be powerful, there are some restrictions. In a way, the name of the language feature already gives it away: operator *overloading*. That is, you can only *overload existing* operators. This implies the following:

- You *cannot invent new* operators such as ?, ===, or <>.

- You *cannot change* the number of operands, associativity, or precedence of the existing operators, nor can you alter the order in which the operands to an operator are evaluated. The only exception as of C++23 is that overloaded subscript operators, [ ], can take any number of operands (including zero), even though the built-in array subscript operator always takes a single operand.

- As a rule, you *cannot override* built-in operators. The signature of an overloaded operator thus typically involves at least one class type. We will discuss the term *overriding* in more detail in the next chapter, but in this case, it means you cannot modify the way existing operators operate on fundamental types or array types. In other words, you cannot, for instance, make integer addition perform multiplication. While it would be great fun to see what would happen, we're sure you'll agree that this is a fair restriction.

These restrictions notwithstanding, you have some freedom when it comes to operator overloading. But it's not because you *can* overload an operator that it necessarily follows that you *should*. When in doubt, always remember the following key guideline:

▓ **Tip** The main purpose of operator overloading is to increase both the ease of writing and the readability of code that uses your class. The fact that overloaded operators make for more compact code should always come second. Compact yet incomprehensible or even misleading code is no good to anyone. Making sure your code is both easy to write and easy to read is what matters. One consequence is that you should, at all costs, avoid overloaded operators that do not behave as expected from their built-in counterparts.

Obviously, it's a good idea to make your version of a standard operator reasonably consistent with its normal usage, or at least intuitive in its meaning and operation. It wouldn't be sensible to produce an overloaded + operator for a class that performed the equivalent of a multiplication. But it can be more subtle than that. Suppose we defined the equality operator for Box objects like this:

```
bool Box::operator==(const Box& aBox) const { return volume() == aBox.volume(); }
```

Seems sensible, and it's nicely analogous to the < operator we defined before. Still, this unconventional definition of operator == could easily lead to confusion. Suppose, for example, that we create these two Box objects:

```
Box oneBox { 1, 2, 3 };
Box otherBox { 1, 1, 6 };
```

Would you then consider these two boxes "equal"? Most likely the answer is that you don't. After all, they have significantly different dimensions. If you order a box with dimensions 1 × 2 × 3, you would not be pleased if you receive one with dimensions 1 × 1 × 6. Nevertheless, with our definition of operator==(), the expression oneBox == otherBox would evaluate to true. This could easily lead to misunderstandings and therefore bugs.

This is how most programmers would expect an equality operator for Box to be defined:

```
bool Box::operator==(const Box& otherBox) const
{
  return m_width == otherBox.m_width
     && m_length == otherBox.m_length
     && m_height == otherBox.m_height;
}
```

Which definition you use will depend on your application and how you expect Boxes to be used. But in this case, we believe it is best to stick with our second, more intuitive, definition of operator==(). The reason is that it probably leads to the least number of surprises. When programmers see ==, they think "is equal to," not "has same volume as." If need be, you can always introduce a member function called hasSameVolumeAs() to check for equal volumes. Yes, hasSameVolumeAs() involves more typing than ==, but it does ensure your code remains readable and predictable—and that is far more important!

Most of the remainder of this chapter is about teaching you similar conventions regarding operator overloading. You should deviate from these conventions only if you have a good reason.

▨ **Caution** One concrete consequence of our key guideline for operators is that you should never overload the logical operators && or ||. If you want logical operators for objects of your class, overloading & and | instead is generally preferable. The reason is that overloaded && and || will never behave quite like their built-in counterparts. Recall from Chapter 4 that if the left operand of the built-in && operator evaluates to false, its right operand does not get evaluated. Similarly, for the built-in || operator, the right-side operand is never evaluated if the left-side operand evaluates to true. You can never obtain this *short-circuit evaluation* with overloaded operators.[1] Because an overloaded operator is essentially equivalent to a regular function, all operands to an overloaded operator are always evaluated before entering the function's

---

[1] Prior to C++17, it was not even guaranteed that the left operand of an overloaded && or || operator would be evaluated before the right operand like it is for the built-in operators. That is, the compiler was allowed to evaluate the right operand before it even started evaluating the left operand. This would have made for another potential source of subtle bugs. This was also the reason that prior to C++17 overloading the comma operator (,) was generally discouraged.

body. For overloaded && and || operators, this means that both the left and right operands will always be evaluated. Because users of any && and || operator will expect the familiar short-circuit evaluation, overloading them would thus easily lead to some subtle bugs. When overloading & and | instead, you make it clear not to expect short-circuit evaluation.

Operator Function Idioms

The remainder of this chapter is all about introducing commonly accepted patterns and best practices regarding the when and how of operator overloading. There are only a few real restrictions for operator functions. But with great flexibility comes great responsibility. We will teach you when and how to overload various operators and the various conventions C++ programmers typically follow in this context. If you adhere to these conventions, your classes and their operators will behave predictably, which will make them easy to use and thus reduce the risk of bugs.

All the binary operators that can be overloaded always have operator functions of the form that you've seen in the previous section. When an operator, Op, is overloaded and the left operand is an object of the class for which Op is being overloaded, the member function defining the overload is of the following form:

```
ReturnType operator Op(Type right_operand) const;
```

In principle, you are entirely free to choose ReturnType or to create overloads for any number of parameter Types. It is also entirely up to you to choose whether you declare the member function as const. Other than the number of parameters, the language imposes nearly no constraints on the signature or return types of operator functions. For most operators, though, there are certain accepted conventions, which you should as much as possible try to respect. These conventions are nearly always motivated by the way the default built-in operators behave. For comparison operators such as <, >=, and !=, for instance, ReturnType is typically bool. And because these operators normally do not modify their operands, they usually are defined as const members that accept their argument either by value or by const reference—but never by non-const reference. Besides convention and common sense, however, there is nothing stopping you from returning a string from operator<() or from creating a != operator that doubles a Box's volume when used, or even one that causes a typhoon halfway around the world. You'll learn more about the various conventions throughout the remainder of this chapter.

You can implement most binary operators as nonmember functions as well, using this form:

```
ReturnType operator Op(const ClassType& left_operand, Type right_operand);
```

ClassType is the class for which you are overloading the operator. Type can be any type, including ClassType. As can be read from Table 13-1, the only binary operator that cannot be implemented as a nonmember function this way is the assignment operator, operator=().

If the left operand for a binary operator is of class Type, and Type is not the class for which the operator function is being defined, then the function must be implemented as a global operator function of this form:

```
ReturnType operator Op(Type left_operand, const ClassType& right_operand);
```

We'll give you some further guidelines for choosing between the member and nonmember forms of operator functions later in this chapter.

You have no flexibility in the number of parameters for most operator functions—either as class members or as global functions. You *must* use the number of parameters specified for the particular operator. Unary operators defined as member functions don't usually require a parameter. The post-increment and post-decrement operators are exceptions, as you'll see. The general form of a unary operator function for the operation Op as a member of the ClassType class is as follows:

```
ClassType& operator Op() const;
```

Naturally, unary operators defined as global functions have a single parameter that is the operand. The prototype for a global operator function for a unary operator Op is as follows:

```
ClassType& operator Op(const ClassType& obj);
```

We won't go through examples of overloading every operator, as most of them are similar to the ones you've seen. However, we will explain the details of operators that have particular idiosyncrasies when you overload them. We'll begin by wrapping up the discussion on comparison operators.

Supporting All Comparison Operators

Having implemented < and == for the Box class, that only leaves >, <=, >=, and !=. Of course, you could simply plow on and define these as well. And there would be nothing wrong with that. All it takes is an extra ten functions. Easy peasy. C++20, however, introduced a far more appealing alternative—and it's out of this world!

If you overload the spaceship operator, <=>, for your class, you automagically get complete support for all four *relational operators* (<, >, <=, and >=), free of charge. And if you overload ==, you similarly get a working != operator as well. There's thus rarely a need to define custom <, >, <=, >=, or != operators anymore in modern C++. The only comparison operators that you still have to overload are <=> and/or ==. Moreover, quite often, the compiler can even generate their definitions for you. But before we explain when the compiler can take this off your hands, let's first see how you define <=> and == operators yourself. As always, we use the Box class as an example.

```
// Box.cppm
export module box;

import std; // For std::partial_ordering (see Chapter 4)

export class Box
{
public:
  // ...
  // Same constructors and member functions as in Ex13_02, except no operator<.

  std::partial_ordering operator<=>(const Box& otherBox) const
  {
    return volume() <=> otherBox.volume();
  }
  std::partial_ordering operator<=>(double otherVolume) const
  {
    return volume() <=> otherVolume;
  }
```

```
  bool operator==(const Box& otherBox) const
  {
    return m_length == otherBox.m_length
        && m_width  == otherBox.m_width
        && m_height == otherBox.m_height;
  }

private:
  double m_length {1.0};
  double m_width {1.0};
  double m_height {1.0};
};
```

An overload of the <=> operator should return one of the three comparison category types defined by the <compare> Standard Library module: std::partial_ordering, weak_ordering, or strong_ordering (see Chapter 4). Here we opted for std::partial_ordering.

As argued before, we do not consider two boxes with the same volume to be equal, unless they also have the same dimensions. Labeling them *equivalent makes sense, yes,* but they are not *equal* (see also Chapter 4 for the difference between "equivalent" and "equal"). So that rules out std::strong_ordering.

Which leaves partial_ordering and weak_ordering. In Chapter 4 you saw that comparing two floating-point values with operator <=> results in a value of type partial_ordering (because one or both operands could be not-a-number). While we do not expect Boxes to ever have dimensions that are not-a-number, there is nothing in place to prevent this either (exceptions could help with this; see Chapter 16). Which means that, at least in theory, the volume() of a Box could be not-a-number as well. And so, in theory, comparing two Boxes could result in std::partial_ordering::unordered. Not to mention that the input to Box::operator<=>(double) could just as easily be not-a-number as well, of course. This is why partial_ordering is not only the easiest, but also a fitting choice for both our overloads of <=>.

▨ **Tip** There will be times where you do prefer a strong ordering for comparisons that involve comparing floating-point values—if need be, under the precondition that these values are never not-a-number. The std::strong_order() function can then be of help; when passed two floating-point numbers, be it not-a-number or not, std::strong_order() always produces a sensible value of type std::strong_ordering. (It even strongly orders different not-a-number values on most architectures, although in practice, you'll mostly not care about this possibility.)

What matters most in our example, though, is that by defining just *three* operator functions (instead of the *seventeen* we would've needed otherwise!), our latest Box class now has *full* support for all *seven* comparison operators (<, >, <=, >=, ==, !=, and <=>). That is, not only can you now compare two Boxes using any of these operators, but you can also compare Boxes with values of type double (and vice versa!) using <, >, <=, >=, or <=>. The following program confirms this:

```
// Ex13_03.cpp - Overloading <=> and == to fully support all comparison operators
import std;
import box;

int main()
{
  const std::vector boxes {Box {2.0, 1.5, 3.0}, Box {1.0, 3.0, 5.0},
```

```
                        Box {1.0, 2.0, 1.0}, Box {2.0, 3.0, 2.0}};
    const Box theBox {3.0, 1.0, 4.0};

    for (const auto& box : boxes)
      if (theBox > box)   // > works
        std::println("{} is greater than {}", to_string(theBox), to_string(box));
    std::println("");

    for (const auto& box : boxes)
      if (theBox != box)  // != works
        std::println("{} is not equal to {}", to_string(theBox), to_string(box));

    std::println("");

  for (const auto& box : boxes)
      if (6.0 <= box)      // Yes, even double <= Box works!!
        std::println("6 is less than or equal to {}", to_string(box));
}
```

The last few lines of this program prove that even `6.0 <= box` indeed works (pardon the pun) out of the box. This is remarkable since we no longer defined any operator with `double` as the first operand type. The reason that `6.0 <= box` works is that, whenever a C++20 compiler fails to find a dedicated `<=` operator, it attempts to rewrite expressions of the form `x <= y` to either `is_lteq(x <=> y)` or `is_gteq(y <=> x)`[2], in that order (see Chapter 4 for these named comparison functions). The expression `6.0 <= box` is therefore evaluated as if by `is_gteq(box <=> 6.0)` (notice the swapping of the operand order!).

The compiler analogously rewrites all expressions containing `<`, `>`, or `>=` in terms of operator `<=>` (provided of course no dedicated operator is found).

The compiler does *not*, however, rewrite expressions containing `==` or `!=` in terms of `<=>`. In general, doing so could lead to suboptimal performance[3]. Luckily, the compiler does rewrite expressions containing `!=` in terms of operator `==`, so at least we no longer have to supply an overload for `!=`.

▓ **Tip**   Even if the compiler will never do it, you yourself are free to express `==` in terms of `<=>`. In fact, in many cases that will work just fine.

---

[2] In actuality, the compiler will not use the named comparison functions `std::is_lteq()` or `std::is_gteq()`. These are just meant for us, mere humans, to make our code readable. But the generated code will be equivalent.
[3] Consider the `==` and `!=` operators of `std::string`. Now suppose you are comparing the strings "Little Lily Lovelace likes licking luscious lemon lollipops" and "Little Lily Lovelace likes lasagna". Simply by comparing their length, operators `==` and `!=` can then instantly determine that these two strings cannot possibly be equal. Operator `<=>`, however, has to work harder; to order these two strings, it has to compare at least 29 characters. Unlike `==` and `!=`, the `<=>` operator cannot stop after comparing the lengths of the strings. "lasagna" comes before "licking luscious lemon lollipops", naturally, but not because it's a shorter string. This illustrates why rewriting `==` and `!=` expressions in terms of `<=>` may lead to suboptimal performance.

In the case of the Box class, however, we already argued why we prefer a true equality operator over a has-equal-volume operator. And so we plugged in the equality operator from earlier. From the output of Ex13_03 you will be able to see that the compiler indeed uses the == operator to evaluate theBox != box, and not the <=> operator; otherwise, the output would not have contained the line "Box(3.0, 1.0, 4.0) is not equal to Box(2.0, 3.0, 2.0)" (both Boxes have the same volume, 12).

▒ **Tip**   You can also create overloads of the == operator that compare objects of your class with values of other types. And here too one overload per type suffices, as the compiler will swap the order of the operands in == and != expressions for you if needed.(We will ask you to work out an example of this in the exercises at the end of this chapter.)

▒ **Caution**   The <utility> module of the Standard Library offers a set of operator templates in the std::rel_ops namespace that define operators <=, >, >=, and != for any type T in terms of T's < and == operators. This solution has its fair share of flaws, though, and should no longer be used.

Defaulting Comparison Operators

Compared to earlier versions of C++, having to implement at most two comparison operators is tremendous progress. Nevertheless, even defining two operators quickly turns into a boring, repetitive chore. And what is worse, it is an *error-prone*, boring, repetitive chore. Consider for instance the == operator you wrote for the Box class in Ex13_03 (moved out of the class definition here for illustration purposes):

```
bool Box::operator==(const Box& otherBox) const
{
   return m_length == otherBox.m_length
       && m_width  == otherBox.m_width
       && m_height == otherBox.m_height;
}
```

Now image that Box had a dozen more member variables. Or that you had to define the same operator for a dozen more classes. Boring and repetitive, right? Now image you are adding a member variable to the Box class, say a few months later. How easy would it then be to forget to update this == operator? Believe us, we have encountered many out-of-date comparison operators already in legacy code (as well as some subtle bugs that were caused by them!).

It's a good thing, then, that we know someone who truly excels at churning out repetitive code: our trusty old friend, the C++ compiler. And he does not even consider this boring at all. All you have to do is ask nicely, and he'll happily generate (and, more importantly, forever maintain!) your comparison operators for you. The required syntax is analogous to the one you use for defaulted constructors (see Chapter 12):

```
bool Box::operator==(const Box& otherBox) const = default;
```

Of course, you can, and often will, default these operators directly in-class. In that case, you omit the Box:: prefix. A defaulted == operator compares all member variables in order of their declaration—precisely like the == operator you originally wrote for Box. So for the Box class, defaulting the == operator works out perfectly. You can find a Box class that is simplified along these lines in Ex13_03A.

> ▓ **Caution** If not all member variables of `MyClass` have an accessible non-deleted `==` operator, defaulting `==` for `MyClass` will result in an implicitly deleted operator `==`. That is, `= default` then has the same effect as adding `= delete` (see also Chapter 12 for this syntax).

While in principle you can default all seven comparison operators (`==`, `!=`, `<=>`, `<`, `>`, `<=`, and `>=`), it normally again suffices to default only `<=>` and/or `==`. Normally, you will never default any of the other five operators.[4] In fact, typically, you'll only have to default one operator, `<=>`, as implied by the following Tip:

> ▓ **Tip** Whenever you default the `<=>` operator, the compiler adds a defaulted `==` operator as well. So if the default behavior for all comparison operators suits you, you only have to default one single operator function anymore: `<=>`. Easy peasy lemon squeezy!

Let's focus now on defaulting the `<=>` operator. In an attempt to further reduce the size of the Box class of Ex13_03A, for instance, you could default its `<=>` operator like this (or directly inside the class definition, of course):

```
std::partial_ordering Box::operator<=>(const Box& otherBox) const = default;
```

In fact, you could even save yourself some more typing and use `auto` as the return type here instead (see also Chapter 8). The compiler then deduces the return type based on the `<=>` operators of the class's member variables. Because all three member variables of the Box class are doubles, the compiler would then indeed deduce `std::partial_ordering` for the following definition:

```
auto Box::operator<=>(const Box& otherBox) const = default;
```

But what does a defaulted `<=>` operator do exactly? Naturally, the defaulted `<=>` operator for Box will not compare boxes by their `volume()`. The day that the compiler can figure out that Boxes should be compared by their volume is the day that we should scramble to deactivate Skynet. No, instead this defaulted `<=>` operator performs a *member-wise lexicographical comparison*. In other words, it compares all corresponding member variables of the left and right operands in the order of their declaration, using their respective `<=>` operators. And as soon as it then finds a pair of variables that is not equivalent, the result of their comparison is returned.

To clarify, for the Box class, the generated `<=>` function would thus be equivalent to this:

```
std::partial_ordering Box::operator<=>(const Box& otherBox) const
{
  // See Chapter 4 for the 'if (initialization; condition)' syntax
  if (std::partial_ordering order = (m_length <=> otherBox.m_length); std::is_neq(order))
    return order;
```

---

[4] Defaulted `!=` and `<`, `>`, `<=`, or `>=` operators are evaluated in terms of `==` and `<=>`, respectively, as always. The only reason you would ever define or default these operators in modern C++ is to allow taking the address of these functions. In practice, however, you mostly use function objects in C++ (see Chapter 19), and there's scarcely ever a need to work with function pointers.

```
  if (std::partial_ordering order = (m_width <=> otherBox.m_width); std::is_neq(order))
    return order;
  return m_height <=> otherBox.m_height; // return even if both heights are equivalent...
}
```

That is clearly quite a lot of code already. If member-wise lexicographical comparison suits you, it is therefore truly a blessing that the compiler can generate (and maintain!) it for you. For our Box class, however, we will not be using a defaulted <=> operator; we will stick to our volume-based definition instead. The reason is that that definition fits better with the way we currently use Boxes in our applications.

■ **Tip** In practice you will often not care precisely how your objects are ordered—as long as they are ordered in an efficient and consistent way. A defaulted <=> operator is then typically perfectly adequate. If the goal is simply to sort a collection of Box objects for more efficient processing, for instance, or to use them as keys for ordered associative containers (see Chapter 20), then you really do not care whether Boxes are sorted lexicographically or by volume. In fact, for applications such as these, the stronger lexicographical order is even preferred over the weaker volume-based order!

■ **Caution** If not all member variables of MyClass have an accessible non-deleted <=> operator, 'auto MyClass::operator<=>(const MyClass&) const = default;' again results in a deleted <=> operator. As explained next, you could then be better off not using auto as the return type.

The previous warning is especially relevant today. Because the spaceship operator <=> was introduced only in C++20, many class types will not support it yet. All fundamental types do already, as do all relevant types of the Standard Library. But user-defined types generally will not yet support <=>.

But it's not all bad news. Luckily, many legacy types do support (at least) operators < and ==. And, luckily, the compiler is capable of synthesizing defaulted <=> operators that compare variables of such legacy types using their == and < operators instead of their missing <=> operators. Your only job then is to help the compiler out by specifying which comparison category it should use for the defaulted <=> operator. That is, if a defaulted <=> operator is to use == and < to compare member variables of legacy types, you cannot use auto as the return type; you then have to explicitly specify std::partial_ordering, weak_ordering, or strong_ordering as the return type.

That concludes what we wanted to say about the comparison operators. In summary:

■ **Tip** To allow any comparisons *between two objects of your own class*, you only need two operators (be it explicitly or implicitly): <=> and ==. Both are typically implemented as a member function. Whenever the default lexicographic comparison is okay, you should default these operator overloads, so the compiler will generate (and *maintain!*) their definitions for you. When you default <=>, the compiler moreover automatically defaults == as well, saving you one more line of typing. You can also have the compiler auto-deduce the return type of a defaulted <=> operator, but only if all member variables support <=>. Otherwise, you should specify partial_ordering, weak_ordering, or strong_ordering explicitly, to allow the compiler to synthesize a <=> operator based on the < and == operators of the class's member variables.

To allow any comparisons between an object of your class *and values of some other type*, you again only have to overload <=> and/or ==. And you no longer need nonmember functions for this; the compiler conveniently swaps the operand order for you where needed. Operators for comparisons between different types can never be defaulted, though. Not until Skynet becomes self-aware, at least...

It's high time we turn our attention to other operators. We begin with the most common family of overloads for the << operator.

Overloading the << Operator for Output Streams

Compared to streaming to std::cout, C++23's std::print() functionality is both more compact and more efficient (and just as safe). We therefore haven't really used the stream output operator << yet in this edition of the book. Regardless, output in C++ is still often handled through streams. Not only to stream to standard output, mind you, but also to files, network sockets, and so on. It remains important that you understand how to overload the streaming operators.

Of course, to stream a Box to std::cout, you could always convert it to a string first, analogous to what you did in Ex13_03 earlier:

```
std::cout << to_string(theBox) << " is greater than " << to_string(box);
```

But this is not ideal, neither in syntax nor performance (creating the transient std::string object, as always, comes at a small cost). But now that we know how to overload operators, we could make stream output statements for Box objects feel more natural by overloading the << operator for output streams. This would then allow us to simply write this:

```
std::cout << theBox << " is greater than " << box;
```

But, how do we overload this << operator? As a first step, we'll add parentheses to our running example to clarify the associativity of the << operator:

```
((std::cout << theBox) << " is greater than ") << box;
```

The innermost << expression will be evaluated first. So, the following is equivalent:

```
auto& something{ (std::cout << theBox) };
(something << " is greater than ") << box;
```

Naturally, the only way this could ever work is if something, the result of the innermost expression, is again a reference to a stream. To clarify things further, we can also use function-call notation for operator<<() as follows:

```
auto& stream1{ operator<<(std::cout, theBox) };
(stream1 << " is greater than ") << box;
```

Using a few more similar rewrite steps, we can spell out every step the compiler takes to evaluate the entire statement:

```
auto& stream0 = std::cout;
auto& stream1 = operator<<(stream0, theBox);
auto& stream2 = operator<<(stream1, " is greater than ");
auto& stream3 = operator<<(stream2, box);
```

While this is quite verbose, it makes clear the point we wanted to make. This particular overload of operator<<() takes two arguments: a reference to a stream object (left operand) and the actual value to output (right operand). It then returns a fresh reference to a stream that can be passed along to the next call of operator<<() in the chain. This is an example of what we called *method chaining* in Chapter 12.

Once you understand this, deciphering the function definition that overloads this operator for Box objects should be straightforward:

```
export std::ostream& operator<<(std::ostream& stream, const Box& box)
{
  stream << std::setprecision(1) << std::fixed; // Same as .1f format specifier
  stream << "Box(" << box.getLength() << ", "
                   << box.getWidth() << ", " << box.getHeight() << ')';
  return stream;
}
```

The first parameter identifies the left operand as an std::ostream object, and the second specifies the right operand as a Box object. The standard output stream, std::cout, for instance, is of type std::ostream. Because we cannot add the << operator overload as a member of std::ostream, we have no choice but to define it as a nonmember function instead. Because the dimensions of a Box object are publicly available, we do not have to use a friend declaration. The value that is returned is, and always should be, a reference to the same stream object as referred to by the operator's left operand.

To configure the formatting of the three floating-point numbers, we first insert the std::setprecision() and std::fixed stream manipulators into the stream (see also Chapter 2). Since streams use the exact same concepts as std::print() and std::format() (concepts such as precision, width, fill characters, fixed formatting, and so on), you should have no trouble figuring out what these manipulators do. Most manipulators influence the formatting of all subsequent values inserted into the stream. This is why we only had to insert std::setprecision() and std::fixed into std::cout once. The only exception to this rule is std::setw(), which only determines the width of the next formatted field, after which a stream's width property resets back to default (zero).

To test our << operator, you can add its definition to the box module of Ex13_03A. In the main() function of Ex13_03A, you can then replace all std::println() statements with equivalent statements that use the << operator (std::endl inserts a newline character and "flushes" any buffered text further down the stream):

```
std::cout << theBox << " is greater than " << box << std::endl;
```

You can find the resulting program in Ex13_04.

■ **Note** Overloading the stream extraction >> for std::istreams (such as std::cin) is completely analogous to overloading the stream insertion operator for std::ostreams (such as std::cout). We'll ask you to do this in the exercises at the end of the chapter.

▓ **Note**   The << and >> operators of the stream classes of the Standard Library are prime examples of the fact that overloaded operators do not always have to be equivalent to their built-in counterparts—recall that the built-in << and >> operators perform bitwise shifts of integers! Another nice example is the convention to use the + and += operators to concatenate strings, something you have already used repeatedly with std::string objects. The fact that until now you may not have given much thought to how and why such expressions work just proves that, if used judiciously, overloaded operators can lead to very natural coding.

Overloading the Arithmetic Operators

We'll explain how you overload the arithmetic operators by looking at how you might overload the addition operator for the Box class. This is an interesting example because addition is a binary operation that involves creating and returning a new object. The new object will be the sum (whatever you define that to mean) of the two Box objects that are its operands.

What might the sum of two Box objects mean? There are several possibilities we could consider, but because the primary purpose of a box is to hold something, its volumetric capacity is of primary interest, so we might reasonably presume that the sum of two boxes is a new box that could hold both. Using this assumption, we'll define the sum of two Box objects to be a Box object that's large enough to contain the two original boxes stacked on top of each other. This is consistent with the notion that the class might be used for packaging because adding several Box objects together results in a Box object that can contain all of them.

You can implement the addition operator in a simple way, as follows. The m_length member of the new object will be the larger of the m_length members of the objects being summed, and a m_width member will be determined in a similar way. If the m_height member is the sum of the m_height members of the operands, the resultant Box object can contain the two Box objects. By modifying the constructor, we'll arrange that the m_length member of an object is always greater than or equal to the m_width member.

Figure 13-2 illustrates the Box object that will be produced by adding two Box objects. Because the result of this addition is a new Box object, the function implementing addition must return a Box object. If the function that overloads the + operator is to be a member function, then the declaration of the function in the Box class definition can be as follows:

```
Box operator+(const Box& aBox) const;        // Adding two Box objects
```

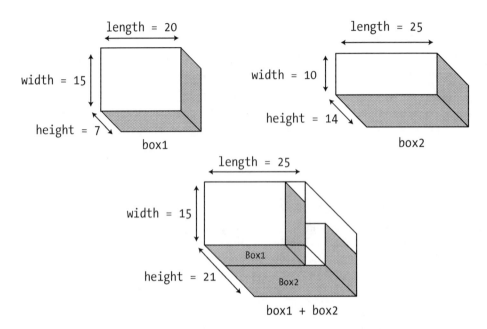

Figure 13-2. *The object that results from adding two Box objects*

The aBox parameter is const because the function won't modify the argument, which is the right operand. It's a const reference to avoid unnecessary copying of the right operand. The function itself is specified as const because it doesn't alter the left operand. The definition of the member function in Box.cppm will be as follows:

```
// Operator function to add two Box objects
Box Box::operator+(const Box& aBox) const
{
  // New object has larger length and width, and sum of heights
  return Box{ std::max(m_length, aBox.m_length),
              std::max(m_width, aBox.m_width),
              m_height + aBox.m_height };
}
```

As is conventional for an arithmetic operator, a local Box object is created and returned to the calling program. Of course, as this is a new object, returning it by reference must never be done. The box's dimensions are computed using std::max(), which simply returns the maximum of two given arguments. It is instantiated from a function template in the <algorithm> module. This template works for any argument type that supports operator<(). An analogous std::min() function template to compute the minimum of two expressions exists as well.

We can see how the addition operator works in an example. We'll start from a box module similar to that of previous examples again:

```cpp
// Box.cppm
export module box;
import std;

export class Box
{
public:
  Box() = default;        // Default constructor
  Box(double length, double width, double height)
    : m_length{ std::max(length,width) }
    , m_width { std::min(length,width) }
    , m_height{ height }
  {}

  double volume() const; // Function to calculate the volume

  // Accessors
  double getLength() const { return m_length; }
  double getWidth() const  { return m_width; }
  double getHeight() const { return m_height; }

  // Functions that add full support for comparison operators
  std::partial_ordering operator<=>(const Box& aBox) const;
  std::partial_ordering operator<=>(double value) const;
  bool operator==(const Box& aBox) const = default;

  Box operator+(const Box& aBox) const;   // Function to add two Box objects

private:
  double m_length {1.0};
  double m_width {1.0};
  double m_height {1.0};
};

// ... Include definitions of
//      - the operator<=>() and volume() member functions of Ex13_03A
//      - the to_string() nonmember function of Ex13_03A
//      - the new operator+() member function
```

The first important difference is the second constructor, which uses std::min() and max() to ensure a Box's length is always larger than its width. The second difference, of course, is the addition of the declaration of operator+().

Here's the code to try it:

```
// Ex13_05.cpp - Using the addition operator for Box objects
import std;
import box;

auto createUniformPseudoRandomNumberGenerator(double max)
{
  std::random_device seeder;         // True random number generator to obtain a seed (slow)
  std::default_random_engine generator{seeder()};      // Efficient pseudo-random generator
  std::uniform_real_distribution distribution{1.0, max}; // Generate in [1, max) interval
  return std::bind(distribution, generator);           //... and in the darkness bind them!
}

int main()
{
  const double limit {99};          // Upper limit on Box dimensions
  auto random { createUniformPseudoRandomNumberGenerator(limit) };

  const std::size_t boxCount {20}; // Number of Box objects to be created
  std::vector<Box> boxes;          // Vector of Box objects

  // Create 20 Box objects
  for (std::size_t i {}; i < boxCount; ++i)
    boxes.push_back(Box{ random(), random(), random() });

  std::size_t first {};            // Index of first Box object of pair
  std::size_t second {1};          // Index of second Box object of pair
  double minVolume {(boxes[first] + boxes[second]).volume()};

  for (std::size_t i {}; i < boxCount - 1; ++i)
  {
    for (std::size_t j {i + 1}; j < boxCount; j++)
    {
      if (boxes[i] + boxes[j] < minVolume)
      {
        first = i;
        second = j;
        minVolume = (boxes[i] + boxes[j]).volume();
      }
    }
  }

  std::println("The two boxes that sum to the smallest volume are {} and {}",
               to_string(boxes[first]), to_string(boxes[second]));
  std::println("The volume of the first box is {:.1f}", boxes[first].volume());
  std::println("The volume of the second box is {:.1f}", boxes[second].volume());
  std::println("The sum of these boxes is {}", to_string(boxes[first] + boxes[second]));
  std::println("The volume of the sum is {:.1f}", minVolume);
}
```

We got the following output:

```
The two boxes that sum to the smallest volume are Box(39.8, 4.9, 17.0) and Box(24.7, 8.8,
25.6)
The volume of the first box is 3341.7
The volume of the second box is 5586.6
The sum of these boxes is Box(39.8, 8.8, 42.6)
The volume of the sum is 14964.9
```

You should get a different result each time you run the program. Refer to Chapter 12 for an explanation of the createUniformPseudoRandomNumberGenerator() function.

The main() function generates a vector of 20 Box objects that have arbitrary dimensions from 1 to 99. The nested for loops then test all possible pairs of Box objects to find the pair that combines to the minimum volume. The if statement in the inner loop uses the operator+() member to produce a Box object that is the sum of the current pair of objects. The operator<=>() member is then (implicitly) used to compare the resultant Box object to the value of minVolume (remember, the compiler essentially rewrites boxes[i] + boxes[j] < minVolume to std::is_lt(boxes[i] + boxes[j] <=> minVolume)). The output shows that everything works as it should. We suggest you instrument the operator functions and the Box constructors just to see when and how often they are called.

Of course, you can use the overloaded addition operator in more complex expressions to sum Box objects. For example, you could write this:

```
Box box4 {box1 + box2 + box3};
```

This calls the operator+() member twice to create a Box object that is the sum of the three, and this is passed to the copy constructor for the Box class to create box4. The result is a Box object box4 that can contain the other three Box objects stacked on top of each other.

Implementing One Operator in Terms of Another

One thing always leads to another. If you implement the addition operator for a class, you inevitably create the expectation that the += operator will work too. If you are going to implement both, it's worth noting that you can implement + in terms of += very economically.

First, we'll define += for the Box class. Because assignment is involved, convention dictates that the operator function returns a reference:

```
// Overloaded += operator
Box& Box::operator+=(const Box& aBox)
{
  // Updated object has larger length and width, and sum of heights
  m_length = std::max(m_length, aBox.m_length);
  m_width  = std::max(m_width, aBox.m_width);
  m_height += aBox.m_height;
  return *this;
}
```

This is straightforward. You simply modify the left operand, *this, by adding the right operand according to the definition of addition for Box objects. The convention to return a reference-to-this from compound assignment operators is motivated by the fact that it enables statements that use the result of an assignment expression in a bigger expression. You already saw this in action for the << stream operator, and you will encounter it again when we discuss the overloading of increment and decrement operators.

You can now implement operator+() using operator+=(), so the definition of operator+() simplifies to the following:

```
// Function to add two Box objects
Box Box::operator+(const Box& aBox) const
{
  Box copy{*this};
  copy += aBox;
  return copy;
}
```

The first line of the function body calls the copy constructor to create a copy of the left operand to use in the addition. The operator+=() function is then called to add the right operand object, aBox, to the new Box object. This object is then returned.

Ex13_06 contains a box module that started from that of Ex13_05, but with the addition operators implemented as described in this section. With this new definition of Box, you can easily modify the main() function of Ex13_05 as well to try the new += operator. In Ex13_06.cpp, for instance, we did this as follows:

```
int main()
{
  // Generate boxCount random Box objects as before in Ex13_05...

  Box sum{0, 0, 0};                  // Start from an empty Box
  for (const auto& box : boxes)  // And then add all randomly generated Box objects
    sum += box;

  std::println("The sum of {} random boxes is {}", boxCount, to_string(sum));
}
```

▓ **Tip** Always implement a binary arithmetic operator *op*() in terms of the corresponding arithmetic assignment operator *op=*().

Member vs. Nonmember Functions

Both Ex13_05 and Ex13_06 define operator+() as a member function of the Box class. You can, however, just as easily implement this addition operation as a nonmember function. Here's the prototype of such a function:

```
Box operator+(const Box& aBox, const Box& bBox);
```

Because the dimensions of a Box object are accessible through public member functions, no friend declarations are required. But even if the values of the member variables were inaccessible, you could still just define the operator as a friend function. And that begs the question: Which of these options is best? A member function? A nonmember function? Or a friend function?

Of all your options, a friend function is generally seen as the least desirable. While there is not always a viable alternative, friend declarations undermine data hiding and should therefore be avoided when possible.

The choice between a member function and a nonfriend nonmember function, however, is not always as clear-cut. Operator functions are fundamental to class capability, so we mostly prefer to implement them as class members. This makes the operations integral to the type, which puts this right at the core of encapsulation. Your default option should probably be to define operator overloads as member functions. But there are at least two cases where you should implement them as nonmember functions instead.

First, there are circumstances where you have no choice but to implement them as nonmember functions, even if this means you must resort to friend functions. These include overloads of binary operators for which the first argument is either a fundamental type or a type different from the class you are currently writing. We have already seen examples of both categories:

```
bool operator<(double value, const Box& box);      // double cannot have members
ostream& operator<<(ostream& stream, const Box& box);  // cannot add ostream members
```

▓ **Note**   Once one of the overloads of an operator needs to be a nonmember function, you might decide to turn all other overloads into nonmember functions as well for consistency. For instance, suppose you define a multiplication operator for the Box class (left as an exercise to you):

```
bool operator*(double, const Box&); // Must be nonmember functionbool
operator*(const Box&, double); // Symmetrical case often done for consistency
```

Only the first of these two overloads really needs to be a nonmember function. Your compiler will only ever attempt to swap the operand order for the operators <, >, <=, >=, ==, !=, and <=> (see earlier).[5] To obtain mixed-type support for any other binary operator (operators such as +, -, *, /, %, |, and &), you still need at least one nonmember function. Turning the function for the other operand order into a nonmember function as well, though, allows you to nicely group these declarations together in your source code.

But there is one more reason you might sometimes prefer nonmember functions over member functions, and that is when implicit conversions are desired for the left operand of a binary operator. We'll discuss this case in the next subsection.

---

[5] Technically, the compiler will only reorder the arguments of <=> and ==. But since it will also rewrite <, >, <=, >=, and != in terms of <=> or ==, it's usually as if the compiler reorders the arguments of all comparison and equality operators.

Operator Functions and Implicit Conversions

As noted earlier in this and previous chapters, allowing implicit conversions from double to Box is not a good idea. Because such conversions would lead to unpleasant results, the corresponding single-argument constructor for Box should really be explicit. But this is not the case for all single-argument constructors. The Integer class you worked on earlier during the exercises in Chapter 12, for instance, provides a good example. At its essence, this class looked like this:

```
class Integer
{
public:
  Integer(int value = 0) : m_value{value} {}
  int getValue() const { return m_value; }
  void setValue(int value) { m_value = value; }
private:
  int m_value;
};
```

For this class, there is no harm in allowing implicit conversions. The main reason is that Integer objects are much closer to ints than Boxes are to doubles. Other examples of harmless (and convenient!) implicit conversions you already know about are those from string literals to std::string objects or T values to std::optional<T> objects.

For classes that allow implicit conversions, the general guideline for overloading operators as member functions typically changes. Consider the Integer class. Naturally, you'd like binary arithmetic operators such as operator+() for Integer objects. And, of course, you'd like them to work also for additions of the form Integer + int and int + Integer. Obviously, you could still define three operator functions like we did for the + operator of Box—two member functions and one nonmember one. But there is an easier option. All you need to do is define one single nonmember operator function as follows:

```
Integer operator+(const Integer& one, const Integer& other)
{
  return one.getValue() + other.getValue();
}
```

Put this function together with our simple class definition of Integer in a integer module. Add similar functions for -, *, /, and %. Because int values implicitly convert to Integer objects, these five operator functions then suffice to make the following test program work. Without relying on implicit conversions, you would've needed no less than 15 function definitions to cover all possibilities!

```
// Ex13_07.cpp - Implicit conversions reduce the number of operator functions
import std;
import integer;

int main()
{
  const Integer i{1};
  const Integer j{2};
  const auto result = (i * 2 + 4 / j - 1) % j;
  std::println("{}", result.getValue());
}
```

The reason you need to use nonmember functions to allow implicit conversions for either operand is that the compiler never performs conversions for the left operand of member functions. That is, if you'd define operator/() as a member function, an expression such as 4 / j would no longer compile.

▓ **Tip**   Operator overloads should be implemented mostly as member functions. Only use nonmember functions if a member function cannot be used or if implicit conversions are desired for the first operand.

Overloading Unary Operators

So far, we have only seen examples of overloading binary operators. But you can overload unary operators as well. For the sake of illustration, assume a common operation with boxes is to "rotate" them in the sense that their width and length are swapped. If this operation is indeed frequently used, you could be tempted to introduce an operator for it. Because rotation involves only a single Box—no additional operand is required—you'd have to pick one of the available unary operators. Viable candidates are +, -, ~, !, &, and *. From these, operator~() seems like a good pick. Just like binary operators, unary operators can be defined either as a member function or as a regular function. Starting again from the Box class from Ex13_03A, the former possibility would look like this:

```
class Box
{
public:
  // Constructors
  Box(double l, double w, double h) : m_length{l}, m_width{w}, m_height{h} {}

  Box operator~() const
  {
    return Box{m_width, m_length, m_height}; // Width and length are swapped
  }

  // Remainder of the Box class as before...
};
```

As convention dictates, operator~() returns a new object, just like we saw for the binary arithmetic operators that do not modify their left operand. Defining the Box "rotation" operator as a nonmember function should come easy by now as well:

```
Box operator~(const Box& box)
{
  return Box{ box.getWidth(), box.getLength(), box.getHeight() };
}
```

With either of these operator overloads in place, you could write code like the following:

```
Box someBox{ 1, 2, 3 };
std::println("{}", to_string( ~someBox ));
```

You can find this example in Ex13_08. If you run that program, you'll get this result:

```
Box(2.0, 1.0, 3.0)
```

■ **Note** Arguably, this operator overload violates our key guideline from earlier in this chapter. While it clearly leads to very compact code, it does *not* necessarily make for natural, readable code. Without looking at the class definition it is doubtful that any of your fellow programmers would ever guess what the expression ~someBox is doing. So, unless the notation ~someBox is commonplace in the world of packaging and boxes, you may be better off defining a regular function here instead, such as rotate() or getRotatedBox().

Overloading the Increment and Decrement Operators

The ++ and -- operators present a new problem for the functions that implement them for a class because they behave differently depending on whether they prefix the operand. You need two functions for each operator: one to be called in the prefix case and the other for the postfix case. The postfix form of the operator function for either operator is distinguished from the prefix form by the presence of a dummy parameter of type int. This parameter only serves to distinguish the two cases and is not otherwise used. The declarations for the functions to overload ++ for an arbitrary class, MyClass, will be as follows:

```cpp
class MyClass
{
public:
  MyClass& operator++();          // Overloaded prefix increment operator

  const MyClass operator++(int);  // Overloaded postfix increment operator

  // Rest of MyClass class definition...
};
```

The return type for the prefix form normally needs to be a reference to the current object, *this, after the increment operation has been applied to it. Here's how an implementation of the prefix form for the Box class might look:

```cpp
Box& Box::operator++()           // Prefix ++operator
{
  ++m_length;
  ++m_width;
  ++m_height;
  return *this;
}
```

This just increments each of the dimensions by one and then returns the current object.

For the postfix form of the operator, you should create a copy of the original object *before* you modify it; then return the *copy* of the original after the increment operation has been performed on the object. Here's how that might be implemented for the Box class:

```
const Box Box::operator++(int)   // Postfix operator++
{
  auto copy{*this};              // Create a copy of the current object
  ++(*this);                     // Increment the current object using the prefix operator...
  return copy;                   // Return the unincremented copy
}
```

In fact, the previous body could be used to implement any postfix increment operator in terms of its prefix counterpart. While optional, the return value for the postfix operator is sometimes declared const to prevent expressions such as theObject++++ from compiling. Such expressions are inelegant, confusing, and inconsistent with the normal behavior of the operator. If you don't declare the return type as const, such usage is possible.

■ **Tip** Always implement the postfix increment operator operator++(int) in terms of the prefix increment operator operator++().

The Ex13_09 example, part of the online download, contains a small test program that adds the prefix and postfix increment and decrement operators to the Box class of Ex13_04 and then takes them for a little test-drive in the following main() function:

```
int main()
{
  Box theBox {3.0, 1.0, 3.0};

  std::println("Our test Box is {}", to_string(theBox));

  std::println("Postfix increment evaluates to the original object: {}",
               to_string(theBox++));
  std::println("After postfix increment: {}", to_string(theBox));

  std::println("Prefix decrement evaluates to the decremented object: {}",
               to_string(--theBox));
  std::println("After prefix decrement: {}", to_string(theBox));
}
```

The output of this test program is as follows:

```
Our test Box is Box(3.0, 1.0, 3.0)
Postfix increment evaluates to the original object: Box(3.0, 1.0, 3.0)
After postfix increment: Box(4.0, 2.0, 4.0)
Prefix decrement evaluates to the decremented object: Box(3.0, 1.0, 3.0)
After prefix decrement: Box(3.0, 1.0, 3.0)
```

▪ **Note** The value returned by the postfix form of an increment or decrement operator should always be a copy of the original object before it was incremented or decremented; the value returned by the prefix form should always be a reference to the current (and thus incremented or decremented) object. The reason is that this is precisely how the corresponding built-in operators behave with fundamental types.

Overloading the Subscript Operator

The subscript operator, [ ], provides very interesting possibilities for certain kinds of classes. Clearly, this operator is aimed primarily at selecting one of a number of objects that you can interpret as an array, but where the objects could be contained in any one of a number of different containers. You can overload the subscript operator to access the elements of a sparse array (where many of the elements are empty), an associative array, or even a linked list. The data might even be stored in a file, and you could use the subscript operator to hide the complications of file input and output operations.

The Truckload classes from Chapter 12, for example, could support the subscript operator. A Truckload object contains an ordered set of objects, so the subscript operator could provide a means of accessing these objects through an index value. An index of 0 would return the first object in the list, an index of 1 would return the second, and so on. The inner workings of the subscript operator would take care of iterating through the list to find the required object.

The operator[]() function for the Truckload class needs to accept an index value as an argument that is a position in the list and to return the pointer to the Box object at that position. The declaration for the member function in the TruckLoad class is as follows:

```cpp
class Truckload
{
public:
  // Rest of the class as before...
  SharedBox operator[](std::size_t index) const;   // Overloaded subscript operator
  // ...
};
```

You could implement the function like this:

```cpp
SharedBox Truckload::operator[](std::size_t index) const
{
  std::size_t count {};         // Package count
  for (Package* package{m_head}; package; package = package->m_next)
  {
    if (count++ == index)       // Up to index yet?
      return package->m_box;    // If so return the pointer to Box
  }
  return nullptr;
}
```

The for loop traverses the list, incrementing the count on each iteration. When the value of count is the same as index, the loop has reached the Package object at position index, so the smart pointer to the Box object in that Package object is returned. If the entire list is traversed without count reaching the value of index, then index must be out of range, so nullptr is returned.

If you add the array subscript operator to the Truckload class in the Exercise 12-7 solution, you can use the following program to exercise this new operator:

```cpp
// Ex13_10.cpp - Using the subscript operator
import std;
import truckload;

// Add the createUniformPseudoRandomNumberGenerator() function from Ex13_05 here.

int main()
{
  const double limit {99.0};      // Upper limit on Box dimensions
  auto random{ createUniformPseudoRandomNumberGenerator(limit) };

  Truckload load;
  const std::size_t boxCount {16};    // Number of Box objects to be created

  // Create boxCount Box objects
  for (std::size_t i {}; i < boxCount; ++i)
    load.addBox(std::make_shared<Box>(random(), random(), random()));

  std::println("The boxes in the Truckload are:");
  load.printBoxes();

  // Find the largest Box in the Truckload
  double maxVolume {};
  std::size_t maxIndex {};
  std::size_t i {};
  while (load[i])
  {
    if (*load[i] > maxVolume)
    {
      maxIndex = i;
      maxVolume = load[i]->volume();
    }
    ++i;
  }

  std::println("\nThe largest box is: {}", to_string(*load[maxIndex]));

  load.removeBox(load[maxIndex]);

  std::println("\nAfter deleting the largest box, the Truckload contains:");
  load.printBoxes();
}
```

When we ran this example, it produced the following output:

```
The boxes in the Truckload are:
 Box(36.5,82.2,17.1) Box(61.7,4.0,14.7) Box(19.9,64.3,64.5) Box(56.5,77.1,56.3)
 Box(61.9,35.2,67.5) Box(52.6,38.1,47.7) Box(2.7,50.0,38.0) Box(59.3,66.7,57.5)
 Box(34.4,95.6,65.9) Box(33.0,88.8,74.8) Box(21.3,77.9,19.6) Box(22.8,24.5,50.1)
 Box(71.0,29.3,20.9) Box(12.4,47.4,11.7) Box(7.1,70.5,34.9) Box(26.3,41.2,53.4)

The largest box is: Box(56.5,77.1,56.3)

After deleting the largest box, the Truckload contains:
 Box(36.5,82.2,17.1) Box(61.7,4.0,14.7) Box(19.9,64.3,64.5) Box(61.9,35.2,67.5)
 Box(52.6,38.1,47.7) Box(2.7,50.0,38.0) Box(59.3,66.7,57.5) Box(34.4,95.6,65.9)
 Box(33.0,88.8,74.8) Box(21.3,77.9,19.6) Box(22.8,24.5,50.1) Box(71.0,29.3,20.9)
 Box(12.4,47.4,11.7) Box(7.1,70.5,34.9) Box(26.3,41.2,53.4)
```

The main() function now uses the subscript operator to access pointers to Box objects from the Truckload object. You can see from the output that the subscript operator works, and the result of finding and deleting the largest Box object is correct.

▓ **Caution** In the case of Truckload objects, the subscript operator masks a particularly inefficient process. Because it's easy to forget that each use of the subscript operator involves traversing at least part of the list from the beginning, you should think twice before adding this operator in production code. Especially if the Truckload object contains a large number Boxes, using this operator could be catastrophic for performance. It is because of this that the authors of the Standard Library decided not to give their linked-list class templates, std::list<> and std::forward_list<>, any subscript operators either. Overloading the subscript operator is best reserved for those cases where it can be backed by an efficient element retrieval mechanism.

To solve this performance problem of the Truckload array subscript operator, you should either omit it or replace the linked list of Truckload::Packages with a std::vector<SharedBox>. The only reason we used a linked list in the first place was for educational purposes. In real life, you should probably never use linked lists. A std::vector<> is almost always the better choice. We'll postpone implementing this version of Truckload until the exercises in Chapter 20.

▓ **Tip** New in C++23 is that overloaded subscript operators can take any number of input parameters (zero even, if you're feeling playful). A multidimensional subscript operator is particularly useful if your class models some higher dimension data collection, such as a matrix. Here is an example of a typical two-dimensional subscript operator:

```
double Matrix::operator[](std::size_t row, std::size_t column) const
{
  return m_data[row * m_num_columns + column];
}
```

You invoke a multidimensional subscript operator by passing the correct number of arguments:

```
Matrix m{ 5, 6 };    // Constructs a matrix with 5 rows and 6 columns
// ...
std::println("Element at row 3, column 4: {}", m[2, 3]); // m[2, 3], not m[2][3]!
```

Modifying the Result of an Overloaded Subscript Operator

You'll encounter circumstances in which you might want to overload the subscript operator and use the object it returns, for instance, on the left of an assignment or call a function on it. With your present implementation of operator[]() in the Truckload class, a program compiles but won't work correctly if you write either of these statements:

```
load[0] = load[1];
load[2].reset();
```

This will compile and execute, but it won't affect the items in the list. What you want is that the first pointer in the list is replaced by the second and that the third is reset to null, but this doesn't happen. The problem is the return value from operator[](). The function returns a *temporary copy* of a smart pointer object that points to the same Box object as the original pointer in the list but is *a different pointer*. Each time you use load[0] on the left of an assignment, you get a *different* copy of the first pointer in the list. Both statements operate but are just changing *copies* of the pointers in the list, which are copies that won't be around for very long.

This is why the subscript operator normally returns a reference to a value inside a data structure instead of a copy of that value. Doing this for the Truckload class, however, poses one significant challenge. You can no longer return nullptr from operator[]() in the Truckload class because you cannot return a reference to nullptr. Obviously, you must never return a reference to a local object in this situation either. You need to devise another way to deal with an invalid index. The simplest solution is to return a SharedBox object that doesn't point to anything and is permanently stored somewhere in global memory.

You could define a SharedBox object as a static member of the Truckload class by adding the following declaration to the private section of the class:

```
static inline SharedBox nullBox {};    // Pointer to nullptr
```

Now we can change the definition of the subscript operator to this:

```
SharedBox& Truckload::operator[](std::size_t index)
{
  std::size_t count {};                 // Package count
  for (Package* package{m_head}; package; package = package->m_next)
  {
    if (count++ == index)               // Up to index yet?
      return package->m_box;            // If so return the pointer to Box
  }
  return nullBox;
}
```

It now returns a reference to the pointer, and the member function is no longer const. Here's an extension of Ex13_10 to try the subscript operator on the left of an assignment. We have simply extended main() from Ex13_10 to show that iterating through the elements in a Truckload list still works:

```
int main()
{
  // All the code from main() in Ex13_10 here...

  load[0] = load[1];          // Copy 2nd element to the 1st
  std::println("\nAfter copying the 2nd element to the 1st, the list contains:");
  load.printBoxes();

  load[1] = std::make_shared<Box>(*load[2] + *load[3]);
  std::println("\nAfter making the 2nd element a pointer to the 3rd plus 4th, "
               "the list contains:");
  load.printBoxes();
}
```

You can find the complete program in Ex13_11.cpp. The first part of the output is similar to the previous example, after which the output is as follows:

```
After copying the 2nd element to the 1st, the list contains:
Box(85.5,33.0,56.9) Box(85.5,33.0,56.9) Box(78.3,5.4,13.9) Box(69.1,31.6,78.1)
Box(41.6,30.0,14.8) Box(23.8,22.1,97.8) Box(97.8,33.4,74.0) Box(88.4,8.3,65.7)
Box(19.8,13.7,14.6) Box(77.6,72.1,35.0) Box(87.7,51.6,15.4) Box(90.5,3.5,8.3)
Box(65.6,29.6,91.7) Box(88.8,16.5,73.7) Box(64.3,2.7,30.7) Box(69.9,51.5,85.9)
Box(29.0,20.5,76.4) Box(72.8,19.2,49.1) Box(59.9,56.3,8.9)

After making the 2nd element a pointer to the 3rd plus 4th, the list contains:
Box(85.5,33.0,56.9) Box(78.3,31.6,92.0) Box(78.3,5.4,13.9) Box(69.1,31.6,78.1)
Box(41.6,30.0,14.8) Box(23.8,22.1,97.8) Box(97.8,33.4,74.0) Box(88.4,8.3,65.7)
Box(19.8,13.7,14.6) Box(77.6,72.1,35.0) Box(87.7,51.6,15.4) Box(90.5,3.5,8.3)
Box(65.6,29.6,91.7) Box(88.8,16.5,73.7) Box(64.3,2.7,30.7) Box(69.9,51.5,85.9)
Box(29.0,20.5,76.4) Box(72.8,19.2,49.1) Box(59.9,56.3,8.9)
```

The first block of new output shows that the first two elements point to the same Box object, so the assignment worked as expected. The second block results from assigning a new value to the second element in the Truckload object; the new value is a pointer to the Box object produced by summing the third and fourth Box objects. The output shows that the second element points to a new object that is the sum of the next two. Just to make it clear what is happening, the statement that does this is equivalent to the following:

```
load.operator[](1).operator=(
  std::make_shared<Box>(load.operator[](2)->operator+(*load.operator[](3))));
```

Much clearer, isn't it?

▓ **Caution**   The somewhat clumsy workaround we used in this section to deal with invalid indexes to a subscript operator—returning a non-`const` reference to a special "null object"—has one critical flaw. Perhaps you can already guess what this is? Hint: If supplied with an invalid index, the `operator[]()` function returns a *non-const reference* to `nullBox`. Exactly. The fact that this reference is non-`const` implies that there is nothing to prevent the caller from modifying `nullBox`. In general, allowing the user to modify the objects that are accessed through the operator is exactly what we set out to do. But for the special `nullBox` object, this exposes a grave risk. It allows a careless caller to assign a non-null value to the `nullBox` pointer, which would essentially cripple the subscript operator! The following illustrates how things could go wrong:

```
Truckload load(std::make_shared<Box>(1, 2, 3));       // Create load with single box
...
load[10] = std::make_shared<Box>(6, 6, 6);            // Oops: assigning to nullBox...
...
auto secondBox = load[100];                           // Access nonexistent Box...
if (secondBox)                                        // nullBox is no longer null!
{
  std::println("{}", secondBox->volume());           // Prints 216 (6*6*6)
}
```

As this example shows, one accidental assignment to a nonexistent eleventh element causes unexpected and undesirable behavior. The `Truckload` now appears to have a box with dimensions {6, 6, 6} at index 100. (Note that this will even break the subscript operator for all `Truckload` objects all at once. Because `nullBox` is a static member of `Truckload`, it is shared between all objects of this class.)

Because of this dangerous loophole, you should never use the technique we used here in real programs. In Chapter 16, you will learn about a more appropriate mechanism for dealing with invalid function arguments: exceptions. Exceptions will allow you to return from a function without having to invent a return value. (Note that the `std::optional<>` vocabulary type in Chapter 9 is less an option here, because the whole idea is to allow the use of `operator[]()` calls to the left of an assignment.)

Function Objects

A *function object* or *functor* is an object of a class that overloads the function call operator, which is (). A function object can be passed as an argument, thus providing a powerful way to pass functions around. We will dig much deeper into this topic in Chapter 19. Here we'll just quickly show you how to overload the function call operator and give you a first idea how function objects work with a basic example.

Suppose we define a `ComputeVolume` class like this:

```
class ComputeVolume
{
public:
  double operator()(double x, double y, double z) const { return x * y * z; }
};
```

The function call operator in a class looks like a misprint. It is operator()(). But with this operator overload in place, you can use a ComputeVolume object to compute a volume:

```
ComputeVolume computeVolume;                          // Create a functor
double roomVolume { computeVolume(16, 12, 8.5) }; // Room volume in cubic feet
```

The computeVolume object represents a function, one that can be called using its function call operator. The value in the braced initializer for roomVolume is the result of calling operator()() for the computeVolume object, so the expression is equivalent to computeVolume.operator()(16, 12, 8.5). Because function call operators often do not modify any member variables of the functor object, they are often defined as const member functions.

Of course, you can define more than one overload of the operator()() function in a class:

```
class ComputeVolume
{
public:
  double operator()(double x, double y, double z) const { return x*y*z; }
  double operator()(const Box& box) const { return box.volume(); }
};
```

Now a ComputeVolume object can return the volume of a Box object as well:

```
Box box{1.0, 2.0, 3.0};
std::println("The volume of the box is {}", computeVolume(box));
```

Naturally, this example will not convince you at all yet of the usefulness of function objects. But what if we told you that you have already encountered some very useful function objects earlier? Remember createUniformPseudoRandomNumberGenerator()? That function created and used no less than four different function objects. The random device, the pseudo-random number generator, the uniform distribution, and the result of std::bind()—all these were objects that represent a function. The pseudo-random number generator, for instance, represents a function that returns a different number each time it is invoked. To accomplish this, the object stores certain data inside its member variables. This data is first initialized based on a given seed value (from a truly random source, ideally) and then updated each time a new number is generated (to get it ready for generating the next number). This is not possible using a regular function, as a regular function cannot store data. At best a regular function can use global or static variables, but these do not suffice in general (especially not in multithreaded applications!). You need a function object for this!

If you are still not convinced that representing callable functions as objects is a powerful concept, or if it's all still a bit too abstract, we refer you to Chapters 19 and 20. In Chapter 19, you will learn all about the versatility of function objects (in particular, lambda expressions), and in Chapter 20, you'll see just how powerful they are in combination with Standard Library algorithms and containers.

■ **Note**   Unlike most operators, function call operators must be overloaded as member functions. They cannot be defined as regular functions. The function call operator is also the only operator next to the subscript operator that can have as many parameters as you want and that can have default arguments.

■ **Tip** New in C++23 is that function call operators can be static member functions. The advantage, in essence, is that compilers can more easily generate optimal code for function objects with `static` function call operators because it's then more obvious that no `this` pointer needs to be passed around for these function objects. Both function call operators in our `ComputeVolume` example, for instance, could thus benefit from a `static` specifier (as always, if you add `static` you need to remove `const` from the member function declaration).

Overloading Type Conversions

You can define an operator function as a class member to convert from the class type to another type. The type you're converting to can be a fundamental type or a class type. Operator functions that are conversions for objects of an arbitrary class, `MyClass`, are of this form:

```
class MyClass
{
 public:
   operator OtherType() const;      // Conversion from MyClass to OtherType
   // Rest of MyClass class definition...
};
```

`OtherType` is the destination type for the conversion. Note that no return type is specified because the target type is always implicit in the function name, so here the function must return an `OtherType` object.

As an example, you might want to define a conversion from type `Box` to type `double`. For application reasons, you could decide that the result of this conversion would be the volume of the `Box` object. You could define this as follows:

```
class Box
{
public:
   operator double() const { return volume(); }

   // Rest of Box class definition...
};
```

■ **Note** Unlike most operators, conversion operators *must* be overloaded as member functions. They cannot be defined as regular functions. They are also the only operators where the `operator` keyword is not preceded by a return type (instead, the return type comes *after* the `operator` keyword).

Suppose we have the following highly advanced mathematical function:

```
void square(double x) { return x * x; }
```

Then the type conversion operator member function of Box would be called if you wrote this:

```
Box box {1.0, 2.0, 3.0};
square(box);
```

This causes an implicit conversion to be inserted by the compiler. But squaring a Box? Clearly, implicitly converting boxes to numbers may lead to strange and potentially undesired situations. This is similar to what we encountered in Chapter 12 with non-explicit converting constructors. You can prevent implicit calls of a conversion operator function by adding the explicit specifier to its declaration. In the Box class, you could, and probably should, write this:

```
explicit operator double() const { return volume(); }
```

Now the compiler will not use this member for most implicit conversions to type double. The only implicit conversions an explicit cast operator allows are those of the following form:

```
double boxVolume{ box }; // Calls conversion operator, even if marked explicit
```

If need be, you can always still invoke the conversion operator function explicitly as follows (explicit casts work irrespective of whether the operator is marked explicit).

```
square(static_cast<double>(box));
```

Potential Ambiguities with Conversions

When you implement conversion operators for a class, it is possible to create ambiguities that will cause compiler errors. You have seen that a constructor can also effectively implement a conversion—a conversion from type Type1 to type Type2 can be implemented by including a constructor in class Type2 with this declaration:

```
Type2(const Type1& theObject);  // Constructor converting Type1 to Type2
```

This can conflict with this conversion operator in the Type1 class:

```
operator Type2() const;       // Conversion from type Type1 to Type2
```

The compiler will not be able to decide which constructor or conversion operator function to use when an implicit conversion is required. To remove the ambiguity, declare either or both members as explicit.

Overloading the Assignment Operator

You have already encountered several instances where one object of a nonfundamental type is seemingly overwritten by another using an assignment operator, like so:

```
Box oneBox{1, 2, 3};
Box otherBox{4, 5, 6};
...
oneBox = otherBox;
...
std::println("{}", oneBox.volume());    // Outputs 120 (= 4 x 5 x 6)
```

But how exactly does this work? And how do you support this for your own classes?

You know that the compiler (sometimes) implicitly generates default constructors, copy constructors, and destructors. This is not all the compiler provides, though. Similar to a default copy constructor, a compiler also generates a default *copy assignment operator*. For Box, this operator has the following prototype:

```
class Box
{
public:
    ...
    Box& operator=(const Box& rightHandSide);
    ...
};
```

Like a default copy constructor, the default copy assignment operator simply copies all the member variables of a class one by one (in the order they are declared in the class definition). You can override this default behavior by supplying a user-defined assignment operator, as we'll discuss next.

■ **Note** The assignment operator cannot be defined as a regular function. It is the only binary operator that must always be overloaded as a class member function.

Implementing the Copy Assignment Operator

The default assignment operator copies the members of the object to the right of an assignment to those of the object of the same type on the left. For a Box, this default behavior is just fine. But this is not the case for all classes. Consider a simple Message class that, for whatever ill-advised reason, uses a plain C-style string allocated in the free store. A naïve definition for such a class might look like this:

```
import std;

class Message
{
public:
    explicit Message(const char* text = "")
        : m_text(new char[std::strlen(text) + 1]) // Caution: include the null character!
    {
        std::strcpy(m_text, text);                 // Mind the order: strcpy(destination, source)!
    }
    ~Message() { delete[] m_text; }
    const char* getText() const { return m_text; }
private:
    char* m_text;
};
```

The constructor uses two functions of the C Standard Library: std::strlen() and std::strcpy()[6]. The former gives you the length of a null-terminated string (*not* including the terminating null character!), whereas the latter copies from one null-terminated string to another (*including* the terminating null character).

■ **Note**   Notice again how easy it is to make a mistake with C-style strings (see also Chapter 7). Forget to add 1 to strlen(text) in the member initializer list, for instance, and strcpy() will happily write one character beyond the bounds of the newly allocated array. And once that happens, anything goes. Your program might continue to work fine, mostly; or it may crash, occasionally; or it may just behave totally weirdly, once in a blue moon. Happy debugging!

Aren't you starting to appreciate the std::string class even more? But things are as they are, and Message uses C-style strings, not std::string. For some reason...

You can write the following to invoke the (default) copy assignment operator of Message:

```
Message message;
Message beware {"Careful"};
message = beware;            // Call the assignment operator
```

This snippet will compile and run. But now think about what the default assignment operator of the Message class does exactly during this last statement. It copies the m_text member from the beware Message onto that of the message object. This member is just a raw pointer variable, though, so after the assignment, we have two different Message objects whose m_text pointer refers to the same memory location. Once both Messages go out of scope, the destructors of both objects will therefore apply delete[] on the same location! It's impossible to tell what the result of this second delete[] will be. One likely outcome, though, is a program crash.

So, clearly, the default assignment operator will not do for classes that manage dynamically allocated memory themselves. You have no other option but to redefine the assignment operator for Message. (Besides switching to std::string, obviously. But you can't. For some reason...)

An assignment operator should return a reference, so in the Message class, it would look like this:

```
Message& operator=(const Message& message);    // Assignment operator
```

The parameter should be a reference-to-const and the return type a reference-to-non-const. As the code for the assignment operator will just copy data from the members of the right operand to the members of the left operand, you may wonder why it must return a reference—or indeed, why it needs to return anything. Consider how the assignment operator is applied in practice. With normal usage, you can write this:

```
message1 = message2 = message3;
```

---

[6] Yes, C programmers do seem to like abbreviated function names. Other beauties from the same <cstring> header are strspn(), strpbrk(), strchr(), and strstr(). For obvious reasons, we categorically advise against this practice. Code is not meant to be compact, it's meant to be readable!

These are three objects of the same type, so this statement makes message1 and message2 copies of message3. Because the assignment operator is right-associative, this is equivalent to the following:

```
message1 = (message2 = message3);
```

The result of executing the rightmost assignment is evidently the right operand for the leftmost assignment, so you definitely need to return something. In terms of operator=(), this statement is equivalent to the following:

```
message1.operator=(message2.operator=(message3));
```

You have seen this several times before. This is called method chaining! Whatever you return from operator=() can end up as the argument to another operator=() call. The parameter for operator=() is a reference to an object, so the operator function must return the left operand, which is the object that is pointed to by this. Further, to avoid unnecessary copying of the object that is returned, the return type must be a reference.

Here is a reasonable first attempt at a definition of an assignment operator for Message:

```
Message& operator=(const Message& message)
{
  delete[] m_text;                                // Delete the previous char array
  m_text = new char[std::strlen(message.m_text) + 1]; // Replace it with a new array
  std::strcpy(m_text, message.m_text);            // Copy the text (mind the order!)
  return *this;                                    // Return the left operand
}
```

The this pointer contains the address of the left operand, so returning *this returns the object. This function looks okay, and it appears to work. And in nearly all cases, it really does work just fine. Nevertheless, there is one serious fly left in the ointment. Suppose someone writes this:

```
message1 = message1;
```

The likelihood of someone writing this explicitly is very low, but self-assignment could always occur indirectly. Inside the operator=() function, message and *this then both refer to the same object—message1, in our contrived example. It is informative to spell out what this statement then does exactly. That is, executing message1 = message1 then acts as if you were executing this:

```
delete[] message1.m_text;
message1.m_text = new char[std::strlen(message1.m_text) + 1]; // Reading reclaimed memory!
std::strcpy(message1.m_text, message1.m_text);               // Copying uninitialized memory!
```

The result of this statement is thus that you first apply delete[] on the m_text array of message1, after which std::strlen() attempts to read from that very same array. Because m_text now points to reclaimed free store memory, this is already likely to result in a fatal error. But even if we somehow make it through this statement unharmed, and even if strlen() somehow magically manages to retrieve the correct string length (there's really no telling what strlen() will produce here), even then we are not out of the woods. Or better put, even then self-assignment will still go horribly wrong. After the second statement, message1.m_text now points to a fresh, new array, filled with any number of totally random, uninitialized characters. And these totally random characters may or may not contain a null character. See where this could be heading for the third statement?

To cut a long story short, with our defective assignment operator, self-assigning a Message either crashes or results in a m_text array filled with an indeterminate number of random characters. Neither result is very pleasant. We invite you to give it a try and see what happens for you.

The easiest and safest solution is to always check for identical left and right operands first in a copy assignment operator. An idiomatic copy assignment operator therefore looks as follows:

```
Message& operator=(const Message& message)
{
  if (&message != this)
  {
    // Do as before...
  }
  return *this;      // Return the left operand
}
```

That way, you are always safe. If this now contains the address of the argument object, the function does nothing and just returns the same object.

■ **Tip** A typical user-defined copy assignment operator should start by checking for self-assignment. Forgetting to do so may lead to fatal errors when accidentally assigning an object to itself.

If you put this in the Message class definition, the following code will show it working:

```
// Ex13_12.cpp - Defining a copy assignment operator
import message;
import std;

int main()
{
  Message beware {"Careful"};
  Message warning;

  warning = beware;    // Call assignment operator

  std::println("After assignment beware is: {}", beware.getText());
  std::println("After assignment warning is: {}", warning.getText());
}
```

The output will demonstrate that everything works as it should and that the program does not crash!

▓ **Caution** For each custom copy assignment operator that you implement, you should probably implement a custom copy constructor as well, and vice versa. For the `Message` class, for instance, we now fixed copy assignment, but copy construction will still result in two messages pointing to the same string (and thus will crash):

```
Message warning;
warning = beware;        // Safe, uses correct custom copy assignment operator
Message danger{ beware }; // Danger, danger! Incorrect default copy constructor!
```

Therefore, whenever you do implement custom copy members (and you mostly shouldn't; see Chapter 18), always implement them both—that is, always implement the copy constructor and the copy assignment operator together.

Ex13_12A contains an augmented version of Ex13_12 where a correct copy constructor was added as well.

▓ **Note** You'll encounter another example of a user-defined copy assignment operator in Chapter 17, where you'll work on a bigger example of a `vector`-like class that manages an array of dynamically allocated memory. Based on that example, we'll also introduce a standard, even better technique for implementing a correct, safe assignment operator: the *copy-and-swap idiom*. Essentially, this C++ programming pattern dictates to always reformulate the copy assignment operator in terms of the copy constructor and a `swap()` function.

Copy Assignment vs. Copy Construction

The copy assignment operator is called under different circumstances than the copy constructor. The following snippet illustrates this:

```
Message beware {"Careful"};
Message warning;
warning = beware;              // Calls the assignment operator
Message otherWarning{warning}; // Calls the copy constructor
```

On the third line, you *assign* a new value to a previously constructed object. This means that the *assignment* operator is used. On the last line, however, you *construct* an entirely new object as a copy of another. This is thus done using the copy *constructor*. If you do not use the uniform initialization syntax, the difference is not always that obvious. It is also legal to rewrite the last line as follows:

```
Message otherWarning = warning;  // Still calls the copy constructor
```

Programmers sometimes wrongly assume that this form is equivalent to a copy assignment to an implicitly default-constructed `Message` object. But that's not what happens. Even though this statement contains an equals sign, the compiler will still use the copy constructor here, not an assignment. Assignment operators come into play only when assigning to existing objects that were already constructed earlier.

Deleting the Copy Assignment Operator

As with the copy constructor, you may not always want an overzealous compiler to generate an assignment operator for your class. There could be various reasons for this. Classical design patterns, such as singleton and flyweight, for instance, rely on objects that may not be copied. You can learn about these in specialized literature. Another obvious reason would be that the compiler-generated operator would misbehave, as with our Message class. No copying is always better than faulty copying. You can create a Message class whose objects cannot be copied as follows:

```
class Message
{
public:
  explicit Message(const char* text = "");
  ~Message() { delete[] m_text; }

  Message(const Message&) = delete;
  Message& operator=(const Message&) = delete;

  const char* getText() const { return *m_text; }
private:
  const char* m_text;
};
```

If you plug this new Message class into Ex13_12A, you will notice that Messages indeed can no longer be copied. Of course, when deleting copy members, the same advice goes as when implementing custom versions:

░ **Tip**   To prevent copying, always delete both copy members. Deleting only the copy constructor or deleting only the copy assignment operator is rarely a good idea.

Assigning Different Types

You're not limited to overloading the assignment operator just to copy an object of the same type. You can have several overloaded versions of the assignment operator for a class. Additional versions can have a parameter type that is different from the class type, so they are effectively conversions. In fact, you have even already seen objects being assigned values of a different type:

```
std::string s{"Happiness is an inside job."};
...
s = "Don't assign anyone else that much power over your life."; // Assign a const char[]
```

Having reached the end of this chapter on operator overloading, we are positive that you can figure out how to implement such assignment operators on your own. Just remember, by convention any assignment operator should return a reference to *this!

Summary

In this chapter, you learned how to add functions to make objects of your own data types work with the basic operators. What you need to implement in a particular class is up to you. You need to decide the nature and scope of the facilities each class should provide. Always keep in mind that you are defining a data type—a coherent entity—and that the class needs to reflect its nature and characteristics. You should also make sure that your implementation of an overloaded operator doesn't conflict with what the operator does in its standard form.

The important points from this chapter include the following:

- You can overload any number of operators within a class to provide class-specific behavior. You should do so only to make code easier to read and write.

- Overloaded operators should mimic their built-in counterparts as much as possible. Popular exceptions to this rule are the << and >> operators for Standard Library streams and the + operator to concatenate strings.

- Operator functions can be defined as members of a class or as global operator functions. You should use member functions whenever possible. You should resort to global operator functions only if there is no other way or if implicit conversions are desirable for the first operand.

- For a unary operator defined as a class member function, the operand is the class object. For a unary operator defined as a global operator function, the operand is the function parameter.

- For a binary operator function declared as a member of a class, the left operand is the class object, and the right operand is the function parameter. For a binary operator defined by a global operator function, the first parameter specifies the left operand, and the second parameter specifies the right operand.

- If you overload operators == and <=>, you get operators !=, <, >, <=, and >= all for free. In many cases you can even have the compiler generate the code for you.

- Functions that implement the overloading of the += operator can be used in the implementation of the + function. This is true for all op= operators.

- To overload the increment or the decrement operator, you need two functions that provide the prefix and postfix form of the operator. The function to implement a postfix operator has an extra parameter of type int that serves only to distinguish the function from the prefix version.

- To support customized type conversions, you have the choice between conversion operators or a combination of conversion constructors and assignment operators.

EXERCISES

The following exercises enable you to try what you've learned in this chapter. If you get stuck, look back over the chapter for help. If you're still stuck after that, you can download the solutions from the Apress website (www.apress.com/book/download.html), but that really should be a last resort.

Exercise 13-1. Define an operator function in the Box class from Ex13_05 that allows a Box object to be post-multiplied by a numeric value to produce a new object that has a height that is n times the original object. This should work for both integer and fractional multiples. Demonstrate that your operator function works as it should.

Exercise 13-2. Define an operator function that will allow a Box object to be premultiplied by a numeric value to produce the same result as the operator in Exercise 13-1. Demonstrate that this operator works.

Exercise 13-3. Take another look at your Exercise 13-2 solution. If it's anything like our model solution, it contains two binary arithmetic operators: one to add two Boxes and one overloaded operator to multiply Boxes by numbers. Remember that we said that one thing always leads to another in the world of operator overloading? While subtracting Boxes does not work well, surely if you have operators to multiply with an integer, you'd also want operators to divide by one? Furthermore, each binary arithmetic operator *op*( ) creates the expectation of a corresponding compound assignment operator *op* =( ). Make sure to implement all requested operators using the canonical patterns!

Exercise 13-4. If we allow my_box <= 6.0 and 6.0 <= my_box, then why not allow my_box == 6.0 and 6.0 != my_box? How many operator functions do you need to accomplish this? Extend the Box class of Ex13_03A and try out your latest operator.

Exercise 13-5. If we allow std::cout << my_box, then why not allow std::cin >> my_box? Extend Ex13_04 by adding a stream extraction operator for Box objects. To keep things simple, a Box is represented in a std::istream simply by three consecutive floating-point values.

Exercise 13-6. Create the necessary operators that allow Box objects to be used in if statements such as these:

```
if (my_box) ...
if (!my_other_box) ...
```

A Box is equivalent to true if it has a nonzero volume; if its volume is zero, a Box should evaluate to false. Create a small test program that shows that your operators work as requested.

Exercise 13-7. In Exercise 13-6, we steered you toward a solution with two operators: a type conversion operator and a unary ! operator. Not on purpose, believe us. When we first created the exercise, we still believed that that was the proper solution. But, as it turns out, you really only need one of them. Moreover, and this is less obvious, in idiomatic use, this operator is declared explicit to avoid implicit conversions to type bool in places where this is not desired. Thankfully, inside an if statement or after !, conversions to bool are always performed implicitly, even if the conversion operator is marked as explicit. Simplify your Exercise 13-6 solution and convince yourself that conversions to bool work as desired.

Exercise 13-8. Implement a class called `Rational` that represents a rational number. A rational number can be expressed as the quotient or fraction n / d of two integer numbers, an integral numerator n, and a nonzero, positive integral denominator d. Do not worry about enforcing that the denominator is nonzero. That's not the point of the exercise. You should definitely create an operator that allows a rational number to be streamed to `std::cout`. Beyond that, you are free to choose how many and which operators you add. You could create operators to support multiplication, addition, subtraction, division, and comparison of two `Rational` numbers and of `Rational` numbers and integers. You could create operators to negate, increment, or decrement `Rational` numbers. And what about converting to a `float` or a `double`? There really is a huge number of operators you could define for `Rationals`. The `Rational` class in our model solution supports well over 20 different operators, many overloaded for multiple types. Perhaps you come up with even more rational (as in sensible) operators for your `Rational` class? Do not forget to create a program to test that your operators actually work.

Exercise 13-9. Create your own pseudo-random number generator function object that generates integer values between 0 and 100 and use it to replace the `createUniformPseudoRandomNumberGenerator()` function of `Ex13_06`. To obtain proper pseudo-randomness, you should still seed your generator using the `std::random_device` function object. Hint: In Chapter 12, we gave you a simple mathematical formula that you could use for this.

Exercise 13-10. Take another look at the `Truckload` class from `Ex13_11`. Isn't there an operator missing? The class has two raw pointers called `m_head` and `m_tail`. What will the default copy assignment operator do with these two raw pointers? Mend the assignment for the `Truckload` class and modify the `main()` function to exercise your freshly written operator. Does self-assignment work?

CHAPTER 14

Inheritance

In this chapter, you'll look at a topic that lies at the heart of object-oriented programming: *inheritance*. Inheritance is the means by which you can create new classes by reusing and expanding on existing class definitions. Inheritance is also fundamental to making *polymorphism* possible. We'll discuss polymorphism in the next chapter, so what you'll learn there is an integral part of what inheritance is all about. There are subtleties in inheritance that we'll tease out using code that shows what is happening.

In this chapter, you'll learn

- How inheritance fits into the idea of object-oriented programming

- What base classes and derived classes are and how they're related

- How to define a new class in terms of an existing class

- The use of the `protected` keyword as an access specification for class members

- How constructors behave in a derived class and what happens when they're called

- What happens with destructors in a class hierarchy

- The use of `using` declarations within a class definition

- What multiple inheritance is

- How to convert between types in a class hierarchy

Classes and Object-Oriented Programming

We'll begin by reviewing what you've learned so far about classes and explain how that leads to the ideas we'll introduce in this chapter. In Chapter 12, we explained the concept of a class and that a class is a type that you define to suit your own application requirements. In Chapter 13, you learned how you can overload the basic operators so that they work with objects of your class types. The first step in applying object-oriented programming to solve a problem is to identify the types of entities to which the problem relates and to determine the characteristics of each type and the operations that will be needed to solve the problem. Then you can define the classes and their operations, which will provide what you need to program the solution to the problem in terms of instances of the classes.

Any type of entity can be represented by a class—from the completely abstract such as the mathematical concept of a complex number, to something as decidedly physical as a tree or a truck. A class definition characterizes a *set* of entities that share a common set of properties. So, as well as being a data type, a class can also be a definition of a set of real-world objects, or at least an approximation that is sufficient for solving a given problem.

In many real-world problems, the *types* of the entities involved are related. For example, a dog is a special kind of animal. A dog has all the properties of an animal plus a few more that characterize a dog. Consequently, classes that define the Animal and Dog types should be related in some way. As a dog is a specialized kind of animal, you can say that any Dog *is* also an Animal. You would expect the class definitions to reflect this. A different sort of relationship is illustrated by an automobile and an engine. You can't say that an Automobile *is* an Engine, or vice versa. What you can say is that an Automobile *has* an Engine. In this chapter, you'll see how the *is a* and *has a* relationships are expressed by classes.

Hierarchies

In previous chapters, we defined the Box class to represent a rectilinear box. The defining properties of a Box object were just the three orthogonal dimensions. You can apply this basic definition to the many kinds of rectangular boxes that you find in the real world: cardboard cartons, wooden crates, candy boxes, cereal boxes, and so on. All these have three orthogonal dimensions, and in this way they're just like generic Box objects. However, each of them has other properties such as the things they're designed to hold, the material from which they're made, or the labels printed on them. You could describe them as specialized kinds of Box objects.

For example, a Carton class could have the same properties as a Box object—namely, the three dimensions—plus the additional property of its composite material. You could then specialize even further by using the Carton definition to describe a FoodCarton class, which is a special kind of Carton that is designed to hold food. A FoodCarton object will have all the properties of a Carton object and an additional member to model the contents. Of course, a Carton object has the properties of a Box object, so a FoodCarton object will have those too. Figure 14-1 shows the connections between classes that express these relationships.

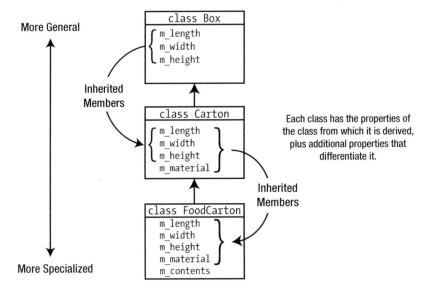

Figure 14-1. *Classes in a hierarchy*

The Carton class is an extension of the Box class. You might say that the Carton class is *derived* from the Box class. In a similar way, the FoodCarton class has been derived from the Carton class. It's common to indicate this relationship diagrammatically by using an arrow pointing toward the more general class in the hierarchy. This notation is used also by the Unified Modeling Language (UML), the de facto standard way for visualizing the design of object-oriented software programs. Figure 14-1 is a simplified UML *class diagram*, with some additional annotations to clarify.

In specifying one class in terms of another, you're developing a hierarchy of interrelated classes. One class is derived from another by adding extra properties—in other words, by *specialization*—making the new class a specialized version of the more general class. In Figure 14-1, each class in the hierarchy has *all* the properties of the Box class, which illustrates precisely the mechanism of class inheritance. You could define the Box, Carton, and FoodCarton classes quite independently of each other, but by defining them as related classes, you gain a tremendous amount. Let's look at how this works in practice.

Inheritance in Classes

To begin with, we'll introduce the terminology that is used for related classes. Given a class A, suppose you create a new class B that is a specialized version of A. Class A is the *base* class, and class B is the *derived* class. You can think of A as being the "parent" and B as being the "child." A base class is sometimes referred to as a *superclass* of a class that is derived from it, and the derived class is a *subclass* of its base. A derived class automatically contains all the member variables of its base class and (with some restrictions that we'll discuss) all the member functions. A derived class *inherits* the member variables and member functions of its base class.

If class B is a derived class defined *directly* in terms of class A, then class A is a *direct base class* of B. Class B is *derived from* A. In the preceding example, the Carton class is a direct base class of FoodCarton. Because Carton is defined in terms of the Box class, the Box class is an *indirect base class* of the FoodCarton class. An object of the FoodCarton class will have inherited members from Carton, including the members that the Carton class inherits from the Box class. Figure 14-2 illustrates the way in which a derived class inherits members from a base class.

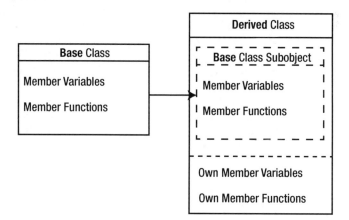

Figure 14-2. *Derived class members inherited from a base class*

As you can see, the derived class has a complete set of member variables and functions from the base class, plus its own member variables and functions. Thus, each derived class object contains a complete base class subobject, plus its own members.

Inheritance vs. Aggregation and Composition

Class inheritance isn't just a means of getting members of one class to appear in another. There's an important idea that underpins the whole concept: derived class objects should be sensible specializations of base class objects. To decide whether this is the case in a specific instance, you can apply the *is a* test, which is that any derived class object *is a* base class object. In other words, a derived class should define a subset of the objects that are represented by the base class. We explained earlier that a Dog class might be derived from an Animal class because a dog *is an* animal; more precisely, a Dog object is a reasonable representation of a particular kind of Animal object. On the other hand, a Table class shouldn't be derived from the Dog class. Although Table and Dog objects share a common attribute in that they both usually have four legs, a Table object can't really be considered a Dog in any way, or vice versa.

The *is a* test is an excellent first check, but it's not infallible. For example, suppose you define a Bird class that among other things reflects the fact that most birds can fly. Now, an ostrich *is a* bird, but it's nonsense to derive a class Ostrich from the Bird class because ostriches can't fly! The problem arises because of a poor definition for Bird objects. You really need a base class that doesn't have the ability to fly as a property. You can then derive two subclasses, one for birds that can fly and the other for birds that can't. If your classes pass the *is a* test, you should double-check by asking whether there is anything we can say about (or demand of) the base class that's inapplicable to the derived class. If there is, then the derivation probably isn't sound. Deriving Dog from Animal is sensible, but deriving Ostrich from Bird as we described it, isn't.

If classes fail the *is a* test, then you probably shouldn't use class derivation. In this case, you could check the *has a* test. A class object passes the *has a* test if it contains an instance of another class. You can accommodate this by including an object of the second class as a member variable of the first. The Automobile and Engine classes that we mentioned earlier are an example. An Automobile object would have an Engine object as a member variable; it may well have other major subassemblies as member variables of types such as Transmission and Differential. This type of relationship is called *aggregation*.

If the child object contained in a parent object cannot exist independently of its parent, their relation is called *composition* instead of aggregation. An example of composition would be the relation between a House and a Room, if Rooms cannot exist without a House. If you delete a House, all its Rooms are typically deleted as well. An example of aggregation is the relation Class-Student. Students generally do not cease to exist if their Class is canceled.

Of course, what is appropriate to include in the definition of a class depends on the application. Sometimes, class derivation is used simply to assemble a set of capabilities so that the derived class is an envelope for packaging a given set of functions. Even then, the derived class generally represents a set of functions that are related in some way. Let's see what the code to derive one class from another looks like.

Deriving Classes

We start again from a basic version of the Box class from earlier chapters:

```
// Box.cppm - defines Box class
export module box;

export class Box
{
public:
```

```
  Box() = default;
  Box(double length, double width, double height)
    : m_length{length}, m_width{width}, m_height{height}
  {}

  double volume() const { return m_length * m_width * m_height; }

  // Accessors
  double getLength() const { return m_length; }
  double getWidth()  const { return m_width; }
  double getHeight() const { return m_height; }

private:
  double m_length {1.0};
  double m_width  {1.0};
  double m_height {1.0};
};
```

We'll define Carton as a derived class using this Box class as the base class. A Carton object will be similar to a Box object but with an extra member variable that indicates the material from which it's made.

```
// Carton.cppm - defines the Carton class with the Box class as base
export module carton;

import std;
import box;

export class Carton : public Box
{
public:
  explicit Carton(std::string_view material = "Cardboard")  // Constructor
    : m_material{material} {}

private:
  std::string m_material;
};
```

We have put this new class in a new module called carton. The import declaration for the box module is necessary because that module defines (and exports) the Box class, which is the base class for Carton. The first line of the Carton class definition indicates that Carton is indeed derived from Box. The base class name follows a colon that separates it from the name of the derived class, Carton in this case. The public keyword is a *base class access specifier* that determines how the members of Box can be accessed from within the Carton class. We'll discuss this further in a moment.

In all other respects, the Carton class definition looks like any other. It contains a new member, m_material, which is initialized by the constructor. The constructor defines a default value for the string describing the material of a Carton object so that this is also the default constructor for the Carton class. Carton objects contain all the member variables of the base class, Box, plus the additional member variable, m_material. Because they inherit all the characteristics of a Box object, Carton objects are also Box objects.

There's a glaring inadequacy in the Carton class in that it doesn't have a constructor defined that permits the values of inherited members to be set (that is, for now, all Cartons will have dimensions 1×1×1). But we'll return to that later. Let's first see how these class definitions work in an example:

```
// Ex14_01.cpp - Defining and using a derived class
import std;
import box;
import carton;

int main()
{
  // Create a Box object and two Carton objects
  Box box {40.0, 30.0, 20.0};
  Carton carton;
  Carton chocolateCarton {"Solid bleached board"};  // Good old SBB
  // Check them out - sizes first of all
  std::println("box occupies {} bytes", sizeof box);
  std::println("carton occupies {} bytes", sizeof carton);
  std::println("chocolateCarton occupies {} bytes", sizeof chocolateCarton);

  // Now volumes...
  std::println("box volume is {}", box.volume());
  std::println("carton volume is {}", carton.volume());
  std::println("chocolateCarton volume is {}", chocolateCarton.volume());

  std::println("chocolateCarton length is {}", chocolateCarton.getLength());

  // Uncomment any of the following for an error...
  // box.m_length = 10.0;
  // chocolateCarton.m_length = 10.0;
}
```

We get the following output:

```
box occupies 24 bytes
carton occupies 56 bytes
chocolateCarton occupies 56 bytes
box volume is 24000
carton volume is 1
chocolateCarton volume is 1
chocolateCarton length is 1
```

The main() function creates a Box object and two Carton objects and outputs the number of bytes occupied by each object. The output shows what you would expect—that a Carton object is larger than a Box object. A Box object has three member variables of type double; each of these occupies 8 bytes on nearly every machine, so that's 24 bytes in all. Both Carton objects are the same size: 56 bytes (with the compiler configuration that we tested, at least). The additional memory occupied by each Carton object is down to the member variable m_material, so it's the size of a string object that contains the description of the material. The output of the volumes for the Carton objects shows that the volume() function is indeed inherited in the Carton class and that the dimensions have the default values of 1.0. The next statement shows that the accessor functions are inherited too and can be called for a derived class object.

Uncommenting either of the last two statements results in an error message from the compiler. The member variables that are inherited by the Carton class were private in the base class, and they are still private in the derived class, Carton, so they cannot be accessed from outside the class. There's more, though. Try adding this function to the Carton class definition as a public member:

```
double cartonVolume() const { return m_length * m_width * m_height; }
```

This won't compile. The reason is that although the member variables of Box are inherited, they are inherited as private members of the Box class. The private access specifier determines that members are totally private to the class. Not only can they not be accessed from outside the Box class, they also cannot be accessed from inside a class that inherits them.

Access to inherited members of a derived class object is not only determined by their access specification in the base class but by *both* the access specifier in the base class and the access specifier of the base class in the derived class. We'll go into that a bit more next.

Protected Members of a Class

The private members of a base class being only accessible to member functions of the base class can be, to say the least, inconvenient. Often you want the members of a base class to be *accessible* from within the derived class but nonetheless *protected* from outside interference. In addition to the public and private access specifiers for class members, you can declare members as protected. Within the class, the protected keyword has the same effect as the private keyword. protected members cannot be accessed from outside the class except from functions that have been specified as friend functions. Things change in a derived class, though. Members of a base class that are declared as protected are freely accessible in member functions of a derived class, whereas the private members of the base class are not.

We can modify the Box class to have protected member variables:

```
class Box
{
public:
  // Rest of the class as before...

protected:
  double m_length {1.0};
  double m_width {1.0};
  double m_height {1.0};
};
```

The member variables of Box still cannot be accessed by ordinary global functions, but they are now accessible within member functions of a derived class.

■ **Tip** Member variables should normally always be private. The previous example was just to indicate what is possible. In general, protected member variables introduce similar issues as public member variables, only to a lesser extent. We'll explore this in more detail in the next section.

The Access Level of Inherited Class Members

In the Carton class definition, we specified the Box base class as public using the following syntax: class Carton : public Box. In general, there are three possibilities for the base class access specifier: public, protected, or private. If you omit the base class access specifier in a class definition, the default is private (in a struct definition, the default is public). For example, if you omit the specifier altogether by writing class Carton : Box at the top of the Carton class definition in Ex14_01, then the private access specifier for Box is assumed. You already know that the access specifiers for class members come in three flavors as well. Again, the choice is the same: public, protected, or private. The base class access specifier affects the access status of the inherited members in a derived class. There are nine possible combinations. We'll cover all possible combinations in the following paragraphs, although the usefulness of some of these will only become apparent in the next chapter when you learn about polymorphism.

First let's consider how private members of a base class are inherited in a derived class. Regardless of the base class access specifier (public, protected, or private), a private base class member *always* remains private to the base class. As you have seen, inherited private members are private members of the derived class, so they're inaccessible outside the derived class. They're also inaccessible to member functions of the derived class because they're private to the base class.

Now, let's look into how public and protected base class members are inherited. In all the remaining cases, inherited members can be accessed by member functions of the derived class. The inheritance of public and protected base class members works like this:

1. When the base class specifier is public, the access status of the inherited members remains unchanged. Thus, inherited public members are public, and inherited protected members are protected in a derived class.

2. When the base class specifier is protected, both public and protected members of a base class are inherited as protected members.

3. When the base class specifier is private, inherited public and protected members become private to the derived class, so they're accessible by member functions of the derived class but cannot be accessed if they're inherited in another derived class.

This is summarized in Figure 14-3. Being able to change the access level of inherited members in a derived class gives you a degree of flexibility, but remember that you can only make the access level more stringent; you can't relax the access level that is specified in the base class.

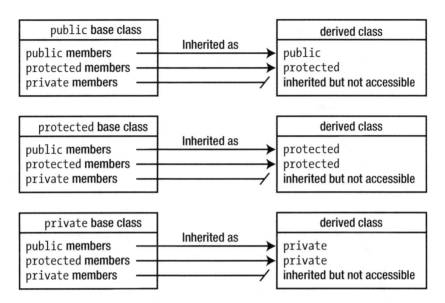

Figure 14-3. *The effect of the base class specifier on the accessibility of inherited members*

Access Specifiers and Class Hierarchies

Figure 14-4 shows how the accessibility of inherited members is affected only by the access specifiers of the members in the base class. Within a derived class, `public` and `protected` base class members are always accessible, and `private` base class members are never accessible. From outside the derived class, only `public` base class members may be accessed, and this is the case only when the base class is declared as `public`.

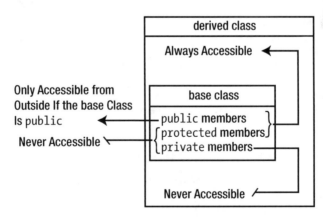

Figure 14-4. *The effect of access specifiers on base class members*

If the base class access specifier is `public`, then the access status of inherited members remains unchanged. By using the `protected` and `private` base class access specifiers, you are able to do two things:

- You can prevent access to `public` base class members from outside the derived class—either specifier will do this. If the base class has `public` member functions, then this is a serious step because the class interface for the base class is being removed from public view in the derived class.

- You can affect how the inherited members of the derived class are inherited in another class that uses the derived class as its base.

Figure 14-5 shows how the `public` and `protected` members of a base class can be passed on as `protected` members of another derived class. Members of a `privately` inherited base class won't be accessible in any further derived class. In the majority of instances, the `public` base class access specifier is most appropriate with the base class member variables declared as either `private` or `protected`. In this case, the internals of the base class subobject are internal to the derived class object and are therefore not part of the public interface for the derived class object. In practice, because the derived class object *is a* base class object, you'll want the base class interface to be inherited in the derived class, and this implies that the base class must be specified as `public`.

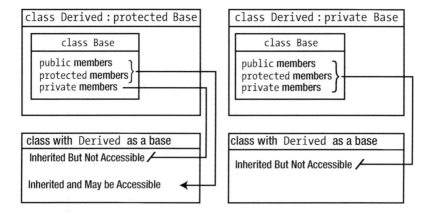

Figure 14-5. *Affecting the access specification of inherited members*

Constructors are not normally inherited for very good reasons, but you'll see later in this chapter how you can cause constructors to be inherited in a derived class.

Choosing Access Specifiers in Class Hierarchies

You have two aspects to consider when defining a hierarchy of classes: the access specifiers for the members of each class and the base class access specifier in each derived class. The `public` members of a class define the external interface to the class, and this shouldn't normally include any member variables. In fact:

> ▓ **Tip**   As a rule, member variables of a class should always be `private`. If code outside of the class requires access to member variables, you should add `public` or `protected` getter and/or setter functions.
>
> (This practice does not extend to structures. `struct`s mostly do not define any member functions at all; they typically consist solely of a set of `public` member variables.)

This widely accepted guideline is motivated by the data hiding principle explained in Chapter 12. If you recall, there were at least four good reasons to only access or modify member variables through a set of well-defined interface functions. Briefly, these were the following:

- Data hiding allows you to preserve the integrity of an object's state.

- It reduces coupling and dependencies with external code, thus facilitating evolution and changes either in a class's internal representation or in the concrete implementation of its interface functions.

- It allows you to inject extra code to be executed for every access and/or modification of member variables. Beyond validity and sanity checks, this may include logging and debugging code, for instance, or change notification mechanisms.

- It facilitates debugging, as most development environments support putting so-called debugging breakpoints on function calls. Putting breakpoints on getters and setters makes it much easier to track which code reads or writes to member variables and when.

Most programmers abide by the rule to avoid `public` member variables at all times. What is often forgotten, though, is that `protected` member variables have many of the same disadvantages as `public` ones:

- There is nothing stopping a derived class from invalidating an object's state, which may invalidate *class invariants*—properties of an object's state that should hold at all times—counted on by code in the base class.

- Once derived classes directly manipulate the member variables of a base class, changing its internal implementation becomes impossible without changing all the derived classes as well.

- Any extra code added to public getter and setter functions in the base class becomes void if derived classes can bypass it.

- Halting a debug session using break points when member variables are modified becomes, at the least, more difficult if derived classes can access them directly, halting when they're read impossible.

Therefore, always make member variables `private`, unless you have a good reason not do so.

> ▓ **Note**   To keep our code samples short, we will at times use `protected` member variables in this book. Such shortcuts have no place in professional-quality code, though.

Member functions that aren't part of the `public` interface of a class should not be directly accessible from outside the class either, which means that they should be `private` or `protected`. Which access specification you choose for a particular function then depends on whether you want to allow access from within a derived class. If you do, use `protected`; otherwise, use `private`.

Changing the Access Specification of Inherited Members

You might want to exempt a particular base class member from the effects of a protected or private base class access specification. This is easier to understand with an example. Suppose you derive the Carton class from the Box class in Ex14_01 but with Box as a private base class. All members inherited from Box will now be private in Carton, but you'd like the volume() function to remain public in the derived class, as it is in the base class. You can restore the public status for a particular inherited member that was public in the base class with a using declaration.

This is essentially the same as the using declaration for namespaces. You can force the volume() function to be public in the derived class by defining the Carton class like this:

```
class Carton : private Box
{
public:
  explicit Carton(std::string_view mat = "Cardboard") : m_material {mat} {}
  using Box::volume;   // Inherit as public
private:
  std::string m_material;
};
```

The class definition defines a scope, and the using declaration within the class definition introduces a name into that class scope. The member access specification applies to the using declaration, so the volume name is introduced into the public section of the Carton class so it overrides the private base class access specification for the volume() member of the base class. The function will be inherited as public in the Carton class, not as private. Ex14_01A in the code download shows this working.

There are several points to note here. First, when you apply a using declaration to the name of a member of a base class, you must qualify the name with the base class name, because this specifies the context for the member name. Second, you don't supply a parameter list or a return type for a member function—just the qualified name. This implies that overloaded functions always come as a package deal. Third, the using declaration also works with inherited member variables in a derived class.

You can use a using declaration to override an original public or protected base class access specifier in a base class. For example, if the volume() function was protected in the Box base class, you could make it public in the derived Carton class with the same using declaration in a public section of Carton. However, you can't apply a using declaration to relax the specification of a private member of a base class because private members cannot be accessed in a derived class.

Constructors in a Derived Class

If you put output statements in the constructors for the Carton class and the Box class of Ex14_01 and rerun the example, you'll see what happens when a Carton object is created. You'll need to define the default Box and Carton class constructors to include the output statements. Creating each Carton object always results in the default constructor of Box being called first, followed by the Carton class constructor.

Derived class objects are always created this way, even when there are several levels of derivation. Every constructor of a derived class always starts by invoking a constructor of its base class. And that base class constructor then invokes the constructor of its base class, and so on, until a class is reached that is not derived from any other class. The effect is that the first constructor to be fully evaluated is that of the most base class constructor, followed by the constructor for the class derived from that, and so on, until finally the constructor for the most derived class is evaluated. This makes sense if you think about it. A derived class object has a complete base class object inside it, and this needs to be created before the rest of the derived class object. If that base class is derived from another class, the same applies.

Although in Ex14_01 the default base class constructor was called automatically, this doesn't have to be the case. You can call a particular base class constructor in the initialization list for the derived class constructor. This will enable you to initialize the base class member variables with a constructor other than the default. It will also allow you to choose a particular base class constructor, depending on the data supplied to the derived class constructor. Let's see it working in another example.

Here's a new version of the Box class:

```cpp
export class Box
{
public:
  // Constructors
  Box(double l, double w, double h) : m_length{l}, m_width{w}, m_height{h}
  { std::println("Box(double, double, double) called."); }

  explicit Box(double side) : Box{side, side, side}
  { std::println("Box(double) called."); }

  Box() { std::println("Box() called."); }   // Default constructor

  double volume() const { return m_length * m_width * m_height; }

  // Accessors
  double getLength() const { return m_length; }
  double getWidth()  const { return m_width; }
  double getHeight() const { return m_height; }

protected:                                    // Protected to facilitate further examples
  double m_length {1.0};                       // later in this chapter (should normally be private)
  double m_width {1.0};
  double m_height {1.0};
};
```

All three Box constructors print a message when called. The Carton class looks like this:

```cpp
export class Carton : public Box
{
public:
  Carton() { std::println("Carton() called."); }

  explicit Carton(std::string_view material) : m_material{material}
  { std::println("Carton(string_view) called."); }

  Carton(double side, std::string_view material) : Box{side}, m_material{material}
  { std::println("Carton(double,string_view) called."); }

  Carton(double l, double w, double h, std::string_view material)
    : Box{l, w, h}, m_material{material}
    { std::println("Carton(double, double, double, string_view) called."); }

private:
  std::string m_material {"Cardboard"};
};
```

This class has four constructors, including a default constructor. You must define this here because if you define any constructor, the compiler will not supply a default default constructor. As always, we declare our single-argument constructor to be explicit to avoid unwanted implicit conversions.

■ **Note**   The notation for calling the base class constructor is the same as that used for initializing member variables in a constructor. This is perfectly consistent. You are essentially initializing the Box subobject of the Carton object using the arguments passed to the Carton constructor.

Here's the code to exercise the derived Carton class:

```
// Ex14_02.cpp - Calling base class constructors in a derived class constructor
import std;
import carton;          // For the Carton class

int main()
{
  // Create four Carton objects
  Carton carton1;                         std::println("");
  Carton carton2 {"White-lined chipboard"}; std::println("");
  Carton carton3 {4.0, 5.0, 6.0, "PET"};   std::println("");
  Carton carton4 {2.0, "Folding boxboard"}; std::println("");

  std::println("carton1 volume is {}", carton1.volume());
  std::println("carton2 volume is {}", carton2.volume());
  std::println("carton3 volume is {}", carton3.volume());
  std::println("carton4 volume is {}", carton4.volume());
}
```

The output is as follows:

```
Box() called.
Carton() called.

Box() called.
Carton(string_view) called.

Box(double, double, double) called.
Carton(double,double,double,string_view) called.

Box(double, double, double) called.
Box(double) called.
Carton(double,string_view) called.

carton1 volume is 1
carton2 volume is 1
carton3 volume is 120
carton4 volume is 8
```

The output shows which constructors are evaluated for each of the four Carton objects that are created in main():

- Creating the first Carton object, carton1, results in the default constructor for the Box class being evaluated first, followed by the default constructor for the Carton class.

- Creating carton2 evaluates the default constructor of Box followed by the Carton constructor with a string_view parameter.

- Creating the carton3 object evaluates the Box constructor with three parameters followed by the Carton constructor with four parameters.

- Creating carton4 causes two Box constructors to be called because the Box constructor with a single parameter of type double that is called by the Carton constructor calls the Box constructor with three parameters in its initialization list.

This is all consistent with constructors being evaluated in sequence from the most base to the most derived. Every derived class constructor calls a base class constructor. If a user-defined derived class constructor does not explicitly call a base constructor in its initialization list, the default constructor will be called.

You can never initialize member variables of a base class in the initialization list for a derived class's constructor. Not even if those members are protected or public. For example, try replacing the fourth and last Carton class constructor in Ex14_02 with the following:

```
// This constructor won't compile!
Carton::Carton(double l, double w, double h, std::string_view material)
  : m_length{l}, m_width{w}, m_height{h}, m_material{material}
  { std::println("Carton(double, double, double, string_view) called."); }
```

You might expect this to work because m_length, m_width, and m_height are protected base class members that are inherited publicly, so the Carton class constructor should be able to access them. However, the compiler will complain that m_length, m_width, and m_height are *not* members of the Carton class. This will be the case even if you make the member variables of the Box class public. If you want to initialize the inherited member variables explicitly, you could in principle do it in the *body* of the derived class constructor. The following constructor definition would compile:

```
// Constructor that will compile!
Carton::Carton(double l, double w, double h, std::string_view material)
  : m_material{material}
{
  m_length = l;  // These should normally be initialized in a base class constructor...
  m_width = w;
  m_height = h;
  std::println("Carton(double, double, double, string_view) called.");
}
```

By the time the body of the Carton constructor begins executing, the base part of the object has been created. In this case, the base part of the Carton object is created by an implicit call of the default constructor of the Box class. You can subsequently refer to the names of the non-private base class members without a problem. Still, if possible, it is always best to forward constructor arguments to an appropriate base class constructor and have the base class deal with initializing the inherited members.

The Copy Constructor in a Derived Class

You already know that the copy constructor is called when an object is created and initialized with another object of the same class type. The compiler will supply a default copy constructor that creates the new object by copying the original object member by member if you haven't defined your own version. Now let's examine the copy constructor in a derived class. To do this, we'll add to the class definitions in Ex14_02. First, we'll add a copy constructor to the base class, Box, by inserting the following code in the public section of the class definition:

```
// Copy constructor
Box(const Box& b) : m_length{b.m_length}, m_width{b.m_width}, m_height{b.m_height}
{ std::println("Box copy constructor"); }
```

■ **Note** You saw in Chapter 12 that the parameter for the copy constructor *must* be a reference.

This initializes the member variables by copying the original values and generates some output to track when the copy constructor is called.

Here's a first attempt at a copy constructor for the Carton class:

```
// Copy constructor
Carton(const Carton& carton) : m_material {carton.m_material}
{ std::println("Carton copy constructor"); }
```

Let's see if this works (it won't!):

```
// Ex14_03.cpp - Using a derived class copy constructor
import std;
import carton;      // For the Carton class

int main()
{
  // Declare and initialize a Carton object
  Carton carton(20.0, 30.0, 40.0, "Expanded polystyrene");
  std::println("");

  Carton cartonCopy(carton);    // Use copy constructor
  std::println("");

  std::println("Volume of carton is {}", carton.volume());
  std::println("Volume of cartonCopy is {}", cartonCopy.volume());
}
```

This produces the following output:

```
Box(double, double, double) called.
Carton(double,double,double,string_view) called.
```

```
Box() called.
Carton copy constructor

Volume of carton is 24000
Volume of cartonCopy is 1
```

All is not as it should be. Clearly the volume of cartonCopy isn't the same as carton, but the output also shows the reason for this. To copy the carton object, you call the copy constructor for the Carton class. The Carton copy constructor should make a copy of the Box subobject of carton, and to do this it *should* call the Box copy constructor. However, the output clearly shows that the *default* Box constructor is being called instead.

The Carton copy constructor won't call the Box copy constructor if you don't tell it to do so. The compiler knows that it has to create a Box subobject for the object carton, but if you don't specify how, the compiler won't second-guess your intentions—it will just create a default base object.

The obvious fix for this is to call the Box copy constructor in the initialization list of the Carton copy constructor. Simply change the copy constructor definition to this:

```
Carton(const Carton& carton) : Box{carton}, m_material{carton.m_material}
{ std::println("Carton copy constructor"); }
```

The Box copy constructor is called with the carton object as an argument. The carton object is of type Carton, but it is also a perfectly good Box object. The parameter for the Box class copy constructor is a reference to a Box object, so the compiler will pass carton as type Box&, which will result in only the base part of carton being passed to the Box copy constructor. If you compile and run the example again, the output will be as follows:

```
Box(double, double, double) called.
Carton(double,double,double,string_view) called.

Box copy constructor
Carton copy constructor

Volume of carton is 24000
Volume of cartonCopy is 24000
```

The output shows that the constructors are called in the correct order. In particular, the Box copy constructor initializes the Box subobject of carton before the body of the Carton copy constructor is entered. By way of a check, you can see that the volumes of the carton and cartonCopy objects are now identical.

The Default Constructor in a Derived Class

You know that the compiler will not supply a default default constructor if you define one or more constructors for a class. You also know that you can tell the compiler to insert a default constructor in any event using the default keyword. You could replace the definition of the default constructor in the Carton class definition in Ex14_02 with this statement:

```
Carton() = default;
```

Now the compiler will supply a definition, even though you have defined other constructors. The definition that the compiler supplies for a derived class calls the base class constructor, so it looks like this:

```
Carton() : Box{} {};
```

If the base class does not have a non-private default constructor, or if its default constructor is deleted (either implicitly or explicitly using = deleted), then a defaulted default constructor of the derived class shall be implicitly deleted. In other words, adding = default to the derived class then has the same effect as adding = delete.

To demonstrate this, you can take the following steps. Start from Ex14_02. Begin by replacing the default constructor of the Carton class with Carton() = default; (as suggested earlier) and removing the explicit constructor of Carton that accepts a string_view (which also relies on the default constructor of Box). Next, remove the line in the main() program that calls the latter constructor, but be sure to keep the line that default-constructs a Carton. After that, you can alter the default constructor from the Box class in one of three ways: you either remove it, replace it with Box() = delete;, or make it private. In any case, the Carton class and carton module will continue to compile just fine (even with the defaulted default constructor), but the default construction of Carton in the main() function will result in a compilation error. This error should normally inform you that your defaulted default constructor for Carton is indeed implicitly deleted.

The different variations of Ex14_02 discussed in this section are available online as Ex14_04 (where the defaulted default constructor of Carton can be invoked without error) and Ex14_04A, Ex14_04B, and Ex14_04C (variations where the inherited default constructor of Box is not defined, deleted, or inaccessible).

Inheriting Constructors

Base class constructors are not normally inherited in a derived class. This is because a derived class typically has additional member variables that need to be initialized, and a base class constructor would have no knowledge of these. However, you can cause constructors to be inherited from a direct base class by putting a using declaration in the derived class. Here's how a version of the Carton class from Ex14_02 could be made to inherit the Box class constructors:

```
class Carton : public Box
{
  using Box::Box;  // Inherit Box class constructors

public:
  Carton(double length, double width, double height, std::string_view mat)
    : Box{length, width, height}, m_material{mat}
    { std::println("Carton(double, double, double, string_view) called."); }

private:
  std::string m_material {"Cardboard"};
};
```

If the Box class definition is the same as in Ex14_02, the Carton class will inherit three constructors: Box(double, double, double), Box(double), and Box(). The constructors in the derived class will look like this:

```
Carton(double length, double width, double height) : Box {length, width, height} {}
explicit Carton(double side) : Box{side} {}
Carton() : Box{} {}
```

Each inherited constructor has the same parameter list as the base constructor and calls the base constructor in its initialization list. The body of each constructor is empty. You can add further constructors to a derived class that inherits constructors from its direct base, as the Carton class example illustrates.

Unlike regular member functions, (non-private) constructors are always inherited using the same access specifier as the corresponding constructor in the base class. So, even though the using Box::Box declaration is part of the implicitly private section of the Carton class, the constructors inherited from Box are both public. If the Box class would have had protected constructors, these would have been inherited as protected constructors in Carton as well.

▓ **Note**   You can put constructor inheritance declarations anywhere within the class definition. In fact, you'd normally put them in the public section of the class definition for clarity. The only reason we put that of the Carton class in its implicitly private section was to illustrate that the location of such a declaration has no effect on the access specifiers of the inherited constructors.

You could try this by modifying Ex14_02 to create the following objects in main():

```
Carton cart;                                        // Calls inherited default constructor
Carton cube { 4.0 };                                // Calls inherited constructor
Carton copy { cube };                               // Calls default copy constructor
Carton carton {1.0, 2.0, 3.0};                      // Calls inherited constructor
Carton cerealCarton (50.0, 30.0, 20.0, "Chipboard"); // Calls Carton class constructor
```

The resulting program is available online as Ex14_05. The output statements in the Box constructors will show that they are indeed called when invoking the inherited constructors.

Destructors Under Inheritance

Destroying a derived class object involves both the derived class destructor *and* the base class destructor. You can demonstrate this by adding destructors with output statements in the Box and Carton class definitions. You can amend the class definitions in the correct version of Ex14_03. Add the destructor definition to the Box class:

```
// Destructor
~Box() { std::println("Box destructor"); }
```

And for the Carton class:

```
// Destructor
~Carton() { std::println("Carton destructor. Material = {}", m_material); }
```

Of course, if the classes allocated free store memory and stored the address in a raw pointer, defining the class destructor would be essential to avoid memory leaks. The Carton destructor outputs the material so you can tell which Carton object is being destroyed by assigning a different material to each. Let's see how these classes behave:

```
// Ex14_06.cpp - Destructors in a class hierarchy
import std;
import carton;    // For the Carton class
```

```
int main()
{
  Carton carton;
  Carton candyCarton{50.0, 30.0, 20.0, "SBB"};      // Solid bleached board

  std::println("carton volume is {}", carton.volume());
  std::println("candyCarton volume is {}", candyCarton.volume());
}
```

Here's the output:

```
Box() called.
Carton() called.
Box(double, double, double) called.
Carton(double,double,double,string_view) called.
carton volume is 1
candyCarton volume is 30000
Carton destructor. Material = SBB
Box destructor
Carton destructor. Material = Cardboard
Box destructor
```

The point of this exercise is to see how the destructors behave. The output from the destructor calls indicates two aspects of how objects are destroyed. First, you can see the order in which destructors are called for a particular object, and second, you can see the order in which the objects are destroyed. The destructor calls recorded by the output correspond to the following actions:

Destructor Output	Object Destroyed
Carton destructor. Material = SBB.	candyCarton object
Box destructor.	Box subobject of candyCarton
Carton destructor. Material = Cardboard.	carton object
Box destructor.	Box subobject of carton

This shows that the objects that make up a derived class object are destroyed in the *reverse* order from which they were created. The carton object was created first and destroyed last; the candyCarton object was created last and destroyed first. This order is chosen to ensure that you never end up with an object in an illegal state. An object can be used only after it has been defined—this means that any given object can only contain pointers (or references) that point (or refer) to objects that have already been created. By destroying a given object *before* any objects that it might point (or refer) to, you ensure that the execution of a destructor can't result in any invalid pointers or references.

The order of destructor calls for a derived class object is thus the reverse of the constructor call sequence for the object. The derived class destructor is called first, and then the base class destructor is called, just as in the example. Figure 14-6 illustrates the case of a three-level class hierarchy.

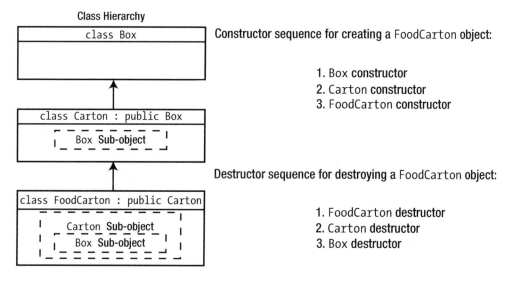

Figure 14-6. *The order of destructor calls for derived class objects*

Duplicate Member Variable Names

It's possible that a base class and a derived class each have a member variable with the same name. If you're really unlucky, you might even have names duplicated in the base class and in an indirect base. Of course, this is confusing, and you should never deliberately set out to create such an arrangement in your own classes. However, circumstances or oversights may lead to unfortunate naming conflicts that cannot always be resolved by renaming the culprit entities. So, what happens if member variables in the base and derived classes have the same names?

Duplication of names is no bar to inheritance, and you can differentiate between identically named members of base and derived classes. Suppose you have a class Base, defined as follows:

```
class Base
{
public:
  Base(int value = 10) : m_value{value} {}     // Constructor

protected:
  int m_value;
};
```

This just contains a single member variable, m_value, and a constructor. You can derive a class Derived from Base as follows:

```
class Derived : public Base
{
public:
  Derived(int value = 20) : m_value{value} {}   // Constructor
  int total() const;                            // Total value of member variables

protected:
  int m_value;
};
```

The derived class has a member variable called m_value, and it will also inherit the m_value member of the base class. You can see that it's already starting to look confusing! We'll show how you can distinguish between the two members with the name m_value in the derived class by writing a definition for the total() function. Within the derived class member function, m_value by itself refers to the member declared within that scope, that is, the derived class member. The base class member is declared within a different scope, and to access it from a derived class member function, you must qualify the member name with the base class name. Thus, you can write the total() function as follows:

```
int Derived::total() const
{
  return m_value + Base::m_value;
}
```

The Base::m_value expression refers to the base class member, and m_value by itself refers to the member declared in the Derived class.

Duplicate Member Function Names

What happens when base class and derived class member functions share the same name? There are two situations that can arise in relation to this. The first is when the functions have the same name but different parameter lists. Although the function signatures are different, this is *not* a case of function overloading. This is because overloaded functions must be defined within the same scope, and each class—base or derived— defines a separate scope. In fact, scope is the key to the situation. A derived class member function will *hide* an inherited member function with the same name. Thus, when base and derived member functions have the same name, you must introduce the qualified name of the base class member function into the scope of the derived class with a using declaration if you want to access it. Either function can then be called for a derived class object, as illustrated in Figure 14-7.

```
class Base
{
public:
  void doThat(int arg);
  ...
};
```

By default the derived class function doThat() would hide the inherited function with the same name. The using declaration introduces the base class function name, doThat, into the derived class's scope, so both versions of the function are available within the derived class. The compiler can distinguish them in the derived class because they have different signatures.

```
class Derived: public Base
{
public:
  void doThat(double arg);
  using Base::doThat;
  ...
};
```

```
Derived object;
object.doThat(2);    // Call inherited base function
object.doThat(2.5);  // Call derived function
```

Figure 14-7. *Inheriting a function with the same name as a member function*

The second possibility is that both functions have the same function signature. You can still differentiate the inherited function from the derived class function by using the class name as a qualifier for the base class function:

```
Derived object;            // Object declaration
object.Base::doThat(3);    // Call base version of the function
```

There's a lot more to this latter case than we can discuss at this point. This subject is closely related to *function overriding*, which in turn is closely related to polymorphism. We explore this in much more depth in the next chapter.

Multiple Inheritance

So far, your derived classes have all been derived from a *single* direct base class. However, you're not limited to this structure. A derived class can have as many direct base classes as an application requires. This is referred to as *multiple inheritance* as opposed to *single inheritance*, in which a single base class is used. This opens vast new dimensions of potential complexity in inheritance, which is perhaps why multiple inheritance is used much less frequently than single inheritance. Because of the complexity, it is best used judiciously. We'll just explain the basic ideas behind how multiple inheritance works.

Multiple Base Classes

Multiple inheritance involves two or more base classes being used to derive a new class, so things are immediately more complicated. The idea of a derived class being a specialization of its base leads, in this case, to the notion that the derived class defines an object that is a specialization of two or more different and independent class types concurrently. In practice, multiple inheritance is rarely used in this way. More often, multiple base classes are used to add the features of the base classes together to form a composite object containing the capabilities of its base classes, sometimes referred to as *mixin* programming. This is usually for convenience in an implementation rather than to reflect any particular relationships between objects. For example, you might consider a programming interface of some kind—for graphics programming, perhaps. A comprehensive interface could be packaged in a set of classes, each of which defines a self-contained interface that provides some specific capability, such as drawing two-dimensional shapes. You can then use several of these classes as bases for a new class that provides precisely the set of capabilities you need for an application.

To explore some of the implications of multiple inheritance, we'll start with a hierarchy that includes the Box and Carton classes. Suppose you need a class that represents a package containing food, such as a carton of cereal. It's possible to do this by using single inheritance, deriving a new class from the Carton class, and adding a member variable to represent the contents (similar to what is shown in Figure 14-1), but you could also do it using the hierarchy illustrated in Figure 14-8.

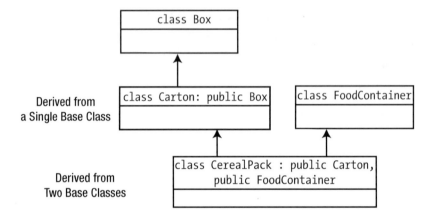

Figure 14-8. *An example of multiple inheritance*

The definition of the CerealPack class looks like this:

```
class CerealPack : public Carton, public FoodContainer
{
  // Details of the class...
};
```

Each base class is specified after the colon in the class header, and the base classes are separated by commas. Each base class has its own access specifier, and if you omit the access specifier, private is assumed, the same as with single inheritance. The CerealPack class will inherit *all* the members of *both* base classes, so this will include the members of the indirect base, Box. As in the case of single inheritance, the access level of each inherited member is determined by two factors: the access specifier of the member in the base class and the base class access specifier. A CerealPack object contains two subobjects, a FoodContainer subobject and a Carton subobject that has a further subobject of type Box.

Inherited Member Ambiguity

Multiple inheritance can create problems. We'll put together an example that will show the sort of complications you can run into. The Box class is the same as in Ex14_02, but we'll extend the Carton class from that example a little:

```
export class Carton : public Box
{
public:
  // Same 4 constructors from Ex14_02 (all containing output statements)...

  // One new constructor
  Carton(double l, double w, double h, std::string_view m, double density, double thickness)
    : Carton{l, w, h, m}
  {
    m_thickness = thickness; m_density = density;
    std::println("Carton(double, double, double, string_view, double, double) called.");
  }

  // Copy constructor
  Carton(const Carton& carton) : Box{carton}, m_material{carton.m_material},
    m_thickness{carton.m_thickness}, m_density{carton.m_density}
  {
    std::println("Carton copy constructor");
  }

  // Destructor
  ~Carton()
  {
    std::println("Carton destructor. Material = {}", m_material);
  }

  double getWeight() const
  {
    return 2.0 * (m_length * m_width + m_width * m_height + m_height * m_length)
                * m_thickness * m_density;
  }

private:
  std::string m_material {"Cardboard"};
  double m_thickness {0.125};    // Material thickness in inch
  double m_density {0.2};        // Material density in pounds/cubic inch
};
```

We've added two member variables that record the thickness and density of the material from which the Carton object is made; a new constructor that allows all member variables to be set; and a new member function, getWeight(), which calculates the weight of an empty Carton object. The new constructor calls another Carton class constructor in its initialization list, so it is a delegating constructor, as you saw in Chapter 12. A delegating constructor cannot have further initializers in the list, so the values for m_density and m_thickness have to be set in the constructor body.

The FoodContainer class will describe relevant properties of the food product, such as breakfast cereal, that can be contained in a carton. The class will have three member variables to store, respectively, the name, volume, and density of the contents. Here's the class definition, which we expose from a module aptly named food:

```
// food.cppm - The FoodContainer class
export module food;
import std;
```

```
export class FoodContainer
{
public:
  FoodContainer() { std::println("FoodContainer() called."); }

  FoodContainer(std::string_view name) : name {name}
  { std::println("FoodContainer(string_view) called."); }

  FoodContainer(std::string_view name, double density, double volume)
    : name {name}, density {density}, volume {volume}
  { std::println("FoodContainer(string_view,double,double) called."); }

  ~FoodContainer() { std::println("FoodContainer destructor"); }

  double getWeight() const { return volume * density; }

protected:
  std::string name {"cereal"};    // Food type
  double volume {};               // Cubic inches
  double density {0.03};          // Pounds per cubic inch
};
```

In addition to the constructors and the destructor, the class has one public member function, getWeight(), to calculate the weight of the contents.

Note that we purposely did not follow our usual conventions: we didn't add an m_ prefix to the names of all member variables, nor did we make these same variables private. We did this solely to illustrate some potential issues later on. You may also have noticed how the two member initializer lists in the constructors of FoodContainer initialize the three member variables with the value of parameters that have the exact same name. This is simply to illustrate that it is possible—and is by no means a recommended approach!

We'll define the CerealPack class with the Carton and FoodContainer classes as public base classes:

```
// cereal.cppm - Class defining a carton of cereal
export module cereal;
import std;
import carton;
import food;

export class CerealPack : public Carton, public FoodContainer
{
public:
  CerealPack(double length, double width, double height, std::string_view cerealType)
    : Carton {length, width, height, "Chipboard"}, FoodContainer {cerealType}
  {
    std::println("CerealPack constructor");
    FoodContainer::volume = 0.9 * Carton::volume();    // Set food container's volume
  }

  ~CerealPack()
  {
    std::println("CerealPack destructor");
  }
};
```

572

This class inherits from both the Carton and FoodContainer classes. The constructor requires only the external dimensions and the cereal type. The material for the Carton object is set in the Carton constructor call in the initialization list. A CerealPack object will contain two subobjects corresponding to the two base classes. Each subobject is initialized through constructor calls in the initialization list for the CerealPack constructor. Note that the volume member variable of the FoodContainer class is zero by default, so in the body of the CerealPack constructor, the value is calculated from the size of the carton. The reference to the volume member variable inherited from the FoodContainer class must be qualified here because it's the same as the name of the function inherited from Box via Carton. You'll be able to trace the order of constructor and destructor calls from the output statements here and in the other classes.

Now we try creating a CerealPack object and calculate its volume and weight with the following simple program:

```
// Ex14_07 - Using multiple inheritance - doesn't compile!
import std;
import cereal;        // For the CerealPack class

int main()
{
  CerealPack cornflakes {8.0, 3.0, 10.0, "Cornflakes"};

  std::println("cornflakes volume is {:.3}", cornflakes.volume());
  std::println("cornflakes weight is {:.3}", cornflakes.getWeight());
}
```

Unfortunately, there's a problem. The program won't compile. The difficulty is that we have foolishly used some nonunique function names in the base classes. The name volume is inherited as a function from Box and as a member variable from FoodContainer, and the getWeight() function is inherited from Carton and from FoodContainer in the CerealPack class. So there's more than one ambiguity problem here.

Of course, when writing classes for use in inheritance, you should avoid duplicating member names in the first instance. The ideal solution to this problem is to rewrite your classes. If you are unable to rewrite the classes—if the base classes are from a library of some sort, for example—then you would be forced to qualify the function names in main(). You could amend the output statement in main() to get the code to work:

```
std::println("cornflakes volume is {:.3}", cornflakes.Carton::volume());
std::println("cornflakes weight is {:.3}", cornflakes.FoodContainer::getWeight());
```

With this change, the program will compile and run, and it will produce the following output:

```
Box(double, double, double) called.
Carton(double,double,double,string_view) called.
FoodContainer(string_view) called.
CerealPack constructor
cornflakes volume is 240
cornflakes weight is 6.48
CerealPack destructor
FoodContainer destructor
Carton destructor. Material = Chipboard
Box destructor
```

You can see from the output that this cereal will give you a solid start to the day—a single packet weighs more than six pounds. You can also see that the constructor and destructor call sequences follow the same pattern as in the single inheritance context. The constructors run down the hierarchy from most base to most derived, and the destructors run in the opposite order. The CerealPack object has subobjects from both legs of its inheritance chain, and all the constructors for these subobjects are involved in the creation of a CerealPack object.

An alternative way of making Ex14_07 compile is by adding casts to a reference to either of the base classes (we cast to a reference and not the class type itself to avoid the creation of a new object):

```
std::println("cornflakes volume is {:.3}", static_cast<Carton&>(cornflakes).volume());
std::println("cornflakes weight is {:.3}",
                        static_cast<FoodContainer&>(cornflakes).getWeight());
```

A working version along these lines is in the code download as Ex14_07A.

It is clearly very inconvenient, however, that users of our current CerealPack class must always disambiguate the volume() and getWeight() members using one of these clumsy workarounds. Luckily you can prevent this from happening, even if renaming the members is not an option (for whatever reason). The using keyword allows you to explicitly stipulate, once and for all, that a CerealPack's volume should always be computed using the volume() member of Carton and its weight using the getWeight() member of FoodContainer. The CerealPack class definition then becomes as follows (see Ex14_07B):

```
export class CerealPack : public Carton, public FoodContainer
{
public:
    // Constructor and destructor as before...

    using Carton::volume;
    using FoodContainer::getWeight;
};
```

Earlier in this chapter, you encountered a similar use of the using keyword to inherit constructors from the base class. In this case, you use it to cherry-pick from which base class a multiple inherited member function needs to be inherited. Now CerealPack users—or breakfast eaters, as they are more commonly known—can simply write this:

```
std::println("cornflakes volume is {:.3}", cornflakes.volume());
std::println("cornflakes weight is {:.3}", cornflakes.getWeight());
```

Clearly, this last option is thus preferred whenever there is a clear answer as to which multiple inherited members should be used. If you disambiguate the inheritance already in the class definition, it saves the users of your class the hassle of fighting against the compiler errors that would otherwise surely follow.

Repeated Inheritance

The previous example demonstrated how ambiguities can occur when member names of base classes are duplicated. Another ambiguity can arise in multiple inheritances when a derived object contains multiple versions of a subobject of one of the base classes. You must not use a class more than once as a direct base class, but it's possible to end up with duplication of an *indirect* base class. Suppose the Box and FoodContainer classes in Ex14_07 were themselves derived from a class called Common. Figure 14-9 shows the class hierarchy that is created.

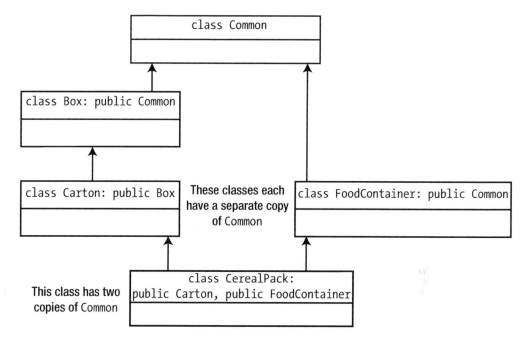

Figure 14-9. *Duplicate base classes in a derived class*

The CerealPack class inherits all the members of both the FoodContainer and Carton classes. The Carton class inherits all the members of the Box class, and both the Box and FoodContainer classes inherit the members of the Common class. Thus, as Figure 14-9 shows, the Common class is duplicated in the CerealPack class. The effect of this on objects of type CerealPack is that every CerealPack object will have two subobjects of type Common. The complications and ambiguities that arise from such repeated inheritance are often referred to as the *diamond problem*—named after the shape of inheritance diagrams such as Figure 14-9.

It is conceivable that you actually want to *allow* the duplication of the Common class. In that case, you must qualify each reference to the Common class member so that the compiler can tell which inherited member you're referring to in any particular instance. You can do this by using the Carton and FoodContainer class names as qualifiers because each of these classes contains a unique subobject of type Common. Of course, to call the Common class constructors when you're creating a CerealPack object, you would also need qualifiers to specify which of the two base objects you were initializing.

More typically, though, you would want to *prevent* the duplication of a base class, so let's see how to do that.

Virtual Base Classes

To avoid duplication of a base class, you must identify to the compiler that the base class should appear only once within a derived class. You do this by specifying the class as a *virtual base class* using the virtual keyword. The FoodContainer class would be defined like this:

```
export class FoodContainer : public virtual Common
{
  ...
};
```

The Box class would also be defined with a virtual base class:

```
export class Box : public virtual Common
{
  ...
};
```

Now any class that uses the FoodContainer and Box classes as direct or indirect bases will inherit the other members of the base classes as usual but will inherit only one instance of the Common class. The derived CerealPack class would inherit only a single instance of the Common base class. Because there is no duplication of the members of Common in the CerealPack class, no qualification of the member names is needed when referring to them in the derived class.

Converting Between Related Class Types

Every derived class object has a base class object inside it waiting to get out. Conversions from a derived type to its base are always legal and automatic. Here's a definition of a Carton object:

```
Carton carton{40, 50, 60, "Corrugated fiberboard"};
```

We have already seen two ways this object can be converted to a base class object of type Box. The first is by means of a copy constructor:

```
Box box{carton};
```

And the second is a copy assignment (see Chapter 13):

```
Box box;
box = carton;
```

Both convert the carton object to a new object of type Box and store a copy of it in box. The assignment operator that is used is the default assignment operator for the Box class. Of course, only the Box subobject part of carton is used; a Box object has no room for the Carton-specific member variables. This effect is called *object slicing*, as the Carton-specific portion is sliced off, so to speak, and discarded.

▓ **Caution**   Object slicing is something to beware of in general because it can occur when you don't want a derived class object to have its derived members sliced off. In the next chapter, you will learn about the mechanism that allows working with pointers or references to base class objects while preserving the members and even behavior of the derived class.

Conversions up a class hierarchy (that is, toward the base class) are legal and automatic as long as there is no ambiguity. Ambiguity can arise when two base classes each have the same type of subobject. For example, if you use the definition of the CerealPack class that contains two Common subobjects (as you saw in the previous section) and you initialize a CerealPack object, cornflakes, then the following will be ambiguous:

```
Common common{cornflakes};
```

The compiler won't be able to determine whether the conversion of cornflakes should be to the Common subobject of Carton or to the Common subobject of FoodContainer. The solution here would be to cast cornflakes to either Carton& or FoodContainer&. Here's an example:

```
Common common{static_cast<Carton&>(cornflakes)};
```

You can't obtain automatic conversions for objects down a class hierarchy—that is, toward a more specialized class. A Box object contains no information about any class type that may be derived from Box, so the conversion doesn't have a sensible interpretation.

Summary

In this chapter, you learned how to define a class based on one or more existing classes and how class inheritance determines the makeup of a derived class. Inheritance is a fundamental characteristic of object-oriented programming, and it makes polymorphism possible (polymorphism is the subject of the next chapter). The important points to take from this chapter include the following:

- A class may be derived from one or more base classes, in which case the derived class inherits members from all of its bases.

- Single inheritance involves deriving a class from a single base class. Multiple inheritance involves deriving a class from two or more base classes.

- Access to the inherited members of a derived class is controlled by two factors: the access specifier of the member in the base class and the access specifier of the base class in the derived class declaration.

- A constructor for a derived class is responsible for initializing *all* members of the class. This normally involves invoking a constructor of the base class to initialize all inherited members.

- The creation of a derived class object always involves the constructors of all of the direct and indirect base classes, which are called in sequence (from the most base through to the most direct) prior to the execution of the derived class constructor.

- A derived class constructor can, and often should, explicitly call constructors for its direct bases in the initialization list for the constructor. If you don't call one explicitly, the base class's default constructor is called. A copy constructor in a derived class, for one, should always call the copy constructor of all direct base classes.

- A member name declared in a derived class, which is the same as an inherited member name, will hide the inherited member. To access the hidden member, use the scope resolution operator to qualify the member name with its class name.

- You can use using not only for type aliases but also to inherit constructors (always with the same access specification as in the base class), to modify the access specifications of other inherited members, or to inherit functions that would otherwise be hidden by a derived class's function with the same name but different signature.

- When a derived class with two or more direct base classes contains two or more inherited subobjects of the same class, the duplication can be prevented by declaring the duplicated class as a virtual base class.

EXERCISES

The following exercises enable you to try what you've learned in this chapter. If you get stuck, look back over the chapter for help. If you're still stuck, you can download the solutions from the Apress website (https://www.apress.com/gp/services/source-code), but that really should be a last resort.

Exercise 14-1. Define a base class called Animal that contains two private member variables: a string to store the m_name of the animal (e.g., "Fido" or "Yogi") and an integer member called m_weight that will contain the weight of the animal in pounds. Also include a public member function, who(), that outputs a message giving the name and weight of the Animal object. Derive two classes named Lion and Aardvark, with Animal as a public base class. Write a main() function to create Lion and Aardvark objects ("Leo" at 400 pounds and "Algernon" at 50 pounds, say) and demonstrate that the who() member is inherited in both derived classes by calling it for the derived class objects.

Exercise 14-2. Change the access specifier for the who() function in the Animal class to protected, but leave the rest of the class as before. Now modify the derived classes so that the original version of main() still works without alteration.

Exercise 14-3. In the solution to the previous exercise, change the access specifier for the who() member of the base class back to public and implement the who() function as a member of each derived class so that the output message also identifies the name of the class. Change main() to call the base class and derived class versions of who() for each of the derived class objects.

Exercise 14-4. Define a Person class containing member variables to store a person's age, name, and gender. Derive an Employee class from Person that adds a member variable to store a personnel number. Derive an Executive class from Employee. Each derived class should define a member function who() that displays information about what it is. Think carefully about proper data hiding and access specifiers in this exercise. In this particular application, privacy concerns prohibit the exposure of personal details, except for the information printed by an object's who() member. Each class can explicitly decide what to expose there. (Name and type will do—something like "Fred Smith is an Employee.") Furthermore, people also aren't allowed to change name or gender, but they are allowed to age and have birthdays. Write a main() function to generate a vector of five executives and a vector of five ordinary employees and display information about them. In addition, display the information about the executives by calling the member function inherited from the Employee class.

CHAPTER 15

Polymorphism

Polymorphism is such a powerful feature of object-oriented programming that you'll use it in the majority of your C++ programs. Polymorphism requires you to use derived classes, so the content of this chapter relies heavily on the concepts related to inheritance in derived classes that we introduced in the previous chapter.

In this chapter, you'll learn

- What polymorphism is and how you get polymorphic behavior with your classes
- What a virtual function is
- What function overriding is and how this differs from function overloading
- How default parameter values for virtual functions are used
- When and why you need virtual destructors
- How you cast between class types in a hierarchy
- What a pure virtual function is
- What an abstract class is

Understanding Polymorphism

Polymorphism is a capability provided by many object-oriented languages. In C++, polymorphism always involves the use of a pointer or a reference to an object to call a member function. Polymorphism only operates with classes that share a common base class. We'll show how polymorphism works by considering an example with more boxes, but first we'll explain the role of a pointer to a base class because it's fundamental to the process.

Using a Base Class Pointer

In the previous chapter, you saw how an object of a derived class type contains a subobject of the base class type. In other words, you can regard every derived class object as a base class object. Because of this, you can always use a pointer to a base class to store the address of a derived class object; in fact, you can use a pointer to any direct or indirect base class to store the address of a derived class object. Figure 15-1 shows how the Carton class is derived from the Box base class by single inheritance, and the CerealPack class is derived by multiple inheritances from the Carton and FoodContainer base classes. It illustrates how pointers to base classes can be used to store addresses of derived class objects.

```
CerealPack cereal;

// You can store the address of
// the cereal object
// in any base class pointer:

Carton* pCarton {&cereal};
Box* pBox {&cereal};
FoodContainer* pFood {&cereal};

// You can store the address of
// a Carton object in a base pointer

Carton carton;
pBox = &carton;
```

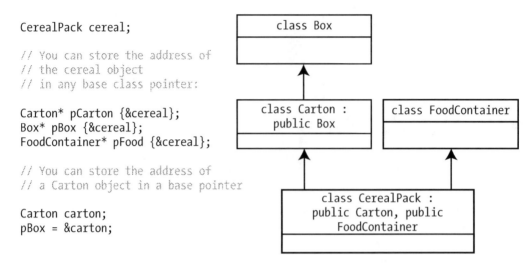

Figure 15-1. *Storing the address of a derived class object in a base class pointer*

The reverse is *not* true. For instance, you can't use a pointer of type Carton* to store the address of an object of type Box. This is logical because a pointer type incorporates the type of object to which it can point. A derived class object is a specialization of its base—it *is a* base class object—so using a pointer to the base to store its address is reasonable. However, a base class object is definitely *not* a derived class object, so a pointer to a derived class type cannot point to it. A derived class always contains a complete subobject of each of its bases, but each base class represents only part of a derived class object.

We'll look at a specific example. Suppose you derive two classes from the Box class to represent different kinds of containers, Carton and ToughPack. Suppose further that the volume of each of these derived types is calculated differently. For a Carton made of cardboard, you might just reduce the volume slightly to take the thickness of the material into account. For a ToughPack object, you might have to reduce the usable volume by a considerable amount to allow for protective packaging. The Carton class definition could be of the following form:

```
class Carton : public Box
{
public:
  double volume() const;

  // Details of the class...
};
```

The ToughPack class could have a similar definition:

```
class ToughPack : public Box
{
public:
  double volume() const;

  // Details of the class...
};
```

Given these class definitions (the function definitions follow later), you can declare and initialize a pointer as follows:

```
Carton carton {10.0, 10.0, 5.0};
Box* box {&carton};
```

The pointer box, of type pointer to Box, has been initialized with the address of carton. This is possible because Carton is derived from Box and therefore contains a subobject of type Box. You could use the same pointer to store the address of a ToughPack object because the ToughPack class is also derived from Box:

```
ToughPack hardcase {12.0, 8.0, 4.0};
box = &hardcase;
```

The box pointer can contain the address of any object of any class that has Box as a base. The type of the pointer, Box*, is called its *static type*. Because box is a pointer to a *base* class, it also has a *dynamic type*, which varies according to the type of object to which it points. When box is pointing to a Carton object, its dynamic type is a pointer to Carton. When box is pointing to a ToughPack object, its dynamic type is a pointer to ToughPack. When box points to an object of type Box, its dynamic type is the same as its static type. The magic of polymorphism springs from this. Under conditions that we'll explain shortly, you can use the box pointer to call a function that's defined both in the base class and in each derived class and have the function that is actually called selected at runtime on the basis of the dynamic type of box. Consider this statement:

```
double volume = box->volume();   // Store volume of the object pointed to
```

If box contains the address of a Carton object, then this statement calls volume() for the Carton object. If it points to a ToughPack object, then this statement calls volume() for ToughPack. This works for any classes derived from Box, if the aforementioned conditions are met. If they are, the expression box->volume() can result in different behavior depending on what box is pointing to. Perhaps more importantly, the behavior that is appropriate to the object pointed to by box is then selected automatically at runtime.

Polymorphism is a powerful mechanism. Situations arise frequently in which the specific type of an object cannot be determined in advance—not at design time or at compile time. Situations, in other words, in which the type can be determined only at runtime. This can be handled easily using polymorphism. Polymorphism is commonly used with interactive applications, where the type of input is up to the whim of the user. For instance, a graphics application that allows different shapes to be drawn—circles, lines, curves, and so on—may define a derived class for each shape type, and these classes all have a common base class called Shape. A program can store the address of an object the user creates in a pointer, shape, of type Shape* and draw the shape with a statement such as shape->draw(). This will call the draw() function for the shape that is pointed to, so this one expression can draw any kind of shape. Let's take a more in-depth look at how inherited functions behave.

Calling Inherited Functions

Before we get to the specifics of polymorphism, we need to explain the behavior of inherited member functions a bit further. To help with this, we'll revise the Box class to include a function that prints the usable volume of a Box object as computed by the familiar volume() function. The new version of the class definition will be as follows (we will comment on the module partitioning later):

```
// Box.cppm - Module partition interface file for the box partition of the boxes module
export module boxes:box;

import std;
```

```
export class Box
{
public:
  Box() : Box{ 1.0, 1.0, 1.0 } {}
  Box(double l, double w, double h) : m_length {l}, m_width {w}, m_height {h} {}

  // Function to print the usable volume of a Box object
  void printVolume() const
  { std::println("Box usable volume is {}", volume()); }

  // Function to calculate the volume of a Box object
  double volume() const { return m_length * m_width * m_height; }

  // 3 public getters, getLength(), getWidth(), and getHeight() (omitted for brevity)

private:
  double m_length, m_width, m_height;
};
```

Next, we'll define a ToughPack class with Box as a base. A ToughPack object incorporates packing material to protect its contents, so its capacity is only 87% of a basic Box object. Therefore, a different volume() function is needed in the derived class to account for this:

```
// ToughPack.cppm - Partition interface file for the tough_pack partition
export module boxes:tough_pack;

import :box;    // Import the box partition for use of Box as base class

export class ToughPack : public Box
{
public:
  // Inherit the Box(length, width, height) constructor
  using Box::Box;

  // Function to calculate volume of a ToughPack allowing 13% for packing
  double volume() const { return 0.87 * getLength() * getWidth() * getHeight(); }
};
```

Conceivably, you could have additional members in the derived ToughPack class. But for the moment, we'll keep it simple, concentrating on how the inherited functions work. The idea here is that you can get the inherited function printVolume() to call the derived class version of volume() when you call it for an object of the ToughPack class.

Thus far, we have always defined each class in its own module. In this chapter, we wanted to show you some other options, though. For Ex15_01, we defined the two classes—Box and ToughPack—in the same module, boxes. And because a single file containing two such massive classes would be truly unwieldy (just kidding—it's to illustrate this interesting possibility), we split this module into two partitions—boxes:box and boxes:tough_pack.

To use Box as a base class of ToughPack, we first had to import the boxes:box partition into the boxes:tough_pack partition. The module import declaration that took care of this looks as follows:

```
import :box;    // Import the box partition for use of Box as base class
```

Because you can only import partitions of the same module, there is no need to specify the boxes module name in this declaration. In fact, you are not even *allowed* to write import boxes:box;—neither within the same module, nor in any other source file. Modules can only be imported in their entirety, and module partitions can only be imported within other files of the same module.

Now that we have these two module partitions—each consisting of a single partition interface file—we still need to create the module's primary interface file. The one file that glues the module together. As explained in Chapter 11, every module needs precisely one primary interface file (a file starting with export module *name*;). For the boxes module this file simply re-exports the module's two partitions:

```
// Boxes.cppm - Primary module interface file
export module boxes;

export import :box;          // Export all partitions
export import :tough_pack;
```

With this primary module interface file in place, we're now ready to see whether invoking the inherited printVolume() function works as one might hope:

```
// Ex15_01.cpp - Behavior of inherited functions in a derived class
import boxes;

int main()
{
  Box box {20.0, 30.0, 40.0}; // Create a box
  ToughPack hardcase {20.0, 30.0, 40.0}; // Create a tough pack - same size

  box.printVolume();          // Display volume of base box (calls volume() for box)
  hardcase.printVolume();     // Display volume of derived box (call volume() for hardcase)
}
```

Unfortunately, when we run the program, we get this rather disappointing output:

```
Box usable volume is 24000
Box usable volume is 24000
```

The derived class object, hardcase, is supposed to have a capacity that is 13% less than that of the base class object (to account for the packing material, remember?), so the program is obviously *not* working as intended. Did the 13% jinx it?

Let's try to establish what's going wrong. The second call to printVolume() in main() is for an object of the derived class, ToughPack, but evidently this is not being taken into account. The trouble is that when the volume() function is called by the printVolume() function of Box, the compiler sets it once and for all as the version of volume() defined in the base class. No matter how you call printVolume(), it will never call the ToughPack version of the volume() function. It will always call the Box version of volume().

When function calls are fixed in this way before the program is executed, it is called *static resolution* of the function call, or *static binding*. The term *early binding* is commonly used as well. In this example, the Box::volume() function is bound to the call inside Box::printVolume() when the program is compiled and linked. Every time printVolume() is called, it uses this statically bound Box::volume() function.

But what if, instead of through printVolume(), you were to call the volume() function for the ToughPack object directly? As a further experiment, let's add statements in main() to call the volume() function of a ToughPack object directly, as well as through a pointer to the base class:

```
std::println("hardcase volume is {}", hardcase.volume());
Box* hardcaseBox {&hardcase};
std::println("hardcase volume through a Box* pointer is {}", hardcaseBox->volume());
```

Place these statements at the end of main(). Now when you run the program, you'll get this output:

```
Box usable volume is 24000
Box usable volume is 24000
hardcase volume is 20880
hardcase volume through a Box* pointer is 24000
```

This is quite informative. You can see that a call to volume() for the derived class object, hardcase, calls the derived class volume() function, which is what you want. The call through the base class pointer hardcaseBox, however, is resolved to the base class version of volume(), even though hardcaseBox contains the address of hardcase[1]. In other words, both calls are resolved statically. The compiler implements these calls as follows:

```
std::println("hardcase volume is {}", hardcase.ToughPack::volume());
Box* hardcaseBox {&hardcase};
std::println("hardcase volume through a Box* pointer is {}",
                              hardcaseBox->Box::volume());
```

A static function call through a pointer is determined solely by the pointer type and not by the object to which it points. In other words, it is determined by the *static type* of the pointer rather than the *dynamic type* of the object. The pointer hardcaseBox has a static type pointer-to-Box, so any static call using hardcaseBox calls a member function of Box.

---

[1] For the nitpickers, yes, because hardcaseBox has type Box* this variable technically does not contain the address of hardcase but that of the Box *subobject* of this ToughPack. And, yes, in general the address of a subobject may very well not be the same as that of the complete object, even if there is only a single base class. But we're not entirely wrong: because Ex15_01's ToughPack is a *standard layout class* (never mind what that means), the address of the Box subobject of a ToughPack object is, in this case, guaranteed to be exactly the same as that of the complete ToughPack object. In other words, the address stored in the hardcaseBox pointer (type Box*) will be exactly the same as the value of the expression &hardcase (type ToughPack*). In technical speak, the ToughPack object and its Box subobject are *pointer-interconvertible*. Once we make the Box class polymorphic in the next section, however— by adding a virtual function—the address of the Box subobject may become different from that of the ToughPack object (it then depends on how your specific compiler arranges the object and its subobject in memory).

> ■ **Note** Any call to a function through a base class pointer that is resolved statically calls a base class function. This applies not only to pointers such as hardcaseBox in our latest example, but also to the (implicit) this pointer in member functions of the base class (such as, for instance, within the Box::printVolume() function earlier).

What we want is that our program resolves which volume() function to call at runtime, not at compile time. What we want is for this to be based on the *dynamic type* of the pointed-to object, and not on the static type of the pointer. So, if printVolume() is called for a derived class object, the derived class volume() function should always be called, not the base class version, even if volume() is called through a base class pointer. This sort of operation is referred to as *dynamic binding* or *late binding*. To make this work, we must tell the compiler that the volume() function in Box and any overrides in the classes derived from Box are special, and that calls to them are to be resolved dynamically. We can obtain this effect by specifying that volume() in the base class is a *virtual function*, which will result in a *virtual function call* for volume().

Virtual Functions

When you specify a function as virtual in a base class, you indicate to the compiler that you want dynamic binding for function calls in any class that's derived from this base class. A virtual function is declared in a base class by using the virtual keyword, as shown in Figure 15-2. Describing a class as *polymorphic* means that it contains at least one virtual function.

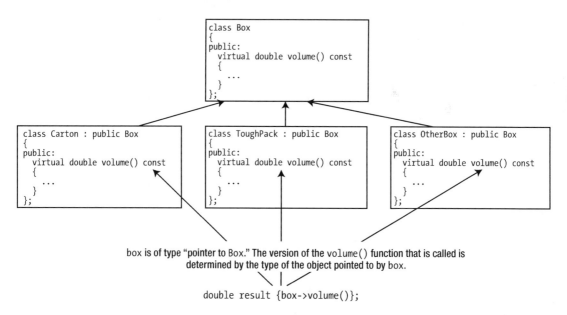

Figure 15-2. *Calling a virtual function*

A function that you specify as virtual in a base class will be virtual in all classes that are directly or indirectly derived from the base. This is the case whether or not you specify the function as virtual in a derived class. To obtain polymorphic behavior, each derived class may implement its own version of the virtual function (although it's not obliged to—we'll look into that later). You make virtual function calls using a variable whose type is a pointer or a reference to a base class object. Figure 15-2 illustrates how a call to a virtual function through a pointer is resolved dynamically. The pointer to the base class type is used to store the address of an object with a type corresponding to one of the derived classes. It could point to an object of any of the three derived classes shown or, of course, to a base class object. The type of the object to which the pointer points when the call executes determines which volume() function is called.

Note that a call to a virtual function using an object is *always* resolved statically. You *only* get dynamic resolution of calls to virtual functions through a pointer or a reference. Storing an object of a derived class type in a variable of a base type will result in the derived class object being sliced, so it has no derived class characteristics. With that said, let's give virtual functions a whirl. To make the previous example work as it should, a very small change to the Box class is required. We just need to add the virtual keyword in front of the definition of the volume() function:

```
export class Box
{
public:
  // Rest of the class as before...

  // Function to calculate the volume of a Box object
  virtual double volume() const { return m_length * m_width * m_height; }

  // ...
};
```

▒ **Caution**   If a member function definition is outside the class definition, you must *not* add the virtual keyword to the function definition; it would be an error to do so. You can only add virtual to declarations or definitions inside a class definition.

To make it more interesting, let's implement the volume() function in a new class called Carton a little differently. Here is the class definition:

```
// Carton.cppm
export module boxes:carton;

import :box;
import std;

export class Carton : public Box
{
public:
  // Constructor explicitly calling the base constructor
  Carton(double l, double w, double h, std::string_view mat = "cardboard")
    : Box{l, w, h}, m_material{mat}
  {}

  // Function to calculate the volume of a Carton object
  double volume() const
  {
    return std::max(getLength() - 0.5, 0.0)
         * std::max(getWidth() - 0.5, 0.0)
```

```
                 * std::max(getHeight() - 0.5, 0.0);
  }
private:
  std::string m_material;
};
```

The volume() function for a Carton object assumes the thickness of the material is 0.25, so 0.5 is subtracted from each dimension to account for the sides of the carton. If a Carton object has been created with one or more dimensions that are less than 0.5 for some reason, we set the carton's volume to 0. The alternative would be risking to end up with a negative volume, or—and this would possibly be even worse (as such a bug could be significantly harder to spot)—a positive volume obtained from the product of two negative values.

We'll keep the remainder of the boxes module of Ex15_01 as it was. So after turning Box::volume() into a virtual function and creating the new module partition for the Carton class, all you still have to do is add export import :carton; to the primary module interface file, and you are ready to try out virtual functions. Here's the code for the source file containing main():

```
// Ex15_02.cpp - Using virtual functions
import std;
import boxes;

int main()
{
  Box box {20.0, 30.0, 40.0};
  ToughPack hardcase {20.0, 30.0, 40.0};       // A derived box - same size
  Carton carton {20.0, 30.0, 40.0, "Plastic"}; // A different derived box

  box.printVolume();         // Volume of Box
  hardcase.printVolume();    // Volume of ToughPack
  carton.printVolume();      // Volume of Carton

  // Now using a base pointer...
  Box* base {&box};          // Points to type Box
  std::println("\nbox volume through base pointer is {}", base->volume());
  base->printVolume();

  base = &hardcase;          // Points to type ToughPack
  std::println("hardcase volume through base pointer is {}", base->volume());
  base->printVolume();

  base = &carton;            // Points to type Carton
  std::println("carton volume through base pointer is {}", base->volume());
  base->printVolume();
}
```

The output that is produced should be as follows:

```
Box usable volume is 24000
Box usable volume is 20880
Box usable volume is 22722.375
```

```
box volume through base pointer is 24000
Box usable volume is 24000
hardcase volume through base pointer is 20880
Box usable volume is 20880
carton volume through base pointer is 22722.375
Box usable volume is 22722.375
```

Notice that we have not added the virtual keyword to the volume() functions of either the Carton or ToughPack class. The virtual keyword applied to the function volume() in the base class is sufficient to determine that all definitions of the function in derived classes will also be virtual. You can optionally use the virtual keyword for your derived class functions as well, as illustrated in Figure 15-2. Whether or not you do is a matter of personal preference. We'll return to this choice later in this chapter.

The program is now clearly doing what we wanted. The call to printVolume() for the box object calls the base class version of volume() because box is of type Box. The next call to printVolume() is for the ToughPack object hardcase. It calls the printVolume() function inherited from the Box class, but the call to volume() in printVolume() is resolved to the version defined in the ToughPack class because volume() is a virtual function. Therefore, you get the volume calculated appropriately for a ToughPack object. The third call of printVolume() for the carton object calls the Carton class version of volume(), so you get the correct result for that too.

Next, you use the pointer base to call the volume() function directly and indirectly through the nonvirtual printVolume() function. The pointer first contains the address of the Box object box and then the addresses of the two derived class objects in turn. The resulting output for each object shows that the appropriate version of the volume() function is selected automatically in each case, so you have a clear demonstration of polymorphism in action.

Requirements for Virtual Function Operation

For a function to behave "virtually," its definition in a derived class must have the same signature as it has in the base class. If the base class function is const, for instance, then the derived class function must also be const. Generally, the return type of a virtual function in a derived class must be the same as that in the base class as well, but there's an exception when the return type in the base class is a pointer or a reference to a class type. In this case, the derived class version of a virtual function may return a pointer or a reference to a more specialized type than that of the base. We won't be going into this further, but in case you come across it elsewhere, the technical term used in relation to these return types is *covariance*.

If the function name and parameter list of a function in a derived class are the same as those of a virtual function declared in the base class, then the return type must be consistent with the rules for a virtual function. If it isn't, the derived class function won't compile. Another restriction is that a virtual function can't be a template function.

In standard object-oriented programming terms, a function in a derived class that redefines a virtual function of the base class is said to *override* this function. A function with the same name as a virtual function in a base class only overrides that function if the remainder of their signatures match exactly as well; if they do not, the function in the derived class is a new function that *hides* the one in the base class. The latter is what we saw in the previous chapter when we discussed duplicate member function names.

This implies that if you try to use different parameters for a virtual function in a derived class or use different const specifiers, then the virtual function mechanism won't work. The function in the derived class then defines a new, different function—and this new function will therefore operate with static binding that is established and fixed at compile time.

You can test this by deleting the const keyword from the definition of volume() in the Carton class and running Ex15_02 again. The volume() function signature in Carton no longer matches the virtual function in Box, so the derived class volume() function is not virtual. Consequently, the resolution is static so that the function called for Carton objects through a base pointer, or even indirectly through the printVolume() function, is the base class version.

▓ **Note**   static member functions cannot be virtual. As their name suggests, calls of static functions are always resolved statically. Even if you call a static member function on a polymorphic object, the member function is resolved using the static type of the object. This gives us yet another reason to always call static member functions by prefixing them with the class name instead of that of an object. That is, always use MyClass::myStaticFunction() instead of myObject.myStaticFunction(). This makes it crystal clear not to expect polymorphism.

Using the override Specifier

It's easy to make a mistake in the specification of a virtual function in a derived class. If you define Volume()—note the capital V—in a class derived from Box, it will not be virtual because the virtual function in the base class is volume(). This means that calls to Volume() will be resolved statically, and the virtual volume() function in the class will be inherited from the base class. The code may still compile and execute but not correctly. Similarly, if you define a volume() function in a derived class but forget to specify const, this function will overload instead of override the base class function. These kinds of errors can be difficult to spot. You can protect against such errors by using the override specifier for every virtual function declaration in a derived class, like this:

```
class Carton : public Box
{
public:
  double volume() const override
  {
    // Function body as before...
  }

  // Details of the class as in Ex15_02...
};
```

The override specification, like the virtual one, only appears within the class definition. It must not be applied to an external definition of a member function. The override specification causes the compiler to verify that the base class declares a class member that is virtual and has the same signature. If it doesn't, the compiler flags the definition containing the override specification as an error (give it a try!).

▓ **Tip**   Always add an override specification to the declaration of a virtual function override. First, this guarantees that you have not made any mistakes in the function signatures at the time of writing. Second, and perhaps even more important, it safeguards you and your team from forgetting to change any existing function overrides when the signature of the base class function changes.

Some argue that adding the override keyword already makes it clear to anyone reading your code that this is a virtual function, and therefore there's no need to apply the virtual keyword to virtual function overrides. Other style guides insist to always add virtual nonetheless because it makes it even more apparent that it concerns a virtual function. There is no right answer. In this book, we'll limit the use of the virtual keyword to base class functions and apply the override specification to all virtual function overrides in derived classes. But feel free to include the virtual keyword to function overrides as well if you feel it helps.

Using final

Sometimes you may want to prevent a member function from being overridden in a derived class. This could be because you want to limit how a derived class can modify the behavior of the class interface, for example. You can do this by specifying that a function is final. You could prevent the volume() function in the Carton class from being overridden by definitions in classes derived from Carton by specifying it like this:

```
class Carton : public Box
{
public:
  double volume() const override final
  {
    // Function body as before...
  }

  // Details of the class as in Ex15_02...
};
```

Attempts to override volume() in classes that have Carton as a base will result in a compiler error. This ensures that only the Carton version can be used for derived class objects. The order in which you put the override and final keywords does not matter—so both override final and final override are correct—but both have to come after const or any other part of the function signature.

▓ **Note** In principle you could declare a member function that is both virtual and final even if it does not override any base class member. This would be self-contradictory, though. You add virtual to allow function overrides, and you add final to prevent them. Note that there is no contradiction in combining override and final. This just states that you disallow any further overrides of the function you are overriding.

You can also specify an entire class as final, like this:

```
class Carton final : public Box
{
public:
  double volume() const override
  {
    // Function body as before...
  }

  // Details of the class as in Ex15_02...
};
```

Now the compiler will not allow Carton to be used as a base class. No further derivation from the Carton class is possible. Note that this time it is perfectly sensible to use final on a class that does not have any base class of its own. What does not make sense, though, is to introduce new virtual functions in a final class, that is, virtual functions that do not override a base class function.

■ **Note**   final and override are not keywords because making them keywords could break code that was written before they were introduced. This means you could use final and override as variable or even class names in your code. This doesn't mean you should, though; it only creates confusion.

Virtual Functions and Class Hierarchies

If you want your function to be treated as virtual when it is called using a base class pointer, then you must declare it as virtual in the base class. You can have as many virtual functions as you want in a base class, but not all virtual functions need to be declared within the most basic base class in a hierarchy. This is illustrated in Figure 15-3.

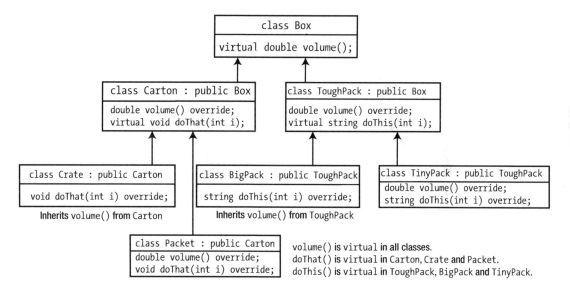

Figure 15-3. Virtual functions in a hierarchy

When you specify a function as virtual in a class, the function is virtual in all classes derived directly or indirectly from that class. All of the classes derived from the Box class in Figure 15-3 inherit the virtual nature of the volume() function, even if they do not repeat the virtual keyword. You can call volume() for objects of any of these class types through a pointer of type Box* because the pointer can contain the address of an object of any class in the hierarchy.

The Crate class doesn't define volume(), so the version inherited from Carton would be called for Crate objects. It is inherited as a virtual function and therefore can be called polymorphically.

A pointer carton, of type Carton*, could also be used to call volume(), but only for objects of the Carton class and the two classes that have Carton as a base: Crate and Packet.

The Carton class and the classes derived from it also contain the virtual function doThat(). This function can also be called polymorphically using a pointer of type Carton*. Of course, you cannot call doThat() for these classes using a pointer of type Box* because the Box class doesn't define the function doThat().

Similarly, the virtual function doThis() could be called for objects of type ToughPack, BigPack, and TinyPack using a pointer of type ToughPack*. Of course, the same pointer could also be used to call the volume() function for objects of these class types.

Access Specifiers and Virtual Functions

The access specification of a virtual function in a derived class can be different from the specification in the base class. When you call the virtual function through a base class pointer, the access specification in the base class determines whether the function is accessible, regardless of the type of object pointed to. If the virtual function is public in the base class, it can be called for any derived class through a pointer (or a reference) to the base class, regardless of the access specification in the derived class. We can demonstrate this by modifying the previous example. Modify the ToughPack class definition from Ex15_02 to make the volume() function protected, and add the override keyword to its declaration to make absolutely sure it indeed overrides a virtual function from the base class:

```
export class ToughPack : public Box
{
public:              // Optional: constructor is inherited as public regardless
  using Box::Box;    // Inherit Box(length, width, height) constructor

protected:
  // Function to calculate volume of a ToughPack allowing 13% for packing
  double volume() const override { return 0.87 * getLength() * getWidth() * getHeight(); }
};
```

The main() function changes very slightly with a commented-out statement added:

```
// Ex15_03.cpp - Access specifiers and virtual functions
import std;
import boxes;

int main()
{
  Box box {20.0, 30.0, 40.0};
  ToughPack hardcase {20.0, 30.0, 40.0};          // A derived box - same size
  Carton carton {20.0, 30.0, 40.0, "Plastic"};    // A different derived box

  box.printVolume();                              // Volume of Box
  hardcase.printVolume();                         // Volume of ToughPack
  carton.printVolume();                           // Volume of Carton
  std::println("");
```

```
// Uncomment the following statement for an error
// std::println("hardcase volume is {}\n", hardcase.volume());

    // Now using a base pointer...
    Box* base {&box};                       // Points to type Box
    std::println("box volume through base pointer is {}", base->volume());
    base->printVolume();

    base = &hardcase;                       // Points to type ToughPack
    std::println("hardcase volume through base pointer is {}", base->volume());
    base->printVolume();

    base = &carton;                         // Points to type Carton
    std::println("carton volume through base pointer is {}", base->volume());
    base->printVolume();
}
```

It should come as no surprise that this code otherwise produces the same output as the last example. Even though volume() is declared as protected in the ToughPack class, you can still call it for the hardcase object through the printVolume() function that is inherited from the Box class. You can also call it directly through a pointer to the base class, base. However, if you uncomment the line that calls the volume() function directly using the hardcase object, the code won't compile.

What matters here is whether the call is resolved dynamically or statically. When you use a class object, the call is determined statically by the compiler. Calling volume() for a ToughPack object calls the function defined in that class. Because the volume() function is protected in ToughPack, the call for the hardcase object won't compile. All the other calls are resolved when the program executes; they are polymorphic calls. In this case, the access specification for a virtual function in the base class is inherited in all the derived classes. This is regardless of the explicit specification in the derived class; the explicit specification only affects calls that are resolved statically.

So, access specifiers determine whether a function can be called based on the *static* type of an object. The consequence is that changing the access specifier of a function override to a more restricted one than that of the base class function is somewhat futile. This access restriction can easily be bypassed by using a pointer to the base class. This is shown by the printVolume() function of ToughPack in Ex15_03.

▨ **Tip** A function's access specifier determines whether you can *call* that function; it plays no role whatsoever, though, in determining whether you can *override* it. The consequence is that you can *override a* private virtual *function* of a given base class. In fact, it is often recommended that you declare your virtual functions private.

In a way, private virtual functions give you the best of two worlds. On one hand, the function is private, meaning it cannot be called from outside your class. On the other hand, the function is virtual, allowing derived classes to override and customize its behavior. In other words, even though you facilitate polymorphism, you are still in perfect control where and when such a private virtual member function is called. This function could be a single step in a more complex algorithm, a step that is to be executed only after all the previous steps of the algorithm have been correctly performed. Or it could be a function that may only be called after acquiring a particular resource, for instance after performing the necessary thread synchronization.

The fundamental idea behind this is the same as with data hiding. The more you restrict access to members, the easier it becomes to ensure that they aren't used incorrectly. Some classic object-oriented design patterns—most prominently the *template method* pattern—are best implemented using private virtual functions. These patterns are a bit too advanced for us to go in to more detail here. Just understand that access specifiers and overriding are two orthogonal concepts, and always keep in mind that declaring your virtual functions private is a viable option.

Default Argument Values in Virtual Functions

Default argument values are dealt with at compile time, so you can get unexpected results when you use default argument values with virtual function parameters. If the base class declaration of a virtual function has a default argument value and you call the function through a base pointer, you'll always get the default argument value from the base class version of the function. Any default argument values in derived class versions of the function will have no effect. We can demonstrate this quickly by altering the previous example to include a parameter with a default argument value for the volume() function in all three classes. Change the definition of the volume() function in the Box class to the following:

```
virtual double volume(int i=5) const
{
  std::print("(Box argument = {})          ", i);
  return m_length * m_width * m_height;
}
```

In the Carton class, it should be as follows:

```
double volume(int i = 50) const override
{
  std::print("(Carton argument = {})       ", i);
  return std::max(getLength() - 0.5, 0.0)
       * std::max(getWidth() - 0.5, 0.0)
       * std::max(getHeight() - 0.5, 0.0);
}
```

Finally, in the ToughPack class, you can define volume() as follows and make it public once more:

```
public:
  double volume(int i = 500) const override
  {
    std::print("(ToughPack argument = {})  ", i);
    return 0.87 * getLength() * getWidth() * getHeight();
  }
```

Obviously, the parameter serves no purpose here other than to demonstrate how default values are assigned.

Once you've made these changes to the class definitions, you can try the default parameter values with the main() function from the previous example, in which you uncomment the line that calls the volume() member for the hardcase object directly. The complete program is in the download as Ex15_04. You'll get this output:

```
(Box argument = 5)          Box usable volume is 24000
(ToughPack argument = 5)    Box usable volume is 20880
(Carton argument = 5)       Box usable volume is 22722.375
```

```
(ToughPack argument = 500)   hardcase volume is 20880

(Box argument = 5)           box volume through base pointer is 24000
(Box argument = 5)           Box usable volume is 24000
(ToughPack argument = 5)     hardcase volume through base pointer is 20880
(ToughPack argument = 5)     Box usable volume is 20880
(Carton argument = 5)        carton volume through base pointer is 22722.375
(Carton argument = 5)        Box usable volume is 22722.375
```

Every time volume() is called except one, the default parameter value is that specified for the base class function, namely 5. The exception is when you call volume() using the hardcase object. This is resolved statically to volume() in the ToughPack class, so the default parameter value specified in the ToughPack class is used. All the other calls are resolved dynamically, so the default parameter value specified in the base class applies, even though the function executing is in a derived class.

Using References to Call Virtual Functions

You can call a virtual function through a reference; reference parameters are particularly powerful tools for applying polymorphism, particularly when calling functions that use pass-by-reference. You can pass a base class object or any derived class object to a function with a parameter that's a reference to the base class. You can use the reference parameter within the function body to call a virtual function in the base class and get polymorphic behavior. When the function executes, the virtual function for the object that was passed as the argument is selected automatically at runtime. We can show this in action by modifying Ex15_02 to call a function that has a parameter of type reference to Box:

```cpp
// Ex15_05.cpp - Using a reference parameter to call virtual function
import std;
import boxes;

// Global function to display the volume of a box
void printVolume(const Box& box)
{
  std::println("Box usable volume is {}", box.volume());
}

int main()
{
  Box box {20.0, 30.0, 40.0};                  // A base box
  ToughPack hardcase {20.0, 30.0, 40.0};       // A derived box - same size
  Carton carton {20.0, 30.0, 40.0, "Plastic"}; // A different derived box

  printVolume(box);                            // Display volume of base box
  printVolume(hardcase);                       // Display volume of derived box
  printVolume(carton);                         // Display volume of derived box
}
```

Running this program should produce this output:

```
Box usable volume is 24000
Box usable volume is 20880
Box usable volume is 22722.375
```

The class definitions are the same as in Ex15_02. There's a new global function that calls volume() using its reference parameter to call the volume() member of an object. main() defines the same objects as in Ex15_02 but calls the global printVolume() function with each of the objects to output their volumes. As you see from the output, the correct volume() function is being used in each case, confirming that polymorphism works through a reference parameter.

Each time the printVolume() function is called, the reference parameter is initialized with the object that is passed as an argument. Because the parameter is a reference to a base class, the compiler arranges for dynamic binding to the virtual volume() function.

Polymorphic Collections

Polymorphism becomes particularly interesting when working with so-called polymorphic or heterogeneous collections of objects—both fancy names for collections of base class pointers that contain objects with different dynamic types. Examples of collections include plain C-style arrays, but also the more modern and powerful std::array<> and std::vector<> templates from the Standard Library.

We'll demonstrate this concept using the Box, Carton, and ToughPack classes from Ex15_03 and a revised main() function:

```cpp
// Ex15_06.cpp - Polymorphic vectors of smart pointers
import std;
import boxes;

int main()
{
  // Careful: this first attempt at a mixed collection is a bad idea (object slicing!)
  std::vector<Box> boxes;
  boxes.push_back(Box{20.0, 30.0, 40.0});
  boxes.push_back(ToughPack{20.0, 30.0, 40.0});
  boxes.push_back(Carton{20.0, 30.0, 40.0, "plastic"});

  for (const auto& box : boxes)
    box.printVolume();

  std::println("");

  // Next, we create a proper polymorphic vector<>:
  std::vector<std::unique_ptr<Box>> polymorphicBoxes;
  polymorphicBoxes.push_back(std::make_unique<Box>(20.0, 30.0, 40.0));
  polymorphicBoxes.push_back(std::make_unique<ToughPack>(20.0, 30.0, 40.0));
  polymorphicBoxes.push_back(std::make_unique<Carton>(20.0, 30.0, 40.0, "plastic"));

  for (const auto& box : polymorphicBoxes)
    box->printVolume();
}
```

The output from this example is as follows:

```
Box usable volume is 24000
Box usable volume is 24000
Box usable volume is 24000

Box usable volume is 24000
Box usable volume is 20880
Box usable volume is 22722.375
```

The first part of the program shows how *not* to create a polymorphic collection. If you assign objects of derived classes in a vector<> of base class objects by value, as always, object slicing will occur. That is, only the subobject corresponding to that base class is retained. The vector in general has no room to store the full object. The dynamic type of the object also gets converted into that of the base class. If you want polymorphism, you know you must always work with either pointers or references.

For our proper polymorphic vector in the second part of the program, we could've used a vector<> of plain Box* pointers—that is, a vector of type std::vector<Box*>—and store pointers to the dynamically allocated Box, ToughPack, and Carton objects in there. The downside of that would've been that we'd have had to remember to also delete these Box objects at the end of the program.

You already know that the Standard Library offers so-called smart pointers to help with this. Smart pointers allow us to work safely with pointers without having to worry all the time about deleting the objects.

In the polymorphicBoxes vector, we store elements of type std::unique_ptr<Box>, which are smart pointers to Box objects. The elements can store addresses for objects of Box or any class derived from Box, so there's an exact parallel with the raw pointers you have seen up to now. Fortunately, as the output shows, polymorphism remains alive and well with smart pointers. When you are creating objects in the free store, smart pointers still give you polymorphic behavior while also removing any potential for memory leaks.

░ **Tip** To obtain memory-safe polymorphic collections of objects, you can store smart pointers such as std::unique_ptr<> and shared_ptr<> inside containers such as std::vector<> and array<>.

Destroying Objects Through a Pointer

The use of pointers to a base class when you are working with derived class objects is very common because that's how you can take advantage of virtual functions. If you use pointers or smart pointers to objects created in the free store, a problem can arise when derived class objects are destroyed. You can see the problem if you add destructors to the various Box classes that display a message. Start from the files from Ex15_06 and add a destructor to the Box base class that just displays a message when it gets called:

```
export class Box
{
public:
  Box() : Box{ 1.0, 1.0, 1.0 } {}
  Box(double l, double w, double h) : m_length {l}, m_width {w}, m_height {h} {}
```

```
~Box() { std::println("Box destructor called"); }

// Remainder of the Box class as before...
};
```

Do the same for the ToughPack and Carton classes. That is, add destructors of the following form:

```
~ToughPack() { std::println("ToughPack destructor called"); }
```

and

```
~Carton() { std::println("Carton destructor called"); }
```

There is no need to change the main() function. The complete program is present in the code download as Ex15_07. It produces output that ends with the following dozen or so lines (the output that you'll see before this corresponds to the various Box elements being pushed and sliced into the first vector<>; but this is not the part we want to dissect here):

```
...
Box usable volume is 24000

Box usable volume is 24000
Box usable volume is 20880
Box usable volume is 22722.375
Box destructor called
Box destructor called
Box destructor called
Box destructor called
Box destructor called
Box destructor called
```

Clearly, we have a failure on our hands. The same base class destructor is called directly for all six objects, even though four of them are objects of a derived class. This occurs even for the objects stored in the polymorphic vector. Naturally, the cause of this behavior is that the destructor function is resolved statically instead of dynamically, just like with any other function. To ensure that the correct destructor is called for a derived class, we need dynamic binding for the destructors. What we need is virtual destructors.

▓ **Caution** You might think that for objects of classes such as ToughPack or Carton calling the wrong destructor is no big deal because their destructors are basically empty. It's not like the destructors of these derived classes perform any critical cleanup task or anything, so what's the harm if they aren't called? The fact of the matter is that the C++ standard specifically states that applying delete on a base class pointer to an object of a derived class results in undefined behavior, unless that base class has a virtual destructor. So while calling the wrong destructor may appear to be harmless, even during program execution, in principle anything might happen. If you're lucky, it's benign, and nothing bad happens. But it might just as well introduce memory leaks or even crash your program.

Virtual Destructors

To ensure that the correct destructor is always called for objects of derived classes that are allocated in the free store, you need *virtual class destructors*. To implement a virtual destructor in a derived class, you just add the keyword virtual to the destructor declaration in the base class. This signals to the compiler that destructor calls through a pointer or a reference parameter should have dynamic binding, so the destructor that is called will be selected at runtime. This makes the destructor in every class derived from the base class virtual, despite the derived class destructors having different names; destructors are treated as a special case for this purpose.

You can see this effect by adding the virtual keyword to the destructor declaration in the Box class of Ex15_07:

```
export class Box
{
public:
  Box() : Box{ 1.0, 1.0, 1.0 } {}
  Box(double l, double w, double h) : m_length {l}, m_width {w}, m_height {h} {}

  virtual ~Box() { std::println("Box destructor called"); }

  // Remainder of the Box class as before...
};
```

The destructors of all the derived classes will automatically be virtual as a result of declaring a virtual base class destructor. If you run the example again, the output will confirm that this is so:

```
...
Box usable volume is 24000

Box usable volume is 24000
Box usable volume is 20880
Box usable volume is 22722.375
Box destructor called
ToughPack destructor called
Box destructor called
Carton destructor called
Box destructor called
Box destructor called
Box destructor called
Box destructor called
```

If it weren't for the output message we added for illustration purposes, the body of the ~Box() destructor would have been an empty {} block. Instead of using such an empty block, though, we recommend you declare the destructor using the default keyword. This makes it much more visible that a default implementation is used. For our Box class, you would then write the following:

```
virtual ~Box() = default;
```

The default keyword can be used for all members the compiler would normally generate for you. This includes destructors but also, as you saw earlier, constructors and assignment operators. Note that compiler-generated destructors are never virtual, unless you explicitly declare them as such.

▦ **Tip** When polymorphic use is expected (or even just possible), your class must have a virtual destructor to ensure that your objects are always properly destroyed. This implies that as soon as a class has at least one virtual member function, its destructor should be virtual as well—be it explicitly due to a `virtual` specifier in its own definition, or implicitly due to a virtual destructor in a base class.

(The only time you do not have to follow this guideline is if the nonvirtual destructor is `protected`, but that is a rather exceptional case.)

▦ **Tip** When you define a derived class, you can add `override` to the destructor. This then prompts a compiler error if there's not at least one base class with a virtual destructor. In fact, you could even add a defaulted destructor with the `override` specifier solely to enforce that a base class's destructor is, and forever remains, virtual. For the `Carton` class, for instance, such a definition would look as follows:

```
~Carton() override = default; // Error if ~Box() is not virtual
```

Converting Between Pointers to Class Objects

You can implicitly convert a pointer to a derived class to a pointer to a base class, and you can do this for both direct and indirect base classes. For example, let's first define a smart pointer to a `Carton` object:

```
auto* carton{ new Carton{ 30, 40, 10 } };  // Normally, you should use smart pointers...
```

You can convert the pointer that is embedded in this smart pointer implicitly to a pointer to Box, which is a direct base class of `Carton`:

```
Box* box_pointer{ carton };
```

The result is a pointer to Box, which is initialized to point to the new `Carton` object. You know from examples Ex15_05 and Ex15_06 that this form of polymorphism also works with references and smart pointers, respectively. A reference to Box, for instance, could be obtained from `carton` as follows:

```
Box& box_reference{ *carton };
```

▦ **Note** As a rule, everything we discuss in this section about pointers applies to references as well. We will not always explicitly repeat this, though, nor will we always give analogous examples for references.

Let's look at converting a pointer to a derived class type to a pointer to an indirect base. Suppose you define a `CerealPack` class with `Carton` as the `public` base class. Box is a direct base of `Carton`, so it is an indirect base of `CerealPack`. Therefore, you can write the following:

```
CerealPack cerealPack{ 30, 40, 10, "carton" };
Box* box {&cerealPack};                       // Implicit cast to pointer-to-base-class
```

This statement converts the address in &cerealPack from type pointer to CerealPack to type pointer to Box. This would not be legal if the Box class was inaccessible. You could also specify the type conversion explicitly using the static_cast<>() operator, but doing so is not required:

```
Box* box {static_cast<Box*>(&cerealPack)};  // Explicit cast to pointer-to-base-class
```

The result of casting a derived class pointer to a base pointer type is a pointer to the subobject of the destination type. It's easy to get confused when thinking about casting pointers to class types. Don't forget that a pointer to a class type can only point to objects of that type or to objects of a derived class type and not the other way around. To be specific, a pointer of type Carton* could contain the address of an object of type Carton (which could be a subobject of a CerealPack object) or an object of type CerealPack. It cannot contain the address of an object of type Box because a CerealPack object is a specialized kind of Carton, but a Box object isn't. Figure 15-4 illustrates the possibilities between pointers to the Box, Carton, and CerealPack objects.

Creating the Pointer:

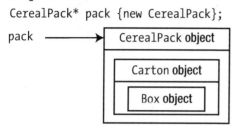

Cast to the Direct Base:

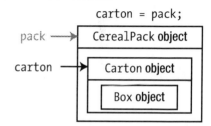

Cast to the Indirect Base:

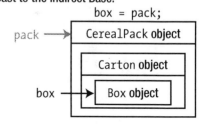

Figure 15-4. *Casting pointers up a class hierarchy*

Despite what we have said so far about casting pointers up a class hierarchy, it's sometimes possible to make casts in the opposite direction. Casting a pointer down a hierarchy from a base to a derived class is different; whether or not a cast works depends on the type of object to which the base pointer is pointing. For a static cast from a base class pointer such as box to a derived class pointer such as carton to be legal, the base class pointer must be pointing to a Box subobject of a Carton object. If that's not the case, the result of the cast is undefined. In other words, bad things will happen.

Figure 15-5 shows static casts from a pointer, box, that contains the address of a Carton object. The cast to type Carton* will work because the object is of type Carton. The result of the cast to type CerealPack*, on the other hand, is undefined because no object of this type exists.

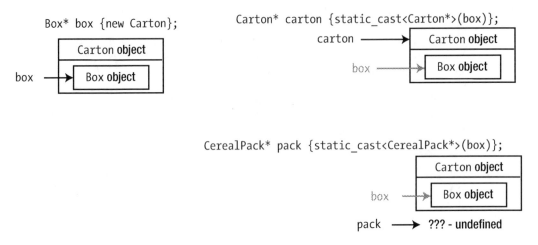

Figure 15-5. *Casting pointers down a class hierarchy*

If you're in any doubt about the legitimacy of a static cast, you shouldn't use it. The success of an attempt to cast a pointer down a class hierarchy depends on the pointer containing the address of an object of the destination type. A static cast doesn't check whether this is the case, so if you attempt it in circumstances where you don't know what the pointer points to, you risk an undefined result. Therefore, when you want to cast down a hierarchy, you need to do it differently—in a way in which the cast can be checked at runtime.

Dynamic Casts

A *dynamic cast* is a conversion that's performed at runtime. The dynamic_cast<>() operator performs a dynamic cast. You can only apply this operator to pointers and references to polymorphic class types, which are class types that contain at least one virtual function. The reason is that only pointers to polymorphic class types contain the information that the dynamic_cast<>() operator needs to check the validity of the conversion. This operator is specifically for the purpose of converting between pointers or references to class types in a hierarchy. Of course, the types you are casting between must be pointers or references to classes within the same class hierarchy. You can't use dynamic_cast<>() for anything else. We'll first discuss casting pointers dynamically.

Casting Pointers Dynamically

There are two kinds of dynamic cast. The first is a "cast down a hierarchy," from a pointer to a direct or indirect base type to a pointer to a derived type. This is called a *downcast*. The second possibility is a cast across a hierarchy; this is referred to as a *crosscast*. Figure 15-6 illustrates these.

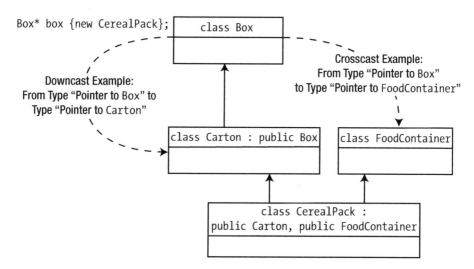

Figure 15-6. *Downcasts and crosscasts*

For a pointer, box, of type Box* that contains the address of a CerealPack object, you could write the downcast shown in Figure 15-6 as follows:

```
Carton* carton {dynamic_cast<Carton*>(box)};
```

The dynamic_cast<>() operator is written in the same way as the static_cast<>() operator. The destination type goes between the angled brackets following dynamic_cast, and the expression to be converted to the new type goes between the parentheses. For this cast to be legal, the Box and Carton classes must contain virtual functions, either as declared or inherited members. For the previous cast to work, box must point to either a Carton object or a CerealPack object because only objects of these types contain a Carton subobject. If the cast doesn't succeed, the pointer carton will be set to nullptr.

The crosscast in Figure 15-6 could be written as follows:

```
FoodContainer* foodContainer {dynamic_cast<FoodContainer*>(box)};
```

As in the previous case, both the FoodContainer class and the Box class must be polymorphic for the cast to be legal. The cast can succeed only if box contains the address of a CerealPack object because this is the only type that contains a FoodContainer object and can be referred to using a pointer of type Box*. Again, if the cast doesn't succeed, nullptr will be stored in foodContainer.

Using dynamic_cast<>() to cast down a class hierarchy may fail, but in contrast to the static cast, the result will be nullptr rather than just "undefined." This provides a clue as to how you can use this. Suppose you have some kind of object pointed to by a pointer to Box and you want to call a nonvirtual member function of the Carton class. A base class pointer only allows you to call the virtual member functions of a derived class, but the dynamic_cast<>() operator can enable you to call a nonvirtual function. If surface() is a nonvirtual member function of the Carton class, you could call it with this statement:

```
dynamic_cast<Carton*>(box)->surface();
```

This is obviously hazardous and in fact little or no better than using static_cast<>(). You need to be sure that box is pointing to a Carton object or to an object of a class that has the Carton class as a base. If this is not the case, the dynamic_cast<>() operator returns nullptr, and the outcome of the call again becomes undefined. To fix this, you can use the dynamic_cast<>() operator to determine whether what you intend to do is valid. Here's an example:

```
Carton* carton {dynamic_cast<Carton*>(box)};
if (carton)
  carton->surface();
```

Because you generally only need the carton variable inside the if branch of such an if statement, it's not uncommon to move the dynamic_cast<> into the condition of the if statement:

```
if (Carton* carton {dynamic_cast<Carton*>(box)})
  carton->surface();
```

This works because any variable definition is also an expression that evaluates to the value of the newly defined variable, in our example to the value of carton.

In fact, coding guidelines typically recommend reducing the scope of the carton variable like this, as it prevents inadvertent use of the nullptr further down the code. That is, if defined inside the condition of an if statement, a variable only exists within the scope of that if statement. (You can still use such a variable, though, inside an else branch of an if-else statement.) After the if statement, it no longer exists.

Note that, if you prefer, you can also make the nullptr check more explicit by splitting of the local variable definition from the nullptr check as follows (refer to Chapter 4 for the if (*initialization*; *condition*) syntax):

```
if (Carton* carton {dynamic_cast<Carton*>(box)}; carton != nullptr)
  carton->surface();
```

Either way, you'll only call the surface() member function if the result of the cast is not nullptr.

▨ **Caution**   A common mistake is to resort to dynamic casts too often, especially in those cases where polymorphism would be more appropriate. If at any time you find code of the following form, know that you may have to rethink the class design:

```
Base* base = ...;      // Start from a pointer-to-Base

// dynamic_cast to any number of derived types in a chain of if-else statements

if (auto derived1 = dynamic_cast<Derived1*>(base); derived1 != nullptr)
  derived1->DoThis();
else if (auto derived2 = dynamic_cast<Derived2*>(base); derived2 != nullptr)
  derived2->do_this();
...
else if (auto derivedN = dynamic_cast<DerivedN*>(base); derivedN != nullptr)
  derivedN->doThat();
```

More often than not, such code should be replaced with a solution based on polymorphism. In our fictional example, you should probably create a function called doThisOrThat() in the Base class and override it in any derived class that warrants a different implementation. This entire block of code then collapses to this:

```
Base* base = ...;    // Start from a pointer-to-Base
base->doThisOrThat();
```

Not only is this much shorter, this will even keep working if at some point yet another DerivedX class is added that derives from Base. This is precisely the power of polymorphism. Your code does not need to know about all possible derived classes, now or in the future. All it needs to know about is the interface of the base class. Any attempt to mimic this mechanism using dynamic casts is bound to be inferior.

While our previous example was clearly fictional, unfortunately we do see such patterns emerge all too often in real code. So, we do advise you to be very cautious about this!

A related symptom of dynamic_cast misuse we sometimes encounter, albeit less frequently, is a dynamic cast of a this pointer. Such ill-advised code might, for instance, look something like this:

```
void Base::DoSomething()
{
  if (dynamic_cast<Derived*>(this))    // NEVER DO THIS!
  {
    /* do something else instead... */
    return;
  }
  ...
}
```

The proper solution here is to make the DoSomething() function virtual and override it in Derived. Downcasting a this pointer is never a good idea, so please don't ever do this! The code of a base class has no business referring to derived classes. Any variation of this pattern should be replaced with an application of polymorphism.

▦ **Tip**   In general, leveraging polymorphism may involve you splitting a function into multiple functions, some of which you can then override. If you're interested, this is again related to the aforementioned *template method* design pattern. You can find more information online or in books about design patterns.

Dynamic Casts and const

Same as with static_cast<>(), you can't remove const-ness with dynamic_cast<>(). If the pointer type you're casting from is const, then the pointer type you are casting to must also be const. If you want to cast from a const pointer to a non-const pointer, you must first cast to a non-const pointer of the same type as the original using the const_cast<>() operator. Recall that using const_cast<>() is rarely recommended, though. Most of the time there is a good reason you have only a const pointer or reference at your disposal, meaning that side-stepping const-ness using const_cast<> may lead to unexpected or inconsistent states.

Converting References

You can apply the dynamic_cast<>() operator to a reference parameter in a function to cast down a class hierarchy to produce another reference. In the following example, the parameter to the function doThat() is a reference to a base class Box object. In the body of the function, you can cast the parameter to a reference to a derived type:

```
double doThat(const Box& box)
{
  ...
  const Carton& carton {dynamic_cast<const Carton&>(box)};
  ...
}
```

This statement casts from type reference to const Box to type reference to const Carton. Of course, it's possible that the object passed as an argument may not be a Carton object, and if this is the case, the cast won't succeed. There is no such thing as a null reference, so this fails in a different way from a failed pointer cast. What happens is that execution of the function stops, and an exception of type std::bad_cast is thrown. You haven't really met exceptions yet, but you'll find out what this means in the next chapter. Suffice to say, if you mistakenly expected box to always be a Carton, and you therefore also did not add code to handle bad_cast exceptions, a failed dynamic_cast<const Carton&> will make your entire program crash.

So, applying a dynamic cast to a reference blindly is clearly risky. You could go ahead and add code to handle the exception (see next chapter), but there's an easier alternative. Simply turn the reference into a pointer using the address-of operator, &, and apply the cast to the pointer instead. Then you can again check the resulting pointer for nullptr:

```
double doThat(const Box& box)
{
  ...
  if (const Carton* carton {dynamic_cast<const Carton*>(&box)})
  {
    ...
  }
  ...
}
```

Calling the Base Class Version of a Virtual Function

You've seen that it's easy to call the derived class version of a virtual function through a pointer or reference to a derived class object—the call is made dynamically. However, what do you do when you actually want to call the base class function for a derived class object?

If you override a virtual base class function in a derived class, you'll often find that the latter is a slight variation of the former. An excellent example of this is the volume() function of the ToughPack class you've been using throughout this chapter:

```
// Function to calculate volume of a ToughPack allowing 13% for packing
double volume() const override { return 0.87 * getLength() * getWidth() * getHeight(); }
```

Obviously, the getLength() * getWidth() * getHeight() part of this return statement is exactly the formula used to compute the volume() in the base class, Box. In this case, the amount of code you had to retype was limited, but this won't always be the case. It would be much better if you could simply call the base class version of this function instead.

A plausible first attempt to do so in our example case might be this:

```
double volume() const override { return 0.87 * volume(); }  // Infinite recursion!
```

If you write this, however, the volume() override is simply calling itself, which would then be calling itself again, which would then be calling itself again.... You get the idea; this would result in what we called infinite recursion in Chapter 8 and therefore a program crash (that is, if your compiler does not already flat out reject this code). The solution is to explicitly instruct the compiler to call the base class version of the function (a ToughPack.cppm with this modification is available in Ex15_08):

```
double volume() const override { return 0.87 * Box::volume(); }
```

Calling the base class version from within a function override like this is common. In some rare cases, though, you may also want to do something similar elsewhere. The Box class provides an opportunity to see why such a call might be required. It could be useful to calculate the loss of volume in a Carton or ToughPack object; one way to do this would be to calculate the difference between the volumes returned from the base and derived class versions of the volume() function. You can force the virtual function for a base class to be called statically by qualifying it with the class name. Suppose you have a pointer box that's defined like this:

```
Carton carton {40.0, 30.0, 20.0};
Box* box {&carton};
```

You can calculate the loss in total volume for a Carton object with this statement (see also Ex15_08):

```
double difference{ box->Box::volume() - box->volume() };
```

The expression box->Box::volume() calls the base class version of the volume() function. The class name, together with the scope resolution operator, identifies a particular volume() function, so this will be a static call resolved at compile time.

You can't use a class name qualifier to force the selection of a particular derived class function in a call through a pointer to the base class. The expression box->Carton::volume() won't compile because Carton::volume() is not a member of the Box class. A call of a function through a pointer is either a static call to a member function of the class type for the pointer or a dynamic call to a virtual function.

Calling the base class version of a virtual function through an object of a derived class can be done analogously. You can calculate the loss in volume for the carton object with this statement:

```
double difference{ carton.Box::volume() - carton.volume() };
```

Calling Virtual Functions from Constructors or Destructors

Ex15_09 illustrates what happens when you call virtual functions from inside constructors and destructors. As always, we start from a Box class with the necessary debugging statements in its relevant members:

```
// Box.cppm
export module boxes:box;
```

```
import std;

export class Box
{
public:
  Box(double length, double width, double height)
    : m_length {length}, m_width {width}, m_height {height}
  {
    std::println("Box constructor called for a Box of volume {}", volume());
  }
  virtual ~Box()
  {
    std::println("Box destructor called for a Box of volume {}", volume());
  }

  // Function to calculate volume of a Box
  virtual double volume() const { return m_length * m_width * m_height; }

  void printVolume() const
  {
    std::println("The volume from inside Box::printVolume() is {}", volume());
  }

private:
  double m_length, m_width, m_height;
};
```

We also need a derived class, one that overrides Box::volume():

```
export module boxes:tough_pack;
import std;
import :box;

export class ToughPack : public Box
{
public:
  ToughPack(double length, double width, double height)
    : Box{length, width, height}
  {
    std::println("ToughPack constructor called for a Box of volume {}", volume());
  }
  ~ToughPack() override
  {
    std::println("ToughPack destructor called for a Box of volume {}", volume());
  }

  // Function to calculate volume of a ToughPack allowing 13% for packing
  double volume() const override { return 0.87 * Box::volume(); }
};
```

The primary module interface file for boxes is trivial as always:

```
export module boxes;
export import :box;
export import :tough_pack;
```

And in this case the main program is trivial as well. All it does is create an instance of the derived class ToughPack and then show its volume:

```
// Ex15_09.cpp - Calling virtual functions from constructors and destructors
import boxes;

int main()
{
  ToughPack toughPack{1.0, 2.0, 3.0};
  toughPack.printVolume();    // Should print a volume equal to 87% of 1x2x3, or 5.22
}
```

This is the resulting output:

```
Box constructor called for a Box of volume 6
ToughPack constructor called for a Box of volume 5.22
The volume from inside Box::printVolume() is 5.22
ToughPack destructor called for a Box of volume 5.22
Box destructor called for a Box of volume 6
```

Focus first on the middle line of this output, which is the product of the toughPack.printVolume() function call. ToughPack overrides volume(), so if you call volume() on a ToughPack object, you expect the version of ToughPack to be used, even if this call originates from inside a base class function such as Box::printVolume(). The output clearly shows that this is also what happens. Box::printVolume() prints out a volume of 0.87 * 1 * 2 * 3, or 5.22, as expected.

Now let's see what happens if you call volume() not from a regular base class member function such as printVolume() but from a base class constructor. The first line in the output shows you that volume() then returns 6. So, it's clearly the original function of Box that gets called, not the overridden version of ToughPack! Why is that? You'll recall from the previous chapter that when an object is constructed, all its subobjects are constructed first, including the subobjects of all its base classes. While initializing such a subobject—for instance, the Box subobject of our ToughPack—the object of the derived class will at most be partially initialized. It would in general be extremely dangerous to call member functions on an object whose subobjects have not yet been fully initialized. This is why all function calls from inside a constructor, including those of virtual members, are always resolved statically.

Conversely, when destructing an object, all its subobjects are destructed in the reverse order in which they were constructed. So, by the time the destructor of the base class subobject is called, the derived class is already partially destructed. It would thus again be a bad idea to call members of this derived object. So, all function calls in destructors are thus resolved statically as well.

▓ **Caution**   Virtual function calls made from inside a constructor or a destructor are always resolved statically. If you, in rare cases, do need polymorphic calls during initialization, you should do so from within an init() member function—often virtual itself—that you then call *after* the construction of the object has completed. This is called the *dynamic binding during initialization* idiom.

How Polymorphic Function Calls Work

As you know, there's no such thing as a free lunch, and this also applies to polymorphism. You pay for polymorphism in two ways: it requires more memory, and virtual function calls result in additional runtime overhead. These consequences arise because of the way that virtual function calls are typically implemented in practice. Luckily, both costs are mostly marginal at best and can mostly be ignored.

For instance, suppose two classes, A and B, contain identical member variables, but A contains virtual functions, whereas B's functions are all nonvirtual. In this case, an object of type A requires more memory than an object of type B.

▓ **Note**   You can create a simple program with two such class objects and use the sizeof operator to see the difference in memory occupied by objects with and without virtual functions.

The reason for the increase in memory is that when you create an object of a polymorphic class type, a special pointer is created in the object. This pointer is used to call any of the virtual functions in the object. The special pointer points to a table of function pointers that gets created for the class. This table, usually called a *vtable* or *virtual function table*, has one entry for each virtual function in the class. Figure 15-7 illustrates this.

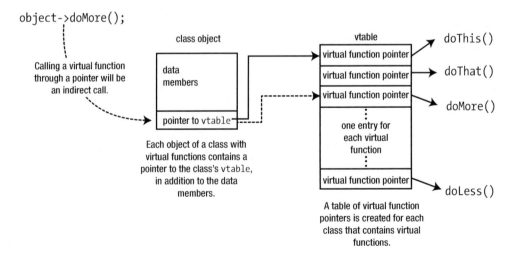

Figure 15-7. *How polymorphic function calls work*

When a function is called through a pointer to a base class object, the following sequence of events occurs:

1. The pointer to the vtable in the object pointed to is used to find the beginning of the vtable for the class.

2. The entry for the function to be called is found in the vtable, usually by using an offset.

3. The function is called indirectly through the function pointer in the vtable. This indirect call is a little slower than a direct call of a nonvirtual function, so each virtual function call carries some overhead.

However, and this is sometimes overlooked, the overhead in calling a virtual function is small and shouldn't give you cause for concern. A few extra bytes per object and ever so slightly slower function calls are small prices to pay for the power and flexibility that polymorphism offers. This explanation is just so you'll know why the size of an object that has virtual functions is larger than that of an equivalent object that doesn't.

░ **Tip**   The only time you should even debate whether the memory overhead of a virtual function table pointer is worth it is when you have to manage a truly large number of objects of the corresponding type at once. Suppose you have a `Point3D` class that represents a point in 3D space. If your program manipulates millions and millions of such points—a Microsoft Kinect, for instance, produces up to 9 million points per second—then avoiding virtual functions in `Point3D` can save you a significant amount of memory. For most objects the cost of a virtual function table pointer is only marginal, though, and well worth the benefits.

Determining the Dynamic Type

Suppose you have a reference to an object of a polymorphic class—which as you recall is a class with at least one virtual function. Then you can determine the dynamic type of this object using the `typeid()` operator. This standard operator returns a reference to a `std::type_info` object that encapsulates the actual type of its operand. Similar in use to the `sizeof` operator, the operand to the `typeid()` operator can be either an expression or a type. Concretely, the semantics of the `typeid()` operator are more or less as follows:

- If its operand is a type, `typeid()` evaluates to a reference to a `type_info` object representing this type.

- If its operand is any expression that evaluates to a reference to a polymorphic type, this expression is *evaluated*, and the operator returns the *dynamic type* of the value referred to by the outcome of this evaluation.

- If its operand is any other expression, the expression is *not evaluated*, and the result is the *static type* of the expression.

The reason we introduce this already more advanced operator to you is because `typeid()` can be a useful learning or debugging aid. It enables you to easily inspect the type of various expressions or to observe the difference between an object's static and dynamic type.

Let's create a program to see this operator in action. We'll again use the Box and Carton classes of Ex15_06. Of course, by now you know that any base class should have a virtual destructor, so naturally we have given the Box class a defaulted virtual destructor. But this small change is not that relevant in this example. Here, we'll use the Box classes to illustrate `typeid()`'s behavior with polymorphic classes.

▓ **Note**   To use the `typeid()` operator, you must always first import the `<typeinfo>` module from the Standard Library (either explicitly or through `import std;`). This makes the `std::type_info` class available, which is the type of the object returned by the operator. Note that there is an underscore in the name of the type but not in that of the module. Go figure!

```cpp
// Ex15_10.cpp - Using the typeid() operator
import std;
import boxes;

// Define trivial non-polymorphic base and derived classes:
class NonPolyBase {};
class NonPolyDerived : public NonPolyBase {};

Box& getSomeBox();              // Function returning a reference to a polymorphic type
NonPolyBase& getSomeNonPoly();  // Function returning a reference to a non-polymorphic type

int main()
{
  // Part 1: typeid() on types and == operator
  std::println("Type double has name {}", typeid(double).name());
  std::println("1 is {}", typeid(1) == typeid(int)? "an int" : "no int");

  // Part 2: typeid() on polymorphic references
  Carton carton{ 1, 2, 3, "paperboard" };
  Box& boxReference = carton;
  std::println("Type of carton is {}", typeid(carton).name());
  std::println("Type of boxReference is {}", typeid(boxReference).name());
  std::println("These are{} equal", typeid(carton) == typeid(boxReference) ? "" : " not");

  // Part 3: typeid() on polymorphic pointers
  Box* boxPointer = &carton;
  std::println("Type of &carton is {}", typeid(&carton).name());
  std::println("Type of boxPointer is {}", typeid(boxPointer).name());
  std::println("Type of *boxPointer is {}", typeid(*boxPointer).name());

  // Part 4: typeid() with non-polymorphic classes
  NonPolyDerived derived;
  NonPolyBase& baseRef = derived;

  std::println("Type of baseRef is {}", typeid(baseRef).name());

  // Part 5: typeid() on expressions
  const auto& type_info1 = typeid(getSomeBox());       // function call evaluated
  const auto& type_info2 = typeid(getSomeNonPoly());   // function call not evaluated
  std::println("Type of getSomeBox() is {}", type_info1.name());
  std::println("Type of getSomeNonPoly() is {}", type_info2.name());
}
```

```
Box& getSomeBox()
{
  std::println("getSomeBox() called...");
  static Carton carton{ 2, 3, 5, "duplex" };
  return carton;
}
NonPolyBase& getSomeNonPoly()
{
  std::println("getSomeNonPoly() called...");
  static NonPolyDerived derived;
  return derived;
}
```

A possible output of this program looks as follows:

```
Type double has name double
1 is an int
Type of carton is class Carton
Type of boxReference is class Carton
These are equal
Type of &carton is class Carton *
Type of boxPointer is class Box *
Type of *boxPointer is class Carton
Type of baseRef is class NonPolyBase
getSomeBox() called...
Type of getSomeBox() is class Carton
Type of getSomeNonPoly() is class NonPolyBase
```

Don't panic if your results look different. The names returned by the name() member function of type_info are not always quite so human readable. With some compilers, the type names that are returned are *mangled names*, which are the names that the compiler uses internally. If that's the case, your results might look more like this:

```
Type double has name d
1 is an int
Type of carton is 6Carton
Type of boxReference is 6Carton
These are equal
Type of &carton is P6Carton
Type of boxPointer is P3Box
Type of *boxPointer is 6Carton
Type of baseRef is 11NonPolyBase
getSomeBox() called...
Type of getSomeBox() is 6Carton
Type of getSomeNonPoly() is 11NonPolyBase
```

You can consult your compiler's documentation on how to interpret these names or possibly even on how to convert them to a human-readable format. Normally, the mangled names themselves should already carry sufficient information for you to follow this discussion.

The Ex15_10 test program consists of five parts, each illustrating a particular aspect of using the typeid() operator. We'll discuss each of them in turn.

In the first part, we apply typeid() on a hard-coded type name. In itself, this is not that interesting, at least not until you compare the resulting type_info to the result of applying typeid() to an actual value or expression, as shown in the second statement of main(). Note that the compiler does not perform any implicit conversions with type names. That is, typeid(1) == int is not legal C++; you have to explicitly apply the typeid() operator, as in typeid(1) == typeid(int).

The second part of the program demonstrates that typeid() can indeed be used to determine the dynamic type of an object of a polymorphic type—the main topic of this section. Even though the static type of the boxReference variable is Box&, the program's output should reflect that typeid() correctly determines the object's dynamic type: Carton.

The third part of the program shows you that typeid() does not work with pointers in quite the same way as it does with references. Even though boxPointer points to a Carton object, the result of typeid(boxPointer) does not represent Carton*; instead, it simply reflects the static type of boxPointer: Box*. To determine the dynamic type of the object pointed to by a pointer, you must dereference the pointer first. The outcome of typeid(*boxPointer) shows that this indeed works.

The program's fourth part illustrates that there is no way to determine the dynamic type of objects of nonpolymorphic types. To test this, we quickly defined two simple classes, NonPolyBase and NonPolyDerived, both trivially nonpolymorphic. Even though baseRef is a reference to an object of dynamic type NonPolyDerived, typeid(baseRef) evaluates to the static type of the expression instead, which is NonPolyBase. You can see the difference if you turn NonPolyBase into a polymorphic class, such as by adding a defaulted virtual destructor like this:

```
class NonPolyBase { public: virtual ~NonPolyBase() = default; };
```

If you then run the program again, the output should show that typeid(baseRef) now resolves to the type_info value for the NonPolyDerived type.

▓ **Note** To determine the dynamic type of an object, the typeid() operator needs so-called runtime type information (RTTI for short), which is normally accessed through the object's vtable.[2] Because only objects of polymorphic types contain a vtable reference, typeid() can determine the dynamic type only for objects of polymorphic types. (This, by the way, is also why dynamic_cast<> works only for polymorphic types.)

In the fifth and final part, you learn that the expression passed as an operand to typeid() is evaluated if and only if it has a polymorphic type; from the program's output, you should be able to read that the getSomeBox() got called, but getSomeNonPoly() did not. In a way, this is logical. In the former case, typeid() needs to determine the dynamic type because getSomeBox() evaluates to a reference to a polymorphic type. Without executing the function, the compiler has no way of determining the dynamic type of its result. The getSomeNonPoly() function, on the other hand, evaluates to a reference to a nonpolymorphic type. In this case, all the typeid() operator needs is the static type, which is something the compiler already knows at compile time simply by looking at the function's return type.

---

[2] Some compilers don't enable runtime type identification by default, so if this doesn't work, look for a compiler option to switch it on.

▓ **Caution** Because this behavior of typeid() can be somewhat unpredictable—sometimes its operand is evaluated, sometimes it is not[3]—we advise you to never include function calls in the operand to typeid(). If you only apply this operator to either variable names or types, you will avoid any nasty surprises.

Pure Virtual Functions

There are situations that require a base class with a number of classes derived from it and a virtual function that's redefined in each of the derived classes, but where there's no meaningful definition for the function in the base class. For example, you might define a base class, Shape, from which you derive classes defining specific shapes, such as Circle, Ellipse, Rectangle, Hexagon, and so on. The Shape class could include a virtual function called area() that you'd call for a derived class object to compute the area of a particular shape. The Shape class itself, though, cannot possibly provide a meaningful implementation of the area() function, one that caters, for instance, to both Circles and Rectangles. This is a job for a *pure virtual function*.

The purpose of a pure virtual function is to enable the derived class versions of the function to be called polymorphically. To declare a pure virtual function rather than an "ordinary" virtual function that has a definition, you use the same syntax but add = 0 to its declaration within the class.

If all this sounds confusing in abstract terms, you can see how to declare a pure virtual function by looking at the concrete example of defining the Shape class we just alluded to:

```
// Generic base class for shapes
class Shape
{
public:
  Shape(const Point& position) : m_position {position} {}
  virtual ~Shape() = default; // Remember: always use virtual destructors for base classes!

  virtual double area() const = 0;       // Pure virtual function to compute a shape's area
  virtual void scale(double factor) = 0; // Pure virtual function to scale a shape

  // Regular virtual function to move a shape
  virtual void move(const Point& position) { m_position = position; };

private:
  Point m_position;        // Position of a shape
};
```

The Shape class contains a member variable of type Point (which is another class type) that stores the position of a shape. It's a base class member because every shape must have a position, and the Shape constructor initializes it. The area() and scale() functions are virtual because they're qualified with the virtual keyword, and they are pure because the = 0 following the parameter list specifies that there's no definition for these functions in this class.

---

[3] With some popular compilers, we kid you not, you may even notice that typeid() evaluates its operand *twice*. In our example, that means that the line getSomeBox() called... might appear twice in the output. This is a compiler bug, of course. But still it's all the more reason never to apply typeid() to a function call.

A class that contains at least one pure virtual function is called an *abstract class*. The Shape class contains two pure virtual functions—area() and scale()—so it is most definitely an abstract class. Let's look a little more at exactly what this means.

Abstract Classes

Even though it has a member variable, a constructor, and even a member function with an implementation, the Shape class is an incomplete description of an object because the area() and scale() functions are not defined. Therefore, you're not allowed to create instances of the Shape class; the class exists purely for the purpose of deriving classes from it. Because you can't create objects of an abstract class, you cannot pass it by value to a function; a parameter of type Shape will not compile. Similarly, you cannot return a Shape by value from a function. However, pointers or references to an abstract class can be used as parameter or return types, so types such as Shape* and Shape& are fine in these settings. It is essential that this should be the case to get polymorphic behavior for derived class objects.

This raises the question, "If you can't create an instance of an abstract class, then why does the abstract class contain a constructor?" The answer is that the constructor for an abstract class is there to initialize its member variables. The constructor for an abstract class will be called by a derived class constructor, implicitly or from the constructor initialization list. If you try to call the constructor for an abstract class from anywhere else, you'll get an error message from the compiler.

■ **Tip** Because the Shape constructor is only intended for constructors in derived classes, we could have declared it in the protected section of the Shape class as well. However, while doing so does clarify the intent, it also effectively inhibits constructor inheritance. Remember that when inheriting a constructor, you always inherit the access specifier of the base class along with it, irrespective of which section of the derived class you put the inheritance declaration in. As a rule, we therefore prefer to declare constructors of abstract base classes in the public section.

Any class that derives from the Shape class must define both the area() function and the scale() function. If it doesn't, it too is an abstract class. More specifically, if any pure virtual function of an abstract base class isn't defined in a derived class, then the pure virtual function will be inherited as such, and the derived class will also be an abstract class.

To illustrate this, you could define a new class called Circle, which has the Shape class as a base. Suppose you export the Shape class from a shape module, then you can create a new shape.circle module that exports Circle as follows:

```
export module shape.circle;
import shape;
import std;

// Class defining a circle
export class Circle : public Shape
{
public:
  Circle(const Point& center, double radius) : Shape{center}, m_radius{radius} {}

  double area() const override {
    return m_radius * m_radius * std::numbers::pi;
  }
```

```
void scale(double factor) override { m_radius *= factor; }

private:
  double m_radius;    // Radius of a circle
};
```

The area() and scale() functions are defined, so this class is not abstract. If either function were not defined, then the Circle class would be abstract. The class includes a constructor, which initializes the base class subobject by calling the base class constructor.

Of course, an abstract class can contain virtual functions that it does define and functions that are not virtual. An example of the former was the move() function in Shape. It can also contain any number of pure virtual functions.

■ **Note**   For all boxes modules in this chapter, we defined each class in its own module partition. For shapes we decided to mix things up again and define each class back in its own separate module. That is, the identifier shape.circle is that of a module, *not* that of a partition. Module partitions always have identifiers of the form module:partition (mind the colon!). The difference is that the shape.circle module can be imported from any source file, whereas partitions can only be imported from source files belonging to the same module. As a user of these modules, you therefore always get all Box types at once—as a package deal, if you will—whereas you have to import the different Shape types separately. To get the best of both worlds, you could define an additional umbrella module that allows you to easily import several related modules at once. For example:

```
export module shapes;
export import shape.circle;
export import shape.rectangle;
// ... same for any other module exporting a shape class
```

How you package your types (and functions) into modules is entirely up to you. If a set of types is always used together, you'll probably want to group them in the same module. But if types can or typically are used independently, it may make more sense to create separate modules.

An Abstract Box Class

Let's look at a working example that uses an abstract class. For this, we'll define a new version of the Box class with the volume() function declared as a pure virtual function. As a polymorphic base class, it needs a virtual destructor as well:

```
export module boxes:box;
export class Box
{
public:
  Box(double l, double w, double h) : m_length {l}, m_width {w}, m_height {h} {}
  virtual ~Box() = default;                 // Virtual destructor
  // The usual getLength(), getWidth(), and getHeight() (omitted for brevity...)

  virtual double volume() const = 0;        // Function to calculate the volume
```

```
private:
  double m_length, m_width, m_height;
};
```

Because Box is now an abstract class, you can no longer create objects of this type. Even though the constructor is public, invoking it from anywhere but a constructor of a derived class will result in a compiler error.

The Carton and ToughPack classes in this example are essentially the same as seen several times before. They both define the volume() function, so they aren't abstract, and we can use objects of these classes to show that the virtual volume() functions are still working as before:

```
// Ex15_11.cpp - Using an abstract class
import std;
import boxes;

int main()
{
  // Box box{20.0, 30.0, 40.0};                // Uncomment for compiler error

  ToughPack hardcase {20.0, 30.0, 40.0};        // A derived box - same size
  Carton carton {20.0, 30.0, 40.0, "plastic"}; // A different derived box

  Box* base {&hardcase};                        // Base pointer - derived address
  std::println("hardcase volume is {}", base->volume());

  base = &carton;                               // New derived address
  std::println("carton volume is {}", base->volume());
}
```

This generates the following output:

```
hardcase volume is 20880
carton volume is 22722.375
```

Declaring volume() to be a (pure) virtual function in the Box class ensures that the volume() member functions of the Carton and ToughPack classes are also virtual. Therefore, you can call them through a pointer to the base class, and the calls will be resolved dynamically. The output for the ToughPack and Carton objects shows that everything is working as expected.

▓ **Note**   Because the Box::volume() is now a pure virtual function without a function body definition, you obviously can no longer invoke it with static binding. You also can no longer implement the volume() member of the ToughPack class like we did in Ex15_10:

```
double volume() const override { return 0.87 * Box::volume(); }
```

Without a definition of Box::volume(), you'll again have to spell out getLength() * getWidth() * getHeight() here.

▓ **Tip**   A little-known fact about pure virtual functions—so much so that we maybe shouldn't even mention it here—is that pure virtual functions can have a function body definition. That is, these definitions for Box and its volume() would be perfectly valid:

```
class Box
{
// ...
virtual double volume() const = 0;    // Pure virtual function...
// ...
};

// Definition for pure virtual function... (always out-of-class)
double Box::volume() const { return m_length * m_width * m_height; }
```

The Box class remains abstract, though, and all derived classes are still required to override volume(). This implies that the body of Box::volume() will never be executed through dynamic binding (think about it). So why define it then? Well, despite it being pure virtual, you can still invoke Box::volume() through *static* binding. Such invocations will typically appear in derived classes, and more specifically, in the functions that override that same pure virtual function. With Box::volume() defined as outlined; for instance, the definition of the ToughPack's volume() member in Ex15_11 could have remained the same as in Ex15_09:

```
// Statically invoking pure virtual base class function in overriding function...
double ToughPack::volume() const override { return 0.87 * Box::volume(); }
```

Abstract Classes as Interfaces

Sometimes an abstract class arises simply because a function has no sensible definition in the context of the class and has a meaningful interpretation only in a derived class. However, there is another way of using an abstract class. An abstract class that contains only pure virtual functions—no member variables or other functions—can be used to define what in object-oriented terminology is often called an *interface*. It would typically represent a declaration of a set of related functions that supported a particular capability—a set of functions for communications through a modem, for example. While other programming languages such as Java and C# have specific class-like language constructs for this, in C++ you define an interface using an abstract class consisting solely of pure virtual functions. As we've discussed, a class that derives from such an abstract base class must define an implementation for each virtual function, but the way in which each virtual function is implemented is specified by whoever is implementing the derived class. The abstract class fixes the interface, but the implementation in the derived class is flexible.

Because the abstract Shape and Box classes from the previous section have member variables, they're not really interface classes. An example of an interface would be the following Vessel class, defined in Vessel.cppm. All it does is specify that any Vessel has a volume, which may be obtained from its (pure virtual) volume() member function:

```
// Vessel.cppm - Abstract class defining a vessel
export module vessel;
```

```
export class Vessel
{
public:
  virtual ~Vessel() = default;          // As always: a virtual destructor!
  virtual double volume() const = 0;
};
```

There could be any number of classes implementing the Vessel interface. All would implement the interface's volume() function in their own way. Our first Vessel class will be, naturally, our beloved Box class:

```
export module boxes:box;
import vessel;

export class Box : public Vessel
{
public:
  Box(double l, double w, double h) : m_length {l}, m_width {w}, m_height {h} {}

  double volume() const override { return m_length * m_width * m_height; }

private:
  double m_length, m_width, m_height;
};
```

This makes any classes derived from Box valid Vessels as well. You can, for instance, use the Carton and ToughPack classes from earlier (although you can use Box::volume() again in ToughPack, if you want).

Of course, you can also add another class derived from Vessel. One example would be a class that defines a can. Here is a class definition you can place in Can.cppm:

```
// Can.cppm - Class defining a cylindrical can of a given height and diameter
export module can;
import vessel;
import std;

export class Can : public Vessel
{
public:
  Can(double diameter, double height)
    : m_diameter {diameter}, m_height {height} {}

  double volume() const override
  {
    return std::numbers::pi * m_diameter * m_diameter * m_height / 4;
  }

private:
  double m_diameter, m_height;
};
```

This defines Can objects that represent regular cylindrical cans, such as a beer can. You can find the program that glues everything together in Ex15_12.cpp:

```
// Ex15_12.cpp - Using an interface class and indirect base classes
import std;
import vessel;
import boxes;
import can;

int main()
{
  Box box {40, 30, 20};
  Can can {10, 3};
  Carton carton {40, 30, 20, "Plastic"};
  ToughPack hardcase {40, 30, 20};

  std::vector<const Vessel*> vessels {&box, &can, &carton, &hardcase};

  for (const auto* vessel : vessels)
    std::println("Volume is {:.6}", vessel->volume());
}
```

This generates the following output:

```
Volume is 24000
Volume is 235.619
Volume is 22722.4
Volume is 20880
```

This time around, we used a vector of raw pointers to Vessel objects to exercise the virtual functions. The output shows that all the polymorphic calls of the volume() function work as expected.

You have a three-level class hierarchy in this example, as shown in Figure 15-8.

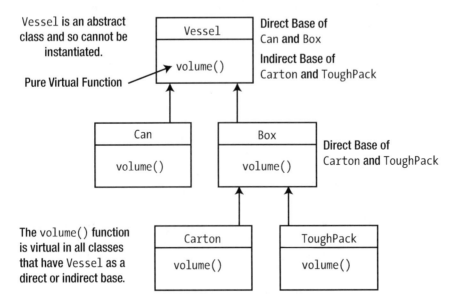

Figure 15-8. *A three-level class hierarchy*

Recall that if a derived class fails to define a function that's declared as a pure virtual function in the base class, then the function will be inherited as a pure virtual function, and this will make the derived class an abstract class. You can demonstrate this effect by removing the const and override keywords from either the Can or the Box class. This makes the function different from the pure virtual function in the base class, so the derived class inherits the base class version, and the program won't compile.

Summary

In this chapter, we covered the principal ideas involved in using inheritance. These are the fundamentals that you should keep in mind:

- Polymorphism involves calling a (virtual) member function of a class through a pointer or a reference and having the call resolved dynamically. That is, the particular function to be called is determined by the object that is pointed to or referenced when the program is executing.

- A function in a base class can be declared as virtual. All occurrences of the function in classes that are derived from the base will then be virtual too.

- You should always declare the destructor of classes intended to be used as a base class as virtual (often this can be done in combination with = default). This ensures correct selection of a destructor for dynamically created derived class objects. It suffices to do so for the most base class, but it does not hurt to do it elsewhere either.

- You should use the override qualifier with each member function of a derived class that overrides a virtual base class member. This causes the compiler to verify that the functions signatures in the base and derived classes are, and forever remain, the same.

- The final qualifier may be used on an individual virtual function override to signal that it may not be overridden any further. If an entire class is specified to be final, no derived classes can be defined for it anymore.

- Default argument values for parameters in virtual functions are assigned statically, so if default values for a base version of a virtual function exist, default values specified in a derived class will be ignored for dynamically resolved function calls.

- The dynamic_cast<> operator is generally used to cast from a pointer-to-a-polymorphic-base-class to a pointer-to-a-derived-class. If the pointer does not point to an object of the given derived class type, dynamic_cast<> evaluates to nullptr. This type check is performed dynamically, at runtime.

- A pure virtual function has no definition. A virtual function in a base class can be specified as pure by placing = 0 at the end of the member function declaration.

- A class with one or more pure virtual functions is called an *abstract class*, for which no objects can be created. In any class derived from an abstract class, all the inherited pure virtual functions must be defined. If they're not, it too becomes an abstract class, and no objects of the class can be created.

EXERCISES

The following exercises enable you to try what you've learned in this chapter. If you get stuck, look back over the chapter for help. If you're still stuck after that, you can download the solutions from the Apress website (https://www.apress.com/gp/services/source-code), but that really should be a last resort.

Exercise 15-1. Define a base class called Animal with two member variables: a string member to store the name of the animal (e.g., "Fido") and an integer member, weight, that will contain the weight of the Animal in pounds. Also include a public member function, who(), that returns a string object containing the name and weight of the Animal object, as well as a pure virtual function called sound() that in a derived class should return a string representing the sound the animal makes. Derive at least three classes—Sheep, Dog, and Cow—with the class Animal as a public base and implement the sound() function appropriately in each class.

Define a class called Zoo that can store the addresses of any number of Animal objects of various types in a vector<> container. Write a main() function to create a random sequence of an arbitrary number of objects of classes derived from Animal and store pointers to them in a Zoo object. To keep things simple, work with std::shared_ptr<> pointers to transfer and store Animals into the Zoo. (Later, in Chapter 18, we'll teach you about move semantics, which will allow you to use unique_ptr<> smart pointers for this as well.) The number of objects should be entered from the keyboard. Define a member function of the Zoo class that outputs information about each animal in the Zoo, including the text of the sound they all make.

Exercise 15-2. Start from the solution in Exercise 15-1. Because Cows are notoriously self-conscious about their weight, the result of the who() function of this class must no longer include the weight of the animal. Sheep, on the other hand, are whimsical creatures. They tend to prefix their name with "Woolly"—that is, for a Sheep called "Pete" who() should return a string containing "Woolly Pete". Besides that, it should also reflect a Sheep's true weight, which is its total weight (as stored in the Animal base object) minus that of its wool (known by the Sheep itself). Say that a new Sheep's wool by default weighs 10% of his total weight.

Exercise 15-3. Can you think of a way to implement the requirements in Exercise 15-2 without overriding who() in the Sheep class? (Hint: Perhaps Animal::who() could call polymorphic functions to obtain the name and weight of an Animal.)

Exercise 15-4. Add a function herd() to the Zoo class you made for Exercises 15-2 or 15-3 that returns a vector<Sheep*> with pointers to all Sheep in the Zoo. The Sheep remain part of the Zoo. Define a function called shear() for Sheep that removes their wool. The function returns the weight of the wool after correctly adjusting the weight members of the Sheep object. Adjust the program in Exercise 15-2 so that it gathers all Sheep using herd(), collects all their wool, and then outputs information in the Zoo again.

Hint: To extract an Animal* pointer from a given shared_ptr<Animal>, you call the get() function of the std::shared_ptr<> template.

Extra: In this chapter, you learned about two different language mechanisms that could be used to herd() Sheep, that is, two techniques to differentiate Sheep* from other Animal* pointers. Try both (leaving one commented out).

Exercise 15-5. You may have wondered why for the herd() function in Exercise 15-4 we asked you to switch from using Animal shared_ptr<>s to raw Sheep* pointers. Shouldn't that have been shared_ptr<Sheep> instead? The main problem is that you cannot simply cast a shared_ptr<Animal> to a shared_ptr<Sheep>. These are unrelated types as far as the compiler is concerned. But you are correct; it probably would've been better to use shared_ptr<Sheep>, and we were probably underestimating your capabilities there. All you really need to know is that to cast between shared_ptr<Animal> and shared_ptr<Sheep> you mustn't use the built-in dynamic_cast<> and static_cast<> operators, but instead the std::dynamic_pointer_cast<> and std::static_pointer_cast<> Standard Library functions. For instance, let shared_animal be a std::shared_ptr<Animal>. Then std::dynamic_pointer_cast<Sheep>(shared_animal) results in a std::shared_ptr<Sheep>. If shared_animal points to a Sheep, the resulting smart pointer will refer to that Sheep; if not, it will contain nullptr. Adapt the Exercise 15-4 solution to properly use smart pointers everywhere.

Exercise 15-6. Start from the Shape and Circle classes we used earlier to introduce abstract classes. Create one more Shape derivative, Rectangle, that has a width and a height. Introduce an extra function called perimeter() that computes a shape's perimeter. Define a main() program that starts by filling a polymorphic vector<> with a number of Shapes (a hard-coded list of Shapes is fine; there's no need to generate them randomly). Next, you should print out the total sum of their areas and perimeters, scale all Shapes with a factor 1.5, and then print out these same sums again. Of course, you haven't forgotten what you learned in the first half of this book, so you shouldn't put all code inside main() itself. Define the appropriate amount of helper functions!

Hint: For a circle with radius r, the perimeter (or circumference) is computed using the formula $2\pi r$.

CHAPTER 16

▨ ▨ ▨

Runtime Errors and Exceptions

Exceptions are used to signal errors or unexpected conditions in a program. While other error-handling mechanisms do exist, exceptions generally lead to simpler, cleaner code, in which you are less likely to miss an error. Particularly in combination with the *RAII principle* (short for "resource acquisition is initialization"), we will show that exceptions form the basis of some of the most effective programming patterns in modern C++.

In this chapter, you'll learn

- What an exception is and when you should use exceptions

- How you use exceptions to signal error conditions

- How you handle exceptions in your code

- What happens if you neglect to handle an exception

- What RAII stands for and how this idiom facilitates writing exception-safe code

- When to use the noexcept specifier

- Why to be extra careful when using exceptions inside destructors

- What types of exceptions are defined in the Standard Library

Handling Errors

Error handling is a fundamental element of successful programming. You need to equip your program to deal with potential errors and abnormal events, and this can often require more effort than writing the code that executes when things work the way they should. Every time your program accesses a file, a database, a network location, a printer, and so on, something unexpected could go wrong—a USB device is unplugged, a network connection is lost, a hardware error occurs, and so on. Even without external sources of errors, your code is likely not-bug free, and most nontrivial algorithms do fail at times for ambiguous or unexpected inputs. The quality of your error-handling code determines how robust your program is, and it is usually a major factor in making a program user-friendly. It also has a substantial impact on how easy it is to correct errors in the code or to add functionality to an application.

Not all errors are equal, and the nature of the error determines how best to deal with it. You don't usually use exceptions for errors that occur in the normal use of a program. In many cases, you'll deal with such errors directly where they occur. For example, when a user enters data, mistakes can result in erroneous input, but this isn't really a serious problem. It's usually quite easy to detect such errors, and the most appropriate course of action is often simply to discard the input and prompt the user to enter the

© Ivor Horton and Peter Van Weert 2023
I. Horton and P. Van Weert, *Beginning C++23*, https://doi.org/10.1007/978-1-4842-9343-0_16

data again. In this case, the error-handling code is integrated with the code that handles the overall input process. Generally, exceptions should be used if the function that notices the error cannot recover from this. A primary advantage of using exceptions to signal errors is that the error-handling code is separated completely from the code that caused the error.

The key is that the name *exception* is aptly chosen. Exceptions should be used only to signal *exceptional* conditions. Events that you do not expect to occur in the normal flow of your program and that require special attention. You should certainly never use exceptions during the nominal execution of a program—for instance, to return a result from a function. In a function that verifies whether the user entered the correct password to decrypt a file, you don't use an exception to signal that the password is incorrect. Instead, you simply return false. Users entering the wrong password once or twice is perfectly normal (you only really start paying attention the third time, right, to avoid getting locked out?). If reading the file goes wrong due to a disk read failure, however, then maybe you could consider throwing an exception.

▨ **Tip** Exceptions are by no means the only mechanism to signal errors. As seen in Chapter 9, C++23's std::expected<>, in particular, can be a worthy alternative at times. At the end of the day, though, exceptions do remain the most scalable, non-intrusive, non-repetitive mechanism around for most applications. A lot of fear of exceptions (and, believe us, there is a lot of that going around!) is misguided. When you use it for exceptional circumstances only, the impact of exceptions on performance (in both time and space) is almost always negligible. Exceptions also do not lead to more resource leaks than any of the alternatives; exceptions or not, if you don't use RAII techniques (as explained in this chapter), you *will* leak resources. Even the fact that uncaught exceptions (see later) lead to the termination of your program is mostly a good thing (continuing after an unexpected failure may lead to or increase data corruption, data loss, hardware failure, and so on). So don't be too hasty to discard exceptions as your primary error handling mechanism!

Understanding Exceptions

An *exception* is a temporary object, of any type, that is used to signal an error. In theory, an exception can be of a fundamental type, such as int or const char*, but it's usually and more appropriately an object of a class type. The purpose of an exception object is to carry information from the point at which the error occurred to the code that is to handle the error. In many situations, more than one piece of information is involved, so this is best done with an object of a class type.

When you recognize that something has gone wrong in the code, you can signal the error by *throwing* an exception. The term *throwing* effectively indicates what happens. The exception object is tossed to another block of code that *catches* the exception and deals with it. Code that may throw exceptions must be within a special block called a try block if an exception is to be caught. If a statement that is not within a try block throws an exception or a statement within a try block throws an exception that is not caught, the program terminates. We'll discuss this further a little later in this chapter.

A try block is followed immediately by one or more catch blocks. Each catch block contains code to handle a particular kind of exception; for this reason, a catch block is sometimes referred to as an exception *handler*. All the code that deals with errors that cause exceptions to be thrown is within catch blocks that are completely separate from the code that is executed when everything works as it should.

Figure 16-1 shows a try block, which is a normal block between braces that is preceded by the try keyword. Each time the try block executes, it may throw any one of several different types of exception. Therefore, a try block can be followed by several catch blocks, each of which handles an exception of a different type. A catch block is a normal block between braces preceded by the catch keyword. The type of exception that a catch block deals with is identified by a single parameter between parentheses following the catch keyword.

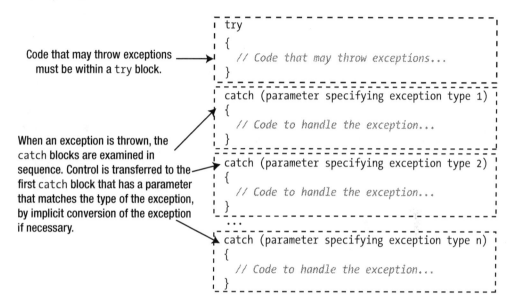

Code that may throw exceptions must be within a try block.

When an exception is thrown, the catch blocks are examined in sequence. Control is transferred to the first catch block that has a parameter that matches the type of the exception, by implicit conversion of the exception if necessary.

```
try
{
    // Code that may throw exceptions...
}

catch (parameter specifying exception type 1)
{
    // Code to handle the exception...
}

catch (parameter specifying exception type 2)
{
    // Code to handle the exception...
}
...

catch (parameter specifying exception type n)
{
    // Code to handle the exception...
}
```

Figure 16-1. *A try block and its catch blocks*

The code in a catch block executes only when an exception of a matching type is thrown. If a try block doesn't throw an exception, then none of the catch blocks following the try block is executed. A try block always executes beginning with the first statement following the opening brace.

Throwing an Exception

It's high time you threw an exception to find out what happens when you do. Although you should always use class objects for exceptions (as you'll do later in the chapter), we'll begin by using basic types because this will keep the code simple while we explain what's going on. You throw an exception using a *throw expression*, which you write using the throw keyword. Here's an example:

```
try
{
    // Code that may throw exceptions must be in a try block...

    if (test > 5)
        throw "test is greater than 5";    // Throws an exception of type const char*

    // This code only executes if the exception is not thrown...
}
```

```
catch (const char* message)
{
  // Code to handle the exception...
  // ...which executes if an exception of type 'char*' or 'const char*' is thrown
  std::println(R"(message caught - value is "{}")", message);
}
```

If the value of test is greater than 5, the throw statement throws an exception. In this case, the exception is the literal "test is greater than 5". Control is immediately transferred out of the try block to the first handler for the type of the exception that was thrown: const char*. There's just one handler here, which happens to catch exceptions of type const char*, so the statement in the catch block executes, and this displays the value of the caught exception. Notice that we used a raw string literal (see Chapter 7) to avoid having to escape the double quote characters, ", in the format string.

Let's try exceptions in a working example that will throw exceptions of type int and const char*. The output statements help you see the flow of control:

```
// Ex16_01.cpp - Throwing and catching exceptions
import std;

int main()
{
  for (int i {}; i < 5; ++i)
  {
    try
    {
      if (i < 2)
        throw i;

      std::println("i not thrown - value is {}", i);

      if (i > 3)
        throw "Here is another!";

      std::println("End of the try block");
    }
    catch (int i)      // Catch exceptions of type int
    {
      std::println("i caught - value is {}", i);
    }
    catch (const char* message)    // Catch exceptions of type char*
    {
      std::println(R"(message caught - value is "{}")", message);
    }

    std::println("End of the for loop body (after the catch blocks) - i is {}", i);
  }
}
```

This example produces the following output:

```
i caught - value is 0
End of the for loop body (after the catch blocks) - i is 0
i caught - value is 1
End of the for loop body (after the catch blocks) - i is 1
i not thrown - value is 2
End of the try block
End of the for loop body (after the catch blocks) - i is 2
i not thrown - value is 3
End of the try block
End of the for loop body (after the catch blocks) - i is 3
i not thrown - value is 4
message caught - value is "Here is another!"
End of the for loop body (after the catch blocks) - i is 4
```

The try block within the for loop contains code that will throw an exception of type int if i (the loop counter) is less than 2, and an exception of type const char* if i is greater than 3. Throwing an exception transfers control out of the try block immediately, so the output statement at the end of the try block executes only if no exception is thrown. The output shows that this is the case. You only get output from the last statement when i has the value 2 or 3. For all other values of i, an exception is thrown, so the output statement is not executed.

The first catch block immediately follows the try block. All the exception handlers for a try block must immediately follow the try block. If you place any code between the try block and the first catch block or between successive catch blocks, the program won't compile. The first catch block handles exceptions of type int, and you can see from the output that it executes when the first throw statement is executed. You can also see that the next catch block is not executed in this case. After this handler executes, control passes directly to the last statement at the end of the loop.

The second handler deals with exceptions of type char*. When the exception "Here is another!" is thrown, control passes from the throw statement directly to this handler, skipping the previous catch block. If no exception is thrown, neither of the catch blocks is executed. You could put this catch block before the previous handler, and the program would work just as well. On this occasion, the sequence of the handlers doesn't matter, but that's not always the case. You'll see examples of when the order of the handlers is important later in this chapter.

The statement that identifies the end of a loop iteration in the output is executed regardless of whether a handler is executed. Throwing an exception that is caught doesn't end the program—unless you want it to, of course—in which case you terminate the program in the catch block. If the problem that caused the exception can be fixed within the handler, then the program can continue.

The Exception-Handling Process

From the example, you should have a fairly clear idea of the sequence of events when an exception is thrown. Some other things happen in the background, though; you might be able to guess some of them if you think about how control is transferred from the try block to the catch block. The throw / catch sequence of events is illustrated conceptually in Figure 16-2.

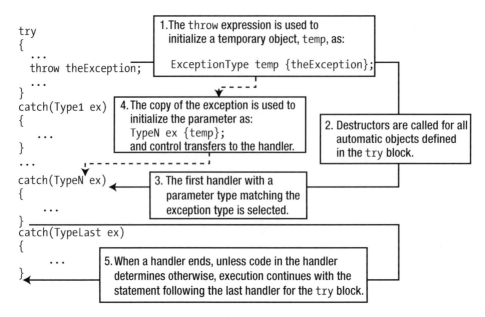

Figure 16-2. *The mechanism behind throwing and catching an exception*

Of course, a try block is a statement block, and you know that a statement block defines a scope. Throwing an exception leaves the try block immediately, so at that point all the automatic objects that have been defined within the try block prior to the exception being thrown are destroyed. The fact that none of the automatic objects created in the try block exists by the time the handler code is executed is most important; it implies that you must not throw an exception object that's a pointer to an object that is local to the try block. It's also the reason why the exception object is copied in the throw process.

Because the throw expression is used to initialize a temporary object you can throw *objects* that are local to the try block but not *pointers* to local objects. The copy of the object is used to initialize the parameter for the catch block that is selected to handle the exception.

A catch block is also a statement block, so when a catch block has finished executing, all automatic objects that are local to it (including the parameter) will be destroyed. Unless you transfer control out of the catch block using, for instance, a return statement, execution continues with the statement immediately following the last catch block for the try block. Once a handler has been selected for an exception and control has been passed to it, the exception is considered handled. This is true even if the catch block is empty and does nothing.

Code That Causes an Exception to Be Thrown

At the beginning of this discussion, we said that try blocks enclose code that may throw an exception. However, this doesn't mean that the code that throws an exception must be physically between the braces bounding the try block. It only needs to be logically within the try block. If a function is called within a try block, any exception that is thrown and not caught within that function can be caught by one of the catch blocks for the try block. An example of this is illustrated in Figure 16-3. Two function calls are shown within the try block: fun1() and fun2(). Exceptions of type ExceptionType that are thrown within either function can be caught by the catch block following the try block. An exception that is thrown but not caught within a function may be passed on to the calling function the next level up. If it isn't caught there, it can be passed one up to the next level; this is illustrated in Figure 16-3 by the exception thrown in fun3() when it is called by fun1(). There's no try block in fun1(), so exceptions thrown by fun3() will be passed to the function that called fun1(). If an exception reaches a level where no further catch handler exists and it is still uncaught, then the program is typically terminated (we'll discuss what happens after an uncaught exception in more detail later).

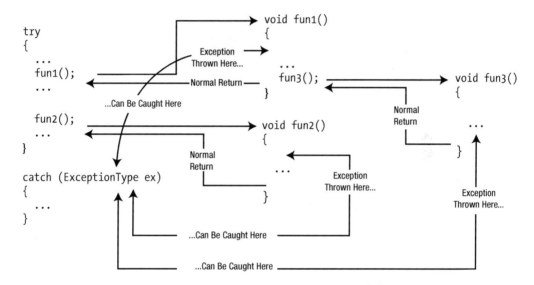

Figure 16-3. *Exception thrown by functions called within a try block*

Of course, if the same function is called from different points in a program, the exceptions that the code in the body of the function may throw can be handled by different catch blocks at different times. You can see an example of this situation in Figure 16-4.

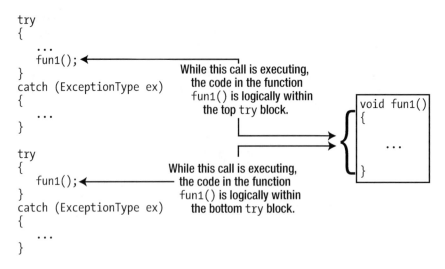

Figure 16-4. *Calling the same function from within different try blocks*

As a consequence of the call in the first try block, the catch block for that try block handles any exceptions of type ExceptionType thrown by fun1(). When fun1() is called in the second try block, the catch handler for that try block deals with any exception of type ExceptionType that is thrown. From this you should be able to see that you can choose to handle exceptions at the level that is most convenient to your program structure and operation. In an extreme case, you could catch all the exceptions that arose anywhere in a program in main() just by enclosing the code in main() in a try block and appending a suitable variety of catch blocks.

Nested try Blocks

You can nest a try block inside another try block. Each try block has its own set of catch blocks to handle exceptions that may be thrown within it, and the catch blocks for a try block are invoked for exceptions thrown only within that try block. This process is shown in Figure 16-5.

```
try
{
    ...         // outer try block

    try
    {
      ...      // inner try block
    }
    catch (ExceptionType1 ex) ◄──────────
    {
      ...
    }
    ...

}
catch (ExceptionType2 ex)◄───────────
{
    ...
}
```

This handler catches `ExceptionType1` exceptions thrown in the inner `try` block.

This handler catches `ExceptionType2` exceptions thrown in the outer `try` block, as well as uncaught exceptions of that type from the inner `try` block.

Figure 16-5. *Nested try blocks*

Figure 16-5 shows one handler for each try block, but in general there may be several. The catch blocks catch exceptions of different types, but they could catch exceptions of the same type. When the code in an inner try block throws an exception, its handlers get the first chance to deal with it. Each handler for the try block is checked for a matching parameter type, and if none matches, the handlers for the outer try block have a chance to catch the exception. You can nest try blocks in this way to whatever depth is appropriate for your application.

When an exception is thrown by the code in the outer try block, that block's catch handlers handle it, even if the statement originating the exception precedes the inner try block. The catch handlers for the inner try block can never be involved in dealing with exceptions thrown by code within the outer try block. The code within both try blocks may call functions, in which case the code within the body of the function is logically within the try block that called it.

Class Objects as Exceptions

You can throw any type of class object as an exception. However, the idea of an exception object is to communicate information to the handler about what went wrong. Therefore, it's usually appropriate to define a specific exception class that is designed to represent a particular kind of problem. This is likely to be application-specific, but your exception class objects almost invariably contain a message of some kind explaining the problem and possibly some sort of error code. You can also arrange for an exception object to provide additional information about the source of the error in whatever form is appropriate.

Let's define a simple exception class. We'll do so in a module with a fairly generic name, troubles, because we'll be adding more exception types to this module later:

```
// Troubles.cppm - Exception classes
export module troubles;
import std;
```

```
export class Trouble
{
public:
  explicit Trouble(std::string_view message = "There's a problem")
    : m_message {message}
  {}
  std::string_view what() const { return m_message; }
private:
  std::string m_message;
};
```

Objects of the Trouble class simply store a message indicating a problem and are thus ideally suited as simple exception objects. A default message is defined in the parameter list for the constructor, so you can use the default constructor to get an object that contains the default message. Whether you should be using such default messages is another matter entirely, of course. Remember, the idea is usually to provide information regarding the cause of the problem to aid with problem diagnosis. The what() member function returns the current message. To keep the logic of exception handling manageable, your functions should ensure that member functions of an exception class don't throw exceptions. Later in this chapter, you'll see how you can explicitly signal that a member function will never throw exceptions.

Let's find out what happens when a class object is thrown by throwing a few. As in the previous examples, we won't bother to create errors. We'll just throw exception objects so that you can follow what happens to them under various circumstances. We'll exercise the exception class with a simple example that throws some exception objects in a loop:

```
// Ex16_02.cpp - Throw an exception object
import std;
import troubles;

void trySomething(int i);

int main()
{
  for (int i {}; i < 2; ++i)
  {
    try
    {
      trySomething(i);
    }
    catch (const Trouble& t)
    {
      // What seems to be the trouble?
      std::println("Exception: {}", t.what());
    }
  }
}

void trySomething(int i)
{
  // There's always trouble when 'trying something'...
  if (i == 0)
    throw Trouble {};
```

```
    else
        throw Trouble {"Nobody knows the trouble I've seen..."};
}
```

This produces the following output:

```
Exception: There's a problem
Exception: Nobody knows the trouble I've seen...
```

Two exception objects are thrown by trySomething() during the for loop. The first is created by the default constructor for the Trouble class and therefore contains the default message string. The second exception object is thrown in the else clause of the if statement and contains a message that is passed as the argument to the constructor. The catch block catches both exception objects.

The parameter for the catch block is a reference. If you don't specify the parameter for a catch block as a reference, it'll be copied upon being caught—quite unnecessarily. The sequence of events when an exception object is thrown is that first the object is used to initialize a temporary object and the original is destroyed because the try block is exited and the object goes out of scope. This temporary object is then passed to the catch handler—by reference if the parameter is a reference. If you want to observe these events taking place, just add a copy constructor and a destructor containing some output statements to the Trouble class.

Matching a Catch Handler to an Exception

We said earlier that the handlers following a try block are examined in the sequence in which they appear in the code, and the first handler whose parameter type matches the type of the exception will be executed. With exceptions that are basic types (rather than class types), an exact type match with the parameter in the catch block is necessary. With exceptions that are class objects, implicit conversions may be applied to match the exception type with the parameter type of a handler. When the parameter type is being matched to the type of the exception that was thrown, the following are considered to be a match:

- The parameter type is the same as the exception type, ignoring const.

- The type of the parameter is a direct or indirect base class of the exception class type, or a reference to a direct or indirect base class of the exception class, ignoring const.

- The exception and the parameter are pointers, and the exception type can be converted implicitly to the parameter type, ignoring const.

The possible type conversions listed here have implications for how you sequence the catch blocks for a try block. If you have several handlers for exception types within the same class hierarchy, then the most derived class type must appear first and the most base class type last. If a handler for a base type appears before a handler for a type derived from that base, then the base type is always selected to handle the derived class exceptions. In other words, the handler for the derived type is never executed.

Let's add a couple more exception classes to the module containing the Trouble class and use Trouble as a base class for them. Here's how the contents of the module file will look with the extra classes defined:

```
// troubles.cppm - Exception classes
export module troubles;
import std;
```

```
export class Trouble
{
public:
  explicit Trouble(std::string_view message = "There's a problem") : m_message {message} {}
  virtual ~Trouble() = default;    // Base classes must have a virtual destructor!

  virtual std::string_view what() const { return m_message; }
private:
  std::string m_message;
};

// Derived exception class
export class MoreTrouble : public Trouble
{
public:
  explicit MoreTrouble(std::string_view str = "There's more trouble...")
    : Trouble {str}
  {}
};

// Derived exception class
export class BigTrouble : public MoreTrouble
{
public:
  explicit BigTrouble(std::string_view str = "Really big trouble...")
    : MoreTrouble {str}
  {}
};
```

Note that the what() member and the destructor of the base class have been declared as virtual. Therefore, the what() function is also virtual in the classes derived from Trouble. It doesn't make much of a difference here, but it would in principle allow derived classes to redefine what(). Remembering to declare a virtual destructor in a base class *is* important, though. Other than different default strings for the message, the derived classes don't add anything to the base class. Often, just having a different class name can differentiate one kind of problem from another. You just throw an exception of a particular type when that kind of problem arises; the internals of the classes don't have to be different. Using a different catch block to catch each class type provides the means to distinguish different problems. Here's the code to throw exceptions of the Trouble, MoreTrouble, and BigTrouble types, as well as the handlers to catch them:

```
// Ex16_03.cpp - Throwing and catching objects in a hierarchy
import std;
import troubles;

int main()
{
  for (int i {}; i < 7; ++i)
  {
    try
    {
      if (i == 3)
        throw Trouble{};
```

```
      else if (i == 5)
        throw MoreTrouble{};
      else if (i == 6)
        throw BigTrouble{};
    }
    catch (const BigTrouble& t)
    {
      std::println("BigTrouble object caught: {}", t.what());
    }
    catch (const MoreTrouble& t)
    {
      std::println("MoreTrouble object caught: {}", t.what());
    }
    catch (const Trouble& t)
    {
      std::println("Trouble object caught: {}", t.what());
    }

    std::println("End of the for loop (after the catch blocks) - i is {}", i);
  }
}
```

Here's the output:

```
End of the for loop (after the catch blocks) - i is 0
End of the for loop (after the catch blocks) - i is 1
End of the for loop (after the catch blocks) - i is 2
Trouble object caught: There's a problem
End of the for loop (after the catch blocks) - i is 3
End of the for loop (after the catch blocks) - i is 4
MoreTrouble object caught: There's more trouble...
End of the for loop (after the catch blocks) - i is 5
BigTrouble object caught: Really big trouble...
End of the for loop (after the catch blocks) - i is 6
```

Inside the for loop, objects of type Trouble, MoreTrouble, and BigTrouble are thrown as an exception. These objects are constructed at the moment they are thrown, as is often the case with exceptions. The type of object that is thrown depends on the value of the loop variable, i. Each of the catch blocks contains a different message, so the output shows which catch handler is selected when an exception is thrown. In the handlers for the two derived types, the inherited what() function still returns the message. Note that the parameter type for each of the catch blocks is a reference, as in the previous example. One reason for using a reference is to avoid making an unnecessary copy of the exception object. In the next example, you'll see another, more crucial reason why you should always use a reference parameter in a handler.

Each handler displays the message contained in the object thrown, and you can see from the output that each handler is called to correspond with the type of the exception thrown. The ordering of the handlers is important because of the way the exception is matched to a handler and because the types of your exception classes are related. Let's explore that in a little more depth.

Catching Derived Class Exceptions with a Base Class Handler

Exceptions of derived class types are implicitly converted to a base class type for the purpose of matching a catch block parameter, so you could catch all the exceptions thrown in the previous example with a single handler. You can modify the previous example to see this happening. Just delete or comment out the handlers for the two derived classes from main() in the previous example:

```cpp
// Ex16_04.cpp - Catching exceptions with a base class handler
import std;
import troubles;

int main()
{
  for (int i {}; i < 7; ++i)
  {
    try
    {
      if (i == 3)
        throw Trouble{};
      else if (i == 5)
        throw MoreTrouble{};
      else if (i == 6)
        throw BigTrouble{};
    }
    catch (const Trouble& t)
    {
      std::println("Trouble object caught: {}", t.what());
    }
    std::println("End of the for loop (after the catch blocks) - i is {}", i);
  }
}
```

The program now produces this output:

```
End of the for loop (after the catch blocks) - i is 0
End of the for loop (after the catch blocks) - i is 1
End of the for loop (after the catch blocks) - i is 2
Trouble object caught: There's a problem
End of the for loop (after the catch blocks) - i is 3
End of the for loop (after the catch blocks) - i is 4
Trouble object caught: There's more trouble...
End of the for loop (after the catch blocks) - i is 5
Trouble object caught: Really big trouble...
End of the for loop (after the catch blocks) - i is 6
```

The catch block with the parameter of type const Trouble& now catches all the exceptions thrown in the try block. If the parameter in a catch block is a reference to a base class, then it matches any derived class exception. So, although the output proclaims "Trouble object caught" for each exception, the output corresponds to objects of other classes that are derived from Trouble.

The dynamic type is retained when the exception is passed by reference. To verify this is indeed so, you could obtain the dynamic type and display it using the typeid() operator. Just modify the code for the handler to the following:

```
catch (const Trouble& t)
{
  std::println("{} object caught: {}", typeid(t).name(), t.what());
}
```

Remember, the typeid() operator returns an object of the type_info class, and calling its name() member returns the class name. With this modification to the code, the output shows that the derived class exceptions still retain their dynamic types, even though the reference in the exception handler is to the base class. For the record, the output from this version of the program looks like this:

```
End of the for loop (after the catch blocks) - i is 0
End of the for loop (after the catch blocks) - i is 1
End of the for loop (after the catch blocks) - i is 2
class Trouble object caught: There's a problem
End of the for loop (after the catch blocks) - i is 3
End of the for loop (after the catch blocks) - i is 4
class MoreTrouble object caught: There's more trouble...
End of the for loop (after the catch blocks) - i is 5
class BigTrouble object caught: Really big trouble...
End of the for loop (after the catch blocks) - i is 6
```

▨ **Note** If your compiler's version of the typeid() operator results in mangled names, the names of the exception classes in your program's output may look less pleasing to the eye. This was discussed in Chapter 15. For illustration's sake, we will always show the results in an unmangled, human-readable format.

Try changing the parameter type for the handler to Trouble so that the exception is caught by value rather than by reference:

```
catch (Trouble t)
{
  std::println("{} object caught: {}", typeid(t).name(), t.what());
}
```

This version of the program produces the output:

```
End of the for loop (after the catch blocks) - i is 0
End of the for loop (after the catch blocks) - i is 1
End of the for loop (after the catch blocks) - i is 2
class Trouble object caught: There's a problem
End of the for loop (after the catch blocks) - i is 3
End of the for loop (after the catch blocks) - i is 4
```

```
class Trouble object caught: There's more trouble...
End of the for loop (after the catch blocks) - i is 5
class Trouble object caught: Really big trouble...
End of the for loop (after the catch blocks) - i is 6
```

Here, the Trouble handler is still selected for the derived class objects, but the dynamic type is not preserved. This is because the parameter is initialized using the base class copy constructor, so any properties associated with the derived class are lost. Only the base class subobject of the original derived class object is retained. This is an example of *object slicing*, which occurs because the base class copy constructor knows nothing about derived objects. As explained in Chapter 14, object slicing is a common source of error caused by passing objects by value. This leads us to the inevitable conclusion that you should *always* use reference parameters in catch blocks:

■ **Tip** The golden rule for exceptions is to always *throw by value and catch by reference* (reference-to-const, normally). In other words, you mustn't throw a new'ed exception (and definitely no pointer to a local object), nor should you ever catch an exception object by value. Obviously, catching by value would result in a redundant copy, but that's not the worst of it. Catching by value may slice off parts of the exception object. The reason this is so important is that this might slice off precisely that valuable piece of information that you need to diagnose which error occurred and why!

Rethrowing Exceptions

When a handler catches an exception, it can *rethrow* it to allow a handler for an outer try block to catch it. You rethrow the current exception with a statement consisting of just the throw keyword:

```
throw;    // Rethrow the exception
```

This rethrows the existing exception object without copying it. You might rethrow an exception if a handler that catches exceptions of more than one derived class type discovers that the type of the exception requires it to be passed on to another level of try block. You might want to register or log the point in the program where an exception was thrown, before rethrowing it. Or you may need to clean up some resources—release some memory, close a database connection, etc.—before rethrowing the exception for handling in a caller function.

Note that rethrowing an exception from the inner try block doesn't make the exception available to other handlers for the inner try block. When a handler is executing, any exception that is thrown (including the current exception) needs to be caught by a handler for a try block that *encloses* the current handler, as illustrated in Figure 16-6. The fact that a rethrown exception is not copied is important, especially when the exception is a derived class object that initialized a base class reference parameter. We'll demonstrate this with an example.

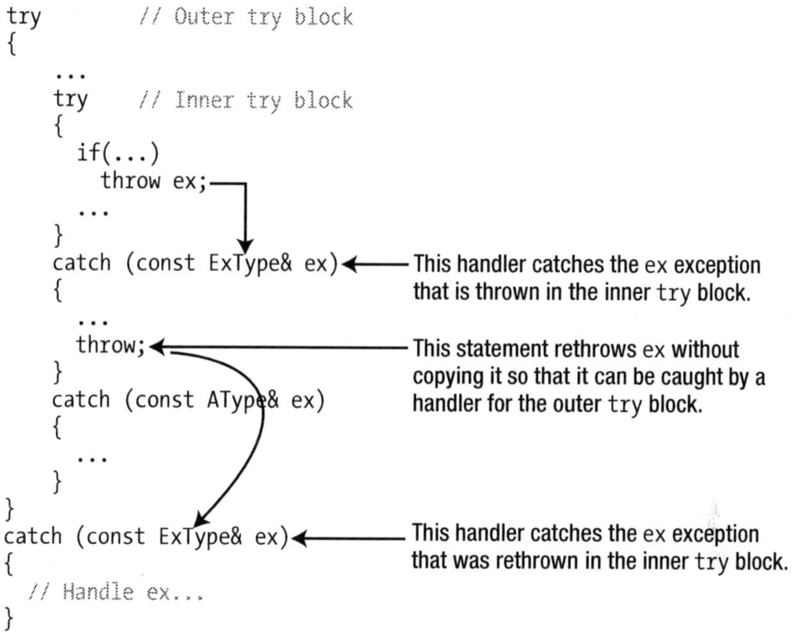

```
try         // Outer try block
{
    ...
    try     // Inner try block
    {
      if(...)
        throw ex;
      ...
    }
    catch (const ExType& ex)          This handler catches the ex exception
    {                                 that is thrown in the inner try block.
      ...
      throw;                          This statement rethrows ex without
    }                                 copying it so that it can be caught by a
    catch (const AType& ex)           handler for the outer try block.
    {
      ...
    }
}
catch (const ExType& ex)              This handler catches the ex exception
{                                     that was rethrown in the inner try block.
  // Handle ex...
}
```

Figure 16-6. *Rethrowing an exception*

This example throws Trouble, MoreTrouble, and BigTrouble exception objects and then rethrows some of them to show how the mechanism works:

```cpp
// Ex16_05.cpp - Rethrowing exceptions
import std;
import troubles;

int main()
{
  for (int i {}; i < 7; ++i)
  {
    try
    {
      try
      {
        if (i == 3)
          throw Trouble{};
        else if (i == 5)
          throw MoreTrouble{};
        else if (i == 6)
          throw BigTrouble{};
      }
```

```
    catch (const Trouble& t)
    {
      if (typeid(t) == typeid(Trouble))
        std::println("Trouble object caught in inner block: {}", t.what());
      else
        throw;      // Rethrow current exception
    }
  }
  catch (const Trouble& t)
  {
    std::println("{} object caught in outer block: {}", typeid(t).name(), t.what());
  }
  std::println("End of the for loop (after the catch blocks) - i is {}", i);
  }
}
```

This example displays the following output:

```
End of the for loop (after the catch blocks) - i is 0
End of the for loop (after the catch blocks) - i is 1
End of the for loop (after the catch blocks) - i is 2
Trouble object caught in inner block: There's a problem
End of the for loop (after the catch blocks) - i is 3
End of the for loop (after the catch blocks) - i is 4
class MoreTrouble object caught in outer block: There's more trouble...
End of the for loop (after the catch blocks) - i is 5
class BigTrouble object caught in outer block: Really big trouble...
End of the for loop (after the catch blocks) - i is 6
```

The for loop works as in the previous example, but this time there is one try block nested inside another. The same sequence of exception objects as the previous example objects is thrown in the inner try block, and all the exception objects are caught by the matching catch block because the parameter is a reference to the base class, Trouble. The if statement in the catch block tests the class type of the object passed and executes the output statement if it is of type Trouble. For any other type of exception, the exception is rethrown and therefore available to be caught by the catch block for the outer try block. The parameter is also a reference to Trouble so it catches all the derived class objects. The output shows that it catches the rethrown objects and they're still in pristine condition.

You might imagine that the throw statement in the handler for the inner try block is equivalent to the following statement:

```
throw t;      // Rethrow current exception
```

After all, you're just rethrowing the exception, aren't you? The answer is no; there's a crucial difference. If you make this modification to the program code and run it again, you'll get this output:

```
End of the for loop (after the catch blocks) - i is 0
End of the for loop (after the catch blocks) - i is 1
End of the for loop (after the catch blocks) - i is 2
Trouble object caught in inner block: There's a problem
End of the for loop (after the catch blocks) - i is 3
```

642

```
End of the for loop (after the catch blocks) - i is 4
class Trouble object caught in outer block: There's more trouble...
End of the for loop (after the catch blocks) - i is 5
class Trouble object caught in outer block: Really big trouble...
End of the for loop (after the catch blocks) - i is 6
```

The statement with an explicit exception object specified is throwing a new exception, not rethrowing the original one. This results in the original exception object being copied, using the copy constructor for the Trouble class. It's that vexing object slicing problem again! The derived portion of each object is sliced off, so you are left with just the base class subobject in each case. You can see from the output that the typeid() operator identifies all the exceptions as type Trouble.

■ **Tip**   Always throw by value, catch by reference-to-const, and rethrow using a throw; statement.

Unhandled Exceptions

If a thrown exception is not caught, either directly or indirectly (that is, it does not have to be caught within the same function, as we discussed earlier), then the program is terminated instantly. And you really should expect such a termination to be fairly abrupt. Destructors for static objects will not get called anymore, for one; there is no guarantee that the destructors of any objects still allocated on the call stack will be executed. In other words, the program essentially instantly *crashes*.

■ **Note**   In actuality, if an exception goes uncaught, std::terminate() is called, which, by default, calls std::abort(), which, in turn, by default, triggers the abrupt termination of the program. This sequence of events for an uncaught exception is shown in Figure 16-7.

You can override the behavior of std::terminate()[1] by passing a function pointer to std::set_terminate(). However, this is rarely recommended and should be reserved for (pun intended…) exceptional cases. There is also not that much you are allowed to do in a terminate handler. Acceptable uses include making sure that certain critical resources are properly cleaned up or writing a so-called *crash dump* that your customers can then send to you for further diagnosis. These topics are too advanced for this book to warrant further discussion. Whatever you do, though, you must never attempt to keep your program running once std::terminate() got triggered. std::terminate(), by definition, is invoked after an *irrecoverable error*; any attempt to recover results in

---

[1] You can also alter the default behavior of std::abort() on most platforms (notable exception are POSIX-based platforms) by installing a signal handler for the SIGABORT signal. But we won't go into that here. Signals are more the realm of C than of C++. Still, if you interact with third-party components that may call std::abort() either directly, or, say, through C-style assert() statements (see also Appendix A), hooking into the lower level termination procedures may be preferrable over installing a termination handler.

undefined behavior. Your terminate handler must always end with one of two function calls: either `std::abort()` or `std::_Exit()`.[2] Both functions end the program without performing any further cleanup (the difference between the two is that `std::_Exit()` allows you to decide which error code the terminated process returns to the environment).

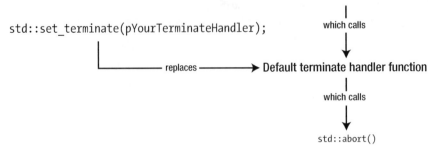

Figure 16-7. *Uncaught exceptions*

Terminating the program after an uncaught exception may sound harsh, but what other alternative is there really? Remember, you normally throw an exception if something unexpected and unrecoverable has happened that needs further attention. If it then turns out that there is no code in place to appropriately deal with this error, what other course of action is there? The program is inherently in some unexpected, erroneous state, so carrying on as if nothing had happened would generally just lead to more, and potentially far worse, errors. Such secondary errors may furthermore be much harder to diagnose. The only sensible course of action is to halt the execution.

Catching All Exceptions

You can use an ellipsis (`...`) as the parameter specification for a `catch` block to indicate that the block should handle any exception:

```
try
{
  // Code that may throw exceptions...
}
catch (...)
{
  // Code to handle any exception...
}
```

---

[2] You shouldn't even call `std::exit()` from a terminate handler because that again may result in undefined behavior. Consult a Standard Library reference if you want to know the subtle differences between the various program termination functions.

This catch block handles an exception of any type, so a handler like this must always be last in the sequence of handlers for a try block. Of course, you have no idea what the exception is, which, as we explain shortly, often precludes you from properly handling the error. Note that even though you don't know anything about it, you can still rethrow the exception as you did in the previous example.

You can modify the previous example to catch all the exceptions for the inner try block by using an ellipsis in place of the parameter:

```cpp
// Ex16_06.cpp - Catching any exception
import std;
import troubles;

int main()
{
  for (int i {}; i < 7; ++i)
  {
    try
    {
      try
      {
        if (i == 3)
          throw Trouble{};
        else if (i == 5)
          throw MoreTrouble{};
        else if (i == 6)
          throw BigTrouble{};
      }
      catch (const BigTrouble& bt)
      {
        std::println("Oh dear, big trouble. Let's handle it here and now.");
        // Do not rethrow...
      }
      catch (...)    // Catch any other exception
      {
        std::println("We caught something else! Let's rethrow it.");
        throw;       // Rethrow current exception
      }
    }
    catch (const Trouble& t)
    {
      std::println("{} object caught in outer block: {}", typeid(t).name(), t.what());
    }
    std::println("End of the for loop (after the catch blocks) - i is {}", i);
  }
}
```

This produces the following output:

```
End of the for loop (after the catch blocks) - i is 0
End of the for loop (after the catch blocks) - i is 1
End of the for loop (after the catch blocks) - i is 2
We caught something else! Let's rethrow it.
```

```
class Trouble object caught in outer block: There's a problem
End of the for loop (after the catch blocks) - i is 3
End of the for loop (after the catch blocks) - i is 4
We caught something else! Let's rethrow it.
class MoreTrouble object caught in outer block: There's more trouble...
End of the for loop (after the catch blocks) - i is 5
Oh dear, big trouble. Let's handle that here and now.
End of the for loop (after the catch blocks) - i is 6
```

The last catch block for the inner try block has an ellipsis as the parameter specification, so any exception that is thrown but not caught by any of the other catch blocks of the same try block will be caught by this catch block. Every time an exception is caught there, a message displays, and the exception is rethrown to be caught by the catch block for the outer try block. There, its type is properly identified, and the string returned by its what() member is displayed. Exceptions of class BigTrouble will be handled by the corresponding inner catch block; as they are not rethrown there, they do not reach the outer catch block.

▨ **Caution** If your code will throw exceptions of different types, it may be tempting to use a catch-all block to catch them all at once. After all, it's less work than enumerating catch blocks for every possible exception type. Similarly, if you're calling functions that you're less familiar with, quickly adding a catch-all block is much easier than researching which exception types these functions may throw. This is rarely the best approach though. A catch-all block risks catching exceptions that need more specific handling, or sweeping unexpected, dangerous errors under the rug. They also do not allow for much error logging or diagnosis. All too often we encounter patterns such as this in code:

```
try
{
    doSomething();
}
catch (...)
{
    // Oops. Something went wrong... Let's ignore what happened and cross our fingers...
}
```

The comments usually don't actually contain the part about ignoring the error and crossing your fingers, but they might as well. The motivation behind such patterns is generally "Anything is better than uncaught exceptions." The truth of the matter is that this is mostly just a symptom of a lazy programmer. There is no substitute for proper, thought-through error-handling code when it comes to delivering stable, fault-tolerant programs. And like we said in the introduction of this chapter, writing error-handling and recovery code will take time. So while catch-all blocks may be tempting shortcuts, it's usually preferred to explicitly check which exception types may be raised by the functions that you call and, for each, to consider whether you should add a catch block and/or leave it to a calling function to handle the exception. Once you know the exception type, you can usually extract more useful information from the object (like with the what() function of our Trouble class) and use this for proper error handling and logging. Note also that, especially during development, a program crash is actually better than a catch-all. Then at least you learn about potential errors, instead of blindly ignoring them, and can adjust your code to properly prevent them or recover from them.

Make no mistake, we do not mean to say that catch-all blocks should never be used—they certainly have their uses. Catch-all blocks that rethrow after some logging or cleanup, for instance, can be particularly useful. We just want to caution you against using them as an easy, subpar substitute for more targeted error handling.

Functions That Don't Throw Exceptions

In principle, any function can throw an exception, including regular functions, member functions, virtual functions, overloaded operators, and even constructors and destructors. So, each time you call a function somewhere, anywhere, you should learn to think about the potential exceptions that might come out and whether you should handle them with a `try` block. Of course, this does not mean every function call needs to be surrounded by a `try` block. As long as you are not working in `main()`, it is often perfectly acceptable to delegate the responsibility of catching the exception to the callees of the function.

Sometimes, though, you know full well that the function you are writing won't ever throw an exception. Some types of functions even should never throw an exception at all. This section briefly discusses these situations and the language facilities that C++ provides for them.

The noexcept Specifier

By appending the `noexcept` keyword to the function header, you specify that a function will never throw exceptions. For instance, the following specifies that the `doThat()` function will never throw:

```
void doThat(int argument) noexcept;
```

If you see a `noexcept` in a function's header, you can be sure that this function will never throw an exception. The compiler makes sure that if a `noexcept` function *does* unwittingly throw an exception that's not caught within the function itself, the exception will not be propagated to the calling function at runtime. Instead, the C++ program will treat this as an irrecoverable error and call `std::terminate()`. As discussed earlier in this chapter, `std::terminate()` always results in an abrupt termination of the process.

Note that this does not mean that no exceptions are allowed to be thrown within the function itself; it only means that no exception will ever escape the function. That is, if an exception is thrown during the execution of a `noexcept` function, it must be caught somewhere within that function and not rethrown. For example, an implementation of `doThat()` of the following form would be perfectly legal:

```
void doThat(int argument) noexcept
{
  try
  {
    // Code for the function...
  }
  catch (...)
  {
    // Handles all exceptions and does not rethrow...
  }
}
```

The noexcept specifier may be used on all functions, including member functions, constructors, and destructors. You will encounter concrete examples later in this chapter.

In later chapters, you'll even encounter several types of functions that should always be declared as noexcept. This includes swap() functions (discussed in Chapter 17) and move members (discussed in Chapter 18).

■ **Note** Unlike for instance in Java, in C++ you cannot specify what types of exceptions a non-noexcept function may throw. You used to be able to do so by appending throw(exception_type1, ..., exception_typeN) to a function header, but this syntax has been removed from the language.

Exceptions and Destructors

Starting with C++11, destructors are normally implicitly noexcept. Even if you define a destructor without a noexcept specification, the compiler will normally add one implicitly. This means that should the destructor of the following class be executed, the exception will never leave the destructor. Instead, std::terminate() shall always be called (in accordance with the implicit noexcept specifier added by the compiler):

```
class MyClass
{
public:
  ~MyClass() { throw BigTrouble{}; }
};
```

It is in principle possible to define a destructor from which exceptions may be thrown. You could do so by adding an explicit noexcept(false) specification. But since you should normally never do this,[3] we won't discuss or consider this possibility any further.

■ **Tip** Never allow an exception to leave a destructor. All destructors are normally[4] noexcept, even if not specified as such explicitly, so any exception they throw will trigger a call to std::terminate().

---

[3] If you're not careful, even throwing from a noexcept(false) destructor may very well still trigger a call to std::terminate(). Details are again out of scope. Bottom line: Unless you really know what you're doing, never throw exceptions from a destructor!

[4] Concretely, the compiler implicitly generates the noexcept specification for a destructor without an explicit noexcept(...) specification unless the type of one of the subobjects of its class has a destructor that is not noexcept.

Exceptions and Resource Leaks

Making sure all exceptions are caught prevents catastrophic program failure. And catching them with properly positioned and sufficiently fine-grained catch blocks allows you to properly handle all errors. The result is a program that always either presents the desired result or can inform the user precisely what went wrong. But this is not the end of the story! A program that appears to be functioning robustly from the outside may still contain hidden defects. Consider, for instance, the following example program (it uses the same troubles module as Ex16_06):

```cpp
// Ex16_07.cpp - Exceptions may result in resource leaks!
import std;
import troubles;

double computeValue(std::size_t x);           // A function to compute a single value
double* computeValues(std::size_t howMany);   // A function to compute an array of values

int main()
{
  try
  {
    double* values{ computeValues(10'000) };
    // Unfortunately we won't be making it this far...
    delete[] values;
  }
  catch (const Trouble&)
  {
    std::println("No worries: I've caught it!");
  }
}

double* computeValues(std::size_t howMany)
{
  double* values{ new double[howMany]; }
  for (std::size_t i {}; i < howMany; ++i)
    values[i] = computeValue(i);
  return values;
}

double computeValue(std::size_t x)
{
  if (x < 100)
    return std::sqrt(x);   // Return the square root of the input argument
  else
    throw Trouble{"The trouble with trouble is, it starts out as fun!"};
}
```

If you run this program, a Trouble exception is thrown as soon as the loop counter in computeValues() reaches 100. Because the exception is caught in main(), the program does not crash. It even reassures the user that all is well. If this was a real program, you could even inform the user about what exactly went wrong with this operation and allow the user to continue. But that does not mean you are out of the woods! Can you spot what else has gone wrong with this program?

The computeValues() function allocates an array of double values in the free store, attempts to fill them, and then returns the array to its caller. It is the responsibility of the caller—in this case main()—to deallocate this memory. However, because an exception is thrown halfway through the execution of computeValues(), its values array is never actually returned to main(). Therefore, the array is never deallocated either. In other words, we have just leaked an array of 10,000 doubles!

Assuming computeValue() inherently leads to the occasional Trouble exception, the only place where we can fix this leak is in the computeValues() function. After all, main() never even receives a pointer to the leaked memory, so there is little that can be done about it there. In the spirit of this chapter thus far, a first obvious solution would be to add a try block to computeValues() as follows (you can find this solution in Ex16_07A):

```
double* computeValues(std::size_t howMany)
{
  double* values{ new double[howMany] };
  try
  {
    for (std::size_t i {}; i < howMany; ++i)
      values[i] = computeValue(i);
    return values;
  }
  catch (const Trouble&)
  {
    std::println("I sense trouble... Freeing memory...");
    delete[] values;
    throw;
  }
}
```

Notice that values was defined outside the try block. Otherwise, the variable would be local to the try block, and we could not refer to it anymore from within the catch block. If you redefine computeValues() like this, no further changes are required to the rest of the program. It will also still have a similar outcome, except that this time the values array is not leaked:

```
I sense trouble... Freeing memory...
No worries: I've caught it!
```

While this computeValues() function with the try block makes for a perfectly correct program, it is not the most recommended approach. The function's code has become about twice as long and about twice as complicated as well. The next section introduces better solutions that do not suffer these shortcomings.

Resource Acquisition Is Initialization

One of the hallmarks of modern C++ is the *RAII idiom*, short for "resource acquisition is initialization." Its premise is that each time you acquire a resource you should do so by initializing an object. Memory in the free store is a resource, but other examples include file handles (while holding these, other processes often may not access a file), mutexes (used for synchronization in concurrent programming), network connections, and so on. As per RAII, *every* such resource should be managed by an object, either allocated on the stack or as a member variable. The trick to avoid resource leaks is then that, by default, the destructor of that object makes sure the resource is always freed.

Let's create a simple RAII class to demonstrate how this idiom works:

```cpp
class DoubleArrayRAII final
{
public:
  explicit DoubleArrayRAII(std::size_t size) : m_resource{ new double[size] } {}
  ~DoubleArrayRAII()
  {
    std::println("Freeing memory...");
    delete[] m_resource;
  }

  // Delete copy constructor and assignment operator
  DoubleArrayRAII(const DoubleArrayRAII&) = delete;
  DoubleArrayRAII& operator=(const DoubleArrayRAII&) = delete;

  // Array subscript operator
  double& operator[](std::size_t index) noexcept { return m_resource[index]; }
  const double& operator[](std::size_t i) const noexcept { return m_resource[i]; }

  // Function to access the encapsulated resource
  double* get() const noexcept { return m_resource; }

  // Function to instruct the RAII object to hand over the resource.
  // Once called, the RAII object shall no longer release the resource
  // upon destruction anymore. Returns the resource in the process.
  double* release() noexcept
  {
    double* result = m_resource;
    m_resource = nullptr;
    return result;
  }

private:
  double* m_resource;
};
```

The resource—in this case the memory to hold a double array—is acquired by the constructor of the RAII object and released by its destructor. For this RAII class, it's critical that the resource, the memory allocated for its array, is released only once. Without adding custom copy members, we therefore mustn't allow copies to be made of an existing DoubleArrayRAII; otherwise, we end up having two DoubleArrayRAII objects pointing to the same resource. You accomplish this by deleting *both* copy members (as shown in Chapters 12 and 13).

An RAII object often mimics the resource it manages by adding the appropriate member functions and operators. In our case, the resource is an array, so we define the familiar array subscript operators. Besides these, additional functions typically exist to access the resource itself (our get() function) and often also to release the RAII object of its responsibility of freeing the resource (the release() function).

With the help of this RAII class, you can safely rewrite the computeValues() function as follows:

```
double* computeValues(std::size_t howMany)
{
  DoubleArrayRAII values{howMany};
  for (std::size_t i {}; i < howMany; ++i)
      values[i] = computeValue(i);
  return values.release();
}
```

If anything goes wrong now during the computation of the values (that is, if an exception is thrown by computeValue(i)), the compiler guarantees that the destructor of the RAII object is called, which in turn guarantees that the memory of the double array is properly released. Once all values have been computed, we again hand over the double array to the caller as before, along with the responsibility of deleting it. Notice that if we hadn't called release() prior to returning, the destructor of the DoubleArrayRAII object would still be deleting the array.

▓ **Caution** The destructor of the DoubleArrayRAII object is called regardless of whether an exception occurs or not. Therefore, had we called get() instead of release() at the last line of the computeValues() function, we would still be deleting the array that is being returned from the function. In other applications of the RAII idiom, the idea is to always release the acquired resources, even in case of success. For instance, when performing file input/output (I/O), you normally want to release the file handle at the end, irrespective of whether the I/O operations succeeded or failed.

The resulting program is available as Ex16_07B. Its outcome demonstrates that even though we have not added any complicated exception-handling code to computeValues(), the memory is still freed:

```
Freeing memory...
No worries: I've caught it!
```

▓ **Tip** Even if your program does not work with exceptions, it remains recommended to always use the RAII idiom to safely manage your resources. Leaks due to exceptions can be harder to spot, true, but resource leaks can manifest themselves just as easily within functions with multiple return statements. Without RAII, it is simply too easy to forget to release all resources prior to every return statement, especially, for instance, if someone who did not write the function originally returns to the code later to add an extra return statement.

Standard RAII Classes for Dynamic Memory

In the previous section, we created the DoubleArrayRAII class to help illustrate how the idiom works. Also, it is important that you know how to implement an RAII class yourself. You will almost certainly create one or two RAII classes at some point in your career to manage application-specific resources.

Nevertheless, there are Standard Library types that perform the same job as DoubleArrayRAII. In practice, you would therefore never write an RAII class to manage arrays.

The first such type is std::unique_ptr<T[]>. Using this familiar smart pointer template (covered first in Chapter 4), you can write computeValues() as follows:

```
double* computeValues(std::size_t howMany)
{
  auto values{ std::make_unique<double[]>(howMany) };  // type unique_ptr<double[]>
  for (std::size_t i {}; i < howMany; ++i)
      values[i] = computeValue(i);
  return values.release();
}
```

In fact, with std::unique_ptr<>, an even better option would be to write it like this:

```
std::unique_ptr<double[]> computeValues(std::size_t howMany)
{
  auto values { std::make_unique_for_overwrite<double[]>(howMany); }
  for (std::size_t i {}; i < howMany; ++i)
      values[i] = computeValue(i);
  return values;
}
```

If you return the unique_ptr<> itself from computeValues(), you will have to slightly adjust the main() function accordingly. If you do, you'll notice that you no longer need the delete[] statement there. That's yet another potential source of memory leaks eliminated! Unless you are passing a resource to, for instance, a legacy function, there is rarely any need to release a resource from its RAII object. Just pass along the RAII object itself!

▨ **Note** If you attempt to return a DoubleArrayRAII object from computeValues() like this, you will run into a compiler error referring to its deleted copy constructor. To return a DoubleArrayRAII from a function, you first need to enable *move semantics* for this class (as was done for, for instance, std::unique_ptr<>). We explain this further in Chapter 18.

Because the resource we are working with is a dynamic array, you could simply use a std::vector<> instead as well:

```
std::vector<double> computeValues(std::size_t howMany)
{
  std::vector<double> values;
  for (std::size_t i {}; i < howMany; ++i)
      values.push_back( computeValue(i) );
  return values;
}
```

In this case, a vector<> is probably the most appropriate choice. After all, a vector<> is specifically designed to manage and manipulate dynamic arrays. Whichever you prefer, the main message of this section remains as follows:

▓ **Tip**   All dynamic memory should be managed by an RAII object. The Standard Library offers both smart pointers (such as `std::unique_ptr<>` and `shared_ptr<>`) and dynamic containers (such as `std::vector<>`) for this purpose. In the case of smart pointers, `make_unique()` and `make_shared()` should always be used instead of `new` / `new[]` as well. One important consequence of these guidelines is that the `new`, `new[]`, `delete`, and `delete[]` operators generally have no place in a modern C++ program. Be safe: always, always use an RAII object!

Standard Library Exceptions

Quite a few exception types are defined in the Standard Library. They're all derived from the `std::exception` class that is defined in the `<exception>` module, and they all reside in the `std` namespace. For reference, the hierarchy of the standard exception classes is shown in Figure 16-8.

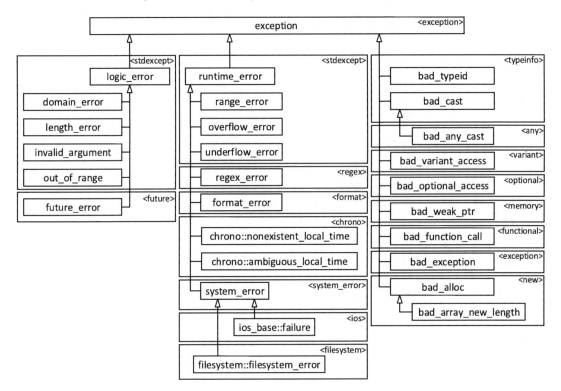

Figure 16-8. *Standard exception class types and the modules in which they are defined*

Many of the standard exception types fall into two groups, with each group identified by a base class that is derived from `exception`. Both these base classes, `logic_error` and `runtime_error`, are defined in the `<stdexcept>` module. For the most part, Standard Library functions do not throw `logic_error` or runtime_error objects directly, only objects of types derived from these. The exceptions that derive from them are listed in the first two columns of Figure 16-8. The rules for categorizing types in either branch of the exception hierarchy are as follows:

- The types that have logic_error as a base are exceptions thrown for errors that could (at least in principle) have been detected before the program executed because they are caused by defects in the program logic. Typical situations in which logic_errors are thrown include calling a function with one or more invalid arguments or calling a member function on an object whose state doesn't meet the requirements (or *preconditions*) for that particular function. You can avoid these types of errors in your program by explicitly checking the validity of the arguments or the object's state prior to the function call.

- The other group, derived from runtime_error, is for errors that are generally data dependent and can only be detected at runtime. Exceptions derived from system_error, for instance, generally encapsulate errors originating from calls onto the underlying operating system, such as failing file input or output. File access, as any interaction with hardware, can always fail in ways that cannot a priori be predicted (think disk failures, unplugged cables, network failures, and so on).

There are a lot of exception types in Figure 16-8; and we are not going to grind through where they all originate. Your library documentation will identify when a function throws an exception. We only mention some exception types here that are thrown by the operations that you're already familiar with:

- The std::out_of_range exception type is used when accessing array-like data structures with an invalid index (usually defined as lying outside the valid range [0, size-1]). Various member functions of std::string throw this exception, as do the at() accessors of, for instance, std::vector<> and std::array<>. The corresponding overloads of the array access operators (operator[]()) do not perform bounds checking on the index. Passing an invalid index to these operators thus leads to undefined behavior.

- Code behind functions such as std::format() and std::print() uses std::format_error to signal syntactical errors in replacement fields. Nevertheless, you can rest assured that most of these functions never throw std::format_error at runtime. The reason is that the format string verification of std::format(), print(), and println() happens entirely at compile time. There are also string formatting functions that don't verify their format string at compile time, though (and for which the format string is therefore not required to be constexpr). Examples include std::vformat() and std::vprint_unicode() (they all have a v in their name). When passed an invalid format string, these functions do throw std::format_error at runtime.

- A std::bad_typeid exception is thrown if you apply the typeid() operator on a dereferenced null pointer to a polymorphic type.

- A std::bad_cast exception is thrown by a dynamic_cast<T&>(expr) operation if expr cannot be cast to T&. An exception can occur only when casting to a reference type T&. When failing to cast to a pointer type T*, dynamic_cast<T*>(expr) simply evaluates to nullptr instead.

- The value() member of the std::optional<> and std::expected<> vocabulary types throw, respectively, a std::bad_optional_access and std::bad_expected_access when called on an object that doesn't hold a value. The related * and -> operators

655

never throw exceptions, and neither does error(). Using these on an object without a value or error results in undefined behavior (in practice, this means you will read junk data).

- A std::bad_alloc exception (or one of a type derived from bad_alloc) may be thrown by operators new and new[]. Operator new[], for instance, throws a std::bad_array_new_length exception if it's passed a negative or excessively large array size. But even with valid inputs, either operator may throw a bad_alloc exception if memory allocation fails. Possible causes are corruption of the free store, or a lack of available memory. And by extension, any operation that requires dynamic memory allocation may throw bad_alloc exceptions as well. Notable examples of such operations include, for instance, copying or adding elements to std::vector<> or std::string objects.

The Exception Class Definitions

You can use a standard exception class as a base class for your own exception class. Since all the standard exception classes have std::exception as a base, it's a good idea to understand what members this class has because they are inherited by all the other exception classes. The exception class is defined in the <exception> module like this:

```
namespace std
{
  class exception
  {
  public:
    exception() noexcept;                          // Default constructor
    exception(const exception&) noexcept;          // Copy constructor
    exception& operator=(const exception&) noexcept; // Assignment operator
    virtual ~exception();                          // Destructor
    virtual const char* what() const noexcept;     // Return a message string
  };
}
```

This is the public class interface specification. A particular implementation may have additional non-public members. This is true of the other standard exception classes too. The noexcept that appears in the declaration of the member functions specifies that they do not throw exceptions, as we discussed earlier. The destructor is noexcept by default. Notice that there are no member variables. The null-terminated string returned by what() is defined within the body of the function definition and is implementation dependent. This function is declared as virtual, so it will be virtual in any class derived from exception. If you have a virtual function that can deliver a message that corresponds to each exception type, you can use it to provide a basic, economical way to record any exception that's thrown.

A catch block with a base class parameter matches any derived class exception type, so you can catch any of the standard exceptions by using a parameter of type exception&. Of course, you can also use a parameter of type logic_error& or runtime_error& to catch any exceptions of types that are derived from these. You could provide the main() function with a try block, plus a catch block for exceptions of type exception:

```
int main()
{
  try
```

```
{
  // Code for main...
}
catch (const std::exception& ex)
{
  std::println("{} caught in main: {}", typeid(ex).name(), ex.what());
  return 1;  // Return a nonzero value to indicate failure
}
}
```

The catch block catches all exceptions that have exception as a base and outputs the exception type and the message returned by the what() function. Thus, this simple mechanism gives you information about any exception that is thrown and not caught anywhere in a program. If your program uses exception classes that are not derived from exception, an additional catch block with ellipses in place of a parameter type catches all other exceptions, but in this case, you'll have no access to the exception object and no information about what it is.

Making the body of main() a try block like this should only be a last-resort fallback mechanism. More local try blocks are preferred because they provide a direct way to localize the source code that is the origin of an exception when it is thrown. Also, letting the program crash after an unexpected failure is not necessarily a bad thing. If you, for instance, configure your program to write crash dumps (also called *core dumps*) upon uncaught exceptions—or if the operation system supports this out of the box—you will often get more information about the source of the error from a crash dump than you can extract from a caught exception object. Rethrowing unhandled exceptions from main() after logging what you can from them is then also an option, of course.

The logic_error and runtime_error classes each only add two constructors to the members they inherit from exception. Here's an example:

```
namespace std
{
  class logic_error : public exception
  {
  public:
    explicit logic_error(const string& what_arg);
    explicit logic_error(const char* what_arg);

  private:
    // ... (implementation specifics, no doubt including a std::string member variable)
  };
}
```

runtime_error is defined similarly, and all the subclasses except for system_error also have constructors that accept a string or a const char* argument. The system_error class adds a member variable of type std::error_code that records an error code, and the constructors provide for specifying the error code. You can consult your library documentation for more details.

Using Standard Exceptions

There is no reason why you shouldn't use the exception classes defined in the Standard Library in your code and a few very good reasons why you should. You can use the standard exception types in two ways: you can either throw exceptions of standard types in your code or use a standard exception class as a base for your own exception types.

Throwing Standard Exceptions Directly

Obviously, if you are going to throw standard exceptions, you should only throw them in circumstances consistent with their purpose. This means you shouldn't be throwing bad_cast exceptions, for instance, because these have a specific role already. Throwing an object of type std::exception is also less interesting as it is far too generic; it does not provide a constructor you can pass a descriptive string to. The most interesting standard exception classes are those defined in the <stdexcept> module, derived from either logic_error or runtime_error. To use a familiar example, you might throw a standard out_of_range exception in a Box class constructor when an invalid dimension is supplied as an argument:

```
Box::Box(double length, double width, double height)
  : m_length {length}, m_width {width}, m_height {height}
{
  if (length <= 0.0 || width <= 0.0 || height <= 0.0)
    throw std::out_of_range{"Zero or negative Box dimension."};
}
```

The body of the constructor throws an out_of_range exception if any of the arguments are zero or negative. The out_of_range type is a logic_error and is therefore well suited for this particular use. Another candidate here would be the more generic std::invalid_argument exception class. If none of the predefined exception classes suits your need, though, you can derive an exception class yourself.

Deriving Your Own Exception Classes

A major point in favor of deriving your own classes from one of the standard exception classes is that your classes become part of the same family. This makes it possible for you to catch standard exceptions as well as your own exceptions within the same catch blocks. For instance, if your exception class is derived from logic_error, then a catch block with a parameter type of logic_error& catches your exceptions as well as the standard exceptions with that base. A catch block with exception& as its parameter type always catches standard exceptions—as well as yours, as long as your classes have exception as a base.

You could incorporate the Trouble exception class and the classes derived from it into the standard exception family quite simply, by deriving it from the exception class. You just need to modify the class definition as follows:

```
class Trouble : public std::exception
{
public:
  explicit Trouble(std::string_view message = "There's a problem");
  const char* what() const noexcept override;

private:
  std::string m_message;
};
```

This provides its own implementation of the virtual what() member defined in the base class. Because it is a redefinition of a base class member, we added override to the declaration of what(). We have also removed the virtual specifier, as per our convention. More interestingly, though, we have added a noexcept specification to signal that no exception will be thrown from what(). In fact, we have to. Any override of a noexcept function must be noexcept as well. It is also worth mentioning that noexcept must always be specified after const and before override.

The definition for the member function must include the same exception specification that appears for the function in the class definition. The what() function thus becomes the following (virtual or override must not be repeated, but noexcept is):

```
const char* Trouble::what() const noexcept { return m_message.c_str(); }
```

▓ **Note**   We purposely did not add the noexcept specifier to the constructor of Trouble. This constructor, inevitably, has to copy the given error message into the corresponding std::string member variable. This, in turn, inevitably involves the allocation of a character array. And memory allocation can always, at least in principle, go awry and throw a std::bad_alloc exception.

For a more concrete example, let's return once more to the Box class definition. For the constructor defined in the previous section, it could be useful to derive an exception class from std::out_of_range to provide the option of a more specific string to be returned by what() that identifies the problem causing the exception to be thrown. Here's how you might do that:

```
export module dimension_error;
import std;

export class DimensionError : public std::out_of_range
{
public:
  explicit DimensionError(double value)
    : std::out_of_range{"Zero or negative dimension: " + std::to_string(value)}
    , m_value{value} {}

  // Function to obtain the invalid dimension value
  double getValue() const noexcept { return m_value; }
private:
  double m_value;
};
```

The constructor provides for a parameter that specifies the dimension value that caused the exception to be thrown. It calls the base class constructor with a new string object that is formed by concatenating a message and value. The to_string() function is a template function that is defined in the <string> module; it returns a string representation of its argument, which can be a value of any numeric type. The inherited what() function will return whatever string is passed to the constructor when the DimensionError object is created. This particular exception class also adds a member variable to store the invalid value, as well as a public function to retrieve it, such as to use it in a catch block.

Here's how this exception class could be used in the Box class definition:

```
// Box.cppm
export module box;
import std;
import dimension_error;

export class Box
{
public:
```

659

```
Box(double l, double w, double h) : m_length {l}, m_width {w}, m_height {h}
{
  if (l <= 0.0 || w <= 0.0 || h <= 0.0)
    throw DimensionError{ std::min({l, w, h}) };
}

double volume() const { return m_length * m_width * m_height; }
private:
  double m_length {1.0};
  double m_width {1.0};
  double m_height {1.0};
};
```

The Box constructor throws a DimensionError exception if any of the arguments are zero or negative. The constructor uses std::min() to determine the dimension argument that is the minimum of those specified—that will be the worst offender. Note the use of a so-called initializer list to find the minimum of three elements. The resulting expression std::min({l, w, h}) is certainly more elegant than std::min(l, std::min(w, h)), wouldn't you agree?

The following example demonstrates the DimensionError class in action:

```
// Ex16_08.cpp - Using an exception class
import std;
import box;

int main()
{
  try
  {
    Box box1 {1.0, 2.0, 3.0};
    std::println("box1 volume is {}", box1.volume());
    Box box2 {1.0, -2.0, 3.0};
    std::println("box2 volume is {}", box2.volume());
  }
  catch (const std::exception& ex)
  {
    std::println("Exception caught in main(): {}", ex.what());
  }
}
```

The output from this example is as follows:

```
box1 volume is 6
Exception caught in main(): Zero or negative dimension: -2.000000
```

The body of main() is a try block, and its catch block catches any type of exception that has std::exception as a base. The output shows that the Box class constructor is throwing a DimensionError exception object when a dimension is negative. The output also shows that the what() function that DimensionError inherits from out_of_range is outputting the string formed in the DimensionError constructor call.

Incidentally, did you notice how Ex16_08.cpp does not import the dimension_error module, even though it catches and handles a DimensionError exception? It does not have to because we are catching the exception by reference-to-const-std::exception, not by reference-to-const-DimensionError. And to make the virtual what() function of std::exception work, all the compiler needs to know is the definition of the std::exception class in the Standard Library's <exception> module, which is imported indirectly through std. This makes sense; polymorphism means not having to know the concrete dynamic type of an object. So, you do not have to import the module that our concrete exception type belongs to either. That would defeat the purpose of polymorphism. So a Box can throw any exception object it likes as long as its type derives from std::exception, and the main() program does not need to know what that derived type will be.

▓ **Tip** When throwing exceptions, always throw objects, never fundamental types. And the class of these objects should always derive from std::exception, either directly or indirectly. Even if you declare your own application-specific exception hierarchies—which often is a good idea—you should use std::exception or one of its derived classes as the base class. Many popular C++ libraries already follow this same guideline. Using only a single, standardized family of exceptions makes it much easier to catch and handle these exceptions.

Stack Traces

A std::exception can tell you *what* went wrong (through the aptly named what() function). What a std::exception cannot tell you, however, is *where* things went wrong. That is, there is no (standard) way for you to find out *where* in the code the exception was thrown. Naturally, this complicates diagnosis, especially if the same exception may originate from multiple locations.

This limitation may surprise you if you're used to, say, Java or C#. In these and many other languages exceptions inherently carry a *stack trace*—something their runtimes are all too keen to throw into your face if you ever let an exception go uncaught. An exception's stack trace is a snapshot of the function call stack at the moment the exception was thrown. It typically contains not only precisely where in the code—in which source file, in what function, at what line number—the exception was thrown, but also what other functions were executing at that moment and where. Having that information available (in your program's log files, for instance) is clearly a big help in diagnosing unexpected errors.

As of C++23, you can emulate the same in standard C++ by embedding a std::stacktrace object in your exception objects. The following defines such an exception class:[5]

```
// Tracing.cppm - A custom exception class that carries a stack trace
export module tracing;
import std;
```

---

[5] As before with our Trouble classes, copying message or trace could technically trigger a secondary exception if the system is out of memory. We refer you to the exercises in Chapter 18 for a (partial) solution to this imperfection.

```
export class TracingException : public std::exception
{
public:
  TracingException(std::string_view message,
      std::stacktrace trace = std::stacktrace::current()) //<-- Magic happens here!
    : m_message{ message }
    , m_trace{ trace }
  {}

  const char* what() const noexcept override { return m_message.c_str(); }
  const auto& where() const noexcept { return m_trace; }

private:
  std::string m_message;
  std::stacktrace m_trace;
};
```

The constructor of TracingException uses a clever trick that hinges on a std::stacktrace parameter with std::stracktrace::current() as the default argument value. While you could, in principle, create or obtain your own std::stacktrace object and then pass that to the TracingException constructor, you're not supposed to do so in typical use. The intention is to let the compiler generate a default argument value through std::stracktrace::current() instead. Before we divulge precisely why this trick is so clever, it's instructive to show it in action first.

```
// Ex16_09.cpp - Embedding a stack trace in an exception
import std;
import tracing;

int f3() { throw TracingException{ "Something's amiss!" }; } // Obtains a stack trace!
int f2() { return f3(); }
int f1() { return f2(); }

int main()
{
  try
  {
    f1();
  }
  catch (const TracingException& ex)
  {
    std::println("Exception of type {} caught: {}; trace:\n{}",
        typeid(ex).name(), ex.what(), ex.where());
  }
}
```

Ex16_09 simply calls f1(), catches any TracingException that comes out, and if so, prints out what went wrong and where. Note that you should be able to print a std::stacktrace object directly through std::println() (if your library does not support this yet—it was a later addition to C++23—you can convert the stacktrace to a string first using the std::to_string() non-member function, analogous to the one we defined for our Box classes earlier in the book).

The printed stack trace will show, in reverse order, what functions were active at the moment things went amiss. On our test system, the output looked as follows:

```
Exception of type class TracingException caught: Something's amiss!; trace:
0> D:\Beginning C++23\Examples\Chapter 16\Ex16_09\Ex16_09.cpp(5): Ex16_09!f3+0x32
1> D:\Beginning C++23\Examples\Chapter 16\Ex16_09\Ex16_09.cpp(6): Ex16_09!f2+0x9
2> D:\Beginning C++23\Examples\Chapter 16\Ex16_09\Ex16_09.cpp(7): Ex16_09!f1+0x9
3> D:\Beginning C++23\Examples\Chapter 16\Ex16_09\Ex16_09.cpp(13): Ex16_09!main+0x18
[...]
```

The first lines of this output inform you that something went amiss in f3() at line 5 of Ex16_09.cpp. Reading the remainder of the trace bottom to top moreover tells you that at that time, main() was calling f1() on line 13 of Ex16_09.cpp, f1() was calling f2() on line 7, and f2() was calling f3() on line 6.

▓ **Tip** Embed a stack trace in all your exceptions. Obviously, doing so adds some cost to throwing exceptions, but since exceptions should only occur exceptionally, this should not be a cause for concern.

▓ **Tip** The primary advantage of using a default argument expression to obtain the current stack trace in TracingException's constructor is that it prevents the exception's constructor from always appearing at the top of the stack trace. Default argument expressions are always evaluated at the calling site. The f3() function of Ex16_09, for instance, thus behaves exactly as if you had written it as follows:

```
int f3() { throw TracingException{ "...", std::stacktrace::current() }; }
```

If you initialize TracingException's m_trace with std::stacktrace::current() in any of the more obvious manners—be it in the constructor's member initializer list, in the constructor's body, or directly in the declaration of m_trace—std::stacktrace::current() always becomes evaluated inside the TracingException constructor instead, adding an extra entry to the stack trace. And when looking at a stack trace, you surely don't want the first line to always reference the exception's constructor—that first line should tell you where the exception was thrown! (Added advantage of having a std::stacktrace parameter, incidentally, is that it leaves the door open for more advanced usage where you do obtain the stack trace somewhere else, and only later forward the std::stacktrace object to the exception.)

Summary

Error handling is an integral part of programming in C++. Several operators throw exceptions, and you've seen that they're used extensively within the Standard Library to signal errors. Therefore, it's important that you have a good grasp of how exceptions work, even if you don't plan to define your own exception classes. The important points that we've covered in this chapter are as follows:

- Exceptions are objects that are used to signal errors in a program.

- Code that may throw exceptions is usually contained within a try block, which enables an exception to be detected and processed within the program.

- The code to handle exceptions that may be thrown in a try block is placed in one or more catch blocks that must immediately follow the try block.

- A try block, along with its catch blocks, can be nested inside another try block.

- A catch block with a parameter of a base class type can catch an exception of a derived class type.

- A catch block with the parameter specified as an ellipsis will catch an exception of any type.

- If an exception isn't caught by any catch block, then the std::terminate() function is called, which immediately aborts the program execution.

- Every resource, including dynamically allocated memory, should always be acquired and released by an RAII object. This implies that, as a rule, you should normally no longer use the keywords new and delete in modern C++ code.

- The Standard Library offers various RAII types you should use consistently; the ones you already know about include std::unique_ptr<>, shared_ptr<>, and vector<>.

- The noexcept specification for a function indicates that the function does not throw exceptions. If a noexcept function does throw an exception it does not catch, std::terminate() is called.

- Even if a destructor does not have an explicit noexcept specifier, the compiler will almost always generate one for you. This implies that you must never allow an exception to leave a destructor; otherwise, std::terminate() will be triggered.

- The Standard Library defines a range of standard exception types in the <stdexcept> module that are derived from the std::exception class.

- By embedding a std::stracktrace in your exception objects, you grant the code that handles them the opportunity to not only report and/or log *what* went wrong, but also *where* and under which circumstances.

EXERCISES

The following exercises enable you to try what you've learned in this chapter. If you get stuck, look back over the chapter for help. If you're still stuck after that, you can download the solutions from the Apress website (https://www.apress.com/gp/services/source-code), but that really should be a last resort.

Exercise 16-1. Derive your own exception class called CurveBall from the std::exception class to represent an arbitrary error and write a function that throws this exception approximately 25% of the time. One way to do this is to generate a random integer between 1 and 100 (both inclusive) and, if the number is less than or equal to 25, throw the exception. Define a main() function to call this function 1,000,000 times, while recording the number of times an exception was thrown. At the end, print out the final count. Of course, if all went well, this number should fluctuate somewhere around 250,000.

Tip: If you prefer to generate a random Boolean directly (instead of going through generating a random integer first), you should check out the std::bernoulli_distribution in your favorite Standard Library reference. (This classical distribution is named after Jacob Bernoulli, a 17ᵗʰ century Swiss pioneer in the field of probability.)

Exercise 16-2. Define another exception class called TooManyExceptions. Then throw an exception of this type from the catch block for CurveBall exceptions in the previous exercise when the number of exceptions caught exceeds ten. Observe what happens if you neglect to catch the exception.

Exercise 16-3. Remember our conundrum with Ex13_11 in Chapter 13? In the Truckload class of that example, we were challenged with defining an array subscript operator (operator[]) that returned a Box& reference. The problem was that we had to return a Box& reference even if the index provided to the function was out of bounds. Our ad hoc solution involved "inventing" a special null object, but we already noted that this solution was severely flawed. Now that you know about exceptions, you should be able to finally fix this function once and for all. Choose an appropriate Standard Library exception type and use it to properly reimplement Truckload::operator[]() from Ex13_11. Write a small program to exercise this new behavior of the operator.

Exercise 16-4. Pick any number of Standard Library exception types from Figure 16-8 and write a program that causes each of them to be raised in turn (without actually throwing them yourself, of course). You should catch each of these exceptions and output the what() messages they contain, before moving on to triggering the next exception.

Exercise 16-5. Create a function called readEvenNumber() intended to read an even integer from the std::cin input stream. About 25% of the time, something really odd happens inside readEvenNumber(), resulting in a CurveBall exception. You can simply reuse code from Exercise 16-1 for this. Normally, however, the function verifies the user input and returns an even number if the user enters one correctly. If the input is not valid, however, the function throws one of the following exceptions:

- If any value that is not a number is entered, a NotANumber exception is thrown.

- If the user enters a negative number, a NegativeNumber exception is thrown.

- If the user enters an odd number, the function throws an OddNumber exception.

You should derive these new exception types from `std::domain_error`, one of the standard exception types defined in the `<stdexcept>` module. Their constructors should compose a string containing at least the incorrectly entered value and then forward that string to the constructor of `std::domain_error`.

Hint: After attempting to read an integer number from `std::cin`, you can check whether parsing that integer succeeded by using `std::cin.fail()`. If that member function returns `true`, the user entered a string that is not a number. Note that once the stream is in such a failure state, you cannot use the stream anymore until you call `std::cin.clear()`. Also, the nonnumeric value the user had entered will still be inside the stream—it is not removed when failing to extract an integer. You could, for instance, extract it using the `std::getline()` function defined in `<string>`. Putting this all together, your code might contain something like this:

```
if (std::cin.fail())
{
  std::cin.clear();    // Reset the failure state
  std::string line;    // Read the erroneous input and discard it
  std::getline(std::cin, line);
  ...
```

Once the `readEvenNumber()` helper is ready, use it to implement `askEvenNumber()`. This function prints user instructions and then calls `readEvenNumber()` to handle the actual input and input verification. Once a number is read correctly, `askEvenNumber()` politely thanks the user for entering the number (the message should contain the number itself). For any `std::exception` that `readEvenNumber()` throws, `askEvenNumber()` should at least output `e.what()`. Any exception that is not a `domain_error` is to be rethrown, and `askEvenNumber()` has no idea how to handle these. If the exception is a `domain_error`, however, you should retry asking for an even number, unless the exception is a `NotANumber`. If a `NotANumber` occurs, `askEvenNumber()` stops asking for numbers and simply returns.

Finally, write a `main()` function that executes `askEvenNumber()` and catches any `CurveBalls` that may come out. If it catches one, it should output "…hit it out of the park!" because that's what you do when life throws you a curveball!

Exercise 16-6. The `Exer16_06` directory contains a small program that calls upon a C interface to a fictitious database system (the interface is actually a simplified version of the C interface of MySQL). As is common with C interfaces, our database interface returns so-called handles to various resources—resources that need to be freed again explicitly once you're done using them by calling another interface function. In this case, there are two such resources: the connection to the database and the memory allocated to store the result of a SQL query. Carefully read the interface specification in `DB.h` to learn how the interface should be used. Since this is an exercise, in the `Exer16_06` program, these resources may leak under certain conditions. Can you spot any conditions under which the resources are leaked? Since this is an exercise in a chapter on exceptions, these conditions will mostly involve exceptions.

Hint: To appreciate how subtle error handling can be, ever wondered what `std::stoi()` does when passed a string that does not contain a number? Check a Standard Library reference—or write a small test program—to find out. Suppose you have customers living at number 10B or 105/5. What will happen in our program? And what if a Russian customer lives at к2, that is, a house whose official address has a street "number" starting with a letter? Similarly, what if for some customers the house number is not filled in? That is, what if the house number stored in the database is an empty string?

To fix the resource leaks in our program, you could add explicit resource cleaning statements, add some more `try-catch` blocks, and so on. For this exercise, however, we'd like you to create and use two small RAII classes instead: one that ensures an active database connection is always disconnected and one that releases the memory allocated for a given query result. Note that if you add cast operators to the RAII classes to implicitly convert to the handle types they encapsulate (and/or to a Boolean), you may not even have to change much of the remainder of the code!

Note: With the approach we suggested for this exercise, the main program still uses the C interface, only now it does so while immediately storing all resource handles in RAII objects. This is certainly a viable option, one that we have used in real-life applications. An alternative approach, though, is to use the *decorator* or *wrapper* design pattern. You then develop a set of C++ classes that encapsulates the entire database and its query functionalities. Only these decorator classes are then supposed to call upon the C interface directly; the remainder of the program simply employs the members of the C++ decorator classes. The interface of these decorator classes is then designed such that memory leaks are not possible; all resources that the program can ever access shall always be managed by an RAII object. The C resource handles themselves are normally never accessible for the rest of the program. Working out this alternative approach would take us too far from the main topic of this chapter (exceptions), but it is one to keep in mind if ever you have to integrate a C interface within a larger C++ program.

CHAPTER 17

■ ■ ■

Class Templates

Both function and class templates are used extensively throughout the C++ Standard Library to provide powerful generic utilities, algorithms, and data structures. You learned about templates that the compiler uses to create functions in Chapter 10; this chapter is about templates that the compiler uses to create classes. Class templates are a powerful mechanism for generating new class types.

With this chapter, you are also nearing the end of our series of chapters on defining your own classes. Besides introducing class templates, we will also include some slightly off-topic contemplations on coding style. With these sidebars we want to incite you to reason about aspects of your code that go beyond mere functional correctness. We will advocate that writing code should be about more than just making sure it computes the correct values. Your code should be easy to read and maintain, it should be robust against unexpected conditions and exceptions, and so on. Naturally, we will also teach you a few standard techniques along the way to help you accomplish these fundamental nonfunctional requirements.

In this chapter, you'll learn

- What a class template is and how to define one

- What an instance of a class template is and how it is created

- How to define templates for member functions of a class template outside the class template definition

- What a partial specialization of a class template is and how it is defined

- How a class can be nested inside a class template

- Why it pays to invest in high-quality code that is not just correct but also easy to maintain and robust against failure

- What the "copy-and-swap" idiom is and how to use it to write exception-safe code

- How to use the "const-and-back-again" idiom to avoid duplicating overloaded member functions

Understanding Class Templates

A class template is based on the same idea as a function template (see Chapter 10). It is a *parameterized type* that constitutes a recipe for creating a family of class definitions. Just like a recipe is not edible, a class template definition in itself has no executable code associated with it. It's only when the compiler *instantiates* concrete class definitions from a class template that it gives rise to actual code. Before your program can use variables of type std::vector<int>, for instance, the compiler has to instantiate a vector<int> class from the vector<> class template. In doing so, the compiler ensures that only one *instance* is created per unique set of template arguments. Within the same executable, all variables of type std::vector<int> thus share the same class definition. This process is illustrated in Figure 17-1.

© Ivor Horton and Peter Van Weert 2023
I. Horton and P. Van Weert, *Beginning C++23*, https://doi.org/10.1007/978-1-4842-9343-0_17

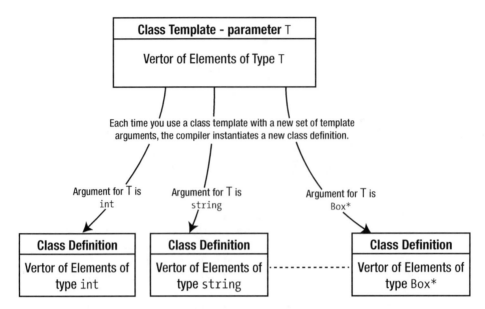

Figure 17-1. Class template instantiation

By creating separate, specialized class definitions for each set of template arguments, the compiler is capable of generating highly specific, highly optimized code for each situation.

You already have ample experience *using* classes that are instantiated from class templates—class templates such as vector<> and array<> (Chapter 5), unique_ptr<> and shared_ptr<> (Chapter 6), optional<> and span<> (Chapter 9), and so on. Even string (Chapter 7) and string_view (Chapter 9) are nothing but type aliases for basic_string<char> and basic_string_view<char>, so whenever you used variables of these types the compiler first had to instantiate the corresponding class definitions from their respective templates as well.

In this chapter we take the logical next step and show you how to *define* class templates of your own. We will start off easy and walk you through how to create a basic template.

Defining Class Templates

The general form of a class template looks like this:

```
template <template parameter list>
class ClassName /*final*/ /*: parent classes (inheritance)*/
{
  // List of access specifiers and member declarations...
};
```

Like most templates in C++[1], a class template is prefixed by the `template` keyword, followed by a list of template parameters between angle brackets. The class template itself then always begins with the `class` (or `struct`) keyword followed by the class template's name, and the body of the definition between curly brackets. You write the code for the body of the template just as you'd write the body of an ordinary class, except that some of the member declarations and definitions will be in terms of the template parameters that appear between the angle brackets. Just like a regular class, the whole definition ends with a semicolon.

Just like regular classes, classes instantiated from templates can benefit from inheritance; they can inherit members from one or more base classes, declare or override virtual functions, and so on. The syntax used for this is precisely the one you saw in Chapter 14. To prevent any further classes deriving from an instance of your template, you can add the `final` keyword as well (as seen in Chapter 15). Once you're past the template parameter list, a class template definition really is completely analogous to a regular class definition, except that you typically use template parameter names here and there as placeholders for whatever types of values are plugged in during template instantiation.

As with function templates, the template parameter list of a class template can contain any number of parameters of two kinds—*type parameters* and *non-type parameters*. Figure 17-2 illustrates the options for both kinds. The argument corresponding to a type parameter is always a type, whereas the argument for a non-type parameter can be any constant expression that is compatible with the type of the parameter. Template type parameters are much more commonly used than non-type parameters, so we'll explain these first and defer discussion of non-type parameters until later in this chapter.

---

[1] Abbreviated function templates (see Chapter 10) and generic lambdas (Chapter 18) are the only templates that are not preceded by the template keyword. There is no abbreviating the syntax for class templates or for the templates of their members, though.

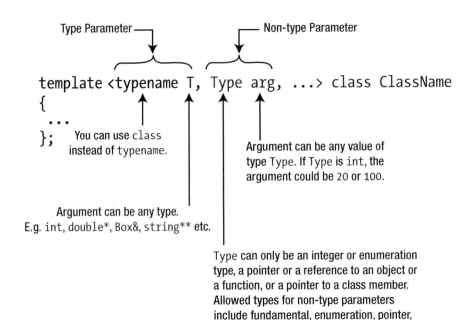

Figure 17-2. *Class template parameters*

▓ **Note**   There's technically a third possibility for template parameters as well. A template parameter can also be a *template* where the argument then must be an instance of a class template. A detailed discussion of these rarely used *template template parameters* (yes, that's two times the word *template*) would be a little too advanced for this book, though.

Template Type Parameters

As with function templates, you can introduce template type parameters either using the typename keyword (see Figure 17-2) or using the class keyword. In this context, typename and class are again synonymous. As before, we mostly prefer typename because class tends to connote a class type and in most cases a template type argument can be any type, not just a class type. If we do still use the class keyword here, we do so to explicitly mark those type parameters that can effectively only be assigned certain class types as arguments. In Chapter 21, you will see better techniques to explicitly encode such type constraints, though.

Conventionally type parameter names start with a capital letter to distinguish them from regular variable names. T in particular is a popular name for a template type parameter. But none of that is required, and you can use whatever name you want. Using more descriptive parameter names than T is often even advisable, especially if your template has multiple type parameters.

A Simple Class Template

Let's take an example of a class template for dynamic arrays that perform bounds checking on index values to make sure that they are legal. The Standard Library already provides such a template—std::vector<>, that is, which does bounds checking in its at() members—but building a limited container class template is an effective basis from which you can learn how templates work.

In outline, the definition of our class template will be as follows:

```
template <typename T>
class Array
{
  // List of access specifiers and member declarations...
};
```

The Array<> template has just one type parameter, T. You can tell that it's a type parameter because it's preceded by the keyword typename. Whatever is "plugged in" for the parameter when the template is instantiated—int, double*, string, or whatever—determines the type of the elements stored in an object of the resultant class. Since this obviously does not necessarily have to be a class type, we have used the keyword typename rather than class.

The definition in the body of the template will be much the same as a class definition, with constructors, member functions, and member variables that are specified as public, protected, or private. You can use T to define member variables or to specify the parameter or return types for member functions, either by itself or in types such as T*, const T&, or std::vector<T>.

The very least we need by way of a class interface is an overloaded subscript operator, as well as a constructor, a destructor, and copy members. We need the latter three because the space for the array will need to be allocated / deallocated dynamically. Since it's desirable that the number of elements in an Array<T> object can be determined (for instance to iterate over them in a for loop), we will also include a getSize() accessor. With this in mind, the initial definition of the template looks like this:

```
template <typename T>
class Array
{
public:
  explicit Array<T>(std::size_t size);            // Constructor
  ~Array<T>();                                    // Destructor
  Array<T>(const Array<T>& array);                // Copy constructor
  Array<T>& operator=(const Array<T>& rhs);       // Copy assignment operator
  T& operator[](std::size_t index);               // Subscript operator
  const T& operator[](std::size_t index) const;   // Subscript operator-const arrays
  std::size_t getSize() const noexcept;           // Accessor for m_size

private:
  T* m_elements;       // Array of elements of type T
  std::size_t m_size;  // Number of array elements
};
```

The body of the template looks much like a regular class definition, except for the type parameter T in various places. It has for example a member variable, m_elements, of type *pointer to* T (equivalent to *array of* T). When the template is instantiated to produce a concrete class definition, T is replaced by the template type argument that was passed to Array<>. In the instance of the template for type double, for instance, m_elements will be of type double*, or *array of* double.

The first constructor is declared as explicit to prevent its use for implicit conversions. The second constructor is the copy constructor. Together with the copy assignment operator it allows Array<T> objects to be deep-copied from others, which is something you can't do with ordinary arrays. If you wanted to inhibit this capability, you should declare these members with = delete to prevent the compiler from supplying the default (as shown in Chapter 13).

The subscript operator has been overloaded on const. The non-const version of the subscript operator applies to non-const array objects and returns a non-const reference to an array element. Thus, this version can appear on the left of an assignment. The const version is called for const objects and returns a const reference to an element; obviously this version cannot appear on the left of an assignment.

The copy members both accept a parameter of type const Array<T>&. This type is *reference to const* Array<T>. When a class is synthesized from the template this is a reference to the class name for that particular class. With T as type double, for example, this would then be const Array<double>&. More generally, the class name for a specific instance of a template is formed from the template name followed by the template arguments between angle brackets. The template name followed by the list of parameter names between angle brackets is called the *template ID*.

It's not essential to use the full template ID within a template definition. Within the body of the Array template, Array by itself will always be taken to mean Array<T>. This means we can simplify the class template as follows:

```
template <typename T>
class Array
{
public:
  explicit Array(std::size_t size);   // Constructor
  ~Array();                           // Destructor
  Array(const Array& array);          // Copy constructor
  Array& operator=(const Array& rhs); // Copy assignment operator

  // Other members remain the same...
};
```

Defining Member Functions of a Class Template

The syntax for defining members outside of the template body is a little different from what applies to a normal class. The clue to understanding this syntax is to realize that external definitions for member functions of a class template are themselves templates. This is true even if a member function has no dependence on the type parameter T. So even getSize(), for instance—which always returns the same value of type std::size_t, irrespective of the value of T—needs a template definition of the following form.

```
// Template for getter to retrieve the m_size member of Array<T>
template <typename T>
std::size_t Array<T>::getSize() const noexcept
{
    return m_size;
}
```

The parameter list for the template that defines a member function must always match that of the class template. That is, you cannot, for instance, omit template parameters that the member function template seemingly does not need (such as T in the getSize() template). Besides, you do need the template type parameter to qualify to which class template (Array<T>) the member template belongs.

All member function definitions that you'll write in this section are templates that are inextricably bound to the Array<> class template. They are *not* function definitions; they're *templates* to be used by the compiler when the code for one of the member functions of the class template needs to be generated.

▓ **Note** The definition of a member template needs to be available to all source files that require its instantiation. You therefore almost always put member template definitions in the same file as the corresponding class template definition. If the template is exported from a module, this implies you normally put all member template definitions in the module interface as well. This is similar to function template definitions (see Chapter 10), but unlike regular member definitions (and unlike regular function definitions, for that matter), which you can freely move to an implementation file.

We continue by defining templates for the constructors of Array<> classes.

Constructor Templates

When you're defining a constructor template outside a class template definition, its name must be qualified by the class template name in a similar way to a member function of an ordinary class. However, this isn't a function definition; it's a *template* for a function definition, so that must be expressed as well. Here's the definition of the constructor template:

```
template <typename T>
Array<T>::Array(std::size_t size) : m_elements{ new T[size] {} }, m_size{ size }
{}
```

The first line identifies this as a template and specifies the template parameter as T. Splitting the template function declaration into two lines, as we've done here, is not necessary if the whole construct fits on one line, but it is often done for clarity regardless. The template parameter is essential in the qualification of the constructor name because it ties the definition to the class template. Note that you don't need a template argument list after the constructor name. Once past the ::, any occurrence of Array will again be taken to mean Array<T>.

In the constructor template you must allocate memory in the free store for an m_elements array that contains size elements of type T. If T is a class type, a public default constructor must exist in the class T; otherwise, the instance of this constructor template won't compile.

To copy an Array<T>, you must create an array of T elements with the same size and then copy over all T elements. The template for copy constructors does just that:

```
template <typename T>
Array<T>::Array(const Array& array) : Array{ array.m_size }
{
  for (std::size_t i {}; i < m_size; ++i)
    m_elements[i] = array.m_elements[i];
}
```

The body of this function template assumes that the assignment operator works for type T.

▨ **Note** The operations that a template performs on objects of type T *implicitly* place requirements on the definition of type T when T is a class type. In this section we mentioned two such requirements already: for the `Array<T>::Array(std::size_t)` constructor to work, objects of type T must be *default constructible*; for the copy constructor to work, they additionally need to be *copy assignable*. In Chapter 21 you will learn how to *explicitly* communicate such restrictions to the users of your template.

The Destructor Template

In many cases a default destructor will be okay in a class generated from a template, but this is not the case here. The destructors must release the memory for the m_elements array, so its definition will be as follows:

```
template <typename T>
Array<T>::~Array() { delete[] m_elements; }
```

We are releasing memory allocated for an array, so we must use the delete[] form of the operator. Failing to define this template would result in all classes generated from the template having major memory leaks.

Subscript Operator Templates

The operator[]() function template is equally straightforward. We just have to ensure illegal index values can't be used. For an index value that is out of range we can throw an exception:

```
template <typename T>
T& Array<T>::operator[](std::size_t index)
{
  if (index >= m_size)
    throw std::out_of_range {"Index too large: " + std::to_string(index)};
  return m_elements[index];
}
```

An exception of type std::out_of_range is thrown if the value of index is too large. We could define an exception class to use here, but it's easier to borrow the std::out_of_range class type from the Standard Library. This exception type is thrown already if you index a string, vector<>, or array<> object with an out-of-range index value, so our usage here is consistent with that. Note that index already cannot be negative because it is a value of type size_t, an *unsigned* integer type.

In a first, natural implementation, the body of the template for the const versions of the subscript operator would be identical to that of the non-const versions:

```
template <typename T>
const T& Array<T>::operator[](std::size_t index) const
{
  if (index >= m_size)
    throw std::out_of_range{ "Index too large: " + std::to_string(index) };
  return m_elements[index];
}
```

Introducing duplicate definitions for the const and non-const overloads of a member function, though, is considered bad practice. It is a particular instance of what is more generally referred to as *code duplication*. Because avoiding code duplication is key in making sure your code remains maintainable, we'll contemplate this a bit more before we move on to the final class member template—that for the assignment operator.

CODE DUPLICATION

Writing the same or similar code more than once is rarely a good idea. Not only is it a waste of time, such *duplicated code* is undesirable for a number of reasons—most notably because it undermines the maintainability of your code base. Requirements evolve, new insights are gained, and bugs are discovered. So, more often than not, your code will need to be adjusted several times after it is written. Having duplicated code snippets then implies you always have to remember to adjust all copies of that same code. Believe us when we say that this is a maintenance nightmare! The principle of avoiding code duplication is also called the *Don't Repeat Yourself* (DRY) principle.

Even if the duplicated code is just a few lines, it is often already worthwhile rethinking it. Consider, for instance, the duplicated operator[]() templates we just proposed for the Array<> template. Now imagine that you want to change the type of exception thrown or change the message passed to the exception. Then you have to change it in two places. Not only is this tedious, it is also really easy to forget one of these duplicates—especially if this were code written by someone else, or that you no longer remember the details of. This unfortunately occurs a lot in practice; changes or bug fixes to duplicated code are made in only one or some of the duplicates, while other duplicates live on containing the original now-incorrect version. If each piece of logic appears only once in your code base, this cannot happen!

The good news is that you already know most of the tools you need to battle code duplication. Functions are reusable blocks of computations, templates are instantiated to functions or classes for any number of types, a base class encapsulates all that is common to its derived classes, and so on. All these mechanisms were created precisely to make sure you do not have to repeat yourself!

A traditional approach to eliminate the code duplication between the const and non-const overloads of a member function is to implement the non-const version in terms of its const twin. While this sounds simple enough in principle, the resulting code may, nay *will*, seem daunting at first. So prepare yourself. For our operator[]() template, for instance, the classical implementation of this idiom looks as follows:

```
template <typename T>
T& Array<T>::operator[](std::size_t index)
{
   return const_cast<T&>(static_cast<const Array<T>&>(*this)[index]);
}
```

Ouch! We warned you that it would get scary, didn't we? The good news is that C++17 has introduced a little helper template, std::as_const(), that can make this code more bearable:

```
template <typename T>
T& Array<T>::operator[](std::size_t index)
{
   return const_cast<T&>(std::as_const(*this)[index]);
}
```

Nevertheless, since this is your first encounter with the idiom, let's rewrite this still nonobvious `return` statement into some smaller steps. That will help us explain what is going on:

```
template <typename T>
T& Array<T>::operator[](std::size_t index)
{
  Array<T>& nonConstRef = *this;        // Start from a non-const ref
  const Array<T>& constRef =            // Convert to const reference
          std::as_const(nonConstRef);
  const T& constResult = constRef[index]; // Obtain the const result
  return const_cast<T&>(constResult);    // Convert to non-const result
}
```

Because this template generates non-const member functions, the `this` pointer has a pointer-to-non-const type. So in our case, dereferencing the `this` pointer gives us a reference of type `Array<T>&`. The first thing we need to do is add `const` to this type. As of C++17, this can be done using `std::as_const()`. Given a value of type T&, instances of this function template produce a value of type `const T&`.

Once we have our reference-to-const, we simply call the overloaded function again with the same set of arguments. In our case, we call the `[ ]` operator function again with the same `size_t` argument, `index`. The only difference is that this time we call the overloaded function on the reference-to-const variable, which means that the `const` overload of the function—`operator[](size_t) const`—gets called. If we didn't add `const` to the type of `*this` first, we'd simply be calling the same function again, which would trigger infinite recursion.

Because we now call the function on a `const` object, it typically returns a reference to a `const` element as well. If it didn't, it would break `const` correctness. But what we need is a reference to a non-`const` element. In a final step, we must therefore strip away the `const`ness of the result before returning it from the function. And the only (clean) way to remove `const` in C++ is by using a `const_cast<>` (see Chapter 12).

Paraphrasing J. R. R. Tolkien, we propose to call this idiom "const-and-back-again." You first go from non-const to const (using `std::as_const`) and then back again to non-const (using a `const_cast<>`). Note that this idiom is one of the few cases where it is recommended to use a `const_cast<>`. In general, casting away `const`ness is considered bad practice. But eliminating code duplication using the const-and-back-again idiom is a widely accepted exception to this rule.

■ **Tip** Use the const-and-back-again idiom to avoid code duplication between the const and non-const overloads of a member function. In general, it works by implementing the non-const overload of a member in terms of its const counterpart using the following pattern:

```
ReturnType MyClass::myFunction(Arguments)
{
  return const_cast<ReturnType>(std::as_const(*this).myFunction(Arguments));
}
```

▓ **Note** The const-and-back-idiom is clearly a big help in reducing code duplication of member functions overloaded on const. The only downside is that you still have to write two functions. As of C++23, an even more economical code duplication reduction option presents itself; you can fold multiple member function overloads into a single template by parameterizing the explicit object parameter (see Chapter 12 for an introduction to this new syntax). The only downside is that to express such a template, you first need to master more advanced concepts, such as *member function templates, forwarding references*, and *(perfect) forwarding*—constructs that only few C++ developers are truly fluent with. We'll therefore not go in too much detail here. But just to give you a taste, here is how you could apply this novel C++23 idiom to replace both overloads of operator[] in the Array<> template of our running example:

```
template <typename T>
template <typename Self>
decltype(auto) Array<T>::operator[](this Self&& self, std::size_t index)
{
  if (index >= self.m_size)
    throw std::out_of_range {"Index too large: " + std::to_string(index)};
  return std::forward_like<Self>(self.m_elements[index]);
}
```

The first template parameter list is there because Array<> is a class template. For every instantiation Array<T>, this outer template effectively instantiates a new template for operator[] members of the class Array<T>. For T equal to std::string, for instance, this secondary template becomes:

```
template <typename Self>
decltype(auto) Array<std::string>::operator[](this Self&& self, std::size_t index)
{
  if (index >= self.m_size)
    throw std::out_of_range {"Index too large: " + std::to_string(index)};
  return std::forward_like<Self>(self.m_elements[index]);
}
```

The type parameter Self, in turn, parameterizes the type of the explicit object parameter self (see Chapter 12). Because Self is a template type parameter, the syntax Self&& introduces what is known as a *forwarding reference*. (This syntax should not to be confused with the syntax for rvalue references you'll learn about in Chapter 18, which, very confusingly, also uses &&, but then preceded by a concrete type...) The forwarding reference Self&& may bind to any Array<T> reference type—including Array<T>& and const Array<T>& (and Array<T>&&: see Chapter 18). Clearly, instantiating the secondary template with Self equal to const Array<T>& effectively instantiates a const member function overload.

The final ingredient to this more advanced idiom is *(perfect) forwarding*. When `Self` is bound to `Array<T>&`, we want to return a reference of type `T&`. Yet when `Self` is bound to `const Array<T>&`, we want to return a reference of type `const T&`. (And, naturally, when `Self` is bound to the for-now-mysterious `Array<T>&&` reference type—explained in Chapter 18—we want to return a reference of type `T&&`.) In other words, we always want to return a reference type of the exact same form as `Self`. And that is precisely what `std::forward_like<>()` does; it casts its function parameter to a reference type whose form matches that of its template type parameter. Another expression of the same family which you'll often need in templates such as this is `std::forward<Self>(self)`. You can look up *perfect forwarding* online to know more about this.

A lot to take in? Worry not. The more traditional `const`-and-back-again idiom will mostly do just fine avoiding duplication between `const` and non-`const` function overloads, and is far easier to remember and to get right. And on that note, it's high time we return to the main quest line: defining templates for member functions of class templates.

The Assignment Operator Template

There's more than one possibility for how the assignment operators could work. The operands must be of the same `Array<T>` type with the same `T`, but this does not prevent the `m_size` members from having different values. You could implement the assignment operators so that the left operands retain the same value for their `m_elements` member whenever possible. That is, if the right operand has fewer elements than the left operand, you could just copy sufficient elements from the right operand to fill parts of the array for the left operand. You could then either leave the excess elements at their original values or set them to the value produced by the default `T` constructor.

To keep it simple, however, we'll just make a left operand allocate a new `m_elements` array always, even if the previous array would be large enough already to fit a copy of the elements of the right operand. To implement this, the assignment operator functions must release any memory allocated in the destination object and then do what the copy constructors did. To make sure the assignment operators do not `delete[]` their own memory, they must first check that the objects are not identical (see Chapter 13). Here's the definition:

```
template <typename T>
Array<T>& Array<T>::operator=(const Array& rhs)
{
  if (&rhs != this)               // If lhs != rhs...
  {                               // ...do the assignment...
    delete[] m_elements;          // Release any free store memory

    m_size = rhs.m_size;          // Copy the members of rhs into lhs
    m_elements = new T[m_size];
    for (std::size_t i {}; i < m_size; ++i)
      m_elements[i] = rhs.m_elements[i];
  }
  return *this;                   // ... return lhs
}
```

CHAPTER 17 ░░░ CLASS TEMPLATES

Remember, checking to make sure that the left operand is not identical to the right is essential here; otherwise, you'd free the memory for the m_elements member of the object pointed to by this and then attempt to copy it to itself when it no longer exists! Every assignment operator of this form must start with such a safety check. When the operands are different, you release any free store memory owned by the left operand before creating a copy of the right operand.

You can find the full source code of the Array<> template in Ex17_01.

░░░ **Note** Did you notice how we repeated ourselves here? Perhaps take a second look at the assignment operator template if you missed it. The template begins by repeating the logic of the destructor template, followed by that of the copy constructor template. So we are in clear violation of the DRY principle here. But that is not the only thing amiss with this template, as we explain in the upcoming sidebar. The good news, though, is that you can solve both issues in one go using the *copy-and-swap idiom*.

EXCEPTION SAFETY AND COPY-AND-SWAP

Assignment operators instantiated from the template we just proposed will work perfectly in the nominal case. But what if something goes wrong? What if an error occurs during its execution and an exception is thrown? Can you perhaps locate the two places in the function template's code where this might happen? Try to do so before reading on.

We annotated the two potential sources of exceptions inside the body of our function template in the following code snippet:

```
template <typename T>
Array<T>& Array<T>::operator=(const Array& rhs)
{
  if (&rhs != this)
  {
    delete[] m_elements;

    m_size = rhs.m_size;
    m_elements = new T[m_size]          // may throw std::bad_alloc
    for (std::size_t i {}; i < m_size; ++i)
      m_elements[i] = rhs.m_elements[i]; // may throw any exception
  }                                      // (depends on T whether it may)
  return *this;
}
```

The first potential source is operator new[]. In Chapter 16, you learned that operator new[] throws a std::bad_alloc exception if free store memory cannot be allocated for some reason. While unlikely, especially on today's computers, this could absolutely happen when rhs is a particularly large array that doesn't fit twice in the available memory.

> ■ **Note** Free store memory allocation failures are rare these days because physical memory of most devices is large and virtual memory even larger. Because of this, checking for bad_alloc is omitted in most code. Nevertheless, given that we are implementing a template for classes whose sole responsibility is to manage arrays of elements, properly handling memory allocation failures does seem appropriate in this particular case.

The second potential source of exceptions is m_elements[i] = rhs.m_elements[i]. Since the Array<T> template can be used with any type, T may very well be a class type whose assignment operator throws an exception if the assignment fails. One likely candidate already is again std::bad_alloc. As witnessed by our own assignment operator template, a copy assignment often involves memory allocation. But in general this could be any exception type. It all depends on the definition of the assignment operator of type T.

> ■ **Tip** As a rule, you should assume that *any* function or operator you call might throw an exception. Consequently, consider how your code should behave if and when this occurs. The only exceptions to this rule, as you know from Chapter 16, are functions annotated with the noexcept keyword and most destructors (destructors are generally implicitly noexcept).

Once you have identified all potential sources of exceptions, you must analyze what would happen if exceptions are in fact thrown there. It would again be good practice for you to do so now, before reading on. Ask yourself, what exactly would happen to the Array<> object if an exception occurs in either of these two locations?

If the new[] operator in our example fails to allocate new memory, the m_elements pointer of the Array<> object becomes what is known as a *dangling pointer*—a pointer to memory that has been reclaimed. The reason is that right before the failing new[], delete[] was already applied on m_elements. This means that even if the caller catches the bad_alloc exception, the Array<> object has become unusable. Worse, actually, its destructor is almost certainly going to cause a fatal crash because it'll again apply delete[] on the now-dangling m_elements pointer.

Assigning nullptr to m_elements after the delete[] like we recommended in Chapter 6 would in this case only be a small patch on the wound. As none of the other Array<> member functions—for instance, operator[]—checks whether m_elements is nullptr, it would again only be a matter of time before a fatal crash occurs.

If one of the individual assignments performed inside the for loop fails, we are only slightly better off. Supposing the culprit exception is eventually caught, you are left with an Array<> object where only the first some m_elements have been assigned a correct new value, while the rest is still default-initialized. And there is no way of knowing how many have succeeded.

When you call a member function that modifies an object's state, you typically want one of two things to happen. Ideally, the function fully succeeds and brings the object into its desired new state. As soon as any error prevents a complete success, however, you really do not want to end up with an object in some unpredictable halfway state. Leaving a function's work half-finished mostly means that the object becomes unusable. Once anything goes wrong you instead prefer the object to remain in, or revert to, its initial state. This all-or-nothing quality of functions is formally known as *strong exception safety*.

For your assignment operators to be strongly exception-safe, you must ensure that whenever an assignment fails to allocate or copy all elements, that the `Array<>` object then still (or again) points to the same m_elements array as it did prior to the assignment attempt, and that m_size has remained untouched as well.

Like we said in Chapter 16, writing code that is correct when nothing goes wrong (the so-called happy scenario) is often only half of the work. Making sure that your code behaves reliably and robustly when faced with unexpected errors can be at least as hard. Proper error handling always starts from a cautious attitude. That is, always be on the lookout for possible sources of errors and make sure you understand the consequences of such errors. Luckily, once you have located and analyzed the problem areas—and you'll get better at spotting these over time—there exist standard techniques to make your code behave correctly after an error. Let's see how this might be done for our example.

The programming pattern that can be used to guarantee the desired all-or-nothing behavior for our assignment operator is called the *copy-and-swap idiom*. The idea is simple. If you have to modify the state of one or more objects and any of the steps required for this modification may fail and/or throw an exception, then you should follow this simple recipe:

1.   *Copy* the objects. (Often this concerns only one object, but in general it can be any number of objects.)

2.   Start modifying the copies. All this time, the original objects remain untouched!

3.   Once all modifications are successful, replace—or *swap*—the original objects with the now fully modified copies.

As soon as anything goes wrong, either while copying the originals or during any of the subsequent modification steps, you abandon all copied, possibly half-modified objects and let the entire operation fail. The original objects then remain as they were.

While this idiom can be applied to virtually any code, it is often used within a member function. For assignment operators, the application of this idiom looks like this:

```
template <typename T>
Array<T>& Array<T>::operator=(const Array& rhs)
{
   Array<T> copy{rhs}; // Copy...        (could go wrong and throw an exception)
   swap(copy);         // ... and swap! (noexcept)
   return *this;
}
```

We have effectively rewritten the assignment in terms of the copy constructor. Note that a self-assignment test is no longer required in a copy-and-swap assignment operator either (swapping an object with a copy of itself is perfectly safe), although there is no harm in adding one either.

In a way, this is a degenerate instance of the copy-and-swap idiom. In general, the state of the copied object may need any number of modifications between the copy and the swap stages of the idiom. These modifications are then always applied to the copy, never directly to the original object (*this, in our case). If either the copy step itself or any of the additional modification steps that follow throw an exception, the stack-allocated `copy` object is automatically reclaimed, and the original object (`*this`) remains unchanged.

Once you are done updating the copy, you swap its member variables with those of the original object. The copy-and-swap idiom hinges on the assumption that this final step, the swapping, can be done without any risk for exceptions. That is, it must not be possible that an exception occurs at a point where some member variables are already swapped and others not. Luckily, implementing a `noexcept` swap function is almost always trivial.

By convention, the function to swap the contents of two objects is called `swap()` and is implemented as a nonmember function in the same namespace as the class whose objects it is swapping. (We know, in our `operator=()` template we used `swap()` as a member function. Be patient, we're getting to that!) The Standard Library also offers the `std::swap<>()` template that can be used to swap values or objects of any copyable data type. For now, you can think of this function template as if it were implemented like this:[2]

```
template <typename T>
void swap(T& one, T& other) noexcept
{
  T copy(one);
  one = other;
  other = copy;
}
```

At this point, applying this template to `Array<>` objects would not be particularly efficient. All the elements of the objects being swapped would be copied several times. Besides, we could never use it to swap `*this` and `copy` in our copy assignment operator—do you see why?[3] We'll therefore create our own, more effective `swap()` function for `Array<>` objects. Similar specializations of `std::swap<>()` exist for many Standard Library types.

Because the member variables of `Array<>` are private, one option is to define `swap()` as a friend function. Here, we'll take a slightly different approach, one that is also followed by standard container templates such as `std::vector<>`. The idea is to first add an extra member function `swap()` to `Array<>` as follows:

```
template <typename T>
void Array<T>::swap(Array& other) noexcept
{
  std::swap(m_elements, other.m_elements); // Swap two pointers
  std::swap(m_size, other.m_size);         // Swap the sizes
}
```

---

[2] The actual `swap<>()` template is different in two aspects. First, it moves the objects if possible using move semantics. You'll learn all about move semantics in the next chapter. Second, it is only conditionally `noexcept`. Concretely, it is `noexcept` only if its arguments can be moved without exceptions. Conditional `noexcept` specifications are a significantly more advanced language feature we do not cover in this book.

[3] The reason we cannot use the `std::swap()` from within our copy assignment operator is that `std::swap()` in turn would use the copy assignment operator. In other words, calling `std::swap()` here would result in infinite recursion!

You then use this `swap()` member to implement the conventional nonmember `swap()` function:

```
template <typename T>
void swap(Array<T>& one, Array<T>& other) noexcept
{
    one.swap(other);      // Forward to public member function
}
```

You can find the full source code of the `Array<>` template updated to employ copy-and-swap in Ex17_01A.

▨ **Tip**   Always implement the assignment operator in terms of the copy constructor and a noexcept `swap()` function. This basic instance of the copy-and-swap idiom will ensure the desired all-or-nothing behavior for your assignment operators. While `swap()` can be added as a member function, convention dictates that making objects swappable involves defining a nonmember `swap()` function. Following this convention also ensures that the `swap()` function gets used by various algorithms of the Standard Library.

The copy-and-swap idiom can be used to make any nontrivial state modification exception-safe, either inside other member functions or simply in the middle of any code. It comes in many variations, but the idea is always the same. First copy the object you want to change, then perform any number (zero or more) of risky steps on that copy, and only once they all succeed commit the changes by swapping the state of the copy and the actual target object.

Class Template Instantiation

The compiler instantiates a class template as a result of a definition of an object that has a type produced by the template. Here's an example:

```
Array<int> data {40};
```

When this statement is compiled, a definition for the `Array<int>` class is created where every occurrence of T in the template is substituted with `int`. But there's one subtlety. The compiler compiles *only* the member functions that your program *uses*, so you basically may not get the entire class that would be produced by a simple substitution for the template parameter. On the basis of just the definition for our object, data, the instantiated `Array<int>` class would thus be equivalent to the following:

```
class Array<int>
{
public:
    explicit Array(std::size_t size); // Constructor
    ~Array();                         // Destructor
```

```
private:
  int* m_elements;              // Array of type int
  std::size_t m_size;           // Number of array elements
};
```

You can see that the instantiated class only has two member functions: the constructor and the destructor. The compiler won't create instances of anything that isn't required to create or destruct the object, and it won't include parts of the template that aren't needed in the program.

Of course, the declaration of data causes the constructor Array<int>::Array(std::size_t) to be called as well, so after instantiating the class definition the compiler also instantiates a definition for the constructor for the Array<int> class from the corresponding member template:

```
Array<int>::Array(std::size_t size) : m_elements{ new int[size]{} }, m_size{ size }
{}
```

Once the data object inevitably goes out of scope, the compiler analogously instantiates the destructor for the Array<int> class as well.

▓ **Note**   This so-called *lazy instantiation* trait of member function templates implies that you can in fact create and use an Array<T> object for a type T whose objects cannot be copied (such as for instance Array<std::unique_ptr>), as long as you do not use the copy constructor or copy assignment operator. It also implies, though, that coding errors in class member templates may go undetected until you first use them. We will give you some pointers in the next subsection on how you can quickly test for such errors.

If the instantiation of a class template arises as a by-product of declaring an object, it is referred to as an *implicit instantiation* of the template. This terminology also distinguishes it from an *explicit instantiation* of a template, which as seen in the next subsection behaves a little differently.

Explicit Template Instantiation

You have already seen how to explicitly instantiate *function* templates in Chapter 10. You can also *explicitly* instantiate a class template without defining an object of the template type. The effect of an explicit instantiation of a template is that the compiler creates the instance determined by the parameter values that you specify. To instantiate a class template, just use the template keyword followed by the class (or struct) keyword, the template class name, and the template arguments between angle brackets.

This definition, for instance, explicitly creates an instance of the Array template for type double:

```
template class Array<double>;
```

Explicitly instantiating a class template not only generates the complete class type definition, it also instantiates all member functions of the class from their templates. This happens regardless of whether you call the member functions, so the executable may contain code that is never used.

■ **Tip**   You can use explicit instantiation to quickly test whether a class template and all its member templates can be instantiated without errors for a given type. It saves you the trouble of writing code that creates an object for the corresponding instance and then calls all its member functions one by one. Once you're satisfied that all templates instantiate and compile fine, you can remove such explicit class template instantiations again.

Testing the Array Class Template

It's high time we tried out the Array<> template in a working example. We begin by collecting the class template and the templates for its member functions in a module interface file called Array.cppm:

```cpp
// Array.cppm - Array class template definition
export module array;
import std;

export template <typename T>
class Array
{
    // Definition of the Array<T> template...
};

// Optional: (exported) template for non-member swap(Array<T>&, Array<T>&) functions

// Definitions of the templates for member functions of Array<T>...
```

Notice that the export keyword goes in front of the template keyword, and not in front of the class keyword. This expresses that you are, effectively, exporting a template, rather than defining a template for exported classes (the latter is not allowed).

As with regular out-of-class member definitions, none of the templates for the members of Array<T> may be exported; only the class template itself can be exported. Because they are templates, however, you must not move these member templates to a module implementation file. The compiler needs these templates to be part of the module interface to instantiate them when consumers of the module supply new values for the type parameter T.

With our array module complete, we now need a program that declares some arrays using the template and tries them. For old times' sake, our example will create an Array<> of Box objects. You can use this box module:

```cpp
export module box;

export class Box
{
public:
  Box() : Box{ 1.0, 1.0, 1.0 } {}
  Box(double l, double w, double h) : m_length {l}, m_width {w}, m_height {h} {}

  double volume() const { return m_length * m_width * m_height; }
private:
  double m_length, m_width, m_height;
};
```

We'll use some out-of-range index values in the example as well, just to show that it works:

```cpp
// Ex17_01(A).cpp - Using a class template
import array;
import box;
import std;

int main()
{
  try
  {
    const std::size_t numValues {20};
    Array<double> values {numValues};

    for (std::size_t i {}; i < numValues; ++i)
      values[i] = static_cast<double>(i + 1);

    std::print("Sums of pairs of elements:");
    std::size_t lines {};
    for (std::size_t i {numValues - 1}; i >= 0; --i)
    {
      if (lines++ % 5 == 0) std::println("");
      std::print("{:5g}", values[i] + values[i-1]);
    }
  }
  catch (const std::out_of_range& ex)
  {
    std::println("\nout_of_range exception object caught! {}", ex.what());
  }

  try
  {
    const std::size_t numBoxes {5};
    Array<Box> boxes {numBoxes};
    for (std::size_t i {} ; i <= numBoxes ; ++i)
      std::println("Box volume is {}", boxes[i].volume());
  }
  catch (const std::out_of_range& ex)
  {
    std::println("\nout_of_range exception object caught! {}", ex.what());
  }
}
```

This example will produce output similar to this:

```
Sums of pairs of elements:
   39   37   35   33   31
   29   27   25   23   21
   19   17   15   13   11
    9    7    5    3
```

```
out_of_range exception object caught! Index too large: 18446744073709551615
Box volume is 1
Box volume is 1
Box volume is 1
Box volume is 1
Box volume is 1

out_of_range exception object caught! Index too large: 5
```

The main() function creates an object of type Array<double> that implicitly creates an instance of the class template with a type argument of double. The number of elements in the array is specified by the argument to the constructor, numValues. The compiler will also create an instance of the template for the constructor definition.

A first for loop initializes the elements of the values object with values from 1 to numValues. The expression values[i] in the loop's body results in an instance of the subscript operator function being created. This instance is called implicitly by this expression as values.operator[](i). Because values is not const, the non-const version of the operator function is instantiated and called. If you used the const-and-back-again idiom, this will in turn instantiate and call the const overload of the operator.

The explicit conversion to double in that same loop body is there only because otherwise compilers (where std::size_t is a 64-bit integer type) may warn you that not all std::size_t values are convertible to double without loss of precision. Silly compilers... numValues would have to be just a tad larger than 20 before we run into any real trouble; the first integer that cannot be represented exactly by an IEEE double precision floating-point number is 9,007,199,254,740,993. And besides, even if numValues were that large, we'd probably run into more significant issues long before we experience any loss of precision; an array of that many doubles would require roughly 72 petabytes of memory... Long story short, this particular type conversion is more than safe!

The second for loop in the try block then outputs the sums of successive pairs of elements, starting at the end of the array. The code in this loop also calls the subscript operator function, but because the instance of the function template has already been created, no new instance is generated.

Clearly, the values[i-1] expression has an illegal index value when i is 0, so this causes an exception to be thrown by the operator[]() function. The catch block catches this and outputs a message to the standard error stream. You can see from the output that the index took on a very large value, which indeed suggests that it originated by decrementing an unsigned zero value. When the exception is thrown by the subscript operator function, control is passed immediately to the catch block. The illegal element reference is therefore not used. Of course, the for loop ends immediately at this point as well.[4]

The next try block then defines an Array<> object that can store Box objects. The compiler generates a second instance of the class template, Array<Box>, because the template has not been instantiated for Box objects previously. The statement also calls the constructor to create the boxes object, so an instance of the function template for the constructor is created. The constructor for the Array<Box> class calls the default constructor for the Box class when the m_elements member is created in the free store. All the Box objects in the m_elements array therefore have the default dimensions of 1×1×1.

The volume of each Box object in boxes is output in a final for loop. The boxes[i] expression calls the overloaded subscript operator, so the compiler instantiates this template a second time as well. When i has the value numBoxes the subscript operator function throws an exception because an index value of numBoxes is beyond the end of the m_elements array. The catch block following the try block catches the exception. Because the try block is exited, all locally declared objects will be destroyed, including the boxes object.

---

[4] Which in a way is fortunate, because the same developer that carelessly passed an invalid index to values[i-1] also mistakenly wrote an otherwise indefinite for loop. Do you see why?

Non-Type Class Template Parameters

A non-type parameter looks like a function parameter—a type name followed by the name of the parameter. Here's an example:

```
template <typename T, std::size_t size>
class ClassName
{
  // Definition using T and size...
};
```

This template has a type parameter, T, and a non-type parameter, size. The definition is expressed in terms of these two parameters and the template name.

You cannot use just any type as the type of a non-type template parameter. Most class types in particular are not allowed[5]. That is, you cannot use types such as Box or std::string for a non-type template parameter. The type of a non-type template parameter is nearly always a fundamental type (size_t, long, bool, char, float, and so on—only not void), enumeration type, pointer type, or reference type (this includes pointers and references to functions).

If you need it, the type for a non-type parameter can also be the type name of a preceding type parameter:

```
template <typename T,     // T is the name of the type parameter
          T value>        // T is also the type of this non-type parameter
class ClassName
{
  // Definition using T and value...
};
```

The parameter T must appear before its use in the parameter list, so value couldn't precede the type parameter T here. Of course, using a type parameter as the type of a non-type parameter implicitly restricts the arguments for T to the aforementioned types that are allowed for non-type parameters.

To illustrate how you could use non-type parameters, we'll add a non-type parameter to the Array template of Ex17_01 to allow flexibility in indexing the array:

```
template <typename T, int startIndex>
class Array
{
public:
  explicit Array(std::size_t size);          // Constructor
  ~Array();                                  // Destructor
  Array(const Array& array);                 // Copy constructor
  Array& operator=(const Array& rhs);        // Assignment operator
  void swap(Array& other) noexcept;          // noexcept swap() function
  T& operator[](int index);                  // Subscript operator
  const T& operator[](int index) const;      // Subscript operator-const arrays
  std::size_t getSize() const noexcept { return m_size; } // Accessor for size
```

---

[5] As of C++20, you can in principle use certain class types (a specific subset of *literal classes*, to be exact), but the restrictions on these class types are so severe we won't discuss this possibility.

690

```
private:
  T* m_elements;       // Array of elements of type T
  std::size_t m_size;  // Number of array elements
};
```

This adds a non-type parameter, startIndex, of type int. The idea is that you can specify that you want to use index values that vary over a given range. For example, if you dislike that array indexes in C++ start at 0 and not at 1, you should instantiate Array<> classes for which startIndex equals 1. You could even create Array<> objects that allows index values from –10 to +10. You would then specify the array with the non-type parameter value as –10 and the argument to the constructor as 21 because the array would need 21 elements.

As index values can now be negative, the parameter for the subscript operator functions has been changed to type int. Notice that the size of the array will still always be a positive number, so the type of the m_size member can remain std::size_t.

Templates for Member Functions with Non-Type Parameters

Because you've added a non-type parameter to the class template definition, the templates that define its member functions need to be changed as well. They now all need the same two parameters as the class template—even the ones that do not use the new non-type parameter. The parameters are part of the identification for the class template, so to match the template they must have the same parameter list. The template for the primary Array<> constructors, for instance, must be updated as follows:

```
template <typename T, int startIndex>
Array<T, startIndex>::Array(std::size_t size) : m_elements{new T[size] {}}, m_size{size}
{}
```

The template ID is now Array<T, startIndex>, so this is used to qualify the constructor name. This is the only change from the original definition apart from adding the new template parameter to the template.

Most other member templates need little more than this same update of their template parameter list and template ID. We will not spell them all out here. You can find the updated definitions in Ex17_02.

The only template that requires more significant changes—and at the same time the only template to truly use the non-type template parameter startIndex in its body—is that for the const subscript operators:

```
template <typename T, int startIndex>
const T& Array<T, startIndex>::operator[](int index) const
{
  if (index < startIndex)
    throw std::out_of_range {"Index too small: " + std::to_string(index)};

  if (index > startIndex + static_cast<int>(m_size) - 1)
    throw std::out_of_range {"Index too large: " + std::to_string(index)};

  return m_elements[index - startIndex];
}
```

As said, the index parameter is now of type int to allow negative values. The validity checks on its value now verify that it's between startIndex and startIndex + m_size - 1. Careful: Because size_t is an unsigned integer type, you must explicitly convert m_size to int; if you don't, the other values in the expression will be implicitly converted to size_t, which will produce a wrong result if startIndex is negative. The choice of messages for the exceptions has also been changed.

If you hadn't used the const-and-back-again idiom in Ex17_01, you would have had to apply all these same changes to the template for the non-const subscript operator overloads as well. Whereas now, after the obligatory update of the template parameters and ID, you only need to change the type of its index parameter to int. This just goes to show how much it pays to never repeat yourself!

```cpp
template <typename T, int startIndex>
T& Array<T, startIndex>::operator[](int index)
{
  return const_cast<T&>(std::as_const(*this)[index]);
}
```

The following example exercises the new features of our latest Array<> class template. To build it, assemble all updated template definitions in a new array module and use the box module from Ex17_01:

```cpp
// Ex17_02.cpp - Using a class template with a non-type parameter
import array;
import box;
import std;

int main()
{
  try
  {
    try
    {
      const std::size_t size {21};                         // Number of array elements
      const int start {-10};                               // Index for first element
      const int end {start + static_cast<int>(size) - 1};  // Index for last element

      Array<double, start> values {size};                  // Define array of double values

      for (int i {start}; i <= end; ++i)                   // Initialize the elements
        values[i] = i - start + 1;

      std::print("Sums of pairs of elements:");
      std::size_t lines {};
      for (int i {end}; i >= start; --i)
      {
        if (lines++ % 5 == 0) std::println("");
        std::print("{:5g}", values[i] + values[i-1]);
      }
    }
    catch (const std::out_of_range& ex)
    {
      std::println("\nout_of_range exception object caught! {}", ex.what());
    }

    // Create array of Box objects
    const int numBoxes {9};
    Array<Box, -numBoxes / 2> boxes { static_cast<std::size_t>(numBoxes) };
```

```
    for (int i { -numBoxes / 2 }; i <= numBoxes/2 + numBoxes%2; ++i)
      std::println("Volume of Box[{}] is {}", i, boxes[i].volume());
  }
  catch (const std::exception& ex)
  {
    std::println("{} exception caught in main()! {}", typeid(ex).name(), ex.what());
  }
}
```

This displays the following output:

```
Sums of pairs of elements:
   41    39    37    35    33
   31    29    27    25    23
   21    19    17    15    13
   11     9     7     5     3

out_of_range exception object caught! Index too small: -11
Volume of Box[-4] is 1
Volume of Box[-3] is 1
Volume of Box[-2] is 1
Volume of Box[-1] is 1
Volume of Box[0] is 1
Volume of Box[1] is 1
Volume of Box[2] is 1
Volume of Box[3] is 1
Volume of Box[4] is 1
class std::out_of_range exception caught in main()! Index too large: 5
```

The nested try block starts by defining constants that specify the range of index values and the size of the array. The size and start variables are used to create an instance of the Array<> template to store 21 values of type double. The second template argument corresponds to the non-type parameter and specifies the lower limit for the index values of the array. The size of the array is specified by the constructor argument.

The for loop that follows assigns values to the elements of the values object. The loop index, i, runs from the lower limit start, which will be –10, up to and including the upper limit end, which will be +10. Within the loop the values of the array elements are set to run from 1 to 21.

A second for loop then outputs the sums of pairs of successive elements, starting at the last array element and counting down. The lines variable is used to output the sums, five to a line. As in Ex17_01, sloppy control of the index value eventually results in a values[i-1] expression, which throws an std::out_of_range exception. The handler for the nested try block catches it and displays the message you see in the output.

The statement that creates an array to store Box objects is in the outer try block of main(). The type for boxes is Array<Box, -numBoxes / 2>, which demonstrates that expressions are acceptable as argument values for non-type parameters in a template instantiation. The type of such an expression must either match the type of the parameter, or at least be convertible to the appropriate type by means of an implicit conversion.

You do need to take care if such an expression includes the > character. Here's an example:

```
Array<Box, numBoxes > 5 ? numBoxes : 5> boxes{42};   // Will not compile!
```

The intent of the expression for the second argument that uses the conditional operator is to supply a value of at least 5, but as it stands, this won't compile. The > in the expression is paired with the opening angle bracket and closes the parameter list. Parentheses are necessary to make the statement valid:

```
Array<Box, (numBoxes > 5 ? numBoxes : 5)> boxes{42};  // OK
```

Parentheses are also likely to be necessary for non-type argument expressions that involve the right shift operator >> (though not for operators ->, <=>, and >=).

The final for loop throws another exception, this time because the index exceeds the upper limit. The exception is caught by the catch block for the body of main(). The output shows that the exception is identified as type std::out_of_range. This again confirms there is no object slicing when catching the exception by reference to a base class (see Chapter 16).

CODE READABILITY

It's time for another sidebar on code quality. For Ex17_02, we used the following implementation of the operator[]() template for our Array<> class template:

```
template <typename T, int startIndex>
const T& Array<T, startIndex>::operator[](int index) const
{
  if (index < startIndex)
    throw std::out_of_range {"Index too small: " + std::to_string(index)};

  if (index > startIndex + static_cast<int>(m_size) - 1)
    throw std::out_of_range {"Index too large: " + std::to_string(index)};

  return m_elements[index - startIndex];
}
```

While there is nothing functionally wrong with this code, chances are fairly high that you had to think at least twice to convince yourself that the conditions in the if statements were correct, in particular that of the second one. If so, you may find the following version easier to understand:

```
template <typename T, int startIndex>
const T& Array<T, startIndex>::operator[](int index) const
{
  // Subtract startIndex to obtain the actual index into the m_elements array.
  // If startIndex is 0, conventional 0-based array indexing is used.
  const int actualIndex = index - startIndex;

  if (actualIndex < 0)
    throw std::out_of_range {"Index too small: " + std::to_string(index)};

  if (actualIndex >= m_size)
    throw std::out_of_range {"Index too large: " + std::to_string(index)};

  return m_elements[actualIndex];
}
```

By first computing actualIndex, we have greatly simplified the logic in both if conditions. All that remains is comparing actualIndex with the actual bounds of the m_elements array. In other words, all that remains is to check that actualIndex lies in the half-open interval [0, m_size), which is something any C++ programmer is much more accustomed to than working with a startIndex. It follows that it now becomes much more apparent that the conditions are correct.

We've also purposely added the "If startIndex is 0..." line of comment to make it easier for readers of the code to convince themselves that the computation of actualIndex itself is correct. In general, it often helps to substitute edge cases such as 0 when validating such computations.

While, admittedly, this may not yet have been the most convincing example, the lesson we want to convey here is that professional coding is about much more than simply writing correct code. Writing readable, understandable code is at least as important. In fact, doing so already goes a long way toward avoiding bugs and keeping your code base maintainable.

■ **Tip** Once you have written a piece of code, small or big, you should get into the habit of taking a step back and placing yourself in the shoes of a person who must read and understand your code later. This could be a colleague tasked with fixing a bug or making a small change, or it could be you in a year or two (trust us, more than likely, you will not remember writing it anymore!). Ask yourself, can I not rewrite the code to make it more readable? Easier to understand? Should I not clarify things by adding some more code comments? At first, you may find this difficult and time-consuming or even fail to see the point. But believe us, after a while, this will become a second nature, and one day you will find yourself mostly writing high-quality code from the start.

Arguments for Non-Type Parameters

An argument for a non-type parameter must be a compile-time constant expression. This means you can't use an expression containing a non-const integer variable as an argument for Array<>, which is a slight disadvantage, but the compiler will validate the argument, which is a compensating plus. For example, the following statements won't compile:

```
int start {-10};
Array<double, start> values{ 21 };    // Won't compile because start is not const
```

The compiler will generate a message to the effect that the second argument here is invalid. Here are correct versions of these two statements:

```
const int start {-10};
Array<double, start> values{ 21 };    // OK
```

Now that start has been declared as const, the compiler can rely on its value, and both template arguments are now legal. The compiler applies standard conversions to arguments when they are necessary to match the parameter type. For example, if you had a non-type parameter declared as type std::size_t, the compiler converts an integer literal such as 10 to the required argument type.

You cannot modify the value of a parameter within any of the member function templates. The value of a non-type template argument is statically hardwired into the instantiated class type, and is thus effectively treated as a constant. Consequently, a non-type parameter cannot be used on the left of an assignment or have the increment or decrement operator applied to it.

Non-Type Template Arguments vs. Constructor Arguments

Besides the fact that template arguments must be compile-time constants, there are some other disadvantages to the definition of Array<> we have been using as an example for non-type template parameters:

```
template <typename T, int startIndex>
class Array;
```

Non-type parameter arguments in a class template are part of the type of an instance of the template. Every unique combination of template arguments produces another class type. This means that the type of an array of double values indexed from 0 will be different from that of an array of double values indexed from 1. This has at least two undesirable consequences. First, you may get a lot more compiled code in your program than you might have anticipated (a condition known as *code bloat*); and second, you won't be able to intermix elements of the two types in an expression. The following code would not compile, for instance:

```
Array<double, 0> indexedFromZero{10};
Array<double, 1> indexedFromOne{10};
indexedFromOne = indexedFromZero;
```

■ **Note**   In principle, you could resort to advanced techniques such as adding member function templates to our Array<> class template to facilitate intermixing related instantiations of the Array<> template. These are templates for member functions that add extra template parameters—such as a different start index—on top of the two existing template parameters of the class. We discussed member function templates earlier already when we created one combining the definitions of all different overloads of operator[ ].

It would be much better to provide flexibility for the range of index values by adding a parameter to the constructor rather than using a non-type template parameter. Here's how that would look:

```
template <typename T>
class Array
{
public:
  explicit Array(std::size_t size, int startIndex=0);
  // Other member functions as before...
private:
  T* m_elements;       // Array of elements of type T
  std::size_t m_size;  // Number of array elements
  int m_start_index;   // Starting index value
};
```

The extra member variable, m_start_index, stores the starting index for the array specified by the second constructor argument. The default value for the startIndex parameter is 0, so normal indexing is obtained by default. Of course, you would have to update the copy constructor and the swap() method as well to take this extra member into account.

Default Values for Template Parameters

You can supply default argument values for both type and non-type parameters in a class template. This works in a similar way to default values for function parameters. If a given parameter has a default value, then all subsequent parameters in the list must also have default values specified. If you omit an argument for a template parameter that has a default value specified, the default is used, just like with default parameter values in a function. Similarly, when you omit the argument for a given parameter in the list, all subsequent arguments must also be omitted.

The default values for class template parameters are written in the same way as defaults for function parameters—following an = after the parameter name. You could supply defaults for both the parameters in the version of the Array template with a non-type parameter. Here's an example:

```
template <typename T = int, int startIndex = 0>
class Array
{
  // Template definition as before...
};
```

If a class template has default values for any of its parameters, they only need to be specified in the first declaration of the template in a source file, which usually will be the definition of the class template. You must not specify the default values in the templates for the member functions; the compiler will use the argument values used to instantiate the class template.

You could omit all the template arguments to declare an array of elements of type int indexed from 0.

```
Array<> numbers {101};
```

The legal index values run from 0 to 100, as determined by the default value for the non-type template parameter and the argument to the constructor. You must still supply the angled brackets, even though no arguments are necessary. The other possibilities open to you are to omit the second argument or to supply them all, as shown here:

```
Array<std::string, -100> messages {200}; // Array of 200 string objects indexed from -100
Array<Box> boxes {101};                  // Array of 101 Box objects indexed from 0
```

Class Template Argument Deduction

You'll recall from Chapter 10 that for function templates, more often than not, you do not have to specify any template arguments—not even for template parameters without a default value. In most cases, the compiler can deduce all function template arguments from the function arguments. You saw function template argument deduction in action, for instance, in Ex10_01:

```
template<typename T> T larger(T a, T b);    // Function template prototype

int main()
{
  std::println("Larger of 1.5 and 2.5 is {}", larger(1.5, 2.5));
  ...
```

You did not have to specify the template type argument using larger<double>(1.5, 2.5). The compiler conveniently deduced the type argument double by matching the type, double, of the two function arguments with the two occurrences of T in the template's function parameter list.

For a long time, no deduction existed for class template arguments. You always had to explicitly specify all arguments without a default value (even if that happened to be zero arguments, as seen in the previous section). Of course, there is not always another choice. Consider the variable definition you encountered in Ex17_01:

```
const std::size_t numValues {20};
Array<double> values {numValues};
```

You could try to omit <double> from the type of this variable as follows:

```
const std::size_t numValues {20};
Array values {numValues};   /* Will not compile (cannot deduce value for T) */
```

But doing so will result in a compilation error. The compiler cannot possibly deduce the value of the template type parameter T from this constructor invocation. All it has to work with is numValues, a size_t argument passed to a size_t constructor parameter. The template parameter T never even enters this equation and neither does the type double, so how could the compiler possibly deduce anything here? It's thus only fair that you have to specify the template argument double yourself in such cases.

Suppose, however, that you add an *initializer list constructor* to the Array<> template. The template for this constructor would look as follows:

```
template <typename T>
Array<T>::Array(std::initializer_list<T> elements)
   : m_elements {new T[elements.size()]}, m_size {elements.size()}
{
   // std::initializer_list<> has no operator[], but can be used in range-based for loop.
   for (std::size_t i {}; const T& element : elements)
      m_elements[i++] = element;
}
```

You briefly encountered the std::initializer_list<> class template at the end of Chapter 2. In short, objects of type std::initializer_list<T> can get created automatically from a braced initializer list with values of type T. This occurs when you invoke an initializer list constructor, for instance. (Refer to Chapter 2 should you need more examples.) Invoking initializer list constructors, however, should hold no secrets; you have done so plenty of times already with std::vector<>. Here is an example:

```
std::vector<float> floats{ 1.0f, 2.0f, 3.0f, 4.0f };
```

This, as you know, creates a vector initialized with a dynamic array containing the four given float values. If you add the initializer list constructor we showed earlier to the Array<> template of Ex17_01, you can analogously create Array<> objects as follows (see also Ex17_03.cpp):

```
Array<int> integers{ 1, 2, 3, 4, 5 };
Array<double> doubles{ 1.0, 2.0, 3.0, 4.0, 5.0 };
```

Only, this time, you *can* omit the template argument list as follows:

```
Array integers{ 1, 2, 3, 4, 5 };           // Deduced type: Array<int>
Array doubles{ 1.0, 2.0, 3.0, 4.0, 5.0 };  // Deduced type: Array<double>
```

From these constructor invocations, the compiler *can* deduce the template type arguments (int and double, respectively). It can, because this time the template type parameter T *is* part of the constructor's signature. By matching the type of the constructor's elements parameter (initializer_list<T>) with the types of the arguments (initializer_list<int> and initializer_list<double>, respectively), the compiler can easily deduce correct type arguments for T.[6]

Class template argument deduction (or CTAD for short) can save you some typing when constructing values of either your own generic types or any number of Standard Library types such as std::pair, std::tuple, std::vector, and so on. Always remember, though, that CTAD only applies to constructor invocations; you must still always specify the complete template ID when using a class template instance as the type of a function parameter or member variable, as the return type of a function, and so on.

▓ **Note**   CTAD is deliberately not enabled for the popular smart pointer types std::unique_ptr<> and shared_ptr<>. That is, you cannot write the following:

```
std::unique_ptr smartBox{ new Box{1.0, 2.0, 3.0} };       // Will not compile!
```

The motivation is that, in general, the compiler cannot deduce whether a value of type Box* points to either a single Box or an array of Boxes. As you'll recall, pointers and arrays are closely related and can mostly be used interchangeably. When constructed with a Box*, the compiler therefore has no way of knowing whether to deduce either unique_ptr<Box> or unique_ptr<Box[]>. To initialize smart pointer variables, the recommended approach thus remains the use of std::make_unique<>() and std::make_shared<>(). Here's an example:

```
auto smartBox{ std::make_unique<Box>(1.0, 2.0, 3.0) };
```

▓ **Caution**   If you compile and run the Ex17_01 program with the Array<> template of Ex17_03 (that is, the template with the additional initializer list constructor), you will notice that the output of Ex17_01 changes. The reason is that this statement in the main() function of Ex17_01 started doing something completely different:

```
Array<double> values{ numValues };   // Now uses the initializer list constructor!
```

Where before it created an Array<> containing 20 times the double value 0.0 (numValues is equal to 20), it now suddenly creates an Array<> containing only a single double value, 20.0. When you invoke a constructor using the braced initializer syntax, the compiler always picks an initializer list constructor if possible. We cautioned you about the analogous phenomenon already with std::vector<> in Chapter 5. If you'll recall, the solution to this predicament is to use rounded brackets instead for these specific cases:

```
Array<double> values( numValues ); // Uses Array(size_t) constructor as before
```

---

[6] Detailing the precise built-in template argument deduction rules or explaining how to override or augment them with *user-defined deduction guides* would lead us too far for this basic introduction. The good news though is that the built-in rules mostly work just fine!

Class Template Specialization

You might encounter situations where a class template definition won't be satisfactory for every conceivable argument type. For example, you can compare string objects by using overloaded comparison operators, but you can't do this with null-terminated strings. If a class template compares objects using the comparison operators, it will work for type string but not for type char*. To compare objects of type char*, you need to use the comparison functions that are declared in the <cstring> header. One option to deal with situations like this is to define a *class template specialization*, which provides a class definition that is specific to a given set of arguments for the template parameters.

Defining a Class Template Specialization

Suppose it was necessary to create a specialization of the first version of the Array<> template for type const char*. Perhaps because you'd like to initialize the elements of the array with pointers to the empty string ("") rather than null pointers. You'd then write a specialization of the class template definition as follows:

```
template <>
class Array<const char*>
{
  // Definition of a class to suit type const char*...
};
```

This definition of the specialization of the Array template for type const char* must be preceded by the original template definition or by a declaration for the original template.

Because all the parameters are specified, this is called a *complete specialization* of the template. The set of angle brackets following the template keyword is then empty. A complete class template specialization is a class definition, not a class template. Instead of using the template to generate the class from the template for const char*, the compiler uses the specialization you define for that type instead. Thus, a class template specialization provides a way to predefine instances of a class template to be used by the compiler for specific sets of arguments for the template parameters.

There is no requirement for a class template specialization to have the same members as the original template. The specialization's class can alter, add, or omit members without restraint. For instance, in principle, you could define a specialization for arrays of doubles as follows:

```
template <>
class Array<double>
{
public:
  // Constructor, destructor, copy members, ...

  double& operator[](std::size_t index);        // Subscript operator
  double operator[](std::size_t index) const; // Subscript operator-const arrays

  double sum() const;
  double average() const { return sum() / m_num_values; }
  std::size_t count() const noexcept { return m_num_values; }
```

```
private:
  std::size_t m_num_values;
  double* m_values;
};
```

The `const` subscript operator of this class returns by value and not by reference-to-`const` as the generic `Array<>` template. The class also has extra `sum()` and `average()` members, and it uses different names for the `getSize()`, `m_size`, and `m_elements` members. It stands to reason that creating a specialization with an inconsistent interface like this is rarely a good idea, though.

■ **Note**   In Chapter 10, we cautioned you to never specialize function templates, and to use function overloading instead. Class template specialization, on the other hand, is perfectly safe.

Partial Template Specialization

If you were specializing the version of the template with two parameters of Ex17_02, you may only want to specify the type parameter for the specialization, leaving the non-type parameter open. You could do this with a *partial specialization* of the `Array<>` template that you could define like this:

```
template <int startIndex>                // Because there is a parameter...
class Array<const char*, startIndex>     // This is a partial specialization...
{
  // Definition to suit type const char*...
};
```

This specialization of the original template is still a template. The parameter list following the `template` keyword must contain the parameters that need to be specified for an instance of this template specialization—just one in this case. The first parameter is omitted because it is now fixed. The angle brackets following the template name specify how the parameters in the original template definition are specialized. The list here must have the same number of parameters as appear in the original, unspecialized template. The first parameter for this specialization is `const char*`. The other parameter is specified as the corresponding parameter name in this template.

Apart from the special considerations you might need to give to a template instance produced by using `const char*` for a type parameter, it may well be that pointers in general are a specialized subset that need to be treated differently from objects and references. For example, to compare objects when a template is instantiated using a pointer type, pointers must be dereferenced; Otherwise, you are just comparing addresses, not the objects or values stored at those addresses.

For this situation, you can define another partial specialization of the template. The parameter is not completely fixed in this case, but it must fit within a particular pattern that you specify in the list following the template name. For example, a partial specialization of the `Array` template for pointers would look like this:

```
template <typename T, int startIndex>
class Array<T*, startIndex>
{
  // Definition to suit pointer types other than const char*...
};
```

The first parameter is still T, but the T* between angle brackets following the template name indicates that this definition is to be used for instances where T is specified as a pointer type. The other two parameters are still completely variable, so this specialization will apply to any instance where the first template argument is a pointer.

Class Templates with Nested Classes

A class can contain another class nested inside its definition. A class template definition can also contain a nested class or even a *nested class template*. A nested class template is independently parameterized, so inside another class template it creates a two-dimensional ability to generate classes. Dealing with templates inside templates is outside the scope of this book, but we'll introduce aspects of a class template with a nested class.

Let's take a particular example. Suppose you want to implement a stack, which is a "last in, first out" storage mechanism. A stack is illustrated in Figure 17-3. It works in a similar way to a plate stack in a self-service restaurant. It has two basic operations. A *push operation* adds an item to the top of a stack, and a *pop operation* removes the item from the top of the stack. Ideally, a stack implementation should be able to store objects of any type, so this is a natural job for a template.

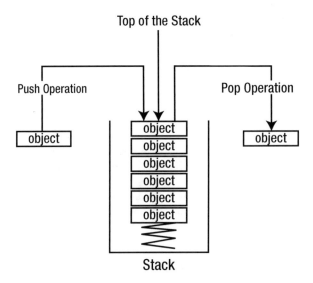

Figure 17-3. *The concept of a stack*

The parameter for a Stack template is a type parameter that specifies the type of objects in the stack, so the initial template definition will be as follows:

```
template <typename T>
class Stack
{
  // Detail of the Stack definition...
};
```

If you want the stack's capacity to grow automatically, you can't use fixed storage for objects within the stack. One way of providing the ability to automatically grow and shrink the stack as objects are pushed on it or popped off it is to implement the stack as a linked list. The nodes in the linked list can be created in the free store, and the stack only needs to remember the node at the top of the stack. This is illustrated in Figure 17-4.

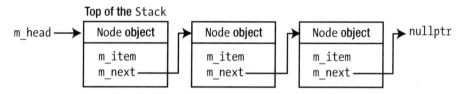

A Stack object only needs to store a pointer to the node at the top.

In an empty stack, the pointer to the top of the stack will be null, because no nodes exist.

```
m_head = nullptr;
```

Figure 17-4. *A stack as a linked list*

When you create an empty stack, the pointer to the head of the list is nullptr, so you can use the fact that it doesn't contain any Node objects as an indicator that the stack is empty. Of course, only the Stack object needs access to the Node objects that are in the stack. The Node objects are just internal objects used to encapsulate the objects that are stored in the stack, so there's no need for anyone outside the Stack class to know that type Node exists.

A nested class that defines nodes in the list is required in each instance of the Stack template, and because a node must hold an object of type T, the Stack template parameter type, you can define it as a nested class in terms of T. We can add this to the initial outline of the Stack template:

```
template <typename T>
class Stack
{
  // Rest of the Stack class definition...
private:
  // Nested class
  class Node
  {
  public:
    Node(const T& item) : m_item {item} {} // Create a node from an object

    T m_item;                              // The object stored in this node
    Node* m_next {};                       // Pointer to next node
  };
};
```

The Node class is declared as private, so we can afford to make all its members public so that they're directly accessible from member functions of the Stack template. A Node object stores an object of T by value. The constructor is used when an object is pushed onto the stack. The parameter to the constructor is a const reference to an object of type T, and a copy of this object is stored in the m_item member of the new Node object. The rest of the Stack class template to support the linked list of Node objects shown in Figure 17-4 is as follows:

```
template <typename T>
class Stack
{
public:
  Stack() = default;                // Default constructor
  ~Stack();                         // Destructor

  Stack(const Stack& stack);        // Copy constructor
  Stack& operator=(const Stack& rhs); // Copy assignment operator
  void swap(Stack& other) noexcept;   // noexcept swap() function

  void push(const T& item);         // Push an object onto the stack
  T pop();                          // Pop an object off the stack
  bool isEmpty() const noexcept;    // Empty test

private:
  // Nested Node class definition as before...

  Node* m_head {};      // Points to the top of the stack
};
```

As we explained earlier, a Stack<> object only needs to "remember" the top node so it has only one member variable, m_head, of type Node*. There's a default constructor, a destructor, a copy constructor, and a copy assignment operator function. The destructor and copy members are essential here because nodes are created dynamically using new, and their addresses are stored in raw pointers. The swap() function is used to implement the copy-and-swap idiom for the assignment operator, the push() and pop() members transfer objects to and from the stack, and the isEmpty() function returns true if the Stack<> object is empty. We'll discuss the definitions of all member function templates for the Stack<> type in the next subsection.

Function Templates for Stack Members

We'll start with the constructors. The default constructor is defaulted within the class template, so the compiler will generate one for you if and when needed. The copy constructor must replicate a Stack<T> object, which can be done by walking through the nodes and copying them one by one, as follows:

```
template <typename T>
Stack<T>::Stack(const Stack& stack)
{
  if (stack.m_head)
  {
    m_head = new Node {*stack.m_head}; // Copy the top node of the original
    Node* oldNode {stack.m_head};      // Points to the top node of the original
    Node* newNode {m_head};            // Points to the node in the new stack
```

```
    while (oldNode = oldNode->m_next)   // If m_next was nullptr, the last node was copied
    {
      newNode->m_next = new Node{*oldNode};  // Duplicate it
      newNode = newNode->m_next;             // Move to the node just created
    }
  }
}
```

This copies the stack represented by the stack input argument to the current Stack object, which is assumed to be empty (the m_head member variable starts out initialized to nullptr). It does this by replicating the m_head of the argument object, then walking through the sequence of Node objects, copying them one by one. The process ends when the Node object with a null m_next member has been copied.

The isEmpty() functions simply check whether the m_head member points to an actual Node or is nullptr:

```
template <typename T>
bool Stack<T>::isEmpty() const noexcept { return m_head == nullptr; }
```

The template for the swap() function is implemented as follows:

```
template <typename T>
void Stack<T>::swap(Stack& other) noexcept
{
  std::swap(m_head, other.m_head);
}
```

(For completeness, you could add the conventional template for nonmember swap(Stack<T>&, Stack<T>&) functions as well. We do not show it here, but it is part of Ex17_04.)

The template for the assignment operator then uses the corresponding swap() function to implement the copy-and-swap idiom we introduced earlier in this chapter:

```
template <typename T>
Stack<T>& Stack<T>::operator=(const Stack& stack)
{
  auto copy{rhs}; // Copy...        (could go wrong and throw an exception)
  swap(copy);     // ... and swap!  (noexcept)
  return *this;
}
```

The template for the push() operation is fairly easy as well:

```
template <typename T>
void Stack<T>::push(const T& item)
{
  Node* node{ new Node{item} }; // Create the new node
  node->m_next = m_head;        // Point to the old top node
  m_head = node;                // Make the new node the top
}
```

The Node object encapsulating item is created by passing the reference to the Node constructor. The m_next member of the new node needs to point to the node that was previously at the top. The new Node object then becomes the top of the stack, so its address is stored in m_head.

The pop() operation is slightly more involved, though. The first question you need to answer is, what should happen if pop() is invoked on an empty stack? Because the function returns a T object by value, you can't easily signal an error through the return value. One obvious solution is to throw an exception in this case, so let's do that. Once that corner case is taken care of, you know that the function has to perform at least the following three actions:

1. Return the T item stored in the current m_head.

2. Make m_head point to the next Node in the linked list.

3. Delete the old m_head Node that is no longer required now.

It takes some figuring out in which order these actions should be performed. If you're not careful, you may even run into crashes. Here is a working solution, though:

```
template <typename T>
T Stack<T>::pop()
{
  if (isEmpty())              // If it's empty pop() is not valid so throw exception
    throw std::logic_error {"Stack empty"};

  auto* next {m_head->m_next}; // Save pointer to the next node
  T item {m_head->m_item};     // Save the T value to return later
  delete m_head;               // Delete the current head
  m_head = next;               // Make head point to the next node
  return item;                 // Return the top object
}
```

The key is that you mustn't delete the old m_head without first extracting all information from it that you still need—in this case both its m_next pointer (which is to become the new m_head) and its T item (the value that you have to return from the pop() function). Once you realize this, the rest writes itself.

In the destructor, you face a similar problem. (Remember this for later!) Clearly, it needs to release all dynamically allocated Node objects belonging to the current Stack object. From the pop() template you know not to delete any Nodes without first copying what you still need from it:

```
template <typename T>
Stack<T>::~Stack()
{
  while (m_head)
  {                            // While current pointer is not null
    auto* next{ m_head->m_next }; // Get the pointer to the next node
    delete m_head;             // Delete the current head
    m_head = next;             // Make m_head point to the next node
  }
}
```

Without the temporary pointer next to hold the address stored in m_head->m_next, you couldn't move m_head along anymore to the next Node in the list. At the end of the while loop, all Node objects belonging to the current Stack object will have been deleted and m_head will be nullptr.

That's all the templates you need to define the stack. If you gather all the templates into a module interface file, Stack.cppm, you can try it with the following code:

```cpp
// Ex17_04.cpp - Using a stack defined by a class template with a nested class
import stack;
import std;

int main()
{
  std::string words[] {"The", "quick", "brown", "fox", "jumps"};
  Stack<std::string> wordStack;              // A stack of strings

  for (const auto& word : words)
    wordStack.push(word);

  Stack<std::string> newStack{wordStack};  // Create a copy of the stack

  // Display the words in reverse order
  while (!newStack.isEmpty())
    std::print("{} ", newStack.pop());
  std::println("");

  // Reverse wordStack onto newStack
  while (!wordStack.isEmpty())
    newStack.push(wordStack.pop());

  // Display the words in original order
  while (!newStack.isEmpty())
    std::print("{} ", newStack.pop());
  std::println("");

  std::println("\nEnter a line of text:");
  std::string text;
  std::getline(std::cin, text);              // Read a line into the string object

  Stack<char> characters;                    // A stack for characters

  for (std::size_t i {}; i < text.length(); ++i)
    characters.push(text[i]);                // Push the string characters onto the stack

  while (!characters.isEmpty())
    std::print("{}", characters.pop());      // Pop the characters off the stack

  std::println("");
}
```

Here's an example of the output:

```
jumps fox brown quick The
The quick brown fox jumps

Enter a line of text:
A whole stack of memories never equal one little hope.
.epoh elttil eno lauqe reven seiromem fo kcats elohw A
```

You first define an array of five objects that are strings, initialized with the words shown. Then you define an empty Stack object that can store string objects. The for loop then pushes the array elements onto the stack. The first word from the array will be at the bottom of the wordStack stack and the last word at the top. You create a copy of wordStack as newStack to exercise the copy constructor.

In the next while loop, you display the words in newStack in reverse order by popping them off the stack and outputting them in a while loop. The loop continues until isEmpty() returns false. Using the isEmpty() function member is a safe way of getting the complete contents of a stack. newStack is empty by the end of the loop, but you still have the original in wordStack.

The next while loop retrieves the words from wordStack and pushes them onto newStack. The pop and push operations are combined in a single statement, where the object returned by pop() for wordStack is the argument for push() for newStack. At the end of this loop, wordStack is empty, and newStack contains the words in their original sequence—with the first word at the top of the stack. You then output the words by popping them off newStack, so at the end of this loop, both stacks are empty.

The next part of main() reads a line of text into a string object using the getline() function and then creates a stack to store characters:

```
Stack<char> characters;    // A stack for characters
```

This creates a new instance of the Stack template, Stack<char>, and a new instance of the constructor for this type of stack. You then peel off the characters from text and push them onto this new stack in a for loop. The length() function of the text object is used to determine when the loop ends. Finally, the input string is output in reverse by popping the characters off the stack. You can see from the output that our input was not even slightly palindromic, but you could try, "Ned, I am a maiden" or even "Are we not drawn onward, we few, drawn onward to new era."

A BETTER STACK?

In this chapter we have already illustrated a few times that you should not necessarily be satisfied with your code just because it is correct. We have advised you to shun code duplication, to be on the lookout for code that throws exceptions, and to always strive for robust and readable code. With this in mind, let's review the Stack<> class template we wrote in this section and see whether we can improve it.

A first obvious improvement, of course, would be to use std::unique_ptr<Node> instead of a raw Node* pointer for the m_head and m_next member variables, as advocated in Chapter 16. That way you could not possibly forget to apply delete anymore. We'll leave that improvement as an exercise for you to try on your own, although we do recommend that you wait with this until after Chapter 18.

Let's instead keep our pointers raw for now and review the template for the destructors. Is there anything else that strikes you as suboptimal there?

We already noted the similarities between the destructor and pop() earlier. That is, both had to set aside a temporary next pointer, delete m_head, and then move m_head along to the next node.

This is code duplication as well, albeit somewhat less obvious. You can eliminate it using the following, alternative implementation of the destructor template that leverages the existing isEmpty() and pop() functions instead of directly manipulating the pointers itself:

```
template <typename T>
Stack<T>::~Stack()
{
  while (!isEmpty()) pop();
}
```

Because this is trivially readable and therefore far less prone to errors, you should definitely use this new version. In case you are worried about performance, today's optimizing compilers will likely generate the same code for both versions—after inlining the isEmpty() and pop() function calls, it becomes trivial for a compiler to rework the code to exactly what we wrote in the original version. You can find this implementation in Ex17_04A.

We understand that initially it will not always be easy to improve your code like this. And, at first, doing so may seem to take up a lot of your time. Unfortunately, we also cannot give you a fixed set of rules that dictate when code is good, bad, or good enough. But with sufficient practice you will see that this will come more and more naturally. In the long run, applying the principles you learn about here will improve your productivity as a programmer substantially. You will find yourself consistently producing elegant, readable code, which will contain less bugs and be easier to maintain and adapt.

We would now like to conclude these digressions on producing high-quality code with one of our favorite quotes, from one of the pioneers of computer science, Donald E. Knuth:

Computer programming is an art,
because it applies accumulated knowledge to the world,
because it requires skill and ingenuity,
and especially because it produces objects of beauty.
A programmer who subconsciously views himself as an artist
will enjoy what he does and will do it better.

Dependent Names Nuisances

When a compiler encounters a template, it is supposed to perform certain checks immediately. A template may therefore give rise to compilation errors before it is instantiated, or even when it is never instantiated at all. Because the compiler obviously cannot check everything without knowing the v10alues of the template arguments, other checks are only performed after the template is instantiated. This is called *two-phase compilation* or *two-phase (name) lookup*.

To see this for yourself you can add a function template of the following form to any source file and then try to compile it:

```
template <typename T>
void someFunction() { T::GOs6xM2D(); kfTz3e7l(); }
```

Your compiler is supposed to parse this template definition and check it for programming errors. We chose gibberish names GOs6xM2D and kfTz3e7l because that is what all names look like to a compiler until it can match them to a declaration of entities such as functions, variables, or types.

GOs6xM2D is said to be a *dependent name* because in order to resolve it the compiler needs to know the value of the template type parameter T. The name GOs6xM2D, in other words, is *dependent on* T. Is it the name of a static function? A function pointer? Function object? Or maybe it is the name of a nested type? Or perhaps GOs6xM2D is simply a typo and should've been GOs6xN2B instead? The compiler cannot possibly know just by looking at the template definition. In fact, while unlikely, GOs6xM2D may even refer to different kinds of entities altogether for different values of T. The compiler therefore assumes this particular statement is valid and defers any further checks until the template is instantiated.

kfTz3e7l, on the other hand, is clearly not a dependent name. The compiler is supposed to resolve the name kfTz3e7l prior to instantiation and verify whether kfTz3e7l() is a valid statement. So unless a function-like entity named kfTz3e7l happens to exist in your code, your compiler is supposed to flat out reject this function template, even if it is never instantiated.

■ **Note**   Not all compilers (fully) implement two-phase lookup and defer more (if not most) checks until templates are instantiated. It is therefore possible that your compiler does not take notice of the undeclared kfTz3e7l name in our earlier example until you effectively use the template. If so, you may also not need some or any of the workarounds we discuss in the next two subsections either.

Of course, whether your compiler rejects *invalid* templates early or only at instantiation time rarely matters. The issue that we want to address here, however, is that compilers sometimes reject seemingly *valid* templates as well, prior to instantiation—templates that would produce perfectly valid code when textually substituting all type parameter names with actual types. This is one of the most vexing quirks of C++: Your template looks perfectly correct to you, and yet the compiler spits out a flood of baffling error messages.

The reason this sometimes happens always boils down to the same thing: the compiler tries to make sense of an uninstantiated template and somehow misinterprets dependent names. To correct this, you then need to know some simple—yet far from obvious—syntactic workarounds. We now outline two fairly common situations where your compiler may get confused like that, and then show you what workarounds you can use to make it parse your templates correctly.

Dependent Type Names

Suppose you have a class template of the following form (similar to the Stack<> template from before).

```
template <typename T>
class Outer
{
public:
  class Nested { /* ... */ };  // Or a type alias of form 'using Nested = ...;'
  // ...
};
```

■ **Note**   Nested types and type alias members are actually quite common in the Standard Library. Examples include vector<>::iterator, optional<>::value_type, and shared_ptr<>::weak_type.

Now try to define the following function template (see Ex17_05A.cpp):

```
template <typename T>
void someFunction() { Outer<T>::Nested* nested; /* ... */ }
```

With one of our compilers, this gives the following error (without any further information):

```
error: 'nested' was not declared in this scope
   17 |  void someFunction() { Outer<T>::Nested* nested; /* ... */ }
      |                                          ^~~~~~~
```

Silly compiler… Of course, nested is not declared yet in that scope; the statement that you are rejecting *is the declaration* of nested! So, what is going on? Why did our compiler get confused here?

The problem is that inside the body of a template, a compiler generally does not interpret dependent names such as T::name or MyClass<T>::name as type names. In our example, the compiler reads the body's opening statement as a multiplication of two variables, Outer<T>::Nested and nested. In the compiler's mind, nested must be a non-dependent name, just like kfTz3e7l was in our earlier example. And, the compiler subsequently finds no declaration for nested in the surrounding scope—hence the baffling error message.

To make the compiler interpret dependent names such as Nested as type names, you must explicitly mark them as such using the typename keyword. The template from Ex17_05A, for instance, can be fixed as follows:

```
template <typename T>
void someFunction() { typename Outer<T>::Nested* nested; /* ... */ }
```

Now the compiler correctly parses its opening statement as intended: as the declaration of a variable nested of type pointer-to-Outer<T>::Nested.

Does this mean that you always have to add typename in front of a dependent type name? Not quite. Sometimes your compiler does recognize a dependent name as that of a type by default. (In fact, a C++23-compliant compiler will do so more than ever before!) When a dependent name is used as the return type of a function, inside a cast expression, or after the keyword new, for instance, any compiler should understand that that name can only refer to a type. Here is an example (see also Ex17_05B).

```
template <typename T>    // T assumed to define nested Base and Derived types / aliases
T::Base someOtherFunction()
{
   typename T::Base* b{ new T::Derived{} };               // Or: auto* b{ ... }
   const typename T::Derived& d{ static_cast<T::Derived&>(*b) };// Or: const auto& d{ ... }
   /* ... */
   return b;
}
```

You do still need the typename to disambiguate the names on the left here. As indicated, placeholder types such as auto, auto*, or auto& can often be a more compact alternative, though.

Knowing exactly when typename is either optional or required in front of a dependent type name is not that important. We don't know the complete set of rules either to be honest. The main takeaway from this section should instead be that you learn to recognize errors caused by misinterpreted dependent type names, and that you know how to work around them by adding typename. In practice, that means you basically have two options: you can either play it safe and add typename in front of all (or most) dependent type names, or you can add as few as possible and rely on the compiler to tell you when you missed one. Now that you understand the problem, both these pragmatic approaches will work just fine.

Dependent Base Classes

Dependent name nuisances also arise when you combine templates with inheritance. More specifically, they arise when you use a dependent type as a base class. In its most common form, this occurs when you define class templates that look like this (available in Ex17_06.cpp):

```
template <typename T>
class Base
{
public:
  void baseFun() { /* ... */ }
protected:
  int m_base_var{};
};

template <typename T>
class Derived : public Base<T>
{
public:
  void derivedFun();
};
```

There is nothing special about this setup at all. Derived<T> classes inherit from Base<T> classes, and they all have some basic, very realistic members.

Now suppose you define the template for the member functions of the derived classes as follows:

```
template <typename T>
void Derived<T>::derivedFun()
{
  baseFun();
  std::println("{}", m_base_var);
}
```

While some compilers might accept this definition, they are actually not supposed to. One of the compilers we tested had this to say:

```
<source>:22:3: error: use of undeclared identifier 'baseFun'
  baseFun();
  ^
<source>:23:22: error: use of undeclared identifier 'm_base_var'
  std::println("{}", m_base_var);
```

Silly compiler... Clearly these identifiers are declared in the Base<> class template, right? So what is going on this time?

The base class of Derived<T>, Base<T>, is obviously dependent on T. Prior to instantiation, the compiler cannot reliably check names baseFun() and m_base_var. After all, at any given location where Derived<> is instantiated for, say, type MyType, a class template specialization Base<MyType> may be defined that does not have baseFun() and m_base_var members. Or for which baseFun is the name of a variable, and m_base_var that of a type. Conceptually, baseFun and m_base_var *should* therefore be treated as dependent names, right? Still, the errors make it clear that the compiler treats them as non-dependent names instead. The question thus becomes: Why are baseFun() and m_base_var treated as non-dependent names?

The problem is that, if we extend the reasoning from the previous paragraph, the compiler might as well not check for any non-dependent names inside member function templates such as that of Derived<T>::derivedFun(). After all, an unknown class template specialization of Base<> can introduce any member it wants. It could, for instance, define a class named std with a static println() function, stultifying any attempts at verifying the std::println() statement.

Because not checking anything would be impractical (you'd have to wait until the template is instantiated to discover even the most basic mistakes), the C++ standard prescribes to check names in all member templates of Derived<T> without considering the possibility that these names could be defined by Base<T>—be it by the primary Base<> template or a specialization. The downside is that we run into startling errors whenever we do access public or protected members of a dependent base class.

There are at least three ways you can work around these errors. In the following we illustrate two:

```
template <typename T>
void Derived<T>::derivedFun()
{
  this->baseFun();                       // Or Base<T>::baseFun();
  std::println("{}", this->m_base_var);  // Or Base<T>::m_base_var
}
```

By adding this-> in front of baseFun() and m_base_var, you signal the compiler that both baseFun and m_base_var are to be interpreted as names of members. And because the compiler finds no such members in the definition of Derived<T> itself, the standard dictates that to assume baseFun and m_base_var refer to members of Base<T>. This effectively turns baseFun and m_base_var into dependent names, telling the compiler to defer all further checks until later.

A second, more obvious, way to turn baseFun and m_base_var into dependent names is to add Base<T>:: in front of them. Both options work, and both are used in practice.

If having to add this-> or Base<T>:: in front of all member accesses annoys you, a third option is to signal to the compiler which members will always come from Base<T> by adding using declarations to the class template definition itself. For our example, this looks as follows:

```
template <typename T>
class Derived : public Base<T>
{
public:
  using Base<T>::baseFun;  // Take care: <T> is not optional for Base<T>
  void derivedFun();       // (Only Derived is taken to mean Derived<T>)
protected:
  using Base<T>::m_base_var;
};
```

As tedious as this may still be, the advantage of this approach is that you only have to add these using declarations once, at the level of the class template. After that, you can use these base class members without special attention in all member function templates. (In our example there is only one member function, yet in general there could be many.)

Summary

If you understand how class templates are defined and used, you'll find it easy to understand and apply the capabilities of the Standard Library. The ability to define class templates is also a powerful augmentation of the basic language facilities for defining classes. The essential points we've discussed in this chapter include the following:

- A class template defines a family of class types.

- An instance of a class template is a class definition that is generated by the compiler from the template using a set of template arguments that you specify in your code.

- An implicit instantiation of a class template arises out of a definition for an object of a class template type.

- An explicit instantiation of a class template defines a class for a given set of arguments for the template parameters.

- An argument corresponding to a type parameter in a class template can be a fundamental type, a class type, a pointer type, or a reference type.

- The type of a non-type parameter can be any fundamental type, enumeration type, pointer type, or reference type.

- If modifying an object takes multiple steps, and one of those steps can throw an exception, you risk leaving the object in an unusable, half-modified state. The copy-and-swap idiom allows you to sidestep this problem. You simply copy the object, modify the copy, and then only if that succeeds, you swap() the actual object with that copy. Swapping can mostly be done very efficiently, and without risk of exceptions.

- Always use the copy-and-swap idiom to implement the copy assignment operator in terms of the copy constructor and a (noexcept) swap() function.

- Use the const-and-back-again idiom to implement non-const overloads in terms of const overloads of the same member function to avoid having to repeat yourself. This is an example of the DRY principle, which advocates avoiding code duplication at all costs.

- A complete specialization of a class template defines a new type for a specific, complete set of parameter arguments for the original template.

- A partial specialization of a class template defines a new template that is to be used for a specific, restricted subset of the arguments for the original template.

- When defining templates, you often have to add the typename keyword in front of a dependent type name to make the compiler parse it as such.

- To refer to the members of a dependent base class from within the definitions of the members of a derived class, you must force the compiler to treat these names as dependent ones.

EXERCISES

The following exercises enable you to try what you've learned in this chapter. If you get stuck, look back over the chapter for help. If you're still stuck after that, you can download the solutions from the Apress website (https://www.apress.com/gp/services/source-code), but that really should be a last resort.

Exercise 17-1. The Array<> template of Ex17_01 is in many ways similar to std::vector<>. One obvious shortcoming is that the size of an Array<T> needs to be fixed at construction time. Let's remedy that and add a push_back() member function that inserts a single element of type T after all existing elements. To keep things simple, your version of push_back() could allocate a new, larger array to hold size + 1 elements each time it is invoked. Also, make sure an (empty) Array<> can be default-constructed. Write a small program to exercise the new functionality.

Extra: It shouldn't be hard to make push_back() strongly exception-safe. That is, if any operation during push_back() should go wrong and throw an exception, make sure that no memory is leaked and the original Array<> is left as is, discarding the new element.

Exercise 17-2. Define a template for classes that represent pairs of values of possibly different types. The values can be accessed using getFirst() and getSecond() member functions, and updated only through setFirst() and setSecond(). Make sure a pair of an int and a std::string can be created and used as follows:

```
Pair<int, std::string> pair{ 122, "abc" };
pair.setFirst(pair.getFirst() + 1);
std::println("pair equals ({}, {})", pair.getFirst(), pair.getSecond());
```

Make sure pairs can be default-constructed as well. Will CTAD work for the Pair<> template?

Next, make sure pairs can be compared using operators ==, <, >=, and so on, based on a *lexicographical* comparison. That is, pairs should be ordered using the same logic as used when sorting two-letter words, except that now the words do not consist of two letters but two different values. Suppose you have the following three pairs:

```
const Pair<int, std::string> pair1{ 0, "def" };
const Pair<int, std::string> pair2{ 123, "abc" };
const Pair<int, std::string> pair3{ 123, "def" };
```

Then the expressions pair1 < pair2 and pair2 < pair3 should both evaluate to true. The first because 0 < 123; the second because "abc" < "def". The second values of the Pairs are looked at only if the first ones compare equal using ==.

Hint: Do you really need much code for this?

Finally, since we seem to be testing your operator prowess, make sure Pairs can be streamed to output streams such as std::cout.

Create a small program to proof that your templates work as required.

Note: Pair<> is similar to the standard std::pair<> template, except that std::pair<> does not use getters and setters, and instead simply has public member variables first and second (and in that respect is more like a typical structure; see Chapter 12).

Exercise 17-3. Define a template for one-dimensional sparse arrays that will store objects of any type so that only the elements stored in the array occupy memory. The potential number of elements that can be stored by an instance of the template should be virtually unlimited. The template might be used to define a sparse array containing elements of type double with the following statement:

`SparseArray<double> values;`

Define the subscript operator for the template so that element values can be retrieved and set just like in a normal array. If an element doesn't exist at an index position, the subscript operator should add a default-constructed object to the sparse array at the given index and return a reference to this newly added object. Because this subscript operator modifies the object, there cannot really be a const overload of this operator. Similar to various Standard Library containers, you should define an at(size_t) member function as well, overloaded on const, that instead of adding a default-constructed value throws an appropriate exception if no value exists for the given index. Because it would still be nice to know in advance whether an element exists at a given index, also add an elementExistsAt() member to check for this.

There are many ways to represent a sparse array and some more efficient than others. But since this is not the essence of the exercise, we propose you keep things simple. Don't worry about performance yet; you'll learn about more efficient data structures and algorithms offered by the Standard Library in later chapters—including even container types that are nearly equivalent to your SparseArray<>, namely, std::map<> and std::unordered_map<>. For now, we propose you simply represent the sparse array as an unsorted vector<> of index–value pairs. For the individual pairs, you can use std::pair<> (the Pair<> class template defined in the previous exercise is less suited for what you'll need here because of the way it hides its first and second components).

Take the SparseArray template for a spin with a main() function that stores 20 random element values of type int at random index positions within the range 32 to 212 in a sparse array with an index range from 0 to 499. Output the values of all inserted elements along with their index positions.

Exercise 17-4. Define a template for a linked list type that allows the list to be traversed in both directions, meaning backward from the end of the list as well as forward from the beginning. Naturally, you should use the iterator design pattern you learned about in Chapter 12 for this (see also Exercises 12-7 and 12-8). To keep things simple, elements stored in the list cannot be modified while traversing the list. Elements can be added using push_front() and push_back() to use member names analogous to those of Standard Library containers. Also add clear(), empty(), and size() functions that do the same as those of standard containers (see Chapters 5 and 20). Apply the template to a program that stores individual words from some arbitrary prose or poetry as std::string objects in a linked list and then displays them five to a line, in sequence and in reverse order.

Exercise 17-5. Use the linked list and sparse array templates to produce a program that stores words from a prose or poetry sample in a sparse array of up to 26 linked lists, where each list contains words that have the same initial letter. Output the words, starting each group with a given initial letter on a new line.

CHAPTER 18

▓ ▓ ▓

Move Semantics

This chapter complements and completes several key topics discussed in the middle parts of the book. In Chapters 12 and 13, for instance, you gained insight into the mechanics behind the copying of objects, that is, copy constructors and assignment operators. And from Chapter 8 you know to prefer pass-by-reference over pass-by-value to avoid undue copying of parameters. And for a long time, that was basically all you needed to know. C++ offered facilities to copy objects, and if you wanted to avoid costly copies, then you simply used either references or pointers. Starting with C++11, however, there has been a powerful new alternative. You can no longer only copy objects; you can now also *move* them.

In this chapter, we'll show you how *move semantics* allows you to efficiently transfer resources from one object into another, without *deep copying*. We also wrap up our treatment of the *special class members*— of which you already know the default constructor, destructor, copy constructor, and copy assignment constructor.

In this chapter, you'll learn

- What the difference is between lvalues and rvalues

- That there's another kind of reference: rvalue references

- What it means to move an object

- How to provide so-called move semantics for objects of your own types

- When objects are moved implicitly and how to explicitly move them

- How move semantics leads to code that is both elegant and efficient

- What impact move semantics has on various best practices regarding defining your own functions and types

- The "rule of five" and "rule of zero" guidelines

Lvalues and Rvalues

Every single expression is either an *lvalue* or an *rvalue* (sometimes written *l-value* and *r-value* and pronounced like that). An lvalue evaluates to some persistent value with an address in memory in which you can store something on an ongoing basis; an rvalue evaluates to a result that is stored only transiently.

Historically, lvalues and rvalues are so called because an *l*value expression typically appears on the *left* of an assignment operator, whereas an *r*value could appear only on the *right* side. If an expression is not an lvalue, it is an rvalue.[1] An expression that consists of a single variable name is always an lvalue.

▓ **Note** Despite their names, lvalues and rvalues are classifications of *expressions*, not of values.

Consider the following statements:

```
int a {}, b {1}, c {-2};
a = b + c;
double r = std::abs(a * c);
auto p = std::pow(r, std::abs(c));
```

The first statement defines variables a, b, and c as type int and initializes them to 0, 1, and -2, respectively. From then on, the names a, b, and c are all lvalues.

In the second statement, at least in principle, the result of evaluating the expression b + c is briefly stored somewhere, only to copy it into the variable a right after. When execution of the statement is complete, the memory holding the result of b + c is discarded. The expression b + c is therefore an rvalue.

The presence of transient values becomes far more apparent once function calls are involved. In the third statement, for instance, a * c is evaluated first and kept somewhere in memory as a temporary value. This temporary then is passed as an argument to the std::abs() function. This makes that a * c is an rvalue. The int that is returned by std::abs() itself is transient as well. It exists only for an instant, just long enough to be implicitly converted into a double. Similar reasoning applies to the return values of both function calls in the fourth statement—the value returned by std::abs(), for instance, clearly exists only momentarily to serve as an argument to std::pow().

▓ **Note** Most function call expressions are rvalues. Only function calls that return a reference are lvalues. One indication for the latter is that function calls that return a reference can appear on the left side of a built-in assignment operator just fine. Prime examples are the subscript operators (operator[]()) and at() functions of your typical container. If v is a vector<int>, for example, both v[1] = -5; and v.at(2) = 132; would make for perfectly valid statements. v[1] and v.at(2) are therefore clearly lvalues.

When in doubt, another good guideline to decide whether a given expression is an lvalue or an rvalue is the following. If the value that it evaluates to persists long enough for you to take and later use its address, then that value is an lvalue. Here's an example (a, b, and c are ints as before, and v a vector<int>):

```
int* x = &(b + c);          // Error!
int* y = &std::abs(a * c);  // Error!
int* z = &123;              // Error!
int* w = &a;                // Ok!
int* u = &v.at(2);          // Ok! (u contains the address of the third value in v)
```

---

[1] The C++ standard defines three additional expression categories with the names glvalue, prvalue, and xvalue. But trust us, you really do not need to know all these gory details. Our brief, more informal, discussion here will serve you just fine!

The memory that stores the result of the expressions b + c and std::abs() is reclaimed immediately after the surrounding statements have finished executing. If they were allowed to exist, the pointers x and y would therefore already be dangling before anyone even had the opportunity to look at them. This indicates that these expressions are rvalues. The example also illustrates that all numeric literals are rvalues. The compiler will never allow you to take the address of a numeric literal.

Granted, for expressions of fundamental types, the distinction between lvalue and rvalue rarely matters. This distinction only becomes relevant for expressions of class types and even then only when, for instance, passed to functions that have overloads specifically defined to accept the result of an rvalue expression or when storing objects in containers. The only way for you to truly appreciate these little theory lessons is therefore to bear with us until the next section. There's just one more concept left to introduce first.

Rvalue References

A reference is a name that you can use as an alias for something else. That much you already know from Chapter 6. What you don't know yet—how could you?—is that there are two kinds of references: *lvalue references* and *rvalue references*.

All references that you've worked with thus far are *lvalue references*. Normally, an lvalue reference is an alias for another variable; it is called an lvalue reference because it normally refers to a persistent storage location in which you can store data so it can appear on the left of an assignment operator. We say "normally" because C++ does allow reference-to-const lvalue references—so variables of type const T&—to be bound to temporary rvalues as well. We established as much in Chapter 8 already.

An *rvalue reference* can be an alias for a variable, just like an lvalue reference, but it differs from an lvalue reference in that it can also reference the outcome of an rvalue expression, even though this value is generally transient. Being bound to an rvalue reference extends the lifetime of such a transient value. Its memory will not be discarded as long as the rvalue reference is in scope. You specify an rvalue reference type using *two* ampersands following the type name. Here's an example:

```
int count {5};
int&& rtemp {count + 3};    // rvalue reference
std::println("{}", rtemp);  // Output value of expression
int& rcount {count};        // lvalue reference
```

This code will compile and execute, but it is definitely *not* the way to use an rvalue reference, and you should never code like this. This is just to illustrate what an rvalue reference is. The rvalue reference is initialized to be an alias for the result of the rvalue expression count + 3. The output from the next statement will be 8. You cannot do this with an lvalue reference—at least not unless you add a const qualifier. Is this useful? In this case, no, indeed it is not recommended at all; but in a different context, it is very useful. It's high time you found out when and why, don't you agree?

Moving Objects

In this chapter's running example , you'll be working with an Array<> class template similar to that of Ex17_01A. Not unlike std::vector<>, it is a template for classes that encapsulate and manage dynamically allocated memory. The definition of this Array<> class template looks like this:

```
template <typename T>
class Array
{
public:
```

```
explicit Array(std::size_t size);                    // Constructor
~Array();                                            // Destructor
Array(const Array& array);                           // Copy constructor
Array& operator=(const Array& rhs);                  // Copy assignment operator
void swap(Array& other) noexcept;                    // noexcept swap function
T& operator[](std::size_t index);                    // Subscript operator
const T& operator[](std::size_t index) const;        // Subscript operator-const arrays
std::size_t getSize() const noexcept { return m_size; } // Accessor for m_size

private:
  T* m_elements;        // Array of elements of type T
  std::size_t m_size;   // Number of array elements
};
```

The implementation of all members can remain the same as in Ex17_01A. For now, the only thing we add is an extra debug output statement in the copy constructor to track when an Array<> is being copied:

```
// Copy constructor
template <typename T>
Array<T>::Array(const Array& array)
  : Array{array.m_size}
{
  std::println("Array of {} elements copied", m_size);
  for (std::size_t i {}; i < m_size; ++i)
    m_elements[i] = array.m_elements[i];
}
```

Because the Array<> template of Ex17_01A employs the copy-and-swap idiom, this output statement also covers the cases where a given Array<> is copied through its copy assignment operator. To refresh your memory, the following is a possible definition of this copy-and-swap assignment operator template. It rewrites copy assignment in terms of the copy construction and a noexcept swap() function:

```
// Copy assignment operator
template <typename T>
Array<T>& Array<T>::operator=(const Array& rhs)
{
  Array<T> copy{ rhs }; // Copy ...       (could go wrong and throw an exception)
  swap(copy);           // ... and swap! (noexcept)
  return *this;         // Return lhs
}
```

Using this Array<> class template, we now compose a first example to underline the cost of copying:

```
// Ex18_01.cpp - Copying objects into a vector
import array;
import std;

// Construct an Array<> of a given size, filled with some arbitrary string data
Array<std::string> buildStringArray(const std::size_t size)
{
  Array<std::string> result{ size };
```

```
  for (std::size_t i {}; i < size; ++i)
    result[i] = "You should learn from your competitor, but never copy. Copy and you die.";
  return result;
}

int main()
{
  const std::size_t numArrays{ 10 };   // Fill 10 Arrays with 1,000 strings each
  const std::size_t numStringsPerArray{ 1'000 };

  std::vector<Array<std::string>> vectorOfArrays;
  vectorOfArrays.reserve(numArrays);   // Inform the vector<> how many Arrays we'll be adding

  for (std::size_t i {}; i < numArrays; ++i)
  {
    vectorOfArrays.push_back(buildStringArray(numStringsPerArray));
  }
}
```

▦ **Note**   This example uses a member function of std::vector<> that you haven't encountered yet: reserve(std::size_t). Essentially, it tells the vector<> object to allocate sufficient dynamic memory to accommodate for the given number of elements. These elements can then be added using push_back(), for instance, without any additional re-allocations of the underlying dynamic array.

▦ **Caution**   v.reserve(n) tells a vector v to reserve enough room for a total of n elements, and not for n *extra* elements (an easy mistake to make). So when you're about to add n extra elements to a non-empty vector, the correct use is therefore v.reserve(v.size() + n).

The program in Ex18_01.cpp constructs a vector<> of ten Arrays, each containing 1,000 strings. The output of a single run normally looks as follows:

```
Array of 1000 elements copied
Array of 1000 elements copied
Array of 1000 elements copied
... (10 times in total)
```

▦ **Note**   It is even possible that your output shows that the Array<> is copied *20* times. The reason is that during each execution of buildStringArray() your compiler might first create the variable result that is defined locally in that function's body and then copy that Array<> for the first time into the object that is returned by the function. After that, this temporary return value is then copied a second time into an Array<> that is allocated by the vector<>. Most optimizing compilers, however, implement the so-called (named) return value optimization that eliminates the former copy. We'll further discuss this optimization later in this chapter.

■ **Tip** If Ex18_01 does perform 20 copies for you, the most likely cause is that your compiler is set to use a nonoptimizing *debug* configuration. If so, switching to a fully optimizing *release* configuration should resolve the issue. Consult your compiler documentation for more information.

The for loop of the main() function calls buildStringArray() ten times. Each call returns an Array<string> object filled with 1,000 string objects. Clearly, buildStringArray() is an rvalue, as the object it returns is transient. In other words, your compiler arranges for this object to be stored temporarily (almost certainly somewhere on the stack) before it passes it on to the push_back() function of vectorOfArrays. Internally, the push_back() member of this vector<> then uses the Array<string> copy constructor to copy this rvalue into an Array<string> object inside the dynamic memory managed by the vector<>. In doing so, all 1,000 std::strings stored by the Array<string> get copied as well. That is, for each of the ten times that such a transient Array<> is copied into vectorOfArrays, the following happens:

1. The Array<> copy constructor allocates a new block of dynamic memory to hold 1,000 std::string objects.

2. For each of the 1,000 string objects this copy constructor has to copy, it calls the copy assignment operator of std::string. Each of these 1,000 assignments in turn allocates one additional block of dynamic memory in which the 73 characters (chars) from the source string are then copied.

In other words, your computer must perform ten times 1,001 dynamic memory allocations and a fair amount of character copying. In itself this is not a disaster, but it surely feels like all this copying ought to be avoidable. After all, once push_back() returns, the temporary Array<> that buildStringArray() had returned gets deleted and together with it all the strings it used to contain. This means that in total we have copied no less than ten Arrays, 10,000 string objects, and 730,000 characters, only to throw away the originals an instant later!

Imagine being forced to manually copy a 10,000-sentence book—say one of the thicker *Harry Potter* novels—only to watch someone burn the original immediately afterward. What a total waste of effort! If no one needs the original anymore, why not simply reuse the original instead of creating a copy? To wrap up the *Harry Potter* analogy, why not give the book a shiny new cover and then pretend that you copied all the pages?

What you need, in other words, is a way to somehow "move" the original strings from inside the transient Array<> into the newly created Array<> object that is held by the vector<>. What you need is a specific "move" operation that does not involve any excessive copying. And if the original Array<> object is to be torn down in the process, so be it. We know it to be a transient object anyway, destined for a *Harry Potter* bonfire.

Defining Move Members

Thankfully, modern C++ offers precisely what you want. C++11's move semantics allow you to program in a natural, intuitive style, while at the same time avoiding any unnecessary, costly copy operations. You even do not have to alter the code of Ex18_01.cpp at all. Instead, you extend the Array<> template to ensure that the compiler knows how to instantly *move* a transient Array<> object into another Array<>, without effectively copying any of its elements.

For this we'll take you back to an earlier example, Ex18_01.cpp. There you studied the following statement:

```
vectorOfArrays.push_back(buildStringArray(numStringsPerArray));
```

Given a statement such as this, any C++11 compiler is well aware that copying the result of buildStringArray() is just silly. After all, the compiler knows full well that the object being passed to push_back() here is a temporary one, scheduled to be deleted right after. So, the compiler *knows* that you'd prefer not to copy the pushed Array<>. Clearly that's not the problem. Rather, the problem is that the compiler has no other option *but* to copy this object. After all, all it has to work with is a copy constructor. The compiler cannot just magically "move" a temporary Array<> object into a new Array<> object—it needs to be told how.

Since the code to construct a *copy* of an object is defined by the *copy constructor* of its class (see Chapter 12), it's only natural that the code to construct a new object from a *moved* object is defined by a constructor as well—a *move constructor*. We discuss how you can define such a constructor next.

■ **Note**   Under the right circumstances, the move members that we're about to introduce will be generated by the compiler, though clearly not for our Array<> template. For the Array<> template you need to define them yourself explicitly. We'll explain why that is later in this chapter.

Move Constructors

Here is, one last time, the template for the Array<> copy constructor:

```
// Copy constructor
template <typename T>
Array<T>::Array(const Array& array)
  : Array{array.m_size}
{
  std::println("Array of {} elements copied", m_size);
  for (std::size_t i {}; i < m_size; ++i)
    m_elements[i] = array.m_elements[i];
}
```

It's an instance of this constructor template that the push_back() function uses in Ex18_01, which is why each evaluation of this statement involves 1,001 dynamic memory allocations and a whole lot of string copying:

```
vectorOfArrays.push_back(buildStringArray(numStringsPerArray));
```

The goal is to write precisely this same line of code but have push_back() use some different constructor instead—one that does not copy the Array<> and its std::string elements. Instead, this new constructor should somehow *move* all these strings into the new object, without actually copying them. Such a constructor is aptly called a *move constructor*, and for the Array<> template, you can declare one as follows:

```
template <typename T>
class Array
{
public:
  explicit Array(std::size_t arraySize);  // Constructor
  Array(const Array& array);         // Copy constructor
  Array(Array&& array);              // Move constructor

  // ... other members like before
};
```

The type of the move constructor's parameter, Array&&, is an rvalue reference. This makes sense; after all, you want this parameter to bind with temporary rvalue results—something regular lvalue references will not do. An lvalue-reference-to-const parameter would, but its const-ness precludes moving anything out of it. When choosing between overloaded functions or constructors, your compiler will always prefer to bind an rvalue argument to an rvalue reference parameter. So whenever an Array<> is constructed with an Array<> rvalue as the only argument (such as our buildStringArray() call), the compiler will call the move constructor rather than the copy constructor.

All that remains now is to actually implement the move constructor. For Array<>, you might do so using this template:

```
// Move constructor
template <typename T>
Array<T>::Array(Array&& moved)
  : m_size{moved.m_size}, m_elements{moved.m_elements}
{
  std::println("Array of {} elements moved", m_size);
  moved.m_elements = nullptr; // Otherwise destructor of moved would delete[] m_elements!
}
```

When this constructor is called, moved will be bound to the outcome of an rvalue, in other words, a value that is typically about to be deleted. In any case, the calling code no longer needs the contents of the moved object anymore. And since no one needs it anymore, there's certainly no harm in you prying the m_elements array out of the moved object to reuse it for the newly constructed Array<> object. That saves both you and your computer the hassle of copying all the T values.

You thus begin by copying the m_size and the m_elements members in the member initializer list. The key here is that you realize that m_elements is nothing but a pointer of type T*. That is, it's a variable containing the address of a dynamically allocated array of T elements. And copying such a pointer is not the same as copying the entire array and all its elements. Far from it. Copying a single T* pointer is much, much cheaper than copying an entire array of T values!

▓ **Note** This is the difference between what is called a *shallow copy* and a *deep copy* (as seen also in Chapter 12). A *shallow copy* simply copies all members of an object one by one, even if these members are pointers to dynamic memory. A *deep copy*, on the other hand, copies all dynamic memory referred to by any of its pointer members as well.

Simply performing a member-by-member shallow copy of the moved object is rarely enough for a move constructor. In the case of Array<>, you probably already guessed why. Having two objects point to the same dynamically allocated memory is rarely a good idea, as we explained at length in Chapter 6. The following assignment statement in the body of the Array<> move constructor is therefore of the utmost importance as well:

```
moved.m_elements = nullptr;    // Otherwise destructor of moved would delete[] elements!
```

If you do not set moved.m_elements to nullptr there, you end up with two different objects pointing to the same m_elements array. Your newly constructed object, clearly, but also the transient Array<> object moved. That object still points to the same array as well. That would put you right in the middle of the highly volatile minefield that we cautioned you about in Chapter 6, complete with dangling pointers and multiple deallocations! By setting the m_elements pointer of the moved object to null, the destructor of the temporary object bound to moved will effectively perform delete[] nullptr, which as you know is harmless. Phew! Mines defused.

You should plug this move constructor into the Array<> template of Ex18_01 and then run the program again (the resulting program is available in Ex18_02). The output then normally becomes as follows (if not, make sure sufficient compiler optimizations are enabled):

```
Array of 1000 elements moved
Array of 1000 elements moved
Array of 1000 elements moved
... (10 times in total)
```

Instead of 10,000 string objects and three-quarters of a million char values, only ten pointers and ten size_t values have now been copied. As performance improvements go, that's not too shabby! Certainly it's well worth the effort of defining a few extra lines of code, wouldn't you agree?

Move Assignment Operators

Just like a copy constructor is normally accompanied by a copy assignment operator (see Chapter 13), a user-defined move constructor is typically paired with a user-defined *move assignment operator*. Defining one for Array<> should be easy enough for you at this point:

```
// Move assignment operator
template <typename T>
Array<T>& Array<T>::operator=(Array&& rhs)
{
  std::println("Array of {} elements moved (assignment)", rhs.m_size);

  if (&rhs != this)              // prevent trouble with self-assignments
  {
    delete[] m_elements;         // delete[] all existing elements

    m_elements = rhs.m_elements; // copy the elements pointer and the size
    m_size = rhs.m_size;

    rhs.m_elements = nullptr;    // make sure rhs does not delete[] m_elements
  }
  return *this;                  // return lhs
}
```

The only new thing here is the rvalue reference parameter rhs, designated using the double ampersands: &&. The operator's body itself simply contains a mix of elements that you've already seen before, either in the copy assignment operators from Chapter 13 or in the move constructor of Array<>.

If present, the compiler will use this assignment operator rather than the copy assignment operator whenever the object on the right side of the assignment is a temporary Array<> object. One case where this would occur is in the following snippet:

```
Array<std::string> strings { 123 };
strings = buildStringArray(1'000);     // Assign an rvalue
```

The Array<std::string> object returned by buildStringArray() is again clearly a temporary object, so the compiler realizes that you'd prefer not to copy it and will therefore pick the move assignment over the copy assignment operator. You can see this assignment operator in action if you add it to the Array<> template of Ex18_02 and use that together with this program:

```
// Ex18_03.cpp - Defining and using a move assignment operator
import array;
import std;

// Construct an Array<> of a given size, filled with some arbitrary string data
Array<std::string> buildStringArray(const std::size_t size);

int main()
{
  Array<std::string> strings { 123 };
  strings = buildStringArray(1'000);     // Assign an rvalue to strings

  Array<std::string> more_strings{ 2'000 };
  strings = more_strings;                // Assign an lvalue to strings
}
```

You can use the same definition of the buildStringArray() function as in Ex18_01 and Ex18_02. The output of this program should reflect that assigning an rvalue to the strings variable indeed results in a call to the move assignment operator, whereas assigning the lvalue more_strings to the same variable results in a call to the copy assignment:

```
Array of 1000 elements moved (assignment)
Array of 2000 elements copied
```

Explicitly Moved Objects

The main() function of Ex18_03.cpp ended with the following two statements:

```
  ...
  Array<std::string> more_strings{ 2'000 };
  strings = more_strings;               // Assign an lvalue to strings
}
```

Running Ex18_03 revealed that this final assignment resulted in the more_strings Array<> being copied. The reason is that more_strings is an lvalue. A variable name is always an lvalue (remember this, it's important!). In this case, however, the fact that more_strings gets copied is actually quite unfortunate. The culprit assignment is the very last statement of the function, so there's clearly no need for more_strings to persist afterward. And even if the main() function would have continued beyond this point, it would still be perfectly plausible that this assignment would be the last statement to reference more_strings. In fact, it is fairly common for a named variable such as more_strings to no longer be needed once its contents have been handed over to another object or to some function. It would be a real shame if "handing over" a variable such as more_strings could be done only by copying just because you gave the variable a name?

Naturally, C++11 foresees a solution for this. You can turn any lvalue into an rvalue reference simply by applying one of C++11's most vital Standard Library functions: std::move(). To see its effect, you should first replace the final two lines of main() in Ex18_03.cpp with the following and then run the program again (this variant is available in Ex18_04):

```
  ...
  Array<std::string> more_strings{ 2'000 };
  strings = std::move(more_strings);     // Move more_strings into strings
}
```

If you do, you will notice that more_strings is indeed no longer copied:

```
Array of 1000 elements moved (assignment)
Array of 2000 elements moved (assignment)
```

Move-Only Types

No discussion of std::move() is complete without an honorary mention of std::unique_ptr<>— undoubtedly the type whose variables you'll be moving the most in modern C++ programming. As explained in Chapter 6, there must never be two unique_ptr<> smart pointers pointing to the same address in memory. Otherwise, both would delete (or delete[]) the same raw pointer twice, which is a perfect way to initiate a tragic failure of your program. It is thus only fortunate that neither of the two lines that are commented out at the end of the following code snippet compiles:

```
std::unique_ptr<int> one{ std::make_unique<int>(123) };
std::unique_ptr<int> other;

// other = one;                      /* Error: copy assignment operator is deleted! */
// std::unique_ptr<int> yet_another{ other }; /* Error: copy constructor is deleted! */
```

What would compile, however, are these two lines:

```
other = std::move(one);                              // Move assignment operator is defined
std::unique_ptr<int> yet_another{ std::move(other) }; // Move constructor is defined
```

That is, while both copy members of std::unique_ptr<> are deleted (as explained in Chapters 12 and 13), both its move assignment operator and its move constructor are present. This is an outline of how you'd normally accomplish this:

```
namespace std
{
  template <typename T>
  class unique_ptr
  {
    ...
    // Prevent copying:
    unique_ptr(const unique_ptr&) = delete;
    unique_ptr& operator=(const unique_ptr&) = delete;
```

```
    // Allow moving:
    unique_ptr(unique_ptr&& source);
    unique_ptr& operator=(unique_ptr&& rhs);
    ...
  };
}
```

To define a move-only type, you always start by deleting its two copy members (like we taught you in Chapter 13). By doing so, you implicitly delete the move members as well (more on this later), so to allow uncopiable objects to be moved you must explicitly define the move members. Often, but not in the case of unique_ptr<>, it would suffice to use = default; to define the two move members and have the compiler generate them for you.

Extended Use of Moved Objects

An lvalue expression by definition evaluates to a persistent value, which is a value that remains addressable after the execution of the lvalue's parent statement. This is why the compiler normally prefers to copy the value of an lvalue expression. We just told you, however, how you can overrule this preference with std::move(). That is, you can force the compiler to pass any object to a move constructor or move assignment operator, even if it's not a temporary object. This raises the question, what happens if you keep using an object after it has been moved? Here's an example (if you want, you can try this in Ex18_04):

```
  ...
  Array<std::string> more_strings{ 2'000 };
  strings = std::move(more_strings);       // Move more_strings into strings

  std::println("{}", more_strings[101]);  // ???
}
```

In this specific case, you already know what will happen. After all, you've written the code for the move assignment operator of Array<> yourself. Once moved, an Array<> object will contain an m_elements pointer that is set to nullptr. Any further use of a moved Array<> would then trigger a null pointer dereference, resulting in the tragic, gruesome death of your program. This example nicely underlines the rationale behind this guideline:

■ **Caution** As a rule, you should only move an object if you are absolutely sure it is no longer required. Unless otherwise specified, you're not supposed to keep on using an object that was moved. By default, any extended use of a moved object results in undefined behavior (read: it'll often result in crashes).

This guideline applies to objects of Standard Library types as well. Completely analogous to Arrays, for instance, you must never simply keep using a moved std::vector<>. Doing so could very well end equally badly. You might hope that a moved vector<> is equivalent to an empty one. And while this may be so for some implementations, in general, the C++ standard does not specify at all in which state a moved vector<> should be. What is (implicitly) allowed, however—and this is something that not too many developers will know—is this:

▓ **Tip**   If need be, you can safely revive a move()'d vector<> by calling its clear() member. After calling clear(), the vector<> is guaranteed to be equivalent to an empty vector<> again and thus safe for further use.

In the rare cases where you do want to reuse moved Standard Library objects, you should always check the specification of their move members. When a std::optional<T> object that contains a T value is moved, for instance, it will still contain a T value—a T value that is now moved (we covered std::optional<> in Chapter 9). Similar to a vector<>, the optional<> can safely be reused after calling its reset() member. Smart pointers are a scarce exception:

▓ **Tip**   The Standard Library specification clearly stipulates that you may continue using smart pointers of type std::unique_ptr<> and std::shared_ptr<> after moving out the raw pointer, and this without first calling reset(). For both types, move operations always set the encapsulated raw pointer to nullptr.

A Barrel of Contradictions

Many find move semantics confusing at first, and understandably so. We hope this section can somewhat spare you from this fate, as it aims to alleviate some of the most common sources of confusion.

std::move() Does Not Move

Make no mistake, std::move() does not move anything. All this function does is turn a given lvalue into an rvalue reference. std::move() is effectively nothing more than a type conversion, not at all unlike built-in cast operators static_cast<>() and dynamic_cast<>(). In fact, you could almost implement your own version of the function like so (somewhat simplified):

```
template <typename T>
T&& move(T& x) noexcept { return static_cast<T&&>(x); }
```

Clearly, this moves nothing. What it does do, however, is make a persistent *lvalue* eligible for binding with the *rvalue* reference parameter of a move constructor or assignment operator. It's these member functions that are then supposed to move the members of the former lvalue into another object. std::move() only performs a type cast to make the compiler pick the right function overload.

If no function or constructor overload exists with an rvalue reference parameter, an rvalue will happily bind with an lvalue reference instead. That is, you can move() all you want; but if there's no function overload standing ready to receive the resulting rvalue, it's all in vain.

To demonstrate this, we'll again start from Ex18_04.cpp. As you may recall, this latest variant of our running example ended with these statements:

```
  ...
  Array<std::string> more_strings{ 2'000 };
  strings = std::move(more_strings);     // Move more_strings into strings
}
```

Obviously, the intent of this final statement is to move the 2,000 `strings` of `more_strings` into `strings`. And in `Ex18_04`, this worked flawlessly. But now see what happens if you remove the declaration and definition of the move assignment operator from its `Array<>` template. If you then run the `main()` function of `Ex18_04.cpp` once more, unaltered, the last line of the output reverts to this:

```
...
Array of 2000 elements copied
```

It does not matter that you still call `std::move()` in the body of `main()`. If there's no move assignment operator for `Array<>` to accept the rvalue, the copy assignment operator will be used instead. So, always remember, adding `std::move()` is of no consequence if the function or constructor that you invoke has no overload that efficiently handles an rvalue!

An Rvalue Reference Is an Lvalue

To be precise, the *name* of a named variable with an rvalue reference type is an lvalue. Let's show what we mean by this, as it turns out that many struggle with this idiosyncrasy at first. We'll keep on milking the same example, naturally, so take `Ex18_04` once again (make sure it contains the original `Array<>` template where the move assignment operator is still defined) and change the last two lines of the program to the following:

```
  ...
  Array<std::string> more_strings{ 2'000 };
  Array<std::string>&& rvalue_ref{ std::move(more_strings) };
  strings = rvalue_ref;
}
```

Notwithstanding that the `rvalue_ref` variable clearly has an rvalue reference type, the output of the program will show that the corresponding object is copied:

```
Array of 1000 elements moved (assignment)
Array of 2000 elements copied
```

Every variable name expression is an lvalue, even if the type of that variable is an rvalue reference type. To move the contents of a named variable, you must therefore always add `std::move()`:

```
  strings = std::move(rvalue_ref);
```

While you'd normally not create an rvalue reference in the middle of a block of code like `rvalue_ref` in our latest example, the analogous situation does occur regularly if you define function parameters that are rvalue references. You can find an example of this in the next section.

Defining Functions Revisited

In this section, we'll study how move semantics has influenced best-practice guidelines for defining new functions, complementing what you saw earlier in Chapter 8. We'll answer questions such as these: How does move semantics affect the choice between pass-by-reference and pass-by-value? Or, to return an object by value without copying, should I use `std::move()` or not? You'll find both answers coming up. We kick off by investigating how and when to pass arguments by rvalue reference to regular functions, that is, to functions that are neither move constructors nor move assignment operators.

Pass-by-Rvalue-Reference

In Exercise 17-1, you were tasked with defining a `push_back()` member function template for `Array<>`. If all went well, you applied the copy-and-swap idiom and created a function similar to this:

```
template <typename T>
void Array<T>::push_back(const T& element)
{
  Array<T> newArray{ m_size + 1 };        // Allocate a larger Array<>
  for (std::size_t i {}; i < m_size; ++i) // Copy all existing elements...
    newArray[i] = m_elements[i];

  newArray[m_size] = element;   // Copy the new one...

  swap(newArray);               // ... and swap!
}
```

While this is by no means the only way to implement `push_back()`, it is definitely one of the cleanest and most elegant options. More important, it is 100 percent robust and safe in the face of exceptions. In fact, if this exercise were part of an exam of Chapter 17, this is what we would be grading you on:

1. To avoid redundant copies of the arguments passed to `push_back()`, you defined the template using a reference-to-`const` parameter—precisely like we taught you in Chapter 8.

2. In the function body, you used the copy-and-swap idiom to make sure that the `push_back()` member behaves as desired even if the function body were to throw an exception (`std::bad_alloc`, for instance, or any other exception that T's copy assignment may throw). We refer you to Chapter 17 for a detailed discussion of copy-and-swap.

The part we'd like to draw your attention to here is the blatant amount of copying that this function performs. First, all existing elements are copied into the new, larger `Array<>` and then the newly added `element` as well. While still excusable for a Chapter 17 exam, in your Chapter 18 exam, such needless copying will start costing you grades. And in this case, it is not because copying on an exam is cheating, but because you should at least try to *move* all these elements instead!

Fixing the loop that copies all existing elements appears easy enough. Simply apply `std::move()` to turn the `m_elements[i]` lvalue into an rvalue. Doing so clearly avoids all copies, provided that the template argument type T has an appropriate move assignment operator:

```
for (std::size_t i {}; i < m_size; ++i)    // Move all existing elements...
  newArray[i] = std::move(m_elements[i]);
```

> ■ **Caution**   If the sidebar sections in Chapter 17 taught you anything, however, it's that appearances can be deceiving. Yes, adding `std::move()` like this works like a charm in the nominal case. But that's not the end of it. In general, this implementation is ever so slightly flawed. We'll reveal what this minor imperfection is later in this chapter. For now, this initial version will do its job just fine. Adieu, gratuitous copying!

Now that all existing elements have been move()'d, let's focus our attention on the newly added element. Omitting all irrelevant parts, this is the code we will consider next:

```
template <typename T>
void Array<T>::push_back(const T& element)
{
...
  newArray[m_size] = element;              // Copy the new element...
...
}
```

Your first instinct might be to simply slap another `std::move()` onto `element`, like so:

```
template <typename T>
void Array<T>::push_back(const T& element)
{
...
  newArray[m_size] = std::move(element);   // Move the new element... (???)
...
}
```

This will not work, though, and with good reason. `element` is a reference to a const T, meaning that the caller of the function expects the argument not to be modified. Moving its contents into another object is therefore completely out of the question. This is also why the `std::move()` type conversion function will never cast a const T or const T& type to T&&. Instead, `std::move()` converts it to the rather pointless type const T&&—a reference to a transient value that you're not allowed to modify. In other words, because the type of `element` is const T&, the type of `std::move(element)` is const T&&, meaning that assigning the latter expression still goes through the copy assignment operator, despite the `std::move()`.

But of course you still want to cater to those cases where the caller does not need the `element` argument anymore—that is, for those cases where `push_back()` is called with an rvalue. Luckily, you cannot only use rvalue reference parameters for move constructors and move assignment operators; you can use them for any function you want. And so, you could easily add an extra overload of `push_back()` that accepts rvalue arguments:

```
template <typename T>
void Array<T>::push_back(T&& element)
{
...
  newArray[m_size] = std::move(element);   // Move the new element...
...
}
```

▨ **Caution**   When passing an argument such as `element` by rvalue reference, never forget that inside the function's body the expression `element` is again an lvalue. Remember, any named variable is an lvalue, even if the variable itself has an rvalue reference type! In our `push_back()` example, this means that the `std::move()` in the function's body is very much required to compel the compiler into choosing T's move assignment operator rather than its copy assignment operator.

The Return of Pass-by-Value

The introduction of move semantics has caused a significant shift in how you can and should define the parameters of certain functions. Before C++11, life was easy. To avoid copies, you simply always passed objects by reference, just like we taught you in Chapter 8. Now that support for move semantics is prevalent, however, pass-by-lvalue-reference is no longer always your best option. In fact, it turns out that passing arguments by value is back on the table, at least in some specific cases. To explain when and why, we'll build further on the same `push_back()` example as just now.

In the previous subsection, we created two separate overloads of `push_back()`, one for `const T&` and one for `T&&` references. For your convenience, you can find this variant in Ex18_05A. While using two overloads is certainly a viable option, it does imply some tedious code duplication. One way to work around this duplication is to redefine the `const T&` overload in terms of the `T&&` one like so:

```
template <typename T>
void Array<T>::push_back(const T& element)
{
  push_back(T{ element });      // Create a temporary, transient copy and push that
}
```

But there is an even better, more compact way, one where one single function definition is all you need. Somewhat surprisingly, this single `push_back()` definition will use *pass-by-value*. You'd probably never have guessed to replace two *pass-by-reference* overloads with one single definition that uses *pass-by-value*, but once you see it in action, you'll surely appreciate the sheer elegance of this approach. If we again omit the irrelevant, this is what your new `push_back()` would look like:

```
template <typename T>
void Array<T>::push_back(T element)  // Pass by value (copied lvalue, or moved rvalue!)
{
...
  newArray[m_size] = std::move(element); // Move the new element...
...
}
```

Provided you only use types that support move semantics (such as Standard Library types), this function always does precisely what you want. It does not matter what kind of argument you pass it: lvalue arguments are copied, once, and rvalue arguments are moved. Because the function parameter is of value type T, a new object of type T is created whenever `push_back()` is called. The beauty is that in order to construct this new T object, the compiler will use a different constructor depending on the kind of argument. If the function's argument is an lvalue, the `element` argument is constructed using T's copy constructor. If it's an rvalue, however, `element` will be constructed using T's move constructor.

▧ **Caution**   The only reason that using pass-by-value is interesting for push_back() is that the Array<> always and inevitably hangs on to a copy of element (the only copy if the caller invoked it with an rvalue reference, or a new copy if the caller invoked it with an lvalue reference). Arguments that a (member) function only reads from should still be passed by reference-to-const!

▧ **Tip**   For a generic container such as Array<>, you probably still want to consider the possibility that the type T does not provide a move constructor or assignment operator. For such types, the push_back(T) function we outlined earlier actually copies any given argument twice. Remember, std::move() does not move unless T has a move assignment operator. If it doesn't, the compiler will quietly resort to the copy assignment operator to evaluate newArray[m_size] = std::move(element). In real life, a container like Array<> would thus mostly still have both overloads of push_back()—one for lvalues and one for rvalues.[2]

For nontemplated functions that inherently copy any lvalue input, though, the use of a single function with a pass-by-value parameter is almost always a wonderfully compact alternative. Concrete examples would be functions with signatures such as setNumbers(std::vector<double> values) or add(BigObject bigboy). The traditional reflex would be to use pass-by-reference-to-const, but by passing the arguments by value instead, you can kill two birds with one stone. If defined like this, the same single function can handle both lvalues and rvalues with near-optimal performance!

To demonstrate that this effectively works, simply add the push_back(T) function we laid out here into the Array<> template of Ex18_04. Now that Array<> supports push_back(), it also makes sense to add a default constructor that creates an empty Array<>:

```
export template <typename T>
class Array
{
public:
  Array();                              // Default constructor
  explicit Array(std::size_t size); // Constructor
// ...
  void push_back(T element);           // Add a new element (either copied or moved)
// ...
};
```

All other members can remain as they were in Ex18_04. With this, you can compose the following example program (the definition of buildStringArray() can be taken from Ex18_04 as well):

```
// Ex18_05B.cpp - Use of a pass-by-value parameter to pass by either lvalue or rvalue
import array;
import std;
```

---

[2] You can use more advanced template techniques such as member function templates and perfect forwarding to fold overloads for lvalue and rvalue reference parameters into a single template, thus sidestepping any code duplication. We've briefly shown an example of perfect forwarding in the previous chapter.

```
// Construct an Array<> of a given size, filled with some arbitrary string data
Array<std::string> buildStringArray(const std::size_t size);

int main()
{
  Array<Array<std::string>> array_of_arrays;

  Array<std::string> array{ buildStringArray(1'000) };
  array_of_arrays.push_back(array);                    // Push an lvalue

  array.push_back("One more for good measure");
  std::println("");

  array_of_arrays.push_back(std::move(array));    // Push an rvalue
}
```

In main(), we create an Array of Arrays of strings, aptly named array_of_arrays. We begin by inserting an Array<> of 1,000 strings into this container. This Array<> element, aptly named array, is clearly pushed as an lvalue, so we expect it to be copied. That is a good thing; we still need its contents for the remainder of the program. At the end of the program, we add array a second time, but this time we first convert it into an rvalue by applying std::move() to the variable's name. We do so in the hopes that the Array<> and its string array will now be moved instead of copied. Running Ex18_05B confirms that this is indeed the case; in total, array is copied only once (provided compiler optimizations are enabled):

```
Array of 1000 elements copied
Array of 1000 elements moved (assignment)

Array of 1001 elements moved
Array of 1000 elements moved (assignment)
Array of 1001 elements moved (assignment)
```

The various move assignments occur in the body of the push_back() function. In between adding array as an lvalue and adding it again as an rvalue, we inject one extra string into it to be able to differentiate the two Array<> elements added to array_of_arrays. Note that in the process of pushing this additional string none of the 1,000 preexisting string elements inside array are copied either. They are all moved to a larger string Array<> through the move assignment operator of std::string!

In the following tip, we summarize the various guidelines regarding function parameter declarations that you have encountered throughout the book, mainly in Chapter 8 and here:

▓ **Tip** For fundamental types and pointers, you can simply use pass-by-value. For objects that are more expensive to copy, you should normally use a const T& parameter. This prevents any lvalue arguments from being copied, and rvalue arguments will bind just fine with a const T& parameter as well. If your function inherently copies its T argument, however, you should pass it by value instead. Lvalue arguments will then be copied when passed to the function, and rvalue arguments will be moved. The latter guideline presumes that the parameter types support move semantics—as all types should these days. In the less likely case that the parameter type lacks proper move members, you should stick with pass-by-reference. More and more types support move semantics these days, though—not in the least all Standard Library types—so pass-by-value is most certainly back on the table!

Return-by-Value

The recommended way for returning an object from a function has always been to return it by value; even for larger objects such as a vector<>. As we'll discuss shortly, compilers have always been good at optimizing away any redundant copies of objects that you return from a function. The introduction of move semantics therefore doesn't change anything for the best practices. There are many misconceptions in this area (believe us, there are!), though, so it remains well worth reviewing this aspect of defining functions as well.

Many sample programs in this chapter were built around the following function:

```
Array<std::string> buildStringArray(const std::size_t size)
{
  Array<std::string> result{ size };
  for (std::size_t i {}; i < size; ++i)
    result[i] = "You should learn from your competitor, but never copy. Copy and you die.";
  return result;
}
```

This function returns an Array<> by value. Its last line is a return statement with the lvalue expression result, the name of an automatic, stack-allocated variable. Performance-conscious developers often get worried when they see this. Won't the compiler use Array<>'s copy constructor to copy result into the object that is being returned? They need not be worried, at least not in this case. Let's review how a modern C++ compiler is supposed to handle return-by-value (slightly simplified, as always):

- In a return statement of the form return name;, a compiler is *obliged* to treat name *as if it were an rvalue expression*, provided name is either the name of a locally defined automatic variable *or* that of a function parameter.

- In a return statement of the form return name;, a compiler is *allowed* to apply the *named return value optimization* (NRVO), provided name is the name of a locally defined automatic variable (so *not* if it is that of a function parameter).

For our example, NRVO would entail that the compiler stores the result object directly in the memory designated to hold the function's return value. That is, after applying NRVO, no memory is set aside anymore for a separate automatic variable named result.

The first bullet implies that using std::move(result) in our example would be, at the very least, redundant. Even without the std::move(), the compiler already treats result as if it is an rvalue. The second bullet moreover implies that return std::move(result) would prohibit the NRVO optimization. NRVO applies solely to statements of the form return result;. By adding std::move(), you would instead force the compiler to look for a move constructor. Doing so would introduce two potential issues—the first of which can be very severe indeed:

- If the type of the object that you return has no move constructor, then adding std::move() causes the compiler to fall back to the copy constructor! Yes, that's right. Adding *move()* can cause a *copy* where otherwise the compiler would probably have applied NRVO.

- Even if the returned object can be moved, adding std::move() can only make matters worse—never better. The reason is that NRVO generally leads to code that is even more efficient than move construction (move construction typically still involves some shallow copying and/or other statements; NRVO does not).

So, adding std::move() at best makes things a little bit slower, and at worst it causes the compiler to *copy* the return value where it otherwise would not!

▓ **Tip** If value is either a local variable (with automatic storage duration) or a function parameter, you should never write `return std::move(value);`. Always write `return value;` instead.

Note that for `return` statements such as `return MyClass{...};`, `return value + 1;` or `return buildStringArray(100);` you never have to worry about adding `std::move()` either. In these cases, you are already returning an rvalue, so adding `std::move()` would at best be redundant. In fact, in cases such as these—where the returned rvalue has no name—a conforming compiler is not even allowed to copy or move anymore; instead, it *must* apply *return value optimization* (RVO).

▓ **Note** The general process where, when returned from a function, an object is neither copied nor moved, is also called *copy elision*. It encompasses both return value optimization (RVO) and named return value optimization (NRVO). Copy elision enables zero-cost pass-by-value semantics.

Does this mean that you should never use `std::move()` when returning a value? Alas, no. Life with C++ is rarely that easy. Mostly, returning by value without `std::move()` is what you want, but certainly not always:

- If the variable value in `return value;` has *static or thread-local storage duration* (see Chapter 11), you need to add `std::move()` if moving is what you want. This case is rare, though.

- When returning an object's *member variable*, as in `return m_member_variable;`, `std::move()` is again required if you do not want the member variable to be copied.

- If the `return` statement contains any other lvalue expression besides the name of a single variable, then NRVO does not apply, nor will the compiler treat this lvalue as if it were an rvalue when looking for a constructor.

Common examples for the latter case are `return` statements of the form `return array[i];`, or `return condition ? var1 : var2;`. While perhaps not obvious, a conditional expression such as `condition ? var1 : var2` is in fact an lvalue. Because it's clearly no variable name, though, the compiler forsakes NRVO and will not implicitly treat it as an rvalue either. It will, in other words, look for a copy constructor to create the returned object (either var1 or var2). To avoid this, you have at least three options. Any of the following `return` statements will at least attempt to move the value that is returned:

```
return std::move(condition ? var1 : var2);
```

```
return condition ? std::move(var1) : std::move(var2);
```

```
if (condition)
  return var1;
else
  return var2;
```

Out of these three, the last one is most recommended. The reason is again that it allows a clever compiler to apply NRVO (at least in theory). The former two forms preclude NRVO.

Defining Move Members Revisited

Now that you are a move semantics expert, we can give some more advice on how to properly define your own move constructors and move assignment operators. Our first guideline—that is, to always declare them as noexcept—is particularly important. Without noexcept, your move members are not nearly as effective. (The noexcept specifier was explained in Chapter 16.)

Always Add noexcept

It is important that all your move members have a noexcept specifier, assuming they do not throw, of course; though, in practice, move members rarely do. Adding noexcept is so important that we'll even go out of our way to explain why this is so. The reason is that we firmly believe that knowing why a guideline exists makes you remember it all the better!

For this, let's pick up where we left off earlier with Ex18_05B. In this example, you defined the following push_back() function for Array<>:

```cpp
template <typename T>
void Array<T>::push_back(T element)   // Pass by value (copy of lvalue, or moved rvalue!)
{
  Array<T> newArray{ m_size + 1 };         // Allocate a larger Array<>
  for (std::size_t i {}; i < m_size; ++i) // Move all existing elements...
    newArray[i] = std::move(m_elements[i]);

  newArray[m_size] = std::move(element);   // Move the new one...

  swap(newArray);                          // ... and swap!
}
```

Looks good, right? Running Ex18_05B also confirmed that all redundant copies are gone. So, what's wrong with this definition then? In Chapter 17, we cautioned you to look beyond apparent correctness. For one, we urged you to always consider what happens in case of unexpected exceptions. Any idea as to what could be wrong with push_back()? It might be good for you to reflect on this for a moment.

The answer is that, while unlikely, the move assignment operator of T could, in principle, throw an exception. This is especially relevant here since the Array<> template should work for any type T. Now consider what happens if such an exception occurred in the middle of the function's for loop, or even while moving the new element.

In a way, adding the std::move() in the for loop has undermined the workings of the copy-and-swap idiom. With copy-and-swap it is crucial that the object being modified (*this, typically, in the case of a member function) remains in pristine, untouched condition right up to the final swap() operation. Any modification prior to the swap() does not get undone in case of an exception. So if an exception occurs inside push_back() while moving one of the objects in the elements array, there's nothing in place to restore any earlier objects that were already moved into newArray.

It turns out that no matter what you try, if a move member may throw, there is no way for you to safely move the existing elements into the new array without copying. If only there was a way for you to know that a given move member never throws any exceptions. After all, if moving never throws, safely moving existing elements into a larger array becomes feasible. And, you know of such a way already! We introduced it in Chapter 16: the noexcept specifier. If a function is noexcept, you know for a fact that it will never throw an exception. In other words, what you want to somehow express in push_back() is this:

```
template <typename T>
void Array<T>::push_back(T element)  // Pass by value (copy of lvalue, or moved rvalue!)
{
  Array<T> newArray{ m_size + 1 };         // Allocate a larger Array<>
  for (std::size_t i {}; i < m_size; ++i) // Move elements (copy if not noexcept)...
    newArray[i] = move_assign_if_noexcept(m_elements[i]);

  newArray[m_size] = move_assign_if_noexcept(element);  // Move (or copy) the new one...

  swap(newArray);                          // ... and swap!
}
```

The move_assign_if_noexcept() function we need here to accomplish an efficient yet safe push_back() template should act as std::move(), yet only if the move assignment operator of T is specified to be noexcept. If not, move_assign_if_noexcept() should turn its argument into an lvalue reference instead, thus triggering the use of T's copy assignment.

This is where we hit a minor bump in the road:

▓ **Caution** The Standard Library only provides std::move_if_noexcept(), but reading the fine print reveals that this function is intended to conditionally invoke either a move *constructor* or a copy *constructor*, depending on whether the move *constructor* is noexcept. The Standard Library offers no equivalent for conditionally invoking a move assignment operator.

While implementing such a move_assign_if_noexcept() function is certainly possible, it requires a technique that is somewhat way too advanced for a beginner's book; concretely, it requires *template metaprogramming*. Before we go there, here's an important conclusion already:

▓ **Caution** If nothing else, what the Array<>::push_back() function should teach you is to never give in to the temptation to implement your own container classes unless this is absolutely necessary (and it rarely is!). Getting them 100 percent right is deceptively hard. Always use containers of the Standard Library instead (or those of other tested and tried libraries such as Boost). Even with the move_assign_if_noexcept() function in place, your Array<> class can hardly be called optimal. You'd need to rework it considerably using more advanced memory management techniques to even get remotely close to a fully optimized std::vector<>!

The upcoming sidebar briefly explains how you could implement the move_assign_if_noexcept() function required for our exception-safe push_back() member (the result is in Ex18_06). It involves template metaprogramming, so it is not for the faint-hearted. So please feel free to skip straight ahead to the next regular subsection, where we'll demonstrate the effect of adding noexcept to move members when using your types in Standard Library containers.

IMPLEMENTING MOVE_ASSIGN_IF_NOEXCEPT

Template metaprogramming typically involves making decisions based on template arguments (which, as you know, are often type names) to control the code that is generated by a template when it is instantiated by the compiler. In other words, it involves writing code that is evaluated at compile time whenever the compiler generates a concrete instance of the corresponding template. In the case of move_assign_if_noexcept(), what we essentially need to encode is the equivalent of a regular C++ if-else statement that expresses the following logic for the function's return type:

"If rvalues of type T&& can be assigned without throwing,
then the return type should be an rvalue reference (that is, T&&);
otherwise, it should be an lvalue reference instead (const T&)."

T here is the template type argument to move_assign_if_noexcept(). Without further ado, this is how you'd convey precisely this logic using some of the template metaprogramming primitives—called *type traits*—provided by the <type_traits> Standard Library module:

```
std::conditional_t<std::is_nothrow_move_assignable_v<T>, T&&, const T&>
```

To a template metaprogrammer, this reads almost word for word as what we said earlier. It takes some (read: a lot of) getting used to, though, which obviously is something we don't have time for now. Which is why we won't dwell on this any further. The aim of this sidebar, after all, is just to give you a quick first taste of what is possible with template metaprogramming.

With the previous meta-expression, composing a fully functioning move_assign_if_noexcept() function is actually not that hard anymore:

```
template<typename T>
std::conditional_t<std::is_nothrow_move_assignable_v<T>, T&&, const T&>
move_assign_if_noexcept(T& x) noexcept
{
   return std::move(x);
}
```

The function body is trivial; all template meta-magic happens in the return type of the function. Depending on the properties of type T—more concretely, depending on whether T&& values can be assigned without throwing—the return type will be either T&& or const T&. Note that in the latter case, it does not matter that the std::move() in the function's body still returns an rvalue reference. If the return type in the template's instantiation for type T is const T&, then the rvalue reference that is returned from the function body gets turned right back into an lvalue reference.

Moving Within Standard Library Containers

Naturally, all container types of the Standard Library are optimized to move objects whenever possible, just like you did for the Array<> container template. This means that any implementation of std::vector<> faces challenges analogous to those you faced with push_back(). Namely, how does one guarantee internal integrity in the presence of exceptions when moving existing elements into a newly allocated, larger array? How does one guarantee the desired all-or-nothing behavior—a behavior the C++ standard normally requires for all container operations?

We can deduce how the Standard Library implementers approached these challenges using the following variant of Ex18_05B:

```
// Ex18_07.cpp - the effect of not adding noexcept to move members
import array;
import std;

// Construct an Array<> of a given size, filled with some arbitrary string data
Array<std::string> buildStringArray(const std::size_t size);

int main()
{
  std::vector<Array<std::string>> v;

  v.push_back(buildStringArray(1'000));

  std::println("");

  v.push_back(buildStringArray(2'000));
}
```

Instead of adding the Array<>s to an Array<>, we now add them to a std::vector<>. More concretely, we add two rvalues of type Array<>&& to a single vector<> (the implementation of buildStringArray() is the same as always). One possible sequence of events is this (provided you started with an Array<> template where the move members do not yet have the necessary noexcept specifiers, that is):

```
Array of 1000 elements moved

Array of 2000 elements moved
Array of 1000 elements copied
```

From this output[3], you clearly see that when adding the second element (the Array<> with 2,000 elements), the first element gets copied (the Array<> with 1,000 strings). The push_back() member of std::vector<> does this while transferring all existing elements to a larger dynamic array, similar to what we did earlier in Array::push_back().

▓ **Note** The Standard Library specification does not explicitly prescribe when and how often a vector<> should allocate a larger dynamic array as you add more elements. So, it could in principle be that with Ex18_07.cpp you do not yet see the Array<> of 1,000 elements being copied. If so, just add more push_back() statements to add extra Array<>&& elements. Because the Standard Library does require a vector<> to store all its elements in one contiguous dynamic array, eventually the vector<> inevitably has to allocate a larger array and then transfer all its existing elements into that.

---

[3] This output may again slightly differ from compiler to compiler, or from compiler configuration to compiler configuration. The array of 1,000 elements will always be copied, though, which is the main takeaway here.

The reason that the Array<> is *copied* rather than *moved* is that the compiler deemed moving to be unsafe. That is, it could not deduce that moving is possible without throwing. Naturally, if you now add noexcept to your Array<> move constructor template and run Ex18_07 again, you'll find that the Array<> and its 1,000 strings are no longer copied:

```
Array of 1000 elements moved

Array of 2000 elements moved
Array of 1000 elements moved
```

■ **Tip** Standard containers and functions typically only exploit move semantics if the corresponding move members are declared with noexcept. Whenever possible—and it almost always is—it is therefore crucial that all your move constructors and move assignment operators are declared noexcept.

The "Move-and-Swap" Idiom

Before we move on to the final section of this chapter, we'll first revisit the implementation of the Array<> move assignment operator. When we defined it earlier, near the beginning of the chapter, you didn't know enough yet to implement this operator in a clean and elegant manner. Going back to this definition, isn't there something that strikes you as suboptimal? We'll throw in the noexcept specifier to get things going, as shown here:

```cpp
// Move assignment operator
template <typename T>
Array<T>& Array<T>::operator=(Array&& rhs) noexcept
{
  std::println("Array of {} elements moved (assignment)", rhs.m_size);

  if (&rhs != this)            // prevent trouble with self-assignments
  {
    delete[] m_elements;       // delete[] all existing elements

    m_elements = rhs.m_elements; // copy the elements pointer and the size
    m_size = rhs.m_size;

    rhs.m_elements = nullptr;  // make sure rhs does not delete[] m_elements
  }
  return *this;                // return lhs
}
```

What if we told you that you're looking for code duplication?

If you look closely, you'll find that the function contains not one but two accounts of duplication:

- First, it contains the same logic as the destructor to clean up any existing members. In our case, this is just a single delete[] statement, but in general, this could require any number of steps.

- Second, it contains the same logic as the move constructor to copy all members and to set the m_elements member of the moved object to nullptr.

In Chapter 17, we told you that it's always good practice to avoid duplication as much as reasonably possible. Any duplication, even that of only one or a couple of lines of code, is just another opportunity for bugs—either now or in the future. Just imagine that one day you add an extra member to Array<>; it would then be easy to forget to update all places where they're copied one by one. The fewer places you need to update, the better.

For copy assignment operators, you are already familiar with the standard technique to solve the analogous problem: the copy-and-swap idiom. Fortunately, you can use a similar pattern for move assignment operators as well:

```
// Move assignment operator
template <typename T>
Array<T>& Array<T>::operator=(Array&& rhs) noexcept
{
  Array<T> moved(std::move(rhs));  // move...       (noexcept)
  swap(moved);                     // ... and swap  (noexcept)
  return *this;                    // return lhs
}
```

This move-and-swap idiom eliminates both accounts of duplication. Any existing elements are deleted by the destructor of the automatic variable moved, and the responsibility of copying the members and assigning nullptr is delegated to the move constructor. The key is not to forget the explicit std::move() of rhs in the function body. Remember, and we cannot repeat this enough, a variable name is always an lvalue, even the name of a variable with an rvalue reference type!

Take care not to go too far in weeding out duplication. Given earlier guidelines, you may be tempted to reduce code duplication even more and combine the copy and move assignment operators into one single assignment operator of the following form:

```
// Assignment operator
template <typename T>
Array<T>& Array<T>::operator=(Array rhs)  // Copy or move...
{
  swap(rhs);        // ... and swap!
  return *this;     // Return lhs
}
```

At first sight, this looks like a nice and elegant improvement. Whenever the right side of an assignment is a temporary object, the rhs value argument to this assignment operator will be constructed and initialized using the move constructor. Otherwise, the copy constructor is used. The problem, however, is that it violates another guideline, which is that the move assignment operator should always be noexcept. Otherwise, you risk that the copy assignment is still used by containers and other Standard Library templates that move only when noexcept is present.

The following guideline thus summarizes our advice regarding defining assignment operators:

▓ **Tip**   If you define them at all (see the next section), always define separate copy and move assignment operators. The latter should be noexcept, the former typically not (copying typically risks triggering a bad_alloc exception, at the least). To avoid additional duplication, the copy assignment operator should use the traditional copy-and-swap idiom, and the move assignment operator should use the analogous move-and-swap idiom we introduced here. Finally, the copy assignment operator should always use pass-by-reference-to-const, not pass-by-value. Otherwise, you risk running into compiler errors because of ambiguous assignments.

Special Member Functions

There are six *special member functions*, and you now know all of them:

- The default constructor (Chapter 12)

- The destructor (Chapter 12)

- The copy constructor (Chapter 12)

- The copy assignment operator (Chapter 13)

- The move constructor (this chapter)

- The move assignment operator (this chapter)

The quality that makes them "special" is that, under the right circumstances, the compiler is kind enough to generate them for you. It's interesting to note what the compiler generates starting from a basic class definition such as this:

```
class Data
{
  int m_value {1};
};
```

What you actually get is the following:

```
class Data
{
public:
  Data() : m_value{1} {}                      // Default constructor
  Data(const Data& data) : m_value{data.m_value} {}                    // Copy constructor
  Data(Data&& data) noexcept : m_value{std::move(data.m_value)} {} // Move constructor

  ~Data() {}                              // Destructor (implicitly noexcept)

  Data& operator=(const Data& data)   // Copy assignment operator
  {
    m_value = data.m_value;
    return *this;
  }
  Data& operator=(Data&& data) noexcept   // Move assignment operator
  {
    m_value = std::move(data.m_value);
    return *this;
  }

private:
  int m_value;
};
```

Default-generated move members are something we haven't discussed yet, so we'll start there. Once they are covered, the remainder of this section then reviews when exactly you should define your own versions of these special functions.

Default Move Members

Analogous to the two default copy members (see Chapters 12 and 13), compiler-generated move members simply move all non-`static` member variables one by one in the order in which the member variables are declared in the class definition. If the class has base classes, their move constructors or move assignment operators are called first, again in the order in which the base classes are declared. An implicitly defined move member, finally, is always `noexcept`, as long as the corresponding member function is `noexcept` for all base classes and non-`static` member variables.

So, no surprises there. *If* the move members are defined by the compiler, they behave exactly as you'd expect. But now the remaining questions are: *When* does the compiler generate these default move members? And why did it, for instance, not do so for our `Array<>` class template? The answer is as follows:

▓ **Tip**   As soon as you declare either a destructor or any of the four copy or move members, the compiler will no longer generate any missing move members.

While this rule may appear fairly restrictive at first, it actually makes a lot of sense. Consider our original `Array<>` template. The compiler observes that you explicitly defined the destructor, copy constructor, and copy assignment operator. The only sensible reason for you to do so is because the compiler-generated defaults would be wrong. From this, the compiler, in turn, can draw only one sensible conclusion: If it were to generate default move members, they would almost certainly be wrong as well (note that for `Array<>`, this reasoning is most definitely sound!). When in doubt, generating no default move members at all is clearly always better than generating incorrect ones. After all, the worst that could happen to an object without move members is that it gets copied from time to time—a fate that pales in comparison to what might happen to objects with incorrect move members!

The Rule of Five

Naturally, whenever you define a move constructor, you should also define its companion, the move assignment operator—and vice versa. From Chapter 13 you'll recall that the same holds when defining the copy members. These observations are generalized in the so-called rule of five. This best-practice guideline concerns the following five special member functions: the copy constructor, copy assignment operator, move constructor, move assignment constructor, and destructor. In other words, it applies to *all* special member functions except for the default constructor. The rule goes as follows:

▓ **Rule of Five**   If you declare any of the five special member functions other than the default constructor, then you should normally declare all five of them.

The motivation, not by chance, is analogous to that in the previous subsection. As soon as you need to override the default behavior for any one of these five special functions, you almost certainly need to do so for the other four as well. For instance, if you need to `delete` or `delete[]` a member variable memory in the destructor, it stands to reason that a shallow copy of the corresponding member would be extremely dangerous. The converse is perhaps less obvious but generally holds as well.

Notice that the rule of five does not state that it is required to actually provide explicit *definitions* for all five special member declarations. Deleting or defaulting a member also counts as a declaration. It is thus perfectly okay to use `= delete;` at times (for instance, when creating uncopiable types) or even `= default;` (typically combined with some `= delete;` declarations—for instance, to create move-only types, as shown earlier in this chapter).

The Rule of Zero

The rule of five governs *what* to do if and when you declare your own special member functions. It does not say anything, however, about *when* you should do so. This is where the *rule of zero* comes in:

░ **Rule of Zero**   Implement the special member functions as little as possible.

In a way, the rule of zero is what mathematicians would call a corollary of the rule of five (a *corollary* is a logical consequence of an already proven proposition). After all, the rule of five stipulates that defining any special member function instantly means defining five of them, as well as perhaps a swap() function, as you already know. Even with the copy-and-swap and move-and-swap idioms, defining five members always involves writing a significant amount of code. And a significant amount of code means a significant number of opportunities for bugs and a significant maintenance overhead.

The usual motivational example is to consider the impact of adding a new member variable to an existing class. In how many places then do you need to add a line of code? One more line in the member initializer list of the copy constructor? And one in the move constructor as well? And, oh yes, we almost forgot about the extra line in swap()! Whatever the count is, nothing beats zero! That is, in an ideal world, all you'd have to do to add a new member variable is to add the corresponding declaration to the class definition. Nothing more, nothing less.

Fortunately, adhering to the rule of zero is not as hard as it might seem at first. In fact, all you generally need to do is follow the various guidelines regarding containers and resource management that we advocated in earlier chapters:

- All dynamically allocated objects should be managed by a smart pointer (Chapter 4).

- All dynamic arrays should be managed by a std::vector<> (Chapter 5).

- More generally, collections of objects are to be managed by container objects such as those provided by the Standard Library (see also Chapter 20).

- Any other resources that need cleanup (network connections, file handles, and so on) should be managed by a dedicated RAII object as well (Chapter 16).

If you simply apply these principles to all member variables of your class, none of these variables should be so-called raw or naked resources anymore. That normally implies that none of the five special member functions that the rule of five speaks about requires an explicit definition anymore either.

One consequence of respecting the rule of zero is that applying the rule of five becomes reserved almost exclusively for when you define either a custom RAII or container type. With these custom RAII and container types in place, you can then compose higher-level types that mostly need no explicit copy, move, or destructor declarations of their own anymore.

There is one special member function that is not governed by the rules of five and zero: the default constructor. You can typically avoid having to define a default constructor by initializing all member variables in your class definition. We did this, for instance, for the Data class at the beginning of this section:

```
class Data
{
  int m_value {1};
};
```

But as soon as you declare any constructor, even one that is not a special member function, you know from Chapter 12 that the compiler will no longer generate a default constructor. Which is why it's a good thing indeed that the rule of zero does not preclude defaulting a default constructor like this:

```
class Data
{
public:
  Data() = default;
  Data(int val);

private:
  int m_value {1};
};
```

Summary

This chapter, in more ways than one, wrapped up that which we started in Chapters 12 and 13. You learned what move semantics is and how it allows for natural, elegant, and—most importantly, perhaps—efficient code. We taught you how to facilitate moving for your own types. The idea of move operations is that since the argument is temporary, the function doesn't necessarily need to copy data members; it can instead steal the data from the object that is the argument. If members of the argument object are pointers, for example, the pointers can be transferred without copying what they point to because the argument object will be destroyed and so doesn't need them.

The important points and best-practice guidelines from this chapter include the following:

- An rvalue is an expression that typically results in a temporary value; an lvalue is one that results in a more persistent value.

- `std::move()` can be used to convert an lvalue (such as a named variable) into an rvalue. Take care, though. Once moved, an object should normally not be used anymore.

- An rvalue reference type is declared using a double ampersand, &&.

- The move constructor and move assignment operator have rvalue reference parameters, so these will be called when the argument is a temporary object or any other rvalue.

- If a function inherently copies one of its inputs, passing this argument by value is preferred, even if this concerns an object of a class type. By doing so, you can cater to both lvalue and rvalue inputs with one single function definition.

- Automatic variables and function parameters should be returned by value and without adding `std::move()` to the `return` statement.

- Move members should normally be `noexcept`; if not, they risk not being invoked by Standard Library containers and other templates.

- The rule of five entails that you either declare all copy members, move members, and the destructor together, or none of them at all. The rule of zero urges you to strive to define none at all. The means to achieve rule of zero compliance, you already know: always manage dynamic memory and other resources using smart pointers, containers, and other RAII techniques!

EXERCISES

The following exercises enable you to try what you've learned in this chapter. If you get stuck, look back over the chapter for help. If you're still stuck after that, you can download the solutions from the Apress website (www.apress.com/book/download.html), but that really should be a last resort.

Exercise 18-1. Define move operators for the Truckload class (the last time you encountered this class was in Exercise 16-3) and provide a small test program to show that it works.

Exercise 18-2. Another class that desperately needs to be upgraded with moving capabilities is the LinkedList<> template you defined for Exercise 17-5. It could even do with more brushing up than just the two special move members. Can you tell what else would be needed for a modern LinkedList<> type? Write a quick program that demonstrates the newly added moving capabilities.

Exercise 18-3. Now that we're digging in the code that you created earlier already, what about the two RAII types you created (or should have created) during Exercise 16-6 when wrapping a C-style API to a fictional database management system? If you recall, one managed a database connection and ensured this connection was always timely severed, whereas the other encapsulated a pointer to the result of a database query whose memory had to be deallocated whenever the user was done inspecting this result. Obviously, you do not want these objects to be copied (why not?). Add the appropriate measures to prevent this.

Exercise 18-4. Like any RAII type (just think of std::unique_ptr<> for an example), the two types you worked on in Exercise 18-3 could surely benefit from move members. Modify the solution of the exercise accordingly, including a few extra lines in the main() function, to prove that your solution works. Is what you did earlier in Exercise 18-3 still needed now? Also, Exercise 16-6 used a Customer class. Does this type perhaps need move members as well?

Exercise 18-5. When implementing move members, the swap()-like std::exchange() function often comes in handy. Consult a Standard Library reference to get acquainted with this useful utility and then give it a try in the move members of the RAII classes in Exercise 18-4.

Exercise 18-6. To conclude, look back at the constructors of the Trouble and TracingException exception classes from Chapter 16. Notice anything suboptimal? How would you improve TracingException knowing what you know now? Give it a try. Hypothetically, what could still go wrong, and how could you fix it?

CHAPTER 19

■ ■ ■

First-Class Functions

C++ has economy-class functions, business-class functions, and first-class functions, all with varying degrees of comfort, space, privacy, and onboard service... No, of course that's not what the term *first-class* means.[1] Let's start over.

In computer science, a programming language is said to offer *first-class functions* if it allows you to treat functions like any other variable. In such a language, for instance, you can assign a function as a value to a variable, just like you would an integer or a string. You can pass a function as an argument to other functions or return one as the result of another function. At first sight, you may find it difficult to imagine the applicability of such language constructs, but they are immensely useful and powerful.

This chapter introduces what C++ has to offer in this area, ranging from function pointers and function objects to anonymous functions and closures that are defined by means of lambda expressions (not to worry, all these fancy terms will become clear to you before this chapter is over). The introduction of lambda expressions in C++11 in particular has thoroughly reshaped C++. It lifted the expressivity of the language to a whole new level. This was, in no small part, due to the heavy use of first-class function parameters throughout the Standard Library. The function templates of its generic algorithms library (which is a topic of the next chapter) are a prime use case for lambda expressions.

In this chapter, you'll learn

- What a function pointer is and what you use it for

- The limitations of function pointers and how to overcome them using standard object-oriented techniques and operator overloading

- What a lambda expression is

- How you define a lambda expression

- What a lambda closure is and why it is more powerful than an anonymous function

- What a capture clause is and how you use it

- How you pass any first-class function as an argument to another function

- How `std::function<>` allows you to represent any first-class function as a variable

---

[1] The term does have a somewhat similar origin. In the 1960s, Christopher Strachey (the same computer language pioneer who first formalized the concepts of lvalues and rvalues, by the way) coined the term when he labeled procedures (functions) as second-class citizens in the programming language ALGOL: "They always have to appear in person and can never be represented by a variable or expression...."

Pointers to Functions

You are familiar already with pointers to data, variables that store the address of those regions in memory containing values of other variables, arrays, or dynamically allocated memory. A computer program is more than just data alone, however. Another essential part of the memory allotted to a computer program holds its executable code, consisting of blocks of compiled C++ statements. Naturally, all compiled code belonging to a given function will typically be grouped together as well.

A *pointer to a function* or *function pointer* is a variable that can store the address of a function and therefore point to different functions at different times during execution. You use a pointer to a function to call the function at the address it contains. An address is not sufficient to call a function, though. To work properly, a pointer to a function must also store the type of each parameter as well as the return type. Clearly, the information required to define a pointer to a function will restrict the range of functions to which the pointer can point. It can only store the address of a function with a given number of parameters of specific types and with a given return type. This is analogous to a pointer that stores the address of a data item. A pointer to type int can only point to a location that contains a value of type int.

Defining Pointers to Functions

Here's a definition of a pointer that can store the address of functions that have parameters of type long* and int and return a value of type long:

```
long (*fun_ptr)(long*, int); // Variable fun_ptr (pointer to function that returns long)
```

This may look a little weird at first because of all the parentheses. The name of the pointer variable is fun_ptr. It doesn't point to anything because it is not initialized. Ideally, it would be initialized to nullptr or with the address of a specific function. The parentheses around the pointer name and the asterisk are essential. Without them, this statement would declare a function rather than define a pointer variable because the * will bind to the type long:

```
long *fun_ptr(long*, int);    // Prototype for a function fun_ptr() that returns long*
```

The general form of a pointer to a function definition is as follows:

```
return_type (*pointer_name)(parameter_types);
```

The pointer can only point to functions with the exact same return_type and parameter_types as those specified in its definition.

Of course, you should always initialize a pointer when you declare it. You can initialize a pointer to a function to nullptr or with the name of a function. Suppose you have a function with the following prototype:

```
long findMaximum(const long* array, std::size_t size);   // Returns the maximum element
```

Then you can define and initialize a pointer to this function with this statement:

```
long (*fun_ptr)(const long*, std::size_t) { findMaximum };
```

Using auto will make defining a pointer to this function much simpler:

```
auto fun_ptr{ findMaximum };
```

You could also use auto* to highlight the fact that fun_ptr is a pointer:

```
auto* fun_ptr{ findMaximum };
```

This defines fun_ptr as a pointer to any function with the same parameter list and return type as findMaximum() and initializes it with the address of findMaximum(). You can store the address of any function with the same parameter list and return type in an assignment. If findMinimum() has the same parameter list and return type as findMaximum(), you can make fun_ptr point to it like this:

```
fun_ptr = findMinimum;
```

> ■ **Note** Even though the name of a function already evaluates to a value of a function pointer type, you can also explicitly take its address using the address-of operator, &. The following statements, in other words, have the same effect as the earlier ones:
>
> ```
> auto* fun_ptr = &findMaximum;
>
> fun_ptr = &findMinimum;
> ```
>
> Some recommend to always add the address-of operator because in doing so you make it more obvious that you're creating a pointer to a function.

To call findMinimum() using fun_ptr, you just use the pointer name as though it were a function name. Here's an example:

```
long data[] {23, 34, 22, 56, 87, 12, 57, 76};
std::println("Value of minimum is {}", fun_ptr(data, std::size(data)));
```

This outputs the minimum value in the data array. As with pointers to variables, you should ensure that a pointer to a function effectively contains the address of a function before you use it to invoke a function. Without initialization, catastrophic failure of your program is almost guaranteed.

To get a feel for these newfangled pointers to functions and how they perform in action, let's try one out in a working program:

```
// Ex19_01.cpp - Exercising pointers to functions
import std;

long sum(long a, long b);          // Function prototype
long product(long a, long b);      // Function prototype

int main()
{
  long(*fun_ptr)(long, long) {};   // Pointer to function

  fun_ptr = product;
  std::println("3 * 5 = {}", fun_ptr(3, 5));  // Call product() thru fun_ptr

  fun_ptr = sum;        // Reassign pointer and call sum() thru fun_ptr twice
  std::println("3 * (4+5) + 6 = {}", fun_ptr(product(3, fun_ptr(4, 5)), 6));
}
```

```
// Function to multiply two values
long product(long a, long b) { return a * b; }

// Function to add two values
long sum(long a, long b) { return a + b; }
```

This example produces the following output:

```
3 * 5 = 15
3 * (4+5) + 6 = 33
```

This is hardly a useful program, but it does show how a pointer to a function is defined, assigned a value, and used to call a function. After the usual preamble, you define and initialize fun_ptr as a pointer to a function, which can point to either of the functions sum() or product().

fun_ptr is initialized to nullptr, so before using it, the address of the function product() is stored in fun_ptr. The product() function is then called indirectly through the pointer fun_ptr in the output statement. The name of the pointer is used just as if it were a function name and is followed by the function arguments between parentheses, exactly as they would appear if the original function name were being used. It would save a lot of complication if the pointer were defined and initialized like this:

```
auto* fun_ptr{ product };
```

Just to show that you can, the pointer is changed to point to sum(). It is then used again in a ludicrously convoluted expression to do some simple arithmetic. This shows that you can use a pointer to a function in the same way as the function to which it points. Figure 19-1 illustrates what happens.

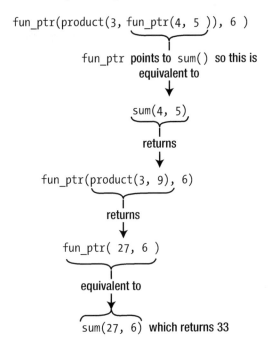

Figure 19-1. Execution of an expression using a function pointer

Callback Functions for Higher-Order Functions

Pointer to function is a perfectly reasonable type, which means a function can have a parameter of this type as well. The function can then use its pointer to function parameter to call the function to which the argument points when the function is called. You can specify just a function name as the argument for a parameter that is a "pointer to function" type. A function passed to another function as an argument is referred to as a *callback function*; the function that accepts another function as an argument is a *higher-order function*. Consider the following example:

```
// Optimum.cppm - A function template to determine the optimum element in a given vector
export module optimum;
import std;

export template <typename T>
const T* findOptimum(const std::vector<T>& values, bool (*compare)(const T&, const T&))
{
  if (values.empty()) return nullptr;

  const T* optimum{ &values[0] };
  for (std::size_t i {1}; i < values.size(); ++i)
  {
    if (compare(values[i], *optimum))
      optimum = &values[i];
  }
  return optimum;
}
```

This higher-order function template generalizes the findMaximum() and findMinimum() functions we alluded to earlier. The function pointer you pass to the compare parameter determines which "optimum" is computed. The parameter's type forces you to pass a pointer to a function that takes two T values as input and returns a Boolean. This pointed-to function is expected to compare two T values and evaluate whether the first one is somehow "better" than the second one. The higher-order findOptimum() function then repeatedly calls the given comparison function through its compare parameter and uses the results to determine which, out of all the T values in its vector argument, is best or optimal.

The key point is that you, as the caller of findOptimum(), determine what it means for one T value to be better or more optimal than the other. If you want the minimum element, you pass a comparison function equivalent to the less-than operator; if you want the maximum element, you pass one equivalent to the greater-than operator; and so on. Let's see this in action:

```
// Ex19_02.cpp - Using function pointers as callback functions
import std;
import optimum;

// Comparison function prototypes:
bool less(const int&, const int&);
template <typename T> bool greater(const T&, const T&);
bool longer(const std::string&, const std::string&);
```

```
int main()
{
  std::vector<int> numbers{ 91, 18, 92, 22, 13, 43 };
  std::println("Minimum element: {}", *findOptimum(numbers, less));
  std::println("Maximum element: {}", *findOptimum(numbers, greater<int>));

  std::vector<std::string> names{ "Moe", "Larry", "Shemp", "Curly", "Joe", "Curly Joe" };
  std::println("Alphabetically last name: {}", *findOptimum(names, greater<std::string>));
  std::println("Longest name: {}",          *findOptimum(names, longer));
}

bool less(const int& one, const int& other) { return one < other; }

template <typename T>
bool greater(const T& one, const T& other) { return one > other; }

bool longer(const std::string& one, const std::string& other)
{
  return one.length() > other.length();
}
```

This program prints out these results:

```
Minimum element: 13
Maximum element: 92
Alphabetically last: Shemp
Longest name: Curly Joe
```

The first two calls to findOptimum() demonstrate that this function can indeed be used to find both the minimum and maximum numbers in a given vector. In passing, we illustrate that a function pointer may point to the instantiation of a function template such as greater<>() as well. All you have to do is explicitly instantiate the template by specifying all its template arguments between < and >.

The second half of the example is perhaps even more interesting. The default comparison operators of std::string, as you know, compare strings alphabetically. As in a phone book, Shemp would therefore always appear last. But there are times where you prefer to compare strings in a different manner. Adding callback parameters to functions such as findOptimum() facilitates this. We illustrate this capability in Ex19_02 by looking for the longest string, by passing a pointer to longer() to findOptimum().

This example showcases the tremendous value of higher-order functions and callbacks in your never-ending battle against code duplication. If it weren't for first-class functions, you would have had to write at least three distinct findOptimum() functions already only to make Ex19_02 work: findMinimum(), findMaximum(), and findLongest(). All three would then have contained the same loop to extract the corresponding optimum from a given vector. While for beginners it may be a great exercise to write such loops at least a couple of times, this soon gets old and certainly has no place in professional software development. Luckily, the Standard Library offers a vast collection of generic algorithms similar to findOptimum() that you can reuse instead, and all will accept similar callback functions that allow you to tune them to your needs. We'll discuss this in more detail in the next chapter.

▒ **Note**   First-class callback functions have plenty more uses beyond serving as the argument to higher-order functions. Callbacks are actively used in other aspects of day-to-day object-oriented programming as well. Objects often store callback functions in their member variables. Callback functions can serve any number of purposes. Callbacks could constitute user-configurable steps in the logic, or signal other objects that some event has occurred. Callbacks in all their forms facilitate various standard object-oriented idioms, most notably variations on the classical Observer pattern. Discussing object-oriented design falls outside of the scope of this book, though; there are other excellent books that specialize in this. You can find a basic example of a callback member variable in the exercises at the end of the chapter.

Type Aliases for Function Pointers

As we're sure you will agree, the syntax required to define a function pointer variable is rather horrendous. The less you have to type this syntax, the better. The auto keyword can help, but there are times when you do want to specify the type of a function pointer explicitly; for instance, when a function pointer is used as a function parameter or as an object's member variable. Because "pointer to function" is just a type like any other, however, you can define an alias for such types using the using keyword (see Chapter 3).

As an example, why don't we consider the definition of the callback parameter in the findOptimum() function template of Ex19_02:

```
bool (*compare)(const T&, const T&)
```

Unfortunately, this type contains a template type parameter, T, which complicates matters a bit. Let's simplify that for a moment and instead start with a concrete instantiation of this type template:

```
bool (*string_compare)(const std::string&, const std::string&)
```

You obtain the type of this variable by copying the entire variable definition and dropping the variable name, string_compare:

```
bool (*)(const std::string&, const std::string&)
```

Quite a mouthful this type is, so it's well worth creating an alias for. With the modern syntax based on the using keyword, defining an alias for this type is as straightforward as this:

```
using StringComparison = bool (*)(const std::string&, const std::string&);
```

The right side of this assignment-like declaration simply matches the type name; the left side is a name of your choosing. With this type alias in place, declaring a parameter such as string_compare immediately becomes a lot less tedious and a lot more readable:

```
StringComparison string_compare
```

One nice thing about the using syntax for type aliases is that it extends gracefully to templated types. To define an alias for the type of the compare callback parameter of Ex19_02, all you need to do is generalize the StringComparison definition in the most natural way; you simply prepend it with the template keyword, as always, followed by a template parameter list between angular brackets:

```
template <typename T>
using Comparison = bool (*)(const T&, const T&);
```

This defines an *alias template*, which is a template that generates type aliases. In the optimum module, you could use this template to simplify the signature of findOptimum():

```
export template <typename T>
using Comparison = bool (*)(const T&, const T&);
export template <typename T>
const T* findOptimum(const std::vector<T>& values, Comparison<T> compare);
```

Of course, you must not forget to export the alias template from the module as well.

Once imported, you can also use the alias template to define a variable with a concrete type:

```
Comparison<std::string> string_compare{ longer };
```

░ **Note** For historical reference, this is how you would define StringComparison using the old typedef syntax (see also Chapter 3):

```
typedef bool (*StringComparison)(const std::string&, const std::string&);
```

With the alias name needlessly appearing in the middle, this syntax is again far more complex than the one that uses the using keyword. Defining an alias template, moreover, is not even possible with typedef. Our conclusion from Chapter 3 thus stands, and stronger than ever: to define a type alias, you should always use using; typedef has no place in modern C++.

Function Objects

Just like pointers to data values, pointers to functions are low-level language constructs that C++ has inherited from the C programming language. And just like raw pointers, function pointers have their limitations, which can be overcome using an object-oriented approach. In Chapter 6 you learned that smart pointers are the object-oriented answer to the inherently unsafe raw pointers. In this section we introduce a similar technique where objects are used as a more powerful alternative to plain C-style function pointers. These objects are called *function objects* or *functors* (the two terms are synonymous). Like a function pointer, a function object acts precisely like a function; but unlike a raw function pointer, it is a full-fledged class type object—complete with its own member variables and possibly even various other member functions. We'll show you that function objects are hence far more powerful and expressive than plain C-style function pointers.

Basic Function Objects

A *function object* or *functor* is an object that can be called as if it were a function. The key in constructing one is to overload the function call operator, as was briefly introduced in Chapter 13. To see how this is done, we will define a class of function objects that encapsulate this simple function:

```
bool less(int one, int other) { return one < other; }
```

Quickly recapping what you saw in Chapter 13, here is how you define a class with an overloaded function call operator:

```
// Less.cppm - A basic class of functor objects
export module less;

export class Less
{
public:
  bool operator()(int a, int b) const { return a < b; }
};
```

This basic functor class has only one member: a function call operator. The main thing to remember here is that the function call operator is denoted with operator() and that its actual parameter list is specified only *after* an initial set of empty parentheses. Beyond that, this is just like any other operator function.

With this class definition, you can create your very first function object and then call it as if it were an actual function like so:

```
Less less;                   // Create a 'less than' functor...
bool is_less{ less(5, 6) }; // ... and 'call' it
std::println(is_less ? "5 is less than 6" : "Huh?");
```

Of course, what is being "called" is not the object but rather its function call operator function. If you're into self-harm and code-obscuring, you could thus also write less.operator()(5,6) instead.

▓ **Tip**   Because the function call operator of Less clearly needs no this pointer, C++23 allows you to define it as a static member function (as noted also in Chapter 13). less.operator()(5,6) then becomes equivalent to Less::operator()(5,6). static operators thus facilitate optimizations that eliminate a functor's this pointer, particularly if a functor's body is not inlinable (for instance, because it is not exported from the module interface). They also enable expressions such as &Less::operator(), enabling you to easily use the operator in contexts that require a function pointer. We recommend you define all function call operators that don't use the this pointer as static members.

Granted, creating a functor just to call it right after is not very useful at all. Things become a bit more interesting already if you use a functor as a callback function. To demonstrate this, you'll first have to generalize the findOptimum() template of Ex19_02 since currently it only accepts a function pointer for its callback argument. Of course, creating an extra overload specifically for the Less type would defeat the purpose of having a higher-order function with a callback in the first place. And there's also no such thing as one single type that encompasses all function object class types. The most common way to generalize a function such as findOptimum() is therefore to declare a second template type parameter and use it as the type of the compare parameter:

```cpp
// Optimum.cppm - a function template to determine the optimum element in a given vector
export module optimum;
import std;

export template <typename T, typename Comparison>
const T* findOptimum(const std::vector<T>& values, Comparison compare)
{
  if (values.empty()) return nullptr;

  const T* optimum{ &values[0] };
  for (std::size_t i {1}; i < values.size(); ++i)
  {
    if (compare(values[i], *optimum))
      optimum = &values[i];
  }
  return optimum;
}
```

Because Comparison is a template type parameter, you can now invoke findOptimum() with compare arguments of any type you like. Naturally, the template's instantiation will then only compile if the compare argument is a function-like value that can be called with two T& arguments. And you know of two categories of arguments that might fit this bill already:

- Function pointers of type bool (*)(const T&, const T&) (or similar types, such as for instance bool (*)(T, T)). Therefore, if you were to plug this new definition of findOptimum<>() into Ex19_02, this example would still work precisely like before.

- Function objects of a type like Less that have a corresponding function call operator.

Both options are demonstrated in our next example:

```cpp
// Ex19_03.cpp - Exercising the use of a functor as callback functions
import std;
import optimum;
import less;

template <typename T>
bool greater(const T& one, const T& other) { return one > other; }

int main()
{
  Less less;      // Create a 'less than' functor

  std::vector numbers{ 91, 18, 92, 22, 13, 43 };
  std::println("Minimum element: {}", *findOptimum(numbers, less));
  std::println("Maximum element: {}", *findOptimum(numbers, greater<int>));
}
```

758

Standard Function Objects

You can customize many templates of the Standard Library by providing them with a first-class function, similar to what you did with findOptimum<>() in examples Ex19_02 and Ex19_03. For regular functions you can mostly use a plain function pointer, but for built-in operators that is not an option. You cannot create a pointer to a built-in operator. Of course, it's easy to quickly define either a function (as in Ex19_02) or a functor class (Less in Ex19_03) that emulates the operator's behavior, but doing so for every operator all the time would become tedious very fast.

Of course, this did not escape the designers of the Standard Library either. The <functional> module of the Standard Library therefore defines a series of function object class templates, one for every built-in operator you may want to pass to other templates. The class template std::less<>, for instance, is fundamentally analogous to the Less template of Ex19_03. You could thus replace the definition of the less variable in Ex19_03 with this one:

```
std::less<int> less;    // Create a 'less than' functor
```

▓ **Tip**   As of C++14, the recommended way to use the function object types of the <functional> module is by omitting the type argument as follows:

```
std::less<> less;    // Create a 'less than' functor
```

Functors of type std::less<> (or std::less<void>, which is equivalent) generally produce more efficient code than those of type std::less<T> with T different from void. The reason is that unlike std::less<T>, std::less<> defines a function call operator *member function template*, capable of instantiating specialized operators for any pair of argument types. This matters especially for *heterogeneous* comparisons where the argument types differ. The specialized instantiations of std::less<>'s operator template can then avoid potentially costly implicit conversions of their input arguments (such as, for instance, the conversion of string literals to std::string when comparing with a std::less<std::string> functor). Long story short, if you simply always omit the type argument, you're guaranteed that the compiler can generate optimal code under all circumstances. Plus, it saves you some typing, so it's a clear win-win!

Table 19-1 lists the complete set of templates. As always, all these types are defined in the std namespace.

Table 19-1.   *The Function Object Class Templates Offered by the <functional> Module*

Comparisons	less<>, greater<>, less_equal<>, greater_equal<>, equal_to<>, not_equal_to<>, compare_three_way<>
Arithmetic operations	plus<>, minus<>, multiplies<>, divides<>, modulus<>, negate<>
Logical operations	logical_and<>, logical_or<>, logical_not<>
Bitwise operations	bit_and<>, bit_or<>, bit_xor<>, bit_not<>

We could use `std::greater<>` to replace our `greater<>` function template of `Ex19_03`. Now isn't that great?

```
std::vector numbers{ 91, 18, 92, 22, 13, 43 };
std::println("Minimum element: {}", *findOptimum(numbers, std::less<>{}));
std::println("Maximum element: {}", *findOptimum(numbers, std::greater<>{}));
```

This time we created the `std::less<>` and `greater<>` function objects as temporary objects directly inside the function call expression itself, rather than storing them first in a named variable. You can find this variant of the program in `Ex19_03A`.

Parameterized Function Objects

Perhaps you've already noticed that, in fact, none of the function objects that you have seen thus far has been more powerful than a plain function pointer. Why go through all the trouble of defining a class with a function call operator if defining a plain function is so much easier? Surely, there must be more to function objects than this?

Indeed there is. Function objects only truly become interesting once you start adding more members—either variables or functions. Building on the same `findOptimum()` example as always, suppose you want to search not for the smallest or largest number but instead for the number that is nearest to some user-provided value. There is no clean way for you to accomplish this using functions and pointers to functions. Think about it, how would the callback's function body ever get access to the value that the user has entered? There is no clean way for you to pass this value along to the function if all you have is a pointer. If you use a function-like object, however, you can pass along any information you want by storing it in the object's member variables. The easiest is if we just show you how you might do this:

```
// Nearer.cppm
// A class of function objects that compare two values based on how close they are
// to some third value that was provided to the functor at construction time.
export module nearer;
import std;    // For std::abs()

export class Nearer
{
public:
  explicit Nearer(int value) : m_value(value) {}
  bool operator()(int x, int y) const
  {
    return std::abs(x - m_value) < std::abs(y - m_value);
  }
private:
  int m_value;
};
```

Every function object of type `Nearer` has a member variable `m_value` in which it stores the value to compare with. This value is passed in through its constructor, so it could easily be a number that was entered by the user earlier. Of course, the object's function call operator has access to this number as well, which is the part that would not have been possible when using a function pointer as a callback. Note that this is also the first function call operator you've encountered that cannot be static.

This program illustrates how to use the Nearer functor class:

```cpp
// Ex19_04.cpp - Exercising a function object with a member variable
import std;
import optimum;
import nearer;

int main()
{
  std::vector numbers{ 91, 18, 92, 22, 13, 43 };

  int number_to_search_for {};
  std::print("Please enter a number: ");
  std::cin >> number_to_search_for;

  std::println("The number nearest to {} is {}",
    number_to_search_for, *findOptimum(numbers, Nearer{ number_to_search_for }));
}
```

A possible session then might go like this:

```
Please enter a number: 50
The number nearest to 50 is 43
```

■ **Note**   In Chapter 13 we explained an example of real-world function objects that go even a step further than the Nearer class of Ex19_04: the pseudo-random number generators of the <random> module. These objects do not simply store some (immutable) member variables, they even alter them upon each invocation of their function call operator so that they can return a different (seemingly random) number each time. This just goes to shows how much more powerful than function pointers function objects can be.

Lambda Expressions

Ex19_04 clearly demonstrates a couple of things. First, it shows the potential of passing a function object as a callback. Given that it can have any number of members, function objects are certainly much more powerful than plain function pointers. But that's not all that we can learn from Ex19_04. Indeed, if there's one more thing that Ex19_04 clearly exposes, it's that defining a class for a function object requires you to write quite some code. Even a simple callback class such as Nearer—which has only one member variable—quickly takes about ten lines of code already.

This is where *lambda expressions* come in. They offer you a convenient, compact syntax to quickly define callback functions or functors. And not only is the syntax compact, lambda expressions also allow you to define the callback's logic right there where you want to use it. This is often much better than having to define this logic somewhere in the function call operator of some class definition. Lambda expressions thus generally lead to particularly expressive yet still very readable code.

A *lambda expression* has a lot in common with a function definition. In its most basic form, a lambda expression basically provides a way to define a function with no name, an *anonymous function*. But lambda expressions are far more powerful than that. In general, a lambda expression effectively defines a full-blown function object that can carry any number of member variables. The beauty is that there's no need for an explicit definition of the type of this object anymore; the compiler generates this type automatically for you.

Practically speaking, you'll find that a lambda expression is different from a regular function in that it can access variables that exist in the enclosing scope where it is defined. Thinking back to Ex19_04, for instance, a lambda expression there would be able to access number_to_search_for, the number that was entered by the user. Before we examine how lambda expressions get access to local variables, though, let's first take one step back again and begin by explaining how you can define a basic *unnamed* or *anonymous function* using a lambda expression.

Defining a Lambda Expression

Consider the following basic lambda expression:

```
[] (int x, int y) { return x < y; }
```

As you can see, the definition of a lambda expression indeed looks very much like the definition of a function. The main difference is that a lambda expression starts with square brackets instead of a return type and a function name. The opening square brackets are called the *lambda introducer*. They mark the beginning of the lambda expression. There's more to the lambda introducer than there is here—the brackets are not always empty—but we'll explain this in more depth a little later. The lambda introducer is followed by the *lambda parameter list* between round parentheses. This list is exactly like a regular function parameter list (ever since C++14, default parameter values are even allowed). In this case, there's two int parameters: x and y.

▓ **Tip**   For lambda functions without parameters, you may omit the empty parameter list, ( ). That is, a lambda expression of form [ ]( ) {...} may be further shortened to [ ] {...}. An empty lambda initializer, [ ], must not be omitted, though. The lambda initializer is always required to signal the start of a lambda expression.

The body of the lambda expression between braces follows the parameter list, again just like a normal function. The body for this lambda contains just one statement, a return statement that also calculates the value that is returned. In general, the body of a lambda can contain any number of statements. The return type defaults to that of the value returned. If nothing is returned, the return type is void.

It's educational to have at least a basic notion of how lambda expressions are compiled. This will aid you later in understanding how more advanced lambda expressions behave. Whenever the compiler encounters a lambda expression, it internally generates a new class type. In the case of our example, the generated class will be similar to the Less class you defined in Ex19_03. Slightly simplified, such a class might look something like this:

```
class __Lambda8C1
{
public:
  auto operator()(int x, int y) const { return x < y; }
};
```

A first notable difference is that the implicit class definition will have some unique, compiler-generated name. We picked __Lambda8C1 here, but your compiler could use whatever name it wants. There's no telling what this name will be (at least not at compile time), nor is there any guarantee it will still be the same the next time you compile the same program. This somewhat limits the way in which these function objects can be used, but not by much—as we'll show you in one of the next subsections.

Another point worth noting first is that, at least by default, a lambda expression results in a function call operator() with a return type equal to auto. You first encountered the use of auto as a return type in Chapter 8. Back then, we explained to you that the compiler then attempts to deduce the actual return type from the return statements in the function's body. There were some limitations, though: auto return type deduction requires that all return statements of the function return a value of the same type. The compiler will never apply any implicit conversions—any conversions need to be added by you explicitly. This same limitation therefore applies to the body of a lambda expression.

You do have the option to specify the return type of a lambda function explicitly. You could do this to have the compiler generate implicit conversions for the return statements or simply to make the code more self-documenting. While clearly not necessary here, you could supply a return type for the previous lambda like this:

```
[] (int x, int y) -> bool { return x < y; }
```

The return type is specified following the -> operator that comes after the parameter list and is type bool here.

▓ **Note**   If a lambda expression has an empty lambda initializer, [ ], you can make the implied function call operator static by adding the static keyword after the function parameter list as follows (the static specifier goes before the trailing return type if one is present):

```
[] (int x, int y) static { return x < y; }
```

As always, doing so may in principle lead to more optimal performance. But since lambda expressions are typically inlined (at which point any self-respecting compiler will realize the this pointer is redundant regardless), adding static to lambda expressions is perhaps less likely to make a difference.

Naming a Lambda Closure

As you know, a lambda expression evaluates to a function object. This function object is formally called a *lambda closure*, although many also refer to it informally as either a *lambda function* or a *lambda*. You don't know a priori what the type of the lambda closure will be; only the compiler does. The only way to store the lambda object in a variable is thus to have the compiler deduce the type for you:

```
auto less{ [] (int x, int y) { return x < y; } };
```

The auto keyword tells the compiler to figure out the type that the variable less should have from what appears on the right of the assignment—in this case a lambda expression. Supposing the compiler generates a type with the name __Lambda8C1 for this lambda expression (as shown earlier), this statement is then effectively compiled as follows:

```
__Lambda8C1 less;
```

Passing a Lambda Expression to a Function Template

You can use less just like the equivalent functor of Ex19_03:

```
auto less{ [] (int x, int y) { return x < y; } };
std::println("Minimum element: {}", *findOptimum(numbers, less));
```

This works because the callback parameter of the findOptimum() template of Ex19_03 is declared with a template type parameter, which the compiler can substitute with whatever name it picked for the lambda closure's generated type:

```
template <typename T, typename Comparison>
const T* findOptimum(const std::vector<T>& values, Comparison compare);
```

Rather than first storing a lambda closure in a named variable, though, it is far more common to directly use a lambda expression as a callback argument as follows:

```
std::println("Minimum element: {}",
  *findOptimum(numbers, [] (int x, int y) { return x < y; })
);
```

Ex19_05 is yet another variant of Ex19_02 and Ex19_03, only this time one that uses lambda expressions to define all its callback functions:

```
// Ex19_05.cpp - Using lambda expressions as callback functions
import std;
import optimum;

int main()
{
  std::vector numbers{ 91, 18, 92, 22, 13, 43 };
  std::println("Minimum element: {}",
            *findOptimum(numbers, [](int x, int y) { return x < y; }));
  std::println("Maximum element: {}",
            *findOptimum(numbers, [](int x, int y) { return x > y; }));

  // Define two anonymous comparison functions for strings:
  auto alpha{ [](std::string_view x, std::string_view y) { return x > y; } };
  auto longer{
     [](std::string_view x, std::string_view y) { return x.length() > y.length(); } };

  std::vector<std::string> names{ "Moe", "Larry", "Shemp", "Curly", "Joe", "Curly Joe" };
  std::println("Alphabetically last name: {}", *findOptimum(names, alpha));
  std::println("Longest name: {}", *findOptimum(names, longer));
}
```

The result will be the same as before. Clearly, if you only need to sort strings on their length once, a lambda expression is more convenient than defining a separate longer() function and far more interesting than defining a Longer functor class.

▦ **Tip** Using a standard functor type is generally more compact and readable than a lambda expression. For instance, you can readily replace the first lambda expressions in Ex19_05.cpp with std::less<> and std::greater<> as follows (see also Ex19_05A):

```
std::println("Minimum element: {}", *findOptimum(numbers, std::less<>{}));
std::println("Maximum element: {}", *findOptimum(numbers, std::greater<>{}));
```

Generic Lambdas

A *generic lambda* is a lambda expression where at least one placeholder type, such as auto, auto&, or const auto& is used as a parameter type. Doing so effectively turns the function call operator of the generated class into a *template*. Precisely as if you would have used the abbreviated function template syntax (see Chapter 10) for this member function. In Ex19_05, for instance, you could replace the definitions of the alpha and longer variables with the following (best not to use plain auto as a placeholder here because strings would needlessly be copied during sorting):

```
auto alpha{ [](const auto& x, const auto& y) { return x > y; } };
auto longer{ [](const auto& x, const auto& y) { return x.length() > y.length(); } };
```

This generates two unnamed functor classes, each with a member function template that instantiates function call operators. Inside findOptimum(), these operator templates are then instantiated with const string& for both parameter types. You can further underline the fact that these lambdas are effectively generic by adding the following line to Ex19_05 (see Ex19_05B):

```
// The generic alpha functor works for any types that allow > comparison:
std::println("{} {} {}", alpha(1, 2), alpha(3.0, 4.0), alpha(5, 6.0));
```

This will instantiate the function call operator template of the generic alpha closure three more times: once to compare two ints, once to compare two doubles, and once to compare an int to a double.

▦ **Note** Our generic lambda functor alpha is thus very similar to a functor of type std::greater<> (instantiated with an empty template argument list), although the latter is still slightly more effective in certain edge cases.

As of C++20, you can use a non-abbreviated syntax to define generic lambdas as well. That is, you can explicitly list and name template parameters prior to the function parameter list. Here is an example:

```
auto alpha = []<typename T>(const T& x, const T& y) { return x > y; };
```

With this new definition, compilation of the expression alpha(5, 6.0) will fail because the compiler cannot unambiguously deduce the correct type for the template type parameter T.

The Capture Clause

As we've said before, the lambda introducer, [], is not necessarily empty. It can contain a *capture clause* that specifies how variables in the enclosing scope can be accessed from within the body of the lambda. The body of a lambda expression with nothing between the square brackets can work only with the arguments and with variables that are defined locally within the lambda. A lambda with no capture clause is called a *stateless lambda expression* because it cannot access anything in its enclosing scope.

If used in isolation, a *capture default* clause applies to all variables in the scope enclosing the definition of the lambda. There are two capture defaults: = and &. We'll discuss both of them in turn next. The capture clause can contain only one of the capture defaults, never both.

Capturing by Value

If you put = between the square brackets, the body of the lambda can access all automatic variables in the enclosing scope by value. That is, while the values of all variables are made available within the lambda expression, the values stored in the original variables cannot be changed. Here's an example based on Ex19_04:

```
// Ex19_06.cpp
// Using a default capture-by-value clause to access a local variable
// from within the body of a lambda expression.
import std;
import optimum;

int main()
{
  std::vector numbers{ 91, 18, 92, 22, 13, 43 };

  int number_to_search_for {};
  std::print("Please enter a number: ");
  std::cin >> number_to_search_for;

  auto nearer { [=](int x, int y) {
    return std::abs(x - number_to_search_for) < std::abs(y - number_to_search_for);
  }};
  std::println("The number nearest to {} is {}",
              number_to_search_for, *findOptimum(numbers, nearer));
}
```

The = capture clause allows all the variables that are in scope where the definition of the lambda appears to be accessed by value from within the body of the lambda expression. In Ex19_06, this means that the lambda's body has, at least in principle, access to main()'s two local variables—numbers and number_to_search_for. The effect of capturing local variables by value is rather different from passing arguments by value, though. To properly understand how capturing works, it's again instructive to study the class that the compiler might generate for the lambda expression of Ex19_06:

```
class __Lambda9d5
{
public:
  __Lambda9d5(const int& arg1) : number_to_search_for(arg1) {}

  auto operator()(int x, int y) const
  {
    return std::abs(x - number_to_search_for) < std::abs(y - number_to_search_for);
  }
```

```
private:
  int number_to_search_for;
};
```

The lambda expression itself is then compiled as follows:

```
__Lambda9d5 nearer{ number_to_search_for };
```

It should come as no surprise that this class is completely equivalent to the Nearer class we defined earlier in Ex19_04. Concretely, the closure object has one member per local variable of the surrounding scope that is used inside the lambda's function body. We say that these variables are *captured* by the lambda. At least conceptually, the member variables of the generated class have the same name as the variables that were captured. That way, the lambda expression's body appears to have access to variables of the surrounding scope, while in reality it is accessing the corresponding member variables that are stored inside the lambda closure.

▓ **Note**   Variables that are not used by the lambda expression's body, such as the numbers vector in Ex19_06, are never captured by a default capture clause such as =.

The = clause causes all variables to be captured by value, which is why the number_to_search_for member variable has a value type (in this case, type int). This number_to_search_for member contains, in other words, a *copy* of the original local variable with the same name. While this implies that the value of the original number_to_search_for variable is in a sense available during the function's execution, you cannot possibly update its value. Even if updates to this member were allowed, you'd only be updating a copy. To avoid any confusion, the compiler therefore even arranges it so that by default you cannot update number_to_search_for at all from within the lambda's body—not even the copy that is stored in the closure's member variable. It does so by declaring the function call operator, operator(), as const. You'll recall from Chapter 12 that you cannot modify any of the member variables of an object from within one of its const member functions.

▓ **Tip**   In the unlikely event that you do want to alter a variable that was captured by value, you can add the keyword mutable to the definition of a lambda expression, right after the parameter list. Doing so causes the compiler to omit the const keyword from the function call operator of the generated class. Remember that you'd still only be updating a *copy* of the original variable. If you want to update the local variable itself, you should capture it by reference. Capturing variables by reference is explained next.

Capturing by Reference

If you put & between the square brackets, all variables in the enclosing scope are accessible by reference, so their values can be changed by the code in the body of the lambda. To count the number of comparisons performed by findOptimum(), for instance, you could use this lambda expression:

```
unsigned count {};
auto counter{ [&](int x, int y) { ++count; return x < y; } };
findOptimum(numbers, counter);
```

All variables within the outer scope are available by reference, so the lambda can both use and alter their values. If you plug this code snippet into Ex19_06, for instance, the value of count after the call to findOptimum<>() will be 5.

For completeness, this is a class similar to the one that your compiler would generate for this lambda expression:

```
class __Lambda6c5
{
public:
  __Lambda6c5(unsigned& arg1) : count(arg1) {}
  auto operator()(int x, int y) const { ++count; return x < y; }
private:
  unsigned& count;
};
```

Note that this time the captured variable count is stored in the closure's member variable by reference. The ++count increment in this operator() will compile, even though that member function is declared with const. Any modification to a reference leaves the function object itself unaltered. It is the variable that the count reference refers to that is modified instead. The mutable keyword is therefore not needed in this case.

Capturing Specific Variables

You can identify specific variables in the enclosing scope that you want to access by listing them in the capture clause. For each variable, you can choose whether it should be captured either by value or by reference. You capture a specific variable by reference by prefixing its name with &. You could rewrite the previous statement as follows:

```
auto counter{ [&count](int x, int y) { ++count; return x < y; } };
```

Here, count is the only variable in the enclosing scope that can be accessed from within the body of the lambda. The &count specification makes it available by reference. Without the &, the count variable in the outer scope would be available by value and not updatable. The lambda expression in Ex19_06, in other words, could also be written as follows:

```
auto nearer { [number_to_search_for](int x, int y) {
  return std::abs(x - number_to_search_for) < std::abs(y - number_to_search_for);
}};
```

▓ **Caution**   You mustn't prefix the names of the variables that you want to capture by value with =. The capture clause [=number_to_search_for], for example, is invalid; the only correct syntax is [number_to_search_for].

When you put several variables in the capture clause, you separate them with commas. You can freely mix variables that are captured by value with others that are captured by reference. You can also include a capture default in the capture clause along with specific variable names that are to be captured. The capture clause [=, &counter], for instance, would allow access to counter by reference and any other variables in the enclosing scope by value. Analogously, you could write a clause such as [&, number_to_search_for], which would capture number_to_search_for by value and all other variables by reference. If present, the capture default (= or &) must be the first item in the capture list.

▓ **Caution**   The capture default, if used, should always come first. Capture clauses such as [&counter, =] or [number_to_search_for, &] are not allowed.

▓ **Caution**   If you use the = capture default, you are no longer allowed to capture any specific variables by value; similarly, if you use &, you can no longer capture specific variables by reference. Capture clauses such as [&, &counter] or [=, &counter, number_to_search_for] are therefore not allowed.

Capturing the this Pointer

In this penultimate subsection on capturing variables, we'll discuss how to use a lambda expression from within the member function of a class. Sadistically beating the findOptimum<>() example to death one last time, suppose you defined this class:

```
// Finder.cppm - Small class that uses a lambda expression in a member function
export module finder;
import std;

export class Finder
{
public:
  double getNumberToSearchFor() const;
  void setNumberToSearchFor(double n);

  std::optional<double> findNearest(const std::vector<double>& values) const;
private:
  double m_number_to_search_for {};
};
```

A fully functional implementation of the Finder example is available under Ex19_07. The getter and setter are of no particular interest, but to define findNearest(), you of course want to reuse the findOptimum<>() template from earlier. A reasonable first attempt at this might look as follows:

```
std::optional<double> Finder::findNearest(const std::vector<double>& values) const
{
  if (values.empty())
    return std::nullopt;
  else
```

```
    return *findOptimum(values, [m_number_to_search_for](double x, double y) {
      return std::abs(x - m_number_to_search_for) < std::abs(y - m_number_to_search_for);
    });
}
```

Unfortunately, though, your compiler won't be too happy with this. The problem is that this time m_number_to_search_for is the name of a member variable rather than that of a local variable. And member variables cannot be captured, neither by value nor by reference; only local variables and function arguments can. To give a lambda expression access to the current object's members, you should instead add the keyword this to the capture clause, like so:

```
    return *findOptimum(values, [this](double x, double y) {
      return std::abs(x - m_number_to_search_for) < std::abs(y - m_number_to_search_for);
    });
```

By capturing the this pointer, you effectively give the lambda expression access to all members that the surrounding member function has access to. That is, even though the lambda closure will be an object of a class other than Finder, its function call operator will still have access to all protected and private members of Finder, including the member variable m_number_to_search_for, which is normally private to Finder. When we say *all* members, we do mean all members. Next to member variables, a lambda expression thus has access to all member functions as well—whether public, protected, or private. Another way to write our example lambda is therefore as follows:

```
return *findOptimum(values, [this](double x, double y) {
  return std::abs(x - getNumberToSearchFor()) < std::abs(y - getNumberToSearchFor());
});
```

■ **Note**   Precisely like in the member function itself, there is no need to add this-> when accessing a member. The compiler takes care of that for you.

Together with the this pointer, you can still capture other variables as well. You can combine this with a & or = capture default and/or any sequence of captures of named variables. Examples of such capture clauses are [=, this], [this, &counter], and [x, this, &counter].

■ **Caution**   The = capture default technically still implies that the this pointer is captured, but this behavior was deprecated in C++20 and should no longer be relied upon. That is, in older code, you may still encounter expressions such as this:

```
return *findOptimum(values, [=](double x, double y) {  // Captures this (deprecated)
    const double n = m_number_to_search_for;
    return std::abs(x - n) < std::abs(y - n);
  });
```

In C++20 code, you should always capture the this pointer explicitly, never implicitly through = (your compiler will likely warn you if you do not).

Capturing Extra Variables

So far, all variables that we captured into a lambda closure were available, with the same name, in the scope surrounding the lambda expression. But you can also introduce new variables in a capture clause, variables that do not exist in the surrounding scope. In general, the syntax for this looks as follows:

```
[..., name = initializer, ...](...) { ... };
```

This effectively introduces an auto-typed member variable called name in the implicitly generated closure class. The type of name is deduced from the type that results from evaluating *initializer*, which can be any expression and may refer to any variable available in the surrounding scope.

Just as an example, in Ex19_07, instead of capturing the this pointer to gain access to m_number_to_search_for, you could also use the following capture clause:

```
return *findOptimum(values, [n = m_number_to_search_for](double x, double y) {
   return std::abs(x - n) < std::abs(y - n);
});
```

This captures the value of m_number_to_search_for in a variable called n, making the latter available in the lambda expression's function body.

▨ **Tip** To capture the result of *initializer* in an auto&-typed reference variable instead, you add & in front of its name. Building on the same example, if m_number_to_search_for were some larger object you'd rather not copy, you could capture a reference to it like this: [&n = m_number_to_search_for].

▨ **Tip** A common use of initialized lambda captures is to capture move-only variables in a lambda closure. Suppose that uncopiable is a variable of type std::unique_ptr<MyClass>. Then you could move uncopiable into a lambda closure as follows:

```
auto lambda = [moved = std::move(uncopiable)] { /* may use moved */ };
```

In fact, you'll often see this used as follows:

```
auto lambda = [uncopiable = std::move(uncopiable)] { /* may use uncopiable */ };
```

That is, an initialized capture variable can have the same name as a variable in the surrounding scope.

The std::function<> Template

The type of a function pointer is very different from that of a function object or lambda closure. The former is a pointer, and the latter is a class. At first sight, it might thus seem that the only way to write code that works for any conceivable callback—that is, a function pointer, function object, or lambda closure—is to use either auto or a template type parameter. This is what we did for our findOptimum<>() template in earlier examples. The same technique is heavily used throughout the Standard Library, as you will see in the next chapter.

Using templates does have its cost. You risk template code bloat, where the compiler has to generate specialized code for all different types of callbacks, even when it's not required for performance reasons. It also has its limitations. What if you needed a vector<> of callback functions—a vector<> that is potentially filled with a mixture of function pointers, function objects, and lambda closures?

To cater to these types of scenarios, the <functional> module defines the std::function<> template. With objects of type std::function<>, you can store, copy, move, and invoke any kind of function-like entity—be it a function pointer, function object, or lambda closure. The following example demonstrates precisely that:

```cpp
// Ex19_08.cpp
// Using the std::function<> template
import std;

// A global less() function
bool less(int x, int y) { return x < y; }

int main()
{
  const int a{ 18 }, b{ 8 };

  std::function<bool(int,int)> compare;

  compare = less;              // Store a function pointer into compare
  std::println("{} < {}: {}", a, b, compare(a, b));

  compare = std::greater<>{};  // Store a function object into compare
  std::println("{} > {}: {}", a, b, compare(a, b));

  int n{ 10 };                 // Store a lambda closure into compare
  compare = [n](int x, int y) { return std::abs(x - n) < std::abs(y - n); };
  std::println("{} nearer to {} than {}: {}", a, n, b, compare(a, b));

  // Check whether a function<> object is tied to an actual function
  std::function<void(const int&)> empty;
  if (empty)                   // Or, equivalently: 'if (empty != nullptr)'
  {
    std::println("Calling a default-constructed std::function<>?");
    empty(a);
  }
}
```

The output looks as follows:

```
18 < 8: false
18 > 8: true
18 nearer to 10 than 8: false
```

In the first part of the program, we define a std::function<> variable compare and assign it three different kinds of first-class functions in sequence: first, a function pointer; then, a function object; and finally, a lambda closure. In between, all three first-class functions are always called. More precisely, they are indirectly invoked through the compare variable's function call operator. A std::function<> itself is, in other words, a function object—one that can encapsulate any other kind of first-class function.

There is only one restriction for the function-like entities that can be assigned to a given std::function<>. They must all have matching return and parameter types. These type requirements are specified between the angular brackets of the std::function<> type template. In Ex19_08, for instance, compare has type std::function<bool(int,int)>. This indicates that compare will only accept first-class functions that can be called with two int arguments and that return a value that is convertible to bool.

■ **Tip**   A variable of type std::function<bool(int,int)> can store any first class function that is *callable* with two int arguments. This implies that functions with signatures such as (long, long), (const int&, const int&), or even (double, double) are acceptable as well. Similarly, the return type must not be exactly *equal* to bool. It suffices that its values can be *converted* into a Boolean. So, functions that return int or even double* or std::unique_ptr<std::string> would work as well. You can try this by playing with the signature and return type of the less() function in Ex19_08.cpp.

The general form of a std::function<> type template instantiation is as follows:

```
std::function<ReturnType(ParamType1, ..., ParamTypeN)>
```

The ReturnType is not optional, so to represent functions that do not return a value, you should specify void for the ReturnType. Similarly, for functions without parameters, you must still include an empty parameter type list, (). Reference types and const qualifiers are allowed for any of the ParamTypes, as well as for the ReturnType. All in all, it's a natural way of specifying function type requirements.

A default-constructed std::function<> object does not contain any callable first-class function yet. Invoking its function call operator would then result in a std::bad_function_call exception. In the last five lines of the program, we show you how you can verify whether a function<> is callable. As the example shows, there are two ways: a function<> implicitly converts to a Boolean (through a nonexplicit cast operator), or it can be compared to a nullptr (even though in general a function<> need not contain a pointer).

The std::function<> template forms a powerful alternative to the use of auto or template type parameters. The prime advantage of these other approaches is that std::function<> allows you to name the type of your first-class function variables. Being able to name this type facilitates the use of lambda-enabled callback functions in a much wider range of use cases than just higher-order function templates: std::function<> may, for example, be used for function parameters and member variables (without resorting to templates) or to store first-class functions into containers. The possibilities are limitless. You'll find a basic example of such a use in the exercises later.

■ **Tip** Functors stored inside `std::function<>` must be copiable, even if you never copy the `std::function<>` object. C++23 therefore introduced `std::move_only_function<>`, a non-copiable, move-only generic function container similar to `std::function<>` that can hold move-only functors. Added bonus is that you can also tune the signature of `std::move_only_function<>`'s function call operator by adding, for instance, `const` or `noexcept` specifiers to the function signature specification. (The function call operator of `std::function<>` is always `const`, even though it will happily call non-`const` members on an underlying functor.)

■ **Tip** When a stateless lambda closure is to be stored inside a `std::function<>` or `std::move_only_function<>`, you may want to specify it to be `static` (see earlier). This gives the function container a better chance at optimizing the storage and later invocation of the implicit function call operator.

Summary

This chapter introduced first-class functions in all their forms and flavors—from plain C-style function pointers over object-oriented functors to full-blown closures. We showed that lambda expressions offer a particularly versatile and expressive syntax, not just to define anonymous functions but also to create lambda closures capable of capturing any number of variables from their surroundings. Like function objects, lambda expressions are much more powerful than function pointers; but unlike function objects, they do not require you to specify a complete class—the compiler takes care of this tedious task for you. Lambda expressions really come into their own when combined, for instance, with the algorithms library of the C++ Standard Library, where many of the higher-order template functions have a parameter for which you can supply a lambda expression as the argument. We'll return to this in the next chapter.

The most important points covered in this chapter are as follows:

- A pointer to a function stores the address of a function. A pointer to a function can store the address of any function with the specified return type and number and types of parameters.

- You can use a pointer to a function to call the function at the address it contains. You can also pass a pointer to a function as a function argument.

- Function objects or functors are objects that behave precisely like a function by overloading the function call operator.

- Any number of member variables or functions can be added to a function object, making them far more versatile than plain function pointers.

- Function objects are powerful but do require quite some coding to set up. This is where lambda expressions come in; they alleviate the need to define the class for each function object you need.

- A lambda expression defines either an anonymous function or a function object. Lambda expressions are typically used to pass a function as an argument to another function.

- A lambda expression always begins with a lambda introducer that consists of a pair of square brackets that can be empty.

- The lambda introducer can contain a capture clause that specifies which variables in the enclosing scope can be accessed from the body of the lambda expression. Variables can be captured by value or by reference.

- There are two default capture clauses: = specifies that all variables in the enclosing scope are to be captured by value, and & specifies that all variables in the enclosing scope are captured by reference.

- A capture clause can specify specific variables to be captured by value or by reference.

- Variables captured by value will have a local copy created. The copy is not modifiable by default. Adding the `mutable` keyword following the parameter list allows local copies of variables captured by value to be modified.

- You can specify the return type for a lambda expression using the trailing return type syntax. If you don't specify a return type, the compiler deduces the return type from the first return statement in the body of the lambda.

- You can use the `std::function<>` template type that is defined in the `<functional>` module to specify the type of a function parameter that will accept any first-class function as an argument, including a lambda expression. In fact, it allows you to specify a named type for a variable—be it a function parameter, member variable, or automatic variable—that can hold a lambda closure. This is a feat that would otherwise be very hard, as only the compiler knows the name of this type.

EXERCISES

The following exercises enable you to try what you've learned in this chapter. If you get stuck, look back over the chapter for help. If you're still stuck after that, you can download the solutions from the Apress website (www.apress.com/book/download.html), but that really should be a last resort.

Exercise 19-1. Define and test a lambda expression that returns the number of elements in a `vector<string>` container that begin with a given letter. The vector is always the same, and should therefore not be passed as a function argument. Invoke the lambda function for a couple of letters.

Exercise 19-2. Throughout this book, you've already defined various sort functions, but they always sorted elements in ascending order and always according to the evaluation of the < operator. Clearly, a truly generic sorting function would benefit from a comparison callback, completely analogous to the `findOptimum<>()` templates that you worked with throughout this chapter. Take the solution to Exercise 10-6 and generalize its `sort<>()` template accordingly. Use this to sort a sequence of integers in descending order (that is, from large to small); to sort a sequence of characters alphabetically, ignoring the case ('a' must rank before 'B', even though 'B' < 'a'); and a sequence of floating-point values in ascending order but ignoring the sign (5.5 should thus precede -55.2 but not -3.14).

Exercise 19-3. In this exercise, you will compare the performance of two sorting algorithms. Given a sequence of n elements, quicksort should in theory use about $n \log_2 n$ comparisons on average, and bubble sort n^2. Let's see whether you can replicate these theoretical results in practice! Start by recycling the quicksort template from the previous exercise (perhaps rename it `quicksort()`?). Then you should extract the bubble sort algorithm from `Ex5_09` and generalize it to work for any element type and comparison callback as well. Next, you define an integer comparison functor that counts the number of times it is called (it can sort in any which order you prefer). Use it to count the number of comparisons that both algorithms need to sort, for instance, sequences of 500, 1,000, 2,000, and 4,000 random integer values between 1 and 100. Do these numbers agree, at least more or less, with the theoretical expectations?

Exercise 19-4. Create a generic function that collects all elements of a `vector<T>` that satisfy a given unary callback function. This callback function accepts a T value and returns a Boolean value that indicates whether the element should be part of the function's output. The resulting elements are to be collected and returned in another vector. Use this higher-order function to gather all numbers greater than a user-provided value from a sequence of integers, all capital letters from a sequence of characters, and all palindromes from a sequence of strings. A palindrome is a string that reads the same backward and forward (for example, `"racecar"`, `"noon"`, or `"kayak"`).

Exercise 19-5. As noted earlier, callback functions have many more interesting uses beyond serving as the argument to higher-order functions. They are used frequently in more advanced object-oriented designs as well. While creating a full-blown, complex system of intercommunicating objects would lead us too far astray, one basic example of how this could work should get you started. Begin by recovering the `Truckload` class from Exercise 18-1. Create a `DeliveryTruck` class that encapsulates a single `Truckload` object. Add `DeliveryTruck::deliverBox()` that not only applies `removeBox()` on its `Truckload` but also notifies any interested party that the given Box is delivered. It does so, of course, by calling a callback function. In fact, make it so that a `DeliveryTruck` can have any number of callback functions, all of which are to be called whenever a Box is delivered (the newly delivered Box is then to be passed to these callbacks as an argument). You could store these callbacks in a `std::vector<>` member, for instance. New callbacks are added through a `DeliveryTruck::registerOnDelivered()` member. We'll leave it to you to choose the appropriate types, but we do expect that all known flavors of first-class functions are supported (that is, function pointers, function objects, and lambda closures). In real life, such callbacks could be used by the trucking company to accumulate statistics on delivery times, to send an email to the customer that his Box has arrived, and so on. In your case, a smaller test program suffices. It should register at least these callback functions: a global `logDelivery()` function that prints information about the delivered Box to standard output, and a lambda expression that counts the number of times any Box is delivered.

Note: What you are to implement in this exercise is a variation of the often-used Observer pattern. In the terminology of this classical object-oriented design pattern, the `DeliveryTruck` is called the *observable*, and the entities that are being notified through the callbacks are called the *observers*. The nice thing about this pattern is that the observable does not need to know the concrete type of its observers, meaning that both can be developed and compiled completely independently from each other.

CHAPTER 20

■ ■ ■

Containers and Algorithms

The Standard Library offers an immense number of types and functions, and this number only increases with the release of every new version of the C++ standard. We could not possibly introduce the full range and scope of the Standard Library here in this book. For a contemporary overview of all the possibilities, details, and intricacies of this vast and growing library, we highly recommend the forthcoming *C++23 Standard Library Quick Reference* by Peter Van Weert and Marc Gregoire. Good online references exist as well, but these make it harder to quickly get a feeling of every single feature that the Standard Library has to offer.

Nevertheless, no introduction of C++ would be complete without at least a brief discussion of *containers* and *algorithms*, as well as the glue that binds them: *iterators*. Rarely is a program written in C++ without either of these concepts. And no doubt the same will soon be true for the *views* and *range adaptors* of C++20's <ranges> module. The goal of this chapter is thus to give you a high-level overview of these concepts. We'll focus on the underlying principles and ideas, as well as common usage idioms, rather than listing and showcasing every individual function and capability. Our goal is not to provide you with an exhaustive reference; for that we refer you to the aforementioned reference works. Instead, we aim to sufficiently arm you to be able to read, understand, and effectively browse such references.

In this chapter, you'll learn

- What containers the Standard Library has to offer beyond std::vector<> and std::array<>

- What the differences are between all container types, their advantages and disadvantages, and how to choose between them

- How to traverse the elements of any container using iterators

- What Standard Library algorithms are and how to use them effectively

- What the difference is between a range and a view

- How range-based algorithms and range adaptors allow you to perform complex algorithmic operations in an even more compact and elegant manner

Containers

We already introduced two of the most commonly used containers in Chapter 5: std::array<T,N> and std::vector<T>. Of course, not all containers store their elements in an array. There are countless other ways to arrange your data, each tailored to make one or the other operation more efficient. Arrays are great for linearly traversing elements, but they do not really lend themselves to quickly finding a particular element. If you're looking for the proverbial needle in a haystack, linearly traversing all stalks may not be the fastest way to go about it. If you organize your data such that all needles automatically group themselves in a

© Ivor Horton and Peter Van Weert 2023
I. Horton and P. Van Weert, *Beginning C++23*, https://doi.org/10.1007/978-1-4842-9343-0_20

common region, retrieving needles becomes much easier. This is where sets and maps come in (collectively called *associative containers*). Before we introduce these, though, let's first take a broader look at the different *sequence containers*.

Sequence Containers

A *sequence container* is a container that stores its elements sequentially, in some linear arrangement, one element after the other. The order in which the elements are stored is determined entirely by the user of the container. Both std::array<> and std::vector<> are sequence containers, but the Standard Library defines three more such container types. Each of the five sequence containers is backed by a different data structure. In this section, we'll briefly introduce each of them in turn.

Arrays

Both std::array<T,N> and std::vector<T> are backed by a single built-in array of T elements, precisely the kind you learned to use in Chapter 5. The advantage of using the containers is that they are easier to use than the built-in arrays and near impossible to misuse.

The key difference between std::array<> and std::vector<> is that the former is backed by a *statically* sized array, whereas the latter is backed by a *dynamic* array allocated in the free store. For an array<>, you therefore always need to specify the number of elements at compile time, which somewhat limits the possible use cases of this container. A vector<>, on the other hand, is capable of dynamically growing its array as you add more and more elements. It does this in much the same way as you did inside the push_back() function of our Array<> template in Chapter 18—only using more efficient techniques.

You know both these sequence containers already quite well from Chapter 5. The main thing we still want to add at this point is how you can add or delete elements in the middle of a vector<> (using insert() or erase()), rather than simply at the end (using push_back() or pop_back()). We can only do so, though, after we have introduced iterators, so we discuss this later in this chapter.

Lists

Out of all data structures that are used instead of an array, the simplest undoubtedly is the *linked list*. You already encountered linked lists at least twice in this book, first in Chapter 12 while working on the Truckload class and again while implementing a Stack<> template in Chapter 17. If you recall, a Truckload was essentially a container of Box objects. Internally, it stored each individual Box inside an object of a nested class called Package. Next to a Box, each Package object contained a pointer to the next Package in the list, thus linking together a long chain of tiny Package objects. We refer you to Chapter 12 for more details. The Stack<> class in Chapter 17 was essentially analogous, except that it used the more generic term Node instead of Package as the name for its nested class.

The Standard Library <forward_list> and <list> modules offer two container types that are implemented in a similar manner:

- std::forward_list<T> stores T values in a so-called singly-linked list. The term *singly-linked* refers to the fact that each node in the linked list has only a single link to another node—the next one in the list. This data structure is completely analogous to that of your Truckload and Stack<> types. Looking back, the Truckload class could simply have used a std::forward_list<std::shared_ptr<Box>>, and creating the Stack<T> template would've been much easier with a plain std::forward_list<T>.

- std::list<T> stores T values in a *doubly-linked list*, where each node not only has a pointer to the next node in the list but has one to the previous node as well. For Exercise 12-7 you created a Truckload class backed by an analogous data structure.

In theory, the key advantage of these linked list containers compared to the other sequence containers is that they facilitate insertions and removals of elements in the middle of the sequence. If you insert an element in the middle of a vector<>—as said, we'll show you how to do this later—the vector<> must first move all elements beyond the point of insertion one position to the right. Moreover, if the allocated array is not large enough to hold any more elements, a new larger array will have to be allocated and all elements moved into that one. With a linked list inserting an element in the middle involves virtually no overhead at all. All you need to do is create a new node and rewire some next and/or previous pointers.

The key disadvantage of linked lists, however, is that they lack the *random access* capability. Both array<> and vector<> are called *random-access containers* because you can instantly jump to any element with a given index. This capability is exposed through the array subscript operator, operator[], of both array<> and vector<> (and their at() function as well, of course). But with a linked list you cannot access any element in the list without first traversing an entire chain of nodes containing other elements (for a forward_list<>, you must always start at the first node of the list—the so-called *head*; for a list<>, you can start at either end). Being able to efficiently insert in the middle of a list means little if you must first linearly traverse half of the list to get there!

Another disadvantage is that linked lists typically exhibit particularly poor memory locality. The nodes of a list tend to become scattered around in free store memory, making it much harder for a computer to quickly fetch all elements. Linearly traversing a linked list is therefore much, much slower than linearly traversing an array<> or vector<>.

The combination of these disadvantages makes for this observation:

▨ **Tip**   While linked lists make for great practice in programming with pointers and dynamic memory, the need to use them in production code occurs only very rarely. A vector<> is nearly always the better choice. Even when elements need to be inserted in or removed from the middle at times, a vector<> normally remains the more efficient choice (today's computers are very good at moving blocks of memory around!).

In all our years of C++ programming, we have never used linked lists in practice. We will therefore not discuss them any further here.

Deque

The fifth and final sequence container is called std::deque<>. The term *deque* is short for *double-ended queue* and is pronounced /dɛk/, precisely like the word *deck* (as in a deck of cards). It is somewhat of a hybrid data structure with the following advantages:

- Just like array<> and vector<>, deque<> is a *random access container*, meaning it has constant-time operator[] and at() operations.

- Just like a list<>, a deque<> allows you to add elements in constant time at both ends of the sequence. A vector<> only supports constant-time additions to the back of the sequence (inserting in the front at least requires all the other elements to be moved one position to the right).

- Unlike a vector<>, the elements of a deque<> are never moved to another bigger array when adding to or removing from either the front or the back of the sequence. This means that T* pointers (and iterators; see later) to elements stored inside the container remain valid, provided you do not insert into or remove from the middle of the sequence using the functions explained later in this chapter.

In our experience, the latter advantage is mainly what makes a deque<> useful at times (the need to insert at both ends of a sequence occurs surprisingly seldom), particularly in more complex scenarios where other data structures store pointers to data that is stored inside a deque<>. For day-to-day use—and this accounts for well over 95 percent of the cases—your go-to sequence container should remain std::vector<>, though.

The following example shows basic use of a deque<>:

```cpp
// Ex20_01.cpp - Working with std::deque<>
import std;

int main()
{
  std::deque<int> my_deque;   // A deque<> allows efficient insertions
  my_deque.push_back(2);      // to both ends of the sequence
  my_deque.push_back(4);
  my_deque.push_front(1);

  my_deque[2] = 3;            // A deque<> is a random-access sequence container

  std::print("There are {} elements in my_deque: ", my_deque.size());

  for (int element : my_deque) // A deque<>, like all containers, is a range
    std::print("{} ", element);
  std::println("");
}
```

This code needs no further explanation. It produces this output:

```
There are 3 elements in my_deque: 1 2 3
```

At the end of Ex20_01, we looped over the elements of my_deque, printing them one at a time. We did this to illustrate that a deque<>, like any container, can be used in a range-based for loop. But std::println() can print containers directly as well (see Chapter 5). The output statements of Ex20_01, for instance, are more or less equivalent to this statement:

```cpp
std::println("There are {} elements in my_deque: {:n}", my_deque.size(), my_deque);
```

The n formatting flag, as introduced in Chapter 5, suppresses the square brackets that by default surround a formatted sequence container. As always, you cannot suppress the commas that separate the individual elements in standard formatting, though. The output of the println() statement therefore becomes as follows:

```
There are 3 elements in my_deque: 1, 2, 3
```

Key Operations

All standard containers—not just sequence containers—provide a similar set of functions, with analogous names and behaviors. All containers have empty(), clear(), and swap() functions and nearly all have a size() function (the only exception is std::forward_list<>). All containers can be compared using == and != and all except the unordered associative containers can be compared using <, >, <=, >=, and <=>. Like we said in the introduction of this chapter, however, it is not our intention to provide you with a detailed and complete reference. For that, we already referred you to other sources. What we do want to give you here is a brief overview of the key distinguishing operations of the various sequence containers.

With the exception of the fixed-size std::array<>, you can freely add or remove as many elements as you want to or from the front, the back, or even somewhere in the middle of the sequence. The following table shows some of the most important operations that the five sequence containers—vector<> (**V**), array<> (**A**), forward_list<> (**F**), list<> (**L**), and deque<> (**D**)—offer to insert, remove, or access their elements. If a square is filled, the corresponding container supports the operation.

Operation	V	A	L	F	D	Description
push_front() prepend_range() pop_front()	□	□	■	■	■	Adds or removes elements at the front of the sequence.
push_back() append_range() pop_back()	■	□	■	□	■	Adds or removes elements at the back of the sequence.
insert() insert_range() erase()	■	□	■	■	■	Inserts or removes elements at arbitrary positions. As explained later in this chapter, you indicate the positions at which to insert or remove elements using iterators. (Note: The corresponding members for forward_list<> are called insert_after(), insert_range_after(), and erase_after().)
front()	■	■	■	■	■	Returns a reference to the first element in the sequence.
back()	■	■	■	□	■	Returns a reference to the last element in the sequence.
operator[] at()	■	■	□	□	■	Returns a reference to the element at a given index.
data()	■	■	□	□	□	Returns a pointer to the start of the underlying array. This is useful to pass to legacy functions or C libraries.

Stacks and Queues

This section covers three related class templates: std::stack<>, std::queue<>, and std::priority_queue<>. They are called *container adaptors* because they are technically not containers themselves. Instead, they encapsulate one of the five sequential containers (by default either a vector<> or deque<>) and then use that container to implement a specific, very limited set of member functions. For instance, while a stack<> is typically backed by a deque<>, this deque<> is kept strictly private. It will never allow you to add or remove elements from the front of the encapsulated deque<>, nor will it allow you to access any of its elements by index. Container adaptors, in other words, employ the data-hiding principle introduced in Chapter 12 to force you to use the encapsulated containers only in a very specific way. For these specific yet common use cases of sequential data, using one of the adaptors is therefore safer and less error-prone than directly using the containers themselves.

LIFO vs. FIFO Semantics

A std::stack<T> represents a container with *last-in first-out* (LIFO) semantics—the last T element that goes in will be the first one to come out. You can compare it to a stack of plates in a self-service restaurant. Plates are added to the top, pushing down the other plates. A customer takes a plate from the top, which is the last added plate on the stack. You already created your own Stack<> template in Chapter 17.

A std::queue<> is similar to a stack<> but instead has *first-in first-out* (FIFO) semantics. You can compare it to a queue at a nightclub. A person who arrived before you will be allowed to enter before you (provided you do not grease the bouncer, that is—though there's no greasing a queue<>!).

The following example clearly shows the difference between both container adaptors:

```
// Ex20_02.cpp - Working with stacks and queues
import std;

int main()
{
  std::stack<int> stack;
  for (int i {}; i < 10; ++i)
    stack.push(i);

  std::print("The elements coming off the top of the stack:    ");
  while (!stack.empty())
  {
    std::print("{} ", stack.top());
    stack.pop();    // pop() is a void function!
  }
  std::println("");

  std::queue<int> queue;
  for (int i {}; i < 10; ++i)
    queue.push(i);

  std::print("The elements coming from the front of the queue: ");
  while (!queue.empty())
  {
    std::print("{} ", queue.front());
    queue.pop();    // pop() is a void function!
  }
  std::println("");
}
```

The program shows canonical use of both adaptors, first of a stack and then of a queue. Even though the same ten elements are added to both in the same order, the output confirms that they will be taken out in opposite orders:

```
The elements coming off the top of the stack:    9 8 7 6 5 4 3 2 1 0
The elements coming from the front of the queue: 0 1 2 3 4 5 6 7 8 9
```

Note that the pop() function does not return any element. You must typically first access these elements using top() or front(), depending on which adaptor you use. (Unsurprisingly, the same holds by the way for all pop_front() and pop_back() members of the various sequence containers.)

std::stack<> and queue<> provide only a few member functions beyond those used in the example. Both have the conventional size(), empty(), and swap() functions, but that is about it. Like we said, the interface of these adaptors is specifically tailored for one specific use and for that use alone.

▓ **Caution** Lacking begin() and end() functionality (see later), stacks and queues are not ranges. This means, for instance, that you cannot use them in range-based for loops or with any of the algorithms we discuss later in this chapter. You can also not inspect the contents of a stack or queue beyond the top() element of a stack or the front() and back() elements of a queue. (You can, however, print container adaptors directly with std::print() and format() functions.)

▓ **Tip** Container adaptors are typically used to manage elements that represent tasks that need to be executed in a setting where executing all tasks at once is unfeasible. If independent or consecutive tasks are scheduled, then a queue<> is often the most natural data structure to use. Tasks are then simply executed in the order in which they are requested. If the tasks represent subtasks of other scheduled or suspended tasks, then you normally want all subtasks to finish first before initiating or resuming their parent tasks. A stack<> is then the easiest approach (note that this is also how C++ executes functions—using a call *stack*!).

FIFO and LIFO are thus useful for most simple task scheduling applications; for more complex scenarios, priority-based scheduling may be required. This is what std::priority_queue<> provides, which is the container adaptor that we'll briefly introduce next.

Priority Queues

The final container adaptor is std::priority_queue<>, defined by the same <queue> module as queue<>. You can compare a priority queue to how a queue works at a *real* night club; that is, certain groups of guests will get in before others. Guests that have a higher priority—VIPs, good-looking ladies, even daft nephews of the nightclub's owner—take precedence over those with lower priority. Another analogy is the queue at your local supermarket or bus stop, where disabled people and pregnant women can cut the line.

Similar to the other adaptors, elements are added to a priority_queue<> through push() and taken out via pop(). To access the next element in the queue, you use top(). The order in which elements exit a priority_queue<T> is determined by a comparison functor. By default, the std::less<T> functor is used (see Chapter 19). You can override this comparison functor with your own. We refer you to a Standard Library reference for more details on how to use a priority queue.

> ▪ **Caution** In common speech it is normally the element with the *highest* priority that takes precedence. In a `priority_queue<>`, however, the front (or better yet, the `top()`) of the queue will by default be the element that compares *lowest* using `<`. To make the element with the highest priority rise to the `top()` first you can override the default comparison functor by `std::greater<>`. You do so by instantiating the template as follows: `std::priority_queue<T, std::vector<T>, std::greater<>>` (the first optional template type parameter determines the underlying sequence container).

Associative Containers

The C++ Standard Library offers two kinds of *associative containers*: sets and maps. We now discuss both in turn.

Sets

A *set* is a container in which each element can appear at most once. Adding a second element equal to any of the elements that is already stored in a set has no effect. It's easiest to show this with a quick example:

```
// Ex20_03.cpp - Working with sets
import std;

int main()
{
  std::set<int> my_set;

  // Insert elements 1 through 4 in arbitrary order:
  my_set.insert(1);
  my_set.insert(4);
  my_set.insert(3);
  my_set.insert(3);   // Elements 3 and 1 are added twice
  my_set.insert(1);
  my_set.insert(2);

  std::println("There are {} elements in my_set: {:n}", my_set.size(), my_set);
  std::println("The element 1 occurs {} time(s)", my_set.count(1));

  // Like all containers, sets are ranges...
  int sum {};
  for (int x : my_set) sum += x; // ... and can thus be used in a range-based loop
  std::println("The sum of the elements is {}", sum);

  my_set.erase(1);    // Remove the element 1 once
  std::println("After erase(1), my_set holds {} elements: {:n}", my_set.size(), my_set);

  my_set.clear();     // Remove all elements
  std::println("After clear(), my_set holds {} elements: {:n}", my_set.size(), my_set);
}
```

Executing this code produces the following output:

```
There are 4 elements in my_set: 1, 2, 3, 4
The element 1 occurs 1 time(s)
The sum of the elements is 10
After erase(1), my_set holds 3 elements: 2, 3, 4
After clear(), my_set holds 0 elements:
```

▓ **Note** If you omit the :n format specifiers from Ex20_03, you'll notice that by default formatted associative containers are surrounded by curly braces, {...}, and not square braces, [...], like arrays and sequential containers are.

There are no "push" or "pop" members for set containers. Instead, you always add elements through insert() and remove them through erase(). You can add any number of elements, and in any order. Adding the same element a second time, though, has no effect. Even though in Ex20_03 we add the values 1 and 3 to my_set twice, the output clearly shows that both elements are stored in the container only once.

You'll often use set containers to manage or gather a collection of duplicate-free elements. They also excel at efficiently checking whether they contain a given element. To check whether a given element is contained in a set or not, you can use its contains(), count(), or find() members. contains() returns a Boolean; count() always returns 0 or 1 for a set container (see Ex20_03); find() returns an iterator. We'll discuss find() some more later, after you've had a thorough introduction to iterators.

The Standard Library offers three types of set containers: std::set<>, std::flat_set<>, and unordered_set<>. In essence, they all provide the exact same functionality. You could, for instance, replace the std::set<> in Ex20_03 with either std::flat_set<> or std::unordered_set<> and the example will work about the same. Internally, though, they use very different data structures to organize their data. We now look at the different flavors of sets in a bit more detail.

▓ **Tip** We only discuss std::set<>, flat_set<>, and unordered_set<>. The Standard Library also offers std::multiset<>, flat_multiset<>, and unordered_multiset<>, though. Unlike set containers, multiset containers (also known as *bags* or *msets*) may contain the same element more than once (for these containers, count() may thus return numbers higher than 1). Apart from that, they share the exact same functionality and benefits of their set counterparts (fast element checks and retrieval, analogous underlying data structures, etc.). If you can work with sets, you can work with multisets as well.

Ordered Sets

Given that one of the set types is named std::unordered_set<>, it stands to reason that the elements of the others—std::set<> and std::flat_set<>—are *ordered*. This is also apparent from Ex20_03: even though you added the elements 1 through 4 in some arbitrary order, the output corroborates that the container somehow organizes its elements such that they become ordered—and for good reason. Ordering your data makes it much easier to quickly find a given element. Just imagine how long it would take you to find the definition of *capricious* in a dictionary if all words were scrambled in some arbitrary order!

▒ **Tip**   By sorting their elements, ordered sets have logarithmic `insert()`, `erase()`, `find()`, `contains()`, and `count()` operations. If the term "logarithmic" means nothing to you, it implies that even for a sizable set of, say, 100 million elements, these operations never take more than 26 to 27 steps to complete ($\log_2(100{,}000{,}000) \approx 26.5$). It therefore takes a truly immense number of elements for logarithmic operations to become noticeably slower than operations that finish in constant time.

By default, `std::set<T>` and `flat_set<T>` order their elements using `<`. If T is a class type, by default, it has to overload either operator `<` or operator `<=>` (see Chapter 13). We said "by default" because you can override the way a `set<>` orders its elements by supplying a different comparison operator. You could, for instance, replace the definition of `my_set` in Ex20_03 with the following:

```
std::set<int, std::greater<>> my_set;
```

The elements of `my_set` then become sorted from highest to lowest. The second type argument of the `std::set<>` class template is optional (it defaults to `std::less<T>`). You can specify any first-class function type (see Chapter 19) whose instances, when invoked, compare two T elements and return `true` if the element passed to its first parameter should precede that passed to the second. Ordered containers typically default construct the comparison operator, but if need be, you could pass it yourself to the constructor of `set<>` as well. You need to, for instance, if you want to use a function pointer (which is why you'd typically create a functor type instead when customizing an associative container).

```
std::set<int, bool(*)(int, int)> my_set{ &myComparisionFunction };
```

Flat Sets

C++23 added `std::flat_set<>` to the Standard Library. Even more so than `std::unordered_set<>`, `std::flat_set<>` is a drop-in replacement for `std::set<>`, only with different time- and space-efficiency properties. For those who know their data structures: a `std::set<>` is backed by a *balanced tree* (typically a *red-black tree*), while a `flat_set<>` is simply backed by an ordered sequential container.

Like `std::stack<>`, `queue<>`, and `priority_queue<>`, `std::flat_set<>` is a *container adaptor*, meaning it uses an underlying random-access sequence container to store its elements. By default, the type of this container is `std::vector<>`, but if you want you could use a `deque<>` as well like this:

```
std::flat_set<int, std::less<>, std::deque> my_flat_set;
```

Unlike `std::stack<>`, `queue<>`, and `priority_queue<>`, though, `std::flat_set<>` has a full-fledged container API, mostly mirroring that of `std::set<>`. Flat sets, for one, are ranges, and therefore usable in range-based `for` loops and with algorithms.

▒ **Tip**   Flat sets consume less memory and provide faster element lookup and iteration than tree-based sets (in no small part due to their superior memory locality). Tree-based sets, on the other hand, are better at inserting and erasing elements, especially if elements cannot be moved efficiently and/or if the number of elements grows (for flat sets, inserting or erasing elements has a linear instead of logarithmic worst-case complexity).

The only way to know for sure which set type is better for your application, though, is to measure their performance on real, representative inputs. But before you go there, please make sure that it is worth the effort; after all, for most applications, either option will perform more than adequately. The same goes for the question of whether to use an ordered or an unordered set, in fact, as discussed next.

Unordered Sets

Unlike ordered sets, an `unordered_set<>`, naturally, does not order its elements—at least not in any order that is of any particular use to you. Instead, it is backed by a *hash table* or *hash map*. All operations of an `unordered_set<>` consequently usually run in near-constant time, making them potentially even faster than a regular `set<>`. For most common variable types—including all fundamental types, pointers, strings, and smart pointers—an `unordered_set<>` is again a drop-in replacement for `std::set<>` or `std::flat_set<>` (as long as your code does not rely on the ordering of the elements, of course). Before you can store objects of your own class types in an unordered associative container, though, you must first define a *hash function*. You can consult your Standard Library reference on how to do this.

▓ **Tip**   Benchmarks suggest that unordered sets are generally faster than ordered sets for many realistic data sets and operations (except for iterating over all elements, in which flat sets are, for obvious reasons, unbeatable). As said, the only way to know which data structure is optimal is to measure. To measure is to know. But before you measure, know that in most cases either option will perform more than adequately. So, if writing a comparison operator is easier than writing an effective hash function—and it usually is—you should probably simply stick with ordered associative containers until performance measurements show that further optimizations are warranted.

Maps

A *map* or *associative array* container is best thought of as a generalization of a dictionary or phone book. Given a specific *key* (a word or name of a person), you want to store or quickly retrieve the associated *value* (a definition or phone number). Keys in a map need to be unique; values do not (a dictionary allows for synonyms, and a phone book in principle allows for different people to share the same phone number).

Analogous to `std::set<T>`, `flat_set<T>`, and `unordered_set<T>`, the Standard Library offers three map types: `std::map<Key,Value>`, `flat_map<Key,Value>`, and `unordered_map<Key,Value>`. Unlike most container templates, these map templates need at least two template type arguments: one to determine the type of the keys and one to determine the type of the values. Let's clarify this with a quick example:

```
// Ex20_04.cpp - Basic use of std::map<>
import std;

int main()
{
  std::map<std::string, unsigned long long> phone_book;
  phone_book["Joe"] = 202'456'1111;
  phone_book["Jill"] = 202'456'1111;
  phone_book["Francis"] = 39'06'6982;
  phone_book["Charles"] = 44'020'7930'4832;
```

```
    std::println("The pope's number is {}", phone_book["Francis"]);

    for (const auto& [name, number] : phone_book)
      std::println("{} can be reached at {}", name, number);
}
```

This produces the following result (notice how the elements become ordered on their keys):

```
The pope's number is 39066982
Charles can be reached at 4402079304832
Francis can be reached at 39066982
Jill can be reached at 2024561111
Joe can be reached at 2024561111
```

In Ex20_04, phone_book is defined as a map<> with keys of type std::string and values of type unsigned long long (people rarely have negative phone numbers). It uniquely associates strings with numbers. No two keys can be the same. The example also confirms that no such restriction exists for the values; the same phone number can be inserted multiple times.

You typically use a map in much the same way as an array or random-access sequential container: through its array subscript operator, []. Only with maps you do not (necessarily) address the values by contiguous integers (oft-called indices); instead, you can in principle use keys of any type you like.

Most of what applies to std::set<> applies to std::map<> as well. Both containers order their elements; both are backed by a balanced tree; both allow you to configure their comparison operator; both have analogous flat and unordered counterparts—std::flat_map<> and std::unordered_map<> (the latter being a textbook *hash table* or *hash map*); and so on. There is little point in us repeating these properties and their consequences in more detail. In what follows, we focus on topics specific to maps instead. First, we elaborate on how to iterate over their elements, and then, while developing a slightly larger example, we further zoom in on the somewhat peculiar behavior of their [] operator.

▓ **Note**   Of course, std::multimap<>, flat_multimap<>, and unordered_multimap<> exist as well. All three allow multiple values to be associated with the same key. std::multimap<K, V> is, in other words an alternative for std::map<K, std::vector<V>>, but with different time and space efficiencies.

Elements of a Map

To traverse the elements of its phone_book container, Ex20_04 uses a syntax that you have not yet seen before:

```
    for (const auto& [name, number] : phone_book)
      std::println("{} can be reached at {}", name, number);
```

This syntax has been possible since C++17. It is instructive to see how you'd express this loop using more familiar C++11 syntax:

```
    for (const auto& element : phone_book)
      std::println("{} can be reached at {}", element.first, element.second);
```

In fact, it is even more instructive to spell out the long-winded type name of element:

```
for (const std::pair<const std::string, unsigned long long>& element : phone_book)
    std::println("{} can be reached at {}", element.first, element.second);
```

This tells you that elements contained in a map container are effectively key-value pairs. You've briefly encountered the std::pair<> type before during the Chapter 17 exercises. It is a basic template for classes that model a pair of values, possibly of different types. You access the two values contained in a pair<T1,T2> through the public member variables first (of type T1) and second (type T2).

Clearly, though, the auto [ ] syntax is far less verbose than accessing the key and value items through first and second explicitly. This syntax introduces a *structured binding declaration*, or *structured binding* for short. To further illustrate it, consider the following snippet:

```
std::pair my_pair{ false, 77.50 };    // Deduced type: std::pair<bool, double>
auto [my_bool, my_number] = my_pair;
```

Prior to C++17, you always had to write this in a more verbose way:

```
std::pair<bool, double> my_pair{ false, 77.50 };
bool my_bool = my_pair.first;
double my_number = my_pair.second;
```

Or, alternatively, using the std::tie() Standard Library function:

```
bool my_bool;
double my_number;
std::tie(my_bool, my_number) = my_pair;
```

Either way, structured bindings are clearly far more elegant. The loop in Ex20_04 moreover shows that you can combine the auto [ ] syntax quite naturally with const and & as well. We'll use structured bindings again in the somewhat larger example that we assemble in the next subsection.

■ **Tip** Structured bindings don't just work for std::pair<>. They also work for any other type with only public member variables (including, most struct types; see Chapter 12), for C-style arrays, and for specific classes such as std::array<> and std::tuple<> (std::tuple<> is a generalization of std::pair<> for any number of elements). You can even make them work for your own class types by specializing a series of templates, but you'll have to look that up; we won't cover that here.

Counting Words

Enough with the tiny toy examples. Let's look at an example use of std::map<> with some more body to it. A possible use case for a map is to count unique words in a string. Let's see how this works with an example based on Ex8_17. We'll use the following type aliases and function prototypes:

```
// Type aliases
using Words = std::vector<std::string_view>;
using WordCounts = std::map<std::string_view, std::size_t>;
```

```
// Function prototypes
Words extractWords(std::string_view text, std::string_view separators = " ,.!?\"\n");
WordCounts countWords(const Words& words);
void showWordCounts(const WordCounts& wordCounts);
std::size_t maxWordLength(const WordCounts& wordCounts);
```

The extractWords() function is a slight variation of the function with the same name in Ex8_17; you should therefore have no trouble at all defining it on your own. The function extracts all individual words from a given text. A word is defined as any sequence of characters different from the given separators.

Our main point of interest here is the countWords() function. Its job, as you may have guessed, is to count the number of times each individual word occurs in the input vector<>. To count all unique words, the function uses a std::map<std::string_view, std::size_t>. In this map the words are the keys and the value associated with each key is the number of times that the corresponding word occurs in the vector words. The function thus has to insert a new key/value pair into the map each time it encounters a new word. And whenever that same word is seen again, its count needs to be incremented. Both of these operations can be implemented using a single line of code:

```
WordCounts countWords(const Words& words)
{
  WordCounts result;
  for (const auto& word : words)
    ++result[word];
  return result;
}
```

The following line does all the work:

```
++result[word];
```

To understand this, we need to explain the workings of the array index operator, operator[], of a map container a bit better:

- If a value is already associated with the given key, the operator simply returns an lvalue reference to that value. Applying the ++ operator to this reference then increments the value that was already stored within the map to 2 or higher.

- If no value is associated with the given key yet, though, the operator first inserts a new key/value pair into the map. The value of this new element is zero-initialized (or default constructed, if it concerns an object of a class type). Once the new element is inserted, the operator then returns a reference to this zero-initialized value. In countWords(), we then instantly increment the resulting size_t value to 1.

The maxWordLength() function from Ex8_18 needs to be changed slightly, because we want it to use the words stored in the map. For brevity, we'll only output words later that appear more than once in the output, so we best ignore these here already as well:

```
std::size_t maxWordLength(const WordCounts& wordCounts)
{
  std::size_t max{};
  for (const auto& [word, count] : wordCounts)
    if (count >= 2 && max < word.length()) max = word.length();
  return max;
}
```

Finally, all words that occur at least twice are output with a showWordCounts() function.

```cpp
void showWordCounts(const WordCounts& wordCounts)
{
  const std::size_t field_width{maxWordLength(wordCounts) + 1};
  const std::size_t words_per_line{5};

  std::size_t words_in_line{}; // Number of words in the current line
  char previous_initial{};
  for (const auto& [word, count] : wordCounts)
  {
    if (count <= 1) continue;  // Skip words that appear only once

    // Output newline when initial letter changes or after 5 per line
    if ( (previous_initial && word[0] != previous_initial)
         || words_in_line++ == words_per_line)
    {
      words_in_line = 0;
      std::println("");
    }
    // Output "word (count)", where word has a dynamic field width
    std::print("{:>{}} ({:2})", word, field_width, count);
    previous_initial = word[0];
  }
  std::println("");
}
```

The fact that we used a map<> automatically ensures that all words are sorted in alphabetical order, making it easy for us to print them out alphabetically as well. In particular, showWordCounts() groups words that begin with the same letter on the same line. Beyond this, showWordCounts() does not really contain much you haven't seen several times before in similar output functions. So, we believe we can skip any further explanations and fast-forward to seeing it all working in a complete example:

```cpp
// Ex20_05.cpp - Working with maps
import std;

// Type aliases
using Words = std::vector<std::string_view>;
using WordCounts = std::map<std::string_view, std::size_t>;

// Function prototypes
Words extractWords(std::string_view text, std::string_view separators = " ,.!?\"\n");
WordCounts countWords(const Words& words);
void showWordCounts(const WordCounts& wordCounts);
std::size_t maxWordLength(const WordCounts& wordCounts);

int main()
{
  std::string text;     // The string to count words in
```

```
// Read a string from the keyboard
std::println("Enter a string terminated by *:");
getline(std::cin, text, '*');

Words words{ extractWords(text) };
if (words.empty())
{
  std::println("No words in text.");
  return 0;
}

WordCounts wordCounts{ countWords(words) };
showWordCounts(wordCounts);
}

// The implementations of the extractWords(), countWords(), showWordCounts(),
// and maxWordLength() functions as discussed earlier.
```

If you compile and run this program, a possible session could go as follows:

```
Enter a string terminated by *:
Nobody expects the Spanish Inquisition! Our chief weapon is surprise! Surprise and fear.
Fear and surprise. Our two weapons are fear and surprise - and ruthless efficiency! Our
three weapons are fear, and surprise, and ruthless efficiency, and an almost fanatical
devotion to the Pope. Our four, no, among our weapons are such elements as fear, surpr- I'll
come in again.*
        Our ( 4)
        and ( 7)        are ( 3)
 efficiency ( 2)
       fear ( 4)
    ruthless ( 2)
    surprise ( 4)
        the ( 2)
    weapons ( 3)
```

Iterators

You first encountered the concept of iterators in Chapter 12, where we employed an iterator to traverse all Boxes of a given Truckload container in a nice and elegant manner. To do so, you simply asked the Truckload object for an Iterator object, after which you could use this iterator's getFirstBox() and getNextBox() members to retrieve all Boxes in a straightforward loop:

```
auto iterator{ my_truckload.getIterator() };
for (auto box { iterator.getFirstBox() }; box != nullptr; box = iterator.getNextBox())
{
  std::println("{}", to_string(*box));
}
```

This iterator concept is actually a classical and widely applied object-oriented design pattern. One used extensively by the Standard Library as well, as you'll discover throughout this chapter. Before we go there, however, let's first reflect some more on why an iterator is such an attractive pattern.

The Iterator Design Pattern

Iterators allow you to traverse a set of elements contained within any container-like object in an effective, uniform manner. This approach has several advantages, as discussed next.

The Truckload example from earlier is an excellent starting point. If you recall, internally a Truckload object used a (singly) linked list to store its Boxes. Concretely, a Truckload stored each individual Box inside its own dedicated instance of a nested class called Package. Next to a Box, each Package object contained a pointer to the next Package in the list. We refer you to Chapter 12 for more details, in case you forgot. Or, better yet, do not reach back to Chapter 12 just yet! Our main point here is precisely that you do not need to know anything of a Truckload's internal wiring to iterate over all its Boxes. All you need to learn as a user of the Truckload class is the straightforward public interface of its Iterator class.

Library writers typically define Iterators with analogous interfaces for all their container types. This is the case, for instance, for all containers of the Standard Library, as we'll discuss shortly. With this approach, it thus becomes possible to traverse different containers in precisely the same way—be it an array, linked list, or even some more complex data structure. You then no longer need to know at all how a particular container works internally to inspect its elements! Among other thing, this leads to code that is as follows:

- Easy to write and understand.

- Bug-free and robust. Compared to traversing pointers within potentially complex data structures, there is considerably less room for errors when using an iterator.

- Efficient. For instance, as discussed earlier in this chapter, one important limitation of a linked list data structure is that you cannot jump to an arbitrary element with a given index without first traversing all other elements prior to this element. In a Truckload, for example, you can only get to the Box you need by following a whole lot of next pointers starting from the head of the list. This means that a loop of the following form would be particularly inefficient:

```
for (std::size_t i {}; i < my_truckload.getNumBoxes(); ++i)
{
  std::println("{}", to_string(*my_truckload[i]));
}
```

  In such a loop, each invocation of the array subscript operator [ ] would involve traversing the linked list of the iterator, starting from the first Package (the head of the list) all the way until the ith Package. That is, with each iteration of the for loop, obtaining a reference to the ith Box would take longer and longer. An Iterator's getNextBox() function does not suffer from this problem, as it always contains a pointer to a Package, from which the next Box can always be retrieved in constant time.

- Flexible and maintainable. You can readily change the internal representation of a container without having to worry about breaking any external code traversing its elements. For instance, after this chapter, it should be straightforward to reimplement the Truckload class in terms of a vector<> instead of a custom linked list, while still preserving the same public functions, both for the class itself and for its Iterator class.

- Easy to debug. You could add extra debugging statements and assertions to the iterator's member functions. Typical examples are out-of-bounds checks. Library writers mostly add such checks conditionally, such that they are or can be enabled for less-efficient build configurations that facilitate debugging. None of this would be possible if external code was manipulating the internal pointers or arrays directly.

■ **Note**   It should come as no surprise that iterators share many of these advantages with the concept of data hiding we explained in Chapter 12. Data hiding is precisely what iterators and other object-oriented design patterns do. They hide complexity and implementation details from the users of an object behind a familiar, easy-to-use public interface.

Another clear advantage of uniform iterators is that they facilitate the creation of function templates that work for iterators of any container type—functions that can operate on any range of elements, irrespective of whether these elements are contained within for instance a vector, a list, or even a set. As all iterators have analogous interfaces, these function templates thus do not need to know about the inner workings of the containers anymore. It's precisely this idea, combined with first-class functions (see Chapter 19), that powers the higher-order functions of the Standard Library's algorithms library that we will discuss in the final parts of this chapter.

Iterators for Standard Library Containers

All container types of the Standard Library—and with them those of most third-party C++ libraries—offer iterators that are completely analogous. No matter which containers you work with, you can always traverse the elements they store in the same manner. You create new iterator objects through functions with the same name, you access the element an iterator currently refers to in the same manner, and you advance to the next element in the same manner. The public interface of these iterators is slightly different from that of the Truckload Iterators we discussed earlier, but the general idea remains the same.

Creating and Working with Standard Iterators

The most common way to create an iterator for a given container is by invoking its begin() member function. Every single standard container provides this function. Here's an example:

```
std::vector letters{ 'a', 'b', 'c', 'd', 'e' };  // Deduced type: std::vector<char>
auto my_iter{ letters.begin() };
```

The type of an iterator for a container of type ContainerType is always ContainerType::iterator, which is either a concrete type or a type alias. Our my_iter variable definition in full would thus be as follows:

```
std::vector<char>::iterator my_iter{ letters.begin() };
```

It's safe to say that container iterator types are a prime example where C++11's auto type deduction truly has made all our lives a lot easier!

Through the magic of operator overloading (see Chapter 13) every iterator provided by the Standard Library containers mimics a pointer. For example, to access the element that our my_iter iterator currently refers to, you apply its dereference operator:

```
std::println("{}", *my_iter);        // a
```

Since begin() always returns an iterator that points to the first element in the container, this statement will simply print out the letter a.

Just like with a pointer, a dereferenced iterator results in a reference to the actual element stored inside the container. In our example, *my_iter therefore results in a reference of type char&. As this expression is clearly an lvalue reference, you can also use it, for instance, on the left side of an assignment:

```
*my_iter = 'x';
std::println("{}", letters[0]);      // x
```

Naturally you can do more with an iterator than access the first element of the container. As you'll recall from Chapter 6, pointers support the arithmetic operators ++, --, +, -, +=, and -=, which you could use to move from one element in an array to the next (or previous). You work with vector<> iterators in precisely the same manner. Here's an example:

```
++my_iter;                           // Move my_iter to the next element
std::println("{}", *my_iter);        // b

my_iter += 2;                        // Move my_iter two elements further
std::println("{}", *my_iter--);      // d
std::println("{}", *my_iter);        // c (iterator altered using the post-decrement
                                     //    operator in the previous statement)
auto copy{ my_iter };                // Create a copy of my_iter (pointing at c)
my_iter += 2;                        // Move my_iter two elements further
std::println("{}", *copy);           // c (copy not affected by moving my_iter)
std::println("{}", *my_iter);        // e
std::println("{}", my_iter - copy);  // 2
```

This code, which you can find in its totality in Ex20_06, should really explain itself at this point, as all this is completely analogous to working with pointers. This even applies to the last line in our example, which is perhaps a bit less obvious than the others. That is, subtracting two vector<> iterators results in a value of a signed integer type that reflects the distance between the two iterators.

▓ **Tip** Iterators also provide a member access operator (informally, arrow operator), ->, to access the member variables or functions of the element they refer to. That is, suppose string_iter is an iterator that refers to an element of type std::string; then string_iter->length() is short for (*string_iter).length()—again just like it is with a pointer. We will see more concrete examples later in the chapter.

Different Flavors of Iterators

The iterator that we used for the example in the previous subsection is a so-called random-access iterator. Out of all iterator categories, random-access iterators offer the richest set of operations. All iterators returned by standard containers support operators ++, *, and ->, as well as == and !=. But beyond that, there are some differences. Any limitations are easily explained from the nature of the data structures behind the various containers:

- The iterators for a std::forward_list<> do not support --, -=, or -. The reason is that there is no (efficient) way for an iterator to go back to the previous element. Each node in a singly-linked list only has a pointer to the next element in the list. Such iterators are referred to as *forward iterators*. Other containers that may only support forward iterators are the unordered associative containers.

- The iterators for a std::list<>, on the other hand, do support the -- decrement operators (both pre- and post-decrement). Going back to the previous node in a doubly-linked list is trivial. Jumping multiple elements at once still cannot be done efficiently, though. To discourage such use, std::list<> iterators do not feature, for instance, the +=, -=, +, or -- operators. The iterators for the tree-based ordered associative containers have the same limitations, as traversing the nodes of the underlying tree data structure is similar to traversing those of a doubly-linked list. This category of iterators is termed *bidirectional iterators*—for obvious reasons.

- The only iterators to offer +=, -=, +, and -, as well as the comparison operators <, <=, >, >=, and <=> are *random-access iterators*. All random-access sequence containers (std::vector<>, array<>, and deque<>) offer random-access iterators, as do the flat associative containers that decorate them (std::flat_set<>, flat_multiset<>, flat_map<>, and flat_multimap<>).

▓ **Note**   Knowing and understanding these terms becomes important only when consulting your Standard Library reference, most particularly its section on the generic algorithms library that we discuss later in this chapter. The reference of each algorithm template will specify which type of iterators it expects as input—a forward iterator, bidirectional iterator, or random-access iterator.

These three iterator categories form a hierarchy. That is, every random-access iterator is also a valid bidirectional iterator, and every bidirectional iterator is also a forward iterator. So to an algorithm that requires, for instance, a forward iterator, you could most certainly pass a random-access iterator as well. For completeness, your Standard Library reference may also employ the terms *input iterator* and *output iterator* in this context. These are more theoretical concepts that refer to iterators with even fewer requirements than a forward iterator. In practice, every iterator created by a standard container is thus always a valid input or output iterator.

▓ **Note**   As noted earlier, the std::stack<>, queue<>, and priority_queue<> container adaptors do not offer any iterators at all—not even forward iterators. Their elements can be accessed only through the top(), front(), or back() functions (whichever is applicable).

Traversing Elements of a Container

From Chapter 6, you know how to traverse an array using pointers and pointer arithmetic. To print out all elements in an array, for instance, you may use the following loop:

```
int numbers[] { 1, 2, 3, 4, 5 };
for (int* pnumber {numbers}; pnumber < numbers + std::size(numbers); ++pnumber)
{
  std::print("{} ", *pnumber);
}
std::println("");
```

You could traverse all elements of a vector in precisely the same manner:

```
std::vector numbers{ 1, 2, 3, 4, 5 };  // Deduced type: std::vector<int>
for (auto iter {numbers.begin()}; iter < numbers.begin() + numbers.size(); ++iter)
{
  std::print("{} ", *iter);
}
std::println("");
```

The problem with this loop is that it uses two operations that are exclusive to random-access iterators: < and +. This loop would thus not have compiled had numbers been, for instance, of type std::list<int> or std::set<int>. The following is a more conventional way of expressing this same loop:

```
for (auto iter {numbers.begin()}; iter != numbers.end(); ++iter)
{
  std::print("{} ", *iter);
}
```

This new loop is equivalent to the one we used before, only this time it works for any standard container. Conceptually, iterators returned by a container's end() member point to "one past the last element." Once an iterator is incremented up to the point that it equals the container's end() iterator—that is, once an iterator is incremented past the container's last element—you should therefore clearly abort the loop. While it is undefined what would happen, no good can come from dereferencing an iterator that points beyond the bounds of the actual container.

▓ **Tip**   In C++ you normally use iter != numbers.end() instead of iter < numbers.end() because forward and bidirectional iterators are not required to support comparisons by means of <. You also normally use ++iter instead of iter++ because pre-increment operators tend to be more efficient (recall from Chapter 13 that post-increment operators normally have to create and return a copy of the iterator before moving it to the next element).

The following example uses a loop exactly like this to traverse all elements contained in a list<>:

```cpp
// Ex20_07.cpp - Iterating over the elements of a list<>
import std;

int main()
{
  std::print("Enter a sequence of positive numbers, terminated by -1:");

  std::list<unsigned> numbers;

  while (true)
  {
    signed number{-1};
    std::cin >> number;
    if (number == -1) break;
    numbers.push_back(static_cast<unsigned>(number));
  }

  std::print("You entered the following numbers:");
  for (auto iter {numbers.begin()}; iter != numbers.end(); ++iter)
  {
    std::print("{} ", *iter);
  }
  std::println("");
}
```

A possible session then might go like this:

```
Enter a sequence of positive numbers, terminated by -1: 4 8 15 16 23 42 -1
You entered the following numbers: 4 8 15 16 23 42
```

Of course, each container is a range as well, and ranges can be used in range-based for loops (see Chapter 5). The for loop of Ex20_07, for instance, could be replaced by the following much simpler range-based for loop:

```cpp
for (auto number : numbers)
{
  std::print("{} ", number);
}
```

░ **Tip** To iterate over all elements in a container, always use a range-based for loop. You should only use a more verbose and complex iterator-based loop if you explicitly need access to the iterator for more advanced processing in the loop's body or if you only want to iterate over a subrange of the container's elements.

We will see examples where the loop's body needs access to the iterator later.

Const Iterators

All iterators that we have used thus far have been *mutable* (or *non*-const) iterators. You can alter the element that a mutable iterator refers to simply by dereferencing it or, for elements of a class type, through its member access operator ->. Here's an example:

```
// Ex20_08.cpp - Altering elements through a mutable iterator
import std;
import box; // From Ex11_04

int main()
{
  std::vector boxes{ Box{ 1.0, 2.0, 3.0 } }; // A std::vector<Box> containing 1 Box

  auto iter{ boxes.begin() };
  std::println("{} ", iter->volume());        // 6 == 1.0 * 2.0 * 3.0

  *iter = Box{ 2.0, 3.0, 4.0 };
  std::println("{} ", iter->volume());        // 24 == 2.0 * 3.0 * 4.0

  iter->setHeight(7.0);
  std::println("{} ", iter->volume());        // 42 == 2.0 * 3.0 * 7.0
}
```

There is nothing new or surprising about this example yet. The point we wanted to make is that besides mutable iterators of type *ContainerType*::iterator (see earlier), each container also offers const *iterators* of type *ContainerType*::const_iterator. Dereferencing a const iterator results in a reference to a const element (const Box& in our example), and its -> operator only allows you to either access member variables as const or invoke const member functions.

There are two ways you typically obtain a const iterator:

- By calling cbegin() or cend() instead of begin() or end(). The c in the names of these member functions refers to const. You can try this by changing begin() to cbegin() in Ex20_08.

- By invoking begin() or end() on a const container. If the container is const, these functions return a const iterator; only if the container itself is mutable will the result be a mutable iterator as well. (You saw in Chapter 12 how to accomplish this effect through function overloading by defining one overload of the same function that is const and one that is not.) You can give this a try as well by adding the keyword const in front of the declaration of the boxes vector<> in Ex20_08.

If you turn iter in Ex20_08 into a const iterator in either of these two ways, the lines containing the statements *iter = Box{ 2.0, 3.0, 4.0 }; and iter->setHeight(7.0) will no longer compile. Altering an element through a const iterator is not possible.

■ **Tip**   Just like it is good practice to add const to your variable declarations whenever possible, you should also use const iterators whenever applicable. This prevents you or anyone else from accidentally altering elements in contexts where that is not desired or expected.

The for loop in Ex20_07, for instance, simply prints out all elements in the container. This certainly is not supposed to alter these elements. You could therefore write the loop like this:

```
for (auto iter{ numbers.cbegin() }; iter != numbers.cend(); ++iter)
{
   std::print("{} ", *iter);
}
```

░ **Note**   Set and map containers *only* provide const iterators. For these types, begin() and end() always return const iterators, even when invoked on a non-const container. As always, these restrictions are easily explained by the nature of these containers. A std::set<>, for example, orders its elements. If you allow a user to alter the value of such an element through an iterator, mid-traversal, maintaining this ordering invariant obviously becomes infeasible. This is also why the iterators of map containers point to std::pair<const Key, Value> elements; once inserted into a map, you are no longer supposed to alter a key.

Inserting in and Erasing from Sequence Containers

In Chapter 5, we introduced push_back() and pop_back()—functions you can use to add elements to and remove elements from, respectively, most sequence containers. There was only one restriction: these functions only allow you to manipulate the very last element of the sequence. Earlier in this chapter you also saw push_front() in action, a similar function that some sequence containers provide to add elements to the front of the sequence. This is all well and good, but what if you need to insert or remove elements in or from the middle of the sequence? Shouldn't this be possible as well?

The answer is that you can insert and remove elements wherever you want! And now that you know about iterators, we are finally ready to show you how. That is, to indicate where to insert or which elements to remove, you need to provide iterators. All sequence containers except std::array<> offer various insert() and erase() functions that accept either iterators or iterator ranges to this end.

We'll start off with something simple and add a single element to the beginning of a vector:

```
std::vector numbers{ 2, 4, 5 };      // Deduced type: std::vector<int>
numbers.insert(numbers.begin(), 1); // Add single element to the beginning of the sequence
std::println("{}", numbers);         // [1, 2, 4, 5]
```

The element you provide as insert()'s second argument is inserted *right before* the position referred to by the iterator you provide as its first argument. The output of this snippet is therefore [1, 2, 4, 5].

Naturally, you can insert() new elements at any position you want. The following, for instance, adds the number 3 right in the middle of our numbers sequence:

```
numbers.insert(numbers.begin() + numbers.size() / 2, 3); // Add in the middle
std::println("{}", numbers);                             // [1, 2, 3, 4, 5]
```

The insert() function moreover has a couple of overloads that allow you to add multiple elements at once. A common use of these used to be to append one vector<> to another:

```
std::vector more_numbers{ 6, 7, 8 };
numbers.insert(numbers.end(), more_numbers.begin(), more_numbers.end());
std::println("{}", numbers);     // [1, 2, 3, 4, 5, 6, 7, 8]
```

Like with all overloads of insert(), the first argument again indicates the position *right after* where the new elements are to be added. In this case, we selected the end() iterator, which means we're inserting right before "one past the end" of the current sequence—or, in other words, right after the last element. The two iterators passed to the function's second and third parameters indicate the range of elements to insert. In our example, this range corresponds to the entire more_numbers sequence.

▦ **Note**   Ranges of elements are indicated using half-open intervals in standard C++. In Chapter 7, you saw that many member functions of std::string accept half-open character intervals specified through std::size_t indexes. Container members such as insert() and erase() similarly work with half-open intervals indicated by means of iterator pairs. If you provide two iterators, from and to, then that range encompasses all elements in the half-open interval [from, to). That is, the range includes the element of the from iterator but not that of the to iterator. This also implies that you can safely use end() iterators for the to iterator—which is fortunate, because these one-past-the-end iterators do not point to any element, and should thus never be dereferenced. Virtually all algorithm templates of the <algorithm> and <numeric> modules (discussed later in this chapter) have overloads that accept half-open iterator ranges as well.

As much fun as it is to work with iterator pairs (it's not...), though, C++23 has introduced functions such as insert_range() and append_range() that are more convenient for inserting ranges into existing containers. We can easily illustrate this with our running example:

```
std::vector some_more{ 9, 10 };
// numbers.insert(numbers.end(), some_more.begin(), some_more.end()); // Ugh
// numbers.insert_range(numbers.end(), some_more);   // Shorter
numbers.append_range(some_more);                     // Shortest
```

The opposite of insert() is called erase(). The following sequence of statements removes, one by one, the same elements we added earlier using insert() and append_range():

```
numbers.erase(numbers.end() - 5, numbers.end());      // Erase last 5 elements
numbers.erase(numbers.begin() + numbers.size() / 2);  // Erase the middle element
numbers.erase(numbers.begin());                       // Erase the first element
std::println("{}", numbers);    // [2, 4, 5]
```

The overload of erase() with two parameters deletes a range of elements; the one with a single parameter deletes only a single element (remember this distinction; it'll be important again later in this chapter!).

The complete source for the example we used throughout this section can be found in Ex20_09.

▦ **Note**   Most containers offer similar insert() and erase() functions (the only exception is std::array<>). Naturally, set and map containers will not allow you to indicate *where* to insert() an element (only sequence containers do), but they do allow you to erase() elements that correspond to either an iterator or iterator range. Consult your Standard Library reference for more details.

Altering Containers During Iteration

In past sections we showed you how to iterate over elements in a container as well as how to insert() and erase() elements. The logical next question is then, what if you insert() or erase() elements *while* you are iterating over a container?

Unless otherwise specified (consult a Standard Library reference for details), any modification to a container is said to *invalidate* all iterators that were ever created for that container. Any further use of an invalidated iterator results in undefined behavior, which translates to anything from unpredictable results to crashes. Consider the following function template (recall from Chapter 10 that the use of the auto& placeholder as a parameter type makes this an abbreviated function template definition):

```
void removeEvenNumbers(auto& numbers)
{
  auto from{ numbers.begin() }, to{ numbers.end() };
  for (auto iter {from}; iter != to; ++iter)              /* Wrong!! */
  {
    if (*iter % 2 == 0)
      numbers.erase(iter);
  }
}
```

The intent is to write a template that removes all even numbers from containers of a variety of types—be it vector<int>, deque<unsigned>, list<long>, set<short>, or unordered_set<unsigned>.

The problem is that this template contains two serious yet fairly realistic bugs, both triggered by the erase() in the loop's body. Once you modify a sequence (for instance through erase()) you should generally stop using any existing iterators. Yet the loop in removeEvenNumbers() ignores that. Instead, it simply soldiers on using both the to and iter iterators, even after invoking erase() on the container to which both these iterators refer. There's no telling what will happen should you execute this code, but it most certainly will not be what you might've hoped for.

More specifically, once you call erase() a first time, the to iterator no longer points "one past the last element," but (at least in principle) "two past the last element." This means that your loop probably dereferences the actual end() iterator, with all its catastrophic consequences. You can solve this rather easily by requesting a new end() iterator after each iteration of the for loop as follows:

```
  for (auto iter {numbers.begin()}; iter != numbers.end(); ++iter)  /* Still wrong!! */
  {
    if (*iter % 2 == 0)
      numbers.erase(iter);
  }
```

This new loop is still very much wrong, though, as it continues to use the iter iterator after invoking erase(). This, in general, will end in disaster as well. For a linked list, for instance, erase() will likely deallocate the node that iter refers to, meaning it becomes highly unpredictable what the upcoming ++iter will do. For a std::set(), an erase() might even reshuffle the entire tree to put its elements back nicely in order. Any further iteration then becomes risky business as well.

Does this mean that you cannot remove multiple individual elements from a container without restarting each time from begin()? Fortunately not, as that would be particularly inefficient. It just means that you have to follow this pattern:

```
void removeEvenNumbers(auto& numbers)      /* Correct! */
{
  for (auto iter {numbers.begin()}; iter != numbers.end(); )
  {
    if (*iter % 2 == 0)
      iter = numbers.erase(iter);
    else
      ++iter;
  }
}
```

Most erase() and insert() functions return an iterator that you can use to continue the iteration with. This iterator will then refer to one element past the one that was just inserted or erased (or be equal to end(), if the latter concerned the last element in the container).

▧ **Caution**   Do not deviate from the standard pattern we just laid out. For instance, the iterator returned by either erase() or insert() should itself not be incremented anymore, which is why we moved the for loop's classic ++iter statement into the else branch in the loop's body!

▧ **Tip**   This pattern is relatively easy to get wrong, and for sequence containers it is even quite inefficient. Later in this chapter we will introduce both the classical *remove-erase* idiom and the newer erase() and erase_if() nonmember functions, both of which you should use over such error-prone loops whenever possible. To insert() elements while iterating over a sequence, however, you still need to write loops of this form explicitly yourself.

The following example takes the removeEvenNumbers() template we just developed for a spin. Even though it does so using a vector<int> container, we could've used any of the aforementioned types as well:

```
// Ex20_10.cpp
// Removing all elements that satisfy a certain condition
// while iterating over a container
import std;

std::vector<int> fillVector_1toN(int N); // Fill a vector with 1, 2, ..., N
void removeEvenNumbers(auto& numbers);

int main()
{
  const int num_numbers{15};

  auto numbers{ fillVector_1toN(num_numbers) };

  std::println("The original set of numbers: {:n}", numbers);
```

```
  removeEvenNumbers(numbers);

  std::println("The numbers that were kept: {:n}", numbers);
}

std::vector<int> fillVector_1toN(int N)
{
  std::vector<int> numbers;
  for (int i {1}; i <= N; ++i)
    numbers.push_back(i);
  return numbers;
}
```

The following is the outcome of this program.

```
The original set of numbers: 1, 2, 3, 4, 5, 6, 7, 8, 9, 10, 11, 12, 13, 14, 15
The numbers that were kept: 1, 3, 5, 7, 9, 11, 13, 15
```

Iterators for Arrays

Iterators behave like pointers—so much so that any pointer is a valid iterator as well. To be more precise, any raw pointer may serve as a random-access iterator. This observation will allow the generic algorithm templates we discuss in the next section to iterate over arrays and containers alike. In fact, array pointers can be used in any context where one would otherwise use iterators. Recall the following statements from Ex20_09:

```
std::vector more_numbers{ 6, 7, 8 };
numbers.insert(numbers.end(), more_numbers.begin(), more_numbers.end());
```

Now suppose the more_numbers variable was defined as a built-in array instead. Then one way to append these numbers is by exploiting the array-pointer duality, combined with pointer arithmetic and the std::size() function, as introduced in Chapter 5:

```
int more_numbers[] { 6, 7, 8 };
numbers.insert(numbers.end(), more_numbers, more_numbers + std::size(more_numbers));
```

While perfectly sound, there is a nicer and more uniform way as well. For that, you use the std::begin() and std::end() nonmember function templates:

```
int more_numbers[] { 6, 7, 8 };
numbers.insert(numbers.end(), std::begin(more_numbers), std::end(more_numbers));
```

These function templates do not only work for arrays; they also work for any container:

```
std::vector more_numbers{ 6, 7, 8 };
numbers.insert(std::end(numbers), std::begin(more_numbers), std::end(more_numbers));
```

When used with containers, thanks to the way name resolution works in C++ for nonmember functions, you even do not have to explicitly specify the `std::` namespace:

```
std::vector more_numbers{ 6, 7, 8 };
numbers.insert(end(numbers), begin(more_numbers), end(more_numbers));
```

Not surprisingly, `cbegin()` and `cend()` nonmember functions exist as well, which create the corresponding `const` iterators for either arrays or containers:

```
std::vector more_numbers{ 6, 7, 8 };
int even_more_numbers[]{ 9, 10 };
numbers.insert(end(numbers), cbegin(more_numbers), cend(more_numbers));
numbers.insert(end(numbers), std::cbegin(even_more_numbers), std::cend(even_more_numbers));
```

The compactness and uniformity of this syntax makes it our preferred way of specifying ranges in the remainder of this chapter. There is nothing wrong though with using the (c)begin() and (c)end() member functions for containers instead.

▓ **Tip**   C++23's `numbers.append_range(even_more_numbers)` also works for C-style arrays (with known bounds), and is even better here because it completely hides all iterator pair manipulation.

Algorithms

The generic algorithms of the Standard Library combine the strengths of various concepts explored earlier in this book, such as function templates (Chapter 10), first-class and higher-order functions (Chapter 19), and iterators (earlier this chapter). You'll find that these algorithms are particularly powerful and expressive when combined with C++11's lambda expressions (Chapter 19).

▓ **Note**   Combined, the `<algorithm>` and `<numeric>` modules of the Standard Library offer well over 100 algorithms, more than we could possibly cover here. We instead focus on the most commonly used ones (here and in the exercises at the end of the chapter), as well as common patterns that are recurring in many algorithms. Once you master these, working with the other algorithms is nearly always analogous. We invite you to browse a Standard Library reference afterward to get a feeling of which algorithms are available.

In this section we begin by introducing the traditional *iterator pair–based algorithms*. As of C++20, we expect that these will be gradually phased out and replaced with the functionally equivalent *range-based algorithms* we introduce in the final section of this chapter. Iterator-based algorithms will remain ubiquitous in legacy code for some time to come, though.

A First Example

Some of the higher-order functions defined in Chapter 19 already come close to some of the standard algorithms. Remember the findOptimum() template? It looked as follows:

```
template <typename T, typename Comparison>
const T* findOptimum(const std::vector<T>& values, Comparison compare)
{
  if (values.empty()) return nullptr;

  const T* optimum{ &values[0] };
  for (std::size_t i {1}; i < values.size(); ++i)
  {
    if (compare(values[i], *optimum))
    {
      optimum = &values[i];
    }
  }
  return optimum;
}
```

While already quite generic, this template still has two unfortunate limitations:

- It works only for elements that are stored inside a container of type vector<>.

- It works only if you want to consider all elements of the given collection. Considering only a subset of these elements is not possible yet without copying them all in a new container first.

You can resolve both shortcomings rather easily by generalizing the template even further using iterators:

```
template <typename Iterator, typename Comparison>
Iterator findOptimum(Iterator begin, Iterator end, Comparison compare)
{
  if (begin == end) return end;

  Iterator optimum{ begin };
  For (Iterator iter{ ++begin }; iter != end; ++iter)
  {
    if (compare(*iter, *optimum))
    {
      optimum = iter;
    }
  }
  return optimum;
}
```

This new version does not suffer the two aforementioned issues:

- Iterators can be used to traverse the elements of all container and array types alike.

- The new template readily works with subranges by simply passing only part of a complete [begin(), end()) iterator range.

The <algorithms> module offers an algorithm exactly like this. Only it is not called findOptimum(), but std::max_element(). And where there's a max_element(), there's of course a min_element(). Let's see them both in action by adjusting some of the examples of the previous chapter:

```cpp
// Ex20_11.cpp - Your first algorithms: std::min_element() and max_element()
import std;

int main()
{
  std::vector numbers{ 91, 18, 92, 22, 13, 43 };
  std::println("Minimum element: {}", *std::min_element(begin(numbers), end(numbers)));
  std::println("Maximum element: {}", *std::max_element(begin(numbers), end(numbers)));

  int number_to_search_for {};
  std::print("Please enter a number: ");
  std::cin >> number_to_search_for;

  auto nearer { [=](int x, int y) {
    return std::abs(x - number_to_search_for) < std::abs(y - number_to_search_for);
  }};

  std::println("The number nearest to {} is {}",
     number_to_search_for, *std::min_element(begin(numbers), end(numbers), nearer));
  std::println("The number furthest from {} is {}",
     number_to_search_for, *std::max_element(begin(numbers), end(numbers), nearer));
}
```

The first thing that jumps from this example is that for min_element() and max_element(), the comparison callback function is optional. Both offer an overload without this third parameter—both of which use the less-than operator, <, to compare elements. Besides that, these standard algorithms do precisely what you'd expect:

```
Minimum element: 13
Maximum element: 92
Please enter a number: 42
The number nearest to 42 is 43
The number furthest from 42 is 92
```

▪ **Tip** The <algorithm> module also provides std::minmax_element(), which you can use to obtain both minimum and maximum elements within a given range at once. This algorithm returns a pair<> of iterators, with the expected semantics. You could therefore replace the last two statements in Ex20_11 with this:

```cpp
const auto [nearest, furthest] {
  std::minmax_element(begin(numbers), end(numbers), nearer) };
```

```
std::println("The number nearest to {} is {}", number_to_search_for, *nearest);
std::println("The number furthest from {} is {}", number_to_search_for,
                                                                  *furthest);
```

We refer you to earlier in this chapter for an introduction to the pair<> template and auto [] syntax.

Finding Elements

The Standard Library provides various algorithms to search for elements within a range of elements. In the previous subsection we introduced min_element(), max_element(), and minmax_element(). The two related algorithms that you'll probably use most often are std::find() and find_if(). The first, std::find(), is used to search a range for an element that equals a given value (it compares values with the == operator). The second, find_if(), instead expects a first-class callback function as an argument. It uses this callback function to determine whether any given element satisfies the desired characteristics.

To try them, let's reach back to an old favorite: the Box class. Because std::find() needs to compare two Boxes, you'll need a variant of Box with an overloaded operator==(). The box module from Ex13_03 for instance will do just fine:

```
// Ex20_12.cpp - Finding boxes.
import std;
import box;        // From Ex13_03

int main()
{
  std::vector boxes{ Box{1,2,3}, Box{5,2,3}, Box{9,2,1}, Box{3,2,1} };

  // Define a lambda functor to print the result of find() or find_if():
  auto print_result = [&boxes] (auto result)
  {
    if (result == end(boxes))
      std::println("No box found.");
    else
      std::println("Found matching box at position {}", result - begin(boxes));
  };

  // Find an exact box
  Box box_to_find{ 3,2,1 };
  auto result{ std::find(begin(boxes), end(boxes), box_to_find) };
  print_result(result);

  // Find a box with a volume larger than that of box_to_find
  const auto required_volume{ box_to_find.volume() };
  result = std::find_if(begin(boxes), end(boxes),
             [required_volume](const Box& box) { return box > required_volume; });
  print_result(result);
}
```

The output is as follows:

```
Found matching box at position 3
Found matching box at position 1
```

Both `find()` and `find_if()` return either an iterator to the found element or the end iterator of the range if no element is found that matches the search criteria.

▓ **Caution**   If no element is found, the end iterator of the range to search is returned, not the end iterator of the container. Even though in many cases these are the same (in `Ex20_12` they are), this is not always true.

Several variants are provided by the standard. The following list shows a few of them. Consult a Standard Library reference for more details.

- `find_if_not()` is similar to `find_if()`, only it searches for the first element for which the given callback function returns `false` (rather than `true`).

- `find_first_of()` searches a range of elements for the first element that matches any element from another given range.

- `adjacent_find()` searches for two consecutive elements that are equal or that satisfy a given predicate.

- `search()` / `find_end()` search for a range of elements in another range of elements. The former returns the first match, while the latter returns the last match.

- `binary_search()` checks whether a given element is present in a sorted range. By exploiting the fact that the elements in the input range are sorted, it can find the desired element faster than `find()`. Elements are compared using either the `<` operator or a user-provided comparison callback.

▓ **Caution**   Earlier in this chapter, we explained that set and map containers are really good at finding elements themselves already. Because they know the internal structure of their data, they can find elements much faster than any generic algorithm ever could. These containers therefore offer a `find()` member function that you should always use instead of the generic `std::find()` algorithm. In general, whenever a container offers member functions that are functionally equivalent to an algorithm, you should always use the former.

Handling Multiple Output Values

find(), find_if(), find_if_not()—these three algorithms all search for the first element that meets a particular requirement. But what if you're interested in finding all of them instead? If you glance through all algorithms that the Standard Library has to offer, you'll find that there is no algorithm with a name like find_all(). Luckily, there are at least three algorithms that would allow you to obtain all elements in a given range that satisfy a given condition:

- std::remove_if() can be used to remove all elements that do *not* satisfy the condition. We discuss this algorithm in the next subsection.

- std::partition() rearranges the elements in a range such that those elements that satisfy a callback condition are moved to the front of the range and those that do not are moved to the back. We'll leave this option for you to try later in the exercises.

- std::copy_if() can be used to copy all elements you need to a second output range.

```
// Ex20_13.cpp - Extracting all odd numbers.
import std;

std::set<int> fillSet_1toN(int N);    // Fill a set with 1, 2, ..., N

int main()
{
  const int num_numbers{20};

  const auto numbers{ fillSet_1toN(num_numbers) };

  std::vector<int> odd_numbers( numbers.size() ); // Caution: not { numbers.size() }!
  auto end_odd_numbers{ std::copy_if(begin(numbers), end(numbers), begin(odd_numbers),
                                   [](int n) { return n % 2 == 1; }) };
  odd_numbers.erase(end_odd_numbers, end(odd_numbers));

  std::println("The odd numbers are: {:n}", odd_numbers);
}
```

The fillSet_1toN() is analogous to the fillVector_1toN() function of Ex20_10. Coding this should be routine by now.

Let's instead focus our attention on the three lines of the program that matter: those that copy all odd numbers from numbers to odd_numbers. The first two arguments of std::copy_if() are *input iterators*. They determine the range of elements that potentially need to be copied. The callback function in the fourth argument then determines which of these elements are effectively copied. Of particular interest here, though, is the third argument of copy_if(). It is your first example of an *output iterator*—an iterator that determines where an algorithm writes its output. Its workings are best explained through some code. After inlining all function calls (including that of the lambda expression), the copy_if() statement of Ex20_13 acts as follows:

```
auto output_iter{ begin(odd_numbers) };
for (auto input_iter{ begin(numbers) }; input_iter != end(numbers); ++input_iter)
    if (*input_iter % 2 == 1)
      *output_iter++ = *input_iter;        // <-- working of an output iterator
// return output_iter;
auto end_odd_numbers = output_iter;
```

810

Each element that the algorithm has to output gets assigned to the position that the output iterator points to at that moment. Remember that dereferencing an iterator results in a (lvalue) reference. In our example, this means that the expression *output_iter is of type int&. After each assignment the output iterator is incremented, getting it ready to receive the next output.

If you use a plain output iterator, it is crucial that the target range—the vector<> odd_numbers in Ex20_13—is large enough to hold all elements that the algorithm will output. Because you do not always know in advance how many elements that will be, you may be forced to allocate a buffer of memory that is larger than required. This is what you see in Ex20_13 as well: odd_numbers is initialized with a dynamic array of numbers.size() elements (all zeros). As this is large enough to hold all numbers, it is most definitely large enough to hold all odd numbers. But it will turn out to be twice as large than actually required. For that purpose, the std::copy_if() algorithm returns an iterator into the output range that points one past the last element that was copied. You can use this iterator to erase all superfluous elements from the target container, precisely like it's done in Ex20_13.

▩ **Caution**　Take care not to forget the second argument to the call to erase()! It must be the end iterator of the container. If you forget this second argument, erase() will just erase the single element pointed to by the iterator passed as the first argument. (In Ex20_13, in other words, only one of the original zeros would then be erased from odd_numbers!)

Many algorithms copy or move output into a target range analogously to std::copy_if() (std::copy(), move(), replace_copy(), replace_copy_if(), remove_copy()—the list goes on...). With all these algorithms you could, in principle, use the same pattern of conservatively allocating an overly large target range, which you then shrink to its proper size using the iterator returned by the algorithm.

This pattern, however, while still useful at times, is clearly clumsy, verbose, and quite error-prone. Luckily, there is a better way. For Ex20_13, you could use the following two statements instead (see Ex20_13A):

```
std::vector<int> odd_numbers;
std::copy_if(begin(numbers), end(numbers), back_inserter(odd_numbers),
             [](int n) { return n % 2 == 1; });
```

With this technique, there is no need to over-allocate and thus no need to erase() any redundant elements afterward either. Instead, you create a special "fake" iterator through the std::back_inserter() function. In our example, each element that copy_if() assigns through this special output iterator is effectively forwarded to the push_back() function of odd_numbers—the container you passed to back_inserter() when you created the iterator. The end result is the same—all odd numbers are added to odd_numbers—but this time you did so with less code and, more importantly, code that is much clearer, and that leaves considerably less room for error.

▩ **Tip**　The <iterator> module defines the back_inserter(), front_inserter(), and inserter() functions that create "fake" output iterators that forward to, respectively, push_back(), push_front(), and insert() whenever a value is assigned to these iterators after dereferencing. Use these whenever an algorithm needs to output values into a container.

The Remove-Erase Idiom

Often you need to delete all elements from a container that satisfy specific conditions. With the removeEvenNumbers() function of Ex20_10 earlier in this chapter, we showed you how you can do this using a rather complex for loop that iterates over all the elements of the container, checks whether an element satisfies the conditions, and if so calls erase() on the container to remove the element. Implementing it this way, however, can be both inefficient and error-prone. Take a vector<> as an example. If you remove an element from the middle of the vector<>, all subsequent elements need to be shifted down to fill the gap of the removed element. That is very inefficient (it exhibits quadratic complexity). Also, when removing elements from the container while you are iterating over that same container, you need to take extra care that the iterator is correctly handled, as discussed earlier. This is prone to errors. The remove-erase idiom, as well as the higher-level helper functions discussed in the next subsection, are therefore far more effective methods to remove elements from containers.

As the name suggests, the *remove-erase idiom* typically involves an invocation of a remove() or remove_if() algorithm, followed by an invocation of an erase() member function of a container.

░ **Caution**   Algorithms such as remove() and remove_if() do not actually remove any elements from a container. They can't because they only have access to iterators. Without access to the container or its member functions, algorithms cannot possibly erase() any elements. Instead, such algorithms operate by moving all elements that are to be kept to the front of the input range.

When you apply algorithms such as remove() and remove_if() to the full range of a sequence container, all elements that should be erased thus flock to the tail of the sequence. To this end, remove() and remove_if() return an iterator to the first element that should be erased. You generally use this iterator as a first argument to the erase() method of the container to erase any excess elements. First you remove(), then you erase(). Hence the name of the idiom: remove-erase.

Let's see how the remove-erase idiom works with some actual code. You can use the same program as Ex20_10, only this time you replace the removeEvenNumbers() with this version:

```
void removeEvenNumbers(std::vector<int>& numbers)
{
  // Use the remove_if() algorithm to remove all even numbers
  auto first_to_erase{ std::remove_if(begin(numbers), end(numbers),
                                [](int number) { return number % 2 == 0; }) };
  // Erase all elements including and beyond first_to_erase
  numbers.erase(first_to_erase, end(numbers));
}
```

The output of the resulting program (available in Ex20_14) should then remain the same:

```
The original set of numbers: 1, 2, 3, 4, 5, 6, 7, 8, 9, 10, 11, 12, 13, 14, 15
The numbers that were kept: 1, 3, 5, 7, 9, 11, 13, 15
```

It may be instructive to see what happens if you remove the line that calls `numbers.erase()` from `removeEvenNumbers()`. If you do that, the output almost certainly becomes the following:

```
The original set of numbers: 1, 2, 3, 4, 5, 6, 7, 8, 9, 10, 11, 12, 13, 14, 15
The numbers that were kept: 1, 3, 5, 7, 9, 11, 13, 15, 9, 10, 11, 12, 13, 14, 15
```

As you can see, `remove_if()` simply moves all elements that are to be kept (odd numbers 1 till 15) to the front of the range, leaving the back of the range in disarray. That is, the algorithm does not go to the trouble of nicely moving all even numbers to the back of the range as well. Doing so would only be a waste of time. The back of the range is meant to be erased, so it's okay if there's odd numbers left there.[1] Algorithms such as `remove()` and `remove_if()` are always meant to be followed by a call to `erase()`. Always. You can use `std::partition()` if you also want the even numbers to move to the back of the range.

▓ **Caution** Take care—and we cannot repeat this enough—not to forget the second argument to the call to `erase()`! It must be the end iterator of the container. If you forget this second argument, `erase()` will just erase the single element pointed to by the iterator passed as the first argument. In `Ex20_14`, for instance, only the number 9 would then be removed.

Erase Functions

Compared to loops where you either increment an iterator or assign it the result of `erase()` (as in the original `removeEvenNumbers()` function of `Ex20_10`), the algorithm-based remove-erase idiom is already a big step forward. But it remains somewhat error-prone (it's ever so easy to forget the second argument of `erase()`!), and it for sure remains rather wordy (two function invocations just to remove some elements?). C++20 therefore added nonmember function templates `std::erase(Container, Value)` and/or `std::erase_if(Container, Function)`. Using `std::erase_if()` you can, for instance, simplify `removeEvenNumbers()` from `Ex20_14` as follows:

```cpp
void removeEvenNumbers(std::vector<int>& numbers)
{
  std::erase_if(numbers, [](int number) { return number % 2 == 0; });
}
```

Neat, right? The resulting program is available in `Ex20_14A`.

▓ **Tip** There are no `std::erase()` nonmember functions for sets or maps, only `std::erase_if()` functions. You should use the `erase()` *member* functions of these containers instead.

---

[1] In general, elementsto the front of the range using std::move(). If your container contains objects of a class type, algorithms such as `remove()` and `remove_if()` thus leave moved elements at the back of the range. From Chapter 18 you know that these elements should then typically not be used anymore. So you best `erase()` them as soon as possible.

> ■ **Note**   It's not because `std::erase()` and `std::erase_if()` exist now that you no longer need to know the remove-erase idiom. Of course, `std::erase()` and `std::erase_if()` should replace all eponymous applications of the idiom—that is, invocations of `std::remove()` or `remove_if()` followed by an invocation of `erase()`. But the same idiom applies to other algorithms as well—algorithms for which no `std::erase()`-like equivalents exist yet. We refer you to Exercise 20-8 for an example.

Sorting

Another key operation for arrays and sequence containers is sorting their elements. You may need this to present these elements to the user in a sorted order, but often also as a prerequisite for further algorithmic processing (such as with `std::binary_search()`, `std::merge()`, `std::set_intersection()`, and so on).

The `std::sort()` algorithm sorts a range of elements. The first two arguments passed to the algorithm are the begin and end iterators of the range to sort. The third argument passed is an optional comparator. If no comparator is given, the elements are sorted in ascending sequence. That is, if applied to a range of strings, the strings will be sorted lexicographically. The following example sorts a range of strings twice, first lexicographically and then according to the length of each string:

```cpp
// Ex20_15.cpp - Sorting strings
import std;

int main()
{
  std::vector<std::string> names{"Frodo Baggins", "Gandalf the Gray",
    "Aragon", "Samwise Gamgee", "Peregrin Took", "Meriadoc Brandybuck",
    "Gimli", "Legolas Greenleaf", "Boromir"};

  // Sort the names lexicographically
  std::sort(begin(names), end(names));
  std::println("Names sorted lexicographically: {:n}", names);

  // Sort the names by length
  std::sort(begin(names), end(names),
    [](const auto& left, const auto& right) { return left.length() < right.length(); });
  std::println("Names sorted by length: {:n}", names);
}
```

The output is as follows:

```
Names sorted lexicographically:
Aragon, Boromir, Frodo Baggins, Gandalf the Gray, Gimli, Legolas Greenleaf, Meriadoc
Brandybuck, Peregrin Took, Samwise Gamgee

Names sorted by length:
Gimli, Aragon, Boromir, Peregrin Took, Frodo Baggins, Samwise Gamgee, Gandalf the Gray,
Legolas Greenleaf, Meriadoc Brandybuck
```

Other sorting-related algorithms include `std::stable_sort()` (which guarantees not to reorder equal elements such as the equally-long strings `"Peregrin Took"` and `"Frodo Baggins"` in Ex20_15), `std::partial_sort()` / `partial_sort_copy()` (to sort only the first few elements), and `std::is_sorted()`. The opposite of `std::sort()`, in a way, is `std::shuffle()`, which permutes elements in a random order.

Parallel Algorithms

One of the most notable additions to the C++17 Standard Library are the parallel versions of most algorithms. Virtually every computer today has multiple processing cores. Even the most modest of phones has multiple processing cores these days. By default, an algorithm only uses one of these cores. All other cores then risk sitting by idly, envious of that one core that gets to have all the fun. That would be a real shame. When processing larger amounts of data, algorithms run much faster if they can divide the work among all available cores. With C++17, doing this became easy as pie. All you have to do in Ex20_15 to sort the fellowship in parallel, for instance, is tell the algorithm to use the *parallel execution policy*, like so:

```
std::sort(std::execution::par, begin(names), end(names));
```

(The `<execution>` Standard Library module offers other execution policies as well, but we won't discuss them here.)

Naturally, with only nine members in the fellowship, you are unlikely to notice any difference. Parallel execution would make a lot more sense, though, if for instance Saruman or Sauron were to sort the names of their troops.

Nearly every algorithm can be parallelized this way. It costs you close to nothing, and the gains can be significant. So, always keep this option in mind when processing larger data sets.

▓ **Tip**   The `<algorithm>` module also defines the `for_each()` algorithm, which you now could use to parallelize many regular range-based `for` loops. Do take care, though, that each iteration of the loop can execute independently, or you'll run into data races. Data races and other aspects of concurrent programming, however, are outside the scope of this book.

▓ **Note**   The range-based algorithms we discuss next do not (yet?) have parallelized overloads. To parallelize algorithmic execution, you must still resort to the traditional iterator pair–based algorithms we discussed here.

Ranges and Views

Looking back at the advantages of the iterator pattern—easy, robust, efficient, flexible, maintainable, debuggable—you may notice that we did not include, "leads to compact and elegant code." And it's true; as any C++ developer will attest, working with iterator pairs can lead to verbose and clumsy code. It's heaps better than directly manipulating the underlying data structures, but still not as compact and elegant as you would like it to be. And that is where C++20's ranges and views come in. They add a powerful extra layer of abstraction on top of iterators that allows you to manipulate data ranges far more comfortably and elegantly than ever before.

In what follows, we start with the basics, which are the modern *range-based* alternatives to the traditional iterator pair-based algorithms.

Range-Based Algorithms

How often have you written begin(*container*), end(*container*) by now? Enough to be totally fed up with it, we wager (just imagine how we felt after years of dabbling with iterator pairs!). It is indeed needlessly tedious. Consider for instance Ex20_15, where you wrote this:

```
std::sort(begin(names), end(names));
```

Intuitively, you want to sort names. You want to sort a container. A range of values. Having to translate between that intent and pairs of iterators all the time becomes dreary very quickly. And it leads to awkward and verbose code. Iterator pairs are useful and powerful, but they are too detailed, too low level.

In C++20, most algorithms in the std namespace received equivalent templates in the std::ranges namespace that allow you to work directly with ranges instead of iterator pairs. Thanks to this, our earlier std::sort() statement can and should now be written far more elegantly as follows:

```
std::ranges::sort(names);
```

Valid ranges include containers, statically-sized arrays, strings, string views, std::span<>s (see Chapter 9), and so on—basically anything that supports begin() and end(). Internally, range-based algorithms still work with iterators, but you, as the user of the library, are no longer constantly exposed to it. Which is as it should be. A good, easy-to-use API hides implementation details (details such as iterators... which in turn hide all kinds of other lower-level details...).

In Ex20_11A, Ex20_12A, Ex20_13B, Ex20_14B, and Ex20_15A, you can find all earlier algorithm examples, but this time expressed using range-based algorithms instead of iterator pair–based algorithms. Most of these are perfectly straightforward, except perhaps Ex20_14B. Unlike std::remove_if(), std::ranges::remove_if() returns a std::ranges::subrange<> object. This subrange represents the range of elements that you should erase. You can consult your Standard Library reference for all members of subrange<>, but for our example it suffices to know that, as a range, it provides begin() and end():

```
void removeEvenNumbers(std::vector<int>& numbers)
{
  // Use the remove_if() algorithm to remove all even numbers
  const auto range_to_erase
    { std::ranges::remove_if(numbers, [](int number) { return number % 2 == 0; }) };
  // Erase all elements of the returned subrange
  numbers.erase(range_to_erase.begin(), range_to_erase.end());
}
```

Note that in this case, the std::erase_if() function we introduced in Ex20_14A remains still more compact and elegant. The range-based algorithms still win from their iterator pair counterparts, though, reducing[2] the need for the tiresome begin()-end() argument pairs.

And frankly, if this were all ranges had to offer in C++20, we would have been over the moon already. But there is much, much more. The <ranges> module offers an entirely new and very powerful kind of ranges called *views*. Before we move on to views, though, first a quick word on yet another very nice feature of range-based algorithms, called *projection*.

---

[2] Incidentally: yes, Standard Library designers, erase_range() members would be nice for these specific cases as well....

░ **Note** Just like with iterators (see earlier), you have different kinds of ranges: forward ranges, bidirectional ranges, random-access ranges, and so on. Their classification mostly mirrors that of the underlying iterators. This distinction only becomes important when reading the specifications of range-based algorithms, though. `std::ranges::sort()`, for instance, only works for random-access ranges. You therefore cannot apply this range-based algorithm to, say, a `std::list<>`[3].

Projection

Unlike their counterparts in the `std` namespace, many if not most `std::ranges` algorithms support an extra feature called *projection*. Suppose that you want to sort a sequence of Boxes, and that you want to sort them not by their volume but by their height. In C++17 you could accomplish this as follows:

```
std::sort(begin(boxes), end(boxes),
    [](const Box& one, const Box& other) { return one.getHeight() < other.getHeight(); });
```

As of C++20, you can replace this with the following:

```
std::ranges::sort(boxes, std::less<>{}, [](const Box& box) { return box.getHeight(); });
```

Before an element is passed to the comparison function, it is first passed through a projection function. In this case, the projection function transforms all Boxes into their heights before handing them off to the generic `std::less<>{}` functor. The `std::less<>{}` functor, in other words, always receives two values of type `double`, blissfully unaware that we are actually sorting Boxes and not doubles.

The optional projection parameter can even be a pointer to a (parameterless) member function, or to a (public) member variable. The sheer elegance of this is best illustrated with an example:

```
std::ranges::sort(boxes, std::less<>{}, &Box::getHeight);
// Or std::ranges::sort(boxes, std::less<>{}, &Box::m_height); should m_height be public
```

Projection then happens either by invoking the given member function on each object, or by reading the value of the given member variable from each object.

Views

Verbosity is not the only downside of the classical iterator-pair–based algorithms. They also do not compose well. Suppose that you are given a container of Boxes called boxes and that you want to obtain pointers to all Boxes in boxes that are large enough to hold some volume, `required_volume`. Because the output should consist of Box* pointers rather than copies of Boxes, you cannot use `copy_if()` as in Ex20_13. So you consult your Standard Library reference and learn that the `std::transform()` algorithm can convert a range of elements of one type (Box) into a range of elements of another type (Box*). But much to your surprise, you cannot find a `transform_if()` algorithm to transform only a subset of elements. Prior to C++20, you always needed at least two steps to accomplish such a task. Here is one option:

---

[3] Linked list containers do provide `sort()` member functions that you can use instead.

```
std::vector<Box*> box_pointers;
std::transform(begin(boxes), end(boxes), back_inserter(box_pointers),
               [](Box& box) { return &box; });
std::vector<Box*> large_boxes;
std::copy_if(begin(box_pointers), end(box_pointers), back_inserter(large_boxes),
             [=](const Box* box) { return *box >= required_volume; });
```

You first transform all Boxes into Box* pointers, and then you copy only those that point to a Box that is large enough. Clearly this is an excessive amount of code for such a simple task. An excessive amount of code that is moreover not as performant as it should be:

- If most Boxes cannot hold required_volume, collecting all Box* pointers in a temporary vector first is clearly wasteful.

- Even though taking the address of a Box is still cheap, in general the transformation function could be arbitrarily expensive. Applying it to all elements may be inefficient then.

To address these issues, you may want to *first filter* out irrelevant objects, and *only then transform only* the few Boxes that pass the muster. To accomplish this purely with algorithms, you had to resort to more advanced intermediate containers such as std::vector<std::reference_wrapper<Box>>. We won't go there now, but our point should be clear: composing algorithms quickly becomes verbose and awkward.

And these types of problems, where several algorithmic steps must be composed, occur surprisingly often. With range-based algorithms, you can solve them very effectively, often even in several different ways. The key innovation that facilitates this is a powerful new concept called *views*.

■ **Caution** Before we introduce views it is worth noting that, contrary to what you might think at first (or at least, contrary to what *we* thought at first), you cannot readily solve our gather-all-pointers-to-large-enough-Boxes challenge using the projection feature of std::ranges::copy_if(). While the following expression may look perfectly reasonable, it does not compile:

```
std::ranges::copy_if(
    boxes,                                                    // Input range
    back_inserter(large_boxes),                              // Output iterator
    [=](const Box* box) { return *box >= required_volume; }, // Condition
    [](Box& box) { return &box; }                            // Projection functor
);
```

The problem is that copy_if()'s projection function (which in our case converts a Box& reference into Box* pointer) is applied before passing an element to the condition function (which for us tests whether a Box is sufficiently large), and *not* before writing to copy_if()'s output iterator. In our erroneous expression, copy_if() essentially attempts to cram Box *values* into a vector of Box* *pointers*, which of course won't work.

818

Views vs. Ranges

Views and ranges are similar concepts. In fact, every view is a range, but not all ranges are views. Formally, a *view* is a range for which the cost of moving, destruction, and copying (if copying is at all possible) is independent of the number of elements in the view, and therefore mostly negligible. A container, for instance, is a range but not a view. The more elements there are in a container, the more costly it becomes to copy and destroy it. The string_view and span<> classes introduced in Chapter 9, on the other hand, are implementations of the view concept. Creating and copying objects of these types is virtually free, no matter how large the underlying range is. As views go, though, they are still fairly straightforward. They simply reproduce the exact same elements as this underlying range, completely unaltered, and in the same order.

The views offered by the <ranges> module are far more powerful. They allow you to alter the way underlying ranges are perceived. Think of it as viewing the world through rose-colored glasses. When viewing a range of Boxes through a transform_view, for instance, you may instead see a range of heights, volumes, Box* pointers, or even pink fluffy unicorns dancing on rainbows. And when viewing a range of Boxes through a filter_view, you may suddenly see a lot fewer Boxes. Perhaps you see only large Boxes, only cubic Boxes, or only pink Boxes with yellow polka dots. Views allow you to alter the way subsequent algorithmic steps perceive a given range, which parts of this range they perceive, and/or in which order.

The following statements, for instance, create a transform_view and a filter_view, respectively:

```
std::ranges::transform_view volumes_view{ boxes, &Box::volume };
std::ranges::filter_view big_box_view{ boxes,
                         [=](const Box& box) { return box >= required_volume; } };
```

Like the projection function, the transform and filter functions can be any first-class function, including member function pointers or lambda expressions.

As with any range, you can then traverse the elements of a view by means of iterators, either explicitly by invoking begin() and end(), or implicitly through a range-based for loop.

```
for (auto iter{ volumes_view.begin() }; iter != volumes_view.end(); ++iter) { /* ... */ }
for (const Box& box : big_box_view) { /* ... */ }
```

What is important here is that there is virtually no cost associated with creating these views, neither in time nor in space—irrespective of the number of Boxes there are. Creating a transform_view does not yet transform any elements; this is done only at the time an iterator over the view is dereferenced. And, similarly, creating a filter_view does not yet do any filtering; this is only done while incrementing the view's iterators. In technical speak, a view and its elements are mostly only generated *lazily*, or *on demand*.

Range Adaptors

In practice, you will not often create these views directly using their constructors as we did in the previous section. Instead, you will mostly use the *range adaptors* in the std::ranges::views namespace, in combination with the overloaded bitwise OR operator, |. In general, the following two expressions are equivalent:

```
std::ranges::xxx_view{ range, args }    /* View constructor */
range | std::ranges::views::xxx(args)   /* Range adaptor + overloaded | operator */
```

Because `std::ranges::views` is quite the mouthful, the Standard Library also defines `std::views` as an alias for `std::ranges::views`. Using range adaptors, the two views from before can be created as follows:

```
auto volumes_view{ boxes | std::views::transform(&Box::volume) };
auto big_box_view{
  boxes | std::views::filter([=](const Box& box) { return box >= required_volume; }) };
```

The advantage of this notation is that you can chain operator | invocations to compose multiple views. Our gather-all-pointers-to-large-enough-Boxes problem, for instance, can be solved quite easily using range adaptors.

```
std::ranges::copy(
    boxes | std::views::filter([=](const Box& box) { return box >= required_volume; })
          | std::views::transform([](Box& box) { return &box; }),
    back_inserter(large_boxes)
);
```

Notice how easy it is now to filter before we transform? Of course, if you prefer to instead perform the transformation step first, you can simply swap the order of the `filter()` and `transform()` adaptors. The `filter()` adaptor then also needs to be adapted to work with Box* pointers instead of Box& references. We invite you to give it a try (Ex20_16 contains our solution that adapts boxes with `filter()` first, so you can start from there).

▓ **Note**   A chain of range adaptors is called a *pipeline*, and | is commonly referred to as the *pipe character* or *pipe operator* in this context. This | notation mirrors that used by most UNIX shells to connect the output of one process to the input of a next process.

For completeness, here are yet two more ways to solve our running problem using range-based algorithms and view adaptors:

```
using namespace std::ranges::views;

std::ranges::copy_if(    /* Transform using adaptor before filtering in copy_if() */
    boxes | transform([](Box& box) { return &box; }),        // Input view of boxes
    back_inserter(large_boxes),                              // Output iterator
    [=](const Box* box) { return *box >= required_volume; } // Condition for copy_if()
);

std::ranges::transform(  /* Filter using adaptor before transforming using algorithm */
    boxes | filter([=](const Box& box) { return box >= required_volume; }),
    back_inserter(large_boxes),        // Output iterator
    [](Box& box) { return &box; }      // Transform functor of transform()
);
```

Range Factories

Besides range adaptors, the <ranges> module also offers *range factories*. As the name suggests, these are constructs that do not adapt a given range, but instead produce a new range out of thin air. The following example shows one such range factory in action, in combination with several view adaptors, some of which will be new to you as well.

```
// Ex20_17.cpp - Range factories and range adaptors
import std;

bool isEven(int i) { return i % 2 == 0; }
int squared(int i) { return i * i; }

int main()
{
  using namespace std::ranges::views;

  for (int i : iota(1, 10))    // Lazily generate range [1,10)
    std::print("{} ", i);
  std::println("");

  for (int i : iota(1, 1000) | filter(isEven) | transform(squared)
                             | drop(2) | take(5) | reverse)
    std::print("{} ", i);
  std::println("");
}
```

It produces the following output:

```
1 2 3 4 5 6 7 8 9
196 144 100 64 36
```

Both loops invoke the oddly named range factory std::ranges::views::iota() (its name is explained in the upcoming note). Similar to what the pipe operator | does given a range adaptor, invoking the iota(from, to) factory function constructs a iota_view as if by std::ranges::iota_view{from, to}. This view represents a range that, conceptually, contains the numbers from (inclusive) to to (exclusive). As always, creating a iota_view costs nothing. That is, it does not actually allocate or fill any range. Instead, the numbers are generated lazily while iterating over the view.

▒ **Note** The name iota refers to the Greek letter iota, written ι. It is an homage to the classical programming language, APL, developed by Turing Award winner Kenneth E. Iverson in the 1960s in his influential book *A Programming Language* (this title is where the acronym APL itself stems from). The APL programming language used mathematical symbols to name numeric functions, one of which was ι. In APL, ι3, for instance, would produce the array {1 2 3}.

The first loop simply prints the contents of a small iota() range, but in the second loop we decided to show off and pipe a much larger iota() range through a rather long adaptor pipeline first. The filter() and transform() adaptors you already know; drop(n) produces a drop_view that drops the first n elements of a range (drop(2) in Ex20_17 thus drops elements 4 and 16, the first two squares of even numbers); take(n) produces a take_view that takes the first n elements of a given range and discards the rest (take(5) in Ex20_17 thus discards squares 256 and beyond); and reverse produces a view that reverses a given range. We invite you to play with Ex20_17 to see the effect of the different adaptors, what happens if you change their order, and so on.

░ **Note**   Unlike most range adaptors, std::ranges::views::reverse is a variable, not a function.

As always, you can consult a Standard Library reference for an overview of all available views, range adaptors, and range factories that the <ranges> module provides. Combined with the range adaptors you will encounter in the exercises shortly; however, we do believe we covered the ones you will use the most.

Writing Through a View

As long as a view (or any range for that matter) is based on non-const iterators, dereferencing its iterators will result in lvalue references. In the following program, for instance, we use a filter_view to square all even numbers of a given range:

```
// Ex20_18.cpp - Writing through a view
import std;

bool isEven(int i) { return i % 2 == 0; }

int main()
{
  std::vector numbers { 1, 2, 3, 4, 5, 6, 7, 8, 9, 10 };

  for (int& i : numbers | std::views::filter(isEven))
    i *= i;

  std::println("{}", numbers);
}
```

The result will be the following:

```
[1, 4, 3, 16, 5, 36, 7, 64, 9, 100]
```

If you add const in front of the definition of the numbers variable in Ex20_18 then the compound assignment in the for loop will no longer compile. The same if you replace numbers with, for instance, std::ranges::views::iota(1, 11), which is an inherently read-only view (since the elements of this view are only generated on the fly and then discarded, writing to them makes no sense).

Turning Ranges into Containers

A view is no container. It holds no elements. So, whenever you keep a view around, you need to make sure that any underlying data persists as well. While this certainly is a viable option, there will be times where you want to store all elements in a view for future retrieval. Prior to C++23, doing so was somewhat awkward because no dedicated functionality existed to convert a range into container, or to insert its elements into one. Thankfully, C++23 more than rectified this situation. The next example lists the different means at your disposal to store the elements of a range into a container:

```cpp
// Ex20_19.cpp - Converting ranges to containers
import std;

bool isOdd(int i) { return i % 2 == 1; }

int main()
{
  auto view{ std::views::iota(1, 11) }; // Could be any view/range...

  // std::ranges::to<>() range conversion:
  auto deque{ std::ranges::to<std::deque<int>>(view) }; // Any container
  auto vector{ std::ranges::to<std::vector>(view) };    // Deducing element type
  auto set{ deque | std::ranges::to<std::unordered_set>() }; // Pipe syntax
  auto longs{ set | std::ranges::to<std::vector<long>>() };  // Element type conversion

  // Constructors with std::from_range tag:
  std::vector v{ std::from_range, set | std::views::filter(isOdd) };

  // xxx_range() members:
  std::vector<int> v1;
  v1.assign_range(view | std::views::reverse); // Assign 10, 9, 8, 7, ..., 1
  v1.append_range(std::views::repeat(-1, 3));  // Append 3 times -1
  v1.insert_range(v1.begin() + 5, set);        // Insert any range

  // Same operations, but now using pre-C++23 iterator-pair based functions:
  auto odds{ set | std::views::filter(isOdd) };
  std::vector<int> v2{ odds.begin(), odds.end() };

  std::vector<int> v3;
  const auto atoi{ view | std::views::reverse };
  v3.assign(atoi.begin(), atoi.end());
  const auto repeated = std::views::repeat(-1, 3);
  v3.insert(v3.end(), repeated.begin(), repeated.end());  // No append()!
  v3.insert(v3.begin() + 5, set.begin(), set.end());
}
```

The code should be self-explanatory. To convert a range into a new container, your options always include std::ranges::to<>() (which is particularly useful at the end of a pipeline) or a container constructor where you pass the special std::from_range value as the first argument (to avoid ambiguities with overload resolution). And as said before, to add a range's elements to an existing container, all standard containers now also offer various members ending with _range(). You can consult a Standard Library reference to know which container offers which members.

From the final lines of Ex20_19, you can clearly see that without these extra constructors and members (added in C++23), getting the elements of a range into a container goes significantly less smoothly. Especially when you are working with views or pipelines. To use iterator pairs, you must always first store the range into a named variable to call begin() and end() on it.

▨ **Tip** All range-to-container conversion options apply to all ranges, not just to views. In Ex20_19, for instance, we used `std::ranges::to<>` to convert a sequence container into a set container and vice versa (even with a different element type) and inserted the elements of a set into a vector.

Summary

This chapter provided you with a solid first introduction to some of the most important, most frequently used features of the Standard Library: containers, iterators, algorithms, views, and range adaptors. Containers organize your data using various data structures, each with its strengths and limitations. Typical containers, particularly sequential containers, do not offer much functionality beyond adding, removing, and traversing elements. More advanced operations to manipulate the data that is stored inside these containers are instead provided in the form of an impressive collection of generic, higher-order function templates called algorithms. Combined with views and range adaptors, range-based algorithms, in particular, constitute an extremely powerful, elegant toolbox for manipulating arbitrary data ranges.

Our goal here was never to make you an expert user of all the different container and algorithm templates yet. For that, considerably more pages are required than we had left for this book. To actively start using the features that you learned about in this chapter, you'll need to regularly consult a Standard Library reference—one that lists all member functions of the various containers, as well as the many algorithm templates that exist (there are more than 100 of them in total!). Even the most seasoned C++ developer regularly needs guidance from a good reference book or website.

In this chapter, we instead aimed to convey a broad bird's-eye overview, focused on general principles, best practices, and common caveats to watch out for, with guidelines on choosing between the rich set of features that the Standard Library has to offer, typical use cases, and standard idioms. In short, it contained everything that you cannot readily extract from a typical reference work. The most important points covered in this chapter are the following:

- Sequence containers store data in a straightforward user-determined linear order, one element after the other.

- Your go-to sequential container should be `std::vector<>`. The practical use for the other sequential containers in real-life applications, and `list<>`, `forward_list<>`, and `deque<>` in particular, is typically limited.

- The three container adaptors—`std::stack<>`, `queue<>`, and `priority_queue<>`— all encapsulate a sequential container, which they use to implement a limited set of operations that allow you to inject and later take out elements. Their difference mostly lies in the order in which these elements come out again.

- Sets are duplicate-free containers and are good at determining whether they contain a given element.

- Maps uniquely associate keys with values and allow you to quickly retrieve a value given their keys.

- Both sets and maps come in two flavors: ordered and unordered. The former is particularly interesting if you need a sorted view of your data as well; the latter has the potential to be more efficient but may come with the complexity of having to define an effective hash function first (we did not cover hash functions here, but you can read all about it in your favorite Standard Library reference).

- As of C++23, the ordered associative containers in turn also come in two flavors: regular and flat. The former is backed by a balanced tree and allows for fast element addition and removal; the latter adapts a sorted sequential container and allows for fast element traversals, for one.

- You—and the standard algorithms as well—can use iterators to enumerate the elements of any given container without having to know how this data is physically organized.

- Iterators in C++ typically make heavy use of operator overloading to look and feel like pointers.

- The Standard Library offers more than 100 different algorithms, most in the `<algorithms>` module. We made sure that the ones you'll likely use most often are covered either in the main text or in the following exercises.

- All algorithms operate on half-open ranges of iterators, and many accept a first-class callback function. Mostly you'll call an algorithm with a lambda expression if its default behavior does not suit you.

- Algorithms that retrieve a single element from a range (`find()`, `find_if()`, `min_element()`, `max_element()`, and so on) do so by returning an iterator. The end iterator of the range is then always used to denote "not found."

- Algorithms that produce multiple output elements (`copy()`, `copy_if()`, and so on) should normally always be used in conjunction with the `std::back_inserter()`, `front_inserter()`, and `inserter()` utilities provided by the `<iterator>` module.

- To remove elements from a container, you should use the `std::erase()` or `std::erase_if()` functions (or the `erase(key)` member functions for sets and maps). Applying the remove-erase idiom is generally no longer required in C++20, except for certain lesser-used algorithms.

- You can take advantage of the multiprocessing capabilities of current hardware by passing the `std::execution::par` execution policy as the first argument to most (iterator pair–based) algorithms.

- In C++20, most algorithms in the `std` namespace received counterparts in the `std::ranges` namespace that allow you to directly manipulate ranges instead of iterator pairs.

- The `<ranges>` module introduces various views, as well as the means to easily produce and compose them. Views produced when piping a range to a range adaptor alter the way the next stage in your algorithm perceives a range; they may transform elements, filter out elements, or rearrange them. Views produced by range factories generate new elements on the fly. Creating views and passing them around is very cheap: views and/or their elements are always generated lazily.

- To convert a view into a container, or a container into one of another type, you can use `std::ranges::to<>()`.

EXERCISES

The following exercises enable you to try what you've learned in this chapter. If you get stuck, look back over the chapter for help. If you're still stuck after that, you can download the solutions from the Apress website (www.apress.com/book/download.html), but that really should be a last resort.

Exercise 20-1. In practice, we would never recommend you implement your own linked list data structure to store Boxes in Truckload. At the time, it made perfect sense to practice nested classes and working with pointers; but normally, you should follow our advice from earlier in this chapter and simply use a vector<> instead (a polymorphic vector<>, to be precise—see Chapter 15). If you need a sequence container, a vector<> is almost always the way to go! Eliminate the linked list from the Truckload class in Exercise 19-5 according to this guideline. Notice how you can now adhere to the rule of zero as well (see Chapter 18)? You can plug the result in the test program in Exercise 18-1 to see that it all still works.

Note: Normally, you'd probably also not easily create your own Iterator type, and even less so one whose API differs from the conventional iterator API. But, unlike the underlying list, changing Iterator is a breaking API change. A daunting task, given how much Truckload is used in our vast code bases. Therefore, and for the sake of the exercise, we ask you to rework the Iterator class, preserving its API.

Exercise 20-2. Replace both instances of your self-defined Stack<> in Ex17_04A with an instance of std::stack<>.

Exercise 20-3. Rework your solution to Exercise 17-5 by replacing all instances of your SparseArray<> and linked list template types with standard containers. Carefully think about which container types would be most appropriate!

Note: If you want extra practice, you can do the same for the solutions in Exercises 17-3 and 17-4 as well.

Exercise 20-4. Research the partition() algorithms and use one to reimplement the removeEvenNumbers() function of either Ex20_10 or Ex20_14.

Exercise 20-5. Not all Standard Library algorithms are defined by the <algorithms> module. Some are defined by the <numeric> module as well. One such example is accumulate(). Research this algorithm and use it to implement an algorithm-like function template that computes the average of a given iterator range. Exercise your newly implemented template with a little test program.

Exercise 20-6. Another algorithm that is defined by the <numeric> module is the iota() algorithm, which you can use to fill a given range with values M, M+1, M+2, and so on. Use it to rework the fillVector_1toN() function of Ex20_10.

Exercise 20-7. Speaking of Ex20_10, you of course know that instead of filling a vector with numbers from 1 to N, you could have used an appropriate view. And instead of removing elements from that vector, you could have used another view. Rework Ex20_10 to work with views.

Exercise 20-8. `erase()` and `erase_if()` are not the only algorithms for which the remove-erase idiom is applicable. Another example is `std::unique()`, which is used to remove duplicates from a presorted range of elements. Write a little program that fills a `vector<>` with a considerably large number of random integers between 0 and 10'000, sorts this sequence, removes the duplicates, and then prints out the number of remaining elements.

Exercise 20-9. Parallelize your solution to the previous exercise.

Exercise 20-10. Near the end of Ex20_15A, we sort a range of strings on their length. Come up with a way to rewrite this algorithm invocation without (directly) using the < operator. (And, no, by that we do not mean you should use <=> instead, or use > and then `reverse()`...).

Exercise 20-11. Write a function that determines whether a given integer is a prime number. If you're lost on how to do this, you can always distill a prime test from Ex6_05. Now use this function to print out the first 100 prime numbers in reverse order. Do so without the use of any container. Of course, it goes without saying that you get bonus points for using algorithms and range factories in the prime test function as well.

Hint: You already used the `iota(from,to)` range factory, but `iota(from)` is valid as well. The latter factory call produces a view that, conceptually, contains an *infinite* number of consecutive values, starting with `from`. Because a view's elements are only generated lazily, having a view that is, at least conceptually, infinitely large is no problem. Just make sure you do not attempt to exhaustively read all elements of such a view because that might take a while...

Exercise 20-12. Research the `take_while()` and `drop_while()` range adaptors and use them to alter your solution to Exercise 20-11 to output all prime numbers smaller than 1,000.

Exercise 20-13. Replace the loop in the `maxWordLength()` function of Ex20_05 with an appropriate algorithm. Try to come up with a few alternative solutions.

Exercise 20-14. In this exercise, you'll need several previously unseen views, so have a Standard Library reference at the ready. You begin by creating, in one statement, a vector filled with all multiples of 3 between 5 and 50. Don't count upfront how many elements the vector will contain. This should not *take a while*, especially if you're doing the exercises in order (was that a hint?). From this, create, again in one statement, a container that associates each of the multiples with the string `"zip zip"` (*repeating* the word *zip*... Could that be a hint within a hint?). Use a different technique to create the map than you used to create the vector. Iterate over the map once to turn all values into `"zap zap"` (not a hint...), and once to turn them into `"zop zop"` (not a hint either...). Use a different technique for each iteration, of which one leverages a final previously unseen view.

Exercise 20-15. This exercise and the next two are, in a way, what we have been working toward for some time now. They combine string formatting (Chapter 2), working with strings (Chapter 7), constant expressions (Chapters 8 and 12), inheritance (Chapter 14), exceptions (Chapter 16), class template specialization (Chapter 17), and iterator manipulation and range algorithms (this chapter).

We already told you several times that you cannot only make streams (such as `std::cout`) work with objects of your own class types (by overloading `<<`), but `std::print()` and `std::format()` functions as well. And now you are finally ready to see for yourself. The goal of these exercises is thus to ensure that

```
std::println("My new box, {:.2}, is fabulous!", box)
```

does the same as

```
std::println("My new box, Box({:.2}, {:.2}, {:.2}), is fabulous!",
                    box.getLength(), box.getWidth(), box.getHeight());
```

Like most of the Standard Library, the formatting framework of `<print>` and `<format>` is defined in terms of templates. By default, the templates that power the `std::print()` and `std::format()` functions can only be instantiated for fundamental types and specific Standard Library types (strings, containers, and so on). But you can add specializations of your own to allow these templates to be instantiated for your own types as well. Because function template specialization is flawed (as seen in Chapter 10), the mechanism chosen to allow customization of `std::print()` and `std::format()` is class template specialization (Chapter 17).

For every argument of type T that a function such as `std::println()` has to format, it creates an object of type `std::formatter<T>` and then invokes two of its member functions in sequence: first `parse()`, and then `format()`. The job of `parse()` is to scan for the format specification string (such as `":.2"`), extract information from it ("the field width has to be 2"), and store that in the member variables encapsulated by the formatter (say, a `m_field_width` member of type `std::optional<unsigned>`). These member variables are then read by `format()` while producing the desired output string representing a given runtime argument of type T. (This two-phase approach, btw, allows you to, in general, call `parse()` only once, and `format()` repeatedly...)

Creating a full specialization for `std::formatter<T>` can be quite some work, especially if you have to parse more complex format specifier syntax. So, when possible, you'll want to take a shortcut and leverage existing formatters. Because formatting a Box basically boils down to formatting three fields of type `double`, we're sure you can guess which formatter you may want to leverage here. If you make sure that `std::formatter<Box>` inherits from that class, you can have the inherited `parse()` member take care of all the parsing, and then use the inherited `format()` member in your own `format()` function to format the length, width, and height components of the Box.

(If you're disappointed that you don't get to write a function: patience, we'll get to that in the next exercise. One step at a time...)

Your `format()` member must accept two inputs: a Box, obviously, and a *format context* of type `std::format_context`. `format()` is to write the correct sequence of characters to an *output iterator* (obtained from `context.out()`), and then return an output iterator pointing to where any remaining output should go. To get you started, here is the outline of the `format()` function:

```
auto format(const Box& box, std::format_context& context)
{
    auto iter = context.out(); // Get the output iterator
```

```
/* Output characters whilst advancing the output iterator... */
context.advance_to(iter);  // Prepare context for further output
iter = /* format, say, the length: leverage the base class! */;
/* And so on... */
return iter; // Pointing one beyond the last outputted character
}
```

Complete the `std::formatter<Box>` class template specialization and write a short test program that shows that it works.

To get a feeling of working with output iterators, output at least some of the characters one by one through the output iterator. As instructive as that may be, though, doing so gets old quite fast. We recommend you also take a look at `std::format_to()`. It's a function of the same family as `std::format()`, except that it formats to an output iterator instead of a string. Like the `format()` functions themselves, as well as all standard algorithms that write to an output iterator (as seen earlier in this chapter), `std::format_to()` returns an output iterator that points one character past the output that it already wrote.

Exercise 20-16. In the previous exercise, you learned how to create a `format()` function for custom formatters. For the parsing, you still fully relied on an existing `parse()` function, though. While that was very convenient, at times you'll need to parse custom format specifiers as well. Or, and this is perhaps even more likely, to parse a combination of default specifiers and custom ones.

Your next goal is to create a new Box formatter that now also support a formatting flag n, analogous to the flag with the same name for formatting ranges (Chapter 5). If n is specified at the end of the format specifier (to keep things simple), it means that `"Box(...)"` should be dropped from the output. That is, the formatter should then produce only `"length, width, height"`.

Of course, for this to work, your formatter needs a `parse()` function now as well. `parse()` operates on a `std::format_parse_context`. While this context has some more member functions as well (look those up if you're interested), in this exercise, we'll simply treat it as a range of characters. That is, like most range objects, a `std::format_parse_context` offers `begin()` and `end()` members. Take our previous running example again:

```
std::println("My new box, {:.2}, is fabulous!", box);
```

While parsing this format string, `std::println()` at some point creates a `std::formatter<Box>` and then invokes its `parse()` function with a context object. This context is then a range—or, more specifically, a view—that points to a substring `".2}..."` (the view may or may not extend past the closing `}`). As said before, the job of `parse()` is then to go over that string, extract all information from it ("field width should be 2"), store that in members of the formatter (to be used by `format()` later on), and return an iterator that points to the closing brace. Whenever the context points to an invalid replacement field (unknown specifiers, missing braces, etc.), `parse()` should throw a `std::format_error` (see Chapter 16).

Minor complication: For empty replacement fields of the form `"{}"`, the formatting framework is allowed to pass an empty view as well. In that case, `parse()` should return the `begin()` iterator of the context. Or the `end()` iterator, naturally...

Like we already explained in Chapter 12, functions such as `std::print()`, `std::println()`, and `std::format()` always evaluate `parse()` entirely at compile time. This implies that `parse()` needs to be a function that the compiler is willing to evaluate from an immediate function (from a `consteval` constructor, to be precise). Revisit Chapter 12 if you forgot how to do this. Otherwise your formatter can only be used by string formatting functions that parse the format string at runtime, such as `std::vprint_unicode()`, `std::vformat()`, and so on (we also mentioned these briefly before in Chapter 16).

We won't ask you to parse all possible formatting options for type `double`, because that's truly a daunting job (maybe you could try with a subset one day?). Instead, we suggest that your `parse()` function extracts the format string (`".2"` in the running example) and stores that in a member. Afterward, `format()` can use this string to format the Box, for instance using a statement of the following form (the format string cannot be a constant expression here, so you'll need a `vformat()` function):

```
std::vformat_to(output iterator, format string,
                std::make_format_args(box length, width, height));
```

Don't forget to also look for the extra format specifier n!

One final complication. Because `parse()` has to be evaluated at compile time, it cannot allocate memory in the runtime free store (as explained in Chapter 8). This means that you cannot store `".2"` in, say, a `std::string` or a `std::vector<char>`. Instead, you'll have to statically allocate a character array in the formatter's member variables that is sufficiently large to hold any format specifier string imaginable (100 characters should be plenty, no?).

Hint: This being the chapter on ranges and algorithms, you can expect to need some range-based algorithms in the suggested `parse()` function. Our solution uses three: `std::ranges::empty()`, `std::ranges::find()`, and `std::ranges::copy()`.

Exercise 20-17: A final idea would be to combine the approaches of the previous two exercises. This combined approach is likely more efficient than what we did in Exercise 20-16 (which still involves runtime parsing of format string). The goal is precisely the same as in Exercise 20-16, but instead of extracting a format string and storing that in a member variable for use with `vformat()` function, you should now construct a temporary `std::string` object (recall from Chapter 8: `constexpr` functions can allocate dynamic arrays, as long as they delete them as well), put a string such as `".2}"` in there (mind the closing brace!), take out any non-standard specifiers (that is, n), create a temporary `std::format_parse_context` from the resulting temporary string, and then pass that context to the `parse()` function of a `std::formatter<double>` sub-object similar to what you did in Exercise 20-15. To mix things up even more, maybe don't use inheritance this time, but come up with another approach (which we'll dub "composition") that, at least in principle, could lend itself to using multiple helper formatters?

CHAPTER 21

■ ■ ■

Constrained Templates and Concepts

Templates define parameterized families of C++ entities such as functions (Chapter 10) or class types (Chapter 17). In practice, templates are mostly parameterized on seemingly arbitrary types. Yet most templates cannot be instantiated for just any type; at least not without error. The binary `std::max<>()` function template, for instance, can only be instantiated for types that support the `<` operator. And the `std::vector<>` and `std::optional<>` class templates may not be instantiated for reference types, `void`, or array types. Most of your own templates have similar restrictions as well, whether you realized it or not.

One thing all these templates have in common is that the restrictions on their template type arguments are all *implicit* and stem from how values of dependent types are used, often deep inside the templates' code. There is nothing *explicitly* preventing you from invoking `max<>()` for values without a `<` operator, or from attempting to create objects of types such as `vector<int[]>` or `optional<int&>`. It's just that doing so will result in a flood of oft-incomprehensible template instantiation errors. And without any indication in a template's head, how are you supposed to know what parameters can and cannot be used? Safe from dissecting the template's code, your best bet is to look for code comments or online API documentation—which as we all know are often lacking.

In this chapter, you'll learn

- What a concept is and what the qualities are of well-designed concepts

- How to define your own concepts

- How to work with the concepts that the Standard Library has to offer

- How to explicitly encode restrictions on template type parameters using constraints and why doing so makes your templates easier to use

- What constraint-based function template overloading is and how it allows you to specialize your algorithms or data structures for select families of types

- That concepts can be used outside of the context of templates to constrain placeholder types such as `auto`, `auto*`, `const auto&`

All language and library features you learn about in this chapter were introduced in C++20.

© Ivor Horton and Peter Van Weert 2023
I. Horton and P. Van Weert, *Beginning C++23*, https://doi.org/10.1007/978-1-4842-9343-0_21

Unconstrained Templates

All templates you defined so far, as well as all templates of the Standard Library that predate C++20, are *unconstrained templates*. Even though such templates almost always carry *implicit* requirements on their template arguments, there is nothing in their definition that *explicitly* states what these requirements are. This makes it hard to discover how these templates can or should be used. And to add insult to injury, whenever you do accidentally use a template with an unsuitable type argument, your compiler typically unloads a boatload of baffling errors onto you. As an (extreme) example, we invite you to try and compile the following innocent-looking program.

```
// Ex21_01.cpp - Class template instantiation errors
import std;

class MyClass { /* just a dummy class */ };

int main()
{
  std::vector<int&> v;

  MyClass one, other;
  auto biggest{ std::max(one, other) };

  std::set<MyClass> objects;
  objects.insert(MyClass{});

  std::list numbers{ 4, 1, 3, 2 };
  std::sort(begin(numbers), end(numbers));
}
```

One of the compilers we fed this program to back in 2020 produced nearly 2,000 (!) lines of error messages, and the runner-up barely managed to keep it below 500. Somewhere deep down in this jungle of errors lie, at best, some indirect clues to what you did wrong. Best of luck weeding through all that if you're new to a template!

But course you are not new to these particular templates. So before reading on, do you know what we did wrong in all four cases?

As we mentioned in the introduction of this chapter, vector<> cannot be instantiated for reference types (much like you cannot create a dynamic array of references using new int&[...]), and the binary overloads of std::max() only work for objects that support operator <. And with Chapter 20 fresh in mind, you know not to insert objects that do not support < into an *ordered* set either.

Only the last case of Ex21_01 is perhaps a bit less obvious. What could possibly be wrong with trying to sort a list of integers? If you look at the generated flood of errors, chances are it looks something like this:

```
[...]
error: invalid operands to binary expression (...)
std::__lg(__last - __first) * 2,
          ~~~~~~ ^ ~~~~~~~
note: candidate: [...]
[...]
note: candidate: [...]
[...]
```

```
[...] note: in instantiation of function template specialization
'std::__sort<std::_List_iterator<int>, __cxx::__ops::_Iter_less_iter>' requested here
std::__sort(__first, __last, _cxx::__ops::__iter_less_iter());
       ^

[...] note: in instantiation of function template specialization [...] requested here
std::sort(begin(numbers), end(numbers));
      ^

[...]
```

Whenever you misuse an unconstrained template such as std::sort(), the compiler blindly instantiates blobs of code from a myriad of templates, tries to compile them all, and then starts whining about every little statement or expression that it could not compile—of which, in general, there will be many. In our heavily redacted error listing for std::sort(begin(numbers), end(numbers)), we only highlighted one such error (there were several): "invalid operands to binary expression"? What binary expression?

The fact of the matter is, you don't care. You don't care about precisely which expressions failed to compile, which candidates the compiler dismissed for each of these (the many "candidate" notes in the error listing), or to which lines in the many layers of template code all these errors can be traced. All you care about is *where* in *your* code you did something wrong, *what* you did wrong, and, ideally, how you can fix it.

To find out *where* in your code you made a mistake, you typically need to work your way down the flood of irrelevant diagnostic messages. That is, the most interesting information is often located at the end of such an error listing. Finding out *what* you did wrong is often even harder. One thing you can always do is take a look at the declaration of an instantiated template. In our case, we traced it back to a call of std::sort(), whose declaration may look something like this:

```
template<typename _RandomAccessIterator>
void sort(_RandomAccessIterator first, _RandomAccessIterator last);
```

We're in luck. The person who wrote this particular implementation of the Standard Library knew better than to use T as the name for this template type parameter. So from this name we can infer that std::sort() expects random-access iterators (see Chapter 20). Yet from Chapter 20, you know that std::list<> only provides bidirectional iterators. Directly jumping to a particular point in a linked list is not possible; you must always linearly traverse a chain of nodes. This is why linked list iterators do not support the +, -, +=, -=, or [ ] operators—some of which the implementation of std::sort() is bound to use.

▩ **Tip**   You should use the sort() member functions of list containers instead to sort their elements.

Constrained Templates

So the reason we get that many errors when compiling code such as Ex21_01.cpp is thus that the compiler first fully instantiates all relevant templates, as well as all templates used by these templates, and so on. This often results in a significant amount of code, littered with invalid declarations and/or statements. When compiling this, the compiler then encounters many different problems. The resulting error messages moreover mostly only point to vague, circumstantial symptoms, originating from some deep, dark corners of the template's internals. Working your way back from these messages to their root cause (the invalid template argument) can at times be challenging.

Compare this, if you will, to invoking a regular function such as this getLength() function:

```
std::size_t getLength(const std::string& s) { return s.length(); }
```

When you then invoke getLength(1.23f), for instance, the compiler does not distract you by stating that 1.23f has no length() member. Instead, it simply informs you that you cannot invoke getLength() with argument 1.23f because a float cannot be converted to a std::string. Clear and to the point. In fact, the compiler does not even look at the function body for this at all. All the information it needs is available in the function's signature. And that information is readily available there for you as well.

By adding *constraints* to the parameters of a template, you can achieve the same qualities for templates, namely that:

- It is instantly clear from the head of the template which template arguments are allowed and which are not.

- A template is only instantiated if the template arguments satisfy all constraints. You should thus never again see the countless and obscure errors you get from improperly instantiated templates. The intent is that once all constraints of a template are satisfied, the instantiated code always compiles without error.

- Any violation of a template's constraints, conversely, results in an error message that is much closer to the root cause of the problem, namely that you tried to use a template with improper template arguments.

All algorithms in the std::ranges namespace, for instance, are *constrained function templates*. As a sneak preview, the constrained versions of std::sort(), defined in the std::ranges namespace, look something like this (somewhat simplified):

```
template <std::random_access_iterator Iter>
void sort(Iter first, Iter last);

// See Chapter 10 for the abbreviated function template syntax...
void sort(std::ranges::random_access_range auto&& r);
```

The std::random_access_iterator<> and std::ranges::random_access_range<> *concepts* express *type constraints* on the type parameters of these templates. Even though we are yet to explain what concepts and type constraints are, we're sure you can more or less image their semantics in the sort() example. No need to look at the body of the templates anymore to know what types you are allowed to instantiate these templates with; the template header tells you. If nothing else, adding constraints to your templates thus clearly leads to more *self-documenting code* already.

But these constraints are not only meant for you. They also save the compiler from the fruitless efforts of trying to compile code instantiated with invalid template arguments, which in turn saves you from having to wade through the resulting error floods. As an example, you can replace the std::sort() statement in Ex21_01 with one that uses the constrained std::ranges::sort() template:

```
std::list numbers{ 4, 1, 3, 2 };
std::ranges::sort(numbers);
```

With one of the compilers we tried, we got a sequence of compiler errors that began as follows:

```
[...] error: no matching function for call [...]
std::ranges::sort(numbers);
^~~~~~~~~~~~~~~~~
[...] note: candidate template ignored: constraints not satisfied [...]
[...] note: because 'std::list<int> &' does not satisfy 'random_access_range'
```

While we still omitted some clutter (a process your IDE can surely help with as well, by the way), these errors are actually about as good as you can reasonably expect. The first message clearly tells you precisely *where* you did something wrong, while the subsequent notes do a fairly adequate job explaining *what* you did wrong. It's particularly impressive if you compare these messages to those we received from the unconstrained std::sort() template instantiation earlier.

At this point, the main conclusion of this chapter should already be clear: always use constrained templates if available, and always constrain your own templates (or at least those that you intend to reuse throughout your code base, or share with others). Before we can show you how to add constraints to your own templates, though, we must first introduce the language feature of choice to express their requirements: concepts.

■ **Tip** Always use the algorithms in the std::ranges namespace over those in the std namespace. Not only to operate on ranges directly (see Chapter 20), but also when working with explicit iterator pairs. Thanks to the constraints on their template parameters, these algorithms should result in better error messages if you make a mistake. An added bonus is that many std::ranges algorithms accept an optional projection function parameter (see also Chapter 20).

Concepts

Conceptually, a *concept* is a named set of *requirements*. We distinguish three categories of requirements:

- *Syntactic requirements.* For i to be a random-access iterator, for instance, expressions such as i + n, i -= n, and i[n] should all be valid for integral n.

- *Semantic requirements.* It's not because an object offers the necessary operators to make i + n, i -= n, and i[n] compile that these operators also behave like we expect from a random-access iterator. i[n], for instance, should be equivalent to *(i + n), i -= n to i += -n, and i += n to n times ++i (for positive n). --i after ++i should bring you back to where you started, &(i += n) should equal &i, and so on. There are often many more semantic than syntactic requirements.

- *Complexity requirements.* Expressions such as i + n and i -= n are required to evaluate in constant time, irrespective of the size of n. Implementations are therefore not allowed to implement these operators in terms of operators ++ or --.

The only requirements that we can put into actual code, however, are the syntactic ones. These are also the only kind of requirements that a compiler can decidedly enforce (automatically validating semantic or complexity requirements is very hard at best, and provenly impossible in general). But that does not mean these other requirements are of any less importance—on the contrary, the implied semantic and complexity requirements of a concept are often far more important than the syntactic ones.

▓ **Tip**   Explicitly specify all non-obvious semantic and complexity requirements of a concept in the form of code comments and/or other code documentation.

▓ **Caution**   Avoid concepts that carry solely syntactic requirements such as "has a + operator." Random-access iterators, numbers, strings, and so on all have + operators, yet clearly model totally different concepts. The intent of a concept is first and foremost to model some *semantic* notion (such as "an iterator," "a number," "a range," or "totally ordered") with *semantic* requirements ("behaves as a built-in pointer," or "adheres to arithmetic properties such as commutativity, transitivity, or associativity"). The fact that we can only approximate this by encoding and enforcing the syntactic aspects of a concept does not take anything away from that.

Concept Definitions and Expressions

A *concept definition* is a template for a named set of *constraints*, where each constraint prescribes one or more requirements for one or more template parameters. In general, it has the following form:

```
template <parameter list>
concept name = constraints;
```

Analogous to other templates, a concept's parameter list specifies one or more template parameters. As always, these parameters will mostly be type parameters, although non-type template parameters are technically allowed as well (with the usual restrictions). Unlike other templates, however, concepts are never instantiated by the compiler. They never give rise to executable code. Instead, concepts should be seen as functions that the compiler evaluates at compile time to determine whether a set of arguments satisfies the given constraints.

The constraints in the body of a concept definition are logical expressions that consist of conjunctions (&&) and/or disjunctions (||) of one or more constant expressions of type bool (and exactly bool; no type conversions are allowed). A *constant expression*, as you know from Chapter 8, is any expression that the compiler can evaluate at compile time. Here is a straightforward example:

```
template <typename T>
concept Small = sizeof(T) <= sizeof(int);
```

We say that a type T *models* a concept if it satisfies its constraints expression. A type T thus models Small<> if the physical size of T objects is no larger than that of a single int.

To verify whether a given type models a concept, you use a *concept expression*. A concept expression consists of a concept name followed by a template argument list between angle brackets. Expressions such as Small<char> and Small<short>, for instance, evaluate to true, whereas Small<double> and Small<std::string> generally evaluate to false.

Concepts are often entirely or at least partially defined in terms of concept expressions of other concepts. Here are some examples:

```
template <typename I>
concept Integer = SignedInteger<I> || UnsignedInteger<I>;

template <typename Iter>
concept RandomAccessIterator = BidirectionalIterator<Iter>
    && /* Additional syntactical requirements for random-access iterators... */;
```

A type I thus models Integer<> if it models either SignedInteger<> or UnsignedInteger<> (both hypothetical concepts). And for a type to model RandomAccessIterator<>, it must first model the BidirectionalIterator<> concept as well. Of course, ultimately you need more than concept expressions alone. You eventually need to express the actual syntactical requirements of a concept, such as the alluded requirements specific to RandomAccessIterator<>. For this, you typically use a *requires expression*.

Requires Expressions

A requires expression takes one of these forms:

```
requires { requirements }
requires (parameter list) { requirements }
```

Its optional parameter list is analogous to that of a function definition (although default argument values are not allowed). You use it to introduce typed variables local to the body of the requires expression (regular variable declarations are not allowed there). In that body, you then form expressions out of these parameter names. Mind you, the parameters of a requires expression never get bound to actual arguments, nor do the expressions in its body ever get executed. All the compiler does with these expressions is check whether they form valid C++ code. This will all become clear with the examples in the upcoming sections.

The body of a requires expression next consists of a sequence of *requirements*. Each requirement ends with a semicolon and is a *simple requirement*, a *compound requirement*, a *type requirement*, or a *nested requirement*. We now look at each of these requirement types in turn.

Simple Requirements

A *simple requirement* consists of an arbitrary C++ expression statement and is satisfied if the corresponding expression would compile without errors if it were part of real, executable code. The following example shows a more complete version of the RandomAccessIterator<> concept definition from before:

```
template <typename Iter>
concept RandomAccessIterator = BidirectionalIterator<Iter>
  && requires (Iter i, Iter j, int n)
    {
      i + n; i - n; n + i;
      i += n; i -= n;
      i[n];
      i < j; i > j; i <= j; i >= j;
    };
```

This requires expression consists of ten simple requirements. It evaluates to true if all corresponding expressions are valid. In this example, all expressions apply some operator to two parameter names, but any form of expression may be used instead, including literals, function calls, constructor invocations, type conversions, class member accesses, and so on. All variables you use in these expressions must either be global variables or variables introduced in the parameter list. That is, you cannot declare local variables in the usual way as follows:

```
requires (Iter i, Iter j)
{
  int n;                               /* Error: not an expression statement */
  i + n; i - n; n + i; i += n; i -= n; i[n]; /* Error: undeclared identifier n */
  i < j; i > j; i <= j; i >= j;
}
```

░ **Tip** To better express the actual requirements, you should add a const qualifier to the type of each parameter of a requires expression that is not used in any expression that effectively requires it to be non-const. If need be, you can introduce both const and non-const variables of the same type. Here is how you could refine the definition of RandomAccessIterator<> along these lines:

```
template <typename Iter>
concept RandomAccessIterator = BidirectionalIterator<Iter>
  && requires (const Iter i, const Iter j, Iter k, const int n)
    {
        i + n; i - n; n + i; i[n];     // Required to work on const operands
        k += n; k -= n;                // Only these (left) operands must be non-const
        i < j; i > j; i <= j; i >= j; // Required to work on const operands
    };
```

Compound Requirements

A *compound requirement* is similar to a simple requirement; only besides asserting that a given expression must be valid, a compound requirement can also prohibit this expression from ever throwing an exception and/or constrain the type that it evaluates to. A compound requirement can take the following forms.

```
{ expr };                       // expr is a valid expression (same as expr;)
{ expr } noexcept;              // expr is valid and never throws an exception
{ expr } -> type-constraint;   // expr is valid and its type satisfies type-constraint
{ expr } noexcept -> type-constraint;
```

The first form, { expr };, is completely equivalent to the corresponding simple requirement. The noexcept keyword, however, adds the requirement that *expr* must be known never to throw. In other words, for a noexcept requirement to be fulfilled, any function that *expr* invokes must be noexcept (either explicitly or implicitly; see Chapter 16). As an example of such a compound requirement, here is a concept for types whose destructors must not throw:

```
template <typename T>
concept NoExceptDestructible = requires (T& value) { { value.~T() } noexcept; };
```

Because destructors are mostly implicitly noexcept (see Chapter 16), nearly all types model NoExceptDestructible<>. Note that even fundamental types such as int or double act as if they have a public destructor, precisely to facilitate generic expressions such as this.

░ **Caution** There is no semicolon after the expression inside the curly braces of a compound requirement. As always, there is a semicolon after the complete compound requirement though. Take care not to forget the curly braces around the expression either (especially since -> can be a valid operator as well!).

The most common use of compound requirements is to constrain the type to which expressions evaluate. In our RandomAccessIterator<> example, for instance, it is not enough for the iterators to support all ten required operators; we also expect i + n to result in a new iterator, i < j to be convertible to bool, and so on. With that in mind, here is an updated definition:

```
template<typename Iter>
concept RandomAccessIterator = BidirectionalIterator<Iter>
    && requires(const Iter i, const Iter j, Iter k, const int n)
      {
        { i - n } -> std::same_as<Iter>;
        { i + n } -> std::same_as<Iter>;   { n + i } -> std::same_as<Iter>;
        { k += n }-> std::same_as<Iter&>;  { k -= n }-> std::same_as<Iter&>;
        { i[n] }  -> std::same_as<decltype(*i)>;
        { i < j } -> std::convertible_to<bool>;
        // ... same for i > j, i <= j, and i >= j
      };
```

std::same_as<> and std::convertible_to<> are two concepts commonly used to express the *type constraints* in compound requirements. Being aptly named, their use should be fairly self-explanatory. The compound requirements in RandomAccessIterator<> now assert that i - n, i + n, and n + i must all result in a new iterator of type Iter (operators + and - operate on a const Iter and leave i unchanged), that k += n and k -= n should evaluate to a value of type reference-to-Iter (for class type iterators, for example, these operators are expected to return *this), and that the type of i[n] should be the same as that of *i. decltype() is a special operator that results in the type of a given expression. The four comparison operators, finally, have to evaluate to a type that is (implicitly or explicitly) convertible to bool.

■ **Caution**   The -> arrow in a compound requirement must always be followed by a *type constraint* (defined shortly), never by a *type*. While tempting, the following syntax is *not* allowed:

```
requires(const Iter i, const Iter j, Iter k, const int n)
{
    { i - n } -> Iter;  /* Error: Iter is a type, not a type constraint! */
    // ...
};
```

A *type constraint*, like a concept expression, consists of a concept name followed by zero or more template arguments between angle brackets. What is peculiar about a type constraint, however, is that you always specify one less template argument than there are template parameters in the concept definition. For unary concepts, the template argument list thus becomes empty in a type constraint. Such empty argument lists, <>, can, and typically are, omitted. The following, for instance, could be the start of a concept for random-access containers:

```
template<typename Container>
concept RandomAccessContainer = requires (Container c)
{
    { c.begin() } -> RandomAccessIterator;  // Short for RandomAccessIterator<>
    // ...
};
```

Even though our RandomAccessIterator<> concept has one type parameter, it takes zero arguments when used in a type constraint. The standard std::same_as<> or std::convertible_to<> concepts similarly have two template parameters, yet in the concept definition of RandomAccessIterator<> earlier we always specified only a single argument.

The way this works is that the type of the expression on the left of -> is plugged in front of any arguments already specified in the type constraint. The concept expression that is actually evaluated for a compound requirement of the form { *expr* } -> *concept*<*Args*...>; is therefore *concept*<decltype(*expr*), *Args*...>.

Type Requirements and Nested Requirements

Type requirements and nested requirements, lastly, have the following forms:

```
typename name;       // name is a valid type name
requires constraints;  // same as in 'template <params> concept = constraints;'
```

Both are relatively straightforward. Next, we sketch part of a possible String<> concept that uses both a type and a nested requirement (std::ranges::range<> and std::integral<> are concepts defined by the Standard Library—their semantics should be obvious):

```
template <typename S>
concept String = std::ranges::range<S> && requires(S& s, const S& cs)
{
  typename S::value_type;
  requires Character<typename S::value_type>;
  { cs.length() } -> std::integral;
  { s[0] } -> std::same_as<typename S::value_type&>;
  { cs[0] } -> std::convertible_to<typename S::value_type>;
  { s.data() } -> std::same_as<typename S::value_type*>;
  { cs.data() } -> std::same_as<const typename S::value_type*>;
  // ...
};
```

■ **Note** All but the first occurrence of the typename keyword in the String<> concept definition are required to make the compiler parse the template correctly. The reason, as you may remember from Chapter 17, is that S::value_type is a dependent type name. You may also note that instead of defining an extra integer variable like we did in RandomAccessIterator<>, we took a shortcut here and simply used the integer literal 0 in the s[0] and cs[0] expressions.

The first requirement in String<>'s requires expression is a *type requirement*. It is fulfilled if S::value_type names a nested class, an enumeration type, or a type alias.

The second requirement is a *nested requirement* consisting of a single constraint that requires the (dependent) type S::value_type to model Character<>. Because this constraint only refers to the template type parameter S, you could lift it out of the requires expression as well. A nested requirement is only necessary if its constraints refer to variables introduced by the parameter list of a surrounding requires expression.

■ **Tip** Another common use for type requirements is to check whether a given class template can be (explicitly) instantiated for a given type. Such type requirements then have the following form:

```
typename MyClassTemplate<Args...>;  // MyClassTemplate can be instantiated with Args...
```

For completeness, the Character<> concept we used in String<> could be defined as follows:

```
template <typename C>
concept Character = std::same_as<std::remove_cv_t<C>, char>
                 || std::same_as<std::remove_cv_t<C>, char8_t>
                 || std::same_as<std::remove_cv_t<C>, char16_t>
                 || std::same_as<std::remove_cv_t<C>, char32_t>
                 || std::same_as<std::remove_cv_t<C>, wchar_t>;
```

To be consistent with standard concepts such as std::integral<> (all character types model std::integral<> as well, by the way), we prefer both Character<C> and Character<const C> to be true for all character types C. To this end, we use the standard *type trait* std::remove_cv_t<> to strip any qualifiers such as const from type C. You should think of type traits as compile-time functions that operate on types. In this case, std::remove_cv_t<> converts one type into another type. Both remove_cv_t<char> and remove_cv_t<const char>, for instance, evaluate to type char. Note that the definition of Character<> also illustrates once more that std::same_as<> is actually a binary concept.

Asserting That a Type Models a Concept

When defining your own class types, you will want to verify that they model certain concepts. Conversely, when defining new concepts, you will want to verify that they are modeled by certain types. You can accomplish either by means of *static assertions*. In general, static_assert(*expr*); is a special declaration that results in a compilation error if the constant expression *expr* evaluates to false. And since concept expressions are constant expressions like any other, you can use them in static assertions as well. Here is an example that applies this idea to confirm that our earlier concept definitions do in fact work.

```
// Ex21_02.cpp - Asserting that a type models a concept
import std;

template <typename Iter>
concept BidirectionalIterator = true; // Feel free to further work out all requirements...

// Include here these (sometimes partial) concept definitions from before:
// NoExceptDestructible<>, String<>, Character<>, and RandomAccessIterator<>.

static_assert(NoExceptDestructible<std::string>);
static_assert(NoExceptDestructible<int>);
static_assert(String<std::string>);
static_assert(!String<std::vector<char>>);
static_assert(Character<char>);
static_assert(Character<const char>);
static_assert(RandomAccessIterator<std::vector<int>::iterator>);
static_assert(!RandomAccessIterator<std::list<int>::iterator>);
static_assert(RandomAccessIterator<int*>);
```

Standard Concepts

The Standard Library offers a rich set of concepts as well. Most concepts we defined earlier, for instance, have a counterpart in the Standard Library. `NoExceptDestructible<>` is equivalent to `std::destructible<>` from the `<concepts>` module (including the noexcept requirement), `RandomAccessIterator<>` is nearly the same as `std::random_access_iterator<>` from the `<iterator>` module, and `RandomAccessContainer<>` is generalized to `std::ranges::random_access_range<>` in the `<ranges>` module (not all ranges are containers).

In essence, these standard concepts are built similarly to ours. `std::random_access_iterator<>`, for instance, is defined in terms of `std::bidirectional_iterator<>` and `std::totally_ordered<>`, where the latter combines all typical requirements for a type's `<`, `>`, `<=`, `>=`, `!=`, and `==` operators. Yet overall, the concepts of the Standard Library will be better/more refined than those that we worked out thus far. They underwent thorough scrutiny during standardization and were perfected along many iterations, and by learning from real-world use of earlier prototypes. Hence our advice:

▓ **Tip** Whenever possible, use existing concepts defined by the Standard Library or other established libraries, not just for consistency and interoperability but also because writing useful concepts is deceptively hard and can take many iterations to get exactly right.

The Standard Library offers over 100 concepts, far more than we can reasonably cover in this book. Instead, we conclude this section with a brief overview of the most important categories of concepts, and in which modules you can find them. Throughout the remainder of this chapter and its exercises we also try to give at least one example from each of the most commonly used categories. For a full list of all concepts and detailed specifications, however, you should consult a Standard Library reference.

The `<concepts>` module offers core language concepts (`same_as<>`, `derived_from<>`, `convertible_to<>`,...), arithmetic concepts (`integral<>`, `floating_point<>`, ...), concepts for common object operations (`copyable<>`, `assignable_from<>`, `default_initializable<>`, ...), comparison concepts (`totally_ordered<>`, `equality_comparable<>`, ...), and concepts for function-like entities (`invocable<>`, `predicate<>`, `equivalence_relation<>`, ...). If you are not specifically working with either iterators or ranges, `<concepts>` is the best place to start your quest for appropriate concepts.

The `<iterator>` module offers a wide range of iterator concepts (`input_or_output_iterator<>`, `forward_iterator<>`, `random_access_iterator<>`, ...), indirect variants of some concepts from `<concepts>` (`indirectly_copyable<>`, `indirect_binary_predicate<>`, ...), as well as other common requirements for iterator-based algorithms (`swappable<>`, `sortable<>`, ...). Generally speaking, `indirect_concept<Iter>` is equivalent to `concept<iter_value_t<Iter>>`, where `iter_value_t<Iter>` results in the type of the value that an iterator of type `Iter` points to. Other type traits offered by the `<iterator>` module that are useful when defining iterator requirements include `projected<>` and `iter_difference_t<>`.

The `<ranges>` module, finally, rather unsurprisingly offers the `range<>` and `view<>` concepts, as well as various refinements thereof. Many of the refinements of `range<>` mirror those of the related iterator concepts: `input_range<>`, `bidirectional_range<>`, and so on.

▓ **Note** Our `String<>` concept has no direct equivalent in the Standard Library, no doubt because most string algorithms can easily be generalized to accept any range, and not just ranges of characters. Algorithms such as the classical Boyer-Moore string search algorithm, for instance, are generalized by the Standard Library in such a way that they could in principle operate on any range (see `std::search()` and `std::boyer_moore_searcher<>`).

Requires Clauses

You can constrain template type parameters by adding a *requires clause* in between the template parameter list and the template's body. Combined, the template's parameter list and optional `requires` clause form the *template head*. The general outline for a *constrained template* thus becomes as follows:

```
template <parameter list> requires constraints
template body;
```

The `constraints` component in a template's `requires` clause is completely analogous to that of a concept definition (or that of a nested requirement in a `requires` expression for that matter). It is, in other words, a conjunction or disjunction of one or more constant expressions of type `bool`.

As a first basic example we will constrain an old favorite from Chapter 10: the `larger<>()` template.

```
template <typename T> requires constraints
const T& larger(const T& a, const T& b) { return a > b ? a : b; }
```

You always begin by analyzing what the requirements are of a template. Syntactically, `larger<T>()` only requires two things: that you can compare two values of type `T` using the `>` operator, and that the result of this comparison is implicitly convertible to `bool`. A first (rarely good) option is to encode precisely that minimal set of requirements as an *ad hoc constraint* directly in the template's `requires` clause:

```
template <typename T>
requires requires (const T x)  { {x > x} -> std::convertible_to<bool>; }
const T& larger(const T& a, const T& b) { return a > b ? a : b; }
```

The keyword `requires` appears twice in a row here because we used a `requires` *expression*—which is a constant expression of type `bool` you can use outside of concept definitions as well—inside a template's `requires` *clause*. Clearly, the `requires requires` syntax is beyond awkward. Normally, though, you won't use it very often. Normally, you give the part starting at the second occurrence of `requires` a name by means of a concept definition, and then use a concept expression instead of the unnamed `requires` expression.

The ad hoc constraint in our example, moreover, is purely syntactic, and has little to no correlation to any semantic notion. Once your minimal set of requirements are clear, it is therefore typically better to look for suitable concepts that prescribe them (often together with other, related requirements). The standard concept to constrain to types with comparison operators, for instance, is `std::totally_ordered<>`:

```
template <typename T>
requires std::totally_ordered<T>
const T& larger(const T& a, const T& b) { return a > b ? a : b; }
```

This concept expression adds more requirements than are strictly needed. `std::totally_ordered<T>` requires *all* comparison and equality operators of `T` (`<`, `>`, `<=`, `>=`, `==`, and `!=`) to exist and behave as expected; not just its `>` operator. But semantically (mathematically) speaking, a total order is precisely what you want for `larger<>()`: If values of type `T` are only partially ordered, for instance, then there may not be a larger of two values.

⬛ **Note** Speaking of partial orderings, you should know that float, double, and long double also model std::totally_ordered<>, despite the existence of incomparable not-a-number values (see Chapters 4 and 13). From what we can gather, totally_ordered<> implicitly adds the *precondition* to not pass not-a-number values to the corresponding arguments of the instantiated function. Or, in other words, if T is constrained by totally_ordered<>, the behavior of using not-a-number T values is, at least in principle, undefined. This is perfectly acceptable for our larger<>() template, by the way. The notion "larger" loses all meaning when not-a-number values are involved.

Other examples of preconditions are: "do not use numbers that lead to overflow," "do not use nullptr," "first <= last," "do not use graphs with cycles," and so on. Where concepts constrain types, preconditions constrain values. Even though preconditions are mostly orthogonal to types and concepts (not all operations that operate on the same types will have the same preconditions), totally_ordered<> illustrates that the semantical implications of a concept can bring about preconditions for template instantiations as well.

In general, imposing more requirements than strictly needed—like we did by requiring std::totally_ordered<T> for larger<T>()—stimulates the creation of types with predictable, coherent sets of operations, which is something we advocated in the chapter on operator overloading as well. Requiring more than presently needed also ensures that you can still evolve the implementation of a template without having to worry about using operations that are not covered by overly narrow requirements in the template's head. In general, you want to avoid having to add requirements to the head of a template post factum because doing so might break existing code.

⬛ **Tip** Always specify meaningful semantic requirements. The preferred tools for constraining type parameters are concepts. Properly designed concepts correlate to clean, semantic notions, and impose requirements for complete, coherent sets of operations.

Sometimes requirements involve more than one template parameter. As an example, here is a constrained version of one of the other larger<>() templates in Chapter 10:

```
template <typename T1, typename T2>
requires std::totally_ordered_with<T1, T2> && std::common_with<T1, T2>
decltype(auto) larger(const T1& a, const T2& b) { return a > b ? a : b; }
```

For types T1 and T2 to model std::totally_ordered_with<>, operators <, >, <=, >=, ==, and != should all exist and behave as expected for operands of either type, possibly mixed. Note that this requirement implies that both T1 and T2 must model std::totally_ordered<> as well.

For types T1 and T2 to model std::common_with<T1, T2>, T1 and T2 must furthermore have a *common type*, a type to which both types implicitly convert. The common type of int and double, for instance, is double. The common type of two class types is their most specific common base class. And so on. Clearly, if T1 and T2 have no common type, there is no way to determine a suited return type for the larger() template. (Note that in our current implementation, we rely on the semantics of the conditional operator ?: to determine the return type for us.)

▦ **Tip**   Constrain all template parameters, especially for templates that are exported from their module. Unconstrained parameters should be the exception.

Shorthand Notation

Up until now, you introduced every template type parameter with the typename keyword (or with the class keyword, when you were feeling frisky). But since the introduction of concepts, you can introduce a type parameter with a *type constraint* as well. Here is an example:

```
template <std::totally_ordered T>
const T& larger(const T& a, const T& b) { return a > b ? a : b; }
```

You encountered type constraints already after the -> arrow of compound requirements, so it should come as no surprise that a template parameter of the form *concept<args...>* T is equivalent to a regular type parameter typename T with a constraint *concept<T, args...>* added to the template's requires clause. For unary concepts such as std::totally_ordered<>, the empty angle brackets, <>, are generally omitted from a type constraint.

▦ **Tip**   Use the shorthand notation for type parameters with a single constraint. This makes the template head more compact and readable. If the requirements consist of a conjunction of constraints, it depends: sometimes you can lift one conjunct to a type constraint in a clean and meaningful way (see Ex21_04 later for an example); other times, it is clearer to keep all constraints together in a requires clause.

The shorthand notation also applies to concepts with multiple arguments. Concepts for which this works nicely include std::convertible_to<> and std::derived_from<>, as outlined by these hypothetical examples:

```
template <std::derived_from<SomeBaseClass> T>
void foo(const T& x);

template <std::convertible_to<SomeType> T>
void bar(const T& x);
```

▦ **Note**   std::derived_from<> constraints are the equivalent of bounded type parameters in Java (where the syntax is T extends SomeBaseClass) and generic type constraints in C# (of the form where T : SomeBaseClass).

If a type constraint spans multiple template parameters, you can use the shorthand notation as well by referring to type parameters defined further to the left. Whether or not doing so is still more elegant than simply adding the requirement to a requires clause, though, is debatable. In the next example, for instance, we would argue that the shorthand notation isn't an improvement.

```
template <typename T1, std::totally_ordered_with<T1> T2>
requires std::common_with<T1, T2>
decltype(auto) larger(const T1& a, const T2& b) { return a > b ? a : b; }
```

Constrained Function Templates

As a further exercise on constraining function templates, we now review the iterator-based findOptimum<>() template we used as an illustration in Chapter 20. It was defined as follows:

```
template <typename Iterator, typename Comparison>
Iterator findOptimum(Iterator begin, Iterator end, Comparison compare)
{
  if (begin == end) return end;

  Iterator optimum{ begin };
  for (Iterator iter{ ++begin }; iter != end; ++iter)
  {
    if (compare(*iter, *optimum)) optimum = iter;
  }
  return optimum;
}
```

As always, the first step is to establish the minimal requirements for the two parameters of this template. We invite you to take a moment to think about this...

There are already quite some requirements, even for such a simple template. Clearly, values of type Iterator should be iterators of some sort. More specifically, they should support prefix increments (++), equality comparisons (== and !=), dereferencing (using the unary * operator), and copy construction and assignment (to initialize and update optimum). Next, values of type Comparison should be first-class functions that accept two values. Their function arguments are not of type Iterator, though, but of whatever element type these iterators refer to (that is, the type of *iter and *optimum).

Once the requirements are clear, you should map them onto existing concepts. And since we are working with iterators, the <iterator> module is the obvious place to start. Can you find the appropriate concepts for our template? (You will need a Standard Library reference for this.)

Because findOptimum<Iterator>() reads from both *iter and *optimum, Iterator has to model at least std::input_iterator<>. But that alone is not enough for several reasons. First, input_iterator<> does not require iterators to be comparable with == or !=, nor does it require them to be copyable. Second, input iterators are allowed to be *one-pass iterators*. With a one-pass iterator, you can iterate over the (implied) sequence of elements only once, and you can only access the current element for as long as you have not already advanced the iterator. In our case, if Iterator iterators were (copyable) one-pass iterators, there would thus be no guarantee that we could still dereference optimum after incrementing iter. The range and its elements may then simply be gone. The level of refinement for constrained iterators after input_iterator<> is forward_iterator<>. This concept adds equality comparability, copyability, and the *multi-pass* guarantee, and is therefore perfectly suited to constrain our Iterator parameter. (All bidirectional iterators, random-access iterators, and contiguous iterators are forward iterators as well.)

The most appropriate concept to constrain Comparison is a bit harder to find: std::indirect_strict_weak_order<>. The full declaration of our template thus becomes as follows:

```
template <std::forward_iterator Iterator,
          std::indirect_strict_weak_order<Iterator> Comparison>
Iterator findOptimum(Iterator begin, Iterator end, Comparison compare);
```

In indirect_strict_weak_order, strict refers to the fact that Comparison relations should evaluate to false for equal elements (< and >, for instance, are *strict* relations, <= and >= are not), weak puts the relation somewhere between a partial and a strong order, and indirect, as noted earlier, denotes that Comparison functions do not compare Iterator values, but rather the values that these iterators refer to. You could equivalently write this constraint with the "direct" strict_weak_order<> concept instead, but then you would have to first transform the Iterator type yourself using iter_value_t<> or iter_reference_t<> from the <iterator> module. Here is how you could do that:

```
template <std::forward_iterator Iterator,
          std::strict_weak_order<std::iter_reference_t<Iterator>,
                                 std::iter_reference_t<Iterator>> Comparison>
Iterator findOptimum(Iterator begin, Iterator end, Comparison compare);
```

■ **Note**   For function templates, you can also add a *trailing requires clause*, which is a requires clause that appears after the function parameter list. You can even combine a trailing requires clause with a regular requires clause and/or constraints specified using the shorthand notation. The following are all equivalent declarations for a template of findOptimum<> functions.

```
// All constraints moved to a trailing requires clause
template <typename Iter, typename Comp>
Iter findOptimum(Iter begin, Iter end, Comp compare)
  requires std::forward_iterator<Iter> && std::indirect_strict_weak_order<Comp, Iter>;

// Combination of regular and trailing requires clauses
template <typename Iter, typename Comp> requires std::forward_iterator<Iter>
Iter findOptimum(Iter begin, Iter end, Comp compare)
  requires std::indirect_strict_weak_order<Comp, Iter>;

// A trailing return type constraining an abbreviated template's parameter type
template <std::forward_iterator Iter>
Iter findOptimum(Iter begin, Iter end, auto compare)
  requires std::indirect_strict_weak_order<decltype(compare), Iter>;
```

Constrained Class Templates

Constraining class templates is completely analogous to constraining function templates. And since most class templates, even the most basic ones, cannot be instantiated for just any type either, it is good practice to constrain most class template parameters as well.

In Chapter 17, we developed a simple Array<> template. You may recall that while doing so, we already mentioned most of the requirements for its type parameter. It's now just a matter of translating these requirements into constraints, and preferably into concept expressions. Here is the outline of such a constrained Array<> template:

```
template <typename T> requires std::default_initializable<T> && std::destructible<T>
class Array
{
public:
  explicit Array(std::size_t size = 0);
  ~Array();
  // ...
};
```

To create a dynamic array of type T with operator new[ ], this type needs to be default-initializable. This rules out types without an accessible default constructor, as well as reference types and types such as void. To be able to later delete[ ] this array again, the type's destructor must be public and non-deleted as well. (As mentioned before, std::destructible<> additionally requires this destructor to be noexcept, but that is something we are most definitely okay with.)

These are templates for two members of Array<> that rely on these constraints:

```
template <typename T> requires std::default_initializable<T> && std::destructible<T>
Array<T>::Array(std::size_t size) : m_elements {new T[size] {}}, m_size {size}
{}

template <typename T> requires std::default_initializable<T> && std::destructible<T>
Array<T>::~Array() { delete[] m_elements; }
```

The main thing to note here is that you must repeat the requires clause of a constrained class template in the definitions of the templates for its members (even though at least one major compiler allows you to omit this, the C++ standard requires you to repeat the entire template head).

Constrained Class Members

Sometimes some members have more requirements than others. So too with our Array<> template. Array<T>'s copy members, for instance, require type T to have a public and non-deleted copy assignment operator. In a class template, this translates to additional requires clauses for specific members. A fully constrained Array<> template might therefore look as follows:

```
template <typename T> requires std::default_initializable<T> && std::destructible<T>
class Array
{
public:
  explicit Array(std::size_t size = 0);
  ~Array();
  Array(const Array& array) requires std::copyable<T>;
  Array& operator=(const Array& rhs) requires std::copyable<T>;
  Array(Array&& array) noexcept requires std::movable<T>;
  Array& operator=(Array&& rhs) noexcept requires std::movable<T>;
  void push_back(T value) requires std::movable<T>;
  // ...
};
```

To define the template for a constrained class member you must repeat both the requires clause of the template class's head (if any) and the extra requires clause of the member. Only the former can be part of the member template's head, though; the latter should be specified as a trailing requires clause. For the template for the copy constructor of Array<T>, for instance, you thus have to specify its two requires clauses as follows:

```
template <typename T> requires std::default_initializable<T> && std::destructible<T>
Array<T>::Array(const Array& array) requires std::copyable<T>
  : Array{ array.m_size }
{
  std::ranges::copy_n(array.m_elements, m_size, m_elements);
}
```

Notice also that we replaced the for loop from Chapter 17 with a call to copy_n(). The standard copy algorithms often copy arrays much faster than a naïve for loop does.

Of course, constraining these members does not stop you from using Array<> objects for uncopyable and/or unmovable types. Doing so remains perfectly possible as long as the compiler does not have to instantiate any members whose constraints are violated (see also Chapter 17). We demonstrate this by creating and moving some Array<std::unique_ptr<int>> variables in the following example. Uncommenting the line that attempts to copy such an Array<>, however, will result in a constraint violation.

```
// Ex21_03.cpp - Violating constraints of uninstantiated class members
import array;
import std;

// Assert that Array<std::unique_ptr<int>> is a valid type
static_assert(requires { typename Array<std::unique_ptr<int>>; });

int main()
{
  Array<std::unique_ptr<int>> tenSmartPointers(10);
  Array<std::unique_ptr<int>> target;
  // target = tenSmartPointers;   /* Constraint not satisfied: copyable<unique_ptr> */
  target = std::move(tenSmartPointers);
  target.push_back(std::make_unique<int>(123));
}
```

> ■ **Note** Because our current implementation of Array<> (indirectly) uses copy and move *assignments* in the copy and move *constructors* (and copy-and-swap techniques for both assignment operators), it would technically suffice to require assignable_from<T&, const T> and assignable_from<T&, T> instead of copyable<T> and movable<T>, respectively. But that would prohibit us from later optimizing the constructors to use some form of construction instead (first default-initializing all objects only to immediately overwrite them as we do now is not particularly efficient). And, besides, it never hurts to require semantically consistent sets of operations.

Constraint-Based Overloading

Sometimes the same functionality, algorithm, or data structure can or should be implemented differently depending on the type of values it operates on. As seen in Chapter 10, overloading is one way to deal with this. But the basic overloading techniques seen in Chapter 10 do not suffice if multiple related types require similar treatment (beyond pointer or reference types, that is, because then you can specialize for, say, T* or T& types). With the introduction of requires clauses in C++20, you can finally overload for different groups of types in a general, easy, readable way. You simply define multiple versions of the same template, only with different constraints. The compiler then instantiates the most appropriate template, based on which constraints are satisfied by the template arguments.

> ■ **Tip** constexpr if statements are a viable alternative and/or powerful complement to function template overloading; see Chapter 10.

As an example of constraint-based function template overloading, we will implement our own version of std::distance<>(), a template for functions that determine the distance between two arbitrary iterators.

```
// Ex21_04.cpp - Constraint-based function template overloading
import std;

// Precondition: incrementing first eventually leads to last
template <std::input_or_output_iterator Iter> requires std::equality_comparable<Iter>
auto distanceBetween(Iter first, Iter last)
{
  std::print("Distance determined by linear traversal: ");
  std::iter_difference_t<Iter> result {};
  while (first != last) { ++first; ++result; }
  return result;
}

template <std::random_access_iterator Iter>
auto distanceBetween(Iter first, Iter last)
{
  std::print("Distance determined in constant time: ");
  return last - first;
}

int main()
{
    std::list l{ 'a', 'b', 'c' };
    std::vector v{ 1, 2, 3, 4, 5 };
    float a[] = { 1.2f, 3.4f, 4.5f };

    std::println("{}", distanceBetween(cbegin(l), cend(l)));
    std::println("{}", distanceBetween(begin(v), end(v)));
    std::println("{}", distanceBetween(a, a + std::size(a)));
}
```

In Ex21_04.cpp, we define templates for two flavors of distanceBetween() functions: an inefficient one that works for any iterator type, and an efficient one that only works for random-access iterators. The only differences in the head of these templates are the constraints on their Iter parameter.

The first template uses std::input_or_output_iterator<>, the most general concept for iterators. All iterator types model std::input_or_output_iterator<>. Because that concept does not require iterators to be comparable using == or !=, you must add that requirement separately as well. This template also nicely shows how you can complement the shorthand notation (the input_or_output_iterator type constraint in the parameter list) with some extra constraints in a requires clause.

The second template uses std::random_access_iterator<>. Random-access iterators, as you well know, are the only iterators that support the subtraction operator. This allows you to compute the distance between two such iterators instantly in one single expression. Given the complexity requirements of std::random_access_iterator<>, this expression should moreover evaluate in constant time—and thus be much faster than the while loop of the first template.

Both templates are for functions that accept two arguments of the same type, so both templates are considered by the compiler for all three calls of distanceBetween<>() in the main() function of Ex21_04.

When the constraints for only one template are satisfied, the compiler simply instantiates that one template. That much is clear. This is what happens for the first call of distanceBetween<>() in Ex21_04: Because the iterators of std::list<> aren't random-access iterators, their type only satisfies the constraints of the first template. The program's output confirms that this is what happens:

```
Distance determined by linear traversal: 3
Distance determined in constant time: 5
Distance determined in constant time: 3
```

This output also makes clear that for the other two calls, the compiler instantiates the second template. (Yes, raw pointers are valid random-access iterators as well!) The question is, why? After all, all random-access iterators are input iterators, and they all support equality comparison as well. So for these last two calls, the constraints of both templates are satisfied. This begs the question: How did the compiler choose between a template with satisfied constraint std::random_access_iterator<Iter>, and one with satisfied constraints std::input_or_output_iterator<Iter> && std::equality_comparable<Iter>?

Out of all templates with satisfied constraints, the compiler picks the one template with the *most specific* constraints; or, more formally, the template whose constraints *subsume* (or *imply*) those of all other templates. If no such template can be found, compilation will fail with an ambiguity error.

To determine whether one constraint expression subsumes another, both expressions are first *normalized*. This basically means that all concept expressions are recursively expanded, ultimately leaving two big logical expressions with conjunctions and disjunctions of constant bool expressions. One such expression then subsumes the other if it can be proven to logically imply the other.

random_access_iterator<Iter>, for instance, first expands to bidirectional_iterator<Iter> && totally_ordered<Iter> && ..., which in turn expands to forward_iterator<Iter> && ... && equality_comparable<Iter> && ..., and so on. This process is applied to the constraints of both templates in Ex21_04 until no concept expressions are left. Once done, the compiler can easily determine that the conjunction of constraints for the first template is a subset of that of the second one. In other words, the latter subsumes the former and is therefore more specific.

▓ **Caution** The compiler's constraint subsumption solver only compares atomic expressions *syntactically*; it *never* reasons about them *semantically*. For instance, sizeof(T) > 4 will not subsume sizeof(T) >= 4, even though it is semantically speaking more specific.

Constraint normalization also only expands concept expressions; never type trait expressions. Type trait expressions std::is_integral_v<T> or std::is_floating_point_v<T> will therefore not subsume std::is_fundamental_v<T>. This is why you should always use concept expressions such as std::integral<T> over seemingly equivalent type trait expressions such as std::is_integral_v<T>.

The compiler's constraint subsumption solver, finally, only reasons about logical conjunction (&&) and disjunction (||), not about logical negation (!). It never expands expressions of the form !*concept expression* either. This implies that it won't deduce, for instance, that !integral<T> subsumes !signed_integral<T>.

░ **Tip**   Constraint-based template overloading or specialization is possible with other kinds of templates as
well, such as class templates and constrained class member templates. The principle is always the same. Out
of several templates with different satisfied sets of constraints, the compiler will instantiate the one whose
constraints logically subsume all other constraints.

Constraining Auto

Type constraints can also be used to constrain placeholder types such as auto, auto*, and auto&. Basically,
wherever you can use auto, you can use *type-constraint* auto as well: to define local variables, to introduce
function return type deduction, for the abbreviated template syntax, in generic lambda expressions, and so
on. Whenever the type deduced for a constrained placeholder type does not satisfy its type constraint, the
compiler emits an error. Here is an example:

```
template <typename T>
concept Numeric = std::integral<T> || std::floating_point<T>;

Numeric auto pow4(const Numeric auto& x)
{
  const Numeric auto squared{ x * x };
  return squared * squared;
}
```

Due to the abbreviated template syntax, pow4() is a template. Constrained placeholder types are useful
outside of templates as well. Here is a small example:

```
bool isProperlySized(const Box& box)
{
  const Numeric auto volume{ box.volume() };
  return volume > 1 && volume < 100;
}
```

With the constrained placeholder type Numeric auto, you effectively state that as far as this function
body is concerned, it does not really matter what the exact type of volume is; the only requirement is that
it models Numeric<>. Like with an unconstrained auto, this definition keeps on compiling fine—that is,
without errors or inadvertent type conversions—even if Box::volume() is changed to return double or int
instead of float. Compared to unconstrained placeholder types, however, type constraints make the code
more self-documenting, and they generally lead to more useful error messages should the constraint ever
become violated. After all, these errors will then point to the definition of a variable rather than to the place
where an unsupported operation is attempted on that variable.

Of course, type constraints may take arguments here as well, as shown by this example:

```
bool isProperlySized(const Box& box)
{
  const std::totally_ordered_with<int> auto volume{ box.volume() };
  return volume > 1 && volume < 100;
}
```

Summary

In this chapter, you learned about constraints and requirements, concept definitions and concept expressions, `requires` expressions and `requires` clauses, and how to apply these notions to constrained templates, constraint-based specialization, and constrained placeholder types. Nearly all language features you encountered in this chapter are newly introduced in C++20. What you should remember from this chapter includes the following:

- You should, as a rule, constrain all template parameters with a type constraint and/ or a `requires` clause. Doing so makes your code more self-documenting and may vastly improve the error messages you get when accidentally using a constrained template with invalid arguments.

- A concept is a named set of requirements that you typically define in terms of concept expressions and `requires` expressions.

- A well-defined concept always corresponds to a proper semantic notion and prescribes not only syntactic but also semantic and complexity requirements, and always on a complete, semantically coherent set of operations.

- Constraint-based template overloading allows you to easily define different templates for different sets of types. When the constraints of multiple templates are satisfied, the compiler instantiates the one with the most specific constraints.

- You can refine placeholder types such as `auto`, `auto*`, or `const auto&` by adding a type constraint in front of the `auto` keyword. The motivation is the same as with constrained templates: self-documentation and better error messages.

EXERCISES

These exercises enable you to try some of what you've learned in this chapter. If you get stuck, look back over the chapter for help. If you're still stuck, you can download the solutions from the Apress website (`https://www.apress.com/gp/services/source-code`), but that really should be a last resort.

Exercise 21-1. Compound requirements are nothing but syntactic sugar that allow you to combine multiple requirements into one using a more convenient syntax. Rewrite the compound requirements of the `RandomAccessIterator<>` concept definition from Ex21_02 in terms of equivalent simple and nested requirements.

Optional bonus exercise: `noexcept` is also an operator that can be used in constant expressions of the form `noexcept(expr)`. Such a `noexcept` expression evaluates to `true` if the given expression is known not to throw. With this knowledge, it should be easy to also rephrase the `NoExceptDestructible<>` concept of Ex21_02 such that it no longer uses compound requirements.

Exercise 21-2. Unlike the algorithms in the `std` namespace, the algorithms in the `std::ranges` namespace allow the type of the second iterator of an iterator pair to be different from that of the first iterator. This second iterator is called the *sentinel in the Standard Library*. As said, these same algorithms also support an optional projection parameter. Generalize `findOptimum<>()` (seen earlier in this chapter) accordingly. Do not forget to constrain your template type parameters (see the hint that follows). The `<iterator>` module is again a good place to start.

Hint: `std::projected<>` (part of the `<iterator>` module) is a type trait for which, in essence, `std::projected<Iter, ProjectionFunction>` gives you the type that results from applying a function of type `ProjectionFunction` to a dereferenced iterator of type `Iter`. The use of `std::projected<>` also constrains `ProjectionFunction`, which is why at first sight most algorithms in the `std::ranges` appear to leave the corresponding type unconstrained.

Exercise 21-3. While uncommon, concepts can be used to constrain non-type template parameters as well. Create a `medianOfSorted<>()` template that computes the median of any fixed-size `span<>` (see Chapter 9), assuming the input span is sorted. For odd span sizes, the median is then simply the middle element; for even span sizes, the median is the mean of the two middle elements. Also, make sure that the template does not instantiate for empty spans.

Exercise 21-4. `std::advance<>()` is a function template from the `<iterator>` module that, given an iterator and an offset, results in a new offsetted iterator. The expression `std::advance(iter, 5)` therefore evaluates to an iterator that is 5 positions further in the iteration order than `iter`. And, for iterators that support it, `std::advance(iter, -1)` is an iterator that points one position earlier than `iter`. Being a very old template, `std::advance<>()` is unconstrained. Create a constrained equivalent that not only works for all kinds of iterators but also has the optimal time complexities in all cases. To keep things interesting, you are not allowed to use `std::advance<>()` or `std::ranges::advance<>()`. (Don't look at their implementation for inspiration!).

Exercise 21-5. Generalize your solution to Exercise 21-3 such that `medianOfSorted()` works for any pre-sorted range (that is, not just for fixed-size spans as in Exercise 21-3) with appropriate and sufficiently complete type constraints. This time, don't use `std::span<>`. Also, generalize it such that `medianOfSorted()` also works for element types where you cannot compute an average (that is, that not support division by two). For non-arithmetic types, you may simply pick the first of the two obvious candidates as the median.

Tip: Take a look at the existing range constraint (`std::ranges::sized_range<>`, but also others, such as the requirements on the range's iterators) and range operations `std::ranges::size()`, `std::ranges::begin()`, and `std::ranges::advance()`. (Instead of `std::ranges::advance()`, you could also use your solution to Exercise 21-4!).

Exercise 21-6. In Chapter 18, we created `move_assign_if_noexcept<>()` using some basic template metaprogramming techniques. As is often the case, concepts allow you to accomplish the same thing in a much more accessible way. Define an appropriate concept and use it to create a version of `move_assign_if_noexcept<>()` that does not use any type traits.

APPENDIX A

■ ■ ■

Preprocessing, ODR, Linkage, and Header Files

In this appendix, we discuss some additional aspects of managing source code in multiple files—aspects that mostly become relevant when working with nonmodular code. From Chapter 11, you already know how to organize C++ entities of larger programs into composable, self-contained modules. But modules were only introduced in C++20. Prior to C++20, programs were organized in header files and source files. In this appendix, we discuss how nonmodular program files interact and how you manage and control their contents.

Including header files is significantly more intricate and low level than importing module files. To understand how you properly divide C++ declarations and definitions in headers and source files, you first need to know the one definition rule, as well as the different types of linkage a name can have in C++. And because the inclusion of header files is both performed and controlled using low-level preprocessing directives, we must first introduce preprocessing as well.

In this appendix, you'll learn

- What a translation unit is

- What preprocessing is and how to use the preprocessing directives to manage code

- How you can define macros, and why C++ typically offers better alternatives

- How to pick and choose what code to compile depending on the active compiler, target platform, or compiler configuration

- The debugging help you can get from the assert() macro of the Standard Library

- That ODR is short for One Definition Rule, and why it is especially important to understand these fundamental rules when managing nonmodular code

- What linkage is and when it matters

- How you organize declarations and definitions in header and source files in nonmodular C++

- The advantages of modules over legacy header and source files

© Ivor Horton and Peter Van Weert 2023
I. Horton and P. Van Weert, *Beginning C++23*, https://doi.org/10.1007/978-1-4842-9343-0

Translation: From Source to Executable

Creating an executable from a set of C++ source code files is basically a three-phase process[1]: *preprocessing*, *compilation*, and *linking* (see also Chapter 1).

First, the *preprocessor* prepares and modifies each source file according to instructions that you specify by *preprocessing directives*. It recursively analyzes, executes, and then removes all these directives from the source code. The output of the preprocessor is called a *translation unit*, and it consists purely of C++ declarations and statements.

Next, the *compiler* processes each translation unit independently to generate an object file. An object file contains the machine code for the definitions it encountered in the translation unit, as well as references to *external entities*—entities that were used by, but not defined in, the translation unit. Examples of external entities include entities that are defined and exported by an imported module (see Chapter 11). Later in this appendix, you will encounter other examples of external entities as well.

The *linker* combines all object files of a program to produce the final executable. It establishes all necessary connections between all object files for all source files. If an object file contains references to an external entity that is not found in any of the other object files, no executable will result, and there will be one or more error messages from the linker.

The combined process of preprocessing source files, compiling translation units, and linking object files is referred to as *translation*.

▨ **Note**   For your convenience, the preprocessing and compilation stages are typically performed by one and the same executable (often referred to as "the compiler"), but most compiler systems allow you to invoke the preprocessor separately as well, should you choose to.

Even though the introduction of modules (see Chapter 11) has had a significant impact on how we translate source code into executables today, the overall three-stage process has remained more or less the same. All source files—including module files—are still preprocessed into translation units and subsequently compiled into binary object files, which are then ultimately all linked together to form an executable. The biggest difference is that with modules the preprocessor no longer textually copy-pastes the source of the entire module interface into each translation unit that imports it. Instead, as explained also in Chapter 11, the compiler relies on a precompiled binary of the module's interface to process any translation unit that consumes it. We'll have more to say about the differences between including headers and importing modules later in this appendix.

Before we can properly explain these differences, though, we first need to explain how header inclusion works exactly. And for that, you need to understand how preprocessing works, and how you can control it using the different preprocessing directives.

Preprocessing Directives

All preprocessing directives begin with the symbol #, so they are easy to distinguish from C++ language declarations. Table A-1 shows the complete set.

---

[1] Formally, translation actually consists of *nine* distinct phases, not three. Before preprocessing, for instance, there are three more stages: roughly, first all Unicode characters are escaped, then all code comments are removed, and finally lines split using \ are glued together. (You will see an example of using \ later in this appendix.) There is little point in knowing all nine formal phases of translation, though, which is why we simplify matters here and compress them into three informal ones.

Table A-1. *Preprocessing Directives*

Directive	Description
#define	Defines a macro.
#undef	Deletes a macro previously defined using #define.
#if	Start of a conditional preprocessing block. May be followed by any number of #elif, #elifdef, or #elifndef directives, in turn optionally followed by at most one #else directive. Either way, the entire preprocessing block must be terminated with a single #endif directive.
#else	else for #if. Can only be used once after each #if, #ifdef, or #ifndef.
#elif	Shorthand for #else #if. #elif is not only shorter, but also more practical: #else #if needs both a line break between #if and #else (any characters on the same line as #else are ignored), and an extra #endif (you need one terminating #endif directive per #if directive).
#ifdef	Equivalent to #if defined(...). Start of a conditional preprocessing block whose if branch is processed if a macro with the given identifier is defined.
#ifndef	Equivalent to #if !defined(...). Start of a conditional preprocessing block whose if branch is processed if no macro with the given identifier is defined.
#elifdef	Equivalent to #elif defined(...): see #elif and #ifdef (new in C++23).
#elifndef	Equivalent to #elif !defined(...): see #elif and #ifndef (new in C++23).
#endif	Signals the end of a conditional preprocessing block.
#error	Outputs a compile-time error message and stops the compilation. Typically part of a conditional preprocessing block (for obvious reasons).
#warning	Outputs a compile-time warning message (new in C++23). Often part of a conditional preprocessing block.
#line	For use by automatic code generation tools that translate other source files into C++ code. Overrides the line number you obtain through functionality such as __LINE__, std::source_location::line(), and std::stacktrace_entry::source_line() for all subsequent lines of code to start at a given integer value. An optional second string argument further redefines the file name you obtain through functionality such as __FILE__, std::source_location::file_name(), and std::stacktrace_entry::source_file(). We introduce the __LINE__ and __FILE__ macros and their C++ counterpart std::source_location later in this chapter; std::stracktrace was discussed in Chapter 16.
#include	Injects the entire contents of a given file into the current translation unit.
#pragma	Offers vendor-specific features. Example uses of the #pragma directive include the suppression of compiler warnings, the configuration of compiler optimizations, and so on. You can consult your compiler documentation for a list of supported pragmas and their syntax.

Preprocessing is a low-level mechanism that originates from C, and is becoming less and less relevant with current C++. The capabilities of C++ often provide much more effective and safer ways of achieving the same result as the preprocessing directives of Table A-1. Modules, for instance, provide a far more satisfying way of organizing your code in multiple, self-contained files than you can achieve using #include directives. And constants and function templates are far safer and more powerful than the macros you define with the #define directive. We will signal these and other alternatives offered by C++ throughout this appendix.

Most preprocessing directives nonetheless do still have their uses, even in modern C++, albeit only sporadically. For instance, when your code has to be compatible with different compilers, or if you target multiple operating systems, the occasional conditional preprocessing block tends to be unavoidable. And of course you will still encounter preprocessing directives in virtually any legacy header or source file. So you for sure still need at least a basic notion of what the different preprocessing directives do.

We begin by explaining how you define macros using the #define directive.

Defining Preprocessor Macros

A #define directive specifies a *macro*. A macro is a text rewrite rule that instructs the preprocessor which text replacements to apply to the source code prior to handing it over to the compiler. We distinguish two types of macros: *object-like macros* and *function-like macros*.

Defining Object-Like Macros

The simplest form of the #define preprocessing directive is the following:

```
#define IDENTIFIER sequence of characters
```

This *object-like* macro effectively defines IDENTIFIER as an alias for sequence of characters. IDENTIFIER must conform to the usual definition of an identifier in C++; that is, any sequence of letters and digits, the first of which is a letter, and where the underline character counts as a letter. A macro identifier does not have to be in all caps, although this is certainly a widely accepted convention. sequence of characters can be any sequence of characters, including an empty sequence or a sequence that contains whitespace. In fact, object-like macros with empty replacement sequences are relatively common; we discuss this option further in a subsection shortly.

The most obvious use for #define, surely, is to specify some identifier that is to be replaced in the source code by a non-empty substitute string during preprocessing. Here's how you could define PI to be an alias for a sequence of characters that represents a numerical value:

```
#define PI 3.1415
```

Even though this PI macro *looks* like a variable, it has nothing to do with one. PI is a symbol, or *token*, that is to be exchanged for the specified sequence of characters by the preprocessor before the code is compiled. To the preprocessor, 3.1415 is not a numerical value. It is merely text. A string of characters. No validation at all takes place during preprocessing on whether this sequence forms a valid number. If you accidentally wrote 3,1415, or 3.1415, or 3.14*!5 as the replacement sequence, the substitution would still occur and almost certainly result in invalid C++ code. The preprocessor blindly replaces text, without any safety checks on the character sequence on its right size.

Moreover, if your code contains any C++ entity (a variable, function, type, and so on) named PI, the preprocessor will blindly replace all occurrences of this identifier with 3.1415. Suppose that you didn't know about the PI macro, and you wrote the following otherwise correct C++ statement.

```
const double PI = std::numbers::pi;
```

Then all the preprocessor sees is a token PI, which it has been instructed to replace by the character sequence 3.1415. The preprocessor neither knows nor cares that this token occurs on the left of a C++ assignment. It simply replaces tokens with text. And, so, this is what it hands over to the compiler:

```
const double 3.1415 = std::numbers::pi;
```

Similarly, if the macro was called `pi` instead of `PI`, the preprocessor would just as happily rewrite your code into this equally nonsensical statement.

```
const double PI = std::numbers::3.1415;
```

In either case, the compiler will produce a series of cryptic error messages. And, believe us, if you truly have no knowledge of the culprit macros, such errors can be particularly baffling. We will discuss an all too realistic example of such a scenario soon, in the section on function-like macros.

While the `#define` directive is often used to define *symbolic constants* such as `PI` in C, it should be clear by now why you should never, ever do this in C++. It is much better and safer to define a constant variable, like this (and even better and safer, of course, to use predefined constants such as those of the standard `<numbers>` module introduced in Chapter 2, but that's beside the point):

```
constexpr double PI { 3.14159265358979323846 };
```

▨ **Caution**   Never use a macro in C++ when a `const` or `constexpr` variable (or variable template) will do. Using a `#define` directive has at least three major disadvantages: there's no type checking support, it doesn't respect scope, and the identifier name cannot be bound within a namespace.

Even though the preprocessor will happily rewrite perfectly correct C++ into complete and utter gibberish if you're not careful, it is actually not entirely agnostic about C++'s syntax. It replaces identifiers only when they are tokens; never if they are part of a longer identifier, a string literal, or a code comment. That is, with our earlier macro definition, the preprocessor will not replace the PI character sequences in C++ identifiers such as `ALPHA_PI_ALPHA`, in string literals such as `"What famous scientist is born on PI day (March 14)?"`[2], or in C++ code comments such as `/* PI = icRT */` or `// The millionth digit of PI is 5`.

Here's an example program that uses some object-like macro definitions:

```
// ExA_01.cpp - Defining object-like macros
import std;

#define POINTER_SIZE sizeof(int*) * BITS_PER_BYTE
#define BITS_PER_BYTE 8

int main()
{
  std::println("{}", POINTER_SIZE);   // 32 or 64, normally
}

// The next macro (while providing a perfectly valid definition for "main")
// is never applied, because it is not defined yet when the preprocessor
// processes the line "int main()".
#define main Of chief or leading importance; prime, principal.
```

---

[2] The answer is Albert Einstein (born on Pi Day in 1879). Did you also know that Stephen Hawking passed away on Pi Day in 2018? And that he was born 8 January 1942, precisely 300 years after Galileo Galilei died on that exact same day—8 January 1642? Coincidence? We believe so...

With these macros, the preprocessor first replaces any occurrence of POINTER_SIZE with the character sequence sizeof(int*) * BITS_PER_BYTE, which it then further rewrites to sizeof(int*) * 8. That is, after expanding a macro, the preprocessor processes the resulting character sequence again from the start, replacing more tokens where needed. This process continues until there are no more tokens left to replace.

As you know from Chapter 2, the sizeof operator evaluates to the number of bytes that is used to represent a type or variable. We arbitrarily choose the type int* in ExA_01, but any other pointer type would do as well. For a 32-bit program, any pointer occupies 4 bytes, or 32 bits; for a 64-bit program, any pointer occupies 8 bytes, or 64 bits. The output of ExA_01 therefore typically reads either 32 or 64.

The preprocessor processes a file from top to bottom, executing directives and performing text replacements as it goes along. This is why at the moment that the preprocessor reaches the line with int main(), there is no macro defined yet with identifier main. This macro only becomes defined a few lines later, and is therefore never applied.

Note also that we purposely defined the BITS_PER_BYTE macro *after* the POINTER_SIZE macro to illustrate the order in which text replacements occur. That is, the preprocessor does not yet process the right side of a macro definition when executing a #define directive; it only does so after each macro expansion.

Defining Empty Macros

There's no restriction on the sequence of characters that is to replace the identifier. It can even be absent, in which case the identifier exists but with no predefined substitution string—the substitution string is empty. If you don't specify a substitution string for an identifier, then occurrences of the identifier in the code will be replaced by an empty string; in other words, the identifier will be removed. Here's an example:

```
#define VALUE
```

The effect is that all occurrences of VALUE that follow the directive will be removed.

More often than not, however, you do not define empty object-like macros to perform text replacement. In our example, the same directive also defines VALUE as an identifier whose existence can be tested by other directives, and then used for conditional compilation. The single most common use of this technique in standard C++ is probably the management of header files, as you'll see near the end of this appendix. Another typical use is conditional compilation based on macros set by the compiler or build system. Such macros may, for instance, signal properties of the target platform (such as the operating system, address size, and so on), or certain compiler settings (toggling of debug builds), and so on. You will see examples of conditional compilation shortly, after a brief introduction to function-like macros.

Defining Function-Like Macros

Besides object-like macros, you can also define *function-like* text-replacement macros with #define directives. Here's an example:

```
#define MAX(A, B) A >= B ? A : B
```

While this macro looks an awful lot like a function, it most certainly isn't one. There are no argument types, nor is there a return value. A macro is not something that is called, nor does its right side necessarily specify statements to be executed at runtime. Our sample macro simply instructs the preprocessor to replace all occurrences of MAX(anything1, anything2) in the source code with the character sequence that appears in the second half of the #define directive. During this replacement process, all occurrences of the macro's parameter identifier A in A >= B ? A : B are replaced by anything1, and all occurrences of B are replaced with anything2. The preprocessor makes no attempt at interpreting or evaluating the anything1 and anything2 character sequences; all it does again is blind text replacement. Suppose, for instance, that your code contains this statement:

```
std::cout << MAX(expensive_computation(), 0) << std::endl;
```

Then the preprocessor expands it to the following source code before handing it over to the compiler:

```
std::cout << expensive_computation() >= 0 ? expensive_computation() : 0 << std::endl;
```

This example exposes two problems:

- The resulting code will not compile. If you use the ternary operator ?: together with the streaming operator <<, the C++ operator precedence rules (see Chapter 3) tell us that the expression with the ternary operator should be between parentheses. A better definition of our MAX() macro would therefore be the following:

  ```
  #define MAX(A, B) (A >= B ? A : B)
  ```

  Even better would be to add parentheses around all occurrences of A and B to avoid similar operator precedence problems there as well:

  ```
  #define MAX(A, B) ((A) >= (B) ? (A) : (B))
  ```

  The bottom line is, though, that making sure that even the simplest of macros always expands to valid code can be surprisingly hard.

- The expensive_computation() function is called up to two times. If a macro parameter such as A appears more than once in the replacement, the preprocessor will blindly copy the macro arguments more than once. This undesired behavior with macros is not only harder to avoid, but also harder to discover (given that it compiles without error).

These are just two of the common pitfalls with macro definitions. We therefore recommend you create function-like macros only if you have a good reason for doing so. While some advanced scenarios do call for macros, C++ mostly offers superior alternatives. Macros are popular among C programmers because they allow the creation of function-like constructs that work with any parameter type. But you already know that C++ offers a much better solution for this: function templates. After Chapter 10, it should be a breeze for you to define a C++ function template that replaces the C-style MAX() macro. C++ function templates inherently avoid both of the shortcomings of macro definitions we listed earlier.

▓ **Caution**   Never use preprocessor macros where a function template will do. Instead, you should always use either (overloaded) C++ functions or function templates. Function templates are far superior to preprocessor macros for defining blueprints of functions that work for any argument type. C++ functions are type safe, respect scope, can be overloaded, their names can be bound to a namespace, and they are much easier to debug than macros. Function arguments, moreover, are never evaluated more than once.

▓ **Note**   Because of all the aforementioned downsides of macros, macros cannot even be exported from C++ modules. Another solid reason to always define proper variables, functions, and templates instead of macros in modern C++.

Preprocessor Operators

For completeness, Table A-2 lists the two operators you can apply to the parameters of a function-like macro.

Table A-2. *Preprocessor Operators*

#	The so-called stringification operator. Turns the argument in a string literal containing its value (by surrounding it with double quotes and adding the necessary character escape sequences).
##	The concatenation operator. Concatenates (pastes together, similar to what the + operator does for the values of two std::strings) the values of two identifiers.

The following toy program illustrates how you might use these operators:

```
// ExA_02.cpp - Working with preprocessor operators
import std;

#define DEFINE_PRINT_FUNCTION(NAME, COUNT, VALUE) \
  void NAME##COUNT() { std::println(#VALUE); }

DEFINE_PRINT_FUNCTION(fun, 123, Test 1 "2" 3)

int main()
{
  fun123();
}
```

Before we get to the use of both preprocessor operators, ExA_02.cpp shows one additional thing: macro definitions are not really allowed to span multiple lines. By default, the preprocessor simply replaces any occurrences of the macro's identifier (possibly taking a number of arguments) with all the characters it finds on the same line to the right of the identifier. However, it is not always practical to fit the entire definition on one single line. The preprocessor therefore allows you to add line breaks, as long as they are immediately preceded by a backslash character. All such escaped line breaks are discarded from the substitution. That is, the preprocessor first concatenates the entire macro definition back into one single line (in fact, it does so even outside of a macro definition).

■ **Note** In ExA_02.cpp, we added the line break before the right side of the macro definition, which is probably the most natural thing to do. But since the preprocessor always just stitches any sliced lines back together, without interpreting the characters, such escaped line breaks can really appear anywhere you want. Not that this is in any way recommended, but this means you *could* in extremis even write the following, perfectly valid C++ program (equivalent to ExA_02.cpp):

```
import std;

#define DEFINE_PRINT_FUNC\
TION(NAME, COUNT, VALUE) v\
oid NAME##COUNT() { std::pr\
intln(#VALUE); }
```

```
DEFINE_PRINT_FUNCTION(fun, 123, Test 1 "2" 3)
```

```
\
i\
nt\
 ma\
in()\
{fun1\
23();}\
```

Mind you, if you do splice identifiers like this, for whatever crazy reason, take care not to add unwanted whitespace characters at the beginning of the next line, as these are not discarded by the preprocessor when it puts the pieces back together.

Enough about multi-line macros and line breaks, though; it's time to get back to the topic at hand: preprocessor operators. The macro definition in ExA_02 uses both ## and #:

```
#define DEFINE_PRINT_FUNCTION(NAME, COUNT, VALUE) \
  void NAME##COUNT() { std::println(#VALUE); }
```

With this definition, the line DEFINE_PRINT_FUNCTION(fun, 123, Test 1 "2" 3) in ExA_02.cpp expands to the following function definition:

```
void fun123() { std::println("Test 1 \"2\" 3"); }
```

The tokens fun and 123 are concatenated with ##. Without the ## operator, you'd have the choice between either NAMECOUNT or NAME COUNT. In the former, the preprocessor would not recognize NAME or COUNT; with the latter, our example macro would expand to fun 123, which is not a valid function name. (C++ identifiers may not contain spaces.)

Without the # operator, then, your best attempt at turning VALUE's value into a string literal would be "VALUE", but that does not work for two reasons. First, "VALUE" would simply result in the string literal "VALUE", as the preprocessor again does not replace occurrences of macro parameter identifiers inside literals, identifiers, or code comments. And even if we ignore that minor inconvenience, there would be no way for you to inject the required escape characters (\) in front of characters such as double quotes in more complex cases such as our deviously crafted Test 1 "2" 3.

Because the preprocessor runs first, the definition of the fun123() function will be present by the time the C++ compiler gets its hands on the code. This is why you can call fun123() in the program's main() function, where it produces the following result:

```
Test 1 "2" 3
```

ExA_02 thus illustrates that you are by no means limited to specifying only variable- or function-like constructs with macros. That is, you can also use macros to generate entire function definitions, or even entire class definitions if you want to.

Undefining Macros

You may want the macro resulting from a #define directive to be applied only to *part* of a program file. Putting the macro definition in a scope delimited by curly braces ({ and }), however, does not work. Preprocessing macros do not respect scoping, as illustrated by the following example.

```
{
    #define PI 3.14159265358979323846264338327950288
    // ...
}
// All occurrences of PI in code from this point are still replaced!
```

What you can do, however, is nullify a definition for an identifier using the #undef directive. You can negate a previously defined macro with this directive:

```
#undef IDENTIFIER
```

IDENTIFIER is no longer defined following this directive, so no substitutions for IDENTIFIER occur below that line anymore. The following code fragment illustrates this:

```
#define PI 3.14159265358979323846264338327950288
// ...
#undef PI
// PI is no longer defined from here on so no substitutions occur.
// Any references to PI will be left in the code below.
```

Between the #define and #undef directives, preprocessing replaces appropriate occurrences of PI in the code with 3.14159265358979323846264338327950288. Elsewhere, occurrences of PI are left as they are. The #undef directive also works for function-like macros. Here's an example:

```
#undef MAX
```

▧ **Tip** Functions of the native API of the Windows operating system are made available through headers such as <Windows.h>. One well-known annoyance with this and other Windows headers is that, by default, they define min() and max() preprocessing macros analogous to our MAX() macro earlier. (The #include directive and how it may introduce macro definitions into a source file is discussed later in this appendix.) For starters, these macros suffer from the same issue as any function-like macro: unlike functions, their arguments are potentially evaluated twice, which may inadvertently lead to poor performance. At least as annoying, though, is that the min() and max() macros injected by the Windows headers invalidate otherwise perfectly correct C++ expressions such as std::max(0, my_val) because they instruct the preprocessor to rewrite these expressions into utter nonsense like

```
std::((0) > (my_val) ? (0) : (my_val))
```

One solution is to undefine both macros after including one of these Windows headers as follows:

```
#include <windows.h>
#undef min
#undef max
```

Another solution[3] is to define the NOMINMAX macro prior to the #include directive, like so:

```
#define NOMINMAX
#include <Windows.h>
```

This causes the Windows headers to no longer define the min() and max() macros in the first place, using the conditional compilation techniques we discuss in the next section.

Conditional Compilation

The logical #if works in essentially the same way as an if statement in C++. Among other things, this allows conditional inclusion of code and/or further preprocessing directives (including macro definitions!) in a file, depending on whether preprocessing identifiers have been defined or based on identifiers having specific values. This is particularly useful when you want to maintain one set of code for an application that may be compiled and linked to run in different hardware or operating system environments. You can define preprocessing identifiers that specify the environment for which the code is to be compiled and select either code or #include or #define directives accordingly.

Testing Whether Identifiers Are Defined

You can use the #if defined directive to test whether a given identifier has been defined and include code or not in the file depending on the result:

```
#if defined MY_IDENTIFIER
  // The code here will be placed in the source file if MY_IDENTIFIER has been defined.
  // Otherwise it will be omitted.
#endif
```

All the lines following #if defined up to the #endif directive will be kept in the file if the identifier, MY_IDENTIFIER, has been defined previously and will be omitted if it has not. The #endif directive marks the end of the text that is controlled by the #if defined directive. You can use the abbreviated form, #ifdef, if you prefer:

```
#ifdef MY_IDENTIFIER
  // The code here will be placed in the source file if MY_IDENTIFIER has been defined.
  // Otherwise it will be omitted.
#endif
```

---

[3] A third, in this case less elegant, solution is to resort to expressions such as (std::max)(0, my_val). By adding an extra pair of parentheses around std::max, you turn this qualified name into a single token in the eyes of the preprocessor, which prevents the unwanted macro expansion.

Similarly, you can use the #if !defined or its equivalent #ifndef to test for an identifier not having been defined:

```
#if !defined MY_IDENTIFIER
   // The code down to #endif will be placed in the source file
   // if MY_IDENTIFIER has NOT been defined. Otherwise, the code will be omitted.
#endif
```

Suppose you put the following code in your program file:

```
// Code that sets up the array data[]...

#ifdef CALC_AVERAGE
   double average {};
   for (std::size_t i {}; i < std::size(data); ++i)
     average += data[i];
   average /= std::size(data);
   std::println("Average of data array is {}", average);
#endif

// rest of the program...
```

If the CALC_AVERAGE identifier has been defined by a previous preprocessing directive, the code between the #ifdef and #endif directives is compiled as part of the program. If CALC_AVERAGE has not been defined, the code won't be included.

Because the compiler does not even get to see code that is part of a conditional block for which the condition is not met, it may even contain statements that it would not know how to compile at all. This is why such techniques are often used to conditionally compile code based on macros that are only defined for a particular compiler, or when targeting a particular operating system, processor type, and so on. The idea is that code in these blocks then only compiles and/or works when these macros are effectively defined.

Besides testing whether a given macro is defined, you can more generally use the #if directive to test whether any constant expression is true. Let's explore that a bit further.

Testing for Specific Identifier Values

The general form of the #if directive is as follows:

```
#if constant_expression
```

The constant_expression must be an integral constant expression that does not contain casts. All arithmetic operations are executed with the values treated as type long or unsigned long, though Boolean operators (||, &&, and !) are definitely supported as well. If the value of constant_expression evaluates to nonzero, then lines following the #if down to the #endif will be included in the code to be compiled. The most common application of this uses simple comparisons to check for a particular identifier value. For example, you might have the following sequence of statements:

```
#if ADDR == 64
   // Code taking advantage of 64-bit addressing...
#endif
```

The statements between the #if directive and #endif are included in the program only if the identifier ADDR has been defined as 64 in a previous #define directive.

▦ **Tip** There is no cross-platform macro identifier to detect whether the current target platform uses 64-bit addressing. Most compilers, however, do offer some platform-specific macro that it will define for you whenever it's targeting a 64-bit platform. A concrete test that should work for the Visual C++, GCC, and Clang compilers, for instance, would look something like this:

```
#if _WIN64 || __x86_64__ || __ppc64__
  // Code taking advantage of 64-bit addressing...
#endif
```

Consult your compiler documentation for these and other predefined macro identifiers.

Multiple-Choice Code Selection

The #else directive works in the same way as the C++ else statement, in that it identifies a sequence of lines to be included in the file if the #if condition fails. This provides a choice of two blocks, one of which will be incorporated into the final source. Here's an example:

```
#if ADDR == 64
  std::println("Standard 64-bit addressing version.");
  // Code taking advantage of 64-bit addressing...
#else
  std::println("Legacy 32-bit addressing version.");
  // Code for older 32-bit processors...
#endif
```

One or the other of these sequences of statements will be included in the file, depending on whether ADDR has been defined as 64.

There are special forms of #if for multiple-choice selections. This is the #elif directive, which has the following general form:

```
#elif constant_expression
```

C++23 introduced #elifdef and #elifndef as shorthand for #elif defined and #elif !defined, which you'll then typically use in conditional compilation blocks introduced by #ifdef.

The nice thing about the #elif directives is that, unlike with the nearly equivalent #else #if constructs, you still only need one single #endif to end the conditional compilation block. Here is an example of how you might use this:

```
#if LANGUAGE == ENGLISH
  #define Greeting "Good Morning."
#elif LANGUAGE == GERMAN
  #define Greeting "Guten Tag."
#elif LANGUAGE == FRENCH
  #define Greeting "Bonjour."
```

```
#else
  #define Greeting "Ola."
#endif
  std::println(Greeting);
```

With this sequence of directives, the output statement will display one of a number of different greetings, depending on the value assigned to LANGUAGE in a previous #define directive.

▓ **Caution**   Any undefined identifiers that appear after the conditional directives #if and #elif are replaced with the number 0. This implies that, should LANGUAGE for instance not be defined in the earlier example, it may still compare equal to ENGLISH, GERMAN, or FRENCH should any of these three either be undefined as well, or explicitly defined to be zero.

Another possible use is to include different code depending on an identifier that represents a version number:

```
#if VERSION == 3
  // Code for version 3 here...
#elif VERSION == 2
  // Code for version 2 here...
#else
  // Code for original version 1 here...
#endif
```

This allows you to maintain a single source file that compiles to produce different versions of the program depending on how VERSION has been set in a #define directive.

▓ **Tip**   Your compiler likely allows you to specify the value of preprocessing identifiers by passing a command-line argument to the compiler. (If you're using a graphical IDE, there should be a corresponding properties dialog somewhere.) That way, you can compile different versions or configurations of the same program without changing any code.

Testing for Available Headers

Each version of the Standard Library provides a multitude of new header files. These new features and functionalities allow you to write code that would otherwise have taken you a lot more effort, or that would otherwise have been far less performant or robust. On the one hand, you therefore normally always want to use the best and latest that C++ has to offer. On the other hand, though, your code is sometimes supposed to compile and run correctly with multiple compilers—either multiple versions of the same compiler or different compilers for different target platforms. This sometimes requires a way for you to test, at compile time, which headers the current compiler can access to enable or disable different versions of your code.

The __has_include() macro can be used to check for the availability of any header file, be it part of either the Standard Library or some other external library, or one of your own headers. Here is an example:

```
#if __has_include(<execution>)
  #include <algorithm> // Or 'import <algorithm>;' and 'import <execution>;' (see later)
  #include <execution>

  // ... Definitions that use std::for_each(std::execution::par, ...)
  // (Note: Chapter 20 explains how to use parallel execution policies)
#elif __has_include(<tbb/parallel_for.h>)
  #include <tbb/parallel_for.h>

  // ... Definitions that use tbb::parallel_for(...) from Intel's TBB library
#else
  #error("Support for parallel loops is required for acceptable performance")
  // ... Alternative is to provide definitions that use slower, sequential for loops
#endif
```

We're sure that you can figure out how this works from this example outline alone, at least as far as the conditional compilation is concerned. (The #include directive is discussed in more detail later.)

Testing for Available Language Features

With the __has_include() macro from the previous section, you can check whether some Standard Library header exists, but it does not tell you anything about the content of that header. New versions of C++ regularly add functionality to existing headers as well. C++20, for instance, added the unseq execution policy object to C++17's <execution> header. The condition __has_include(<execution>) from before tells you nothing about whether this new policy is supported. Other examples of new C++20 functionality in existing headers include the extension of std::make_shared<>() (see Chapter 6) to support the creation of shared arrays, and the addition of the std::lerp<>() and midpoint<>() linear interpolation[4] functions to <cmath> (see Chapter 2). How do you know whether your code can take advantage of these features, or that it should instead fall back to potentially less effective alternatives?

As of C++20, you can test whether your compiler supports a particular Standard Library feature using the macros defined in the <version> header. Here is how you could test for the different features we mentioned in the previous paragraph. For brevity, we omit the actual conditional blocks and #endif directives.

```
#if __cpp_lib_execution                      // The <execution> header exists (C++17)
#if __cpp_lib_execution >= 201902L    // <execution> defines unseq policy (C++20)

#if __cpp_lib_shared_ptr_arrays              // std::shared_ptr<> supports arrays (C++17)
#if __cpp_lib_shared_ptr_arrays >= 201707L // std::make_shared<>() supports arrays (C++20)

#if __cpp_lib_interpolate        // std::lerp<>() and midpoint<>() added to <cmath> (C++20)
#ifdef __cpp_lib_interpolate          // Equivalent to previous
#if __cpp_lib_interpolate >= 201902L // Equivalent to previous (201902L is initial value)
```

---

[4] "lerp" is a contraction of "linear interpolation" commonly used in computing and mathematical jargon.

Once a Standard Library implementation fully supports a new library feature, the corresponding *feature testing macro* is either defined or updated. From then on, that macro rewrites to an integer number that denotes the month in which the corresponding feature was officially added to the C++ standard. This number increases whenever that feature is updated significantly. For instance, because the specification for the <execution> header was first added to the C++ standard in March 2016, `__cpp_lib_execution` will always be defined as a value that is higher or equal to 201603L by a Standard Library that provides this header. If your implementation added support for the unseq policy, though, the macro will have been redefined to expand to the value 201902L, which denotes February 2019, the month in which this policy was added to the draft of the C++20 standard.

The <version> header defines about 200 *library feature test macros* like this, so you'll forgive us that we don't cover them all. You can consult a Standard Library reference should you ever need to know what macros are available, and what their possible values are.

▨ **Caution** Because macros are not exported from modules, importing the std or std.compat modules does not suffice to gain access to the library feature testing macros. As discussed in more detail later in this chapter, you therefore need to use either import <version>; or #include <version> instead.

Of course the Standard Library is not the only thing that evolves, so does the C++ language itself. Analogous macros therefore exist to test whether your compiler already supports a given language feature. `__cpp_lambdas`, for instance, is defined if your compiler supports lambda expressions (see Chapter 18), `__cpp_concepts` is defined if it supports concepts (Chapter 21), and so on. These *language feature test macros* (there's about 70 of them at the moment) are implicitly defined in every translation unit, without including any header file or importing any module.

Most feature test macros are object-like. The only exception is `__has_cpp_attribute()`. You can use this function-like macro to test whether your compiler supports a given C++ attribute, such as the [[fallthrough]] attribute we discussed in Chapter 4. Here is how you could define a FALLTHROUGH macro that only expands to an actual fallthrough statement, [[fallthrough]];, if your compiler is known to support it; otherwise, the (still self-documenting) identifier FALLTHROUGH is simply removed by the preprocessor.

```
#ifdef __has_cpp_attribute
  #if __has_cpp_attribute(fallthrough)
    #define FALLTHROUGH [[fallthrough]];
  #else
    #define FALLTHROUGH
  #endif
#else
  #define FALLTHROUGH
#endif
```

Note that, to be fully compatible with older compilers, we first have to check whether the `__has_cpp_attribute` macro itself is defined. Without this macro, there is no reliable, standardized means to check whether your compiler supports the [[fallthrough]] attribute.

▨ **Note** Even though the feature test macros have only been added to the official standard in C++20, several major compilers have been supporting these macros since about 2013. Unfortunately, though, not all major compilers followed suit on this at the time, so to be fully compatible with older legacy compilers, you may still have to rely on non-standard means.

Standard Preprocessing Macros

There are several more standard predefined preprocessing macros besides the feature test macros discussed in the previous section. Table A-3 list some useful examples.

Table A-3. *Predefined Preprocessing Macros*

Macro	Description
__DATE__	The date when the source file was preprocessed as a character string literal in the form Mmm dd yyyy. Here, Mmm is the month in characters, (Jan, Feb, etc.); dd is the day in the form of a pair of characters 1 to 31, where single-digit days are preceded by a blank; and yyyy is the year as four digits (such as 2021).
__TIME__	The time at which the source file was compiled, as a character string literal in the form hh:mm:ss, which is a string containing the pairs of digits for hours, minutes, and seconds separated by colons.
__LINE__	The line number of the current source line as a decimal integer literal. (Note: This macro is superseded by the functionality of C++'s <source_location>, as explained shortly.)
__FILE__	The name of the source file as a character string literal (superseded by <source_location>).
__func__ [5]	The name of the current function as a character string literal (superseded by <source_location>).
__cplusplus	A number of type long that corresponds to the highest version of the C++ standard that your compiler supports. This number is of the form yyyymm, where yyyy and mm represent the year and month in which that version of the standard was approved. At the time of writing, possible values are 199711 for nonmodern C++, 201103 for C++11, 201402 for C++14, 201703 for C++17, 202002 for C++20, and 202302 for C++23). Compilers may use intermediate numbers to signal support for earlier drafts of the standard as well. More fine-grained testing for supported language features may be accomplished by the feature test macros we discussed in the previous section.

Note that each of the macro names in Table A-3 start, and most end, with two underscore characters. You can use the date and time macros to record when your program was last compiled with a statement such as this:

```
std::println("Program last compiled at {} on {}", __TIME__, __DATE__);
```

When this statement is compiled, the values displayed by the statement are fixed until you compile it again. Thus, the program outputs the time and date of its last compilation. These macros can be useful for use in either about screens or log files.

The __LINE__ and __FILE__ macros expand to reference information relating to the source file. You can modify the current line number using the #line directive, and subsequent line numbers will increment from that. For example, to start line numbering at 1000, you would add this directive:

```
#line 1000
```

---

[5] Technically, __func__ is not a macro, but a static local variable that is implicitly defined within every C++ function body. We decided to list it in Table A-3 anyway because you often use it together with the macros __LINE__ and __FILE__.

You can use the #line directive to change the string returned by the __FILE__ macro. It usually produces the fully qualified filename, but you can change it to whatever you like. Here's an example:

```
#line 1000 "The program file"
```

This directive changes the line number of the next line to 1000 and alters the string returned by the __FILE__ macro to "The program file". This doesn't alter the filename, just the string returned by the macro. Of course, if you just wanted to alter the apparent filename and leave the line numbers unaltered, the best you can do is to use the __LINE__ macro in the #line directive:

```
#line __LINE__ "The program file"
```

It depends on the implementation what exactly happens after this directive. There are two possible outcomes: either the line numbers remain unaltered or they are all decremented by one. (It depends on whether the value returned by __LINE__ takes the line on which the #line directive appears into account.)

You may wonder why you would want to use the #line directive to change the line number and/or filename. The need for this is rare, but one example is a program that maps some other language into C or C++. An original language statement may generate several C++ statements, and by using the #line directive, you can ensure that C++ compiler error messages identify the line number in the original code, rather than the C++ that results. This makes it easier to identify the statement in the original code that is the source of the error.

■ **Tip** The C++ Standard Library offers a better, more powerful alternative to the __LINE__ and __FILE__ macros. The following snippet shows a typical use:

```
void logError(std::string_view errorMessage,
              std::source_location location = std::source_location::current())
{
  std::println("{}:{}:{} - An unexpected error occurred in {}: {}",
               location.file_name(), location.line(), location.column(),
               location.function_name(), errorMessage);
}
```

When invoked from the main() function in ExA_03.cpp (available online), logError("OOPS!"); produces output of the following form: "ExA_03.cpp:14:3 - An unexpected error occurred in main(): OOPS!". Because default argument values are evaluated at the calling site, line 14 refers to the line at which logError() is invoked from within main()—and so *not* to the line at which the logError() function itself is defined. With __LINE__, __FILE__, and __func__, you'd have to turn logError() into a macro as well to obtain a similar result, and even then you wouldn't have access to the column number of the source location (at least not in a standardized way). Another advantage is that you can readily store std::source_location objects and pass them around.

■ **Tip** As of C++23 logging or capturing a complete std::stacktrace instead of a std::source_location may be even more informative. See Chapter 16 for details.

Including Files

The final preprocessing directive we introduce is #include. The #include directive takes the contents of a given file and injects that into the current file. To illustrate this, you can create a file called inclusivity. quote with the following three lines of code:

```
std::println("We are trying to construct a more inclusive society.");
std::println("We are going to make a country in which no one is left out.\n"
             "\t\t\t\t- Franklin D. Roosevelt");
```

You can then inject these three lines into an actual program with an #include directive as follows:

```
// ExA_04.cpp - Introducing the #include directive
import std;

int main()
{
#include "inclusivity.quote"
}
```

▓ **Note**   Do not add a semicolon after an #include directive.

In the translation unit that the preprocessor hands over to the compiler for this source file, the #include directive will be gone. It's replaced with the content of the inclusivity.quote file. When executed, ExA_04 therefore outputs the following inspirational and all-too-relevant quote on inclusivity:

```
We are trying to construct a more inclusive society.
We are going to make a country in which no one is left out.
                    - Franklin D. Roosevelt
```

Of course, the way we used #include in ExA_04 is not how you would normally use this directive. You normally use #include to include header files. You also normally put all your #include directives near the top of a file, and not in the middle of a function body. But ExA_04 does nicely illustrate what an #include directive is—a crude, low-level construct that instructs the preprocessor to look for a file with a given name, take its contents, and copy-paste it into the translation unit at the exact spot where it found the #include directive. Nothing more, nothing less. As we will see later, this has a significant impact on the remainder of the translation process, as well as on how you should compose and structure your header files.

Understanding Header Inclusion

Later in this appendix we will show you how to correctly compose header files of your own. Before we can do this, though, you first need to understand the limitations (in particular, the *one definition rule*) and some more underlying concepts (such as *external linkage*). Nevertheless, we believe it is beneficial to already give you an intuitive feeling of how header inclusion works here. This should make it easier for you to follow the upcoming, more theoretical, sections that we need to explain these limitations and concepts.

Consider this #include directive, which you can use to gain access to the Standard Library's basic mathematical functions (see Chapter 2 for an introduction to some of these functions).

```
#include <cmath>
```

In a first step, the preprocessor replaces this #include directive with the contents of the <cmath> Standard Library header. Where exactly this header file is located is implementation defined.

Like with macro text replacement before, though, any included body of text is immediately preprocessed as well, which often leads to the contents of more files being injected into the translation unit. And so on, until no more preprocessing directives are left.

This is also what happens after including <cmath>. Even though <cmath> is arguably one of the more straightforward Standard Library headers[6], a <cmath> header typically contains #include directives for several more headers, which in turn rely on even more headers, and so on. In the Standard Library implementation we looked at, a single #include directive for <cmath> alone, fully expanded, resulted in about 6,000 (!) lines of code (over 10,000 if you include code comments) being injected into our translation unit. Which is massive, given that you typically only want to call one or two simple math functions, such as std::abs() or std::sqrt().

This immediately illustrates one of the primary disadvantages of #include directives: they generate a tremendous amount of work for the preprocessor, compiler, and linker, all of which have to process code over and over again for countless C++ entities, most of which are typically not even used by your application. The good news, though, is that, even though this obviously puts pressure on your compilation times, the impact of #includes on the eventual size of your executable is usually limited. For the most part, code for entities that you do not use does not make it into the final binary.

This should give you enough of a feeling of how header inclusion works. In short, including even a single header can often inject thousands of lines of code into a translation unit, consisting of hundreds of entity declarations and definitions. The exact implications on which declarations and definitions you are therefore allowed to put in your own header files, and how you should do this robustly, is something we can only properly explain once you know more about the one definition rule and the different types of linkage. But first, some additional notes on the syntax of the #include directive.

Double Quotes vs. Angle Brackets

Here is how you included your own source file named inclusivity.quote into the translation unit for ExA_04.cpp.

```
#include "inclusivity.quote"
```

This syntax differs slightly from the one used to include Standard Library headers (more on this shortly), which as you know from the previous section looks as follows:

```
#include <cmath>
```

---

[6] Although you should never underestimate the complexity and ingenuity that goes into defining efficient, numerically stable mathematical primitives!

The concrete difference between specifying a filename between double quotes or between angled brackets lies in the locations in which the preprocessor will search for a file with that name. The precise locations the preprocessor uses for this are implementation-dependent and should be described in your compiler documentation. Usually, though, the idea is that you use angle brackets for headers of external libraries, and double quotes for files that are stored next to the current source file.

```
#include <some_external_header.h>
#include "some_local_header.h"
```

Usually, when a filename is between double quotes, the preprocessor first searches the current directory (typically either the directory that contains the source file that is being compiled, or one of its parent directories). Eventually, though, if the file is not found there, the preprocessor is required to fall back to searching the same directories that it would search had the name been between angled brackets.

When a name is between angle brackets, then, the preprocessor by default typically only searches the directories that it knows contain the Standard Library headers, although sometimes this is automatically combined with directories that contain headers native to the target operating system as well. Most compilers allow you to provide other directories for the preprocessor to search as well, though. The idea is that these additional *include directories* then contain the headers of any external (often third-party) library that your program may rely on.

▓ **Tip**   Most third-party libraries make their APIs available through header files that are located in a directory called `include`.

If a header file is located in some subdirectory, either relative to the current working directory or to any of the additional `include` directories, you normally put the relative path for the header file between quotes or braces. Here is an example.

```
#include "subdirectory/in/current_directory/myheader.h"
#include <subdirectory/in/external_library_include_directory/some_header.h>
```

Using the assert() Macro

Before we explain the one definition rule and how to create your own header files, there is one more standard macro we want to introduce: `assert()`. This preprocessor macro enables you to test logical expressions in your program. By default, writing a line of the form `assert(expression)` results in code that causes the program to be terminated with a diagnostic message if `expression` evaluates to `false`. We can demonstrate this with this simple example:

```
// ExA_05.cpp - Demonstrating assertions
import std;        // Importing a module does not import macros: see later
#include <cassert> // import <cassert>; is not guaranteed to work: see later

int main()
{
  int y {5};
```

```
for (int x {}; x < 20; ++x)
{
  std::println("x = {}\ty = {}", x, y);
  assert(x < y);
}
}
```

assert() is defined in the cassert header—one of the 27 headers that the C++ Standard Library inherited from the C Standard Library. You can recognize these headers by the prefix c in their name. To use their macros, you must always include the correct header via an #include directive. (We'll have more to say about this later in the section on header units.) To include a Standard Library header, as explained in the previous section, you surround its name with angle brackets:

```
#include <cassert>
```

If you compile ExA_05 using a debug configuration (one where NDEBUG is not defined; see next section), then you should see an assertion message in the output when the value of x reaches 5. When an assertion is triggered—which in our example occurs when x < y evaluates to false—the program is terminated. Concretely, the assert() macro calls the std::abort() function from the Standard Library, which effectively terminates the program immediately. Right before terminating, though, assert() outputs a diagnostic message on the standard error stream, std::cerr. The message typically contains the condition that failed and also the filename and line number in which the failure occurred. This is particularly useful with multifile programs, where the source of the error is pinpointed exactly.

Assertions are often used for critical conditions in a program where, if certain conditions are not met, disaster will surely ensue. You would want to be sure that the program wouldn't continue if such errors arise. You can use any logical expression as the argument to the assert() macro, so you have a lot of flexibility.

Using assert() is simple and effective, and when things do go wrong, it provides sufficient information to pin down where the program has terminated.

▓ **Caution** assert() is for detecting programming errors, not for handling errors at runtime. It is for asserting facts that you, as a programmer, are 111% convinced should never, ever occur. The logical expression of an assertion should thus never be based on something beyond your control (such as whether opening a file succeeds). Your program should include code to handle any and all error conditions that might be expected to occur occasionally—however unlikely their occurrence may be. As seen in Chapter 16, exceptions are an effective means of signaling and/or handling such runtime errors in C++.

▓ **Note** assert() is the last commonly used C Standard Library macro without a replacement in C++ (examples of superior C++ constructs include the function templates of <cmath>, std::min() and max(), std::numeric_limits<>, std::source_location, nullptr, and so on). In C++26, they aim to introduce *contracts*, which should allow us to phase out the more primitive assert() macro as well.

Switching Off assert() Macros

You can switch off the preprocessor assertion mechanism when you recompile the program by defining NDEBUG at the beginning of the program file:

```
#define NDEBUG
```

This causes all assertions in the translation unit to be ignored. If you add this #define at the beginning of ExA_05.cpp, you'll get output for all values of x from 0 to 19 and no diagnostic message. Note that this directive is effective only if it's placed *before* the #include directive for <cassert>.

▩ **Tip** Most compilers also allow you to define macros such as NDEBUG globally for all source and header files at once (for instance, by passing a command-line argument or by filling in some field in your IDE's configuration windows). Often NDEBUG is defined that way for fully optimizing "release" configurations, but not for the configurations that are used during debugging. Consult your compiler's documentation for more details.

▩ **Caution** If NDEBUG is defined, the logical expression passed to assert() is not evaluated. Because it is then removed by the preprocessor, this expression is not even part of the compiled code anymore. Because assertions are typically turned off for optimizing compilations, evaluation of the logical expression should thus never cause any side effects.

Static Assertions

Static assertions, unlike the assert() macro, are part of the C++ language. That is, they are no Standard Library addition but built into the language. The assert() macro is for checking conditions *dynamically, at runtime*, whereas static assertions are for checking conditions *statically, at compile time*. You already encountered an example use of static assertions in Chapter 21, where we added assertions to verify that a given type models a given concept—a technique that is useful both when developing a new class type and when developing a new concept.

In general, a static assertion is a statement of either of the following forms:

```
static_assert(constant_expression);
static_assert(constant_expression, error_message);
```

static_assert is a keyword, constant_expression must produce a result at compile time that can be converted to type bool, and error_message is an optional string literal. If constant_expression evaluates to false, then the compilation of your program should fail. The compiler will abort the compilation and output a diagnostics message that contains error_message if you provided it. If you did not specify an error_message, the compiler will generate one for you (usually based on constant_expression). When constant_expression is true, a static assertion does nothing.

As a brief example, suppose that your program does not support 32-bit compilation, for instance because it needs to address more than 2GB of memory to process larger data sets. Then you could put the following static assertion anywhere in your source file:

```
static_assert(sizeof(int*) > 4, "32-bit compilation is not supported.");
```

Adding this static assertion will thus ensure that you cannot inadvertently compile as a 32-bit program.

■ **Note**   Prior to C++20, static assertions were often used to restrict type parameters of templates, typically in an attempt to produce more legible error messages in case these templates were ever inadvertently instantiated for unsupported type arguments. (See Chapters 10 and 21 for a discussion on how notoriously unclear and verbose template instantiation errors can be.) Here is an example:

```
template<typename T>
T average(const std::vector<T>& values)
{
  static_assert(std::is_arithmetic_v<T>,
                "Type parameter for average() must be arithmetic.");
  // ... Code that applies operators + and / to T values
}
```

`std::is_arithmetic_v<T>` is a constant expression based on a type trait from the `<type_traits>` module. (You encountered type traits in Chapters 10 and 21.) It evaluates to `false`, thus triggering the static assertion, whenever the template is instantiated for a template type argument T that is anything but a floating-point or integral type.

From Chapter 21, however, you know that type constraints and requires clauses are far more powerful and effective for constraining template type parameters. Here is how you would therefore write the previous example in C++20:

```
// There is no std::arithmetic<> concept, so we define one ourselves
template <typename T>
concept Arithmetic = std::integral<T> || std::floating_point<T>;

template <Arithmetic T>
T average(const std::vector<T>& values)
{
  // ... Code that applies operators + and / to T values
}
```

The One Definition Rule

The *one definition rule* (ODR) is an important concept in C++. Despite its name, ODR is not really one single rule; it's more like a set of rules. Our exposition of these rules won't be exhaustive, nor will it use the formal jargon you'd need for it to be 100% accurate. Our main intent is to familiarize you with the general ideas behind the ODR restrictions. This will help you to better understand how to organize the code of your program in header and source files and to decipher and resolve the compiler and linker errors you'll encounter when you violate an ODR rule.

ODR Within a Translation Unit

In a given translation unit, no variable, function, class type, enumeration type, or template must ever be *defined* more than once. You can have more than one *declaration* for any such entity, but there must never be more than one *definition* that determines what it is and causes it to be created. If there's more than one definition within the same translation unit, the code will not compile.

▥ **Note** A *declaration* introduces a name into a scope. A *definition* not only introduces the name but also defines what it is. In other words, all definitions are declarations, but not all declarations are definitions.

To familiarize yourself with the error messages that ODR violations produce, you can try to compile the following program.

```
// ExA_06.cpp - Defining the same function twice
import std;

double power(double x, int n);
double power(double x, int n);          // Redundant declaration (harmless)

int main()
{
  for (int i {-3}; i <= 3; ++i)          // Calculate powers of 8 from -3 to +3
    std::println("{:10}", power(8.0, i));
}

double power(double x, int n)            // A first definition
{
  if (n == 0)        return 1.0;
  else if (n > 0)    return x * power(x, n - 1);
  else /* n < 0 */   return 1.0 / power(x, -n);
}

double power(double x, int n);           // Another redundant declaration (harmless)

double power(double x, int n)            // A second, more efficient definition (error!)
{
  if (n < 0) return 1.0 / power(x, -n); // Deal with negative exponents
  if (n == 0) return 1.0;               // Base case of the recursion
  const double y{ power(x, n / 2) };    // See Exercise 8-8 for an explanation
  return y * y * (n % 2 == 1 ? x : 1.0);
}
```

ExA_06.cpp contains a number of declarations and definitions for one and the same function: power(). You may recognize this function from Chapter 8. We refer you to Exercise 8-8, in particular, for an explanation of the less-obvious recursive definition at the bottom of ExA_06.cpp.

From Chapter 8, you'll also recall why `main()` can call `power()`, even though the definition of this function is not known to the compiler when it processes the body of `main()` (a compiler processes a source from top to bottom). To invoke a function, the compiler only needs to know its prototype, which is contained in non-defining declarations as well. Remember this, as this will prove important in understanding how the separation of code in header and source files works (this, in combination with *external functions*, which we discuss in one of the next sections).

While it's certainly odd to declare the same function more than once like we did in `ExA_06.cpp`, it is perfectly allowed by C++. You can have as many *declarations* for the same function as you want within a translation unit, as long as they are all equivalent, and no more than one of these declarations is a *definition*.

Obviously, the problem with `ExA_06.cpp` thus lies with its two definitions of `power(double, int)`. How is the compiler to know which of these definitions it should generate machine code for in the object file? The naïve implementation at the top? Or the more efficient one at the bottom? And so, compilation of `ExA_06.cpp` fails with an error—and rightfully so!

Of course, only a true scatterbrain would explicitly define the same entity twice within the same file. But duplicate definitions do make it into the same translation unit at times by (indirectly) including an improperly created header file more than once. We discuss the techniques you should use to prevent this later in this appendix.

ODR Within a Program

The ODR rules do not only apply within one translation unit. They also stipulate that regular functions and variables must be defined once and only once *within an entire program*. As a rule, no two definitions of the same function or variable are allowed, even if they're identical and appear defined in different translation units. Naturally, violations against this aspect of the ODR rules are only discovered during the linking stage of translation.

Exceptions to this rule are *inline functions* and *inline variables*. In fact, for inline functions and inline variables that are not defined in a module file, a definition *must* appear once and only once *in every translation unit* that uses them. All definitions of a given inline function or variable within different translation units of a program have to be identical, though. One traditionally uses inline functions and variables to define variables or functions in header files, something which with regular functions and variables would almost certainly lead to ODR violations. We show you how to define inline entities later, when we are ready to discuss header files.

The program-wide ODR rules for class types (see Chapter 12), enumeration types (Chapter 3), and templates (Chapters 10 and 17) are similar to those of inline functions and variables. That is, unless they are defined in a module file, one and only one definition is required for these entities *within every translation unit* that uses them. Note that, in a way, the compiler does preserve an ODR-like behavior for templates by instantiating each template only once for any given combination of template arguments.

While multiple definitions of the same class type are thus allowed, its member functions and variables do have to obey the same ODR rules as regular functions and variables. In other words, non-inline class members must have only one single definition within the entire program. This is one of the reasons why in nonmodular code you generally put the definitions for a class's members in a source file, while the class definition itself is placed in the corresponding header file. We will see an example of this later.

ODR and Modules

In a fully modular program, you are far less likely to ever run into issues with ODR. In fact, the only way you can get ODR violations in modular code is when you export the same entity from multiple modules—something you should be able to avoid by properly organizing your names in namespaces (see Chapter 11).

A first, obvious, reason that ODR violations are far less likely with modules is that import declarations are fundamentally different from #include directives. Any definition you place in a header gets copy-pasted into every translation unit that includes it, either directly or indirectly. Because this inherently copies declarations many times over, you clearly must always be watchful for ODR violations in the nonmodular setting. The content of a module interface file, however, is never duplicated. An import declaration is part of the C++ language, and therefore does not have to be processed and removed by the preprocessor. It simply tells the C++ compiler to make the declarations from a given module visible and/or reachable within the consuming translation unit (see Chapter 11); no definitions are ever copied when importing a module. Any duplicate definition in modular code will therefore be one by your hand.

The second reason that you are far less likely to run into ODR issues with modular code stems from the fact that non-exported entities in a named module A are always different from non-exported entities in module B, even if these entities appear to have the exact same name or signature. Formally, module-local entities are said to have *module linkage*, whereas local entities in nonmodular source files generally have *external linkage* by default. We discuss these and other types of linkage further in the next section.

The Different Types of Linkage

Entities defined in one translation unit often need to be accessed from code in another translation unit, even in nonmodular code. Functions and class types are obvious examples of where this is the case, but you can have others—variables defined at global scope that are shared across several translation units, for instance, or the definitions of type aliases or enumeration types. Because the compiler processes one translation unit at a time, such references can't be resolved by the compiler. Only the linker can do this when all the object files from the translation units in the program are available.

The way that a name in a translation unit is handled in the compile/link process is determined by a property called *linkage*. The linkage of a name expresses where in the program code the entity it represents can be defined and/or accessed. Every name that you use in a program either has linkage or doesn't. A name has linkage when you can use it to access something in your program that is *outside* the scope in which the name is declared. If this isn't the case, it has no linkage. If a name does have linkage, then it can have *internal linkage*, *module linkage*, or *external linkage*.

Determining Linkage for a Name

The linkage for each name in a translation unit is determined *after* the contents of any header files have been inserted into the source file that is the basis for the translation unit. The linkage possibilities have the following meanings:

- *Internal linkage*: The entity that the name represents can only be accessed from within the same translation unit. For example, the names of non-inline, non-exported, const-qualified variables defined at global or namespace scope have internal linkage by default.

- *External linkage*: A name with external linkage can be accessed from other translation units in addition to the one in which it is defined. In other words, the entity that the name represents can be shared and accessed throughout the entire program. In nonmodular code, most names that are declared at global or namespace scope have external linkage by default—including those of functions, enumerations, classes, templates, and inline or non-const variables. Naturally, all entities that are exported from a module have external linkage as well.

- *Module linkage*: An entity name with module linkage is accessible only in translation units of the same named module. The name of any non-exported entity that is declared at global or namespace scope within the purview of a module file (in other words, anywhere after the module file's optional global module fragment; see Chapter 11) has module linkage by default.

- *No linkage*: When a name has no linkage, the entity it refers to can be accessed only from within the scope that applies to the name. All names that are defined within a block—local names, in other words—have no linkage.

External Functions

In a program made up of several files, the linker establishes (or *resolves*) the connection between a function call in one source file and the function definition in another. When the compiler compiles a *call* to the function, it only needs the information contained in a function prototype to create the call. The compiler either extracts this prototype from a (precompiled) module interface file (see Chapter 11), or from any function *declaration* present in the current translation unit itself (often after including it from a header file). Either way, the compiler doesn't care whether the function's *definition* occurs in the same translation unit, or in any other translation unit. If a function is not defined within the translation unit in which it is called, the compiler flags the call as external and leaves it for the linker to sort out.

We should clarify this with an example. For this, we'll adapt ExA_06.cpp and move one of the definitions of its power() function to a different translation unit. The other definition of power() we simply discard (although it may be instructive for you to move that definition to a second source file as well, and study the ODR-related linker errors you then get during linking).

```cpp
// ExA_07.cpp - Calling external functions
import std;

double power(double x, int n);    // Declaration of an external power() function

int main()
{
  for (int i {-3}; i <= 3; ++i)  // Calculate powers of 8 from -3 to +3
    std::println("{:10}", power(8.0, i));
}
```

Even though power() is called by main(), no definition of this function is present in the ExA_07 translation unit. But that's okay. Like we said, all the compiler needs to carry out a call to power() is its prototype. Because function names have external linkage by default, the compiler simply makes note of a call to an externally defined power() function inside the object file for the ExA_07 translation unit. It then becomes the linker's job to hook up—or *link*—this call with a definition. If the linker doesn't find the appropriate definition in one of the other translation units of the program, it will signal this as a translation failure.

To make the ExA_07 program translate correctly, you'll thus need a second translation unit with the definition of power(). We of course pick the more efficient implementation and discard the slower one.

```
// Power.cpp
// The power function called from ExA_07.cpp is defined in a different translation unit
double power(double x, int n)
{
  if (n < 0) return 1.0 / power(x, -n); // Deal with negative exponents
  if (n == 0) return 1.0;               // Recursion base case
  const double y{ power(x, n / 2) };    // See Exercise 8-8 for an explanation
  return y * y * (n % 2 == 1 ? x : 1.0);
}
```

By linking the object files of the ExA_07 and Power translation units, you obtain a program that is otherwise completely equivalent to that of ExA_06 (after first removing the slower definition of power() there as well, of course).

Notice that in order to use the power() function, we still had to supply the compiler with a prototype in the beginning of ExA_07.cpp. It would be very impractical if you had to do this explicitly for every externally defined function, and that you moreover had to repeat these same prototypes over and over again in every source file that wants to call them. This is why, in nonmodular code, function prototypes are typically gathered in header files, which you can then conveniently #include into your translation units. Here is a sneak preview of how this works.

```
// Power.h
// Your first header file containing a declaration of an external power() function
double power(double x, int n);
```

```
// ExA_07A.cpp
// Calling external functions that are declared in a header file
import std;
#include "Power.h"

int main()
{
  for (int i {-3}; i <= 3; ++i)  // Calculate powers of 8 from -3 to +3
    std::println("{:10}", power(8.0, i));
}
```

The only difference between ExA_07A and ExA_07 is that we moved the declaration of power() to a header file, Power.h, which we subsequently included in ExA_07A.cpp. By including Power.h, the preprocessor obviously produces the exact same translation unit for ExA_07A.cpp as it did for ExA_07.cpp, and so the compiler does not even notice the difference between both programs. You, the developer, however, now only have to type the prototype of power() twice—once for the declaration in the header file, and once for the definition in the source file—which is clearly a step forward, compared to having to type it once in every source file in which you want to call the function. Of course this gain is even greater if you need copies of entire class definitions in every translation unit that uses the class, but we'll get to that.

This naïve header file, Power.h, is perfectly correct and safe (albeit somewhat unconventional), yet only because it does not contain any definitions. If your header does contain definitions (class definitions, template definitions, inline definitions of variables or functions, and so on), things become slightly more involved. Without additional precautions, header inclusion would then quickly lead to ODR violations, whereby the same definition is inadvertently included in the same unit multiple times. Later in this appendix we explain how you can avoid such issues.

Before we show you how to create more advanced header files, though, we first continue with the various types of linkage, moving on now from external functions to external variables.

External Variables

Suppose that in ExA_07.cpp, you wanted to replace the magic constants -3 and 3 using an externally defined variable power_range, like so:

```
for (int i {-power_range}; i <= power_range; ++i)      // Calculate powers of 8
    std::println("{:10}", power(8.0, i));
```

The first step is to create an extra source file called Range.cpp containing the variable's definition:

```
// Range.cpp
int power_range{ 3 };           // A global variable with external linkage
```

Non-const variables have external linkage by default, just like functions do. So other translation units will have no problem accessing this variable. The interesting question, though, is this: How do you declare a variable in the consuming translation unit without it becoming a second definition? A reasonable first attempt would be this:

```
// ExA_08.cpp - Using an externally defined variable
import std;

double power(double x, int n);   // Declaration of an external power() function
int power_range;                 // Not an unreasonable first attempt, right?

int main()
{
  for (int i {-power_range}; i <= power_range; ++i)   // Calculate powers of 8
    std::println("{:10}", power(8.0, i));
}
```

The compiler will have no problem with this declaration of power_range. The linker, however, will signal an error! We recommend you give this a try as well to familiarize yourself with this error message. In principle (linker error messages do not always excel in clarity), you should then be able to deduce that we have supplied two distinct definitions for power_range: one in Range.cpp and one in ExA_08.cpp. This, of course, violates the one definition rule!

The underlying problem is that our declaration of the power_range variable in ExA_08.cpp is not just any old variable declaration; it's a variable *definition*:

```
int power_range;
```

In fact, you might've already known this would happen. Surely, you'll remember that variables generally contain garbage if you neglect to initialize them. Near the end of Chapter 3, however, we also covered *global* variables. And global variables, as we told you, will be initialized with zero, even if you omit the braced initializer from their definition. In other words, our declaration of the global power_range variable in ExA_08.cpp is equivalent to the following definition:

```
int power_range {};
```

And ODR does not allow for two definitions of the same variable. The compiler therefore needs to be told that the definition for the global variable power_range will be external to the current translation unit, ExA_08. If you want to access a variable that is defined *outside* the current translation unit, then you must declare the variable name using the extern keyword:

```
extern int power_range;    // Declaration of an externally defined variable
```

This statement is a declaration that power_range is a name that is defined elsewhere. The type must correspond exactly to the type that appears in the definition. You can't specify an initial value in an extern declaration because it's a declaration of the name, not a definition of a variable. Declaring a variable as extern implies that it is defined in another translation unit. This causes the compiler to mark the use of the externally defined variable. It is the linker that makes the connection between the name and the variable to which it refers.

Within any block in which this declaration appears, the name power_range refers to the variable defined in another file. The declaration can appear in any translation unit that needs access to power_range. You can place the declaration either at global scope so that it's available throughout the entire translation unit, or within a block, in which case it is available only within that local scope.

■ **Tip** You're allowed to add extern specifiers in front of function declarations as well. For example, in ExA_08.cpp you could've declared the power() function with an explicit extern specifier to call attention to the fact that the function's definition will be part of a different translation unit:

```
extern double power(double x, int n);
extern int power_range;
```

While entirely optional, our advice is to add extern in front of any declaration for an externally defined function, unless that declaration occurs in a header or module interface file. Doing so is not just consistent, but also far clearer for the person reading the code.

---

const Variables with External Linkage

Given its nature, you'd want to define the power_range variable from Range.cpp of ExA_08 as a global constant, rather than as a modifiable global variable:

```
// Range.cpp
const int power_range {3};
```

A const variable, however, has internal linkage by default, which makes it unavailable in other translation units. You can override this by using the extern keyword in the definition:

```
// Range.cpp
extern const int power_range {3}; // Definition of a global constant with external linkage
```

The extern keyword tells the compiler that the name should have external linkage, even though it is const. When you want to access power_range in another source file, you must declare it as const and external:

```
extern const int power_range;       // Declaration of an external global constant
```

You can find this in a fully functioning example in ExA_08A.

Global variables can be useful for constant values that you want to share because they are accessible in any translation unit. By sharing constant values across all of the program files that need access to them, you can ensure that the same values are being used for the constants throughout your program. As with external functions, though, if a global variable is required in multiple nonmodular files, you generally place them in a header file. You'll see an example of this later in this appendix.

▓ **Tip**   As mentioned in Chapter 3, coding and design guidelines typically dictate that global variables are to be avoided. Global constants, though—global variables declared with the const keyword —are a noble exception to this rule. It is recommended to define all your constants only once (in a header or module file), and global variables are perfectly suited for that.

Internal Names

If there's a way to specify that names should have external linkage, surely there must be ways to specify that they should have internal linkage as well, right? And of course there are. Two even! Yet neither is the one you'd expect!

Let's first illustrate when and why you'd need this possibility. Perhaps you noticed that upon every recursive call of power() in ExA_07, the function checks whether its argument n is positive or negative. This is somewhat wasteful because the sign of n, of course, never changes. One option is to rewrite power() in the following manner:

```
// Power.cpp - A slightly optimized power function

double localHelper(double x, unsigned n)
{
  if (n == 0) return 1.0;                     // Recursion base case
  const double y{ localHelper(x, n / 2) }; // See Exercise 8-8 for an explanation
  return y * y * (n % 2 == 1 ? x : 1.0);
}

double power(double x, int n)
{
  return n >= 0 ? localHelper(x, static_cast<unsigned>(n))
              : 1.0 / localHelper(x, static_cast<unsigned>(-n));
}
```

The power() function itself is now no longer recursive. Instead, it calls the recursive helper function localHelper(), which is defined to work only for positive (unsigned) exponents n. Using this helper, it's easy to rewrite power() in such a way that it checks whether the given n is positive only once.

In this case, localHelper() could in principle be a useful function in its own right—best renamed then to become an overload of power() specific for unsigned exponents. For argument's sake, however, suppose we want localHelper() to be nothing more than a local helper function, one that is only to be called by power(). You'll find that the need for this occurs quite often; you need a function to make your local code clearer or to reuse within one specific translation unit, but that function is too specific for it to be exported to the rest of the program for reuse.

Our localHelper() function currently has external linkage as well, just like power(), and can therefore be called from within any translation unit. Worse, the one definition rule implies that no other translation unit may define a localHelper() function with the same signature anymore either! If all local helper functions always had external linkage, they'd all need unique names as well, which would make it very hard indeed to avoid name conflicts in larger programs.

What we need is a way to tell the compiler that a function such as localHelper() should have internal linkage rather than external linkage. Given that extern gives names external linkage, an obvious attempt would be to add an intern specifier in front of the definition. And that just might've worked, if not for the little detail that there's no such keyword in C++. Instead, in the (very) old days, the way to mark a name (function or variable name) for internal linkage was by adding the static keyword. Here's an example:

```
static double localHelper(double x, unsigned n) // localHelper() now has internal linkage
{
  if (n == 0) return 1.0;                        // Recursion base case
  const double y{ localHelper(x, n / 2) };       // See Exercise 8-8 for an explanation
  return y * y * (n % 2 == 1 ? x : 1.0);
}
```

While this notation will still work, this use of the static keyword is no longer recommended. The only reason that this syntax, which originates from C, is not (or no longer, for those who know their history) deprecated or removed from the C++ Standard is that you'll still find it a lot in legacy code. Nevertheless, the recommended way to define names with internal linkage in C++ is through unnamed namespaces.

▓ **Caution**   Never use static anymore to mark names that should have internal linkage; always use unnamed namespaces instead.

Unnamed Namespaces

You declare an *unnamed namespace* with the following code:

```
namespace
{
   // Code in the namespace, functions, etc.
}
```

Declaring an entity within an unnamed namespace effectively has the same effect as declaring it as static in the global namespace, except that static can only be applied to variables or functions. Within a translation unit, you refer to entities of its unnamed namespace as if they were defined in the global namespace (even if they technically are not). Here is how you would therefore normally create a local helper function in the Power.cpp source file of our running example (the result is available from ExA_09).

```
// Power.cpp - A local helper function with internal linkage
namespace
{
  double localHelper(double x, unsigned n)    // localHelper() has internal linkage
  {
    if (n == 0) return 1.0;                      // Recursion base case
    const double y{ localHelper(x, n / 2) }; // See Exercise 8-8 for an explanation
    return y * y * (n % 2 == 1 ? x : 1.0);
  }
}

double power(double x, int n)                 // power() has external linkage
{
  return n >= 0 ? localHelper(x, static_cast<unsigned>(n))
              : 1.0 / localHelper(x, static_cast<unsigned>(-n));
}
```

Entities with internal linkage are never accessible from outside the translation unit. Similar to the fact that the parameter names x in localHelper() and power() refer to two distinct entities, any function declaration with prototype double localHelper(double, unsigned) in a translation unit other than Power will now no longer name the same entity. You can try this by altering the main source file of ExA_07 as follows:

```
// ExA_09A.cpp
// Attempting to call a function with internal linkage from a different translation unit
import std;

double localHelper(double x, unsigned n); // Declares an external localHelper() function

int main()
{
  for (unsigned i {0}; i <= 5; ++i)        // Calculate positive powers of 8
    std::println("{:10}", localHelper(8.0, i));
}
```

The declaration in ExA_09A now declares an external function localHelper()—a function for which the linker will not find a definition.

▓ **Tip** All names declared inside an unnamed namespace have internal linkage (even names defined with an extern specifier...). If a function, global variable, class, enumeration, or template is not supposed to be accessible from outside a particular translation unit, you should therefore always define it in an unnamed namespace, especially in nonmodular code (see also the next section). Using a static specifier for this purpose is no longer recommended (and was only ever possible for function and variable definitions anyway).

Module-Local Names

Each module in a way forms its own self-contained little universe in which the ODR applies. Naturally, names of exported entities have external linkage, which means that two modules exporting the same entity constitutes an ODR violation (technically even if you never import both modules in the same file). But names of non-exported entities by default have module linkage if they are declared at global or namespace scope in the purview of a module file; not external linkage. This means that if multiple modules for example each define a module-local function with the same prototype, these are not seen as the same entity by the linker, and thus will not lead to a violation of any ODR rule. The following example illustrates the implications of module linkage.

```
// ModuleA.cppm
export module A;
void logError(std::string_view error) { /* ... */ }
// Code that uses the module-local logError() in case of error...
// Other module files of module A can call this same function.
// No additional declaration is required in module implementation files
// because this interface file is implicitly imported there (see Chapter 11).
// In module partition files either an 'import A;' declaration
// or an additional declaration of logError() is required, though.

// ModuleB.cppm
export module B;
void logError(std::string_view error) { /* ... */ }
// Code that uses the module-local logError() in case of error...
// Analogous to module A. Because both logError() names have module linkage,
// these functions are seen as independent, different entities,
// and can therefore never cause any ODR issues--not even if you import
// both A and B into the same source file.

// ModuleCSource.cpp
module C;
void logError(std::string_view error) { /* ... */ }
// Code that uses the module-local logError() in case of error...
// Other module files of module C can call this same function,
// provided they add a declaration first.
```

If you only need a particular entity in one module translation unit, you can still give its name internal linkage by declaring it in an unnamed namespace. A concrete example for which this would have been applicable is the local from_roman(char) helper function in the from_roman.cpp source file of Ex11_02. You can even imagine that singling internal linkage gives the compiler and linker slightly less work, or even that it may facilitate certain optimizations such as inlining (see also later in this appendix). That notwithstanding, using unnamed namespaces to avoid ODR violations is somewhat less crucial in modular code. After all, you are far less likely to encounter ODR violations by inadvertently defining two identical entities within the same module than you are within an entire program (modules are typically much smaller and under full control of the same developer or team of developers).

Organizing Nonmodular Code

Now that you understand preprocessing directives, the ODR rules, and the different types of linkage, we are finally ready to explain how you correctly organize nonmodular code in headers and source files.

▓ **Note** If your compiler supports it, we highly recommend you always use modules in new code, and gradually convert existing code to modules whenever possible. (The final section of this appendix further reinforces this recommendation.) But this is not always an option (even as we are writing this, no compiler fully supports modules yet), and even if it is, you will likely still have to work in legacy, nonmodular code for a long time to come. So, either way, it for sure remains important to understand how headers and source files interrelate.

We already gave you a sneak peek at how header inclusion works in ExA_07A, where we included the following basic header file to avoid having to repeat the prototype of power() in every source file in which you want to call this external function.

```
// Power.h
// Your first header file containing a declaration of an external power() function
double power(double x, int n);
```

Including a header file (such as Power.h) that does not contain any *definitions* never leads to issues with the one *definition* rule (ODR). Without duplicate definitions, there are no ODR violations—that much is clear. In what follows, we look at the two types of ODR violations that occur if you do add definitions to a header file in a naïve way, and of course we teach you how to avoid these issues.

Preventing Duplication of Header File Contents

For your first non-trivial header file, it is only fitting that we start with the first module file that you ever created: math.cppm (see Ex11_01). This is how you naïvely convert that module interface file into a header file.

```
// BadMath.h - The start of your very first proper header file
auto square(const auto& x) { return x * x; }    // An abbreviated function template

const double lambda{ 1.303577269034296391257 }; // Conway's constant

enum class Oddity { Even, Odd };
bool isOdd(int x) { return x % 2 != 0; }
auto getOddity(int x) { return isOdd(x) ? Oddity::Odd : Oddity::Even; }
```

If you include this header twice into the same translation unit, though, you violate the most obvious ODR rule: no two definitions of the same entity are allowed within the same translation unit, ever. In fact, after preprocessing, you basically end up in exactly the same situation as in ExA_06 earlier.

```
// ExA_10.cpp - Including the same definitions twice
import std;
#include "BadMath.h"
#include "BadMath.h"

int main()
{
  std::println("{}", square(1.234));
}
```

Of course, only a true scatterbrain (the same scatterbrain that explicitly defined the same function twice in ExA_06) would explicitly include the same header twice into the same source file like this. But, as we explained earlier, each header that you include typically includes several more headers, and this process can go on many levels deep. Even in the most basic of programs, there is therefore a good chance that you might include header files more than once in the same translation unit indirectly. In some situations this may even be unavoidable.

Adding a definition to a header file therefore clearly opens the door to ODR violations through indirect header inclusion. Our challenge thus is: How can we close that door again?

A first, obvious idea would be to simply move all definitions to a source file, leaving only non-defining declarations in a header file. But, unfortunately, that idea only works for functions and variables; it does not work for classes, enumeration types, type aliases, templates, and so on. For all these other entities, a definition—one and only one—needs to be present (or at least visible or reachable; see Chapter 11) in every translation unit that uses these entities. For this reason, you cannot move the definitions of square() (a template) or Oddity (a type definition) out of the BadMath.h header file of ExA_10, for instance, and into some source file. This is entirely analogous to why in Ex11_01 you could not move these same definitions out of the interface of the math module, and into a module implementation file.

So, what do we have so far? On the one hand, each header file unavoidably gets included more than once into some translation unit, eventually. Which, in combination with the basic ODR rules, suggests that you should never define any entities in a header. Yet, on the other hand, when you define a type or template you often want to use it in more than one translation unit. While defining Box classes over and over again has been barrels of fun, you normally want to define a given class only once, and then reuse that same definition throughout your program. Which, in nonmodular C++, means you have no choice *but* to define it in a header file, to then include it where needed.

In standard, idiomatic C++, the solution to this apparent stalemate is to surround each header file with an *#include guard*. This pattern is based on a clever use of the #ifndef and #define preprocessing directives. You have already seen that you don't have to specify a value when you define a macro:

```
#define MY_IDENTIFIER
```

This creates MY_IDENTIFIER, so it exists from here on and represents an empty character sequence. You also know that you can use the #ifndef directive (short for #if !defined) to test whether a given identifier has been defined and include code or not in the file depending on the result:

```
#ifndef MY_IDENTIFIER
  // The code down to #endif will be placed in the source file if MY_IDENTIFIER
  // has NOT been defined. Otherwise, the code will be omitted.
#endif
```

All the lines following #ifndef down to the #endif directive will be omitted entirely from the file if the identifier, MY_IDENTIFIER, has been defined previously. It will no longer be considered by the preprocessor, and thus not by the compiler either. If MY_IDENTIFIER is defined, it is as if that entire block of code were never there. And so, more to the point: if MY_IDENTIFIER is defined, it is as if any potentially duplicate entity definitions in that conditional code block were never there.

These observations form the basis for the #include guards that you can use to ensure that the contents of header files are never duplicated in a translation unit. Applied to the BadMath.h header from before, this pattern looks as follows:

```cpp
// BetterMath.h - A second, better attempt at creating a header file
#ifndef BETTER_MATH_H
#define BETTER_MATH_H

auto square(const auto& x) { return x * x; }      // An abbreviated function template

const double lambda{ 1.303577269034296391257 }; // Conway's constant

enum class Oddity { Even, Odd };
bool isOdd(int x) { return x % 2 != 0; }
auto getOddity(int x) { return isOdd(x) ? Oddity::Odd : Oddity::Even; }

#endif   // The end of the #include guard
```

Naturally, you can choose any unique identifier instead of BETTER_MATH_H, as long as you use a different identifier in each header. Different naming conventions are used, although most base these names on the name of the header file itself. In this appendix we'll use identifiers of the form HEADER_NAME_H.

To show the effects of an #include guard, we now include BetterMath.h twice in the same translation unit and walk you through what happens.

```cpp
// ExA_10A.cpp
// Including the same header twice in the same translation unit without violating ODR
import std;
#include "BetterMath.h"
#include "BetterMath.h"

int main()
{
  std::println("{}", square(1.234));
}
```

The first #include directive will include the various C++ entity definitions in BetterMath.h because at that point BETTER_MATH_H is not yet defined. In the process, though, the preprocessor defines the macro BETTER_MATH_H. Any subsequent #include directive for BetterMath.h in the same translation unit will thus no longer include any code at all because BETTER_MATH_H will have been defined previously. It is as if that second #include directive was never there at all. Have another look at the #include guard in BetterMath.h, and we're sure you'll appreciate the cleverness of this trick.

▓ **Tip**   Surround all your headers with an #include guard to eliminate the potential for violating the one definition rule when that header is included twice into the same translation unit.

■ **Tip** Most compilers offer a #pragma preprocessing directive to achieve the same effect as the relatively verbose #include guard pattern. Simply placing a line containing #pragma once at the beginning of a header file generally suffices to prevent duplication of the header's contents as well. While nearly all compilers support this #pragma, it is not standard C++, so for this appendix we'll continue to use #include guards in header files.

Defining Functions and Variables in Headers

While #include guards prevent duplicate definitions *within a single translation unit,* they do not prevent violations of the program-wide ODR rules when you include the same variable or function definition into *multiple translation units of the same program.* Suppose you have a program that, next to the BetterMath.h header of ExA_10A, consists of the following five files:

```
// Hypot.h - Declaration of an external math::hypot() function
#ifndef HYPOT_H
#define HYPOT_H

namespace math
{
  // Computes the length of the hypotenuse of a right-angle triangle
  double hypot(double x, double y);
}

#endif
```

```
// Hypot.cpp - Definition of the math::hypot() function
#include "BetterMath.h"  // For the square() function template definition
#include "Hypot.h"
#include <cmath>          // For std::sqrt()

// Caution: See Chapter 11 for why you should always use std::hypot()
// over this naïve definition (based on the Pythagorean Theorem)!
double math::hypot(double x, double y) { return std::sqrt(square(x) + square(y)); }
```

```
// Pow4.h - Declaration of a math::pow4() function
#ifndef POW4_H
#define POW4_H

namespace math
{
  // Same as std::pow(x, 4)
  double pow4(double x);
}

#endif
```

```
// Pow4.cpp - Definition of the math::pow4() function
#include "BetterMath.h"  // For the square() function template definition

namespace math
{
  double pow4(double x) { return square(square(x)); }
}
```

```
// ExA_11.cpp
import std;
#include "Hypot.h"
#include "Pow4.h"

int main()
{
  std::println("{}\t{}", math::hypot(3, 4), math::pow4(5));
}
```

The Hypot.cpp and Pow4.cpp source files define hypot() and pow4(), respectively. Both are functions in the math namespace, as declared in the corresponding header files. Refer to Chapter 11 for the different ways you can define entities within a namespace after declaring them first in an interface file. Whether this interface file is the module's interface file or an included header makes no difference for this.

The main point that we want to make with ExA_11, though, is this: Because Hypot.cpp and Pow4.cpp both contain an #include directive for BetterMath.h, both their translation units contain a definition for the isOdd() and getOddity() functions. This violates the program-wide ODR rule that stipulates that only one definition of the same function is allowed in the entire program. And since a C++ preprocessor considers each translation unit independently, no amount of #include guards or #pragmas can protect you from this.

▓ **Note**   The #include guards surrounding Hypot.h and Pow4.h are not really required, because neither header contains a definition. It is common practice, though, to add an #include guard (and/or a #pragma once directive) to all your headers, even to those where it is strictly speaking not required. The reason is because that guideline is both easy to remember and safe.

▓ **Note**   Recall that the program-wide ODR rules only restrict the definitions of functions and non-const variables. In ExA_11, for instance, only the definitions of isOdd() and getOddity() therefore violate ODR. Multiple definitions for the same type or template (such as the enum class Oddity or the square() template) are allowed by the ODR rules (and often even required), as long as they are all identical and there is at most one such definition per translation unit. The reason that the lambda variable does not violate ODR in ExA_11 is because it is qualified as const, which gives its name internal linkage in both translation units in which it is included. The resulting definitions for lambda are therefore not seen as two definitions of the same external entity, but rather as independent definitions of two different constants, each internal to its respective translation unit.

Does this mean that you can never define functions and non-const global variables in a header? That you should always define functions and variables in a source file instead? Of course not. And we already gave away the answer in the section on ODR; the program-wide ODR rules only apply to regular functions and regular variables; they do not apply to *inline functions* and *inline variables*. For inline entities, multiple definitions are allowed within a program, as long as they are all identical, and no two definitions appear within the same translation unit—just like for type and class definitions.

But before we show you how you can create inline definitions in header files, perhaps first a brief discussion on when and why you would want to place certain definitions in a header file in the first place— besides to avoid having to type the same declarations twice, which is already a perfectly understandable sentiment in its own right.

Inlining

Defining a function in a header file may result in better runtime performance. Roughly speaking, a function call involves pushing a record on the call stack, getting things ready such that the function body has access to the values of all arguments, jumping to the location in memory where the compiled code for the function body is located, evaluating the function's statements, popping the record of the call stack again, and in doing so somehow retrieving the function's return value (if any). So quite a lot of work. If the compiler has access to the function definition, however, it can simply copy-paste the code from the function body into the calling function and avoid all these extra steps. That is, the compiler can then for instance rewrite an expression such as isOdd(something()) into (something() % 2 != 0), and by doing so, avoid the (relatively speaking) far more expensive function call of isOdd(). This compiler optimization is called *inlining*.

▓ **Tip**   For most functions, the overhead of a function call is either negligible compared to the time it takes to execute the function body, and/or they are never called often enough for inlining to make any difference in the overall performance of the program. You should therefore only consider facilitating compilation-time inlining of function calls for functions that are both small (as in, consist of only one or a few statements), and are likely to be called many times in time-critical code. Prime examples where inlining can make a difference include basic primitives such as std::abs() or our own isOdd(), and function members such as size() or operator[]() for containers (see Chapter 20). These functions are clearly not only very small, they are also very likely to be used inside loops that process a lot of data. In general, though, our advice is to not worry about optimizations such as inlining unless performance profiling tells you to!

Inline Functions and Variables in Headers

To define an inline function or variable, all you have to do is add the inline keyword in front of the definition. Here is how you do this in our running example.

```cpp
// ProperMath.h - Your first, proper header file
#ifndef PROPER_MATH_H
#define PROPER_MATH_H

auto square(const auto& x) { return x * x; }  // An abbreviated function template

const inline double lambda{ 1.303577269034296391257 };       // Conway's constant
```

```
enum class Oddity { Even, Odd };
inline bool isOdd(int x) { return x % 2 != 0; }
inline auto getOddity(int x) { return isOdd(x) ? Oddity::Odd : Oddity::Even; }
```

```
#endif
```

This header, `ProperMath.h`, is finally a fully ODR-safe equivalent of the math module of `Ex11_01` (you can find this header in `ExA_12`). The `#include` guard prevents ODR violations when you (indirectly) include the header multiple times into the same single translation unit, and by turning `isOdd()` and `getOddity()` into `inline` functions, you have ensured that you can safely include `ProperMath.h` not just in one translation unit, but in as many different translation units of the same program as you want.

Implicitly instantiated instances of a function template (see Chapter 10) are inline by default. Even though you are allowed to explicitly add `inline` in front of the definition of `square()` in `ProperMath.h` if you want to, there is no real need to do this.

Whether you add `inline` to constants such as `lambda` is not that important either.[7] As argued earlier, without the `inline` specifier that we added to the definition of `lambda` in `ProperMath.h`, you simply end up with a local copy of this variable in each translation unit in which it is included. The reason is that the names of non-inline, `const` variables have internal linkage by default. Take care, though—had the `lambda` variable not been `const`, the `inline` specifier would no longer have been optional, because then `lambda` would've had external linkage!

The order in which you specify `const` and `inline` in front of a variable definition does not matter.

▦ **Note**   The `inline` keyword is merely a suggestion to the compiler to inline a function, nothing more. If the compiler concludes that it would be more efficient not to inline a particular call, it will still ignore your suggestion and generate a function call instead. Conversely, if it believes this to be more efficient, the compiler will happily inline any non-inline function definition that is present in the same translation unit as well.

▦ **Caution**   Defining functions and variables in a header file comes at a cost, especially during development. Each time you change a definition in a header file, all translation units in which that header is included will need to be recompiled. If you change a definition in a source file, on the other hand, only that source file needs to be recompiled. (In both cases, the program must be linked again.) Because function definitions change far more often than their prototypes, defining functions in source files rather than in header files generally speeds up development tremendously.

Modules do not suffer from this last issue nearly as much as headers do, so the considerations are different. We discuss this further in the next section.

---

[7] The only noticeable difference between an inline constant and a non-inline constant at the global or namespace scope occurs when you take the address of this constant in different translation units, and then compare these. In the former case, there is only one (external) variable, which means it has the same address in all compilation units; in the latter case, there is one (internal) variable per translation unit, which means the address will be different in each compilation unit.

Inline Functions and Variables in Modules

As you know, modules are designed to be self-contained, independent, composable units (see Chapter 11). One of the key goals in designing the modules language feature was that modules should reduce compilation times, both when creating an executable from scratch, and when re-creating one after some changes during development. The latter is often referred to as *incremental compilation*. These concerns led to the restriction that, as long as the interface of a module does not change, you should be able to work inside that module and recompile its files as often as you want, without ever having to recompile any of the external translation units that import it. Only if you change the exported interface of a module should you have to rebuild its binary interface file, and then recompile all translation units that consume this interface.

As a consequence, your compiler is by default not allowed to inline a call to a function that is imported from a different module. By default, a function's definition is not part of a module's interface, not even if that definition appears in a module interface file. The definition of an exported function only becomes part of the module interface if you explicitly mark it as `inline`, and only then is the compiler allowed to inline this definition in consuming translation units[8].

Mind you, marking a function as `inline` in a module interface does imply that any consequent change to its function body necessitates recompilation of consuming translation units, so even in modular code you should still only consider using `inline` for functions that are small, whose definition is unlikely to change, and that are likely to be called a significant amount of times in time-critical code.

Defining Classes in Headers

So far, we mostly focused on definitions of functions and variables in this appendix, mostly because they are compact. Of course, nonmodular C++ code contains class definitions at least as often. In this section, we briefly explore how header and source files that define classes and their members typically look.

Because you need access to the definition of a class in every translation unit in which objects of that class are used, classes themselves are generally defined in header files. Take this header, for instance, which contains a definition of an old-time favorite: the Box class (see Chapter 12 and beyond).

```
// Box.h - Your first header file with a class definition
#ifndef BOX_H
#define BOX_H

class Box
{
public:
  Box();
  Box(double length, double width, double height);

  double getLength() const;
  double getWidth() const;
  double getHeight() const;
```

---

[8] Compiler vendors will likely add a switch to allow you to overrule this default behavior and give the compiler the green light to inline any exported functions it deems fit, regardless of whether you specified them as inline. The idea is then that you would rely on the default behavior during development to reduce recompilation times, but use that compiler switch for the final, fully optimized binary that is intended for your users.

```
  double volume() const;

private:
  double m_length;
  double m_width;
  double m_height;
};

#endif
```

Because member definitions have to obey the same ODR rules as regular functions and variables, we kept things safe and easy in this first version of the header and defined all member functions in a source file. Besides the #include directive at the top, and the lack of a module declaration, this source file looks precisely like the analogous module implementation files (see Chapter 12).

```
// Box.cpp
#include "Box.h"

Box::Box() : Box{1.0, 1.0, 1.0} {}
Box::Box(double length, double width, double height)
  : m_length{length}, m_width{width}, m_height{height}
{}

double Box::getLength() const { return m_length; }
double Box::getWidth() const  { return m_width; }
double Box::getHeight() const { return m_height; }

double Box::volume() const
{
  return m_length * m_width * m_height;
}
```

Here is a small test program to show you that this nonmodular separation of interface and definition works.

```
// ExA_13.cpp - Including a class definition from a header
import std;
#include "Box.h"

int main()
{
  Box boxy{ 1, 2, 3 };
  std::println("{}", boxy.volume());
}
```

Note that this main() function is again able to call the volume() member function, even though no definition of this member is present in its translation unit. The reason that this works, of course, is again because the compiler simply flags this call as an external function call, after which the linker matches it to the correct definition in the Box translation unit. You should remove the definition of volume() from Box.cpp to see what errors the linker then produces.

Inline Class Members

You can also define class member functions directly in the header file, but only if you use inline definitions. To illustrate your options, you can remove the Box.cpp source file of ExA_13 and replace the Box.h header file with this version.

```cpp
// Box.h - Inline class member definitions
#ifndef BOX_H
#define BOX_H

class Box
{
public:
  Box() = default;    // In-class definition, and thus implicitly inline
  Box(double length, double width, double height);

  // In-class member definitions are implicitly inline
  double getLength() const { return m_length; }
  double getWidth() const  { return m_width; }
  double getHeight() const { return m_height; }

  double volume() const;

private:
  double m_length {1.0};
  double m_width {1.0};
  double m_height {1.0};
};

// Out-of-class member definitions must be explicitly marked as inline
inline Box::Box(double length, double width, double height)
  : m_length{length}, m_width{width}, m_height{height}
{}

inline double Box::volume() const
{
  return m_length * m_width * m_height;
}

#endif // End of the #include guard
```

In nonmodular code, all in-class member definitions are implicitly inline. This is why inline is not needed in front of the defaulted default constructor or the three getters of Box in Box.h. (You can add inline there, if you want to, but you do not have to.) When defining a member out-of-class, however, its definition is inline only if you explicitly mark it as such. Without the inline specifier in front of the definition of either the non-default constructor or Box::volume(), ODR would thus prohibit you from including Box.h in more than one translation unit of the same program. (Perhaps give that a try as well?).

Modules vs. Headers

We already covered most of the advantages that modules offer over headers. We start this final section of the book by recapitulating.

- Modules result in *reduced compilation times* because every module file is processed by the compiler only once. Header files, on the other hand, are included and processed over and over again in every translation unit that consumes them, directly or indirectly.

- Modules result in *faster incremental recompilation* as well, because only changes to the module's interface trigger recompilations of consuming translation units. Changes to the bodies of non-inline functions, or changes to local entities, require only the module file itself to be recompiled.

- Modules are *self-isolating*, in the sense that only changes to a module's interface can ever impact the compilation of other translation units. Header files often leak declarations and definitions of local entities into the including translation units, as well as #include directives for lower-level headers, or dangerous macro definitions—all of which may lead to inadvertent name clashes or other compilation issues. Just think of the havoc that the min() and max() macros defined by the Windows API headers often wreak in C++ code!

- The order in which you import modules never matters, where with headers it could. The reason is that a module interface is never impacted by any macro definitions in the importing translation unit, nor does it ever inject any new ones.

- With modules, you can easily and naturally *define all entities directly in one file*. There is no need for constructs such as #include guards, #pragmas, unnamed namespaces, or inline specifiers—at least not to avoid ODR violations. (You may occasionally still want to add inline to improve performance, though.) Mind you, there can still be value in separating a module's interface from its implementation. This may allow you to present a more compact, cleaner overview of the interface, for instance, or to hide confidential implementation details when shipping libraries to customers. But at least with modules, when you do create multiple files, it will be for the right reasons, and not because of a fear of ODR violations or of increased recompilation times.

All this combined should make one thing crystal clear: if your compiler and build automation systems support it, you should *always* use modules to organize new code. No question about it.

Since modules were only introduced in C++20, though, there is decades' worth of *nonmodular* C++ code out there. While we patiently wait for the C++ ecosystem to fully embrace modules, you can keep using all nonmodular functionality as well.

You can perfectly use modular and nonmodular source files side by side. In nonmodular source files you can simply mix import declarations and #include directives. We already did so tacitly in several of the examples in this chapter. In module files you can use #include directives as well, but you shouldn't just interleave them with the import declarations. In module files, #include directives instead belong in the *global module fragment*. We discuss this further next.

Using Headers in Module Files: Global Module Fragments

In a module file—be it a module interface file or a module implementation file—any #include directives should normally go in its *global module fragment*. You can, in principle, use #include directives in the remainder of the module file as well, but then all included entities gain module linkage (see earlier), which is generally not what you want. Entities declared in header files, as a rule, are associated with the *global module*, and should not be dragged into another module like that.

Conceptually, all C++ entities declared in nonmodular source files are part of one large implicit, module referred to as the *global module*. To use these entities in a named module, you include the necessary headers in a global module fragment.

Here is the typical layout of a module file with a global module fragment:

```
module;                     // Start of the global module fragment

#define NOMINMAX            // Only preprocessor directives in the global module fragment
#include <Windows.h>        // Any number of #includes of nonmodular code

/*export */module myModule; // Start of the module purview

import std;                 // Import of C++ Standard Library module
import myOtherModule;       // Import of module

// Module code that consumes entities from <Windows.h>, std, and myOtherModule...
```

A global module fragment comes *before* the module declaration of a module file. In fact, other than comments, nothing but a global module fragment may appear before the module declaration. The section of the module file that starts with the module declaration is formally called the *module purview*.

The global module fragment may only contain preprocessor directives, such as #include and #define. Nothing else. The global module fragment may not contain any function declarations, no variable definitions, no import declarations, nothing. All regular declarations belong in the module purview.

▓ **Note**   The module; line at the start of a global module fragment may seem redundant. The reason they made it compulsory is to make it easier for compilers and build systems to quickly determine whether a given file is a module file or not (without having to process any of the #include directives).

▓ **Caution**   Never add module import declarations to a header file. By design, build systems should be able to discover module dependencies without full preprocessing. This implies that import declarations are not allowed to originate from either an #include directive or a macro expansion. This also explains why all import declarations in a module's purview have to appear before any other declarations (as seen in Chapter 11). All these limitations are put in place specifically to facilitate efficient dependency discovery, which is something build systems need to do when deciding in which order they should compile a larger number of program files.

Using Headers as Modules: Header Units

When mixing #include directives and import declarations as outlined earlier, you'll be faced with the typical disadvantages of #include directives: increased (re)compilation times, macro and local definition leakage, #include order dependencies, and so on. Disadvantages you don't have with import declarations. The good news is that compilers can turn many if not most header files into importable module units, meaning you can just start importing instead of include legacy headers—all without changing any code. This is what we explore in this final section.

In the section on organizing nonmodular code we turned a module interface file into a header file, side-stepping the various ODR issues that this brings as we went along. But of course, you are normally faced with the opposite task: turning nonmodular code into modules to leverage the advantages that we listed earlier. As an example, recall ProperMath.h from ExA_12.

```
// ProperMath.h - Your first, proper header file
#ifndef PROPER_MATH_H
#define PROPER_MATH_H

auto square(const auto& x) { return x * x; }          // An abbreviated function template

const inline double lambda{ 1.303577269034296391257 };  // Conway's constant

enum class Oddity { Even, Odd };
inline bool isOdd(int x) { return x % 2 != 0; }
inline auto getOddity(int x) { return isOdd(x) ? Oddity::Odd : Oddity::Even; }

#endif
```

Your first option, of course, is simply to plow on, remove the #include guards, add the module declaration, add export keywords where desired, and rename the header file. If the header file is paired with a source file, you must add a matching module declaration there as well. On the whole, this is a fairly straightforward process for most headers.

While rewriting your code like that is certainly a viable option—especially in the longer term—it does still takes some effort. You may not always have the time to convert all code at once. Also, sometimes the same source code may still need to work for other programs in which you cannot yet use modules—for instance, because these programs use an older compiler to target different platforms. Or perhaps the header files in question are part of a third-party library out of your control.

In cases like that, there is generally a second option as well. Clearly the steps required to turn nonmodular program files into module files are fairly predictable and repetitive, at least for most headers (and source files). And if there is one thing that computers do better than humans, it's predictable, repetitive jobs. The language therefore allows you to compile and subsequently import most header files as if they were interface files of a module. The general syntax you use to import such a synthesized module looks as follows.

```
import "some/local_path/local_header.h";
import <some/external_path/external_header.h>;
```

That is, instead of a module name (see Chapter 11), you can also specify the name (or, in general, the relative path) of a header file in an import declaration, surrounded with either double quotes or angle brackets. The way the compiler resolves these path names will be analogous to the way the preprocessor resolves those of #include directives (see earlier).

An `import` declaration that names a header file acts as if it imports some compiler-generated module, whose interface is extracted from the header file. The synthesized translation unit that specifies this interface is referred to as a *header unit*. In this header unit, all declarations within the original header file become exported. The only difference between the two following import declarations is therefore that the former makes an `isOdd()` function available to the importing unit, whereas the latter does not. Of course, this difference only exists because in the `math` module of `Ex11_01` we choose not to export the module-local `isOdd()` function.

```
import "ProperMath.h"; // Imports a module whose interface is synthesized from ProperMath.h
import math;           // Imports the hand-written math module of Ex11_01
```

The exact steps you need to create a header unit—and in doing so, making your header *importable*—are vendor specific. It could be that the header unit is generated implicitly, or it could be that you have to take extra steps compiling the header unit first. You should consult your compiler's documentation for this.

▧ **Tip** Your compiler may have an option to implicitly treat `#include <header>` directives as if they were `import <header>;` declarations. This option typically exists at least for all importable C++ Standard Library headers (more on this in the next subsection), but possibly also for your own headers or those of other dependencies. Since this can significantly speed up translation, without reworking any code at all, this may be worth looking into.

Standard Library Header Units

For most of the book we have treated the C++ Standard Library as one large module named `std`. As one should in C++23. In reality, though, the Standard Library is defined in over 100 distinct header files. As you know from earlier in this chapter, you can include individual headers as well using the following syntax:

```
#include <print> // Injects code for std::print(), println(), and so on...
```

Most headers of the C++ Standard Library should be importable as well (the implementation should effectively ensure that suitable header units are either available or generated on the fly):

```
import <print>;  // Imports std::print(), println(), ... from header unit
```

Because `import` declarations are generally more efficient, we recommend you use these over `#include` directives (yet still only if you cannot yet import the `std` module, of course...).

The only Standard Library headers that are not guaranteed to be importable are those that originate from the C Standard Library (those whose names begin with the prefix `c`). Headers with commonly used C library facilities include `<cmath>` (see Chapter 2) and `<cassert>` (see earlier). Safe from importing the `std` or `std.compat` umbrella modules (which import all functionality of the C Standard Library as well), the only way to gain access to this functionality is therefore through `#include` directives.

Overall, simply importing `std` or `std.compat` remains by far the most convenient way to use the Standard Library. But even then, you may occasionally still need an `#include` directive for Standard Library functionality: to use macros defined by the C++ headers that originate from the C Standard Library, to be exact. We discuss this in the next section.

Modules and Macros

You cannot export a macro from a module. Or, in other words, when importing a proper module (that is, not a header unit), you never import any macro definitions. To reuse macros between different source files, they therefore still have to be defined in header files.

Header units, however, *do* export macros. They export all preprocessing macro definitions defined in the corresponding header at the end of the preprocessing phase. For example, unlike import std; (std is a proper module, not a header unit), import <version>; (which does import a header unit) will import all library feature test macros we discussed earlier. You only ever really need #include directives for headers that are not importable; for importable headers import declarations remain preferred.

▓ **Caution** Because the headers of the Standard Library offering C library facilities are not guaranteed to be importable (they may be, but it's not guaranteed), and because importing std or std.compat does not import any macros, you should use #include directives to gain access to their macros. This is why in ExA_04 earlier we used this directive:

```
#include <cassert>
```

▓ **Caution** Header units are not impacted by which macros are defined at the point where the import declaration occurs. That is, defining a NOMINMAX macro prior to a hypothetical import <Windows.h>; declaration, for instance, would not work to prevent min() and max() from being imported. (We discussed the Windows.h example before in the section on undefining macros.) Nor will defining _UNICODE give you access to the Unicode version of the Windows API macros. Like with all module interface units, a header unit is only compiled once. So any macros that configure what the header defines (and thus what its header unit exports) should be defined at the moment that the header unit is synthesized, not when you import it. One option is to pass the necessary flags to your compiler when synthesizing the header unit. (Consult your compiler documentation for details.)

Summary

This appendix discussed various topics, most of which are particularly relevant in nonmodular code. The important points from this chapter include the following:

- The preprocessing phase executes directives to transform the source code in a translation unit prior to compilation. When all directives have been processed, the translation unit will only contain C++ code, with no preprocessing directives remaining.

- You can use the #define directive to define object- or function-like text replacement macros. In C++, you should mostly use variables or function templates instead, though.

- You can use conditional preprocessing directives to control which blocks of code make it into a translation unit. This is particularly convenient if the same program files should compile with different compilers, or for different target platforms.

- You insert the entire contents of any file into another file using an #include directive. The files that you include this way will nearly always be header files.

- The assert() macro enables you to test logical conditions during execution and issue a message and abort the program if the logical condition is false. You can use static_assert() to similarly check conditions at compile time.

- Each entity in a translation unit must have only one definition. If multiple definitions are allowed throughout a program, they must still all be identical. Multiple definitions are not allowed for functions, member functions, or global, non-const variables, though, unless they are specified to be inline.

- A name can have internal linkage, meaning that the name is accessible throughout a translation unit; external linkage, meaning that the name is accessible from any translation unit; module linkage, meaning that the name is accessible from any translation unit of the same named module; or it can have no linkage, meaning that the name is accessible only in the block in which it is defined.

- You use header files to contain definitions and declarations required by other headers or your source files. A header file can contain template and type definitions, enumerations, constants, function declarations, inline function and variable definitions, and named namespaces. By convention, header filenames use the extension .h.

- Your source files will typically contain the definitions for all non-inline functions and variables declared in the corresponding header. This also typically includes the definitions of class members.

- You can use conditional preprocessing directives in the form of an #include guard to ensure that the contents of a header file are never duplicated within a translation unit. Most compilers also support the more convenient #pragma once directive for this same purpose.

- In new code you should always use modules, and existing code should gradually be made modular.

- Header units, which are module interface units that the compiler generates based on a legacy header file, can help leverage the advantages of modules without reworking existing code.

- The module declaration may be preceded by a global module fragment, containing preprocessor directives. The global module fragment is where you normally mainly add #include directives for headers that are not importable as modules (such as the C headers of the Standard Library).

EXERCISES

The following exercises enable you to try what you've learned in this chapter. If you get stuck, look back over the chapter for help. If you're still stuck after that, you can download the solutions from the Apress website (https://www.apress.com/gp/services/source-code), but that really should be a last resort.

Exercise A-1. Define your own ASSERT() macro that, like a built-in static_assert() declaration optionally does, accepts two arguments: a condition and a message. If the given condition evaluates to false, it should print the given message to std::cerr and then call std::abort(), a function declared in the <cstdlib> header. Define your function-like macro in an ASSERT.h header file and use it to replace the assertion in ExA_03.cpp.

Exercise A-2. Make the `ASSERT()` macro in Exercise A-1 do nothing (not even evaluate the given expression) if the object-like NDEBUG macro is defined. Define NDEBUG to test that it works.

Exercise A-3. Create an exception class derived from `std::logic_error` that, next to the inherited `what()` function, adds a `where()` function that returns a reference to a `std::source_location`. This `source_location` facilitates pinpointing where exactly the exception was thrown. Make sure that users of the class can, but do not have to, explicitly create the `source_location` object themselves. In the spirit of this chapter, you should define the new class in a header file and its members in a source file. Write a small test program to show that it works.

Exercise A-4. In Exercise A-3's solution, move all member definitions from the source file to the header file. For the class's constructors, you should use in-class definitions; for its `where()` function, use an out-of-class definition. Make sure, that at least in principle, the header could be included in any number of translation units.

Exercise A-5. Write a program that calls two functions, `print_this(std::string_view)` and `print_that(std::string_view)`, each of which calls a third function, `print(std::string_view)`, to print the string that is passed to it. Define each function and `main()` in separate source files and create header files to contain the prototypes for `print_this()` and `print_that()`. For the sake of the exercise, don't put the prototype of `print()` in its own header (although one normally would, to avoid having to duplicate the function's prototype).

Exercise A-6. Modify the program in Exercise A-5 so that the definition of `print()` is inside a header file that is included in the source files of both `print_this()` and `print_that()`.

Exercise A-7. Modify the program in Exercise A-6 so that `print()` uses a global integer variable to count the number of times it has been called. Output the value of this variable in `main()` after calls to `print_this()` and `print_that()`. Then do the same with the program in Exercise A-6, and work around any issues you may encounter without moving the definition of `print()`.

Index

© Ivor Horton and Peter Van Weert 2023
I. Horton and P. Van Weert, *Beginning C++23*, https://doi.org/10.1007/978-1-4842-9343-0

▧ T

▧ U

▓ V

▓ W

▓ X, Y

▓ Z

Printed in the United States
by Baker & Taylor Publisher Services